General Reports of the XVIIIth Congress of the International Academy of Comparative Law/Rapports Généraux du XVIIIème Congrès de l'Académie Internationale de Droit Comparé

Karen B. Brown • David V. Snyder
Editors

General Reports of the XVIIIth Congress of the International Academy of Comparative Law/ Rapports Généraux du XVIIIème Congrès de l'Académie Internationale de Droit Comparé

Editors
Karen B. Brown
George Washington University Law School
2000 H Street
Washington, DC 20052
USA
karenbrown@law.gwu.edu

David V. Snyder
American University
Washington College of Law
4801 Massachusetts Ave. NW
Washington, DC 20016
USA
dsnyder@wcl.american.edu

ISBN 978-94-007-2353-5 e-ISBN 978-94-007-2354-2
DOI 10.1007/978-94-007-2354-2
Springer Dordrecht Heidelberg London New York

Library of Congress Control Number: 2011942913

Printed on acid-free paper

Springer is part of Springer Science+Business Media (www.springer.com)

Preface

In the international and comparative law worlds, the quadrennial congress of the International Academy of Comparative Law (IACL) presents the opportunity to tackle the captivating legal issues of our times. The 18th World Congress of the IACL was held in Washington, DC in July 2010, featuring sessions and plenary meetings that considered more than 30 issues of extraordinary import to legal thinkers. These included topics covering a spectrum of modern themes, such as Religion and the Secular State, the Role of Practice in Legal Education, Complexity of Transnational Sources, Catastrophic Damages, Class Actions, Climate Change and the Law, Corporate Governance, Surrogate Motherhood, Same Sex Marriage, Jurisdiction in Intellectual Property Matters, Age Discrimination, Protection of Foreign Investment, Public-Private Partnerships, The Exclusionary Rule in Evidence, Corporate Criminal Responsibility, Regulation of Corporate Tax Avoidance, and the Regulation of Private Equity, Hedge Funds, and State Funds. The congress was co-sponsored by the IACL and the American Society for Comparative Law (ASCL) and was hosted by American University Washington College of Law, Georgetown University Law Center, and George Washington University Law School.

The IACL chose the topics for the congress in conjunction with the organizing committee, which consisted of faculty from the law schools listed above and members of the ASCL. General reporters and national reporters were selected by the IACL and the national committees. All of the reports were made available on the congress website in advance of the congress. Many of the topics have been published in a volume containing all of the topic reports relating to one nation. A vertical volume containing the general report and all of the national reports will be also be published for many of the topics. The publication of all of the general reports in this single volume is an invaluable resource for academics, researchers, practitioners, students, and all others wishing to be informed about the current trends and future developments in pivotal areas of the law.

We would like to thank the host law schools, the IACL, and the ACSL for financial and moral support for the congress. We would also like to express our gratitude for the devoted efforts of all members of the organizing committee, particularly Ms. Jennifer Dabson, Director of Continuing Legal Education at American University Washington College of Law. Professor Dr. J. H. M. van Erp, a member of the organizing committee of the 17th Congress and President of the Netherlands Comparative Law Association, provided much-needed advice and assistance, for which we are especially grateful. Finally, we want to express our deep appreciation to the IACL leadership, especially the secretary-general, Prof. Dr. h.c. Jürgen Basedow; the president, Professor George Bermann; and the deputy secretary-general, Dr. Katrin Deckert.

Professor Karen B. Brown
George Washington University Law School
Washington, DC
(Member of the Steering Committee)

Professor David V. Snyder
American University
Washington College of Law
Washington, DC
(Chair of the Steering Committee)

Steering Committee, 18th International Congress of Comparative Law, Washington, DC, July 2010

David V. Snyder, Professor of Law and Director, Business Law Program, American University Washington College of Law (Chair)

Susan L. Karamanian, Associate Dean for International and Comparative Legal Studies, The George Washington University Law School (Vice Chair)

George A. Bermann, Gellhorn Professor of Law & Jean Monnet Professor of European Union Law, Columbia Law School and President, International Academy of Comparative Law

Karen B. Brown, Donald Phillip Rothschild Research Professor of Law, The George Washington University Law School

Jennifer Dabson, Director, Office of Continuing Legal Education, American University Washington College of Law

James V. Feinerman, James M. Morita Professor of Asian Legal Studies and Co-Director, Georgetown Law – Asia, Georgetown University Law Center

Fernanda G. Nicola, Associate Professor, American University Washington College of Law

Mathias Reimann, Hessel E. Yntema Professor of Law, University of Michigan

Franz Werro, Professor of Law, Georgetown University Law Center and Faculté de droit, University of Fribourg (Switzerland)

Préface

Tous les quatre ans le Congrès de l'Académie Internationale du Droit Comparé (AIDC) rassemble des participants du monde entier pour discuter de thèmes moderns relatifs à toutes les disciplines du droit. Le XVIIIème Congrès a eu lieu à Washington, D.C. en juillet 2010 où les membres ont traité de plus de 30 séances qui s'occupaient des sujets très importants. L'éventail de ces thèmes était très grand: la religion et l'état laïque, le rôle de la pratique dans la formation des juristes, la complexité des sources transnationales, les dommages catastrophiques, les actions collectives, changement climatique et la loi, le gouvernement d'entreprises, la gestation pour autrui, la compétence et la loi applicable en matière de la propriété intellectuelle, l'interdiction de la discrimination à cause de l'âge dans les relations du travail, la protection des investissements étrangers, les partenariats publiques privés, l'exclusion de certains moyens de preuve, la responsabilité pénale des personnes morales, la réglementation des fonds spéculatifs, et l'évasion fiscale. Le Congrès s'est tenu sous les auspices de l'AIDC et la Société Américaine de Droit Comparé (SADC) et était subventionné par les facultés de droit American University Washington College of Law, Georgetown University Law Center, and George Washington University Law School.

Les thèmes du congrès sont choisis par l'AIDC, en collaboration avec les organisateurs dont les facultés de droit ci-dessus et les membres de SADC faisaient partis. Les rapporteurs généraux et nationaux étaient sélectionnés. Tous les rapports étaient accessibles sur le site internet du congrès. La plupart des rapports sont publiés en volumes dits volumes verticaux de rapports – le rapport général et les rapports nationaux sur un thème particulier. La publication de tous les rapports généraux dans un seul volume donne une ressource inestimable.

Nous remercions les facultés de droit accueillants, l'AIDC et le SADC qui sont nos principaux soutiens financiers. Nous remercions aussi de tous leurs efforts les membres du comité d'accueil, surtout Madame Jennifer Dabson, le chef du Continuing Legal Education à l'American University Washington College of Law. Prof. Dr. J.H.M. van Erp, membre du comité accueillant du XVIIème Congrès et le Président de l'Association néerlandaise de droit comparé nous a beaucoup aidé et nous le remercions infiniment. Finalement, remerciements profonds aux dirigeants de l'AIDC, surtout le Secrétaire-Général, Prof. Dr. Dr. h.c. Jürgen Basedow, le Président, Prof. George Bermann, et le Député Secrétaire-Général, Dr. Katrin Deckert.

Professor Karen B. Brown
George Washington University Law School
Washington, DC
(Member of the Steering Committee)

Professor David V. Snyder
American University
Washington College of Law
Washington, DC
(Chair of the Steering Committee)

Contents

Religion and the Secular State[1]

1

Javier Martínez-Torrón and W. Cole Durham, Jr.

1.1 Introduction

Every state adopts some posture toward the religious life existing among its citizens. While some states continue to maintain a particular religious (i.e., non-secular) orientation, most have adopted some type of secular system. Among secular states, there are a range of possible positions with respect to secularity, ranging from regimes with a very high commitment to secularism to more accommodationist regimes to regimes that remain committed to neutrality of the state but allow high levels of cooperation with religions.[2] Not surprisingly, comparative examination of the secularity of contemporary states yields significant insights into the nature of pluralism, the role of religion in modern society, the relationship between religion and democracy, and more generally, into fundamental questions about the relationship of religion and the state.

To impose manageable limits on the general topic, the National Reporters were requested to focus on a number of recurring tension points in the relationship of religion and the state: (1) the general social context; (2) the constitutional and legal setting; (3) religious autonomy (and autonomy of the state from religion); (4) legal regulation of religion as a social phenomenon; (5) state financial support for religion; (6) civil effects of religious acts; (7) religion and education; (8) religious symbols in public places; and (9) tensions involving freedom of expression and offenses against religion.[3] The aim has been to obtain a picture of the solutions provided by different countries to the overarching problem of how the secular state deals with religion or belief in a way that preserves the reciprocal autonomy of state and religious structures and guarantees the fundamental human right involved.

It is as difficult to define what is secular as it is to define what is religious.[4] The terms describe adjacent but opposite areas of social space, each being the negation of the other, and yet each being intertwined with the other in vital ways. In what follows, our aim is to provide perspective on the wealth of ways that modern states interact with religion. Comparative analysis identifies a range of types of secular states, and recognizes that the idea of the secular state is a flexible one

[1] I.B., La religion et l'état laïque. The current essay is a shortened version of the original General Report, which is available at http://www.iclrs.org/index.php?blurb_id=975&page_id=3. The full version contains more detailed footnoting to the various country reports that could not be included here.

[2] For more extensive analysis of types of religion-state configurations, see W. Cole Durham Jr. and Brett G. Scharffs, *Religion and the Law: National, International and Comparative Perspectives* (Austin/Boston/Chicago/New York/Netherlands: Wolters Kluwer Law and Business, 2010), 114–122.

[3] The discussion of the sixth of these topics (civil effects of religious acts) has been dropped from the current version of this General Report, but is available in the full version as indicated in note 1 above.

[4] See W. Cole Durham, Jr. and Elizabeth A. Sewell, "Definition of Religion," in James A. Serritella et al. (eds.), *Religious Organizations in the United States: A Study of Legal Identity, Religious Freedom and the Law* (Durham: Carolina Academic Press, 2006).

J. Martínez-Torrón
Department of Law and Religion, Complutense University School of Law, Madrid, Spain
e-mail: jmtorron@der.ucm.es

W.C. Durham, Jr. (✉)
J. Reuben Clark Law School, Brigham Young University, Provo, UT, USA
e-mail: durhamc@lawgate.byu.edu

K.B. Brown and D.V. Snyder (eds.), *General Reports of the XVIIIth Congress of the International Academy of Comparative Law/Rapports Généraux du XVIIIème Congrès de l'Académie Internationale de Droit Comparé*, DOI 10.1007/978-94-007-2354-2_1, © Springer Science+Business Media B.V. 2012

that is capable of accommodating the ever-increasing pluralism that is the hallmark of modern life.

As the Canadian Report suggests, there are "four key principles constituting any model of secularism..."[5] These are "the moral equality of persons; freedom of conscience and religion; State neutrality towards religion; and the separation of Church and State."[6] It is clear, however, that these features can be blended in many ways. The nature of the secular state can vary considerably, depending on which of these elements is given most prominence and how each is interpreted.

As a general matter we discern two broad patterns. The first can be described as secularism, in which secularization is sought as an end itself. Secularism in this sense is an ideology or system of belief. In its harshest forms, it goes to the extreme of persecuting and repressing religion, as was all too often the case when communism was in power in former socialist bloc countries. More typically it takes the form of what the Canadian report refers to as a "'strict' or 'rigid' conception of secularism [that] would accord more importance to the principle of neutrality than to freedom of conscience, attempting to relegate the practice of religion to the private and communal sphere, leaving the public sphere free from any expression of religion."[7]

The alternative approach, which we refer to as "secularity," is a more flexible or open arrangement that places greater emphasis on protecting freedom of conscience.[8] Secularity favors substantive over formal conceptions of equality and neutrality, taking claims of conscience seriously as grounds for accommodating religiously-motivated difference. Separation in this model is clearly recognized as an institutional means for facilitating protection of freedom of religion or belief, rather than as an ideal endstate in itself. The secular state is understood as a framework for accommodating pluralism, including individuals and groups with profoundly differing belief systems who are nonetheless willing to live together in a shared social order.

The question running through this General Report and through many of the National Reports is which of these two archetypes—secularism or secularity—best describes particular legal systems and whether one or the other of these better describes broader patterns of historical convergence across legal systems. There is a tendency to see French *laïcité* and its spin-offs in Turkey and some former French colonies as an example of the former, and the approach in many common law jurisdictions (U.S., U.K., Australia, New Zealand, etc.) as an example of the latter. It is important in reflecting on this question, however, to remember that no system is static. Even confessional states cannot escape internal and international dialogue concerning optimal ways to configure the relationship between religion and the state. The features exhibited by specific legal systems at particular moments in their history typically reflect a political equilibrium that takes into account a variety of historical, sociological, and philosophical factors, to say nothing of current political debates and shifts in political power. Thus, it is better to think of particular systems (even those that would normally be thought of as confessional or religiously aligned states) not so much as instances of particular configurations of state and religion, but as living systems tending toward or away from other possible models. For modern secular states, the question is whether they tend more toward secularism or more toward secularity.

1.2 The Global Social Setting

The individual National Reports provide a wealth of data about the religious demography of their respective countries which provides the context for understanding the nature of their particular religion-state systems. It is not possible to replicate that information in any detail here. However, it is possible to note a number of significant global trends and patterns.

The first point is that religion is here to stay. Even staunch advocates of the secularization thesis have conceded in light of the data that religion is not withering away. Second, the trend is toward greater religious pluralization virtually everywhere. At the global level, no religion has a majority position; all are minorities. Even in countries that at one point had relative religious homogeneity, the percentage of adherents to the dominant religion is declining. Third, while pluralization is increasing, traditional religions continue to hold a very significant place in many soci-

[5] Canada II.

[6] *Id.*

[7] *Id.*

[8] *Id.*

eties. They typically have deep roots, and have generally played a significant role in molding a country's history and shaping and preserving national identity. Because of their centrality in culture, traditional religions can easily become a significant factor in nation building. More generally, politicians often cater to religious groups to garner support. Despite their dominant position, however, prevailing religions often feel threatened and motivated to find ways to strengthen their position in society. As a result, reactions to issues of religious rights are often colored by identity politics, fear of immigrants, and security concerns.

A fourth point has to do with the status of religious freedom protection around the world. Most countries have affirmed their commitment to freedom of religion or belief, either by ratifying the applicable international instruments, or by including appropriate provisions in their constitutions, or (in most cases) both. However, there are substantial deviations in the extent to which these norms are respected in practice. In the last few years, valuable empirical work has begun to emerge that assesses implementation of religious liberty norms worldwide.[9] This research indicates that while 48% of 198 countries and territories have low restrictions on religion, 20% have moderate restrictions, and 32% have high or very high restrictions. Since some of the most populous countries on earth were among those with the highest restrictions, it turns out that only 15% of global population lives in countries with low levels of restrictions; 16% lives in countries with moderate levels of restriction, and 70% lives in countries with high or very high levels of restrictions.

The research distinguishes between governmental restrictions and social restrictions (e.g., hostile acts by individuals) on religion. Both India and China are countries listed as having very high restrictions on religion. Interestingly, however, China has high governmental restrictions but its level of social restrictions is not much higher than that in the United States, Japan or Italy. On the other hand, India has substantially lower levels of government restrictions (moderate to high—somewhat higher than France and Mexico, but lower than Turkey and Russia), yet has very high levels of social restrictions.

Suffice it to say that despite wide and near universal lip service to the ideal of religious freedom, most people on earth live in countries where high or very high levels of restriction are in place. This is a concern not only because the statistics suggest systematic shortfalls in achieving fundamental human rights protection but also because related empirical work shows that there is very strong statistical data showing that low levels of governmental and social restrictions on religion are correlated with and appear to be causal factors accounting for the presence of numerous other social goods. For example, low levels of restrictions on religion are correlated with high levels of protection of other human rights, with higher per capita income (for men and women), better health and education, lower degrees of conflict in society, higher literacy rates, and so forth.[10] Religious freedom correlates with greater religious engagement, which in turn generates social capital that benefits society in many ways. In contrast, and perhaps somewhat surprisingly, high levels of governmental restriction are not only correlated with but appear to be a causal factor of heightened religious violence in society.[11] In short, there appears to be significant empirical evidence that a secular state can best advance a wide variety of secular objectives by protecting the fundamental right to freedom of religion or belief. Secularism is more likely to impose restraints on religion than secularity; to that extent secularity may prove to be more socially beneficial.

1.3 Constitutional and Legal Context

1.3.1 Constitutional Overview

By the time that international human rights were being codified in the aftermath of World War II, freedom of religion or belief emerged as an axiomatic feature of the international human rights regime, memorialized in Article 18 of the Universal Declaration of Human

[9] See, e.g., Pew Forum on Religion and Public Life, Global Restrictions on Religion (17 December 2010), available at http://pewforum.org/Government/Global-Restrictions-on-Religion.aspx; Brian J. Grim and Roger Finke, *The Price of Freedom Denied: Religious Persecution and Conflict in the Twenty-First Century* (Cambridge: Cambridge University Press, 2011).

[10] Grim and Finke, *supra* note 9, at 205–206.

[11] *Id.* at 202–222.

Rights,[12] Article 18 of the International Covenant on Civil and Political Rights (ICCPR),[13] in the 1981 United Nations Declaration on the Elimination of All Forms of Intolerance and of Discrimination Based on Religion or Belief,[14] and in a variety of other international instruments.[15]

Most modern constitutions have provisions affirming the right to freedom of religion or belief. This right is recognized in the overwhelming majority of the world's constitutions, including virtually every European constitution and the constitution of every independent country in the Western Hemisphere. All the national reports we received addressed countries with religious freedom provisions. While there are of course disputes about the universality of human rights norms, freedom of religion or belief has come to be recognized by most nations of the world (and by most religions) as a principle that has universal validity.

1.3.2 Comparative Perspectives: The Religion-State Identification Continuum

To grasp the full range of possible religion-state configurations, it is useful to think of them being spread out along a continuum stretching from positive identification of the state with religion (e.g., theocracies, established churches) through a posture of state neutrality and extending to negative identification (e.g., state persecution or banning of religion). It turns out that if this continuum is curved, with the two endpoints at one end and the middle at the other, as in the accompanying diagram, there is a rough correlation between the position on the identification continuum with the degree of religious freedom experience in the relevant country.[16]

The various positions along this "loop" need to be understood as Weberian ideal types; no state structure corresponds exactly with any of the described positions. Indeed, it is probably best to think of the various positions along the loop as contested equilibrium points reached in different societies at different times. In this sense, the loop structure can be used to map not only the current positions of various states, but also the range of discourse arguing for alternative positions at a given time in a particular country. Most of the reporting countries are positioned toward the "non-identification" middle position on the loop, but even so, the various configurations vary widely. The loop structure provides a way of suggesting how the various systems covered by the reports compare with each other.

Moving along the loop, a number of the reporting countries have "established religions," though most at this point fit comfortably in the "tolerant" rather than "monopoly" mode. The United Kingdom provides the interesting example of a country with two established churches: the Church of Scotland and the Church of England.[17] Sweden, which had long had an established church, decided at the initiative of the church to disestablish, effective 1 January 2000. In some countries, what was once an established church has evolved into a people's church (folk church). For example, in Finland, the Evangelical Lutheran Church is now an institution separate from the state, with its own legal status. The evolution of major churches toward folk churches in this sense can be seen in a number of countries. Armenia, for example, may follow this model. The constitution clearly separates religion from the state, but there is a powerful ethnic identification with the Armenian Apostolic Church, and the majority of Armenians (ironically including even atheists) are steadfast supporters of the Church. Serbian identification with the Orthodox Church may be another example.

The category of "religious status systems" was developed to address systems that recognize multiple religious legal systems, typically in matters of family and personal law. The impulse behind such systems is tolerant, in that they aim at respecting the differing

[12] G.A. Res. 217 (A(III), 10 December 1948, U.N. Doc. A/810, at 71 (1948)).

[13] G.A. Res. 2200A, U.N. GAOR, 21st Sess., Supp. no. 16, at 52, 55, U.N. Doc A/6316 (1966), 999 U.N.T.S. 171 (1976) (Art. 18).

[14] Adopted 18 January 1982, G.A. Res 55, 36 U.N. GAOR Supp. (No. 51), U.N. Doc. A/RES/36/55 (1982).

[15] *American Declaration of the Rights and Duties of Man*, art. III, O.A.S.res. XXX, Adopted by the Ninth International Conference of American States, Bogota (1948): *Novena Conferencia Internacional Americana, 6 Actas y Documentos* (1953), 297–302.

[16] The accompanying diagram is taken from Durham and Scharffs, *supra* note 2, at 117. See discussion there for a fuller analysis of the varying religion-state configurations that it represents.

[17] United Kingdom III. The UK Reporter notes that "[t]e Welsh Church Act 1914 disestablished the Church of England in Wales." For a more detailed analysis of the current state of establishment in the UK, see Anthony Bradney, *Law and Faith in a Skeptical Age* (London: Routledge, 2009), Chapter 3.

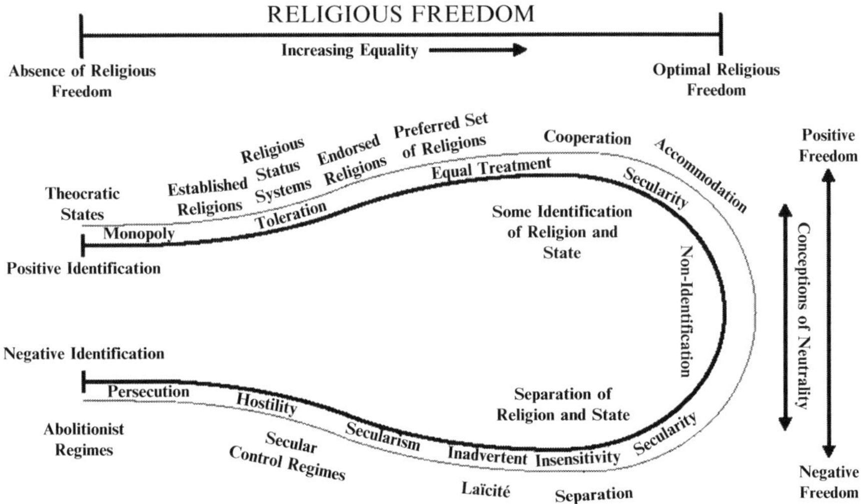

religious norms of different communities. However, they often lead to complications in fact. Thus, in Israel, different laws govern marriage of Jews, Muslims, Druze, and others. But if a Jewish couple is not sufficiently orthodox, they may not be able to be granted a Jewish marriage. In India, a provision of the constitution as originally adopted following partition called for "endeavors . . . [to] secure for the citizens a uniform civil code throughout the territory of India."[18] In fact, however, a dual system of marriage laws remains "under which individuals can make a choice between the secular and the religious matrimonial laws."[19]

The Canadian system flirted with allowing a version of the religious status system approach to operate through Canada's mediation and arbitration system. Specifically, the Ontario government considered a proposal that would allow creation of a "Shari'a Court" to operate on consent of the parties using arbitration provisions of Ontario's laws. A government study of the proposal "concluded that Ontario should allow individuals to choose religious arbitration as a reflection of Canada's multicultural society as long as minimal safeguards, concerning such things as the legitimacy of consent and judicial review procedures, were put into place."[20] Ultimately, the Ontario government rejected the proposal, and amended the province's arbitration act to require that all family arbitrations . . . be conducted exclusively in accordance with Ontario or Canadian law.[21] The effect of the ruling was not to preclude settling "family matters according to religious norms, or before religious authority," but merely to hold that such actions "will not be automatically legally binding or enforceable before a state court of law."[22]

"Endorsed religions" are often a first step away from an official or established church. Instead of declaring that there is an official religion in the state, a constitution acknowledges the special role of a particular religion, but then goes on to affirm the religious freedom of other groups. Sometimes the recognition of religion is placed in a preamble; other times it is located in the body of a constitution. This pattern is evident in many predominantly Roman Catholic or Eastern Orthodox countries.

The "preferred religions" model refers to countries that do not establish or endorse any particular religion, but single out one or a number of religions for favored treatment or recognition. This is sometimes done by distinguishing traditional religions and giving them special status or privilege. Alternatively, this may be done by establishing "multi-tier" regimes that give different groups varying levels of recognition. In theory, the distinctions should be based on objective factors, but typically the effect is to favor traditional groups. Sometimes the distinctions are evident at the level of the constitution; in other systems the distinctions are adopted as part of legislation dealing with religious matters.

[18] India VIII.

[19] *Id.*

[20] Canada VIIB.

[21] *Id.*

[22] *Id.*

Probably the most common arrangement among the national reports is the cooperation model. Most European systems are evolving in this direction. Even separationist France in fact provides significant levels of cooperation in supporting religious schools and in helping with the maintenance of pre-1905 religious buildings. India's "positive conception of equal treatment" and secularism without a wall of separation also appears to fit into this model. Under this model, the state maintains a posture of neutrality toward religion, but no particular religions are singled out for benefits or unfavorable treatment and the state has friendly and cooperative relations with religious communities. Most significantly, this type of religion-state configuration is not averse to state funding of religious activities. In part this grows out of a belief that freedom of religion is not only a defensive right against state interference, but a positive right to state action enabling exercise of religious freedom.

The fundamental point is that cooperation systems respect fundamental baselines of protecting individual religious freedom for all, and the fundamental commitment to neutrality and equality in religious affairs, but understanding these notions in a way that allows the state flexibility to cooperate in a variety of ways with religious communities. The willingness to cooperate with religion distinguishes this approach from secularism. Its willingness to help the support of a variety of communities inclines it toward secularity.

Accommodationist systems are similar in many ways to cooperationist systems, except that they impose tighter constraints on direct funding of religious activity. In the financial area, they are comfortable with tax exemption schemes, because these reflect private choice in the allocation of resources. An accommodationist tends to be more comfortable than a strict separationist with religion as part of national culture. There is thus more willingness to accommodate religious symbols in public settings, to allow tax, dietary, holiday, Sabbath and other kinds of religion-based exemptions and so forth.

Moving further around the "loop," one encounters several constitutional approaches that take a more strictly secular approach to religion-state relations. Many of the states covered by national reports specifically declare themselves to be secular or *laic* in their constitutions. Some prohibit the creation, recognition or establishment of any religion. Others mandate the "separation" of religion and the state. Still others declare the state to be secular, or in French, *laïque*. Stress on formal versions of neutrality and equality can lead to similar results. Not surprisingly, some constitutions include two or more of these types of provisions. For example, Article 14 of the Constitution of the Russian Federation reads as follows: "The Russian Federation is a secular state. No religion may be established as a state or obligatory one. Religious associations shall be separated from the State and shall be equal before the law." Particularly when one recalls that Article 28 of the Russian Constitution also includes a provision on freedom of conscience, it seems clear that the Russian constitution has covered all the secular bases. The contrast between the full range of secularist constitutional provisions in Russia on the one hand and the various forms of state cooperation and accommodation on the other is a reminder of how difficult it is in general to assess the actual nature of religion-state relations on the basis of constitutional provisions alone.

One of the major models of the secular state is that suggested by the French experience, and the French notion of laïcité. As is the case with other positions on the identification continuum, this is really better thought of as a range of positions, signified by various debates going on in French society, and within a number of other countries where the role of religion in the public sphere is an issue (e.g., secular Turkey). There are no doubt versions of *laïcité* that are compatible with the more open notion of secularity. For example, the Italian Constitution declares its own form of laicism, in which the state guarantees safeguards for religious freedom. Further, although churches are seen as separate from the state sphere in Italy, the state enters pacts with the Catholic Church and agreements with other denominations to promote coordination.

This version of *laïcité* is linked with the secular side of the Enlightenment and with the experience of the French Revolution as a revolt against the *ancien régime*, including the religious *ancien régime*. It is often as much about freedom *from* religion as it is about freedom *of* religion. It sees intolerance as a peculiar vice of religion, not recognizing that secularism itself can be as guilty of intolerance as its religious counterparts. At a minimum, it is about confining religion to the private sphere, where it poses no threat to dominance in politics or to capture of state institutions. Any return of religion to public space is viewed as threatening the Enlightenment project as a whole.

It is a short step from extreme forms of secularism/*laïcité* to regimes that have more affirmatively hostile religion-state relationships. What starts as neutrality and formal equality hardens into a view of law that sees itself as compromised if relevant religious differences are taken into account. Allowing flexibility for believers to act according to conscience comes to be viewed as a form of discrimination in favor of religion. State action that intentionally discriminates against religion continues to be seen as wrongful (violating neutrality and equality values), but "neutral and general laws" that have incidental effects imposing heavy burdens on believers are taken to be a normal feature of life in democracy. Equal treatment thus passes over into unintentional disadvantaging. Legislators become better at crafting neutral-seeming laws, and in the end, constraints against overt hostility disappear.

"Secular control regimes" constitute a secular counterpart to established religions. Two versions can be imagined. In the first, secular rulers exploit religion for political gain. Examples would include political leaders catering to religious groups in an effort to contribute to nation building, or simply to attract political support. The second type of secular control regime emphasizes freedom from religion, either for ideological reasons, or to prevent religious communities from becoming a competing source of legitimacy within society. Stalin's anti-religious terror was prompted both by ideological concerns (anti-religious Marxism) and by fears of counterrevolutionary forces in society. Contemporary China would constitute another example.

Besides helping to map different types of relationships between religion and the state (including secular states), the schematization described above helps to bring out several other features of religion-state relations. First, there are a range of different types of relationship which correlate with high degrees of religious freedom. Indeed, what the static diagram cannot make clear is that in fact, different points along the identity continuum may be optimal in different social settings. For example, in countries where religious communities have experienced decades of persecution, as was the case in countries that lived under Soviet hegemony, a cooperation model might be not only optimal but necessary for religious institutions to be revitalized. On the other hand, where religious institutions have been strong and controlling, a position such as French *laïcité* may be vital to carve out space for broader freedom of religion. A significant "margin of appreciation" is necessary not only because different configurations will have different practical effects; they may also have different social meanings.

Second, while freedom and equality norms can sometimes be in tension with each other, for the most part, increasing protection of equality in religion-state relations and increasing freedom go together.

Third, in the optimal "middle range" of the continuum, differing conceptions of freedom may be at work behind different religion-state configurations. Cooperationist regimes (and cooperationist models of the secular state) reflect positive conceptions of freedom, in that they assume that the state should help actualize the conditions of freedom. Separationist regimes (and separationist conceptions of the secular state), by contrast, assume a negative conception of freedom according to which religious freedom is maximized by minimizing state intervention in the religious sphere (and religious intervention in the public sphere).

Fourth, in a similar vein, the different types of configurations reflect different assumptions about what state neutrality means. One model of neutrality is state inaction. A state that is totally separate and gives no aid to religion could be seen as being neutral among all religions. A second model is neutrality as impartiality (e.g., the impartiality of an unbiased umpire). This model calls for the state to act in formally neutral and religion blind ways. This corresponds to a strict version of separation that does not allow religious factors to be taken into account in assessing legal policies and state implementation schemes. A third model views the state a the monitor of an open forum. This is like the model of neutrality as impartiality, except that it allows imposition of time, place and manner restrictions that set the boundaries within which religious debate and competition occur, but does not allow the state to be involved in shaping the substance of religious value systems. The first three models of neutrality correspond to differing versions of separationist or strictly secular states. A fourth model calls for substantive equal treatment and corresponds to accommodations positions that allow conscientious beliefs to be taken into account in shaping and interpreting public policies. A fifth model is a "second generation rights version" of the fourth, which views affirmative actualization of substantive rights as an affirmative or positive obligation of the state, and thus corresponds to the cooperationist position.

1.3.3 Other Constitutional Issues Involving Religion

An number of constitutional issues that govern religion-state relations in various details fit into this larger framework, and are affected by where a regime seeks to position itself along the identification continuum. Thus, as indicated earlier, most countries have ratified the key international instruments governing freedom of religion or belief. Many have constitutional provisions indicating that international treaties override ordinary legislation. But the international instruments tend to be read in ways that are consonant with the applicable type of religion-state system. One of the issues that has been explicit in international instruments since the 1960s is that the right to freedom of religion or belief protects not only religious believers, but atheists, humanists and other forms of conscientious secular beliefs. Not surprisingly these notions are taken more seriously among the more laicist states, including former communist states that have particularly high numbers of non-believers.

The scope of permissible limitations on freedom of religion also tends to vary depending on the type of religion-state configuration. Most identify the protection of public safety, order, health, morals, or the fundamental rights and freedoms of others as legitimating grounds for imposing limitations on manifestations of religion. Some, but not all, of these are clear that in order to override religious freedom claims, it must be possible to demonstrate that even limitations based on these legitimating grounds must be "necessary" in the sense of being narrowly tailored to the end being pursued and proportionate to the seriousness of the right being limited, as required by the international instruments.

Most constitutions have provisions prohibiting discrimination based on religion. In some states this takes the form of a broad provision stating that all citizens are equal before the law, which the state then interprets to protect against all forms of discrimination, including discrimination which is religiously based.

1.3.4 The Legal Setting

In addition to constitutional provisions, virtually all states have laws designed to implement general commitments to religious freedom. These include laws that specify how religious communities can acquire legal entity status, through registration, incorporation, or other legal means. One of the significant developments in this area over the past decade has been the emergence of a series of cases, most notably in the European Court of Human Rights, affirming the right to acquire entity status if a religious community so desires, and the right to operate without such status if it does not. This right embraces the right for a group to acquire legal personality authorizing it to carry out the full range of religious and belief activities.

In general, states that facilitate access to legal entity status are acting in a manner consistent with the ideal of secularity. States that incline toward secular control, either out of continuation of earlier patterns of restriction or because of present desires to control religious groups, comport at best with secularism and more typically with secular control orientations. Generally, cooperation rights—including access to public funding—are keyed not to registration rules governing access to base-level legal entity status but to some higher-level qualifications. Thus, cooperation regimes are generally fairly open to flexible registration rules, and in that sense, are consistent with secularity. Pressure for tightened control frequently increases as one moves toward preferred, endorsed and established religions—here not because of secularism, but because of increased religious control authorized by the religion-state regime.

Where cooperation is allowed, the need to manage the flow of funds and other aspects of cooperation often leads to the emergence of a multi-tiered religion state system. At the base level of the structure is a registration system that allows religious communities to receive basic legal entity status, and in some cases qualification for indirect support through tax exemptions and the deductibility of contributions. A number of states, such as Austria and Romania, have an intermediate status for smaller religious communities that gives them some heightened status vis-à-vis ordinary non-profit organizations, but not the benefits of full financial and other benefits of the highest level of recommendation. In a number of countries, particularly those with a significant Catholic population, there is a pattern of bilateral agreements between the state and various religious communities. For the Catholic Church, these take the form of concordats; for others they are agreements designed to be similar in principle to the Catholic Concordats, but without the full attributes of transnational agreements with another sovereign state. The Italian national report characterizes Italy's arrangement as a four tier system where non-recognized associations receive no benefits but have complete freedom, recognized churches receive tax benefits, denominations with agreements have additional privileges, and the Catholic Church has special status at the highest tier. Spain has developed a variation on the agreement system whereby for religions other than Roman Catholicism, agreements are entered into not with a single denomination, but with a federation of denominations. Depending on the nature of the cooperation that is being managed, the number of "tiers" in any national structure may vary. In Serbia there is only a two-tier system which differentiates between recognized and unrecognized churches. Traditional churches are recognized and given religious instruction rights.

The difficulties with the multi-tiered systems are three-fold. While the intention behind the agreement systems is good (the aim is to equalize denominations by bringing them up to the level of the Roman Catholic Church), the implementation typically falls short of the aim. In the first place, full equalization with the Catholic Church is not possible, because no other Church controls its own country, enabling it to enter into formal treaties with other states. Even leaving that aside, there is a tendency, particularly where the Catholic Church is overwhelmingly dominant, for the Catholic Church to receive more extensive benefits than other groups. Second, there is a flaw in the structure of the agreement system that is only partially rectified by Spain's federation model. Once the state has entered into a certain number of agreements, it is very difficult for smaller groups not yet covered to mobilize the political will with the state to form further agreements. Third, while the differential benefits associated with the various tiers are supposedly based on objective factors, there is a substantial risk that some level of impermissible religion-based discrimination may occur in administering these systems.

1.4 Religious Autonomy

International human rights instruments and many constitutions generally take individual freedom of religion or belief as the starting point. But in most traditions, religion is very much a communal matter, involving joint practices, shared belief, a common ritual life, and a shared common life. With that in mind, it is particularly important that the individual right includes the "freedom, either individually or in *community* with others and in *public* or private, to manifest his religion or belief . . . ."[23] The freedom of individual belief cannot be fully realized without the prior freedom of communal belief. To the extent belief systems are subjected to coercion or manipulation from external sources, they are not fully and authentically themselves. It is for this reason that protection of the religious autonomy or independence of the religious community is such a vital element of freedom of religion or belief.[24] Whether conceptualized as deriving from individual freedom, or being grounded directly in the rights of the community, freedom of religion without institutional autonomy cannot be full religious freedom.

Most of the national reports indicate strong support for the idea of religious or institutional autonomy. What is at issue here is not the freedom of individual or personal autonomy, but "the right of religious communities (hierarchical, connectional, congregational, etc.) to decide upon and administer their own internal religious affairs without interference by the institutions of government."[25] A variety of different metaphors are used to describe the notion. Some of the reports refer to implementation of a model of "separate spheres" that is linked to notions of lack of state competence in religious matters and to state neutrality. The German national report speaks in a similar vein of maintaining equidistance of the state from various religious communities, and of withdrawing from religious issues. Others focus on a "prohibited intervention" model, which underscores the freedom of the religious community.

In some constitutions, the right to religious autonomy is addressed directly. In others, constitutional provisions address only individual rights, but collective rights to autonomy and self-determination are addressed at the level of civil codes or other statutes. Still others address the issue primarily in case law or in agreements with major denominations. In any event,

[23] International Covenant on Civil and Political Rights, art. 18(1) (emphasis added).

[24] For an extensive collection of comparative studies of this theme, see Gerhard Robbers (ed.), *Church Autonomy: A Comparative Survey* (Frankfurt: Peter Lang, 2002).

[25] Mark E. Chopko, "Constitutional Protection for Church Autonomy: A Practitioner's View," in Robbers, *supra* note 24, at 96.

religious autonomy entails broad protection for religious communities to govern themselves. This includes both the right to specify doctrine (which includes beliefs about structuring of the religious community) and the right to self-determination and self-management in internal affairs. Prominent among the self-determination rights are rights to autonomy in religious ritual practice, the right to establish places of worship, the ability to establish the group's own organization and hierarchy, the right to create other legal persons pursuant to statute or canon law, the right to select, manage and terminate personnel, the right to communicate with religious personnel and the faithful, including the right to confidential communications; the right to establish educational and charitable organizations; the right to receive, produce and distribute information through the media; the right to own and sell property; the right to solicit and expend funds; and so forth.

A more sensitive and disputed area has to do with the implication of religious autonomy rights for employment disputes involving religious personnel. A set of cases on this topic was pending before the European Court of Human Rights at the time this Report was written. The general rule in this area is that religious communities have broad discretion in determining the terms on which they hire, retain, and terminate religious personnel. Religious employers are typically exempted from rules that proscribe discrimination on the basis of religion for the same reason that other expressive organizations (e.g., political parties, advocacy groups, and the like) are not required to hire individuals with opposed views. These rules are particularly clear when a religious body itself is hiring someone who fulfills a pastoral or teaching type role. The question gets somewhat more difficult when the employer is a religiously affiliated entity (a school, a broadcasting station, a newspaper, a hospital, a hostel or housing for the elderly, etc.) or where the employee has a less clearly religious role (a pastor or other minister, a religion teacher, a history teacher, a math teacher, a secretary to a religious leader, a news broadcaster, an individual who makes religious clothing, a truck driver at the warehouse of a religious charity, a janitor at a church-owned gymnasium).

The question is how strong religious autonomy protections are in such situations. From a secular perspective, it is all too easy to say that normal anti-discrimination rules should apply unless both the employer and the employee are engaged in religious conduct that makes religious qualifications vital to the job. But that is far too simple, and fails to understand what a serious issue this is for a religious community. From the religious perspective, it may well be that the religious status of all the employees may be extremely significant. The religious employer cannot know in advance which of its employees will have the type of spiritual impact it hopes to foster. It can be very concerned about unspoken messages that are communicated by someone who is not loyal to the religious institution. Non-adherents of the faith may substantially alter the ambience of the workplace. Misconduct by such personnel may disrupt trust relations in the workplace, and could affect the religious community's sense of whether the individual is qualified or worthy to carry out a particular task. It is for that reason that appropriate exemptions for religious employers are appearing in various jurisdictions.

Even assuming that a particular case involves a dispute between a type of employer and a type of employee whose relationship would be appropriately covered by religious autonomy protections, are there other constraints that should set limits on the scope of religious autonomy rights? A leading U.S. case involved the suspension and ultimate defrocking of the bishop who had led the Serbian Orthodox Church in the United States and Canada for many years.[26] The claim was that the leaders of the Serbian Orthodox Church who had taken this action had not followed their own rules for such cases and had acted arbitrarily. Earlier dicta had suggested that while in general, courts are required to defer to hierarchical authority in resolving religious disputes, they might review arbitrary action by such tribunals. The U.S. Supreme Court rejected this reasoning on the ground that "it is the essence of religious faith that ecclesiastical decisions are reached and are to be accepted as matters of faith whether or not rational or measurable. Constitutional concepts of due process, involving secular notions of 'fundamental fairness' or impermissible objectives, are therefore hardly relevant to such matters of ecclesiastical cognizance."[27] The national report from Netherlands, in contrast, suggests that while religious communities should be given broad autonomy in the employment dispute context, "this does not mean that churches can act at will. Fairness, acting in good faith, [and] following fair

[26] Serbian Eastern Orthodox Diocese v. Milivojevich, 426 U.S. 696 (1976).

[27] *Id.* at 714–715.

procedure[s] are elements that courts can and will use in reviewing church decisions."

1.5 Legal Regulation of Religion as a Social Phenomenon

Religious communities and their individual members live in modern societies that are governed by laws. Because laws have generally developed against the background of the local culture, often including religious culture, there are many ways in which religious norms and legal norms automatically align.[28] Obvious examples include the calendar, religious holidays, days of rest, and so forth. Core criminal law notions such as murder, theft, kidnaping, and the like also overlap with religious teachings. But in contemporary pluralistic states, it is not at all uncommon for religious communities to develop beliefs that are in tension with at least some legal norms. The theologian H. Richard Niebuhr, in his classic text, *Christ and Culture*,[29] identified five types of relationships between religious communities and the larger culture. As summarized by Professor Angela Carmella,[30] these range along a continuum from countercultural to acculturated responses.

> [A]t one end, he places those manifestations of religion most separate and distinct from the dominant culture, and at the other end, those manifestations most engaged in, and most similar to, surrounding culture. . . . In between . . . Niebuhr places three other responses. One, which Niebuhr calls the dualist response, considers faith to be in tension with culture, yet accepts that life is lived in and through culture, not separate from it; another, the synthesis response, places faith above culture, and acknowledges that although the culture may have virtues, faith inspires its adherents to go beyond them toward perfection; finally, the conversionist response sees faith transforming culture through love.[31]

Because many of the classic cases involving freedom of religion or belief are asserted by countercultural groups, the importance of freedom of religion for other types of interaction with culture is often overlooked. Professor Carmella gives the example of a counseling center affiliated with a Protestant seminary. All of the counselors were theologically trained and were members of the clergy. The center applied for a building permit to construct offices in a local church. Under the applicable law, religious uses were exempt from the land use law, so the counselors assumed they would have no trouble obtaining the building permit. In fact, the zoning board denied the permit on the ground that the counseling center was not a religious activity.[32] Had the center been seeking a building permit for pastoral counseling, the exemption probably would have applied. But because the center was acculturated, it no longer looked like it deserved or needed special freedom of religion protection. Similar issues can arise for each of the various types of religious relationship to culture.

Further complexity emanates from the vast set of legal norms that religious communities are expected to obey in modern administrative and regulatory states. These norms may target specific religious groups, either to grant certain privileges or to discriminate against them. More typically, in systems operating in good faith, legal or regulatory norms may be adopted that happen to run counter to specific beliefs of the community. For example, legislators desiring to encourage humane treatment of animals may publish regulations concerning animal slaughter which make preparation of kosher or halal food for Jews and Muslims illegal.

The national reports grapple with these complexities, and specify different ways that states regulate religious phenomena. It is not possible in this general report to address this range of phenomena in detail. In part, analysis of the religion-state identification continuum above goes a considerable distance toward providing comparative analysis of the types of state approaches to regulating religious phenomena that exist. In this section, we focus on a different set of issues: what are the major approaches that states take toward determining whether laws, regulations and other state actions that affect religion are permissible. Of course, some states and officials operate in lawless, arbitrary and discriminatory ways that are inconsistent with the rule of law (and typically with the

[28] See Netherlands VII (noting that "[t]he law in general has developed against the background of a Western culture based on a morality influenced by Christianity.") The same point can be made about law with different background cultures. See, e.g., national reports of India, Japan and Sudan.

[29] H. Richard Niebuhr, *Christ and Culture* (New York: Harper & Brothers, 1951).

[30] Angela C. Carmella, "A Theological Critique of Free Exercise Jurisprudence," *George Washington Law Review* 60 (1992): 782–808.

[31] *Id.* at 786–787.

[32] *Id.* at 788–789.

requirements of the constitutions under which they operate). These are problematic cases, but our focus here is on systems that are seeking to operate legally, subject to the rule of law. What deserve attention as a matter of comparative law are the different standards that are applied as a matter of international and constitutional law in determining the breadth or narrowness of religious freedom protections.

The key question in this domain is whether religious freedom protections are sufficiently strong to generate exemptions from ordinary legislation. A number of jurisdictions hold that constitutional protections of the right to freedom of religion or belief require the judiciary to read ordinary legislation so as not to conflict with the constitutional religious freedom norm. This has the effect of creating an exemption for the conscientious claimant. Germany's freedom of religion provisions are read in this way,[33] as are Hungary's.[34] Japan's courts also appear to interpret the Japanese constitution in this manner.[35] This approach typically involves proportionality analysis to determine if the state interests involved are of a kind and with sufficient weight to outweigh the religious freedom claim. Prior to 1990, the United States Supreme Court applied a functionally similar "strict scrutiny" test according to which state action that burdened religion was impermissible unless justified by a compelling state interest that could not be advanced by less restrictive means.[36]

Canada has one of the more sensitive constitutional tests in this area. Under the Canadian test, the government must "prove that, on a balance of probabilities, the infringement is reasonable and can be demonstrably justified in a free and democratic society. To this end, two requirements must be met. First, the legislative objective being pursued must be sufficiently important to warrant limiting a constitutional right. Next, the means chosen by the state authority must be proportional to the objective in question . . . . The first stage of the proportionality analysis consists in determining whether [there is] a rational connection with the objective [of the action] . . . . The second stage of the proportionality analysis is often central to the debate as to whether the infringement of a right protected by the *Canadian Charter* can be justified. The limit, which must minimally impair the right or freedom that has been infringed, need not necessarily be the least intrusive solution."[37] This test seems more precise than the United States' compelling state interest test; it is likely to provide very strong protection for religious freedom. The Canadian report describes a recent case in which a private party was able to invoke a religious freedom claim in order to override a contractual obligation.[38]

At the other end of the spectrum are regimes that hold that any legislation that is formally adopted and complies qualitatively with the rule of law (i.e., is not unduly vague, is not open to arbitrary enforcement, is not retroactive, and so forth) will override religious freedom claims. Australia appears to have this type of system, there being in that country "no general or constitutional exemption from ordinary laws for religions."[39] Sweden also disallows conscientious objection exemptions from military service or contractual clauses.[40] The U.S. Supreme Court moved to a similar position in 1990, in *Employment Division, Department of Human Resources of Oregon v. Smith.*[41] In that case, the Supreme Court jettisoned the standard "compelling state interest" test, and held instead that any neutral law of general applicability sufficed to override free exercise claims.[42]

To be sure, the revised standard was qualified in certain important respects. First, the Court made it clear that "the First Amendment obviously excludes all 'governmental regulation of religious *beliefs* as such.' "[43] In particular, "government may not compel affirmation of religious belief;"[44] it may not "punish the expression of religious doctrines it believes to be false;"[45] and it may not "impose special disabilities on the basis of religious views or religious status."[46] Thus,

[33] Germany VII.

[34] Hungary VIII.

[35] Japan VII.

[36] Sherbert v. Verner, 374 U.S. 398 (1963); Wisconsin v. Yoder, 406 U.S. 205 (1972).

[37] Multani v. Commission Scolaire Marguerite-Bourgeoys and Attorney General of Quebec, 1 S.C.R. 256, 2006 SCC 6 (2006) (Supreme Court of Canada), paras. 42–43, 49–50.

[38] Canada V.A.

[39] Australia VI.

[40] Sweden VII.

[41] 494 U.S. 872 (1990).

[42] *Id.* at 879–81, 884.

[43] *Id.* at 877 (citing *Sherbert,* 374 U.S. at 402).

[44] *Id.* (citing Torcaso v. Watkins, 367 U.S. 488 (1961)).

[45] *Id.* (citing United States v. Ballard, 322 U.S. 78, 86–88 (1944)).

[46] *Id.* (citing McDaniel v. Paty, 435 U.S. 618 (1978); Fowler v. Rhode Island, 345 U.S. 67, 69 (1953)).

the classic bar to state interference with inner beliefs (as opposed to outer conduct) was not abandoned. Second, the Court expressly reaffirmed its line of religious autonomy cases, emphasizing that "government may not . . . lend its power to one or the other side in controversies over religious authority or dogma."[47] Third, the Court indicated that in a number of prior cases involving "hybrid situations," free exercise claims, when coupled with other constitutional protections such as freedom of expression or parental rights, were sufficient to bar application of neutral and general laws. Fourth, the Court did not overrule use of the compelling state interest analysis in unemployment compensation cases following the earlier *Sherbert* precedent, where the loss of employment was not linked to criminal activity. The Court rationalized retention of strict scrutiny analysis in this context because it involved "individualized governmental assessment of the reasons for the relevant conduct,"[48] noting that "where the State has in place a system of individual exemptions, it may not refuse to extend that system to cases of 'religious hardship' without compelling reason."[49] Finally, implicit in the idea of "neutral and general laws" is the notion that non-neutral and non-general laws that intentionally target and discriminate against religious groups or religious activities remain subject to strict scrutiny.[50] In each of these situations, First Amendment protections remained what they had been prior to the *Smith* decision. Despite these exceptions, *Smith* held that in the main, "neutral law[s] of general applicability" would suffice to overrule free exercise claims.

It is important to note, however, that the United States in fact remains closer to being a "strict scrutiny" jurisdiction than the Supreme Court decisions might lead one to believe. First, Congress passed the Religious Freedom Restoration Act of 1993[51] ("RFRA"). This restored the compelling state interest test as a matter of ordinary legislation. While this measure was held unconstitutional as applied to the states in 1997,[52] it has remained intact in the federal setting.[53] Various other pieces of federal legislation have reasserted the compelling state interest test in areas where there is specific federal authority to act.[54] Even more significantly, 25 of the 50 states have expressly retained a heightened scrutiny approach, either by passing a state RFRA, or as a result of judicial interpretations of religious freedom provisions of state constitutions.[55] Moreover, only a handful of states have expressly followed the *Smith* decision. All in all, this means that the United States remains closer to being a country that requires exemptions than might be thought.

Another possible position on the exemption issue is that exemptions may be permissible if granted by the legislative branch. Australia appears to allow this possibility, as does the Czech Republic. Legislative tax exemption schemes are common, as are schemes that exempt ritual slaughter from normal rules applied to slaughter of animals. Still another prominent example is provisions involving conscientious objection to military service. Newer sets of statutory exemptions are emerging with respect to health care, insurance, and discrimination issues.

1.6 State Financial Support for Religion

State financial support of religion is one of the most significant issues when examining the relations between religion and the secular state. Assuming that in Western societies there is a dividing line between

[47] *Id.* (citing Presbyterian Church in U.S. v. Mary Elizabeth Blue Hull Memorial Presbyterian Church, 39U.S. 440, 445–452 (1969); Kedroff v. St. Nicholas Cathedral, 344 U.S. 94, 95–119 (1952); Serbian Eastern Orthodox Diocese v. Milivojevich, 426 U.S. 696, 708–725 (1976)).

[48] *Id.* at 884.

[49] *Id.* (quoting Bowen v. Roy, 476 U.S. 693, 708 (1986)).

[50] This was confirmed in *Church of Lukumi Babalu Aye, Inc. v. Hialeah*, 508 U.S. 520 (1993).

[51] The Religious Freedom Restoration Act of 1993, 42 U.S.C. §§ 2000bb et seq. (2007).

[52] City of Boerne v. Flores, 521 U.S. 507 (1997).

[53] Gonzales v. O Centro Espirito Beneficente Uniao Do Vegetal, 546 U.S. 418 (2006).

[54] Religious Liberty and Charitable Donation Protection Act of 1998, Pub. L. No. 105–183, 112 Stat. 517 (1998) (amending 11 U.S.C. 544, 546, 548, 707, 1325 (1994)); Religious Land Use and Institutionalized Persons Act of 2000, 42 U.S.C. §§ 2000 cc et seq.; American Indian Religious Freedom Act Amendment of 1994, Pub. L. No. 103–344, 108 Stat. 3125 (1994) (codified at 42 U.S.C. § 1996a (2007)).

[55] For further details, see W. Cole Durham Jr. and Robert T. Smith, "Religion and the State in the United States at the Turn of the Twenty-First Century," in *Law and Justice, The Christian Law Review* (United Kingdom: The Edmund Plowden Trust, 2009) Number 162. The total count of states opting for heightened scrutiny reached 25 when Tennessee passed a state RFRA in early 2010.

the legitimate competences of state and religion, it seems logical that public money should be used for secular purposes. The issue, then, consists in analyzing to what extent contemporary states perceive that funding of religion can be fit into their secular purposes.

There is a first important fact: virtually all states analyzed in the national reports grant some type of financial support to religion—or, more precisely, to religious denominations or communities—either directly or indirectly, whatever their constitutional principles are with regard to religion. Even in countries with a remarkably anti-clerical history or with a specific prohibition of funding religion, the state provides indirect forms of financing, such as tax benefits or subsidies for welfare activities run by religious groups on equal conditions to other non-profit organizations, chaplaincies in public institutions, support of religious schools or funding for the preservation or restoration of worship places of historic or cultural value (e.g. Armenia, France, Ireland, Japan, Kazakhstan, Mexico, Philippines, Uruguay, Ukraine, Ireland, USA).

State financing of religion is not always dependent on the constitutional or legal context that defines the state's general attitude towards religion and religious freedom. Logical internal coherence of state financing systems is not necessarily the rule. Very often, financial support is determined by historical circumstances, by social pressure or political negotiation. Thus, some states that in theory are separatist, such as France or the US, provide indirect financial support for religion more generously than states that define themselves as cooperationist (e.g. Spain). Another separationist state in theory, Turkey, pays for the salaries of the imams of Sunni Islam—but not for the clergy of other religions.

What this universal support of religion reveals is that states do not find any contradiction between their secular character and some sort of public funding of religion—not even those states that adopt a strict principle of separation or secularism as a constitutional sign of identity. At the same time, while the state's fundamental attitude towards religion does not necessarily determine whether there is or is not financial support for religion, or even whether the amount of financial support is greater or less, it may have an impact on the theoretical justification of funding of religion, on the criteria used to select the beneficiaries of state funding, and on the ways the state chooses to fund religion.

1.6.1 Justification of State Funding of Religion

The theoretical justification of state funding of religion in nations with an established church or with a specially protected church (e.g. England, Scotland, Finland, Greece) does not face particular problems with respect to the established churches. As these privileged churches are closely linked to the history, the sociological structure and sometimes the political organization of those nations, their public funding does not call for a particular justification but is assumed as something "natural", even when it is achieved through the general state budget. The challenge that these states have faced lately is rather how to reconcile their traditional ways of supporting national churches with the respect for the rights of people that are not members of those churches. Even if there is an established church, those who are not members should not be required to pay taxes for the support of a church that is not their own. More sophisticated jurisdictions have methods for channeling support so that tax payments do not flow from an adherent of one religion to support for a different religion, except where there is a normal, secular justification for the support in question. Moreover, there are concerns with the implications of the principle of equality, which is gaining more and more momentum in constitutional and international law. In this context, a key issue is the extent to which other legally recognized religious denominations should be granted the same or at least similar benefits to those given to the national church.

In other states that adopt a constitutional or legal perspective that combines the principles of neutrality towards religions and cooperation with religion (e.g. Germany, Spain, Italy), the theoretical justification of financial support of religion turns on the idea that religion is a positive social factor and therefore deserves public funding as well as other social factors deemed positive, such as cultural, educational, humanitarian or health initiatives and activities (see, e.g., Colombia). The understanding of religion as a positive social factor, on the other hand, is not derived only from the fact that institutionalized religion is an expression of the exercise of a constitutional right but also from the fact that religious denominations actually make positive contributions to society, for instance through constituting a source of morals for citizens or taking care of social services that otherwise should be provided by the state (thus saving public effort and resources). This does not mean that non-religious institutions or initiatives must be considered negative social factors or viewed as having an inferior status, for religion and other types of belief are normally put on the same level from the perspective of constitutional freedoms. Perhaps as a consequence of this balanced approach, the trend is to apply some of the typical methods of funding religion, especially tax benefits, to other non-profit activities or institutions. The German Constitution, in particular, foresees that religious denominations and other organizations promoting a certain philosophy of life (*Weltanschauung*) can acquire the same legal and economic status in comparable circumstances.[56]

This justification of public financing of religion is applicable also to separationist states. Here the basic idea is that the secularity of the state does not require discrimination against religion where the support of secular objectives may have the incidental effect of benefiting religion. After all, the state has competence to address all sorts of social factors within its territory, and religion is, no doubt, another social factor—and indeed a very significant one. In addition, it is important to note that historical circumstances have played in some states a determining role in the structuring of economic aid to religion, particularly when confiscation of church property took place in the past. Thus, the 1905 law in France determined that churches built before that date would pass to be the property of the state—and the state would take care of them—but would be operated by the Catholic Church, which is a peculiar but efficient way to support the maintenance of many Catholic places of worship in that country. In Eastern Europe, the massive confiscation of ecclesiastical property under communist regimes has led to a complex, and unfinished, process of restitution of property and economic compensation to the relevant churches. In other countries, such as Germany, Belgium, Spain or Colombia, compensation for confiscation of ecclesiastical property in the nineteenth century played a role in granting economic aid to the major church in the past, and still plays a role in maintaining some forms of public funding for those churches.

1.6.2 Criteria Used to Grant Financial Support

The nature of the justification of state funding of religion influences the criteria used to select the beneficiaries and to distribute funding. Among these criteria, we can mention historical roots or social acceptance—which may be applied together with certain registration procedures or the negotiation of specific cooperation agreements with the state—and the promotion of or compliance with certain moral or civic values. These criteria have been applied in various ways in different countries and sometimes have led to the recognition of different tiers of cooperation with religious denominations.

Thus, within Europe, some countries grant special "upper-tier" levels of state economic cooperation to those religions that demonstrate that they have deep roots in the territory. Germany, for instance, grants the status of public law corporation to those religious denominations, and organizations promoting philosophical views of life, that provide a guarantee of permanence; this status implies, among other things, the possibility—upon request of the relevant religion—that the state authorities collect ecclesiastical taxes from their members on behalf of the church. Switzerland, inspired by German law, has a system of recognition of churches under public law at the cantonal level that entails the possibility of levying taxes and of receiving state subsidies. Portugal, also inspired by German law, recognizes the status of "rooted religion" to those religions that can give a "guarantee of durability", with the effect that they should in principle be granted the right to enter into a negotiation process that would conclude with the adoption of a specific cooperation agreement with the state.[57] In Spain, almost all expressions of state economic cooperation are reserved to those religions that have been recognized as having "well-known roots" (*notorio arraigo*) and have subsequently signed a cooperation agreement with the state authorities. Something similar occurs in Italian law. Belgium has a remarkable degree of economic cooperation with "recognized religions", a category that requires, among other criteria, a relatively high number of members and settlement in the country for a long period. Since 1993, also organizations

[56] See Article 137 of the Weimar Constitution, integrated into the current German *Grundgesetz*.

[57] See the Portuguese *Lei da Liberdade Religiosa* of 2001, art. 37.

providing "moral non-confessional assistance" can enjoy the same cooperation. The Czech Republic has a specific category of registered religious communities, those "with special rights." This status is granted by the Ministry of Culture and entails a privileged position in different areas, including economic cooperation in the form of state subsidies for ministers' salaries. Two different tiers of registered religions exist also in Serbia, with tax exemptions being reserved for those religions in the upper tier.

On the other hand, a number of European countries (e.g. Czech Republic, Slovakia, Estonia, Latvia, Portugal[58]) and other countries outside of Europe (e.g. Mexico, Peru, Colombia) link eligibility for certain tax benefits to ordinary registration of religious communities, but requirements for registration may vary considerably from one country to another.[59] Portugal is an example of easy registration[60] while the Slovak Republic, with a requirement of proving membership of 20,000 Slovak citizens, is the opposite. (It should be noted, however, that Slovakian law grants a religion, immediately after registration, the same rights and privileges enjoyed by the so-called "historical churches." The restrictiveness of Slovakian law means that it in effect has only an "upper tier" when it comes to recognizing religious organizations. This presents obvious problems for new or smaller groups).

In a number of jurisdictions, the process of determining eligibility for financial or tax benefits is separated from the process of granting basic legal entity status to religious communities and groups. This makes it possible to have more relaxed criteria for granting legal entity status, while maintaining adequate controls to assure that financial benefits are not abused. Thus, in the United States, religious organizations can generally acquire legal entity status without difficulty. Legal entity status is granted at the state level, and while there are differences in the types of entities available in different states, the underlying principle is flexibility and respect for religious autonomy. A variety of forms are available, affording religious groups latitude in the types of legal structures they elect to use. Tax exempt status is determined separately by tax authorities. Even then, religious groups face less burdensome filing, reporting and auditing requirements out of respect for the religious freedom rights of religious organizations.[61] In Australia, any institution that fulfills the constitutional definition of religion is entitled to tax benefits. In England and Wales, as in Canada, all religious groups that register as charities are entitled to some tax benefits, and the same rule applies to other groups pursuing "the promotion of religious or racial harmony or equality and diversity". However, while advancement of religion is a charitable purpose, in England and Wales it is necessary for a charity to show that it is for the public benefit to be registered and there is no longer an automatic presumption that a religion is for the public benefit. This has led, for example, to the rejection of the Church of Scientology's application for charitable status. Disclosure of the assets of a charity and their use, and independent certification of accounts, may be requirements to be granted charitable status (Scotland).

Compliance with certain principles or standards set by secular law is sometimes required as a condition to obtain public funding either of a religion in general or for particular activities—especially those aimed at providing social services—run by religious institutions. In Australia, for example, agencies that receive funding for the provision of some forms of welfare are contractually bound to comply fully with anti-discrimination laws and religious schools must reach certain educational standards. In Sweden, since 1998, the state may provide financial subsidies to a registered religious denomination only upon condition that the denomination contributes to the maintenance and development of fundamental values of the society; this includes the fight against all forms of racism and other discrimination, as well as against violence and brutality, contribution to equality between men and women, and the requirement that its members and staff are guided by ethical principles which correspond with the fundamental democratic values of the society.

[58] See, in addition to the national reports, the Portuguese *Lei da Liberdade Religiosa* of 2001, art. 32.

[59] This is illustrated in detail in the relevant section of national reports.

[60] See the Portuguese *Lei da Liberdade Religiosa* of 2001, arts. 32–36.

[61] For more background on the U.S. system, see Durham and Scharffs, *supra* note 2, at 420–23, 472–73.

By and large, we can affirm that full implementation of equality is the main challenge in the application of criteria for the selection of state funding of religion in most countries. Greater equality, both between religious and non-religious institutions and between different religious institutions or communities, seems to be the prevailing trend even among states with an official or privileged church. When applied to religious institutions, equality means that the beneficiaries of public funding must be determined according to objective and non-discriminatory criteria, and not according to a state judgment on the doctrines or moral value of religious communities as such. In fact, equality is often duly implemented with respect to a large percentage of religious denominations—especially those accepted as historical or traditional in the country—and most states analyzed in national reports do not have a discriminatory approach to public financing of religion. The real problem is rather a lack of sensitivity towards the situation and needs of residual minority groups, particularly when they lack historical roots or appear as "new" or "atypical" in the country. This situation tends to be even more frequent when direct funding is involved (Spain, Estonia).

In addition, it is interesting to note that, with different profiles, major churches often enjoy privileged state funding over other religious communities in a number of countries, especially in those with state churches (e.g. Finland, Norway), with especially recognized churches (e.g. Greece) or with concordats with the Catholic Church (e.g. Spain, Italy, Portugal, Argentina, Colombia[62]). This fact has often been justified by reference to the historical role or social predominance of those churches and to the rule that unequal situations call for unequal treatment. In practice, the privileged status of major churches has often been positive for religious minorities, for the recognition of the "untouchable" status of the former, together with contemporary concerns about the consequences of the equality principle, has contributed to raising the level of state economic cooperation with minority religions. This is true especially with respect to countries with major Christian churches (Spain, Italy, Portugal, Colombia, Sweden, Finland); in predominantly Islamic countries the trend towards equality is not so visible or not existing at all (Sudan, Turkey).

1.6.3 Methods for Providing State Financial Support of Religion

Typically the methods of state funding of religion have been divided into two categories: direct and indirect economic aid.

1.6.3.1 Direct Economic Aid

The first category comprises different channels through which states may provide economic resources directly to religious communities.

One of them consists in budgetary provisions in favor of one or several religions for the payment of clergy's salaries, for the construction and maintenance of places of worship or institutions for the education of the clergy or the formation of other religious structures etc. Separationist countries, such as the US, Kazakhstan, Ireland, Philippines or Uruguay, usually prohibit this type of economic cooperation, but not all separationist countries do the same. Turkey, for instance, pays for the salaries of Sunni imams; and France pays for the preservation of Catholic churches existing when the Law of 1905 was enacted. These structures are state property but most often are operated by the Catholic Church and destined for Catholic worship. Countries with a close connection between the state and a national church use this system (Sweden, Finland, Greece), as do some countries (e.g. Germany, Switzerland, Belgium) that abide by the principle of neutrality but construe it to allow a high degree of cooperation with traditional churches.

Some of these latter countries use in addition another form of economic aid to religion, which is granted to some religious communities with qualified legal status: the possibility of levying taxes or fees on their members and utilizing the assistance of state structures for collection of the resulting revenues (Germany, Switzerland, Sweden, Finland).

In some Latin-American countries, budgetary provisions in favor of the Catholic Church have been kept (Colombia, Argentina, Peru; also, in Europe, and as a consequence of its peculiar constitutional system, Andorra). In Europe there is an interesting tendency in some predominantly Catholic countries that have drawn

[62] The same applies to other countries, as Andorra, in which the preferential treatment of the Catholic Church derives from the Constitution rather than from a Concordat.

on state budgets in the past to move towards a third method of direct financing of religion: the so-called "tax-assignment" or "tax check-off" system (Spain, Italy, Slovak Republic, Portugal, Hungary[63]). This system allows taxpayers to donate a percentage of their income tax to the religious community of their choice among a list of religious communities that have been recognized as having a qualified legal status. The percentage of income tax that is at the disposal of taxpayers varies depending on the countries (from 0.5% in Portugal to 2% in Slovakia); the resulting amount of taxpayers' choices is given directly by the state, every year, to the relevant religious representatives. Note that both the tax levying systems and the tax assignment systems channel funds from believers to their own religious denomination,[64] and that in both cases, the channeling is voluntary—taxpayers can opt in (tax assignment) or out (tax levying) of the respective systems.

1.6.3.2 Indirect Economic Aid

The most frequent channel to provide indirect economic aid to religious communities is through tax benefits, in particular the exemption from paying certain taxes that is granted to religious institutions and the privileged tax treatment that is recognized to donations made by individuals or corporations to religious institutions. Virtually every state provides one or both of these two varieties of tax benefits, although the system does not work identically in all countries. For instance, in some countries the control and record of eligible institutions for tax benefits is in the hands of tax authorities and religious communities are subject to essentially the same rules as other charities (this is frequent in common law countries, such as England and Wales, USA or Australia), while in other countries there is a specific registry of religious communities, normally run by the Ministry of Justice, Culture or Interior, that determines their eligibility for legal entity status, and tax benefits are linked to acquisition of that status.

In the latter countries, the legal requirements to register as a religious entity and qualify for tax benefits are diverse. For example, Portugal has a very flexible system but Slovakia has a very rigid system, as mentioned above; in Spain, registration of religious entities is very easy but does not give access to tax benefits, which are reserved for those religious denominations which have signed a formal cooperation agreement with the state (at the moment, only the Catholic Church, as well as three federations of Protestant, Jewish and Islamic communities). In countries that keep a specific registry for religious groups there is a tendency to grant them the same tax benefits—no more, no less—recognized to other non-profit organizations involved in providing different social services.

In addition to tax benefits, there are a variety of channels that are widespread throughout the world and are normally considered as indirect public financing of religion. Among these we can mention state funding of religious schools or religious instruction in public schools (this is frequently the case in European and some Latin-American countries); state funding of religious hospitals or eldercare facilities; and payment of chaplaincies in military centers, hospitals or penitentiaries (this is the only public funding that the state may grant to religious denominations in the Philippines). Although the public money invested in these activities goes, no doubt, to religious institutions, it is doubtful that these channels of indirect cooperation can be put on the same level as tax benefits, for their main purpose is not to finance religion but rather to fund public services and to facilitate citizens' exercise of religious freedom, which is not the same thing.

Thus, when some states pay for the expenses of religious schools or hospitals, or the expenses generated by religious denominational instruction in public schools, they are not strictly financing religious denominations as such but rather paying for a public service run by non-state institutions and, in the case of religious instruction, responding to the legitimate choices of parents with respect to the religious or moral orientation of their children's education. Similarly, the purpose of chaplaincies in hospitals, military centers or penitentiaries is to make religious assistance possible in difficult circumstances in which citizens do not have free access to the worship places or ministers of their choice. In other words, it is an active way of removing the barriers to the exercise of a fundamental freedom. We can add analogous observations with respect to subsidies sometimes granted in India for pilgrimages or public religious celebrations. The same can be said with

[63] See, in addition to the relevant country reports, the Portuguese *Lei da Liberdade Religiosa* of 2001, art. 32.

[64] On the other hand, note also that in the tax-assignment systems taxpayers are not asked about their religious affiliation but just about their will to donate a certain percentage of their income tax for the support of a religious community. Therefore, nothing prevents a taxpayer to choose as beneficiary a religious community different from his own, although in practice this is unusual.

respect to the public money that is often invested in the preservation or restoration of religious places that are part of the historical heritage of a country—the financing of religion that it can produce is but a side effect of what is directly intended, i.e. the protection of cultural heritage, which is no doubt a legitimate competence, and a duty, of contemporary secular states.

1.6.4 Benefits and Problematic Aspects of State Financial Support of Religion

The comparative analysis of funding of religion in different countries shows a diversified panorama of systems. As in other aspects of the relation between state and religion, there is no uniformity; nor are there pronounced trends toward convergence, apart from efforts to respect choice, to avoid using coercive tax mechanisms to urge adherents of one tradition to support others, and to have some secular justification (sometimes in addition to religious justifications) for the support given. There is, however, a common element: virtually all the contemporary states understand the need to use public funds (or to waive public funds that would be raised but for exemptions) to assist with the financing of religion in one way or an other. A variety of reasons move states to reach this conclusion. Among them: (1) the affirmation of broad (though not unlimited) state authority to address matters of social relevance, including many manifestations of religion that extend into the secular sphere; (2) an argument of comparative treatment with other non-profit activities and institutions (funding the latter and not funding religion would seem blatantly discriminatory); and (3) the conviction that financing religious institutions is a way of facilitating the exercise of a fundamental right, freedom of religion or belief, which constitutes a legitimate secular interest.

Behind these other arguments is a more basic practical intuition, that facilitating the financial operation of religious organizations is justifiable because on balance, organizations that foster religions and beliefs are a beneficial force in society. This idea, on the other hand, can be understood in a material sense—religious institutions provide social services that save much state activity, effort and money—or in a more spiritual sense—religions are a significant source of morals and the moral dimension of citizens is indispensable for a strong and well-structured society.

It is then logical that secular states do not feel threatened in their secularity by the use of public money to finance religion, especially in a political landscape characterized globally by interventionist states, which control a large part of individual lives and are accustomed to financing a variety of activities deemed to be part of welfare societies. Public funding of religion constitutes a challenge rather than a threat to the secular state—the challenge of finding the appropriate criteria for funding.

This leads us to the problematic aspects of public financing of religion, which co-exist with its indubitable benefits. Two aspects are particularly important and therefore need special attention, for they constitute a deviation from the use of public money for secular purposes. First, public financing can be used by the state to try to control religion and therefore can threaten the autonomy of religious communities, which is a substantial part of religious freedom. And second, state economic support of religion can be used in a discriminatory way, i.e. to favor some religions at the expense of others—which is, after all, another way to try to control religious life in society in addition to being an affront to the dignity of those that suffer the discrimination. In this respect, it is perhaps acceptable that historical or sociological considerations be acknowledged as social realities and be taken into account in justifying proportionate differences in state economic cooperation with different religious communities, at least where such considerations are linked to objective considerations calling for differential treatment. Such justifications are often asserted in Europe and Latin America, noting that unequal situations call for unequal measures. But it is unacceptable to use the history of a country or the social influence of some major religions as justification in itself for denying access to exemptions or funding to other minority or less traditional groups as a method of control that impairs their ability to exercise the full range of their right to freedom of religion or belief on equal terms with other members of society.

1.7 Civil Effects of Religious Acts

(This section, which focused on the civil effects of religious marriage, has been eliminated due to publication space constraints. It can be accessed as indicated in note 1 above).

1.8 Religious Education

The school system may be—and often is—a significant instrument for the religious education of the youth and therefore constitutes an important subject for analysis from the perspective of the relation between religion and the secular state. There are two main topics that we should face here. One is the functioning and legal status of private schools with a religious ethos, for they are an effective way for religious communities to disseminate their doctrines and educate their younger members in their moral and religious values; indeed some religious denominations, such as the Catholic Church, have traditionally showed a strong interest in ensuring the freedom of religious institutions to operate their own schools. The other topic is whether religious instruction should be provided in public schools, and if so, whether this should be conducted as denominational or non-denominational religious instruction. The diverse approaches of states to these two areas reveal more generally their attitude towards the role of religion in society vis-à-vis the state—and also towards who is ultimately responsible for the education of the youth: the society itself or state authorities.

1.8.1 Private Schools

Private schools, including those with a religious ethos and run by religious institutions, are permitted to operate in almost all states, although their actual significance within the educational landscape varies considerably depending on the country. In some countries the presence of religious schools is very important (e.g. the Netherlands, where approximately two-thirds of the schools are in private hands, almost always with a religious ethos). Indeed, the religious presence can be even overwhelming, as is the case in Ireland, where the vast majority of schools are Catholic, controlled by ecclesiastical institutions, and integrated within the state system. In other countries the percentage of private schools is substantial (e.g. Australia or Spain, where they cover approximately one-third of schools), and in some others it is insignificant—e.g. Finland or Switzerland, where almost all schools are public and private schools are looked at with a certain distrust by many people, considering that they are not as effective for the social integration of students. Some former communist countries have a predominantly public conception of the school system. Thus, Ukraine permits "spiritual educational centers"—which in practice are run by churches—and grants them some tax benefits, but studies in these centers are not officially approved by the state. In Kazakhstan, there is the theoretical possibility of establishing private schools but the government's administrative restrictions determine that, in practice, all schools are public and state controlled. The opposite occurs in Turkey, where the system should be in theory almost entirely secular and state controlled, but in practice many schools are run by Muslim groups (religious minorities find doing so much more difficult).

Very often the state recognition—and funding—of private schools is subject to compliance with some minimum educational standards aimed at guaranteeing that education received in private and public schools have a comparable quality.[65] Sometimes these standards include also respect for or promotion of certain civic values that are considered particularly important (Sweden). In any event, the big question with regard to private education—especially religious schools—is the funding granted by the state.

In some countries, funding of private schools has been typically understood as incompatible with the separation of state and religion (e.g. USA, Kazakhstan). The assumption is that because such institutions tend to be pervasively sectarian in practice, any substantial support would inevitably support the religious instruction that they often provide to their students. In the USA, however, the Supreme Court has allowed state funding for other expenses, such as transportation of students to parochial schools (*Everson*, 1947[66]) and even state vouchers given by local authorities to parents to cover the tuition of their children in public or private schools, when the public funding is open to all and is not aimed at supporting a particular sectarian type of school (*Zelman*, 2002[67]). In some countries, such as Australia, the state has traditionally granted generous funding for private religious schools. However, this issue has recently become contentious,

[65] Thus, for instance, in Germany and Australia. In Japan, the issue of the educational quality of private schools does not seem to be an issue, for some religious schools enjoy a predominant prestige in the country.

[66] Everson v. Board of Education, 330 U.S. 1 (1947).

[67] Zelman v. Simmons-Harris, 536 U.S. 639 (2002).

and there is an ongoing debate about whether it is compatible with state neutrality and about which criteria should be used to assure that public funding does not discriminate against minorities.

In contrast, many European countries, whatever their constitutional system of church-state relations is, do not find that public funding of private schools is at all incompatible with the secular nature of the state. This attitude is grounded, on the one hand, on the right of parents to have their children educated in accordance with their religious or philosophical convictions; and, on the other hand, on the understanding that education is a public service that the state must control but can be performed by state institutions or by private institutions (religious or not). The result has been a widespread system of state funding of private schools in Europe, normally generous and sometimes on an equal footing with public schools (e.g. the Netherlands, Belgium, Sweden, Slovakia, and also Czech Republic in the case of church schools). In some cases, private religious schools have been integrated within the state system and largely funded with public money, as in Ireland or the United Kingdom, but churches have been allowed to keep a relatively high degree of control over the operation of these schools.

In large parts of Europe, the real issue under discussion often has been not whether private religious schools should be publicly funded or not—this is taken for granted—but rather what the conditions for eligibility for public funding should be. The focus in these debates has been on guaranteeing minimum quality standards, on preventing private schools from becoming in practice ghettos that isolate certain students from the rest of society, and on prohibiting discriminatory policies by school authorities on the ground of religion or belief. These issues have also been discussed outside of Europe, with a variety of solutions. Thus, for instance, with respect to student admission policies, France and India forbid schools funded with public money from rejecting students on the ground of religion. In New Zealand private schools funded by the state must reserve 5% of their admissions for students not adhering to the school's religious ethos. The Netherlands have adopted a solution more favorable to the school ethos, and religious schools can choose their own policies of admission as far as they are applied in a consistent manner. In Ireland, this issue is controversial, and the traditional respect for the policies followed by Catholic schools in the admission of students and the hiring of teachers is under revision, for many consider it to be discriminatory in practice.

By and large, we can affirm that, with a few exceptions, the trend is to see private schools—including those with a religious ethos—as a "normal" part of the educational landscape of the country. Whether they should be funded with public money is a different question, whose answer sometimes depends on two coordinates: on the one hand, the understanding of state neutrality in religious matters; and on the other hand, the notion of the state role in education and also the very notion of public service. In general, an inclusive concept of state neutrality, together with a reliance on spontaneous societal channels to intervene in the management of education and other public services, tends to favor liberal funding of private schools, but there are significant exceptions. For instance, France does not have particular problems with the funding of religious schools, while the United States does. In both cases, their attitude is probably linked to their respective political histories: church-state relations in France along the nineteenth century and the twentieth century interpretation of the establishment clause by the Supreme Court in the US. Once again, history proves to be crucial to understand many of the solutions—and apparent inconsistencies—adopted by different states in their relations with religion.

1.8.2 Religious Instruction in Public Schools

1.8.2.1 Denominational Religious Instruction

In many European countries there is denominational religious instruction in public schools. France is one of the few exceptions.[68] This is seen as a natural cooperation of the state with churches and, even more important, as a guarantee of the parents' rights to determine the religious and moral education of their children (Finland stresses also that it is a right of the students). For these reasons, the state recognizes the autonomy of the relevant churches to select the teachers that are qualified for this type of education and often pays for the expenses this generates. Significant is the example

[68] However, there is religious confessional instruction organized by public authorities in the region of Alsace-Moselle, which did not join the separation system after it was returned to France in 1918.

of Ireland, where the government and the courts have found public funding of religious education—and of Catholic chaplaincies in schools—to be fully compatible with the constitutional prohibition of endowment of religion. Another common element is that denominational religious instruction is normally understood as voluntary, and must be requested by the students or their parents. Some countries, such as Latvia, specifically require a written application. Ireland, where most schools are in the hands of Catholic institutions, has clearly affirmed the students' right to refuse religious instruction, although it does not seem easy to put into practice. Exceptions to the voluntary character of denominational religion courses in Europe are Greece, where Orthodox religious instruction is provided as a compulsory subject, although non-Orthodox students are exempted; and Russia, where this matter is decentralized but many regions have imposed mandatory Orthodox religious instruction in public schools (according to the Russian national report, approximately 70% of students in public schools receive Orthodox religious instruction).

Out of these common features, there are a variety of systems in Europe. For instance, some countries, such as Hungary, do not include religious instruction as part of the school curriculum, and in others, such as the Netherlands, its inclusion in the curriculum or not depends on local authorities. Finland, although including these courses in the curriculum, emphasizes the need to distinguish religious instruction from religious practices or observance. Some countries not only include confessional religious instruction in school curricula but also make it mandatory for all schools to offer some kind of religious instruction, although the students—or their parents—are free to choose it or to take alternative courses on secular ethics, civil education or the like (e.g. Germany, Belgium, Slovakia, Serbia). In some countries that have a concordat with the Holy See, schools are obliged to provide Catholic instruction, though students are always free to take it or not. The offering of similar courses for other qualified religions is not mandated but only possible upon request of a minimum number of students (e.g. Italy, Spain, Czech Republic, Malta).

Outside of Europe the panorama is more diverse and, as one could expect, the states' attitudes towards religious instruction are heavily influenced by their respective political or judicial history. For instance, the United States is well known for excluding confessional religious education from public schools, considering it incompatible with the judicial interpretation of the constitutional establishment clause—although this does not preclude the possibility of controversies with respect to mandatory subjects with a potential doctrinal dimension, as the debate about creationism and evolutionism in public schools demonstrates. In Latin America religious denominational education is excluded from public schools in those countries that experienced anti-clerical political shifts at certain points in their histories. This is the case in Mexico, Uruguay and Argentina. In the latter country, religious instruction was eliminated long ago by General Peron at the national level, but it has been later reintroduced by some provinces. In other countries where institutional relations with the Catholic Church have a stronger basis, a system similar to that of Germany or Spain is followed (e.g. Colombia, Chile and Peru). In Africa, Muslim education is mandatory in Northern Sudan, even in Christian schools. In Asia, Japan and South Korea exclude confessional education from public schools. In South Korea, where students are not free to choose their school but are assigned one by draw, the courts have declared unconstitutional the expulsion of a student from a Christian school who openly criticized religious instruction. India prohibits denominational religious education when schools are totally funded by the state but not when they are partly or not funded at all, so long as the free consent of students to this type of education is guaranteed. New Zealand permits religious instruction in the school premises but out of the school curriculum and teaching hours, without economic aid from the state. In some other countries, as diverse as Switzerland, Brazil, Australia and Canada, this matter has long been decentralized and depends on the decision of regional or local authorities, although the tendency is to allow some kind of religious instruction upon request of the parents.

1.8.2.2 Non-denominational Religious Education

In the last decades a different type of religious education has been gaining momentum in various countries: a neutral, non-denominational teaching that is normally conceived as an instrument to foster respect for and understanding of religious pluralism—a need that is increasingly felt in many contemporary societies.

A number of countries have introduced, or are in the process of introducing this type of non-confessional teaching about religions with different profiles and often not in competition, but in parallel, with confessional religious instruction. This is the case in Sweden and the Netherlands, for example, where this teaching is mandatory and the law provides that great care should be taken to ensure its real neutrality and objectivity. In Switzerland and Australia the tendency is the same, although the decision corresponds to the regional authorities and the subject has not always been imposed as compulsory for students. In some provinces of Canada this education has been introduced as a mandatory subject and has been declared constitutional by the courts as far as it meets certain specific requirements that guarantee its neutrality. In Estonia the subject has been included in the school curricula as an elective. There have been attempts to make it mandatory, but there is the fear that it could lead in practice to the imposition of predominantly Christian views.[69] This is the situation in Ukraine, where there is religious teaching that is neither strictly sectarian nor entirely neutral, for it is focused on the basics of Christian values; however, students are entitled to opt out. Kazakhstan is currently studying how to introduce this teaching in an appropriate way. Japan and South Korea, strongly opposed to sectarian religious instruction in public schools, find neutral teaching about religion not objectionable. Turkey imposes this subject as compulsory in all public schools, and opt-outs are possible only for non-Muslim students (Muslims constituting the vast majority). In practice, however, the teaching is not neutral and there is a strong emphasis on the doctrines of Sunni Islam to the detriment of other religions. For this reason, the European Court of Human Rights declared this teaching contrary to religious freedom since opt-outs on religious grounds are not permitted.[70]

1.8.2.3 Practical Problems in the Implementation of Religious Education

The main problems of non-denominational religious education are quite clear: it requires a high degree of academic and moral qualification in teachers; and in addition, objectively, neutrality is very difficult to achieve in this particularly sensitive area. An obvious risk is that teaching about religion that in theory is non-confessional becomes in practice indoctrination in a certain religion or non-religious worldview, or is used by governments for that purpose. This explains why international organizations are promoting different initiatives that serve as orientation to states interested in this type of education.[71]

Denominational religious education, from the perspective of the secular state, has generated controversies around three particular points.

One is derived from the fact that, in some countries, schools must offer confessional religion courses but, as the acceptance of this teaching is voluntary for students, those who decide not to take the courses are bound to choose alternative subjects such as secular ethics, civic education, comparative and neutral study of religions, or the like. This approach has been criticized from different angles. Some have argued that including sectarian religious teaching in the school curriculum unnecessarily forces non-religious students to take some alternative courses that otherwise they would not need. Other times the reasoning has gone in the opposite direction: secular ethics or non-confessional study of religions are important school subjects that should not be just an alternative to confessional religious instruction. On the contrary, they should be mandatory for all students and sectarian religious course should not be a cause for exemption. It has also been argued that the need to opt out may imply in practice a certain stigmatization of students not attending religion courses (this is the reason why Canadian courts have declared Christian instruction in public schools unconstitutional in Ontario, despite the fact that parents were given the possibility of opting out[72]). One way or an other, the aim of these arguments seems

[69] This possibility was examined by the European Court of Human Rights in *Folgerø et al. v. Norway*, June 29, 2007.

[70] Zengin v. Turkey, App. No. 1448/04 (ECtHR, 9 October 2007).

[71] See, for instance, the *Toledo Guiding Principles on Teaching about Religions and Beliefs*, prepared by the OSCE/ODIHR Advisory Council of Experts on Freedom of Religion or Belief, Warsaw 2007, where the difficulties of this type of religious education, together with detailed recommendations to make it efficient and actually neutral, are well explained. The text is available in http://www.osce.org/publications/odihr/2007/11/28314_993_en.pdf.

[72] The European Court of Human Rights has faced this type of issues in *Saniewski v. Poland* (App. No. 40319/98, declared inadmissible on 26 June 2001) and *Grzelak v. Poland* (App. No. 7710/01, Chamber Judgment of 15 June 2010).

to be the same: to take denominational religious education out of school curricula (and out of state funding), in contradiction with the long established tradition of many countries.

A second controversial point is the guarantee of equal rights to religious minorities. Usually, the organization of religion courses is attentive to the students that are members of major or at least traditional religions, while minority religions are often neglected. This is, no doubt, an important issue, as is everything related to the implementation of the principle of equality in the area of fundamental rights. However, the predictable difficulties to extend this system of religious instruction to religious minorities have been sometimes used to undermine the legitimacy of the system as applied to religious majorities and to propose its elimination. This is perhaps more difficult to understand, especially considering that, as indicated above, religion courses are designed not only to satisfy the wishes of religious communities but also to ensure the fundamental right of parents to decide on the religious education of their children. The proportionate extension to minorities of the benefits that many states grant to major religions is one of the challenges that the secular state must face, and the solution does not seem to be their elimination for all. There are of course practical or even technical difficulties in the implementation of equality, but often it is just a matter of political will.

The third controversial point generated by denominational religious instruction has been the selection of the persons that are qualified to teach religion courses, especially in those countries where teachers are hired and paid by the state. Typically the relevant religious communities are recognized as having the competence to assess the qualification of teachers. Normally the religious authorities grant permits to a number of persons, according to specific and well-described academic criteria, and then schools may choose among them. In Spain some problems have been raised when teachers have had their ecclesiastical permit withdrawn not because of lack of academic qualification but because they engaged in public behavior contrary to the moral principles of the Catholic Church. The Constitutional Court has supported the position of the Catholic bishops, holding that only they are competent to say who can teach religion on behalf of the Catholic Church and recognizing that publicly known immoral conduct may have a negative educational impact on students, which only the ecclesiastical authorities are in a position to evaluate.[73] Certainly, it seems difficult to see how to take a different stance without impairing religious autonomy, particularly in the case of churches with a clear hierarchical structure.

1.9 Religious Symbols in Public Places

One of the major areas where the difference between secularity and secularism has been evident in various legal systems around the world is in attitudes toward religious symbols in public space. Key debates have focused on the wearing of attire that has religious significance, the display of religious symbols such as the crucifix in schools and other public buildings, and the permissibility of symbolic displays and monuments in public settings.

1.9.1 Religious Attire

Probably the most controversial of these issues has centered on the right to wear Islamic head coverings. A challenge to Turkish regulations banning headscarves in public universities ultimately reached the European Court of Human Rights, where a grand chamber in a controversial decision held that the ban did not violate the right to freedom of religion or belief.[74] A subsequent case sustained expulsion of a Muslim girl from a French public school for failing to participate in physical education classes without a headscarf.[75] The Court's judgments in these cases determined that the relevant states had not exceeded their margin of appreciation, in part because of the importance of secularism (*laïcité*) in the legal systems of Turkey and France.

While this issue was significant in some of the countries covered by national reports, it was not a major issue for most. Several indicated that their citizens were free to wear religious symbols if they so desired.[76] A number of countries noted that both

[73] See the Constitutional Court decisions 38/2007, of 15 February 2007; and 80/2007, of 19 April 2007; *but see*, decision 51/2011 of 14 April 2011 (going in the opposite direction).

[74] Şahin v. Turkey, App. No. 44774/98 (ECtHR (Grand Chamber), 10 November 2005).

[75] Dogru v. France, App. No. 27058/05 (ECtHR, 4 December 2008).

[76] Andorra XI; Chile IV.C; Colombia XI; Estonia IX; Peru X; Philippines XI; Russia XI; Ukraine XI; Uruguay XII. The same would be true in the United States today, although there have been cases striking down older laws targeting Catholic nuns and priests that imposed constraints on the wearing of religious garb in school settings.

students and teachers may wear religious garb.[77] A number noted that restrictions in this area would be viewed as measures inconsistent with religious freedom.[78] The Czech reporter mentioned that in fact, Muslim headscarves were no different than head coverings routinely worn by Czech women in the countryside. The Israel report indicated that his country had no restrictions in this area, and that religious head coverings were a "normal part of the landscape." The Netherlands reporter commented that "Dutch neutrality in the public domain is not interpreted such that the public domain should be void of any religious expression. On the contrary, the plurality of religious expressions is respected." In a similar vein, the Italian report indicated that *laicità* as understood in Italy allows wearing of religious symbols in schools, hospitals, public offices and by public employees, and that Italy respects the signs and symbols of all religions.

A number of other countries respect the right of individuals to wear religious symbols, but emphasize that there are limits. Thus, the Finnish national report indicated that individuals are free to wear religious symbols except where doing so might constitute a hazard to safety or might injure the religious feelings of others. Similarly, Sweden has no rules against wearing religious garb in public, and indeed, doing so would be protected by religious freedom norms under Swedish law. However, in educational settings, restrictions may be imposed where necessary to avert threats to the order and security of the school, or where allowing the clothing would impair the pedagogic mission of the school.

In short, there is an array of responses to the issues of wearing religious symbols. Of course, many of the countries that see no difficulty in accommodating Muslim headgear do not face concerns with the rise of political Islam that have triggered concerns elsewhere. Moreover, some are countries with strong identification with prevailing religions that might be sympathetic to the use of religious symbols in their own traditions. Nonetheless, the fact that wearing of religious headgear is so easily accommodated in many countries raises questions about the necessity of bans, even in the public settings where such bans typically apply. It is not clear that wearing the headscarf would be as likely to become a political statement if secularism's bans would be replaced by secularity's accommodations.

1.9.2 Display of Religious Symbols in Public Settings

As noted by Malta's national report, many European countries where display of crucifixes or other religious symbols is common were at the time of this writing "awaiting the grand chamber decision in *Lautsi*," then pending before the European Court of Human Rights. The Grand Chamber rejected the Court's previous ruling that requiring the display of crucifixes in Italian public schools violated the rights of Italian pupils and their parents to freedom of religion or belief.[79] The Italian national report indicated that the crucifix case had become the center of "a lively debate around the preservation of Italian identity." The validity and constitutional legitimacy of the decrees mandating crucifixes in the classroom, which date back to the fascist era, were disputed. Some argued that the display of crucifixes is inconsistent with the notion of *laicità* and its commitment to cultural and religious pluralism. But this was reported to be a minority view, both among legal scholars and the Italian populace. The majority view, holding that *laicità* should be able to acknowledge and give "constitutional relevance to the Catholic cultural tradition of the country," was ultimately vindicated by the European Court, following the reasoning of some Italian courts that "the crucifix represents a sign of national identity and cannot be considered a threat to freedom of conscience: on the contrary, it allows all children, and especially the extra-communitarian ones, to perceive the values of tolerance written into the constitution."

The issue of public display of religious symbols is arguably more difficult because the choice to make a public display is by definition a public choice, whereas clothing decisions always have an individual choice element. At the same time, however, a decision not to display or to discontinue a display that has been customary risks offending majority groups in the population. It may be the case (and indeed is likely) that every possible public decision will appear non-neutral to some portion of the citizenry.

In part because of Russia's distinctive history over the past century, and its importance both as a center of Christian Orthodoxy and as a center of atheism, the Russian experience has some unique features.

---

[77] Australia X; Italy VIII; Netherlands XVI.

[78] Czech Republic XI; Sweden XI.

[79] Lautsi v. Italy, App. No. 30814/06 (ECtHR, 3 November 2009), reversed by; the Grand Chamber opinion of 18 March 2011.

Apparently, there is no law governing the use of institutional symbols. There are in fact a large number of religious symbols in public space, but this is not necessarily the sign of a confessional state. Constitutional guarantees of the separation of church and state in Russia do not need to be understood as requiring a separation in social life. At the same time, there is a concern in Russia about the increasing clericalization of public institutions.

1.9.2.1 Monuments and Temporary Displays

Regulation of monuments is challenging because of the interface of history—acknowledging and memorializing particularly significant moments, persons and ideas—and religious life. Erection of a monument can be simultaneously a reminder of secular history and values and assertion of religious values as well. Installing a new monument may stir political sensitivities, but once one has been in place for a substantial period of time, the controversy may fade.

Many if not most countries maintain landmark registers, and not surprisingly, churches are often designated as protected landmarks. Armenia, for example, noted that there are many monuments and historic buildings which are under state protection. One of the challenges in this area is that historic preservationists typically want to maintain structures exactly as they have always been, but religious usage may change. Alters may need to be repositioned to correspond to new forms of worship; the population center of a church may change, so that the church may wish to move to a new location; and so forth. As important as the state's interest in protecting history is, it is hard to say that it overrides the value of protecting the religious freedom of the community that gave rise to the history in the first place.

Over the past few years, the United States has seen recurrent controversies over monuments inscribed with the Ten Commandments. The United States report draws attention to two cases about such monuments that were decided in opposite ways.[80] A key difference lies in whether a monument is merely acknowledging and memorializing history, or whether there is a subtext aimed at imposing a particular religious point of view. If the latter is the case, the monument lacks a secular purpose and cannot withstand establishment clause scrutiny. One of the dilemmas is that the effort to show that the monument is primarily secular may lead those defending the monument to water down the religious values that they wish to memorialize. As with the other symbol cases, the deeper question is whether notions of state neutrality and separation of church and state can be read in a way that leaves more room to accept authentic religiosity without empowering it to impose itself on others.

1.10 Freedom of Expression and Offenses Against Religion

One of the most sensitive issues in the relationship between religion and secular states concerns treatment of offensive expression targeting religion and religious sensitivities. The Danish cartoons controversy in 2005 helped sensitize the rest of the world to the fact that for a variety of reasons, including religiously grounded taboos on pictorial depictions of the Prophet Mohammed, Muslims have much higher sensitivities regarding offensive speech and insults concerning their religion.[81] But of course, Muslims are not alone in having sensitivities in this area.

Beginning in 1999, and in every year since, the Organization of the Islamic Conference ("OIC") has drafted and secured passage of resolutions addressing "defamation of religion" in United Nations settings. These resolutions were first passed in the U.N. Human Rights Commission, and subsequently in the U.N. Human Rights Council. In large part because of the visibility given the issue by the Danish cartoons controversy, the General Assembly began considering the issue in, and has passed a resolution entitled "Combating Defamation of Religions" in each year since—albeit with declining majorities in most years.

Broad defamation laws, particularly criminal ones, have come under extreme criticism in recent years from a very broad array of U.N. and regional human rights leaders. For example, in December 2008, the four freedom of expression rapporteurs of the U.N., the Organization for Security and Cooperation in Europe (OSCE), the Organization of the American States (OAS), and the African Commission on Human

[80] United States II.

[81] For an excellent analysis of this controversy, see Jytte Klausen, *The Cartoons That Shook the World* (New Haven: Yale University Press, 2009).

and Peoples' Rights (ACHPR) issued a joint statement urging international organizations to stop supporting the idea of defamation of religions because "it does not accord with international standards accepted by pluralistic and free societies. . . Restrictions on freedom of expression to prevent intolerance should be limited in scope to advocacy of national, racial or religious hatred that constitutes incitement to discrimination, hostility or violence."[82]

Many countries continue to have blasphemy, heresy and apostasy legislation on the books. As recently as April 2010, the Indonesian Constitutional Court rejected challenges to Indonesia's blasphemy and heresy law, although the Court did recognize that the legislation in question needed reform. In many countries, however, while such legislation is still extant, it is seldom applied. In Canada, in a 1990 case involving holocaust denial, the Supreme Court upheld, by a narrow majority of 4–3, the constitutionality of Section 319(2) of Canada's criminal code, which aimed at suppressing the willful promotion of hatred against identifiable groups. In contrast, a number of countries have repealed earlier blasphemy legislation. Hungary repealed this legislation during its communist era. The United Kingdom abrogated the common law crime of blasphemy in 2008. The trend is clearly toward replacing blasphemy legislation, which typically protects injury only to the dominant religion in a country, with hate speech legislation that covers insults to any religion, ethnic, or racial group, but is narrowly crafted to minimize adverse impacts on freedom of speech.

For those who have shifted from blasphemy-type legislation to hate speech, a number of techniques are evident to minimize adverse impacts on freedom of expression. Thus, the Czech legislation qualifies the notion of hate speech by stressing that the speech in question must be extreme. In Canada, the fact that statements were made in the course of private conversations or that statements were made in good faith to advance an opinion on a religious subject has been recognized as a defense. Also, hatred convictions can be obtained only if the state can prove beyond a reasonable doubt that the accused willfully promoted hatred against a group identifiable by color, race, religion or ethnic origin, where the promotion of hatred means that individuals are to be "despised, scorned, denied respect and made subject to ill-treatment on the basis of group affiliation." Stringent standards of mens rea, requiring intent, are necessary. Strict intent requirements are necessary under many hate speech provisions. Another approach is suggested by the Philippines, which makes it clear that mere criticisms of other religions cannot be regulated by a board charged with regulating television content.

In general, one can discern a shift toward both secularity and secularism in the trends evident in this field. On the one hand, there is a clear shift, in line with secularism, away from older blasphemy legislation. On the other hand, continued protection of hate speech against religious targets, the broadening of such legislation to cover all and not just dominant groups, and the efforts to draw the balance of such legislation more carefully to protect freedom of expression (including religious expression), all signal efforts to communicate that efforts will be made to protect the religious (and belief) sensitivities of all members of society.

1.11 Conclusion

In general, the national reports suggest that there is remarkable diversity in the configuration of religion-state relations around the world, even within regional blocs. This appears to be the natural consequence of the fact that religion, religious pluralism, and experience at the religion-state interface is embedded in the distinctive history of each country. Every country faces tensions in this area, and each has reached its own equilibrium position—a position which tends to shift over time in response to particular incidents, argumentation within the country, concerns about identity politics, and efforts to more effectively protect human rights.

If we accept that religious pluralism is a positive reality, or at least a reality that is unavoidably present in every country that we know, it seems reasonable to propose that constitutional and legal provisions should guarantee certain minimum standards of protection of freedom of religion or belief, in line with existing standards that most countries have accepted.

[82] Joint Declaration on Defamation of Religions and Anti-Terrorism and Anti-Extremism Legislation, Frank La Rue, UN Special Rapporteur on Freedom of Opinion and Expression, Miklos Haraszti, OSCE Representative on Freedom of the Media, Catalina Botero, OAS Special Rapporteur on Freedom of Expression, and Faith Pansy Tlakula, ACHPR Special Rapporteur on Freedom of Expression, page 2 (10 December 2008), available online at http://www.osce.org/documents/rfm/2008/12/35705_en.pdf.

There is a tendency to speak of the idea of a "secular state" as thought this term has a univocal meaning. In fact, however, practice tends to be the result of historical circumstances that are different in different countries. In many cases, secular states were born in the course of rebellion against the hold that major religions had on society, and these historical experiences have shaped their view of the secular state and the need to protect it against dominant religions in the past, just as the effort to implement human rights norms has affected more recent history. This has often led to systems characterized by what we have termed secularism or *laïcité*. On the other hand, experience in other countries has taken the need to deal with existing pluralism as the starting point. This has been more likely to generate systems we have described in terms of secularity. Because of differences of historical experience, we can hardly expect logical internal coherence when we apply the notion of the secular state in different areas. States that may appear the same from the perspective of the great constitutional principles may adopt rather different interpretations of their constitutional ideas as they apply them in concrete areas. This is not necessarily a negative, but confirms the famous saying from Justice Oliver Wendell Holmes, that the life of the law has not been logic but experience.

It is worth noting, however, that sociological shifts evident around the world indicate that pluralism is growing everywhere. This may suggest that there is a need to shift focus from defending the secular state against religion to finding ways to secure peaceful coexistence of the many religions that are found in every society. Protection of freedom of religion or belief has long been a powerful tool to that end. This needs to be taken into account in dealing with pressing contemporary issues about how to handle the influx of immigrants in various parts of the world. Sensitivity to accompanying religious differences can substantially reduce tensions in this area.

There is also a need to recognize that the idea of the secular state should not be thought of as an end in itself, but as an instrumental means toward the creation of states that can help those holding different worldviews—even deeply divided ones—to find peaceful ways to live together. In an often quoted phrase from the European Court of Human Rights' decision in *Serif v. Greece*,[83] although it is true "that tension is created in situations where a religious any other community becomes divided, it considers that this is one of the unavoidable consequences of pluralism. The role of the authorities in such circumstances is not to remove the cause of tension by eliminating pluralism, but to ensure that the competing groups tolerate each other . . . ." In achieving this objective, there is much to be said for reinterpreting the ideal of the secular state in terms of secularity, rather than secularism.

[83] App. No. 38178/97 (ECtHR, 14 December 1999), § 53.

2 Complexity of Transnational Sources[1]

Silvia Ferreri

2.1 The Subject

The title assigned to the IC session on Comparative Law and Unification of laws (*Droit comparé et unification du droit*) at first seemed rather enigmatic, a very broad topic, with great potential for development in a variety of directions, and suggesting many different lines of research. I had been informed that the reports to be collected by me concerned the "*Complexity of Transnational Sources/Complexité des sources transnationales*:" without an explanatory subtitle this could mean several different things and I had to make up my mind about the approach to take in such a broad field of investigation. I needed to define a line to propose to our reporters: the problem crosses borders between the competences of different disciplines such as Conflict of Laws/Private International Law (including procedural issues such as enforcement of foreign judgments), International Law (treaty law), European Union law, Uniformation of the Law and Private Law, to name but a few.

Indeed, the Austrian Reporter points out that conflict of laws aspects are sometimes underestimated since "... Private International Law is still regarded by practice and in legal education as a special branch, which only touches upon some cases. Further, Private International Law is conceived as a difficult branch of law, which is true, and where there is a high degree of uncertainty as to what interests – party autonomy versus fundamental rights – ought to prevail, which is understandable."[2] One factor contributing to the complexity is the increasing existence of mandatory rules: the mechanisms of conflict of laws are complicated by the interplay between both locally and internationally mandatory rules.[3] Some observers also emphasize the increasing number of provisions on conflict of laws that are incorporated in instruments concerning the substantive aspects of an issue: control over changes in conflict of laws questions is lost in a plethora of specific documents that omit to harmonize their solutions with treaties of wider scope, such as the Rome Convention of 1980 on the law applicable to contractual obligations (now European regulation Rome I).[4]

[1] I.C. La complexité des sources transnationales.

Silvia Ferreri (✉)
Dipartimento di Scienze Giuridiche, University of Turin, Turin, Italy
e-mail: silvia.ferreri@unito.it

[2] B. Verschraegen, *Austrian report.*

[3] B. Verschraegen, quoted above, and Jan Smits, *Netherlands' report* ("courts often have to find their way in a complex web of rules on conflict of laws, international conventions on the law applicable to transnational relationships, domestic rules of a mandatory character limiting or affecting the applicability of international provisions, and a large variety of private codes of conduct ..."). Indeed mandatory rules may prevent the application of uniform acts, if they are deemed in conflict with policies that are qualified as "mandatory": see, for example, Kazuaki Sono, "The Rise of Anational Contract in the Age of Globalization," *Tulane Law Review* 75 (2001): 1185 ff.

[4] E.-M. Kieninger, K. Linhart, *German Report* (reference to O. Remien, "Einheit, Mehrstufigkeit und Flexibilität im europäischen Privat- und Wirtschaftsrecht," *RabelsZ* 62 (1998): 627, at p. 633: the author argues the need to "coordinate single conflict of laws provisions within substantive legal instruments with pre-existing sources of conflict of laws, such as e.g. bringing provisions in EU directives in line with the – at the time – Rome Convention of 1980); E. M. Kieninger, "Der grenzüberschreitende Verbrauchvertrag zwischen Richtilinienkollisionsrecht und

K.B. Brown and D.V. Snyder (eds.), *General Reports of the XVIIIth Congress of the International Academy of Comparative Law/Rapports Généraux du XVIIIème Congrès de l'Académie Internationale de Droit Comparé*,
DOI 10.1007/978-94-007-2354-2_2, © Springer Science+Business Media B.V. 2012

The research project was organized on the basis of national affiliation: a solution that may seem paradoxical since we were invited to reflect on "*transnational*" *data*, as was pointed out by our Canadian reporters who argued that there was a contradiction in looking at sources acting **across** borders from a perspective within national boundaries.[5] However the traditional academic approach is based on contributions by observers residing in different States, and that is the starting point,[6] although we also had the opportunity to read responses by some institutional actors such as UNCITRAL[7] and OHADA,[8] working at international or supranational level.[9]

We are thus in a position to benefit also from the views of lawyers involved in projects aiming to limit diversity, and to increase coordination and simplification of the law at international level.

I should add that investigating the response of local judges and practitioners to these issues seemed to make sense since "judges still swear to observe their constitution and State's legislation," as I was once told by a French colleague who was presenting the response of legal practitioners regarding "transnational" issues. Taking account of the views of legal practitioners touches, then, on a sensitive point.

Our Canadian reporters in the end also agreed to an investigation of the subject based on national reports: after all "globalization cannot exist without the state."[10]

2.2 Scope of Project

I started my investigation by first excluding one aspect: I thought it would not be very productive or useful to cover once more an area which we had already investigated in relation to our Utrecht congress (*Contract with no governing law in private international and non-State law*): in 2006 we had been invited to reflect on the effectiveness of "non-State law", that is, on sources of law that are not supported by the coercive power of the State.

A number of reporters on that occasion explained what weight would be given in their legal systems to *International Restatements* of Legal Principles in the field of contract law such as UNIDROIT or PECL compilations, collections of rules drawn from cross-border commercial practice, to INCOTERMS, model contracts, usages of international trade such as those set out in the *Uniform Customs and Practice for Documentary Credits* (*UCP*), and to guidelines drawn up by multinational corporations.

In Utrecht we had already noted the fact that the classical range of normative tools traditionally managed by lawyers was not limited to legislation or case-law enforced by the State, but that many more means were available to govern transactions thanks to the work of bodies such as the International Chamber of Commerce, UNCITRAL, UNIDROIT, and FIDIC:

Rome I-Verordnung," in *Die richtige Ordnung, Festschrift für Jan Kropholler* (2008), 499. The German reporters also point to the specific experience of R. Wagner who acted as Head of the Department of Private International Law at the German Justice Ministry ("Die Haager Konferenz für Internationales Privatrecht zehn Jahre nach der Vergemeinschaftung der Gesetzgebungskomptenz in der justiziellen Zusammenarbeit in Zivilsachen," *RabelsZ* 73 (2009): 215 ff.): the increase in competences of the EU has affected the individual States' capacity to participate (in some fields) in negotiations taking place within the Hague Conference.

[5] H. Dedek, A. Carbone, "Transnational law, however, is, even and particularly in a private law context, by its definition "beyond", some might even say "after" or "without," the state. Does it make sense to approach through a national lens a discourse whose subject is, by its very nature, meta-jurisdictional?": see *Canadian report*.

[6] The reports submitted were presented by: 14 AFRICAN Member States of the OHADA, summarized by S. Mancuso (University of Macau; Centre for African Laws and Society, Xiangtan University); AUSTRIA (Bea Verschraegen, Law Faculty of the University of Vienna); CANADA (H. Dedek, A. Carbone, Faculty of Law, McGill University, Montreal); GERMANY (E. Kieninger and K. Linhart, Würzburg); HUNGARY (G. Suto Burger); JAPAN (Tetsuo Morishita, Sophia University, Tokyo); NETHERLANDS (J. M. Smits, Tilburg University); PORTUGAL (L. de Lima Pinheiro, University of Lisbon); SERBIA (J. Perovic, University of Belgrade, Faculty of Economics); SPAIN (G. García Cantero, Zaragoza University); SWITZERLAND (A. Fötschl, Swiss Institute of Comparative Law, Lausanne); USA (W. Ewald, University of Pennsylvania Law School); VENEZUELA (Z. Marin).

[7] UNCITRAL, report by Luca Castellani.

[8] OHADA, report by Salvatore Mancuso.

[9] "Supranational" may be appropriately used to indicate aggregations of States where the power to legislate in some matters is delegated to specific institutions and a central court is empowered to interpret the normative instruments adopted within this framework and to deliver judgments that are enforceable in the member States (as is the case with the EU).

[10] Quotation of Harry W. Arthurs (Toronto, Ontario) (Harry W. Arthurs, "*Globalization of the Mind: Canadian Elites and the Restructuring of Legal Fields*," *Canadian Journal of Law & Society* 12 (1997): 219 at 221): with Roderick A. Macdonald (teaching in Montreal, Quebec) mentioned as one of the Canadian "pioneers of legal pluralism theory."

their influence being more obvious where arbitration proceedings are involved rather than the state courts' jurisdiction since state judges exhibit a higher level of caution, of reserve, towards normative products not implemented by the State.

In the meantime the EU has also implemented a scheme to explore the possibility of codifying the European law of contract: if not immediately, at least in the future through the controversial "tool box" of the *Common frame of reference* (DCFR). This fact adds a further element to the plan to move, in some areas, from the State level of legislation to a higher level, be it regional, international or transnational.[11] We are not now in a position to foresee what will be the final result of this project because it is meeting with some resistance and concerns expressed by even the more open-minded observers.[12]

Obviously we do not imply that the field of *lex mercatoria* is outdated: it continues to be relevant and important.

The reporter from Japan mentioned that in his country a study in "soft law" was recently carried out on "norms that, although not part of the formal law provided by the state and whose enforceability is not guaranteed in the courts, are perceived by both state and private parties as having some binding force and are, in fact, obeyed."[13] The study resulted in a 5-volume publication, including one book specifically dedicated to "Soft Law on International Issues."

Thus, although all the concerns expressed in a well-known article by Lord Mustill in the late 1980s[14] may not have been resolved, in fact the field of *lex mercatoria* and *soft law* continues to grow.

Rather than reconsidering and updating the question of how the State's rules can be integrated by paradigms created outside the classical *fora* of legislative production, it seemed more productive to turn the focus of our investigation to the difficulties that lawyers belonging to a specific national legal system meet when they have to deal with such multilayered normative material. This pragmatic level of observation, rather than the classical theoretical approach, shall be my starting point.

It is no easy task to find a path through local conflict of law rules, the foreign law identified by those rules, and the special instruments overriding that legislation because of some international undertaking stipulated by the State of *renvoi*, especially if there is a need to interpret the international instrument in the light of the specific case-law of the State involved. This case-law is usually accessible only in the local language, not the same as the language of the judge involved with the original case that started the whole machinery off.[15]

If we turn our minds back a number of years, for instance, to consider the UNIDROIT Congress of Rome in 1987 on *International Uniform Law in Practice* (Oceana 1988) it is obvious that progress has certainly been made. Today any legal practitioner, even a solo practitioner working in a small State mostly with domestic litigation, is aware that the relationship between law and State is looser than in the past. It is clear to all that in e-commerce any electronic transaction that may occur from any ordinary personal computer is rather loosely bound by the national law; other sources of law become relevant. Even the more conservative, traditional lawyers must accept the obvious fact that national legislations are permeable to other sources of law. Not only because

[11] Jan Smits, reporting on the subject from the Netherlands, comments on this point by referring to the fact that "The Dutch government supports the use of this DCFR as a non-binding instrument to make existing directives more consistent, but does not regard it as a step towards a European Civil Code": we learn this in a letter sent by "the Dutch Minister of Justice … after Parliament raised questions about an article in a Dutch newspaper", claiming that the European Commission was trying to introduce a European Civil Code "through the backdoor".

[12] Jan Smits acutely observes that even a codification of European contract law would not resolve the problem of fragmentation in Europe since "even if the European competence to introduce a binding European Civil Code existed, this would not end the present fragmentation … One only needs to think of closely connected areas of procedural and administrative law (that will remain national) and competition law (that is largely European), leaving aside that a European Civil Code in whatever form will probably not contain rules on immovable property, family law and the law of succession".

[13] See "Summary of the Project" by Nobuhiro Nakayama available at http://www.j.u-tokyo.ac.jp/coelaw/: Japan report by Tetsuo Morishita, footnote 10.

[14] Lord Justice Michael Mustill, "The New Law Mercatoria: The First Twenty-Five Years," *Journal of International Arbitration* (1988): 86.

[15] Martin Wolff once famously said "a conscientious judge will be glad if the rules of Private International Law allow him to apply the law of his own country … Even if he knows the foreign language he is never sure that his interpretation of, say, a foreign code is correct … He is acting as a judge, but he knows no more and often less about the foreign law than first-year students in the country in question": Martin Wolff, *Private International Law* (Oxford: Clarendon, 1950), 17–18.

of our growing inclination to globe-trotting (attending congresses in Utrecht, then in Washington, and further afield; producing and buying products globally),[16] but also because many relationships occur in an "unsubstantial" way, in a meta-physical area, not really attached to any place in particular. The internet explosion has certainly encouraged transactions detached from any local law.[17] A certain porosity in national systems of law is undeniable.

It may still be true that "the legal profession, typical of most professions, is most comfortable with and inclines towards the familiar … (and) faced with the option of drafting clients' contractual obligations with reference to existing and long-established domestic law, the practitioner will choose to shun the application of a novel uniform law … if at all possible."[18]

There is evidence of this attitude in the national reports. The Canadian report indicates that "… the treatment and application of the CISG in Canadian courts has been lamentable, the courts always deferring back to a homeward trend. It has either been the case that the CISG has been overlooked altogether, or that, when it has been considered, it has been interpreted in light of common law principles, thus undermining the international character and goal of uniformity the Convention seeks to achieve"[19] ("a homeward trend" is what John Honnold diagnosed some years ago[20]). The Serbian report,[21] the reports from Hungary,[22] from Portugal,[23] and from Venezuela[24] all agree that the

[16] A Canadian judge of the Supreme Court of Canada (Justice La Forest), speaking about enforcement of foreign judgments is quoted saying: "Modern means of travel and communications have made many … nineteenth century concerns appear parochial. The business community operates in a world economy and we correctly speak of a world community even in the face of decentralized political and legal power. Accommodating the flow of wealth, skills and people across state lines has now become imperative. Under these circumstances, our approach to the recognition and enforcement of foreign judgments would appear ripe for reappraisal" (in *Morguard Investments Ltd.* v. *De Savoye* [1990] 3 S.C.R. 1077 (at pp.1095–1096), 76 D.L.R. (4th) 256, quoted by Dedek and Carbone). This opening towards complexity may seem just a little overstated – Lord Denning would say the "heroics" of this statement might seem disproportionate – considering "that the judgment did not deal with an international, but with an inter-provincial conflict, the enforcement of an Alberta judgment in British Columbia." But we also learn that "La Forest's call for the acceptance of a "world community" and a more cosmopolitan understanding of the law … [was] later repeated in different contexts."

[17] A. Fischer-Lescano, G. Teubner, "Regime-Collisions: The Vain Search for Legal Unity in the Fragmentation of Global Law," *Michigan Journal of International Law* 25 (2004): 999 ff. 8 available on line at: http://papers.ssrn.com/sol3/papers.cfm?abstract_id=873908

[18] J. P. Carter, *The Experience of the Legal Profession*, in UNIDROIT, *International Uniform Law in Practice*, proceedings of the 3rd Congress on Private Law held by UNIDROIT, Rome (September 1987) (Dobbs Ferry, NY: Oceana, 1988), 411 ff. (at 415).

[19] Canadian Report: "In the case of the CISG, judges have not only been eschewing complexity; they might not even be aware of it. If any positive changes in Canadian CISG jurisprudence are to take place, there must be an increase in awareness of the Convention among both counsel and judges".

[20] Honnold, *Documentary History of the Uniform law for the International Sale of Goods*, 1989; ID., "The Sales Convention in Action – Uniform International Words: Uniform Application?," *Journal of Law and Commerce* 8 (1988): 207 (at the Symposium organized by the University of Pittsburgh School of Law for entry into force of the CISG in 1988).

[21] Serbian Report (J. Perovic) "Although the application of the CISG as a ratified international convention has the priority over national laws, the courts of Serbia are not very familiar with its application even in simple cases of direct application specified in article 1.1.a CISG. Generally speaking, the first instance courts in most cases do not apply the CISG at all; instead, the judges determine the applicable law by virtue of the rules of private international law which usually means the application of Serbian substantive law under which they consider the Serbian Code on Obligations and not the CISG, although all the conditions for the application of the CISG are met. On the other hand, in the appeal proceedings the High Commercial Court expressed different views regarding the application of the CISG. … Contrary to the regular court practice, the CISG is well known and widely implemented in the Serbian arbitration practice".

[22] G. Suto Burger (pp. 7–8): according to "one of the most well known handbooks « *in the Hungarian judicial practice unfortunately, there are cases where the court forgot about the obvious duty to apply the CISG (Legf. B. Pf. III. 20.998/1995.) In a dispute over a sale and purchase agreement between a Hungarian and an Austrian party the court applied the rules of the Austrian ABGB at a time when the CISG has already entered into force in both Hungary (January 1st, 1988) and Austria (January 1st, 1989)* » … There are some problems with the wording of the cases. The Metropolitan Court of Appeals issued a decision stating "*Because both Germany and Hungary have ratified the CISG, based on the conflict of laws rules, German law is applicable*". After this misleading explanation, the court applied the CISG in the given dispute."

[23] Portugal report, Luís de Lima Pinheiro: "when interpreting and filling gaps of international sources the Portuguese courts resort normally to domestic law instead of following the criteria applicable to the interpretation and filling of gaps of international conventions. Instead of aiming to a uniform interpretation and gap filling, through an autonomous interpretation and the resort to the principles underlying the rules of the convention, they simply apply the rules of internal source".

[24] Venezuelan Report (Zhandra Marin, answer to question 8) "Venezuelan judges do not have much training or knowledge in

binding nature of the Vienna convention is still underestimated in court practice. In choosing between the option of treading traditional paths, well-known to the local lawyer, and engaging in applying international instruments (some even 20 years old), the appeal of the well-worn route is still strong.[25] In Germany, E. Jayme, in an article of 1975, showed examples of cases in which not only local courts but also higher Regional Courts (*Oberlandesgerichte* – OLG) and the German Supreme Court (BGH) "have decided … without applying a convention that would have been applicable."[26]

But there are now fields of law where the transnational rules have overtaken any national legislation, areas where the domestic legislator is running after innovation rather than breaking ground. In these fields even the most traditional lawyer is drawn to see the relevance of extra-national sources.

2.3 A Tapestry Woven with Many Normative Threads

The normative resources that are to be managed, in many cases, and in various situations (also when advising clients), can be visualized as a complex tapestry woven with many threads intertwined in an intricate pattern.[27]

Several levels of specialization are overlaid, one on top of the other: private international law leads us to a foreign law, but that may be displaced by a convention ruling in a uniform way on the matter; then, in turn, the foreign State may have ratified the international instrument with some reservation and ruled on some exception; the local case-law may differ from that of other States; administrative restrictions may limit the effect of the would-be uniform legislation; and trade usages may interfere with its application. The roads to be followed to reach the solution have many sharp turns, and bridges and tunnels and overpasses and subways and crossways.

However, this does not necessarily mean that we should complain about complexity. Simplicity is not perforce a value in itself; the illusion that the law could simply be reduced to what the national Parliament had established (as some nineteenth century lawyers believed) lasted only for a brief moment in history: most western legal systems have known the complexity of interaction between *jus civile* and *jus praetorium*/*jus honorarium*, between *canon law* and *civil law*, between *mercantile* and *maritime* laws and the ordinary practice of state courts, or between *jus commune* and *local statutes* (*placita principorum*).

The notion that, even within a single State, the law has more than one matrix and that several jurisdictions may co-exist with distinct repositories of rules to be applied is not in any way new. The reduction of the law to "one main source," the positivistic approach of the first half of the nineteenth century, had a very short life after Napoleon and it may have been an illusion in itself to begin with, as many scholars have found, identifying customs that were consistently followed in certain sections of society, despite all the talk of the "paramount" character of Parliament-made legislation.

---

the area; therefore it is easier to apply the forum law, a national law or even to assume that the case is domestic rather than international. Striking as it is, this last situation is very common: neither the judge nor the parties realize that the contract in front of them is international".

[25] In Japan a specific difficulty is mentioned by Tetsuo Morishita: "under Japanese Court Law, all proceedings in Japanese courts shall be conducted in Japanese. All documents, including foreign laws, cases and expert opinions, which may be necessary to identify foreign laws, as well as transactional documents such as contracts, need to be translated into Japanese before they are submitted to Japanese courts"; and, in relation to "Japan's accession to CISG", it should be remembered that: "Many foreign cases on CISG are available in English. Most … Japanese academics consider that judges, not parties, have to find laws and to research cases by themselves. If so, when Japanese judges apply CISG, judges need good English ability to research foreign cases. Because it is difficult to require all judges to have such English ability, it could be an idea to set up [a] special department of courts in the future" (answer to question 5).

[26] E.-M. Kieninger, K. Linhart, *German Report* (quoting Jayme, *Staatsverträge zum Internationalen Privatrecht*, *Berichte der Deutschen Gesellschaft für Völkerrecht* (*BerGesVölkR*) 16 (1975): 12–13.

[27] J. Smits, Netherlands' *Report*: "courts often have to find their way in a complex web of rules on conflict of laws, international conventions on the law applicable to transnational relationships, domestic rules of a mandatory character limiting or affecting the applicability of international provisions, and a large variety of private codes of conduct, guidelines, restatements of trade usages and practices, as well as collections of principles by non-governmental organisations". According to the German Report (by Kieninger, Linhart): "In an article on European Private and Commercial Law *Remien* has pointed out that this particular area of law is characterized by a complex multi-level structure (*Mehrstufigkeit*)"(O. Remien, "Einheit, Mehrstufigkeit und Flexibilität im europäischen Privat- und Wirtschaftsrecht," *RabelsZ* 62 (1998): 627 ff., at pp. 627–647). A title suggesting the complexity of the matter introduces a work by M. Reimann, *Conflict of Laws in Western Europe, A Guide Through the Jungle* (Irvington: Transnational Publishers, 1995).

The effort to justify the effectiveness of other, non-State sources, by allowing their silent incorporation into contracts, by tacit inclusion in some State pieces of legislation and by other covert devices, was early recognized as a thin veil, too thin to mask the underlying reality.

Comparativists predicted quite some time ago that the compact image of one State-coherent legal system would break down: observing legal phenomena across national borders inevitably led the researcher to see that the various legal formants were often in disagreement within one State, and that similarities occurred more often between similar formants in different States than between the various components in the same State[28]: the "dogma" of the "unitary" character of the law in one State was early dissolved in the eyes of comparative law scholars.

In a number of countries – we are reminded by our Canadian reporters – legal pluralism was associated with anthropological studies on colonialism, with the situation of imported Western "law" clashing with indigenous systems of normativity: law, custom, and religion.[29] Legal pluralism, however, has "long moved beyond … this field of application and has developed into a discourse that inquires into the general phenomenon of the multiplicity of normative orders in societies …. In an age of global migration, legal pluralism has been connected with concepts of multiculturalism and diversity:"[30] socio-legal theories have investigated the subject for some time.[31]

In international law, since 2006, many authors have commented on the report by the study group of the International Law Commission concerning the *Fragmentation of International Law.*[32] But fragmentation is not at all new in this field.[33] As early as 1975, Erik Jayme had pointed out that some agreements among States are drawn up and ratified without prior consideration to the work carried out by other organizations or conferences in the same area.[34]

Some theorists – especially in the field of social studies – have emphasized this aspect of the law, i.e. the evidence that the State does not have full control of production of norms. *Globalization* is the password, to the point that it can be considered as a distinguishing feature of our times: positive evaluation is made of *legal pluralism* and its *enriching effect* on the State's system.[35] A whole wave of academic production has

[28] For instance, students in Rodolfo Sacco's classes were exposed to the theory of *legal formants* in the 1970s; in 1979 the theory of legal formants was fully propounded, and in 1980 it was published in a systematic form in the Italian *Introduzione al diritto comparato,* later translated into English for the *American Journal of Comparative Law* as "Legal Formants: A Dynamic Approach to Comparative Law," *American Journal of Comparative Law* 39, no. 1 (1991): 1–34. Previously Sacco had introduced the subject in articles published in French: see R. Sacco, "Définitions savantes et droit appliqué dans les systèmes romanistes," *Revue internationale de droit comparé* 47 (1965): 827 ff.), and *Droit commun de l' Europe et composantes du droit,* in Cappelletti (ed.), *Nouvelles perspectives d'un droit commun de l' Europe* (Leyden: Sijthoff, 1978).

[29] Paul Schiff Berman, "Global Legal Pluralism," *Southern California Law Review* 80 (2006): 1155 (at 1158); in the report by OHADA (by S. Mancuso) we read "that stratigraphical analysis of African law applied to the present situation of development of African law [shows] a new layer … in African law. It is the law made by the Westerners (mostly Europeans) for the Africans. … The OHADA law represents the most advanced example of this new layer of African law".

[30] Dedek and Carbone, *Canadian Report*: "Canada has experienced the clash between Western law and the laws of the Canadian aboriginal peoples. With a long history of liberal immigration policies, modern Canadian society is one of the most diverse in the world, which brings up numerous questions of – from the perspective of state law – the necessary and permissible degree of "accommodation": studies on legal pluralism as the "paradigm of legal science" date since the late 1970s": references are to Roderick A. Macdonald, "Pour la reconnaissance d'une normativité juridique implicite et «inférentielle»," *Sociologie et Sociétés* 18 (1986): 47; Roderick A. Macdonald and Martha-Marie Kleinhans, "What is Critical Legal Pluralism?" *Canadian Journal of Law and Society* 12 (1997): 25.

[31] In Canada we are referred to Jean-Guy Belley, *Conflit Social et Pluralisme Juridique en Sociologie du Droit* (LL.D. Thesis, Université de droit, d'économie et de sciences sociales de Paris (Paris 2), 1977).

[32] *Fragmentation of International Law: Difficulties arising from the Diversification and Expansion of International Law*, report by the Study Group of the International Law Commission finalized by Martti Koskenniemi, UN A/CN.4/L.682 (13 April 2006).

[33] Jan Smits, Netherlands' report, with reference to Anne-Charlotte Martineau, "The Rhetoric of Fragmentation: Fear and Faith in International Law," *Leiden Journal of International Law* 22 (2009): 1.

[34] E.-M. Kieninger, K. Linhart, *German Report* quoting E. Jayme, "Staatsverträge zum Internationalen Privatrecht, Berichte der Deutschen Gesellschaft für Völkerrecht," *BerGes VoelkR* 16 (1975): 7

[35] G. Teubner has written extensively on the effects of globalization: several of his articles have gained large popularity ("Breaking Frames: the Global Interplay of Legal and Social Systems," *American Journal of Comparative Law* 45 (1997): 149 ff.; Andreas Fischer-Lescano & Gunther Teubner,

explored this view, which is diametrically opposed to the older illusion of the unity of the legal system.

We read in the Canadian report that we may "use the insights of legal pluralism to help us understand the complex and ubiquitous phenomenon we call globalization as a proliferation of contending legal orders."[36]

Yet, some feeling of frustration, of disappointment, of a missed goal, or a sense of anxiety may filter through in some legal spheres: if judicial decisions must reach the same results under similar circumstances ("like cases are to be decided alike"), the multiplicity of sources of law may render this result less certain, and the combining of many prescriptions deriving from a variety of normative bodies may bring greater risk. The chances of getting lost are greater, and predictability becomes more unlikely.

The fact that simplification of the applicable rules was once envisaged (one compact *corpus* of coherent written rules, emanating from one legitimate authority) makes the prospect of coping with fragmented pieces of rules, expressed through various different specific languages, a great deal less appealing, at least at the level of practice.[37]

We are not seeing ecclesiastics or aristocrats being governed by different rules from the bourgeois, as under ancient constitutions, but we have contracts governed by rules that differ according to which parties are involved (business or consumers), according to the choice of applicable law and *depeçage*, and according to the subject matters involved: a fragmented picture supersedes the idea of a general contract law.

A number of institutions have strived for some kind of uniformity, either in the field of conflict of laws (such as the Hague Conference of Private International Law) or in the area of substantive provisions of civil and commercial law (through the offices of various U.N. agencies such as UNCITRAL, or by non-Governmental bodies such as UNIDROIT). But their work has not been rewarded by real simplification: in reality the many efforts by numerous players have produced the paradox of an increase in number of instruments.

This discovery is not completely unexpected: in 1988 J. Putzeys (a colleague from Belgium specialized in transport law) had already reported in Rome on the "Droit uniforme désuniformisé." In relation to the field of transport law, he listed an increasing number of instruments of uniformation since 1946. In his words *« à partir de 1946 c'est le délire … sans avoir la prétention d'être exhaustif nous avons relevé … 85 conventions dans le seul domaine des transports, sans parler évidemment des innombrables traités bilatéraux ou régionaux dans les matières les plus diverses, mais toujours liés aux transports (fiscaux, sociaux, administratifs …). »*[38] Labeling the Warsaw system as a "*patchwork législatif*" was in itself illustrative.

The growth in number of international instruments has continued, even in fields such as Human Rights where one might expect a certain stability to have been reached.[39] The creation of courts charged with guaranteeing, at a supranational level, respect for international obligations makes cases of disagreement between them obnoxious.

A number of reporters mentioned (with some dismay, perhaps even a feeling of being overcome) the number of EU directives enacted in the last 20 years: the overwhelming impression is not expressed only by lawyers belonging to States that have recently joined the Union (and who may be shocked by the effort required to comply with such a huge *acquis*

"Regime-Collisions: The Vain Search for Legal Unity in the Fragmentation of Global Law," *Michigan Journal of International Law* 25 (2004): 999 at 1004).

[36] Harry W. Arthurs, "Globalization of the Mind: Canadian Elites and the Restructuring of Legal Fields," *Canadian Journal of Law and Society* 12 (1997): 219 at 221. Robert Wai (Toronto) sees "global legal pluralism" as offering "an excellent conceptual framework for understanding normative contestation among the different state and non-state normative orders of contemporary global society"("The Interlegality of Transnational Private Law," *Law and Contemporary Problems.* 71 (2008): 107 at 110). Peer Zumbansen (Toronto) has called the phenomenon "a radical challenge to all theorizing about law as it reminds us of very fragility and unattainedness of law" (Peer Zumbansen, *Transnational Law*, in Jan Smits (ed.) *Encyclopedia of Comparative Law* (Cheltenham: Edward Elgar, 2006), 738 ff., at 739.

[37] Jan Smits, (Netherlands' report): apart from systematic purity, "consistency serves the important goal of establishing equality before the law (and thereby legal certainty): only if rules and principles are applied in a uniform way, similar cases are treated alike".

[38] J. Putzeys, *Le droit uniforme désuniformisé*, in UNIDROIT, "International Uniform Law in Practice," In: *Proceedings of the 3rd Congress on Private Law* held by UNIDROIT, Rome (September 1987) (Dobbs Ferry, NY: Oceana, 1988), 440 at 442.

[39] OHADA report, S. Mancuso, mentions: "the African Chart for the protection of human rights, directly derived from the 1948 Universal Declaration of Human Rights"

communautaire),[40] but also by older members of the club.

What was the reaction in everyday experience? In some judicial settings, a certain contradiction can be detected between lip-service paid to the *enrichment* deriving from legal pluralism, and actual judicial practice that sometimes ignores complexity simply by oversight, by leaving aside solutions deriving from the international source rules that ought be applied – according to the relationship between sources of law.

The reporters from Canada (Helge Dedek and Alexandra Carbone) were explicit in commenting on this duplicity: on several occasions, the courts in the different provinces of Canada have declared their openness towards legal pluralism, but in everyday practice their actual record as to the application of foreign law, or even international law written in binding treaties, is not wholly commendable.[41]

The reporters distinguish between "cultural attitude" (both of academic studies and courts) and technical application. While culturally Canadians are fairly open to other experiences, when they have to deal pragmatically with sources belonging to foreign States or with international conventions (and less formal normative instruments) some obstacles prevent a satisfying performance. Helge Dedek and Alexandra Carbone mention a certain difficulty even in identifying the treaties that have been actually incorporated into Canadian law (because of the dualist approach Canada has adopted towards international texts), and they mention some disregard of foreign sources both by litigants and judges.

It should be clear that the issue of a discrepancy between good intentions and modest effects is considered also by other reporters: but the Canadian reporters seem to have expressed the point in the most striking and effective manner. The reporter from Hungary (Suto Burger) was also fairly outspoken about the under-representation of the Vienna Convention in Hungarian case-law on the sale of goods.[42] Similar critical remarks were made by the Serbian reporter (Jelena Perovic). The USA report states that trial courts have little experience in dealing with transnational cases.[43]

We are informed that in Austria "lower courts … do not always recognise the Private International Law-implications of cases or do not always solve the conflict problems properly … problems caused by fragmentation and proliferation are to a great extent located by many in European Union law and International Public law. This may be due to the fact that there are only few experts on Private International Law in Austria."[44] The remark is all the more noteworthy as it applies to countries professing high fidelity to international commitments and not pleading – as is the case for some African Countries[45] – unusual difficulty in accessing documents

[40] Report by Garcia Cantero, Spain ("l'existence d'environ 20.000 directives … représente l'argument décisif à propos de l'interêt préminent en Espagne pour le droit de l'Union Européenne"); Jan Smits (Netherlands), mentions "directives implemented in the 27 member States and sets of soft law prepared with the support of the European Commission (while regulations are enforced in the field of private international law on insolvency, judicial and extra-judicial documents, evidence, enforcement of foreign decisions, on the law applicable to non contractual and contractual obligations)". Also the Serbian reporter refers to the daunting duty of gradually transposing EU directives in view of future membership of the EU (Jelena Perovic report); in Hungary (G. Suto Burger): "the government … has set out the training of judges for community law. The National Judicial Council has paid also special attention to trainings of community laws especially in respect of administrative leaders in the last years, with special attention to this decision and the new, important tasks the judges were to receive with the EU accession."

[41] Looking at judicial practice in Canada there seems to be a divergence between general declarations and actual application of the ideas professed: while the Canadian judiciary exhibits an open mind towards legal pluralism and the interaction of several sources of law, it is also possible to detect cases – at the level of appeal courts – where the CISG should have been applied as governing law, and neither the parties nor the judge seem to have realized that such was the case, so that the decision is based only on Canadian law even if the sale was actually international (and, of course, Canada has ratified the CISG): a case of contradiction between good intentions and poor performance.

[42] Quoting from a textbook on International Sale of goods by Sandor and Vékás, 2005.

[43] USA Report (EWALD), par. III: "the sheer geographical size of the United States means that, even when cases involving foreign law arise, they constitute only a minor fraction of the business of the judiciary. The state courts deal with some 40 million cases annually; and the federal courts with a further 300,000. It follows that the caseload of a typical American judge is overwhelmingly domestic."

[44] "… Most lawyers dealing with civil law claim that they deal with conflict cases only rarely, with the exception of international family and succession law:" Beata Verschraegen, *Austrian Report*.

[45] OHADA Report, S. Mancuso (answer to question 7): "… most of the reporters refer to the problem – well known in Africa – of the lack of information about the law in force. In countries like Central African Republic, Comoros or Guinea-Bissau there is a serious difficulty even in the information and knowledge of the national law …."

incorporating the international treaties, or in consulting the existing case-law applying these treaties to actual litigation.

It is perhaps worth mentioning that the Vienna Convention of 1980, the CISG, is considered a very successful document: the fact that it is fairly often ignored in the very country where it was signed is all the more significant.

2.4 Transnational, International or Extra-National Sources?

The title of our session used the adjective "transnational" which is often associated with customs and practices spontaneously followed across borders by some sections of society, apart from a State's endorsement (the obvious example being mercantile usages enforced in arbitral awards). However, it seemed necessary not to limit our attention only to *lex mercatoria* or to mechanisms of soft law, and wiser to also consider the classical tools that govern transnational cases: that is, international treaties and conventions.

Even these more institutional means and more classical instruments are liable to cause uncertainty at the level of application: a look at the practice of trials before ordinary State courts may reveal contradictory solutions being reached because of the wealth of instruments adopted in the field of commercial law or transport law or even in relation to human rights. Judges often omit to use the proper international instrument: either by ignoring (or being unaware of) the international text which is applicable to the case in hand, or by reducing its content to the local law (reading the international provision as if it meant the same thing as the national legislation that the judge is familiar with).[46] We should not forget that often judges do not have immediate access to international texts, but only to the local statutes that incorporate them into the national legislation. They often rely on translations that may often remind the local judge of local concepts, institutions, and lines of reasoning. Some procedures of incorporation which convert the international text into a national piece of legislation hide the origin of the document and encourage a municipal approach to the rules in force.[47]

Academic studies have increasingly revealed the fragmentation of international sources. In addition to the UN and its agencies, regional organizations also promote the drafting of treaties; these treaties reproduce, or sometimes anticipate, agreements which are broader in scope, sometimes *universal conventions* which are meant to be ratified by a large number of participants. An example of this is found in human rights conventions, where there are large numbers of both regional and world instruments.

This point was raised specifically by the reporter for Africa, who described the situation of the OHADA member countries and mentioned the coming into force of the *African Chart for the Protection of Human Rights* (1981, in force since 1986) together with the UN *Universal Declaration of Human Rights* of 1948 (in competition also with various regional instruments such as the *European Convention on Human Rights* of 1950). Many provisions coincide, but there are also some discrepancies between the two documents. A specific court (the African Court on Human and

[46] Luís de Lima Pinheiro (Portugal Report), answer to question 7: « In the Portuguese system the principle *iura novit curia* applies both to internal sources and to supranational sources. The court is also under a duty to ascertain the content of foreign law *ex officio* (Article 348(1) and (2) of the Civil Code). In practice there is a judicial trend to maximize the scope of application of the *lex fori*, and the courts often ignore the supranational or foreign sources where they are not pleaded by the parties."

[47] Several reporters commented on this issue: some uncertainty about treaties in force is observed in Canada because of the dualistic system that requires – as in many other countries, such as Italy for instance – a domestic act of legislation to incorporate the international text in the national legal system. This domestic legislation often omits to mention the origin of the provision so that the reader may be quite unaware of the original international nature of the document, sometimes implementation may "also be inferred by the fact that new legislation is approved which is in compliance with the international courses, without explicitly declaring that international obligations are carried out. These circumstances cause uncertainty in the judiciary about the real status of international commitments so that courts sometimes refer to international law as "relevant and persuasive" in order to avoid to state whether they are actually bound by it." The same report makes the point that the Vienna convention on the sale of goods (CISG) was included in Canadian law by a Uniform Act that "merely adopted the CISG as domestic law with the Convention text appended as a Schedule", giving jurists little guidance or assistance in understanding the CISG. Also in Hungary (SUTO BURGER), "Hungarian law is based on a dualistic system; therefore, all international and similar conventions must be published by a Hungarian statute having full binding force."

People's Rights)[48] has been empowered since 2005 to revise decisions by appeal courts from the various States in order to guarantee uniform application.

Increasing numbers of international commitments may strengthen the bonds between a group of States. To duplicate a universal declaration by means of a treaty between a more limited circle of participants may bring the commitment closer to the minds of people, and reinforce the will to respect the obligations undertaken. But it may also cause uncertainty. It may happen that a State signs a regional convention without denouncing a previous more comprehensive treaty; or a State may be a party to several regional coalitions, or different courts may be in charge of guaranteeing respect for conventions which have almost the same aim.

As an example, to focus our attention in preparing the report, reference was made – once more – to a well-known experience in the field of the sale of goods. A long list of international texts have aimed to regulate the field of international commerce in the Nordic countries,[49] the socialist countries,[50] and western Europe, by means of the Hague Convention of 1964, then by the United Nations Vienna Convention of 1980 (CISG) which has been approved by almost everyone, with the exception of the United Kingdom (as often happens), Ireland and Portugal.

There were problems, when the Vienna Convention followed the Hague Convention, between States that had signed both instruments, but at different times; for example, between Italy and Germany that exited from the older treaty at different dates, to accede to the new one. The Nordic countries joined the Vienna Convention, making some reservations in order to preserve the previous agreement between them: but their uniformity was affected at first by the fact that Denmark did not adopt the new version of the Scandinavian sale of goods and later by the fact that some of the Northern States have become part of the EU and others have not (as in the case of Norway). As a consequence, the 99/44 EC directive on certain guarantees in the sale of goods to consumers is applicable to some transactions between Nordic buyers and sellers, but not to all of them.

Although it is tempting to consider this "patchwork" of rules as a temporary phenomenon, it is nevertheless true that not all conventions can move from the level of regional agreement to become documents of universal application. Ernst Rabel started his effort to unify the law of sale in the 1930s and the struggle to combine several international commitments in the same area is still ongoing. The Vienna convention has been extremely successful (at least in terms of the number of States where it is in force), but it still lacks the UK's ratification, and is subject to reservation by other States. This process lasted from the 1950s (at least) to 1980 and has still not cleared the field of uncertainty.

The US reporter[51] very appropriately specified that, from his point of view, that of a federal State, we should distinguish between *transnational* and *transborder* relations. In the USA lawyers are well trained to deal with the combination of sources belonging to different States of the federation, and to cope with the interaction of federal and State laws. However dealing with international instruments or foreign substantive laws is still an exercise which can cause difficulty. The records concerning the application of CISG in US courts are not very satisfactory: the low numbers of cases decided lead the observers to suspect that in many cases the parties opt out of the convention and in some cases they may ignore the binding force of the convention. Greater difficulty derives from the fact that means to cope with diversity at national level are not quite as effective across different cultures: no Restatements, no UCC, no national law schools, and no common legal background are available beyond national borders.

The same distinction made by the US reporter can probably be shared by others who practice law in federal jurisdictions. The reporter from Japan quite

---

[48] Protocol of the *African Chart of Human and People's Rights*, creating the African Court on Human and People's Rights, adopted in 1998, in Ouagadougou (Burkina Faso), in force since 2004.

[49] The Scandinavian Sale of Goods Act has been implemented in Finland, Norway and Sweden in the late 1980s, replacing the previous legislation of the beginning of the century and modeled on the Swedish Sale of Goods Act of 1905 (also reproduced in Denmark, 1906): J. Ramberg, *The New Swedish Sales Law*, in Bonell, *Saggi, Conferenze e Seminari*, Centro Studi e Ricerche di diritto comparato e straniero, vol. 28 (Roma, 1997); J. Lookofsky, *Understanding the CISG in Scandinavia*, Copenhagen, 1996; ID., "Alive and Well in Scandinavia: CISG Part II," *Journal of Law and Commerce* 18 (1999): 289–299, http://www.cisg.law.pace.edu/cisg/biblio/lookofsky1.html.

[50] The *Bilateral Terms for Delivery of Goods* of 1948 between member States of the CMEA (Council for Mutual Economic Assistance, COMECON) was followed by the *Multilateral Terms for Delivery of Goods* of 1958 and then further replaced by a new version in 1968 (Z, Stalev, The *Uniform CMEA Law and its Uniform Application*, in UNIDROIT, *International Uniform Law in Practice*, *cit.* (Oceana, 1988), 231 ff.)

[51] Ewald's report (USA).

reasonably points out the fact that Japan does not belong to any regional circuit: and this circumstance at least simplifies the normative background.[52]

2.5 A Closer Look at the Questions

The questions I proposed to our reporters were meant to clarify two main points: "How bad is the problem?" and then "What can be done about it?"

First of all, in an attempt to understand how the problem is perceived, we considered (question 1) whether concern about fragmentation of international sources (such as regional versus universal conventions, codes of conduct and trade usages) is expressed in the various countries, and if so, by whom.

2.5.1 Academic Literature

Concern about difficulty with combination of texts, stratification of documents having similar content, and the interaction of courts created to guarantee the implementation and interpretation of international treaties, has been widely addressed in academic studies. Therefore the first question aimed to ascertain whether other components of the legal community shared this concern. Overall, the answers seem to incline towards the negative.

Apart from replies by institutional actors such as UNCITRAL[53] and OHADA[54] where the problem is well understood and efforts of cooperation are ongoing, the views of national reporters show a certain skepticism about the degree of awareness that various actors have of the problem.[55]

The general impression conveyed by many reporters is that practicing lawyers are more concerned with local issues: they might also consider questions raised by contacts with legal sources not belonging to their State, but rather episodically, on a case-by-case basis,

[52] Tetsuo Morishita (Japan's report): "Comparing to European countries, the fragmentation of law is not so material and has not caused serious problems in Japan. … First, Japan doesn't belong to a regional framework such as [the] European Union. There is no international body which creates rules that Japanese government has to automatically accept with binding force. The lack of such regional framework makes the layer of norms which may be applied in Japanese courts relatively simple."

[53] Report by L. Castellani, answer to question 1: "UNCITRAL has a mandate to coordinate global and regional activities relating to the unification and harmonization of international trade law (United Nations General Assembly Resolution 2205 (XXI), para. 8, line a) which aims at preventing the fragmentation of international sources in this area … A report on coordination of work is prepared yearly by the Secretariat and submitted to the Commission. Moreover, activities of promotion of UNCITRAL texts and of dissemination of related information may impact on the fragmentation of sources of international trade law".

[54] Report for OHADA (S. Mancuso): "As it is well known Africa is the continent with the highest number of regional organizations. … There is a general concern in the OHADA member countries about the issue of fragmentation of international sources, even if some of them (Chad, Gabon, Guinea Bissau and Senegal) seem not having directly experimented the problem in their daily practice. … A particular case of potential conflict between regional organizations and their legal instruments could affect DRC [Democratic Republic of Congo] once its process of membership to OHADA will be completed, since DRC is also member of the Southern African Development Community (SADC). …".

[55] Report for Japan (Tetsuo Morishita): "… a lot of academic literature about the fragmentation of international sources, but as far as this Reporter knows, no significant concern has been expressed in executive branches or by practitioners. …"; Report for Portugal (Luís de Lima Pinheiro): "To the knowledge of the reporter the concern with the fragmentation of sources has only been expressed *en passant* by one academic author concerning Private International Law"; Report from Spain (Garcia Cantero): "d'une manière progressive l'interêt suscité chez les cercles les plus spécialisés, se répand surtout dans la doctrine juridique. Peut-être il faudra faire une distinction: en effet, l'interêt pour le droit étranger se concentre d'abord autour du droit communautaire et moins sur les autres traités internationaux …"; Report for Hungary (SUTO BURGER, p. 1): "The topic receives more attention in legal literature … but … no complete monograph was published in the last decade in Hungary that would focus on this problem …"; Venezuela's Report (Zhandra Marin, p. 1): "the concern is expressed by literature, law schools and private associations mainly. The case-law is scarce. … if the parties have elected a forum it is not likely to be Venezuela. This is the consequence of many factors … If Venezuela is the elected forum, it is probable that the parties will choose an arbitration forum instead of the judicial one … judges are not at ease with transnational law. Even though our private international law statute compels them to apply it, they simply look for an escape and they end up using a better known law…"; Austrian Report (Beata Verschraegen, p. 2): "In *Austria*, the complexity of various transnational (legal) sources gives cause for concern. The main dilemma probably is that Private International Law is still regarded by practice and in legal education as a special branch, which only touches upon some cases…." African member States of OHADA (MANCUSO): "Almost all the national reporters agree to assign a fundamental role to the doctrine in detecting and evidencing the cases of fragmentation and conflict of the sources of law. …. A remarkably lower role seems to be played by the State administrations, who are only marginally involved in the application of the transnational sources of law."

in connection with some limited issue.[56] Responsibility for describing the whole network of possible interactions between local and transnational sources is not taken by any other leading actors of the legal world.

For many European reporters the problems connected with enforcement of EU law are in the forefront of worries as far as extra-national sources are concerned.[57] The Reporter from the Netherlands points out the dilemma that many governments have had to face: whether to incorporate directives in their civil codes (in order to preserve the unity of approach that is the *raison d'être* of the code) or to implement them as separate legislation, because they have a different conceptual origin, are phrased in a different language and provide distinct remedies:[58] unfortunately both of the two options have disadvantages.[59]

2.5.2 Support by the Executive

If we look separately at the different formants involved in defining the situation of the various States (in relation to the fragmented complex of sources), it appears that the administration, the executive power, is often reported as being in charge of the task of keeping records of all treaties and international agreements and of updating the list of commitments binding the State.[60] But it may seem surprising that the replies suggest that a clear picture of instruments in force is not always readily available.

For a number of reasons connected with the mechanism of incorporation of international engagements, based on the dualistic system adopted, we learn for instance that in Canada "[T]he question of whether or not an international treaty has been implemented into domestic legislation is a source of confusion for Canadian courts, as there are different *degrees* of implementation. ... At one end of the spectrum is explicit implementation ... whereby the international agreement is incorporated directly into the legislation either in the body or as a schedule. Alternatively, implementing legislation may contain a preamble signalling that its purpose is to fulfill a treaty obligation. However, "there is no rule that Parliament or legislature must expressly refer to a treaty in legislation implementing it" and other, less obvious forms of implementation are possible ... It should be further noted that Canada's federal system requires that each province implement a treaty individually when the subject matter falls within the province's jurisdiction. In these cases, the federal government may enter into an international agreement, but cannot guarantee that it will properly be implemented into domestic law by the provinces."

In some countries the support guaranteed to legal practitioners by the executive power is considered as rather poor: such is the situation in Venezuela.[61] For the area of the OHADA states, the reporter[62] indicates

[56] Jan Smits, Netherlands' Report, par. 3: "fragmentation is almost always perceived in the Netherlands ... not as a general phenomenon cutting across several areas ..., but as something that is only observed in separate areas of the law..."; Andreas Fötschl, Switzerland's Report: "the concern is addressed in connection to particular branches of the law or in respect to particular instruments ... Already in 1977 Prof. Paul Volken ... thoroughly examined conflicts of conventions ..." mostly in the area of private international law.

[57] Report for Spain, Garcia Cantero: "l'interêt pour le droit étranger se concentre d'abord autour du droit communautaire et moins sur les autres traités internationaux ... " (answer to question 1).

[58] Jan Smits: "The Dutch legislature, well aware of the risk of fragmentation, made the reasoned choice to incorporate European directives into the Civil Code .... Implementation inside the Civil Code allows one to scrutinise the consequences of the directive for national law, including 'where national law, in view of the coherence of the national legal system, is to be adjusted in a more far reaching way than the directive would possibly oblige it to.' Only by giving directives such a greater field of application (so-called 'supererogatory implementation') than strictly necessary, a 'coherent system' can be maintained".

[59] Jan Smits: "The solution to implement directives outside of the Civil Code would lead to 'patchwork' policies ... Thus, provisions that the European legislature only intended to affect consumer contracts, were sometimes given a more extensive application and now also cover other types of contracts. ... This implementation strategy has the important advantage of allowing the national Civil Code to retain its role as the major codification of private law. However, one can still question whether this strategy really enhances overall consistency. ... It was therefore observed in Dutch doctrine that with the fundamental choice for implementation inside the Civil Code, the Code has become a sandcastle, with European law as an incoming tide...Other doubtful consequence of the present approach is that the Civil Code needs permanent updating and that it is often unclear which provisions are of European origin".

[60] Question 3 was :"Has the executive power in your country kept a strict monitoring of all international engagements which were undertaken and made use of clauses of exemption/reservation (to preserve previous international engagements) when signing new instruments?"

[61] Venezuela report (Zhandra Marin, answering to the question whether the executive keeps updated records of treaties): "In this particular moment I believe this kind of topics are not a priority for the Venezuelan Executive power".

[62] S. Mancuso, report (emphasis added).

differences between the various members of the organization but he points out that: "The Constitution of Benin reserves the task of monitoring all international engagements which were undertaken to the executive power [as in Niger and Congo] ... but there is no evidence that this work has been really done, and also in Gabon and Togo the executive power does not seem to make use of this power. ... In Burkina Faso, Comoros, Equatorial Guinea and Guinea-Bissau the position of the executive power is not known, and in this last country also because most of the international agreements that are signed by the country are not published in the *Boletim Oficial* (Official Journal); while in the Comoros the lack of any systematic knowledge of the conventions to which the country is part prevents the executive to from exercising its prerogatives."

Elsewhere assistance in ascertaining the status of international texts is fairly reliable. In particular, an important change has occurred in Hungary in comparison with the past experience of the socialist period: the new legislation (replacing the previous) "the Treaties Act [Act No L of 2005] obliges the minister responsible for foreign policy to maintain a register of international treaties and conventions to which Hungary has acceded and keep the original copies thereof. The register of treaties contains all data specified in the Treaties Act. ... It is an important rule of the Treaties Act that the minister responsible for foreign policy is *obliged to publish the register on the homepage of its ministry*."[63]

In Austria, a distinction is made between different situations, as "the Austrian Federal Ministries, especially the Federal Ministry of Justice are very well informed on the international engagements, they observe exemption clauses and reservations", but "... whether other authorities keep track of the developments depends on several factors: work load, lacking staff, priorities set, urgencies and frequency of dealing with conflict issues."[64] In Japan, "the engagement of international treaties are under strict monitoring by the Cabinet and the Diet."[65] How far these data are accessible by legal practitioners is not specified. The same is true in Portugal: "At the national level, the most significant measure is the compulsory impact assessment prior to the decision on the signing of each new legal instrument ... Among other information, that assessment comprises exhaustive identification of all legal acts related with the subject of the instrument at stake."[66]

The task of keeping a clear record of all the binding international rules on a certain subject, of updating it with new provisions and deleting old rules, is not always carried out in accordance with a general standard: it depends very much on each State. The most flattering report is perhaps that of the Netherlands: "The Dutch government has made a good start by providing information on all international agreements the Netherlands has concluded on a special website, including the exemptions and reservations it makes. It now refers to 6,500 treaties ratified since 1961 and it considerably enhances the accessibility of relevant sources."[67] The report from Switzerland is also fairly positive in terms of access generally granted to the database containing all the conventions and agreements entered into by the country.[68] The German Report is the most detailed as regards the internal procedures governing the signing and ratifying of international instruments: mechanisms are devised in order to guarantee that a reasonable level of compatibility between various commitments is kept.[69]

[63] G. Suto Burger (reference to http://www.kulugyminiszterium.hu/szerzodes/main.aspx). Also "Hungarian law is based on a dualistic system; therefore, all international and similar conventions must be published by a Hungarian statute having full binding force" (p. 7) (emphasis added).

[64] Beata Verschraegen, report.

[65] Tetsuo Morishita, report.

[66] "Such analysis is carried out by the competent Ministries according to the subject matter, in cooperation with the Ministry of Foreign Affairs, which is responsible for the overall coordination of foreign policy": Portugal Report, by Luís de Lima Pinheiro.

[67] J. Smits, Netherlands Report, par. 3.3: "This *Verdragenbank* is available at http://www.minbuza.nl/nl/Onderwerpen/Verdragen. The database contains links to the full text consolidated versions of the treaties (in so far as published after 1981)".

[68] A. Fötschl, answer 3: the reporter adds that "before ratification ... the relevant departments verify if the convention is in conflict with other international obligations ... But it seems that there exists no legal rule that would command such verification". A complicate mechanism is involved in the field of conflict of laws as Switzerland is bound by the Lugano Convention of 1988 and its provisions are to be combined with the instruments binding the European member states next door, within the UE: a system of "collection and exchange of judgments" and reports between EFTA and UE have become necessary.

[69] Kieninger, Linhart, German Report: information is offered concerning the three sets of rules relevant in this area: Common Rules for the Federal Ministries (*Gemeinsame Geschäftsordnung der Bundesministerien – GGO*), Guidelines for the Administration of International Treaties (*Richtlinien für die Behandlung völkerrechtlicher Verträge – RvV*), Guidelines for the Drafting of Statutes Ratifying International Treaties and Treaty-related Regulations (*Richtlinien für die Fassung von Vertragsgesetzen und vertragsbezogenen Verordnungen – RiVeVo*). The whole complex of provisions reflect a significant effort to keep a clear image of international commitments and a uniform approach of the institutions involved in the procedure.

One possibly unexpected fact that deserves some mention is that "in Guinea-Bissau the Faculty of Law of the University of Bissau proposed to create a database of the International Law Treaties and Conventions signed by the country and in force therein, also in order to investigate the existing overlaps among the different international legal instruments to which the country is part, being them at international, regional or sub-regional level."[70]

2.5.3 The Judiciary

If we look at the situation at the level of judicial power,[71] we learn that sometimes meetings and seminars are organized to inform judges on the application of European law,[72] especially in countries that have recently acceded to the EU,[73] but no reporter mentioned any event especially dedicated to the problem of combining together many international sources (and less official normative *corpora* such as *lex mercatoria*), to illustrate all the levels of relevant provisions that may come into play. The main concern seems to be classification of international instruments in relation to national ones (questions of hierarchical positions between State constitution and treaties, subordinate legislation, etc.): without describing the network of various sources that can be found outside national borders and the problems arising from their different level of specificity, their range of applicability, the duration of their enforceability, and the existence of different international courts whose competences may overlap.

Comfort at least can be taken from the fact that EU law is widely recognized as an important source[74] and the case-law is translated into all the 23 official languages of the Member States. Several reporters mentioned the training program for judges that started in 2002 within the European Judicial Network (EJN).[75] It is designed to enable judges from various European countries to interact in civil and commercial matters.

[70] OHADA report, by S. Mancuso.

[71] Question 4 of the questionnaire was: "Has the judiciary in your country provided special training for judges to increase their ease and proficiency in dealing with sources of law which were not generated in their legal system?"

[72] Cp. Austrian report, Beata Verschraegen: "The legal training of judges focuses on knowledge of law in various fields of law, with regard to cross border-issues especially on EU-law. Special knowledge on conflict rules is realised on the basis of "learning by doing" when facing specific problems in specific cases and additional focussed learning". In Portugal (de Lima Pinheiro): "The training of judges and state's attorneys takes place in the "Centro de Estudos Judiciários" through specialized courses …. This includes a course on "European and International Law" that is aimed at familiarizing them with international and European Community instruments.. … Furthermore, the "Centro de Estudos Judiciários" has been organizing several events addressed to acting judges and state's attorneys in order to increase their proficiency in dealing with international and EC Community sources". According to the Netherlands' report (Jan Smits, footnote 53): "At the 2006 annual meeting of the most important professional association of Dutch lawyers (the *Nederlandse Juristen-Vereniging*), the influence of European law on national law was widely discussed, but the participants were not unanimous in their view on how to deal with the fragmentation it causes". In Germany (Kieninger, Linhart's Report): "the European Law Academy, also located in Trier, Germany, offers mostly courses on European Union Law for judges and other legal practitioners" (while for the general training of judges "the *Deutsche Richterakademie* (DRA), located in Trier, is providing for continuous current information on the application of international or foreign legal provisions": the most interesting aspect may lie in the courses that deal with the international courts, since there the problem of interaction between several instruments may be highlighted, http://www.deutsche-richterakademie.de).

[73] Hungary's Report (G. Suto Burger), answer 4: "Except for the law of the European Union and human rights conventions, there is currently no special training for judges for international legal sources … the government of the Republic of Hungary … has set out the training of judges for community law. The National Judicial Council has paid also special attention to trainings on community laws especially in respect of administrative leaders in the last years … As of 1998, community law trainings were organized for the leaders of the courts to underline the importance of such trainings and to assist in providing an efficient education to the judges. Until the end of January 2003, all judges have participated on trainings regarding the basis of community laws. In a Follow up, supporting trainings were organized, in which numerous (1296) judges have participated. … The National Judicial Council decided that simultaneously with these fundamental measures a legal educational-advisor team must also be trained. This institution that was established in the summer 2002, currently employs 57 judges. …".

[74] Hungary's Report (Suto Burger): the problem of fragmentation "is currently less important than others relating to the obligatory harmonization of laws … partial steps were made in relation to norms of international source, such as international conventions … and the implementation of the law of the European Union".

[75] Council Decision 2001/470 establishing a European Judicial Network in Civil and Commercial matters, *OJ EC* L 174/25. The network has been particularly active in the field of private international law.

But if we look beyond European sources, information becomes less systematic.

The reporter from Venezuela is rather outspoken: "Professors' Associations maintain a continuous effort to dictate forums, courses, conferences, symposiums, workshops, directed to the judiciary, in order to keep them trained in such matters. Disregarding these efforts, they [the judges] **seldom assist** to these events."[76]

An interesting insight is offered by the reporter for Japan: apart from the initial effort to send young judges abroad,[77] and to assist them by providing research material concerning foreign sources,[78] "the Justice Reform Council … has published its recommendation in 2001" suggesting in particular that: "The arbitration system (including international commercial arbitration) should be coordinated quickly, paying heed to international trends."[79] According to our reporter, therefore, "arbitration is considered as an option to increase the proficiency of Japanese legal system to deal with international cases. Also, law schools … expected to play some role to increase the proficiencies of legal professionals to deal with transnational legal matters. Unfortunately, however, Japanese law schools tend to pay more attention to teach basic laws and technique to pass the bar exam, because the passing rate of the bar exam is limited to about 30% and law schools are in severe competitions to gain a higher passing rate."

In the USA, the situation of judges is not satisfactory either: "Although newly-appointed federal judges receive some basic instruction (from the United States Judicial Conference) in how to deal with issues of foreign law, and although some federal courts (e.g. the Southern District of New York), because they deal with a significant number of cases involving multinational corporations, have become familiar with the application of foreign law, still this falls short of their skill in dealing with the law of one of the American states. As for judges in the state court systems, their formal training in the application of foreign legal materials is minimal."[80]

When we look at the African countries belonging to OHADA, we find various situations: from the case of Burkina Faso, DRC (Dem. Rep. Congo), Gabon, Guinea-Bissau, Ivory Coast, Senegal and Togo which "do not have any kind of training activity for the judges with regard to this kind of sources of law," to the situation of a "training school dedicated to judges called Ecole Nationale de la Magistrature in Benin and Niger …, and the Institut National de Formation Judiciaire in Mali, or through courses organized directly by the government in the case of Chad, Congo and Equatorial Guinea."[81]

More systematic assistance is offered by the training school for judges created by the OHADA treaty (*École Régionale Supérieure de la Magistrature*–ERSUMA).[82] In the area where the organization is involved, where uniform acts have been adopted (general business law, company law and pooling of economic interest, securities law, bankruptcy law, credit collection and enforcement law, accounting law, arbitration law and contracts for the carriage of goods by road), the idea inspiring the creation of the ERSUMA is "to make up for the insufficient level of specialization of the judges, and also for the absence of a system of continuous formation and to

[76] Zhandra Marin, report for Venezuela, answer to question 4 (emphasis added).

[77] Tetsuo Morishita: "The Supreme Court of Japan, who is in charge of personnel matters of judges, sends tens of judges of relatively younger generation to study abroad. Such experience of studying abroad helps the judges to deal with sources of law which are not generated in Japan. However, it should be pointed out that there is no other training system which is available to all judges to increase their proficiency in dealing with laws other than Japanese laws. Unfortunately, in the Reporter's view, it should be admitted that some judges don't have sufficient ability to deal with cases containing the issues relating to conflict of laws and foreign laws".

[78] Tetsuo Morishita, *ibidem:* "the administrative office of the Supreme Court may give some assistance for research of foreign laws to each judge when necessary. Some academics pointed out that an institution which would have a good ability to help judges to research foreign laws and the global framework of nations to cooperate with such research should be established [Akira Mikazuki, *Application of Foreign Law and Courts* (written in Japanese: *Gaikokuho no Tekiyo to Saibansyo*) in Takao Sawaki and Yoshimitsu Aoyama (ed.) *Theory of International Civil Procedure* (*Kokusai Minjisosyoho no Riron*) (Yuhikaku, 1987) 239, at 280. In this article, Prof. Mikazuki introduced the Max Planck Institute as a good example]. No such institution or global framework has existed in relation to Japan".

[79] The English version of the Recommendation is available at http://www.kantei.go.jp/foreign/policy/sihou/singikai/990612_e.html.

[80] US Report, W. Ewald, par. III (*The diversity of transnational sources*).

[81] OHADA report, by S. Mancuso (in Mali the Supreme Court has an agreement with the French Cour de Cassation to provide to Malian judges a continuous training that can provide them also a comparative perspective).

[82] OHADA Treaty, Art. 41.

the lack of sufficient legal formation in the member countries."[83] The school is dedicated to training legal professionals in OHADA law.

No governing body of the legal profession seems to have taken up the concerns expressed by the academic world; they all seem rather absorbed by local issues, and by national concerns.

In our exploration of the current situation, to detect differences that may occur, it seemed useful to check whether a higher level of awareness existed in countries that have specialized judges dealing with international commerce: this was done in question 5 in the list put to our reporters.[84] The reply seems to be that in the large majority of cases no specialized jurisdiction in commercial matters exists, and that the real difference lies between state judges and arbitration: arbitrators have more familiarity with international documents and especially with usages and practices of the business world that only rarely find their way into the ordinary practice of courts.[85]

The Venezuelan reporter expressed concern about the fact that a specialized court in international commercial law may develop an independent trend and lose contact with the rest of the judiciary.[86] That may be the reason why only a few instances are reported of courts that are particularly qualified in international transactions. They may be a further element of fragmentation, within the domestic judiciary.

In Hungary, however, where the tradition of a special institution for international arbitration of the socialist period has left its mark, we learn from the Hungarian reporter that "There is no state administrated special judicial institution in Hungary to deal with international commercial cases. … In the first place however, international commercial cases are decided on the basis of an arbitration clause by an arbitration body. The Permanent Arbitration Court attached to the Hungarian Chamber of Commerce and Industry is the most frequently used and most well-known arbitration court in Hungary."[87]

The US reporter confirmed that "most American courts are *generalist* courts, expected to handle a full range of criminal and civil cases. In particular, there do not exist courts specifically designed to deal with questions of trans-national law;"[88] in Spain, no specialized judicial court is in charge of international commercial law;[89] "in Japan, there is no specialized judicial institution which deals with international commercial cases."[90] The same is true of Portugal [91] and Switzerland.[92] In Germany "there is not one specialized institution, that deals with international commercial cases. There is, however, a rather limited specialization of court divisions concerning international or transnational law": this specialization is more evident in the field of family law, for the recognition and enforcement of foreign judgments, where international awards are involved.[93]

---

[83] See Alhousseini Mouloul, *Comprendre l'OHADA*, 2nd ed. (Conakry, 2009), 42. Thimotée Somé, *A formação dos magistrados africanos pela OHADA*, in 6 *Boletim da Faculdade de Direito de Bissau*, (supplement) (2004), at 9.

[84] "Does the fact that in some countries a specialized judicial institution deals with international commercial cases affect the functioning of justice under this profile? Would you assess the records of these judicial institutions as an improvement?"

[85] Sometimes an indirect process of reception occurs through the medium of a decision by a state court: when it recognizes (by the exequatur) an arbitration decision in a certain field. The recognition opens a trend of aknowledgment for usages that were incorporated in the arbitral award (Goldman, *Nouvelles réflexions sur la Lex mercatoria*, in *Etudes P. Lalive* (Basel: Helbing & Lichtenhahn, 1993), 241).

[86] Zhandra Marin, answer to question 5: "… having a specialized judicial institution would positively affect the international commercial cases. Having specialized, updated judges on this area would be a great improvement for our subject. On the other hand, if this institution is to exist, it is important to maintain its judges linked to the rest of the judiciary's reality. Having a separate instance does not mean having judges isolated from the rest of the judicial power, elaborating decisions incoherent and not homogeneous with the rest of the legal system".

[87] Suto Burger (Hungary's report adding that "Although its proceedings and awards are not public, … some of its decisions are published in the legal literature in forms of summaries without names. Accordingly, the most important decisions of this arbitration court are available in form of summaries and have an effect on legal professionals. Parties of a state court trial would cite such decisions in their filings as legal argumentation").

[88] Ewald's Report, par. 3.

[89] García Cantero: "Cet organe n'est pas prévu en droit espagnol".

[90] Considering the cost and difficulties of translation in Japanese the reporter adds that "In the Reporter's opinion, Japan should consider to set up special division of the court in which case could be heard in English" (Tetsuo Morishita).

[91] Luís de Lima Pinheiro: "In Portugal there is no specialized judicial institution to deal with international commercial cases".

[92] A. Fötschl, answer 5 ("there is no specialized judicial institution for international commercial cases").

[93] kieninger, Linhart, *German Report*, p. 13: for implementation of the Hague Convention on International Child Abduction of 1980 (OLG Köln) or the European Custody Convention (OLG Schleswig-Holstein), for international arbitral awards (OLG Karlsruhe). An experiment has been started in some Laender at

In Austria we find the Commercial Court of Vienna.[94] One of the competences of this court is to receive the results of investigations on trade customs by the Austrian Federal Economic Chamber (AFEC).[95] The president of the Commercial Court "used to publish the trade customs in a separate monograph. For quite some years now, the administration of the index has been delegated to specific judges.[96]" The importance of the fact that trade customs are included in the publication is obvious at the litigation level since: "Whenever a party refers to a trade custom which is not entailed in the index, the court requests the AFEC to make a poll ... by a questionnaire with a statement of facts made anonymous to all relevant trade businesses."[97]

As far as African countries are concerned, generally there is not "a specific jurisdiction in the OHADA member countries which deals with international commercial cases. When they should arise they are solved by the ordinary courts or by the commercial courts where existing (Congo, DRC, Guinea-Bissau,[98] Mali)." On the other hand, the OHADA treaty has set up a rather ambitious system at the supranational level of the organization, with a Court that has broader jurisdiction than the European Court of Justice within the EU (that is only accessible by the courts on a preliminary ruling). "The Common Court of Justice and Arbitration (*Cour Commune de Justice et d'Arbitrage* – CCJA) has jurisdiction as judge of last instance in all matters related to commercial law in which the application of any OHADA norm is involved, with the only exception related to the application of criminal sanctions. ... The national jurisdictions remain therefore competent to judge at first and at second instance on cases related to application of uniform acts.[99] Consequently, the CCJA exercises the function of judge of appeal against the judgments of the courts of appeal of the member States, as well as against the judgments of first instance of the national courts which are not subject to appeal at national level."[100]

The mechanism which was set up in Africa embodies a project which was often considered in the harmonization/uniformation process also in other geographical contexts: the idea of an international court competent to guarantee uniform interpretation of uniform acts was advocated at the UNCITRAL New York Congress of 1992 (UNCITRAL 25th anniversary) by L. Sohn (George Washington University), under the title of "Uniform laws require uniform interpretation. Proposals for an international tribunal to interpret uniform legal texts."[101]

The origin of the proposal goes back a long way, to Hans Wehberg at the beginning of the twentieth century,[102] and it was advanced again when the

the beginning of 2010, within the project "Law – made in Germany": the Regional Courts (*Landgerichte*) of Köln, Bonn and Aachen, the Higher Regional Court (*Oberlandesgericht*) of Köln have nominated Chambers or Senates where the trial can be conducted in the English language.

[94] Handelsgericht Wien (*Report* for Austria: B. Verschraegen).

[95] Wirtschaftskammer Österreichs (Wkö; http://wko.at/awo/chamberinfo.htm): it is, by law, the representative of the entire *Austrian* business community.

[96] However, due to the high rate of crew change among judges these judges first try to deal with the files and by the time they could spend some attention to the updating of the index on the trade customs, they are upgraded, start working at another court or are absent for other reasons (e.g. maternity or paternity leave) (B. Verschraegen, reference to E.M. Weiss, *Handelsbräuche in Österreich*, supplement 7a, 1991).

[97] B. Verschraegen, p. 13: "The entire procedure turns out to be very time-consuming for all the persons concerned. However, according to judges that were questioned for the purpose of this contribution, parties at stake seem to be quite pleased with this procedure. A questionnaire is only sent on the occasion of a concrete court procedure during which the judge at stake requests the AFEC whether a trade custom exists".

[98] In Guinea Bissau the commercial court was created in July 2008, but there is no record yet about its activity.

[99] OHADA Treaty, Art. 13: in the Report by S. Mancuso.

[100] OHADA Treaty, Art. 14, par. 3 and 4. Cp. Mancuso: "In the exercise of its jurisdictional function the CCJA is a supranational court whose decisions are considered as *res judicata* and can be enforced in the territory of every Member State. It is a sort of "transnational court" created through the agreement of the OHADA member States to function as supreme court in all the cases involving the application of the Treaty and the uniform acts; consequently all the supreme courts of the member States are deprived of their judicial power whenever the application of OHADA law is involved.... The CCJA judgments are final and close the case definitely. They are not subject to any appeal". The Court functions also as an international arbitration center dealing with arbitration under its own rules (basically modeled on the ICC rules).

[101] UNCITRAL Colloquia, *Uniform Commercial Law in the Twenty-First Century*, 18–22 May 1992, New York, http://www.uncitral.org/pdf/english/texts/general/Uniform_Commercial_Law_Congress_1992_e.pdf, 50 ff.

[102] According to L. Sohn the 1911 proposal was for an international tribunal that would deal with "disputes relating to questions of private international law (on appeal from national courts); and private claims based on international treaties establishing uniform laws (on appeal from national courts)".

Permanent Court of International Justice was created (1920).[103] A first experiment was carried out in 1931 through a Protocol (signed at the Sixth session of the Conference on Private International Law) recognizing the jurisdiction of the Permanent Court of International Justice (over disputes regarding the interpretation of conventions prepared by the Hague Conferences on Private International Law); the Protocol "was ratified by only a few States, and was never resorted to by any State."[104]

The solution put forward in New York in 1992 was based on the model of the Hague International Court of Justice: according to the proposal, States would accept the jurisdiction of a "tribunal, parallel to the International Court of Justice, to deal with the problems created by inconsistent interpretations of international agreements containing a variety of uniform laws, codes of conduct and declarations." The jurisdiction of the tribunal "would be specified in a protocol which would contain an amendable list of multilateral conventions, and a State ratifying the protocol would accept the jurisdiction of the tribunal with respect to at least one or, if possible, more conventions, and would be encouraged to make additional acceptances from time to time." In cases where States were reluctant to reach such a solution, they would at least agree to devolve the interpretation of a uniform text to the international court when national courts reached conflicting interpretations.[105] The power to invest the tribunal with an advisory opinion on the interpretation of a convention would lie in the national court "on request of one of the private parties to the dispute … allowed to present their views to the tribunal."

The project, at world level, repeatedly met with objections connected with the failed experiences of some previous UN conventions, such as the CMR, *Conv. Marchandises par route* (a text drawn up within the ECE, the UN *Econ. Comm. for Europe*). Some of these older documents did in fact lay down the competence of the Court of International Justice to interpret uniform acts, but the States never used the opportunity to ask for the uniform interpretation of the Court, so that the rule fell into oblivion.[106] Implementation of the proposal at world level has in the past been qualified as "entirely unrealistic."[107]

The OHADA experience is thus particularly interesting because of its special character and the scope of its competence.[108]

Still in regard to courts, one of the questions proposed to national reporters[109] concerned a further possible divergence in practice between administrative courts and ordinary courts, bearing in mind the rather "reserved" attitude in the past of the French *Conseil d'Etat* towards European legislation.[110] In general, the reporters did not point out any significant difference in this

[103] *Première rencontre des Organisations s'occupant de l'unification du droit*, in UNIDROIT, *Annuaire de droit uniforme*, 1956: the idea was to assign competence to the court in the field of conflict of laws, copyright, patents, commercial and maritime law.

[104] L. Sohn, *Proposals for an International Tribunal to Interpret Uniform Legal Texts*, *cit.*, p. 51.

[105] According to L. Sohn, the advantage of the solution proposed would have been to avoid the creation of a number of courts, each competent for specific subjects, with a consequent constant increase in their number, subject after subject. "The authors of the statute of the proposed international tribunal would be able to draw on the experience of the Court of Justice of the European Community, of the International Centre for Settlement of Investment Disputes … of the arbitral panels established under the Canada-United States Claims tribunal, and of the several less-known tribunals functioning in various areas of the world" (ID., p. 52).

[106] Cp. the discussion between J. Putzeys and R. Loewe in *International Uniform Law in Practice*, Proceedings of the UNIDROIT Congress on *International Uniform Law in Practice*, Rome (1987), (Oceana, 1988), 529.

[107] F. Enderlein, *Uniform Law and its Application by Judges and Arbitrators*, *ibidem*, (1988), 329 ff., at p. 352., while L. RÉCZEI in 1992 judged Sohn's idea in New York to be "difficult but not impossible".

[108] The court was created by the founding treaty, but "the formation of this institution was made through the application of the political agreements called "N'Djamena agreements" of 18 April 1996, that distributed the different positions among some States (the presidency of the court was assigned to Senegal, the first vice-presidency to the Central African Republic …). The new text of the Treaty in October 2008, by Art. 31 has restored the full force of the criteria provided in the Rules of Procedure adopted under Art. 19 of the Treaty" (OHADA report by S. Mancuso).

[109] Question (6) asked: "Is there a difference in attitude towards transnational sources among administrative courts (where they exist), courts dealing with civil law matters, criminal law and commercial courts in your country?"

[110] The well-known "Acte clair" doctrine discouraged administrative courts in France, for a fair period of time, from proposing preliminary rulings to the ECJ : e.g. Conseil d'Etat, Cohn/Bendit case, decision of 22 December 1978 (in *Rev. trim. dr. eur.*, (1979): 157. In general terms: P. PESCATORE, *Interpretation of Community Law and the Doctrine of "Acte Clair"*, in *Legal Problems of an Enlarged Community* (London, 1972), 27).

respect[111]: a more cautious attitude by the administrative courts might have been expected, but this prediction was not confirmed in the data provided by national reporters.[112]

Some writers made mention of the fact that administrative courts may be less likely to meet problems involving extra-national sources.[113] This expectation is perhaps reflected in the training of judges: administrative judges receive a shorter period of education in the field of international law, in some countries.[114]

2.5.4 Jura novit curia?

Finally, in relation to question 7, the possibility that application of the rule *jura novit curia* (instead of the principle allocating to parties the burden of proof regarding the foreign or transnational rule applicable to their case) could make a difference with respect to the application of foreign law,[115] did not obtain a clear answer: there seems to be no firm opinion about which solution facilitates application by the court of the relevant foreign sources.

Cooperation between the court and the parties involved in litigation is the more commonly found solution: if parties really care about the application of extranational sources, they have to take an active role.

It is generally held that civil law countries favor the *iura novit curia* rule: the court must investigate applicable law, even if the sources involved are external to the national legal system; in the common law world, generally the issue of application of foreign law is treated as a matter of fact to be proved by the parties.

But the Canadian and the USA reports reveal that in both experiences there have been corrections of the approach that would generally be expected. We learn

[111] In Switzerland (A. Fötschl, answer 6): "there seems to be no difference in attitude towards transnational sources amongst different types of courts. It is rather the frequency of being confronted with transnational sources that might lead to a different attitude. ... dealing with the European Convention for Human Rights has become a habit for criminal and administrative courts...". In Hungary (SUTO BURGER): "Only labour courts are separated from the general courts ... we cannot identify any discrepancy in transnational sources among courts. ... courts dealing with a criminal case would be reluctant to make use of transnational sources (such as human rights) unless they are forced to do so by a domestic material or procedural rule. Courts dealing with criminal cases tend to cite international (human rights) principles more often, but their decisions are not based on these. A study has been conducted in support of this theory in relation to the European Court of Human Rights (Strasbourg), because its most important case law is available in Hungarian. ... There is a visible reluctance to apply this case law; in certain cases, judges refuse the application. ... judges dealing with commercial matters face transnational sources more often, which makes them more open towards such sources. But also among these judges, one may identify a special legal culture, a legal formalism that is typical for post-communist states. Because of this, one can hardly find cases and only relating to certain international conventions where a judge bases its decision only on an international norm, although these conventions are made national law by their publication in Hungary ...". In Spain (Garcia Cantero, answer to question 6): "il y a des Tribunaux *contencioso-administrativos*, cependant ils ne font pas partie de l'Administration, mais du Pouvoir Judiciaire. En tout cas, ces dernières Cours à l'heure actuelle sont de plus en plus sensibles aussi à l'application du Droit communautaire (par ex. Droit des contrats publiques, responsabilité par contamination etc.)". In the Report for the OHADA member states S. Mancuso mentions the fact that "Most of the francophone countries member of the OHADA have administrative jurisdictions. They are not present in DRC, Guinea-Bissau, Equatorial Guinea and Niger, while in the Comoros it has never really worked. No one of the national reporters referred about any difference in attitude towards transnational sources among administrative courts, courts dealing with civil law matters, criminal law and commercial courts". But in Venezuela (Zhandra MARIN, answer to question 6): "Civil and Commercial courts are more inclined to apply transnational law than the rest of the courts. The difference between courts applying Public Law and Private Law, regarding *lex mercatoria*, is noticeable".

[112] The reporter from Portugal (L. De Lima Pinheiro) pointed out that "The most remarkable shortcoming in the application of supranational sources by Portuguese courts is the reluctance to ask the Court of Justice of the European Union for preliminary rulings .... To my knowledge only a tax court has once asked for a preliminary ruling of the Court of Justice of the European Union".

[113] L. De Lima Pinheiro: "In Portugal there is a division between judicial courts (dealing with civil law, criminal law and commercial law matters), on one hand, and administrative and tax courts, on the other hand. Judicial courts are more concerned with the application of international sources than administrative and tax courts. Nevertheless, all of them are often concerned with the application of European Community law. It cannot be said that there is a difference of attitude towards international and European Community sources".

[114] In Portugal (L. De Lima Pinheiro), "The training of judges and state's attorneys takes place in the "Centro de Estudos Judiciários" .... This includes a course on "European and International Law"... . This course is annual for judges and state's attorneys of judicial courts and lasts a trimester for judges and state's attorneys of administrative and tax courts".

[115] Question 7 asked: "Do you think that the efficiency of judges in dealing with cases raising complex interaction of sources may be affected by the fact that the judge himself/herself has to find the applicable law (*iura novit curia*) in opposition to the situation in which the parties themselves have to plead and prove the law to the court?"

that in Canada: "in the common law jurisdictions, judicial notice is taken of international law, and thus it need not be directly pleaded. In Quebec, the matter is governed by article 2807 of the Civil Code of Quebec, which provides that international law must be pleaded. This rule exists as a way to facilitate matters for the judge by providing him or her with sources of law that are otherwise not readily available."[116]

In the USA report[117] we read that: "the traditional approach was to treat the determination of foreign law as essentially a question of fact. This had several consequences. First, the foreign law needed to be proved in accordance with the rules of evidence .... Secondly, the determination of foreign law, being a question of fact, was for the jury to decide. And, thirdly, the scope of review by an appellate court was restricted, so that a mistaken determination of foreign law could be set aside only if it could be shown to be clearly erroneous.

In the USA, in 1966 the situation in the federal courts was changed by the adoption of Rule 44.1 of the Federal Rules of Civil Procedure. That rule states:

> A party who intends to raise an issue about a foreign country's law must give notice by a pleading or other writing. In determining foreign law, the court may consider any relevant material or source, including testimony, whether or not submitted by a party or admissible under the Federal Rules of Evidence. The court's determination must be treated as a ruling on a question of law
> .....

In essence, this Rule 44.1 does two things: it gives the judge (rather than the jury) the ultimate responsibility for determining foreign law, and it gives the judge considerable discretion in deciding how that determination is to be made. ...[118] Importantly, because the judge's finding is now classified as a question of law rather than of fact, it can be reviewed and argued on appeal".

Therefore here we find a move towards the *"jura novit curia"* position.

In addition to the peculiarity of the situation where a mixed law jurisdiction (Quebec) limits judicial notice in international matters, while a common law country (USA) moves towards a wider responsibility of the judge in cross-border cases, it is also worth mentioning that the switch has not brought about the results that might have been hoped for. The Canadian reporters[119] indicate that: "Taking these rules into consideration, one would assume that once counsel has raised the CISG in its pleadings, the courts would have no trouble ascertaining the situations in which it is in fact applicable law. As the jurisprudence shows, this is not the case. The CISG has been in Canada for over 17 years, and yet, there is no evidence that it has had a significant impact on Canadian legal practice ....."[120]

A sort of midway solution is recorded in other countries too: although it is the courts that have to seek the applicable law, the parties are not exempted from active participation, even if the law to be applied is not foreign, but international, that is: *binding* on the citizens of the signatory State.

Thus in Hungary[121]: "The court knows the law *ex officio* (*iura novit curia*), but in the practice this obligation of the court is likely only to cover written national law. Hungarian law is based on a dualistic system; therefore, all international and similar conventions must be published by a Hungarian statute having full binding force. Accordingly, courts must know these sources of law and apply them. ... International sources nevertheless, may have interpretations and/or precedents in foreign countries that were not discovered by Hungarian national courts. In this relation, parties may plead and prove the content and/or the interpretation of a statute to the court, but the court won't be bound by such interpretation".

In Switzerland[122] "the principle *jura novit curia* prevails ... In private international law, Switzerland follows a system that might be characterized by its

---

[116] Canadian *Report*, p. 45.

[117] USA *Report* by Ewald, par. IV. "techniques for dealing with the complexity of trans-national law", last but one page.

[118] "In the ordinary case, the judge will expect the attorneys to produce some sort of evidence supporting their view of the relevant foreign law. The evidence may come in the form of testimony in open court by an expert witness, or in an affidavit; it may come from an attorney accredited in the foreign legal system, or from a domestic scholar of comparative law. Some judges will press the parties to produce witnesses; others (using Rule 706(a) of the Federal Rules of Evidence) may appoint their own expert .... As Rule 44.1 makes clear, the evidence need not be presented in open court; the judge is moreover free to accept or to reject the evidence, and also to undertake independent research".

[119] H. Dedek, A. Carbone, Canadian *Report*.

[120] Furthermore "... English translations of foreign case law are readily available, and thus «the blame for any lack of international case law to assist in an interpretation of the Convention lies squarely with legal practitioners»".

[121] Suto Burger Hungary report.

[122] A. Fötschl, answer 7.

mixed nature: the content of the applicable law has to be determined by the Swiss court *ex officio*. The court may demand the cooperation of the parties. For patrimonial claims the burden of proof on the foreign law can be transferred to the parties. But also in this case the court has a duty to cooperate ...".

In Germany, the judge, who is expected to know the law, including conflict of laws (according to §293 of the German Code of Civil Procedure), may "ask for written opinions (*Gutachten*) either by university professors, specialized in Private International Law or Comparative Law, or by members of the Max-Planck-Institute for Comparative and Private International Law in Hamburg"; this solution has proved to be "useful and efficient. Unnecessary costs can be avoided in cases where the judge was mistaken in his assumption that the law of a foreign country is applicable in his case, by for example failing to follow a *renvoi*."[123]

In Portugal[124] "the principle *iura novit curia* applies both to internal sources and to supranational sources. The court is also under a duty to ascertain the content of foreign law *ex officio* (Article 348(1) and (2) of the Civil Code). In practice there is a judicial trend to maximize the scope of application of the *lex fori*, and the courts often ignore the supranational or foreign sources where they are not pleaded by the parties".

In Spain the statute ruling on the matter deviates from the civil law tradition, but case-law mitigates the letter of the legislation: "La nouvelle Lec2000 n'a pas changé, à première vue, le droit antérieur en vigueur en Espagne: Art. 281. 2: «Le droit étranger sera l'objet de preuve [...] Le droit étranger devra être prouvé quant à son contenu et à sa vigueur, et le Tribunal pourra utiliser tous les moyens nécessaires à l'objet de sa connaissance et de son application». Mais si la règle c'est que le droit étranger doit être prouvé par la partie qui l'a invoqué dans le procès, l'art. 281.2 Lec2000 établit, encore, une modération ou plutôt une nuance: «Le Tribunal ou le Juge sont autorisés à faire toute sorte de démarches ou de recherches pour mieux arriver à connaître le droit étranger applicable; la connaissance personnelle du Juge n'est pas exclue». La jurisprudence sur cette règle est très abondante ...."[125]

The traditional civil approach is still followed in Japan: "Japanese academics consider that judges, not parties, have to find laws and to research cases by themselves. ...."[126]

Thus we find that cooperation between judge and parties is generally required, and this compromise is all the more necessary in Africa[127]: there we find that "all the OHADA member countries belong to the civil law legal tradition (with the sole exception of the Anglophone part of Cameroun), therefore the *iura novit curia* principle has great influence in these legal systems.

There is a general understanding that the efficiency of judges in dealing with cases involving complex interaction of sources is affected by the fact that the judge has to find the law applicable to the case. The reasons vary, but most of the reporters refer to the problem – well known in Africa – of the lack of information about the law in force. In countries such as Central African Republic, Comoros or Guinea-Bissau it can also be extremely difficult to obtain information and knowledge about national law; but even where such information exists, the lack of documentation on the different sources of law (scarcity of libraries, no law journals or doctrinal commentaries to laws, poor access to internet resources, difficulty in getting written sources from abroad, poor training of judges) means that it is simply impossible for the judge to have access to (or sometimes even to learn about, in time) legal materials that are different from those of the country.

A further consequence of this situation is that even the parties themselves – or their lawyers – are sometimes unaware of the existence of different rules from domestic rules, that may be applicable to their case."[128]

[123] Kieninger, Linhart, *German report*: in addition "the database "IR-Online" (*Internationale Rechtshilfe online*) provides an overview on the international sources of law existing in the fields of service of documents abroad, taking of evidence abroad, abolishing the requirement of legalisation, or on information of foreign law, created by the European Union, the Council of Europe or under the auspices of the Hague Conference on Private International Law as well as bi- and multilateral international agreements Germany is a party of. This collection is accompanied by the German primary and secondary sources of law ... (*Ausführungsgesetze*) or the so-called *Denkschriften*".

[124] L. de Lima Pinheiro.

[125] Garcia Cantero.

[126] Tetsuo Morishita.

[127] OHADA Report, by S. Mancuso.

[128] "Sometimes the burden of proof can help: in Benin (but the situation may also be similar in other countries) the application of the *iura novit curia* principle is limited to national law .... At other times, day to day practice comes to the aid of the judge, since application of the *iura novit curia* principle does not prevent lawyers from supporting their arguments by inserting in

2.5.5 Judicial Strategies

In the final questions submitted to the national reporters, the focus was on the strategies that courts may adopt when faced with the use of a complex network of non-national rules.[129]

The question on this point owes something to the experience of a number of lawyers who reported strategic "ways out" practiced by judges when faced with complicated issues of foreign law.[130]

Another very striking result emerging from the reports is that judges tend to shun not only foreign sources (or a-national instruments such as trade usages and commercial practices), but also international sources, if they feel unfamiliar with them.

For instance, we learn that in Canada,"courts are criticized as having a narrow understanding of when an international treaty has been implemented into Canadian law, thereby restricting its role in Canadian domestic law. As a result of this narrow interpretation, Canadian courts continue to put Canada in conflict with public international law. When domestic courts are confronted with the task of applying an international agreement, they sometimes employ the "doctrine of legitimate expectations" or the "presumption of conformity" to temper the ambiguity that surrounds the domestic application of international law. ....[131] The general attitude in Canadian courts is that international human rights law should be treated as "relevant and persuasive" in deciding *Charter* cases. This is an approach compatible with the "presumption of conformity" whereby the courts interpret legislation so as not to put Canada in violation of its international agreements".

In Venezuela, "Venezuelan judges do not have much training or knowledge in the area; therefore it is easier to apply the forum law, a national law or even to assume that the case is domestic rather than international. Striking as it is, this last situation is very common: neither the judge nor the parties realize that the contract in front of them is international".

In Portugal,[132] "when interpreting and filling gaps of international sources the Portuguese courts normally resort to domestic law instead of following the criteria applicable to the interpretation and filling of gaps of international conventions. Instead of aiming for a uniform interpretation and gap filling, through an autonomous interpretation and the resort to the principles underlying the rules of the convention, they simply apply the rules of internal source".

An interesting comparison may be drawn with the situation in Hungary,[133] although a warning should be given first. In Hungary, "prior to the judicial reform of 1997, it was practically impossible to perform any research relating to the courts' activity. Not only were decisions inaccessible,[134] but no statistics or reviews were published ... . The Act N° XC of 2005 on the freedom of electronic information provides ... that the decisions of the *Supreme Court and the Appellate Courts* on the merits of the cases must be published in the Court Decisions Compilation, together with the first instance decisions serving as basis of these, in digital anonym version. .... Decisions made after July 1st, 2007 are available and researchable in a digital archive

their file a copy of the law whose application is claimed, for the benefit of the judge. In Congo there is an effort in improving the training of the judges who are appropriating more and more of the international legal sources, limiting therefore the burden of proof imposed to the parties to prove the law of other countries whose application is claimed in a Congolese case" (Mancuso's Report).

[129] Question 8: "Are there detectable common strategies that the judges seem to use to elude complexity (e.g. by the presumption that the foreign law is the same as the local law or by a presumed waiver of foreign sources if the party has not pleaded their applicability immediately)?"

[130] See e.g.: R. Miner, "The Reception of Foreign Law in the U.S. Federal Courts," *American Journal of Comparitive Law* 43 (1995), 581 ss., p. 585 quoting the presumptions applied by some courts that "the foreign law is the same as the forum's common law, that the foreign law is identical to the forum law, that foreign law is based on generally recognized principles of civilized nations, and ... that the party by not proving the foreign law has essentially acquiesced to the forum law".

[131] "The "doctrine of legitimate expectations" is based on the idea that, when a state commits itself to an international treaty, it creates an expectation among its citizens that it will comply with the international undertaking. ... The "presumption of conformity" requires the courts to interpret domestic law in a manner that is consistent with Canadian treaty obligations. The presumption is based on the idea that Canada's legislature does not purposefully or lightly violate its international obligations. The presumption of conformity thus creates a framework in which Canadian courts can apply treaties that have not been implemented, but have been ratified. ...".

[132] L. de Lima Pinheiro.

[133] G. Suto Burger, emphasis added by general reporter.

[134] The most important decisions of the Supreme Court were published as a selection with simplified content prior to this date "for enabling the unified decision making": as had been common in the socialist praxis of several East European States.

by anyone. Decisions prior to that date are not accessible. … As of July 1st, 2007, published decisions may be analyzed in a limited manner inasmuch as a complete analysis is *only available relating to higher courts*."

Under these circumstances we observe that: "… judges in many cases tend towards an easier solution of cases and try to reduce the issues to some of the provisions of Hungarian law… . Moreover … judges tend to apply the most relevant rules of domestic law without considering broader contexts. Of course, this is a tendency that may not be true to all judges. … Even those international norms that are made part of the domestic law (especially in respect of legal principles) need time until courts apply these. Even more time is necessary until the interpretation of such norms is made in international context instead of by purely domestic rules. … As a general formula, one can state that the longer the given rule is part of domestic law and the more often judges have to apply the international convention, [the more] judges tend to base their judgments only on these conventions. As an example, in a case the Supreme Court declared that in a dispute governed by the COTIF, domestic rules may only be applied to an extent the convention does not have any provisions in relation of the issue in question.[135] The same firmness is not identifiable in the case … relating to the UNIDROIT Convention on International Financial Leasing."[136]

In the Netherlands "courts also have techniques available to elude complexity. Although Dutch law does not accept the basic rule of the *lex fori* as a general principle, there are several rules that come close. … De Boer has suggested accepting the theory of 'facultative choice of law' in Dutch law.[137] It means that the courts only need to apply conflict of laws if one of the parties asks for it. If this request is not made, the courts must apply the *lex fori*. The recent draft statute of 2009 … explicitly rejects this view, meaning that the courts will have to apply foreign law at their own initiative wherever necessary. Their task is of course facilitated by the possibility to ask for information under the European Convention on Information on Foreign Law (1968). However, it is more likely that the parties (or their lawyers) provide the court with expert opinions or that the court looks into foreign law itself."[138]

In the USA[139]: "What if the court is unable to determine to its own satisfaction precisely what foreign law requires? Sometimes the foreign law will be unclear, and in some cases indeterminable. There is no universally agreed answer to what happens in this situation. One possibility is to dismiss the case altogether. But this can be a harsh outcome; so judges will sometimes resort to a presumption that the foreign law is identical to the law of the forum, or that the parties have agreed to waive the application of foreign law, or that general principles of equity are to be applied. … the system deals with the issue by using the traditional mechanism of adversarial proceedings, relying upon the attorneys to research and argue the issues of foreign law".

The difficulties met in well-resourced western or European countries are surpassed by those encountered by the OHADA member States. "… There is a general difficulty to answer to this question since it presupposes a detailed analysis of the related jurisprudence, while in Africa (including the OHADA member countries) there is a general lack of publication of the

---

[135] Courts' Decisions BH1999.21, quoted by the Hungarian reporter. "The "*per se*" application of the provisions of the COTIF/CIM as well as the CMR is well identifiable in many decisions of the Supreme Court".

[136] As to the causes of the reluctant attitude of some judges faced with non-domestic sources of law Suto Burger, comments: "Those judges who became judges before the political system … changed may decide complex commercial cases without any obligatory additional training. An additional argument is usually that they have too many cases to deal with at the same time. Furthermore, it is a question how easily a judge may access foreign norms and adhering literature, which usually is only available in a foreign language, which older judges may not speak. One may conclude that judges with lower personal ambitions are reluctant to deal with complex cases with international elements …. A slight tendency may be identified which shows that courts identify and deal with such cases well. Nevertheless, there is no statistic on this tendency yet. This tendency however, may be identified in the first place relating to the European Human Rights Convention, because organizations exercise strong professional control and high quality legal literature is available".

[137] Th. M. de Boer, *Facultative Choice of Law*, vol. 257 of *Recueil des cours de l'Académie de droit international* (Gravenhage: Martinus Nijhoff, 1996), 225.

[138] The Dutch government indicates that this possibility is facilitated by the internet: TK 2009–2010, 32137, nr. 3, p. 9. An example showing the difficulty in dealing with these issues refers to "the statute on the law of conflicts in case of divorce of 1981 …".

[139] Ewald's report, last page.

judgments … In the Comoros the judge tends to apply the law that he knows better, due also to the serious problems about knowledge of legal materials present in that country.

In Niger there is a tendency for the judges to apply the national law over the international convention, mainly because they know their domestic law better than the international legal instruments.

The strategy of presuming a waiver of foreign sources if the party has not pleaded their applicability immediately is used in Congo, since under the Congolese jurisprudence the parties are requested to claim immediately the application of a foreign law otherwise the judge will not take it into consideration. More rarely the judges tend to consider the Congolese law similar to the foreign one, due to the differences that Congolese law has with others in many domains."[140]

2.6 Suggestions as to "What Can Be Done About the Problem?"

A specific question[141] about proposals to improve the problem of multiple sources of law, scattered at different levels of normativity, did not return a great deal of material. Not much guidance seems to derive from legal scholarship.[142] No easy solution appears available.

At the institutional level, within the international organizations involved in the production of law that will influence the lives of citizens of the different States, some efforts are underway to reach a higher level of coordination. Within UNCITRAL[143] we find "a mandate to coordinate global and regional activities relating to the unification and harmonization of international trade law (United Nations General Assembly Resolution 2205 (XXI)…) … A report on coordination of work is prepared yearly by the secretariat and submitted to the Commission". UNCITRAL also provides "activities of promotion of UNCITRAL texts and of dissemination of related information" that may impact on the fragmentation of sources of international trade law.[144]

In relation to this point the German report reminds us of the need for at least three institutions to work in close connection: UNCITRAL, UNIDROIT and the Hague Conference of Private International Law. Since the past separation between conflict of laws profiles and substantive law issues is no longer observed (but conventions on specific subjects deal with all the aspects connected with them), Hans van Loon has insisted on the need for close cooperation,[145] and this has already brought some improvement.

In Africa, Equatorial Guinea is promoting "the merger of the African organizations of legal and/or economic integration, also to reduce the economic efforts requested to each member country to keep alive all these organizations."[146]

---

[140] An instance of "presumption" allowing a homeward trend is also referred to by the Serbian reporter in connection with the CISG (Jelena PEROVIC, Report) considering "a decision of the High Commercial Court of 9 June 2004, where the Court decided to apply the national Code to the contract of international sale of goods concluded between the party with the place of business in Slovenia and the party with the place of business in Serbia. Since the contract did not contain a choice of law clause, the Court held that the parties *implicitly expressed that choice by choosing the court in Serbia*. … the Court appreciated as one of the main indicators of the parties' intention that the substantive law to their contract is to be the law of Serbia. Having that in mind, the Court concluded that the decision of the 1st instance court to apply the Code of Obligations of Serbia as a substantial law to the contract was correct".

[141] Question 2: "Which proposals have been put forward in your legal system to cope with the problem, and by whom?"

[142] Jan SMITS, Netherlands' Report, Par. 3.3. "… Although the problems associated with [the rise of private regulation] – and with the multiplication of sources generally – are acknowledged in the Dutch literature, one cannot say that the doctrine provides courts with strategies to deal with them. This means that courts often have to find their way in a complex web of rules …" (emphasis added).

[143] Castellani's report, answer to question 1.

[144] *Ibidem*: "Thus, training is offered regularly and specific tools have been developed. While training is offered to all relevant stakeholders (lawyers, government officials, lecturers, etc.) specific activities for the judiciary are carried out in certain fields, such as cross-border insolvency, where this target group has been identified as particularly relevant by funding institutions (other inter-governmental or non-governmental organizations)".

[145] E.-M. Kieninger and K. Linhart, *German Report*; H. van Loon, *Unification of private international law in a multi-forum context*, in Kieninger (ed.), *Denationalisierung des Privatsrechts?, Symposium anlässlich des 70. Geburtstages von Karl Kreuzer*, Tübingen, 2005, 33, at p. 43: the Würzburg symposium of 2004 concerned the "Denationalization of Private Law".

[146] OHADA report, by S. Mancuso. In addition, "OHADA and CEMAC (*Communauté Economique et Monétaire des Etats de l'Afrique Centrale)* recognized the need to have a close cooperation with reference to law-making policies to keep each other informed about projects of legislative acts in progress within each organization, with the objective of reducing the risks of conflicts of supranational laws", considering that "the domain belonging to the harmonization of business law in Africa under OHADA has been maintained voluntarily flexible …."

In the area of conflict of laws, one of the reporters[147] suggested that "[R]egarding the matter of protection of minors, ... the fragmentation of sources and plurality of regimes could, to a large extent, be prevented if the matter had been left to the Hague Conventions: duplicating the professional field of an existing organization with a long tradition does not improve results".

The Swiss report joins in, under this heading, anticipating future conflicts between several Hague conventions concerning minors and the Rome III proposal: with the added complexity of the Lugano level for Switzerland. The same reporter reminds us that Paul Volken suggested as long ago as 1977 that techniques be adopted to avoid conflicts in conventions not only by cooperation between the institutions (with UNCITRAL in an eminent position), but also by providing a "self-disciplined sphere of application" in the conventions and by instructing judges "to apply conventions in a way that concurrences are avoided."[148]

At the level of individual States, we can detect both initiatives "from above" in the legislative field and "horizontal" initiatives, involving training and education.

In several cases, the old solution of codification seems to be gaining popularity: in Portugal, in the form of a new codification of Private International Law encompassing choice of law, jurisdiction and recognition of judgments.[149] In the Netherlands: "... debate was heavily influenced by the old plan (going back to 1947, when work on the new Dutch Civil Code started) to codify Dutch private international law in a separate book (Book 10) of the Dutch Civil Code ... codification was presented as an answer to the existing plurality of sources: this plurality would even provide an incentive to codify. This is also the view of the Dutch government that sent a draft statute for a new Book 10 to Parliament in September 2009.[150] The draft explicitly refers to the aim of bringing coherence among national, European and international rules and to facilitate the incorporation of future European rules. Reference in this context is made to Belgium, where private international law was codified in 2004."[151]

These efforts seem insufficient to provide a definitive answer to a much larger problem. For one thing, in Europe the field of conflict of laws is increasingly influenced by legislation written at the EU level. This means that national codes may have to be continuously updated (although the fact that these EU instruments are usually regulations rather then directives means that the contradictions we have already mentioned about incorporation of European directives in the domestic law are less evident).[152]

[147] Portugal Report, L. de Lima Pinheiro, p. 2 (references to Ulrich Spellenberg – "IntVerfREhe", *in J. von Staudingers Kommentar zum Bürgerlichen Gesetzbuch, Einführungsgesetz zum Bürgerlichen Gesetzbuch/IPR*, Berlin, 2005, Vorbem zu Art 1, no. 20, and Bertrand Ancel and Horatia Muir Watt, "L'intérêt supérieur de l'enfant dans le concert des juridictions : le Réglement Bruxelles II bis," *Critical Review* (2005) 94: 569–605, 574. For a convergent view, see Erik Jayme, "Zum Jahrtausendwechsel: Das Kollisionsrecht zwischen Postmoderne und Futurismus," *IPRax* (2000) 20: 168–171, 169. Opposing, see Marianne Andrae, "Zur Abgrenzung des räumlichen Anwendungsbereichs von EheVO, MSA, KSÜ und autonomem IZPR/IPR," *IPRax* (2006) 26: 82–88, 88–89.

[148] This obvious precaution does not seem to be always observed: the German reporters (p. 3–4) mention similar recommendations conveyed by D. Janzen (the conventions should define clearly their scope and avoid too specific or short-lived subjects, they should give directions for their interpretation, they should be consistent in their definitions, etc.): D. Janzen, *Der UNCITRAL-Konventionenentwurf zum Recht der Internationalen Finanzierungsabtretung*, *Symposium* in Hamburg 1998, *RabelsZ* 1999, p. 368 ff.

[149] See de Lima Pinheiro (n. 3) p. 373; Moura Ramos, loc. cit.; Maria Helena Brito, *O Direito Internacional Privado no Código Civil – perspectivas de reforma*, vol. II of *Estudos Comemorativos dos 10 Anos da Faculdade de Direito da Universidade Nova de Lisboa* (Coimbra: Almedina, 2008), 355–380, 379–380.

[150] J. Smits, mentioning: TK 2009–2010, 32137 (*Vaststelling en invoering van Boek 10 van het Burgerlijk Wetboek*).

[151] See e.g. TK 2005–2006, Aanhangsel, nr. 892 and TK 2009–2010, 32137, nr. 3, p. 4.

[152] See above, comments e.g. by J. SMITS, p. 10: "European directives are implemented as much as possible inside the Dutch Civil Code ..., even though this cannot take away the causes of increasing incoherence. Also the disperse rules on private international law are structured in a new part of the Civil Code, even though it is no longer in the power of the national legislature to create a coherent system. In my view, the strategy of the Dutch legislature is therefore clearly wrong: it should accept it has no longer the power to create a coherent system through legislation and seek new strategies to deal with the various legal regimes that exist on its territory. These strategies will have to take into account the multilevel structure of present-day private law. It must be accepted that the responsibility for coherence and unity of the legal system is no longer in the hands of one institution".

See also, Jelena Perovic (Serbia): "the text of directives should not be introduced in the Code of Obligations, especially not integral texts. The influence of directives may be seen only in ... amending the Code of Obligations where necessary in order to adapt certain provisions of the Code to the adequate requirement of a relevant directive. The Code of Obligations which represents a permanent source of the law of obligations and a specific monument of legal culture should not be exposed to frequent changes, what is exactly the domain of directives which are prompt to adapt to the dynamics of commercial relations".

Again, as regards codification efforts, we have been informed about projects to collect trade usages and practices in accessible forms, notably in the case of the ICC/CCI, but also in the case of the *Austrian* Federal Economic Chamber (AFEC)/Wirtschaftskammer Österreichs (WKÖ).[153]

Concerning the area of training and education, several reporters mention ongoing efforts to improve the familiarity of legal practitioners with extra-national sources, by way of work-experience in foreign or international courts, with the assistance of the European Commission (European Judicial Training Network, EJTN)[154] or within networks of cooperation between States.[155]

Another possible solution is "to enhance coordination among the various actors involved in the multilevel system."[156]

An occasional reference was made to the assistance provided in Germany by the Max Planck Institute as a possible influencing factor in more efficient application of foreign sources.[157] In Switzerland judges dealing with complex cases involving questions of international private law can seek assistance from the Swiss Institute of Comparative Law which might "write opinions about existing transnational instruments or a particular convention and its application."[158]

The German reporters also reminded us of a proposal already put forward in 2004 within the European setting: in order to improve the awareness of the European Court of Justice about the need for an "interplay between comparative law, European Law, Conflict of Laws and Private and Commercial Law" (instead of "focusing predominantly on European law aspects and interests"), O. Remien suggested that, firstly, in the course of deciding on a preliminary ruling (by means of art. 234 EC, now art. 267 TFUE), the ECJ could be assisted by the national court referring the question: the court might "deliver an outline of how its own domestic law would handle the legal issue in question"; and secondly, other States could file memoranda and experts in comparative law could submit *amici curiae* opinions, indicating possible solutions from a comparative law perspective.[159]

Law schools have increased their classes on international subjects and on foreign law: in Canada the Law Faculty of McGill University (Montreal, Quebec) "since 1998, has offered an integrated, comparative, 3-year curriculum, known as the McGill Programme, that teaches even first-year introductory courses, such as Contractual and Extra-contractual Obligations, from a comparative perspective. The ultimate aspiration of this programme … is to transcend the fixation on the study of law as the study of "legal systems" – to overcome the traditional Western bias of conceptualizing law as nothing but a "system" … to free the educational discourse about law from its positivistic constraints."[160] Obviously the tendency to a comparative approach is most encouraged in a mixed jurisdiction.[161]

In the end, we may agree that "most of all, however, we need to rethink our view of private law as a national

---

[153] B. Vershraegen, Austrian Report.

[154] Working sometimes in cooperation with the Council of the Bars and Law Societies of the European Union (CCBE) and the Council of the Notariats of the European Union (CNUE).

[155] In Austria (Verschraegen's report): "The reaction by universities and professional legal associations has been to deepen the knowledge on EU – law, but also to advise students to study abroad and to strengthen cooperation of Austrian practitioners with those from other EU – countries". The German Report includes a paragraph on *Länder*-Academies *(Justizakademien)*: the lists of events involving judges from various European countries is rather impressive (especially in connection with the Eastern European area).

[156] Such as the Open Method of Coordination (OMC), accepted as a method of governance at the 2000 Lisbon European Council and since then applied in various areas.

[157] Japan's report: "Some academics pointed out that an institution which would have a good ability to help judges to research foreign laws and the global framework of nations to cooperate with such research should be established", quoting Akira Mikazuki, *Application of Foreign Law and Courts* (written in Japanese).

[158] A. Fötschl, answer n. 8.

[159] Remien, "*Einheit, Mehrstufigkeit und Flexibilität im europäischen Privat- und Wirtschaftsrecht*," *RabelsZ* (1998) 62: 627 ff., at 633.

[160] Canadian Report: "The programme attempts to understand global legal diversity as a cultural plurality by, for example, using the heuristic tool of the "tradition", as most notably suggested by H. Patrick Glenn. Conceptualizing "law" as "tradition" allows, according to Glenn, for a "normative engagement" with otherness (as opposed to the hierarchic dominance of the positivist, "systemic" approach), while explaining, at the same time, the necessity to sustain diversity. …".

[161] Nicholas Kasirer "has underlined that the pluralist philosophy behind this experiment is very closely linked to the particular legal consciousness of *Quebec,* a mindset that Kasirer described as characterized by the experience of being "mixed", interstitial, and in flux": Nicholas Kasirer, "Legal Education as Métissage," *Tulane Law Review* (2003) 78: 481.

and coherent system."[162] The suggestion is to proceed "from the idea of adapting legal cultures. There is no coercion between the cultures but proactive cooperation. Finding this normative compatibility is a task for the judges searching the law. But for this goal we have to leave aside the traditional sentence that a judge may not innovate the law. Interlegality leads to the building of new law."[163]

For my part, the answer does not seem to have changed since 1987, when I proposed at the UNIDROIT congress in Rome that scholars and law schools should avoid maintaining and creating artificial divisions and distinctions where the actual solutions practiced in each jurisdiction were not different. We often present legal rules as conflicting, or far from one another, even if practical cases may in the end receive similar answers. The way we approach problems along traditional lines of teaching or of analysis may emphasize inconsistencies between different traditions rather than stress similarities that may occur at the operational level. "We must react against the habit of dramatising differences expressing legal rules through conceptual tools which make them unnecessarily rigid. It is for scholars to restate rules, stressing more the operative side so that artificial barriers are not built up by theoretical classifications."[164]

Comparative lawyers are in a position to lift the veil hiding reality. They can introduce students to the general features of different legal systems, so that lawyers are not misled by the different classifications that are sometimes used to qualify facts (for example, in common law and civil law jurisdictions, with the tortious rather than proprietary approach to some remedies to recover personal property); they can also illustrate certain areas of the law, where similar needs suggest similar answers.

The suggestion to intervene early in the process of education, made in 1987, was welcomed (by J. Honnold), but also attracted some skeptical comments: in particular by practitioners involved in the process of making the law uniform. They had the impression that starting early in teaching foreign law, or rather the foreign way of thinking about law, would not overcome the usual set of difficulties in persuading States to ratify and enforce international instruments of uniform law.[165] Gerold Herrmann (senior legal officer of UNCITRAL) was especially skeptical, particularly about the proposal to "start very early with education and professional training". In an ironic reply he mentioned his 6-year-old son to whom he said he was "reading every night two pages of summary records of the *travaux préparatoires* of one of the important unification projects ...". He concluded by saying that "My anticipation is that in about 25 years we will still be discussing the same problems and that unification will still be as important as it is today". He was right. Education takes a long time to bear results, and requires a consistent approach.[166]

In the meantime, teaching has changed: many more exchange programmes have been established between universities, and classes include increasing numbers of foreign students.

[162] See Smit, "Plurality of Sources in European Private Law, or: How to Live With Legal Diversity?," in *The Foundations of European Private Law*, ed. R. Brownsword, H. Micklitz, L. Niglia and S. Weatherill (Oxford: Hart Publishing, 2010).

[163] A. Fötschl, answer 7 (the reporter mentions the "order for the judge to find law in Switzerland that is in conformity with the European Rules ... the national judge may find law *contra legem* if no political will to the contrary was expressed by the legislator").

[164] That was my suggestion in Rome, at the UNIDROIT congress (*International Uniform in Practice*, *cit*., p. 292). I was obviously not the only one to encourage a comparative approach, see: G. Reinhart (Heidelberg University), *Le droit comparé et le perfectionnement juridique dans le domaine du droit privé*, *ibidem*, p. 264 ff.

[165] G. Herrmann, in UNIDROIT, *International Uniform Law in Practice*, *cit.*, p. 543–544.

[166] Discussions concerning the harmonization of the European law of contract often turn on the alternative between, on the one hand, speeding up unification by outright codification and, on the other side, educating lawyers of the different European States to each other's perspective. A classical example: O. Lando supports the first solution (O. Lando, "Principles of European Contract Law, An alternative or Precursor of European Legislation," *American Journal of Comparative Law* (1992) 40: 573–585; O. Lando, "Why *Codify* the European Law of Contract?," *European Review of Private Law* (1997) 5: 525, 526–27), while A. Flessner seems to lean towards the second option (see the *Rechtseinheitlichung durch Rechtswissenschaft und Juristenausbildung*, in the Congress proceedings of the 1991 Hamburg meeting on *Alternativen zur Legislatorischen Rechtsvereinheitlichung*, in *RabelsZ. für ausl. und int. Privatrecht*, 1992, p. 217 ss., at p. 243). The German report mentions opposition by K. Kreuzer to a project of codification of civil law across borders (*Entnationalisierung des Privatrechts durch globale Rechtsintegration?*, in *Festschrift 600 Jahre Würzburger Juristenfakultät*, 2002, 247 ff., at 286).

In the span of time between my experience in 1987 and today's experience, I can add that working in international teams such as the European *Acquis Group on Principles of European Contract law* has increased my comprehension of how scholars from different backgrounds approach problems. I cannot say that I can actually predict what their answers are going to be to issues presented to them, but I can follow their reasoning, and also make myself understood when I raise an objection or I present a different way of seeing the problem. I also see that this kind of communication is easier and more obvious for younger colleagues in our (élite) group.

I should only add that one of the reporters mentioned a fact that in my view is particularly revealing: in the case-law on the CISG "in one case, a court cited 40 foreign court decisions and arbitral awards. Two decisions have each cited two foreign cases, and several cases have cited a single foreign decision. More recently, a court referred to 37 foreign court decisions and arbitral awards."[167] When foreign decisions are easily accessible and translated into one of the languages that most lawyers have struggled to learn, judges and parties do refer to them.[168] In this sense the work done by UNCITRAL through CLOUT (*Case Law on UNCITRAL Texts*) and the *Digest of Case Law,* which summarizes existing judicial and arbitral cases, is probably the best effort made to date, to encourage readers to keep abreast with change.

[167] Tetsuo Morishita, arguing about the need in Japan to have a specialized court in international commercial law, whose judges may feel confident in English, and referring to http://www.cisg.law.pace.edu/cisg/text/digest-art-07.html#a.

[168] I noticed the enthusiasm in quoting foreign decisions (written in German) also in Italian judgments published in the UNILEX collection (unilex.org) and I was somewhat puzzled (since knowledge of German is not so common in our courts), as I mentioned at the UNCITRAL Congress on the 25th anniversary of the CISG, in Vienna, March 2005, "Some Remarks Concerning the Implementation of the CISG by the Courts (the Seller's Performance)," *Pittsburgh Journal of Law and Commerce* (2005–2006) 25(2): 223–240.

The Role of Practice in Legal Education[1]

3

Richard J. Wilson

This general report represents a synthesis of national reports, as well as observations and conclusions.[2]

3.1 An Overview of Issues for the General Report

3.1.1 A Brief Taxonomy, and Some Issues in Theories of Comparison

The submitted reports may be said to reflect what Prof. Mathias Reimann criticizes as the "Country and Western tradition" of comparative law more generally, in which the emphasis is on Europe and its scholars who focus their comparative attentions on the operation of private law within "nation state legal systems and Western capitalist societies." That tendency, he suggests, is in "dire need of a major overhaul."[3] Here, the individual national reporters could have no way of knowing who would respond on the topic under review, and most of the legal education under study here is within the public realm. Yet the Reimann critique must be taken seriously if true and accurate comparisons are to take place within the academy.

Moreover, the particular data-set reported here (again, through no fault of the individual national reporters) generally skews toward those countries in which the role of the teaching of theory within the academy has long reigned supreme over that of the teaching of practice. It does not allow, on its face, for any general conclusions as to the global prevalence and trend in growth of what I will call a pedagogy of practice within the legal academy. I have written elsewhere on the reasons for the absence of practical training within the academy in Western Europe.[4] While my focus in that article was on clinical legal education, the critique applies broadly to the theory-focused legal education that historically predominates in continental Europe as well as in the United States, where the Langdellian case-method of 1870, the verifiable child of German legal science, remains the dominant pedagogy. The national report of Germany specifically engages my critique and provides the beginnings of an international dialog on the topic.

Whatever the shortcomings in the sample, however, I have developed a careful analysis of the national reports, in both narrative and schematic form, in the attached tables. Table 3.2, with explanations, provides the real meat of this report, as it portrays the ways in which the national reports present information on the extent of the teaching of practice within legal education. Table 3.1 is necessary only in order to give context and potential explanation for the data in Table 3.2. For example, as

[1] I.D., Le role de la pratique dans la formation des jurists.

[2] Reports were submitted for Australia, Belgium, Canada (Quebec Province), Czech Republic, England and Wales, France, Germany, Greece, Hungary, Ireland, Italy, New Zealand, Portugal, Switzerland, Taiwan, Turkey, and Venezuela.

[3] Mathias Reimann, "The Progress and Failure of Comparative Law in the Second Half of the Twentieth Century," *American Journal of Comparative Law* 50 (2002): 671, 685.

[4] Richard J. Wilson, "Western Europe: Last Holdout in the Worldwide Acceptance of Clinical Legal Education," *German Law Review* 10 (2009): 823.

R.J. Wilson (✉)
American University, Washington College of Law,
Washington, DC, USA
e-mail: rwilson@wcl.american.edu

K.B. Brown and D.V. Snyder (eds.), *General Reports of the XVIIIth Congress of the International Academy of Comparative Law/Rapports Généraux du XVIIIème Congrès de l'Académie Internationale de Droit Comparé*,
DOI 10.1007/978-94-007-2354-2_3, © Springer Science+Business Media B.V. 2012

Table 3.1 General structure of legal education

		Number LS							
Country	Pop. (M)	Pub	Priv	Bar size(TH)	Grads/year	Grad% prac	Control	Cost/yearUS$/€	Nat. entry exam
Australia	22.3	28[a]	2	3.8B 34.5S	?	Most	Local	$8,000–35,000	yes
Belgium	10.8	12	0	15.8	1,600	Minority	Local	€ 80–837	No
Canada (Quebec)	7.8	6 (civ)	0	23[c]	800	?	Leg.	$ 1,200–1,800	Fr.
Czech Rep.	10.5	4	9	---	1,479 (pub)	65	Min. Ed.	$ 2,500–3,000	Yes/Priv.
England/Wales	62 (UK)	103[e]		15B 115S	13,800	60	Bar, Univ.	$ 5,300–16,400	U/ LNAT
France	65.5	< 50	<10[h]	47.7[i]	?	?	State	€ 8,970[j]	---
Germany	81.7	42	1	147	6,300 1st ex.	50	Local/Univ.	€ 100Pu 9,900Pri	Priv.
Greece	11.3	3	0	>89[l]	1,500	---	State	–0-	---
Hungary	10	6[n]	2	---	3,190	Majority	Leg.	$ 700–1,000	Yes
Ireland	4.5	12[p]	7[q]	2B 8S	1,500	66–73	HEA/Bar	€22,000[r]	Yes
Italy	60.3	47	8+8[u]	200	15,448	Minority	State/courts	€ 1,320–10,000	Priv/Self/ pub
New Zealand	4.3	6	0	10.5	1,400[v]	?[w]	CLE	$ 3,600	NCEA (2002)
Portugal	10.6	5	6	26	1,500	70	Leg.	€ 1,000–4,000	H.S. Exam
Switz.	7.7	9	1 DL	8	1,400	70	Local Coord.	€ 700–1,400	H.S. Exam
Taiwan	23	17	19[x]	5	3,000[y]	Most 70%	Min. Ed.	$ 1,460–2,830	Yes
Turkey	72.5	17	27	---	4,200	Most 76%	State	$ 200	Yes
Venez.	28.7	7	>13[aa]	143	7,000	---	State	$ -0-–3,700	Yes/Vol.

Explanation of Data
Table 1 displays data about the general structure of legal education
Entry Key
Yes or no = responded generally
--- = general reporter did not find responsive data in the report
? = national reporter does not have the data
Acronyms used in the Table come from the national reports
Column Explanations
Column 1 – "Pop (M)" – National population, in millions. I did not ask for national populations. All population figures are taken from estimates by the Population Division of the United Nations Department of Economic and Social Affairs, as of July of 2009
Columns 2–3 – "Number LS" – number of law schools, public and private
Column 4 – "Bar Size (Th)" – Size of bar, including all practicing members, at last count, in thousands
Column 5 – "Grads/year" – Grads in last recorded year
Column 6 – "Grad % prac." – estimated percentage of graduates who will engage in practice as an advocate
Column 7 – "Control" – refers to who controls or governs legal education generally: legislature, courts, etc., as well as the level at which that authority is exercised: national or local
Column 8 – "Cost yr, US$/€" – estimated cost of enrollment per year. Some reporters gave estimated total cost. In all countries with state control and support of legal education, the state, nationally or locally, subsidizes the cost of legal education, either to the university or directly to the student
Column 9 – "Nat. Entry Exam" – whether there is some other requirement beyond graduation from secondary school or undergraduate school, excluding national graduation exams within those levels
Columns 10–11 – "Degrees/years" – this refers to the number of years of schooling required for basic admission to practice law as an advocate. The first degree is, almost without exception, taken after completion of secondary education, not after a general undergraduate B.A. or B.S. The second degree is a masters degree, but may be required for practice, particularly in Bologna process countries
Column 12 – "Comp Grad Exam" – whether there is some comprehensive examination prior to or following graduation from law school
Columns 13–15 – "Apprenticeship" – this cluster tells the term of an apprenticeship or trainee period, whether some course of study is required during that period, and whether there is some form of examination during or after the traineeship. The apprenticeship is managed by the bar unless otherwise indicated
Columns 16–18 – "Professoriate" – this group discusses full-time (FT) and part-time (PT) professors, and whether the full-time faculty can engage in the private practice of law while employed by the university (PrPr)
Column 19 – "Future" is a column to give one of two pithy words of summary from the national reports on the future of practice in the academy
Note – Due to the complexity of national curricula, no column indicates that information. As a general conclusion, however, one notes that much of the curriculum is more required than elective, and that required courses are often designated by a body outside of the law schools themselves, such as national legislation or a national regulatory agency. Nor did I include reference to rules regarding student practice of law, as such rules were both rare or non-existent

Degrees/years			Apprenticeship			Professoriate			
1st(af.H.S.)	2d	Compgrad exam	Term	Course	Exam	FT	PT	FTPrPr	Future
5 or 2-3 gr		yes	1yr reader	PLT/1 mo (L.S.)	Yes	Most	Growing	---	Strong/Americanized
3	2	No	3 years[b]	Yes (L.S.)	Yes	Most	Growing	Yes	---
---	---	---	6 months	Yes	Yes	Most	Yes	Yes	---
3	2	Yes[d]	3 years	---	Yes	55%	45%	---	More practice
3 (1–4 grad)[f]	--	---	12 months + pupilage	BPTC LPC	No[g]	Most	---	---	Increasing, E, not R
3	1–2	CAPA	18 months	---	---	100	---	Yes	---
4	---	Yes	2 years[k]	Yes	Yes (Cts)	100	---	Rare	---
4	---	---	18 months	---	Yes[m]	100	---	Yes	Legal aid by bar
5		---	3 years	---	Yes[o]	Most	Growing	Some	Needs refining
3	1–3	yes[s]	1 year[t]	1 year	Yes (Bar)	Most	---	---	More – Increasing
3	2	Dissert.	2 year	Yes (L.S.)	Yes	---	Most	Yes	More in LLM stage
4	---	1st year & yes	18 weeks	PLSC	Yes	Core	Contract	---	---
4		no	2 years	Yes 6 months	Yes	10%	Most	Yes	Not needed
3	1–2		1 year	Yes	Yes	Core	Lecture	Yes	---
4–5	[3–4]	Yes[z]	5 months	1 month	No	41%	59%	No	More prac/ Not like American
4		no	1 year	Yes	Some	Most	---	---	---
5		Comp/Univ.	3 months[ab]	---	---	---	---	---	More in future

[a]14 of these schools have been founded since 1989
[b]Includes pro deo obligation to accept legal aid cases
[c]47% of the bar is female
[d]Includes diploma paper
[e]No public/private distinction noted. All schools listed in appendix to national report
[f]Also includes option to read law without attending law school
[g]Entry is competitive
[h]This is a reference to combined business and law schools with a commercial focus
[i]Not from this report; from report of Italy, at 11
[j]Estimated average total cost
[k]Supported by state stipend
[l]Actual number significantly smaller
[m]Written and oral stages
[n]Four new schools between 1995 and 2002
[o]Administered by government, not bar
[p]Seven Universities and five institutes of technology
[q]Five colleges and two professional legal bodies
[r]Estimated total cost
[s]Often preceded by “grind” preparation course
[t]Called pupilage or “deviling”
[u]Includes 8 “e-schools” by distance learning
[v]28% increase from 2002 to 2006
[w]Decreasing percentage as enrollment rises, due to wide choice of career options
[x]Increase in total schools by 28 since 2000
[y]Only 494 passed bar – see next note
[z]Very low pass rate – estimated at 8%, rising to 22% in recent year
[aa]Many schools founded since 1990
[ab]Done as Community Service

Table 3.2 Practice in legal education – courses and methods

Country	Foreign language	Research	Rhetoric/ Writing	Drafting	Ethics	Cases	PBL	Seminars	Simulation	Moots	Extern Intern	Clinic[a]
Australia	---	R	---	E	R	---	---	E	E	E	E	Some
Belgium	English (LLM)	E	E	E	R/E	Yes	E	E	E	E	E	V/law shops
Canada (Quebec)	English expected	---	---	---	R	---	---	---	E	E	E	E/V Pro Bono
Czech Rep.	Yes	---	N	---	E	---	---	E	---	---	---	1[b]/E
England/Wales	No	R	R	E	R (B)/E	R	E	E	E	E	E	Many/E
France	English – E (business)	No	---	---	---	---	---	---	---	---	---	No/V
Germany	One	"Legal methods"	E	E	E	Yes .Exams	---	E	E	E	R (3 mo)	1/E
Greece	---	---	---	---	No	---	Yes	Yes	---	E	E	No
Hungary	English/Some German	---	2-E	---	Yes	Yes	---	E	---	Yes/E	R (6–8 wks)	5[c]/E
Ireland	No	R	R	R	Yes	R	---	R	E	E	E	2/E
Italy	Yes/English	---	---	---	---	---	---	---	---	No	20%	No
New Zealand	---	R	R	R	R	---	E	---	E	E	2/E	1/E
Portugal	---	---	---	---	E	Yes	---	---	---	---	No	No
Switz.	Yes/English	R	R Oral - E	---	E	Yes	---	No	E	E	R/LLM V/St.	V/St. run
Taiwan	No	E	---	E	Yes	---	---	---	Trial Process	Yes	Yes/Ct & Pros.	Legal Aid/V
Turkey	---	---	---	---	No	Yes	Yes	Yes/E	---	Yes/Virtual	Visits	Yes/Private
Venez.	No	R	E	---	Yes	Yes	---	---	---	---	R	Práctica Jur -R

Key
R – Required
E – Elective
B – Bar or Professional Requirement before admission to practice; not an academic offering
Yes or No – Mentioned in report
--- – Not mentioned in report
Numbers indicate number of schools identified as using course or method
[a]No column included on student practice - ranges from absolute bar to no limitations at all
[b]Charles University Refugee Clinic, not mentioned in report
[c]Some of the five schools have multiple clinical offerings

the New Zealand report notes, legal education is divided into three broad stages: a first academic phase, a second professional training phase, and a third post-admission phase of ongoing or continuing legal education, often required in many countries.[5] The reports themselves all reflect the first two stages: a period of formal training is followed by a required period of apprenticeship in every reporting country. The apprenticeship period is required before a student who has graduated from law school can be admitted to practice as an advocate, and often before he or she can move on to specialized training for either the judiciary or prosecution services. It is often within the apprenticeship phase of training that the trainee-lawyer is said to gain an exposure to training in the actual practice of law.

English, it can be argued, has become the *lingua franca* of international and comparative law.[6] This is important not only in its own right, but because it strongly relates to information in both the national reports and in general on comparative legal education. It is obvious from the national reports that English has become an important tool for teaching law in a globalized world, and as a common root language for students across borders. Many of the reports note a trend toward a more globalized curriculum,[7] and law courses in English seem to offer a kind of common denominator for whether schools will attract a global study body. In Belgium, France, Germany, Hungary, Italy and Switzerland, at least some courses are offered in English. (see Table 3.2, "Foreign Language" column).

A second issue in conducting a comparative study is the frame of reference for comparison itself. Comparative law has struggled mightily with this theme throughout its existence, and modern comparative study of legal education and the legal profession is not immune to this critique. Some of that, in turn, has to do with the existing literature on the topic, and prior frames of reference. First, then, let us briefly review the English-language literature on comparative legal education and the legal professions.

Literature on comparative legal education is sparse at best, and where it exists, it tends toward comparisons of U.S. and classic European systems. In 1965[8] and 1970,[9] comprehensive bibliographies on comparative legal education were published in the United States. The later bound volume is significantly larger, and contains over 100 pages of annotated entries on legal education around the world, under the heading of "Comparative Legal Education." These materials are organized by region and country, and make no further subject-matter distinctions within countries. In 1993, another volume appeared, this time on international legal education,[10] but bibliographies appear to be otherwise limited to country-specific materials.

Comparative materials on the legal professions share much the same fate, aside from the general observation that legal professions and legal education are often treated as separate fields of study, as though the two were completely unrelated. The definitive series of books on *Lawyers in Society*, edited by Richard Abel and Philip Lewis in the late 1980s,[11] remain the best single collection on comparative legal professions, but their work focuses primarily on the sociology of law rather than purely comparative perspectives. Now more than 20 years old, this collection still remains as the best comparative source on these topics, but it too is limited largely to comparison of lawyers in Europe and the United States. A more recent volume represents a kind of sequel, but again focuses on Europe and North America, with additional chapters on Australia, Korea, Mexico and Latin America generally.[12] The late Mauro Capelletti's multi-volume

[5] New Zealand national report, at 1. While many reports make mention of continuing legal education requirements, my focus here is on legal education itself, so there will be no discussion of CLE.

[6] An interesting new title, published in May of 2010, suggests that English can be reduced, in turn, to "Globish," with a reductive vocabulary of some 1500 essential words used for business purposes. Robert McCrum, *Globish: How the English Language Became the World's Language* (New York: W.W. Norton & Co., 2010).

[7] See, e.g., Belgium Report, at 10; Greece Report, at 17; Italy Report, at 6.

[8] Doris Yendes Alspaugh, *A Bibliography of Materials on Legal Education* (New York: New York University School of Law, 1965).

[9] Dusan J. Djonovich, *Legal Education: A Selective Bibliography* (Dobbs Ferry: Oceana, 1970).

[10] International Legal Education Bibliography (Donald B. King ed. 1993) (loose-leaf document prepared for the Section on International Legal Exchanges of the Association of American Law Schools).

[11] Richard L. Abel and Philip S.C. Lewis, *Lawyers in Society,* 4 vols (Berkeley: University of California Press,1989).

[12] William L.F. Felstiner ed., *Reorganization and Resistance: Legal Professions Confront a Changing World* (Oxford: Hart, 2005).

series on access to justice, completed in the 1970s, contained more information on a wider range of countries, but on a narrower topic.[13] There is, to my knowledge, only one volume exclusively devoted to the legal professions in the global south, primarily Africa and Latin America, but also including Malaysia, and that volume is now nearly 30 years out of date.[14]

The most recent volumes on comparative legal professions take a more cultural perspective,[15] while challenging the dominant paradigms of comparison through the traditional civil v. common law structures.[16] Prof. Garth, for example, suggests that perspectives grounded in institutional economics, such as the writings of Ugo Mattei, or with market-oriented grounding, provide better alternative frameworks for analysis than the traditional comparativists. Each alternative "defines the object of study differently, and each provides very different insights about what it means to be a 'lawyer' or 'jurist' in different places."[17] Other comparativists suggest abandonment of the common-law-versus-civil-law paradigm entirely, in favor of broad factors such as prestige, power or efficiency as motivators on the part of the receiving countries in the "legal transplant" process, while imposition through colonialism or imperialism is the primary tool of the exporting countries.[18] Prestige and power, politics and economics, patriarchy and paternalism may also provide significant structural frameworks for the analysis of the persistence of tradition within legal education.[19]

In this study, for example, there is no analysis of the implications for legal education of the economic and sociological phenomenon known as "big law," or the growth of the enormous, multi-national law firm. The biggest 100 global law firms, mostly based in the United States, but also found in England, the Netherlands, Spain, France, Australia and Canada, averaged over 1,000 lawyers per firm in 2008 for the first time.[20] In 2009, the biggest U.S. firm, Baker & McKenzie, topped out at just short of 4,000 lawyers in 39 countries.[21] Its gross revenues of $2.1 billion rank it higher than the GDP of 32 countries of the world in 2009, by World Bank measures of GDP. Recent studies show that the particular organizational structures of these firms, as well as the lawyering skills needed to perform well within firm culture, may require us to change our views of the legal profession and the ways in which legal education trains future lawyers.[22] Market-driven decisions erode lawyer's ethics and can make the practice of law more a business than a profession.[23] And the lure of big money goes with big law – starting salaries for new associates, even during the recession and with delayed start dates, have stayed in the neighborhood of $160,000 per year in the U.S. And even though big law laid off lawyers, deferred new hires, and slashed the size of incoming classes of associates,[24] revenue per partner in the biggest firms in

[13] Mauro Cappelletti ed., *Access to Justice,* 4 vols. (Milan/Alphen aan den rijn: A. Giuffrè/Sijthoff and Noordhoff 1978–1979).

[14] C.J. Dias et al., eds., *Lawyers in the Third World: Comparative and Developmental Perspectives* (Uppsala/New York: Scandinavian Institute of African Studies/International Center for Law in Development, 1981).

[15] See, e.g., Ralph Grillo et al., eds., *Legal Practice and Cultural Diversity* (Farnham: Ashgate, 2009).

[16] Bryant Garth, "Comparative Law and the Legal Profession: Notes Toward a Reorientation of Research," in *Lawyers' Practice and Ideals: A Comparative View,* ed. John J. Barceló III and Roger C. Cramton (The Hague/Boston: Kluwer Law International, 1999), 227.

[17] Id. at 228.

[18] Gianmaria Ajani, "By Chance and Prestige: Legal Transplants in Russia and Eastern Europe," American Journal of Comparative Law 43 (1995): 93, 112–114; Michele Graziadei, "Comparative Law as the Study of Transplants and Receptions," in *The Oxford Handbook of Comparative Law*, ed. Mathias Reimann and Reinhard Zimmermann (Oxford: Oxford University Press 2006), 441, 355–461.

[19] See, e.g., Duncan Kennedy, "The Political Significance of the Structure of the Law School Curriculum," *Seton Hall Law Reviews* 14 (1983–1984): 1; generally, Ugo Mattei, "Why the Wind Changed: Intellectual Leadership in Western Law," *American Journal of Comparative Law* 42 (1994): 195.

[20] *The Global 100: Most Lawyers*, 30 American Lawyer 171 (Oct. 2008). The German national reporters also note the growth of "big law" in that country.

[21] *The Am Law 100, 2010*, 32 American Lawyer 137 (May 2010).

[22] Richard Susskind, *The End of Lawyers? Rethinking the Nature of Legal Services* (2009) (British perspective); Thomas Morgan, *The Vanishing American Lawyer* (2010) (American perspective).

[23] See, e.g., John J. Barceló III and Roger C. Cramton, eds., *Lawyers' Practice and Ideals: A Comparative View* (The Hague/Boston: Kluwer Law International, 1999), with six chapters on legal ethics in the profession, and Milton Reagan Jr., *Eat What You Kill: The Fall of a Wall Street Lawyer* (Ann Arbor: University of Michigan Press 2005).

[24] *No Answers Easy: Am Law 100 Firms Laid Off Thousands of Lawyers in 2009*, 32 American Lawyer 108 (May 2010).

2009 still averaged just over $1 million, with the top firm's partners taking in $4 million each.[25] While this report lends itself to the traditional construct of comparison by civil law/common law distinctions, these economic factors are profoundly changing the face of the bar, and raising troubling questions about legal education's relationship to – and arguably its profound disconnection from – the contemporary practice of law.

3.1.2 Definitional Issues

Before beginning a detailed discussion of the data, then, I will provide some definitional framework for common reference. At the heart of the matter is the question of what constitutes the "practice" of law; put another way, what is the legal "profession" and what do law professionals do? A related question is what terminology should be used for one who engages in the practice of law.

When using those terms in the United States, the usage is relatively straightforward. In *Black's Law Dictionary*, a "lawyer" is defined as "a person learned in the law; as an attorney, counsel or solicitor; a person licensed to practice law." Even there, several synonyms are offered: attorney, counsel or solicitor. In the U.S., however, the term "solicitor" is not used, as the bar is unitary; the last half of the definition is better. A lawyer is, simply, one who holds a license to practice law, that license having been issued by the highest bar authority in the state in which the law school graduate sat for a state bar examination and passed the related "character and fitness to practice" element of the licensing process. Once a lawyer has her license, she can appear in any state court within that jurisdiction, and without much more than payment of an additional licensure fee, can appear in the federal courts as well.

Lawyers in the U.S. engage in the practice of law, whether they are self-employed, or employed by a law firm, as in-house counsel in a business entity, by government, prosecution services, or as court personnel other than judges. The area of practice focus matters little for lawyers in the U.S., and lawyers rarely take on the role of judge immediately after law school graduation; judicial positions are gained later in one's career by either nomination or non-partisan popular election. One can readily see that the term "lawyer" captures the vast majority of the legal profession, other than the judiciary and most of the teaching profession. A lawyer is, in short, a provider of general legal services. While some law school graduates do not actively practice law, the vast majority take a bar exam and become licensed in some state, usually within the first year after their graduation from law school. In the U.S., a notary is not legally educated, and serves simply as a qualified public official who certifies that a document has been sworn under oath to be true and accurate. Legal secretaries often act as notaries after taking a short course and obtaining a notary certificate; a small fee may be charged for notary services.

The U.S. definition of law practice and membership in the legal profession does not hold true almost anywhere else in the world, and certainly not within the civil law world. As was apparent from the reports (and the general reporter's prior knowledge), many law school graduates from Europe and other parts of the world do not go on to become licensed practitioners after law school graduation. While many national reports were not able to make accurate estimates, most reports suggested that somewhere between 60 and 75% of all law school graduates go on to pursue a law license, and are now in practice. (See Table 3.1, column marked "Grad % prac."). Only one country report, Italy, suggested that a "minority" of law grads go on to licensure,[26] while several suggested that "most" graduates obtain licenses. In many parts of Europe, such graduates of law school without licensure are referred to as "jurists," and they will be designated as such hereafter. In-house counsel for corporations or businesses often fall into this category, and may not need formal licensure to advise their business clients.

For those with legal training who go on to licensure and then into private or public practice, the most common term is "advocate," although countries that are part of the British tradition (England & Wales, Ireland and Australia) continue to make distinctions between two categories of training and practice: solicitor and barrister. The barrister is most associated with those who appear in court to plead a client's case, while a solicitor traditionally engages in out-of-court advisory

[25] *The Am Law 100, 2010: 2009 Profits Per Partner/By Location*, 32 American Lawyer 157 (May 2010). The top firm, in PPP, was New York's Wachtell, Lipton, Rosen & Katz, with $4,300,000 each for 86 equity partners.

[26] Bar leaders in the Netherlands hold a similar view; see below.

work, but those distinctions are blurring, despite maintenance of the hierarchy of barrister over solicitor. Here, I will use the term advocate or lawyer when referring to individuals licensed for the private or public practice of law within a national jurisdiction. In his study comparing lawyers and law practice between the common law and civil law tradition, however, American scholar Richard Abel found accurate comparisons of the legal professions to be "acutely problematic" across the civil and common law, but not impossible.[27]

There are, however, categories of the legal profession that are not associated with the traditional practice of law. These include, most typically, notaries, prosecutors, judges or magistrates, and sometimes bailiffs. For those statuses, special additional training may be required in addition to or distinct from the traditional apprenticeship stage before entry into law practice, and such forms of the legal profession often have their own guilds or bar associations apart from advocates. Positions in these fields are normally begun after law school, are life-long specialized careers, and are not considered to be engaged in law "practice." The same may be true in some countries for specialized training in a particular area of law, especially in fields such as tax or real estate law. Thus, as the French report notes (in my own translation from the original French), "law studies offer numerous possibilities: the professions of advocate, notary, magistrate, in-house counsel, bailiff, realtor, insurer, judicial administrator, appraiser, banker, different positions within the public sphere (professors, hospital directors, lieutenants and commissioners of police, work inspectors, customs inspectors, tax controllers, etc.)" and others.[28] One may or may not have a formal license to practice law in order to engage in some of these functions, and sometimes one must have more than formal legal education and an apprenticeship to hold such positions, but all are available with a law school diploma.

The European distinctions between law practice and other legal roles, however, do not appreciably differ from the functions carried out by U.S. jurists and advocates, and legal education still has, as its primary function, "the formation of skilled lawyers," as noted in the Belgian report.[29] That report goes on to suggest that because the skills of a lawyer remain a "tricky" question, the inclusion of skills training in law school curricula remains difficult, as there is "no general accepted 'standard' for implementing practice in curricula."[30] That may well be true in Belgium, and more broadly in continental Europe, but it is not true in England and Wales, nor in the United States, where the bar and the academy together have sharpened answers to the question of what baseline skills a lawyer needs in order to competently engage in the practice of law.

No generally accepted standard for the teaching of practice exists on the Continent for a number of reasons. First, very little time has been devoted by the legal academy there to the question of what a lawyer does in practice, as most law school academics do not practice law themselves, and the topic holds little academic interest. More than 20 years ago, Richard Abel noted that "students of comparative law . . . have paid little or no attention to lawyers," at least in English-language studies. He noted in 1988 that "very little has been written in English on lawyers outside of the common law world."[31] Second, and a corollary of the first, issues of practice on the Continent are best designed and taught by the bar or bench during the separate period of apprenticeship, as it is the bar or bench that is best equipped to teach skills.[32] Third, it is assumed that issues of practice can and will be taught adequately during the period of formal apprenticeship, a period of immersion in the world of law practice, often accompanied by classes intended to expose students to practice issues. All of the reporting countries in this study provide for some period of apprenticeship, although the time period for such training varies radically, from as short as 18 weeks, in New Zealand, to as long as 3 years, in Belgium, the Czech Republic and Hungary. (see Table 3.1, first column under "Apprenticeship" heading). Finally, it is assumed that if the apprenticeship does not adequately prepare the new advocates for practice, they will get that training on the job, through training programs conducted by the law firms by which the advocate will be employed.

[27] Richard I. Abel, "Lawyers in the Civil Law World," in *Lawyers in Society: Vol. 2, The Civil Law World,* ed. Richard I. Abel & Philip S.C. Lewis 1, 5 (Berkeley: Univ. of California Press, 1988).

[28] French report, at 8.

[29] Belgian report, at 9.

[30] Ibid.

[31] Abel, *Lawyers in the Civil Law World*, supra n. 27, at 1.

[32] Note that three jurisdictions – Australia, Belgium and Italy – report that law school faculty design and teach the courses offered during the apprenticeship period.

The French report hints that practical training is easy for recent graduates to pick up; the report seems to suggest that, for starting in-house counsel, such training can occur in "less than 2 months, if the new recruit demonstrates such a mind or natural potential to reinforce [such training] quickly."[33] If there is little current scholarship on what lawyers do in practice on the Continent, there is even less, empirical or otherwise, on the question of what actually happens during the apprenticeship period or with other forms of on-the-job training, except very anecdotally. One can fairly conclude, I believe, that the legal academy, in both Europe and United States, knows very little about what happens after formal academic training is over, whether in an apprenticeship or in practical, on-the-job training. Indeed, one can make the case that the legal academy, not only in Europe but throughout the world, is strangely balkanized from the law profession and law practice itself, and that legal education's age-old romance with doctrinal issues – whether through codes or cases – comes at the expense of actually knowing, and helping students to learn, what lawyers need to know and do in their professional work. If the national reports are a reflection of the broader world of law teaching, that is certainly the case in continental Europe and Latin America today, after millennia of teaching law as science through an overwhelmingly mandated doctrinal curriculum, via dogmatic lecture and rote memorization to huge classrooms of students.[34] Law teaching, we might note, is no less tradition-bound and doctrinally focused in the United States or throughout the common law system. U.S. history is simply shorter, and the historical direction is discernibly more toward a greater role for practice within the academy.

It is not the purpose of this report to call for legal education to exclusively or *only* teach practice. To focus legal education on practice skills exclusively might well, as the French national report notes, "suppress any systematic or synthetic thinking."[35] Rather, the purpose of the report is simply to document the extent to which legal education today gives attention to what might be called a pedagogy of practice, *in addition to* imparting the skill of careful and logical legal reasoning.

The recent report of the Carnegie Foundation for the Advancement of Teaching, *Educating Lawyers: Preparation for the Profession of Law*,[36] critiquing legal education in the United States today, suggests that the role of legal education should be to focus on what it calls the "three apprenticeships": training for thinking, performing and professional conduct. The first apprenticeship is intellectual or cognitive, and is the traditional apprenticeship that dominates legal education throughout the world today. The second apprenticeship is "the forms of expert practice shared by competent practitioners," and must be taught by "quite different pedagogies" than those by which theory is taught. The third, an apprenticeship of "identity and purpose," inculcates values for which the legal profession is responsible.[37] While the Carnegie Report authors do not explicitly so conclude, one can make the case that these apprenticeships are universal; they are or should be common to the mission of legal education throughout the world. It may be that the traditional apprenticeship period following law school in many countries contributes to construction of the three essential apprenticeships, but the question remains as to whether legal education lives up to its promise to prepare skilled, competent beginning lawyers.

One final issue deserves explication, that of what constitutes the scope or range of the teaching of practice in legal education. Is the teaching of practice primarily focused on the content of the subject matter offered within a school's curriculum, or is the teaching of practice a question of teaching methodology?

[33] French report, at 9.

[34] If taken as accurate, this was certainly true 15 years ago, when the great comparative scholar, John Henry Merryman, wrote that in Western Europe, "[q]uestions about teaching objectives and methods are considered uninteresting or not open to discussion. One teaches as professors have always taught; one's purposes are the same purposes as they have always been; questions about such matters do not arise." John Henry Merryman, "Legal Education There and Here: A Comparison," in *Civil Law,* ed. Ralf Rogowski, 79, 85 (1996). And later, he opines that in "the civil law world, the educational focus is primarily on substance; method is deemphasized." Id., at 91. This seems no less true in Latin America today. See, Juny Montoya, "The Current State of Legal Education Reform in Latin America: A Critical Appraisal," *Journal of Legal Education* 59 (2010): 545 (commenting that in Latin America, the "teaching of law has inherited medieval, dogmatic methods and later incorporated a further, inner dogmatism shaped by the ideology of codification." Id., at 546).

[35] French report, at 14.

[36] William M. Sullivan et al., *Educating Lawyers: Preparation for the Profession of Law* (San Francisco: Carnegie Foundation, 2007).

[37] Id., at 27–29.

This report, and hopefully the questionnaire itself, left ample room for broad inclusion of both content and method in the teaching of practice.

Methods of teaching practice are often referred to as "active" or "experiential" methods, as they engage the student in some activity other than passive listening. They may be hypothetical or real, but all involve activity: doing, rather than merely thinking.[38] In this sense, active or experiential learning goes beyond not only the classic lecture method, but also the "Socratic-case" method in U.S. legal education, developed from roots at Harvard Law School in the late nineteenth century. The case method, although grounded in the study of cases as precedents, was designed by Dean Langdell pursuant to the notion that a few essential principles of law could be discovered in the cases through a scientific method. This concept was borrowed from German legal science, then seen as a guiding force by many American academics.[39] It is, as such, a method of legal analysis or legal thinking, and the use of cases is simply another context for critical legal reasoning; it is grounded in thinking, and not in doing. Nonetheless, because at least six national reports from the civil law tradition[40] included the study of cases as a method for teaching of practice, five civil law countries list seminars,[41] and another three civil law countries[42] use what is commonly called problem-based learning, I have included those three methods or course contexts along the continuum of the teaching of practice. (see Table 3.2, columns headed "Cases," "Seminars" and "PBL")

Thinking of the teaching of practice as flowing along a continuum of courses or subjects might be helpful in approaching this topic within the report.[43] The constellation of courses moves from the more passive to the more active in engaging the student in the learning process. Courses or subjects such as a foreign language, cases, problem-based learning and seminars are all included here, but all involve either teaching or learning contexts only of legal thinking or analysis. The mere fact that a student is speaking in class can arguably make a subject active, but it is not yet experiential; that is, students are largely using their cognitive, analytical skills rather than other, less cognitive processes such as judgment, creativity, interpersonal skills or time-efficiency. Another set of courses engages the students in activities that are experiential in the sense that they simulate lawyering tasks through replication in often-complex and lengthy hypothetical situations. These include such courses as legal research, legal rhetoric, legal drafting, or other simulation courses (examples might include courses on client interviewing or counseling, trial practice, or on alternative dispute resolution methods such as negotiation, mediation or arbitration). Those courses are listed in Table 3.2 as well, although there is one catch-all category called "Simulation" that is intended to capture subject-matters taught through simulation or role-play, but beyond the most basic lawyering skills.[44]

This is not to say, of course, that all courses or subjects on the continuum are of equal weight or strength as teaching methods. Each has come under significant criticism, particularly when compared to the benefits of work with actual clients in the clinical context.

---

[38] Julian Webb, a British scholar, draws more subtle distinctions between experiential learning and practical or experiential knowledge. The experiential model "places a premium on the know how rather than the know what aspects of learning." Julian Webb, "Where the Action Is: Developing Artistry in Legal Education," *International Journal of Legal Profession* 2 (1995): 187, 190–191.

[39] See, Laura I. Appleman, "The Rise of the Modern American Law School: How Professionalization, German Scholarship, and Legal Reform Shaped Our System of Legal Education," *New England Law Review* 39 (2005): 251 (arguing that German legal science, as adopted by Langdell, was "less about individual German courses and more about a specific scholastic ideology – a way of thinking about learning – focusing on scholarship and research as the definition of one's professional career . . . The scientific method, emphasized by such German scholars as Leopold von Ranke, emphasized long hours in the library and absolute fidelity to sources." Id., at 274); Howard Schweber, "The 'Science' of Legal Science: The Model of the Natural Sciences in Nineteenth-Century American Legal Education," *Law and History Review* 17 (1999): 421 (suggesting the science was a natural science inherited from the British, but arguing that "Langdell's 'legal science' was emphatically not based on the experience of legal practice." Id., at 461).

[40] Belgium, Hungary, Portugal, Switzerland, Turkey and Venezuela. Germany notes that cases are used in state examinations.

[41] Belgium, Czech Republic, Greece, Hungary and Turkey.

[42] Belgium, Greece and Turkey. Among the common law countries, England & Wales and New Zealand also listed PBL as a context for teaching practice.

[43] I first suggested the existence of a "passive-to-active pedagogical continuum" for legal education in Richard J. Wilson, "The New Legal Education in North and South America," *Stanford Journal of International Law* 25 (1989): 373, 420–422 .

[44] One course listed in the German report as "Legal Methods," appeared to fall within this category, but the German national reporter clarified that this is not a skills course. He noted that skills courses are offered on an optional basis.

Moots, for example, have been justifiably criticized. Although mooting is seen, in Canada and elsewhere, as "one of the rites of passage of undergraduate legal education," moots inappropriately shift focus "away from finding a 'good outcome' towards discovering a 'winning formula' with little attention paid to the actual consequences. [Mooting] is incomplete and naïve when it comes to dealing with real life problems and real life clients."[45] By contrast, problem based learning, or PBL, a method often used in medical training, can provide opportunities for cooperative and collective work, if conducted properly. It also emphasizes the process dimensions of learning by encouraging student groups to "think about *how* they went about the task they were assigned, to reflect on what problem-solving techniques they are developing and what worked and did not work to produce good results."[46] The same is true of the experiential context of clinical education, in which the cycle of planning, doing, reflection and abstract conceptualization is central to the clinical enterprise.[47]

Another Canadian scholar criticizes the difference between role-play or simulation's artificially constructed learning contexts and those of clinical work:

> These arise because a student caseworker who engages with the contexts of poverty law with a "live client" must confront contingencies which often cannot be adequately replicated in a simulated exercise. When a client is facing homelessness, deportation or other dire consequences of poverty, a host of issues may surround and enmesh the legal issues, including the need for an interpreter, the need for psychological assistance, the need for medical treatment, the need for food, the need for shelter and so on... It is clearly a very different enterprise ... to prepare a distressed non-English-speaking client for next Monday's deportation proceedings than it is to dissect and prepare questions based upon the facts gleaned from a five page "transcript" of an "interview" for a role-played direct examination.[48]

There also are courses or options that involve the actual doing of a lawyer's work. These technically include only clinical courses, but here will include externships as well, as the two are sometimes included together within the ambit of clinical legal education.[49] A number of national reports noted that students may make visits to local courts or other legal institutions. These are not externships in the sense in which this report means the term. As one British source notes, "observation exercises (e.g., court visits, watching practitioners either in life or on video or film) being essentially passive," do not qualify as clinical experiences.[50] An externship (sometimes also called an internship; the terms seem interchangeable) is the placement of a student within a legal institution or law office, under the supervision of an employee of that office who works within the legal profession, allowing the student to observe and occasionally take part in the work of that person or office, hopefully for credit within the law school but sometimes on a volunteer basis. There should be some oversight of the student's work in the office by a faculty member of her school, and in law schools such as my own, externships are rarely taken for credit without an accompanying externship seminar, often with people from the same subject area. Simulations[51] and externships[52] have their strong defenders, and are included here within the

[45] Julie Macfarlane, "What Does the Changing Culture of Legal Practice Mean for Legal Education?," *Windsor Y.B. Access to Just*. 20 (2001): 191, 195.

[46] Id., at 203–204 (emphasis in original).

[47] Steven Hartwell, a clinical teacher, suggests ways in which experiential learning can be incorporated into the traditional, and much larger, doctrinal class. Steven Hartwell, "Six Easy Pieces: Teaching Experientially," *San Diego Law Review* 41 (2004): 1011.

[48] Rose Voyvodic, "Considerable Promise and Troublesome Aspects: Theory and Methodology of Clinical Legal Education," *Windsor Y.B. Access Just* 20 (2001): 111, 117–118.

[49] See, e.g., Elliott S. Milstein, "Clinical Legal Education in the United States: In-House Clinics, Externships, and Simulations," *Journal of Legal Education* 51 (2001): 375. The massive bibliography on clinical legal education compiled by Profs. Sandy Ogilvy and Karen Czapanskiy also includes externships and in-house clinics (those housed within a law school) within the definitional scope of clinical legal education. J.P. Ogilvy and Karen Czapanskiy, "Clinical Legal Education: An Annotated Bibliography 3d ed.," *Clinical Law Review* 12 (2005): 5, also available on-line at http://faculty.cua.edu/ogilvy/Index1.htm, visited on 21 May 2010.

[50] Andrew Boone, Michael Jeeves and Julie Macfarlane, "Clinical Anatomy: Towards a Working Definition of Clinical Legal Education," *The Law Teacher* 21 (1987): 61, 65.

[51] Deborah Maranville, "Passion, Context and Lawyering Skills: Choosing Among Simulated and Real Clinical Experiences," *Clinical Law Review* 7 (2000): 123 (United States); Russell Stewart, "Making Simulations Stimulating," *Journal of Professor of Legal Education* 3 (1985–1986): 51.

[52] For a very recent and comprehensive treatment of externship programs, see James Backman, "Externships and New Lawyer Mentoring: The Practicing Lawyer's Role in Educating New Lawyers," *BYU Journal of Public Law* 24 (2009): 65. As noted above, other significant works on externships can be found in the Ogilvy and Czapanskiy bibliography, id.

realm of experiential learning because they are forms of active student experience.

In the questionnaire, I defined clinical legal education to mean "a course within the law school, for credit, in which the student provides legal advice or other legal services to persons who could not otherwise afford counsel." This is a rather simplified definition, but was intended to be inclusive. By contrast, a Canadian scholar says that clinical legal education can be described as "a process, or method, of teaching that is '. . .a curriculum-based learning experience, requiring students in role, interacting with others in role, to take responsibility for the resolution of a potentially dynamic problem,' and in which the student performance is subjected to intensive critical review."[53] Earlier, the same author cautions on over-inclusion regarding the scope of a definition of clinical legal education:

> [T]here appears to be a tendency to label many law-related activities students engage in outside of the classroom, including such traditional activities as legal research and mooting, as "clinical." This usage has been traced to associations of this term with innovative or novel programs which depart from the case method, but may have little else in common, or with instructional methods which appear to be primarily focused on skills.[54]

Another effort at defining clinical education, this time British, calls for five essential elements: (1) active participation; (2) interaction in role; (3) dynamic nature of the problem; (4) student responsibility for outcome; and (5) relation to the curriculum.[55]

Elsewhere, I have defined a legal clinic as ideally having the following five components: (1) academic credit for participation, within the law school curriculum; (2) students provide legal services to actual clients with real legal problems, within a framework permitted by local statute, bar or court rules permitting limited student practice, advice or other legal services;[56] (3) clients served by the program are legally indigent; they generally cannot afford the cost of legal representation or come from traditionally disadvantaged, marginal or other underserved communities; (4) students are closely supervised by an attorney licensed to practice law in the relevant jurisdiction; and (5) case-work by students is preceded or accompanied by a law school course, for credit, on the skills, ethics and values of law practice, as well as the necessary predicate doctrinal knowledge needed for the cases or matters to be handled by the clinic.[57] All of these elements may not be present in every law school clinic, but, as noted, they represent an ideal. My definition elaborates on that used in the first comprehensive report on what American clinical teachers call the "live-client, in-house clinic," within law schools. That report defined "clinical education" as

> first and foremost a method of teaching. Among the principal aspects of that method are these features: students are confronted with problem situations of the sort that lawyers confront in practice; the students deal with the problem in role; the students are required to interact with others in attempts to identify and solve the problem; and, perhaps most critically, the student performance is subjected to intensive critical review. . . If these characteristics define clinical teaching, then the live-client clinic adds to the definition the requirement that at least some of the interaction in role be in real situations rather than in make-believe ones.[58]

There is one way in which I fundamentally disagree with the last definition and the ones offered by the Canadian and British scholars. Clinical education is, at once, much more than a powerful instructional method. It is, as well, a learning context immersed in society, as well as a stance before the law. It cannot be done individually, and must be done with an awareness of issues of justice and equality; its fundamental democratic elements are central to its mission. As element four of my definition above notes, true clinical work privileges a focus on the poor, the disadvantaged and the marginalized – vast populations which simply are not served by the majority of the legal profession. This unique role of clinics, with its opportunities to make clinical

[53] Voyvodic, supra, n. 48, at 126; internal quote from Boone, Jeeves and Macfarlane, supra, n. 50, at 68.

[54] Id. at 122.

[55] Boone, Jeeves and Macfarlane, supra, n. 50, at 65.

[56] Within the U.S. clinical movement, an increasing number of clinics are involved in project-based work, without representation of individual clients. This is sometimes referred to as cause-based work, and may involve long or short-term work on a specific legal issue such as, e.g., prolonged and unfair detention of immigrant populations or the growing problem of gang-related violence in urban communities.

[57] Wilson, supra n. 4, at 829–830.

[58] Report of the Subcommittee on Pedagogical Goals of In-House, Live-Client Clinics, "Report of the Committee on the Future of the In-House Clinic," *Journal of Legal Education* 42 (1992): 511.

students "provocateurs for justice," marks perhaps its greatest divergence from the dominant pedagogies in legal education.[59]

3.2 The Paradigms of Practice in Legal Education: The National Reports and Beyond

3.2.1 The Prevailing Paradigm in the National Reports

If one were to generalize about the structure of legal education, as represented in the national reports, one would be looking at the universe of legal education in the civil law tradition, mostly in continental Western Europe. There, legal education is mostly public, generally accessible and inexpensive as a field of undergraduate study. Costs for legal education run from a low of no tuition or fees to a cost of no more than €2,000 per year. Many national reports from those countries indicate that either state of local governments provide additional direct support to students through expense stipends. The Greek report indicates that the state "provides for books, access to libraries, food discounts for public transportation, as well as housing for economically deprived students."[60] Germany provides a government stipend to anyone in the apprenticeship stage of training. Private schools in the civil law countries are considerably more expensive, with tuitions up to the €9–10,000 range, but still far less than private legal education in the common law countries.

The prevailing paradigm is taught in a highly structured curriculum, with mandatory courses making up the majority of offerings. Teachers are generally full-time, hold doctoral degrees in law, and only rarely practice law outside of the academy. They are scholars first.[61]

While there is little trend data requested in the questionnaire, there is a strong suggestion that the number of law students, and the size of the national bar commensurately, has grown dramatically over recent decades. This seems most evident outside of Europe, where, for example, the total number of law schools has expanded by 28 in Taiwan since 2000, or in Venezuela, where some 13 law schools have come into existence since 1990. Many of these schools are private, exclusive (requiring entrance exams or merit-based screening) and a good deal more expensive than public law schools.

The prevailing paradigm reveals that the structure of legal education has changed dramatically in Western Europe in the last decade, with many law schools moving toward the uniform structure suggested by the Bologna Process. Forty-six participating countries, including the entire European Union membership, signed onto the 1998 Sorbonne Declaration and the 1999 Bologna Declaration, along with several additional communiqués over the past decade, all collectively referred to today as the Bologna Process, with a goal to create a so-called European Higher Education Area (EHEA) by the year 2010.[62] Seven of the reporting countries[63] have adopted the two-tiered system of legal study recommended by Bologna, with a first, general and undergraduate term of law studies of 3 years followed by a focused masters program of 1 to 2 years duration. Only after taking the second degree may the student move on to formal licensure.[64]

One more aspect of the national reports from civil law countries, not revealed in the Tables, is the extent to which curricula in these schools have been internationalized. This move to the globalization of legal

[59] See, e.g., Jane H. Aiken, "Provocateurs for Justice," *Clinical Law Review* 7 (2001): 287; Stephen Wizner, "The Law School Clinic: Legal Education in the Interests of Justice," *Fordham Law Review* 70 (2002): 1929; Lucie E. White, "The Transformative Potential of Clinical Legal Education," *Osgoode Hall Law Journal* 35 (1997): 635.

[60] Greek Report, at 4.

[61] The Belgian report suggests an economic disincentive to practice, that being the need for the law professor practitioner to carry malpractice insurance, an additional expense that inclines universities "not [to] tend to promote real counseling." Belgium Report, at 14.

[62] Laurel S. Terry, "The Bologna Process and Its Impact in Europe: It's So Much More than Degree Changes," *Vanderbilt Journal of Transnational Law* 41 (2008): 107, 113–114.

[63] Belgium, Czech Republic, England and Wales, France, Ireland, Italy, Switzerland. The common law jurisdictions also have other variants to legal study, including both post-graduate and traditional apprenticeship routes involving no formal instruction at all.

[64] Some have argued that this structure makes European legal education more like that of the United States, with our nearly uniform practice of 4 years of undergraduate study, followed by 3 years of law. The analogy is strained, I believe, because in Europe, even the first 3 years are within the field of law, albeit general subjects, while undergraduate education in the United States is in the liberal arts or sciences, so entering law students may have a degree in engineering, math, physics or even music.

education has been much-examined in the literature, and is one of the few aspects of the field to which significant scholarship has been devoted. As the Italian report put it so nicely, "something is moving in Italy, and more generally in Europe."[65] There, as in many other European countries, there is an active and well-established program of student exchange through programs such as Erasmus and Socrates, founded in 1987.[66] The Italian report notes a number of student exchange programs outside of Europe, with shared or joint degree programs with "American Schools, Latin American Schools or Law Schools of China, Japan and Australia."[67] This was typical of many reports. More and more schools offer required courses in EU law, as is true in Ireland, while in Belgium some schools make International or European Law required courses at the Masters level. The Greek report notes that the "internationalization of legal studies" has "blurred the dividing line between the two legal education traditions" of the common and civil law.[68]

A second aspect of internationalization is technological. Several of the national reports include reference to distance-learning legal education, including Italy's report of a total of eight "e-learning" law schools in the country, with Switzerland and the Netherlands (see section that follows) each reporting one such school. (See Table 3.1, column marked "Number LS" and accompanying notes) England, for example, also reports an increase in the use of "e-learning simulation software" for use in particular courses,[69] while Switzerland notes that a private organization has made a business of offering training in legal uses of the internet.[70]

All of the reporting countries here require a period of apprenticeship for licensure after academic study, usually organized by the legal profession, but sometimes by the law schools or the courts. That apprenticeship varies in length from 18 weeks, in New Zealand, to 3 years in several countries, and it is usually organized and run by the nationally organized and unified bar. This apprenticeship almost always includes some period of time devoted to practical courses and exams, either on the individual subjects or more broadly through a general bar examination. Only Turkey reports no requirement for a final bar examination before entry into the profession, while Taiwan puts its extremely rigorous bar examination after graduation and before entry into the apprenticeship. Another country with rigorous entry requirements is Germany, with two formal state examinations, one after law school and another after completion of the *Referendariat*, or apprenticeship. The second exam is designed to establish one's qualifications as a judge, the most demanding branch of legal study.[71] That same trend is reflected in the shift to English-language courses and degrees, noted above.

Given the dominant paradigm of Western European legal education, together with the prevalence of the apprenticeship period, it is easy to see why there are so few reported practice elements within the curricula of these countries. What is most surprising, in this reporter's view, is the absence of even the most fundamental courses in legal research or legal writing and oral advocacy that have become so much a mainstay in the common law tradition. If one examines the columns on "Research" and "Rhetoric/Writing" in Table 3.2, one can see that only Switzerland and Germany (and Venezuela, outside of Europe) require either of both within the civil law tradition.

Again, looking within the prevailing paradigm here, one sees virtually no situation in which any element of practice, or any methodology focused on practice, is made mandatory. Only Belgium and Quebec's civil law faculties make the teaching of legal ethics mandatory, among the many options. In fact, the teaching of ethics, either as a doctrinal subject or within other doctrinal coverage, appears to be one of the most frequent practical subjects taught, at least among those that are listed here. Only the reports of Greece and Turkey indicate that the subject is not taught at all, of those reports that address that subject. (See Table 3.2, column headed "Ethics") On the methodological end, several of the civil law jurisdictions use moots or externships for their students. In fact, the popularity of international moot court competitions in Europe, starting with the historic Jessup International Law moot court competition, seem to be another element in the globalization of law phenomenon noted above.

[65] Italian Report, at 6.

[66] More information on the Erasmus program can be found at http://ec.europa.eu/education/lifelong-learning-programme/doc80_en.htm, visited on May 25, 2010.

[67] Italian Report, at 6.

[68] Greek Report, at 3.

[69] England & Wales Report, at 19.

[70] Switzerland Report, at 7.

[71] German Report, at 3.

Finally, clinical legal education is conspicuous by its absence in the Western European countries. Only one private law school in Germany offers a legal clinic; Belgium and Switzerland offer volunteer clinical work, usually organized by students themselves and without law school credit. Outside of continental Europe, the picture changes rapidly. Venezuela makes clinical legal education a requirement prior to graduation, through a national program of *Práctica Jurídica*, or Legal Practice. In the "new" Europe, clinics can be noted in the Czech Republic and Hungary. Turkey, riding the intersection of Europe and Asia, also offers clinical legal education at its private law schools. Clinics also operate in Quebec, probably due to the presence of clinical programs at other law schools in Canada.[72] The extent to which student practice in court is permitted within a jurisdiction is also not found in the Tables, but it was mentioned in several reports. The range was incredibly broad, from the general rule that students could not appear at all in court until licensed, through countries where law school graduates can appear provisionally in court during the apprenticeship phase of training, to countries where there are no limitations on popular access to the courts, thus permitting students to appear in any case.

On the whole, then, practice is largely absent from undergraduate legal training in the prevailing paradigm, as summarized in Table 3.2. Narrative statements support this conclusion. The Belgian report notes that "the focus on legal practice is substantially higher in the Master curriculum than in the Bachelor curriculum. This is due to a more generous staffing in the Master curriculum and to a smaller number of students."[73] Later, the same report notes that while universities stress importance of teaching practice in legal education, "few advertise a clear concept, which suggests that a lot depends on individual professors to integrate practice in their courses."[74] The report also suggests that more practice elements of cooperative or collaborative work by students are not included in the regular curriculum because of "the problem of fair evaluation of the results."[75]

[72] Clinics had a presence in Canada in 1987, although it had "not yet become a significant element in Canadian law schools." James C. Hathaway, "Clinical Legal Education," *Osgoode Hall Law Journal* 25 (1987): 239, 240.

[73] Belgium Report, at 8.

[74] Id. at 10–11.

[75] Id. at 12.

The German report suggests that its *Referendariat*, or apprenticeship period, "shares the key characteristics of clinical legal education" as set out by the author above.[76] The report goes on to note that elements of practice in German law schools have "gained a growing importance within the last years and nowadays [are] mandatorily offered to a minor extent." It further suggests that the civil law tradition in general "pays a higher attention to written documents than to oral presentations (no 'jury system'!)".[77] This is presumably suggested as a reason why there is less focus on the teaching of trial practice skills within the academy there.

The Hungarian report indicates that because the state controls legal education's content, "the current regime of governmental regulations barely deals with the role of practice in legal education," with the only exception being the apprenticeship period.[78] The same report closes by noting a 2002 empirical study taken among students at the University of Szeged Faculty of Law. The student poll identified problems with teaching methods among the three most serious defects of legal education. (The other two were the number of students and the subjectivity of exams). Some 54% of the students said that "the lack of practical legal education" was a serious defect in their educations.[79] Italy's report, too, notes that "practical aspects of legal education, notwithstanding the most recent reforms, have not become part of our system."[80] Although the teaching of practice is "permitted by the regulations, it is not yet common in the ordinary curriculum of the law student," by virtue of a traditional and structured approach to the curriculum.[81] As a result, "elements of practice are almost totally absent in the teaching of law in Italy."[82]

The Swiss report notes the historical roots of university legal education as far back as the sixteenth century, thus making modern law schools "embedded" in a "tradition and culture with rather little contact to legal practice."[83] Optimistically, the report notes,

[76] German Report, at 12.

[77] Id. at 18.

[78] Hungary Report, at 5.

[79] Id. at 10.

[80] Italy Report, at 6.

[81] Id. at 8.

[82] Id. at 9.

[83] Switzerland Report, at 5.

"practice elements are however gaining importance," and reasons for this may include "decline of esteem for pure academic [study] and pressure on law schools to 'be useful,' [and] increased sense of competition between law schools, demands from students and lawyers."[84]

3.2.2 Beyond the National Reports: A Sketch of Data on Practice in Legal Education in the United States and the Netherlands

There were no national reports from either the United States or the Netherlands. This report offers a short sketch of each.

3.2.2.1 Practice in Legal Education in the United States

In 2009, the United States had a population of about 309 million people, with a bar of about 1.18 million lawyers and law school graduates numbering 43,588 the same year.[85] The United States has a total of exactly 200 accredited law schools today, with 70 public and 130 private law schools, thus reversing the paradigm in Western Europe, where public legal education prevails. Private school tuitions averaged just over $34,000 during 2008, and $16, 800 for in-state residents at public schools.[86] Again, even at public law schools, legal education is a good deal more expensive in the U.S. than is generally the case in European public law schools, even for non-residents. In the United States, the phenomenon of rising private school tuitions, particularly at elite and top-ranked law schools, pushes students toward higher paying jobs with large law firms and away from public service jobs.[87] The U.S. Congress recently made public service jobs more attractive by adopting loan forgiveness legislation for those with publically-financed debt who work in the public sector for a 10-year period.[88]

Control of legal education is largely in the hands of state legislatures, bar associations, and the American Bar Association, which holds the all-powerful law school accreditation authority, although it is a voluntary membership organization representing less than half of all licensed lawyers in the U.S. State bar associations, state supreme courts, and occasionally state law control lawyer admission and discipline on a local basis, and licensure is good only in the state in which the graduate takes a bar examination, although some elements of the exam may be transferable. While reciprocity between state bars is generally open, there are some desirable states with no reciprocity, due to high lawyer populations, so admission to practice in those states can only be through taking a bar examination. Examples include California, Florida and Washington state.

The number of lawyers going into the private practice of law in the United States has dropped over the past few years. As of February, 2010, about 60% of graduates were going into private practice at a law firm. Because another 13.5% went to work in business as in-house counsel, and 5.7% went into public interest practice, the total in the practice of law is still nearly 80% in all. Another 10% of graduates went to work in government, while 8.7% took clerkships with judges, assisting in writing decisions and orders in courts. Finally, about 3.5% take academic positions, while 1.3% took legal jobs in the military.[89]

As noted above, law school is a graduate course of study, after a 4 year liberal arts or sciences degree. Law school is normally 3 years in duration, and is normally required before one can sit for the bar examination.[90]

[84] Ibid.

[85] American Bar Association, *National Lawyer Population by State* (2009), at http://abanet.org/marketresearch/resource.html, visited on May 24, 2010.

[86] National Association of Legal Career Professionals, *Law School Tuition 1985–2008.*

[87] See, e.g., ABA Commission on Loan Repayment and Forgiveness, Lifting the Burden: Law Student Debt as a Barrier to Public Service (2003).

[88] Philip G. Schrag, "Federal Student Loan Repayment Assistance for Public Interest Lawyers and Other Employees of Governments and Nonprofit Organizations," *Hofstra Law Review* 36 (2007): 27.

[89] National Association of Legal Career Professionals, *Market for Law Graduates Changes with Recession: Class of 2009 Faced New Challenges* (2010), at 2.

[90] Remarkably, a number of states still permit law office study as a means of legal education, but state bar examiners have made reciprocity for such degrees quite difficult, and such programs are nearly moribund. See, e.g., *District of Columbia Court of Appeals v. Feldman*, 460 U.S. 462 (1983) (refusing to review, on constitutional grounds, a decision by the District of Columbia bar not to seat applicant, who read law in Virginia and therefore did not graduate from an ABA accredited law school, a threshold requirement for bar application in the District).

Admission to law school is uniformly controlled by the law schools themselves, although selection of a law school is a complex interaction of factors for both applicant and school. All law school applicants take the Law School Aptitude Test (LSAT), and applications are reviewed based on test scores, undergraduate grade averages and other factors.[91]

Legal education is generally elective after the first year, unlike its European counterparts. During their first year, students uniformly take doctrinal courses familiar to the civil law tradition – Property, Contracts, Torts, Civil Procedure, Constitutional Law and Criminal Law and Procedure – but law school courses after these are almost uniformly elective. In addition to the doctrinal offerings, however, all law schools include a mandatory first year program in Legal Writing or Legal Rhetoric, usually in both semesters. Such programs normally include components on legal research and writing in various legal contexts, including appellate brief-writing. In the second semester, most such courses add an element of oral advocacy in a moot court exercise that combines written and oral advocacy. A strong driving force in course selection beyond required courses are the so-called "bar" courses: material that will be included in any bar examination. These include such subjects as Evidence, Corporations, Tax and other private law subjects.

Faculty at U.S. law schools are generally full-time, if hired on a tenured or tenure-track basis. Private practice is permitted on a limited and often pro bono basis, but few law teachers other than clinicians engage in practice outside of law school. Tenure, a concept best known in U.S. and Canadian universities, allows professors to hold their positions after a qualifying term, usually 4 to 6 years of service, with a proven record in teaching, scholarship and service. After a grant of tenure, removal from a professorial position can be accomplished only for cause.[92] The use of tenure outside of law schools has been in constant decline since the early 1970s, and even within legal education, many faculty positions are now contractual or adjunct positions, providing for the teaching of a single course. A recent report on clinical legal education indicates that about 20% of all clinical teachers are tenured or tenure-track, with another 13.1% holding positions of "clinical tenure," usually a lesser status within law faculties than full tenure. More than 20% hold positions under long-term contracts that are routinely renewed.[93]

During the last 2 years of law school, students may but are not generally required to take courses relating to practice. A growing number of U.S. law schools have adopted some form of mandatory experiential learning, and a very few have mandatory clinical programs.[94] Virtually every law school publishes a student-edited law review periodical, and many schools have several such reviews, to which admission is limited to those with high grades or demonstrated research and writing abilities. Every school offers participation in a wide array of moot court competitions, including some that go beyond appellate advocacy and into such areas as client counseling and mediation. Almost every school also offers some form of experiential learning through simulations or role-plays, either throughout entire courses or as an element of a doctrinal course. Externships or other clinical offering are available at almost every school on an elective basis. The most recent report on clinical legal education found that 131 reporting schools offered a total of 809 distinct in-house, live-client clinics, for an average of 6.2 clinics per school.[95] The same report indicated that the reporting schools had a total of 895 distinct field placement programs, for an average of 6.8 per reporting school.[96]

The role of practice in legal education has been an issue for the legal academy since U.S. Supreme Court Chief Justice Warren Berger publically criticized law schools for failing to adequately prepare

[91] A recent Supreme Court ruling allows narrow consideration of race as a factor in law school admission, permitting a form of accommodation for historic discrimination against minorities. *Grutter v. Bollinger*, 539 U.S. 306 (2003).

[92] In 1972, the U.S. Supreme Court held that tenure is a vested property interest for its recipient, and that removal of tenure must be accompanied by due process protections. *Perry v. Sindermann*, 408 U.S. 593 (1972).

[93] David A. Santacroce and Robert R. Kuehn, *Survey of Applied Legal Education (Center for Applied Legal Education), Report on the 2007–2008 Survey*, Available at http://ssrn.com/abrstract=1586009, at 15.

[94] An admittedly anecdotal list of some 30 law schools that have mandatory participation in an experiential course , or mandatory pro bono service by students, can be found at http://www.albanylaw.edu/sub.php?navigation_id=1737, visited on May 25, 2010. Of the listed programs, eight require participation in a clinic.

[95] Santacroce & Kuehn, *supra* n. 93, at 8.

[96] Id. at 9.

lawyers for practice.[97] Several influential reports shifted the terrain of legal education towards a greater role for the teaching of practice, beginning with the so-called "MacCrate Report," named for Robert MacCrate, the chair of an American Bar Association committee charged with reform. The ABA's *Report of the Task Force on Law Schools and the Profession: Narrowing the Gap*, published in 1992, began a steady march towards the inclusion of requirements in law school accreditation criteria dealing with the teaching of practice – skills, ethics and values – as recommended in the MacCrate Report, as well as standards dealing with the status of clinical teachers within the law school academic hierarchy. More recent reports continue that momentum, including the above-mentioned report of the Carnegie Foundation, *Educating Lawyers*, published in 2007, as well as the Clinical Legal Education Association (CLEA) report on *Best Practices for Legal Education: A Vision and A Road Map*, authored by Prof. Roy Stuckey and others, and published in the same year. These newer reports promise to keep the role of practice central to the mission of legal education in the United States.

3.2.2.2 Practice in Legal Education in the Netherlands[98]

The population of the Netherlands in 2009 was about 16.6 million, with a small national bar numbering only about 15,500 lawyers. Legal education in the Netherlands is all public, with nine law schools ranging in size from large (Leiden, Utrecht and Amsterdam), and medium (Tilburg, Rotterdam and Groningen), to small (Maastricht, Nijmegen and the Free University of Amsterdam, a distance-learning school). Like other continental countries, legal education is inexpensive, with tuitions costing a net of about €2,000 per year. Placement in law schools is after high-school qualification for university, and is controlled by a central government authority; law schools have no direct role in the selection of their students. The program of study for all Dutch law schools has moved to the Bologna standard of 3 years of undergraduate study and 1 year of Masters specialization, with both degrees being required for the graduate to move on to the apprenticeship. A special "Togamaster" program is offered at the Masters level for lawyers wishing to focus on national law practice. No comprehensive graduation exam is required, but most law schools require a Masters thesis for graduation.

Data from 1995 indicate that only about 45% of those who start law school finish, and there are less than 1,000 graduates leaving Dutch law schools each year for formal training. Many lawyers noted the dramatic increase in the number of women lawyers and law students, with a current enrollment of about 65% women. The apprenticeship period is 3 years with a 9-month course of study in the first year organized by local bars in the area where new graduates will practice. These courses vary slightly, but include an element of simulated trial practice, including oral advocacy, and all are accompanied by examinations, though no comprehensive national bar exam is given. The number of graduates moving into the training period after law school graduation is on the decline, with estimates than only 20 to 33% of all graduates go on for formal licensure. Jurists without licensure may still appear in most court proceedings, as licensure is not required for practice in many Dutch national courts. One of the most interesting developments in the Netherlands, in parallel with the apprenticeship program, is the commencement of what is called, in English, the Law Firm School (LFS). The School was created in 2009 by 14 of the largest law firms in Amsterdam, in the belief that an organized curriculum on business-related subjects, together with more focus on skills, will better prepare new associates for their roles within these international firms. The LFS has gone through three cycles of training, with some 80–90 trainees per session, and a pass rate of 80% for the combination of bar and LFS courses was largely due to the challenge of the performance aspects of the Litigation course, in which trainees use a simulated case file to prepare for trial and make preliminary arguments.

The professoriate in the Netherlands is generally full-time professionals, although private practice is permitted and common for many faculty members. The program of study in law school is generally highly

[97] See, e.g., Warren R. Burger, "Some Further Reflections on the Problem of Adequacy of Trial Counsel," *Fordham Law Review* 49 (1980): 1.

[98] All data from this section can be found in Richard J. Wilson, *The Public Interest Mission of Law School Clinics in Dutch Legal Culture: Rare Birds in the Formalist Tradition of European Legal Education*, a paper delivered to the Law and Society Association Annual Meeting, (Chicago, May 27, 2010) (unpublished manuscript on file with the author).

structured and required, much like the rest of Europe, with the lecture predominating as the method of instruction. Unlike other European countries, it is not unusual for senior academics or practitioners to move into judicial positions after significant practice experience.

Unlike many other countries in continental Europe, clinical legal education shows a stronger presence in the Netherlands. For historic reasons, the traditional *rechtswinkels*, or law shops, continue to operate, often for university credit. Begun during the social movements of the 1960s, these clinical programs peaked at some 90 offices during the 1970s, some affiliated with law schools and some based in the surrounding communities. They were and are usually operated by volunteer student organizations with little faculty oversight, and their numbers have gradually declined over the years. As the national program of legal aid grew and strengthened, many of the law shops were taken over by the government-funded program. Today, four law schools provide law school credit for student participation in law shops.

Another domestic law clinic of relatively long standing is the Legal Clinic at Maastricht, which opened in 1988, 6 years after the law faculty itself opened. It continues to operate today with five non-faculty advocates on staff, all women, and a male office program director of faculty rank. The clinic has its own building, with a separate entrance for clients, and provides space for meetings, files, support staff and participating students, who sit communally in an area known as "the garden." Four to 13 undergraduate law students participate in clinic at any time, and provide legal services across a broad range of civil and criminal cases during an immersion period of 8 weeks, or one-half of a semester. Because they are well-known in the community, and because of liberal practice rules, clinic students often appear in the local courts, although faculty may make more difficult arguments or take cases with protracted trials. Before entry into the clinic, the students take a number or required pre-requisite courses, including Communications, Evidence and other substantive courses. The clinic charges for its services in order to offset costs, and it recoups much of its operating cost through fees charged directly to clients or to the national legal aid program.

The two newest clinics in the Netherlands are both international in scope. The Amsterdam International Law Clinic has operated for about 10 years, having been founded by a senior Dutch faculty member who returned from a visiting faculty position in the United States during which he learned much about clinical legal education and watched clinics work. The clinic takes only LLM students who can speak English, and English is the common language for clinic work-product and operation. Twelve students participate in the clinic each semester, with project work being done for local law firms, NGOs and other organizations, all having to do with issues of international law. The clinic does limited legal work on litigation matters, mostly providing policy or legal analysis of an issue for law firms or NGOs. Oversight of student work is provided by a part-time clinical director and the founding professor, with additional voluntary assistance provided by faculty within the international law department in their areas of specialty. Most student time is spent on case-work in clinic, but the group sometimes meets for discussion of organizational and ethical issues. The clinic has a small office of its own, and has posted some of its work on a public web-site.[99] Like the Maastricht clinic, the Amsterdam clinic charges fees for its services, with a base rate of €1,500 per case. Fees have been waived in some instances and have been as high as €3,000 in others.

The newest clinic in the Netherlands is at the law faculty of the University of Utrecht, where a new Clinic on Conflict, Human Rights and International Justice opened in the fall of 2009. The clinic was founded by two senior members of the faculty, one from the field of human rights and one from international criminal law. The clinic works on international cases and matters, with a total current enrollment of 18 LLM students working in teams of six, either at international justice institutions in The Hague or for the Inter-American Court of Human Rights in San José, Costa Rica. Student team work is overseen by the senior faculty and by doctoral students who supervise clinic teams. As set up, the clinic permits students to sign up for either one semester or two, and it also includes an externship component at the Hague international justice institutions for students not participating in the clinic. This range of clinical opportunities puts the Netherlands far ahead of other continental European countries in clinical offerings.

[99] A number of the Amsterdam clinic's reports can be found at http://www.jur.uva.nl/ailc/object.cfm/objectid=DAB99ACD-19B3-4DF6-975BC275A03C2DDB, visited on May 26, 2010.

3.2.3 The Minority Paradigm: National Reports and the United States

It should not surprise readers of this report that the "minority paradigm" presented in the national reports – the clustering of common issues that are found in a congruent group of reports – includes the reporting common law jurisdictions. This section, then, provides a kind of profile of legal education, and the role of practice therein, in five jurisdictions: Australia, England & Wales, Ireland, New Zealand and the United States.[100]

Legal education in the minority paradigm tends to include a greater number of private institutions for law teaching, with a commensurate rise in costs of legal education. While legal education can be obtained somewhat less expensively at some public law schools in these jurisdictions, at costs varying from US$3,600 per year in the all-public law schools of New Zealand, to up to US$82,000 per year in British schools. (See Table 3.1, Column headed "Cost/year US$/€") The U.S., too, has high costs for private legal education, with tuitions averaging just over $34,000 in 2008. These costs compare quite unfavorably with the generally lower, and publically subsidized, costs of public legal education in continental Europe, and cause one to speculate whether the private market provides a qualitative product that is measurably superior to that of the public institutions. Privatized legal education also tends to be more selective, with either national or local entry examinations (See Table 3.1, Column headed "Nat. Entry Exam"), and commensurately smaller classes with lower student/faculty ratios (although this information is anecdotal and not reported in national reports here). The Australian report offers a useful construct in noting the "gatekeeper" function for access to the legal profession through examinations, which, in its report, refers to the examinations at the close of legal education or on entry into the bar. In its analysis, the Australian report suggests that the bar plays a much greater role in deciding on admission in the common law jurisdictions, as compared with the state's more prominent role in civil law jurisdictions such as Germany and Japan. The report also notes the implicit gate-keeping role of the market in deciding access, which certainly seems to be true in the roll-backs in big firm hiring discussed in the U.S. section above.[101]

The civil and common law construct seems less true across the range of entry controls now used, where the national reports here indicate roles for the bar, the state and the law schools themselves in designing and administering a virtual phalanx of tests for entry into and graduation from law school, through apprenticeship course exams, and on to a possible final bar exam before full licensure. Testing seems to have emerged as a common factor in both the prevailing and minority paradigms for supply control of the practicing bar. The professoriate in these countries, all lying within the developed world, tends toward full-time employment for a core or majority of teachers, with little information reported on the extent to which professors are permitted to practice outside of their teaching responsibilities. (See Table 3.1, Columns headed "Professoriate")

The length of law school seems to vary widely within the minority paradigm. In this reporter's view, this may lie within the deeply embedded history of the Inns of Court in England, the traditional route into the bar in that country since the Middle Ages, by contrast with continental entry through the university that developed in the same time period.[102] One route lay through practice, the other through theory. Thus, today the common law jurisdictions, which only "recently" (within the last 100 years!) moved into the university, provide a greater array of options for entry, and across widely varying periods of from no formal schooling at all (the reader, or apprentice, in a law firm only – still an option in England, and at least in theory, in a few states of the United States); a 5 year undergraduate career in Australia; the standard Bologna formulation of 3 plus 1–3 in Ireland (See Table 3.1, Column headed "Degree/years"); and a 7 year period of combined undergraduate study (4 years) and graduate study in law (3 years) in the U.S. England too offers law as a form of graduate study, as one of many options.

[100] Canada might have been included in this group if the provinces other than Quebec had submitted a report. As noted above, the primary focus of the Quebec report was on civil law aspects of that jurisdiction.

[101] Australia Report, at 2–3.

[102] H.D. Hazeltine, "Ancient and Mediaeval Legal Profession and Legal Education," in *Encyclopedia of the Social Sciences,* ed., Edwin R.A. Seligman and Alvin Johnson (New York: MacMillan, 1933), 324 329–333.

It is within the realm of the role of practice in legal education that the real differences appear in the minority paradigm, by contrast with the prevailing paradigm in these reports. In all five of the common law jurisdictions, the teaching of practice performs a core function within legal education. One need only glance at Table 3.2 to see the differences between the number of required courses and active methods used in the common law jurisdictions reporting here. All include some element of required research, rhetoric or drafting, and all require a course on ethics. (See Table 3.2, columns with those headings) Similarly, the use of active teaching methods such as simulation, moot courts, externships and clinics seem significantly higher in each of the four common law reports, as well as in the United States. One explanation for this difference may well lie in the distinct cultural histories mentioned in the previous paragraph. Another may lie in the economies of scale between private versus public legal education; smaller schools with more resources can afford to provide more focused and individualized training than schools with hundreds of students in a lecture hall for the majority of their classes. And yet some data militate against this conclusion. In Australia and New Zealand, for example, public legal education dominates, and both countries require a period of apprenticeship or pupilage, and yet both countries provide a rich array of practice offerings within law school. Australia's report indicates that clinics are "generally not mandatory," and that there are "some optional programs" including externships.[103] However, a supplemental submission from one of the Australian national reporters indicates that there is shared commitment to a goal, by 2011, "to have all 31 of Australia's law schools making available to students at least one clinical education or pro bono program to help them develop professionalism and to understand the responsibility of lawyers to the broader community." The same author notes that as of 2004, 23 Australian universities had "some type of clinical program, many in conjunction with the communities close to the university."[104] This seems more than "some" schools!

One aspect of legal education that remains largely unexplored in most national reports, whether in common law or civil law jurisdictions, is that of outcome or benchmark measures as assessment tools. These are elaborated in greatest detail in the text and Annexes to the national report of England & Wales. There, benchmark statements have been widely adopted by higher education institutions in general. Such statements are designed, as for example in the case of the Quality Assurance Agency, to "set out the minimum achievement which a student should demonstrate before they are awarded an honours degree in law."[105] The benchmarks are set out in terms of skills that the student should be able to demonstrate before graduating, such as basic knowledge of legal principles, application of principles to problem-solving, research and manipulation of legal sources, critical judgment, autonomy and ability to learn, written and oral communication, and numeracy skills such as statistics, the internet and email. Similar benchmarks are set out for training barristers and trainee solicitors.[106] Similar efforts are now under way in the United States, where basic lawyering competencies have been identified, and efforts have moved toward more formative rather than summative assessment. In summative assessment, the typical assessment method in most law schools, a single exam is given at the end of a course to test students' comprehension of course material. Formative assessment provides feedback and assessment during the process, all along the way, and experiential learning provides an ideal context for such work.[107]

Despite the level of practice teaching now offered, some country reports in the minority paradigm seem apologetic for not having more. The Irish national report, for example, states that "more advanced law practice skills (e.g., law office management, client interviewing, etc.) are largely absent from the curriculum."[108] Later in its report, it notes that historically, Ireland and other common law jurisdictions offered legal education that was "theory-based and took place exclusively in lecture halls. Law, however, is a quasi-academic and quasi-vocational discipline." The author nonetheless concludes that Ireland "still lags far behind" in offering practice training in the academy.[109]

[103] Australia Report, at 18.

[104] The Hon. Michael Kirby AC CMG, "Foreword," in *Community Engagement in Contemporary Legal Education: Pro Bono, Clinical Legal Education and Service-Learning* ed. Patrick Keyzer ii, iv (Ultimo: Halstead Press, 2009).

[105] England and Wales Report, at Annex 3, Section 2.1.

[106] Id. at Annexes 4A and 4B, 5.

[107] See the Carnagie Foundation report, supra, n. 39, at Chapter 5, *Assessment and How to Make it Work*, p. 162, 172.

[108] Ireland Report, at 9.

[109] Ireland Report, at 13.

Similarly, although legal clinics internships are offered at a number of schools in England and Wales, as are the required courses in basic research, writing and ethics, the British report concludes that issues of "legal practice are tackled primarily at the post academic stages of training."[110] The same report concludes that the teaching of practice is "emerging primarily as a voluntary additional activity rather than a core component" of the law schools' curricula.[111] At bottom, then, many of the reporting countries, whether within the prevailing or minority paradigm, call for a greater role of the teaching of practice within legal education.

3.3 Other Noteworthy Aspects of Legal Education from the National Reports

3.3.1 Relationship of Population to Bar Size, and Bar Size to Law Graduates

There appears to be little relationship in these reports between national populations and the size of the bar, or between the size of the bar and the number of law schools and law graduates, other than the trend toward growth of the legal profession noted above. Some jurisdictions of relatively similar size have vastly different lawyer populations and law schools. The United States, for example, is assumed to have one of the largest per capita lawyer populations in the world. In 2009, the estimated U.S. population was 309.3 million, and the number of practicing lawyers stood at 1.18 million,[112] yielding 1 lawyer for around every 260 persons in the country. France, England & Wales, and Italy, with relatively equal populations of just over 60 million, yield per capita lawyer populations of 1:1373, 1:476 and 1:301 respectively,[113] while Germany, with a total population of just over 80 million, has more than three times the licensed lawyers as neighboring France, for a ratio of 1:505. Venezuela has the highest ratio with 1 lawyer for every 200 persons, while Taiwan seems to have the lowest, with 1 lawyer for every 4,600 persons. Can we say that there are too many or too few lawyers in any of these countries? Using raw data such as this often leads to false conclusions. We can say that bar size is increasing, or that enrollments in law schools have trended upwards over time (as the Abel & Lewis study also notes[114]) but because this report gathers no trend data, such conclusions are anecdotal at best.

One data set that is useful in that cluster is that comparing the number of graduates per year with the overall size of the bar. (Table 3.1, column headed "Grads/ year") In the case of some of the larger bars, there is a corresponding large number of recent graduates, as in England and Wales, with 13,800 graduates in the last recorded year, and Italy, with 15, 448 graduates. These numbers contribute to the high per capita population of lawyers in those countries. Taiwan seems, at first glance, to have a similarly high number of graduates, at 3,000, until one accounts for the dramatically low bar passage rate, which *rose* to 22% in a recent year, yielding newly admitted lawyers totaling only 494. (see n. 22 to Table 3.1) Similarly, Germany appears to be controlling the supply end of the lawyer population by having limited the number of lawyers who pass the first state exam to 6,300 in the last reported year, a number that seems low compared to total lawyer population in that country. In the United States, by contrast, there were 43,588 J.D. degrees awarded in 2009.[115] This continues a long upward trend in new lawyers, but seems roughly proportional to the total and lawyer populations. These graduates, of course, face a different employment market than in prior years with the global recession, something that has yet to be fully felt in Europe, but was noted in some reports.[116]

3.3.2 Demographics and Legal Education

Only one national report made mention of the gender demographic within the bar: the Quebec report notes

[110] England & Wales Report, at 16.

[111] Id., at 19.

[112] ABA data, at n. 85, supra.

[113] Data extrapolated by dividing size of bar, in thousands (Table 3.1, Column headed "Bar Size (Th)") into total population, in millions (Table 3.1, first Column headed "Pop. (M)").

[114] Abel, *Lawyers in the Civil Law World*, supra n. 27, at 31–35.

[115] American Bar Association, *Enrollment and Degrees Awarded: 1963–2008*, at http://www.abanet.org/legaled/statistics/charts/stats%20-%201.pdf, visited on May 25, 2010.

[116] National Association of Legal Career Professionals, *Market for Law Graduates Changes with Recession: Class of 2009 Faced New Challenges* (2010) (finding the job market "significantly harder" for 2009 graduates than for classes in immediately preceding years), available at www.nalp.org.

that 47% of the province's 23,000 practicing advocates are female.[117] I also noted a dramatic rise in women in the legal profession and law schools in my summary of the situation in the Netherlands, a phenomenon universally noted by bar and legal education leaders. Again, I did not request demographic data as to gender, racial or ethnic composition of legal education, but this single data point summarizes, in a nutshell, a phenomenon that has been analyzed extensively in *Lawyers in Society*, written in 1995,[118] and its "sequel," a 2005 study that calls the feminization of the bar the "most important change" in the nature of the legal profession worldwide. It calls the "single most important dimension of that change" the fact that "women have a more difficult time achieving career goals than men."[119] The Menkel-Meadow study cited here offers extensive theoretical explanations for both the phenomenon and its implications. The Ireland report notes special entrance provisions for "mature" students (over 23),[120] and the New Zealand national report noted that some of its law schools give "equity considerations" to particular cohorts, such as Maori and Pacific Island students.[121]

3.3.3 Near-Elimination of *Numerus Clausus* Provisions

In *Lawyers in Society*, the lawyers noted the decline in but persistence of *numerus clausus*, or admission quotas imposed by law or rule, as one of the ways in which the supply end of the legal profession was controlled.[122] Notably, only one report, that of Greece, notes a *numerus clausus* for the bar there, although some reports in civil law jurisdictions indicate limits on other elements of the legal professions such as notaries.

[117] The report also notes that 53% of Quebec's notaries are women. Canada (Quebec) Report, at 14.

[118] Carrie Menkel-Meadow, "Feminization of the Legal Profession: The Comparative Sociology of Women Lawyers," in *Lawyers in Society: An Overview*, ed. Richard L. Abel and Philip S.C. Lewis (Berkeley: University of California Press, 1995), 221.

[119] William L.F. Felsteiner, "Introduction," in *Reorganization and Resistance*, supra, n. 12, at 1,7. Perhaps not coincidentally, Felsteiner notes that the study that elaborates most on women lawyers is that on Canada. Ibid.

[120] Ireland Report, at 4.

[121] New Zealand Report, at 6.

[122] Richard L. Abel, *Lawyers in the Civil Law World*, supra, n. 27, at 10–11.

3.3.4 Practice-Related Issues on the National Bar Examination

As an ultimate observation, the general reporter notes that a number of national reports include mention of practice questions on the final bar examination for aspiring advocates. Italy's exam, for example, includes "the drafting of two attorney's opinions" on interpretation of code provisions,[123] while the Hungarian bar includes resolution of hypothetical questions in both the written and oral phases of the bar exam.[124] In Greece, practical questions may include "drafting a law suit or preparing arguments for a hypothetical case."[125] These steps replicate a phenomenon that also occurs in the Netherlands, as noted above, and in the United States, where an increasing number of states include practice-related hypothetical "case files" on their bar examination. Such tests recognize the importance of the resolution by lawyers of real-world problems, and not merely abstract knowledge of rules without context.

3.4 The Pedagogy of Practice in the Rest of the World

It is neither possible nor appropriate for a report of this nature to fully document the extent to which practice can be found in legal education in the some 180 countries of the world not covered by this report. Instead, I will provide a "lightning round" tour of new developments worthy of note, mostly on a regional basis, but noting particular developments within individual countries. I might remind readers here of the immense on-line bibliography on clinical legal education mentioned previously, which includes a section on "Non-U.S. Clinical Programs,"[126] and note at the outset that a new book broadly covers the global reach of clinical legal education.[127]

[123] Italy Report, at 11.

[124] Hungary Report, at 3.

[125] Greece Report, at 7.

[126] See, Ogilvy and Czapanskiy, supra n. 49.

[127] Frank Bloch, ed., *The Global Clinical Movement: Educating Lawyers for Social Justice* (Oxford: Oxford University Press, 2010).

3.4.1 Central and South America

The tradition of required or optional practical training as part of legal education is deeply ingrained in Latin American legal culture, where clinics have existed in Chile and some other countries of the Southern Cone since the late 1960s and early '70s.[128] Clinics became mandatory in Colombia in 1971 by virtue of government decree. A similar decree governs mandatory clinical participation in Nicaragua and other Central American countries.[129] A clinical experience was designed to "familiarize the student with the exercise of professional skills before judicial functionaries."[130] As early as 1961, law professors meeting in Lima, Peru adopted a conference resolution calling for law teaching to be "'active'; there should be 'an intimate copenetration between doctrinal and practical teaching, the latter meaning various aspects of professional formation, not merely procedural techniques.'" Practical teaching was to include "solution of practical cases and problems, and legal aid clinic work."[131] In 1999, clinical students from the Public Interest Clinic at the Center for Investigation and Economic Studies (Spanish acronym "CIDE") in Mexico City won an appeal in a criminal case involving the false accusation and conviction for murder of 22 indigenous persons in the village of Acteal, in remote Chiapas State.[132] This tradition of commitment to what is called *Práctica Jurídica* (Law Practice) in our Venezuelan national report, *Consultorios Jurídicos* (Law Clinics) in other Latin American countries, and *Bufetes Populares* (People's Law Firms) in Nicaragua and Cuba, have a long-standing tradition within the last 2 years of the largely required legal education curriculum, normally of 5 years in duration. There is a growing literature on clinical legal education in Spanish, much of it arising from the Public Interest Law clinics established with Ford Foundation donations in the 1990s.[133] Another more recent anthology was published in Mexico in 2007.[134]

3.4.2 Central and Eastern Europe and Russia

A similar trend can be noted in Central and Eastern Europe, where clinical legal education emerged strongly after the fall of the Soviet Union. The destabilization of the old guard in legal education, coupled with a desire for European integration and donor focus on clinical legal education, led to the rapid growth of clinical legal education offerings in such countries as Hungary, the Czech Republic and Turkey, among our nationally reporting countries.[135] Perhaps no other country has a more developed infrastructure for clinics than Poland, which began its first clinical programs at Jagiellonian University of Krakow in 1997, with money from the Ford Foundation, then rapidly spread throughout the nation. Today, the Polish clinics have a sophisticated national network of 25 clinical programs with their own website.[136] Enthusiasm for clinics has flowed into neighboring Ukraine, which has a similar website and network of 14 clinics.[137] Perhaps the greatest achievement, however, is the widespread acceptance of clinical legal education in Russia. Although their national website is in Russia, the U.S. development group, the Agency for International Development (AID) indicates that Russia has implemented over 160

[128] Richard J. Wilson, "Three Law School Clinics in Chile, 1970–2000: Innovation, Resistance and Conformity in the Global South," *Clinical Law Review* 8 (2002): 801.

[129] Richard J. Wilson, "Criminal Justice in Revolutionary Nicaragua: Intimations of the Adversarial in Socialist and Civil Law Traditions," *University of Miami Inter-American Law Review* 23 (1991–1992): 269, 340–341.

[130] Richard J. Wilson, "The New Legal Education in North and South America," *Stanford Journal of International Law* 25 (1989): 375, 384.

[131] Quoted in Id., at 394.

[132] Marc Lacey, *Mexico Court Orders 22 Tied to '97 Killings Freed*, New York Times, Aug. 12, 2009; José Antonio Caballero, *Acteal y la Enseñaza del Derecho (Acteal and Law Teaching)*, El Universal.com, 13 Aug. 2009 (in Spanish).

[133] See, e.g., Defensa Jurídica del Interés Público: Enseñaza, Estrategias, Experiencias (Judicial Defense of the Public Interest: Teaching, Strategies, Experiences) (Felipe González and Felipe Viveros eds. 1999) (there are now five or six volumes in this series).

[134] Enseñaza Clínica del Derecho: Una Alternativa a los Métodos Tradicionales de Formación de Abogados (Clinical Teaching in Law: An Alternative to Traditional Methods for Training Lawyers) (Marta Villareal and Christian Courtis, eds., 2007).

[135] See generally, Richard J. Wilson, "Training for Justice: The Global Growth of Clinical Legal Education," *Penn State International Law Review* 22 (2004): 421 (noting donor activity in the region from the American Bar Association and the Soros Foundation, among others).

[136] *Legal Clinics in Poland: Legal Clinics Foundation*, at http://www.fupp.org.pl/index_eng.php, visited on May 29, 2010.

[137] *Ukrainian Association of Legal Clinics*, at http://www.legalclinics.org.ua/eng/clinics/liga.php, visited on May 29, 2010.

clinical programs, with "informal associations of specialized law school clinics providing free assistance to juveniles, refugees and prisoners."[138]

3.4.3 Asia, Africa and the Middle East

Asia and Africa remain the biggest challenges for new methodologies in legal education, both because theirs are radically different legal cultures, often with colonial traditions that persist today, and in the case of Africa, serious economic underdevelopment. In Oceania, nearby Asia, the longest running programs have been in common law jurisdictions, such as the reports we have here from Australia and New Zealand. Within Asia itself, the oldest established program is that of India, a common law jurisdiction with strong clinical roots. The first clinical program began at Delhi University as early as 1969, when the Delhi Legal Aid Clinic came into being, and clinics have thrived there ever since.[139] In neighboring China, clinics have developed quickly as part of a general reform of legal education and the legal profession there within the past decade. According to one local source, nearly 90 law schools had established clinical programs as of 2008.[140] Clinics have withstood the test of time and sustainability in several Asian countries that have survived prolonged conflicts or radically conservative traditions: Cambodia,[141] Japan,[142] and even war-torn Afghanistan.[143]

In sub-Saharan Africa, the strongest clinical programs are in South Africa and Nigeria. The South African experience with legal aid clinics predates the end of apartheid, and clinics are thriving throughout the country today.[144] In Nigeria, the most populous of the African countries, clinical legal education has a later start but is gaining a strong foothold, with a nationwide network of law school clinics already established.[145] In the Middle East region, Israel has always had a strong clinical history,[146] while neighboring Lebanon has just opened its first clinic,[147] and again, as in Afghanistan, Iraq is introducing the concept of clinical legal education into its universities.[148]

3.5 Conclusion: A Global Role for a Pedagogy of Practice?

While many lessons can be drawn from the quick sketch of a pedagogy of practice around the world today, there are several significant lessons that stand out by contrasting these countries with those reporting here, particularly for those who are skeptics as to the teaching of skills within a law school. First, although the reports here, by virtue of their geographic distribution, put the civil law countries of the European continent into the prevailing paradigm with stunted programs of practice in legal education, there is no inherent aversion to the teaching of practice skills within the civil law tradition more broadly. Virtually all of the programs examined here are jurisdictions

[138] *Rule of Law and Human Rights Projects*, U.S. AID/Russia, at http://russia.usaid.gov/programs/democratic_dev/rule_of_law_and_human_rights/, visited on May 29, 2010.

[139] N.R. Madhava Menon, "Clinical Legal Education: Concept and Concerns," in *A Handbook of Clinical Legal Education*, ed. Dr. N.R. Madhava Menon (Lucknow : Eastern Book Co, 1998), 1, 18–19.

[140] Zhen Zhen, *Clinical Legal Education in China – Current Situation and its Future of China's Clinical Legal Education* (2008), conference paper published at http://www.mcgeorge.edu/Experiential_Education_in_China/Published_Resources.htm, visited on May 30, 2010.

[141] *Student Legal Clinics*, Open Society Justice Initiative, at http://www.soros.org/initiatives/justice/focus/legal_capacity/projects/legal-clinics, visited on June 2, 2010 (mentioning a legal clinic established in Cambodia).

[142] Peter A. Joy et al., "Building Clinical Legal Education Programs in a Country without a Tradition of Graduate Professional Legal Education: Japan Educational Reform as a Case Study," *Clinical Law Review* 13 (2006–2007): 417.

[143] Ele Pawelski, "Defining Justice in Afghanistan: Development of a National Legal Aid System," *Windsor Review of Legal and Social Issues* 27, no. 98 (2009): 185, 206 (describing an established legal clinic at Herat University).

[144] Willem De Klerk, "University Law Clinics in South Africa," *South African Law Journal* 122 (2005): 929; David McQuoid-Mason, "Street Law as a Clinical Program: The South African Experience with Particular Reference to the University of KwaZulu Natal," *Griffith Law Review* 17 (2008): 27.

[145] Olugbenga Oke-Samuel, "Clinical Legal Education in Nigeria: Developments and Challenges," *Griffith Law Review* 17 (2008): 139, 144 (noting clinics at 8 law schools in Nigeria); the national network is NULAI, or the Network of University Legal Aid Institutions, with participating clinical programs at http://www.nulainigeria.org/law_clinic.htm, visited on June 2, 2010.

[146] Yuval Elbashan, *Teaching Justice, Creating Law – The Legal Clinic as Laboratory*, paper presented at the UCLA/IALS Sixth International Clinical Conference (October 2005) (Elbashan is director of the legal clinic at Hebrew University of Jerusalem).

[147] See *Student Legal Clinics*, supra n. 141, noting establishment of a clinic in Lebanon.

[148] Haider Ala Hamoudi, "Toward a Rule of Law Society in Iraq: Introducing Clinical Legal Education into Iraqi Law Schools," *Berkeley Journal of International Law* 23 (2005): 112.

with deep historical links to the civil law, and yet clinical legal education is thriving.[149] There is no inherent common law "preference" for clinical legal education. Second, undergraduate students are not too young to assume responsibility for real cases with real clients. In most of the countries examined here, the students involved in providing legal services to real clients are in their third to fifth year of undergraduate legal education, making them somewhere between 20 and 23 years old, assuming they have attended school continuously, which is often not the case. They are, for pedagogical purposes, adult learners.[150]

Third, one cannot ignore the close connection between the increased use of clinical programs in the developing world and the absence of an effective state-funded legal aid system in these countries. Because of the economic disincentives for the bar to handle legal aid cases on a pro bono basis, a credible argument can be made that the provision of legal services was moved into the law schools so that the most rudimentary legal needs of the poor could be met. The German report notes this connection, arguing that one of the reasons it does not have clinical offerings is that Germany enjoys "a very elaborate system of legal aid ('*Prozesskotenhilfe*') providing for a relatively easy and cheap access to justice for everybody."[151] A similar historical connection is noted in a new book.[152] However, neither the historical connection of the two themes nor the existence of a strong legal aid program offer convincing arguments against a stronger role for a pedagogy of practice within the academy. The primary purpose of a clinical program is, or should be, pedagogical, not the provision of basic legal services. When clinics take on excessive case loads, as they inevitably will when they become the primary legal services provider for the poor, they put at risk both their essential pedagogical mission and their obligations of competent service to clients. Students simply cannot be adequately supervised except in the most routine clerical tasks in legal services provision, and their bad habits may well carry over into practice, while clients may be ill-served by unsupervised neophyte lawyers. The bar and the state both abdicate their responsibilities to equal access to justice by foisting the justice mission on law schools alone. Moreover, law clinics, as noted in the U.S. summary, provide legal services across a wide range of subjects; their scope of services vastly exceeds the fundamental legal aid mission.

Fourth, many of the global changes in the direction of a pedagogy of practice are the result of donor efforts from the developed north, the so-called western world.[153] This does not mean that clinical legal education is an exclusively American export. Many of the national reports note – some with enthusiasm or admiration and others with open hostility or simple resignation – a tendency in their jurisdiction toward the "Americanization" of legal education. This observation, however, is hardly limited to clinical legal education or even to more active methods generally. As the preceding section shows, clinics have taken on a momentum of their own, and many of the reforms in the pedagogy of practice come from "South-South" exchanges, such as South Africa to Nigeria, Chile to Mexico, or Hungary to China. This is not, in my view, American legal imperialism,[154] but native common sense.

Finally, legal clinics need not be expensive. The experience of the rest of the world, mostly from the global South, demonstrates that while donor funds may be required to begin a clinical program in the developing world, the programs are often, indeed usually, self-sustaining within law schools after foreign donors withdraw, with indigenous resources and support, along with strong student and faculty backing,

[149] The fine work of Prof. Philip Genty, from Columbia University in the U.S., does not suggest otherwise, although it astutely notes that the approach to clinical legal education must be different, and culturally sensitive, in countries of the civil law tradition. Philip M. Genty, "Overcoming Cultural Blindness in International Clinical Collaboration: The Divide Between Civil and Common Law Cultures and its Implications for Clinical Education," *Clinical Law Review* 15(2008–2009): 131.

[150] See Wilson, *Three Law School Clinics in Chile*, supra n. 128, at 569–573 (arguing that adult learning theory applies to students in the 20–25 year age range, based on empirical study).

[151] German Report, at 25.

[152] Frank S. Bloch and Mary Anne Noone, "Legal Aid Origins of Clinical Legal Education," in *The Global Clinical Movement,* supra, n. 127.

[153] See Wilson, *Training for Justice*, supra, n. 135.

[154] This is not to suggest that the U.S. does not engage in legal imperialism on some fronts. As noted at the outset, the emergence of big law may represent some elements of market-controlled imperialism directed almost entirely from the United States and the U.K. beginning with the Reagan-Thatcher connection and continuing with law and economics theories. See, e.g., Ugo Mattei, "A Theory of Imperial Law: A Study of U.S. Hegemony and the Latin Resistance," *Indiana Journal of Global Legal Studies* 10 (2003): 383.

providing the continued momentum for practical education. If this is true in the countries of the global South, it can be no less true in the affluent north, particularly in the G-20 countries, where relatively, resources abound.

It is not my purpose, after all of this focus on clinical legal education, to suggest that learning by doing through actual practice is the *only* answer to the reform of legal education, but it certainly is *an* answer, and one that has been widely, indeed universally, adopted. Clinical legal education is also a powerful bellwether, a portent of a future for legal education that is very different from its traditional past. Indeed, some continue to argue that learning "substantive knowledge of the law is usually denominated 'education,' while acquiring practical skills is ordinarily called 'training'."[155] Clinical legal education is one of a spectrum of subjects and methods that involve learning by doing, experiential learning that lies at the theoretical core of adult learning, or andragogy, a subject almost completely absent from theoretical study among legal educators.[156] We would all be better teachers if we studied andragogy more closely. Experiential learning has as legitimate a place in the pantheon of education as doctrine itself, and the role of practice in legal education is growing around the world every day, as well it should.

[155] James R. Maxeiner, "Integrating Practical Training and Professional Legal Education," in *The Internationalization of Law and Legal Education*, ed. Jan Klabbers and Mortimer Sellers (New York: Springer, 2009) 38.

[156] Malcolm S. Knowles, Elwood F. Holton III and Richard A. Swanson, *The Adult Learner*, 5th ed. (1998); Frank S. Bloch, "The Andragogical Basis of Clinical Legal Education," *Vanderbilt Law Review* 35 (1982): 321.

Catastrophic Damages: Liability and Insurance[1]

4

Pablo Salvador Coderch, Sonia Ramos González, and Rosa Milá Rafel

4.1 Introduction

The main features of catastrophic harms have been stressed by the majority of the twenty reports received by our research team. The starting point for the general report is a unified concept of catastrophe, the newest classification of catastrophic events and damages, and the increasing statutory definitions of catastrophe found in a raft of regulations on catastrophe prevention, emergency response and insurance. Our report accepts the basic distinction between natural and man-made catastrophes. Most catastrophes are mixed, as harms might derive both from natural events and human acts or omissions, and that is why the law of torts still has a role to play, even though it is ill-equipped to deal with mass torts and even less so with catastrophic harms. Depending on geographical situation, some countries are more prone to natural catastrophes than others, and their national statutory regulations are typically designed to cover them by specific measures of public relief and reconstruction and very specifically by compulsory insurance systems and compulsory coinsurance and reinsurance systems.

At the academic meeting held in Washington D.C. on the 26th of July 2010, participants converged in three different but related lines of thought, which we will expand upon in this general report:

Firstly, some participants emphasized the idea that catastrophic harms are a social construct, almost a cultural concept, and even the worst natural disaster is defined both by geology and culture. This idea was held by the reporters from Poland, China, Japan, Slovenia and Italy.

> Section 3 of the Japanese Emergency Response Act (August 30, 2007) refers to 'serious social damage' when defining "emergency event" (Yonemura, *Japanese Report*), and Section 8(1) of the Slovenian Act on Protection against Natural and Other Disasters, refers to "harm to cultural heritage and environment" when identifying harms associated with catastrophes (Sladič, *Slovenian report*).

Secondly, and in the context of catastrophic harms, one of the main distinctions relevant to private insurance and insurance and reinsurance law is economic. The private insurance industry is mainly affected by those harms that happen to occur in developed countries, but is less affected by those harms that occur in developing ones, where the population does not massively resort to private insurance. Consequently, governmental or even international aid or intervention becomes the main legal tool in developing countries to deal with catastrophic harms, acting as an insurance of last resort.

> The Chinese reporter applies this distinction to his own country: "China is a developing country, and many disasters which involve large-scale loss are usually redressed through the administrative process. For example, in the Sichuan Earthquake of 2008 and Yushu Earthquake of 2010, compensation for the victims and the rehabilitation of the city were mainly secured through public finance under the direction of the local and central government, and only a small fraction of loss was paid by private insurance companies".

[1] II.A.1, Les dommages catastrophiques – responsabilité civile et assurances.

P. Salvador Coderch (✉) • R. Milà Rafel
Private Law Department, Pompeu Fabra university, Barcelona, Spain
e-mail: pablo.salvador@upf.edu; rosa.mila@upf.edu

S. Ramos González
Private Law Department, University of Lleida, Lleida, Spain
e-mail: sonia.ramos@upf.edu

K.B. Brown and D.V. Snyder (eds.), *General Reports of the XVIIIth Congress of the International Academy of Comparative Law/Rapports Généraux du XVIIIème Congrès de l'Académie Internationale de Droit Comparé*,
DOI 10.1007/978-94-007-2354-2_4, © Springer Science+Business Media B.V. 2012

Thirdly, the meeting raised the concept of polarization as one of the basic features of catastrophic harms hypothetically relevant to the Law of Torts. This notion was explained as follows: in purely natural catastrophic harms, there is by definition no human causation and consequently neither negligence nor strict liability applies. However, in mixed catastrophic harms, negligence or even intentional causation of the harm seems to be prevalent. Individuals and legal entities are blamed for their contribution to the harm and strict liability – understood as non-fault liability – is almost absent.

When confronted with this hypothesis, most of the reporters who responded did not agree with the idea that strict liability plays no role in compensating catastrophic harms.

For instance, the Chinese reporter, Xuefeng, contends that "it is difficult to say [that] the standard of liability is fault liability or strict liability in the abstract meaning". The Norwegian reporter, Rosaeg, does not agree with this third approach, because he "sees no reason why there cannot be strict liability if there is no human causation. Under EU Law based on international systems, for example, there is strict liability for the carrier of passengers if the perfectly seaworthy vessel sinks in an unexpected gale".

4.2 Harms and Catastrophes: Defining 'Catastrophic Harms'

4.2.1 Definition of "Catastrophic Harms"

4.2.1.1 Classic Concept of Catastrophe

As professor Olivier Moréteau writes in his outstanding report on US Law, "catastrophe", from the Greek καταστροφή (*katastrophé*), "describes an upheaval but also an end or an outcome" and "denotes total 'ruin' or radical 'overturning'".[2] Dr. Eugenia Dacoronia, author of the Greek report, adds that the verb *katastrepho* means in ancient Greek "to turn something upside down", "[t]hus, catastrophe means the complete destruction, a big accident".

4.2.1.2 Modern Concept of Catastrophe

To illustrate the modern concept of catastrophe, several features can be highlighted[3]:

A single event or a series of events, usually sudden and unexpected.

This idea is also captured by national reports when referring to "inevitable event" (Rosaeg, *Norwegian Report*[4]), "unavoidable event" (Novotná, *Slovakian Report*), "extraordinary and irresistible event or combination of events" (Majda, *Polish Report*), "unforeseeable" natural catastrophe (Wagner, *German Report*) or "events of extraordinary occurrence" (Tamayo, *Colombian Report*).

Causing an important number of victims.

"[I]t is fair to say that one is confronted with catastrophic loss when there is an important number of victims and when one single event causes this loss. One can also refer to mass loss ..." (Dubuisson\Bernauw, *Belgian Report*). In the same sense, "[t]he central feature of a catastrophe is that many people are affected at the same time, by one and the same cause or a series of related causes" (Wagner, *German Report*) and catastrophic damages are "[a]ll sort of damages that are caused by events leading to heavy destruction, loss and ruining of the general order"(Yavuz, *Turkish Report*).[5]

The American insurance industry offers a quantitative approach by defining a catastrophe as any event that causes $25 million or more in insured property losses and affects a large number of insured and insurers (Moréteau, *United States Report*).

[2] Moréteau, *United States Report*. From the Latin *catastropha*, can be understood as well "as a *coup de théâtre*, something of an unforeseen happy or unhappy event that turns the situation around at the end of a play, be it a comedy or a tragedy".

[3] In most national reports the word disaster is used as a synonym of catastrophe (Bernauw/Dubuisson, *Belgian Report*; Chang, *Taiwanese Report*; Majda, *Polish Report*; Mendelson, *Australian Report*; Moréteau, *United States Report*; Sladič, *Slovenian Report*; Yonemura, *Japanese Report*). Others are "public calamity", "major accident" or "mass loss" (Bernauw/Dubuisson, *Belgian Report*); "collective emergencies" or "national emergency" (Arbour, *Canadian Report*); "major risk" (Wagner, *German Report*), "emergency" (Mendelson, *Australian Report*; Novotná, *Slovakian Report*; *Xuefeng, Chinese Report*); "urgent event" (Mendelson, *Australian Report*), "extraordinary harms" (Kerschner, *Austrian Report*); "extraordinary event" (Novotná, *Slovakian Report*); and "serious accident" (Sinde/Veloso, *Portuguese Report*). The following adjectives have been also used to qualify the term "catastrophe" or "catastrophic harm": "major" (Bernauw/Dubuisson, *Belgian Report*; Moréteau, *United States Report*); "unexpected" (Xuefeng, *Chinese Report*); "huge", "sudden", "unexpected", "very terrible", "extraordinary", "irresistible", "unavoidable" and "tremendous" (last eight adjectives are mentioned in Majda, *Polish Report*; Novotná, *Slovakian Report*; Chang, *Taiwanese Report*; Xuefeng, *Chinese Report*).

[4] Lov nr. 72/1996 om petroleumsvirksomhet § 7–3.

[5] See also Xuefeng, *Chinese Report*.

Victims are seriously harmed.

The German national report stresses the idea that "(…) it is essential that the victims do not suffer trivial harm only but that each one or the vast majority is affected seriously. If, for example, the population of a particular area suffered from a light cough for two days due to contamination of the air, this will not be categorized as a "catastrophe". Matters would be different if the same group sustained serious harm, like some irreversible loss of bodily functions" (Wagner, *German Report*).

Disrupting normal community life.

This idea is explained in the Mexican report when identifying the consequences of a catastrophe: "The community faces the loss of its members, infrastructure or environment, so that the social structure becomes misadjusted and . . . the fulfillment of the essential activities of the society [is impossible], affecting the fulfillment of the primary necessities of living" (Hegewisch, *Mexican Report*). In other words, "[t]he perception of what is catastrophic harm is general rather than individual, with victims needing and expecting a greater amount of solidarity than in the case of an individual incident, due to challenging social disruption" (Moréteau, *United States Report*).[6]

Triggering the need for a significant and coordinated public response.[7]

"[T]he normal or local means cannot cope with [the catastrophe or disaster], irrespective of its cause. In general in this context most disaster events are defined by the need for external assistance" (Dubuisson/Bernauw, *Belgian report*). "A catastrophe within the meaning of [the German Civil Defence and Catastrophic Relief Act (1997)] is an occurrence which poses a risk to or harms the life, health or support of many people, private property … or the natural environment …, such that the provision of help and protection requires the cooperation of several units and agencies of the home protection service under common leadership" (Wagner, *German report*). This characteristic is also mentioned in the Canadian Report when it affirms that "Ministry of Civil Security must itself establish a national civil protection plan designed to provide support if the magnitude of a major disaster risk exceeds the capacity of local authorities to manage it" (Arbour, *Canadian report*). In the United States, "Federal Emergency Management Agency [1979] is meant to support local governments in situations where they happen to be overwhelmed" (Moréteau, *United States Report*).[8]

In some cases, a previous political decision qualifying the event as a catastrophe is necessary to trigger the relief and compensation mechanisms.

Both the Portuguese and the Belgian Reports illustrate this idea with several examples. In Portugal, the "Fund for Calamities" provides compensation to farmers for any damage not covered under their crop insurance, when an "agricultural disaster of climatic origin" has been declared. This is also the case with the "emergency account", established with the purpose of enabling measures of assistance "to people affected by catastrophes or calamities", and with the "municipal emergency fund", designed to provide financial aid to local authorities (Sinde/Veloso, *Portuguese Report*). In Belgium, the application of the Act of July 12, 1976 on the compensation of certain damages to private property caused by natural catastrophes depends on a political decision (Dubuisson/Bernauw, *Belgian report*).

From an insurance point of view, catastrophic risks have specific traits: low probability of occurrence and high amount of losses expected.[9] In this context, "[t]he characteristic of a catastrophe", add Prof. Bernauw and Prof. Dubuisson, Belgian reporters, "consists of the fact that it simultaneously hits all or a large part of all insure[d] [parties]".

To summarize, all these features are captured by the definition of disaster used by the United Nations' International Strategy for Disaster Reduction:

"A serious disruption of the functioning of a community or a society involving widespread human, material, economic or environmental losses and impacts, which exceeds the ability of the affected community or society to cope using its own resources.[10]"

4.2.1.3 Concept of Catastrophic Harm

Nowadays, accepted kinds of harm in the Law of Torts invariably include property damages and death or personal injuries. Apart from that, only under certain

[6] See also Yavuz, *Turkish Report*, according to which catastrophes are "[n]atural, technological and mankind sourced supernatural events that affect the communities by stopping and interrupting the normal life and the activities of the people which create physical, economical and social damages".

[7] It is the wording of the definition of "emergency" within the *Victorian Emergencies Act of 2004*. See Mendelson, *Australian Report*.

[8] The United Nations Department of Humanitarian Affairs also defines a national disaster as an "event for which the capacity to respond is beyond the ability of the national or regional authorities alone" http://www.un.org/ha/moreha.htm (last visited June 25, 2010).

[9] AA.VV, *Natural Catastrophes Insurance Cover. A Diversity of Systems* (Madrid: Consorcio de Compensación de Seguros, 2008), 20.

[10] http://www.preventionweb.net/english/professional/terminology/v.php?id=475, quoted by Bernauw/Dubuisson, *Belgian Report*.

circumstances may economic losses, pain and suffering and environmental law be compensated.

> In Norway, pain and suffering can be only compensated in case of gross negligence resulting in bodily harm or infringement.[11]

Specifically in the context of catastrophic harms a fifth category has to be considered: social or cultural damages are very often associated with a catastrophe, but are rarely compensated. So, the traditional distinction between property damages (plus economic losses) and personal injury (plus pain and suffering) is insufficient to cope with cultural damages. Some national reporters have emphasized the idea that catastrophic harms are a social construct, almost a cultural concept, and that even the worst natural disaster is defined both by geology and culture.

Few national reports take into account the social and cultural damages associated with a catastrophe. The Polish national report holds that "the widened meaning of 'harm' includes also environmental, social or cultural damage".[12] The Chinese report explains that "environmental damages and political or cultural damages are usually not regarded as harm under civil law, but may be regarded as harm in other branches of law, for example, environmental law or criminal law". Furthermore, Section 3 of the Emergency Response Act of the People's Republic of China (August 30, 2007) refers to "serious social damage" when defining "emergency event".[13] The Japanese reporter points out that "the traditional definition of harm can be interpreted to encompass resultant cultural and moral disadvantages, as long as they are able to be estimated economically".[14] Section 8(1) of the Slovenian Act on Protection against Natural and Other Disasters, refers to "harm to cultural heritage and environment" when identifying harms associated with catastrophes.[15]

4.2.2 Statutory Definitions of Catastrophe

Statutory definitions of 'catastrophe', 'catastrophic harm' or 'disaster' are found in several legal instruments dealing with prevention and compensation of damages caused by catastrophes. Public catastrophic law is specifically enacted to cope with prevention, emergency and relief action after the catastrophe, but also with victim compensation. On the other hand, insurance law often defines catastrophic harms in order to exclude them from coverage under the insurance policy.

Five comprehensive statutory definitions of catastrophe or its synonyms have been selected:

'Major disaster' (Section 42 of the United States Code § 5122, 2007):

> "[M]eans any natural catastrophe (including any hurricane, tornado, storm, high water, winddriven water, tidal wave, tsunami, earthquake, volcanic eruption, landslide, mudslide, snowstorm, or drought), or, regardless of cause, any fire, flood, or explosion, in any part of the United States, which in the determination of the President causes damage of sufficient severity and magnitude to warrant major disaster assistance under this chapter to supplement the efforts and available resources of States, local governments, and disaster relief organizations in alleviating the damage, loss, hardship, or suffering caused thereby.[16]"

Catastrophe (Section 8(1) Slovenian Act on Protection against Natural and Other Disasters):

> "[I]s an event or a series of events caused by unsupervised natural and other forces which affect or endanger the lives and health of persons, animals and property, causes harm to cultural heritage and environment to such an extent that special forces, means and measures are to

---

[11] Røsæg, *Norwegian Report.*

[12] Majda, *Polish Report.*

[13] Xuefeng, *Chinese Report.*

[14] Yonemura, *Japanese Report.*

[15] Sladič, *Slovenian report.*

[16] See also Section 13 (1) of the Queensland Disaster Management Act of 2003 (Australia), which defines disaster as "a serious disruption in a community, caused by the impact of an event that requires a significant coordinated response by the State and other entities to help the community recover from the disruption". According to Section 13(2) of the same Act "serious disruption means:
(a) loss of human life, or illness or injury to humans; or
(b) widespread or severe property loss or damage; or
(c) widespread or severe damage to the environment."

And see Section Two of the Japanese Act on Special Financial Support to Deal with the Designated Disaster of Extreme Severity (1962), which defines "disaster of extreme severity":

> "When a disaster exerts overwhelming influence on the national economy and leaves individual victims and local governments in need of specific financial support, the disaster is designated a disaster of extreme severity by a cabinet order."

be used in order to control them as ordinary activities, forces and means are insufficient.[17]"

Natural catastrophes (Section 1 Colombian Decree No. 3990 of 2007, on the operation of the Health System's Fund for Solidarity and Guarantee):

"[A]re those changes in the physical environment which can be identified in time and space, causing massive and indiscriminate serious damages to the population and affecting the community as a whole, such as earthquakes, seaquakes, volcanic eruptions, landslides, floods and avalanches.[18]"

National emergency (Section 3 Canadian Emergencies Act, 1985):

"[U]rgent and critical situation of a temporary nature" that (a) seriously endangers the lives, health or safety of Canadians and is of such proportions or nature as to exceed the capacity or authority of a province to deal with it, or (b) seriously threatens the ability of the Government of Canada to preserve the sovereignty, security and territorial integrity of Canada and that cannot be effectively dealt with under any other law of Canada.[19]"

Calamity (Section 2, 1° Belgian Royal Decree of February 28, 2003, creating a coordination council for emergency relief aid abroad[20]):

"[Is] an event caused by man or a natural phenomenon of such an extent that the emergency services of the country struck are not able to render the required assistance and endangering the life or health of the population, excluding cases of armed conflicts.[21]"

A few statutes define catastrophes or disasters through a list of events. Section 2 of the Taiwanese Disaster Prevention and Protection Act (2000) defines disaster as

hazards caused by any of the following disasters:

"(1) Natural disasters including windstorm, flooding, earthquake, drought, frost, and debris flow; and;

---

[17] Sladič, *Slovenian Report*. See also Section 2 of the Turkish Code, No. 5902, regulating the Structural Formation and the Administration of Catastrophe and the Emergency Situations, which defines catastrophes as:

"[I]ncidents which stop or suspend the regular life and activities of the whole society or certain sections or require urgent response."

And Section 3 of the Slovakian Act No. 42/1994 Coll. on civil protection of population, which defines catastrophe as:

"An extraordinary event, which leads to an augmentation of destructive factors and their subsequent accumulation caused by natural disaster or technological disaster."

And, finally, Section 3 (1&2) of the Portuguese Law No. 27/2006, of July 3, regarding the Framework Law for Civil Defence, defines catastrophe as a:

"[S]erious accident or series of serious accidents capable of causing levels of material damage and, possibly, victims, which greatly affect living conditions and socio-economic conditions in areas of or throughout national territory."

[18] See also Section 3 of the Polish Act on Natural Disasters (2002), which defines "natural disaster" as:

"[A] natural catastrophe … which causes a threat for the life or health of a great number of people, for property … or for [the] environment. In this case aid or protection may be undertaken only by introducing extraordinary means in co-operation of many authorities and specialized services."

[19] See also Section 3 of the Emergency Response Act of the People's Republic of China (August 30, 2007), which defines an "emergency event" as:

"[A] natural disaster, accidental disaster, public health event or social safety event, which takes place by accident, has caused or might cause serious social damage and needs the adoption of emergency response measures. According to such factors as degree of social damage and extent of effects, the natural disasters, accidental disasters and public health events shall be divided into four levels: especially serious, serious, large and ordinary, except as otherwise provided for by law or administrative regulation or the State Council."

And Section 3 of the South Australia Emergency Management Act 2004, which defines emergency as "a disruption to essential services or to services usually enjoyed by the community".

[20] In case of a catastrophe or calamity and a permanent support service.

[21] See also Section 2§1, 1° of the Belgian Act of July 12, 1976 on the compensation of certain damages caused to private property by natural catastrophes, which defines catastrophes as:

"Natural events with extraordinary force or unforeseeable violence or that have caused important losses, in particular earthquakes or landslides, tidal waves or other floods of a calamitous nature, hurricanes or other storm winds."

And Section 6§2 of the Belgian Royal Decree of February 16, 2006 on emergency and intervention plans, which defines an emergency situation as:

"[E]very event that causes detrimental effects for social life such as serious disturbance of public safety, serious threat of human life or health or material interests, where coordination of disciplines is required to remove the threat and to limit the damaging consequences."

(2) Major fire, explosion, public gas, fuel pipe line and power transmission line failure, air crash, shipwreck and land traffic accidents, toxic chemical materials disaster.[22]"

4.2.3 Classification of Catastrophic Events and Damages

Three basic classifications can be made when referring to catastrophic events or accidents and its consequences. First of all, catastrophic harms can result from natural events or disasters, but there are, of course, accidents caused by human agency traditionally covered by the Law of Torts. Within this first common category, there are purely natural catastrophic harms (Krakatoa, 1883; meteorite in Tunguska, Siberia, 1908; Eyjafjallajökull, Iceland, 2010), purely man-made catastrophes (Minamata Disease, 1956; Bhopal, 1984[23]) and mixed catastrophic harms, that is to say, those originated by a natural event, but aggravated by human agency (earthquakes in Haiti and Chile, 2010).

The United Nations' International Strategy for Disaster Reduction defines socio-natural hazard as "[t]he phenomenon of increased occurrence of certain geophysical and hydrometeorological hazard events, such as landslides, flooding, land subsidence and drought, that arise from the interaction of natural hazards with overexploited or degraded land and environmental resources"[24]

Secondly, further distinctions can be made when we take into account the duration and lapse in time of the cause and the losses of the catastrophe. Regarding the cause, there are single-event accidents (terrorist strikes or earthquakes) and accidents spread over time (asbestos exposure, leakage, pollution). And, any of these different causes can result in harmful consequences that can be either instantaneous (volcanic eruption), latent (contamination of blood products with HIV or with HCV) or spread over time (environmental damages).

4.3 Insurance System

4.3.1 The Practice of Insurance Coverage of Catastrophic Harms

In catastrophic harms, one of the key distinctions marking private insurance and reinsurance law apart is economic. The private insurance industry is mainly affected by those harms that happen to occur in developed or emerging countries, but is less affected by those harms that occur in developing countries, which do not massively resort to private insurance. Consequently, public relief measures and reconstruction become the main legal tool in developing countries to deal with catastrophic harms.

The Chinese reporter, Xuefeng, applies this distinction to his own country: "China is a developing country, and many disasters which involve large-scale loss are usually redressed through the administrative process. For example, in the Sichuan Earthquake of 2008 and Yushu Earthquake of 2010, the compensation for the victims and the rehabilitation of the city were mainly secured through public finance under the direction of the local and central government, and only a small fraction of loss was paid by private insurance companies".

4.3.1.1 Characteristics of Catastrophic Risk from an Insurance Perspective

From an insurance perspective, catastrophic risks are cumulative risks, given that catastrophes affect a large number of people and inflict serious harm on each victim at the same time, involving a large number of claims concentrated in a short period of time. Moreover, catastrophic risks have a low frequency of occurrence.[25]

"[Catastrophes]' insurability is problematic, as spreading the onus for the losses amongst the insureds no longer operates … From an insurance and compensation point of view, the fact that the event (i) simultaneously ("single-event disaster") affects (ii) a large number of victims or prejudiced persons ("mass disaster") is thus characteristic of a catastrophe.[26]"

[22] Article 1105 of the Colombian Commercial Code contains, by way of example, a list of catastrophic events that are considered catastrophic, such as civil or international war, riots, strikes, and subversive movements and volcanic eruptions, earthquakes and other convulsions of nature (Tamayo, *Colombian Report*).

[23] See Section 4.4.4. of this general report.

[24] http://www.preventionweb.net/english/professional/terminology/v.php?id=7830

[25] AA.VV, *Natural Catastrophes Insurance Cover. A Diversity of Systems* (Madrid, Consorcio de Compensación de Seguros, 2008), 20.

[26] Bernauw/Dubuisson, *Belgian Report.*

These specific characteristics make the catastrophic risk very costly to insure, and consequently, most insurance companies usually exclude coverage of catastrophic harms from their policies. Nevertheless, insurance companies usually offer specific coverage of catastrophic risks through an endorsement to the insurance policy, subject to payment of an extra premium.

"Cumulative risks are costly to insure because the insurer stands to lose enormous funds if disaster strikes. This explains the dominance of exclusionary clauses which, however, run counter to the interests of the insureds. To accommodate such interests, insurers offer the inclusion of these risks into the insurance cover in exchange for an extra premium" (Wagner, *German Report*).

According to the Chinese National report, "[t]he catastrophic risk will get special and separate treatment in the process of premium rating, because its probability is very low and its amount of loss once happened may be huge. In devising the policy, the insurance company can exclude the coverage for the risk [when] the magnitude of loss is huge and is difficult to predict by probability. As for risks where the magnitude of loss is huge and the probability is low, the insurance company can treat it as additional coverage and charge additional premium" (Xuefeng, *Chinese Report*).

4.3.1.2 Catastrophic Risks Most Excluded from Standard Form Insurance Policies

Most insurance companies' standard forms exclude catastrophic harms. The most excluded natural catastrophes are earthquakes and floods, although other natural catastrophes are also excluded depending on their significance in the region (e.g. tsunamis in China[27] or fire in Australia[28]).

Besides this, standard insurance policies usually exclude coverage for man-made catastrophic harms caused by war, armed conflicts, terrorism and nuclear accidents. Moving down one rung in order of importance, riots and strikes may also be excluded, although technological and industrial risks or toxic damages are usually not excluded, suggesting that insurance companies do not consider them catastrophes.

It is remarkable that the exclusion of natural catastrophic risks is less common in life, accident and health insurance contracts in certain countries such as Austria and China:

"In personal insurances there is seldom an exclusion of natural catastrophes [life, accident and health insurance policies], whereas in the insurance against material damage … some natural catastrophes are excluded" (Kerschner, *Austrian Report*).

"The standard form of life, accident and health insurance policies usually excludes the death, injury or disease resulting from the events as follows: war, military action, riot, armed revolt; nuclear reaction, nuclear radiation, nuclear pollution" (Xuefeng, *Chinese Report*).

4.3.2 Regulation on Insurance Coverage of Catastrophic Harms

The legal systems under study deal with insurance coverage of catastrophic harms in three different ways. Some do not include any general ruling on the matter, a few contain a default rule excluding catastrophic risks from the private contract, while a third group of systems has enacted regulations in order to increase the insurability of catastrophic risks historically recurrent in its territory[29]:

4.3.2.1 Lack of General Legal Regulation on Insurability of Catastrophic Risks

Most of the national statutory bodies of law analyzed in this report do not include any general rule governing either the insurability or uninsurability of catastrophic risks: the choice to include or exclude such coverage in the insurance policy is ultimately left to the parties. Insured risk is contractual risk. This appears to be the case with Australia, Austria, China, Germany, Italy, Mexico, Poland, Portugal, Slovakia and Slovenia.

According to the German report, "[i]n the absence of statutory provisions limiting the exposure of the insurer (…) the insurance policies used in practice, or rather the standard business terms of the insurance industry, routinely exclude damage caused by emergencies and catastrophes from the scope of coverage" (Wagner, *German Report*).

Article 45.2 of the Portuguese Insurance Contract Law sets down that the "insurance contract may exclude the cover, among other items, of risks related to war, insurrection or terrorism" (Sinde/Veloso, *Portuguese Report*).

4.3.2.2 Legal Exclusion from Insurance Coverage as a Default Rule

(a) **General Exclusion**

Some legal systems contain a default rule excluding catastrophic risks from the private insurance contract,

[27] Xuefeng, *Chinese Report*.

[28] Mendelson, *Australian Report*.

[29] Please note, however, that some legal systems, such as the Spanish one, might belong to more than one group.

unless the parties agree otherwise. This is the case with Colombia and Spain.

- According to Article 1105 of the Colombian Commercial Code, "catastrophic harms are in principle excluded from insurance coverage (…)." However, the same Article allows the parties to enter into a particular agreement to "cover catastrophic harms under commercial insurance policies".[30] This Section contains an open-ended list of examples of catastrophic harms legally excluded from coverage, such as war, riots, strikes, volcanic eruptions and earthquakes.
- In addition, Article 44.1 of the Spanish Insurance Contract Act[31] excludes "war risks" and "extraordinary risks" from the coverage of the private insurance contract, unless otherwise agreed. Please note, however, that some natural catastrophes, terrorism and armed conflicts are subject to compulsory coverage by a public entity, as we explain in Section 4.3.2.3.b of this report.

In particular, Article 44.1 states that "The insurer does not cover property and personal damages caused by armed conflict (…), or by extraordinary risks, unless otherwise agreed".

Although the Spanish Insurance Contract Act does not provide a definition of "extraordinary risks" it seems undisputed that catastrophic risks are extraordinary risks. In fact, a former drafting of Article 44 included an open list of extraordinary risks, comprising civil and international war, riot, popular uprisings, terrorism, earthquakes and floods. Moreover, the Spanish doctrine uses the term "extraordinary risk" as a synonym of "catastrophic risks".[32]

Since both property and personal damages caused by extraordinary risks are mentioned in this legal text, the rule laid down in Article 44.1 applies not only to property insurance contracts, but also life, medical and personal accident insurance contracts.[33]

(b) **Exclusions of certain catastrophic risks**

Other legal systems have enacted regulations excluding certain specific catastrophic risks from coverage under the private insurance contract, unless the parties agree to the contrary. Some examples can be found in Belgian, Greek, Quebec and Taiwanese law.

- According to Section 9 of the Belgian Land Insurance Contract Act (1992) "the risk of war and assimilated events are in principle excluded from the insurance cover".[34] The same rule applies in Greece, as prescribed by Section 13 of the Greek Insurance Contract Act (1997): "If the insured risk materializes as a result of war events or actions, civil war, riots or popular revolt, then no insurance coverage is provided".[35]
- In fire insurance contracts, section 2486 of the Quebec Civil Code provides that: "[a]n insurer who insures a property against fire is not liable for damage due to fires or explosions caused by foreign or civil war, riot or civil disturbance, nuclear explosion, volcanic eruption, earthquake or other cataclysm". And, in relation to property insurance contracts, section 2465 of the same Code establishes that: "[t]he insurer is not liable to indemnify for injury resulting from natural loss (…)".[36]
- In Taiwan, Section 23 of the Model Clauses of Commercial Property Insurance Policy lists the following excluded risks: "(1) damages caused by radiation, (2) damages incurred by nuclear devices, (3) war, (4) volcanic eruptions (…)".[37]

4.3.2.3 Legal Duty to Offer Insurance Coverage for Certain Specific Catastrophic Risks Historically Recurrent in Particular Areas

Many of the legal systems covered by this report have enacted regulations in order to increase the insurability of catastrophic risks, given that insurance companies usually exclude such coverage, and governments are anxious to ensure that victims receive economic compensation from private sources and not from public funds.

In this context, governments have imposed a legal duty to offer insurance coverage for certain specific

[30] Tamayo, *Colombian Report.*

[31] Act n. 50 of October 8, 1980, regarding the Insurance Contract, modified by Act n. 21 of December 19, 1990 and Act n. 30 of November 8, 1995.

[32] Fernando Sánchez Calero, "Comentario al art. 44" in Fernando Sánchez Calero (Dir.), *Ley de Contrato de Seguro. Comentarios a la Ley 50/1980, de 8 de octubre, y a sus modificaciones,* , 3rd ed. (Cizur Menor (Navarra): Thomson Aranzadi, 2005), 790, 788–805.

[33] Fernando Sánchez Calero, "Comentario al art. 44", *op. cit.*, 791.

[34] Bernauw/Dubuisson, *Belgian Report.*

[35] Dacoronia, *Greek Report.*

[36] Arbour, *Canadian Report.*

[37] Chang, *Taiwanese Report.*

catastrophic risks historically recurrent in their territories. This third group comprises areas such as Taiwan, Turkey, Belgium, Norway, California, United States of America, Australia, Spain, and France.

Typical natural catastrophic risks, such as flooding, storms, earthquakes, volcanic eruptions and tsunamis have diverse effects on different geographical areas. California is earthquake prone, but in Florida the most conspicuous risk is hurricane. In the same vein, storms and floods pose a significant risk in Norway, while earthquakes are the most significant in Turkey and Japan. It is therefore reasonable in such areas for the law to impose the aforementioned legal duty on insurers.

Countries to have established this legal duty can be classified in different groups depending on: (a) the risk covered; (b) the public, private or mixed nature of the insurer; and (c) the voluntary or mandatory nature of the purchase.

(a) **Risks covered**

Some countries have established the duty to offer insurance coverage for a single risk. For instance, earthquake risk is subject to compulsory coverage in California,[38] Turkey[39] and Taiwan,[40] while this also applies to terrorism risk in the United States of America,[41] Australia[42] and France.[43]

Other legal systems, such as Norway, Spain, Belgium and Japan, have enacted regulations with a close-ended list of compulsory covered risks:

- Property in Norway that is insured against fire is also insured against damage caused by natural events, provided the damage to the item in question is not covered by other insurance. Natural damage is understood to be damage directly caused by a natural event such as landslide, avalanche, storm, floods, storm surge, earthquake or volcanic eruption. (Section 1 of Norwegian Natural Damage Insurance Act, 1989).[44]
- The Spanish Insurance Compensation Consortium only covers:
  (a) The following natural risks: earthquake, seaquake, extraordinary flood, volcanic eruption, windstorm or tornado, and sidereal bodies and meteorite falls.
  (b) Those caused violently by terrorism, rebellion, sedition, and riot.
  (c) Interventions of the Army and the Police in peacetime

(Section 6 of Act n. 7 of October 29, 2004, on the Spanish Insurance Compensation Consortium[45] Act 7/2004).[46]

- The Belgian Land Insurance Contract Act (1995) and the Royal Decree regulating insurance against fire and other risks (1992), in relation to simple risks, set up a mechanism whereby cover will be compulsorily extended for certain perils (storm, labor conflict, natural catastrophes, and terrorism[47]) in the context of fire insurance contracts for a small private risk.[48]
- The Japanese Earthquake Insurance Act (1966) sets up specific and compulsory governmental reinsurance for all household earthquake insurance policies. In order to qualify for this

[38] Moréteau, *United States Report*.

[39] Yavuz, *Turkish Report*.

[40] Since 2001, according to Section 138 of the Taiwanese Insurance Law Act all dwelling fire insurance policies must cover earthquake risk. Chang, *Taiwanese Report* and AA.VV, *Natural Catastrophes Insurance Cover. A Diversity of Systems* (Madrid, Consorcio de Compensación de Seguros, 2008), 155.

[41] Sections 102 and 103 (a) (3) Terrorism Risk Insurance Act of 2002. 15 U.S.C. § 6701 (2006). Moréteau, *United States Report*.

[42] In response to the reluctance of Australian insurance companies to insure businesses for loss or damage caused by terrorism, the Australian Terrorism Insurance Act 2003 imposed insurance coverage for damages caused to commercial property and business activities by acts of terrorism (Section 8). Mendelson, *Australian Report*.

[43] In France, terrorism risk is mandatorily included in the coverage of property and casualty polices. Section 9 of the French Act against terrorism (1986).

[44] Røsæg, *Norwegia Report*. See also AA.VV, *Natural Catastrophes Insurance Cover. A Diversity of Systems* (Madrid: Consorcio de Compensación de Seguros, 2008), 122–123.

[45] Regulation *n.* 300 of February 20, 2004 develops Act 7/2004.

[46] According to Section 6.3 of the Act 7/2004 and Section 6 of the Regulation 300/2004, damages will not be compensated by the Consortium when arising from the following events:
(a) Defective condition of the insured product itself or the lack of its maintenance.
(b) War and armed conflicts.
(c) Events declared as a catastrophe or a national calamity by the Government because of its intensity and severity.
(d) Nuclear catastrophes.

[47] The Belgian Act of April 1, 2007 introduced the compulsory coverage of terrorism risk.

[48] Bernauw/Dubuisson, *Belgian Report*.

reinsurance, insurance companies are under the obligation to offer, in relation to their household fire and multi-risk polices, coverage for property damage caused to buildings and contents used totally or partially as a dwelling, resulting in fire, destruction, burial, translocation, and caused by an earthquake, volcanic eruption or tsunami. The coverage should nevertheless be limited to 30–50% of the sum insured under the main insurance policy to which the earthquake insurance is attached.[49]

By way of exception, France regulates the legal duty to offer insurance coverage with an open-ended list in case of natural catastrophes. According to Section 1 of the French Act of 13 July 1982:

> "Insurance contracts subscribed by any individual or legal entity other than the State guaranteeing coverage for damage by fire or [any] other damage to property [located] in France (…), [cover] the effects of natural catastrophes on the property (…).
>
> Moreover, if the insured is covered against business interruption, this guarantee extends to the effects of natural catastrophes (…). [T]he effects of natural catastrophes are considered to be direct material damage caused decisively by the abnormal intensity of a natural agent when the usual measures (…) would not have prevented it, or could not be adopted. An interministerial decree will declare the state of natural catastrophe."

(b) **Public, Private or Mixed Nature of the Insurer**

A duty to offer coverage for catastrophic risks is generally imposed on private insurance companies. This is the case with France, Japan, Belgium, Taiwan and Norway.

By way of exception, Spain follows a public insurance system of extraordinary risks. The coverage of catastrophic risks is offered by the Spanish Insurance Compensation Consortium, a public entity funded mainly by charging a rate of insurance companies' premiums.[50] The system is managed by the private insurers of property and personal insurance contracts, which charge their clients an additional fee to fulfill this duty. Contribution is compulsory, irrespective of whether the private insurer provides coverage for the extraordinary risks.[51]

Moreover, in other legal systems the duty to offer coverage for certain catastrophic risks is imposed on an entity with both public and private ownership.

- In California, insurers acting in the branch of household policies must offer earthquake coverage to their policyholders directly or through the California Earthquake Authority – CEA, an entity publicly managed but privately funded by private insurance companies.[52] Seventeen insurance companies, representing 70% of the Californian household insurance market, participate in the CEA. CEA products are the standard market policies.
- In Turkey, there has been compulsory earthquake insurance in effect since 2000 to compensate damages to dwellings caused by earthquakes. The authorized insurance companies and their agencies issue the compulsory insurance policies on behalf and in the name of the Natural Catastrophe Insurance Institution (NCII), which is a public legal entity with private participation, aimed at insuring owners against earthquake risks in exchange for an amount of premium determined by the Turkish Government.[53]

(c) **Voluntary or mandatory character of the purchase**

As a general rule, in legal systems where there is a duty to offer insurance coverage, the purchase of such insurance is compulsory for the insured party. The duty is normally linked to the purchase of a first party insurance contract, such as fire insurance and household insurance. In Norway, Taiwan, Belgium, France and Spain, when the insured party willingly purchases first party insurance, the insurer has the duty to include the catastrophic risk within the coverage of the contract, usually through an endorsement to the main policy and subject to payment of an additional premium. In Turkey, the

[49] Yonemura, *Japanese Report*. See also AA.VV, *Natural Catastrophes Insurance Cover. A Diversity of Systems* (Madrid: Consorcio de Compensación de Seguros, 2008), 90–92.

[50] Section 23 Spanish Act 7/2004. See Enrique Barrero Rodríguez, *El Consorcio de Compensación de Seguros,* Tirant lo Blanch-Cuatrecasas, Valencia, 2000), 158–257.

[51] Section 8.1 of the Spanish Act 7/2004 and Section 4 Regulation 300/2004.

[52] AA.VV, *Natural Catastrophes Insurance Cover. A Diversity of Systems* (Madrid: Consorcio de Compensación de Seguros, 2008), 192–198.

[53] Yavuz, *Turkish Report*.

duty to purchase the additional coverage is linked to the ownership of a dwelling in some areas.

Exceptionally, and in relation to earthquake coverage in Japan and California and terrorism coverage in the United States, the purchase of the additional coverage is voluntary for the insured party, meaning they are entitled to reject it.

4.3.2.4 Compulsory Coinsurance and Reinsurance Systems of Extraordinary Risks

In addition to the duty to offer insurance coverage for certain catastrophic risks, the legal systems covered by this report tend to establish a compulsory coinsurance and reinsurance system. In France, Japan, Norway, Taiwan and Turkey, a compulsory coinsurance or reinsurance system is linked to the existence of compulsory coverage for certain catastrophic risks.

- The French natural catastrophes coverage system sets up the *Caisse Centrale de Réassurance* (CCR), a state body authorized to operate in reinsurance to cover risks arising from the effects of natural disasters, with state guarantee (Section 1 of Decree 82–706 of 10 August 1982).[54]
- In Japan, reinsurance is compulsory for all household earthquake insurance policies. Every company that accepts primary earthquake insurance can conclude a reinsurance contract with the Japan Earthquake Reinsurance Co., Ltd. (JER), which also concludes reinsurance contracts with the government and private insurance companies. The share of each depends on the amount of the damages.[55]
- The Taiwanese legal system established the National Residential Earthquake Insurance Program, designed to reinsure earthquake related losses. The Taiwanese Residential Earthquake Insurance Fund (TREIF) has, since 2005, been distributing earthquake insurance risk among the coinsurance pool members, the TREIF itself, other domestic and foreign insurers and reinsurers and capital markets, and the national government.[56]
- Norway also features a compulsory coinsurance system, reflected in the Norwegian Natural Perils Pool, which includes all companies authorized to insure against fire, and manages the compulsory insurance of natural risks.[57]

However, the national reports also reveal other examples of reinsurance. In the United States, a year after Hurricane Andrew hit in August 1992, the Florida Hurricane Catastrophe Fund (FHCF) was set up in order to prevent insurance companies from stopping coverage for hurricane-related losses or from offering hurricane coverage only at unaffordable rates. The FHCF is a state-run mandatory reinsurer that provides reimbursements to insurers writing residential property insurance in the state. The reinsurance program is compulsory for all household insurers authorized to operate in Florida, and covers property damage to dwellings in Florida and their contents, along with additional living expenses, caused by any storm categorized as a hurricane by the National Hurricane Center.[58]

4.3.3 Catastrophic Harm Compensation Funds

Compensation Funds are a second mechanism for compensating damage caused by catastrophes. Considering the wide range of examples given by the legal systems covered by this report, two functional distinctions can be made:

A first relevant distinction relates to i) funds designed to compensate damage caused by catastrophes and not covered by an insurance contract, and ii) those that compensate catastrophic harms regardless of whether they are covered by a private insurance contract. A further distinction can be drawn between natural and man-made catastrophe funds.

Some legal systems have established mechanisms to compensate harms caused by certain specific extraordinary risks only when they are not covered by a private insurance contract. Four examples of these can be found in the national reports.

---

[54] AA.VV, *Natural Catastrophes Insurance Cover. A Diversity of Systems* (Madrid: Consorcio de Compensación de Seguros, 2008), 66–68.

[55] Japanese Earthquake Insurance Act of May 18, 1966. Yonemura, *Japanease Report.*

[56] Chang, *Taiwanese Report.* See also AA.VV, *Natural Catastrophes Insurance Cover. A Diversity of Systems* (Madrid: Consorcio de Compensación de Seguros, 2008), 155–156.

[57] Røsæg, *Norwegian Report*, pp. 2–3. AA.VV, *Natural Catastrophes Insurance Cover. A Diversity of Systems* (Madrid: Consorcio de Compensación de Seguros, 2008), 122.

[58] Moréteau, *United States Report.* AA.VV, *Natural Catastrophes Insurance Cover. A Diversity of Systems* (Madrid: Consorcio de Compensación de Seguros, 2008), 198–199.

- The Norwegian National Fund for Natural Damage Assistance (1961), funded by the State budget, compensates damage to property caused by certain natural disasters, such as flood, storm and tempest, landslide, avalanche, earthquake and volcanic eruption, only when such damage is not covered by a private insurance contract.[59]
- The Austrian Catastrophe Fund (*Katastrophenfonds*) for natural events (1966) is financed by a percentage of the revenues from certain taxes and administered by the Federal Ministry of Finance. The fund's aim is to compensate damage in the event of flood, avalanche, earthquake, landslide, hurricane or hail. The fund deducts any amounts already paid by private insurers from the compensation payable to the victim.[60]
- In Belgium, there is a Natural Catastrophe Fund (*Fond de Calamités*), created by the Act of July 12, 1976, and financed publicly, by cash advances, credits and other budgetary input in the wake of a disaster.[61] The Belgian fund compensates damage to private property caused by natural events previously declared as a disaster by the Government,[62] and only when the losses are not covered by the private insurance contract.
- The German legal system has not established a general fund covering extraordinary risks in cases of catastrophic damages, but has set up ad hoc funds to address the consequences of specific catastrophic events. This is the case of the German "National Solidarity Fund 'Reconstruction'", which was established to provide an ad hoc solution to the consequences of the flooding that plagued East Germany in the summer of 2002. The main feature of this fund is that "private parties were designated as beneficiaries, but only insofar as compensation from insurers or other third parties was not available".

  However, "[t]he regulations enacted on the basis of this statute refrained from explicitly creating rights to compensation in the hands of private parties. Rather, it was left to the discretion of the fund to award compensation in individual cases. The prerogative that payments made by insurers and other third parties should remain the primary source of redress was specified further (…) [R]egulations provided that the fund had discretion to ignore claims against insurers and other third parties where it appeared that it was impossible for the victim to enforce such claims promptly. In these instances, the fund was authorized to compensate the victim in spite of the fact that valid claims against insurers or third parties existed. However, the fund would do so only in exchange for an assignment of these claims by the victim" (WAGNER, *German Report)*.

Another distinction can be drawn between natural and man-made catastrophe funds.

- Two examples of the former are the Greek Special Fund for the Treatment of Sudden needs, regulated by Presidential Decree 227/2007, which is a general public fund for flood, conflagration, earthquakes and other natural disasters[63]; and the Taiwanese Agricultural Compensation Fund for Natural Disasters, which compensates agricultural damages caused by natural disasters including typhoons, storms, hailstones, and earthquake.[64]
- In relation to man-made catastrophes, several examples can be found in the medical and pharmaceutical sectors and in the field of terrorism. The German legal system has set up ad hoc funds to provide compensation for specific man-made catastrophes, such as the Thalidomide case (1971)[65] and the HIV-contaminated blood products (1995).[66] Since 1979,

[59] Røsæg, *Norwegian Report*. AA.VV, *Natural Catastrophes Insurance Cover. A Diversity of Systems* (Madrid: Consorcio de Compensación de Seguros, 2008), 125.

[60] Kerschner, *Austrian Report*. AA.VV, *Natural Catastrophes Insurance Cover. A Diversity of Systems* (Madrid: Consorcio de Compensación de Seguros, 2008), 31.

[61] Bernauw/Dubuisson, *Belgian Report*. AA.VV, *Natural Catastrophes Insurance Cover. A Diversity of Systems* (Madrid: Consorcio de Compensación de Seguros, 2008), 35.

[62] The minimum requirements for such a declaration are:
(a) The exceptional nature of the natural event.
(b) Minimum damage of €1,250,000 to private property in the area affected by the natural catastrophe.
(c) Minimum average damage of €5,000 per individual claim.

See AA.VV, *Natural Catastrophes Insurance Cover. A Diversity of Systems* (Madrid: Consorcio de Compensación de Seguros, 2008), 35.

[63] Dacoronia, *Greek Report*.

[64] Chang, *Taiwanese Report*.

[65] Gesetz über die Errichtung der Stiftung "Hilfswerk für das behinderte Kind", of 17.12.1971, BGBl. I, p. 2018. Wagner, *German Report*.

[66] Gesetz über die humanitäre Hilfe für durch Blutprodukte HIV-infizierte Personen of 24.07.1995, BGBl I, p. 972; Bekanntmachung der Satzung der Stiftung "Humanitäre Hilfe für durch Blutprodukte HIV-infizierte Personen" of 02.08.1995, Banz Nr. 157 of 22.08.1995. Wagner, *German Report*.

Japan has offered a compensation fund for damages caused by drugs, founded by the contributions of drug manufacturers in proportion to their total output and managed by an independent administrative organization (Pharmaceuticals and Medical Devices Agency). The manufacturer of a drug that causes adverse effects must pay an additional contribution the following year.[67] Among the several funds operating under the Belgian legal system, the Belgian Terrorist Attacks Fund (2007) is founded by insurers, reinsurers and the state.[68]

4.4 Tort Law, Catastrophic Harms and Mass Torts

4.4.1 The Role of the Law of Torts in Catastrophic Harms and Mass Torts

In most Common Law and Civil Law jurisdictions, Tort Law has been shaped and developed by case law and by judicial precedent. Tort Law systems typically cover moderate and instantaneous harms, meaning that neither collective nor latent harms have been given a central role in this field of torts. Civil litigation relating to latent damage, creating drawn out episodes of case law, such as asbestos contamination, raises huge problems relating to causation or the expiry of liability limitation periods.[69]

Tort Law is well equipped to adjudicate moderate accidents on a case-by-case basis, but is less able to cope with mass torts and even less so with catastrophic harms. Nevertheless, tort has a role to play in man-made catastrophes or even in natural catastrophes, in which human agency increased, negligently or even intentionally, the intensity and severity of the harm. Consequently, criminal and civil liability has to be taken into account in all jurisdictions, where the Law of Torts operates as a deterrent, although it is rarely the primary source of compensation.

Generally, there is separate procedural treatment for civil and criminal liability. In countries such as China, Italy, Portugal and Spain, the criminal court may decide on both criminal and civil liability.

Ex ante public safety regulation and ex post public measures of relief and reconstruction are the main legal tools to be used in catastrophic harms.[70] It is well known that in cases of moderate harm, private insurance tends to be more efficient than Tort Law, because the costs of administering the latter are higher.

> "Existing data suggest that in the United States the administrative costs of the liability system are large. Many studies find that administrative costs, averaged over settled and litigated claims, approach or exceed the amounts received by victims. That is, for every dollar received by a victim, a dollar or more is spent delivering the dollar to him (…)
>
> The administrative costs associated with provision of accident insurance are much lower than those of the liability system, sometimes less than the 10 percent of what victims receive.[71]"

However, private insurance is not always the most appropriate instrument for addressing compensation for potential catastrophic harms. The magnitude of the risk, its concentration in time and the pool of victims make it difficult, if not impossible, to insure in cases of huge catastrophic harms. As a result, compulsory insurance, compensation funds, public relief, and the government as an insurer of last resort, take precedence over the private insurance of catastrophic harms.

---

[67] Yonemura, *Japanese Report*.

[68] Bernauw/Dubuisson, *Belgian Report*.

[69] On the uneven performance of tort law and insurance when dealing with mass torts, see Albert Azagra Malo, *Daños del amianto:* litigación, aseguramiento y fondos de compensación, Fundación Mapfie, Madrid, 2011. Asbestos litigation and asbestos injuries compensation funds are the manuscript's main case studies.

[70] Perhaps three outstanding examples are:
- The Civil Protection Act of Quebec (February 2001) protects "(…) persons and property against disasters, through mitigation measures, emergency response planning, response operations in actual or imminent disaster situations and recovery operations".
- The Mexican Civil Protection Act (May 12 2000) regulates the national system of civil protection. According to Section 10 of the Act "[t]he aim of the National System is to protect the individual and the society in the event of a disaster caused by natural or human agency, through actions that might reduce or eliminate the loss of lives … the destruction of property, environmental damage and the disruption of the main functions of society, as well as to pursue the recovery of the population and its environment to the conditions of life they had before the disaster".
- The Japanese Act on Special Financial Support to Deal with the Designated Disaster of Extreme Severity (1962) provides for governmental relief in case of a "disaster of extreme severity".

[71] Steven Shavell, *Foundations of Economic Analysis of Law*, (Cambridge, MA: Belknap Press of Harvard University Press, 2004), 281–282.

Against this backdrop, which is prevalent in most economically and legally developed legal systems, classic Tort Law still plays an important role as a safety valve in the field of mixed catastrophic harms and purely man-made catastrophic harms. In this sense, it retains its two main functions:

(a) Deterrence of wrongful and harmful behavior, in that economic and social agents will know in advance that if they fail to comply with safety rules and regulations, or with reasonable social standards, they will be forced to face the consequences of their acts or omissions.
(b) Redress to the victim under the general principle of full compensation, which does not apply under the private insurance system or public remedies, such as funds or public relief.

Moreover, the following mechanisms must also be taken into account when comparing Tort Law with Insurance Law:

(c) Subrogation of the first party insurer against the tortfeasor, enabling the insurer to recover the money paid to the insured, meaning that, the price of the insurance premium will be reduced at the end of the day.
(d) Direct action by the victim against the injurer's insurer is widely recognized only in certain jurisdictions, such as France, Spain,[72] Norway[73] and China.[74] Most jurisdictions, however, allow for direct action in some fields, such as traffic insurance. This is the case with Germany,[75] Japan[76] and Italy.[77]

4.4.2 Man-Made Catastrophes and Standards of Liability Under Tort Law

Under contemporary Tort Law, man-made catastrophic harms have come in for the most attention.

The United Nations' International Strategy for Disaster Reduction offers several examples of man-made technological hazards, which include "industrial pollution, nuclear radiation, toxic wastes, dam failures, transport accidents, factory explosions, fires, and chemical spills".[78]

In purely natural catastrophic harms, by definition, there is no human causation and consequently neither negligence nor strict liability applies.

An example of a pure natural catastrophe might be the case of the enormous meteorite that crashed to the ground in the remote Siberian region of Tunguska, destroying a huge swath of ancient growth forest on June 30, 1908.

However, natural hazards can be worsened by human agency:

"Flooding can also be caused as a result of zoning plans being faulty or not properly monitored. The causes of an earthquake cannot be attributed to anyone, but foreseeable or avoidable consequences of construction defects or poor disaster management can.[79]"

In the context of man-made catastrophes, defendants, either individuals or legal entities, will essentially be held civilly liable under the following standards of liability:

(a) Negligence (i.e. defective building project or building in violation of mandatory safety regulations).
(b) Intentional causation of harm (i.e. terrorism).
(c) Strict liability. Case law traditionally applied this standard to abnormally dangerous activities. Nowadays, most jurisdictions enact legislation to subject certain abnormally dangerous activities to a system of strict liability, although the traditional basis of this standard still acts as a default rule. Some of the most common activities governed by the system of strict liability are the following: environmental pollution; public services; commercialization of defective products; road traffic; air traffic; nuclear power plants; chemical industry; waste management industry; and oil pollution.

  Even though man-made and mixed catastrophes might result from activities subjected to the aforementioned strict liability regimes, individuals and legal entities are mostly held liable because of their negligent or intentional contribution to the harm. That is why strict liability, understood as non-fault liability, is almost absent.

[72] Section 45 of the Spanish Insurance Contract Act n. 50/1980, October 8.

[73] Sections 7-6, 7-7 and 7-8 of the Norwegian Insurance Act n. 69/1989.

[74] Section 65 of the Insurance Act of People's Republic of China (2009).

[75] Section 115 (1) (No. 1) of the German Insurance Contract Act (2008).

[76] Section 16 of the Japanese Automobile Liability Security Act (1955).

[77] Poddighe, *Italian Report*.

[78] http://www.preventionweb.net/english/professional/terminology/v.php?id=507.

[79] Christian Lahnstein, "Catastrophes, Liability and Insurance," *Connecticut Insurance Law Journal* 9 (2002–2003):443–445.

4.4.3 Collateral Source Rule

In the context of man-made catastrophic harms, the victim might have been compensated prior to the tort claim by either its first party insurance company, by a compensation fund, or through Social Security benefits or other public benefits.

The Slovakian[80] and Portuguese[81] reporters illustrate the practical significance of this issue. In Portugal, for instance, there are at least four compensation mechanisms applicable to catastrophic harms: Social Security benefits, benefits for victims of violent crime and domestic violence recognized by law, several compensation funds and, of course, voluntary first party insurance.

In this setting, two questions arise:

(a) Firstly, whether benefits received from a third party preempt tort claims against the tortfeasor. Legal systems do not generally impose a preemption rule, but when accepted it is most commonly applied in cases of compensation funds and public benefits, since these systems are designed ad hoc to work as an alternative mechanism to the tort law system. On the other hand, private insurance and Social Security benefits are often compatible with damage awards.

In this regard, certain Spanish statutory bodies of law do act as bars to tort claims, such as Act n. 35 of December 11, 1995, on assistance to victims of violent crimes or sexual crimes; Act n. 32 of October 8, 1999, on assistance to victims of terrorism; and Regulation n. 9 of May 28, 1993, on assistance to victims of HIV infections in public hospitals; or Act n. 14 of June 5, 2002, on assistance to victims of HVC infections in public hospitals.

Similarly, Section 53 VI, 2nd paragraph of the French Asbestos Injuries Compensation Fund Act nº 2000–1257 recognizes the subrogation of the Fund to proceed against the tortfeasor to recover the money paid to the victim. In contrast, payments from the Australian Victorian Bushfire Fund do not act as a bar to tort claims against any potential tortfeasor of the fire.[82]

(b) If there is no such preemption rule, the second question to be dealt with is whether the amount paid to the victim by a third party should be deducted from the damages awarded. The legal systems under study do not follow a sole pattern.

Some, such as the United States of America, Australia and China follow in principle the collateral source rule, so "compensation from 'collateral sources' is none of the defendant's business and does not go to reduce the defendant's obligation to pay damages".[83]

Some other countries, on the contrary, support the principle that the amount of compensation should be reduced in proportion to any previous payment that compensates the same damage. The Japanese Supreme Court has recently passed a lot of judgments that back this principle.[84]

Whether the collateral source rule applies or not, legal systems recognize that third parties who have already paid the victim will enjoy a right of recourse against the tortfeasor. For example, this principle of subrogation applies either in the United States of America in case of private insurers,[85] or in Germany in the case of Social Security[86] and, as a result, makes first party insurance cheaper than liability insurance. The right of recourse serves a further purpose in cases in which the tort claim is preempted, because it keeps the deterrent function of Tort Law alive.

4.4.4 Relevant Legal Characteristics of Main Global and Local Catastrophes

There are some key features in man-made catastrophes that appear relevant to the Law of Torts. An analysis of the main global and local catastrophes that occurred in the second half of the twentieth century show us the significance of the hidden or long latency of the harm, the signature character of the disease, the primary or secondary character or the injurer linked to its close relation with the tragedy and the consideration of the harm as concentrated or diffuse.

John G. Fleming's classification of mass torts distinguishes three types of disasters: "(1) single-event occurrences which simultaneously inflict injury on many individuals, like airplane crashes or nuclear explosions; (2) serial injuries ("creeping disasters") caused by the same product to numerous victims over a period of time,

[80] Novotná, *Slovakian Report.*

[81] Sinde/Veloso, *Portuguese Report.*

[82] Mendelson, *Australian Report.*

[83] Dan B. Dobbs, *The Law of Torts* (St. Paul, MN: West Group, 2000), 1058.

[84] Yonemura, *Japanese Report.*

[85] Moréteau, *United States Report.*

[86] Wagner, *German Report.*

like asbestos and pharmaceuticals; (3) toxic damage affecting persons or property over a given area".[87]

In the 1950s and 1960s, two examples of catastrophes are relevant. The Thalidomide case dealt with a signature disease since the cause of the damage was clearly identified (a teratogenic drug indicated to prevent nausea during pregnancy) and also its consequences: there was a concrete final number of victims (over 10,000 children) and the harms were massive, but discrete (serious physical impairments consisting of underdeveloped limbs and lack of pelvic bones).

In 1954, Chemie Grünenthal, a German pharmaceutical company, identified a molecule (alpha-phtalimido glutarimide) with sedative and anti-inflammatory properties. The company conducted no biochemical or clinical trials to provide a scientific explanation as to the effectiveness of thalidomide, and the different effects observed among animals and humans. Nevertheless, the company patented the discovery, and in 1957 marketed it as a non-prescription drug specifically indicated to combat nausea during pregnancy. The drug was distributed under different brands in over 50 countries (Germany, United Kingdom, Austria, Canada, Spain…), with the exception of the United States of America, where the FDA did not allow for its distribution due to the aforementioned lack of scientific explanation.

The Thalidomide case yielded significant legal reforms. In Germany, the Thalidomide scandal was solved with a fund set up by statute,[88] and in Europe, product liability frameworks were altered by limiting the state of the art defense. In particular, the German Drug Act of 1976 (Arzneimittelgesetz) imposed on the pharmaceutical company the duty to prove that the defect could not be discovered according to the state of the art (article 84). Afterwards, Directive 85/374/EEC, of 25 July 1985, on Liability for Defective Products extended the same general rule to all producers (article 7.e), but allowed Member States to hold the producer liable even if the state of the art was not such as to enable the existence of a defect to be discovered (article 15.1.b) – accordingly, for instance, Luxembourg and Finland refused to allow the state of the art defense for all products, while Spain did the same for drugs and food. In the United States of America, the Thalidomide tragedy suffered in Europe also gave rise to legal reforms to design a more demanding procedure to obtain authorization to distribute a drug, instead of tackling the state of the art defense.[89]

Another catastrophe took place in Japan from the 1950s to the 1960s. Minamata disease, a neurological disorder resulting from mercury poisoning, was the cause of latent damage and was linked to organic mercury pollution emitted by chemical plants of large corporations. Japanese case law held the managing companies of the chemical plants liable[90] and triggered new legislation on compensation under several sorts of public nuisance.[91]

"Minamata Disease" took place mainly in Kunamoto. Around 1970, the Japanese Government presented data proving that the cause of Minamata Disease was organic mercury. In 1969, the Statute on Special Relief for Pollution-Related Health Damage was enacted (Yonemura, *Japanese Report*).

A highly complex global catastrophe emerged in the 1970s. The asbestos crisis is clearly characterized by the long latency period of its resulting damage. The delay between exposure to asbestos and the development of cancer is generally 20 years or more. The first parties to cause asbestos-related harm were asbestos product manufacturers (primary manufacturing), although the crisis also affected industries that used asbestos in their manufacturing process (second injurers or secondary manufacturing, such as shipbuilding and repair and construction),[92] and even certain industries loosely related to asbestos, like automobile or railroad industries. Moreover, the complexity of this catastrophe is exacerbated by the fact that asbestos not only causes signature diseases, such as mesothelioma and asbestosis, but also diseases (lung cancer, for instance) potentially produced by multiple causes.

Asbestos is a fireproof and insulating material that has been used in developed countries for many industrial purposes during the 20th century. Asbestos was so inexpensive and easy to manipulate that the world industry used it increasingly, peaking in 1980, when 4,800,000 tons were employed worldwide.

---

[87] John G. Fleming, "Mass Torts", *The American Journal of Comparative Law* 42 (1994): 507–508.

[88] Gesetz über die Errichtung der Stiftung "Hilfswerk für das behinderte Kind", of 17.12.1971, BGBl. I, p. 2018. Wagner, *German Report*.

[89] Pablo Salvador Coderch and Antoni Rubí Puig, "Causas de exoneración de la responsabilidad: excepción por riesgos de desarrollo", in Pablo Salvador Coderch and Fernando Gómez Pomar (editors) *Tratado de responsabilidad civil del fabricante*, Civitas, Madrid, 2008, pages 585–593.

[90] The Judgement of Niigata District Court on September 29, 1971 and the Judgement of Kumamoto District Court on March 20th, 1973. Yonemura, *Japanese Report*.

[91] The Act on Compensation of Pollution-Related Health Damage, 1973; The Act on Punishment of Crime to Cause Pollution Harmful for Human Health, 1970; The Air Pollution Control Act, 1968; The Water Pollution Control Act, 1979; The Basic Act for Environmental Pollution Control, 1970. Yonemura, *Japanese Report*.

[92] See Nicholson, W. J., G. Perkel, and I. J. Selikoff, "Occupational Exposure to Asbestos: Population at Risk and Projected Mortality 1980–2030," *American Journal of Industrial Medicine* 3 (1982): 259–311.

In the mid-sixties, after the work of Irving J. Selikoff (1964 and 1965), the scientific community unanimously acknowledged the dangers of asbestos exposure, yet awareness of such dangers did not prevent the industry from using it. Beginning in the seventies, U.S. industry was challenged by massive litigation (a total of 730,000 claimants), leading to the award of substantial damages, both compensatory and punitive, and the bankruptcy of the top manufacturing companies. The regulatory response came long after the litigation crisis: in the US there is no general ban on asbestos, but specific prohibitions. In contrast, the use of asbestos is completely banned in many countries (including New Zealand, Australia, Brazil and Japan). In Europe, complex regulatory activity embraced the prohibition of asbestos (Directive 1999/77/EC, of 26 July 1999), as well as the creation by the national governments of some Member States (France and Belgium) of no-fault compensation funds that go beyond the Social Security system.

In the 1980s, HIV (Human Immunodeficiency Virus) was identified as the cause of AIDS (Acquired Immune Deficiency Syndrome), a disease which can develop, generally, in a 7–10-year period from the infection.[93] Since its origin – the virus came from SIV (Simian Immunodeficiency Virus) affecting chimpanzees – human agency has multiplied the spread of the disease. Among the different causes of transmission – sex, blood transfusion, contaminated hypodermic needles, exchange between mother and baby during pregnancy, childbirth, breastfeeding – the most relevant in terms of the number of tort claims is infection through blood transfusions and blood products at a time when the virus and its mode of transmission were still unknown to the scientific community.

The harm caused could not be handled by tort claims alone. National governments launched ad hoc compensation systems, which were based on the idea of solidarity for victims, but all of them differ in the following aspects: (1) eligibility requirements, either that the victim is hemophiliac (UK, France, US); or was infected during a certain period of time (France, Canada, Germany, US, Spain); or was infected in a public hospital (Spain); and (2) waiver of tort claims following compensation (France, US, Germany, Spain).

On the 3rd of December, 1984, a toxic gas called methyl isocyanate leaked from the pesticide plant owned by Union Carbide India, Limited (UCIL), in Bhopal, India, causing the death of 16,000 people and serious harm to over 500,000 people.[94] It was clearly a man-made technological catastrophe:

Lack of due care during cleaning and maintenance of the plant made impurities come into contact with the stored gas, initiating a chemical reaction that caused overpressure and the subsequent opening of safety valve tanks. In addition, the cooling system and the gas catalyst had been turned off to save costs.

Litigation started on the 7th of December, 1984, when a multi-billion dollar lawsuit was filed in a US court, since UCIL was a subsidiary of Union Carbide Corporation (UCC), an American corporation. In March, the Indian government enacted the Bhopal Gas Leak Disaster Act to ensure that claims were dealt with speedily and equitably. This Act also made the Indian government the only representative of the victims in legal proceedings in India and abroad. Cases were placed under Indian jurisdiction and finally, as a full and final settlement, UCC agreed to pay $470 million to the Indian government to be distributed to claimants.

Another man-made catastrophe arose in the United States in the twenty-first century, namely the terrorist attacks on the World Trade Center and the Pentagon on the 11th of September, 2001. This catastrophe had two main legal effects: the creation of a Victim Compensation Fund, to provide prompt and fair compensation to the victims of the attacks and their families. And, since insurance companies were called on to pay huge amounts and this raised concerns regarding the solvency of the American insurance industry, the Terrorism Risk Insurance Act was passed in 2002 to provide a cap on the losses for which the private insurance industry will be responsible in the event of a major act of terrorism. The Federal government will assume the role of excess liability insurer.[95]

In Australia, the National Health Security Act 2007 (Cth) was enacted by the Commonwealth in response to the potential threat of "naturally occurring epidemics or to terrorist attacks involving chemical, biological and radiological agents".[96] This Act has created a national system of public health surveillance whose functions are to identify and respond to public health events of national significance.

[93] Joan C. Seuba Torreblanca, *Sangre contaminada, responsabilidad civil y ayudas públicas* (Madrid: Civitas, 2002), 74.

[94] Editorial, "Has the World Forgotten Bhopal?," *Lancet* 356 (2000): 1863.

[95] Moréteau, *United States Report.*

[96] Mendelson, *Australian Report.*

Appendix

Questionnaire on Catastrophic Harms

I. Harms and catastrophes: defining "catastrophic harms"

1. May we ask you, please, to provide us with a generic definition of "catastrophic harms" well suited to your own legal culture?

II. Catastrophic harms and statutory law

2. Please specify the main legal requirements present in your own legal systems to construct the concept of legally relevant catastrophic harms.

III. Insurance System

3. Is an event of catastrophic harm, which may severely affect the company or eliminate it, contemplated somehow by insurance policies, or even by statutory law?
4. Does your national legal system distinguish between damages covered by insurance policies and those that are legally excluded?
5. Even if some catastrophic damages may be legally covered by insurance policies, which are the events more commonly excluded by standard forms of insurance policies in your own jurisdiction?
6. Does your country have any legally established fund covering, among others, extraordinary risks? If so, or if there is more than one, please list the most relevant three, adding short comments about contributors, amount of contribution, management and coverage.
7. How do the levels of risk concentration and risk magnitude translate into insurance policies and rates? When answering, please consider which levels make reinsurance or coinsurance a good practice, and the existence of compulsory reinsurance or coinsurance or similar meaningful features you think may be of interest.
8. How does your system distinguish between sudden accidents and long term risks? If so, please, provide us with a very short list of statutory or case law defining latency and distinguishing between sudden accidents and long term risks.
9. Please describe new statutes, if any, in your legal systems triggered by global catastrophes, as the above-mentioned ones, and any new statutes driven by national or local events?
10. Was legal change triggered by case law itself? If so, please cite the leading cases?

IV. The Law of Torts

11. Do "catastrophic harms" generate criminal, administrative, civil or labor liability? If so, what are the main legal sources or the leading case law?
12. Do administrative fines or criminal punishment preempt civil claims?
13. Which standard of liability governs catastrophic harm claims?
14. Are co-injurers jointly, severally or joint and severally liable? If there is a joint and several liability standard, is there a right to contribution and, if so, how is it regulated?
15. Are class actions regulated in your procedural system? If so, please provide brief details of their main features?
16. May the victims or their estates sue the insurance company directly (direct action)? If so, please cite the relevant statute.
17. According to the Collateral Source Rule and if the law does not provide otherwise, any amount of compensation paid to the victim or their estates is not to be taken into account to decrease the liability of the injurer. How is this rule applied in your legal system?
18. Is the State of the Art Defense (Risk of Development) regulated by your own jurisdiction? Is it generally accepted as a defense? Is it excluded for some economic activities or public sectors?

V. Regulatory Agencies and Liability

19. If victims have a tort claim, must they wait until a regulatory agency decision is taken or reviewed, or can victims merge their tort claims with general administrative proceedings? If so, please provide a short list of relevant legal sources and case law.
20. Is there a general preemption clause in your own legal system? Are there specific preemption clauses?

List of National Reporters

Country	National reporter
Australia	Danuta Mendelson, Deakin University
Austria	Ferdinand Kerschner, Universität Wien
Belgium	Bernard Dubuisson, Université Catholique de Louvain
	Kristiaan Bernauw, University of Gent
Canada	Marie-Ève Arbour, Université Laval (Quebec) and Università del Salento (Italy)
Colombia	Javier Tamayo Jaramillo, Javier Tamayo Jaramillo & Asociados
China	Zhou Xuefeng, China-EU School of Law, Beihang University School of Law
Germany	Gerhard Wagner, Universität Bonn
Greece	Eugenia Dacoronia, National and Kapodistrian University of Athens
Italy	Elena Poddighe, Università degli Studi di Sassari

Country	National reporter
Japan	Shigeto Yonemura, Tohoku University
Mexico	Fernando Hegewisch Díaz Infante; Hegewisch Abogados, S.C.
Norway	Erik Rosaeg, Scandinavian Institute of Maritime Law
Poland	Rafal Majda, Université de Lód
Portugal	Jorge Sinde Monteiro and Maria Manuel Veloso Gomes, University of Coimbra
Slovakia	Marianna Novotná, University of Trnava
Slovenia	Jorg Sladič, Law Firm Sladič – Zemljak
Taiwan	Kuan-Chun Chang National Chengchi University
Turkey	Cevdet Yavuz, Marmara Universitesi
United Sates	Olivier Moréteau, Louisiana State University

La gestation pour autrui[1]

5

Françoise Monéger

Ce rapport a été complété après le congrès de Washington. D'abord parce nous avons pris connaissance à Washington du rapport américain que nous n'avions pas reçu, ainsi que du rapport italien, ensuite parce qu'il est apparu lors des discussions, qu'il était dommage que certains pays soient absents. Nous avons ainsi sollicité un rapport pour Israël,[2] pays qui a réglementé la gestation pour autrui dès 1996 et accepté une contribution belge évoquant les questions de droit international privé qui deviennent essentielles dans un tel domaine.

En dépit de plusieurs relances, nous n'avons en effet reçu pour le congrès que 17 rapports sur les 27 promis, nous ferons référence dans cette synthèse, à ces seuls rapports,[3] auxquels il convient d'ajouter les rapports américain, belge, israélien et italien. Il aurait été regrettable de ne pas prendre en considération la situation des Etats-Unis d'Amérique, qui est un condensé de toutes les situations des autres pays puisque comme l'explique Carla Spivack, certains Etats interdisent la pratique des mères porteuses, d'autres la réglementent, d'autres enfin, reconnaissent les parents d'intention. Ces rapports sont de tailles très inégales, il y a des études très complètes en particulier pour le Canada, la Corée, l'Espagne, les Etats-Unis, les Pays-Bas et le Royaume-Uni, d'autres beaucoup plus courtes qui répondent aux questions par oui et par non sans plus d'explications. Certains rapports répondent aux questions posées,[4] d'autres s'en éloignent, en privilégiant un angle d'attaque particulier comme la contribution belge déjà citée.

Les réponses sont en général neutres mais quelquefois les rapporteurs prennent position pour ou contre la gestation pour autrui. C'est ainsi que le rapporteur canadien est très défavorable, le rapporteur polonais, à l'inverse, y est très favorable, de même que le rapporteur serbe, avec un petit peu moins de fermeté.

Beaucoup constatent qu'en tout état de cause la pratique de la gestation pour autrui existe et qu'il suffit de consulter les offres et les demandes via internet pour en être convaincu. C'est pourquoi les questions 1 et 2 qui paraissaient assez simples (« Est-ce que votre droit accepte la gestation pour autrui » et « si oui, quel est le régime juridique ») sont difficiles à synthétiser, puisque la réponse à la question 1, est souvent « non », le droit ne l'accepte pas, mais qu'en réalité, la pratique existe et que le droit doit régler les conséquences de cette pratique quant au statut de l'enfant qui naît et à la protection de la femme qui a mis au monde cet enfant.

Les rapports soulèvent également des problèmes de définition. Nous aurions dû mieux préciser ce qu'il fallait entendre par gestation pour autrui. Dans la terminologie française, l'on distingue en principe la procréation pour autrui, hypothèse où la mère porteuse est à la fois génitrice et gestatrice et la gestation pour autrui où la mère porteuse n'est que gestatrice, l'article

[1] II.A.2, Maternity for Another.

[2] Merci à Talia Einhorn de nous avoir mis en contact avec Carmel Shaley qui a accepté de faire le rapport dans un délai très court.

[3] Allemagne, Argentine, Canada, Corée du Sud, Danemark, Espagne, France, Grèce, Irlande, Macao, Norvège, Pays-Bas, Pologne, Portugal, Royaume-Uni, Serbie, Taïwan.

[4] V. le questionnaire en annexe.

F. Monéger (✉)
Professeur des universités, Conseiller (s.e.)
à la Cour de cassation, France
e-mail: Francoise.Moneger@justice.fr

K.B. Brown and D.V. Snyder (eds.), *General Reports of the XVIIIth Congress of the International Academy of Comparative Law/Rapports Généraux du XVIIIème Congrès de l'Académie Internationale de Droit Comparé*,
DOI 10.1007/978-94-007-2354-2_5,

16–7 du code civil français assimilant d'ailleurs les deux hypothèses pour les interdire.[5] Le terme français « gestation pour autrui » (et non maternité pour autrui) utilisé dans le questionnaire en français est donc plus réducteur que le terme « maternity for another » utilisé dans le questionnaire en anglais. Cette différence terminologique a conduit certains rapporteurs à aborder la maternité pour autrui sous l'angle de l'adoption lorsque la femme remet à la naissance l'enfant qu'elle vient de porter, à un couple qui l'adopte, mais sans que cet enfant n'ait été conçu pour eux. Ce qui est une toute autre problématique.[6] D'autres présentent tout le droit des procréations médicalement assistées, ce qui là encore, déborde la question posée.[7] De plus, certains droits acceptent seulement la gestation pour autrui et refusent la procréation pour autrui.

Les réponses obtenues nous conduisent à concentrer cette synthèse, sur quelques points seulement: les pays qui acceptent la maternité pour autrui et ceux qui l'interdisent, le tourisme procréatif et la tendance dans les projets en cours.

5.1 Les pays qui acceptent la gestation pour autrui

Parmi les droits qui acceptent la pratique, il convient de distinguer deux catégories de pays. Dans la première, il y a ceux qui ont réglementé la maternité pour autrui, dans la seconde, ceux qui n'ont pas légiféré, mais qui ont accepté la pratique et gèrent, à travers leur jurisprudence, les conséquences des naissances.

Il est difficile de placer les Etats-Unis dans l'une ou l'autre catégories. Comme l'explique le rapporteur, les instances fédérales comme « the National Conference of Commisionners on Uniform State Laws (NCCUSL) », et l' « American Bar Association (ABA) » n'ont pas été capables de trouver un consensus et de proposer un modèle unique. La première propose une alternative: la validité ou la nullité des contrats, la seconde retient la validité des contrats en distingant deux hypothèses selon qu'un tribunal intervient ou non.

5.1.1 Les pays ayant élaboré des textes

Ces pays sont peu nombreux: le Canada (quelques provinces), la Grèce, Israël, les Pays-Bas et le Royaume-Uni, et quelques Etats aux Etat-Unis qui ont légiféré sur les contrats. Les dispositions sont contenues à l'intérieur de textes sur les procréations médicament assistées (ci après PMA), la gestation pour autrui étant une des voies offertes en cas d'impossibilité pour une femme, de porter un enfant. En France, la commission mise en place au Sénat pour réfléchir sur la maternité pour autrui avait proposé que cette pratique soit au service exclusif de la lutte contre l'infertilité et soit encadrée comme technique de PMA.

5.1.1.1 Les provinces canadiennes de common law d'Alberta, de Nouvelle Écosse, de Terre Neuve et Labrador[8]

Les soins de santé étant de compétence provinciale, L'Alberta a édicté des dispositions législatives visant directement les contrats de mère porteuse gestationnelle (avec implantation d'un embryon fécondé). La « Family Law Act » de 2003 encadre ces contrats. Selon la « Loi fédérale sur la procréation assistée », seuls les contrats altruistes sont visés, cette loi prévoit dans son article 12 qu'un juge peut déclarer que la mère génétique de l'enfant est la seule mère légale de celui-ci lorsque la mère porteuse y consent. La loi énonce que les contrats ne peuvent pas faire l'objet d'une exécution forcée et que l'existence d'un contrat ne présume pas du consentement de la femme qui accouche pour l'établissement de la filiation de l'enfant.

La Nouvelle Écosse a adopté un règlement en vertu de la « Vitual Statistics Act » du 20 septembre 2007 qui permet au juge, dans le cadre d'une ordonnance d'adoption, d'établir la filiation d'un enfant né à la suite d'une convention de maternité de substitution. Un des deux parents doit avoir un lien génétique avec l'enfant, et la mère porteuse doit consentir à renoncer à ses droits à l'égard de l'enfant.

[5] Art. 16–7: « Toute convention portant sur la procréation pour autrui ou la gestation pour autrui est nulle ».

[6] C'est semble-t-il une des approches du rapport allemand qui envisage l'adoption comme l'une des hypothèses de la « surrogate mother » (rapport, p. 1).

[7] Il en est par exemple ainsi du rapport italien qui présente le texte voté en Italie en 2004 sur l'insémination artificielle et les embryons.

[8] V. le rapport canadien présenté par L. Langevin.

En Terre Neuve et Labrador, selon la « Vital Statistic Act » de 2009, le directeur de l'état civil pourra inscrire les parents intentionnels, comme parents d'un enfant né à la suite d'une convention de mère porteuse si une ordonnance d'adoption a été émise par le tribunal.

5.1.1.2 La Grèce[9]

La loi n° 3089 de 2002 sur la procréation médicalement assistée contient des dispositions à la fois sur les techniques de PMA et sur les conséquences pour la filiation des enfants, dispositions qui ont été incorporées dans le code civil.

La loi permet toutes les méthodes de PMA, sauf le clonage reproductif. Le recours à ces méthodes est possible lorsqu'une procréation naturelle n'est pas possible ou qu'il y a un risque de transmission d'une maladie grave à l'enfant à naître. Les femmes peuvent y recourir jusqu'à l'âge de 50 ans. La PMA est ouverte aux couples de sexe différent, mariés ou vivant en union libre et aux femmes célibataires.

En ce qui concerne spécifiquement la gestation pour autrui, il faut une autorisation judiciaire et après avis médical sur l'impossibilité de la femme à mener à bien une grossesse. M. Papachristos fait état d'une décision récente du tribunal d'Athènes[10] qui a permis à un homme célibataire d'avoir recours aux services d'une mère porteuse, au nom de l'égalité des sexes.

Le contrat doit être conclu entre les parents d'intention et la mère porteuse. Les ovules doivent provenir soit de la mère d'intention soit d'une autre femme, mais pas de la mère porteuse. Celle-ci ne doit pas être rémunérée, elle peut seulement être indemnisée pour ses frais et son manque à gagner, le plafond de cette indemnité étant fixée à 10,000 euros.

Pour éviter le « tourisme procréatif », la loi exige que les deux femmes (mère d'intention et mère porteuse) aient leur domicile en Grèce. Toutefois, le rapporteur remarque que la mère porteuse est souvent une étrangère domiciliée en Grèce, « ce qui suscite, écrit-il, des doutes sur la gratuité de l'offre ».

L'enfant qui naît est automatiquement rattaché à sa mère d'intention sauf si, en dépit de la loi l'enfant est né des ovules de la femme qui l'a porté qui peut alors contester la maternité.

5.1.1.3 Israël[11]

C'est en Israël une loi de 1996 qui a organisé la maternité pour autrui (The Surrogate Mother Agreements). Il y a deux stades dans le processus, le premier est contractuel, le second est juridictionnel. Tout ce qui concerne l'accord entre les parties, entre la femme qui va porter l'enfant et les parents d'intention demeure contractuel, les textes posant des conditions relativement strictes concernant les uns et les autres contrôlées par un comité mis en place par la loi. La mère porteuse ne doit pas être mariée, ni avoir de lien de parenté avec les parents dintention, elle doit avoir la même religion que la mère d'intention, elle peut être ou non la mère génétique et le sperme doit être celui du père d'intention. Seules les personnes résidant en Israël, de sexe différent, et n'ayant pas atteint un certain âge peuvent recourir à ce type de procréation. Le contrat peut prévoir une indemnisation de la mère porteuse.

Le statut de l'enfant, la situation de la femme qui a accouché, la filiation de l'enfant par rapport aux parents d'intention est déterminée par une décision du justice.

5.1.1.4 Les Pays-Bas[12]

Le droit hollandais accepte la maternité pour autrui mais en entourant la pratique de conditions très strictes depuis 1997 dans le cadre des textes sur la fécondation in vitro et de la réglementation des établissements qui pratiquent ce type de fécondation (in Vitro Fertilization, IVF).

C'est une décision judiciaire qui peut seulement transférer des droits de la mère porteuse (et éventuellement de son mari) aux parents d'intention.

Il y a beaucoup de discussions aux Pays-Bas pour savoir si l'on peut admettre en dehors du système de la FIV, que des contrats purement privés soient passés entre des particuliers afin d'organiser les relations entre la mère porteuse et le couple demandeur. Certains estiment que ces contrats n'ont aucune force obligatoire et sont donc nuls, d'autres considèrent qu'ils peuvent être mis en œuvre pour transférer les droits sur l'enfant. Il semble que ces contrats qui sont contraires aux dispositions d'ordre public des textes sur la FIV, peuvent avoir une certaine utilité dans un processus d'adoption.

---

[9] V. le rapport établi par A.C. Papachristos.

[10] N°2827/2008.

[11] Rapport établi par C. Shalev.

[12] Rapport établi par M. Vonk.

Selon l'article 198 du Code civil, la femme qui porte l'enfant est la mère sans que le texte distingue selon qu'elle a donné ses ovules ou non.

5.1.1.5 Le Royaume-Uni[13]

En droit anglais, la maternité pour autrui est régie par deux textes: le « Surrogacy Arrangements Act de 1985 » (SAA) et le « Human Fertilisation and Embryology Act » de 2008 (HFEA). Ces textes visent à la fois le cas de la mère porteuse génitrice, et celui de l'implantation dans son utérus d'un embryon conçu in vitro.

D'après l'article 1 de l'Acte de 1985, aucun contrat de mère par substitution ne peut donner lieu à exécution forcée en cas de conflits entre les parties: la mère porteuse ne pourra pas être contrainte à remettre l'enfant au couple commanditaire. Le rapporteur cite le cas d'une femme devenue stérile à la suite d'une négligence médicale et qui réclamait des dommages et intérêts afin de couvrir les frais d'une mère porteuse. Le juge de la High Court a refusé au motif que des dommages et intérêts ne peuvent être alloués afin de permettre la conclusion d'un contrat dont l'exécution n'était pas autorisée par la loi.

L'article 2 du SAA punit le fait de servir d'intermédiaire rémunéré pour une négociation de contrat de mère par substitution. Mais depuis la réforme de 2008, les organisations à but non lucratif peuvent proposer des services aux candidats potentiels à ce type de contrats.

De plus, lorsque la mère porteuse y consent, le couple commanditaire peut saisir le juge dans les six mois de la naissance de l'enfant pour obtenir un « parental order » (ordonnance relative à l'autorité parentale) afin d'être considéré comme les parents de l'enfant, ce qui aura pour effet de faire cesser la parenté à l'égard de la mère.

Nous évoquerons pour conclure ce paragraphe, la situation aux Etats-Unis qui apparaît assez confuse selon le rapporteur lui-même. Parmi les Etats qui ont pris en considération dans leur législation, les contrats de mère porteuse, six ont refusé de valider les contrats lorsque la femme était rémunérée pour ses services,[14] cinq ont expressement exigé que pour être valable, le contrat ne soit pas être rémunéré,[15] ce qui revient à peu près au même résultat. Ainsi, la plupart des Etats n'ont pas de réglementations, et dans ces Etats, les couples concluent des contrats de ce type avec le risque qu'un tribunal refuse ensuite de le valider pour des raisons d'ordre constitutionnel ou de contrariété à l'ordre public, lorsque par exemple, la femme qui a mis l'enfant au monde refuse de le restituer aux parents d'intention. La liste de ces Etats est longue.[16]

5.1.2 Les pays qui acceptent la pratique

Au Canada, en droit fédéral, la loi sur les PMA de 2004, a interdit et criminalisé les contrats de mères porteuses avec rémunération, sans se prononcer sur les contrats dits altruistes. Les tribunaux, dans les provinces de *common law* ont ainsi, indirectement, reconnu la validité de tels contrats.[17] Il en est de même aux Etats-Unis, dans beaucoup d'Etats, comme nous venons de le remarquer.

En Corée, il apparaît que la pratique est courante depuis des années.[18] Dans un sondage réalisé en 2004 par un chercheur, plus de 80% des personnes interrogées sont toutefois hostiles à la pratique, qu'il s'agisse de contrats rémunérés ou altruistes. Et pourtant, 66% considèrent qu'il faudrait élaborer des textes sur la maternité pour autrui, 37% préférant le recours à une mère porteuse, plutôt que l'adoption d'un enfant.

Le rapporteur mentionne la tendance des coréens à éviter les procès et les tribunaux afin de régler par la médiation les questions d'ordre familial et relève la césure entre les spécialistes de droit de la famille qui affirment la nullité des contrats de mère porteuse, et les spécialistes du droit des contrats qui cherchent au contraire des moyens de valider ce type d'engagement.

En Irlande, il n'y a aucun texte, et il semble que la pratique soit vue avec une certaine faveur.[19] Les conflits éventuels seraient soumis aux juges qui statueraient selon le bien être des enfants.

À Taïwan, l'Artificial Reproduction Act (ARA) promulgué en 2007 n'a pas réglementé la gestation pour autrui[20] pour plusieurs raisons explicitées dans le

[13] Rapport établi par E. Steiner.

[14] Kentuky, Louisiane, Nebraska, New-York, Caroline du Nord et Washington.

[15] Floride, Névada, New Hamshire, Nouveau Mexique et Virginie

[16] V. cette liste dans la note 15 du rapport de C. Spivcack

[17] Par ex., dans l'Ontario, et la Colombie britannique.

[18] Rapport établi par D.-J. Park.

[19] Rapport établi par Dr. M. Harding.

[20] Rapport établi par S.-C.G. Kuo, qui a mis en annexe du rapport le texte de 2007.

rapport, et qui tiennent à la fois aux traditions familiales et au débat entre féministes. Cette absence de réglementation a semble-t-il favorisé un marché potentiel qui attire les sociétés étrangères, en particulier thaïlandaises, qui ont des filiales au Vietnam et au Cambodge et recherchent des parents intéressés par le service de mères porteuses. Un projet établi en 2009 propose un texte sur les mères de substitution, assez restrictif puisque seuls des couples mariés pourraient recourir aux services d'une mère porteuse qui devrait être de nationalité taïwanaise, âgée de 20 ans au moins et ayant déjà eu des enfants.

De même, la loi italienne de 2004 sur l'assistance à la procréation et les embryons, finalement adoptée après quinze années de discussion, n'a pas abordé la question de la gestation pour autrui, et le rapporteur écrit dans la première phrase de son rapport que la pratique est tolérée plutôt que permise.[21]

5.2 Les pays qui refusent la gestation pour autrui

Certains pays ont légiféré pour interdire la maternité pour autrui, le plus souvent lors de la mise en place de textes sur les PMA, d'autres n'ont pas légiféré mais les juges ont fondé l'interdiction sur les principes généraux du droit des contrats.

A. *Les pays qui ont élaboré des textes*

1. En Allemagne,[22] il résulte à la fois de la loi sur la protection de l'embryon et de la loi sur la médiation en matière d'adoption que la pratique des mères porteuses est interdite. Aucune distinction n'est faite selon que la mère porteuse a ou non fourni ses ovocytes pour la conception de l'enfant. Le contrat de mère porteuse est nul comme contraire aux bonnes mœurs et à l'ordre public (art. 134 et 138 du BGB).
2. Au Canada, la loi fédérale sur la procréation assistée de 2004 a interdit la rétribution à la fois des mères porteuses et des intermédiaires et punit le fait d'induire une femme de moins de 21 ans à devenir mère porteuse, ce qui laisse, nous l'avons déjà relevé, le champ libre aux contrats altruistes. De même aux Etats-Unis dans certains Etats déjà cités, des lois ont interdit les contrats rémunérés, ce qui laisse la place aux contrats dits altruistes.

   En revanche, dans une section du Code civil intitulée « De la filiation des enfants nés d'une procréation assistée », le Québec déclare nul de nullité absolue les contrats de mère porteuse, qu'ils soient à titre onéreux ou gratuit.[23] Le rapporteur mentionne que même sans texte spécifique, la convention qui porte atteinte à la dignité de la femme et de l'enfant aurait été interdite au nom de l'ordre public. L'effet de l'article 541 du Code civil est d'empêcher toute possibilité de demander l'exécution forcée d'un tel contrat devant un tribunal. Il n'y a toutefois aucune sanction civile ou pénale pour les intermédiaires. De même, le Code civil ne prévoit pas les conséquences d'un contrat clandestin au regard de l'établissement de la filiation de l'enfant, la filiation sera donc déterminée selon le droit commun, et éventuellement par les règles de l'adoption. De récentes décisions jurisprudentielles ont permis l'adoption d'enfants issus de la pratique de la maternité de substitution.
3. Au Danemark, la loi sur la procréation assistée (Artificial Fertilisation Act de 2006) ne contient pas de dispositions interdisant spécifiquement le contrat de mère porteuse, mais contient plusieurs dispositions qui conduisent à empêcher de tels arrangements.[24] Il en est de même dans la loi sur l'adoption de 2004.
4. En Espagne, l'article 10 de la loi 4/2006 sur les PMA[25] énonce que le contrat de gestation pour autrui est nul, et que la maternité est déterminée par la naissance de l'enfant.
5. Il en est de même en France.[26] Depuis, la loi bioéthique n°94-653 du 29 juillet 1994, la nullité du contrat figure dans le code civil à l'article 16–7, la réforme en 2006 des lois bioéthiques a maintenu le texte.
6. Il semble que Macao[27] ait également élaboré des textes qui figurent dans le code civil interdisant

[21] Rapport établi par Antonello Miranda

[22] Rapport établi par A. Spickhoff.

[23] Art. 541: « Toute convention par laquelle une femme s'engage à procréer et porter un enfant pour le compte d'autrui est nulle d'une nullité absolue ».

[24] Rapport établi par Ph.D. J.R. Hermann.

[25] Rapport établi par M. Perez Monge.

[26] Rapport établi par F. Monéger.

[27] Rapport établi par P. Nunes Correia.

ce type de contrat et prévoyant des sanctions civiles (article 1726 du code civil).

7. Au Portugal,[28] l'article 8 de la loi sur les PMA de 26 juillet 2006 interdit la gestation pour autrui, que le contrat soit à titre gratuit ou à titre onéreux, la mère étant toujours la femme qui porte l'enfant.
8. Enfin, la Serbie a également interdit le recours à des mères porteuses, dans l'article 56 d'une loi de 2009 relative au traitement des infertilités et à l'assistance à la procréation.[29] Le rapporteur se demande si une telle interdiction n'est pas contraire à la Constitution serbe de 2006 qui énonce dans son article 63, la liberté de procréer.[30] Est-ce que la liberté de procréer pour une femme, peut aller jusqu'à lui permettre de procréer pour un autre couple, telle est toutefois la question qu'il faut se poser dans les cas des maternités pour autrui.

B. *D'autres pays n'ont pas élaboré de textes spécifiques mais le principe de la nullité du contrat se trouve dans le code civil*
   1. Il en est par exemple ainsi en Argentine[31]: l'article 242 du Code civil précise que la maternité est établie par la preuve de la naissance et l'article 953 définit l'objet des actes juridiques. Un contrat qui porterait sur le corps humain, puis sur l'enfant né, serait donc nul.

      La jurisprudence française avait adopté la même approche, en se référant aux articles du Code civil sur les obligations avant que le législateur intervienne en 1994.[32]
   2. Il en est de même de la Pologne[33] où il est admis en doctrine que le contrat de mère porteuse serait nul car contraire à l'ordre public en application de l'article 58 §2 du Code civil polonais. De plus l'article 61 de ce code énonce que la mère est la femme qui donne naissance à l'enfant, ce qui ne permettrait pas à la femme qui a donné ses gamètes de faire reconnaître sa maternité.

C. Il est intéressant de comparer les différents droits quant *aux sanctions*. Alors que certains ne prévoient que des sanctions civiles, la nullité du contrat et l'impossibilité de le faire exécuter, ainsi le Québec, Macao, la Norvège, d'autres y ajoutent des sanctions pénales qui peuvent toucher à la fois les protagonistes (le couple d'intention et la mère porteuse) et les intermédiaires. C'est par exemple le cas de la France et de l'Espagne, dont les droits sur la question paraissent très proches, également de la Norvège et du Portugal. En Allemagne, les sanctions pénales ne concernent que les intermédiaires et les médecins.

D. De plus, après la naissance des enfants, les approches jurisprudentielles sont également très différentes. Des juges, au nom de l'intérêt de l'enfant, tentent de régler leur situation en recourant à l'adoption: la femme qui a porté l'enfant consentant à son adoption au profit des parents d'intention. Des exemples de ce type sont cités dans le rapport allemand, canadien, hollandais et polonais. La contribution belge mentionne un arrêt très récent de la Cour d'appel de Liège du 6 septembre 2010 qui a accepté de reconnaître les actes de naissance d'un enfant né en Californie. Les parents d'intention étaient deux hommes et la filiation paternelle a été admise à l'égard de l'un d'eux.

Il y a également beaucoup de jurisprudence citée dans le rapport américain, puisque, en l'absence de dispositions légales, ce sont finalement les juges qui vont régler le sort des contrats et répondre à la question de savoir si la femme qui a accouché peut être contrainte de laisser l'enfant aux parents d'intention et si elle peut recevoir ou non une compensation financière pour la grossesse et la naissance. Le rapporteur fait état de plusieurs théories utilisées par les juridictions américaines pour répondre à ces questions: rechercher l'intention des parties au moment du contrat, respecter les termes du contrat, faire prévaloir la génétique, faire prévaloir la gestation et enfin chercher l'intérêt supérieur de l'enfant.

Il y a au contraire des juges qui ont refusé le contournement des règles mises en place par le législateur. Un jugement de la Cour de Québec (chambre de la

[28] Rapport établi par G. de Oliveira.

[29] Rapport établi par Dr. O. Cvejic Jancic.

[30] « Toute personne doit librement décider si elle procrée ou non ».

[31] Rapport établi par A. Belluscio.

[32] Arrêt d'Assemblée plénière du 31 mai 1991 qui a énoncé que la convention par laquelle la femme s'engage, fût-ce à titre gratuit, à concevoir un enfant pour l'abandonner à sa naissance contrevient tant au principe d'ordre public de l'indisponibilité du corps humain qu'à celui de l'indisponibilité de l'état des personnes. L'arrêt vise les articles 6 (ordre public et bonnes mœurs) et 1128 (choses dans le commerce) du Code civil.

[33] Rapport établi par M. Nesterowicz.

jeunesse) du 6 janvier 2009[34] a « refusé d'entériner la pratique qui consiste à manipuler la finalité des règles du consentement spécial à l'adoption pour contourner les règles de filiation s'appliquant aux contrats de mère porteuse ». Deux autres jugements par la suite ont permis l'adoption au nom du meilleur intérêt de l'enfant.

La jurisprudence française est aussi en ce sens. La Cour de cassation a très clairement énoncé que « la maternité pour autrui, dont le caractère illicite se déduit des principes généraux du Code civil et aujourd'hui de son article 16–7, réalise un détournement de l'adoption »,[35] qui ne peut donc pas être prononcée au profit des parents d'intention. Seule la filiation paternelle de l'enfant peut être établie (lorsque le mari ou le concubin a donné son sperme) mais ensuite l'adoption de l'enfant par son épouse ou compagne sera refusée, même si elle est la mère génétique de l'enfant.

Une telle positon peut paraître extrêmement sévère par rapport aux solutions jurisprudentielles exposées dans les autres rapports.

5.3 Le Tourisme Procreatif

Nous n'avons pas utilisé cette expression dans le questionnaire, mais le tourisme procréatif était indirectement visé dans la question relative aux mères porteuses étrangères et aux enfants qui naissent à l'étranger. Comme plusieurs rapporteurs l'ont souligné, cette question pose de délicats problèmes de droit international privé.[36]

Lorsque les États ont mis en place des textes interdisant et sanctionnant pénalement la maternité pour autrui, la question se pose de savoir à quoi servent de tels textes, s'il suffit pour les couples demandeurs, de se rendre à l'étranger, dans un pays permissif pour revenir avec un enfant dont ils demandent ensuite une reconnaissance juridique.

Les pays qui ont légiféré ont d'ailleurs pris en compte le phénomène, comme c'est le cas du droit grec qui exige que la mère porteuse et la mère d'intention soient toutes deux domiciliées en Grèce, du droit israélien qui pose les mêmes exigences en limitant le champ d'application des textes au territoire d'Israël. Dans la proposition de loi déposée en France, devant le Sénat, il est exigé de même que le couple d'intention et la mère porteuse, soient tous domiciliés en France.

Il est également certain que les pays qui acceptent le recours à des mères porteuses, sont beaucoup plus enclins à reconnaître des situations créées à l'étranger, que ceux qui l'interdisent et qui invoquent alors leur ordre public pour refuser l'établissement de la filiation de l'enfant vis à vis des parents d'intention. De même, on ne peut s'empêcher de constater que les pays de *common law*, sont beaucoup plus « conciliants » que les pays de droit civil, les juges appréciant, cas après cas la situation des enfants sans opposer a priori des principes fondés sur l'ordre public et la fraude.

Le rapport anglais fait état d'une décision de 2008 où un couple d'anglais était allé en Ukraine où la gestation pour autrui contre rémunération est permise. Selon la loi anglaise, la mère porteuse était la mère, alors qu'elle ne l'était pas en droit ukrainien. Le juge Hedley de la High Court, prenant en considération l'intérêt de l'enfant décida, sur la demande des époux commanditaires de prononcer un « parental order » à leur profit, même si, comme l'a constaté le juge, l'ordre public anglais est opposé à la commercialisation de la gestation pour autrui.

En comparaison, la jurisprudence française, s'est montrée dans l'ensemble très stricte. Cette jurisprudence est exposée dans le rapport français. Avant comme après la réforme de 1994, les juges ont refusé le détournement des institutions et l'adoption de l'enfant par la mère d'intention que celle-ci soit génitrice ou non. Si la solution est certaine dans des hypothèses internes, la question est en suspend devant la Cour de cassation pour le cas d'enfants nés à l'étranger selon le droit étranger et ayant un acte d'état civil étranger. Un pourvoi actuellement pendant concerne par exemple un enfant né au Minnesota à la suite d'un contrat de mère porteuse et adopté par un couple de Français. La cour d'appel de Paris a refusé la transcription de l'acte de naissance de l'enfant sur les registres français au nom de l'ordre public international.[37]

La même cour d'appel a annulé la transcription sur les registres d'état civil français des actes de naissance établis en Californie et qui désignent la mère d'intention,

[34] Cité dans la note (2) du rapport.

[35] Cass. Civ. 1ère 9 déc. 2003.

[36] Problèmes évoqués par exemple dans les rapports allemand, canadien, espagnol, français, hollandais, et très développé dans la contribution belge centrée sur les questions de droit international privé.

[37] Cour d'appel de Paris, 26 févr.2009, 1ère chambre C.

comme mère des enfants (des jumelles). La cour précise que « l'absence de transcription n'a pas pour effet de priver les deux enfants de leur état civil américain et de remettre en cause le lien de filiation qui leur est reconnu à l'égard des époux M. par le droit californien ».[38]

Le rapport espagnol fait état d'un cas similaire mais qui concerne deux hommes mariés en Espagne et qui ont eu recours aux services d'une mère porteuse en Californie. Le droit espagnol, à la différence du droit français, permet que les couples de même sexe adoptent un enfant.[39] Le tribunal compétent en matière d'état civil a écarté l'article 10 de la loi espagnole qui interdit le contrat de mère porteuse puisque l'enfant est né en Californie et a permis la transcription des actes américains sur les actes d'état civil espagnol, invoquant l'article 3–1 de la Convention de New York sur les droits de l'enfant.[40]

Le rapporteur fait état des critiques à l'encontre d'une telle décision qui favorise une violation de l'article 10, il suffit en effet d'aller en Californie, ou dans n'importe quel pays qui accepte la maternité pour autrui pour contourner l'interdiction du droit espagnol.

De même, le rapport canadien cite une décision d'août 2009 de la chambre d'adoption du Québec qui concerne également un enfant né en Californie. Dans cette affaire, un couple gay a contracté avec une agence californienne pour retenir les services d'une mère porteuse qui a été inséminée avec le sperme d'un des hommes du couple. Elle a accouché au Québec. Le juge constate que de telles conventions sont légales en Californie. Ensuite, le nom de la mère porteuse apparaît dans le certificat de naissance québécois de l'enfant. Les parties n'ont pas essayé de camoufler leur projet. Enfin, le meilleur intérêt de l'enfant dicte la voie à suivre au juge: les circonstances de naissance de l'enfant ne peuvent être sources de discrimination (art. 523 C.c.Q.). Le juge considère que si le législateur avait voulu interdire le présent projet parental (un couple gay qui fait affaire avec une mère porteuse), il l'aurait clairement exprimé puisqu'il permet à des couples de même sexe d'adopter (art. 539.1 et 578.1 C.c.Q.).

5.4 Les projets en cours

Nous avions posé cette dernière question afin de voir la tendance des législations: vers la légalisation, vers l'interdiction ?

Les réponses sont assez décevantes. Comme nous l'avons relevé, les dispositions sur la maternité pour autrui, qu'il s'agisse de prohibition, ou d'acceptation, figurent dans les législations sur les PMA, ce sont des textes récents qui viennent d'être élaborés.

La question est actuellement posée en France où une réforme des lois bioéthiques de 2006, est en cours. Alors qu'une commission mise en place par le Sénat proposait de légiférer et d'accepter dans des conditions très limitées le contrat de mère porteuse, toutes les autres instances sont d'une opinion contraire, en particulier le Conseil d'État. La loi du 11 mars 2011 a maintenu l'interdiction de la gestation pour autrui.

Le rapporteur taïwanais fait état d'un projet en 2009 de réglementation de la maternité pour autrui. Le projet pose des conditions très restrictives, à la fois pour la femme qui porte l'enfant et pour les couples demandeurs. Le rapporteur doute qu'un tel texte puisse être adopté avant longtemps.

Quelle conclusion en tirer ?

Aucun des rapports reçus n'a présenté une législation très libérale de la gestation pour autrui. Nous n'avons pas eu de rapport venant d'Inde ou d'Ukraine, qui semblent être aujourd'hui deux des pays où un marché des mères porteuses est organisé, avec des agences faisant de la publicité sur internet. Tous les textes présentés dans ces rapports apparaissent très restrictifs. Ils entourent la gestation pour autrui de conditions extrêmement strictes, tant du côté de la femme qui va porter l'enfant, que de celui des parents d'intention, il est en par exemple ainsi en Israël, dernier rapport que nous ayons reçu. Nous avons donc une vue assez partielle des choses, des législations très restrictives qui donnent le plus souvent la préférence à la femme qui a porté l'enfant et qui ne peut pas recevoir de rémunération, où les parents d'intention doivent être des couples hétérosexuels. De telles législations ne vont pas empêcher, dans les pays qui les mettent en place, le

[38]Cour d'appel de Paris, 18 mars 2010, 1ère chambre pôle 1. La Cour de cassation a rejeté les pourvois dans des arrêts du 6 avril 2011. Elle considère que la cour d'appel avait, a bon droit, refusé de transcrire sur les registres français des actes d'état-civil étrangers établis à la suite de gestation pour autrui.

[39]Le droit français ouvre l'adoption aux couples mariés et aux personnes seules, mariées ou non.

[40]General Directorate for Registries and Public Notaries, Resolution of the 18th of February, 2009.

tourisme procréatif, et les juges continueront à être confrontés à la situation de ces enfants nés « hors normes », mais nés quand même.

Peut-on admettre un « marché » des mères porteuses et des enfants ? Jusqu'où peut aller le désir d'enfant ? La gestation pour autrui peut-elle être une technique de procréation médicalement assistée comme une autre, alors qu'une femme participe directement à la procréation ? Une législation prohibitive peut-elle avoir un impact sur la pratique des mères porteuses ? Autant de questions auxquelles il est très difficile de répondre.

Annexe

Questionnaire pour la gestation pour autrui

I. Est-ce que le droit de votre pays accepte la gestation pour autrui?

II. Si la réponse est affirmative, pourriez-vous me préciser le régime juridique:

1. Est-ce que la gestation pour autrui est réalisée sous le contrôle d'un juge?
2. Est-ce purement contractuel, contrat passé entre la mère porteuse et les parents?
3. Quels sont les droits de la femme qui porte l'enfant?
4. Quelle est la filiation de l'enfant:
   Est-ce que cet enfant a une mère (celle qui l'a porté ou celle qui a passé le contrat avec la mère porteuse) ou plusieurs mères (la femme qui a donné ses ovocytes, celle qui a porté l'enfant, celle qui a passé le contrat?)
   Est-ce que l'enfant fait l'objet d'une adoption?
5. Est-ce que la situation juridique est la même lorsque la mère qui porte l'enfant est étrangère et que l'enfant naît à l'étranger?

III. Si la réponse est négative, votre droit a-t-il prévu des sanctions spécifiques?

1. Sanctions civiles?
2. Sanctions pénales

IV. Est-ce que le droit de votre pays est en voie d'évolution?

Quels sont les projets en cours?

Maternity for another

I. Does the Law of your country accept Maternity for another?

II. If the answer is yes, what is the legal situation?

1. Is Maternity for another under the control of a judge?
2. Is it purely contractual?
3. What are the rights of the woman who carries the child?
4. What is the filiation of the baby?
   Who is the mother?
   Does the infant have one or several mothers?
   Is he adopted?
5. Is the situation the same when the carrying mother is a foreign person, or when the baby is born outside the Country?

III. If the answer is no, are they any sanctions?

1. Civil sanctions?
2. Criminal sanctions?

IV. Is your Law about to change?

In which way?

6 Same Sex Marriage[1]

Macarena Sáez

Same sex cohabitation is banned or unrecognized in most of the world.[2] Forty years ago, same sex couples were not legally accepted in any country. In the last 30 years, however, around 20% of countries have granted some rights to same sex couples, making them visible to society. While there are still countries that criminalize sexual relations among two consenting adults of the same sex,[3] other countries are allowing same sex couples to marry and form a family. Between those two poles, many countries have moved or are moving from total rejection of same sex relationships to acceptance of some sort. Countries that have decriminalized sexual relations between individuals of the same sex have shortly thereafter seen a rise in the public debate about formal recognition of same sex couples. At the center of this debate is the role of marriage. While some scholars claim that marriage is essentially heterosexual and the basis for societal structure, others consider the exclusion of same sex couples from marriage unfair discrimination. Both positions are represented in the reports received for this Congress.

6.1 There Are Marriages and There Are *Same Sex* Marriages

All legally sophisticated societies have regulated cohabitation. It has not been individuals themselves who have restricted their sexual encounters, but each community has restricted the types of relationships publicly accepted. Although modern legal systems have functioned on the basis of a separation between a public and a private realm, the way that the private realm has been shaped has been an entirely public affair. Countries not only have traditionally determined a set of legally valuable relationships, but they have also defined duties and rights for each party within a relationship. In this context, the paradigm of the legally valued relationship has been marriage.

Marriage may not mean the same thing in every country but there is a general understanding that certain features are present when we meet a married couple. Generally, it means that the couple went through some formal recognition of their relationship in a particular country and that their union produces legal effects in that country. There is, foremost, an assumption that spouses are legally recognized as family. Most likely, the couple's offspring is legally accepted as

[1] This article was originally published in the American University Journal of Gender, Social Policy & the Law. Macarena Saez, *General Report: Same-Sex Marriage, Same-Sex Cohabitation, and Same-Sex Families Around the World: Why "Same" is so Different*, 19 Am. U. J. Gender Soc. Pol'y & L. 1 (2011).

[2] This report is based on national reports submitted for the following countries: Australia, Austria, Belgium, Canada, Colombia, Croatia, Czech Republic, Denmark, France, Germany, Greece, Hungary, Ireland, Israel, Italy, Japan, New Zealand, Norway, Portugal, Romania, South Africa, Spain, Switzerland, Turkey, United Kingdom, United States, and Uruguay.

[3] The world was reminded again of this disparity after a gay couple in Malawi was sentenced to 14 years of prison for sodomy and indecency. Malawi's President Bingu wa Mutharika issued a pardon to the couple after a visit of UN President Ban Kimoon but made clear that he condemned the couple's behavior. *See* Barry Bearak, *Malawi President Pardons Gay Couple* (NewYork: Times, May 29, 2010), at http://www.nytimes.com/2010/05/30/world/africa/30malawi.html (last visited June 25, 2010).

M. Sáez (✉)
Fellow in International Legal Studies, American University, Washington College of Law, Washington, DC, USA
e-mail: msaez@wcl.american.edu

K.B. Brown and D.V. Snyder (eds.), *General Reports of the XVIIIth Congress of the International Academy of Comparative Law/Rapports Généraux du XVIIIème Congrès de l'Académie Internationale de Droit Comparé*,
DOI 10.1007/978-94-007-2354-2_6, © Springer Science+Business Media B.V. 2012

their own in the country where their union was registered and the couple has rights and obligations towards those children. When one meets a married couple it is safe to assume that some inheritance rights are also recognized. Until recently it was also assumed that marriage required one man and one or more women.[4] In the last 30 years, however, diversity of sex in marriage has become a contested issue.

The Netherlands was the first country to redefine marriage as a union of two individuals regardless of their sex. Instead of enacting a specific statute for same sex marriage, in 2001 the Netherlands amended the rules of marriage in their Civil Code stating that marriage could be contracted by two persons of different sex or of the same sex.[5] With this change, and other later changes, most rules on marriage apply equally to both opposite and same sex marriages.

Originally, however, there were differences between same and opposite sex marriage. Mainly, same sex couples did not have access to international adoptions. The Netherlands, however, amended its statutes in 2005 allowing same sex couples to adopt both locally and internationally.[6] Despite this equality of treatment, it would not be accurate to say that same sex couples can exercise their right to international adoptions just as heterosexual Dutch married couples do. There are still many countries that restrict adoption of their national children to heterosexual couples or single individuals, reducing the pool of countries from which same sex couples can look for adoption.[7]

A second difference referred to the marital presumption of paternity within marriage. In the case of same sex couples, no presumption can be made since it is biologically impossible for the partner of the same sex to be the biological parent of her spouse's child. Dutch legislation expressly established that the presumption of paternity did not operate in the case of same sex couples.[8] Although biologically correct, this exclusion meant that the only possibility of bi-parentage in the case of same sex marriages was through stepchild adoption. The Netherlands eventually changed its regulation in 2001.[9] The female spouse of a woman who gives birth to a child is recognized as the parent of that child, as long as there is no recognizable father, as it would be in the case of a sperm donor. This option, however, is not open to male partners who can only become parents of the same child through step child or joint adoption.[10]

This is the only differential treatment in the Netherlands between same and opposite sex married couples. All couples can also opt for a registered partnership and a married couple can decide to switch their relation to a registered partnership and vice versa.[11]

Belgium[12] became the second country to open marriage to same sex couples in June 2002. Professors Swennen and Leleu explain that the expansion of marriage to same sex couples was controversial and that there was great debate on the issue. The main argument against the expansion of marriage to same sex couples during the discussion of the bill was based on the interest of the State in protecting procreation, a feature exclusive to heterosexual marriages.[13] The central idea was that heterosexual marriage was worthy of special protection because of a natural link to procreation that same sex unions lacked. The compromise at

[4] Polygamy is rejected in many Western world countries and it triggers harsh criticism. Its opponents, however, do not take the position that polygamy is not marriage. The rejection comes out of equality concerns or incompatibility with a liberal state, among others. Adrienne D. Davis, Regulating Polygamy: Intimacy, Default Rules, and Bargaining for Equality, 110 Colulm. L. Rev. 1955 (2010).

[5] Nancy G. Maxwell, "Opening Civil Marriage to Same-Gender Couples: A Netherlands-United States Comparison," 18 Az. J. Int'l & Comp. L. 141 (2001).

[6] Ian Curry-Sumner, All's well that ends registered? The Substantive and Private International Law Aspects of Non-Marital Registered Relationships in Europe, European Family Law Series vol. 11 (Antwerp: Intersentia, 2003), 145–147.

[7] Denis Clifford, Frederick Hertz, and Emily Doskow, *A Legal Guide for Lesbian & Gay Couples*, 15th ed. (Reading: Addison-Wesley, 2010), 113.

[8] Katharina Boele-Woelki, "Registered Partnership and Same-Sex Marriage in The Netherlands," in *Legal Recognition of Same Sex Couples in Europe*, ed. Katharina Boele-Woelki and Angelika Fuchs, 44 (2003).

[9] Kees Waaldijk, Others May Follow: The Introduction of Marriage, Quasi-Marriage, and Semi-Marriage for Same-Sex Couples in European Countries, 38 New Eng. L. Rev 549, 576 (2004).

[10] *Id.*

[11] Wendy W. Schrama, Registered Partnership in the Netherlands, 13 Int'l J. L. Pol'y & Fam. 322 (1999); *see also* Holland South Local Reference Information, "Same-sex Marriage and Registered Partnerships in the Netherlands," *available at* http://hollandsouth.angloinfo.com/countries/holland/gaymarriage.asp (last visited November. 17, 2010).

[12] Frederik Swennen & Yves-Henri Leleu, *National Report: Belgium*, 19 Am. U. J. Gender Soc. Pol'y & L. 57 (2011) [hereinafter Belgium Report].

[13] *Id.* at 66.

the end was to open marriage to same sex couples but deprive it of affiliation effects, including adoption.[14] Advocates of same sex marriage may have been happy to see that marriage was open to same sex couples, but the new regulation was far from reaching equality between opposite and same sex couples. Some scholars described it as an "amputated marriage."[15]

In 2005 Belgium amended its laws to allow adoption by same sex married couples.[16] However, the presumption of paternity that the legal system grants to husbands is still not available to same sex married couples. Since surrogacy is not allowed in Belgium, same sex couples can only become parents through adoption.[17] Thus, the lack of automatic parental recognition for same sex couples remains the only difference between opposite and same sex marriage.

In 2005 Spain[18] became the third country to amend its legislation and open marriage to same sex couples.[19] Law 13/2005 amended the Spanish Civil Code to include in the definition of marriage that this was a union between two people of undefined sex.[20] The justification of the Act was grounded in the right to free development of personality and equality based on article 32 of the Spanish Constitution that states that men and women have the right to enter into marriage with full legal equality.[21]

Professors Martinez de Aguirre and De Pablo Contreras disagree with the direction taken by the Spanish legislature and argue that same sex marriage may be unconstitutional. They consider that a correct interpretation of Article 32 of the Spanish Constitution should not lead to the recognition of same sex marriage.[22] Among other arguments, they claim that a grammatical interpretation of this article depends on the Dictionary of the Spanish Royal Academy's definition of marriage as a long term union between a man and a woman.[23] The word "marriage", therefore, requires the presence of both sexes. Thus a same sex marriage would be a contradiction in terms. Professors Martinez de Aguirre and De Pablo Contreras argue that because the social importance of marriage derives from its heterosexual nature and its link to the procreation of new citizens, same sex unions could not have the same social meaning because they would be structurally incapable of reproduction.[24] In their opinion, the Spanish legislature has changed the constitutional meaning of marriage by changing the core of the concept of marriage. This argument was also used in 2005 to challenge the Act before the Constitutional Tribunal.[25] The decision of this action is still pending. Part III will discuss these arguments in more detail.

Spanish law grants full equality to same sex couples, including adoption without restrictions. In this sense, it goes further than the Dutch and Belgian laws. However, it also maintained the rules on paternity presumptions of the Civil Code. Thus, bi-parentage within same sex marriage can only be achieved through adoption.

Spanish law does not establish rules on marriage of a Spanish citizen with a foreign citizen. The interpretation has been, however, that a Spaniard can marry a foreigner of the same sex even if the partner's country does not recognize same sex marriage.[26]

Almost at the same time as Spain, Canada[27] opened marriage to same sex couples. The Civil Marriage Act, enacted by Federal Parliament, modified the common law definition of marriage by stating that "marriage, for civil purposes, is the lawful union of two persons to

[14] *Id.* at 67.

[15] *Id.* at 65, 70.

[16] *Id.* at 78.

[17] Professor Swennen explained to me that surrogacy was performed in Belgian hospitals, though there was no current regulation on this matter. Furthermore, some judges may not allow adoption of children born from a surrogate mother and international surrogacy is illegal.

[18] Carlos Martínez de Aguirre Aldaz & Pedro de Pablo Contreras, *National Report: Spain*, 19 Am. U. J. Gender Soc. Pol'y & L. 289 (2011) [hereinafter Spain Report].

[19] Law 13/2005, (Spain) (B.O.E., 2005, 157), *available at* http://www.boe.es/boe/dias/2005/07/02/pdfs/A23632-23634.pdf. (last visited June 25, 2010).

[20] Spain Report, *supra* note 18, at 291.

[21] *Id.*

[22] *Id.* at 292.

[23] *Id.* at 294.

[24] *Id.* at 295.

[25] For an account by the Spanish press, see Reuters, *El PP presenta recurso de inconstitucionalidad contra bodas gays*, Sep. 30, 2005, at http://www.20minutos.es/noticia/52467/0/ESPANA/GAYS/RECURSO/. The constitutionality claim can be found at http://www.felgtb.org/files/docs/7cef87591594.pdf (last visited June 27, 2010) (Spain).

[26] *See* Maria Ángeles Rodriguez Vásquez, "Los matrimonios entre personas del mismo sexo en el derecho internacional privado español," *Boletin Mexicano de Derecho Comparado [B.M.D.C]* 41 (2008): 194 (Mex.).

[27] Marie-France Bureau, *National Report: Canada*, 19 Am. U. J. Gender Soc. Pol'y & L. 85 (2011) [hereinafter Canada Report].

the exclusion of all others."[28] Professor Bureau states in her report that the pathway to same sex marriage began in the nineties, with several provinces granting rights to same sex couples that only married couples enjoyed before.[29] The Federal Parliament also took measures aimed at insuring equality for same-sex couples. As an example, Professor Bureau cites the *Loi visant à moderniser le régime d'avantages et d'obligations dans les Lois du Canada*, enacted in 2000.[30] This law amended 68 provisions to insure a uniform application of federal laws to unmarried same sex and opposite sex couples.[31]

Canada seems to have achieved complete equality between same sex and opposite sex marriages. Same sex couples can adopt just as opposite sex couples can. Regarding the paternity presumption within same sex marriage, the rules vary from province to province.[32] In Quebec, however, marriage entails a presumption of paternity that applies both to fathers and to the partner of the woman who gives birth.[33]

There is one restriction applicable to same-sex marriage that relates to freedom of religion. According to article 3 of the Civil Marriage Act, officials of religious groups can refuse to perform marriages that are not in accordance with their religious beliefs. In some provinces this prerogative has been utilized, albeit unsuccessfully, to give civil servants the right to refuse celebrating a civil marriage when it goes against their religious beliefs.[34]

South Africa[35] is an interesting case of legal reform triggered by courts. The Marriage Act of 1961 defined marriage as a union between a man and a woman, but in 2005 the Constitutional Court gave the legislature a year to amend the Marriage Act to include same sex marriage.[36] The reasoning was based on the values of human dignity, equality and freedom.[37] Parliament consequently enacted the Civil Union Act 17 of 2006.[38] Article 1 of the Act states that "unless the context otherwise indicates, 'civil union' means the voluntary union of two persons who are both 18 years of age or older, which is solemnised and registered by way of either a marriage or a civil partnership, in accordance with the procedures prescribed in this Act, to the exclusion, while it lasts, of all others." [39]

Instead of amending the Marriage Act, South Africa opted for the creation of a new set of rules through the Civil Union Act. There are four statutes in South Africa that regulate unions: The Marriage Act, the Customary Marriages Act 120 of 1998, the Civil Union Act, and the Recognition of Customary Marriages Act.[40] Accordingly, couples have several options for civil recognition of cohabitation:

1. Marriage according to the Marriage Act for heterosexual couples.
2. Marriage for same and opposite sex couples according to the Civil Union Act.
3. Civil Partnership for same and opposite sex couples according to the Civil Union Act.
4. Marriage in accordance with the customs and usages traditionally observed among the indigenous African peoples of South Africa, as regulated by the Recognition of Customary Marriages Act.

It is interesting that the political compromise between opposing views on the topic of same sex marriage has led South Africa to an array of alternatives, all of which seem to have the same effects. The same rights and duties, including the right to stepchild adoption and adoption in general, apply to married couples under the Marriage Act, married couples under the

[28] Lois Sur le Mariage Civil [Law on Civil Marriage], R.S.C., ch. 33, Article 2 (2005) (Can.) ("Le mariage est, sur le plan civil, l'union légitime de deux personnes, à l'exclusion de toute autre personne."), *available at* http://www.canlii.org/fr/ca/legis/lois/lc-2005-c-33/derniere/lc-2005-c-33.html (last visited October 22, 2010).

[29] Canada Report, *supra* note 27, at 88.

[30] *Id.* at 89.

[31] *Id.*

[32] The Greenwood Encyclopedia of LGBT Issues Worldwide 60 (Chuck Stewart ed., Greenwood Press 2010).

[33] *Id.*; *see also* Robert Leckey, 'Where the Parents are of the Same Sex': Quebec's Reforms to Filiation, 23 Int'l J. L. Pol'y & Fam. 62, 66 (2009).

[34] Canada Report, *supra* note 27, at 91.

[35] François du Toit, *National Report: South Africa*, 19 Am. U. J. Gender Soc. Pol'y & L. 277 (2011) [hereinafter South Africa Report].

[36] Fourie and Bonthuys v. Minister of Home Affairs, 2006 (3) BCLR 355 (CC) (S. Afr.), *available at* http://www.saflii.org/za/cases/ZACC/2005/19.pdf (last visited October 22, 2010).

[37] *Id.* at 47.

[38] Civil Union Act of 2006, BSRSA (S. Afr.), *available at* http://www.info.gov.za/view/DownloadFileAction?id=67843 (last visited June 28, 2010).

[39] *Id.* at art. 1.

[40] South Africa Report, *supra* note 35, at 281.

Civil Union Act, and registered unions under the Civil Union Act.[41]

Similar to Canada, the Civil Union Act allowed religious denominations to request their designated marriage officers to be exempt for conscientious reasons from registering civil unions of same sex couples.[42]

With regards to parenting, the rules on parental responsibilities are established in the Children's Act 38, 2005. According to this regulation it is possible for the spouse of the biological parent to enter into an agreement by which he or she assumes parental responsibilities of the child.[43] The rules apply equally to same sex and opposite sex couples.

Similar to South Africa, when Norway[44] amended its Marriage Act in 2008 to state that "two persons of opposite sex or of the same sex may contract marriage,"[45] it authorized "marriage solemnizers" to refuse to celebrate a marriage. Clerical solemnizers can refuse to solemnize a marriage if one of the parties is divorced and the previous spouse is still living or if the parties to the marriage are of the same sex.[46] As explained above, this was also the model for Canada and South Africa. This is the only difference between same and opposite sex marriage in Norway. Thus, the spouse of a woman giving birth obtains parental rights over the spouse's biological child at the moment of birth.

In 2009, Sweden amended its regulation and opened marriage to same sex couples.[47] Adoption was already permitted to same sex couples under a civil registered partnership.[48] A distinctive feature of the Swedish experience is that the Swedish church was in favor of the expansion of marriage. In most countries religious denominations have been a strong opposition to same sex marriage.[49]

Portugal,[50] Iceland,[51] and Argentina[52] are the last three countries allowing same sex marriage by passing laws in 2010.

Paragraph 1 of Article 36 of the Portuguese Constitution states that all persons have the right to form a family and marry in conditions of full equality.[53] The second paragraph states that the law will determine the requirements and effects of marriage.[54] These paragraphs were the grounds for a constitutional challenge of the definition of marriage set out by the Portuguese Civil Code. In a case in 2007 presented by two women whose marriage license was denied, the Constitutional Court affirmed that prohibition of same sex marriage was not unconstitutional but that neither was same sex marriage.[55] The court left the legislature to regulate this matter.[56] Three years after this decision, the Portuguese Congress passed Law 9 of 2010, redefining marriage as a contract between two people that intend to form a family through a community of

[41] *Id.* at 285.

[42] Civil Union Act of 2006 at art. 6.

[43] South Africa Report, *supra* note 35, at 285.

[44] Torstein Frantzen, *National Report: Norway*, 19 Am. U. J. Gender Soc. Pol'y & L. 273 (2011) [hereinafter Norway Report].

[45] Marriage Act, § 1 (Nor.) *translated in* http://www.regjeringen.no/en/doc/Laws/Acts/the-marriage-act.html?id=448401 (last visited October 22, 2010).

[46] Norway Report, *supra* note 44, at 274 (citing Marriage Act § 13).

[47] Ministry of Justice (Swed.), Fact Sheet, *Gender Neutral Marriage and Marriage Ceremonies*, May 2009, *available at* http://www.sweden.gov.se/content/1/c6/12/55/84/ff702a1a.pdf (last visited November 10, 2010).

[48] Yvonne C. L. Lee, "Don't Ever Take a Fence Down Until You Know the Reason It Was Put up" – Singapore Communitarianism and the Case for Conserving 377A," *Singapore Journal of Legal Studies* 347 n. 161 (2008) (Sing.).

[49] For media coverage of the Swedish church support of religious same sex marriage, see *Same sex marriage suggested by board of Church of Sweden*, Stockholm News (Swed.), June 13, 2009, *available at* http://www.stockholmnews.com/more.aspx?NID=3407 (last visited October 22, 2010).

[50] The Report on Portugal was prepared by Professor Jorge Duarte Pinheiro [hereinafter Portugal Report].

[51] In June 10, 2010, the Icelandic Parliament unanimously approved a law that allows marriage between same sex partners. *See* Michelle Garcia, *Iceland Legalizes Gay Marriage*, *available at* http://www.advocate.com/News/Daily_News/2010/06/11/Iceland_Legalizes_Gay_Marriage/ (last visited October 22, 2010).

[52] On July 10, 2010, the Senate approved the bill with amendments to the Argentina Civil Code to redefine marriage as a union between two individuals, regardless of their sex. *See* Juan Forero, *Gay rights activists celebrate Argentine vote for same-sex marriage*, Washington Post, July 16, 2010, *available at* http://www.washingtonpost.com/wp-dyn/content/article/2010/07/15/AR2010071501119.html (last visited October 22, 2010).

[53] Portugal Report, *supra* note 50, at 2; *see also* VII Revisão Constitucional [Seventh Revised Constitution] art. 36 (2005), *available at* http://www.parlamento.pt/Legislacao/Paginas/ConstituicaoRepublicaPortuguesa.aspx (last visited October 22, 2010).

[54] *Id.*

[55] Acórdão No. 359/2009, Tribunal Constitucional [Constitutional Court], *available at* http://www.tribunalconstitucional.pt/tc/acordaos/20090359.html (last visited October 22, 2010).

[56] *Id.*

life.[57]Under the new statute all references to husband or wife became applicable to spouses in a gender neutral voice.[58] The Portuguese legislature followed the original model of the Netherlands and Belgium allowing adoption to married couples of different sex only.[59]

Recently, Argentina became the first Latin American country to allow same sex marriage. Article 42 of the new Statute states:

> All references to the institution of marriage established in our legal system will be understood to apply to marriages between two people of the same sex as well as two people of different sex. Members of families from a marriage of two people of the same sex, as well as those of a marriage by two people of different sex will have the same rights and obligations. No regulation of the Argentine legal system shall be interpreted or applied in a way that may limit, restrict, exclude or suppress the exercise or enjoyment of the same rights and obligations to marriages formed by two people of the same sex as well as the one formed by two people of different sex.[60]

In addition to the countries already mentioned, there are countries with federal systems where the regulation of families is a state or provincial matter. Mexico and the United States[61] are notably in this position because parts of their territory have redefined marriage to include same sex couples. The debate over same sex marriage in the United States has been intense both at the legislative and adjudicative level. In his report, Professor Meyer gives an account of how Hawaii started a trend of political and legal fights that is far from being over.[62] This discussion repeated in many states and it reached the federal government with the passing of the Defense Marriage Act (DOMA).[63] Currently, Connecticut, Iowa, Massachusetts, New Hampshire, Vermont, and the District of Columbia issue marriage licenses to same sex couples. [64] Also, New York, Rhode Island, California and Maryland recognize as valid same sex marriages performed in other jurisdictions.[65] In all of them, marriage is treated as a neutral institution where no differences are made between same sex and opposite sex marriages. The only difference of treatment has been reported in Iowa, where hospital staff refused to include in the birth certificate of a child the female spouse of the biological mother. As of November 2011, a law suit is pending on this issue.[66]

Although states may have autonomy to define marriage, the federal benefits granted to married couples are too numerous for marriage to be considered an exclusively state matter.[67] The lack of federal recognition of same sex marriage, therefore, has an impact on the daily lives of same sex couples. There have been several challenges to DOMA. The latest decisions are

---

[57] Portugal Report, *supra* note 50, at 3; *see also* Diário da República, 1ª Série A – N 105–31 de Maio de 2010, Página 1853. Lei n. 9/2010, art. 2 ("…Casamento é o contrato celebrado entre duas pessoas que pretendem constituir família mediante uma plena comunhão de vida, nos termos das disposições deste Código."), *available at* http://www.pgdlisboa.pt/pgdl/leis/lei_mostra_articulado.php?nid=1249&tabela=leis (last visited November 8, 2010).

[58] Diário da República, 1ª Série A – N 105–31 de Maio de 2010, Página 1853. Lei n. 9/2010, art. 2.

[59] Lei N 9/2010 art. 3 (Port.), *available at* http://dre.pt/pdfgratis/2010/05/10500.pdf (last visited October 22, 2010).

[60] Unofficial translation by the author. The original text in Spanish states: "Art. 42. Aplicación. Todas las referencias a la institución del matrimonio que contiene nuestro ordenamiento jurídico se entenderán aplicables tanto al matrimonio constituido por dos personas del mismo sexo como al constituido por dos personas de distinto sexo. Los integrantes de las familias cuyo origen sea un matrimonio constituido por dos personas del mismo sexo, así como un matrimonio constituido por dos personas de distinto sexo, tendrán los mismos derechos y obligaciones. Ninguna norma del ordenamiento jurídico argentino podrá ser interpretada ni aplicada en el sentido de limitar, restringir, excluir o suprimir el ejercicio o goce de los mismos derechos y obligaciones, tanto al matrimonio constituido por personas del mismo sexo como al formado por dos personas de distinto sexo" *available at* http://www.infobae.com/download/55/0345567.pdf.

[61] Report on the United States prepared by Professor David M. Meyer.

[62] *Id.* at 6.

[63] Defense of Marriage Act, Pub. L. No. 104–199, 110 Stat. 2419 (1996).

[64] For a detailed account of the current legislation in each state of the United States, see Sonia Bychkov Green, Currency of Love: Customary International Law and the Battle for Same-Sex Marriage in the United States, Appendix I (The John Marshall Law School, Working Paper Series, March 1, 2010), *available at* http://ssrn.com/abstract=1562234.

[65] *Id.*

[66] Lynda Waddington, *Same-sex couple sues state for right to appear on daughter's birth certificate*, May 13, 2010, http://iowaindependent.com/33946/same-sex-couple-sues-state-for-right-to-appear-on-daughters-birth-certificate (last visited October 22, 2010).

[67] In the U.S. there are more than one thousand benefits granted by the federal government to married couples. Additional State benefits vary and extend the difference of treatment. *See* Barbara J. Cox, *"The Little Project" From Alternative Families to Domestic Partnerships to Same-Sex Marriage*, 15 Wis. Women's L. J. 90 (2000) (citing Office of the General Counsel, General Accounting Office, Report to

from July 8, 2010 by a U.S. District Judge in Massachusetts. In *Massachusetts v. U.S. Department of Health Human Services* and *Gill v. Office of Personnel Management*, Judge Touro ruled that important parts of the DOMA were unconstitutional for violating equal protection principles:

> In the wake of DOMA, it is only sexual orientation that differentiates a married couple entitled to federal marriage-based benefits from one not so entitled. And this court can conceive of no way in which such a difference might be relevant to the provision of the benefits at issue. By premising eligibility for these benefits on marital status in the first instance, the federal government signals to this court that the relevant distinction to be drawn is between married individuals and unmarried individuals. To further divide the class of married individuals into those with spouses of the same sex and those with spouses of the opposite sex is to create a distinction without meaning. And where, as here, 'there is no reason to believe that the disadvantaged class is different, in *relevant* respects' [citing *Romer*, 571 U.S. at 635] from a similarly situated class, this court may conclude that it is only irrational prejudice that motivates the challenged classification. As irrational prejudice plainly *never* constitutes a legitimate government interest, this court must hold that Sect. 3 of DOMA as applied to Plaintiffs violates the equal protection principles embodied in the Fifth Amendment to the United States Constitution.[68]

Also, in September of 2009 members of the House of Representatives introduced the Respect for Marriage Act to repeal the Defense of Marriage Act.[69] As of November 2011, the bill is still under consideration.

The Federal District of Mexico passed a law in December of 2009 amending its State Civil Code. Marriage is now a union between two individuals and all rights and obligations recognized to married couples apply to same sex married couples.[70] The amendment also changed the rule on concubinarian unions to reflect that these unions can now include two female or two male concubines.[71] The Attorney General of Mexico challenged the constitutionality of the statute on the basis that the constitutional mandate is to protect the family defined as a heterosexual and bi-parental institution. He also challenged the rules on adoption because with the expansion of marriage to same sex couples, the statute opened adoption to same sex couples.[72] The Supreme Court upheld the statute, allowing same sex marriage in the Federal District and stating that the Federal Constitution of Mexico provides a vague concept of family. This interpretation leaves the door open to other states to amend their marriage regulations too.[73] The first step towards same sex marriage in the Federal District was the Law of Cohabitation Society (*Ley de Sociedad de Convivencia*) passed in 2006. This statute defined cohabitation society as a legal act formed when two adult individuals of different or same sex, and legally fitted, establish a common household, with the intent to stay together and assist each other.[74]

6.1.1 "Same" Is Different

Most countries reach recognition of same sex marriage after a gradual recognition of same sex couples that starts with the granting of partial material rights. Recognition of marriage as the symbol of full equality is the culmination of these processes. Married same sex couples, however, have not automatically been granted all rights attached to heterosexual marriage. The first and most common difference between opposite and same sex marriage relates to marriage as

---

the Honorable Henry J. Hyde, Chairman, Committee on the Judiciary, House of Representatives, GAO/OCG 97–16 (1997), *available at* www.gao.gov/archive/1997/og97016.pdf (last visited November 8, 2010)).

[68] Gill v. Off. of Personnel Mgmt., 699 F. Supp. 2d 374 (D. Mass. 2010).

[69] H.R. Res. 3567, 111th Cong. (2009), *available at* http://frwebgate.access.gpo.gov/cgi-bin/getdoc.cgi?dbname=111_cong_bills&docid=f:h3567ih.txt.pdf (last visited October 22, 2010).

[70] Gaceta Oficial del Distrito Federal, Dec. 29, 2009, *available at* http://www.metrobus.df.gob.mx/transparencia/documentos/marco%20normativo/decreto%20codigo%20procedimientos%20civil.pdf (Article 146 of the Civil Code for the Federal District states: "Matrimonio es la unión libre de dos personas para realizar la comunidad de vida, en donde ambos se procuran respeto, igualdad y ayuda mutua. Debe celebrarse ante el Juez del Registro Civil y con las formalidades que estipule el presente código.").

[71] *Id.* at art. 291 (stating that "female concubines and male concubines ("concubinas y concubinos") have reciprocal rights and obligations). The former article 291 stated that the female concubine and her male concubine ("la concubina y el concubinario") had reciprocal rights and obligations. http://201.159.134.50/Estatal/DISTRITO%20FEDERAL/Codigos/DFCOD01.pdf (last visited October 18, 2011)

[72] *Id.* at art. 395.

[73] The Supreme Court decision has not been published yet.

[74] Decreto de Ley de Sociedad de Convivencia para el Distrito Federal [Law of Cohabitation Society for the Federal District] art. 2, 136 Gaceta Oficial del Distrito Federal, 16 de Noviembre de 2006 (Mex.).

the gateway to forming a legally recognized family. Countries that were willing to allow marriage between two people of the same sex were not ready to recognize same sex couples as a legitimate parental unit.[75] Many countries have indeed opted for a regime of registered partnership with the specific purpose of distinguishing on one hand an institution that recognizes a union between two individuals, and on the other, an institution that transcends those two individuals and creates legally recognized family ties.

The second common difference between same sex and opposite sex marriages is the treatment of these two institutions by private international law. A country cannot guarantee that marriages performed under its laws will be recognized by other countries. It can, however, regulate what marriages performed abroad, under foreign law, will be recognized in its own territory. It can also restrict the conditions under which foreign nationals can marry within its borders. The Netherlands, for instance, imposed more restrictive rules for same sex than for opposite sex couples on eligibility to marry in Dutch territory.[76] Denmark had done the same with its Registered Partnership Act.[77] Same sex marriage creates a problem in international private law, just as polygamy, surrogacy, or other controversial practices that clash with national regulations do.[78]

The third common difference relates to marriage as a symbol. A point of debate has been whether same sex marriages should be recognized or solemnized by the same officers and through the same procedures than opposite sex marriages. In those countries where civil marriage is achieved through the recognition of a religious ceremony, the desire to protect freedom of religion and allow religious ministers to refuse the solemnization of same sex marriage is understandable. This protection, of course, should not be used as an excuse to create a policy of *de facto* discrimination by leaving same sex couples without any available officer to perform a marriage ceremony. In countries where civil marriage is a strictly secular process, the decision to separate officers and ceremonies does not have any grounds other than a political compromise. Inclusion of same sex couples into the mainstream institution of marriage has come, most of the time, with some type of relinquishing of the symbolism relating to marriage. In some cases, religious ministers are not available. In other cases the officer called to register same sex marriage is different than the one who celebrate heterosexual marriages.

6.2 From Marriage-Like Treatment to Full Invisibility

The redefinition of marriage as a union between two individuals regardless of their sex is a twenty first Century phenomenon. Regulation of same sex cohabitation, instead, is a trend that started earlier, towards the end of the twentieth century. Through legislative changes and judicial review, many countries have granted same sex couples benefits and rights traditionally linked to marriage. Although there are more countries that do not recognize any rights to same sex couples than countries that do, the number of countries affording some form of recognition increases every day.

Countries that recognize the existence of same sex couples and regulate some components of their unions can be divided into three groups:

(a) Full equality of rights between same sex and opposite sex couples but no access to the symbol of marriage.
(b) Recognition of same sex couples as partners with ample recognition of material rights and a narrow access to building family ties.
(c) Recognition of same sex couples as a lawful association between two individuals, narrow or no access to family ties, and limited material rights.

[75] *See* Belgium Report, *supra* note 12, at 70–71; *see also* Portugal Report, *supra* note 50, at 2.

[76] Waaldijk, *supra* note 9, at 579.

[77] Act on Registered Partnership N. 372 was enacted on June 7, 1989 with § 2.2 stating that "A partnership may only be registered provided that (1) one of the parties is habitually resident in Denmark and a Danish citizen, or (2) both parties have been habitually resident in Denmark the 2 years immediately preceding the registration." *See* Boele-Woelki, *supra* note 8, at 215.

[78] For an account on international private law and same sex couples, see Gerard-René de Groot, "Private International Law Aspects Relating to Homosexual Couples," *Electronic Journal of Comparative Law* 13 (2007). Regarding the recognition of Dutch same sex marriage in other countries, see Michael Bogdan, "Some Reflections on the Treatment of Dutch Same-Sex Marriages in Europe and in International Private Law," in *Intercontinental cooperation Through Private International Private Law: Essays in memory of Peter E. Nygh*, ed. Tania Einhorn and Kurt Siehr (The Hague: T.M.C. Asser Press, 2004), 25–35.

6.2.1 Separate but Equal

The United Kingdom[79] is among the few countries in the first category, with three registered partnerships that cover the three legal systems that make up the United Kingdom. Professor Kenneth Norrie states that the Civil Partnership Act of 2004 created "a statutory institution for the legal recognition and regulation of same-sex relationships, which is distinct from but equivalent to the existing institution of marriage...."[80]

Requirements to enter into a marriage and into a civil partnership in the United Kingdom are very similar.[81] The grounds for dissolving a civil partnership are also the same for both institutions, with the exception of adultery.[82] This cause for divorce is the basis for an interesting perspective raised by Professor Norrie regarding the real nature of the difference of treatment between marriage and civil partnerships. In his opinion, whereas marriage is a sexed and religious institution, civil partnership is a de-sexed and secular institution.[83] He doesn't deny that sexual relations are assumed between the parties in a civil partnership but he claims that, legally speaking, the sexual character of the relationship is irrelevant. In fact, the only grounds for divorce that do not apply to partnership dissolution are adultery and sexual impotency.[84]

With regards to the secular nature of registered partnerships, Professor Norrie states that registration of a partnership is exclusively in the hands of civil servants. Marriage, instead, can be performed by civil servants or by religious officers vested with such powers by each recognized religion.[85]

The European Court of Human Rights (ECHR) has divided the distinctions between same and opposite sex couples between material, parental, and other consequences.[86] An analysis of the differences between same sex and opposite sex couples in the United Kingdom leads to the conclusion that it treats marriage and registered partnership equally with regards to material and parental consequences. The distinctions come within the umbrella of what the ECHR called "other consequences."[87] These other consequences are closely tied to the idea of symbolism, which is what Professor Norrie links to religion.[88] Without providing same sex marriage, the United Kingdom gives better treatment to same sex couples than what the Netherlands originally did and Portugal has recently granted. The United Kingdom also treats same sex couples married abroad as civil partners.[89]

In 1989 Denmark[90] was the first country to legally recognize same sex couples through a registered partnership regime open only to same sex couples.[91] Although the original text left most parental rights outside the scope of the act, today the differences between marriage and registered partnership are almost unnoticeable. Since 2009 same sex registered couples have the right to stepchild adoption with certain restrictions.[92] Also, all women have access to assisted reproductive technologies regardless of their sexual orientation and marital status.[93] This change, the Danish report points out, was framed as a health issue rather than a family law one.[94] It had, nevertheless, the

---

[79] Kenneth Norrie, *National Report: United Kingdom*, 19 Am. U. J. Gender Soc. Pol'y & L. 329 (2011) [hereinafter UK Report].

[80] *Id.* at 333; *see also* Civil Partnership Act, 2004, c. 33, *available at* http://www.legislation.gov.uk/ukpga/2004/33.

[81] UK Report, *supra* note 79, at 333.

[82] *Id.*

[83] *Id.* at 334.

[84] *Id.*; *see also* Civil Partnership Act, 2004, c. 33, Part II, Ch. 2.

[85] UK Report, *supra* note 79, at 335.

[86] Schalk and Kopf v. Austria, Application no. 30141/04, Eur. Ct. H.R. (June 24, 2010), *available at* http://cmiskp.echr.coe.int/tkp197/view.asp?item=1&portal=hbkm&action=html&highlight=Schalk%20|%20Kopf&sessionid=63568865&skin=hudoc-en.

[87] *Id.* at 31.

[88] UK Report, *supra* note 79, at 338.

[89] *Id.* at 339–40; *see also* Civil Partnership Act, 2004, c. 33, Part V, Ch. 2.

[90] Annette Kronborg & Christina Jeppesen, *National Report: Denmark*, 19 Am. U. J. Gender Soc. Pol'y & L. 113 (2011) [hereinafter Denmark Report].

[91] Professors Kronborg and Jeppesen point out that although Greenland and the Faroe islands are part of Denmark, they have their own legal systems. Greenland has a registered partnership since 1996 but the Faroe Islands does not have any regulations for same sex couples. *See* Cece Cox, "To Have and To Hold--or Not: The Influence of the Christian Right on Gay Marriage Laws in the Netherlands, Canada, and the United States," 4 *Law and Sexuality* 1, 7 (2005).

[92] Denmark Report, *supra* note 90, at 118.

[93] *Id.* at 118–19.

[94] *Id.* at 119.

effect of diminishing the difference between marriage and registered partnership as the gateway to family formation. Finally, in July 2010, Denmark passed an act that allows same sex couples to adopt under the same conditions than married couples.[95]

Today, the main difference between married couples and registered partnerships lies in what Professor Norrie called the secular feature of same sex unions as opposed to the religious meaning of marriage. Couples concluding a marriage in Denmark can choose to do so in a religious or in a civil ceremony. Registration of a partnership, however, is a strictly secular act.[96]

6.2.2 The Meaning of the Word "Almost:" I Can Treat You as a Spouse but Not as a Parent

Several of the national reports referred to the situation of same sex couples as "almost equal" to married couples. This is the case of the reports from Australia, Austria, and New Zealand. In all these countries same sex couples enjoy property rights, social security, inheritance rights, among others. Their recognition, however, falls short in the area of Family Law, where access to adoption or assisted reproductive technologies is usually limited or not granted to same sex couples. Considering that adoption is the main option that same sex couples have to become parents, the fact that a country grants them all sorts of rights but denies them the access to becoming a family can make the word "almost" lose part of its meaning.

The case of Australia[97] presents an interesting dichotomy. While some Australian jurisdictions continued to criminalize homosexual conduct between males until the 1990s, other states and territories had already begun to legally recognize and protect same sex relationships in specific contexts.[98] Hopes for the introduction of same sex marriage were dashed when the Commonwealth in 2004 amended the Marriage Act of 1961 to define marriage as "the union of a man and a woman to the exclusion of all others, voluntarily entered for life."[99] This statutory definition closed the door to potential attempts to expand the meaning of marriage in the courts. Australian law at present, therefore, seems to firmly reject the notion of same sex marriage. Instead, Australia has used its existing *de facto* legislation to give same sex couples legal protection.[100] Similar to the Canadian approach, the direction taken by Australia has been towards the "equalization" of non married and married couples. At the beginning, this assimilation of married and unmarried couples was aimed at heterosexual couples only. Today, all states and territories have legislation that recognizes and protects *de facto* couples regardless of the sex of the partners.[101] Also, in 2008 the Commonwealth passed comprehensive legislation to equalize treatment of opposite sex as well as same sex *de facto* couples in federal legislation.[102]

What constitutes a *de facto* couple varies slightly from state to state. Dr Witzleb gives a detailed account of these differences, including whether a certain time of cohabitation is required.[103] In states with registered relationships, these couples enjoy full legal protection from the date of registration.[104] Australia has gone above and beyond the Canadian model where unmarried couples have to prove cohabitation for some specific periods of time to enjoy the rights and benefits provided by law.[105]

Adoption is the only area where same sex couples are still treated differently than heterosexual couples. Only the Australian Capital Territory and Western Australia allow same sex couples to apply for joint adoption, and Tasmania allows stepchild adoption.[106] Queensland passed a new adoption statute in 2009 allowing opposite sex *de facto* couples to adopt but continuing to withhold this option from same sex

---

[95] *Id.*; *see also* Lov 2010-05-26 nr. 537 (Den.), *available at* https://www.retsinformation.dk/Forms/R0710.aspx?id=10291 (last visited November 9, 2010).

[96] Denmark Report, *supra* note 90, at 120.

[97] Report on Australia prepared by Dr Normann Witzleb [hereinafter Australia Report]. I want to thank Dr. Witzleb for his edits to this part of the work.

[98] *Id.* at 9.

[99] Marriage Act, 1961, § 5(1) (Austl.), *available at* http://www.comlaw.gov.au/ComLaw/Legislation/ActCompilation1.nsf/0/05431B4AAF75F0F5CA2576E8000392EA?OpenDocument.

[100] Australia Report, *supra* note 97, at 8–10.

[101] *Id.* at 9.

[102] *Id.*

[103] *Id.* at 12.

[104] *Id.* at 11.

[105] Nancy Polikoff, Beyond (Straight and Gay) Marriage 116 (Beacon Press 2008).

[106] Australia Report, *supra* note 97, at 25.

couples.[107] While adoption rights continue to be a sticking point in most jurisdictions, concerns about same sex parenting are not pervasive. This is evidenced by the fact that assisted reproductive technology is available to women regardless of their sexual orientation.[108] Furthermore, Dr Witzleb points out that in most of Australia the same sex partner of a woman who has undergone a fertilization procedure with her partner's consent is legally recognized as the parent of her partner's child.[109]

In New Zealand same sex couples do not have access to marriage but they are recognized through the Civil Union Act of 2004, open to both same and opposite sex couples.[110] The statute allows couples to transition from marriage to civil union and vice versa without the need of a prior divorce.[111] The most important differences between marriage and civil unions are in the area of parental rights. Couples registered in a civil union cannot jointly adopt and do not get parental rights over the child of the other partner.[112] The distinction is not between same sex and opposite sex couples but mainly between married couples and registered civil unions.[113] At the same time, however, New Zealand has followed a similar direction to that of Australia by assimilating married and *de facto* couples. Unmarried couples, regardless of their sex, get recognition of property rights, domestic violence, tax and social security.[114] There are, however, conflicting lower court decisions as to whether "spouses" include unmarried partners too.[115]

Germany follows a model similar to that of Denmark by providing a parallel institution exclusive to same sex couples with limitations in the area of adoption.[116] Dr. Jens Scherpe notes that the Regime of Life Partnership (ELp) enacted in 2001 was meant to be the "functional equivalent" of marriage.[117] But there are still, as he states, important differences between ELp and marriage.

Article 6 of the German Constitution protects marriage and family.[118] The German Constitutional Court (BVerfG) has interpreted this article to protect marriage between a man and a woman.[119] It has also indicated that the special protection afforded to marriage only prevented the legislature from creating a legal regime that was more favorable than marriage but it did not prevent the legislature from providing similar rights to other institutions.[120] As stated in the press release in English for case 1BvR 1164/07:

> For the authority of giving favourable treatment to marriage does not give rise to a requirement contained in Article 6.1 GG to disadvantage other ways of life in comparison to marriage. It cannot be justified constitutionally to derive from the special protection of marriage a rule that such partnerships are to be structured in a way distant from marriage and to be given lesser rights.[121]

Given the jurisprudential development towards recognition of marriage as a heterosexual constitutionally protected institution, Germany opted for the construction of a parallel institution with no cross references to marriage. The legislature wanted to give a clear sign that ELp was a different institution than marriage. Despite this intention, there are more similarities than differences between ELp and marriage.

Similar to the situation of other countries reviewed here, the authority who can register a life partnership in Germany was also a point of debate. The LPartG did not establish the authority who could register life partnerships because this is a state regulated matter.[122] More conservative states left the registration of ELp to public notaries or local authorities and kept civil registrars as the exclusive authority to provide marriage licenses.[123]

---

[107] Adoption Act, 2009, Queensl. Stat. 2009 (Austl.), *available at* http://www.legislation.qld.gov.au/LEGISLTN/ACTS/2009/09AC029.pdf.

[108] Australia Report, *supra* note 97, at 24–25.

[109] *Id.* at 24.

[110] Kenneth Norrie, *National Report: New Zealand*, 19 Am. U. J. Gender Soc. Pol'y & L. 265 (2011) [hereinafter New Zealand Report].

[111] *Id.* at 266–67, 268.

[112] *Id.* at 267–268; *see also* Yuval Merin, *Equality for Same-Sex Couples: The legal recognition of gay partnerships in Europe and the United States* (Chicago: University of Chicago Press 2002), 175.

[113] New Zealand Report, *supra* note 110, at 267.

[114] *Id.* at 268.

[115] *Id.*

[116] Dr. Jens M. Scherpe, *National Report: Germany*, 19 Am. U. J. Gender Soc. Pol'y & L. 151, 154 (2011) [hereinafter Germany Report]; *see also* de Groot, *supra* note 78, at 6.

[117] Germany Report, *supra* note 116, at 154.

[118] *Id.* at 153.

[119] *Id.* (citing Bundesverfassungsgericht [Constitutional Court], July 7, 2009, 1BvR 1164/07 BVerfGE (Ger.)).

[120] Germany Report, *supra* note 116, at 153.

[121] Federal Constitutional Court (Ger.), Press Office, Press Release No. 121/2009, Oct. 22, 2009, *available at* http://www.bverfg.de/pressemitteilungen/bvg09-121en.html.

[122] Germany Report, *supra* note 116, at 170

[123] *Id.*

Substantive differences between marriage and ELp are less noticeable today than when ELp was first enacted. The ELp even establishes kinship between a life partner and the family of the other partner.[124] But as with most countries that have established parallel regimes for same sex couples, the main restriction to civil unions under ELp is parenting. Originally, Germany forbade all access to parenting for couples of the same sex. Today, joint adoption is still unavailable but stepchild adoption is allowed.[125] Same sex couples, however, do not have access to assisted reproductive technologies, including surrogacy, completely forbidden in Germany.[126]

Formally, Austria[127] follows the original registered partnership models of other European countries such as Denmark, the Netherlands, and Norway. Substantively, nonetheless, there are more similarities with the situation of same sex couples in Australia or in Germany: many rights have been granted but access to parenting is restricted.

In 2003 the Austrian Constitutional Court affirmed that the legal definition of marriage as a union between a man and a woman was not unconstitutional and it did not violate the right to family set forth in article 12 of the European Convention of Human Rights.[128] The Court, however, recognized that same sex couples were protected by the right to privacy and should be granted the same rights given to heterosexual unmarried couples.[129] Cohabitation, therefore, should be treated equally regardless of the sex of the parties. On January 1st 2010 the new Registered Partnership Act ("Eingetragene Partnerschaft-Gesetz," EPG) entered into force, open only to same sex couples.[130] According to Professor Aichberger-Beig, "[t]he EPG does not contain a general reference to marriage law. (…) However, the provisions of the Act to a great extent are taken almost verbatim from marriage law. In essence, although under a different name, the Act introduces marriage for same-sex couples."[131]

Some of the differences between marriage and registered partnership in Austria, as it has been the common trend in different countries, relate to treating partnership as a family unit. In addition to keeping parental rights as an exclusive prerogative of marriage, the EPG regulates the change of name after registration only as a "last name." In the case of marriage, instead, the PStG refers to the new last name as the "family name."[132] This is another example of the relevancy of symbolism. Married couples become a unit called family. Registered partners are instead two people associated through a legal contract with limited effects. Consistent with this rationale, registered partners do not have access to joint or stepchild adoption.[133] Assisted reproductive technologies are open to unmarried couples but only of different sex.[134]

The PStG did not replicate marriage regulations that dealt with gender stereotypes. The Austrian legislature assumed that partnership was based on equality between parties and did not consider necessary to regulate in this area. Marriage, instead, is regulated as to insure equality between parties.[135]

In the same tradition of Germany, the Constitution of Switzerland[136] protects the right to marry and to have a family. Here, too, the courts have interpreted marriage as the union between a man and a woman.[137] And just like in Germany and Austria, the legal recognition of same sex couples has come through the enactment in 2004 of a registered partnership statute applicable only to same sex couples (LPart).[138] The statute entered into effect in 2007.[139]

[124] *Id.* at 173.

[125] de Groot, *supra* note 78.

[126] Germany Report, *supra* note 116, at 173; *see also* John A Robertson, Reproductive Technology in Germany and the United States: An Essay in comparative Law and Bioethics, 43 Colum. J. Transnat'l L. 189, 210 (2004).

[127] Dr. Daphne Aichberger-Beig, "Registered Partnership for Same-Sex Couples," *in Austrian Law – An International Perspective*, ed. Bea Verschraegen (Wien: Jan Sramek Verlag, 2010) [hereinafter Austria Report].

[128] *Schalk and Kopf*, *supra* note 86, reaffirms this idea.

[129] Aichberger-Beig, *supra* note 127, at 65.

[130] *Id.* at 68, (citing Eingetragene Partnerschaft-Gesetz [Registered Partnership Act], *available at* http://www.gesetze-im-internet.de/bundesrecht/lpartg/gesamt.pdf).

[131] *Id.*

[132] *Id.* at 71.

[133] *Id.* at 73.

[134] *Id.*

[135] *Id.* at 72–73.

[136] Annelot Peters, *National Report: Switzerland*, 19 Am. U. J. Gender Soc. Pol'y & L. 309 (2011) [hereinafter Switzerland Report].

[137] *Id.* at 311 (citing ATF 119 II 264, 3 mars 1993 (Switz.)).

[138] Loi fédérale sur le partenariat enregistré entre personnes du même sexe [Federal law on the partnership recorded between people of the same sex] (Switz.), *available at* http://www.admin.ch/ch/f/ff/2004/2935.pdf.

[139] Switzerland Report, *supra* note 136, at 311.

The LPart assimilates registered partnership and marriage in many areas: inheritance rights, taxes, hospital visitation, property rights, social security, pensions, immigration and citizenship, tenancy, employment law, and civil and criminal procedure, among others.[140] Registered partnerships have restricted access to parenting and to the symbols of marriage. For example, witnesses are required for the conclusion of a marriage but not for the registration of a partnership.[141] In the case of marriage the parties can adopt a common last name but this is not possible through the LPart.[142] In spite of these differences, registration of both marriages and partnerships take place before the same officers and are recorded in the same registries.[143]

Hungary follows a similar regime to that of Germany and Switzerland, having established a registered civil union regime open only to same sex couples in 2009.[144] The Hungarian Constitution protects the institutions of marriage and the family and, just as the German Constitutional Court, the Hungarian Constitutional Court has concluded that marriage in Hungary means the union between a man and a woman.[145]

In 2007, there was an attempt to pass a registered civil union law very similar to marriage, open to both same and opposite sex couples.[146] The Constitutional Court, however, declared the bill unconstitutional because it was providing opposite sex couples with an institution alternative to marriage. At the same time, it stated that a registered partnership for same sex couples would be constitutional.[147] In 2009, following the recommendations of the Constitutional Court a new registered civil union law was passed, granting to same sex couples rights similar to those enjoyed by married couples.[148] As it has usually been the case in other countries, including Germany, the law excluded same sex partners from adoption and assisted reproductive technologies.[149] In addition to the typical restrictions to access parenting, the law kept some symbols of marriage from registered civil unions. Similar to Austria, the registered civil union did not allow a name change along with registration.[150] This is clearly a matter of symbolism rather than a substantive rights problem because registered civil partners can follow the traditional name change procedure open to anyone in Hungary.

Israel[151] could be viewed as one of the countries that recognizes same sex couples and grants them almost all rights that married couples enjoy. At the same time, it could also be viewed as a country with full invisibility of same sex couples. Although it is true that Israel does not legally recognize same sex couples, this is due to the fact that marriage and divorce are matters of personal law, regulated, therefore, by the religion of the parties or, in the case of foreign nationals, their nationality.[152] Israel is more of a hybrid situation than a case of full invisibility or full recognition. On one hand, marriage is left to religions recognized in Israel. On the other hand, civil courts have jurisdiction to hear cases of interfaith marriages or of people with no religion at all.[153] In the latter case, marriage must take place abroad since no secular marriage institution exists in the country.[154] Religion is not a matter of personal choice; it depends on the rules of each religion, regardless of personal preferences. Since no religion in Israel currently allows same sex marriage, there can be no conclusion of same sex marriages in the country.

Same sex couples and also people who cannot get married due to their lack of religion or because both individuals belong to different religions may decide to conclude their unions outside Israel. Marriages registered abroad are included in the Israeli Population Registry.[155] Although this Registry formally serves only as a statistic gathering center, the reality is that it

[140] A detailed account can be found in the Austria Report, *supra* note 127, at 5–9.

[141] Switzerland Report, *supra* note 136, at 312.

[142] *Id.* at 315.

[143] *Id.* at 312.

[144] András L. Pap & Zsolt Körtvélyesi, *National Report: Hungary*, 19 Am. U. J. Gender Soc. Pol'y & L. 211, 212 (2011) [hereinafter Hungary Report].

[145] *Id.* at 215.

[146] *Id.* at 212.

[147] *Id.* at 213.

[148] *Id.* at 212.

[149] *Id.* at 212.

[150] *Id.*

[151] Report on Israel prepared by Dr. Ayelet Blecher-Prigat [hereinafter Israel Report].

[152] *Id.* at 1–2.

[153] *Id.*

[154] *Id.* at 6.

[155] *Id.* at 6–7.

has been used as a signifier of married marital status. A Supreme Court decision in 2006 mandated the registration of five same sex couples married in Canada.[156] The decision stated that registration was not indicative of the validity of a marriage in Israel.[157] These couples, nonetheless, have access to the same benefits that all married couples enjoy in Israel.[158]

Another factor that makes Israel unique is that parallel to the lack of civil marriage, it has gradually been granting rights, both through legislation and through case law, to unmarried couples or "reputed spouses," along the lines of Australia or Canada.[159] Requirements to be considered reputed spouses vary from one statute to another but in general the definition is very flexible.[160] Some statutes do not even require a minimum time of cohabitation or monogamy.[161] Each specific statute or benefit can have a different scope of application.[162] In many cases, determination of the couples that fall under the category of reputed spouses is a matter of interpretation. For example, there are differing decisions as to whether same sex couples fall within this concept for the purpose of having access to family law courts, and if the Domestic Violence Act applies to them or not.[163] It seems to be uncontested, however, that same sex couples have access to stepchild and joint adoption, and to assisted reproductive technologies.[164] Surrogacy, on the contrary, is open only to heterosexual couples.[165]

6.2.3 Separate and Unequal: Partial Recognition of Same Sex Couples

France, Colombia, Uruguay, and Croatia are among countries that have amended their systems to give formal recognition to same sex couples albeit providing them with limited rights. In these countries, not only are parental rights and the symbolic nature of marriage denied to same sex couples, but they also enjoy limited access to property, succession, and pension rights, to name a few.

In France[166] same and opposite sex couples can sign a *Pacte Civil de Solidarité* (PACS) that provide rights and obligations similar but not equal to marriage.[167] Marriage is an exclusively heterosexual institution.[168] In 2007 the *Cour de Casassion*, reviewing a case of marriage annulment performed in Bordeaux between two individuals of the same sex, affirmed that marriage in France could only exist between a man and a woman.[169] The definition of marriage in France, however, does not expressly require a man and a woman.[170] Professor Hughes Fulchiron gives historical reasons for this omission. It was so evident that marriage could only take place between a man and a woman that there was no need for this requirement to be expressed in the *Code Civil*.[171] In the Preamble of the Civil Code of 1804, however, Portalis did state that marriage was the union between a man and a woman.[172]

Professor Fulchiron makes a distinction between marriage and partnership, with the former statute covering the family and the latter statute covering the couple.[173] This distinction would explain why the rights granted to couples registered under the PACS, unlike marriage, pertain exclusively to the relationship

[156] H.J., 3045/05 Ben-Ari v. The Director of the Population Administration in the Ministry of the Interior (2006) (Isr.) (unpublished decision), *translated in* http://www.scribd.com/doc/22564351/Ben-Ari-v-%D7%92%D7%A8%D7%A1%D7%94-%D7%A1%D7%95%D7%A4%D7%99%D7%AA-Director-of-Population-Administration-official-translation (last visited October 22, 2010).

[157] Israel Report, *supra* note 151, at 8.

[158] *Id.*

[159] *Id.* at 17.

[160] *Id.* at 18.

[161] *Id.* at 19.

[162] *See* Talia Einhorn, "Same-sex family unions in Israel law," *Utrecht L. Rev.* 4, no. 2 (2008): 225.

[163] Israel Report, *supra* note 151, at 19–20.

[164] *Id.* at 24–25.

[165] *Id.* at 25.

[166] Hugues Fulchiron, *National Report: France*, 19 Am. U. J. Gender Soc. Pol'y & L. 123 (2011) [hereinafter France Report].

[167] *Id.* at 124.

[168] *Id.* at 125, 126.

[169] Stéphane X. v. Procureur Général, Cass. 1e civ. (Fr.), March 3, 2007, No. 511, *available at* http://www.courdecassation.fr/publications_cour_26/rapport_annuel_36/rapport_2007_2640/quatrieme_partie_jurisprudence_cour_2653/droit_personnes_famille_2655/mariage_11311.html.

[170] France Report, *supra* note 166, at 126.

[171] *Id.*

[172] *Id.* at 126 n.14.

[173] *Id.* at 132.

between the parties to the PACS and do not create kinship with the partner's family.[174] It would also explain the limited options that PACS partners would have regarding parenting; joint and stepchild adoption are open only to married couples.[175] Assisted reproductive technologies are open to married, PACS, and unmarried couples but only of the opposite sex.[176] Although stepchild adoption is not open to PACS couples, the Court of Cassation has been moving in the direction of slowly allowing a person to adopt the biological child of their same sex partner.[177]

Even if PACS provides legal rights to the couple, it falls short of recognizing rights that affect the couple only. For example, under PACS the foreign partner of a French national cannot apply for the French nationality.[178] The PACS does not grant intestate succession rights nor does it contemplate the option for the partners to change their last name.[179] It provides with a very narrow framework of rights for non married couples, clearly less comprehensive than many equivalent regulations of other European countries.

Colombia[180] seems to follow the same rationale as Australia. Instead of granting rights to same sex couples by giving them access to marriage or registered partnerships, it started to assimilate married and unmarried heterosexual couples. Today in Colombia there is no registered partnership or equivalent regime open to same sex couples. Marriage, as stated in the Constitution, is an exclusively heterosexual institution.[181] In 1990, however, Colombia formally granted some rights to *de facto* heterosexual couples by enacting Law 54. [182] The statute provided several property rights to *de facto* marital unions when cohabitation had been continuous and monogamous for a minimum period of 2 years.[183] This regulation opened the door for the Colombian Constitutional Court to rule in 2007 that any rights granted to *de facto* opposite sex couples under Law 54 had to be granted to same sex couples as well.[184] Following this decision, same sex and opposite sex couples that meet certain legal standards are considered *de facto* marital unions.[185]

Although Law 54 referred only to patrimonial rights of *de facto* marital unions, today these couples enjoy additional rights in the areas of health care, pensions, citizenship, and criminal law, among others.[186] In spite of this assimilation between same and opposite sex unions, there are still several areas where distinctions are legally permitted. These are especially apparent with regards to parenting. Consequently, only heterosexual *de facto* marital unions are allowed to adopt children.[187] There is a pending case before the Constitutional Court challenging the constitutionality of this exclusion but there is precedent from 2001 against granting adoption to same sex couples.[188]

In the late eighties, Uruguay[189] also started regulating heterosexual unmarried couples. Different statutes recognized the existence of the "concubine" and granted rights such as compensation in cases of work related accidents, stepchild adoption, succession rights in special circumstances, and the right to make medical decisions on behalf of the partner, among others.[190]

---

[174] *Id.*

[175] *Id.* at 125.

[176] Nancy D. Polikoff, Recognizing Partners But Not Parents/ Recognizing Parents But Not Partners: Gay and Lesbian Family Law in Europe and the United States, 17 N.Y.L. Sch. J. Hum. Rts. 711, 726 (2000) (citing L-94-653 of 1994, The Bioethics Act (Fr.)).

[177] *See* decision N. 703 of July 8, 2010 (09–12.623), Cass. 1e civ. (Fr.), *available at* http://www.courdecassation.fr/jurisprudence_2/premiere_chambre_civile_568/703_8_16930.html.

[178] Aaron Xavier Fellmeth, State Regulation of Sexuality in International Human Rights Law and Theory, 50 Wm. & Mary L. Rev. 797, 859 (2008).

[179] *Id.*

[180] Daniel Bonilla & Natalia Ramirez, *National Report: Colombia*, 19 Am. U. J. Gender Soc. Pol'y & L. 97 (2011) [hereinafter Colombia Report].

[181] *Id.* at 100.

[182] Law 54 of 1990, art. 1 (Colom.), *available at* http://www.dmsjuridica.com/CODIGOS/LEGISLACION/LEYES/L0054de1990.htm (last visited October 22, 2010).

[183] Colombia Report, *supra* note 180, at 103.

[184] Sentencia C-075/07, Corte Constitucional [Constitutional Court] (2007), *available at* http://www.corteconstitucional.gov.co/relatoria/2007/C-075-07.htm (last visited October 22, 2010).

[185] *Id.* at 103.

[186] *Id.* at 104–109.

[187] *Id.*

[188] *Id.* (citing Sentencia C-814-01, Corte Consitucional [Constitutional Court]), *available at* http://www.corteconstitucional.gov.co/relatoria/2001/C-814-01.htm (last visited October 22, 2010)).

[189] Walter Howard, *National Report: Uruguay*, 19 Am. U. J. Gender Soc. Pol'y & L. 343 (2011) [hereinafter Uruguay Report].

[190] *Id.* at 362–64.

Professor Walter Howard notes that the doctrinal development of *de facto* couples in Uruguay can be traced to 1934 with a decision that recognized that cohabitation had consequences that the legal system could not deny.[191] This recognition of cohabitation, however, did not, and does not amount to the assimilation of married and unmarried couples as in Canada or Australia.

In 2007 Uruguay passed a law to regulate "concubinarian unions." According to this statute, an unmarried couple no matter their sex, identity, and sexual orientation or option, who has continuously lived together in a sexual, exclusive, monogamous, stable and permanent relationship for at least 5 years, will be considered a "concubinarian union."[192] The definition also names restrictions on kinship, age, and state of mind.[193] The effect of the statute is the recognition of same sex unions that until then had been absolutely invisible to the Uruguayan legal system.

De facto couples who fit the definition of a concubinarian union can access a set of rights established in the 2007 statute, mostly on property and succession rights.[194] Couples that do not meet the statute's requirement can still obtain limited rights recognized to unmarried couples prior to the establishment of this Act.[195]

Among its provisions, the 2007 statute provides a more egalitarian regime to claim for alimony after the dissolution of the concubinarian union than the one provided in the case of marriage dissolution. In the latter, a judge can reduce or eliminate the right to alimony of the partner held responsible for the dissolution of his marriage.[196] The concubine's right to alimony, however, is not affected by her or his responsibility in the dissolution of the union.[197]

The concubinarian union regime in many respects mirrors marriage regulation but in most areas it gives limited versions of the rights that married couples enjoy. Although stepchild adoption was provided to unmarried couples, joint adoption may be restricted to heterosexual couples only.[198] The statute that regulates adoption does not expressly ban same sex concubine unions from adoption. Professor Howard, however, thinks that the spirit of the law was to restrict joint adoption to heterosexual couples only.[199]

Croatia,[200] with its 2003 Same Sex Union Statute, is also one of several countries that provide some formal recognition to same sex couples.[201] Article 61 of the Croatian Constitution states that "[t]he family shall enjoy special protection of the State; Marriage and legal relations in marriage, common-law marriage and families shall be regulated by law."[202] This text seems to indicate that different types of families, even those created outside legal marriage, enjoy constitutional protection. Marriage, however, is still confined to heterosexual couples.[203]

According to the Same Sex Union Statute, a same sex union is a "life union of two persons of the same sex (partners) who are not married, who are not in a heterosexual or another same-sex union, and which union lasts for at least 3 years and it is based on the principles of equality of the partners, of mutual respect and help, as well as on emotional ties between the partners."[204] The statue does not require registration of the union and it is limited to the regulation of "financial support between the partners, property rights and the right to mutual help."[205] The Statute applies only to same sex unions but unmarried heterosexual couples can access the same benefits through the Croatian Family Law Act.[206] Same sex couples, therefore, are recognized as an entity that does not fit within family law, regulated outside the Croatian Family Law Act.

[191] Uruguay Report (Spanish version) at 13 (on file with autor) (citing L.J.U., T. V, case 1129, and Salvagno Campos, *La sociedad de hecho en el concubinato more uxorio,* Revista de Derecho, Jurisprudencia y Administración, T. XXXVIII, 221 (1940)).

[192] Uruguay Report, *supra* note 189, at 348; *see also* Law N. 18.246 of Dec. 27, 2007, (Uru.), *available at* http://www.parlamento.gub.uy/leyes/AccesoTextoLey.asp?Ley=18246&Anchor=.

[193] Law N. 18.246 of Dec. 27, 2007, (Uru.) at art 2.

[194] Uruguay Report, *supra* note 189, at 359.

[195] *Id.* at 349.

[196] *Id.* at 350.

[197] *Id.*

[198] *Id.* at 363.

[199] *Id.*

[200] Report on Croatia prepared by Professor Nenad Hlača [hereinafter Croatia Report].

[201] Law on Same Sex Civil Unions, OG RC 116/2003 (2003) (Croat.), *translated in* http://iglhrc.org/cgi-bin/iowa/article/takeaction/resourcecenter/583.html (last visited October 22, 2010).

[202] Constitution of Croatia, art. 61.

[203] Croatia Report, *supra* note 200, at 2.

[204] *Id.* at 3 (citing Article 1 of the OG RC 116/2003).

[205] Croatia Report, *supra* note 200, at 4.

[206] *Id.*

The Czech Republic[207] also provides recognition for same sex couples, with a registered partnership statute of 2006 applicable exclusively to same sex couples. Section 1(1) of this statute states that "[a] registered partnership is a permanent association of two individuals of the same sex established in the manner prescribed by this law."[208] The requirements to enter into a registered partnership are similar to those established for marriage.[209] The benefits, however, are more limited than those for marriage. There are no inheritance rights or joint ownership comparable to those of married couples, there is no creation of kinship but just recognition that for certain matters the partners can act on behalf of each other.[210]

Until recently Ireland[211] did not provide any formal recognition to same sex couples. The Irish Constitution protects marriage using a strong choice of words: "The State pledges itself to guard with special care the institution of Marriage, on which the Family is founded, and to protect it against attack."[212] This protection, although it does not expressly refer to heterosexual marriage, has been interpreted by the Irish High Court as requiring a man and a woman for a legal marriage.[213] In July 2010 the President of Ireland signed the Civil Partnership and Certain Rights and Obligations of Cohabitants Act 2010.[214] The new statute applies only to same sex couples and it provides them with several rights such as household protection, succession, pension, and property rights, among others.[215]

In Ireland there is no formal recognition of families formed by same sex couples and the Supreme Court of Ireland has recently affirmed that "there is no institution of a *de facto* family in Ireland."[216] The decision, however, may be interpreted as a step towards recognition of same sex families since it denied custody to a biological father who was the sperm donor for a lesbian couple.[217] The decision stated that the child lived in a "loving and caring situation for the child."[218]

6.2.4 The Absolute Divide Between Law and Practice: The Invisibility of Same Sex Couples

A majority of countries do not give any formal recognition to same sex couples. A more in depth review of each country, however, may reveal more visibility for same sex couples than what statutes cover. Greece, Italy, and Romania are among the European Union countries that provide no rights to same sex couples. The Council of Europe and the European Court of Human Rights encourage the recognition of same sex couples.[219] These countries, therefore, should soon move towards some type of recognition of same sex couples, even if with limited rights.

In Italy[220] the Constitution states that "the Republic recognizes the rights of the family as a natural society based on marriage."[221] There have been several attempts to recognize same sex couples through registered partnerships regimes but all have failed.[222] Although there is no

[207] Report on the Czech Republic prepared by Professor Michaela Zuklínová [hereinafter Czech Report]. I would like to thank Mr. Peter Polasek for his assistance translating into English relevant parts of Czech's legislation.

[208] Zákon č 115/2006 Sb. (Czech Rep.), *available at* http://www.epravo.cz/top/zakony/sbirka-zakonu/zakon-ze-dne-26-ledna-2006-o-registrovanem-partnerstvi-a-o-zmene-nekterych-souvisejicich-zakonu-15257.html (last visited October 22, 2010).

[209] Czech Report, *supra* note 207, at 1.

[210] *Id.* at 1–2.

[211] Dr. Aisling Parkes, *National Report: Ireland*, 19 Am. U. J. Gender Soc. Pol'y & L. 221 (2011) [hereinafter Ireland Report].

[212] Constitution of the Republic of Ireland, art. 41 (3.1).

[213] Zappone and Gilligan v. Revenue Commissioners and Others, [2008] 2 IR 417.

[214] Civil Partnership Bill, 2009 (Bill No. 44b/2009) (Ir.), *available at* http://www.oireachtas.ie/documents/bills28/bills/2009/4409/b44b09d.pdf (last visited July 16, 2010).

[215] *Id.*

[216] Ireland Report, *supra* note 211, at 223 (citing McD v. L and Anor. [2009] I.E.S.C. 81 (12th October, 2009) (S.C.)), *available at* http://www.supremecourt.ie/Judgments.nsf/60f9f366f10958d1802572ba003d3f45/a6dc1f1e70fed71380257688003laacb?OpenDocument.

[217] Ireland Report, *supra* note 211, at 223.

[218] McD. -v- L. & anor at 81(i) (The Court granted visitation rights to the father.).

[219] *See, e.g.*, Council Resolution A3-0028/94, Resolution on equal rights for homosexuals and lesbians in the EC, 1994 O.J. (C 61), Council Resolution 1728, Discrimination on the basis of sexual orientation and gender identity, April 29, 2010; *Schalk & Kopf v. Austria*, *supra* note 86 (recognizing that same sex couples enjoy family life).

[220] Virginia Zambrano, *National Report: Italy*, 19 Am. U. J. Gender Soc. Pol'y & L. 225 (2011) [hereinafter Italy Report].

[221] Constituzione [Constitution] art. 29 (Italy) ("La Repubblica riconosce i diritti della famiglia come società naturale fondata sul matrimonio. Il matrimonio è ordinato sull'eguaglianza morale e giuridica dei coniugi, con i limiti stabiliti dalla legge a garanzia dell'unità familiare.")

[222] Italy Report, *supra* note 220, at 235.

general recognition of same sex unions, Professor Virginia Zambrano refers to some regulations that grant limited protection as "family" to same sex partners. For instance, articles 4 and 5 of Reg. N. 223/1989 define "family" for the exclusive purpose of gathering vital statistics.[223] Article 4 refers to "famiglia anagrafica," a concept that would also include same sex couples. This definition has "served the purpose of creating special Registries (Registri delle unioni civili) aimed at conferring to cohabitants some administrative rights, especially social housing benefits," and also benefits for inmates, hospital visitations and medical decisions, among others.[224]

Italy follows the civil law tradition where judges are not bound by precedent. This feature is apparent in the many contradictory decisions about the meaning of the anti- discrimination clause set forth in Article 3 of the Italian Constitution.[225] For some judges, this clause is the basis for allowing same sex unions in Italy. For others, instead, there is no constitutional mandate to allow such recognition. As an example of a change in these decisions, Professor Zambrano refers to the decision of a court in Turin where judges held that "there is no reason to distinguish between marriage and same-sex unions, because both have in common the idea of living together."[226] Regardless of different courts' opinions, the view of the Constitutional Court is that marriage is a union between a man and a woman. In a ruling of April 14, 2010, the Court stated that it was a prerogative of the legislature to define marriage and dismissed arguments from three gay couples against decisions of a Venice court and the Turin Court of Appeals that had also interpreted marriage as an exclusively heterosexual institution.[227]

[223] *Id.* at 233.

[224] *Id.*

[225] Constituzione [Constitution] art. 3(Italy) ("Tutti i cittadini hanno pari dignità sociale e sono eguali davanti alla legge, senza distinzione di sesso, di razza, di lingua, di religione, di opinioni politiche, di condizioni personali e sociali. È compito della Repubblica rimuovere gli ostacoli di ordine economico e sociale, che, limitando di fatto la libertà e l'eguaglianza dei cittadini, impediscono il pieno sviluppo della persona umana e l'effettiva partecipazione di tutti i lavoratori all'organizzazione politica, economica e sociale del Paese.").

[226] Italy Report, *supra* note 220, at 234 (citing Corte d'assise Turin, sect. I, ord., 19th November 1999 (Italy)).

[227] *Matrimoni gay, no della Consulta ai ricorsi "Materia di competenza del Parlamento,"* La Republicca (It.), April 14, 2010, *available at* http://www.repubblica.it/cronaca/2010/04/14/news/consulta_matrimoni_gay-3344318/ (last visited Nov. 20, 2010).

Professor Zambrano states that protection of same sex couples has come through contractual law.[228] It is common for same sex couples to enter into contractual obligations to distribute property, care, and make medical decisions on behalf of each other.[229] There are, however, many areas where contracts cannot replace the lack of public regulation. This is especially true with regards to Family Law but it also applies to other areas where no recognition of the partner as a next kin relegates that person to a secondary role in terms of inheritance rights, pensions, and tax, to name a few.[230]

Invisibility of same sex couples may be more evident in Greece[231] where its Parliament enacted in 2008 a "Free Unions Pact" that only applies to unmarried heterosexual partners.[232] The Greek Constitution protects the family using a language that could be interpreted as disconnected from marriage: "Article 21. 1. Family, being the cornerstone of the preservation and advancement of the Nation, as well as marriage, motherhood and childhood, shall be under the protection of the State." [233] According to Professor Alexander Fessas, this means that the Constitution protects all types of families and not only those originated in marriage. Additionally, the Constitution protects marriage without defining it and there seems to be no consensus as to what the constitutional protection of marriage covers.[234] One opinion is that the Constitution protects marriage as the Greek society understands it, including the requirement of opposite sex among the parties. If this was the case, Congress could not redefine marriage to include same sex couples. A different interpretation indicates that marriage can be viewed as a concept "detached of social perceptions,"[235] in constant evolution. According to this interpretation, same sex marriage could enjoy constitutional protection. For now, Greece maintains the traditional interpretation of marriage.

[228] Italy Report, *supra* note 220, at 236.

[229] *Id.*

[230] *Id.* at 237.

[231] Alexander G. Fessas, *National Report: Greece*, 19 Am. U. J. Gender Soc. Pol'y & L. 187 (2011) [hereinafter Greece Report].

[232] *Id.* at 200.

[233] *Id.* at 191.

[234] *Id.* at 191–92.

[235] *Id* at 192.

In Romania[236] there is no civil union or registered partnership for opposite or same sex couples but unions registered in other European countries are recognized as such for purposes of entry to Romania.[237] Thus, while same sex partners are recognized as family members of a European citizen for immigration purposes, no rights derived from such unions are recognized in the country.

Outside the European Union, but with a special interest in joining it, Turkey[238] is also among those countries that deny all rights to same sex couples. The Turkish Constitution does not contain express mention to marriage. It states that family is the foundation of Turkish society but it does not provide any specific definition.[239] Legally, marriage requires the union of a man and a woman and no other form of civil union exists for opposite or same sex couples.[240] There seems to be no cases of same sex couples legally challenging Turkish law. There are, however, several decisions of the Court of Cassation that rule out granting rights to heterosexual unmarried couples because such arrangements would be against morality.[241]

Despite this strict interpretation of the concept of marriage, Professors Başoğlu and Yasan believe that contract law may be used to regulate property between same sex couples and that Turkish torts law allows the surviving same sex partner to recover damages in case of wrongful death of her partner, as long as she can prove that the deceased was her financial provider.[242]

Turkey's official stance on same sex couples is very clear. Gay marriage and same sex families have expressly been rejected by the Turkish government.

Last, a very interesting case of legal invisibility of same sex couples is that of Japan.[243] The Japanese Constitution defines marriage as between a man and a woman by stating that "[m]arriage shall be based only on the mutual consent of both sexes and it shall be maintained through co-operation with the equal rights of husband and wife as a basis."[244] Same sex marriage, therefore, would likely require a constitutional amendment. Regulation of same sex couples through registered partnership would be constitutionally acceptable but according to Professor Teiko Tamaki there have been no attempts, nor even discussions, about recognizing rights to same sex couples.[245]

As with other countries where there is no recognition of rights for same sex couples, gay and lesbian individuals have found alternative means to regulate their relationships. Just as in Italy, Japanese same sex couples can enter into a contractual relationship through a notary deed.[246] Another practice is to use adoption of one partner by the other partner to create kinship and family rights and obligations.[247] As Professor Tamaki states, "[o]nce the ordinary adoption arrangement is successfully made between same-sex couples, they are in a parent-child relationship on the surface with the same legal rights enjoyed by any other natural parent-child relationship and adopted parent-child relationship, the mutual rights and duties of support and succession."[248]

In Japan there are two types of adoption: ordinary adoption (*futsu yo-shi*) and special adoption (*tokubetsu yo-shi*).[249] Ordinary adoption allows an adult to adopt another adult. It is a simple procedure that does not require a court authorization and can be requested before a municipal officer. Professor Tamaki points out that according to statistics, the majority of adoptions are of this kind and special adoptions, which would be the procedure for adopting a child, amount to around 1% of all adoptions.[250] This does not mean, however, that most of these adoptions are done by same sex couples. But even if a small number of couples use this method of forming a family, it is still interesting how pervasive the knowledge of this practice is.[251]

[236] Report on Romania prepared by Professors Cristiana Craciunescu and Dan Lupascu [hereinafter Romania Report].

[237] *Id.* at 3–4

[238] Başak Başoğlu & Candan Yasan, National Report: Turkey, 19 AM. U. J. Gender Soc. Pol'y & L. 319 (2011) [hereinafter Turkey Report].

[239] *Id.* at 320.

[240] *Id.* at 321.

[241] *Id.* at 325 (citing decision 355/6349, 13th Civil Chamber of the Court of Cassation (Turk.), April 24, 2006).

[242] *Id.* at 322.

[243] Teiko Tamaki, National Report: Japan, 19 Am. U. J. Gender Soc. Pol'y & L. 251 (2011) [hereinafter Japan Report].

[244] Kenpō [Constitution] art. 24.

[245] Japan Report, *supra* note 243, at 255.

[246] *Id.* at 260.

[247] *Id.* at 259–60.

[248] *Id.*

[249] *Id.* at 259.

[250] *Id.*

[251] For a description of both adoption and notary deeds by same sex couples in Japan, see Claire Maree, "Same–Sex Partnerships in Japan: Bypasses and Other Alternatives," Women's Studies 33,4 (2004): 541–549.

6.3 The Most Recurrent Arguments for and Against Same Sex Marriage

6.3.1 The Essentialist Arguments

Professors Martínez de Aguirre Aldaz and De Pablo Contreras advance this type of argument by claiming that the correct interpretation of article 32 of the Spanish constitution should have not led to the authorization of same sex marriage.[252] In their opinion, the grammatical interpretation of this article should take the constitutional interpreter to the Dictionary of the Royal Academy of the Spanish Language where marriage is defined as a long term union between a man and a woman.[253] The word "marriage", therefore, would *require* a man and a woman. This argument would be reaffirmed by looking at the etymology of the word matrimony that comes from the Latin "Matri," meaning "mother," and Mony or Monium, meaning "status, role, or function."[254] They argue, therefore, that matrimony is a concept intrinsically linked to becoming a mother and the possibility of procreation.

In opinion of Professors Martínez de Aguirre and De Pablo "[i]f the union is between two men or two women it is then not marriage, but rather another different human and social phenomenon, for the same reason that the sale of something for no money is not a sale but a donation, and saying that a donation is not a sale is not pejorative against the donation, but simply defining substantially different truths, subject to different legal treatment."[255]

A similar argument can be found in the French report. Professor Fulchiron states that in the core of the definition of marriage, the difference of sex is embedded in culture.[256] He claims that even beyond the Judeo Christian culture, marriage has historically been conceived as a union between a man and a woman, regardless of each society's acceptance or not of homosexuality.[257]

[252] Spain Report, *supra* note 18, at 295.

[253] *Id.*

[254] The Random House Dictionary of the English Language (unabridged) 1186, 1247 (2nd ed. 1982).

[255] Spain Report, *supra* note 18, at 295.

[256] France Report, *supra* note 166, at 130.

[257] *Id.*

According to these arguments, there was no need to define marriage as between a man and a woman because it was structurally required to have two sexes for it to exist as such. The reports for Portugal, Greece, Italy, and Uruguay rely on what is known in the civil law tradition as "the theory of the inexistence" to explain why the lack of two opposite sex individuals in a marriage contract did not make that contract null but rather inexistent.[258] The theory of the inexistence was adopted in article 146 of the French Civil Code for the case of lack of consent.[259] It has been used by legal scholars to explain that a marriage between two individuals of the same sex would be inexistent too.[260] Professors Martinez de Aguirre and De Pablo Contreras give the example of a sales contract.[261] If there is no price to be paid, the sales contract is not null; it does not exist as a sales contract and it exists as a donation. Same sex marriage, according to this theory, would not be a marriage but something different that needs to be named differently. That was also the position of a court in Italy to justify its holding that in Italy, though not expressly established by the Civil Code, marriage is a union between a man and a woman. Professor Zambrano explains that the rationale of the court was that "[t]he fact that the Italian legislator, in establishing the eligibility conditions for marriage did not make any reference to the difference of sex was interpreted by these judges as the proof that same sex marriage must be seen as non-existent (*inesistente*) at all."[262] Another example of the ontological position is Sect. 1 of the Michigan Marriage Protection Act of 1996: "Marriage is *inherently* a unique relationship between a man and a woman…"[263]

[258] See Henry Capitant, *Introduction à l'étude du droit civil: Notions générales* (Paris: A. Pedone, 1898), 250–251.

[259] Code civil [C. civ.] Article 146 (Fr.) ("Il n'y a pas de mariage lorsqu'il n'y a point de consentement.").

[260] For a brief account on the theory of the inexistence, see Ricardo Victor Guarinoni, "De lo que no hay. La Inexistencia Jurídica" Cuadernos de Filosofía del Derecho (Spain), Doxa N. 25, 2002. 637–653. Reference to the use of the theory of inexistence in the context of same sex marriage in Germany can be found in W. Müller-Freienfels, "Family Law and the Law of Succession in Germany," *International and Comparative Law Quaterly* 16 (1967): 431.

[261] Spain Report, *supra* note 18, at 295.

[262] Italy Report, *supra* note 220, at 247, referring to Trib. Latina (Italy), 10th June 2005.

[263] Mich. Comp. Laws Serv. § 551.1 (2007) (emphasis added).

Professor Duarte mentions in his report that marriage between two individuals of the same sex was inexistent in Portugal before last May.[264] Now, same sex marriage exists and it is legal.[265] If the argument on the nature of things is right, it would be irrelevant that same sex marriage was legal in Portugal, or in Spain or in any other country. All these countries would be mistaken by calling marriage something that is not marriage. If things are what they are and not a different thing, then it would not be possible for the law to order them to be something different.

There are three different options with regards to the ontological argument. The first option is to take the position that countries that have passed same sex marriage laws have made a conceptual mistake. Under this argument, countries where marriage is a union between a man and a woman should not recognize any effects to same sex marriage because it is not a real marriage. Each country may decide to call a same sex union a marriage and give it the effects of marriage, but because it is structurally not a marriage, no one should be forced to recognize such unions as marriage. This position is not necessarily incompatible with believing in the recognition of rights for same sex couples, but only with the option of opening up marriage to same sex couples. There is, nonetheless, a stronger version of this argument that is incompatible with same sex unions in general. The stronger version is usually based on a faith argument that cannot be disputed because it goes beyond rationality. Some reports tangentially touched on religious bases for regulating marriage but it was not thoroughly advanced by any. I will not refer to this argument here since no report elaborated on these types of arguments.[266]

[264] Portugal Report, *supra* note 50, at 2.

[265] *Id.*

[266] For an overview of such arguments, see John M. Finnis, "Law, Morality, and "Sexual Orientation,"" *Notre Dame Law Review* 69 (1994), 1062–1063 ("At the heart of the Platonic–Aristotelian and later ancient philosophical rejections of all homosexual conduct, and thus of the modern "gay" ideology, are three fundamental theses: (1) The commitment of a man and woman to each other in the sexual union of marriage is intrinsically good and reasonable, and is incompatible with sexual relations outside marriage. (2) Homosexual acts are radically and peculiarly non-marital, and for that reason intrinsically unreasonable and unnatural. (3) Furthermore, according to Plato, if not Aristotle, homosexual acts have a special similarity to solitary masturbation, and both types of radically non-marital act are manifestly unworthy of the human being and immoral.").

The second option is to argue that it is a mistake to affirm that different sex is essential to marriage. Marriage could be defined as a union between individuals emotionally tied to each other. Even if historically the most common definition of marriage has required two individuals of different sex, it would be possible to argue that marriage remains a marriage if more than two people enter into a relationship, or if people of the same sex do so. Professor Fulchiron states that polygamy and same sex are not the same variables in the conceptualization of marriage.[267] Polygamy is marriage, although not accepted by French law, but same sex marriage is not.[268]

The question is, then, what is essential to marriage? Indisputably, it requires the participation of at least two individuals. One person alone cannot marry. It also requires that all parties to the marriage be recognized as individuals by a legal system but it is still marriage if some of the parties to a marriage are legally treated as individuals of lesser value. Also, most legal systems today pose some restrictions on kinship. Are these restrictions essential to marriage? Does marriage require sexual activity between the parties? Does it require emotional support between the parties? There are conflicting answers to these questions and greater issues about family, citizenship and moral values lie behind each position.

In theory there can be essentialist arguments in favor of same sex marriage but essentialists are found primarily on the side of heterosexual marriage advocates.

The third option is to reject essentialism completely and argue that the concept of marriage can mutate from one thing to another. In other words, the law would have the power to define legal concepts. Marriage, thus, may have been a union between a man and a woman but it can now be a union between two individuals of any sex. Marriage can be a union between several men and one woman, or it can be a union between several women and one man, or any combination in between.

It seems that legal systems define and redefine things rather often. Law defines, for legal purposes, life and death. In the Catholic tradition, many women and men baptize the unborn dead fetus and give the fetus a Christian burial. In most Western traditions, however, a dead fetus was never a person. The same happens

[267] France Report, *supra* note 166, at 138.

[268] *Id.*

with death. Law defines the moment of death even if for religious purposes, or even by medical standards, the person may still be alive. Historically, personhood has been legally defined and redefined, sex has been defined and redefined, and many other concepts have been created by laws only to be recreated by different laws. Marriage, therefore, could change too. But there are limits to the process of definition and redefinition, and legal marriage must keep some relation to the social understanding of marriage. At the same time, all legal definitions must respect a framework of human rights. With these restrictions in mind, it would be possible to redefine marriage to include other unions such as those between same-sex couples.

6.3.2 The Teleological Arguments

A second set of arguments that recur in the reports as well as in general literature about marriage relates to the purposes of marriage, or more specifically, the purpose of the state protection of marriage. Many reports assert that refusal to recognize rights to same sex couples have been based on a belief that the state has an interest in protecting heterosexual couples as the only units capable of procreating. That would be the fundamental difference between a couple where both parties are of the same sex and one where they are of different sex. It is not the fact that they will procreate or that in a particular union the goal will be to procreate. It is the general interest of the state to protect associations that will secure procreation. This argument was used in Canada before they granted full recognition of same sex marriage. The Supreme Court of Canada stated then that marriage's "ultimate *raison d'être* (…) is firmly anchored in the biological and social realities that heterosexual couples have the unique ability to procreate, that most children are the product of these relationships, and that they are generally cared for and nurtured by those who live in that relationship."[269] In Belgium this was also an important argument against the recognition of same sex marriage.[270]

A more complex teleological argument is one that links marriage to family in general. The purpose of marriage would not only be to ensure procreation but it would also be to protect family in general by maintaining marriage as the exclusive option to create kinship outside consanguinity. Marriage creates parents who are linked to their children and are also linked to the families of their spouses.

These two reasons are the ones that make Professor Fulchiron affirm that in France, marriage covers the family and PACS is intended to cover the partnership.[271] Marriage would be naturally linked to procreation and to family. This is not the same in the case of same sex couples, who are not naturally linked to procreation.

The question behind the teleological arguments is what the meaning of legal marriage is. Why would a country protect some types of associations over others? Historically, marriage has served several distinct purposes that range from controlling women, controlling sex, controlling offspring, and controlling property, among others.[272] Before the rise of DNA tests, marriage was the most efficient signaling of paternity, and the most efficient tool, therefore, to claim alimony from estranged or irresponsible fathers.

Gradually different countries have been relaxing their rules regarding parenting, but have kept marriage as the ideal of family formation. Countries reviewed for this report show a tension between equality and family rights. Portugal even redefined marriage but was unable to provide adoption rights and access to parenting to same sex couples.[273] Countries such as Denmark or the Netherlands were also hesitant to open the door to parenting to same sex couples, and many countries seem to be ready to equalize all aspects of a same sex relationship with all aspects of marriage but parenting.

There is a recurrent tension between the right to privacy and the right to family. We learn from Professor

[269] Egan v. Canada, (1995) 2 S.C.R. 515 (Can.). Professor Bureau states in the Canada Report that this argument was then abandoned in other decisions such as EGALE Canada Inc. v. Canada, (2003) 13 B.C.L.R.2d 1 (B.C. Ct. App.).

[270] Belgium Report, *supra* note 12, at 66–67.

[271] France Report, *supra* note 166, at 131.

[272] In medieval Europe, marriage was "an institution by which men were confirmed as the masters of their wives on religious and legal grounds. But it was also a union intended to provide for the well-being of both parties and eventually their children. At the peasant level marriage was largely an economic arrangement (…). A bride's dowry consisting of money, goods, animals, or land was essential to the founding of a new household." Marilyn Yalom, *A History of the Wife* (New York: HarperCollins 2001), 47.

[273] Portugal Report, *supra* note 50, at 2.

Aichberger-Beig that the right to private life guaranteed in Article 8 of the European Convention of Human Rights was used by the Austrian Constitutional Court to base its decision to treat unmarried couples of opposite or same sex equally.[274] Countries that accept same sex unions have done so by recognizing that individuals have the right to engage in relationships of their desire. This right, however, seems to end when it clashes with the right to family. Professors Swennen and Leleu state that the constitutional challenge to the legal recognition of same sex marriage in Belgium was based in part in the idea that the law was assimilating different situations: on one hand, people who wish to found a family with a person of the opposite sex, and, on the other, people who wish to enter into a cohabitation regime with a person from the same sex.[275] The claim implies that individuals would have a right to form a partnership with whomever they wish, but that this would be a different situation than wishing to form a family, which could only be done by individuals of opposite sex.

This has been the approach of the ECHR to encourage European countries to recognize rights to same sex couples, and at the same time, maintain that marriage is still a heterosexual institution. Article 8 of the European Convention of Human Rights protects the right to private and family life, whereas Article 12 protects the right to marry and to found a family.[276] Professor Norrie states that the ECHR has been hesitant to use the "right to family life" of Article 8 to decide cases that involve sexual orientation claims. Instead, it has focused its attention on the "right to private life" of the same Article.[277]

There are additional teleological arguments in favor of same sex marriage. The exposition of reasons to introduce same sex marriage (*Exposé des motifs*) in the Belgian Bill stated that "in our contemporary society, marriage is lived and felt as a (formal) relationship between two people, whose primary goal is the creation of a lasting cohabitation. (...)"[278] "Today, the purpose of marriage is essentially to show and affirm the intimate relationship between two people, and marriage loses its procreative character -, there is no reason not to expand marriage to same sex persons."[279]

The argument that the state must protect marriage because of its procreative nature may be the strongest argument against same sex marriage. The state, after all, has an interest in ensuring that new citizens will be born. It has an interest also in ensuring that these new citizens will be raised in loving environments. At the same time, states also have an interest in protecting their own citizens from discrimination and providing an environment that tends toward the pursuit of happiness and self realization. Is it necessary to restrict one in order to protect the other? Is restricting marriage to opposite sex couples the least harmful means to protect procreation? And is it the most effective way to do so?

6.3.3 Marriage as Symbol, but of What?

Several reports refer to the importance of marriage as a symbol, "[s]omething used for or regarded as representing something else."[280] With marriage states are protecting something beyond the solemn act of marriage. Nonetheless, it seems that in some cases the symbol has transcended the idea or thing that it was meant to represent becoming at the same time the signifier and the signified.

Professor Witzleb states, regarding Australia, that "(s)ame-sex marriage is generally no longer needed to achieve equal entitlements and protection before the law. The inequality now lies predominantly in withholding from gay men and lesbians the possibility of giving status to their relationship through an official act celebrating and confirming the existence of that relationship."[281] In South Africa, the Marriage Act remained intact and a different institution, also called marriage but under a different Act, was created.[282]

Registration authority and name change have been recurrent concerns in countries passing registered partnership or civil union regulations. Whether the

[274] Austria Report, *supra* note 127, at 3.

[275] Belgium report, *supra* note 12, at 69.

[276] Council of Europe, Convention for the Protection of Human Rights and Fundamental Freedoms art. 8 and 12, Nov. 4, 1950, E.T.S. No. 5, 213 U.N.T.S. 221.

[277] UK Report, *supra* note 79, at 331.

[278] Belgium Report, *supra* note 12, at 68.

[279] *Id.* at n.49.

[280] The Random House Dictionary of the English Language (unabridged) 1926 (2nd ed. 1982).

[281] Australia Report, *supra* note 97, at 12.

[282] South Africa Report, *supra* note 35, at 280–81.

authority that can register same sex partners (or partners in general) will be the same one that registers marriages was an issue in Denmark and Austria.[283] In Germany those states who opposed ELp left registration to public notaries instead of giving it to the same authority that registers marriages.[284] In Hungary name change was not allowed for registered partners.[285] In Austria registered partnership contemplates the option of name change but as oppose to marriage, the new statute did not refer to this new name as "family name."[286]

The use of marriage as primarily a symbol is found in countries that have created parallel institutions to marriage via registration or recognition of cohabitation and have granted these unions the same rights enjoyed by married couples. United Kingdom and, to great extent, Australia are good examples of this model.[287] If married and unmarried couples or registered partners enjoy the same benefits, rights and obligations, the only added value provided to married couples is a social signifier of their status. As a social signal, the act of marriage is twofold: it facilitates the matching process by acting as a *prima facie* guarantee of commitment, and it is a sign to the rest of society that the relationship between two individuals has an expectancy of a long-term commitment.[288] But why would the State have to facilitate this process for some groups only? It seems that either marriage must stand for something more substantive than a social signifier, or it may well surrender to the fact that it is the standing façade of an old structure that with time has ceded.

If the purposes of marriage—the signified—have lost meaning, the signifier loses meaning too. In those countries where access to parenting is fully restricted to heterosexual married couples, the symbolic nature of marriage makes sense because there is a direct correlation between symbol and purpose: procreation within marriage. Regardless of whether this norm is fair, the symbolism and the substantive objectives behind it are tied together. For example, today marriage makes sense in Romania where only heterosexual couples can marry and no one but married couples can form co-parental families.[289] This, however, is not a statement about the appropriateness of the substantive norm that marriage protects. It may well be that the reasons that lie behind marriage in a particular country do not conform to current standards of treatment of individuals in the eyes of international law or in the eyes of the country's own constitutional values. It can also mean that in practical terms marriage is not fulfilling the purpose that it was meant to carry out. This would be the case, for example, of a country whose statutes recognize only heterosexual married couples but the number of out of wedlock children is almost as large as or larger than the number of children born within marriages. In cases where the purpose of marriage fails, so should the symbol.

Marriage as a symbol can also be analyzed from a different perspective, as the need for legal systems to rely on forms. This is simply the formalist feature of the law. Atiyah and Summers, state that legal reasoning can be formal or substantive. Substantive reasons are those based on "moral, economic, political, institutional or other social consideration[s]."[290] They "serve as primary ingredients of most constitutions, statutes, precedents, and other legally recognized phenomena (…) which give rise to formal reasoning."[291] Formal reasons give judges the power to decide on the bases of a rule that usually excludes any other consideration. "Unlike a substantive reason, a formal reason necessarily presupposes a valid law or other valid legal phenomenon, such as a contract or a verdict."[292]

Formal reasons presuppose that someone else, at a different level, has already weighed all substantive reasons that could be behind the signifier that will replace all other reasons. In this sense, a formal reason has to be created taking into account substantive objectives that the legal system wants to protect. Age requirements to exercise the right to vote or to obtain a driver's

[283] Denmark Report, *supra* note 90, at 120; Austria Report, *supra* note 130, at 6–7.

[284] Germany Report, *supra* note 116, at 167.

[285] Hungary Report, *supra* note 144, at 212.

[286] Austria Report, *supra* note 127, at 7.

[287] UK Report, *supra* note 79, at 333; Australia Report, *supra* note 97, at 6–7.

[288] *See* Robert Rowthorn, "Marriage as a signal," in *The Law and Economics of Marriage and Divorce,* ed. Anthony W. Dnes and Robert Rowthorn (Cambridge: Cambridge University Press, 2002), 141.

[289] Romania Report, *supra* note 236, at 5.

[290] P.S. Atiyah and Robert S. Summers, *Form and substance in Anglo-American law: a comparative study of legal reasoning, legal theory, and legal institutions*, 5 (Oxford: Clarendon Paperbacks, 1987).

[291] *Id.*

[292] *Id.* at 2.

license are examples of formal reasons. Just like voting age, marriage would be "a formal reason for making many decisions."[293] As Atiyah points out, marriage is used as a formal reason to allocate resources, define entitlements, and provide benefits. In his opinion, "[s]o many different questions arise about how we are to treat two parties in some sort of relationship that it is exceedingly convenient and cost-effective to make the answers turn uniformly on one simple formal proposition. Are they married or not?"[294] Formal reasons, however, must change when the substantive reasons that support them change. Marriage used to be evidence of meaningful relationships of one type. Once societies start accepting other meaningful relationships, either these relationships are also included in the formal reason by expanding marriage, or the formal reason loses all meaning. It is no longer efficient for the system to rely on that particular formal marker. Judges often find themselves reviewing a claim that a certain benefit, or a certain share of property, should be granted to the plaintiff as if she were in possession of a marriage certificate that she does not actually have. Individuals urge judges not to look at the formality—the existence of a marriage certificate—but to the substantive reasons that lie behind it.

Marriage used as a legal formal reason is a great argument for expanding the concept of marriage to same sex couples. It reduces claims in courts from gay and lesbian partners requesting the right to hospital visitations, the right to pension benefits, or the right to succession. The formality of marriage, on the contrary, works against assimilation of married and unmarried couples. A system where different forms of association may qualify for legal recognition is certainly more complex than one that attaches rights to a marriage certificate. Nonetheless, Atiyah's assertion that "special rules for long-term cohabitants and also for *intending* long term cohabitants would be an immensely costly and troublesome business"[295] has been already put to test in Canada, Australia, and the United Kingdom, among others. None of the reports have referred to complications, if any, that the change in their regulations may have brought to the adjudicative process.

[293] P.S. Atiyah, Essays on Contract 105 (Clarendon Paperbacks 1986).

[294] *Id.* at 107.

[295] *Id.*

All countries that have opened their legal systems to include same sex couples as legitimate associations worth of recognition (partial or total), have done so after their systems were challenged in court by same sex couples. These trials have been specific to a particular right, as in Colombia, or they have been directly aimed at claiming the right to marry, as in South Africa.

In countries where same-sex couples are invisible in legal statutes, they are very much visible in courts. Judges following their countries' formal signifiers may deny rights to same-sex couples, but these claims show a reality that clashes with the legal construction of emotional associations chosen by such country. What the national reports reviewed here show is that the formality of marriage is often outweighed by substantive reasons in courts.

6.4 Conclusions

Whether scholars and political scientists agree with the direction that family law is taking, it is undeniable that there is a movement towards the recognition of same sex couples as family units, at least in Europe and in the Americas. Same sex marriage, however, is not yet the common type of recognition. Instead, countries have accommodated same sex couples into their legal systems almost as a tacit admission that same sex cohabitation happens, and it has legal consequences that must be regulated. In countries with no recognition of same sex couples, gay and lesbian couples exist and find ways of accommodating at least their basic partnership needs within their legal systems.

These changes in family law pose several challenges both at local and international level. Among these challenges, three can be directly drawn from the country reports reviewed for this work. The first challenge is the relationship between international private law and family law; the second relates to parenting; and the final challenge is the role that international courts play in family law structures.

One of the main obstacles that same sex marriage and registered partnership regimes face in a global world is the recognition of these unions by different countries. The variety of legal regimes for same sex couples will most likely trigger a global change in international private law. Some countries have established rules about how to treat same sex marriages or partnerships performed or recognized abroad.

Most countries, however, have not thought of this issue yet. For a same sex couple, the uncertainty of whether their relationship will be recognized abroad creates a major difference from opposite sex couples.

As long as the majority of countries still define marriage as a union between a man and a woman, a lesbian couple married in Belgium will be less willing to move overseas than a heterosexual couple. At a minimum, same-sex couples thinking of relocation have to weigh arguments that heterosexual couples do not have to consider.

Another challenge that countries face is access to parenting by same sex couples. In some countries the redefinition of marriage as open to same and opposite sex couples has meant that not all marriages are the same. In those countries, as in Portugal, marriage is no longer one single institution but two different institutions that use the same name. In a way, redefining marriage in those terms is like redefining citizenship and having one group of citizens with the right to vote and another group without it.

Countries have moved from strict regulations where only children born within marriage were recognized as legitimate and had access to rights, to regimes where no difference or very little difference is made between children born within marriage and out of wedlock. Countries have also moved from strict adoption laws where only married couples could adopt children to systems in which single individuals can also become adoptive parents. Once parenting is recognized outside marriage, it is difficult to maintain privileges for only one model of parenting.

The complexity of biology must be added to the complexity of adoption regulation. Today procreation is possible in ways unthinkable 50 years ago. If contraception made possible for women to choose if or when to have children, assisted reproductive technologies have made possible for women to choose their family structure. Single women can decide to have a child alone, and lesbian couples can decide to become mothers, all this without emotional ties and even with anonymous sperm donors. In addition to the variety of assisted reproductive technologies, surrogacy is now a reality that opens up the possibility for gay male couples to become fathers too. As stated in this report, some countries treat assisted reproductive technologies as a health issue open to all women regardless of their sexual orientation and marital status.[296] Other countries restrict these technologies to married couples or to heterosexual couples.[297] Surrogacy is forbidden in many countries, others forbid it only if for profit, and other jurisdictions allow it completely.[298] Today there are many more alternatives to become a family than in past generations. Until recently, it was up to each country to determine if the legal concept of family and the social concept of family would coincide or not. In today's culture of universal human rights and international legal regulation, this may not be an exclusively national prerogative. The European Court of Human Rights reinforces this idea in its decision *Schalk and Kopf v. Austria*. Although the Court was not willing to recognize that under the European Convention of Human Rights there was a right for same sex couples to marry, it did change its past interpretation recognizing same sex couples a right to family life.[299]

This is precisely the third challenge that countries are facing with regards to family law. The "national" has become "international" and family law is not isolated from this phenomenon. Traditionally family law has been treated as a local construction that, although regulated by law, transcends its legal conceptualization to ultimately reflect the most intimate cultural values of a nation. For a long time, international law was seen as unrelated to family law. This was reasonable given that families were also shielded from local legal intervention. As inequalities within the family structure have been uncovered, countries have allowed more legal intervention within the family. International law started to intervene when family law issues were presented as human rights issues.

International systems of protection of human rights have evolved from a role of guarantors of a minimal treatment of respect of human rights to a role of authentic interpreters of the concepts of human rights. With this new role, its involvement in shaping family law is inevitable. The *Schalk and Kopf* case recently decided by the ECHR provides a good example of the current intervention of international courts in family law. The Court denied that a heterosexual definition of marriage amounts to discrimination, but it left the door open to revisit this decision as European countries evolve towards more comprehensive definitions of marriage.[300]

[296] This is the case of Denmark. Denmark Report, *supra* note 90, at 118.

[297] Israel Report, *supra* note 151, at 19–20.

[298] Germany Report, *supra* note 116, at 173; *see also* Belgium Report, *supra note* 12.

[299] *Schalk and Kopf*, *supra* note 86, at 94.

[300] *Id*. at 105.

The analysis of same sex couples in different countries shows unease in this area. Changes will keep coming and tensions within countries and among countries regarding same sex couples will continue. It seems that the statement made by Mr. Martin Cauchon as Minister of Justice and Attorney General of Canada in 2002 is still very much pertinent:

> Not just in Canada but around the world, individuals and their governments have debated whether marriage has a continuing value to society, and if so whether and how the state should recognize married relationships in law. The Canadian public, like those in many other countries, are divided on this question. Some feel strongly that governments should continue to support marriage as an opposite-sex institution, since married couples and their children are the principal social unit on which our society is based. Others believe that, for reasons of equality, governments should treat all conjugal relationships—opposite—sex and same-sex—identically. Still others believe that in a modern society, governments should cease to recognize any one form of relationship over another and that marriage should be removed from the law and left to individuals and their religious institutions.[301]

[301] Department of Justice of Canada, Discussion Paper, *Marriage and Legal Recognition of Same Sex Unions*, (November 2002), http://www.justice.gc.ca/eng/dept-min/pub/mar/mar.pdf (last visited October 22, 2010).

7 Consumer Protection in Private International Relationships*

Diego P. Fernández Arroyo

7.1 Introduction

7.2 Emergence of the International Dimension in Consumer Protection

Consumer protection has developed constantly – although in various ways – in recent decades in many countries. Initially, the envisaged protection was predominantly made at a national level, limited to purely internal consumer transactions. The essential purpose of such a limitation seemed to be strongly linked to the traditional notion that these aforementioned transactions represent a reduced sum, the consideration of which did not however prevent consumer protection from becoming a constitutional duty in several legislations. But some phenomena such as the internationalization of the markets, mass tourism and, above all, electronic commerce have increased the global volume of consumer operations to such an extent that it is now absurd to consider them exclusively as questions relating to small, individual transactions. At the same time, these phenomena have led to a kind of democratization of international consumption, which is no longer the rare privilege of the chosen few.

The fact that anyone with access to the Internet can, even without realizing it, enter into genuine international contracts allows us to understand the importance and the necessity of developing the international aspect of consumer protection. If, within each legislation, consumers can be exposed to the rigors of market rules, this weakness is obviously more marked when co-contracting parties are located in a different country and/ or if their transactions are subject to foreign laws and jurisdictions. After the consolidation of "consumer law", there emerges an increasingly powerful "international consumer law" whose categories and concrete responses are, as is often the case in international law, sometimes complicated and very relative but quite indispensable.

In view of the obvious lack of adaptation to general rules as far as international contracts are concerned, this branch of international law has begun to elaborate conflict of laws rules and conflict of jurisdiction rules specifically aimed at international consumption relationships. But the increasing number of these operations, on the one hand, and their singular nature on the other hand, forces legislators to adopt other complementary mechanisms. Consequently, international consumer law cannot be content with good rules of judicial competence, of determining the relevant law and, sometimes of acknowledging and enforcing foreign decisions. All these rules are no doubt necessary. But, in addition to these elements of "classic" private international law, there is a development of mechanisms affecting the procedure, the cooperation and alternative methods of resolving litigation. Basically, one cannot ignore the existence of a "mercantilist" position, which perceives consumer law in general and the protective policies applied by public authori-

*La protection des consommateurs dans les relations privées internationales.

D.P. Fernández Arroyo (✉)
Department of International Law, Complutense University, Madrid, Spain

The Sciences Po School of Law, Paris
e-mail: diexf@hotmail.com

K.B. Brown and D.V. Snyder (eds.), *General Reports of the XVIIIth Congress of the International Academy of Comparative Law/Rapports Généraux du XVIIIème Congrès de l'Académie Internationale de Droit Comparé*, DOI 10.1007/978-94-007-2354-2_7, © Springer Science+Business Media B.V. 2012

ties as obstacles to the freedom of commerce, especially to the functioning of global markets created by electronic commerce.[1] The tension between this position and that which seeks to give a proper substance to rights of the individual in the face of globalization is revealed every time that an effort is made to impose regulation (above all when there is an international attempt at unification or harmonization).[2] The concern to find balanced solutions has long been present in legal literature.[3]

7.3 Comparison of Law in the Context of Internationalization and Privatization

The traditional usage of comparative methodology continues to be useful in teaching, elaborating and in the application of private international law. However, to be useful is not enough. It is in fact necessary to take into account the actual phenomena which require a complementary approach for comparative law, as has already been noticed by several well-known comparativists.[4] The essential considerations that should be borne in mind are, on the one hand, the transfer of law-making power from the State to international or supranational organizations; on the other hand, the transfer of a large part of legal regulation and dispute settlement from the public sector to the private sector. One must be aware of these trends and reversals in order to contribute to a better understanding of private international law and to improve the quality of private international dispute resolution.

Economic integration and international codification greatly influence national legal systems. This is proved by the existence of the supranational legal framework of the European Union (EU) and marked by the communitarization of the law and its collateral effects, for example, the EU's membership of the Hague Conference on Private International Law.[5] Even if elsewhere in the world one cannot speak of a genuinely supranational legal structure, this claim is nonetheless true. Failing to take into account this evolution prevents comprehension of the legal systems and, consequently, prevents interpreting them correctly in the law-making process and in the resolution of real cases.

All these considerations have been taken into account during the elaboration of this Report. It is well known that traditionally the International Academy of Comparative Law appoints one person per subject area, who must write a general report on the basis of information received by national reporters. It goes without saying that the subjects of national laws dealt with in the reports on member States of the EU are likely to be residual and repetitive, as substantive law and private international law in so far as consumer law is concerned come essentially under the law-making power of EU law.[6] In the Americas, for instance, the specific rules of private international law relating to consumer protection are absent in the Latin American countries. The Inter-American Conference on Private International Law is, however, working on this subject and several drafts are on the negotiating table. The Hague Conference, at a universal level, and the Mercosur, at a regional level, are also dealing with this matter. Consequently, in order to write a comparative report as accurately as possible, we have combined international, supranational and national reports, bearing in mind that several national reports were quite limited in their scope.

[1] Critic about this position, N. Reich, "Transnational Consumer Law – Reality or Fiction?," *Penn State International Law Review* 27, 3/4 (2009), 859, 860–861.

[2] Within the framework of the Hague Conference of Private International Law, see the document "The impact of the Internet on the Judgments Project: Thoughts for the Future", Prel. Doc. No 17 of February 2002, Available on the website of the Hague Conference < www.hcch.net > under "Conventions" then "Nr 37" and then "Preliminary Documents." Within the framework of the OAS, see M. J. Dennis, "Diseño de una agenda práctica para la protección de los consumidores en las Américas," in *Protección de los consumidores en América. Trabajos de la CIDIP VII (OEA)*, ed. D.P. Fernández Arroyo and J.A. Moreno Rodríguez, 219 (Asunción: CEDEP/La Ley 2007).

[3] See E. Jayme, "Le droit international privé du nouveau millénaire: la protection de la personne humaine face à la globalisation," *Recueil des Cours* 282 (2000), 9, 25–28, 32–34.

[4] G. A. Bermann, "Le droit comparé et le droit international: alliés ou ennemis?", *RIDC* (2003), 527–529; M. Reimann, "Comparative Law and Private International Law," in *The Oxford Handbook of Comparative Law, ed.* M. Reimann and R. Zimmermann (Oxford: OUP, 2006), 1388 ss.

[5] A. Schulz, "The Accession of the European Community to The Hague Conference on Private International Law," *ICLQ* 56 (2007), 939.

[6] This idea is clearly expressed in the introduction of the French Report: "*dans les relations internationales, la protection est presque intégralement assurée par le droit communautaire, réduisant l'intervention des normes nationales à la portion congrue*". The same may be found in the Polish Report, I.1: "In the Polish legal system the vast majority of legal provisions, both substantive and procedural, protecting consumers involved in international transactions stem, more or less directly, from the law of the European Union" (also at I.2).

7.4 General Context

7.4.1 Rules and Principles in National Constitutions (Consumer Protection as a Category)

Only the most modern constitutions contain specific rules of a more or less complete nature relating to consumer protection,[7] occasionally giving this protection the character of fundamental law.[8] Many of the public legal systems which identify a constitutional rank for consumer protection are to be found in Latin America,[9] others are in Europe.[10] In the Swiss constitution (article 97), for instance, the recognition of consumer protection becomes a reality in the Confederation's obligation to legislate and in the cantonal obligation to organise a process of conciliation or simple and rapid judiciary to resolve disputes whose contentious value does not exceed a sum fixed by the Federal Council.[11] In Africa the projected new Kenyan constitution contains an article on consumer protection, which was adopted in 2004, but which was never put to a referendum and, consequently, has not taken effect.[12]

Among more recent constitutions, the Ecuadorean one of 2008 recognizes the rights of users and consumers (articles 52–55) in the chapter pertaining to the law regarding persons and priority attention groups. Amongst the explicitly acknowledged rights, it is important to emphasize the right to be indemnified for damage caused by the deficiencies of a public service, by the defective quality of a product or the non-compliance of a product with its advertising or its description; in such cases the civil and criminal responsibility of the suppliers is provided for. The 1999 Constitution of the Bolivarian Republic of Venezuela had already foreseen the need to establish in law the procedures needed to defend consumers' rights, damage compensation and penalties for the violation of these rights.[13] But, in our opinion, one of the most interesting cases is that of the Brazilian Constitution of 1988. In addition to describing consumer protection as a fundamental right,[14] and the presence of this category in several articles of the Constitution, the constitutional clauses gave rise to an impressive legislative, doctrinal and judicial development.[15]

In the EU, given the distribution of legislative powers, it is more interesting to note the European rules of law than the treatment reserved for them within the national constitutions. Despite the failure of the so-called "European Constitution" and its ensuing criticism, it is obvious that the regulations concerning the EU's treaties, as a "super State", fulfill a constitutional function inasmuch as they guide and limit for all the regulations and decisions of the EU and its member States. In this sense, the precepts of article 38 of the European Charter of Fundamental Rights,[16] of articles 12 and 169 of the Treaty of the Functioning of the EU (TFEU)[17] serve as "constitutional" regulations in the whole scope of EU law. The first of these articles establishes, in the chapter pertaining to solidarity, the consumers' right to a "high" level of protection. But it is article 12 of the TFEU which most clearly shows the constitutional nature by establishing the obligation to consider the demands of consumer protection in the definition and enforcement of EU policies and actions. This is the present basis for the extraordinary development of protective European regulation, which does not prevent member States from being even more rigorous in their protective efforts. That is to say, that notwithstanding the "high" character

[7]However, more general references such as the restriction of freedom of trade and industry by "*mesures de police sanitaire contre les épidémies et les epizooties*" may be found in old texts. See, for instance, Arts. 31 and 69 of Swiss Constitution of 1874 (Swiss Report, I.1).

[8]See G. A. Rodrigues, "A proteção ao consumidor como um direito fundamental," *RDC* 58 (2006), 75.

[9]In Argentina, Bolivia, Brazil, Colombia, Costa Rica, El Salvador, Ecuador, Guatemala, Honduras, Mexico, Nicaragua, Peru, Venezuela. See J. A. Amaya, *Mecanismos constitucionales de protección al consumidor* (Buenos Aires: La Ley 2004), 38–47. quoted in the Report of Mercosur, note 1.

[10]Among the countries here reported: Spain, Poland, Switzerland and Turkey (partially a European country and candidate to join the EU).

[11]See Swiss Report, I.1.A, notes 2–16 and accompanying text.

[12]See Report of Kenya, I.1, notes 1 and 2 and accompanying text.

[13]Report of Venezuela, I.1.

[14]C. Lima Marques explains that "*cette reconnaissance de l'importance de la protection du consommateur parmi les droits fondamentaux au Brazil est un mandat ... positif d'action ... de l'État ..., un droit fondamental socio-économique qui requiert impérativement une action positive des pouvoirs publics en faveur de la protection du consommateur*" (Brazilian Report, I.1.A).

[15]*Ibid.*

[16]Which has the same legal value than European treaties (Art. 6(1) TEU).

[17]TFEU, adopted into the framework of the "Lisbon Treaty", in force since 1 December 2009. See Report of the EU, I.1.

of protection demanded by the original EU law, the latter merely represents the minimum possible.[18]

Occasionally, national courts apply protective constitutional legislation directly to real cases.[19] And in countries which do not admit such direct application of constitutional legislation relating to this matter, Poland for example,[20] it is accepted, on the one hand, that a person may invoke international and supranational laws of protection when there are no relevant national laws, and on the other hand, that the aforementioned constitutional legislation may serve as a parameter of constitutional validity.[21] And yet, the absence of specific constitutional legislation has not prevented some upper courts from adopting decisions in favor of consumer rights,[22] without necessarily giving their protection the status of "constitutional validity".[23] In fact, many other laws and principles often present in constitutions may be applied in litigation involving consumers.[24] This is the case, amongst others, for the laws and principles relating to competition, those which guarantee access to justice and those which forbid discrimination.[25] Occasionally, it is possible to find in the legislative development of these laws and principles the recognition of a judicial category of consumer protection.[26] In other cases, such a category is directly created by specific legislation.[27]

Totally different and not exclusively attached to consumer protection, is another constitutional question relating to the existence in some States of several legal systems, due to the federal organization of the state. This can be perceived as "an obstacle to a coherent approach"[28] or quite simply as a factor in a certain assimilation of relationships within the state and with those abroad.[29] In some federated States, the latter quite simply represents a division of law-making powers between the federal authority and the state authority to regulate issues relating to consumer protection.[30]

7.4.2 The Relevance of International and Supranational Sources

Despite their obvious importance in international consumer relationships, specific legal solutions for international consumer protection are still relatively rare in much of the world. Generally, with the exception of the EU, the gaps in internal private international law cannot be filled satisfactorily by the actions of international and supranational organizations.

And yet, in addition to the adoption of laws that specifically regulate aspects of the private international law of consumer protection, one cannot ignore the

[18]See Art. 169(4) TFEU.

[19]Thus, in Argentina, the *Cámara Nacional Federal en lo Contencioso Administrativo*, 2nd ch., has said that the protection assured by the Constitution applies even in the absence of a developing act. CNFed.Cont.Adm., 5 November 1998, *Ciancio, José M. c. Enargas, Doctrina Judicial* (1999-2) 1124. Equally interesting is the decision adopted by the same court in *Intergas S.A. c. Enargas*, 18 November 1999, *LexisNexis* nº 8/10280 (Report of Mercosur, note 1). See also, always in Argentina, National Court of Appeal, ch. B, 22 June 2005, *Volpi c. UBS AG*. In Brazil, see STJ – 3.a T. – REsp 170078/SP – rel. Min. Carlos Alberto Menezes Direito – j. 03.04.2001, and the decisions quoted by C. Lima Marques, A.H. Benjamin and B. Miragem, *Comentários ao Código de Defesa do Consumidor*, São Paulo, RT (2006) 75 (See Brazilian Report, I.1.A, note 21).

[20]Art. 76 of Polish Constitution of 1997.

[21]Of particular interest is the decision of the Polish Constitutional Court of 2 December 2008, K 37/07, in which the Court finds contrary to Constitution the rule which required passengers seeking to hold a carrier liable for late arrival or cancellation of a regularly scheduled transportation course to prove previously that the carrier was guilty of intentional misconduct or gross negligence. See Report of Poland, I.1, note 6 and accompanying text. See also decisions mentioned at notes 4 and 5 of the same Report.

[22]See Report of the Czech Republic, I.1; Report of Israel, I.1, spec. notes 1–6 and accompanying text.

[23]For example, in France, consumer protection has been "only" recognized having a general interest, that is to say, being able to limit property rights. See Report of France, I.1.

[24]See, for example, German Report, I.1, and Italian Report, I.1.

[25]See South African Report, I.1. and note 8.

[26]That is the case, in Ethiopia, of the *Trade Practice Proclamation* of 2003 (see Ethiopian Report, I.1, notes 4–9 and accompanying text).

[27]For example, in Greece, Act 2251/1994 on Consumer Protection (see Report of Greece, I.1); in Italy, Consumer Code of 2005 (see Italian Report, I.1); in Japan, Consumer Basic Act and Consumer Contract Act (see Japanese Report, I.1); etc. In South Africa, several texts (*Electronic Communications and Transactions Act* of 2002, *National Credit Act* of 2005 and *Consumer Protection Act* of 2008) offer different notions of consumer (See Report of South Africa, Introduction).

[28]See Report of Australia, I.1. Even if they are not inconsistent the systems in force into one State can be quite different (see UK Report, Introduction).

[29]See Report of Quebec, I.1.

[30]That is the case, already mentioned, of Switzerland. See *supra* note 11. That division between substantial aspects (attributed to the federation or confederation) and procedural aspects (attributed to the sister States) may be found in Argentina. About the organization of law-making power in Canada, see Canadian Report (common law), I.1.

impact of adopting conventions in the domain of international commerce on internal laws relating to consumer protection. For example, agreements put into effect by the World Trade Organization (WTO) have made it possible to define a standard level of "consumer protection".[31] Of course, this does not constitute the only example of an international law causing the regulation of internal law to be modified.[32]

Instruments which are adopted, or which are being drafted, are very varied, as is their insertion in legal systems. Before now, their achievement was only possible at a regional level.

7.4.2.1 Universal Sources

There is no "universal" instrument in effect that contains a specific set of regulations concerning international consumer protection. This does not mean that consumer protection is not of concern to international organizations. On the contrary, 25 years ago the United Nations (UN) adopted one of the guiding principles in this domain with national legislators in mind, particularly those in developing countries,[33] who are always considered and explicitly mentioned when national laws are drafted. In the same way, other laws adopted by the UN may be applied to consumers as is the case of the Legislative Guidelines of the United Nations Commission on International Trade Law (UNCITRAL) concerning operations guaranteed by security rights in 2007 and, exceptionally, by the Vienna Convention of 1980 regarding the international sale of goods.[34] But only now does UNCITRAL envisage the possibility of working on (although non-specifically) international consumer protection, more precisely the bringing into line of different aspects international electronic commercial operations.[35]

For its part, the Hague Conference on Private International Law has often attempted to tackle the international regulation of various aspects of consumer protection. In the area of disputed jurisdictions, the Draft of a "worldwide convention of exequatur" (1999) contained the fairly controversial specific regulation of jurisdiction for consumer contracts.[36] In the area of disputed laws, in its 14th session (1980) the conference adopted the text on the law applicable to consumer sales that was prepared by Arthur T. Von Mehren,[37] which was supposed to become the basis of a future convention or a part of a convention. However, this never happened.[38] Thus, only one among the 39 international instruments adopted by the Conference contained specific provisions for consumers: the Convention of October 2, 1973, on the law applicable to the liability for defective products.[39]

7.4.2.2 Regional Sources

The absence of universal instruments in our subject amplifies the importance of work undertaken in organizations of a regional nature. Indeed, it is at this level that specific instruments have been adopted concerning the different aspects of international consumer law and that new instruments are being prepared. At the same time, increasing commercial relationships within regionally integrated blocks and tighter links between their member States leads to the adoption of laws and

[31] In the Report of Israel, I.2, the author explains how the Standards Law 5713–1953 had to be modified at the request of the WTO, by removing consumer protection from the list of grounds for enacting an official standard. Israeli Report also mentions the Trade Duties and Safeguards Measures Law.

[32] In the Polish Report, the author mentions the Paris Convention of 1962 (of the European Council) on the liability of hotel-keepers concerning the property of their guests, which has provoked the modification of some rules of the Civil Code, particularly to limit the effect of waivers of liability.

[33] Resolution 39/248 of the General Assembly of the UN, adopted in April 1985, on the Guidelines on consumer protection (Doc. NU A/RES/39/248 (1985) 188). See D. Harland, "The UN Guidelines for Consumer Protection: their Impact in the First Decade," in *Consumer Law in the Global Economy*, I. Ramsay (dir.), 2 (Aldershot: Ashgate 1997).

[34] Vienna Convention is not applicable to consumer sales (Art. 2) "unless the seller, at any time before or at the conclusion of the contract, neither knew nor ought to have known that the goods were bought for any such use."

[35] See doc. A/CN.9/706 of 23 April 2010 which contains a summary of a colloquia made by UNCITRAL in cooperation with the Pace Law School Institute of International Commercial Law et la Penn State Dickinson School of Law in Vienna in March 2010, called *A Fresh Look at Online Dispute Resolution and Global E-Commerce: Toward a Practical and Fair Redress System for the twenty first Century Trader (Consumer and Merchant)*.

[36] See Report of the Hague Conference, II.1, and the document "The impact of the Internet on the Judgments Project: Thoughts for the Future", quoted *supra* note 2.

[37] Hague Conference on Private International Law, *Actes et documents de la Quatorzième Session*, t. II, *Ventes aux consommateurs*, pp. II-77-II-179. For a Spanish version, see D.P. Fernández Arroyo and J.A. Moreno (note 2) 39–55.

[38] See Report of the Hague Conference, III.1.

[39] *Ibid.*

policies, which in a more or less indirect way are reflected in consumer relationships.[40]

The EU's case is paradigmatic in this respect. All the typical aspects of private international law of consumers have been scrutinized by the EU legislator: jurisdiction, applicable law, recognition and enforcement of foreign decisions.[41] But the EU initiatives go further than that. The considerable development of material harmonization[42] must be emphasized insofar as it concerns either general aspects of commercial contracts (for example, unfair terms), or specific consumer relationships (for example, time-sharing). Harmonization measures also include specific rules of private international law.[43]

It would be wrong to think that the EU laws, whether private international law or substantive law, are only relevant to their member States.[44] On the contrary, their influence is felt beyond the community borders. Firstly, EU law impacts on the member States of the European Free Trade Association (EFTA) in respect of differently weighted agreements: in the context of private international law, we must mention the Lugano Convention (2007) concerning jurisdiction and the recognition and enforcement judgements, civil and commercial matters.[45] A second sphere of influence is spreading across the States who wish to join the EU, for instance Turkey, which not only bases its rules on jurisdiction and applicable law in the matter of consumer relationships on those adopted by the EU, but has also adopted within its legal framework several European texts relating to substantial law in this domain, the provisions of which are likely to play a mandatory role.[46] A third circle, unlimited in its scope, is gradually taking shape as the world's legislators and academics deem the European regulations to be exemplary models when suggesting laws relating to consumer protection.[47]

In the American hemisphere, even if several texts adopted by the Organization of American States (OAS) within the framework of its Specialized Inter-American Conference on Private International Law (CIDIP) can be applied to litigation wherein consumers are implicated,[48] there are no special instruments in this domain. It is interesting to note that even if the Inter-American Convention on law applicable to international contracts does not explicitly exclude contracts concluded by consumers, the prevailing opinion is that, given the great recognition that the Convention gives to party autonomy, its rules are not applicable to the aforementioned contracts.[49] However, consumer protection is now the main theme of the work undertaken from all possible points of view by CIDIP-VII. Several texts under discussion: a draft convention on

[40]T. Bourgoignie and J. St-Pierre, "Le statut de la politique de protection du consommateur dans les systèmes régionaux économiquement intégrés. Une première évaluation comparative," *Rev. québécois de droit international* 20–1 (2007), 1.

[41]Among other instruments we will pay attention in particular to Regulation 44/2001 on Jurisdiction and the Recognition and Enforcement of Judgments in Civil and Commercial Matters (and to its previous instrument, Brussels Convention of 1968) and to Regulation 593/2008 (Rome I) on the Law Applicable to Contractual Obligations (and to its previous instrument, Rome Convention of 1980).

[42]The EU is working now in the substantial harmonization of consumer law, on the basis of the Proposal of Directive of 8 October 2008 on consumers rights, COM (2008) 614 final. See H. Schulte-Nölke/L. Tichy ed., *Perspectives for European Consumer Law. Towards a Directive on Consumer Rights and Beyond*, (München: Sellier 2010).

[43]Report of the EU, I.2.

[44]In those States, the weight of EU private international law is so heavy that sometimes one forgets that national rules have, notwithstanding their residual character, their own scope of application. See, for instance, Belgian Report, II.1.

[45]Originally adopted in 1988 as a parallel text to the Brussels Convention of 1968 (in its version of 1989, called San Sebastian Convention), the Lugano Convention has been modified in order to adapt it to the text of Regulation 44/2001. The new version is in force in the EU States and in Norway since 1 January 2010. The entry into force in Switzerland should be the 1 January 2011 (see Norwegian and Swiss Reports, I.2).

[46]See Turkish Report, I.2, note 5. See also Y.M. Atamer and H.W. Micklitz, "The Implementation of the EU Consumer Protection Directives in Turkey," *Penn State Int'l Law Review* 27, 3/4 (2009), 551.

[47]See US Report, I.1.B, note 8, and see also L.F. Del Duca, A.H. Kritzer, and D. Nagel, "Achieving Optimal Use of Harmonization Techniques In an Increasingly Twenty-First Century World of Consumer Sales: Moving the EU Harmonization Process to a Global Plane," *Penn State Int'l Law Review* 27, 3/4 (2009), 641; the Ethiopian Report, II.1, mentions a Draft of private international law act of 2003 which reproduces the jurisdiction rules on consumer contracts of the 1978 version of Brussels Convention; Art. 3517 of Civil Code of Quebec follows Art. 5 of the Rome Convention of 1980 (see Report of Quebec, III); etc.

[48]For example, all the conventions dealing with cooperation (in matter of service, proof and information about foreign law, interim measures, recognition and enforcement of judgments, etc.).

[49]The application of these rules may also be excluded taking into account that consumer protection deals either with mandatory rules or with public policy. See *Declaración de Córdoba*, available on www.oas.org. See also J.A. Moreno Rodríguez, "La Convención de México sobre el derecho aplicable a la contratación internacional," in D.P. Fernández Arroyo and J.A. Moreno Rodríguez (note 2) 107, 140–141.

applicable law, originally presented by Brazil, which has received the support of Argentina and Paraguay; a draft model law on jurisdiction and applicable law, proposed by Canada (see below note 80); and a complex project, presented by the United States of America, comprising some Legislative Guidelines and four model laws as appendices (on: ODR, small claims, disputed consumer card payments and government redress for consumers).[50]

Within the framework of Latin American sub-regional integration, Mercosur adopted in 1996 an instrument relating to jurisdiction in consumer relationships, the Santa Maria Protocol, which is not yet in force but which has inspired one of the additional protocols of the draft convention presented by Brazil at CIDIP-VII.[51] Other Mercosur regulations concerning private international law are potentially applicable to consumer litigation.[52] Moreover, Mercosur has drafted some *soft laws* on fundamental consumer rights.[53] The Andean Community has also adopted many rules targeting the material harmonization of consumer protection, of a general nature as well as having a bearing on specific points.[54] Lastly, the constitutional treaty of CARICOM (the Chaguaramas treaty) is the only one amongst the regional treaties in force in the Americas to contain a separate section with provisions relating to consumer protection.[55]

In Africa too, the organizations for economic integration, for instance the Common Market for Eastern and Southern Africa (COMESA) and the East African Community (EAC) have drafted laws that have a direct impact on consumer rights, e.g. the COMESA regulation on competition.[56]

7.4.2.3 Transnational Sources

The limited effectiveness of consumer law has led some authors to suggest developing a sort of transnational consumer law which should have its main roots in auto-regulation.[57] This suggestion –which is attempting to become reality by means of a long list of "non-national" laws–[58] seems to claim that it applies to consumer relationships similar ideas to those based on the *lex mercatoria* debate on professional relationships. The evident differences between these two types of relationship, due to the unequal role of party autonomy on all sides, have attracted some sharp criticism.[59]

7.4.3 The Concept of Consumer

The consumer is defined in a very diverse way in comparative law. Three principal criteria can be used to define what constitutes a consumer, in the knowledge that these criteria can be used individually or in combination.

In the first place, the type of person can be taken into account. Indeed, some legal orders exclusively reserve the description of consumer for physical persons, excluding juridical persons. Others, however, encompass both types. A sub-distinction can be employed for juridical persons: in certain countries, an association may be deemed to be a consumer, but not a corporation (civil or commercial), whereas in others, the description is not limited to a certain type of juridical person.

In the second place, the behavior of a person who purchases goods or services plays an important part in determining the application of protective rules. Following the example of EU law, many legal orders limit the application of consumer law to passive consumers, that is to say, to those who have not taken any particular step to purchase the goods and/ or to those who have been targeted by marketing and advertising campaigns.

---

[50] See http://www.oas.org/dil/CIDIPVII_documents_working_group_consumer_protection.htm where all these documents are available. See also J. M. Velázquez Gardeta, *La protección al consumidor* online *en el derecho internacional privado interamericano. Análisis sistemático de las propuestas presentadas para la CIDIP VII* (Asunción: CEDEP 2009); D. P. Fernández Arroyo, "Current Approaches Towards Harmonization of Consumer Private International Law in the Americas", *Penn State Int'ernational Law Review* 27, 3/4 (2009), 693.

[51] See *infra*, II.1.

[52] Notably in matter of procedure and cooperation. See Report of Mercosur.

[53] Communication on the regional consumer rights of 10 December 1998, and the Charter consumer rights of 15 December 2000, both adopted by Mercosur Council. See R.N. Grassi, "La politique de protection du consommateur dans le système d'intégration régionale du Mercosur," in *L'intégration économique régionale et la protection du consommateur,* ed. Th. Bourgoignie, 339 (Cowansville: Yvon Blais 2009).

[54] Report of the Andean Community, I.2.

[55] T. Bourgoignie and J. St-Pierre (note 40) 18.

[56] See Ethiopian and Kenyan Reports, I.2.

[57] See G.-P. Calliess, *Grenzüberschreitende Verbraucherverträge. Rechtssicherheit und Gerechtigkeit auf dem elektronischen Weltmarkplatz*, (Tübingen: Mohr Siebeck 2006).

[58] Long and very heterogeneous (including some EU rules!). *Ibid.*, at 375–485.

[59] N. Reich (note 1) *passim*.

Finally, some laws consider the purpose for which goods have been purchased in order to determine the application of protective instruments within consumer law. This criterion allows for a flexible appreciation of the notional consumer. Purchases made for professional reasons are excluded from this area of application of consumer law. This element is sometimes combined with the purchaser's expertise: therefore a professional who purchases goods or services for professional reasons, but in an area of activity where he/ she has no experience, may be deemed to be a consumer and may benefit from protective rules.

7.5 Rules of Jurisdiction

7.5.1 Specific Provisions

It goes without saying that the most exhaustive and most "tested" regulation of jurisdiction in consumer law is that of the "Brussels/Lugano system", in force in EU and EFTA countries, whose domain of application extends to jurisdiction and the recognition and enforcement of decisions concerning civil and commercial matters. Although we should make distinctions according to the concrete text that is applicable in each situation,[60] the protection this system guarantees to consumers can be summed up as follows:

- Protection is limited to defined persons (physical persons[61] having concluded a contract "for a purpose which can be regarded as being outside his/ her trade or profession") and to the contracts mentioned in these texts;[62]
- The consumer's co-contractor must be a professional[63];
- The choice of court agreement can only happen when the following conditions have been met[64]: the agreement to choose a court can only occur after the dispute has arisen; the agreement allows the consumer to bring proceedings to other courts not mentioned in the applicable rules, or the consumer and his/ her co-contractor have, at the time of concluding the contract, their domicile or habitual residence in the same contracting country and confer jurisdiction on this country's courts, unless the law of the latter forbids such agreements;
- When there is no valid choice of court, the consumer has the option of bringing the proceedings in the courts where the co-contractor is domiciled or to his/ her own place of domicile ("protection forum"); proceedings may be brought against a consumer by the other party only in the courts of the consumer's domicile.

The EU's Court of Justice case law reveals a restrictive interpretation of the concept of the consumer deserving the protection of the aforementioned rules. This attitude, already present in the Brussels Convention, remains in the interpretation of Regulation 44/2001.[65]

[60] Texts are, for EU member States, 1968 Brussels Convention in its last version of 1996 (in the original version consumer protection was much more restrictive) and Regulation 44/2001 which replaced it and, for all the members of the EU and the EFTA, the 1988 Lugano Convention and its new version of 2007. The application of one text or another depends on, besides the temporary scope rules, the parties, domicile. The 1988 Lugano Convention is parallel to Brussels Convention (Arts. 13–15) and the 2007 Lugano Convention is "parallel" to Regulation 44/2001. Within the EU member States, EU texts have priority (see Art. 64 Lugano Convention of 2007). See EU Report, I.2 and II.1. See also P. Lagarde, "Heurs et malheurs de la protection internationale du consommateur dans l'Union européenne," in *Études Jacques Ghestin*, 511(Paris: LGDJ 2001); A. Bonomi, "Les contrats conclus par les consommateurs dans la Convention de Lugano revise," *DeCITA* 9 (2008), 190; H. Gaudemet-Tallon, *Compétence et exécution des jugements en Europe*, 4th ed., (Paris: LGDJ 2010), 286–301.

[61] This condition is not foreseen in the abovementioned texts (on the contrary, the Regulation Rome I, Art. 6, includes a definition of consumer) but it has been made by the ECJ case law (see judgment of 22 November 2001, C-541-542/99).

[62] In any event, the conclusion of a contract is required (ECJ, 14 May 2009, C-180/06, *Ilsinger*). Regulation 44/2001 and Lugano Convention of 2007 (Art. 15(1.c)) include e-contracts by reference to all the contracts concluded with a person who "by any means directs such activities" to the State of the consumer's domicile.

[63] This condition is not foreseen in the texts but it is generally accepted (Report of the EU, II.1, note 20 and accompanying text).

[64] The acceptance of forum selection clauses could be contradictory, according to some authors, with the Directive 93/13 which forbids the unfair terms in consumer contracts, and which has priority over the Regulation. See Report of the EU, II.1, note 40, quoting P.A. Nielsen, "Art. 17," in *Brussels I Regulation,* ed. U. Magnus and P. Mankowski, 322 (München, 2007), and ECJ, 4 June 2009, C-243/08, *Pannon*. See also the decision of the tribunal of Gent, 4 April 2007, *NjW*, 2008, 174, quoted in the Belgian Report, note 7; Art. 2(7)(λα΄) of the Greek Act 2251/1994, mentioned in the Greek Report, notes 30–31; Art. 385(3) pa. 23 of the Civil Code of Poland (Polish Report, II.1.A); Art. 52 of the Private International Law and Procedure Act of Slovenia (Report of Slovenia, II.1).

[65] See EU Report, II.1, notes 23–25 and accompanying text and the decision already mentioned ECJ of 14 May 2009, *Ilsinger*, par. 58.

It is based on the exceptional nature of grounds of jurisdiction provided for in the section relating to the "jurisdiction over consumer contracts", as much in comparison to the general rule which attributes jurisdiction to the courts where the defendant is domiciled as to the special rule on jurisdiction for contracts.[66]

Grosso modo, when the defendant's domicile is not in a country within the Brussels/Lugano system, the national rules of jurisdiction are applicable. In terms of contracts entered into by consumers, the rules differ from those in the aforementioned system.[67] Thus, in Belgium, in accordance with article 97 (3) of the Code of Private International Law and in Denmark, in accordance with article 245 (2) of the Administration of Justice Act,[68] only the agreement to choose a legal court after the dispute has arisen is binding on the consumers.[69] In Switzerland, the choice of court is possible as long as the consumer is not unfairly deprived of the court protection provided for him/ her in Swiss law.[70] In Germany, article 94 (c) of the Civil Procedure Code (ZPO) – the only provision specifically relating to consumer relationships – establishes the rules of jurisdiction exclusively for door-to-door selling.[71] In Poland, no conditions relative to the type of contract or to the actions of the consumer's co-contractor are necessary for the consumer to bring proceedings in the local courts, provided that the consumer has undertaken the relevant steps to conclude the contract, even if he/she does not have his/her domicile in Poland.[72] In the United Kingdom, whereas Scottish law and the law applicable to inter-UK relationships have adopted rules of jurisdiction for consumer contracts based on the EU model, the determination of jurisdiction by the traditional system of English law does not provide for any specific rule on this topic and is largely at the judge's discretion.[73]

The legal orders of other EU member-states do not contain any specific measure regarding jurisdiction over consumption. This is the case in the Czech Republic,[74] France[75] and Greece.[76] And more importantly yet, in applying article 4 of all the European instruments on jurisdiction, when the defendant is not domiciled in a member State of the "Brussels/Lugano system", the plaintiff can appeal against this to the exorbitant grounds of jurisdiction available within the European States, a right that is absolutely forbidden when the defendant is domiciled in a contracting country (article 3). That is to say that all the grounds, rightly forbidden in principle (plaintiff's nationality, service of process, defendant's property), are perfectly valid against the "foreign" defendant.[77]

Naturally, the European continent is not alone in adopting rules of jurisdiction in matters relating to our subject. The Canadian province of Quebec has introduced jurisdiction in terms of consumer contract in its Civil Code. The basic rule, contained in article 3149, states that the Quebec courts have jurisdiction when the consumer has his/her domicile or residence in Quebec, the waiver of the right to bring proceedings in court not being binding on the consumer.[78] This rule

[66]See EU Report, II.1 and notes 21–22, 26–29 and the accompanying text. See also the decisions of the ECJ of 11 juillet 2002, C-95/00, *Rudolf Gabriel v. Schlank & Schick*, par. 39, and of 3 July 1997, C-269/95, *Benincasa v. Dentalkit*, par. 16–18.

[67]In Italy the Act 218/1995 extends the application of the Brussels Convention and its modifications to all the cases, that is to say, that the rules of the Regulation 44/2001 also apply when the defendant is not domiciled in a EU member State (Italian Report, II.1, which calls that European instrument "law 2001/44"). In Spain, the jurisdiction rules of the Judiciary Power Act have been drafted upon the influence of the Brussels Convention, including rules on consumer contracts; by consequence ECJ case law must be taken into account as to the interpretation of those rules (see Spanish Report, II.1.A).

[68]Danish Report, II.1. Moreover, in Denmark, the Sales Act has a definition of consumer which includes juridical persons.

[69]In the same vein, Art. 4–6(3) of the Civil Procedure Act of Norway (Norwegian Report, II.1.A).

[70]Art. 5 line 2 of Swiss Private International Law Act (PILA). According to Art. 114 line 1 PILA, "*le consommateur ne peut pas renoncer d'avance au for de son domicile ou de sa résidence habituelle*" (Swiss Report, II.1.A).

[71]See Report of Germany, II.1.A.

[72]Art. 1103 of the Civil Procedure Code of Poland, modified in 2008, in force since the 1 July 2009. See Polish Report, II.1.A.

[73]In the UK Report, II.1 (in the notes 26–30 and accompanying text, may be found the restrictive interpretation of the consumer notion whenever the rules based on the European patterns are applied).

[74]See Czech Report, II.1.A, note 7.

[75]See French Report, II.1.A.

[76]See Report of Greece, II.1.

[77]See D. P. Fernández Arroyo, "Compétence exclusive et compétence exorbitante dans les relations privées internationales," *Recueil des Cours* 323 (2006), 197 ss.

[78]However, in the decision *Dell Computer Corp. c. Union des consommateurs* [2007] 2 R.C.S. 801, the Supreme Court of Canada accepted the submission to arbitration abroad, considering that Art. 3149 was not applicable to this case. The law has been modified in order to avoid such decisions. See J. M. Velázquez Gardeta, "Cuando el elemento extranjero se convierte en la excusa imperfecta (*Dell Computer Corp. c. Union des consommateurs*)," *RDC* 73 (2010), 266.

must be applied whilst taking into consideration the general provisions of jurisdiction, which are founded on the links between the defendant or the dispute and the province of Quebec.[79] Outside of Quebec, Canada does not have any specific rules of jurisdiction in this area. However, as we have already noticed Canada has presented a draft model law on jurisdiction and applicable law as regards consumer contracts within the framework of ongoing work at CIDIP-VII (OAS). This draft makes provision for the following grounds of jurisdiction: the defendant's habitual residence, the substantive connection between the forum and the facts of the case, the express choice of court (in certain conditions) and the tacit choice of court; but all these grounds can be swept aside by the court on the basis of *forum non conveniens* doctrine.[80]

At the other extreme of the American continent, the Mercosur in 1996 adopted an international convention named the Santa Maria Protocol on international jurisdiction in consumer relationships[81] which could only become effective after the adoption of another instrument which was to harmonize consumer law within the countries belonging to this organization (Mercosur Common Law for consumer protection), which has never been adopted.[82] The most important provisions of the Protocol are: on the one hand, the option for the consumer to bring actions in the court where he/ she is domiciled, or in the court where the co-contractor is domiciled, or in the place where the contract was concluded, or in the place where the goods were delivered or where the services were provided; on the other hand, the professional, who may only bring proceedings in the courts where the consumer is domiciled, is allowed, in certain conditions, to dispute the complaint, to offer evidence, to resist an appeal, or to set in motion procedural measures which will go before the judges where he/she is domiciled. The Protocol does not contain any arrangements for the choice of court agreements, even to forbid them. Despite the failure of this instrument in the context of specific integration, it recently served as the basis for the "additional Protocol on international jurisdiction for certain contracts and for certain consumer transactions", proposed in 2009 by Argentina, Brazil and Paraguay within the context of CIDIP-VII, as an appendix to the draft Convention on applicable law.[83]

Far from Mercosur, Turkish law regarding jurisdiction contained in article 45 of the Private International Law Act of 2007, reflects a similar attitude: the consumer has several options; on the contrary, the co-contractor can only summons the consumer to appear before the court where the latter is domiciled. However, article 47, which authorizes submission to foreign courts in general, expressly forbids the *derogatio fori* in terms of consumer contracts.[84]

In Japan, a legislative draft dating from 2009 contains rules of jurisdiction in terms of contracts concluded by consumers, of which the general criterion is to recognize the jurisdiction of the Japanese courts when the consumer is domiciled within that country.[85]

7.5.2 Jurisdiction in the Absence of Specific Provisions

When the legal system in question does not provide any specific rule of jurisdiction, court responses can be very unpredictable in the matter of deciding on their jurisdiction regarding consumer contracts. On the one hand, one option consists of applying the same rules of jurisdiction established for contracts. On the other hand, one can equally deny any international dimension to the present situation and treat it as a purely local matter. For the first option, the most representative examples are the United States and Canada (*common law*)[86] and, for the second option, Brazil.

[79] See Report of Quebec, II.1.

[80] See OAS Report, II.1 (insisting on the contradictory character of the North American case law applying the so–called doctrine of online consumer contracts). [Note: On 18 October 2010 Canada withdrew its proposal –see OAS CP/CAJP-2912/10].

[81] Mercosur/CMC/Dec. nº 10/96.

[82] See Report of Mercosur, II.1.

[83] It is worthy to note that none of the Mercosur Member States has specific provision on jurisdiction in respect of our subject. However, in Uruguay, a project of a general Statute on Private International Law is currently submitted for discussion in the Parliament, according to which the Uruguayan Courts would have jurisdiction if the defendant's domicile is in Uruguay, if Uruguayan law is applicable (Art. 56.1 and 2) and, when the consumer is the plaintiff, if the place of conclusion or performance (delivery of goods or services) is in Uruguay (Art. 58.d). The choice of court is forbidden (Art. 59.2). See Report of Uruguay, II.1. The text of the Project is reproduced in *DeCITA* 11 (2009) 429.

[84] According to some authors, the grounds of jurisdiction set out in Art. 45 PILA would be exclusive. See Turkish Report, II.1.

[85] See Japanese Report, II.1 [Note: The Act was promolgated on 2 May 2011].

[86] The common law systems which are reported in this book (Ghana, United Kingdom, Kenya, Australia, Israel…).

In the United States, determination of jurisdiction in terms of consumer contracts is not dissimilar to the general rule: the plaintiff must demonstrate that the defendant has "minimum contacts" with the court; the courts can declare *forum non conveniens* and the choice of court agreements are generally accepted.[87] American case law has made real innovations regarding consumer contracts where contracts are concluded online. Amongst the determining criteria for this, the most famous – and, undoubtedly, the most controversial – is the sliding scale test that had its origins in the *Zippo* case,[88] which was based on the nature of information furnished by the defendant's web-site. In the Canadian system of common law, the choice of court is permitted to a large extent, although the agreements come under very close scrutiny in consumer contracts.[89]

In Brazil, both case law and scholars accept that the jurisdiction of Brazilian courts is based on article 101 (I) of the Code of consumer protection (CDC) – which is not really a rule of international jurisdiction – when the consumer is domiciled in Brazil and brings proceedings in a Brazilian court, even if the products have been purchased abroad (*Panasonic* ruling), if the time-sharing service contract has been fulfilled abroad (*Punta de Leste* case), but only if the consumer is a physical person.[90] The preliminary clauses for agreeing a court have been deemed unfair by the Ministry of Justice[91] and the Superior Court of Justice has described the rule in article 101 (I) of the CDC as a "public policy" rule.[92]

7.5.3 Recognition and Enforcement of Foreign Decisions Relating to Consumption

In general, rules on the recognition and the enforcement of foreign decisions are not very specific in terms of consumer protection. However, if the ground of jurisdiction provided for in this matter is defined as a "protection forum", consistency should lead to a more rigorous assessment of the jurisdiction of the judge of origin when the foreign judgement is recognized. In this sense, the Brussels/Lugano system expressly establishes an exception, in the matter of consumer contracts, to the rule which forbids the aforementioned assessment in the general.[93]

In the same vein, the Swiss Private International Law Act (PILA) establishes specific indirect rules of jurisdiction in the matter of consumer contracts. Thus, article 149 (2) (b) anticipates that the foreign judgement will be recognized provided "that it has been made in the place of domicile or usual residence of the consumer and that the conditions anticipated by article 120 (1) are met". In the same way, the Santa Maria Protocol (Mercosur) points out in article 12 that the grounds of jurisdiction incorporated in the Protocol must be considered to be indirect grounds of jurisdiction when it is a question of applying the Mercosur rules on the recognition and enforcement of decisions.[94] In Quebec, despite the non-binding nature of the choice of court agreements on the consumer, a measure enshrined in the Civil Code (article 3168 duplicates the wording of article 3145 but only for consumers domiciled in Quebec), a foreign decision based on such an agreement can nonetheless have an impact in Quebec, upon condition that the consumer should have brought proceedings in the foreign court or that he/ she should have defended himself/herself on the merits.[95]

That said, even in the absence of a positive rule like the latter, it seems logical that if the consumer deserves protective treatment from the jurisdiction, the enforcement of foreign decisions in this matter should also be subject to stricter monitoring, unless this permits the systematic negation of the outcomes, which would be, in some cases, detrimental to the consumer him/herself.[96] It is obvious that the scrutiny would not be made only

[87]See US Report, II.1.

[88]*Zippo Mfg. Co. v. Zippo Dot Com, Inc.*, 952 F.Supp. 1119 (W.D. Pa. 1997). [Note: Compare with ECJ, 7 December 2010, C-585/08 and C-144/09, *Pammer* and *Hotel Alpenhof*.]

[89]According to the Canadian Report (common law), II.1, "courts assess these contracts with greater scrutiny." See the cases mentioned in notes 37 and 38 of the Report. In a similar sense, see Australian Report, II.1, and the quotation of the decision *Oceanic Sun Special Shipping Line Co Inc vs. Fay* (1988) 165 CLR 197.

[90]See Brazilian Report, II.1.B, notes 95–98 and accompanying text.

[91]Cl. n°. 8, *Portaria* 4/98.

[92]Report of Brazil, *loc. cit.*, notes 105–106.

[93]See Art. 35 of Regulation 44/2001.

[94]Las Leñas Protocol of 1992, in force in the four member States of Mercosur.

[95]See Report of Quebec, II.3.A.

[96]See, under notes 7–9 of Turkish Report, the discussion about the exclusive character or not of the grounds of jurisdiction on consumer contracts in the Turkish Private International Law Act. The admission of such a character would prevent the recognition of any foreign decision on that subject in Turkey.

regarding the jurisdiction of origin. Other grounds, such as violation of due process[97] or violation of public policy, might be also invoked.

It must not be forgotten that, even nowadays, despite the development of international judicial cooperation and the very great acceptance of internationally movement of judicial and arbitral decisions (reflected in most of the reports), some legal orders do not commit themselves to enforcing foreign decisions unless a treaty in force ordains it. This is the case, for example, of Denmark.[98]

7.6 Applicable Law

7.6.1 Specific Conflict of Law Rules on International Consumer Law

Yet again, the best known model is the EU one. Indeed, firstly the Rome Convention of 1980 on the law applicable to contractual obligations (for contracts concluded before December 18th 2009), then the Regulation 593/2008 (known as "Rome I") which "communitarised" it (for contracts concluded after this date), include specific rules to determine the law applicable to consumer contracts in their articles 5 and 6 respectively. Obviously, other (general) rules within each of these texts are also applicable should the case arise.

Contrary to the Regulation 44/2001 and other texts governing the jurisdiction and enforcement of decisions, which leave space for the enforcement of national rules (generally, when the defendant's domicile is not within the Brussels/Lugano system), the Rome Convention and the Regulation Rome I have a universal character. This means that their rules can be applied to all situations which come into their material and temporal scope of application. Thus, the national rules on the law applicable to consumer contracts are only applicable to international litigation if the contract was concluded before the entry into force of the Rome Convention (or the Regulation Rome I). Moreover, we know that we must also take into account the possible application of consumer rules contained in the substantive EU law (notably, the protective guidelines relating to unfair terms, time-sharing, distance contracts, etc.), for which the criteria of application remain problematic.[99]

In spite of the uncertainties generated during the drafting of the Regulation,[100] the real content of article 6 has ultimately remained faithful to its predecessor, although it brings the definition of contracts into line with that of article 15 of Regulation 44/2001 and introduces a modification in order to adapt the provision to electronic contracts. The general rule remains the application of the law of the country of the consumer's habitual residence. Parties can, however, submit the contract to the law of another state, which will be applicable insofar as the choice does not deprive the consumer of the protection guaranteed by the law of his/ her habitual residence, which must be verified *ex officio* by the judge.[101] If the test fails, the law of the habitual residence applies, no means of rectification (exception clause) having been provided. In this way, the EU legislator is trying to find a compromise between the freedom of contract and the protection of the weak party, as did the negotiators involved with the Rome Convention.[102]

At the geographical heart of the EU, but outside it, Switzerland also establishes (article 120 PILA) that the law applicable to consumer contracts is that of the country of the consumer's habitual residence when the contract is concluded. This law will be applicable from the moment that one of the conditions of the article has been met, that is to say when the supplier has received the order in this country, when the finalization of the contract has been preceded by an offer or

[97] See Report of Quebec, II.3.B.

[98] See K. Hertz and J. Lookofsky, *EU-PIL. European Union Private International Law in Contract and Tort*, (København: DJØF Publishing 2009), 137, quoted in Danish Report, note 7.

[99] EU Report, notes 51–59 and accompanying text.

[100] See Regulation proposal, document COM (2005) 650 final.

[101] Although the courts achieve this task in various different ways (see J. Basedow, "Internationales Verbrauchervertragsrecht – Erfahrungen, Prinzipien und europäische Reform," in *Festschrift für Erik Jayme*, I, (München: Sellier 2004), 16), it is clear that this entails a comparison between the chosen law and the law of the consumer's habitual residence. This effort requires to define previously what should be considered as "mandatory" in the law of the habitual residence. See EU Report, notes 66–73 and accompanying text.

[102] This European approach was adopted in Quebec, which Art. 3117 of the Civil Code is based on Art. 5 of the Rome Convention. See the Report of Quebec, III. This approach can also be found in Art. 7 of the Draft Model Law presented by Canada in the framework of CIDIP-VII (OAS).

by advertising in this country or when the consumer has been encouraged by the supplier to go to this country. Swiss law saves its judges from the task of comparing laws, by explicitly ruling out the choice of law clauses.[103] We must mention that article 120 PILA has been referenced by a draft Ethiopian law in 2003. Following this model, the application of Ethiopian law (which contains no consumer protection rules), would still be guaranteed for passive consumers who are domiciled in that country, whereas the consumer from a very protective country would benefit from the application of his/her own law when entering into a contract with an Ethiopian professional (for example, a coffee producer).[104]

This draws the attention on the real protection afforded by the systematic application of the law of the consumer's habitual residence. Everything leads to think that this option can only fulfill its protective function if the law in force in that country contemplates an acceptable level of protection. Such a consideration seems to have formed the basis of the writing of the draft inter-American convention on the law applicable to certain international consumer contracts introduced by Brazil in the context of work on the codification of private international law followed by the OAS (CIDIP).[105] The basic idea consists of applying, amongst the laws connected with the envisaged legal relationship, the most favorable law to the consumer.[106] The draft has already undergone a long process of negotiations, which are reflected in the numerous changes that have been made, including the modification of its structure (placing some rules in various additional protocols). Despite the ensuing criticisms, the draft has received the enthusiastic support of some countries. This support could be seen from the fact that in the draft version presently being discussed – known as the "Buenos Aires Proposal (2009)" – Argentina and Paraguay appear next to Brazil.[107]

The main specific rules of the draft convention set out, for passive consumers (article 4), that the applicable law will be "the law chosen by the parties" who can opt for the law of the consumer's domicile, the law of the place of conclusion, the law of the place of performance or the law of the domicile or seat of the provider of goods or services; such law shall be applicable to the extent that it is more favorable to the consumer. In the case of active consumers (article 5), the parties can choose the law of the place of conclusion of the contract, the law of the place of performance or the law of the consumer's domicile; in the absence of a valid choice, the contract will be governed by the law of the country where the consumer and the professional physically entered into the contract. The draft also includes, in addition to measures relating to "mandatory international norms",[108] the duty of information for the professional and, relating to specific travel and time-sharing contracts, an exception clause known as "hard" according to which "the law specified as applicable in this Convention may not be applicable in exceptional cases, if, considering all the circumstances of the case, the connection of the law indicated as applicable proves to be superficial and the case itself is more closely related to another law, more favourable to the consumer."

---

[103] Swiss Report, III.1. A and B.

[104] The Reporter finds a possible solution for that situation in another provision of the same draft which reproduces Art. 19 PILA (the one which authorizes the application of foreign mandatory rules). See the Ethiopian Report, notes 37–46 and accompanying text. Another example of law relativity on this subject, but which is very different, can be found in the provision enshrined in Art. 9(b) of the Defective Products (Liability) Law, 5740–1980 in Israel, according to which the said law is not applicable when the person having suffered a damage is outside of this State (Israeli Report, III.1).

[105] See the text written by the author of the original project (presented in 2000), C. Lima Marques, "Consumer Protection in Private International Law Rules: The Need for an Inter-American Convention on the Law Applicable to Some Consumer Contracts and Consumer Transactions (CIDIP)," in *Regards croisés sur les enjeux contemporains du droit de la consommation,* ed. T. Bourgoignie, 145 (Quebec: Yvon Blais 2006). See also OAS Report, III.

[106] The most favorable law has been defined in Art. 4(2) in order to reply to the critics made on the apparent uncertainty and the costs that such criterion would entail (See M. Dennis, note 2). The first adopted definition is the one of the law of the consumer's domicile, which could weaken the innovative character of the project, above all if we compare it with the option of introducing substantive presumptions. In any case, comparing possible solutions is a very common activity for the courts. See J. M. Velázquez Gardeta, "El derecho más favorable al consumidor, la mejor solución también para los contratos de consumo online," in *Tendencias y relaciones del derecho internacional privado americano actual*, eds. D.P. Fernández Arroyo and N. González Martín, 29 (México: UNAM/Porrúa/ASADIP 2010).

[107] See C. Lima Marques and M.L. Delaloye, "La Propuesta de 'Buenos Aires' de Brasil, Argentina y Paraguay: El más reciente avance en el marco de la CIDIP VII de protección de consumidores," *RDC* 73 (2010), 224.

[108] One of these adapted to online contracts can be found in Art. 7(2).

Even if it has received the support of certain neighbor States, the draft Brazilian convention does not seem to have convinced the authors of the Uruguay's draft of private international law Act which is rather close to the European model. Indeed, the latter sets out in article 50(5) that the law applicable to consumer contracts will be, in the first instance, that of the country where the goods have been acquired and the services used; if this law cannot be determined, then the law of the consumer's domicile will apply. When the contract is a distance contract or when the professional has made offers or specific advertising in the consumer's domicile, the law of the consumer's domicile is applicable, provided that the consumer has given his/her consent there.[109]

7.6.2 Current Solutions in the Absence of Specific Rules on Applicable Law

When there are no rules provided for the determination of the law applicable to consumer contracts, the available options resemble those mentioned in the absence of rules of jurisdiction. That is to say, either the application of conflict rules for contracts in general (where the dominant trend is to recognize party autonomy),[110] or the ignoring of the international character of the relationship by automatically applying the law of the court.

A remarkable example of the first option is that of the United States, where party autonomy also prevails in consumer contracts.[111] However, it is striking that there is an enormous disparity among the national laws which are potentially applicable to consumer relationships.[112]

The opposite trend, typical of countries like Brazil, consists of denying party autonomy and of automatically applying the *lex fori*. In certain cases, the courts do not seem to have realized the international aspects of the relationships.[113] Moreover, even in the countries where party autonomy is generally accepted, the rules relating to consumer contracts are often considered as mandatory rules, thereby ruling out party autonomy.[114]

7.7 Procedure

Making access to justice easier for consumers by the adoption of favorable rules of jurisdiction is of little use if the countries which have jurisdiction do not take into account the specificity of consumer litigation at a procedural level. International consumer protection can indeed only be guaranteed if consumers have effective access to justice, if they are not discouraged from seizing courts because of the inherent costs of obtaining justice as well as the length of the proceedings.

The right of access to justice for consumers can be achieved through two types of measures, which it is also possible to combine. On the one hand, some countries have adopted special procedures, or have even established special courts to rule on consumer litigation. On the other hand, international consumer protection can be achieved by means of special types of action, such as class or group actions.

7.7.1 Specific Procedures for Consumer Claims

7.7.1.1 The Creation of Special or Specialized Courts

One of the means of guaranteeing the consumer access to justice is, following the example of Australia, Brazil, Israel and Turkey, to create special or specialized courts that are competent in the matter of cross-border litigation. These courts function according to a particular procedure. For example, in Australia, the Small Claims Tribunal (1973), decides on small claims

[109] See Uruguayan Report, III.1.

[110] See Venezuelan Report, II.1.B et III.

[111] See Report of the United States, III.1.

[112] *Ibid.*

[113] See N. de Araujo, "Contratos internacionais e consumidores nas Américas e no Mercosur: Análise da proposta brasileira para uma convenção interamericana na CIDIP VII", *Cadernos do Programa de Pós Graduação em Direito UFRGS* 5 (2006), 107, 119 (with references to the *Panasonic* case, *Superior Tribunal de Justiça*, Resp 63.981, 13 August 2001, *RSTJ*, nº137, 12 (2001), 387). Such attitude can be found everywhere. See the Ethiopian Report, III, which mentions the case *Emma Vakaro v Customs Administration* (Supreme Court of Ethiopia), Civ.app. no. 852/73, *JEL* vol. 5, no 1 (1968) 327.

[114] As in Argentina. See C.D. Iud, "Los acuerdos de prórroga de jurisdicción concluidos por consumidores en el derecho argentine," in: D.P. Fernández Arroyo and J.A. Moreno Rodríguez (note 2) 421, 436. See also the decisions quoted in the French Report, III.1.D, in particular, Cass. Civ. 1e., 23 May 2006, *Époux Richt c/ Commerzbank* (mentioned in note 39).

litigation relating to the supply of goods or services, according to a procedure which takes place without representation by a lawyer unless both parties agree to be represented.[115] In Brazil, where the creation of small claims courts is more recent, dating from 1984, the procedure before the specialized courts (there is no "special" court, but there is a specialization of state and federal common law courts) is free and also takes place without representation, up to a sum corresponding to a minimum of twenty times the person's salary.[116] These courts have been a big hit in Brazil and adjudicate 80% of consumer disputes. Small claims courts have also been introduced in Israel and are based within the Magistrates Courts. The rapid handling of these cases is facilitated by the flexible procedural rules to be followed: these courts are authorized to conduct proceedings in as efficient manner as possible, without complying with the procedural rules applicable in other courts. The court must authorize a party to be represented by a lawyer; another system of free representation – by associations – has also been established.[117] In Turkey there is a dual system. On the one hand, there are consumer courts, before which consumer must lodge any action worth less than 2.446,03 TL. These consumer courts are specialized courts.[118] Above that sum, the consumer has one option. He/ she can indeed resort to arbitral consumer courts.

In two other jurisdictions, Ethiopia and Quebec, such courts also exist but are reserved for domestic claims. In Ethiopia, specialized courts, – named social or *Kebele* courts, and composed of non professional judges – settle small claims, which are defined differently in different States. However, these courts do not have jurisdiction for cross-border disputes. The way they function has moreover been criticized for disregarding the proper administration of justice.[119] Quebec has established a consumer protection Office, apparently with very wide prerogatives[120]; it receives consumer complaints in particular. However, Quebec's consumer protection Act is silent on the role of this Office in international consumer relationships.

A common feature of all these courts is to be open only to physical persons and to provide a very lightweight system of representation, not to say inexistent. Suppressing the use of lawyers allows the overall cost of the proceedings to be reduced.

Nonetheless, these States remain an exception, as in the other States under present scrutiny, consumer disputes are resolved before not specialized courts: for example, in France, the *Tribunal d'instance* has jurisdiction in this kind of cases.[121]

7.7.1.2 The Adoption of a Particular Procedure for Small Claims Settled by Not Specialized Courts

Many countries, however, provide for a particular procedure for small claims, whether peculiar or not to consumer litigation. On this point, it matters little whether the procedures peculiar to small claims be the sole province of consumer litigation or open to any other type of litigation; the most important thing is that consumers can take advantage of a simplified, less expensive and shorter procedure.

With the exception of Regulation 861/2007 of 11 July 2007 establishing a European small claims procedure, which creates a *special* procedure for *cross-border* litigation, no other legal system provides for a special procedure for international consumer litigation. In general, the simplified procedural rules, adopted to settle small claims, are also applicable when the consumer plaintiff neither resides in nor originates from the country where he/she has lodged an action.

In addition to the member States of the EU,[122] where the provisions of aforementioned Regulation 861/2007 apply, it must be noted that a good number of other countries have this kind of procedure. Norway, South Africa, Switzerland and Uruguay have instituted simplified small claims proceedings, all of which are applicable to international consumer relationships.

Moreover, several EU member States use a particular small claims procedure, established before the adoption of Regulation 861/2007 and which remains applicable to claims that are not covered by the scope of application of the aforementioned Regulation. Spain, for instance, distinguishes between two types of procedure, according to

[115] See Australian Report, IV.1.

[116] See Brazilian Report, IV.3.

[117] See Israeli Report, IV.1.

[118] See Turkish Report, IV.1.

[119] See Ethiopian Report, IV.1, particularly note 47.

[120] See Report of Quebec, IV.1.

[121] See French Report, IV.1.

[122] See EU Report, IV.1.

whether the sum comes to a maximum of 30,000 Euros or to a maximum of 9,000 Euros. In the latter case, the procedure is oral and the court seizure is simplified.[123] Denmark and Poland[124] have their own particular rules too.

The definition of what constitutes a small claim, for which the consumer litigation is often archetypal, differs greatly from one country to another. The following table shows the maximum sums that can be demanded in the small claims courts. Unsurprisingly, this sum is quite high in rich countries that are mindful of (international) consumer protection. However, compared to other sums, the threshold defined by Regulation 861/2007 appears ridiculously low. The European procedure for small claims could, by virtue of this, not offer the desired degree of protection.

Mention must be made of the countries that do not provide for any particular procedure intended to facilitate the settlement of small consumer claims. Among the legal orders within this study, five of them[126] do not provide for simplified procedure of any sort.

7.7.2 Particular Procedural Mechanisms (Group Actions)

In addition to specific adjustments in procedural terms, made to enhance consumer access to justice, certain legal orders have adopted certain types of action, especially relevant in consumer litigation which involves, due to using standard contracts, many victims and much damages.

Table recapitulating the monetary thresholds defining small claims (highest to lowest)

Canada(general average for the English-speaking provinces)	25,000	CAD	24,200 USD
Norway	125,000	NOK	19,650 USD
Switzerland	20,000	CHF	18,900 USD
Spain	9,000	EUR	11,380 USD
Brazil	Equivalent to 40 minimum salary installments		11,345 USD
Denmark	50,000	DKK	8,480 USD
Israel	30,000	NIS	7,500 USD
United Kingdom	5,000	GBP	7,500 USD
Scotland	3,000	GBP	4,500 USD
Poland	10,000	PLN	3,100 USD
Northern Ireland	2,000	EUR	3,000 USD
Slovenia	2,000	EUR	2,530 USD
European Union	2,000	EUR	2,530 USD
Uruguay[125]	100	UR	1,790 USD
Turkey	2,446	TRY	1,580 USD
Ethiopia (Addis-Abeba)	–	–	400 USD
Ethiopia (Amhara region)	–	–	120 USD

In the great majority of countries observed, these types of action have not been instituted *for* the consumers, but can be used for consumer litigation. Only Israel has enacted class actions just for consumers, with an amendment to its consumer protection law in 1994.[127] It must, however, be noted that the American proposal to CIDIP-VII (the legislative guidelines) goes in the direction of a special collective action in the matter of consumer litigation,[128] applicable as much to domestic as to international relationships.

[123] See Spanish Report, IV.1.

[124] See among others the detailed Report of Poland, IV.1.

[125] Uruguayan Act 18.507 of 26 June 2009 indicated the amount in float unities, which is not the national currency of Uruguay (amount equivalent in USD as of 1st July 2009). See Report of Uruguay, IV.1.

[126] Chile, Ghana, Kenya, Tunisia, Venezuela.

[127] See Israeli Report, IV.2.

[128] See OAS Report, IV.2.

Observation of the different rules in force within the States having been the subject of a report shows a great variety of these types of action. If one flags up the general features, it is possible to distinguish on one side, actions initiated by physical persons, which group together to bring an action (the American model), put in place in Australia, Canada (all provinces taken together), the United States of America and Denmark, and on the other side, actions which can only be brought by accredited consumer and user associations (the European model). Class action established in Israel results from a hybrid model, as it can be initiated as much by a physical person as by an association for consumer protection.[129]

7.7.2.1 Collective Actions Initiated by a Group of Physical Persons

The North American model, which can be found for example in Canada as well as Australia and, much more recently, Denmark,[130] is based on actions brought by the consumers themselves. As noted by the American reporters, it is moreover the most common means used in the United States[131] to compensate consumers for any damage suffered. Without doubt, it is interesting to note that the United Kingdom does not provide for such an action, to such an extent that an author, quoted by the reporter, maintains that: "as far as England is concerned, the legal system has failed to provide effective solutions to the challenge of finding mechanisms whereby consumers who individually have suffered small losses can group together so that litigation becomes a viable option".[132]

However, bringing class actions raises several difficulties when the "class" includes consumers who are not domiciled in the States in which such an action is brought. This is noted at the same time in the United States Report and both the Canadian Reports (common law and Quebec). Indeed, in international situations, the common character of the question of law or fact (commonality) uniting the class members, as well as the typical character of the claim brought by the class representative (typicality), generally required to bring a class action in the United States, are likely to be difficult to uphold. In Canada, class actions involving foreign consumers can only be allowed once it has been demonstrated that these consumers have a real and substantial connection to the action. There is also some difficulty regarding the fate of the consumers when the class action procedure is described as opting out. Indeed, in these cases, it is no doubt much too ambitious that consumers who live abroad, and who have not declared that they do not wish to be part of the class, are bound by the court decision. This objection does not seem to have been taken into account by the North American proposal to CIDIP-VII relating to the establishment of consumer class actions in the OAS member States, which does not distinguish whether the litigation is international or not.

Lastly, the constitution of a class is sometimes considered as a fundamental consumer right. For example, article 8(1) of the Ontario Consumer Protection Act sets out that one cannot waive in advance its participation in a class action; the introduction of an arbitration clause in a consumer contract subject to Ontario law does not avoid the possibility of a class action. Preference is given to collective appeal, which gives strong protection for the consumers from Ontario.

7.7.2.2 Representative Actions Reserved Solely for Accredited Consumer Associations

Another system of consumer protection which guarantees efficient access to justice is that of representative actions. In this case, consumers themselves are not the plaintiffs; instead an association of consumers and users, which has previously been accredited by a judicial or governmental authority, takes on the defence of the interests of consumers who have suffered damage of common origin. This model is found in many European States, which justifies its description of European model. The *ação coletiva* found in Brazilian law stems from the same model.

In fact the German, Brazilian, Spanish, French, Greek, Italian and Slovenian systems have in common that they provide that consumer interests can be represented before the court by a consumer protection association, therefore by an entity distinct from the consumers themselves. To resume the text of article 422–1 of the French Code for consumption relating to joint representative action: "when several identified consumers, physical persons, have suffered individual damage which have been caused by the behaviour of the same professional, and which have a common origin, any nationally accredited and recognized representative association in the matter of applying the

[129] See Israeli Report, IV.2.

[130] An Act adopted in 2008 has introduced the concept of class action in Danish law. See Report of Denmark, IV.2.

[131] See US Report, IV.2.

[132] J. Hill, *Cross Border Consumer Contracts* (Oxford: OUP, 2008), 164.

measures in the 1st title can, if it has been mandated by at least two of the consumers concerned, seek redress before any court in the name of the consumers. The mandate cannot be solicited by televised or radio broadcast public campaigns, nor by advertising, pamphlets or personalized letters. It must be given in writing by each consumer".[133] Without being totally identical, obviously, this action is close to the *Verbandsklage* of Slovenian law,[134] to the new group action established by article 140-bis of the Italian consumer code,[135] or yet to the *ação coletiva* found in Brazilian law, of which the holders are the Union, the federated States and the municipalities, as well as associations formed more than a year previously and whose object is directly related to consumer protection.[136] Recently added to this list are the *Defensoria Pública*, State owned companies and foundations.

Does it substitute the class action or is it rather a feature of continental civil laws?[137] Are these actions less efficient than action based on the North American model? Appreciation of the practical application of such measures is not easy, as each one responds to different conditions of application. In France, it seems that the joint representation action has not given rise to significant results, and it is even considered that the contribution of this mechanism is practically nil.[138] In Spain, the text is criticized for its lack of clarity,[139] whereas the Italian report spreads a certain optimism in supposing that the putting into action of the new article 140-bis of the consumer code will reinforce consumer protection. This, of course, remains to be seen.

The European Union, for its part, remains rather faint-hearted in this matter. The 2008 green book on collective actions open to consumers[140] has not yet given rise to any proposals for regulations.

7.8 Arbitration and Alternative Dispute Resolution (ADR)

The specificity of consumer litigation requires that we wonder about its means of settlement, and about the viability of dispute settlement mechanisms generally used to resolve commercial disputes. Many legal orders authorize the settlement of consumer litigation by arbitration; some provide as well for special mechanisms to settle disputes.

7.8.1 Arbitration

Arbitration rests on the principle of equality of the parties. And yet, disputes involving consumers depart hypothetically from this principle. It is therefore legitimate to wonder about the arbitrability of such litigation. If international consumer litigation is observed to be arbitrable in most legal orders, nonetheless particular rules, attentive to consumer protection, still apply.

7.8.1.1 Arbitrability of Consumer Litigation

The Principle: The Arbitrability of Consumer Litigation

The question of arbitrability of litigation involving consumers is generally not controversial. The former has indeed been very largely accepted in the national systems reported. Except for Chile[141] and Brazil,[142]

[133] See French Report, IV.2.

[134] See Slovenian Report, IV.2.

[135] See Italian Report, IV.2.

[136] See Brazilian Report and the references in notes 121 and 124: T. Morais da Costa, "Le droit constitutionnel: la protection des droits fondamentaux," in *Introduction au Droit Brésilien,* ed. D. Païva de Almeida, 73 (Paris: L'Harmattan 2006);A. Gidi, "Class Actions in Brazil- A model for Civil Law Countries", *AJCL* 51 (2003) 11.

[137] See the remark made by the author of the French Report, IV.2. and the debate that arose in France relating to this matter: L. Cadiet, "Illusoire renforcement du droit des actions de groupe ?," *JCP G* (1992) I, 3587, § 6; L. Boré, "L'action en représentation conjointe. *Class action* française ou action mort née?," *D.* (1995) 267. See also the German Report, IV.2, which mentions, speaking of UKlag (*Gesetz über Unterlassungsklagen bei Verbraucherrechts- und anderen Verstößen*), that it is ("a kind of class action particularly available for international consumers' disputes").

[138] See French Report, IV.2.

[139] See Spanish Report, IV.2. and the reference made to L. Carballo Piñeiro, *Las acciones colectivas y su eficacia extraterritorial. Problemas de recepción y transplante de las class actions en Europa*, Santiago de Compostela, USC (2009).

[140] Green Paper on Consumer Collective Redress of 27 November 2008 COM(2008) 794 final – (unpublished in the Official Journal).

[141] See Report of Chile: "As a consequence of the foregoing, it would be impossible that these matters might be submitted to international commercial arbitration in Chile."

[142] Two texts seem indeed to bring a contradictory answer. Art. 4 of the Arbitration Act on Adhesion Contracts is generally interpreted as sustaining the arbitrability of such disputes (S. Mendes, "Arbitragem e Direito do Consumidor," *RBA* (2003) 189) whereas Art. 51, IV of the Brazilian Code of Consumption considers the arbitration clauses inserted in consumer contracts as void. See Brazilian Report, IV.1.

which explicitly forbid arbitration clauses in consumer contracts, the other laws, either implicitly or explicitly, authorize the settlement of consumer dispute by means of arbitration. Certainly, in Australia as in Belgium, scholars are divided on what interpretation to give to the absence of specific provision in this respect. According to the Australian reporter, it is possible to interpret article 32 X of the Fair Trade Act as excluding arbitration in matters relating to consumers.[143] A similar interpretation is to be found in article 32 of the Belgian Act on Trade Practice.[144]

When consumer litigation is considered arbitrable, which corresponds to the large majority of laws here studied, the arbitrability is nonetheless subject to certain conditions.

Conditions of Arbitrability

In certain legal orders, the arbitrability of consumer disputes is only admissible if arbitration was agreed after the dispute has arisen. This is the case in the laws of Norway,[145] Denmark[146] and in the Canadian province of Ontario (which constitutes an exception in Canada).

Sometimes, it is a formal condition which applies. Thus, the German (article 1031 ZPO) and Norwegian (article 11 of the law on arbitration, inspired by the German law) laws set out that the arbitration clause must not only be expressly stipulated, but that it must also feature in a separate document, distinct from the contract, which *only* contains the convention of arbitration. This is a means of drawing the consumer's attention in particular and of guaranteeing his/her consent to arbitration, and therefore his /her waiver to State courts. Norwegian law even clarifies that the absence of information given to the consumer on the consequences of an arbitral award can cause the clause to be non-binding on the consumer. The protection can reveal itself to be largely ineffective, insofar as, as has been noted by the German reporter, these instruments only apply if arbitration takes place in these States (in Germany for the application of article 1031 ZPO and in Norway for the application of article 11 of the Norwegian law on arbitration). And yet, given that the choice of seat of the arbitral tribunal can be left in the hands of the party which drafted the clause or of the arbitral tribunal that has been constituted, these protective measures in favour of the consumer can be put aside without too much difficulty. The respect of formal conditions depends sometimes on administrative authorization. Thus, for example, in Alberta, the Fair Trading Act provides that arbitration agreements concluded in these matters which have not received approval of the Ministry cannot be enforced. According to the Canadian reporter (common law), the application of this particular instrument is, however, very limited.[147]

7.8.1.2 Consumer Arbitration Agreement's Regime

The Relative Absence of Specific Rules Relating to International Consumer Arbitration

In States where such litigation is likely to be resolved through arbitration, few of them adopted specific provisions on the matter.[148] Consumer arbitration is therefore subject to the same rules as those applied in matters of commercial arbitration. Also, when international arbitration is governed by a set of rules distinct from those relating to domestic arbitration, the same dichotomy occurs as for consumer arbitration.

This assertion must be put into perspective. In addition to the provisions relating to arbitration, consumer arbitration obeys the rules of consumer law, particularly the provisions relating to unfair terms.

Submission of Arbitration Clauses to the Regime of Unfair Clauses

Even in the absence of specific provisions in their respect, many national reports mention the risk that arbitration clauses, which are concluded before or after a dispute has arisen, are governed by the rules on unfair terms, which can lead, in many cases, to declaring these clauses non-binding on the consumer. Directive 93/13 of 5 April 1993 concerning unfair terms in consumer contracts sets out in this respect that the terms

143 See the Australian Report, V.1.

144 According to Report of Belgium, V.1.

145 See Norwegian Report, V.1.

146 Pursuant to Art. 7(2) of the Arbitration Act of Denmark (553/2005) as modified by 106/2008 Act, the consumer cannot be bound by an arbitration agreement entered into before the dispute has arisen. See Danish Report, V.1.

147 See Canadian Report (common law) and the references mentioned under V.1.

148 One exception: in Spain, the *Real Decreto* 231/2008 organizes an arbitration system which is peculiar to consumer arbitration.

which have the object or effect of "excluding or hindering the consumer's right to take legal action or exercise any other legal remedy, particularly by requiring the consumer to take disputes exclusively to arbitration not covered by legal provisions (....)" (letter q of the annex listing terms) may be declared unfair, in accordance with article 3(1) of the Directive. Thus, in EU law, any arbitration clause inserted into a consumer contract is *a priori* dubious and can be termed an unfair clause. It is nonetheless a question of an option ("can") not an obligation.

Logically, the treatment of arbitration clauses within EU member states having transposed the Directive should be identical. For example, in French law, in the matter of domestic consumer relationships, an arbitration clause preventing the consumer from bringing proceedings before the State courts is deemed unfair and therefore sanctioned by being non-binding on the consumer.[149] On the other hand, when the relationship is international, the arbitration clause concluded in a consumer contract is deemed to be valid, and that is the case, whatever might be the weak position of the consumer.[150] This is also the case in Czech law[151] and in Polish law too, of which article 385(3) point 23 of the Civil Code limits the possibility of submitting a dispute involving a consumer to arbitration and declares, in case of doubt, that such a clause is unfair. In the United Kingdom, article 91 of the English arbitration Act of 1996 establishes that an arbitration agreement is declared unfair (in the sense of the Unfair Terms in Consumer Contracts Regulations 1999) and is, consequently, non-binding as long as the claim does not exceed £5,000 GBP.

Two decisions rendered by the EU Court of Justice must be mentioned, which stated on the one hand, in the *Mostaza Claro*[152] decision, that a court, when an action to annul an arbitral award is brought before it, must determine if the arbitration clause is invalid, notwithstanding the fact the consumer has not invoked the invalidity of the arbitration clause during the arbitral procedure, but only at the stage of annulling the award. On the other hand, in the *Asturcom Telecomunicaciones*[153] case, the Court of Justice decided that when proceedings are brought before a court relating to an action enforcing an arbitral award that has become definitive and rendered without the consumer's participation in the procedure, it must declare *ex officio* if an arbitration clause concluded between the supplier of goods or services and a consumer is unfair.[154]

7.8.2 Alternative Methods of Dispute Settlement

By alternative methods of dispute settlement, we mean all the mechanisms for resolving disputes other than bringing proceedings before a State court or to arbitration (in the traditional sense, that is to say the process by which a third party to the dispute, an arbitral court, gives an award that has the same effect as a judgement). We exclude therefore from this definition of arbitration the systems of online dispute resolution, often known as electronic arbitration, which are not, in the proper meaning of the term, arbitration procedures.

By virtue of their informal, flexible, rapid and generally less costly character, these alternative means (mediation, conciliation, online arbitration) are particularly appropriate for resolving international consumer dispute.

It would be futile to try here to give an exhaustive list of all the possibilities contained in the legal orders which have been reported. Only a few remarkable traits deserve mention.

In the first place, these alternative methods are very generally *optional* for the consumer. It is a question, therefore, of a *supplementary* mechanism put at the consumer's disposal, which can in the case of failure, or if he/ she so wishes, be brought before a State court as of the arising of the dispute.[155]

[149] Art. R. 132–2, 10° of the French Code of Consumption. The author of the French Report notices that "the term belongs however to the 'gray' list of the terms for which the professional is allowed to prove the contrary and not to the 'black' list of terms which are incontestably presumed to be abusive".

[150] See the both decisions rendered by the French Court de cassation mentioned in the French Report: *Jaguar* (1997) and *Rado* (2004).

[151] See the Czech Report, V.1.

[152] *ECJ* of 26 October 2006, C-168-05, *Mostaza Claro v. Centro Movil Milenium SL.*

[153] *ECJ* of 6 October 2009, C-40/08, *Asturcom Telecomunicaciones SL v. Maria Cristina Rodríguez Nogueira.*

[154] See EU Report, V.1.

[155] South Africa seems to be an exception. See South African Report, V.2. See also German law (Art. 15a EGZPO) which can force a consumer to conciliate if the amount in dispute does not exceed 750 Euros. See German Report, V.2.

In the second place, the organizations of these alternative mechanisms are very diverse. It may be a question of a system of public entities. In Denmark and in Norway, consumers can bring matters to the Consumer Complaints Board (Denmark) or to the Consumer Disputes Commission (Norway), which are, in both these countries, independent public entities. Bringing matters to this body is limited to claims for a sum between 800 DKK (approximately 105 Euros) and 100,000 DKK (approximately 13,300 Euros) in Denmark. This "commission" system or "complaints board" is also available for international litigation; it suffices that the Danish or Norwegian courts should have jurisdiction for the litigation which has been brought before them so that these bodies may know of the dispute. In both cases, the procedure is written; the consumer does not appear.[156] In Brazil, mediation is achieved by State or Federation agencies.[157] In Greece, also, a committee for the amicable settlement of disputes, accessible by consumers, has been established in each prefecture.[158] The Ombudsman model is also to be found in different legal orders. In other States, the alternative mechanisms rest with private entities. In Ghana, for example, the law obliges the suppliers of goods and services by electronic means to inform consumers on the electronic trading site of the selected alternative means of dispute resolution.[159]

Thirdly, the *sectorization* of these alternative means must be noted. In many States, consumers have access to a service of litigation regulation that intervenes in a specialized domain. Consultation of the Slovenian, Swiss and Norwegian Reports illustrates this trend toward micro-distribution of litigation according to the sector of activity (banks, insurance, health insurance…).

Lastly, the development of online procedures must be taken into account. This mechanism is essentially established for disputes resulting from, but not solely, electronic commerce. UNCITRAL wants to begin working on the online regulation of disputes in international electronic commercial operations and is taking a particular interest in consumers.[160] The European Union also wishes to promote this means of settlement, notably by launching ECODIR (Electronic Consumer Dispute Resolution Platform).[161] The German and Italian reports also mention local initiatives to implement online dispute resolution mechanism: in the *Land* of Baden-Württemberg, a pilot scheme known as "*Online-Schlichter*" offers an online dispute resolution service relating to internet purchases. In Italy, the Milan Chamber of Commerce has set up a service known as "*RisolviOnline*" in order to settle the same type of disputes.[162] Annex A of the draft submitted by the United States to CIDIP-VII in February 2010 must also be mentioned.

7.9 Cooperation of the Authorities

The question asked to national reporters and regional and international organizations concerns the cooperation between national authorities with the intention of promoting and guaranteeing an efficient protection to cross-border consumers.

It goes without saying that such cooperation is organized in a much more efficient way within regional organizations of economic integration. This is, therefore, these specific reports that should be taken into account.

Before exploring the different mechanisms of integration, we must not forget, at the international level, the Hague Convention of 1965 on the service abroad of judicial and extrajudicial documents in civil or commercial matters which has been very successful. It is also worth mentioning the OECD (Organization for Economic Cooperation and Development) guidelines governing consumer protection against fraudulent and misleading cross-border commercial practices published in 2003[163] that recommended that the member States should establish a framework permitting closer, more rapid and more efficient cooperation between entities charged with monitoring consumer protection. Very little information is, however, available on the application of these guidelines.

Within the European Union, authorities promoting member States' consumer rights are connected by

[156] See Reports of Denmark and Norway, V.2.

[157] See the very detailed Report of Brazil, V.2.

[158] See Greek Report, IV.2.

[159] Pursuant to Art. 47(n) of the Electronic Transactions Act 2008 (Act 772). See Report of Ghana, V.2.

[160] See Secretariat's note of 23 April 2010 on the possible future works on online dispute resolution in electronic commerce transactions, A/CN.9/706. [Note: UNCITRAL WG III has already met for the first time in December 2010.]

[161] See EU Report.

[162] See Reports of Germany and Italy, V.2.

[163] Available at: http://www.oecd.org/dataoecd/24/18/2956424.pdf

different networks created especially to find amicable settlements in European consumer litigation. For example, FIN-NET (Network for the extrajudicial resolution of financial services sector litigation) of which Iceland, Liechtenstein and Norway are also members, or of the EJE network (Network for the extrajudicial resolution of consumer litigation) which have merged to form a single office, ECC-Net (European Consumer Centres Network).[164] Regulation 2004/2006 of 27 October 2004 on consumer protection cooperation aims to create reinforced cooperation between the European Commission and the State authorities, designated by each member State and "responsible for the enforcement of the laws that protect consumers' interests (…) in order to ensure compliance with those laws and the smooth functioning of the internal market and in order to enhance the protection of consumers' economic interests".[165]

As yet, both the systems of integration in Latin America reported here contain few measures of cooperation between authorities. In the Mercosur, cooperation agreements have been concluded, but those are limited to tourism and alerts to defective products (SIMDEC – Mercosur Common Information System about Consumer Protection and Defective Products).[166] An agreement for free service and legal assistance in consumer litigation has also been concluded between Mercosur member States.[167] Within the Andean Community, there does not seem to be any system of cooperation between entities of member States.[168]

Since 2003, OAS has made great efforts in terms of harmonization of international consumer law.[169] Amongst them, there is a very original contribution in the domain of cooperation between authorities which stems from the submission of the legislative guidelines by the United States,[170] in which Annex D (Draft Model Law on Government Redress for Consumers Including Across Borders) suggests measures of cooperation. The aim of this law is to establish within member States judicial authorities in the matter of consumer protection (on the model of the Federal Trade Commission – FTC – in the United States), and to make them responsible for obtaining redress for damage suffered by consumers and to allow them to cooperate with the equivalent authorities of other member States.

More particularly, article 5 of Annex D concerns cross-border cooperation. Notably, it provides that the competent authorities shall notify foreign competent authorities of investigations that affect these foreign countries, so as to alert them of possible wrongdoing in their jurisdiction; share information with the foreign competent authorities and help each other with their investigations.

7.10 Final Considerations

Reading particular reports shows us that international consumer law is in a period of complete transformation. In spite of the universally recognized importance of our subject, it is surprisingly noticeable that a considerable number of States have not yet developed specific rules in this matter. And it is still more striking that where they do exist, rules on electronic commerce do not care about the details of international consumer contracts.

In the States and regions which have adopted rules on the concrete aspects of international private consumer law and created special conflict of laws rules and jurisdiction rules juris, these efforts have been followed by the search for other instruments capable of protecting consumers in procedural spheres, arbitration, alternative means of dispute settlement and international cooperation. But even in a domain like that of rules of applicable law, there is space for new proposals. Without departing from the conflicts methodology, the most interesting is, no doubt, that of replacing the rigid criterion of application of the law of the consumer's habitual residence, as representing the criterion based on the presumption that it is the most favorable to the consumer, for another more flexible and yet more concrete criterion consisting of the most favorable law to the consumer from a substantial point of view. That said, it must be emphasized that in order to achieve an optimal level of protection, no combination of legal mechanisms is sufficient. Apart from the latter, a set of political, economic and educational

[164] See EU Report, V.2.

[165] Art. 1 of Regulation 2004/2006.

[166] See Brazilian Report and the reference quoted: R. A. C. Pfeiffer, "Consumer Defense in Mercosur: A Balance and Recent Challenges," in ed. T. Bourgoignie (note 53) 40.

[167] Dec. CMC/DEC/49/2000 of 15 December 2000.

[168] See Report on the Andean Community, VI.

[169] See OAS Report, I.2.

[170] In its last version of 12 February 2010.

measures must be implemented, without which the best legal instruments are destined to fail.

But in the domain of law, the concern for the subject is not merely legislative. The international dimension of consumer protection attracts more and more attention from the main academic milieus. Part of the increasingly significant work of the sector's principal scholarly institution, *the International Academy of Commercial and Consumer Law,* is dedicated to the international aspects of the subject. It is sufficient to see the work presented at the Bamberg Conference in 2008,[171] a trend which seems to be maintained for the Conference held in Toronto in 2010.

However, the relevance of international consumer law goes beyond the realm of specialists. This is evidenced by the fact that the *International Academy of Comparative Law* has chosen this topic as one of the two subjects of private international law at its quadrennial Congress. The comparativists of the whole world want to know the different ways in which national, supranational and international legislators are striving to guarantee cross-border consumer protection. Indeed, there are few topics which reveal such an aptitude for reflecting on the current challenges of law in general and of private international law in particular. Thus, the tensions between general interests and commercial interests, the limits of traditional mechanisms for resolving disputes, the complementarity of hard and soft law, the development of international and supranational dimensions of legal regulation, the impact of using electronic means, etc., reveal their most surprising manifestations in this domain. The interest of the internationalists is not less than that of the comparativists. Not by chance did the International Law Association, at its Congress in Rio de Janeiro in August 2008, create a specific Committee relating to international consumer law. Henceforth, next to more or less classic matters of international law (international human rights, international commercial arbitration, use of force, space law, climate change, etc.),[172] a new evolving category is emerging that is also full of a transformative power.

[171] 14th Biennial Meeting of the International Academy of Commercial and Consumer Law, Bamberg, Germany (July 30 – August 3, 2008), *Penn State Int'l L. Rev.* 27, 3/4 (2009).

[172] http://www.ila-hq.org/en/committees/index.cfm.

Codification and Flexibility in Private International Law[1]

8

Symeon C. Symeonides

This is an abbreviated version of the first two chapters of an eight-chapter General Report to the 18th International Congress of Comparative Law held in 2010 in Washington, D.C. The full Report on "Recent Private International Law Codifications" focuses on the choice-of-law part of private international law (hereinafter PIL) and explores some general methodological and philosophical themes, as well as the way these codifications resolve tort and contract conflicts. These themes include the tension between legal certainty and flexibility (which is discussed here), the scope and breadth of choice-of-law rules, result selectivism and content-oriented law selection versus state-selection, and the publicization or politicization of PIL.[2]

In preparing the General Report, the author has benefitted from 32 national reports.[3] This Report draws from all of these reports, but also discusses codifications from countries that have not submitted reports, as well as several international conventions and European Union Regulations.

8.1 The New Codification Movement in PIL

8.1.1 National or Sub-National Private International Law Codifications

8.1.1.1 The First Generation

The first codifications of modern PIL were part and parcel of the substantive-law codification movement of the nineteenth century. For example, the French Civil

[2] For the full version of these two chapters, as well as the remaining six chapters, see S. Symeonides, *Recent Private International Law Codifications* (Martinus Nijhoff, forthcoming 2012) [hereinafter referred to as S. Symeonides, *Codifications*).

[3] These reports were submitted by the reporters listed below: Argentina (María Susana Najurieta & María Blanca Noodt Taquela, University of Buenos Aires); Australia (Alice De Jonge, Monash University); Austria (Christiane Wendehorst, University of Vienna); Belgium (Johan Erauw (Gent) & Marc Fallon (Louvain-la-Neuve)); China (Weizuo Chen, Tsinghua University School of Law, Beijing); Croatia (Davor Babić, University of Zagreb); Czech Republic (Monika Pauknerová, Charles University Prague); Denmark (Joseph Lookofsky, University of Copenhagen); England (Christa Roodt, University of Aberdeen); Finland (Ulla Liukkunen, University of Helsinki); France (Benjamin Remy, University of Poitiers); Germany (Peter Mankowski, University of Hamburg); Greece (Evangelos Vasilakakis, University of Thessaloniki); Hungary (Katalin Raffai & Sarolta Szabó, Pázmány Péter, Catholic University); Israel (Talia Einhorn, Ariel University); Japan (Tadashi Kanzaki, Gakushuin University); Macau (Guangjian Tu, University of Macau); Netherlands (Katharina Boele-Woelki & Dorothea Van Iterson, Utrecht University); New Zealand (Tony Angelo, Victoria University of Wellington); Norway (Giuditta Cordero Moss, University of Oslo); Poland (Maksymilian Pazdan, University of Śląski); Portugal (Luís De Lima Pinheiro, University of Lisbon); Quebec (Frédérique Sabourin, Quebec Department of Justice); Scotland (Janeen M. Carruthers & Elizabeth B. Crawford, University of Glasgow); South Korea (Kwang Hyun Suk, Seoul National University); Spain (Carlos Esplugues Mota & Carmen Azcárraga Monzonís, University of Valencia); Switzerland (Andrea Bonomi, Swiss Institute of Comparative Law); Taiwan (Rong-chwan Chen, National Taipei University); Turkey (Zeynep Derya Tarman, Koç University); UNCITRAL (Spiros Bazinas, Senior Legal Officer, UNCITRAL); Uruguay (Cecilia Fresnedo de Aguirre, Catholic University of Uruguay); and Venezuela (Eugenio Hernández-Bretón, Universidad Monteávila, Caracas).

These reports are published in S. Symeonides, *Codifications.* They are referred to hereinafter by the author's name, the country of origin, and the pertinent sections and subdivisions of each report.

S.C. Symeonides (✉)
Willamette University College of Law, Salem, OR, USA
e-mail: symeon@willamette.edu

K.B. Brown and D.V. Snyder (eds.), *General Reports of the XVIIIth Congress of the International Academy of Comparative Law/Rapports Généraux du XVIIIème Congrès de l'Académie Internationale de Droit Comparé*,
DOI 10.1007/978-94-007-2354-2_8, © Springer Science+Business Media B.V. 2012

Code of 1804,[4] the Austrian Civil Code of 1811,[5] the Italian Civil Code of 1865,[6] the Spanish Civil Code of 1889,[7] and the German Civil Code of 1900[8] each contained a handful of broad choice-of-law rules, which then became the models for similar rules in other countries.[9] During the first half of the twentieth century, a handful of other countries in Europe[10] and Asia[11] followed course by including choice-of-law rules in their civil codes, while the codification movement in Latin America gained momentum with an ambitious Pan American "Code of Private International Law," better known as the "Bustamante Code."[12]

This momentum was short-lived, however. During the ensuing decades, the prevailing view in many countries was that PIL did not need to be—nor was susceptible to being—codified. This sentiment seemed to prevail not only in common-law countries such as the United States, where the dismal failure of the First Conflicts Restatement led many to reject not only statutory rules but also Restatement-type non-state rules,[13] but also in European countries, where many scholars expressed serious misgivings about the need or desirability of codifying or re-codifying PIL.[14]

Before the end of the twentieth century, however, those misgivings began to dissipate and were succeeded by a flurry of codification activity. Indeed, the codification movement may have begun in civil law countries, but it has since spread in countries from all legal families and traditions, including England, the epicenter of the common law. In 1982, Sir Peter North, then Law Commissioner for England and Wales, assured his readers that "[c]odes are not monsters . . . [and that], [e]ven if they are, they can be trained."[15] After enacting a statute on tort conflicts,[16] the United Kingdom's decision to adopt the European Union's Rome I and Rome II Regulations on contract and tort conflicts[17] confirmed North's earlier observation that "a most striking feature of the development of private international law over the last century has been that statute law has been the primary instrument of change."[18]

8.1.1.2 The Second Generation

By the 1960s, one could see the signs of a new codification movement, slow at the beginning, but gradually gaining momentum. Although that decade produced only three codifications, the 1970s produced nine, the 1980s also produced nine, the 1990s produced twenty, and the first decade of the twentieth century also produced twenty.

Altogether, the last fifty years have produced 61 national or sub-national codifications or recodifications[19] in 55 jurisdictions.[20] As in the previous generation, some of these codifications form part of new or revised civil codes, especially in the former Soviet republics and eastern European countries. However, the majority of them are free-standing, comprehensive statutes covering not only choice of law, but also jurisdiction and recognition and enforcement of foreign judgments. Perhaps unsurprisingly, Europe has produced the highest number of codifications, a total of 27 (not including the EU regulations). Asia produced

[4]See French Civil Code, Arts.3, 14–15, 309, 311.

[5]See Austrian Civil Code, arts. 4, 33–38, 300.

[6]Originally drafted by Pascuale Mancini, the PIL articles of the Italian Civil Code of 1865 were reproduced as Articles 17–31 of the Italian Civil Code of 1942. *See also* the Civil Code of the Canton of Zurich 1854/56 arts. 1–7.

[7]See Spanish Civil Code, arts. 8–11.

[8]See Introductory Law of the Civil Code of August 15, 1896 (EGBGB), arts. 3–38.

[9]See, e.g., the Japanese Horei (Act No.10) of 1898, which was primarily based on the EGBGB.

[10]See, e.g. the Italian Civil Code of 1942, arts. 17–31; Greek Civil Code of 1940 arts. 4–33.

[11]For example, the Chinese Statute on the Application of Laws of 1918 was based on the Japanese Horei of 1898 and the EGBGB.

[12]See A.S. de Bustamante y Sirvén, *El código de derecho internacional privado y la sexta conferencia panamericana* (Habana: Imprenta Aivisador comercial, 1929): 253. The Bustamante Code was adopted by over a dozen countries.

[13]For the American attitude towards rules, see S. Symeonides, *The American Choice-of-Law Revolution: Past, Present, and Future* (Leiden/Boston: Martinus Nijhoff Publishers, 2006), 411–19, 426–35 (hereinafter S. Symeonides, *Revolution*).

[14]See, e.g., Neuhaus H, "Empfiehlt sich eine Kodifizierung des internationalen Privatrechts?" *RabelsZ* 37 (1973): 453; O. Kahn–Freund, *General Problems of Private International Law* (Leyden: Sijthoff, 1976) 80–84; von Schwind F, "Problems of Codification of Private International Law," *International and Comparative Law Quarterly* 17 (1968): 428, 431.

[15]North P, "Problems of Codification in a Common Law System," *RabelsZ* 46 (1982): 490, at 500.

[16]See infra note 53.

[17]See infra 8.1.2.

[18]North P, "Private International Law: Change or Decay?" *International and Comparative Law Quarterly* 50 (2001): 477, 496.

[19]This list does not include the 14 EU regulations adopted in the last ten years. See infra 8.1.2.

[20]The reason the two counts do not match is because the first count includes re-codifications and six partial codifications.

Table 8.1 Codifications by continent

Africa	Asia	Europe	Latin America	North America
Algeria (1975)	Jordan (1977)	Czechoslovakia (1964)	Ecuador (1970)	Louisiana (1991)
Burkina Faso (1991)	North Yemen (1979)	Poland (1965 & 2011)	Peru (1984)	Quebec (1991)
Tunisia (1998)	United Arab Emirates (1985)	Portugal (1967 & 1977)	Paraguay (1985)	Oregon (2001 & 2009)
	Yemen (1992)	Spain (1974)	Mexico (1988)	
	North Korea (1995 and 2005)	East Germany (1975)	Venezuela (1998)	
	Vietnam (1995)	Hungary (1979)		
	Armenia (1998)	Yugoslavia (1978–1983)		
	Kyrgyzstan (1998)	Austria (1979)		
	Macau (1999)	Germany (1986 & 1999)		
	Azerbaijan (2000)	Switzerland (1987)		
	South Korea (2001)	Finland (1988)		
	Mongolia (2002)	Romania (1992)		
	Qatar (2004)	Latvia (1993)		
	Japan (2007)	United Kingdom (1995)		
	Turkey (2007)	Italy (1995)		
	Taiwan (2010)	Liechtenstein (1996)		
	China (1985, 1987, & 2010)	Belarus (1998)		
		Slovenia (1999)		
		Lithuania		
		Netherlands (2001 & 2011)		
		Russia (2002)		
		Estonia (2002)		
		Moldova (2002)		
		Belgium (2004)		
		Bulgaria (2005)		
		Ukraine (2005)		
		FYROM (2007)		
3	17	27	5	3

17 codifications, followed by Latin America with five, and Africa and North America with three (Table 8.1).

These codifications are listed below in chronological order.[21]

(1) Czechoslovakia (1964)[22];
(2) Poland (1965)[23];
(3) Portugal (1967[24] and 1977[25]);
(4) Ecuador (1970)[26];
(5) Spain (1974)[27];
(6) the former East Germany (1975)[28];
(7) Algeria (1975)[29];

[21] All of these codifications are referred to hereinafter with the country of origin and the abbreviation "codif." regardless of (a) whether they form part of another code, such as a civil code, or (b) their formal designation, such as PIL Act, statute, etc. For full citations to statutory texts, translations, and commentaries on these codifications, the reader is kindly referred to the full version of this Report published in S. Symeonides, *Codifications*.

[22] See Act 97 of 1963 (effective April 1964) on PIL and Procedure. This Act remains in force with minor amendments in the Czech Republic.

[23] See Act of 12 Nov. 1965, effective 1 July 1966, on PIL.

[24] See Portuguese Civil Code arts. 14–65 as revised in 1966.

[25] See Law no. 496/77 (revising 1966 codification in line with Portugal's new constitution).

[26] See Ecuador Civil Code as amended on 29 Sept. 1970, arts. 13–17.

[27] See Spanish Civil Code arts. 8–16 as revised in 1974.

[28] See Act of 5 Dec. 1975, translated into English and discussed in Juenger F, "The Conflicts Statute of the German Democratic Republic: An Introduction and Translation," *American Journal of Comparative Law* 25 (1977): 332.

[29] See Ordinance No. 75-58 of 26 Sept. 1975, amending articles 9 through 24 of the Algerian Civil Code.

(8) Jordan (1977)[30]
(9) Hungary (1979)[31];
(10) The former North Yemen (1979)[32];
(11) The former Yugoslavia (1978–1983)[33];
(12) Austria (1979)[34];
(13) Peru (1984)[35];
(14) Paraguay (1985)[36];
(15) United Arab Emirates (1985)[37];
(16) China (1985,[38] 1987,[39] 1999[40] and 2010[41]);
(17) Germany (1986[42] and 1999[43]);
(18) Switzerland (1987)[44];
(19) Mexico (1988)[45]
(20) Finland (1988)[46];
(21) Louisiana (1991)[47];
(22) Quebec (1991)[48];
(23) Burkina Faso (1991)[49];
(24) Romania (1992)[50];
(25) Yemen (1992)[51];
(26) Latvia (1993)[52];
(27) United Kingdom (1995)[53];
(28) Italy (1995)[54];
(29) North Korea (1995 and 2005)[55];
(30) Vietnam (1995)[56];
(31) Liechtenstein (1996)[57];

[30] See arts. 1–3, 11–29 of Jordanian Civil Code of 1 Aug. 1976 (effective 1 Jan. 1977) J.O. no 2645 of 1 Aug. 1976, arts. 1–3, 11–29.

[31] See Law No. 13 of 1979 on PIL.

[32] See arts. 1–11, 20 23–35 of Civil Code of the Arab Republic of Yemen, promulgated by Law 10 of 21 April 1979 in J.O. of 30 April 1979, French translation with comments by S. Aldeeb Abu-Sahlieh in *Rev. critique DIP* 76 (1987): 650. See also id. at 654 for the codification in the then South Yemen (without any indication as to date of enactment).

[33] The Yugoslav codification was enacted in three installments in 1978, 1979, and 1983. For discussion of the whole, see Sarcevic P, "The New Yugoslav Private International Law Act," *American Journal of Comparative Law* 38 (1985): 283.

[34] See Bundesgesetz vom 15. 6. 1978 über das internationale Privatrecht (IPR-Gesetz), BGBl I 1978/304. For subsequent amendments, see BGBl I No. 119/1998, I No. 18/1999, I No. 135/2000, I No. 117/2003, I No. 58/2004, I No. 109/2009, I No. 135/2009.

[35] See Book X of the Peruvian Civil Code of 1984 (arts. 2046–2111), 129 *Normas Legales*, 128 (Oct. 1984).

[36] See arts. 11–26 of the Civil Code of Paraguay as revised in 1985.

[37] See arts. 1–3, 10–28 of Code of Civil Transactions of the United Arab Emirates (J.O. of UAE, no 185, Dec. 1985, p. 11–361).

[38] See Law of the People's Republic of China on Economic Contracts Involving Foreign Interest of March 21, 1985, and effective July 1, 1985.

[39] See Chapter 8 of General Principles of the Civil Law, Order No. 37 of the President of the People's Republic of China of 12 April 1986, effective 1 January 1987.

[40] See Contract Law of the People's Republic of China of March 15, 1999, effective October 1, 1999.

[41] See Statute of Application of Law to Foreign Civil Relations, adopted at the 17th session of the Standing Committee of the 11th National People's Congress on October 28, 2010, effective April 1, 2011.

[42] See Gesetz zur Neuregelung des IPR vom 25.7.1986, Bundesgesetzblatt I/1986, 810.

[43] See Gesetz zum IPR für außervertragliche Schuldverhältnisse und das Sachenrecht vom 21.5.1999, Bundesgesetzblatt 1999, I, 1026.

[44] Bundesgesetz über das Internationale Privatrecht (IPRG) vom 18. Dezember 1987–Loi féderale sur le droit international privé (LDIP) du 18 décembre 1987, 1988 BB I 5.

[45] See arts. 12–15, 29–34, 2736–38 of Civil Code for the Federal District in Ordinary Matters and for the Entire Republic in Federal Matters, as amended by Decree of 11 Dec. 1987 (effective 8 Jan. 1988), Diario official, 7 Jan. 1988, p.2.

[46] See Hallituksen esitys Eduskunnalle kansainvälisluonteisiin sopimuksiin sovellettavaa lakia koskevaksi lainsäädännöksi, HE 44/1987, p. 25. See also the 1964 Act on Law Applicable to Sale of Goods of International Character; Marriage Act (Act 234/1929, with amendments up to Act 1226/2001); and Code of Inheritance (Act 40/1965 with amendments up to Act 1228/2001).

[47] See Book IV of the Louisiana Civil Code, enacted into law by La. Act No. 923 of 1991, effective January 1, 1992.

[48] See L.Q. 1991, ch. 64 (adopted in 1991, effective 1994) and composing Book Ten of the Quebec Civil Code (arts. 3076–3168).

[49] See arts. 988–1050 of Code of Persons and Family (Law VII 0013 of 19 Nov. 1989, effective 4 Aug. 1990).

[50] See Law No. 105 of 22 Sept. 1992, effective 26 Oct. 1993, on the Settlement of PIL Relations, Official Gazette of Romania No. 245 of 1 Oct. 1992.

[51] See Law of 29 March 1992 on PIL.

[52] See Latvian Civil Code of 1993, arts. 8–25.

[53] See PIL (Miscellaneous Provisions) Act of 8 Nov. 1995 (c 42) (codifying conflicts rules for torts).

[54] See Act No. 218 of 31 May 1995 (Riforma del sistema italiano di diritto internazionale privato).

[55] See minju-juui innin konghwaguk tae'oe minsa kwan'gye bop (The Law of the Democratic People's Republic of Korea on External Civil Relations) of Sept. 6, 1995.

[56] See Civil Code of the Socialist Republic of Viet Nam of 1995, arts. 826–838. For a subsequent revision, see Civil Code of Socialist Republic of Viet Nam (Law of June 14, 2005), arts. 758–777. For international jurisdiction and recognition of foreign judgments and arbitral awards, see Vietnamese Code of Civil Procedure (2004), arts. 405–418, 342–374.

[57] See PIL Act of 1996 in Liechensteinisches Landesgesetzblatt 1996 No. 194.

(32) Armenia (1998)[58];
(33) Belarus (1998)[59];
(34) Tunisia (1998)[60];
(35) Venezuela (1998)[61];
(36) Kyrgyzstan (1998)[62];
(37) Slovenia (1999)[63];
(38) Macau (1999)[64];
(39) Lithuania (2000)[65];
(40) Azerbaijan (2000)[66];
(41) The Netherlands (2001)[67];
(42) South Korea (2001)[68];
(43) Oregon (2001[69] and 2009)[70];
(44) Russia (2002)[71];
(45) Estonia (2002)[72];
(46) Moldova (2002)[73];
(47) Mongolia (2002)[74];
(48) Belgium (2004)[75];
(49) Qatar (2004)[76];
(50) Bulgaria (2005)[77];
(51) Ukraine (2005)[78];
(52) Japan (2007)[79];
(53) Turkey (2007)[80];
(54) Former Yugoslav Republic of Macedonia (FYROM) (2007)[81]; and
(55) Taiwan (2010).[82]

Codification or re-codification projects are currently under way in many other jurisdictions, including Argentina,[83] the Czech Republic,[84] Israel,[85] Mexico,[86] Poland,[87] Puerto Rico,[88] and Uruguay.[89]

[58] See Division 12, arts. 1253–93 of the Civil Code of Armenia of 1998.

[59] See arts. 1093 et seq. of Civil Code of Belarus (Law of 7 Dec. 1998), as amended on 20 June 2008.

[60] See Code of PIL (Law No. 98-97 of 27 Nov. 1998), Official Journal of the Republic of Tunisia, 1 Dec. 1998 p. 2332.

[61] See Act of 6 Aug. 1998 on PIL (Official Gazette No. 36.511) effective 6 Feb. 1999.

[62] See Law of 5 Jan. 1998 revising Civil Code arts. 1167–1208.

[63] See PIL and Procedure Act of 30 June 1999 (Zakon o mednarodnem zasebnem pravu in postopku - ZMSPP) Ur.l. RS, no. 56/1999) in Official Gazette of the Republic of Slovenia 1999/56.

[64] See arts. 13 through 62 of the Civil Code of Macau, as amended in 1999.

[65] See arts. 1.10 through 1.62 of the Civil Code of the Republic of Lithuania of 2000.

[66] See Law of 6 June 2000 on PIL.

[67] See Act of 11 April 2001 (effective 1 June 2001) Regarding Conflict of Laws on Torts, Staatsblad 2001, 190.

[68] See Law 6465 of 7 April 2001, effective 1 July 2001, amending the Conflict of Laws Act of the Republic of Korea.

[69] See Or. Rev. Stat. §§ 81.100–81.135 (2001) (codifying choice of law for contract conflicts).

[70] See Or. Rev. Stat. §§ 31.850–31.890 (2009), effective 1 Jan. 2010 (codifying choice of law for tort conflicts).

[71] See federal law no. 146 of 26 Nov. 2001, enacting Part III of the Civil Code of the Russian Federation, Rossyiskaya Gazeta, n. 49 item 4553, 28/11/2001. The PIL provisions comprise Title VI of Part III, arts. 1186–1224.

[72] See PIL Act of 22 March 2002, effective 1 July 2002, The State Gazette, "Riigi Teataja" I 2002, 35, 217.

[73] See Moldova Civil Code (Law 1107 of 6 June 2002), arts. 1578–1625.

[74] See arts. 539–52 of Mongolian Civil Code, enacted 2 Jan. 2002, effective 1 Sept. 2002.

[75] See Code de droit international privé (Loi du 16 juillet 2004, Moniteur Belge 27 Juillet 2004.

[76] See arts. 10–38 of the Civil Code of Qatar, as amended by Law 22/2004 of 8 Aug. 2004.

[77] See Bulgarian PIL Code (Law No. 42 of 2005 as amended by Law No. 59 of 2007).

[78] See Law of PIL of 23 June 2005, effective 1 Sept. 2005.

[79] See Law No. 10 of 1898 as Newly Titled and Amended on 21 June 2006, effective 1 Jan. 2007, on the General Rules of Application of Laws [Hô no tekiyô ni kan suru tsûsoku-hô].

[80] See Law No. 5718 of 27 Nov. 2007 adopting the Turkish Code of PIL and International Civil Procedure.

[81] See PIL Act of 4 July 2007, effective on 19 July 2008, of the Former Yugoslav Republic of Macedonia.

[82] See Act Governing the Application of Laws in Civil Matters Involving Foreign Elements, promulgated on May 26, 2010, effective on May 26, 2011.

[83] See M.S. Najurieta & M.B. Noodt Taquela, *Argentinean Report*, at I.

[84] For the text of a draft of a new PIL Act of 2009 and an Explanatory Report in Czech, see http://obcanskyzakonik.justice.cz/cz/uvodni-stranka.html.

[85] See T. Einhorn, *Israeli Report*; T. Einhorn, *Private International Law in Israel* (2009).

[86] See Fernández Arroyo D, "What's New in Latin American Private International Law?" *Year Book of Private International Law* 7 (2005): 100–104. For existing and proposed codifications in Latin America in general, see D. Fernández Arroyo, *La codificación del derecho internacional privado en América Latina* (Madrid: Beramar, 1994).

[87] See Pazdan, *Polish Report*, at I-II. The project was completed with the enactment of the PIL Act of 4 Feb. 2001, Ustawa z dnia 4 lutego 2011 r. Prawo prywatne międzynarodowe, Dz U. z dnia 15 kwiethnia 2011 r. nr 80, poz. 432.

[88] See Academia Puertorriqueña de Jurisprudencia y Legislacion, *Proyecto para la Codificación del Derecho internacional privado de Puerto Rico* (S. Symeonides and A. von Mehren, Rapporteurs, 1991). This is now pending before the Puerto Rico legislature as Book VII of the proposed new Puerto Rico Civil Code. The draft code is available at http://www.codigocivilpr.net/.

[89] See Cecilia Fresnedo de Aguirre, *Uruguayan Report*, at I.

8.1.2 European Union Conventions and Regulations

Within the European Union, there has been a dramatic increase of legislative activity regarding PIL matters, which some authors have described as a federalization or Europeanization[90] of PIL amounting to a virtual revolution.[91]

In 2002, the Brussels Convention of 1968[92] was replaced by a Regulation (Brussels I)[93] that is directly binding on member states. In 2003, it was followed by another Regulation known as Brussels II, which covers jurisdiction and judgment recognition in matrimonial matters and matters of parental responsibility,[94] and then by a third regulation that covers maintenance obligations.[95] The 1980 EEC Convention on the Law Applicable to Contractual Obligations was replaced by a Regulation known as "Rome I,"[96] which was revised again in 2008.[97] In 2007, the much-anticipated (if not much-acclaimed) Regulation on the Law Applicable to Non-Contractual Application, known as Rome II, was promulgated.[98] Finally, in the closing days of 2010, we saw the enactment of Rome III, on the law applicable to divorce and legal separation.[99]

The foregoing regulations have displaced the corresponding provisions of several European national codifications on the same subjects. Nevertheless, for the purposes of this Report—which is written from an educational and comparative perspective, rather than from a practitioner's perspective—the superseded provisions remain relevant and are therefore included in this Report.

8.1.3 International PIL Conventions

At the international level, the last fifty-year period has been marked by the proliferation of international and regional PIL conventions and other international instruments. The period began slowly in the 1960s, with only seven conventions, six of which were produced under the auspices of the Hague Conference on PIL. However, the 1970s brought 28 conventions, the 1980s brought 18, as did the 1990s, and the first decade of the twenty-first century brought 30 conventions and similar instruments.[100]

The plurality of PIL conventions, a total of 29, has been produced under the auspices of the Hague Conference. Twenty-two of those conventions are now in force.[101] During the same 50-year period, the Inter-American Specialized Conferences on Private International Law (known by its Spanish acronym, CIDIP[102]) has produced 26 Inter-American PIL conventions, protocols and other instruments.[103]

[90] See Meeusen J, "Instrumentalisation of Private International Law in the European Union: Towards a European Conflicts Revolution?" *European Journal of Migration and Law* 9 (2007): 287; Muir-Watt H, "European Federalism and the 'New Unilateralism,'" *Tulane Law Review* 82 (2008): 1983.

[91] Michaels R, "The New European Choice-of-Law Revolution," *Tulane Law Review* 82 (2008): 1607.

[92] See Brussels Convention on Jurisdiction and the Recognition and Enforcement of Judgments (Brussels I)[1990] O.J. C 189.

[93] See European Community Council Regulation (EC) No. 44/2001 on Jurisdiction and the Recognition of Judgments in Civil and Commercial Matters, [2001] O. J. L.12/1, effective March 1, 2002.

[94] See Council Regulation (EC) 2201/2003, [2003] Official Journal L 338/1 (also known as "Brussels IIa" or "Brussels *IIbis*).

[95] See Council Regulation (EC) No 4/2009 of 18 December 2008 on Jurisdiction, Applicable Law, Recognition and Enforcement of Decisions and Cooperation in Matters Relating to Maintenance Obligations L 7/1 [2009] O.J. 10.1.2009, effective in 2011.

[96] 23 Official Journal of the European Communities No. L 266/1 (1980).

[97] See Regulation (EC) No. 593/2008 of the European Parliament and of the Council of 17 June 2008 on the Law Applicable to Contractual Obligations (Rome I), [2008] OJ L 177/6. *Int'l L.*245 (2008).

[98] See Regulation (EC) No. 864/2007 of the European Parliament and of the Council of 11 July 2007 on the Law Applicable to non-Contractual Obligations (Rome II), [2007] OJ L 199/40.

[99] See Council Regulation (EU) No 1259/2010 of 20 December 2010 implementing enhanced cooperation in the area of the law applicable to divorce and legal separation (OJ n. L 343, p. 10 ff.) (2010). The regulation goes into effect 21 June 21, 2012 in the 14 Member States that currently participate in the enhanced cooperation. In the interim years, other Regulations have been enacted on insolvency, taking of evidence, service of documents, small claims procedure, and enforcement of uncontested claims. Of the 14 Regulations bearing on PIL, this Report covers only the five Regulations that include choice-of-law provisions, namely, Rome I, II, and III, and the Regulations on Maintenance and Insolvency.

[100] Included in this count are the EU regulations listed supra.

[101] For the texts of these conventions and the list of party-States, see the official web site of the Hague Conference at http://www.hcch.net/index_en.php?act=conventions.listing.

[102] The full Spanish name is Conferencia Interamericana sobre Derecho Internacional Privado. The Conference is an arm of the General Assembly of the Organization of American States.

[103] For a list and the texts of these instruments, see the web site of the Organization of American States at http://www.oas.org/dil/CIDIPVI_home.htm and http://www.oas.org/dil/treaties year text.htm#1994.

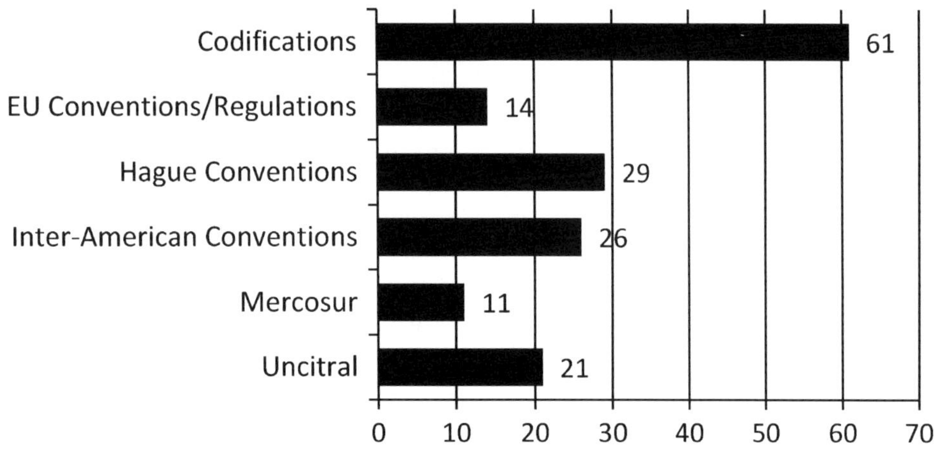

Chart 8.1 PIL codifications, regulations, conventions, protocols, and model laws, 1960–2010

Other international regional organizations have also produced conventions, protocols, and other international instruments bearing on PIL. For example, the MERCOSUR countries (Mercado Común del Sur) of Argentina, Brazil, Paraguay, and Uruguay have produced several such instruments on jurisdiction, judicial assistance, and arbitration, consumer contracts, transportation and traffic accidents, and intellectual property, among other subjects.[104]

The United Nations Commission on International Trade Law (UNCITRAL) has also been very productive during the same period. Although much of UNCITRAL's work is on substantive-law unification or harmonization, it nevertheless affects PIL to the extent it eliminates many conflicts which PIL no longer needs to resolve. Nonetheless, much of UNCITRAL's work on international commercial arbitration, international sale of goods (CISG), security interests, insolvency, international payments, international transport of goods, and electronic commerce has a more direct and significant bearing on PIL.[105]

Finally, mention should be made of the International Institute for the Unification of Private Law, known as UNIDROIT, an independent intergovernmental organization based in Rome.[106] As with UNCITRAL, most of the conventions, model laws, and other instruments produced by UNIDROIT deal with the modernization, harmonization and unification of private *substantive* law. However, some of these instruments have a significant bearing on PIL. For example, a decision to adopt the 1995 UNIDROIT Convention on Stolen or Illegally Exported Cultural Objects,[107] means that the adopting country will resolve conflict of laws involving stolen cultural objects through means other than (and in some instances in addition to) PIL means. In a different way, the UNIDROIT. Principles of International Commercial Contracts of 2004[108] may affect the law applicable to arbitration and, in the long run, the law applicable in the adjudication of certain international contracts.

In conclusion, the last 50-year period between 1960 and 2011, has been an extraordinarily productive period for PIL. During this period we have witnessed the adoption of 61 national PIL codifications[109] in 55 jurisdictions and 101 international or regional conventions, regulations, protocols, model laws, and other international instruments (Chart 8.1).

[104] For a list of and the text of these instruments, see Mercosur's official web site at http://www.mre.gov.py/dependencias/tratados/mercosur/registro%20mercosur/mercosurprincipal.htm.

[105] For a list and the text of UNCITRAL's instruments on these and other topics, see http://www.uncitral.org/uncitral/en/uncitral_texts.html. For UNCITRAL Legislative Guide on Secured Transactions, Supplement on Security Rights in Intellectual Property (2010), see S. Bazinas, *UNCITRAL Report* in Symeonides, *Codifications*.

[106] For the mission and work of UNIDROIT, see its web site at http://www.unidroit.org/.

[107] For the text of this convention, and a list of the countries that have ratified it, see http://www.unidroit.org/english/conventions/1995culturalproperty/main.htm.

[108] For the text, see http://www.unidroit.org/english/principles/main.htm.

[109] This number includes sub-national codifications, such as those of Quebec, Louisiana, and Oregon, as well as partial codifications or re-codifications.

This Report is based on a review of all of these instruments, although it focuses on some of them more than on others.

8.2 Codification and Flexibility

8.2.1 Introduction

The tension between the need for legal certainty and predictability, on the one hand, and the desire for flexible, equitable, and individualized solutions on the other is as old as law itself. Aristotle described it more than 23 centuries ago when he spoke of the role of equity as a corrective of the written law.[110] This tension is cyclical and perpetual but it surfaces with increased intensity during in debates on whether to embark on a codification project. Opponents of codification advance several arguments, some of which depend on timing and context, and some of which remain constant. Among the latter are the arguments of petrification and inflexibility. The petrification argument stands for the proposition that codification arrests the smooth development of the law; it freezes it in time and prevents its adaptation to changing needs.[111] The inflexibility argument asserts that codification usually paints with too broad a brush[112] and is too inflexible to properly resolve certain exceptional or unanticipated cases.[113] These arguments are encountered more frequently in common law systems, where judges are viewed as the principal players, and legislators as only occasional participants in the lawmaking process.[114]

However, as this Report demonstrates, the art or science of codification has advanced significantly in the intervening years and has developed tools for avoiding petrification and for ensuring flexibility. As centuries of codification experience demonstrate, the decision to adopt statutory rules need not result in outlawing judicial discretion. New codifications, more so than the old ones, are replete with examples of express legislative grants of judicial discretion.

In PIL, the codifier who is favorably inclined toward flexibility can choose from a considerable array of tools to that end. Among these tools are:

(a) the use of alternative connecting factors;
(b) the use of escape clauses authorizing courts to deviate from the choice-of-law rules in appropriate circumstances;
(c) the use (either in choice-of-law rules or in the escapes) of composite or "soft" connecting factors, such as the "closest connection" or "strongest connection," namely, factors that do not depend on the location of a single contact but rather on multiple factors and circumstances to be evaluated in the light of each particular case; or
(d) the use of malleable "approaches" or similar formulae that do not directly designate the applicable law but rather provide a list of factors that the court must consider in choosing that law. In some codifications, these formulae are followed by presumptive rules designating the ordinarily applicable law in specified situations, while the formulae in other codifications play a residual role for cases not covered by specific choice-of-law rules.

These tools can be portrayed by a sliding scale like the one shown below. It shows that between the one extreme, the fixed rules of traditional systems, and the other extreme, the American-style ad hoc approaches, there at least three intermediate formulae for controlled flexibility, as well as several combinations among them (Fig. 8.1).

8.2.2 Rules with Alternative Connecting Factors

One characteristic feature of traditional PIL systems was their excessive—and often exclusive—reliance on single and mono-directional connecting factors (such as the *locus contractus* or the *locus delicti*), which were intended to leave little or no discretion to the

---

[110] See Aristotle, *The Nicomachean Ethics*, V. x 4–7.

[111] See, e.g., Currie B, "Comments on *Babcock v. Jackson*," *Columbia Law Review* 63 (1963): 1233, at 1241 ("[N]ew efforts to find short cuts and syntheses should be sternly discouraged. We are beginning to recover from a long siege of intoxication resulting from overindulgence in generalities; for a while, at least, total abstinence should be enforced").

[112] See, e.g., Trautman D, "Reflections On Conflict-of-Laws Methodology," *Hastings Law Journal* 32 (1981): 1612 at 1621 ("[L]egislative direction is inherently incapable of capturing the nuance and sophistication necessary for just and satisfactory choice-of-law solutions.").

[113] See, e.g., Reese W, "Statutes in Choice of Law," *American Journal of Comparative Law* 35 (1987): 395 at 396 ("[n]o legislature, no matter how wise it may be, could envisage all of the almost endless possibilities.").

[114] For the United States in particular, these arguments are discussed in S. Symeonides, *Revolution* 411–19; Symeonides S, "A New Conflicts Restatement: Why Not?," *Journal of Private International Law* 5 (2009): 383, 406–22.

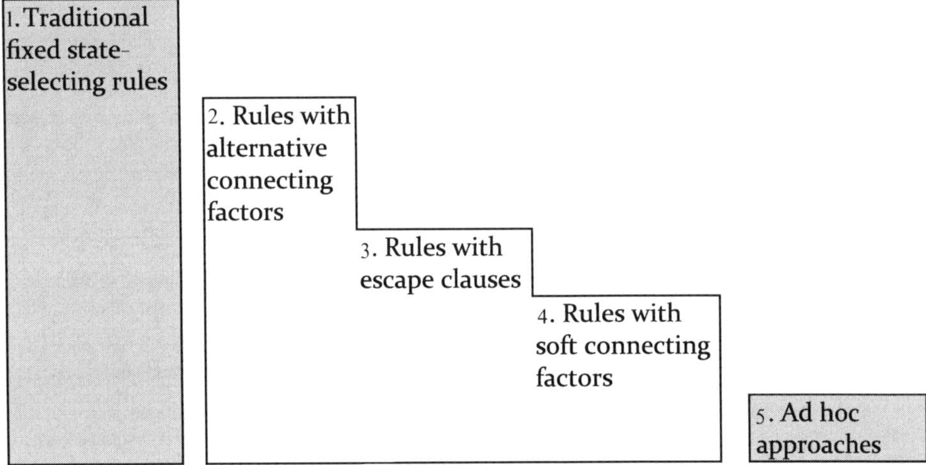

Fig. 8.1 The sliding scale of flexibility

judge in identifying the applicable law. The first small step away from this mind-set was (and remains) the use of "alternative reference rules"—namely, rules that give courts a choice between or among more than one connecting factor in certain well-defined cases.

For example, rather than exclusively subjecting the formal validity of a contract to the *lex loci contractus*, an alternative-reference rule would provide the judge the additional choices of the *lex causae* and the law of the parties' common domicile, habitual residence, or place of business, whichever law upholds the contract. Similarly, rather than *a priori* fixing the *locus delicti* at the place of the injury, other rules give the court or victim a choice between the places of the injurious conduct and the resulting injury.

Although a few of these rules appeared as early as the first part of the twentieth century, they have become much more common in recent codifications. For example, 73 countries have adopted an alternative-reference rule providing that a testament is formally valid if it conforms to the law of the place of making or the testator's domicile, habitual residence, or nationality at either the time of making or the time of death. Many countries have also adopted similar rules governing the form of, or capacity for, other juridical acts, legitimacy, filiation, adoption, marriage, and even divorce.[115] From the judge's perspective, these rules appear inimical to judicial discretion (and thus to flexibility) in that they deny the judge the freedom to choose a law other than the one that produces the pre-selected *result* (e.g., upholding the contract or testament). Nevertheless, from a systemic perspective, these rules provide flexibility in that, although they tie the system to a particular result, they do not tie the system to the law of a particular state.

8.2.3 Rules with Flexible Connecting Factors

The next step in the movement toward flexibility is the replacement of pre-fixed, mono-directional, and rigid connecting factors (such as the *loci contractus* or the *loci delicti*) with open-ended, poly-directional, and flexible connecting factors. These factors do not depend on the location of a single contact, but rather on multiple factors and circumstances to be evaluated in light of each particular case. Because of this attribute, these factors allow the judge considerable discretion in identifying the state of the applicable law.

8.2.3.1 The Closer or Closest Connection

Among recent codifications, the most popular of these flexible connecting factors is the "closer" or "closest connection." With slight variations in verbiage, this factor is used in several recent national codifications and international conventions, as well as in the Rome I

[115] Because these rules are primarily intended to accomplish a particular substantive result, they are discussed later in chapter 3 of this Report, which focuses on result-selectivism. See S. Symeonides, *Codifications*, ch. 3.

and Rome II Regulations. The differences in language include the use of a different adjective ("close" or "strong") in either the comparative ("closer" or "stronger") or the superlative ("closest" or "strongest"),[116] as well as the use of a different noun ("connection," "relationship," "link," or "tie"). Despite these phraseological differences, some of which are the result of variations in translation, these formulations have one thing in common: unlike traditional fixed connecting factors that point directly (and often inexorably) to the state of the applicable law, this connecting factor contemplates a more individualized determination of that state. It allows the court to take account of all pertinent contacts and factors, and, when properly applied, it requires the court to explain why one state's contacts are "closer, "more pertinent," or "more significant" than those of another state.

This "closest connection" factor plays several different roles in the various codifications, and often within different rules of the same codification. Among its various uses are: (1) as the principal connecting factor for, or an escape from, all choice-of-law rules; (2) as a presumption and an escape in contract conflicts and tort conflicts; (3) as an escape in other conflicts; (4) as a tie-breaker or a default rule in certain circumstances; and (5) as a gap-filler for unprovided-for cases.

The closest connection is the principal connecting factor in the codifications of Austria, Bulgaria, Burkina Faso, and China, which anchor all of their choice-of-law rules on this factor.[117] For example, the very first article of the Austrian codification provides that multi-state cases "shall be judged . . . according to the legal order with which the strongest connection exists," and that the codification's choice-of-law rules "shall be considered as expressions of this principle." Although in many cases the flexibility accorded by these general articles is retracted by the more specific articles, the closest connection principle remains the general and residual principle of these codifications and, as explained later, it can serve as an escape from the specific articles in appropriate cases or as a gap-filler for unprovided-for cases.

Six other codifications (Belgium, South Korea, Lithuania, Quebec, Slovenia, and FYROM) use the closer connection factor as the basis for a general escape from all of their rules, but without explicitly declaring that those rules themselves are based on the closer connection factor. These escapes are discussed later.[118] Many more codifications use the closer connection factor as the basis for narrower escapes from only some (rather than all) of the codification's rules. These escapes are also discussed later.[119] For now, though, the discussion turns to codifications that use the closer connection factor as both the basis for a choice-of-law rule and for an escape from that rule.

The closest-connection factor has played a special role in contract conflicts, at least since the days of the 1980 EC Convention on the Law Applicable to Contractual obligations (the Rome Convention). The Rome Convention provided that contracts that did not contain an effective choice-of-law clause were to be governed by the law of the country with which the contract was "most closely connected"[120] and then provided a series of presumptive rules identifying that country for different types of contracts. These rules generally pointed to the habitual residence of the obligor of the "characteristic performance," which itself was another "soft" connecting factor. The Convention also provided, however, that these presumptions were to be disregarded if the contract was "more closely connected with another country."[121]

The Rome Convention has since been replaced by the Rome I Regulation, but the Convention's scheme has been emulated (albeit with variations) in several national codifications, as well as in the Inter-American Contracts Convention.[122] Some countries—such as Denmark[123] and Germany,[124] which were parties to the

[116]The comparative "closer" is used when the decision-maker is to compare with the connection of one other state, usually the connection with the state of the otherwise applicable law. The superlative is used when the decision-maker is to find the "closest" among several connections.

[117]See Austrian codif. art. 1, discussed in Wenderhost, *Austrian Report*, at B.I; Bulgarian codif. art. 2; Burkina Faso codif. art. 1003; Chinese codif. art. 3, discussed in W. Chen, *Chinese Report*, at II.

[118]See infra at 8.2.4.1.

[119]See infra at 8.2.4.2.1.

[120]Rome Convention art. 4(1).

[121]Rome Convention art. 4(5). See also id. art. 6 with regard to employment contracts.

[122]See Inter-American Convention on the Law Applicable to International Contracts of 1994, art. 9.

[123]See Danish Law No. 88 of May 9, 1984, discussed in J. Lookofsky, *Danish Report,* at II.B.

[124]See German codif. arts. 28–30. For a discussion of these articles and their continuing relevance, see P. Mankowski, *German Report*, at I-II, and XIII.

Convention as well as members of the European Union—adopted statutes implementing or emulating the Convention. Emulation was the path chosen by certain countries that later joined the European Union, such as Bulgaria, Estonia, Hungary, Lithuania, and Slovenia.[125] Finally, several countries outside the EU have adopted a model similar to the Convention's or have used the closest-connection factor in similar fashion. These countries include Argentina,[126] Armenia[127] Belarus,[128] China,[129] FYROM,[130] Japan,[131] South Korea,[132] Kyrgyzstan,[133] Quebec,[134] Russia,[135] Switzerland,[136] Taiwan,[137] Turkey,[138] Ukraine,[139] and Venezuela.[140] The Japanese and Quebec codifications have extended the principle of the closest connection to bilateral juridical acts other than contracts, as well as to unilateral acts. Moreover, both codifications articulate the presumption of the characteristic performance in less categorical and more easily rebuttable terms than did the Rome Convention.[141] Finally, in the codification of Macau, the closest connection is the *only* connecting factor, which—unaided by presumptive rules—determines the applicable law for contracts that do not contain an effective choice-of-law clause.[142]

The Rome I Regulation has replaced the Rome Convention's presumptive rules with tighter rules and has deleted the Convention's *explicit* statement that these rules are based on the closest-connection factor. Nevertheless, this factor remains omnipresent, albeit in the background. Not only does it remain the residual connecting factor for contracts in which the applicable law "cannot be determined"[143] through the presumptive rules, but it also provides the basis for an exception from all of those rules (albeit an exception phrased in tighter language than in the Convention). Article 4(3) of Rome I provides that, when it is "clear from all the circumstances of the case that the contract is manifestly more closely connected" with a country other than the country designated by those rules, the law of that other country shall apply.[144]

Many recent codifications assign a similar role to the closest connection in tort conflicts as in contract conflicts. For example, although the text of the Rome II Regulation does not expressly state that its rules are based on the closest-connection factor, Rome II employs several escape clauses based on this factor. These clauses are found in the general rule of Article 4, as well as in the articles dealing with certain specific

[125]See Bulgarian codif. art. 94; Estonian codif. §§ 33, 35, 45; Hungarian codif. art. 29; Lithuanian codif. art. 1.37; Slovenian codif. art. 20. These provisions remain useful for contracts that fall outside the scope of Rome I.

[126]See Argentinian Draft of 2003, art. 72, discussed in M.S. Najurieta & M.B. Noodt Taquela, *Argentinean Report*, at XIII.3.

[127]See Armenian Civil Code art. 1285.

[128]See Belarus codif. art. 1125(4).

[129]The "closest connection" factor is used in Article 5 of the Foreign Economic Contract Law of the People's Republic of China of 1985; Article 145 of the General Principles of Civil Law of 1986, as amended in 2009; Article 269 of the Maritime Code of 1992; Article 188 of the Law of Civil Aviation of 1995 as amended in 2009; Article 126 of the Contract Law of 1999; and Article 5 of the Rules of the Supreme People's Court on Related Issues concerning the Application of Law in Hearing Foreign-Related Contractual Dispute Cases Related to Civil and Commercial Matters of 2007. For pertinent discussion, see W. Chen, *Chinese Report*, at XIII.C.

[130]See FYROM codif. art. 22.

[131]See Japanese codif. arts. 8, 12 (providing presumptive rules for contracts based on the characteristic performance and the assumed closest connection); T. Kanzaki, *Japanese Report* at II.2.

[132]See South Korean codif. Art 26 (providing presumptive rules for contracts based on the characteristic performance and the assumed closest connection); K. Suk, *South Korean Report*, at II.2.

[133]See Kyrgyzstan codif. art. 1199(3).

[134]See Quebec codif.art. 3112–3113. See also id. art. 3107 (regarding trusts). For discussion of arts. 3112–3113 and cases applying them, see F. Sabourin, *Quebec Report* at II.b. and c.

[135]See Russian codif. Art 1211. However, this article provides that its presumptions regarding the closest connection apply "unless it follows otherwise from statute, the terms or nature of the contract, or the totality of the circumstances of the case."

[136]See Swiss codif. arts. 117, 187.

[137]See Taiwanese codif. art. 20. See also id. arts. 17–18 (agency), 43(1) (bills of lading), 44 (securities), 45 (marriage engagement). For discussion, See R. Chen, *Taiwanese Report*, at II, XIII(3).

[138]See Turkish codif. art. 24(4). See also id. arts. 27 (employment contracts), 28(2) (intellectual property contracts), 29(3) (carriage contracts); Z. Tarman, *Turkish Report*, at II.

[139]See Ukranian codif. arts. 44 et seq.

[140]See Venezuelan codif. art. 30; E. Hernández-Bretón, *Venezuelan Report* at II, XIII.

[141]Likewise, the Belgian codification has adopted the closest connection as the residual connecting factor for the interpretation or revocation of wills. See Belgian codif. art. 84; J. Erauw & M. Fallon, *Belgian Report* at II.2.b.

[142]See Macau codif. art. 41, discussed in Tu Guangjian, *Macau Report,* at X. See also id. regarding maritime contracts.

[143]Rome I, art. 4(4).

[144]Rome I, Art 4(3). Similar exceptions are found in arts. 5(3) (contracts of carriage), 7(3) (insurance contracts), and 8(4) (individual employment contracts).

torts.[145] The escapes provide that, if it is "clear from all the circumstances of the case" that the tort is "manifestly more closely connected" with a country other the one whose law is designated as applicable by the above articles, then the law of that country governs.[146] These escapes are available in all EU countries except Denmark. However, because Rome II does not apply to all possible tort conflicts, the choice-of-law rules of those countries remain relevant.[147] Outside the EU, the codifications of Slovenia,[148] Japan,[149] Taiwan,[150] Turkey,[151] and FYROM[152] are among those that employ similar closer-connection escapes in tort conflicts.

The closest connection is used as a connecting factor in miscellaneous other cases as well. For example, the Belgian codification uses this factor for determining the state of the applicable law in certain intellectual property disputes, and for determining rights in certain groups of assets.[153] In the Taiwanese codification, the closest connection is the residual connecting factor for cases involving an agency relationship, bills of lading, and certain rights in securities.[154] In the codification of Burkina Faso, the closer connection triggers an escape from the national law to the domicile law of the decedent in matters of succession.[155] Finally, more than 20 codifications and international conventions provide that in certain cases a court may apply the mandatory rules of a state other than the state of the *lex causae* if the other state has a "close connection" with the case.[156]

The closest-connection factor is also used it as the tie breaker in certain categories of cases, such as cases involving persons with multiple nationalities, domiciles, or habitual residences, or cases involving the effects of marriage or divorce. For example, Article 1262 of the Armenian codification provides that the "personal law" of a person is the law of the state of which the person is a citizen and, in the case of multiple citizenships, the law of the state with which the person is "most closely connected." Close to 20 other codifications provide a similar rule for persons of multiple nationalities.[157] Other codifications, such as that of Ukraine, provide an intermediate tie-breaker by referring to the person's domicile or habitual residence before resorting to the closest connection.[158] The codifications of Bulgaria, Croatia, Japan, North Korea,

[145] In contrast to the preliminary draft, which limited the scope of the escape to cases covered by the general rule, the final text repeats the escape in the articles dealing with products liability (art. 5), unfair competition cases in which the competition affects exclusively the interests of a specific competitor (art. 6(2)), unjust enrichment (art. 10), *negotiorum gestio* (art. 11), and *culpa in contrahendo* (art. 12).

[146] Rome II, arts. 4(3), 5(2), 10(4), 11(4) and 12(2)(c). The first two of these provisions state that a "manifestly closer connection" with another country "might be based in particular on a pre-existing relationship between the parties, such as a contract, that is closely connected with the tort/delict in question."

[147] See, e.g., Austrian codif. art. 48(2); Belgian codif. art. 99; Bulgarian codif. art. 105; Estonian codif. art. 53; EGBGB art. 41; Lithuanian codif. art. 1.43; Slovenian codif. art. 30(2).

[148] See Slovenian codif. art. 30(2) (manifestly closer connection exception to law of contact or injury).

[149] See Japanese codif. arts. 20 and 15 (closer connection exception to the choice-of-law rules for torts, *negotiorum gestio*, and unjust enrichment); T. Kanzaki, *Japanese Report*, at II.

[150] See Taiwanese codif. arts. 25, 28; R. Chen, *Taiwanese Report* at II.

[151] See Turkish codif. art. 34(3) (law of state of closest connection displaces law of state of conduct or injury). For similar escapes on other subjects, see id. art. 24(4) (general contract clause), Art.27(3) (employment contracts), Art.28(2) (contracts on intellectual property rights), Art.29(3) (carriage contracts); Z. Tarman, *Turkish Report*, at II.

[152] See FYROM codif. art. 33(2) (law of state of closest connection displaces law of state of conduct or injury).

[153] See Belgian codif. arts. 93 and 87(2); J. Erauw & M. Fallon, *Belgian Report* at II.2.b.

[154] See Taiwanese codif. arts. 17–19, 43, 44, R. Chen, *Taiwanese Report* at II.

[155] See Burkina Faso codif. art. 1043.

[156] See, e.g., Swiss codif. art. 19; Quebec codif. art. 3079; Belarus codif. art. 1100; Kyrgyzstan codif. art. 1174; Tunisian codif. art. 38; Lithuanian codif. art. 1.11; South Korean codif. art. 7; Russian codif. art. 1192; Argentinean Draft art. 15, Belgium codif. art. 20; Bulgarian codif. art. 46; Ukranian codif. art. 14; Turkish codif. arts. 6, 31; Polish codif. art. 8; Uruguayan Draft art. 6; Czech Draft arts. 25; Dutch codif. art. 7; Rome Convention, art. 7; Inter-American Contracts Convention, art. 11; and the following Hague Conventions on the Law Applicable to: Trusts and on their Recognition, art. 17; Contracts for the International Sale of Goods, art. 17; Succession to the Estates of Deceased Persons, art. 6; International Protection of Adults, art. 20; Certain Rights in Respect of Securities held with an Intermediary, art. 11.

[157] See, e.g., Austrian codif. art. 9; Belarus codif. art. 1103; Belgian codif. art. 3(2); Chinese codif. art. 20; Estonian codif. § 11; EGBGB art. 5; Greek Civ. Code art. 31; Italian codif. art. 19(2); South Korean codif. art. 3(1); Kyrgyzstan codif. art. 1177; Liechtenstein codif. art. 10(1); Lithuanian codif. art. 1.11 (same rule for multiple or indeterminate domiciles); Moldova codif. art. 1589; Macau codif. art. 52; Slovenian codif. art. 10; Taiwanese codif. art. 2; Turkish codif. art. 4; Vietnamese codif. art. 760(3); FYROM codif. art. 11. Some of these codifications contain an exception providing that if one of the nationalities is that of the forum state, that nationality controls.

[158] See Ukranian codif. art. 16.

Vietnam and FYROM provide that, in cases of citizenship in multiple countries, the person's habitual residence provides the tie-breaker—but only if the person is a citizen of such country; if not, the closest connection functions as the tie-breaker.[159] The Dutch codification contains similar rules for the law governing a person's capacity and name.[160]

The closest-connection factor plays a similar role in cases involving the personal or patrimonial effects of marriage or divorce. For example, Articles 36 and 37 of the North Korean codification provide that, if the spouses do not possess the same nationality and do not reside in the same country, the effects of marriage and the availability and effects of divorce shall be determined under the law of the state with which the spouses have the "closest relationship."[161] The Taiwanese codification has the same rules for these two subjects, as well for engagements to marry and for the matrimonial regime.[162] The codifications of Austria, Estonia, Finland, Germany, Japan, South Korea, the Netherlands, Portugal, Slovenia, and Switzerland have a similar rule for the effects of marriage,[163] as does the 1987 Hague Convention on the Law Applicable to Matrimonial Property Regimes.[164] Portugal has a similar rule for the law applicable to adoption, as does Belgium for the filiation of children of same-sex relations.[165]

Several codifications use the closest-connection factor as a last resort when a choice-of-law rule refers to the law of a federal or other plurilegal country with subnational or internal legal systems. These codifications provide that such a reference shall be to the subnational system chosen by that country's rules, but if those rules are inconclusive or non-existent, the reference shall be to the subnational system that has the "closest connection" to the case at hand. For example, Article 18 of the Italian codification provides that, "[i]f reference is made to the law of a State having a non-unified legal system as regards territory or persons, the applicable law shall be determined according to the criteria of that State's legal system," but if it is impossible to establish such criteria, "the legal system shall be applied that appears to be most closely connected to the specific case."[166] Similar rules are found in several Hague Conventions[167] and in the codifications of more than 20 seventeen countries.[168]

Finally, in some codifications, the closest-connection factor plays the role of a gap-filler for cases for which the codification does not provide a choice-of-law rule or in which a particular rule does not provide a clear choice-of-law solution. For example, Article 1186(2) of the Russian Civil Code provides that, if it is impossible to determine the applicable law through the rules provided in the Code or elsewhere in Russian statutes or treaties, the law of the country with which the case is "most closely connected" shall be applied. Similar rules are found in at least ten other codifications.[169]

[159] See Bulgarian codif. Art 48, Croatian codif. Art 11; Japanese codif. art. 38(1); North Korean codif. Art 7; Vietnamese codif. art. 760(2), FYROM codif. Art 11(3).

[160] See Dutch codif. §§ 11, 19.

[161] North Korean codif. art. 37.

[162] See Taiwanese codif. art. 45(2) (effect of engagement to marry), art. 47 (effects of marriage), art. 48(2) (matrimonial regime), art. 50 (divorce).

[163] See Austrian codif. Art 18 (personal effects of marriage); Estonian codif. § 57 (legal consequences of marriage); Finish Marriage Act §§ 128(2), and 129(4) (personal legal effects of marriage and matrimonial regime); German codif. art. 14 (general effects of marriage); Japanese codif. art. 25 (effects of marriage); South Korean codif.. art. 37 (general effects of marriage); Dutch codif. § 36 (non-property effects); Portuguese codif. art. 52 (relations between spouses); Slovenian codif. art. 38(4) (personal and property effects); Swiss codif. art. 48 (effects of marriage). See also Macau codif. arts. 50 and 58. Some of these codifications use the connecting factor of domicile rather than nationality.

[164] See Hague Convention of 1978 on the Law Applicable to Matrimonial Property Regimes, art. 4(3).

[165] See Portuguese codif. art. 60(2); Belgian codif. art. 62(2).

[166] Italian codif. art. 18.

[167] See, e.g., the Hague Conventions on: Conflicts of Laws Relating to the Form of Testamentary Dispositions, art. 1; Law Applicable to Succession to the Estates of Deceased Persons, arts. 19(3)(b), 20; Jurisdiction, Applicable Law, Recognition, Enforcement and Co-operation in Respect of Parental Responsibility, arts. 47(4), 49(b); International Protection of Adults, arts. 45(d),(f), art. 47(b); Hague Protocol on the Law Applicable to Maintenance Obligations, art. 16(d) and (e).

[168] These countries are: Armenia (art. 1256), Austria (art. 5(3)), Belgium (art. 17), Bulgaria (art. 41(4)), Burkina Faso (art. 1007), China (art. 10), Croatia (art. 10), Estonia (§3), Germany (art. 4), Lithuania (Art.1.10(6), The Netherlands (art. 15(2)), Japan (art. 38(3)), South Korea (art. 3(3)), Macau (art. 19), Moldova (art. 1581), Quebec (art. 3077), Russia (art. 1188), Slovenia (art. 9), Taiwan (art. 5), Turkey (art. 2(5)), Ukraine (art. 9), Uruguay (Draft art. 2(2), and FYROM (art. 10).

[169] See, e.g., Armenian codif. art. 1253(2); Austrian codif. art. 1(2); Belarus codif. art. 1093(3); Bulgarian codif. art. 2(2); Burkina Faso codif. art. 1003(3); Chinese codif. art. 3(2); Kyrgyzstan codif. art. 1167(3); Liechtenstein codif. art. 1(2); Moldova codif. art. 1578; Ukranian codif. art. 4(2), FYROM codif. art. 4.

In a more specific context, the closest-connection factor serves as a residual gap-filler for contracts that do not contain an effective choice-of-law clause and in which the applicable law cannot be determined through other criteria, such as the "characteristic performance." This was the case with the Rome Convention and remains so with Rome I and other codifications influenced by them, as noted earlier. See Rome Convention, art. 4(5); Rome I, art. 4(4).

It is worth noting that at least three other codifications employ an even more malleable concept than the closest connection factor for choosing the law governing the unprovided-for cases. The Taiwanese codification—which otherwise relies extensively on the closest-connection factor—states that in unprovided-for cases, the applicable law shall be chosen under the principles derived from "the nature of law."[170] The codifications of Jordan, Slovenia, Qatar, UAE, and Yemen are only slightly more specific. They provide that the "principles of private international law" apply to conflicts for which these codifications do not designate the governing law.[171] The FYROM codification authorizes resort to the same principles, along with the principles of the codification itself and the forum's legal system as a whole.[172] Finally, the Mongolian codification unhesitantly authorizes resort to unspecified "foreign laws" when Mongolian law is silent or unclear.[173]

8.2.3.2 Other Soft Connecting Factors

The extensive use of the closest connection in so many codifications injects a considerable amount of flexibility in the judicial choice-of-law process. To be sure, this is primarily a "geographical" flexibility (as opposed to a content-dependent or policy-based flexibility) and it is very much in keeping with the Savignian objective of seeking the seat of the relationship. Nevertheless, this flexibility allows judges to reach more rational results than those dictated by rules based on fixed connecting factors.

Codifications that are less bound to the Savignian tradition feel freer to employ soft connecting factors that are less geographical and more policy-oriented. The codifications of Louisiana and Oregon, as well as the Puerto Rico draft codification, fall within this category. Under the Louisiana codification, the objective of the choice-of-law process is to identify and apply the law of "the state whose policies would be *most seriously impaired* if its law were not applied" to the particular issue.[174] This phrase is used in the codification's general and residual article (3515), as well as in the general and residual articles in the titles of status (3519), contractual obligations (3537), and delictual and quasi-delictual obligations (3542). Although this objective is legislatively implemented through the specific rules in each of these titles, these specific articles are quite elliptical—they do not cover the entire spectrum of cases. Consequently, cases that fall outside the scope of those articles must be judicially decided under the residual articles by identifying the law of the state of the "most serious impairment."

In the Puerto Rico draft codification, the objective of the choice-of-law process is to identify and apply the law of the state that has the "most significant connection" ("la conexión más significativa")[175] to the parties and the dispute. Although the quoted phrase resembles the "most significant relationship" language of the American Second Restatement[176] and the "closest" or "stronger" connection of codifications discussed above, it differs in that it invites a more qualitative analysis and carries fewer territorial or other physical connotations than the adjectives "stronger" or "closer" used in those codifications. Indeed, the state of the "most significant connection" is to be identified not by considering physical contacts alone, but rather by "(a) considering the policies embodied in the particular rules of law claimed to be applicable, as well as any other pertinent policies of the involved states; and (b) evaluating the strength and pertinence of these policies in the light of:(1) the relationship of each involved state to the parties and the dispute; and (2) the policies and needs of the interstate and international systems."[177] As in the Louisiana codification, the state of the "most significant connection" is legislatively identified through the draft's specific rules and is to be judicially determined in all cases and issues not covered by those rules.

Under the Oregon codifications for torts and contracts, the objective of the choice-of-law process is to identify and apply the law of "the state whose

---

[170] Taiwanese codif. art. 1.

[171] Jordanian codif. art. 25; Slovenian codif. Art 3; Qatar codif. art. 34; UAE codif. art. 23; Yemen codif. art. 34. See also Czech codif. § 10 (providing that, in the absence of an effective choice-of-law, contracts are governed by the law whose application is "in keeping with a reasonable settlement of the respective relationship").

[172] See FYROM codif. art. 4.

[173] See Mongolian codif. art. 540.3.

[174] See La. codif. arts. 3515, 3519, 3537, and 3542 (emphasis added).

[175] Puerto Rico Draft Code, arts. 2, 8, 13, 21, 33, 36, and 45.

[176] See, e.g., American Law Institute, *Restatement of the Law Second, Conflict of Laws* 2d, §§ 145, 188, 222, 283, 291, (1971).

[177] Puerto Rico Draft Code art. 2.

contacts with the parties and the dispute and whose policies on the disputed issues make application of the state's law the *most appropriate* for those issues."[178] Again, this objective is legislatively implemented through specific but elliptical rules, but it remains the goal of the judicial choice-of-law for all cases and issues that are not covered by those rules. Moreover, the quoted phrase provides the basis for a judicial escape from those rules in appropriate exceptional cases, as discussed later.

Finally, as noted earlier, soft connecting factors other than the closest connection are also used for unprovided-for cases in at least six codifications.[179] In a different vein, Section 10 of the Czech codification provides that, in the absence of an effective choice-of-law clause, contracts are governed by the law whose application is "in keeping with a reasonable settlement of the respective relationship."[180]

8.2.4 Escape Clauses

As Aristotle recognized so many centuries ago, any pre-formulated rule, no matter how carefully or wisely drafted, may, "because of its generality,"[181] or because of its specificity, produce results that are contrary to the purpose for which it was designed. In the words of Peter Hay, this "is a natural consequence of the difference between *law making* and *law application*."[182] With some notable exceptions, most modern legislatures seem to be fully aware of the inherent limitations in their ability to anticipate everything. In recent years, those who have codified PIL have recognized these limitations and have taken the previously unprecedented step of expressly granting judges the authority to adjust (or avoid altogether) the application of a rule when the circumstances of the individual case so dictate. In addition to traditional escapes, such as *ordre public* or *fraude à la loi*, this grant of authority takes the form of escape clauses attached to the rules.[183] This section of the Report discusses these escapes. It divides them into two categories: (1) general escapes, which are those that apply to all (or most) choice-of-law rules in a comprehensive PIL codification; and (b) specific escapes, which are those that are attached to a particular choice-of-law rule or small group of rules so as to provide an exception to that rule or rules.

Whether escape clauses are a bolder or more timid step towards flexibility than rules that contain the flexible connecting factors depends on the language, number, and especially the breadth of the escape clauses authorized by each particular system. Thus, escape clauses phrased in terms that suggest that they can be employed only in statistically rare cases are obviously a smaller step toward flexibility than escapes phrased in less categorical language. From a different angle, the use of a general escape qualifying all rules suggests that the legislature is more trusting of judges than the use of a specific escape from only some rules. Generally, however, the basic principles regarding the burden of persuasion suggest that a choice-of-law rule that uses flexible connecting factors accords more discretion than a fixed rule that is accompanied by an escape.

8.2.4.1 General Escapes

Article 15 of the Swiss codification is the prime example of a general escape. It provides that the law designated as applicable by any of the codification's rules is "by way of exception" not to be applied if, "from the totality of the circumstances, it is manifest that the particular case has only a very slight connection to that law and has a much closer relationship to another law."[184] Article 19 of the Belgian codification contains a similarly phrased escape,[185] but also provides more

[178] Or. Rev. Stat. § 31.878 (for torts) (emphasis added); see aldo *id.* § 81.130(for contracts).

[179] See supra notes 170–71 (Taiwan, Slovenia, Qatar, Taiwan, and Yemen).

[180] Czech codif. § 10. For discussion, see M. Pauknerová, *Czech Report* at II.

[181] Aristotle, *Nicomachean Ethics*, V.x 4–7.

[182] Hay P, "Flexibility Versus Predictability and Uniformity in Choice of Law," *Recueil des cours* 26 (1991-I): 281 at 291.

[183] Escape clauses in PIL were the subject of the XIV International Congress of Comparative Law held in Athens in 1994. The general and national reports on this subject were published in D. Kokkini-Iatridou, *Les Clauses d'Exception en matière de Conflits de Lois et de Conflits de Juridictions – ou le principe de proximité* (1994).

[184] Swiss codif. art. 15. For a discussion of this article and cases applying it, see Bonomi, *Swiss Report*, at II; von Overbeck A, "The Fate of Two Remarkable Provisions of the Swiss Statute on Private International Law," *Year Book of Private International Law* 1 (1999): 119; Bucher A, "La clause d'exception dans le contexte de la partie générale de la LDIP," in *Vingt ans LDIP,* ed. A. Bonomi & E. Cashin Ritaine, 59 (2009).

guidance for its judicial deployment. It provides that, in employing this escape, the court should give due consideration to "the need of predictability of the applicable law" and "the circumstance that the relevant legal relationship was validly established in accordance with the private international law of the States with which the legal relationship was connected when it was created."[186] Similar escapes exist in other codifications, including those of South Korea, Lithuania, Quebec, Slovenia, FYROM, and the Netherlands.[187]

Although these escapes differ in their wording, they nevertheless possess several common substantive features noted below, together with their differences.

- All of these escape clauses require a comparative evaluation—specifically, a comparison between the connections of the case to the state whose law is designated as applicable by the codification (e.g., State A) and the connections to another state (e.g., State B). If the connections to State A are "too slight" or attenuated and the connections to State B are "manifestly . . . much closer," then the law of State B displaces that of State A. As the quoted words indicate, the threshold for employing these escapes is intended to be quite high. The escapes are to be employed only in exceptional cases, when the connections of the case to the two states are "manifestly" unequal.
- This required comparison of "connections" suggests that these escapes are intended to provide an exception from only those choice-of-law rules that are themselves based on the principle of the closest connection (known as the "principle of proximity") and not rules that are based on other factors, such as the substantive content of the applicable law. Although some commentators have taken exactly this position,[188] the wording of the escapes is much broader. The escapes speak of "the law designated as applicable" by the codification's other rules, without any particular limitation. Only two escapes are explicit on this point. The first is the Dutch escape. It provides that the law designated as applicable by a choice-of-law "*based on the presumption of a close connection with that law*" shall exceptionally not be applied "if . . . *the close connection assumed in that rule* manifestly exists only to a very small degree and a far closer connection exists with a different law."[189] The second is the Belgian escape, which, as noted earlier, is inoperable against rules that designate applicable law "based on its content."[190]
- The reference to "connections" suggests that the escapes are intended to operate only within the confines of "conflicts justice" and should not be employed solely because of dissatisfaction of the substantive quality of the result produced by the applicable law ("material justice").[191] Nevertheless, courts in some countries have employed the escapes in ways motivated by considerations of material justice.[192] The drafters of the Dutch escape rejected a broader escape based on unfairness or unreasonableness for fear that it may lead to a "better law approach."[193] It remains to be seen, however, whether Dutch courts will adhere to the spirit of the adopted text.
- All of these escapes, except the Lithuanian one, can displace not only a foreign law, but also the law of the forum.

[185] Article 19 of the Belgian codification provides that the law designated as applicable by the codification should not be applied if "it manifestly appears from the totality of the circumstances" that the matter has "only a very slight connection" with the state of the designated law but is "very closely connected" to another state. In such case, the law of the latter state governs. For discussion, see Erauw & Fallon, *Belgian Report*, II.2(d).

[186] Belgian codif. art. 19(2). The article also provides that this escape does not apply in cases of a valid choice of law by the parties or when the codification's designation of the applicable law is "based on its content." Id. art. 19(3).

[187] See South Korean codif. art. 8.1 (discussed in K. Suk, *South Korean Report* at II); Lithuanian codif. art. 1.11.(3); Quebec codif. art. 3082 (discussed in F. Sabourin, *Quebec Report*, at II(a); Slovenian codif. art. 2(1); FYROM codif. art. 3; Dutch codif. art. 8 (discussed in K. Boele-Woelki & D. van Iterson, *Dutch Report*, at 4.1.4).

[188] For the view that the Swiss escape should be so limited, see A. Bucher, supra note 184, at 61–62. For a contrary opinion, see A. von Overbeck, supra note 184, at 130. See also K. Boele-Woelki & D. van Iterson, *Dutch Report* at 4.1.4 (stating that the Explanatory Report to the Dutch draft states that the escape cannot displace choice-of-law rules based on the "favour principle" or the "protection principle").

[189] Dutch Draft § 8 (emphasis added).

[190] Belgian codif. art. 19(3).

[191] For example, this is the prevailing view among Swiss scholars. See Bonomi, *Swiss Report*, at II.1

[192] This seems to be the case in all three Swiss court decisions that have applied the Swiss escape thus far. For a discussion of these cases, see Bonomi *Swiss Report*, at II.1. See also J. Erauw & M. Fallon, *Belgian Report*, II.2(d).

[193] K. Boele-Woelki & D. van Iterson, *Dutch Report*, IV.A.d.25.

- None of these escapes apply when the applicable law is validly chosen by the parties.[194]

Section 1 of the Austrian codification provides a more subtle escape, at least potentially. The first paragraph of this section states the operating principle of the entire codification by providing that "[f]actual situations with foreign contacts shall be judged . . . according to the legal order to which the strongest connection exists." The second paragraph provides that the codification's choice-of-law rules "shall be considered as expressions of this principle." This paragraph is subject to two conflicting interpretations. The first is that it is simply intended to function as a gap-filler, providing guidance for cases for which the codification does not designate the applicable law.[195] The second and more logical interpretation is that this provision is a genuine (albeit oblique) escape, authorizing the court to deviate from the codification's choice-of-law rules if, in the circumstances of a particular case, the court determines that the rule leads to a result that is inconsistent with the general principle of the strongest connection. Austrian court decisions support both interpretations.[196]

Article 2 of the Bulgarian codification is similar but more clearly capable of functioning as a general escape. Paragraph 1 of the article provides that multistate cases are governed by the law of the state that has the closest connection with the legal relation at stake, and that the codification's choice-of-law rules "express this principle." Paragraph 2 then states that, if the governing law cannot be determined through those rules, "the law of the State with which the relationship has the closest connection by virtue of other criteria shall apply."[197] The fact that Paragraph 2 expressly addresses the gap-filling function of the closest-connection principle would render the reference to the same principle in Paragraph 1 superfluous, unless that reference was intended to serve as an authorization for an escape when the state designated by a choice-of-law rule turns out *not* to have the closest connection in the particular case. The codifications of Burkina Faso and China also contain articles with a similar capacity to function as general escapes.[198]

8.2.4.2 Specific Escapes

Specific escapes—namely, escapes that qualify fewer than all of the choice-of-law rules of a particular codification—are much more numerous than general escapes. This is not surprising; after all, the need for legal certainty varies from one area of the law to another. For this reason, the adoption of escape clauses encounters less resistance in some areas of the law (such as torts) than in other areas (such as property) thus making the adoption of specific escapes more palatable to legislators than general escapes.

Escapes Based on the "Closer Connection"

The majority of special escape clauses are based on the principle of the "closer connection" ("proximity principle"). This is not surprising because most of the escapes accompany choice-of-law rules which themselves are based on the principle of closest connection. The typical escape provides that if the state whose law is designated as applicable by a particular choice-of-law rule (based on the closest connection) turns out to have an attenuated connection, and another state has a manifestly much closer connection, the law of the latter state shall govern.

Escape clauses based on this principle can be found in the Rome Convention and now the Rome I Regulation for contracts, and the Rome II Regulation for torts. Article 4(3) of Rome I provides that if it is "clear from all the circumstances of the case" that a contract that does not contain a choice-of-law clause is "manifestly more closely connected" with a country other than that

[194] Each of the escapes contains language to this effect.

[195] The Tunisian codification contains a provision that can function in this fashion. Article 26 provides that, if the codification does not provide a rule for a particular situation, "il dégagera la loi applicable par une détermination objective de la catégorie juridique de rattachement." See also art. 1253(2) of the Armenian codification (providing that if the code does not provide a choice-of-law rule for a particular subject, the court should apply "the law most closely connected" with that subject.).

[196] For a discussion of these cases, see C. Wendehorst, *Austrian Report*, at B.I.

[197] Bulgarian codif. art. 2.

[198] The codifications of China and Burkina Faso also contain articles with a similar to function as general escapes. See Burkina Faso codif. art. 1003 (providing that multistate legal relationships are governed by the law that has the "strongest connection" and that the codification's choice-of-law rules are "considered as the expression of [this] general principle."); Chinese codif. art. 3 (providing the law governing a multistate civil relationship "shall have the closest connection" with such relationship, and that if the codification does not provide for a particular relationship, "the law of the country that has the closest connection with [that] relationship . . . shall be applied.").

indicated by the preceding rules of that article, the law of that other country shall apply.[199] Rome II contains similar escapes in its general rule of Article 4, as well as in the articles dealing with products liability, unfair competition cases in which the competition exclusively affects the interests of a specific competitor, unjust enrichment (Art. 10), *negotiorum gestio*, and *culpa in contrahendo*. The escapes provide that, if it is "clear from all the circumstances of the case" that the tort is "manifestly more closely connected" with a country other the one whose law is designated as applicable by the above articles, then the law of that country governs.[200]

These escapes are now available in all EU countries in which Rome I and Rome II apply, whether or not those countries have similar escapes in their own codifications.[201] Outside the EU, similar escapes can be found in the Hague Sales Convention,[202] and the Taiwanese and Turkish codifications.[203] For torts, escapes similar to those of Rome II can be found in the codifications of Japan, Taiwan, Turkey, and FYROM.[204]

Outside the areas of contracts and torts, escapes based on the closer connection principle are found in the German codification (property), the Finnish Inheritance Code, the Burkina Faso codification (inheritance), and the Hague Conventions on the Law Applicable to Estates.[205] Three other Hague Conventions dealing with maintenance and the protection of children and adults also employ similar (albeit more malleable) escapes. These escapes authorize courts to deviate from the otherwise applicable law and apply the law of another state that has a "*substantial* connection" with the case.[206]

Escapes Based on Other Factors

Among the escapes that are based on factors other than the closer connection, Article 1213 of the Russian Civil Code stands out because it is phrased as an *exception* to the closest connection factor. Article 1213 provides that contracts that do not contain an effective choice-of-law clause are governed by the law of the country with which the contract is "most closely connected." The article then provides several rules presumptively identifying the most closely connected country. However, each of these rules is accompanied by the phrase "unless it otherwise follows from a statute, the terms or the nature of the contract, or *the totality of the circumstances of the case*."[207]

Section 10 of the Czech codification begins by stating that contracts that do not contain an effective choice-of-law clause are governed by the law whose application is "in keeping with a reasonable settlement of the respective relationship"[208] and then designates that law for various types of contracts through eight different paragraphs. However, these paragraphs are introduced with the phrase "as a rule," thus allowing courts to deviate from those rules in appropriate cases.

---

[199] Rome I, art. 4(3). A similar escape is found in Articles 5(3) (contracts of carriage), 7(2) (insurance contracts), and 8(4) (individual employment contracts).

[200] Rome II, arts. 4(3), 5(2), 10(4), 11(4) and 12(2)(c). The first two of these provisions state that a "manifestly closer connection" with another country "might be based in particular on a pre-existing relationship between the parties, such as a contract, that is closely connected with the tort/delict in question."

[201] See, e.g., Austrian codif. §§ 35(3) for contracts and 48(2) for torts; Bulgarian codif. arts. 94(8) for contracts and 105(3) for torts; Estonian codif. art. 34(6) for contracts, 36(3) for employment contracts, 53(1) for torts; German codif., arts. 28(5) for contracts, 30(2), last sentence, 41 for torts; Lithuania codif. art. 1.37(4) for contracts; Romania codif. art. 78(2) for contracts.

[202] See art. 8(3) of the Hague Convention for the Law Applicable to the International Sales of Goods (providing that "where, in the light of the circumstances as a whole . . ., the contract is manifestly more closely connected with a law which is not the law which would otherwise be applicable to the contract . . ., the contract is governed by that other law.")

[203] See Taiwanese codif. art. 20; Turkish codif. art. 24(4) for contracts, art. 27(4) for employment contracts, and art. 28 for contracts relating to intellectual property.

[204] See Japanese codif. art. 15 for negotiorum gestio and unjust enrichment and art. 20 for torts; T. Kanzaki, *Japanese Report*, at II.; Taiwan codif. arts. 25, 28; R. Chen, *Taiwanese Report,* at XII. Turkish codif. art. 34; Z. Tarman, *Turkish Report*, at II, XII.1; FYROM codif. art. 33(2).

[205] See German codif. art. 46; Finnish Code Inheritance § 5(3); Burkina Faso codif. art. 1043; Hague Convention on the Law Applicable to the Estates of Deceased Persons, art. 3.

[206] See Hague Protocol on the Law Applicable to Maintenance Obligations, art. 5; Hague Convention on Jurisdiction, Applicable Law, Recognition, Enforcement and Co-operation in Respect of Parental Responsibility and Measures for the Protection of Children, art. 5(2); Hague Convention on the International Protection of Adults, art. 13(2).

[207] Russian codif. art. 1211 (emphasis added). Articles 1203, 1213, 1217, and 1222 contain similar escapes for cases involving, respectively, certain foreign juridical persons, immovable property contracts, unilateral juridical acts, and unfair competition. The FYROM codification also employs a similar escape in Article 22(2).

[208] Czech codif. § 10. For discussion, see M. Pauknerová, *Czech Report* at II.(1)–(2), XIII.

Article 20 of the Croatian codification is similar,[209] as is Article 106 of the Argentine Draft, which provides that "[e]xceptionally, in the view of the particularities of the case," a marriage celebrated in violation of certain impediments may nevertheless be given effect.[210]

Section 9 of the Dutch codification provides a general escape from its rules in order to protect certain rights acquired under foreign law. Based on the "doctrine of the accomplished fact," this section provides that, when a law that is applicable (according to the choice-of-law rule of a concerned foreign state) attaches certain legal consequences to a particular fact, Dutch law will attribute the same consequences, even if this "would depart from the law that is applicable according to Dutch private international law—to the extent that failure to attach such legal consequences would constitute an unacceptable violation of the parties' justified expectations or of legal certainty."[211]

The English statute of 1995, which applied to tort conflicts other than defamation before the adoption of Rome II, contains a general rule in Section 11 and a multifactor escape in Section 12. The escape provides that the law applicable under the general rule of Section 11 will be displaced "[i]f it appears, in all the circumstances, from a comparison of (a) the significance of the factors which connect a tort or delict with the country whose law would be the applicable law under the general rule; and (b) the significance of any factors connecting the tort or delict with another country, that it is substantially more appropriate for the applicable law for determining the issues arising in the case, or any of those issues, to be the law of the other country[.]"[212]

Article 3547 of the 1991 Louisiana codification provides an escape from all of the codification's articles dealing with tort conflicts (Arts. 3543–46). This article provides that the law applicable under these articles shall not apply if, "from the totality of the circumstances of an exceptional case," it is "clearly evident" under the principles of Article 3542 (the general article for tort conflicts) that the policies of another state would be "more seriously impaired if its law were not applied to the particular issue."[213]

The Oregon codification for contract conflicts articulates its general rule for contracts that do not contain an effective choice-of-law clause in Section 81.130, and then provides a series of presumptive rules for particular types of contracts in Section 81.135. However, the latter section allows a court to deviate from the law designated by those rules if a party demonstrates that the application of that law would be "clearly inappropriate under the principles of [Section] 81.130."[214]

The Oregon codification for tort conflicts articulates its general approach in Section 31.878 and provides particular choice-of-law rules for certain product liability cases in Section 31.872 and for non-product torts in Section 31.875. Both of the latter sections contain escapes that allow the court to deviate from the law designated by these sections if a party demonstrates that the application of the law of another state to a disputed issue is "substantially more appropriate under the principles of [Section] 31.878."[215]

Section 31.875 contains one additional escape for torts in which both the injurious conduct and the resulting injury occurred in a state other than the state in which either the tortfeasor or the victim were domiciled and in which the laws of the parties' home states would not produce the same outcome. In such cases, the applicable law is the law of the state of conduct and

[209] Article 20 introduces several rules designating the applicable law for various contracts with the phrase "if . . . special circumstances of the case do not refer to another law," thus allowing courts to deviate from these rules if the circumstances of the case so warrant. For discussion, see D. Babić, *Croatian Report,* at XIII.2.

[210] See Najurieta & Noodt Taquela, *Argentinian Report* at C.II.

[211] Dutch codif. § 9, discussed in Boele-Woelki & Van Iterson, *Dutch Report* at IV.A.e.

[212] U.K. codif.§ 12; C. Roodt, *English Report,* at B.I(b).

[213] For the history, meaning, and subsequent application of this article, see Symeonides S. "Louisiana's New Law of Choice of Law for Tort Conflicts: An Exegesis," *Tulane Law Review* 66 (1992): 677, 763–66. The Puerto Rico draft code contains several escapes, including one for tort conflicts that is modelled after the Louisiana escape. See Puerto Rico Draft codif. arts. 11 (marriage), 20 (child custody), 24 (matrimonial regimes), 37 (contracts), 45 (torts). For discussion, see Symeonides S. "Codifying Choice of Law for Contracts: The Puerto Rico Projet," in *Law and Justice in a Multistate World: Essays in Honor of Arthur T. von Mehren*, ed. J. Nafziger and S. Symeonides (Ardsley: Transnational Publishers, 2002): 419; Symeonides S. "Revising Puerto Rico's Conflicts Law: A Preview," *Columbia Journal of Transnational Law* 28 (1990): 413.

[214] Or. Rev. Stat. § 81.135. For discussion, see Symeonides S, "Oregon's Choice-of-Law Codification for Contract Conflicts: An Exegesis," *Willamette Law Review* 44 (2007): 205, 235–45.

[215] Or. Rev. Stat. §§ 31.872(3) and 31.875(4). For discussion by the article's drafter, see Symeonides S, "Oregon's New Choice-of-Law Codification for Tort Conflicts: An Exegesis," *Oregon Law Review* 88(2009): 963, 997–1044.

injury. However, an escape provides that if a party demonstrates that, under the circumstances of the particular case, the application of that law to a disputed issue will "not serve the objectives of that law," that issue will be governed by the law selected under the general approach of Section 31.878.[216]

Assessment of Escapes

Although the use of escape clauses is a significant step in the right direction of flexibility, many of the escapes discussed above are phrased in such a tight way as to be employable only in the most extreme cases. This is particularly true of the escapes based on the closest connection. A good example is the general escape of Rome II, found in paragraph 3 of Article 4, which provides an escape from both the *lex loci* rule of paragraph 1 and the common-domicile rule of paragraph 2. As noted earlier, the escape authorizes the court to apply the law of another country if "it is clear from all the circumstances of the case that the tort/delict is manifestly more closely connected with [that other] country."[217] The two problematic features of this escape are that the escape: (a) is phrased in exclusively geographical or quantitative terms that are not correlated to an overarching principle; and (b) does not permit issue-by-issue evaluation.

The reliance on geography is symbolized by the drafters' choice of the adjective "closer" to qualify the word "connection"—rather than, for example, "more significant," which is the critical adjective in the English statute[218] (and, of course, the Restatement (Second)).[219] The finding of a "closer connection" must be based on consideration of "all the circumstances," but, in the absence of any non-quantitative qualifiers, the quoted phrase will be understood in geographical terms. In one sense, it is logical that a system of geographically-based rules would also rely on geography when formulating escapes from those rules. Rome II is such a system because most of its dispositive rules depend on the place in which a single critical event occurred, or in which one or both parties reside. Very few non-geographical factors affect the choice, and the content of the conflicting laws is a factor that appears only in a few narrow exceptions.[220] Having relied on geography in erecting this system, the drafters of Rome II may have felt bound to likewise rely on geography to handle the exceptional cases and overcome the inevitable impasses.

The benefits of such logic, however, will rarely overcome its shortcomings. Escapes should be designed to cure the rule's deficiencies, not to reproduce them. To employ the escape intelligently, a court must know the reasons for which the drafters made the choices embodied in the rule and the goals that the rule seeks to promote. To simply say that one should look for a "closer" connection gives courts little meaningful guidance and creates the risk of degenerating into a mechanical counting of physical contacts. This risk is reduced when the escape is correlated to the overarching principles that permeate the rules, and/or when the escape allows an issue-by-issue evaluation.

For purposes of illustration, not emulation, one can consider the schemes of the Restatement (Second) and the Louisiana codification. The Restatement provides in Section 6 that the goal of the choice-of-law process is to identify the state that has the "most significant relationship." Although the quoted phrase literally appears to contemplate a determination based on geography, the content of Section 6 negates any such inference because it lists a series of substantive policies intended to guide this determination. The subsequent sections of the Restatement provide specific rules, most of which contain an escape authorizing the judge to apply the law of another state if, "*with respect to the particular issue*[,]" that state has a more significant relationship "*under the principles stated in § 6*."[221] Similarly, Article 3542 of the Louisiana codification enunciates the general goal of the choice-of-law process for tort conflicts as one of identifying the state whose policies would be most seriously impaired if its law were not applied. After establishing specific rules based on that goal, the codification also provides an escape clause in Article 3547 that authorizes the judge to apply the law of another state if, "*under the principles of Article 3542*," the policies of that other state

[216] Or. Rev. Stat. § 31.875(3)(b).

[217] Rome II, art. 4(3).

[218] See supra note 212.

[219] See, e.g., Restatement (Second) § 146, infra at text accompanying note 221.

[220] See Symeonides S, "Rome II and Tort Conflicts: A Missed Opportunity," *American Journal of Comparative Law* 56(2008): 173, 181–83.

[221] American Law Institute, *Restatement (Second) of Conflict of Laws*, § 146 (emphasis added).

"would be more seriously impaired if its law were not applied *to the particular issue*."[222]

The italicized phrases signify what is missing from the escape of Article 4(3) of Rome II: issue-by-issue evaluation and correlation to non-geographical overarching principles. For example, suppose that while hunting in Kenya, a French hunter injures a Belgian hunter with whom he has no preexisting relationship. Suppose that Kenya limits the amount of damages to the equivalent of five thousand euros, while France and Belgium impose no ceiling and define the amount of damages in identical ways. In such a case, there is no reason to apply the Kenyan ceiling and every good reason to apply either Belgian or French law. Yet, Article 4(1) of Rome II mandates the application of the Kenyan ceiling, the common-domicile rule of Article 4(2) would be inoperable, and the escape of Article 4(3) would not correct this wrong choice because neither France nor Belgium would be considered to have a "manifestly closer connection" than Kenya.[223]

The failure to allow an issue-by-issue deployment and evaluation is the second major problem with the general escape clause of Rome II and similar escapes. The escape not only avoids the dirty word "issue," but also avoids the phrase "*obligation* arising out of a tort/delict" used earlier in the same article.[224] For the escape to apply, the entire "tort/delict" must be "manifestly more closely connected" with another state, in which case the law of that state will apply to the entire "tort/delict," not to parts or aspects of it. Thus, this is an "all or nothing" proposition; and therein lies its most serious flaw.

In another publication, this author has attempted to illustrate these flaws through six hypothetical scenarios.[225] That discussion will not be repeated here. Its conclusion is that, although the inclusion of an escape clause in Rome II is a significant step in the right direction, the escape would have benefitted from more nuanced and flexible drafting. The drafters' preference for a tight escape that does not swallow the rules is understandable. However, an escape that is so tight as to be rarely utilized, or one that is phrased in broad all-or-nothing terms, is only slightly better than no escape at all.[226] While no one would question the desirability of uniformity and certainty, one can question the extent to which these values should displace all other values of the choice-of-law process, such as the need for sensible, rational, and fair decisions in individual cases. If the American experience has something to offer, it is a reminder that a system that is too rigid (as the First Restatement was) ultimately fails to deliver the promised predictability because, in a democratic society, no system can "mechanize judgment"[227]; to the extent that a system attempts to do so, judges will largely ignore it.[228]

---

[222] La. codif. art. 3547 (emphasis added). For discussion by the article's drafter, see Symeonides S. *Louisiana's New Law of Choice of Law for Tort Conflicts*, supra note 213, at 763–66.

[223] In contrast, the much briefer and simpler escape found in the unenacted Benelux law would have allowed a court to avoid the application of Kenya law by finding that, with regard to the issue of damages, "the *consequences* of a wrongful act belong to the legal sphere of a country other than [Kenya] where the act took place." Traité Benelux portant loi uniforme relative au droit international privé, art. 14 (1969). (emphasis added). Likewise, under the escape of the English statute, a court would compare the "*significance* of the factors" connecting the case with the three countries and conclude that it would be "substantially *more appropriate*" to apply either French or Belgian law "for determining the issues arising in the case, or any of those issues"—here, the issue of damages. English codif. § 12 (emphasis added).

[224] Rome II, art. 4(1) (emphasis added). This phrase could allow a separate evaluation of the potentially multiple obligations that may arise from the same facts, such as (but not only) when the case involves multiple tortfeasors or multiple victims.

[225] See Symeonides S, "The American Revolution and the European Evolution in Choice of Law: Reciprocal Lessons," *Tulane Law Review* 82(2008): 1741, 1773–82.

[226] The reasons for the European Council's and Commission's political preference for certainty over flexibility are obvious. The primary motive behind the movement to draft Rome II, as well as the choice of the particular instrument for its implementation (a regulation as opposed to a directive) was the need to ensure uniformity of choice-of-law decisions within the European Union. See Rome II, recital (6). These two bodies must have concluded that uniformity would be in jeopardy if Rome II were to include too many flexible rules or escape clauses. Although this is plausible, it is not necessarily the best conclusion. The argument that a codification intended for application by the courts of different countries cannot afford to be flexible, is highly overrated. For example, whatever its other faults, the Rome Convention did not fail for being too flexible.

[227] Cavers D, "Restatement of the Law of Conflict of Laws," *Yale Law Journal* 44 (1935): 1478 at 1482.

[228] In Professor Weintraub's words, "[i]ronically Rome II is more likely to succeed in providing reasonable foreseeability if its rules provide sufficient flexibility." Weintraub R, "Rome II and the Tension Between Predictability and Flexibility," *Rivista di diritto internazionale privato e processuale* 19(2005): 561 at 561.

8.2.5 "Approaches"

As used in this context, a choice-of-law "approach" is the antithesis of a choice-of-law "rule." Whereas a rule directly designates the applicable law, an approach does so only indirectly (if at all) by providing a list of principles, policies, and factors through which the court will choose the applicable law after considering the circumstances of the individual case. A rule reflects the legislature's *a priori* choice of law, whereas an approach empowers judges to make the choice *a posteriori* and *ad hoc* within certain general parameters.

The paradigmatic model of an approach is Section 6 of the American Restatement (Second) of Conflict of Laws. It sets forth the guiding principles of the choice-of-law process by stating that "the factors relevant to the choice of the applicable rule of law include (a) the needs of the interstate and international systems, (b) the relevant policies of the forum, (c) the relevant policies of other interested states and the relative interests of those states in the determination of the particular issue, (d) the protection of justified expectations, (e) the basic policies underlying the particular field of law, (f) certainty, predictability and uniformity of result, and (g) ease in the determination and application of the law to be applied."[229] These factors—which are not listed in a hierarchical order and may in fact point in different directions in a given case—provide a guiding, as well as a validating, test for applying almost all other sections of the Restatement, most of which incorporate Section 6 by reference.[230]

This clearly is a very open-ended formula. Conventional wisdom suggests that such a formula has no place in a legislative text. Indeed, a codification is not worth undertaking if the legislature is not prepared to provide more specific direction than restating generalities like those found in Section 6. However, this does not mean that an approach is *incompatible* with codification; an approach is compatible, provided that it is combined with rules. Indeed, the combination of an approach with rules provides a much more versatile tool for attaining an appropriate equilibrium between the competing needs of certainty and flexibility than either an approach or rules alone can accomplish. Rules can provide certainty for those areas of the law (such as property) where certainty is needed most, as well as other areas in which there is a sufficient accumulation of experience to allow adoption of safe and relatively noncontroversial rules. An approach can cover areas in which such experience is lacking and in which the need for certainty is not as pressing. Moreover, an approach can provide the best basis on which to anchor any escapes from the rules for handling exceptional cases.

This combination of rules and approaches is the methodology followed in the two American codifications of Louisiana and Oregon, as well as in the Puerto Rico draft codification. The Louisiana codification employs an approach in Article 3515, the general and residual article for the entire codification. Article 3515 provides that conflicts cases are to be governed by the law of "the state whose policies would be most seriously impaired if its law were not applied" to the particular case, and that state is determined by "evaluating the strength and pertinence of the relevant policies of all involved states in the light of: (1) the relationship of each state to the parties and the dispute; and (2) the policies and needs of the interstate and international systems, including the policies of upholding the justified expectations of parties and of minimizing the adverse consequences that might follow from subjecting a party to the law of more than one state."[231] Similarly, the titles on status, contracts, and torts contain one general, residual and flexible article[232] that enunciates the general approach for that title, and then a varying number of specific articles that implement the general approach for particular fact situations. In contrast, the titles on property, matrimonial property, and successions consist of classic choice-of-law rules (without approaches or escapes) precisely because in those areas the need for certainty outweighs the need for flexibility.[233]

The Oregon codification for torts articulates its general and residual approach in Section 31.878, which calls for the application of the law of the state "whose

[229] Restatement (Second) Conflict of Laws § 6.

[230] See, e.g., Restatement (Second) § 145, which provides that a tort issue is governed by the law of the state that, with respect to that issue, has the most significant relationship to the occurrence and the parties "under the principles stated in § 6."

[231] La. codif. art. 3515.

[232] See La. codif. arts. 3519, 3537, and 3542, respectively.

[233] For discussion of the approach of the Louisiana codification and the balance between certainty and flexibility, see Symeonides S, "The Conflicts Book of the Louisiana Civil Code: Civilian, American, or Original?" *Tulane Law Review* 83(2009): 1041, 1058–70.

contacts with the parties and the dispute and whose policies on the disputed issues make application of the state's law the most appropriate for those issues." The section also provides that the "most appropriate law" is determined by: (1) Identifying the states that have relevant contacts with the dispute and the policies embodied in the laws of those states on the disputed issues; and (2) Evaluating the relative strength and pertinence of those policies with due regard to: (a) The policies of encouraging responsible conduct, deterring injurious conduct and providing adequate remedies for the conduct; and (b) The needs and policies of the interstate and international systems, including the policy of minimizing adverse effects on strongly held policies of other states.[234] The codification provides specific choice-of-law rules for many (but not all) possible tort conflicts or issues, and then provides that cases or issues not covered by the specific rules are governed by the law chosen under the residual approach of Section 31.878.[235]

The Oregon codification for contracts follows a similar combination of rules and approach as the torts codification,[236] whereas the Puerto Rico draft Code follows a similar combination as the Louisiana codification.[237] The English choice-of-law statute discussed earlier also employs a rules/approach combination, except that the approach element is confined to the escape from the rules. Section 11 of the statute states the general rule, which calls for the application of the "country in which the events constituting the tort or delict in question occur."[238] Section 12 contains the escape, which is phrased as an approach in the sense that it calls for an individualized evaluation of a series of factors for determining whether to displace the general rule in a particular case.[239]

For cultural and historical reasons, such rules/approaches combinations are uncommon in the rest of the world, but they do exist. For example, Article 7 of the 1985 Hague Trust Convention provides that a trust that does not contain a valid choice-of-law stipulation is governed by the law of the most closely connected state, which is identified by considering the place of the trust administration designated by the settlor, the situs of the trust assets, the trustee's place of residence or business, the objects of the trust and the places where they are to be fulfilled.[240] The Inter-American Contracts Convention and the Venezuelan codification also employ an approach of sorts for contracts that do not contain a valid choice-of-law clause. Article 9 of the Convention and Article 30 of the Venezuelan codification provide, respectively, that such a contract is governed by the law of the state with which it has the "closest ties" or is "most directly linked" after considering "all objective and subjective elements" of the contract. The Convention provides that the court will also consider "the general principles of international commercial law recognized by international organizations," and "the guidelines, customs, and principles of international commercial law as well as commercial usage and practices . . . in order to discharge the requirements of justice and equity in the particular case."[241] The Venezuela codification calls for consideration of "the General Principles of Business Law accepted by international organizations" and the "norms, customs and principles of International Business Law, as well of generally accepted trade uses and practices, with the purpose of reifying the requirements imposed by justice and fairness in the solution of a concrete case."[242]

8.3 Conclusions

The preceding documentation supports the conclusion that codification in general and PIL codification in particular need not petrify the law nor render it unduly

[234] Or. Rev. Stat. § 31.878. For discussion of this approach, see Symeonides S, "Oregon's New Choice-of-Law Codification for Tort Conflicts: An Exegesis," *Oregon Law Review* 88(2009): 963, 1032–38.

[235] Also, as noted earlier, this section provides the anchor for the escapes contained in some of the specific rules.

[236] For discussion, see Symeonides S, "Oregon's Choice-of-Law Codification for Contract Conflicts: An Exegesis," *Willamette Law Review* 44(2007): 205.

[237] See Symeonides S, "Codifying Choice of Law for Contracts" supra note 213; Symeonides S, "Revising Puerto Rico's Conflicts Law," supra note 213.

[238] PIL (Miscellaneous Provisions) Act § 11(c. 42) (1995).

[239] The text of Section 12 is partly reproduced at text accompanying note 212, supra.

[240] Hague Convention of 1 July 1985 on the Law Applicable to Trusts and on their Recognition, art. 7.

[241] Inter-American Contracts Convention, arts. 9 and 10.

[242] Venezuelan codif. arts. 30 and 31; E. Hernández-Bretón, *Venezuelan Report*, at XIII. For partly similar provisions, see Uruguayan Draft arts. 51 and 13(3) (the latter regarding international trade law); C. Fresnedo de Aguirre, *Uruguayan Report*, at XI.3.

inflexible for exceptional cases. Codification does not necessarily outlaw judicial discretion. Modern PIL codifications employ various tools—such as soft connecting factors, escape clauses, or a combination of rules and residual approaches—which provide controlled dosages of flexibility, and thus help attain an equilibrium between the perpetually competing needs for certainty and flexibility.

To be sure, one may question whether this is equilibrium is the "right" one in every case. For example, one can easily argue that, from the American perspective, most modern PIL codifications are (a) too holistic, i.e., geared to the whole case rather than to aspects or issues of it, or (b) too geographic (e.g., "closer" connection).[243] Even so, one cannot escape the conclusion that modern PIL codifications are much more flexible than the traditional ones, and thus much better for that reason alone.

At the same time—even if relatively modest—the gains of flexibility over rigidity in modern PIL codifications can be instructive for American conflicts law, which has careened in the *opposite* direction without considering any intermediate stops. Indeed, American conflicts law has moved from rigidity to excessive flexibility in an impulsive, rash, and wholesale manner. The starting point was the first conflicts Restatement of 1933 which, although not qualifying as a "codification" under any standard definition, consisted of fixed, rigid, and mechanical choice-of-law rules with no exceptions. Because these rules were poorly conceived and inflexible, judges began deviating from them through several escape devices, such as by manipulating the localization of connecting factors, the characterization of the cause of action or the substance versus procedure dichotomy, misusing the *ordre public* exception, and resorting to *renvoi*.[244] This gradual dissent became an open revolution in the 1960s which, at least in tort and contract conflicts, led to the abandonment of all rules, not just the poorly conceived ones and their replacement with malleable and open-ended approaches.[245]

By the dawn of the twenty-first century, the strong anti-rule sentiment of the first decades of the revolution seems to have lost some of its initial fervor. Although there remains a certain degree of rule-skepticism—which is endemic to the common law tradition—at least there is now a serious debate on whether to undertake a third Restatement or another process of standardization and rule-making.[246] While such an undertaking is far from assured in the immediate future, the experience of foreign systems in drafting new PIL codifications can help sway at least some rule skeptics: If a "true," statutory codification can accommodate the need for flexibility, surely a Restatement can do so much more easily.

Finally, the diverse experiences of American and foreign PIL systems offer two different examples of the perennial, and often cyclical, struggle to attain an equilibrium between certainty and flexibility. During the last fifty years, American and foreign PIL systems have found themselves in different points of this cyclical movement. While American conflicts law has careened from extreme rigidity to extreme flexibility, other PIL systems have moved slowly but steadily from certainty to flexibility.[247] They experienced no revolutions, did not undertake drastic changes, and have not abandoned rules in favor of ad hoc "approaches." Instead, they injected small, controlled doses of flexibility through some new devices, as well as through some old and tested ones. The result is a new equilibrium between certainty and flexibility. One hopes that American conflicts law can draw some inspiration from this experience. It should be possible to construct a new breed of smart and evolutionary rules which will consolidate the substantive and methodological lessons of the revolution, but also provide a modicum of certainty without the rigidity of the traditional rules. The Louisiana and Oregon codifications are reminders that such an undertaking is possible.

[243] For a detailed discussion of this point, see Symeonides S, "The American Revolution and the European Evolution," supra note 225 at 1773–82.

[244] See S. Symeonides, W. Perdue & A. von Mehren, *Conflict of Laws: American, Comparative, International,* 2nd ed. (St. Paul: Thomson/West, 2003):41–103.

[245] See S. Symeonides, *Revolution* 9–121.

[246] See Symeonides S, "A New Conflicts Restatement," supra note 114.

[247] One could argue that the countries that did not have statutory rules at the beginning of this period but have acquired them in the meantime have moved from flexibility to certainty. However, as this chapter of the Report illustrates, the certainty to which they aspired and which they attained was much more pliable than the uncompromising certainty of the first Restatement.

Class Actions[1]

9

Diego Corapi

1. In our world of complex societies, where people daily interact with other anonymous people, where products and services are provided in massive standardized series by large organizations, where the financing of different economic activities is made through impersonal networks, where citizens in their daily life are at times consumers, users, investors, subject to the same kind of opportunities and risks, disputes arising from their interactions must be resolved by procedures different from the traditional bipolar litigation model.

In the nineteenth century the working conditions created by the rising industrial society imposed a dramatic change in labor relations. Trade unionism and employment contracts negotiated in a collective way were the answer. The traditional doctrine of contracts as the expression of the free will of the parties had to be adjusted to this evolution and the solution of conflicts arising from them required different kinds of proceedings.

Now, in the twenty-first century, the conditions created by mass consumption and use of goods and services have imposed a change in contract law granting a collective protection to consumers and investors. To make such protection effective it is not only necessary to adjust the traditional doctrine of contracts as the expression of the free will of the parties and of tort liability based on fault, but it has become also necessary to devise collective redress mechanisms.

In fact, collective redress mechanisms in the cases of consumer protection and mass torts have been introduced in many legal systems. In many other legal systems their introduction is widely discussed and proposals have been prepared.

The goals of collective redress are the same in all jurisdictions. We can take as an example art. 1 of the Israeli Class Action Law of 2006 which spells them out as follows: *1. The goal of this law is to set uniform rules in the matter of the submitting and managing of class actions, in order to improve the defense of privileges, and in doing so particularly promote these: actualizing the privilege of access to the court house, including the types of the population that find it difficult addressing the court as individuals; enforcing the law and deterring its breaking; giving proper assistance to those harmed by the violation of the law; efficient, fair and exhaustive management of suits.*[2]

However, the structure of collective redress mechanisms varies greatly in different jurisdictions.

Also the terminology used to define them is different. Some remarks on it seem necessary.[3]

The term "class action" could be restricted to the US-style procedure whereby many subjects are represented by one single claimant; the term "collective actions" to procedures where different organizations or associations act on behalf of a number of persons (not necessarily their members); the term "test" or "model cases" to procedures in which an individual case may become a precedent for a multitude of other cases.

All such procedures have in common that "at the bottom of these lawsuits there are usually interests of a larger group or even a public interest although they might formally appear as traditional two-party cases."[4]

[1]Les actions collectives.

D. Corapi (✉)
Faculty of Law, University of Rome – Sapienza, Rome, Italy
e-mail: diego.corapi@studiolegalecorapi.it

[2]Quoted by Prof. Michael Karayanni in his report for Israel.

[3]The point is raised by Prof. Astrid Stadler in the introduction to her report for Germany.

[4]I quote again Prof. Stadler's report.

K.B. Brown and D.V. Snyder (eds.), *General Reports of the XVIIIth Congress of the International Academy of Comparative Law/Rapports Généraux du XVIIIème Congrès de l'Académie Internationale de Droit Comparé*,
DOI 10.1007/978-94-007-2354-2_9, © Springer Science+Business Media B.V. 2012

For the purpose of this report it is suggested to reserve the term "class action" for the US style procedure because in that country this redress mechanism was first developed as a specific remedy in cases where significant numbers of persons are involved in situations which present the same questions of law or fact. It was in the US that "class actions" gained an important role and became ingrained in the system as one of its most typical institutions.

A comparative outlook to the procedures envisaged in other jurisdictions may, therefore, be usefully conducted moving from the US style "class action" to discover and understand their convergences and their divergences from it.

2. Any national system of law depends on the culture of its country of origin.

The close link between civil procedural law and the cultural milieu in which it developed is a well-known phenomenon.[5]

Also in the area of collective redress procedures the approach of legislators, judges and lawyers is influenced not only by socio-political and economic factors in general but also by considerations based on their cultural aspect.

The transplant of US style class actions was very strongly opposed also for such cultural reasons.

In the words of an American observer of the civil law world[6]:

The culture of civil law countries considered the class action intellectually untidy. For Continental Europeans all legal institutions, whether substantive, procedural or in the interstices, begin from fundamental premises and structures and work their way patiently towards the details. Rule 23 [of the Federal Rules of Civil Procedure] seemed like a Rube Goldberg artifact – a strange looking melange of pushes and pulls and bells and bumbles. The Rule had some goals, some standards and some procedures, but little in the way of either internal coherence or integration with larger community of means in which it was placed.

This attitude has slowly changed. A vision not only of some unacceptable aspects of US class actions, but also of its positive impacts has been developed.

Consideration has been given to the fact that also in the US criticism of an excessive use of class action procedures and of its sometimes abusive effects has produced in 2005 a reform, the *Class Action Fairness Litigation Act* (CAFA), which transferred to Federal District Courts and subtracted from so called "magnet" state courts interstate class actions, i.e. practically all large class actions.

In analyzing the class action procedure in the US a distinction must be drawn between the aspects which are only a reflection, and a very enhanced one, of typical institutions and rules of American civil procedure and the fundamental character of the class action.

Pre-trial discovery, trial by jury, the way oral testimony is taken and cross examination, the large discretion of judges in case management, punitive damages, the financing of the action by law firms and contingent fees are all aspects which until not long ago simply horrified lawyers formed in civil law jurisdictions and today still leave them very skeptical of the possibility to transplant in to their systems a class action with such paraphernalia.

On the other hand there is a growing perception that the essence of class action US style does not lay in such different procedural and socio-economic characteristics.

In the words of two European observers[7]: "The kernel of the concept" of class action US style is in "an opt-out procedure whereby consumers can be represented by default if given adequate notice of the action."

In the landmark case *Hansberry v. Lee*, 311 US 32 (1940), the Supreme Court approved representative suits as "*due process*" as long as the procedures employed adequately protect absentee interests. In *Phillips Petroleum v. Shutts*, 472 US 797 (1985), the Supreme Court declared not only the constitutionality but also the necessity of the opt-out device.

What impresses lawyers formed outside the US is the way the principle that everyone has an individual right to assert a legal claim[8] and its corollary rule that

[5] De Vos W. "French civil procedure revisited", *Stellenbosch Law Review* 9, no. 2 (1998): 217. On the point Cadiet L. "Culture et droit processuel, Rapport aux Journées Louisianaises de l'Association Henri Capitant, Droit et Culture" Bruxelles 2010, 409

[6] R.B. Cappalli in Cappalli R.B. and Consolo C. "Class Action for Continental Europe? A Preliminary Inquiry", *Temple Int. Comp. Law Journal* 6, (1993): 217 at 219.

[7] Fairgrieve D. and Howells G. "Collective Redress Procedures – European Debates," *ICLQ* 58, (2009): 379.

[8] Art. 24, para. 1 of the 1948 Italian Constitution: "Everyone can act at law for the assertion of his own rights and legitimate interests".

"*nul ne plaide par procureur*"[9] is so candidly disposed of in the class action procedure.

On the other hand, outside the US little attention is given to the fact that in the US *opt-out* system, a class member must usually return to the court a *claim form* stating his or her claim within a defined period, that, in other words, even in an *opt-out* system, a class member must take an active step to benefit from the class judgment.[10]

The adoption of the *opt-out* rule entails some consequences also in the procedural rules which govern a class action.

Judges must certify with great accuracy the requisites of numerosity, commonality and adequacy of representation. The way notification is disposed and effected becomes essential. Case management is the rule. The waiver and the settlement of the action need to be scrutinized and approved by the court. Judges have the power to award a flexible range of remedies, including but not restricted to the awards of damages to identified individuals.

3. The 26 national reports that were sent on this subject give an interesting overall picture of the above situation.[11]

Some countries have introduced or are currently proposing to introduce legislation on collective redress based on the US experience, but even so they either have not introduced the *opt-out* rule or, when they have done it, they have harmonized it with their procedural principles. In no such countries were other aspects of US-style class actions adopted (except when they were already present in their systems: e.g. in common law jurisdictions the rule about no shifting of costs on the losing party).

Other countries have introduced a collective redress action in the form of group action by a representative body or organization.

Finally a third group of countries have only adjusted their existing procedures to the need for collective redress.

All the national reports illustrate their respective situations and even those which are limited to an answer to the questionnaire I sent for guidance are rich with information and thoughtful remarks.

In this general report, therefore, I will confine myself to a survey of the solutions they have presented.

4. Among the countries who have introduced a class action similar to the US one, the rules of countries like Canada and Australia are the nearest to the US ones.

The Australian Federal Act on the matter, in fact, initially structured the procedure as an *opt-out* procedure. However, a Federal Court decision[12] endorsed the validity of clauses of a funding agreement which requested the member of a class to sign the agreement in order to participate in the class action.

This decision admitted the equivalent of an opt-in situation, making possible what the Australian reporter Professor Camille Cameron defines as "closed classes."

It is noticeable that this solution derives from the practice of obtaining financial support for the class action not from law firms (which in Australia are prohibited to stipulate contingent fees), but from other subjects, so called commercial funders.

In Canada the rule in the legislation of most provinces is *opt-out* class action. In some of them, however, there are special provisions requiring non-residents to opt-in and also public authorities, ombudsmen and other organizations may start a class proceeding (although in practice it never happens).

Also Israel, where – as it was remembered above – a Class Action Law was enacted on 2006, has an *opt-out* system.

[9]See prof. Mélina Douchy-Oudot, *Où on est-on avec l'action de groupe*, paper annexed to her report for France.

[10]The point is made by A. Gidi in his report on the US. Antonio Gidi adds that *"the result of this practice is worse than an "opt-in" class action because the class member that does not return the form in effect is a class member bound by the class judgment, is precluded and cannot bring his or her own proceeding and also cannot recover because he or she missed the deadline"*.

[11]The following national reports were sent: Argentina (prof. Guillermo Treacy); Australia (prof. Camille Cameron); Austria (prof. Walter Rechberger); Belgium (prof. Piet Taelman and Stefan Voet); Brazil (prof. Antonio Gidi); Canada (prof. Janet Walker); Danemark (prof. Peter Møgelvang-Hansen); England (prof. Duncan Fairgrieve); Finland (prof. Antti Jokela); France (prof. Melina Douchy Oudot); Germany (prof. Astrid Stadler); Greece (prof. Dimitrios Tsikrikas); Hungary (prof. Petrovichné Wopera Zsuzsa ès Nagy Adrienn); Israel (prof. Michael Karayanni); Italy (prof. Andrea Zoppini); Mexico (prof. Eduardo Ferrer Mac-Gregor, Alberto Benitez and Antonio Gidi); Netherlands (prof. Marie-José van der Heijden); Poland (prof. Janusz Jankowski and prof. Slawomir Cieślak); Portugal (prof. Miguel Teixeira de Sousa); Scotland (prof. Sarah Bleichner); Spain (prof. Regina Garcimartin); Sweden (prof. Per-Henrik Lindblom); Switzerland (prof. Karen Jeanneret-Druckman); Taiwan (prof. Kuan-Ling Shen); USA (prof. Antonio Gidi); Venezuela (prof. Hildegard Rondòn de Sansò).

[12]*Multiplex Funds Management Ltd. V. P. Dawson Nominees Pty Ltd* [2007] FCAFC 200.

5. A number of European countries have recently enacted class action legislation.

Sweden in 2003, Norway in 2005,[13] Denmark in 2008.

Swedish law is based on a mandatory *opt-in* procedure. The Danish and Norwegian rules allow the possibility of using the system with automatic group affiliation coupled with the right to opt-out in certain cases.

In Italy, a new art. 140-bis listed as "Class Action" (*Azione di Classe*) was introduced in the Consumer Code in 2009. The class action had already been introduced by a law of 2007, but never entered into force. The new provision of 2009 not only established its entry into force on January 1, 2010, but also modified the original structure of the action.

While in the previous version the redress was sought by a collective action which could be brought by consumer associations, in the new and final text the action is brought by each single person seeking redress.

The structure is *opt-in* and the class action can be used for the enforcement of "homogenous, individual rights of consumers and users." An association may have standing if the injured party grants it powers.

The choice for the *opt-in* solution allows the application to the class action Italian style of the provisions of the civil procedure code (except for some specificity) with little room for case management. In fact, the persons who *opt-in* do not become technically parties to the proceedings, but only share its results. From a formal procedural point of view, the proceeding remains a bilateral one with only one party representing all the persons who opted in.

Another example of class action based on the US style, but with the *opt-in* solution may be found in Taiwan, where a Consumer Protection Act of 1994 and an Investor Civil Procedure Code of 2003 have regulated two kinds of class action: a class action by statutory assignment (which grants consumers' associations the action for injunctive relief in the protection of public or collective interests) and a class action in which a representative party or an association act by parties' assignment on behalf of persons who opted-in.

Portugal has introduced in 1995 a "civil popular action", by which an individual (as in the class action) or a representative body (as in the collective action) may bring actions related to consumer protection, environment, public health, cultural heritage, and public property.

It appears that the same mechanism may be employed in the protection both of "diffuse interest" and of homogeneous individual interests.

More articulated is the mechanism introduced in the Netherlands. The new Civil Code has provided for a collective action which may be started by associations representing the interested individuals, but only in order to obtain injunctive relief. A Settlement of Mass Damages Act (2005) has introduced a procedure for the collective settlement of mass claims.

According to this procedure, a foundation or association representing the injured persons may request the court to declare that a settlement reached with the infringing party is fair and equitable. The decision binds also the injured persons who were not represented. He who does not wish to be bound by the settlement agreement has to declare it within a term determined by the court. The mechanism works on an *opt-out* basis.

In Spain a law of 2007 has introduced a collective action for consumers' protection, which provides that consumers' associations may claim also for persons not belonging to the association. The same association may also bring action for the protection of diffuse interests.

More recently a new kind of action against gender discrimination was introduced, where again associations have standing.

A somewhat similar mechanism functions in Austria, where on the basis of existing legislation (para. 227(1) of ZPO, which allows the collection of several claims in one action under certain circumstances: *objektive Klagenhäufung*) a kind of collective litigation was developed: several claims of harmed individuals are assigned to an association.

This solution has been defined as "the Austrian model of the class action," but projects for an organic legislative intervention on the matter are pending.

6. An interesting solution has been adopted by the country which was one of the first to introduce a collective redress action: Brazil.

Art. 81 of the Brazilian Consumer Code 1990 provides that:

The protection of consumers' interests or rights may be granted by the Court individually or collectively and the collective protection shall be allowed in case

[13] We have received no report for Norway, but reference to its system is made in the reports for the other Scandinavian countries.

of: I – diffuse interests or rights, meaning transindividual, indivisible interests or rights held by indeterminate persons linked by factual circumstances; II – collective interests or rights, meaning the transindividual, indivisible interests or rights held by a group, category or class of persons linked to each other or to the opposing party by a common legal relationship; or III – homogenous individual interests or rights, meaning those stemming from a common origin.

The wide-ranging object of this action is explained by the circumstance that, according to art. 82 of the same Act, the entities who have collective standing for bringing it are:

I – the office of the Attorney General; II – the Federal, State or Municipal Government and the Federal District; III – entities and agencies of the direct and indirect public administration, including those without legal personality, specifically designed for the protection of the interests and rights protected by the Consumer Code; IV – associations legally incorporated for at least one year, whose institutional purpose include the protection of the interests and rights protected by the Consumer Code.[14]

The circumstance that the Attorney General (*Ministerio Publico*) has standing gives the action a public tinge. The *Ministerio Publico* in Brazil is a completely independent body, which performs its task with vigor.

Another country which has chosen to confer to a public body the action for protection of collective interests of consumers and users is Finland, where an Act, which came into force in 2007, establishes that the Consumer Ombudsman is the primary actor to bring the action as representative of the class. Individuals have a right to act only if the Consumer Ombudsman has decided not to do so.

7. Other countries are experiencing different solutions and are approaching the idea that a more thorough and complete intervention will eventually be needed.

In England the Civil Procedure Rules enacted in 1999 introduced the Group Litigation Order (GLO), a flexible procedure allowing for a register to be established where a number of claims give rise to common or related issues of fact or law.

Exercising powers under a sort of case management, the judge may order that persons which a claimant claims to represent be notified and allowed to *opt-in*. The controversy may then be resolved in a single proceeding. It has to be noticed that persons who opt-in become parties to the proceedings, so that the GLO may be considered as a sort of organized multiparty proceeding.

Germany, too, where legal circles appear to be fiercely opposed to the introduction of class actions or collective redress mechanisms, has enacted in 2005 a test case procedure in the field of securities: the Capital Market Model Case Act (*Kapitalanlage – Musterverfahrensgesetz – KapMuG*).

Where several claims are brought for damages due to false, misleading or omitted public capital market information, upon application of one of the parties and the opting–in of nine other plaintiffs, a model or test case proceeding can be established in order to decide on issues of fact or law which are common to all cases pending and being related to the same dispute.

The court having jurisdiction for the model case proceeding (Higher Regional Court), then has to select the case of one plaintiff as the model case. All other cases pending will be suspended *ex officio* and the decision on the model case will be binding also for them.

In France discussions about group actions are very fervid and many proposals have been put forward also in an official way. Two kind of actions, however, are in existence:

- *l'action d'intérêt collectif,* or *action en cessation d'agissement illicite* which allows consumer associations registered in an official list to bring claims against the infringement of a collective consumer interest or a collective interest of investors. This kind of action is in application of the EC directive on consumer protection;
- *l'action en représentation conjointe*, which is based on a proxy to claim for damages granted to an *association agrée et reconnue représentative sur le plan national.*

Both actions are not much used in practice. The second one, in particular, meets a limit in that "le mandat ne peut être sollicité par voie d'appel public télévisé ou radiophonique, ni par voie d'affichage, de tract ou de lettre personnalisée."[15]

[14]The above English translation of the Consumer Code provisions is taken from the Appendix to Antonio Gidi, "Class Actions in Brazil. A model for civil law countries", *Am. J. of Comparative Law* 51, (2003): 406. Prof. Antonio Gidi's report for Brazil to this Congress makes reference to this article.

[15]This prohibition was applied by a court decision against a group of lawyers who had created a site *classaction.fr*, which offered assistance to other lawyers in the organization of *actions en représentation conjointe*.

8. The reports from Mexico, Venezuela and Argentina indicate that in those countries collective redress proceedings are based on an action of constitutional character (*amparo*) which is envisaged as an action to be employed by public bodies or local communities to protect diffuse and collective interests.

9. The reports of other countries (Belgium, Greece, Hungary, Poland, Scotland, Switzerland) show that the issue of collective redress has aroused interest, debates and proposals for the introduction of new forms of action. But in no such countries were the proposals yet definitively approved.

10. The different solutions presented by the reports for each country offer an impetus also for consideration of one of the fundamental issues which the globalization of economic and social life poses in our time.

It is a common experience that consumers' and investors' contracts very often have a transnational character, that mass damages may be caused by firms who are located and/or operate in countries different from the countries where the consumers or investors live.

Countries like the US which have developed class actions as an effective remedy for the protection of the public have been made aware of this problem especially in the area of international securities litigation. The Court of Appeals for the Second Circuit in *Morrison v. National Australia Bank Ltd.*, 2008 WL 4660742, had elaborated a double test to affirm its jurisdiction: when the fraudulent conduct of a foreign financial institution has specific and relevant consequences within the US (effect test) or, alternatively, when such conduct is performed within the US (conduct test).[16] Its approach has been restricted by the U.S. Supreme Court decision of June 24, 2010 on the same case: on the basis of a general presumption against extraterritoriality of US jurisdiction, it has been excluded that US courts have jurisdiction in foreign cubed litigation, i.e. in collective actions where none of the elements (nationality of claimants, seat of the financial institutions, place of negotiations of the securities) is connected with the US.[17]

This situation makes more and more necessary an integration or, at least, a coordination of different substantive rights and procedural actions of consumers and investors at a transnational level.

How can such integration and/or coordination be reached?

Enormous political and economic problems have, of course, to be solved.

But in order to prepare the ground for their solution, something may be done or, I would say, must be done from a purely legal point of view.

Comparative law scholars are called to the task to analyze the questions which collective redress mechanisms pose in each jurisdiction and to see what kind of solution may be offered.

Studies and essays in this field are already very numerous. I like to mention here one study which represents a generous attempt to give an answer to the difficulty that civil lawyers meet when dealing with "class actions": Antonio Gidi has published in 2005 a class action code, as a model for civil law countries.[18]

11. The reports which came from European countries also confirm one common thread which has been already noticed,[19] namely the desire to find a model of collective redress procedures which is distinct from that of the US class action and which draws upon more specifically European concepts.

The preference for the *opt-in* regime, the role of consumer associations and of public entities (Ombudsman, etc.), the check on the admissibility of the collective claim, the more limited scope of collective redress procedures may be seen as aspects of the different model emerging in European countries, together with the rejection of American procedural devices such as discovery, punitive damages, jury system, and contingency fees.

This process of creating a more harmonized development of collective redress procedures in Europe could be sustained by the EU's policy as it has been indicated in the *Green Paper on Consumer Collective Redress. Com (2008) 794 final.*

[16] See Choi S.J. and Silberman L.J., "The Continuing Evolution of Securities Class Actions Symposium: Transnational Litigation and Global Securities Class Action Lawsuits", *Wis L. Rev.*(2009): 465; Buxbaum H.L. "Multinational Class Actions Under Federal Securities Law: Managing Jurisdictional Conflict", *Col. J. Transnational L* 46 (2007): 14.

[17] For a first commentary of this decision G.T. Conwey III, *U.S. Supreme Court Rejects "Foreign Cubed" Class Actions"* in *blogs.law.harvard.edu.*

[18] Gidi A. "The Class Action Code: A Model for Civil Law Countries", *Arizona Journal of Int. and Comp. Law* 23, (2005): 37.

[19] Fairgrieve D. and Howells G. quoted *supra* at note 7.

Cost and Fee Allocation in Civil Procedure[1]

10

Mathias Reimann

10.1 Introduction: The Topic and Its Limits

This General Report provides a comparative study of the principles and rules governing costs and fees in civil litigation. At the outset, it is appropriate to recognize the contribution of the National Reporters.[2] They supplied most of the information without which this General Report could obviously not have been compiled.

[1] II.C.2, Les règles de repartition des frais.

[2] Camille Cameron (Australia), Marianne Roth (Austria), Ilse Samoy and Vincent Sagaert (Belgium), Silvia Julio Bueno de Miranda and Alexandre Alcino de Barros (Brasil), Patrick Glenn (Canada), Tang Xin and Xiao Jianguo (PR China), Jan Hurdik (Czech Republic), Richard Moorhead (England and Wales), Jarkko Männistö (Finland), Sophie Gjidara-Decaix (France), Burkhard Hess and Rudolf Hübner (Germany), Kalliopi Makridou (Greece), Thorgerdur Erlendsdottir and Sigridur Ingvarsdottir (Iceland), Neela Badami (India), Talia Fisher and Issi Rosen-Zvi (Israel), Alessandra De Luca (Italy), Manabu Wagatsuma (Japan), Gyooho Lee (Korea), Candida Silva Autunes Pires (Macau SAR, PRC), Carlos Sanchez-Mejorada (Mexico), Marco Loos (Netherlands), Anna Nylund (Norway), Andrzej Jakubecki (Poland), Alena Zaytseva (Russian Federation), Greg Gordon (Scotland), Marko Knezevic (Serbia), Nina Betetto (Slovenia), HJ Erasmus (South Africa), José Angel Torres Lana and Francisco Lopez Simo (Spain), Martin Sunnqvist (Sweden), Caspar Zellweger (Switzerland), Fu-mei Sung and Taisan Chiu (Taiwan), Ayse Saadet Arikan (Turkey), James Maxeiner (United States), and José Tadeo Martinez (Venezuela).

M. Reimann (✉)
University of Michigan Law School, Ann Arbor, MI, USA
e-mail: purzel@umich.edu

10.1.1 The Significance of Cost and Fee Rules

The law of costs and fees is a major factor in the decision whether a dispute will result in litigation. In fact, in civil and commercial matters where money is usually the primary object, the financial burden of litigation may well be the single most important consideration in deciding whether to fight in court. Even if a matter is deemed important enough, and even if the chances of success are considered high, a party may not be able or willing to bear the cost of litigation.

In addition, the financial burdens of suing influence litigation strategy. In deciding exactly how to proceed, how much to invest, what risks to take, whether to appeal or not, etc., parties must take into account who will ultimately pay for it all. Thus, an understanding of the rules governing costs and fees is essential for an understanding of the dynamics of civil litigation.

Last, but certainly not least, financial costs and risks of litigation determine who has, and who is being denied, access to justice. Parties who cannot afford to sue (or to defend in court) are effectively excluded from the litigation system. They may well have valid substantive rights or viable defenses but cost barriers can render these rights and defenses practically useless. As we will see, this problem plagues many jurisdictions, albeit to varying degrees.[3]

[3] Infra 10.3.4.

K.B. Brown and D.V. Snyder (eds.), *General Reports of the XVIIIth Congress of the International Academy of Comparative Law/Rapports Généraux du XVIIIème Congrès de l'Académie Internationale de Droit Comparé*,
DOI 10.1007/978-94-007-2354-2_10, © Springer Science+Business Media B.V. 2012

10.1.2 The Importance of Comparative Perspectives

Practically speaking, understanding the rules governing litigation costs is most important at home. Yet, when transboundary litigation is growing fast, and when changes have been in the air in many systems, it is becoming increasingly important also to look beyond one's own jurisdiction. This is true for practitioners and lawmakers as well as for academics.

For legal counsel in transboundary cases, comparing rules on litigation costs is (or at least should be) an important element in choosing a forum (and sometimes the applicable law).[4] This is especially true when drafting a forum selection clause but it also matters more generally when deciding where to file (or whether actually to defend against) a lawsuit.[5] For legislators and policy makers, understanding how other systems deal with litigation costs is valuable when evaluating their own jurisdiction's regime. This is particularly salient if major reforms are being undertaken, as most recently in Belgium (2007) and Portugal (2008), or considered, as is currently the case in the United Kingdom.[6] Finally, for legal scholars, especially those studying international civil litigation, the similarities and differences between the respective rules promise valuable insights. Comparison can indicate common problems (e.g., regarding certain claims), suggest a spectrum of solutions (e.g., ways to improve access to justice), and reveal worldwide trends (e.g., towards deregulation of lawyers' fees). It can even speak to the sense or non-sense of grouping legal systems into families or traditions (e.g. by looking at the degree of correlation between basic cost rules and membership in a particular legal family).

The purpose of this General Report is primarily to gather and organize data and to make sense of them by showing major commonalities and differences across jurisdictions. It is not to advocate concrete solutions to specific problems. While comparison includes pointing out pervasive questions and possible responses, how actually to resolve concrete issues usually involves political choices that comparatists are, contrary to what many of them believe, rarely competent to make.

10.1.3 From Obscurity to Prominence

For many years, there were precious few studies of cost and fee rules from a comparative (and foreign law) perspective[7] – a situation which actually provided the motivation for suggesting the topic to the International Academy of Comparative Law in 2007 for its 2010 Congress. In the meantime, that has changed. Today, there is a growing literature in this field.

Much of the initiative has come from European institutions. Most importantly, as part of the EU Civil Justice Project, a major comparative study of cost and fee rules has recently been undertaken at the University of Oxford.[8] In addition, the Council of Europe and the

[4] See Stefan Vogenauer, Perceptions of Civil Justice Systems in Europe and Their Implications for Choice of Forum and Choice of Contract Law: an Empirical Analysis, in Stefan Vogenauer and Christopher Hodges, eds., *Civil Justice Systems in Europe: Implications for Choice of Forum and Choice of Contract Law* (Oxford: Hart, 2011, forthcoming).

[5] Assuming a choice, it would be an egregious mistake, for example, to file a clear winner in a jurisdiction where each party bears its own costs as opposed to a jurisdiction where the loser has to make the winner whole. In a similar vein, it would be a bad move to file a weak case (perhaps with a view of extracting a settlement) in a jurisdiction where the losing party pays all the costs rather than in system without cost shifting.

[6] See infra note 10.

[7] A major exception was Charles Platto, Economic Consequences of Litigation Worldwide (London: International Bar Association, The Hague, Boston 1999). The book provides valuable data about 20 systems (or regions) some of which were included in writing this General Report. The main problem with the book is that much of the information it provides has already become dated.

[8] Christopher Hodges, Stefan Vogenauer and Magdalena Tulibacka, *Costs and Funding of Civil Litigation: A Comparative Perspective* (Oxford and Portland/Oregon: Hart, 2010) (hereafter cited as Oxford: Costs and Funding). While the book contains only 23 National Reports, the original Study at conducted at the University of Oxford included 34 countries, see Christopher Hodges, Stefan Vogenauer and Magdalena Tulibacka, *Costs and Funding of Civil Litigation: A Comparative Study*, University of Oxford Legal Research Paper Series Paper No. 55/2009 (December 2009), Available at http://ssrn.com/abstract=1511714 (hereafter cited as Oxford: Comparative Study). These countries overlap considerably with the jurisdictions covered in this General Report but each project also considers many jurisdictions not addressed by the other. The Oxford Study encompassed 11 systems not considered here: Bulgaria, Denmark, Estonia, Hong Kong, Hungary, Ireland, Latvia, Lithuania, Portugal, Romania, and Singapore; conversely, this General Report includes 12 systems not addressed by the Oxford Study: Brazil, Iceland, India, Israel, Korea, Macao, Mexico, Serbia, Slovenia, South Africa, Turkey, and Venezuela. Together the two projects thus draw on a total of 46 jurisdictions. The Oxford Study and this General Report also overlap with

European Commission both solicited extensive studies related to this area in recent years.[9] Another, separate, impetus came from the current English reform debate which has resulted in a comprehensive review of the English system.[10] Finally, there are also a few recent publications in English addressing various key jurisdictions, such as England,[11] France,[12] Germany,[13] and Japan[14] as well as occasional comparative studies on a fairly limited scale.[15]

10.1.4 The Database – The Developed Part of the World

This General Report is primarily based on National Reports from 35 jurisdictions.[16] It also draws – to a more limited extent – on the existing studies on costs and fees in civil litigation just mentioned.[17] Additional research provided occasional information on specific points.

The almost three dozen jurisdictions covered by the National Reports represent a substantial portion of the world's legal systems: they hail from all continents; represent civil law, common law, and Asian legal systems as well as various mixed regimes; and they include all major law exporting countries. They are also quite diverse: some are huge (like Russia), others tiny (like Macau); some are highly centralized (like France), others have a federal structure (like Canada); some are liberal and capitalist (like the United States), others authoritarian and socialist (like China). Together, they comprise over 60% of the world population and ca. 90% of the global GDP.

Still, the systems included here do *not* represent the whole world. Serious gaps remain, largely as a result of institutional problems and resource limitations.[18]

regard to the questions they pursue but again, there is enough difference in coverage and thrust for one to complement the other. Overall, the focus of this General Report is somewhat narrower because it deals principally with the *allocation* of costs while the Oxford Study is concerned with *Costs and Funding of Civil Litigation* more broadly.

[9]See especially European Commission for the Efficiency of Justice (CEPEJ), European Judicial Systems: Edition 2006 (2004 data) and European Judicial Systems: Edition 2008 (data 2006) – Efficiency and Quality of Justice (2008); and Jean Albert, Study on the Transparency of Costs of Civil Proceedings in the European Union: Final Report (2007).

[10]Rupert Jackson, Review of Civil Litigation Costs, Final Report (Norwich 2010) (hereafter cited as Jackson Review).

[11]Peter Gottwald, ed., Litigation in England and Germany (Bielefeld: Gieseking-Verlag, 2010).

[12]Dominique Menard, "The Costs Battle: Cost Awards in France after the Enforcement Directive," *Patent World*, 173 (2005), 13–15.

[13]Gottwald, supra note. 11; Gerhard Wagner, "Litigation Costs and Their Recovery: The German Experience," *Civil Justice Quarterly* 28 (2009): 367–66.

[14]Matthew Wilson, "Failed Attempt to Undermine the Third Wave: Attorney Fee Shifting Movement in Japan," *Emory International Law Review* 19 (2005): 1457–88.

[15]See David Root, "Attorney Fee-shifting in America: Comparing, Contrasting, and Combining the "American Rule" and "English Rule"," *Indiana International and Comparative Law Review* 15 (2005): 583–617; see also Andrew Cannon, "Designing Cost Policies to Provide Sufficient Access to Lower Courts. Australia/Germany/Netherlands/Northern Ireland/ England," *Civil Justice Quarterly* 21 (2002): 198–253; Francesco Parisi, "Rent-Seeking through Litigation: Adversarial and Inquisitorial Systems Compared," *International Review of Law and Economics* 22 (2002): 193–216.

[16]Australia, Austria, Belgium, Brazil, Canada, PR China, Czech Republic, England and Wales, Finland, France, Germany, Greece, Iceland, India, Israel, Italy, Japan, Korea, Macau (SAR PRC), Mexico, The Netherlands, Norway, Poland, Russian Federation, Scotland, Serbia, Slovenia, South Africa, Spain, Sweden, Switzerland, Taiwan, Turkey, United States of America, and Venezuela. These Reports are on file with the General Reporter; they are accessible, together with the Questionnaire, under http://www-personal.umich.edu/~purzel/national_reports/. With a few exceptions, this General Report does not provide pinpoint citations to the National Reports; the relevant information can be found in the respective sections which correspond to the Questionnaire.

[17]Information on four additional jurisdictions, for which I had no National Reports, was drawn from Platto, supra note 7, i.e., on Hong Kong, Denmark, New Zealand and Singapore. Since Portugal enacted major reforms in 2008, I also occasionally drew on the Portuguese Reports obtained by the Oxford group, supra note 8, from Barrocas Sarmento Neves, Sociedade de Advogados (Lisboa), available at http://www.csls.ox.ac.uk/documents/ PORTUGAL.doc [cited as Oxford Portuguese Report/Barrocas] and from Henrique Sousa Antunes [cited as Oxford Portuguese Report/Antunes], available at http://www.csls.ox.ac.uk/documents/PORTUGALAC.doc. These additional five jurisdictions bring the number of systems considered to a total of 40.

[18]The recruitment of national reporters by the International Academy of Comparative Law can only charitably be described as haphazard: it is by and large left to the national comparative law groups or organizations whether a reporter is named or not. The process is virtually blind to the importance or representative character of the jurisdictions covered. For the present topic, the International Academy provided names of reporters for 22 countries of which 18 finally submitted a report. Many countries which are highly important by any measure were missing, among them giants like Australia, Brazil, Canada, China, India, Mexico, and Russia (which, incidentally, together comprise almost half of the world's population); this is not to mention smaller, but still important players, like Israel, South Africa, and Switzerland. In order to close these gaps, and to achieve better

Islamic systems are missing, Africa is severely underrepresented, and seriously poor countries are virtually absent.[19] In other words, the picture is by and large limited to the developed part of the globe.[20] To be sure, this is where most civil litigation takes place; it is also likely that most other systems in the world follow any of the major models included here, be it as a result of colonial imposition or post-independence borrowing. Still, it is important to keep in mind that the picture emerging from this General Report shows mainly the situation in the rich and industrialized countries, and that it tells us very little, if anything, about the developing world.

10.1.5 Overview

Beyond this Introduction, this General Report consists of three main parts followed by a Conclusion. Part 10.2 deals with the issue of who pays; it outlines the basic approaches to cost shifting, considers the most important modifications and exceptions, and looks at the underlying policies. Part 10.3 turns to the question of how much; it looks at the three major items – court costs, lawyer fees, and evidence expenses, and conveys a sense of the overall financial burden of civil litigation. Part 10.4 then considers whose money actually pays for litigation costs; in particular, it surveys a variety of special mechanisms that distribute the financial risks of litigation, such as legal aid, litigation insurance, collective actions, success-oriented fees, and third party investment in lawsuits. The Conclusion (10.5) suggests various groupings of legal systems with regard to cost and fee allocation in civil procedure.

representation worldwide, the General Reporter recruited authors for an additional 17 countries, for a total 35. Even these efforts could not cure the lack of representation of the developing world. The problem is in part due to the developing countries' absence from, or weak role in, the International Academy of Comparative Law. In part it is also due to the fact that qualified reporters for the poorer parts of the world are extremely hard to recruit; contacts with the respective countries are scarce and academic institutions there are often poorly connected with the outside world and generally lacking resources.

[19] In terms of per capita GDP, no country covered belongs to the poorer half of the world.

[20] Other available studies do not remedy this problem because they suffer from exactly the same limitations.

10.2 Who Pays? The Basic Rules and Their Reasons

In looking at cost and fee allocation in civil procedure, the first question must be which of the parties has to bear which kinds of litigation expenses.[21] This depends primarily on the basic rules about cost shifting (infra. 1.). Yet, one must also consider the many exceptions and modifications to which these basic rules are often subject (2.). Beyond that, we will look at the avowed policies that underlie the various cost distribution regimes (3.).

10.2.1 The Basic Rule: To Shift or Not to Shift?

Comparative lawyers often think about cost and fee allocation in quasi Shakespearean terms: "to shift or not to shift?." They then tend to divide the world into the systems that shift the winner's litigation costs to the loser –"the English rule" – and the systems that make each side bear its own costs –"the American rule."[22] This dichotomy indeed suggests itself if we look exclusively at the basic principles legal systems *proclaim*: the vast majority of countries claim to adhere to the "loser pays" principle while the United States does not.

Perhaps the most fundamental finding of this General Report is that such a dichotomy is hopelessly simplistic as well as virtually useless. It is hopelessly simplistic because the reality is much more complex: no system makes the winner completely whole (although some come very close), and even in the United States, some costs are shifted to the loser (although usually only a very small part); most jurisdictions operate somewhere in between. The usual dichotomy is virtually useless because what basic principle a legal system proclaims says little about which costs (and which amounts) are actually shifted to the loser: some jurisdictions announcing the "loser pays"

[21] A separate question not pursued in this General Report is how much of the actual expenses are borne by the parties and how much is paid by the state (i.e., the taxpayer), but see infra. 10.3.1.3.

[22] See, e.g., Markus Jäger, Reimbursement for Attorney's Fees (Eleven international publishing, The Hague 2010).

rule arguably charge the loser for no more than in the United States.[23]

The world of cost and fee allocation in civil procedure is much better described as a broad spectrum. On one end are the systems that shift nearly all of the winner's litigation expenses to the loser; in the middle, we find many jurisdictions shifting substantial parts, but not nearly the whole; and at the other end, only a fraction of the winner's costs are recoverable. The exact line-up of the systems on this spectrum is debatable because it depends on the criteria employed. The following division is based on three primary considerations: First, what is the *basic principle* to which a jurisdiction subscribes – to shift or not to shift? Second, *what kinds of expenses* does a system impose on the losing party – all three major categories, i.e., court costs, attorney fees, and the expenses incurred by taking evidence, or only some of them (e.g., no attorney fees)? Third, does a system impose these amounts *in whole or in part* (especially full attorney fees or only a limited amount)?[24] For simplicity's sake, we will divide the systems covered here in three categories – major shifting, partial shifting, and minor shifting – and then proffer more fine-tuned distinctions within these groups where appropriate.

10.2.1.1 Major Shifting

I define systems as "major shifting" if the basic thrust of their rules is to make the winner, at least by and large, whole. In particular, these systems (1) claim to adhere to the "loser pays" principle, (2) shift in all three categories mentioned above (court costs, lawyer fees, and evidence expenses), and (3) impose either the full amounts or at least a sum considered close to it on the loser.[25] In other words, these systems not only proclaim the principle that the loser pays, they are also serious about it. The majority of the jurisdictions included in this General Report fall into this category.

Contrary to widely shared assumptions, the poster child for the major shifters is not England – in fact, it is not even in this category (but rather in the next). Instead, the group consists overwhelmingly of members of the civil law tradition. Its hard core is a handful of "Germanic" jurisdictions in continental Europe: Austria, the Czech Republic, Germany, the Netherlands,[26] and Switzerland. But the club is actually much larger. It also comprises most other continental European systems, both in the East (Poland, Russia, Serbia, Slovenia) and the North (Denmark,[27] Finland, Norway, Sweden) as well as – heavily influenced by the Swiss and German tradition – Turkey. The group of major shifters also contains members clearly way beyond even a broadly defined "Germanic" family, both in Europe (Italy, Spain, after its recent reforms also Belgium and perhaps even Greece[28]) – and beyond (Brazil, Hong Kong,[29] Macau, Venezuela, and Mexico in civil cases[30]). Even the European Union has sometimes embraced a full cost-shifting rule.[31]

Yet, even the systems in this group do not necessarily guarantee the winner *full* compensation for *all* litigation expenses.[32] While they fully shift court costs and (as a rule) the expenses of judicially ordered evidence to the loser, they impose various limits on the recovery of the victorious party's attorney fees. In order to protect the loser from excessive claims, the winner can only charge what was necessary to conduct the litigation. In defining that, jurisdictions vary considerably in two regards: the mode of limitations they employ and the generosity they show to the winner.

[23]"Arguably" because while they may also charge the loser only for court costs, these costs may be substantially higher than in the United States and constitute a larger percentage of the overall litigation expenses; see infra 10.3.1.2.

[24]It is a separate question, of course, whether these categories and impositions amount to a lot or relatively modest amounts of money, i.e., whether shifting costs the loser little or dearly. That depends on how high court costs, attorney fees, expenses of evidence taking, etc. are; see infra. 10.3.

[25]Where the winning party (normally the plaintiff) has advanced these costs (such as filing fees), they must be reimbursed by the loser.

[26]The characterization of the Netherlands as a member of the "Germanic" family of European legal systems is debatable, of course.

[27]Platto, supra note 7, 144.

[28]The membership of Greece in this group is doubtful, see infra. note 38 and text.

[29]Platto, supra note 7, 82–83.

[30]In Mexico, as a general matter, attorney fees are shifted to the loser in civil disputes, but not in commercial cases.

[31]Regulation (EC) No. 861/2007 of the European Parliament and of the Council of 11 July 2007 establishing a European Small Claims Procedure [2007] OJ L 199/1, Recital 29; the costs recoverable by the winner must, however, be "proportionate to the value of the claim" and "necessarily incurred", id.

[32]The results of the Oxford group research support this; see Oxford: Costs and Funding, supra note 8, [72], [20]; Oxford: Comparative Study, supra note 8, II.8, III.65 (regarding lawyers fees), III.81 (recoverability gaps in various systems).

There are three major modes of limiting the loser's liability for the winner's attorney fees. The most common continental European approach is to employ an official (often statutory) tariff for lawyers[33] (as in Austria, Belgium, the Czech Republic, Finland, Germany, Italy, Netherlands, Poland, Serbia, Turkey, Spain and Switzerland). This tariff determines the amount the winner can recover from the loser, even if the winner and his counsel have agreed to a higher or lower rate.[34] The tariff approach is somewhat rigid but provides maximum predictability of the cost the parties are facing in case of defeat.[35] Another approach prevails in a group of Latin countries (Spain, Brazil, Mexico, and Venezuela): recoverable attorney fees are capped by varying percentages of the amount of the claim. This also makes the cost risk fairly foreseeable. Finally, some Nordic systems (Iceland, Norway, Sweden) as well as Russia use a more flexible means of control: the loser has to reimburse the victorious party's attorney fees (which are determined by the market) as long as they are necessary and reasonable. In case of dispute, the court decides what that means in the concrete case, often taking a variety of circumstances into account. This reflects a preference for ex post, judicial, case-by-case determination over an ex ante, legislative, one-size-fits-all solution (and is, in this regard, more in tune with the common law than the civil law tradition).

Certainly, even among the systems providing for major cost shifting, some are more generous to the winner than others. While the statutory tariffs in many countries fully cover the winner's attorney fees in routine cases, in others jurisdictions, they are much lower so that the winner usually chips in. Similarly, in some Latin countries, the percentage cap is set high enough not to create serious problems in most disputes (33% in Spain, 30% in Venezuela[36]) while in others, it is so low that it can render a substantial part of the winner's attorney fees non-recoverable (Brazil 10–20%).[37] Towards the bottom end of the generosity scale, cost shifting is decreasing to a point that is arguably no longer "major." In Greece, for example, while all cost items are shifted, the official tariff for (reimbursable) attorney fees is so low that "they do not cover, even in the slightest, the fee which the litigant in fact paid to his lawyer"[38]; the same must probably be said for Portugal.[39] In terms of practical outcome, these (and arguably other) jurisdictions thus could, and perhaps should, be classified as just partially shifting.

10.2.1.2 Partial Shifting

I define systems as "partially shifting" if their rules purport to compensate the winner for some of the litigation costs but have no ambition to make the victorious party routinely whole. These systems (1) still proclaim the basic principle that "the loser pays," but (2) either leave the amount of recovery to judicial discretion which normally results in merely partial shifting, or (3) shift only court costs and the expenses of evidence taking but not attorney fees. One can perhaps say that while these jurisdictions claim that the loser pays, they do not fully mean it. Almost all jurisdictions not already in the "major shifting" category fall into this group. They form two subgroups to which we must add two – very significant – hybrids.

The first subgroup consists mainly of the British commonwealth tradition (primarily Australia, Canada,

---

[33] It is usually tied to the amount in controversy and then employs a multiplier reflecting various procedural acts or stages. As pointed out by the National Reporter for Italy in her comments on the Draft General Report, tying attorney fees to the procedural stage (as in Germany) instead of to concrete procedural acts (as in Italy) leads to greater predictability because the number of procedural acts within each state may vary from case to case.

[34] The tariff is typically tied to the amount in controversy in a degressive fashion.

[35] In some countries (e.g., Belgium, Italy, Poland), the attorney fee schedule provides a (minimum-maximum) range within which the actual fee must be set, sometimes complemented by a standard fee (as in Belgium).

[36] This, however, requires a "flawless victory" (on all counts) which is not easy to achieve in practice, Venezuelan Report I.1.

[37] In some jurisdictions, the victorious party even has a claim for its own work and other losses related to the litigation (Finland) while such items are not included in most other systems.

[38] Greek Report I.1.

[39] Portugal also limits the recoverable attorney fees to a percentage but pegs it to the "justice fee" (the official court, evidence, etc. costs). Article 41 s. 1 of the 2008 Portuguese Legal Costs Act limits the shiftable attorney fees to between 10 and 25% of the "justice fee", leaving the precise determination to the discretion of the court, see Oxford Portuguese Report/Barrocas, Attachment I. Even if the "justice fee" is substantial, it is hard to imagine that such an amount would be anywhere close to the actual attorney fees in serious cases. This suggests that Portugal shifts only a small part of these fees to the loser and should thus not be considered a system with "major shifting".

England and Wales, New Zealand,[40] and even Scotland as a mixed jurisdiction). This tradition is marked by three characteristic features. First, the "loser pays" principle is not a categorical (and often not a statutory) rule but rather a general guideline, basic expectation, and usual practical outcome. Second, the implementation of this principle is largely left to the discretion of the court, taking all the circumstances of the litigation into account; while this will normally result in cost shifting, the court may decide otherwise.[41] Third, in most cases, the exercise of judicial discretion will result in only partial cost shifting[42]; depending on the jurisdiction and the case, the successful party will thus often bear a considerable share of its own costs.[43] Three further jurisdictions from the (former) British orbit may be included here although they fit the picture only imperfectly because they do not proclaim the loser pays principle in theory. This is true for Israel and South Africa where cost allocation is left entirely in the discretion of the court; in practice, however, winners are usually recovering at least part of their litigation expenses. In a similar vein, the courts in India have complete discretion over cost allocation; whether this generates less actual cost shifting than in the other jurisdictions in this subgroup is hard to tell. Be that as it may, the large role (if not complete predominance) of judicial discretion in the commonwealth tradition makes it difficult for the parties to gauge the financial risks of litigation here as well.

The second subgroup consists of most of the East Asian countries covered in this General Report. They also proclaim the loser-pays principle but most of them (China, Japan, and Taiwan) apply it only to court costs and, except for China, the expenses of taking (court-ordered) evidence, thus excluding attorney fees. Yet, there are some variations and exceptions. To begin with, there are two important modifications in Japan: first, the (court) cost shifting rule is not much used in practice; second, in tort cases for personal injury, part of the attorney fee[44] is shifted from the successful plaintiff to the losing defendant – but not the other way around. Moreover, there is somewhat of an exception to the general approach when it comes to the fourth East Asian jurisdiction covered here: Korea extends the loser-pays principle to attorney fees as well although it also renders these fees only partially recoverable.[45]

Of the two hybrids, France presents the more complex and curious case. Its cost allocation rules are based on a fundamental distinction between the legally inevitable costs of litigation on the one hand and further expenses on the other. The first category (*depens*) comprises the costs the parties (at the outset usually the plaintiff) must pay as a matter of law in order to proceed with the case; they constitute a finite catalog, are regulated by statute, and consist mainly of a variety of fees which must be paid to the lawyer for filing the case and to the court and its officials at various stages and for various purposes.[46] These costs are completely shifted to the losing party as a matter of law. By contrast, expenses not legally necessary – though perhaps practically inevitable – fall into another, open-ended category (*irrépetibles*). They include primarily the lion's share of attorney fees (*honoraires*) which are determined by the market, but also other, incidental (e.g., travel) expenses. Whether, and to what extent, these costs are shifted to the loser is subject to (almost unfettered) judicial discretion. It thus depends on the circumstances of the case, including

[40] Platto, supra note 7, 106.

[41] In England and Wales, Civil Procedure Rule 44.1 contains a long list of factors for courts to take into account.

[42] In England, this is typical for cost shifting on a "standard cost" basis. The courts can hold the losing party fully responsible for the winner's costs but will do so only for special reasons, as under the English principle of "indemnity cost"; see Neil Andrews, Costs and Conditional Fee Agreements in English Civil Litigation, in Gottwald, supra note 11, 185 at 197–198.

[43] The Australian Report estimated that normally, only about 50–60% of the costs will be shifted to the loser in most Australian jurisdictions. The Oxford group mentions "recoverability gaps" of 30–45% for Australia, 25% for Canada, England and Wales, and 33–50% for Scotland (and Singapore), Oxford: Costs and Funding, supra note 8, [20]; Oxford: Comparative Study, supra note 8, III.81. Yet, these figures must also be understood as very rough approximations. Note, however, that the National Reporter for the United Kingdom commented that de facto, in England and Wales, cost shifting is normally total.

[44] Usually 10% of the damages recovered, Japanese Report II.1.

[45] One could thus be tempted to group Korea with the British Commonwealth countries but that would overlook an important difference: contrary to the British tradition, Korea does not leave the amount of recoverable attorney fees to judicial discretion but rather determines it – very much in the civil law style – ex ante through an official tariff (setting an exact, and degressive, percentage).

[46] Such as service of process, taking of evidence, translation of documents, etc. The basic court fees, i.e., the fees for just filing the case itself, are extremely low in France.

the economic situation of the parties, and, of course, the attitude of the judge, and it usually results in partial shifting at best. In a sense then, the French system is a hybrid between the civil law elements of statutory regulation and automatic shifting with regard to the official costs, and a quasi-English practice of discretion-based and partial shifting with regard to lawyer fees and other expenses.

The second hybrid of sorts is Mexico, and it is much simpler. As a general rule, in Mexico attorney fees are shifted in civil cases but not in commercial disputes.[47] Rather than putting Mexico in this middle category, one could thus also say that it belongs partially to the first group of complete shifters and partially to the last of minor (in fact, even non-) shifters.

10.2.1.3 Minor Shifting

The only country squarely in the "minor shifting" group is the United States. It (1) by and large rejects the loser pays principle, and it (2) by and large means it, although (3) cost shifting is not unknown.

The United States is distinct in part simply because it embraces a different ideology than almost all other systems in this study: it does *not proclaim* a loser pays principle.[48] The United States legal system by and large actually enforces the principle that each side bears its own litigation expenses. To be sure, court costs are routinely shifted to the loser,[49] but in practical (i.e., financial) terms, that hardly matters: the use of the courts is very cheap while lawyer time is very expensive. As a result, court costs usually constitute such a trivial fraction of the overall litigation expenses that their shifting is often overlooked altogether. It is also true that some evidence costs can be shifted to the losing party but, again, these usually involve rather insignificant amounts. What really matters in the United States is the general rule that the winner cannot recover lawyer fees which can be, and often are, enormous.[50]

Yet, even with regard to lawyer fees, there are significant (and usually overlooked) exceptions. Most importantly, a large variety of federal and state statutory rules (allegedly over 2000 altogether[51]) do provide for attorney fee shifting. Often, this is meant to encourage private lawsuits in the public interest; thus it works only in a one-way fashion, i.e., merely in favor of certain plaintiffs acting as "private attorney generals" – most famously in antitrust and civil rights cases.[52] Furthermore, courts can and do shift attorney fees for a variety of special reasons, e.g., as a sanction for improper procedural action by one side (see infra. 10.2.2.3). Finally, Alaska deviates from the lower 48 states altogether and generally subscribes to the loser pays principle, even for attorney fees.[53]

Still, cost and fee shifting in the United States is either minor (regarding court costs and some evidence expenses) or limited to special instances (regarding attorney fees). In general, the belief that in principle, each side is responsible for its own litigation expenses is deeply rooted, at least among lawyers. This combination of open rejection of the loser pays principle and actual refusal to shift the lion's share of litigation expenses in the vast majority of cases sets the United States apart from the rest of the systems covered here.

10.2.2 Exceptions and Modifications

While the vast majority of the legal systems covered here (and probably in the world) thus proclaim the loser

[47] There are no court fees in Mexico because free access to justice is considered a constitutional right.

[48] The Oxford group concludes that this principle "is best explained by the critical role it plays in enabling the 'private enforcement' of law" in the interest of "wider public regulatory and observance goals", see Oxford: Costs and Funding, supra note 8, [79]; Oxford: Comparative Study, supra note 8, III.90. The US-American National Report solicited for this General Report does not support this explanation as a major factor, and it is doubtful indeed that this consideration is at the heart of the matter. In most areas in which "private attorney generals" play a significant role, such as antitrust, civil rights or environmental disputes, specific statutes *deviate* from the "American rule" and allow (one-way) cost shifting, see infra. 10.2.1.3.

[49] Still, the Oxford Study, supra note 8, perhaps overlooks court fee shifting when it states that the United States system "does not include cost shifting", at II.8.

[50] Of course, lawyer fees are in large part generated by the extensive discovery common in many cases in the United States, but evidence gathering also entails other expenses, e.g., for hiring expert witnesses, paying stenographers for depositions, or copying (and perhaps translating) massive amounts of documents.

[51] United States Report II.A., citing John F. Vargo, "The American Rule of Attorney Fee Allocation: The Injured Person's Access to Justice," *American University Law Review* 42 (1993): 1567–1629.

[52] I.e., victorious plaintiffs can recover their attorney fees from the defendants but not vice versa. Permitting "qualified one-way costs shifting" has recently also been proposed for England and Wales, see Jackson Review, supra note 10, xvii.

[53] Susanne diPietro and Teresa W. Carns, "Alaska's English Rule: Attorney Fee Shifting in Civil Cases," *Alaska Law Review* 13 (1986):33.

pays principle, they all provide for exceptions and modifications of one sort or another. The variety of the respective rules is bewildering, and considering them in all their detail is unrewarding. Still, there are some recurrent themes that are worth mentioning because they indicate certain underlying policies. Most exceptions and modifications can be grouped into four categories: modifications for special kinds of litigation, exceptions for particular parties, responses to split outcomes, and sanctions for causing unnecessary costs.

10.2.2.1 Special Types of Litigation

To begin with, several jurisdictions, such as Australia, England and Wales, Norway, Scotland, and Turkey, forego or limit cost shifting in small claims cases which are sometimes heard in special courts and according to a simplified procedure. In such cases (and tribunals), court costs tend to be low and legal representation is often not required (and in fact sometimes prohibited, as in South Africa) so that the necessary expenses are likely to be small. Not shifting them imposes no great burden on either side, lowers the financial risks of suing, and thus facilitates access to justice.

A considerable number of jurisdictions make various exceptions from the loser pays principle in family law disputes – either generally (as in England, Norway, and Serbia) or in particular cases, such as divorce proceedings (as in Belgium, China, the Czech Republic, Finland France, and Sweden), child custody (Austria, Finland [with some exceptions], Sweden) or maintenance (Austria, Finland [again, with some exceptions], Greece), or in non-contentious (quasi-administrative) proceedings (Germany and Finland). And indeed, family disputes are special in at least two ways: they are not necessarily (and often not primarily) about money, and the parties are usually related to each other. As a result, making the "loser" pay for the "winner's" litigation expenses (e.g., in a child-custody proceeding) can look like adding insult to injury.

Many systems also exempt cases with a strong social element from cost shifting. This is especially true for labor disputes (England, Italy, Macao, Scotland, Sweden, etc.) but occasionally also for social security cases (e.g., in Italy and Belgium), and consumer litigation (e.g., Turkey, and in certain class actions, Brazil). Some jurisdictions privilege plaintiffs in public interest litigation by protecting them from cost liability if they lose their case (e.g., in Australia [at least sometimes], Brazil, England and Wales, and – in constitutional cases – sometimes Canada).[54]

Japan provides one-way shifting in personal injury cases in favor of victims so that the victorious plaintiff can recover his or her attorney fees from the defendant but not the other way around. The Jackson Review recently recommended the same approach for England and Wales.[55]

10.2.2.2 Party-Based Exceptions

When it comes to cost and fee allocation in *civil* procedure (i.e., in private and commercial litigation), one should think that all animals are equal; yet, in a surprising number of jurisdictions, some animals are clearly more equal than others: while the system generally embraces the loser pays principle, certain parties are not liable for costs even if they lose. This is most understandable with regard to indigents or recipients of social security (as in Belgium, Brazil, Russia, Spain, and Turkey). It becomes a bit more questionable where the state protects itself from cost liability, either in whole (public attorneys in Spain) or in part (particularly limited cost recovery in Greece) or by granting cost immunity to parties affiliated with it (such as soldiers and diplomatic personnel in Turkey).

10.2.2.3 Sanctions for Causing Unnecessary Costs

The general cost shifting principles are frequently trumped by special sanctions for causing expenses without good reason.[56] Even a winner cannot recoup litigation expenses when suing was unnecessary. And each party may be liable to the other for costs caused by certain acts, especially if such acts were procedurally improper.

10.2.2.4 Split Outcomes

A merely partial victory usually has a direct impact on the winner's cost claim against the loser. The systems

[54] In a similar vein, victorious plaintiffs acting in the public interest can sometimes recover their litigation expenses while other plaintiffs cannot.

[55] Jackson Review, supra note 10, 184–193

[56] In civil law jurisdictions, these sanctions tend to be spelled out in statutory form (codes of civil procedure) while in common law systems, they are often a matter of judicial practice when exercising discretion with regard to cost shifting.

covered here differ, however, in exactly how they react to such a situation.

Of course, the simplest reaction to a split outcome is to consider nobody a winner (or both parties losers) and thus to shift no costs at all. Indeed, many systems' first line response to split outcomes is to let each side bear its own expenses. This is true not only in the common law orbit where cost shifting has traditionally been regarded not so much as a matter of right but rather of judicial discretion. It is also the case in many civil law jurisdictions where cost shifting involves considerable judicial discretion, as in France.

Most systems, however, take into account by how much each side won or lost.[57] Exactly how they do so is substantially related to whether recoverable fees and costs are tariff-based or not. The jurisdictions determining costs and fees under a (quasi-) official schedule tend to split the costs fairly precisely. In systems entrusting cost shifting (vel non) primarily to judicial discretion, there is much greater play in the joints, and courts usually eyeball the cost distribution from a broader equity perspective.

10.2.2.5 Settlements

Similar to split-outcome judgments, settlements usually mean that each side prevails in part and thus calls for some kind of cost splitting. As a general rule, settling parties are free to allocate costs as they please, which in practice usually results in each side bearing its own cost. This is also the most common default rule.[58] In the absence of party agreement, several systems also leave cost allocation to the courts (Australia, China, Finland, Iceland, Scotland, Switzerland, Turkey, England and Wales) dividing the burden according to a variety of criteria.

Note that in practice, settlements play a very significant role in most jurisdictions. In the common law orbit, settlement rates are so high that ending litigation by final judgment is clearly the exception[59]; as a result, cost allocation in common law (influenced) jurisdictions is – in reality – *normally* determined by the rules and practices governing settlements, not judgments. But also in the rest of the world, especially in continental Europe and on the Pacific Rim, settlement rates are often significant and can reach well over 50%[60]; thus even there, cost allocation in practice often by-passes the loser-pays principle and results in cost splitting. In other words, while the "American rule" is the *law* only in the United States, it is the prevailing *practice* in a great number of civil cases in the world today.

10.2.3 Policies: Fairness or Instrumentalism

The basic rules on cost and fee allocation, as well as the various exceptions and modifications, reflect certain underlying procedural policies. In the respective jurisdictions, these policies are rarely articulated with great clarity, not to mention sophistication, and one suspects that they are often not clearly understood either.[61] The National Reports thus often had to make informed guesses, stating as best they could what underlies their system's approach. Still, the underlying policies can roughly be divided into two categories: considerations of fundamental fairness to the

[57] See also Oxford: Costs and Funding, supra note 8, [18]; Oxford: Comparative Study, supra note 8, III.75. Venezuela is an exception: cost shifting requires flawless victory. In other words, even losing a small part of the case completely bars any cost recovery in a manner reminiscent of the (now largely defunct) defense of contributory negligence in tort cases.

[58] Some systems (Brazil, Greece, Macau) provide for equal division of costs which would imply that the party with the higher bill can claim part of its costs from the other side.

[59] The National Reports for Australia, Canada, England and Wales, and the United States all indicate settlements rates of at least 90%; the Oxford group confirms that, see Oxford: Costs and Funding, supra note 8, [94–95]; Oxford: Comparative Study, supra note 8, IV.166. The situation in the mixed jurisdictions of Israel and Scotland is similar. The big exception in the common law orbit is India where settlement rates are apparently low. This may be due to the excessive delays in civil proceedings: if a decision cannot be expected for many years down the road, at least the party in the weaker position has little reason to give in by settling.

[60] The information about settlement rates contained in the National Reports was generally patchy. Many Reports did not provide any data for lack of statistical information; some National Reporters proffered good faith estimates while a few others referred to hard data. In a few countries, such as Russia and Turkey, by far most cases go to final judgment. More typically, settlement rates of ca. 15–20% prevail, as in Austria, Germany, Iceland, Norway, or Serbia. Some National Reporters provided much higher numbers, as for China (50–70%), Japan (20–42%) or Switzerland (ca. 50% of all cases with a higher rate in commercial litigation). These numbers roughly match the data provided by the Oxford group, see Oxford: Costs and Funding, supra note 8, [94–95]; Oxford: Comparative Study, supra note 8, IV. 165 (with the exception of Norway for which a settlement rate of 42% is reported).

[61] The Oxford group reaches the same conclusion, see Oxford: Costs and Funding, supra note 8, [73]; Oxford: Comparative Study, supra note 8, IV.123.

winner (infra. 1.) and instrumental goals of encouraging or discouraging litigation (2.). Of course, these policies are not mutually exclusive, and in fact, most systems covered here appear to pursue a mix of them. The United States, however, stands by and large apart in its almost completely instrumentalist position (3.).

10.2.3.1 Basic Fairness

As we have seen, the vast majority of systems embraces the loser-pays principle (supra 10.2.1.1. and 2.). In most of them, this principle reflects primarily an idea of basic fairness in the sense of substantive right: it seems just that the loser must compensate the winner.

10.2.3.2 Instrumentalist Considerations

Most jurisdictions covered here *also* base their cost shifting rules on instrumentalist grounds: these rules are meant to provide incentives for potential litigants to behave in a particular manner.[62] Here we have to distinguish two categories: discouragement of non-meritorious, and encouragement of meritorious, litigation.

In the majority of systems, the loser-pays rule is seen as a means to discourage non-meritorious claims.[63] The underlying logic seems simple enough: since the loser will pay twice (i.e., his or her own as well as the opponent's costs), someone with a dubious claim will also think twice before taking it to court. This General Report is not the place to discuss whether it really works that way. Suffice it to mention that a loser-pays rule also *encourages* parties to sue if they *expect* to win, and that over-optimism in that regard is of course wide spread.[64] In all likelihood, the deterrent effect of the loser-pays rule is not primarily due to the parties' perception of their respective position's merits. Instead, such deterrence is probably mainly the result of general risk averseness: by doubling the stakes, the loser-pays rule scares off parties who, like most, shy away from high downside-risks.

A few systems also see their loser-pays rule as an encouragement of meritorious lawsuits[65]: a party who is right should stand his or her ground even in court without fear of uncompensated litigation costs. To put it differently: access to justice should be free of charge for those with meritorious claims or defenses.[66] Apparently, these systems do not regard litigation as on balance socially undesirable and thus do not wish to discourage it in principle.

10.2.3.3 Pure Instrumentalism

In all this, the United States stands by and large apart: it is not only, as we have seen, the only system covered here which openly rejects the loser-pays principle (supra 10.2.1.3.); it is also the only system that does not justify its basic rule (that each side bears its own expenses regardless of outcome) on fairness grounds – and it would be hard-pressed do so.[67] It is thus the only country predicating its basic cost rule purely on instrumentalist grounds.[68]

---

[62]Only the Reports for Norway and South Africa disclaim such instrumentalist grounds. The Reports for India and Switzerland state that there is no unified or clearly articulated policy.

[63]This is reflected in the National Reports for Austria, Australia, Brazil, Canada, England and Wales, Germany, Greece, Israel, Japan, Korea, Macau, the Netherlands, Norway, Scotland, Sweden, and Venezuela; it is implicit in several others.

[64]All losing plaintiffs were (virtually by definition) over-optimistic and thus potentially encouraged, rather than discouraged, by the loser-pays rule to file a suit which was then proven non-meritorious. Of course, the loser-pays rule will deter litigation if a party recognizes the weakness of the claim.

[65]This is mentioned in the National Report for Germany and intimated in several others emphasizing that the winner deserves to be fully compensated for the vindication of his or her rights.

[66]A few National Reports (especially for Austria, China, and Taiwan) also state that their cost rules are designed to encourage settlement. The loser-pays rule seems ill-designed to do that, except to the extent that it, again, appeals to the parties' risk-averseness. Systems can, and sometimes do, encourage settlement through special cost rules. Some punish a party that refuses to settle, e.g., by imposing the resultant litigation costs, as in Scotland under certain circumstances (if the defender lodges a judicial tender, offering to settle at a certain amount, and the pursuer continues the case and is ultimately awarded less than the defender offered). Others reward parties who do settle, e.g., by waiving part of the court fees as in Portugal.

[67]That is not to say that it is impossible to make fairness arguments in defense of the "American rule". The most obvious such argument is that in many, if not most, cases, litigation outcomes are so unpredictable and luck-driven that both sides run a high risk of defeat which makes it fair for each side to bear its own cost risk. Another argument is that the American rule makes it each side's own business how much money to spend on the litigation. Whether these arguments are ultimately persuasive is of course a matter on which reasonable people can differ.

[68]In his comment on the Draft General Report, the National Reporter for the United States pointed out that "the instrumentalist view in the USA is an after-the-fact justification. It came into being only well after the practice was established."

Moreover, US-American instrumentalism is one-sided: the basic cost rule is meant to lower the risk to the potential loser. This approach is defended primarily as facilitating access to justice, and that implies – at least de facto – encouragement of litigation.[69] Note, however, that the American rule encourages not only lawsuits the plaintiff is confident to win but also the ones the plaintiff thinks he or she may well lose (as long as the matter is not entirely hopeless). In fact, it is the latter effect – the implicit encouragement of weak lawsuits (often with the sole goal to force the defendant to settle) – that sets the rule in the United States apart from pretty much the rest of the world.

Whether the "American Rule" actually facilitates access to justice, and whether it does so in the right (i.e., meritorious) cases, is a question beyond the scope of this General Report. The American National Report raises substantial doubts in this regard. It points out, inter alia, that the American rule can easily end up virtually prohibiting certain meritorious claims: since the plaintiff cannot recover his or her litigation expenses even in case of victory, the amount potentially won must be high enough at least to cover these expenses. Yet, given the high costs of litigation in US-American courts, this is rarely the case for small and even mid-size claims. As a result, these claims become financially impossible to litigate – ironically because of the very cost rule that is supposed to enhance access to justice.[70] In addition, if a case *is* actually litigated, the costs may be so high that even a *winning* plaintiff may pay more in expenses than he would pay as a loser elsewhere.[71]

10.3 How Much? The Financial Risks of Litigation

Whether a system shifts the winner's litigation costs to the loser (in whole or in part) tells only half the story. A realistic picture of what cost shifting means must include the sums at stake. *How much* money are we actually talking about? Only if we look at that question can we understand the actual impact of cost shifting vel non.

The answer we can give here, however, is neither complete nor precise. The data contained in the national reports in response to questions about actual litigation costs in certain types of cases are patchy. While reporters from systems calculating costs according to precise official schedules (such as Germany or Switzerland) could provide exact figures, reporters from jurisdictions without such schedules could only give good faith estimates. A sizeable percentage of national reporters found it impossible to provide any reliable numbers because litigation costs in their systems depend entirely on the circumstances of the case so that generalizations are virtually impossible. Moreover, where actual numbers were provided, they had to be converted into a common currency (USD) according to fluctuating rates. Finally, all these numbers must be evaluated in light of the disparate purchasing power in the respective jurisdictions and, indeed, regions – $ 10,000 is a lot more money in rural China than in downtown London. As a result, the numbers given can only be rough approximations. Still, they show at minimum that among the systems covered, the actual financial impact of cost shifting (vel non) ranges from the truly trivial to the potentially prohibitive.

We will first separately look at the three major cost items in private litigation, i.e., court costs (infra. 1.), attorney fees (2.), and the expenses of taking evidence, e.g., for expert witnesses (3.). Then we will consider the total cost of litigation in order to get a sense of the overall financial burden involved (4.).

10.3.1 Court Costs: Trouble or Triviality?

As we have seen (supra 10.2.1.), court costs are always shifted to the loser – even in the United States. Some jurisdictions, such as Mexico and Venezuela, charge no court costs in order to ease access to justice, others, like France and Sweden, keep them extremely low.[72]

[69]This fits with the usually very low court fees in the United States, see infra. 10.3.1.2.

[70]Such cases are routinely settled; the impossibility of cost-effective litigation normally enhances the bargaining power of defendants and thus tends to lower the price of settlement.

[71]See the tables in the United States Report, VII.

[72]See also Oxford: Costs and Funding, supra note 8, [13]; Oxford: Comparative Study, supra note 8, III.25.

10.3.1.1 Computation

Systems vary greatly as to how court costs are calculated. Most jurisdictions determine them under a schedule by amount in controversy (usually in a degressive fashion) while a few (notably the United States) usually charge a flat fee.[73] In some systems, like Germany, the basic court fee covers virtually the whole proceedings at the particular level, while in others, separate fees are charged at successive stages of the litigation or, as in France and Belgium, for various acts of officials, such as filing, service of process, stamping of documents, etc.; the individual items may look cheap but they tend to add up.

10.3.1.2 Differences in Size

Shifting court costs to the loser can mean vastly different things because the amounts involved vary enormously. For a $ 100,000 lawsuit, Canadian or US-American courts charge at most a few hundred dollars.[74] File the same action in a Brazilian, Greek or Russian court, and you come closer to paying $ 1,000. Take it to a Czech, German or Dutch tribunal, and you will need to put down $ 3,000 – 6,000. Bring the case in Switzerland, and court costs will amount to over $ 10,000.[75]

10.3.1.3 Two Explanations

What explains the huge discrepancies among court fees? While multiple factors will be at play, two are worth at least brief consideration: the amount of work courts perform, and the underlying ideas as to who should pay for the civil justice system.

It is noticeable that common law systems often to charge lower court costs than civil law countries. This may well reflect that common law judges by and large do less work per case than their civil law colleagues. As is well known, common law judges tend to play a more passive role while their civilian brethren are supposed to actively manage and resolve the dispute[76]; in addition, the settlement rate in the common law orbit is very high while civil law judges have to render a great number of final judgments in writing with reasoned opinions. The picture is far from perfect, however: for example, court fees are low in the United States and Canada but quite hefty in the England and Wales; in a similar fashion, they are quite high in Taiwan and in China[77] but surprisingly low in Korea and Japan (at least in small and midsize cases).

Thus, other factors are at work as well. In particular, jurisdictions pursue different policies as to who should pay for the civil justice system. Many countries, such as Germany and Switzerland, but also England and Wales,[78] apparently expect mainly the litigants to pay for using the courts; these systems charge amounts that cover at least a significant part of the civil courts' operating cost – like they would for renting out a government-owned facility. The consequence of this approach is that court cost shifting matters substantially because it can easily involve a significant percentage of the sum in controversy and the equivalent of thousands of dollars. Other jurisdictions, such as Canada, the United States, Japan, and Korea, provide access to the civil courts essentially as a public (i.e., tax-funded) service; they charge merely a small entrance fee – as they would for a state museum or national park. Here, shifting court costs matters much less as it usually involves but a tiny fraction of the amount at stake and at most a few hundred dollars.[79]

---

[73] This has the effect, inter alia, that there is no penalty in terms of court costs for filing a grossly inflated claim which explains, in part, why US plaintiffs often file million dollar lawsuits where parties in other countries would be much more careful not to overstate their claim.

[74] At least in the United States, it is often not worth the time and effort to try to collect the costs from the losing party.

[75] Where court costs are substantial and tied to the amount claimed, parties sometimes save part of them by claiming only part of the amount really at issue, thus filing essentially a test case. This can also be done to save lawyer fees where they are determined by a schedule as well.

[76] See the classic article by John Langbein, "The German Advantage in Civil Procedure," *Chicago Law Review* 52 (1985): 823.

[77] Again, this assumes that the respective approaches to calculation were truly equivalent. In their comment on the Draft General Report, the Chinese Reporters pointed out that they counted "nearly every cent that is spent by both parties during the first instance, second instance, and enforcement procedure."

[78] See Oxford: Costs and Funding, supra note 8, [13]; Oxford: Comparative Study, supra note 8, III.26 (80% of court costs covered by user payments); John Peysner, Litigation Cost Recovery – Tariffs and Hourly Fees in England, in Gottwald, supra note 11, 138 fn. 4; the Jackson Review, supra note 10, recommends to abolish this policy and to fund the courts (largely) through taxpayer money so that the court fees can be lowered and access to justice facilitated, id., 50.

[79] As the National Reporter for Japan pointed out in his comments on the Draft General Report, in cases with particularly large amounts at stake (such as some tort cases for environmental damage or HIV-infected blood products), Japanese court court costs can rise to the level of a barrier to access to justice because they are tied to the amount in controversy.

10.3.2 Attorney Fees: The Lion's Share

As we have seen, the vast majority of systems covered here shifts attorney fees to the loser as well – in most cases either completely or at least a very significant share, although some jurisdictions may make the loser pay for only a small part.[80] At the end of the day, how much attorney fee shifting really matters also depends largely on their magnitude. That magnitude, however, is often very difficult to assess and largely impossible to generalize.

10.3.2.1 Computation

Determining the amount of lawyer fees is a complex business. Two principal approaches must be distinguished. In many systems, especially in continental Europe,[81] shiftable attorney fees are, as mentioned, set by an official schedule tied to the amount in controversy (and sometimes to the court in which the case proceeds) and providing either absolute amounts or a maximum-minimum range. Here, the amount of lawyer fees is set ex ante and thus fairly clear to both winner and loser. Other systems, however, leave the determination of attorney fees by and large to the market. There, lawyer fees vary greatly, depending on the mode of charging (by the hour,[82] flat fee, etc.), location, expertise and reputation, case complexity, and sometimes the client's resources; success fees often further complicate the picture.[83]

10.3.2.2 From Schedule to Market

The complexity of assessing lawyer fees is exacerbated by a general trend away from the former (schedule-based) approach and towards the latter (market-oriented) model. This trend manifests itself in two ways.

First, binding fee schedules are on the decline – several countries have lately departed from official tariffs, albeit to varying degrees. Some trend setting systems have abolished binding schedules altogether – Japan (2003) and Korea (2003) are prime examples. In other jurisdictions, these schedules were relegated to the status of a mere floor above which the parties can freely agree to a higher price, as has lately happened in Germany (2004) and is beginning to happen in Switzerland.[84] Yet other countries rendered them non-binding as a floor but stuck to maximum limits, as in Italy (2006) or leave it to the attorney and his or her client whether to use the official tariff or a market rate, as in the Czech Republic.[85]

Second, prohibitions of success-oriented fees are on the decline[86] – many systems formerly opposed to giving lawyers a stake in the outcome of litigation are now permitting exactly that. England, once staunchly opposed to success-oriented fees, introduced conditional fees in 1990, expanded their use in 1998, and current reform proposals include the introduction of full-fledged contingency fees.[87] Perhaps the most dramatic change in that direction was the recent introduction of outright contingency fees (though only under certain conditions) in Italy (2006) and Germany (2008). Even conservative Switzerland, it seems, is moving in this direction.[88]

This dual trend towards deregulating lawyer fees has been the result of several factors. In some instances, binding schedules were simply deemed incompatible with the status of a free legal profession, as in France. In other jurisdictions, they were thought to violate competition (or antitrust) principles, as in Japan and Korea. In Europe, there were doubts whether such schedules violated the principle of freedom of services in the European Union – as in Italy.[89] In several jurisdictions, a policy of improving

[80] Supra 10.2.1.

[81] Note that this is not true for *all* of continental Europe because many jurisdictions there do not have an official attorney fee schedule, such as France, Spain, and the Scandinavian countries. On the other hand, there is apparently such a schedule in South Africa.

[82] For data on hourly fees in various jurisdictions, see Oxford: Comparative Study, supra note 8, Appendix III.

[83] See infra. 10.4.4.

[84] See Swiss Report IV.2.

[85] There are signs of an incipient counter-trend in England: certain routine cases are handled under a fixed fee, and the recent reform proposals include the introduction of fixed costs in fast track litigation, i.e., cases of up to 25,000 pounds in which trial can be handled in one day, see Jackson Review, supra note 10, xviii, 146–168.

[86] See infra. 10.4.4.

[87] Jackson Review, supra note 10, xviii–xix, 131–133.

[88] See Swiss Report IV.3.

[89] The Italian deregulation came in part as a reaction to decisions rendered by the European Court of Justice, although the Court did *not* declare official fee schedules a per se violation of European law (see Case C-35/99 (*Arduino*) [2002] E.C.R. I-1529-1575; Joined Cases C-94-04 (*Cipolla*) and C-202/04 (*Macrino*),

access to justice (especially for individual clients) drove price deregulation and triggered the permission of success-oriented fees,[90] in others, allowing such fees was meant to compensate for the restriction (or near-elimination) of public legal aid, i.e., constituted a way of privatizing litigation funding.[91] Deregulation was also a response to the increasing international competition from Anglo-American law firms whose prices were subject to precious few official restrictions. Last, but not least, liberating lawyer fees from binding tariffs and from prohibitions of success premiums fit the general trend toward deregulation and trust in market forces that has dominated most of the developed world, certainly until the onset of the financial crisis in 2008, and often beyond.

To be sure, not every jurisdiction covered in this Report has joined the bandwagon, and not everybody involved is necessarily enthusiastic.[92] But the legal systems holding on to traditional regulations and prohibitions are now in the minority, and their number is shrinking. As the German Report put it, "the pressure to change the whole system is growing,"[93] and change points in the direction of free market prices for lawyer fees with few restrictions on success premiums. Since this has long been the situation in the United States, is tempting to speak of – yet another – "Americanization" of law in many parts of the world.[94]

Deregulating lawyer fees has its upsides,[95] but it does make it harder to predict them and it seriously complicates their allocation. Where such fees are fixed by an official schedule, shifting them to the loser is a fairly straightforward matter: the client pays the tariff, and if he wins the lawsuit, recoups what he owes his lawyer from the loser. Since both parties know the amount in advance, full fee shifting is no problem – the amount is fixed so that the winner (and his lawyer) cannot play with the loser's money, and the loser cannot claim unfair surprise. And since fee shifting normally involves few (or no) judgment calls, it can be handled on the clerical level and provides little opportunity for further fighting. By contrast, where the determination of lawyer fees is left to the market (and especially where success-fees are allowed), fee shifting becomes a lot more problematic: now, the winner can make arrangements with his lawyer potentially at the loser's expense, and the loser can often not predict how much he will have to pay. In order to protect the losing party, a legal system must now do one of two things. Either it limits the shiftable fee to a statutorily fixed amount, and since that amount will usually be set on the low side, the winner will often not be made entirely whole; this is true in many jurisdictions, most dramatically in Greece.[96] Or a legal system must install an ex post reasonableness check on the winner's spending which also means that full reimbursement is not guaranteed; this is also true in many countries, especially in the Commonwealth group. Allowing success-fees of course exacerbates the problem. Shifting success premiums makes the loser liable for the reward the winner promised his lawyer; this adds insult to injury as the loser has to pay extra precisely for being defeated. Yet, not shifting success fees denies the winner full recovery of his litigation expenses. Finally, where the shiftable amount is no longer officially fixed ex ante (and especially where it includes some kind of success premium), the loser will often challenge the winner's reimbursement claim as unreasonable – which entails continued fighting even after the main case has been closed.[97]

In short, leaving lawyer fees entirely to the market, and especially allowing success premiums, entails

[2006] E.C.R. I-11421-11478. For a comment, see Martin Ilmer, "Lawyers' Fees and Access to Justice – The Cipolla and Merino Judgment of the ECJ," *Civil Justice Quarterly* 26 (2007): 201.

[90]This was an important factor in Germany, Entscheidungen des Bundesverfassungsgerichts (BVerfGE) 117, 163–202 (2006).

[91]This was clearly the case in England, see United Kingdom, Lord Chancellor's Department, Access to Justice with Conditional Fees (1998); Neil Andrews, Cost and Conditional Fee Agreements in English Civil Litigation, in Gottwald, supra note 11, 185 at 187.

[92]The bar has not necessarily welcomed increased competition through deregulation, see Ilmer, id., at 308 (Italian bar protesting); as the National Reporter for Italy points out in her comments on the Draft General Report, there are efforts to reverse this trend by legislation, and it is conceivable that a more regulated regime will be restored.

[93]German Report, Conclusion.

[94]Cf. L'Américanisation du droit, Archives de philosophie du droit 45 (2001) 7.

[95]For an informative discussion of the advantages and disadvantages of strictly regulated lawyer fees, see Gerhard Wagner, Litigation Costs Recovery – Tariffs and Hourly Fees in Germany, in Gottwald, supra note 11, 149, at 174–184.

[96]See supra 38 and text.

[97]For England, see Martin Ilmer, Lawyer's Fees and Access to Justice, Civil Justice Quarterly 26 (2007) 201, at 207 (with further references). Zuckerman on Civil Procedure (2d ed. London 2006) par. 26.1 et seq.

three major costs: it is incompatible with routine full fee shifting because the winner's agreement with his lawyer cannot automatically determine what the loser owes; it creates predictability problems and thus fairness issues because the amount owed by the loser is not fixed in advance; and it invites second stage litigation because what should reasonably be reimbursed is often debatable.[98]

As a result of the current trends therefore, fewer and fewer legal systems will have fee shifting in the Austrian, German, or Swiss tradition: simple, quick, and usually uncontroversial; and more and more jurisdictions will have cost allocation as in Australia, England or Canada: complex, labor-intensive, and often contested.[99]

10.3.2.3 Absolute and Relative Size

While the computation of lawyer fees is plagued by complexities and uncertainties, especially in market-based systems, a look at the numbers presented in the national reports and culled from various other sources shows two things quite clearly.

First, on the whole, the sums involved in attorney fee shifting are very substantial. Even in jurisdictions with comparably moderate fees, the loser in a $ 100,000 lawsuit, for example, will owe the winner roughly between $ 5,000 and $ 10,000. In more generous jurisdictions, like Switzerland, the debt can easily be twice that amount. And in countries with truly high litigation costs, like Australia or Canada, the loser may owe even more, depending on the complexity of the case and on how much of the lawyer fees the court ultimately awards the winner. Again, generalization is difficult and perhaps not advisable. Suffice it to say that where attorney fees are shifted, it is not at all unusual for the defeated party in a mid-size case to owe the winner 10% of the amount in controversy in lawyer fees alone.[100] Thus, potential liability for them is a very significant part of the overall litigation risk.

Second, in almost all systems, attorney fees invariably exceed court fees. In other words, lawyers are more expensive than courts.[101] This means that attorney fee shifting is practically more important than court cost shifting. How much more important depends on the jurisdiction involved. In this regard, there is a significant difference between continental civil law systems on the one hand and common law regimes on the other. In continental Europe, attorney fees typically exceed court costs by a fairly moderate ratio, typically ranging from just above 1:1 to around 1:6. In common law jurisdictions, attorney fees tend to exceed court fees much more dramatically. The reason for this difference is mainly that court costs are higher in civil law systems than in common law jurisdictions while the opposite tends to be true for lawyer fees.[102] As a result, the comparative importance of shifting court costs and allocating lawyer fees varies. In continental Europe, both elements often matter significantly (though lawyer fee shifting matters more) while in some common law jurisdictions, like Canada or the United States, court costs can constitute such a small item that lawyer fee shifting is all that really counts.

10.3.2.4 Avoiding Attorney Fees

Attorney fees are sometimes avoidable: the majority of legal systems covered in this report broadly permit self-representation, often at all levels; and even the minority of jurisdictions that require representation by a lawyer usually make exceptions for small claims (courts). Where litigants can – de jure and de facto – operate without legal counsel, the importance of attorney fee shifting is of course much diminished.

Yet, whether self-representation is a viable option in reality varies depending on the legal system and the nature of the case involved. In some systems, especially those with a civil law background, judges take a fairly active part in the proceedings and will usually help non-represented parties considerably, particularly in smaller and more routine cases; this is especially

[98] In order to avoid these issues at least in part, England has introduced "fixed costs" for certain types of routine cases and for all fast track trials for under 15,000 pounds; see Oxford: Costs and Funding, supra note 8, [83 fn. 70]; Oxford: Comparative Study, supra fn. 8, IV.145 (incl. fn. 60).

[99] Particularly in England, (second stage) litigation about costs is so notorious and wide spread that insiders often speak of a veritable "cost war", see Andrews, supra note 91, at 204; see also Peysner, supra note 78, 140–141.

[100] This is of course on top of the fee owed to the loser's own lawyer, as well as on top of court costs (supra. 1.) and evidence expenses (infra. 3.) all of which can be very substantial.

[101] This is confirmed by the Oxford group, see Oxford: Costs and Funding, supra note 8, [107]; Oxford: Comparative Study, supra note 8, III.37. and 69.

[102] This is not because common lawyers are more expensive by the hour but because common law procedure is more party-driven and thus requires more lawyer time, see infra. 10.5.2.

true in Asian countries[103]; but it is also the case in Latin America and even in much of continental Europe. As a result, parties there often appear without lawyers, at least in the lower courts. In other jurisdictions, especially from the common law orbit, however, judges are traditionally much more passive and lawsuits are essentially party-driven; this, of course, makes it much harder for laypeople effectively to litigate *pro se*. And everywhere, large and complex cases are usually too difficult to handle without professional assistance.

10.3.3 The Expenses of Evidence: What Price Fact Gathering?

Almost all systems covered in this Report in principle shift the costs of evidence taking to the loser, most in whole, some at least in large part. Yet, again, this basic principle acquires real meaning only once we look more closely at what the costs of evidence taking consist of and in particular, how substantial they are. In this regard, there are significant differences between three kinds of jurisdictions: civil law systems, common law countries in the British tradition, and, as the major exception to the rule of general evidence cost shifting, the United States.

10.3.3.1 Civil Law Systems

All civil law systems impose the costs of evidence taking on the loser. In most cases, however, the impact is relatively slight for two reasons.

First, since fact gathering is largely performed, or at least closely directed, by the judge, the court does most of the work, such as ordering documents, interviewing witnesses, inspecting sites, etc.; and this judicial work is already paid for in form of the – often very substantial – court costs. In other words, court cost shifting already includes much of the cost of evidence taking.

Second, the *additional and separate* costs of evidence are usually low because there is no common-law style discovery. In most cases, they only consist of fees and compensation for witnesses and perhaps the cost of copying documents. The amounts involved here are usually small and do not constitute a significant item in the overall litigation bill. The situation changes to some extent, however, if expert witnesses get involved. In civil law proceedings, expert witnesses are usually appointed by the court, and their fee will also ultimately be borne by the losing party. While expert witnesses are often paid according to an official schedule which remains below market rate, they can still be fairly expensive and thus have an impact on overall costs.

Still, all in all it is fair to say that in civil law systems, evidence cost shifting is usually secondary to both court costs and lawyer fees.

10.3.3.2 Common Law Jurisdictions

In common law jurisdictions in the English tradition, the costs of evidence taking are borne by the loser as well, albeit often only in part. As in civil law proceedings, the impact of this rule is also softened by the fact that a large chunk of these costs is already covered: now, fact gathering is largely performed by the parties' attorneys so that much of the expense of evidence taking is already included in the lawyer fees. Thus, lawyer fee shifting already includes much (if not most) of evidence cost shifting.

In practice, however, shifting the expenses incurred by evidence taking (be it in the form of lawyer fees or other items) is more important in the common law than in the civil law orbit simply because these expenses tend to be higher. This is so mainly for three reasons. First, evidence gathering by the parties' attorneys is more expensive since (common law) attorneys charge more than (civil law) judges. Second, during common law-style discovery, evidence is often taken by both sides (and thus twice) rather than only once by a (civil law) judge. Third, experts tend to cost more in common law jurisdictions because they are hired by the parties and thus at market rates, and because each side usually hires its own instead of relying on just one appointed by the court. As a result, the expenses incurred by evidence taking usually constitute a larger share of the total litigation bill in common law than in civil law systems – which makes shifting these expenses to the loser more crucial.[104]

[103] This is expressly noted in the National Reports for China, Japan, and Korea.

[104] This does not necessarily mean that the loser actually bears a greater amount of these costs than in a civil law court. Remember that most civil law courts routinely shift the total amount while common law judges often chose to shift only a part of the winner's litigation (including evidence taking) costs to the defeated party.

10.3.3.3 The United States Approach

The United States approach to the expenses of evidence taking is sui generis for two reasons. First, the majority of fact gathering costs are *not* shifted to the loser. These costs consist of three major items: the attorney fees generated by the discovery process – which are (under the general US-American rule) borne by each party regardless of outcome; the costs of their expert witnesses – which are also not shifted; and "costs other than attorney fees"[105] – which *are* borne by the loser but comprise merely a variety of minor fees for (non-expert) witnesses, court stenographers, and copying.[106] Thus overall, only a very small, and in fact often trivial, part of the evidence taking costs are shifted. Second, as a result of a uniquely permissive discovery regime,[107] fact gathering in the United States is more extensive – and thus more expensive – than anywhere else in the world. In most cases, the cost of gathering evidence is – often by far – the largest item on the total litigation bill. Thus the practical impact of *not* shifting the lion's share of evidence costs (including expert witness fees) is tremendous: it entails a huge burden for the victor as well as a huge relief for the vanquished. In fact, not shifting the bulk of evidence costs is perhaps *the* defining feature that separates the United States from all other jurisdictions covered here. After all, like *all* other systems, the US-American regime makes the loser pay for court costs; like at least *some* other systems, it normally does not shift attorney fees; but like *no* other system, it makes each party pay for virtually all its own expenses of fact gathering regardless of outcome, and these expenses are normally very high.[108]

10.3.4 The Total Picture: Costs in Four Cases and Their Impact

If court costs (ranging from trivial to substantial), attorney fees (ranging from substantial to astronomical), and expenses of evidence taking (ranging from modest to crushing) are added together, it becomes clear that in most of the legal systems covered here, the overall financial burden of civil litigation is heavy, at least outside of small claims procedures. Unfortunately, it is almost impossible to obtain comparable figures for all these jurisdictions because overall litigation costs depend on a large number of variables including the nature and complexity of the case, the court in which a case is filed,[109] the computation and level of attorney fees, and the method of taking evidence. Still, in response to the General Reporter's request to indicate the total litigation costs for certain claims, most National Reports provided some useful figures.[110] While these figures also have to be taken with a very large grain of salt, they give us some idea of how much it may cost to litigate monetary claims on four levels.

10.3.4.1 Small Claims

Litigating relatively small claims (e.g., roughly the equivalent of $ 1,000) is affordable where they are handled in special small claims courts with a simplified procedure and without legal counsel. This option exists in many systems and seems to generate few problems. Where such an option does not exist, however, and especially where the parties are (by legal requirement or choice) represented by lawyers, litigating small claims is at minimum disconcertingly expensive, often costing over 50% of the amount in controversy (as indicated by the figures for Belgium, China, the Czech Republic, Slovenia, and Switzerland) or outright prohibitive, i.e., costing *more* than the amount in controversy (as signaled by the numbers for Austria, Finland, Iceland, Italy, Spain, Scotland, and possibly also in the Czech Republic, Germany, and the United States). In short, such small claims can usually not be efficiently handled in a regular (full-fledged) civil proceeding if lawyers are employed.

[105] See Federal Rule of Civil Procedure 54(d)(1).

[106] See 28 United States Code § 1920.

[107] Discovery is permissible not only with regard to evidence which is admissible as evidence at trial but also "if the discovery appears reasonably calculated to lead to the discovery of admissible evidence", Federal Rule of Civil Procedure 26(b)(1); this provision thus permits so-called "fishing expeditions".

[108] Under the discovery system in the United States, each side thus has the potential to inflict enormous costs on the other side which can usually not be shifted.

[109] In some systems, like France, Mexico, Serbia, and Russia, there are different courts, and sometimes different cost and cost allocation rules for private and commercial cases; in many other jurisdictions, such as Germany, Norway, and Sweden, family law disputes are subject to special rules and rates; and some systems, like Japan or the United States, treat cases for personal injury differently than, e.g., suits for breach of contract or injunctive relief.

[110] In schedule based-systems, these figures were usually fairly precise; in others, they were based on good faith estimates.

10.3.4.2 Small to Medium Cases

The litigation of small to medium claims (e.g., the equivalent of $ 10,000) raises similar concerns in many systems for which we have data. A few jurisdictions can apparently process such claims at fairly moderate cost, ranging from a few hundred to around two thousand dollars total (figures in that range are given for Belgium, Brazil, China, Greece, Iceland, Korea, Poland, Serbia and Taiwan). In most systems, however, the cost is in the thousands of dollars and thus represents a sizeable percentage of the amount in controversy. And in some jurisdictions, litigation costs closely approach or actually reach the claimed amount (Austria, Finland, Italy, Scotland, and Switzerland are in this category), making it, again, inefficient to litigate such claims at all.

10.3.4.3 Medium to Large Disputes

In suits for medium to large disputes (involving the equivalent of $ 100,000), the absolute cost of litigation is even higher, but the relative cost goes down. While such litigation now often burns up tens of thousands of dollars, no system for which figures were provided exceeded 50% of the amount in controversy, and most ranged between roughly 10% and one third. The two main reasons for these more bearable ratios are the degressive scale of official court cost and lawyer fee schedules as well as more generally, the fact that lawyer time and evidence-taking typically do not increase in a linear fashion with the amount in controversy. Nonetheless, litigating these medium to large disputes is by no means cheap.

10.3.4.4 High-Value Litigation

Unsurprisingly, the litigation of large claims (e.g., $ 1,000,000) is most expensive in absolute terms and cheapest in relation to the amount at stake. It may cost as little as around one percent (this is indicated by the figures given for Belgium, Greece, and, in commercial courts, Serbia) or as much as one third (as in Scotland) of the sum claimed.[111] The more typical ratios, however, range from about 5% to 15%. While this does not threaten to devour the claim, these percentages routinely translate into tens of thousands or dollars and can, in some systems, easily exceed six figures.

10.3.4.5 Litigation Costs and Access to Justice

On the whole, the magnitude of litigation costs in most systems creates three major problems. Not all of these problems occur in all jurisdictions, but most of them are pervasive in most systems.[112] First, outside of special courts with simplified procedures, small and perhaps even midsize claims can often not be efficiently handled because litigating them can easily cost more than their worth.[113] Second, litigating midsize and large claims is frequently so expensive that at least among private individuals, very few can afford to pay for it out of their pocket. Third, in many systems litigation costs in large cases can be exorbitant (as well as highly unpredictable) so that the financial burden (or at least risk) is hard to bear even for deep pocket parties.[114]

Disproportionate costs constitute serious barriers for access to justice.[115] Mere cost-shifting from one side to the other cannot do much to solve this problem. It is true, of course, that under a loser-pays approach, the winning party gets away free (or at least cheaply) – but only at the risk of being hit doubly hard in case of

[111] While no figures were provided for England and Wales or for the United States, common experience suggests that in these systems, litigating a $ 1,000,000 claim could also cost hundreds of thousands of dollars although almost everything would depend on the kind and complexity of the case.

[112] The Oxford group also concluded "that in most states included in this study the costs of litigation are high in relation to the value of the case – sometimes they even exceed the value of the case," Oxford: Costs and Funding, supra note 8, [71]; Oxford: Comparative Study, supra note 8, III.70.

[113] Many National Reports flag this problem; see the Reports for Austria, Brazil, Switzerland, the Czech Republic, Italy, Japan, Mexico, South Africa (at least in unusual or novel cases), Spain (especially in consumer litigation), and Turkey.

[114] Interestingly, *all* National Reports from common law systems (Australia, Canada, England and Wales, and the United States) and mixed jurisdictions (Israel, Scotland, and South Africa) mention this problem. By contrast, only *some* of the civil law based countries report this concern. This indicates that systems with a strong common law element struggle more consistently with cost issues than jurisdictions with a civil law foundation. Given the more lawyer-centered nature of court proceedings in common law (influenced) countries, litigation costs there tend to be higher and, perhaps just as importantly, less predictable, see infra. 10.5.2.

[115] Of course, access to justice is not only a matter of money but depends on a variety of other factors as well though financial costs are an important hurdle for most potential litigants. In some systems, like Italy and India, the main problem is not cost but excessive delay. It is a common maxim in English that "justice delayed is justice denied", and if an injured party cannot enforce its claim through the legal process within a reasonable period of time, even free access to justice provides little help.

defeat. It is also true that if the costs are not (or only partially) shifted, the burden on each side is lighter – but only at the price of having to pay (and often dearly) even when winning hands-down. In either case, rules on cost and fee shifting leave the financial burden of litigation on the parties to the litigation,[116] and these costs can be ruinous, sometimes even for winners.

10.4 Whose Money? Access to Justice Through Mechanisms of Risk Distribution

In reality, however, parties often do not pay for litigation costs with their own money. In response to the problems mentioned, most jurisdictions have developed mechanisms to distribute the financial risk of civil litigation among larger groups. Cost and fee allocation in civil procedure cannot be fully understood without taking these mechanisms into account. They range from traditional legal aid to modern models of litigation as an investment opportunity. Some distribute civil litigation costs more widely than others.[117]

10.4.1 Legal Aid: Assisting the Needy

All systems covered in this General Report provide some form of legal aid. This aid comes in three basic varieties which may be called public, semi-official, and pro bono. Depending on these forms, legal aid is subject to various conditions and limitations.

10.4.1.1 Public Legal Aid

Public legal aid directly funds the parties through state money – usually by waiving court fees, often (though not necessarily) by paying for lawyers,[118] and possibly even by covering the expenses of evidence taking. It thus distributes litigation costs extremely widely: these costs are ultimately borne by the taxpayers in the respective state entity (federation, state, province, etc.).

Public legal aid is offered – at least in principle – in all systems included here, with the exception of the United States[119] and Russia.[120] In many jurisdictions, it is the only kind of legal aid systematically available[121]; in others, it operates in addition to various other forms of assistance (infra. 2. and 3.).[122] Public legal aid is broadly conceived in that it can usually cover both plaintiffs and defendants.

Yet, public legal aid helps only a small segment of all litigants because it is subject to serious restrictions. Their severity and, as a result, the actual availability of legal aid, varies among the systems covered here. Most importantly, *all* jurisdictions impose two very significant limitations. First, only indigent parties are eligible, i.e., parties who fall below a (sometimes statutorily

[116] Some are paid by the state, e.g., where court fees are low.

[117] We leave out here cost distribution by firms through the market to consumers of their services or products because this mechanism is used for virtually all firm costs and thus not particular to civil litigation expenses.

[118] In many systems, lawyers taking on public aid cases are paid only a (sometimes severely) reduced fee; it stands to reason that this will often affect the quality of legal representation.

[119] There is some – very limited – federal funding in support of legal aid efforts but no general public legal aid system. The Oxford group's statement that such a system is not necessary in light of the availability of contingency fees (for indigent parties), is largely (though not completely) untrue, Oxford: Costs and Funding, supra note 8, [22]; Oxford: Comparative Study, supra note 8, III.100. First, contingency fee arrangements are usually available only to plaintiffs, and mainly in tort cases (i.e., not to defendants and not in all forms of litigation). Second, even for tort plaintiffs, a contingency fee arrangement is not viable in low value disputes, as the Oxford Study itself later points out, id. III.113; in fact, this can be true even in high value cases if in light of the necessary investment into litigation, they do not promise sufficient return. Thus the statement in the Oxford Study is true mainly only in the sense that because of the contingency fee system, *some* parties do not need legal aid.

[120] In the United States, there is no generally available public legal aid for private litigation although there are – very limited – federal funds to support legal representation of indigents by lawyers. The federal government and the states do, however, subsidize litigation by providing use of the court system at very low (usually flat) rates (see supra. 10.3.1.2.). As long as parties act *pro se* (i.e., without a lawyer), they thus often face low financial access barriers to justice, especially in small claims courts and procedures. Where this is not a realistic option, the low court costs cannot make up for the high attorney fees common in the United States. In Russia, public legal aid is available only to a very limited extent in certain classes of civil cases (as well as, more generally, in criminal cases). Bar associations sometimes provide legal aid as well, see infra. 10.4.1.3.

[121] This is reported for many civil law countries, including Austria, Belgium, Finland, Germany, Greece, Italy, Korea, Mexico, Russia, Serbia, and Venezuela. In some of these countries, private legal aid is available by way of exception on an ad hoc basis.

[122] This is reported for Brazil, Canada, the Czech Republic, England and Wales, Iceland, India, Israel, Japan, Macau, the Netherlands, Poland, Scotland, and Turkey, although the degree to which private forms of legal aid exist in these countries apparently varies a great deal.

defined) income or wealth threshold; that threshold is mostly so low that public legal aid is normally unavailable to the middle class.[123] Second, all systems require that the applicant's case pass a – variously defined – merits test; in other words, states do not fund long shot litigation. In addition, many systems impose various other kinds of restrictions, such as not covering liability for the other side's expenses in case of defeat, providing only partial or temporary help or excluding certain kinds of disputes.

In several systems, the availability of legal aid for civil litigants has been diminishing as public funds have been in ever shorter supply, especially since the 2008 financial crisis.[124] The French Report speaks of an outright "crise du système d'aide jurisdique."[125] This has increased the pressure to provide semi-official or private forms of legal aid – or to turn to alternative ways of litigation cost distribution altogether

10.4.1.2 Semi-official Assistance

In several jurisdictions, needy parties can receive help from various public institutions, such as clinics operated by law faculties in Iceland, Israel, Mexico, Norway, and the United States; state bureaus in the Czech Republic; or public prosecutors in Poland. In other systems, like Belgium, Brazil, the Czech Republic or Russia, bar associations provide assistance. And help is sometimes available also from various non-governmental organizations, such as trade unions for labor and employment disputes, e.g., in Belgium, Italy, Germany, and the United States, or other non-profit groups, as reported for Israel, Macau, and Poland. This assistance may be limited to legal advice but sometimes also includes free representation in court. The cost of litigation (at least the part absorbed by these institutions) is thus distributed to all those who fund the respective programs through their time or their money.

10.4.1.3 Pro Bono Work

In a number of jurisdictions, legal aid is available in form of pro bono work performed by law firms: these firms provide free advice and representation to particular parties. In effect, pro bono work is funded by all paying clients of the firm.

Pro bono work is a fairly strong tradition in the United States where law firms are under at least a moral obligation to devote a certain percentage of total lawyer time free of charge to litigation in the public interest or to help parties who cannot afford to pay for professional services. Pro bono work is also known in Australia, Brazil, Canada, the Czech Republic, England and Wales, Scotland, Israel, Japan, Norway, Mexico, and, in nascent form, apparently in China; tender beginnings are reported from France as well. Yet, even where pro bono work has become an established practice, as in many common law countries, in terms of providing (free) access to justice for parties in need, it is but a drop in the bucket.

10.4.2 Litigation Insurance: Buying Protection

In most of the systems covered here, the market has responded to the limited availability of legal aid by offering insurance against litigation costs. This is particularly attractive to the middle class and smaller businesses, i.e., potential parties who are too wealthy to qualify for legal aid but not wealthy enough to absorb litigation costs in all but the smallest cases. Litigation insurance also comes in three basic forms which may be labeled package deal, free-standing, and (British) "after-the-event" policies.

10.4.2.1 Package-Deal Insurance

Litigation insurance is frequently part and parcel of policies covering other, standard, risks. It is most commonly included in automobile, home-owner's, and professional malpractice coverage. In some countries, like Finland and Switzerland, it can also be part of commercial liability protection.

Under such policies, the insurer absorbs not only the liability risk but also funds (in part of course in its own interest) litigation triggered by events covered by the policy.[126] In reality, such insurance applies almost exclusively to defendants in tort cases. It can actually cover not only the defendant's own litigation costs but

[123]The same conclusion is reached by the Oxford group; see Oxford: Costs and Funding, supra note 8, [24]; Oxford: Comparative Study, supra note 8, III.103.

[124]This is confirmed by the Oxford group, see Oxford: Costs and Funding, supra note 8, [24]; Oxford: Comparative Study, supra note 8, III.102. For England, see Andrews, supra note 91, at 187.

[125]French Report IV.2.

[126]This usually gives the insurer a say in the selection of the attorney, often also in the litigation strategy, and sometimes even in whether and how to settle a case.

also, where the defendant loses and costs are shifted, liability for the victorious plaintiff's expenses.

Package-deal insurance distributes the litigation costs among all policy holders in the respective category and thus very widely. This keeps the price for coverage fairly low; after all, the number of actual lawsuits is relatively small compared to the number of policies written.

This kind of legal cost insurance is surprisingly common. It is available (in one form or another) in the majority of countries covered here and very popular in a number of them. In these jurisdictions, many middle-class members are thus protected against much of the financial risk of litigation inherent in everyday activities, such as driving a car, owning a home, or engaging in a profession or business.

10.4.2.2 Free-Standing Litigation Insurance

A less common but still fairly wide spread form is free-standing insurance for litigation costs. In many countries, individuals[127] can buy policies protecting them specifically against the financial risk of a lawsuit. In particular, losers are insured both for their own expenses and for having to pay the winner's. This coverage usually extends to both plaintiffs and defendants. Yet, it is mostly limited in two ways. First, it usually covers only certain types of cases – normally the kinds of litigation in which private individuals typically get involved: consumer, landlord-tenant, tort litigation, etc.; family law disputes may or may not be included.[128] Second, the benefits are often capped at a certain amount.

Such free-standing litigation insurance also distributes the cost risk among all policy holders and thus very broadly. Since it also applies to plaintiffs, i.e., the parties who decide to go to court,[129] it implies a higher risk than the merely defendant-oriented package-deal insurance. It is therefore more expensive. Still, the premiums are affordable for most middle-class individuals.[130]

As a result, free-standing litigation insurance is enormously popular in parts of Western Europe, especially where full cost-shifting makes litigation financially dicey. In Germany, almost half of the population (43%)[131] enjoys such coverage. It is also common in France[132] and Iceland, a "widespread industry" in Switzerland, "increasingly popular" in the Netherlands, and known in Belgium,[133] the United Kingdom, and Sweden. Thus, in such countries, the costs of much routine civil litigation are not necessarily borne by middle class individuals in person but rather collectivized through the insurance market.[134] Recent reform proposals encourage the introduction of such insurance for England and Wales as well.[135]

10.4.2.3 British After-the-Event Insurance

A very special form of insuring against litigation costs has developed in Britain. In sharp contrast to the more widespread kinds of litigation insurance (1. and 2.) which is bought *before* anything bad happens (and certainly before litigation is underway), British-style "after-the-event insurance" (ATE) is purchased *after* a dispute has arisen and in fact often even after a lawsuit has been filed. It usually works in tandem with – and it is best understood as a complement to – a "no win, no fee" agreement with one's own lawyer (infra. 10.4.4.2.), creating a "unique and bizarre system."[136]

Lawsuits entail a particularly great financial risk in the British environment of high litigation expenses, low cost predictability, and substantial fee shifting. The parties thus have a strong interest in insuring against the consequences of losing the case in two particular regards: against having to pay their own counsel, and against having to reimburse (at least much of) the opponent's expenses. Regarding the fee of their own lawyer, parties can protect themselves through a "no win, no

[127] This kind of insurance is not reported for businesses.

[128] In many systems, it covers not only civil litigation but also the costs of defending oneself against civil infraction and criminal charges (in practice most often for traffic violations).

[129] Under the respective policies, they usually have to clear that decision with the insurance company which will not provide coverage for bringing frivolous claims.

[130] This may be because the actual litigation rate is still relatively low. The French Report, e.g., states that despite great popularity of litigation insurance, only 2.4% of all new cases filed in 2007, and only ca. 2% of all civil litigation expenses, were actually covered by it, see French Report V.4.

[131] German Report V.4.; Gerhard Wagner, Litigation Costs Recovery – Tariffs and Hourly Fees in Germany, in Gottwald, supra note 11, at 171 fn. 69 cites 41.6% for 2007/2008.

[132] The French Report states that ca. 40% of all households are covered and that this percentage is growing fast, French Report V.4.

[133] Here, it is actually encouraged by tax breaks with a view to facilitate access to justice.

[134] As the Oxford group points out, litigation cost insurance can lower the holder's willingness to settle and thus adversely affect settlement rates, Oxford: Costs and Funding, supra note 8, [276]; Oxford: Comparative Study, supra note 8, IV.167.

[135] Jackson Review, supra note 10, 79.

[136] Peysner, supra note 78, at 137.

fee" agreement.[137] Regarding their liability for the other side's costs, they can protect themselves by buying ATE insurance to cover these costs (up to a certain amount). This insurance is typically bought (usually through their solicitor) at the outset of the litigation. The combination between a no-win-no-fee agreement and ATE insurance thus means that the losing party does not have to pay any attorney fees – its own lawyer receives none, and its opponent's is covered by ATE insurance.[138]

There is more good news, at least from the winner's side: if the case is won, the insured can usually shift the premium to the loser as part of the litigation expenses.[139] And if the case is lost, the insurance premium does not have to be paid at all as the insurer absorbs that risk.[140] Thus, the insured party cannot lose on litigation expenses. This raises concerns regarding fairness to the other party and has led to vociferous debates in the United Kingdom.[141] The Jackson Review thus recommends to render ATE premiums as well as success fees irrecoverable from the loser.[142]

Of course, there is bad news as well: premiums are very high and can easily reach 25% of the amount of coverage. This is so for two fairly obvious reasons. First, after-the-event insurance comes into play often (though not always) when litigation is a certainty so that the risk of cost liability is very high. Second, ATE insurance distributes litigation costs only among real (not merely *potential*) litigants, and even here only among the subset buying such coverage. This pool is much smaller, of course, than for other litigation insurance so that each insured's share of the risk is much higher. In combination with conditional fees, ATE insurance has thus been "the major contributor to disproportionate costs in civil litigation in England and Wales."[143]

10.4.3 Collective Actions: Banding Together

Parties can spread litigation expenses also without resorting to public legal aid or private insurance, i.e., by banding together: they can pursue their interests collectively and thus share the costs. This occurs overwhelmingly on the plaintiff side. Collective actions come in many forms, shapes, and sizes, and the details vary greatly depending on the legal system involved.[144] Roughly speaking, however, they can be put into three major categories: class actions, group actions, and suits by organizations representing collective interests.

10.4.3.1 Class Actions

The (by now) classic form of the class action is its United States variety in which one or several named plaintiffs represent the interests of a large number of similarly situated claimants who will all be bound by the final judgment or settlement unless they have opted out.[145] Similar class actions exist in Australia, Canada, Israel, and apparently also in Russia. In some other jurisdictions, class actions are available for very specific kinds of litigation, such as consumer rights in Brazil and Finland, securities actions in Korea, and actions by non-profit organizations in Sweden. In addition, there has lately been a lively discussion in the European Union and in many of its member states about introducing class actions in particular contexts, especially for consumer claims and antitrust violations.[146]

How exactly litigation costs and fees are allocated in class actions varies considerably across jurisdictions.[147] Under the United States approach and similar models, successful plaintiff attorneys receive (in some cases huge) legal fees which must, however, be approved by the court. These fees are usually charged on a contingency basis (see infra. 10.4.4.1.) and thus come out of the plaintiff's (collective) damage awards, in one form or another. This often results in wide cost

[137]To counterbalance that risk, the lawyer usually receives a success premium on top of his or her usual fee in case of victory.

[138]This is just a rough outline. The details vary greatly because the market offers different models tailored to various kinds of litigation and to the needs of the parties involved.

[139]This is normally permitted in England and Wales, but not in Scotland.

[140]In this regard, ATE insurance is highly similar to a contingency fee arrangment; the main difference is that the insurance company, rather than the plaintiff's lawyer, plays the role of litigation financer.

[141]See Peysner, supra note 78, 137–138; Oxford: Costs and Funding, supra note 8, [22]; Oxford: Comparative Study, supra note 8, III.115.

[142]Jackson Review, supra note 10, XVI, 87.

[143]Jackson Review, supra note 10, XVI.

[144]The situation in the United States is presented and compared with various European models by Samuel Issacharoff, Aggregating Private Claims, in Gottwald, supra note 11, 63–77. For an overview of the situation in Germany, see Astrid Stadler, Aggregate Litigation – Group/Class Actions in Germany, in Gottwald, supra note 11, 79–93.

[145]See especially Federal Rule of Civil Procedure 23.

[146]For an overview, see Matthias Casper, André Jansen, Petra Pohlmann and Reiner Schuler, Auf dem Weg zu einer europäischen Sammelklage (Munich 2009).

[147]In Finland, for example, they are borne by an ombudsman.

distribution among a very large number of claimants. In fact, individual plaintiffs usually do not pay anything out of pocket.[148]

10.4.3.2 Group Actions

The variety of group actions across jurisdictions is even more bewildering than the various forms of class actions. They range from German investor dispute groups which approximate class actions in some regards, to the English *Group Litigation Order*, to Austrian procedures in which consumers assign their rights to the group, and the Greek model which is essentially still a form of joinder of actions. In a similar vein, cost rules vary considerably: in Germany, group members bear the costs according to the relative value of their claims; in the Netherlands, group actions are financed by membership fees; in England and Wales, group members are severally liable for litigations costs, etc.

Yet, all these models have in common that by joining a group, plaintiffs share litigation costs with the other members through one mechanism or another. This enables plaintiffs to litigate their claims more economically than in an individual action. In fact, many such claims, especially in the consumer context, are too small to be pursued on an individual basis at all. In these cases, group actions work like class actions: by defraying litigation costs, they provide access to justice for holders of claims that could otherwise not be judicially enforced.

10.4.3.3 Organizations Pursuing Collective Interests

In a considerable number of jurisdictions, organizations can bring suits in the collective interest, especially to enforce rights of consumers. These suits are usually not for damages to the organization's members but rather pursue injunctive relief: prohibiting certain activities, remedying harmful situations, declaring standard contract clauses void, etc. The respective organizations are usually plaintiffs in their own right and, as such, subject to the general cost rules (i.e., potentially liable to the winner). In some jurisdictions, they are privileged, e.g., by not being liable for the defendant's expenses if they lose in Brazil, or by not having to pay court costs, as in Macau.

To be sure, the primary policy driving lawsuits by organizations acting in the public interest is to overcome the collective action problem. But these suits also spread the financial risks inherent in litigation among all those who finance the respective organizations, be they members or outside donors. Thus, such organization suits facilitate access to justice for claims that would not be brought if single (or a small group of) individuals had to bear the financial risks.

10.4.4 Success-Oriented Fees: Winners Pooling with Losers

By far most jurisdictions included here permit success-oriented lawyer fees in one form or another.[149] Such fees are mostly considered from an incentive perspective: if a lawyer's reward depends (in whole or in part) on the outcome of the case, the lawyer will work harder for the client because their interests align.[150] Sometimes, contingency fees in particular are also understood as a mechanism to provide access to justice: for better or worse, they allow suits by plaintiffs who could not pay for a lawyer if the fee were not taken out of the damages won. Beyond all that, however, success-oriented fees also facilitate access to justice more generally. In contrast to legal aid, litigation insurance, and class actions, they do so not by spreading costs to large numbers of potential or actual litigants but rather by shifting the financial burden to the party who can more easily bear it. Different versions of success-oriented fees accomplish this in slightly different forms.

[148] As is widely known, in many US-style class actions, successful plaintiffs themselves rarely gain much either. In many cases, their individual claims are very small (so that they could not be litigated individually); in others, the class action is really about going after a wrong-doer with little or no pay-out to the plaintiffs (as is typical in securities class actions). In some cases, however, individual plaintiffs may receive considerable benefit, e.g., in class actions for mass toxic torts.

[149] See also the overview provided by the Oxford group, Oxford: Costs and Funding, supra note 8, [132–133]; Oxford: Comparative Study, supra note 8, Appendix VI.

[150] At least with regard to contingency fees in the United States that is not necessarily so, as is well known. Lawyers may actually have an incentive to sell-out their clients' interests, e.g., if a quick settlement reaps substantial awards whereas obtaining more money for the client beyond that point may involve so much time that is not cost-efficient for the lawyer; see Michael Horowitz, Making Ethics Real, Making Ethics Work: A Proposal for Contingency Fee Reform, *Emory Law Journal* 44 (1995): 173.

10.4.4.1 Contingency Fees

Typically, a contingency fee has two characteristics: it is due only if the client wins (otherwise the lawyer gets nothing), and its size is tied to the amount won. Such *quota litis* arrangements are often considered a hallmark of the US-American legal system; they have also been much disparaged especially in continental Europe because giving a lawyer a direct financial interest in the outcome of the litigation appears unethical to many observers on the continent and elsewhere.[151] Yet, contingency fee arrangements are surprisingly common in many parts of the world. Of the jurisdictions surveyed here, almost half (14 out of 35) allow them in one form or another,[152] and the Jackson Review recently recommended that they be allowed in England and Wales as well.[153]

Through a contingency fee arrangement, parties insure themselves against two particularly bad risks: most importantly against having to pay one's lawyer although nothing was gained (the case was lost), and perhaps less importantly, against having to pay one's lawyer a lot although little was gained (the case was won but the result was meager). Parties, in fact usually plaintiffs, insure themselves against these risks by agreeing to pay a lot in case of victory but nothing in case of defeat. This helps both winning and losing plaintiffs to handle the financial risks of litigation for a simple reason: it is much more bearable, both financially and emotionally, to part with a share of the spoils if one wins than it is to pay for one's lawyer's work if one returns from court empty-handed.

10.4.4.2 No-Win-No-Fee Agreements

No-win-no-fee agreements (also known as conditional fee agreements) also make the lawyer's remuneration contingent on the outcome of the case but they differ from the typical contingency fee in that the size of the fee is not (at least not strictly) tied to the sum won (or saved).[154] No-win-no-fee agreements are also very common; they are allowed even in many jurisdictions that prohibit contingency fees, such as Australia, England, Wales, Scotland, Serbia, South Africa, and Venezuela.[155]

In terms of risk sharing, no-win-no-fee agreements work much like contingency fees but they protect only against the first of the two downside risks mentioned before, i.e., having to pay one's lawyer even though the case was lost.[156] The insurance premium essentially consists of paying much upon winning,[157] the benefit lies in owing nothing upon losing. Again, winners and losers form a risk pool which is based on the (at least implicit) understanding that the lucky shield the unlucky from having to suffer insult in addition to injury.

10.4.4.3 Success Premiums (Uplifts)

Success premiums are the mildest form of success-oriented fees. They are permitted in the large majority of the systems covered here (20 out of 35) and very popular in many of them. Jurisdictions often regulate them in various ways, e.g., by limiting them to a percentage of the overall fee.[158]

Success premium agreements are a mechanism of merely partial insurance against the downside risk of having to pay one's lawyer even in case of defeat. The insurance premium clients pay is lower than in the other cases (supra 1. and 2.) because it consists only of

---

[151] They thus remain prohibited in many jurisdictions, especially in Europe. See the long list of (more than a dozen) countries in Oxford: Costs and Funding, supra note 8, [25–26]; Oxford: Comparative Study, supra note 8, III.110.

[152] Canada (including, in practice, Quebec, even though Article 1783 of the Civil Code prohibits advocates from "acquiring litigious rights"), China, Finland (for special reasons only), Germany (as of recently and only as a last resort for access to justice), Greece, Iceland, Israel, Italy (as of recently), Japan, Korea, Mexico, Russia (at least in practice), Slovenia, Taiwan, and, of course, the United States. Oxford: Comparative Study, supra note 8, also reports them to be permitted in Estonia, Hungary, Lithuania, Slovakia, and Spain, id., III.110. Note that contingency fees are often capped by legislation (to a certain percentage) or judicially controlled under a reasonableness test.

[153] Jackson Review, supra note 10, 131–133.

[154] In contrast to contingency fee agreements, no-win-no-fee arrangements are also more common on both the plaintiff and the defendant side.

[155] At least in England, their introduction in 1990 and expansion in 1998 was an attempt by the government to compensate for the drastic cuts in public legal aid, i.e., a result of privatizing litigation funding, see Andrews, supra note 91, at 187.

[156] In other words, they do not protect against the risk of having to pay one's lawyer a lot although the gains were small. At least in theory, a client could still owe fees that render the victory pyrrhic.

[157] Since lawyers have to be paid for their work by someone, they must of course charge more (if they win half their cases, double) under a no-win-no-fee arrangement than otherwise.

[158] The Oxford group reports such caps for Australia, the Czech Republic, and England and Wales, Oxford: Costs and Funding, supra note 8, [25]; Oxford: Comparative Study, supra note 8, III.106.

the additional success fee; the coverage is also more limited because the client still owes the basic (and thus lower) fee win or lose. Even here, however, winners and losers pool the financial risk of litigation by paying extra for victory in order to buy some relief in case of defeat.

In summary, in the great majority of systems included here, success-oriented fees permit litigants (primarily plaintiffs) to shift the burden of having to pay their lawyers from losers to winners. This helps both sides because winners are more willing and able to bear this burden than losers. In all this, lawyers are, so to speak, the brokers for a system of insurance that protects against a major downside risk of litigation. With this protection, parties can face proceedings with somewhat greater equanimity and often gain access to justice they could otherwise not afford.

10.4.5 Outside Investment in Litigation: Sharing the Spoils

A final way of alleviating the financial risks of litigation is to let outside investors take over the case in return for a reward in case of success. While there are various strategies and several hybrids between them, two basic forms can be distinguished: assignment of claims and outside litigation funding.

10.4.5.1 Assignment of Claims

The more traditional strategy is to sell and assign a plaintiff's claim to another party which then pursues it in court. In this case, a new creditor replaces the old one and then sues in his own right. Jurisdictions vary with regard to whether, and to what extent, this is allowed. The civil law tradition has not had a problem with such assignments in principle,[159] although many countries forbid the sale of claims to an attorney.[160] The common law tradition, by contrast, long outlawed the assignment of claims, at least for litigation purposes.[161] Today, common law systems tend to allow the practice but usually continue to consider it illegal with regard to torts claims for personal injury (to the body, feelings, reputation, etc.) – here, only the victim him- or herself can sue. The same is true for the mixed jurisdictions of Israel and South Africa.[162] Legal systems worldwide also vary with regard to whether the sale and assignment of claims (as far as they are allowed) is common or rare.

The sale of a claim for litigation (or collection) purposes transfers the risks of a lawsuit from the assignor to the assignee. Of course, this is not free: the assignee purchases the claim only at a discount. In other words, the old creditor avoids the financial risks of litigation by transferring the difference between par value and discounted price to the new creditor.

This usually amounts to a cost distribution scheme among former creditors. The reason is that purchasers of claims (for litigation or collection purposes) normally buy them en masse knowing that they will win some and lose some, and that they charge the discount rate reflecting the average risk of success to all sellers. To put it differently, the risk is being collectivized among all sellers via the discount rate.

10.4.5.2 Outside Litigation Funding

A more recent strategy is to have the original creditor pursue the claim against the debtor but to bring in a third party to fund the litigation in return for a share in case of success.[163] While, from an enforcement perspective, an assignment strategy makes most sense for a large number of small claims (supra 1.), outside funding is primarily suited for large and

[159] See Wagner, supra note 131, at 172. Some civil law jurisdictions, however, apparently, forbid it, e.g., Korea, Norway, Serbia, Taiwan, and Turkey.

[160] This is indicated in the National Reports for Austria, Italy, Macau, Slovenia, Sweden, Switzerland, and Venezuela. The Reports for China and Switzerland also point out that the sale of just the right to sue is not allowed.

[161] See, for the development and current situation in the United States, the detailed analysis by Tony Sebok, "The Unauthentic Claim," *Vanderbilt Law Review* 64 (2010):61.

[162] Apparently not in Scotland, however.

[163] In recent years, the literature on third-party litigation funding has become a deluge; see, e.g., Michael Abramowitz, On the Alienability of Legal Claims, 114 Yale Law Journal 697 (2004); Isaac M. Marcushammer, Selling Your Torts, 33 Hofstra Law Review 1543 (2009); Marco de Marpurgo, "A Comparative Legal and Economic Approach to Third-Party Litigation Funding," *Cardozo Journal of International and Comparative Law* 19 (no. 2, spring 2011, forthcoming); Jonathan T. Molot, "A Market in Litigation Risk," *University of Chicago Law Review* 76 (2009): 367; M.J. Shukaitis, "A Market in Personal Injury Tort Claims," *Journal of Legal Studies* 16 (1987): 329; US Chamber Institute for Legal Reform, Selling Lawsuits, Buying Trouble: Third Party Litigation Funding in the United States (2009).

complex claims, i.e., for litigation that threatens to be costly but also promises to be rewarding. Such outside litigation funding began in Australia in the 1990s and then spread rapidly, first to other common law jurisdictions, such as Canada, England and Wales, and the United States; later, it also came to several civil law countries as well, such as the Netherlands, Austria, and Germany.[164] Especially in Australia and England, it has grown into an industry of impressive proportions.

Jurisdictions differ, once again, as to whether (and under which circumstances) outside litigation funding is permitted. The civil law tradition apparently has no problem with the phenomenon – perhaps simply because it has not much dealt with it, at least until recently.[165] The common law, by contrast, has traditionally prohibited "maintenance," i.e., third-party help provided for litigants. In most jurisdictions, this prohibition has been greatly relaxed, at least if the third party has a bona fide reason for getting involved. Still, "champerty," the subcategory of "maintenance" in which the third party aids the litigation in return for a share of the spoils in case of success, remains more contested. While some common law systems (e.g., several US states) continue to prohibit it,[166] there has recently been a liberalizing trend. Important signals came from England and Australia when courts overcame the categorical prohibition of "champerty" and allowed outside litigation funding in principle.[167] On the whole, there is little uniformity and much confusion about exactly what kinds of outside involvement in litigation is permitted in common law jurisdictions.[168]

Funding of litigation by outsiders is essentially an equity investment and works much like a contingency fee arrangement: in case of victory, the investor receives a percentage of the spoils; in case of defeat, the plaintiff pays nothing (and will usually be covered regarding his liability for the defendant's costs as well). Outside funding differs from a traditional contingency fee approach mainly in that the investor is not the plaintiff's lawyer but a separate commercial enterprise. This helps to make litigation funding tolerable to jurisdictions which are opposed to letting the litigants' attorneys have a direct financial (*quota litis*) stake in the case.

Like a contingency fee arrangement, outside litigation funding benefits plaintiffs in two principal ways: in return for sharing the prize, it insures them against having to pay potentially huge litigation costs even though the case was lost. And it provides access to justice for parties who cannot themselves fund, or stomach the financial risk, of large-scale, high-stakes litigation.

Outside litigation funding raises a lot of questions to which answers are still in short supply.[169] Whether it will establish itself as a more common and popular response to the high financial risks of complex civil litigation remains to be seen. Future trends will depend largely on whether an international market for such funding continues to develop, what alternative mechanisms will become available (e.g., class actions in continental Europe), and how regulators and courts will react.[170]

---

[164]This is confirmed by the Oxford group, Oxford: Costs and Funding, supra note 8, [27]; Oxford: Comparative Study, supra note 8, III.116. For an overview, see de Marpurgo, supra note 163 (ch. III.B.).

[165]The National Reports from the civil law jurisdictions either indicate that such funding is allowed or contain no response to this particular question; in France, the question is apparently being debated and no final conclusion has been reached; for an overview, see also de Marpurgo, supra note 163 (ch. V.B.). As Gerhard Wagner, supra note 131, at 172, remarked: "It is one of the enigmas of comparative civil procedure that the civil law with its hostility towards contingency fees, has no qualms with the assignment of claims and the funding of litigation through a third party whereas the common law allows contingency fees or at least success fees which involve the personal economic interest of the lawyer in the outcome of the litigation while it bans the promotion of litigation by third parties. It seems that the funding of litigation through outside investors is much more harmless, in terms of public policy, than to allow a lawyer to act, at the same time, as counsel and as entrepeneur operating with a portfolio of claims."

[166]Many (but not all) common law jurisdictions have made an exception for contingency fee agreements between parties and their lawyers.

[167]Giles v. Thompson (1994) AC 142 (England); Campbells Cash and Carry Pty. Ltd. v. Fostif Pty. Ltd., (2006) HCA 41; (2006) ALR 58 (Australia). For a detailed argument that the traditional common law restrictions have become dysfunctional and should thus be lifted, see Sebok, supra note 161.

[168]For an overview of the – highly fragmented – situation in the United States, see Sebok, supra note 161.

[169]Some of these questions are outlined in Oxford: Costs and Funding, supra note 8, [98–99]; Oxford: Comparative Study, supra note 8, III.118.–121.

[170]The Jackson Review, supra note 10, takes a favorable view, see id., 117–124.

10.5 In Conclusion: Grouping Cost and Fee Allocation Systems

One of the major dimensions of comparative law has long been to organize legal systems into groups, families or traditions. As is well known, such classifications are fraught with danger because they tend to oversimplify reality and are often biased in favor of traditional categories.[171] Still, grouping legal systems can be a valuable heuristic device as it can bring similarities and differences into sharper relief and thus provide a sense of how legal systems in the world relate to each other. This is particularly true if such groupings are undertaken in specific contexts, such as cost and fee rules, rather than in an all-encompassing fashion. It is therefore tempting to ask whether the jurisdictions surveyed here can be classified in a plausible manner from a cost allocation perspective.

10.5.1 Regional and Cultural Clusters?

One can indeed identify several regional or cultural clusters. Yet, it requires some temerity and is far from a perfect game. Some clusters are more plausible than others and some conceivable ones don't work out at all.

Perhaps the most plausible cluster consists of a large number of legal systems in Western and Central Europe which are centered around what Zweigert and Kötz labeled "The Germanic Legal Family"[172]: the German-speaking jurisdictions (Germany, Austria, Switzerland), the Netherlands in the West, the Scandinavian systems in the North, and the Central European countries in the East and South East; though geographically distant, Turkey is also part of this cluster. As far as they are covered here, these systems all embrace the loser-pays principle, shift both court costs and attorney fees (more or less completely), and assign judicial discretion a relatively weak role. It is not, however, a perfectly "Germanic" group because some countries clearly from outside of this tradition fulfill the same criteria (e.g., as of recently, Belgium).

By contrast, it is *not* plausible to speak of a "Romanistic Legal Family"[173] in cost and fee allocation matters. The differences among the members of this family are just too fundamental. In France, only the official (court, etc.) costs of civil procedure are allocated to the loser as a matter of law (other costs, especially attorney fees, are left to the judge's discretion); in Italy and Belgium, all costs are routinely shifted (as in the "Germanic" group, supra); in Spain, fee shifting is subject to a cap of 33% of the amount in controversy; etc. Here, diversity triumphs over similarity.

Beyond Europe, there are three other groups that are plausible according to the criteria employed here.

The first group consists of the members of the British Commonwealth tradition, i.e., England and Wales, Australia, and Canada (except Quebec) as well as the mixed jurisdictions of Israel, Scotland, and South Africa: the loser-pays principle prevails, both court costs and attorney fees are usually shifted, but judicial discretion plays a dominant role.

The second category comprises the East Asian legal systems of China, Japan, and Taiwan. They subscribe to the loser-pays rule; but they normally shift only court costs (i.e., not attorney fees); since statutory rules prevail, judicial discretion is fairly weak. Yet, the concept of an Asian legal systems group is somewhat problematic: while Korea fits in some regards, it differs from the other countries in that cost shifting includes attorney fees as well, albeit it only within statutorily defined limits.

Finally, there is, arguably, something that may be called an "Iberian tradition," encompassing Spain, Portugal, and many jurisdictions in Latin America. Here, the loser pays (in principle) all, i.e., both court costs and attorney fees; the latter, however, tend to be shifted only in part as they are often limited by varying percentages of the amount at stake or of the official (court) fees. And while there are statutory rules, judicial discretion plays a considerable role in the individual case. Yet, there are also some significant variations among the countries in this group[174] which may well cast into doubt whether it makes sense to conceive of such an "Iberian tradition."

[171] See Hein Kötz, "Abschied von der Rechtskreislehre?" *Zeitschrift für europäisches Privatrecht* 3 (1998): 493.

[172] Konrad Zweigert and Hein Kötz, *An Introduction to Comparative Law*, 3rd ed. trans. Tony Weir (Oxford: Clarendon Press, 1998): 132.

[173] Id., 74.

[174] For example, as mentioned in Mexico, there is no cost and fee shifting in commercial cases at all, and in Venezuela, cost shifting requires a perfect victory.

If these groupings are at least plausible hypotheses, they should eventually be tested by considering jurisdictions not covered here: e.g., the Baltic States and Hungary in continental Europe, Hong Kong and New Zealand in the British Commonwealth orbit, Vietnam and Cambodia in East Asia, as well as Argentina and Chile in Latin America[175]. If cost and fee allocation in these jurisdictions confirms the existence of the suggested groupings, search for explanations of the intra-group similarities would be in order. It would have to consider the historical connections, look for transplants from major exporting systems within the respective groups (Germany, England, Japan, Spain), and it should consider social, economic, and cultural factors. Such a search for explanations, however, requires a study in its own right and is beyond the scope of this Report.

10.5.2 Civil Law v. Common Law?

While dividing the world into a civil and a common law tradition was a staple of comparative law for most of the twentieth century, this approach has recently been much disparaged.[176] Today, it is almost generally accepted that such a wholesale division is too crude, too private law centered, too tied to outdated views of legal sources, and too blind to the prevalence of variously composed hybrid legal cultures, to serve as a *general* criterion for classifying the world's legal systems. The traditional dichotomy remains useful, however, within many more narrowly defined contexts. One such context is civil procedure. Here, the respective models continue to differ in their basic structures: on the civil law side, a sequential proceeding actively administered by a quasi civil-servant magistrate with the cooperation of the parties; in the common law tradition, a trial-oriented battle fought by the litigants in occasional interaction with a more passive, umpire-like judge. Despite many reforms on both sides, these traditions continue to cast a long shadow.[177]

Cost and fee allocation is an element of civil procedure. It is thus worth asking whether one can meaningfully distinguish a civil and a common law approach to this area. Note that in pursuing that question, what counts as a "civil" or a "common law" jurisdiction must be determined by looking at the respective systems' procedural structures.[178] In that sense, the majority of the jurisdictions covered here, i.e., the continental European, East Asian, and Latin American systems, belong to the civil law tradition; by contrast, the (former) British Commonwealth countries (Australia, Canada, England and Wales, India) and the United States form a common law group to which the mixed jurisdictions of Israel, Scotland, and South Africa can perhaps be added. So, do the similarities and differences in cost and fee allocation we have recorded reflect such a grouping?

From most of the perspectives considered in this Report, the answer is no. Certainly, the acceptance (vel non) of the loser-pays principle does not depend on membership in this or that group: it is true that all civil law systems embrace a loser-pays rule, but so do the clear majority of common law jurisdictions (i.e., all except the United States and arguably India). Certainly, whether only court costs or also attorney fees are shifted has nothing to do with the traditional categories: most

[175] A preliminary look at data available in Platto, supra note 7, and various national reports solicited by the authors of the Oxford Study, supra note 8, suggests that at least the first and third groupings envisaged here make sense. With regard to a Central and Eastern continental European group, Bulgaria, Denmark, Estonia, Hungary, Latvia and Romania all embrace the loser-pays principle and shift both court costs and attorney fees; yet, it appears that in some of these jurisdictions, especially in Denmark and Hungary, judicial discretion does play a fairly significant role. In a similar vein, the information available about further (former) British commonwealth members Hong Kong, New Zealand, Singapore, and also Ireland is compatible with such a grouping; again, however, the role of judicial discretion is apparently weaker in some of these jurisdictions (such as Hong Kong) than in others (such as Ireland).

[176] For a search for an alternative approach, see Ugo Mattei, "Three Patterns of Law: Taxonomy and Change in the World's Legal Systems," *American Journal of Comparative Law* 45 (1997): 5.

[177] Even though the major reform of the English civil justice system in 1998 has shifted much control over the course of litigtion from the parties (and their counsel) to the court, the impact of the reform on the ground has apparently been fairly limited; in particular, it has done little to bring the costs of litigation under control, see Adrian Zuckerman, Court Case Management in England and the Civil Procedure Rules 1998, in Gottwald, supra note 11, 1–13; Peysner, supra note 78, 146–147.

[178] In other words, it does not matter for present purposes what other, traditional criteria suggest, such as the influence of Roman (private) law, the role of codification (and statutes) versus case law, or the emphasis on a more theoretical versus a more practice-oriented legal education.

civil law systems shift both but some do not (China, Japan, Taiwan, and, in a sense, France), and the same is true on the common law side (cf. the United States). Nor does the role of judicial discretion necessarily turn on a jurisdiction's membership in the civil or common law group: while judicial discretion is more pervasive in common law systems, its role is also strong in France, i.e., at the very heart of the civil law culture, and it is a considerable factor in several Latin countries. One cannot even say that the degree of compensation (full v. partial) distinguishes the two groups: to be sure, in many common law and mixed jurisdictions, cost shifting is often incomplete, but that is also true for quite a few civil law systems, such as France or Portugal; in fact, a winner is likely to fare much better in Britain, where in practice most costs are allocated to the loser, than in Greece, where the shiftable amounts of attorney fees are woefully low.

Yet, there are two features that do distinguish civil law systems on the one hand from common law jurisdictions on the other – at least in the sense of general tendencies: the absolute amount of lawyer fees, and their predictability. Since, as we have seen,[179] lawyer fees usually constitute the lion's share of litigation expenses, these are matters of considerable practical importance.

First, it appears that lawyer fees for litigation are, on the whole, higher in the common law than in the civil law systems.[180] This is not because common lawyers charge more per hour than their civilian colleagues[181] but because they do more work when litigating a case – for a more general and a more particular reason.[182] In general, in the more lawyer-driven common law procedure, attorneys have to do a lot of the driving that is performed by the judge in a civil law court. In particular, the different approaches to fact-gathering tend to generate more billable hours in a common law than in the civil law proceeding: not only is common-law style discovery operated by counsel rather than by the judge, it is also by its very nature much more labor-intensive than civil law-style evidence taking[183] – and thus a lot costlier.[184] Small wonder then that complaints about disproportionate lawyer fees are more frequently heard in the common law than in the civil law camp.[185]

Second, the amount of lawyer fees generated by litigation is more predictable in civil law jurisdictions than in common law systems. With regard to about half of the civil law countries surveyed here, this is straightforward: these countries determine (at least the shiftable amount of) lawyer fees under an official schedule (usually tied to the amount in controversy); as a result, one can predict the amount imposed upon the loser with fair accuracy. By contrast, the common law systems included here *all* leave the pricing of lawyer services to the market and then control fee shifting by judicial discretion; as a result, predicting of the how much the loser will have to pay is inevitably a matter of more or less informed guessing.[186] But even in civil law jurisdictions without an official schedule, lawyer fees may well be more predictable than in the common law world. The reason is that in the civil law, the amount of ultimate lawyer fees is

[179] Supra 10.3.2.

[180] Ilmer, supra note 97, at 307, confirms this with regard to England, though without further references.

[181] Hourly rates range widely across both civil and common law jurisdictions, see Oxford: Comparative Study, supra note 8, Appendix III.

[182] As the National Reporter for the United States pointed out in his comments on the Draft General Report, there is – at least arguably – an additional reason, i.e., the different degrees of legal certainty in civil and common law systems: where the law is less certain, it takes more work to decide cases. The hypothesis of significantly differing legal certainty between civil and common law, however, is difficult to generalize and even more difficult to verify. It is true though that in the United States, the high degree of private law fragmentation in the federal system (where most private law is left under the legislative and judicial jurisdiction of the states) diminishes the degree of legal certainty and often increases the legal complexity of disputes.

[183] See supra 10.3.2.; Langbein, supra note 76. To be sure, the extent of permissible discovery varies hugely among common law systems with the United States presenting an extreme case. Yet, even under more restrictive approaches, as in the England and Wales, fact-gathering is usually more labor-intensive than in civil law jurisdictions.

[184] In his comment on the Draft General Report, the National Reporter for the United States proffered an additional argument: in common law countries, the bar tends to have greater control over the litigation system than in civil law countries where the state is more directly involved; the bar thus serves its own interests with less restraint in the former than in the latter.

[185] Supra note 143 and text; see also Jackson Review, supra note 10, 36–39 ("proportionate costs"); Zuckerman, supra note 77, at 14; Andrews, supra note 90, 188–189; Peysner, supra note 78, 145–146.

[186] There are exceptions. In England and Wales, for example, certain cases are handled under a fixed fee, see supra 98; US-style contingency arrangements also make the fee quite predictable, albeit only in terms of a percentage of the amount eventually won (if any).

less dependent on how a case evolves than in the common law – and thus more predictable. This is, again, due to the fact that lawyers are less involved in a civil law proceeding than in a common law litigation. If a case drags on or becomes complex in a civil law court, much of the resultant work will be done by the judge, and that work is already paid for in form of the predetermined court fee[187]; in addition, fact gathering will normally stay within comparatively narrow limits and thus entail fairly moderate cost. By contrast, if a case drags on or becomes complex in a common law court, the lawyers will have to do almost all the resultant work which will translate into fast-growing fees; in particular, discovery can become very time-consuming and thus drive the lawyers' bills to dizzying heights. In short, the chance that lawyer fees spiral out of control as a case evolves is much smaller in a civil law proceeding than in a common law litigation. That keeps the ultimate amount of lawyer fees – at least somewhat – more predictable in Brazil, China or Spain than in Australia, England or the United States.[188]

The magnitude and predictability of attorney fees matter when it comes to allocating them between the parties. Shifting higher fees to the loser is a bigger deal and thus requires more deliberation and circumspection; and the higher the fee, the greater the temptation to shift it only in part. Shifting unpredictable fees raises serious fairness concerns because predictability is one of the hallmarks of due process[189]; and the greater the unpredictability, the greater the need for ex post judicial control. As a result, systems that generate higher attorney fees at lower predictability must struggle harder with shifting them from winner to loser.

To end on a provocative note, one can perhaps say that at least among the common law jurisdictions, the United States has got it right after all: if lawyer fees are unregulated, unpredictable, and high, shifting them to the loser is so fraught with problems that it is better not to undertake it at all.

[187]Court fees do not present a predictability issue because virtually everywhere, they are determined by law in precise amounts tied to the amount at controversy and/or the stage reached by the case.

[188]The greater predictability of lawyer fees in the civil law world is also indicated by the willingness of the various National Reporters to predict the litigation costs in certain kinds of cases. While a clear majority of Reporters from civil law jurisdictions provided numbers, a clear majority of Reporters from common law systems refused to do so because the uncertainty was just too great. Of course, one must not overrate these reactions because much depends on the individual Reporters' willingness to venture a guess (several Reporters from civil law jurisdictions also refused to provide a good faith estimate because too much depends on the circumstancs of the case). Still, it is noteworthy that Reporters even from civil law jurisdictions without official fee schedules apparently felt by and large more comfortable to provide good faith estimates than their common law colleagues. If attorney fees are by and large *considered* more predictable in the civil law systems, this may well reflect that they actually are.

[189]See Burger King Corp. v. Rudzewicz, 471 U.S. 462, 471–72 (1985); World-Wide Volkswagen Corp. v. Woodson, 444 U.S. 286, 297 (1980).

Climate Change and the Law[1]

11

Erkki J. Hollo

11.1 General Remarks

Climate law ranges in the structure of the present Conference under environmental law, agricultural law and to some extent economic environmental law. Ecology in the broad sense of natural processes has a tight relationship with economy and economically oriented administrative tools. Basically many modes of mechanisms which have been introduced to protect the human environment have an economical ground.

The report is based on a questionnaire which is composed of several parts. In the beginning there is a presentation of the reported states and their empirical status under the focus of climate change. The next part deals with main ideology and international sources of climate law, adapted to the national legal system in question. The following part addresses issues concerning national energy and CO_2 policies in terms of the use of renewable sources, recycling of relevant waste, forest management and other. The next part analyzes questions related to the set of legal, economic and political instruments practiced in the legal context, describing also their supranational basis. The last main part focuses on adaptation issues, especially the policies planned or adopted to combat effects caused by global warming.

Altogether, this general report intends to give a picture of the concept and structure of "climate law" – whether it at all is a fruitful basis of organizing legal topics – and specifically to compare national choices of instruments which have been adopted to manage greenhouse gas (GHG) emissions. One aspect is also important for the future, namely how to adapt permanently human activities and needs to the consequences of climate change.

National reports have arrived from following states and regions:

Argentina (reporters: Professors Marcelo Lopez Alfonsin and Alberto)
Australia (reporters: Professors Alex Gardner, David Hodgkinson and Sharon Mascher)
Belgium (reporter: Professor Dr. L. Lavrysen)
Czech Republic (reporter: Professor DrSc. Milan Damohorský)
Finland (reporters Dr. of Law Robert Utter, Associate and Dr. of Law Eero Nordberg)
Germany (reporter: Professor Dr. Hans-Joachim Koch)
Ireland (reporter: Professor Rónán Kennedy)
Israel (reporter: Professor Richard Laster)
Italy (reporters: Professor Dr. Barbara Pozzo and Prof. Giampiero di Plinio)
Japan (reporter: Professor of Law Narumi Hasegawa)
Netherlands (reporter: Professor Dr. Marjan Peeters)
Norway (reporter Professor Hans Christian Bugge)
Poland (reporter: Professor Marek Górski)
Portugal (reporter: Professor Dr. Alexandra Aragão)
Scotland (reporter: Professor Colin T. Reid)
Slovenia (reporter: PhD candidate LL.M. Petra Ferk)
Spain (reporter: Professor of Civil Law Pablo Amat-Llombart)
Taiwan (reporters: Assistant Professor Yen-Lin Agnes Chiu, and PhD Candidate Anton Ming-Zhi Gao)
United States (reporter: Professor Margaret Rosso)

[1] II.D., Changement climatique et la loi.

E.J. Hollo (✉)
Faculty of Law, University of Helsinki, P.O. Box 4, FI 00014 Helsinki, Finland
e-mail: erkki.hollo@helsinki.fi

K.B. Brown and D.V. Snyder (eds.), *General Reports of the XVIIIth Congress of the International Academy of Comparative Law/Rapports Généraux du XVIIIème Congrès de l'Académie Internationale de Droit Comparé*, DOI 10.1007/978-94-007-2354-2_11, © Springer Science+Business Media B.V. 2012

11.2 Section A: Prevention and Management

11.2.1 Part I: Introduction

11.2.1.1 Reasons for Legal Concern

In the first part the intention is to find out to what extent legal orders identify issues related to elements of climate law. Climate is by nature an inconstant system which is far beyond national competences and also beyond scientific knowledge. In that sense climate change in terms of law (climate law) would imply that certain elements of climatic systems and subsystems are connectable to human activities and living conditions. The "natural" part of climate change is to some extent predictable in terms of planetary cycles but here it might be less wise to try to interfere. So, political and consequently legal instruments are still under development and since greenhouse gases are not "pollutants" or even dangerous to mankind, traditional environmental thinking may not be vital or satisfactory. We need more. This makes "climate law", whatever it means, a complex system of strategies and rule which apply to most areas of economy, trade, energy and settlement.[2]

Since the questionnaire has been spread globally, states may belong to different legal and political regimes, others again may have a strong common unifying structure (European Union, EU). There are varieties in the ways the states coordinate the control of GHG emissions with general air pollution measures. The reported states show differences in terms of their governmental structure depending on whether they are centralized or federal states. For some states supranational community law may be relevant (EU, MERCOSUR).

The UN Framework Convention on Climate Change, adopted at the 1992 Rio Earth Summit and in force from March 21, 1994, was designed to achieve "stabilization of greenhouse gas concentrations in the atmosphere at a level that would prevent dangerous anthropogenic interference with the climate system." Parties committed themselves, among other things, to prepare and submit national inventories of GHG emissions and sinks, establish national programs and take measures to mitigate and to adapt to climate change. For developed countries, the goal was to reduce greenhouse gas (GHG) emissions to 1990 levels by the year 2000, but this goal was not legally binding. GHGs are a major cause of climate change. Most important among the GHGs of international concern are carbon dioxide (CO_2), methane (CH_4), nitrous oxide (N_2O), hydrofluorocarbons (HFCs), perfluorocarbons (PFCs), and sulfur hexafluoride (SF_6). Some GHGs, including water vapor and ozone (O_3), occur naturally. Some others are emitted and sequestered by plant or animal respiration and seasonal vegetative cycles. According to scientific studies human activities produce or sequester additional quantities of these gases and affect atmospheric concentrations.

The United Nations Framework Convention on Climate Change (UNFCCC), signed at the Rio Summit 1992, sets an overall framework for intergovernmental efforts to tackle the challenge posed by climate change. The Convention entered into force on 21 March 1994. It recognizes that the climate system is a shared resource whose stability can be affected by industrial and other emissions of carbon dioxide and other greenhouse gases. The Convention enjoys near universal membership, with 192 countries having ratified. Under the Convention, governments shall:

(1) gather and share information on greenhouse gas emissions, national policies and best practices,
(2) launch national strategies for addressing greenhouse gas emissions and adapting to expected impacts, including the provision of financial and technological support to developing countries and
(3) cooperate in preparing for adaptation to the impacts of climate change.

The ultimate objective of the Convention (Art. 2) is to achieve stabilization of greenhouse gas concentrations in the atmosphere at a level that would prevent dangerous anthropogenic interference with the climate system. The reference to the term "dangerous" implies that the prevention of non-severe damage is not part of the UNFCCC framework. Having this in mind, one may ask how far the precautionary principle should reach in terms of obligations for states. On the other hand ambitious and conscious national or regional policies are free to consider how to address scientifically

[2] Since the national reports were prepared mostly during the winter 2009/2010, the latest features of development are not included in those presentations. By setting the policy in the EU of not exceeding 2°C, some reporters see this is an allowance for increasing warming correspondingly. In Copenhagen more stringent limits were proposed but not adopted. Setting the degree limit would in any case be followed up a later review eventually in 2015.

not proved risks. It is rational that states which are not under an imminent threat of changes or disasters due to climate change are not keen to go further than a minimal international commitment would lead to. Islands and low situated countries used to floods and storms surely have a different position. Changes in aquatic and terrestrial ecosystems can be linked to regional climate changes, especially higher temperatures, and other effects on agriculture, forestry, and human health may be related to climate change.

The Intergovernmental Panel on Climate Change (IPCC) came about with the objective to research and to justify practicable models for the mitigation of climate change. According to the IPCC global average air temperatures are rising; 11 of the last 12 years were among the 12 warmest years since 1850. Global average ocean temperatures have increased; sea levels are rising; snow and ice cover have decreased; permafrost is thawing (releasing stored carbon and methane); and precipitation has increased significantly in some areas, with decreases in others. Since climate change is a global problem, coherent international action should equally or with the similar efficiency cover all human activities and areas.

On the other hand the appearance of climate change varies dramatically without scientific evidence of connection to specific human activities. Every country which is not supporting common action is a free-rider and eventually benefits from measures taken by other states. Precaution is therefore an important approach which dominates also the work of the IPCC. The problem for responsible leaders of states is: how far can we burden our citizens with costs for measures which later on may have a wrong basis for calculations. Precaution is therefore strongly connected to political awareness, not only regionally but globally. The IPPC tries to fix numbers for the need of reduction of GHG emissions with the motivation that the reduction based on precaution is directly linked with the protection of mankind. So, a precautionary emission reduction of 25–40% in 2020 is given as a policy goal for developed countries.

Scientists have identified human activities as the major cause of global warming. According to the IPCC, global emissions of GHGs from human activities increased 70% between 1970 and 2004. In comparison with pre-industrial values established in 1750, the "net effect of human activities since 1750 has been one of warming," and human activities (especially use of fossil fuels and agriculture) have increased global atmospheric concentrations of CO_2, CH_4 and N_2O significantly. Without significant improvements in climate change policies and practices, GHG emissions are predicted to increase in the next decades, and warming is projected to continue at the rate of about 0.2°C (0.36°F) per decade.

The text of the Kyoto Protocol to the UNFCCC was adopted at the third session of the Conference of the Parties (COP 3) in Kyoto, Japan, in 1997; it was open for signature from 16 March 1998 to 15 March 1999. By that date the Protocol had received 84 signatures. Today the number of ratifications and approvals is 164. Those Parties that have not yet signed the Kyoto Protocol may accede to it at any time. The Protocol is subject to ratification, acceptance, approval or accession by Parties to the Convention. It entered into force on 16 February 2005 which was the ninetieth day after at least 55 Parties to the Convention deposited their instruments of ratification, acceptance, approval or accession. These parties incorporated Annex I Parties which accounted in total for at least 55% of the total carbon dioxide emissions for 1990 from that group.

There are a number of declarations in connection with the ratification of the Protocol. The European Community declares that its quantified emission reduction commitment under the Protocol will be fulfilled through action by the Community and its Member States within the respective competence of each and that it has already adopted legal instruments, binding on its Member States, covering matters governed by the Protocol. Later on the EU has adopted a treaty in order to share the burden of emission quota among the Member States.

China declared inter alia: "In accordance with the provisions of Article 153 of the Basic Law of the Hong Kong Special Administrative Region of the People's Republic of China of 1990, the Government of the People's Republic of China decides that the United Nations Framework Convention on Climate Change and the Kyoto Protocol to the United Nations Framework Convention on Climate Change shall apply to the Hong Kong Special Administrative Region of the People's Republic of China. The United Nations Framework Convention on Climate Change continues to be implemented in the Macao Special Administrative Region of the People's Republic of China. The Kyoto Protocol to the United Nations Framework Convention on Climate Change shall not apply to the Macao Special Administrative Region of the People's Republic of China until the Government of China notifies otherwise."

In the United States the position was marked by political fear of economic losses. According to the reporter, noting that emissions from developing countries were expected to exceed those of developed countries by 2015, the Senate stated that "the exemption for Developing Country Parties is inconsistent with the need for global action on climate change and is environmentally flawed." The Senate feared "serious harm" to the US economy from "significant job loss, trade disadvantages, [and] increased energy and consumer costs." The US signed the Kyoto Protocol, but it was never sent to the Senate for advice and consent. In 2001, President George W Bush according to the report rejected the Protocol, calling it "fatally flawed in fundamental ways" and "unrealistic" and citing issues of cost, competitiveness, and exemptions for developing countries. In the ensuing years, the US government has addressed climate change. A 2002 proposal set a national goal to reduce GHG intensity by 18% in 10 years through existing programs, voluntary initiatives, and tax incentives, as well as expanded policies for cleaner fuels, energy efficiency, and carbon sequestration. In 2007, the administration promoted low-emissions technologies to meet energy demand and mitigate climate change. In 2008, US officials announced a new national goal – applying incentives to stop growth of GHG emissions by 2025.

The Climate Change Conference in Copenhagen in December 2009 was intended to lead to the adoption of global commitments concerning the target to restrict the warming level to 2 C. This legal commitment was required to save the procedure which was initiated in the Kyoto Protocol. The goal which was in line with the scientific results of the IPCC was strongly supported by the EU and some of its Member States. The political consensus reached in this direction at the Conference led to the expectation that serious measures will not be taken by all Parties involved. In June 2010 some progress in terms of commitment was achieved in the negotiations of Bonn and further efforts will follow before the end of 2010. The present worldwide lack of economic and also political security may slow down the expectations.

11.2.1.2 States' Position in the International Framework

Classification of UNFCCC States

In order to clarify the extent of climate related regulatory instruments national reporters were asked to describe the main national political and legal decisions in two relations, namely first in the general relation of the state to EC Community Law, other Community or regional Law, secondly to the specific position of the state to the UN Climate Change Framework Convention 1992 and the Kyoto protocol. Third and if relevant, the reporters were asked for the reasons of full or partial reluctance to participate in either the UNFCCC or the Kyoto as well as the follow ups of protocols or Conferences of Parties (COP).

Within the framework of the Kyoto Protocol, Parties to UNFCCC are classified as (underlined states have been reported):

- Annex I countries which are industrialized countries and economies in transition (Australia, Austria, Belarus, Belgium, Bulgaria, Canada, Croatia, Czech Republic, Denmark, Estonia, Finland, France, Germany, Greece, Hungary, Iceland, Ireland, Italy, Japan, Latvia, Liechtenstein, Lithuania, Luxembourg, Monaco, Netherlands, New Zealand, Norway, Poland, Portugal, Romania, Russian Federation, Slovakia, Slovenia, Spain, Sweden, Switzerland, Turkey, Ukraine, United Kingdom (Scotland), United States of America).
- Annex II countries which includes developed countries which pay for costs of developing countries (Australia, Austria, Belgium, Canada, Denmark, Finland, France, Germany, Greece, Iceland, Ireland, Italy, Japan, Luxembourg, Netherlands, New Zealand, Norway, Portugal, Spain, Sweden, Switzerland, United Kingdom, United States of America).

The European Union is member of both annexes I and II.

- Developing countries (non-annex countries, as reported): Argentina, Israel, Slovenia, Taiwan.

Annex I countries have ratified the Protocol and they are committed to reduce their emission levels of greenhouse gases to targets that are mainly set below their 1990 levels. They do this mainly by allocating reduced annual allowances to major operators within their borders. Operators within the system may exceed their allocations only if they acquire emission allowances or participate in one of the mechanisms under Kyoto as agreed by all the parties to UNFCCC. Annex II countries are designed as a sub-group of the Annex I countries. The group covers members of the OECD as well as economies in transition in 1992. Developing countries are not required to reduce emission levels unless developed countries supply enough funding and technology.

The UNFCCC did not set direct obligations but declared the following basic notions. The purpose of the UNFCCC in obtaining reductions of greenhouse gases is to avoid restrictions on development of states, because emissions are strongly linked to industrial capacity. The states can sell emissions credits to other states whose operators have difficulty in meeting their emissions targets. States can also get economic profit and advanced technologies for low-carbon investments from Annex II countries. Developing countries are entitled to volunteer and become Annex I countries when they are sufficiently developed. These principles were later concretized as the three Kyoto mechanisms. These are emission trading, joint implementation and clean mechanisms.

State Regimes and Political Position

Since states have a different status in terms of the classifications under the UNFCCC and the Kyoto protocol, basic information was collected about the international position of the reported states. The Member States of the EU have ratified the founding or constitutional treaties of the Community (especially Rome 1957, Maastricht 1992 and Lisbon 2007). The transposition of the treaties between the parties has taken place by national legislation and thus Community law becomes part of national regimes. The EU holds in principle a competence of guidance which is binding for its Member States. Additionally, some Member States go further or have chosen different and more efficient ways of combating air emissions. Under the EU Emissions Trading Directive of 13 October 2003 the Member States were required to establish a system to allow industrial facilities to trade emissions allowances.[3]

Certain regions of states may have self governmental competences as is the case in the United Kingdom and the United States. On the other hand Taiwan has not acquired full sovereignty in international relations but it has developed an independent regime for environment and climate. In European federal states like Germany, Belgium and Spain, the additional question is basically about the division of competences at the state and federal levels. As a curiosity, under the EU burden-sharing agreement (Decision 2002/358/EC), the reduction target for Belgium is 7.5%. The EU burden sharing was followed by an intra-Belgian burden sharing. According to an agreement of March 2004, the Flemish region has a target of – 5.2%, the Walloon region – 7.5% and the Brussels Capital Region +3.475%. To comply with the international/EU reduction target, the federal government, in turn, has to take emission reduction measures within its competence of 4.8 million tons of CO_2-eq and to buy on the international market emission credits covering an emission of 12.3 million tons of CO_2-eq in the period 2008–2012 (a yearly average of 2.46 million tons).

The formal commitment of states and regions to the UNFCCC and the Kyoto Protocol is reported as follows. Both documents have been signed and ratified by Argentina, Belgium, Finland, Germany, Ireland, Israel, Italy, Japan, the Netherlands, Poland, Portugal, Slovenia and the United Kingdom (reported for Scotland). The United States is party to the UNFCCC but has not so far ratified the Kyoto Protocol. Taiwan, due to indicated reasons, is not formally a party to the documents but it has participated in the negotiations and conferences within the framework of an institutional body (Industrial Technology Research Institute, ITRI). It makes efforts of reaching formal admission to the UNFCCC.

The European Community

Belgium is a founding member of the European Community. On the federal level, there is a Federal Government, a Federal Parliament (with two Chambers), a Federal Administration and different federal institutions, such as the Federal Planning Bureau or the Federal Agency for Nuclear Control. The Communities and Regions are invested with legislative power equal to that of the federal legislature.

The Czech Republic, originally as part of Czechoslovakia, joined the European Union in 2004. The Republic acceded to the UNFCCC in 1991 and signed the Kyoto Protocol in 1998; the ratification process for the Protocol was completed in 2001. The state submitted the First National Communication to the Secretariat of the Convention in 1994 with later reviews, the last one in 2001.

Finland joined the European Union in 1995. In 1994 the state became member of the European Economic Area. The state is structured as a central governmental regime.

[3] Directive 2003/87/EC of the European Parliament and the Council of 13 October 2003 establishing a scheme for greenhouse gas emission allowance trading within the Community and amending Council Directive 96/61/EC.

Municipalities have self-governmental power e.g. in land use planning and regional development. The province of the Åland Islands has autonomy and legislative competences in regional matters.

Germany is a founding member of the European Community. The legislative competences are shared between the federal level (Bund) and the States (Länder). The responsibility for international commitments lies mainly with the Bund. Germany was an early starter in efforts to specify emission reduction commitments under the Framework Climate Change Convention and in pursuing what were at the time ambitious reduction targets of its own: the Federal German government aimed to cut greenhouse gas emissions from German sources by 25% by 2005 based on 1990 levels. Subsequent to the Kyoto Protocol, Germany has under the EU burden-sharing scheme agreed to reduce its greenhouse gas emissions by 21% during the period 2008–2012 compared with 1990 levels. This target will be met.

Ireland entered the European Community in 1973. Ireland is a party to the UN Framework Convention on Climate Change and has ratified the 1997 Kyoto Protocol. Under the Kyoto Protocol, Ireland is listed as an Annex 1 party thereby requiring a reduction in Green House Gas emissions during the period 2008–2012. Europe negotiated a special 'bubble' to redistribute the targets requiring an overall reduction of 8%.[4] Under the Burden Sharing Agreement, which divided the obligations among Member States, Ireland is allowed an increase of 13% on 1990 levels.[5]

Italy is a founding member of the European Community. Italy has signed both the UN Climate Change Framework Convention and the Kyoto Protocol. The Kyoto Protocol has been ratified in 2002. The Italian Government has considerably delayed the concrete implementation of the above-mentioned Law, perhaps in the wrong belief that the Kyoto Protocol would have never entered into force. According to the report, notwithstanding the mandatory character of EC law, Italy's attitude towards EC Community environmental law is generally of scarce awareness of what is going on at the EC level. The implementation of EC directives in the environmental field into national law is generally late and characterized by limited comprehension of the important implications on the long run for Italian citizens and business.

The Netherlands, founding member of the European Community, is a party to the UNFCCC (ratified in 1993) and the Kyoto Protocol (ratified in 2002). The reporter claims that the international and European climate dossier has become already extensive and complex, and it is already quite a task to understand the core characteristics, let alone the details of these two legal frameworks.

Poland and Slovenia entered the EU in 2004, Portugal and Spain in 1986.

The United Kingdom (not reported directly) is as a member of the EU and also individually as state a full party to the UNFCCC. It has adopted its first Climate Change Program in 1994.[6] The UK also has ratified the Kyoto Protocol. In allocating responsibility for the EU's collective target of a reduction of greenhouse gas emissions by 8% from 1990 levels the UK's target was 12.5%. The UK's emissions were 18.4% below the 1990 levels in 2007 and are predicted to reach about 23% below those levels by 2010,[7] achieving reductions well in excess of the target.

Scotland is a regional autonomous unit of the United Kingdom, and as such part of the European Union (UK entered the EEC in 1973), but Scotland has since 1999 its own Parliament and Government which have responsibility for many areas of law and policy. The areas of devolved authority include the environment, but exclude most energy matters, while key mechanisms for delivering policy, such as most taxes, are subject to control at the UK level. Scotland is responsible for implementing EU provisions within its area of competence, but all negotiations and agreements at European and international levels are in the hands of the UK government. Climate law thus cuts across the division of responsibilities between Edinburgh, London and the EU.

Other States

Argentina, as a Party to the MERCOSUR (Common Market between the Argentine Republic, the Federal

[4] http://unfccc.int/kyoto_protocol/items/2830.php.

[5] Vinay Ganga, and Simon Armitage, "The Kyoto Protocol, Carbon Credit Trading and their Impact on Energy Projects in Europe and the World," *International Energy Law and Taxation Review* 4: 73.

[6] Climate Change: the UK Programme (Cm 2427, 1994).

[7] Department of Climate Change, The UK's Fifth National Communication under the United Nations Framework Convention on Climate Change (2009).

Republic of Brazil, the Republic of Paraguay and the Republic of Uruguay) participates actively in the development of climate law and adopts it according to effective procedures in force. The MERCOSUR ranges under the Kyoto regime of developing States.

Australia is not a Member State of the EU or any other Community. Thus there is no regional or Community Law which affects the operation of domestic law in Australia. Australia signed and ratified the UNFCCC in 1992. While Australia signed the Kyoto Protocol in 1998, it did not ratify the Protocol until 2007 due to political dispute. One argument was that the Protocol would unfairly hurt the Australian economy, which is heavily reliant on coal for both domestic energy and export income, while countries like India and China were not bound by targets. This position did not change until a Labor Government was elected in November 2007.

Israel is not participating in the climate policy of the EU. Instead, it is interested in being active member within the OECD.

Japan is a centralized state without any political commitment in international communities which might limit sovereignty of the State. According to the Constitution, international treaties where Japan is party must be faithfully observed.

Norway is not member of the EU but of the European Economic Area (EEA). The EEA consists of the 27 EU members plus Norway, Iceland, and Liechtenstein. It means that Norway is party to the EU 'internal market'. Most of EU's secondary legislation in the fields of energy, environment, and climate applies to Norway through the EEA Agreement and has been implemented in Norwegian law. Norway is party to both the UNFCCC and the Kyoto protocol.

Taiwan strives for remaining in accord with global trends and standards. Due to problems in getting recognition of its claims for sovereignty, Taiwan is not formally party to international bodies. The controversies are unsolved since its withdrawal from the United Nations in 1971. As an alternative, Taiwan has adopted a policy of voluntary compliance with international environmental treaties and – under the status of an NGO – regularly attended environmental conferences.

The Unites States became a signatory in June 1992 and ratified the Framework Convention in October 1992. Senate debate on ratification focused on economic costs, effects on competitiveness, and the failure to ask developing countries to reduce emissions. The Senate's advice and consent to ratification occurred, in part, because goals for reduction of emissions were voluntary. Ratification of the Framework Convention moved US climate change policy from "study only" to "study and action," though US action was cautious and limited. In the United States, the Global Change Research Program integrates federal research on climate and change. Non-governmental organizations enhance knowledge and encourage responsible action in the face of climate change. Congress and administrative agencies focus intently on climate change and its causes, while states and local governments develop their own strategies for mitigating and adapting to climate change. The national report declares that global warming is significant for the US. In the last 50 years, US average air temperature increased more than 2°F, and precipitation has also increased 5%, with more rain falling in heavier downpours. Other changes include more frequent and intense extreme weather events (heat waves, droughts), more destructive hurricanes, higher water temperatures, rising sea levels, and stronger winter storms. Impacts of climate change are likely to become more severe, affecting water resources, altering ecosystems, and challenging crop and livestock production.

The Political and Moral Position of States to the UN Climate Change Framework Convention 1992, the Kyoto Protocol and Other Conferences of Parties (COP)

Under the global climate regimes one may observe regional peculiarities and practices depending on the national solution of addressing climate issues. Sometimes the regimes are related to specific regulatory measures, in other cases the emphasis lies on economic on environmental ruling. International conventions allow for certain deviances in the administrative and legislative choices. Within the EU some national reporters explain that the position towards community legislation in general and climate policies in particular is rather restrictive: they stick to the minimum requirements (Ireland, Italy, Poland, and Portugal). The Portuguese reporter says that in Portugal, European Law tends to be accepted in a more or less uncritical and "fatalist" way. The generalized idea is that Portugal cannot determine the evolution of the European Union politics. The influence over the European decision making process is reported as rather weak.

The EU Member States basically comply with the Kyoto and Community mechanisms but most of the States have introduced additional measures. Depending on the structure of the State measures may be part of federal or regional law. In some countries membership in the EU is reported to be of great importance for the development of environmental policy and law in general, and climate policy and law in particular (Belgium). Others follow the general goals of the EU (Finland).

The national report of Scotland emphasizes reasons why regional differences within one nation (UK) should be taken into account when enforcing national commitments. Scotland's interests to some extent diverge from those of the rest of the UK. The population is more scattered and faces harsher climatic conditions than in most of the UK. It has an existing wealth of fossil fuel resources, the exploitation of which is a major industrial activity, but also has outstanding potential for renewable energy generation (wind, wave and tidal, in addition to some hydro-electric potential beyond that already utilized). Political differences also exist, especially over the desirability of an expansion of nuclear power, while Scotland claims to have "the most ambitious climate change legislation anywhere in the world". The proposal of "solving" problems related to climate change by increasing the use of nuclear energy is a common political topic in a great number of States and institutions. The UNFCCC and the protocols do not take position to the choice of energy sources, at least not in this respect.

Some countries report measures that go further than the goal set by the UNFCCC and the Kyoto Protocol. Especially within the EU a number of Member States are proactive and may have developed additional targets and measures than those internationally required (Germany, Netherlands). Germany has committed itself to reduce GHG emissions by 21% during the period from 2008 to 2012. At the national level, the federal Meseberg decisions (August 2007) have been decisive for the development of the integrated energy and climate policy. Argentina has actively participated and participates in the UNFCCC and in the follow ups of protocols and in the COPs. Also activities in the framework of the International Panel for Climate Change (IPCC) are mentioned in the national reports.

Summarizing the situation, the reported States were following at least the minimum formal requirements of both the UNFCCC and the Kyoto Protocol. The United States has not ratified the Protocol but instead it has adopted or plans to adopt other mechanisms to tackle climate change. The background has been elaborated in the national report for the US. Professor Grossman mentions that in the last 50 years, US average air temperature increased more than 2°F and precipitation has also increased 5% with more rain falling in heavier downpours. The US ratified the UNFCCC in 1992.

11.2.1.3 National Climate Policies

Despite the internationally harmonized basis for the targets of climate change mitigation, some states develop further strategies either for coordinating instruments or for promoting the national legislation. Often political lines are drawn between reactive and proactive positions. The EU has adopted an extensive climate and energy policy package aiming at 20% reduction until 2020 coupled with a 20% renewable energy target also for 2020.[8] Under the Kyoto Protocol the EU is only required to cut its emissions by 8% by 2012. These goals entail for Members States the adoption of climate and energy strategies; otherwise the states are not likely to comply with the demands. In addition, by 2020 greenhouse gas emissions in the EU will be reduced to 30% below 1990 levels subject to other industrialized countries agreeing to comparable targets and emerging economies reducing their emissions commensurate with their abilities and resources.

Germany has traditionally made a concerted effort to play a pioneering role also at the EU level – an approach which for competitive reasons large sections of industry greet with skepticism. The Federal German government lays great store in environmentally compatible industry policy in the hope that German industry's leading role in environment technology will make environment protection attractive to industry per se. In the federal system of Germany 16 states (Länder) and approximately 15,000 municipalities have considerable policymaking weight. German constitutional law assigns the individual states a range of legislative powers in matters concerning climate change and the adoption of measures to adapt to its effects. Also, the Länder are reported to bear a great degree of responsibility in law enforcement, including in respect of national law.

[8] See for renewable energy: Directive 2009/28/EC of the European Parliament and of the Council of 23 April 2009 on the promotion of the use of energy from renewable sources and amending and subsequently repealing Directives 2001/77/EC and 2003/30/EC.

Some of these states have developed their own climate change strategies. A milestone in Germany's more recent climate policy came in the form of the Meseberg Decisions on 'integrated energy and climate policy' adopted by the Federal German government in 2007. This climate change program affects all significant emitter groups (industry, transport, buildings and consumers) and comprises 29 measures with quantified CO_2 reduction targets for the period up to 2020. On this basis, Germany aims to cut its greenhouse gas emissions by 40% by 2020 based on 1990 level.

The Netherlands has chosen to adopt a more ambitious approach compared to EU law. In 2009 the following set of climate protection policy goals has been reconfirmed by the central government.[9] The goals include 30% reduction of greenhouse gases in 2020 compared to 1990, 20% renewable energy use in 2020 and an annual energy-saving with 2% in 2011–2020. In December 2009 the Fifth National Communication under the UNFCCC has been submitted by Dutch government to the UNFCCC secretariat. Also this document states an emission reduction target of minus 30% greenhouse gas emissions in the year 2020 compared to 1990. These policy goals go beyond the legally binding commitments for the Netherlands as required by EU law. The ambitious national policy goals have however not been vested in a legal binding document, and it hence remains to be seen whether they will be uphold and complied with. The elections in June 2010 will be crucial for the question whether the more ambitious targets will be upheld.

National reports provide further information about existing strategies and laws aiming at the enforcement of the goals set either by the UNFCC or the EU. In the Czech Republic a National Program to Mitigate the Impacts of Climate Change was prepared and approved in 2004 by the Government.[10] Finland has not yet adopted a political strategy for mitigating climate change; instead allocation and distribution of allowances within the EU ETS sector is governed by the Finnish National Allocation Plan.[11] The same is reported for Italy and Scotland (UK). In the UK climate change mitigation has been given a higher profile in recent years with the publication of the influential Stern Report on the costs of acting, and failing to act, in response to climate change,[12] with legislation in both the UK and Scottish Parliaments[13] and with the reorganization of the UK government to create a Department of Energy and Climate Change.[14] The Stern Review observed that the effects of our actions now on future changes in the climate have long lead times. What we do now can have only a limited effect on the climate over the next 40–50 years. On the other hand, according to the report, what is done in the next 10–20 years can have a profound effect on the climate in the second half of this century and in the next. The United Kingdom has adopted in its Climate Change Act 2008 binding targets for 2020 and 2050, of which the 2020 target is more stringent compared to what this country should do according to EU law. [15]

The Irish regime for mitigating climate change has been set out in the National Climate Change Strategies of 2000 and 2007.[16] Both strategies were designed to comply with the international obligation to reduce emissions under the Kyoto Protocol and the EU Burden Sharing Agreement. In 2007 the National Climate Change Strategy, drawing on the Stern Report, acknowledged an economic motive to taking action against climate change. It stated that "the costs of inaction will greatly outweigh the costs of action, and that progressive climate change policies, based on innovation and investment in low-carbon technology, are consistent with global economic growth."[17]

[9] Letter of 8 September 2009 to the Dutch Parliament, TK 2009–2010, 30 196, nr. 75.

[10] Resolution No. 187/2004.

[11] Emissions Trading Act (Act 683/2004).

[12] Stern Review on the Economics of Climate Change (HM Treasury, 2006); see http://www.occ.gov.uk/activities/stern.htm.

[13] Climate Change Act 2008 and Climate Change (Scotland) Act 2009.

[14] The new department took over responsibilities previously with the Department of the Environment, Food and Rural Affairs and the Department of Business, Innovation and Skills (formerly the Department for Business, Enterprise and Regulatory Reform); see http://www.decc.gov.uk. An Office of Climate Change has existed since 2006: see http://www.occ.gov.uk/.

[15] UK Climate Change Act (http://www.opsi.gov.uk/acts/acts2008/pdf/ukpga_20080027_en.pdf); See for a critical discussion Mark Stallworthy, "Legislating against Climate Change: A UK Perspective on a Sisyphean Challenge," *The Modern Law Review* (2009) 72(3): 412–462.

[16] Both strategies are available from the website of the Department of the Environment, Heritage and Local Government at http://www.environ.ie/en/Environment/Atmosphere/ClimateChange/NationalClimateChangeStrategy/.

[17] National Climate Change Strategy 2007, 7.

In Norway, the problem of climate change has been an important political issue in Norway since the 1987 report of the World Commission on Environment and Development ("Brundtland Commission"). Nearly all political parties, as well as the Norwegian Parliament on many occasions, have defined climate change as a major environmental threat, and policy objectives and measures have been developed by and large with broad political and public support.

In the United States the Energy Policy Act of 1992, a broad statute that outlined a number of energy strategies and programs to reduce harmful emissions, responded to the UNFCCC. Addressing global climate change specifically, the Energy Policy Act established a Director of Climate Protection in the Department of Energy, required a national inventory of aggregate GHG emissions, called for guidelines for voluntary reporting of GHG emissions and reductions, and authorized a Global Climate Change Response Fund to help mitigate and adapt to world climate change. The US submits annual GHG inventory reports to the Convention of the Parties under the Framework Convention. Since the beginning of 2009, the administration under President Obama has made a serious commitment to reduce US emissions of GHGs and to play a leading role in the UN Climate Change Conference. Moreover, the US Congress is considering comprehensive legislation to address the issue of climate change.

As Japan offered to host COP-3 in Kyoto, it naturally assumed its responsibility to take relevant domestic measures to enforce the Protocol's mandate. The Japanese government, immediately after the Protocol was concluded at COP-3, established the Global Warming Prevention Headquarters, headed by the Prime Minister and included all other National Ministers as members. The Law Concerning the Promotion of the Measures to Cope with Global Warming (Climate Change Policy Law) was passed in 1998. It was reformed in 2002, immediately after the Kyoto Protocol was approved in the National Diet. The Headquarters and the Guideline were given a legal status by the reform, which also obliged the government to establish a plan for attaining the targets prescribed in the Kyoto Protocol. This statute laid out the foundation of Japan's official programs to mitigate climate change.

In Australia climate change was a key issue in the 2007 national election with the incoming Labor government committing to a range of climate change mitigation measures. Polls before and after the election have consistently demonstrated that the Australian public want their government to take action on climate change. The current government has accepted that it is in Australia's national interest in mitigating climate change. However, the national regime for mitigating climate change and its related effects is not yet in place. The Government has proposed a domestic emissions trading scheme (ETS) but the legislation to implement the scheme, including the Carbon Pollution Reduction Scheme Bill, has twice been defeated by the Australian Senate. The Carbon Pollution Reduction Scheme Bill is now before the Australian Senate for a third time with second reading of the bill and debate adjourned until May 2010.

11.2.1.4 Empirical Data

Emission Volumes

The reporters were asked to give relevant data information about the intensity of greenhouse gases in their countries. It appeared that the information in most cases is detailed and updated and apt to be used for the enforcement of international programs and strategies. The existence of data does on the other hand not prove that there are all legal implications in force, especially in terms of energy legislation.

As far as the impact of the industrial and other activities on the global load of GHGs some examples may be mentioned here. One has to recall that the reporting basis is somewhat different for Annex I countries and non-Annex I Parties, especially as the forestry sector is concerned. Due to differences in population numbers, comparison may be based either on national totals or emissions per capita. The detailed numbers are available in the national reports. Generally one can observe, having the year 1990 as base, a decrease of GHG emissions. The trend is not stable and also exceptions occur. Large states as China and Brazil are not reported here.

Argentina reports an increase of total GHG emissions from 230,000 ton in the base year 1990 to 282,000 ton in 2000. From the point of view of the sector emissions, Energy contributes to 46.8%, Agriculture and livestock 44.3%, waste management 5.0% and the remainder 3.9% corresponds to Industrial Processes. This high proportion of the farming-livestock sector in the total of the GHG emissions reflects the productive profile of the country.

While Australia has very high per capita emissions (32.3 CO_2-e in 1990 reduced to 28.6 ton CO_2-e in

2007), its national emissions accounted for only 1.5% of global emissions in 2005 with that number projected to decrease to just over 1% of global emissions by 2030.[18] Broken down by economic sector for 2007, of the total 597.2 Mt CO_2-e emissions from all sectors, direct GHG emissions from specific sectors are as follows:

In Belgium, according to the Fourth National Communication on Climate Change under the United Nations Framework Convention on Climate Change (2006)[19] and the 2007 Report on Emissions of Greenhouse gases in Belgium[20], greenhouse gas emissions were estimated to represent 145.8 Mt CO_2-eq in 1990; these emissions have fallen to 143.8 Mt CO_2-eq in 2005 (−2.1%), 135.9 Mt CO_2-eq in 2006 (−6%) and 131.3 Mt CO_2-eq in 2007 (−8.3%)[21]. According to the first estimates, it is also expected that in 2008 and 2009 Belgium will largely meet its Kyoto target, helped in that respect by the financial-economic crisis and the decrease of industrial activity resulting from that crisis. The share of greenhouse gases in Belgium is as follows: CO_2 counts for 85.5%, CH_4 for 5.8%, N_20 for 7.6% and F-gases for 1.1%.

Japan is estimated to emit the equivalent of 1,374 billion tons of CO_2 including non-CO_2 greenhouse gases after they are GWP-adjusted (the Ministry of Environment of Japan), which places Japan at the fifth place among the larger GHG emitters in the World. – According to the Key World Energy Statistics compiled by IEA, as of 2006, Japan's CO_2 emission accounted for 4.3% of the total global CO_2 emission, compared with the U.S.'s 20.3% and EU's 11.6%. Japan's per capita CO_2 emission was 9.49 t-CO_2, about half of the Australia's 19.02 ton and U.S.'s, 19.00 ton; among the smallest emitters within the OECD members, France had the per capita emission volume of 5.97 t-CO_2. – According to the Key World Energy Statistics compiled by IEA, as of 2006, Japan's CO_2 emission accounted for 4.3% of the total global CO_2 emission, compared with the U.S.'s 20.3% and EU's 11.6%. Japan's per capita CO_2 emission was 9.49 t-CO_2, about half of the Australia's 19.02 tons and U.S.'s, 19.00 ton; among the smallest emitters within the OECD members, France had the per capita emission volume of 5.97 t-CO_2.

Finland's national greenhouse gas emissions on a global level can be considered as small in absolute terms (85 Tg CO_2eq in 2003; 70 Tg CO_2 eq in 1990). Greenhouse gas emissions per capita were 16 ton of CO_2eq per person in 2003 and 14 ton of CO_2eq per person in 1990.

Norway's annual emission of GHG is in the order of 55 million tons of CO_2 equivalents. This is a very small part of the global emissions but the average emission of a Norwegian person amounts to nearly 12 ton (close to the OECD average). To fulfill its Kyoto obligations Norway has to reduce its present emission level by 10%.

In Ireland, GHG emissions increased from 55,383.14 Gt CO_2 equivalent in 1990 to 70,650.03 Gt CO_2 equivalent in 2001. Emissions decreased by approximately 3% from 2001 to 68,575.06 Gt COt equivalent in 2003 before rising again in 2004 and 2005. In 2007 emissions decreased by 0.7% to 68,205.15 Gt CO_2 equivalent.[22] The 2007 level is 25% higher than emissions were in 1990.

For the United Kingdom the Greenhouse Gas Inventory[23] shows that the UK as a whole in 2006 produced 652,302.5 kt of carbon dioxide equivalent,[24] of which Scotland's share was 9%. The Scottish contribution of 59,042.7 kt came from the sectors shown below,[25] whilst land use and forestry provided a net sink of carbon dioxide of 4,500 kt. Significant features of the Scottish emissions identified in the Inventory include power generation, where the emissions have

[18] Garnaut Climate Change Review Final Report, Table 3.2.

[19] http://www.climat.be/IMG/pdf/NC4_ENG_LR.pdf.

[20] http://www.climat.be/IMG/pdf/Broeikasgasemissies_2007.pdf.

[21] Belgium's Greenhouse Gas Inventory (1990–2007). National Inventory Report submitted under the United Nations Framework Convention on Climate Change, April 2009, p 9; Rekenhof, Federaal klimaatbeleid. Uitvoering van het Kyotoprotocol. Verslag van het Rekenhof aan de Kamer van Volksvertegenwoordigers, Brussels, June 2009, 7.

[22] National Inventory Reports on greenhouse gas emissions, prepared by the Environmental Protection Agency, are available at http://coe.epa.ie/ghg/nirdownloads.jsp.

[23] Greenhouse Gas Inventories for England, Scotland, Wales and Northern Ireland: 1990–2006 (AEA Report to the Department for Environment, Food and Rural Affairs, The Scottish Government, The Welsh Assembly Government and The Northern Ireland Department of Environment; 2008).

[24] The greenhouse gases measured are CO_2, CH_4 and N_2O with baselines in 1990 and HFCs, PFCs and SF_6 with baselines in 1995.

[25] Based on Table 3.1 and subsequent discussion in the Inventories (note 22, above).

increased since 1990 in contrast to a reduction across the UK as a whole.

Italy's contribution to EC GHG emissions was of 516 CO_2-equivalents (Tg) in 1990 and of 553 CO_2 -equivalents (Tg) in 2007. Italy's GHG emissions are about 7% above 1990 levels in 2007. At International level, Italy's emissions were in 1990 434,687.7 CO_2 – equivalent (Gg) and became 475,302.1 in 2007. Changes in emissions increased of 9.3%. Average annual growth rates was of 0.5 per year.

In the Unites States, total anthropogenic GHG emissions for 2007 were 7,150.1 Tg 25 of CO_2 equivalent (Tg CO_2e), 17% more than in 1990. Total US emissions of GHGs in 2007 were 1.4% higher than in 2006. The increase was due to higher CO_2 emissions resulting from unfavorable weather (more heating and cooling), increased use of fossil fuels for electricity, and reduced hydropower (greater reliance on coal and natural gas). Net emissions, however, were 6,087.5 Tg CO_2e, after reduction of 1,062.6 Tg CO_2e for carbon "sinks" (carbon sequestration from land use, land-use change, and forestry activities). Between 2006 and 2007, GHG intensity (metric tons CO_2e per million dollars of gross domestic product) fell slightly, by 0.6%, a relatively slow rate of improvement; between 2002 and 2007, emissions intensity decreased by 9.8%.

Structure of Emission Sources

The main source of emissions depends highly on the economic structure of each country. Most of those having GHG emission problems are industrialized or energy consuming, others are depending on agricultural and forestal business. One can observe this when studying national surveys and reports. The separation of percentages numbers industry, manufacture and energy production is not always apt for a direct comparison but it seems that e.g. in Australia, the US and Norway industrial production is responsible for at least 25% of the GHG emissions. In other industrialized countries the main source is energy production, in some countries up to 90%. In countries with a large agricultural surface, rural businesses including forestry may cover up to 25%. In others the percentage is around 10% or less.

As a global "middle" Italy gives following numbers: energy 46.8%, agriculture and livestock 44.3%, waste management 5.0% and the remainder 3.9% corresponds to industrial processes. According to the reporter, the high proportion of the farming-livestock sector in the total of the GHG emissions reflects the productive profile of the country. Italian GHG emissions increased since 1990 primarily from: road transport (+25%), electricity (+9.5%) and heat production (+17%) and petrol refining. Italy was able to low CO_2 emissions principally in the manufacturing industries (−11%).

In a central European state as Belgium manufacturing industry (combustion) takes 20.9%, energy industries 20.5%, residential and commercial 20.3%, transport 17.7%, manufacturing industry (process) 9.7%, agriculture 7.8%, others 1.7% and waste 1.4%. In Japan, out of the 1,374 billion t-CO_2 of GHGs emitted in Japan in 2007, the largest share is accounted for by the Energy sector (90.6%), followed by industrial processes (5.7%), agriculture (1.9%) and waste (1.8%). The Energy sector includes energy industries (32.8%), manufacturing industries and construction (27.8%), transport (17.8%) and others: fuel combustion accounts for 99% of the GHG emission in the energy sector.

Transport is in some countries a problem area and may be responsible for even close to 20% of the emissions. Residential emissions are a regionally increasing source of emissions, e.g. In Norway road transport covers 20%, internal shipping 7% and air transport, heating, waste disposal and some other sources together 15%.

Since most of the sources are related to industrial and technical activities, the challenge to slow down the emission trends is to adopt better and more efficient technical practices. Where this option is neglected, one cannot speak of a real political commitment in terms of climate strategies. The situation may be more difficult in "open air" activities and manufacturing but these sectors are relatively low emittents of GHG. One real challenge is the transport sector where e.g. air traffic and fuel policies which in many countries are taken under serious consideration.

Not only CO_2 is a matter of concern. Other greenhouse gases may even cause major problems but their amount of total emission numbers is usually low. For Ireland it is reported that emissions of CO_2 accounted for 67.2% of the national total in 2007, with CH_4 and N_2O contributing 18.7% and 11.7%, respectively. The combined emissions of HFC, PFC and SF_6 accounted for 1.0% of total emissions. In the Czech Republic carbon dioxide (CO_2) is the most important greenhouse gas, contributing 86% to overall emissions, followed by methane (CH_4) with 7.1%, nitrous oxide (N_2O) with 5.7% and F-gases with 1.2%.

In the United States, as in other nations, carbon dioxide is the GHG emitted in the largest quantities. Other GHGs, however, have more global warming potential (GWP). For example, methane has a GWP of 25 (25 times more potent, for equal weights, than CO_2); nitrous oxide, 298. High GWP gases are sulfur hexafluoride (SF6, GWP of 22,200), hydro fluorocarbons (HFCs, 124–14,800), and per fluorocarbons (PFCs, 7390–12,200). Emissions data are often expressed as CO_2 equivalent, a unit of measurement that expresses the GWP of other gases in terms of the warming potential of CO_2. Total anthropogenic GHG emissions for 2007 in the US were 7,150.1 teragrams25 of CO_2 equivalent (Tg CO_2e), 17% more than in 1990. Total US emissions of GHGs in 2007 were 1.4% higher than in 2006.

Specific Reasons for Eventually High Load of GHGs (Energy, Geography, Agriculture, Traffic)

Australia has very high per capita transport emissions (with only five other OECD countries consuming more transport energy per unit of GDP than Australia). Australia's per capita emissions arising from agriculture are also high (more than six times the world average, more than four times the OECD average and third highest in the OECD). The high level of emissions in this sector is a reflection of the large number of cattle and sheep relative to the population.

Belgium is still catching up on the environmental backlog from the past. Energy use, material use and pollutant emission intensities (i.e. per unit of GDP) remain relatively high. Belgium made progress over the last decade in decoupling environmental pressures from economic growth for some conventional pollutants (such as SO_x and NO_x emissions) and for water abstractions. There is, however, still a need to decouple road freight transport from economic growth, as the increase in road freight transport is a major cause for concern. Energy intensity (total primary energy supply per unit of GDP) is still considerably higher than in neighboring countries. Integration of environmental concerns into energy policy is, according to judiciary studies, lagging behind.[26]

[26] L. Lavrysen, "Chapter 2. Belgium" in *The Role of the Judiciary in Environmental Governance. Comparative Perspectives*, L. J. Kotze and A. R. Paterson, 88–90 (Alphen aan den Rijn: Kluwer Law International, 2009).

In Germany, the core components of the Meseberg Energy and Climate Program take in improved energy efficiency, among other things with promotion of combined heat and power, a range of measures targeting electricity consumption, and in buildings. Also, use of renewable energy is to be considerably intensified in the electricity and heating sector. For the transport sector, use of biofuels and the integration of shipping and air transport into the Emissions Trading Scheme will lead to significant reductions in CO_2 emissions. The Meseberg program is less clear as regards ways to reduce greenhouse gas emissions in agriculture – each of the concepts it contains require considerable further enhancement of prevailing (climate change) law.[27]

Geographical and climatic conditions may affect the approach. According to Finland's Fourth National Communication under the UNFCCC reasons are (1) energy intensive industry, (2) energy consumption during long heating period and (3) energy consumption for transport in a large and sparsely inhabited country. In Norway, an important source of GHG emissions in Norway is the very significant off-shore production of oil and gas. This industry has achieved important technological improvements to reduce CO_2 emission, but remains very energy demanding. On the other hand, nearly all electricity in Norway is produced by hydropower. Gas-fired power plants have been introduced only recently. In Italy again, geography and agriculture cannot be considered specific reasons for the high load of GHGs in Italy. The first and principal reason for the high load of GHGs in Italy is the lack of a serious climate change policy. Notwithstanding the various initiatives undertaken, the absence of a serious program to combat climate changes has resulted in a very inappropriate legislation.

In Japan, the GHG emissions in Japan have actually been on the rise since 1990. The total GHG emissions reached 1,374 million t-CO_2 in 2007, an increase by 9.0% over the base year of the Kyoto Protocol. The government attributes the increase to the temporary cessation of some nuclear power facilities due to their

[27] See Bericht zur Umsetzung der in der Kabinettsklausur am 23./24.8.2007 in Meseberg beschlossenen Eckpunkte für ein Integriertes Energie- und Klimaprogramm dated 5.12.2007. The report contains 14 proposals for laws and regulations. See also the background report by BMU, Das Integrierte Energie- und Klimaprogramm der Bundesregierung, Hintergrund of December 2007.

maintenance and mechanical problems, part of which were caused by earthquakes. The operating rates of the nuclear power plants were just over 60% in 2007 and 2008. The major "affirmative" factor, however, is the increase in coal fired power generation.

11.2.2 Part II: Approaches to Mitigation

11.2.2.1 Political and Legal Approaches to Mitigate Climate Change

Under the UNFCCC the three Kyoto mechanisms are the framework for international action, efficiently when Parties agree upon the goals and obligations. The international decision-making process under the UNFCCC has failed to produce a binding agreement with regard to emission reduction targets after the year 2012, and the EU has provided targets only up to 2020. Under the EU Emissions Trading scheme (Directive 2003), Member States were required to establish a system to allow industrial facilities to trade emissions allowances. The solutions are to some extent discretionary, from grand-fathering to auction and open sales. The EU is acting in the Kyoto procedure as well and tries to reach consensus on the need of stringent targets, often in line with the results of the IPCC. Within the EU the positions are not unilateral.

The community legislation of the EU on climate change was mentioned earlier. In addition, a 16% reduction target should be reached in 2020 compared to 2005 following the so-called effort sharing document.[28] The national burden under the Kyoto regime has been transposed into community law by an agreement between the Member States. This agreement settles the legal burden of each Member State. The Kyoto Protocol target for the period 2008–2012 is according to the internal EU burden sharing decision a 6% reduction of greenhouse gas emissions compared to 1990.[29] EU law does not yet regulate in full the use of the Kyoto mechanisms which therefore are under the competence of Member States.

As parties some Member States of the EU have transposed the Kyoto mechanisms into national legislation. In Finland, the use of the Flexible Mechanisms of the Kyoto Protocol is regulated under the Act on the Use of the Flexible Mechanisms of the Kyoto Protocol (Act 109/2007). The Flexible Mechanisms Act, however, basically only distributes the administrative duties between the Ministry for Foreign Affairs of Finland (Clean Development Mechanism) and the Ministry of the Environment (Kyoto Protocol Emissions Trading and Joint Implementation). The Act does not contain further provisions on the mitigation of climate change. The Act does also not provide for any policies and measures concerning mitigation beyond the text of the Kyoto Protocol.

States have randomly adopted positions partly to support politically the international mitigation procedure, partly enacted specified legislation concerning certain measures to reduce GHG emissions. This is the case for instance in Ireland and Italy where national programs create the basis for specified legal activities. In Italy a national program in 1994 had the ambitious target to attain before year 2000 the same level of emissions as in 1990.

Some Member States of the EU – like the UK and Germany – promote further going reductions as currently adopted by the EU (minus 20% in 2020 compared to 1990). The UK has set an emission reduction target of 26% in 2020 compared to 1990 in its Climate Change Act 2008. In Germany an emission reduction target of 40% in 2020 is based on a political agreement of the present government.[30] In the Netherlands, the emission reduction goal of minus 30% in 2020 is also part of a similar the political agreement of the government. [31] In addition, in the fifth national communication to the UNFCCC in 2009 the 30% target has been mentioned. The United Kingdom has been an active participant in climate negotiations, both within the EU and beyond, particularly in trying to influence the

[28] Decision No 406/2009/EC of the European Parliament and of the Council of 23 April 2009 on the effort of Member States to reduce their greenhouse gas emissions to meet the Community's greenhouse gas emission reduction commitments up to 2020.

[29] Council Decision 2002/358/EC of 25 April 2002 concerning the approval, on behalf of the European Community, of the Kyoto Protocol to the United Nations Framework Convention on Climate Change and the joint fulfillment of commitments there under.

[30] Koalitionsvertrag zwischen CDU, FDP and CSU: "Wir werden für Deutschland einen konkreten Entwicklungspfad festlegen und bekräftigen unser Ziel, die Treibhausgas-Emissionen bis 2020 um 40% gegenüber 1990 zu senken."

[31] Coalitieakkoord tussen de Tweede Kamerfracties van CDA, PvdA en ChristenUnie, http://www.regering.nl/Het_kabinet/Beleidsprogramma_2007_2011.

position of the USA. In the summer of 2009 it set out in detail its approach to the Copenhagen conference, seeking a new agreement that is ambitious, effective and fair.[32] The Federal German government also lays great store in environmentally compatible industry policy in the hope that German industry's leading role in environment technology will make environment protection attractive to industry per se. In Germany the core components of the Meseberg Energy and Climate Program take in improved energy efficiency, among other things with promotion of combined heat and power, a range of measures targeting electricity consumption, and in buildings.

Outside the EU the trends are comparable. The US reporter quotes the IPCC which recommended that strategies to combat climate change must include "mitigation, adaptation, technological development (to enhance both adaptation and mitigation) and research" and must include "actions at all levels from the individual citizen through to national governments and international organisations," and concludes that the time is ripe for serious attention to GHG emissions, both nationally and internationally. As of August 2009, 23 states had joined 3 major regional initiatives: 10 states in the Regional Greenhouse Gas Initiative; 7 states and 4 Canadian provinces in the Western Climate Initiative (with 7 states, 2 provinces, and 6 Mexican states as observers); and 6 states plus 1 province in the Midwestern GHG Reduction Accord (with 3 states and 1 province as observers). Regional GHG programs are possible, in part, because the US electric power market is managed by regional transmission organizations created to implement 1980s and 1990s policies of the Federal Energy Regulatory Commission.

In Israel, the Knesset (Parliament) passed a Clean Air Act which enables the Minister of the Environment to set up a comprehensive plan to reduce air pollution. This plan enables the minister to set rules for new plants and for existing plants, for new and old vehicles and for fuels. With this law going into effect in 2011, Israel will be well equipped to handle most aspects of the cause of climate change.

In Argentina, five studies on the mitigation of GHG emissions have been carried out in the framework of climate change mitigation. They cover different components of the main emission sectors. These studies have identified feasible mitigation measures and policies that in a time horizon of 15–20 years would imply a net reduction of emissions of more than 60 million tons of CO_2 eq. per year. These options of mitigation do not include the large hydropower and nuclear facilities that are projected, neither other options of mitigation that were not analyzed in these five studies. According to the report, most of these mitigation options is that their implementation needs additional capital investments in their initiation phase, higher than what is required in the scenarios.

11.2.2.2 Social Awareness and Lobbying

The reliability and efficiency of enforcement to a high degree depends on the response in the public and the respect for the need of measures to mitigate climate change. The reports offer different views to modes of public positions, partly in terms of activities of citizens in local activities, in the manifestations of NGOs and the general awareness in societies supported by information and education. One of the questions touched the issue about awareness of climate change. Generally and officially the results seem to be rather encouraging. In Belgium, the attitude towards climate change problems has dramatically changed in recent years. Since the beginning of this millennium the consequences of global warming can be seen increasingly in daily life. The hot summer of 2006, coupled with very mild winters in recent years and more frequent periods of heavy rain and flooding, are seen as indicators for climate change already now. In Germany, public awareness has been institutionalized especially in land use planning. This places the municipalities under obligations whose fulfillment is of great importance in dealing with climate change. Worthwhile mentioning in this regard is municipal land-use planning within which key climate-relevant stipulations are enacted for urban planning. The reporter refers to judicial authority where 'Think global, act local' is acknowledged as applying to climate change policy as far down as the municipal level. Also in the Netherlands the discussion goes on how far responsibility will be taken by countries themselves, and whether such responsibilities will be vested into binding national law.

In the Czech Republic the State Environmental Policy for 2004–2010 emphasizes the creation and utilization of a program of an interconnected system of education and public awareness throughout all

[32] Department of Energy and Climate Change, The Road to Copenhagen: The UK Government's case for an ambitious international agreement on climate change (Cm 7659, 2009).

environmental sectors. In Italy again, the position of the social society is very fragmentary. There is generally little information. Universities that offer training courses on the subject are few. Consequently, there is no background culture that can provide the basis for creating mass awareness on climate change issues. In Ireland, there is widespread consciousness of the threat posed by climate change and the need to act with urgency. A series of government campaigns to raise awareness, have encouraged people to become aware of their carbon footprint and to take steps to reduce it. Grass roots movements have also played a role in the dissemination of information with Greenhouse Ireland Network (GRIAN),[33] Friends of the Earth and Stop Climate Chaos gaining a significant following.

For Norway, climate change issues are on the agenda of many NGOs in Norway, including the main trade unions and the Confederation of Norwegian Enterprise. It is a major issue for the environmental NGOs. There is much public information about the issue. The public at large is conscious of the problem, but the attitude towards the problem varies. It is seen by many rather as a problem of technological development than a question of individual responsibility for consumption and life-style. There is at present no important appeal or strong drive from the government to reduce individual emissions from private activities and households.

In Australia, the reporter claims that a consistently high portion of Australians are not only concerned about climate change but are prepared to pay for mitigation in higher goods and services prices. According to the Garnaut Climate Change Review Final Report, "[t]here is a much stronger base of support for reform and change on this issue than on any other big question of structural change in recent decades, including trade, tax and public business ownership reform." However, polls indicate that the Australian public does not have a clear understanding of how the mitigation techniques currently proposed by the Australian government, and particularly the proposed ETS, will operate. In Argentina, the nongovernmental organizations (NGOs) contribute to the development of knowledge and the dissemination of the issues related to Climate Change. Their activities and ways of action are diverse, according to their specific interests and characteristics. The NGOs with academic objectives have contributed significantly to the development of knowledge and they have been substantially involved in the enabling of activities of the First and the Second National Communications.

The reporters were also asked how strongly political actors and company groups lobby for a lower profile in national and international contexts. In Germany where a national act was adopted,[34] pressure from the industrial lobby led to the passing of an over-complex national allocations plan in the first trading period. The resulting over-allocation of emissions allowances is reported to have a negative impact on the effectiveness of the emissions trading scheme. In the current, second trading period, pressure from the EU Commission facilitated the authorities to prevent emitters from receiving in the allocation procedure excessive quantities of emissions allowances. In the Netherlands different opinions exist among the major political parties with regard to even the existence of the global warming threat. One fast growing right wing party that is currently high in the polls is reported even to contest the need to take climate protection actions.[35]

In Israel, the major problem in Israel has been the lack of political will to introduce a comprehensive plan for reduction of the individual climate footprint. This is slowly changing as the planning authorities have now allocated a place for the planning and building of a large solar power plant. In addition, there is a law in place requiring the Israel Electric Company to buy power from private individuals who produce energy in their home or business.

11.2.2.3 Evaluation of Compatibility with Global Climate Programs

Most countries, especially the Member States of the EU, tend to enforce the necessary supranational nationally. Some others have developed national programs with more advanced targets. In Finland, there is no

[33] http://www.grian.ie/, http://www.foe.ie/, http://www.stopclimatechaos.ie/.

[34] Federal Greenhouse Gas Emissions Trading Act (TEHG) 2004, Federal Allocation Act 2004 (ZuG), the National Allocation Plan I of 31st March 2004, Federal Allocation Act 2012 2007 and the National Allocation Plan II 14 of 28 August 2006.

[35] This party is called "Partij voor de Vrijheid", the members in Parliament belonging to this Party have submitted several questions to the Dutch government critically questioning the need for a climate policy.

purely national regime for mitigating climate change and related effects in force in Finland. The EU's burden sharing agreement sets a national target for Finland applicable to the period 2008–2012. The EU ETS Directive (Dir. 2003/87/EC) has been implemented through national law and the national allocation plan. For the Czech Republic, the measures evaluated in the Fourth National Communication include the current state of utilization of the flexible mechanisms of the Protocol and participation in the system for trading in emission permits in the framework of the European Union. The basis for policy in creation of measures consists in the National Program to Mitigate the Impacts of Climate Change in the Czech Republic, which was approved by the Government in 2004.

Also for Norway the national choice is compatible with the global programs adopted so far, when taking into account the possible use of the flexible mechanisms of the Kyoto protocol, and the corresponding system of GHG emission trading in the EU (EU-ETS). Norway's climate policy instruments at the state level include compulsory measures such as mandatory emission permits and emission trading for important branches of both land-based and off-shore industry (in accordance with EU-ETS). It also includes several CO_2 taxes, such as CO_2 tax on car petrol, CO_2 tax on emission from off-shore petroleum industry and others. The taxes on new cars vary partly according to their CO_2 emissions. The government provides state aid to construction of new renewable energy plants such as wind farms, and to energy efficiency measures. At the local level, all municipalities are asked to develop a climate action plan as part of the municipal planning, and state guidelines for this have been issued.

The Belgian National Climate Plan 2009–2012[36] elaborated by the National Climate Commission, defines 11 strategic axes, of which 6 sectoral and 5 horizontal. The sectoral axes are the following: (1) optimization of energy production; (2) rational energy use in buildings; (3) adaptation of production processes; (4) development of sustainable means of transport; (5) encouragement of sustainable management of ecosystems in agriculture and forestry, (6) greater efforts in waste management. The horizontal axes are: (7) greater efforts in climate change research; (8) awareness- building among all stakeholders in Belgium; (9) more direct involvement of public authorities in the reduction of GHG emissions; (10) introduction of flexible mechanism; (11) integration of the climate dimension in development cooperation policies. Within these axes various measures are listed, with indication of their phase of implementation.

The German government has spoken out in strong favor of complying with the 2°C target.[37] The Meseberg Energy and Climate Program serves as Germany's contribution to achieving the ambitious targets agreed by the EU heads of state and government under the German EU presidency on 9 March 2007. The Meseberg program is not very clear as regards ways to reduce greenhouse gas emissions in agriculture – each of the concepts it contains require considerable further enhancement of prevailing (climate change) law. The use of renewable energy is to be considerably intensified in the electricity and heating sector. For the transport sector, use of biofuels and the integration of shipping and air transport into the Emissions Trading Scheme will lead to significant reductions in CO_2 emissions.

In Ireland, a new National Climate Change Strategy was launched in 2007 for specified sectors. The large increase in emissions from 1990 to 2001 was driven by emissions from energy use which increased by 45.1% during the 12 year period. The bulk of this increase occurred in the years between 1995 and 2001, when emissions grew by an average of 5.5% annually as Ireland experience unprecedented economic growth. The rate of economic growth slowed down from 2000 to 2004. Each sector concerned is verified by policy measures. The secondary mission was to position Ireland to meet more stringent emission targets in the post 2012 commitment period.[38]

The Australian government's proposed ETS is intended to be compatible with international mechanisms (CDM and JI) as well as other domestic emissions trading schemes in anticipation of developing linkages and recognizing emissions credits generated globally within the domestic scheme. As the ETS is not yet in place it is not possible to evaluate its efficiency with other global programs. In addition to the proposal to cap GHG emissions through an ETS, the

[36] http://www.climat.be/IMG/pdf/NKP_2009-2012.pdf.

[37] Government statement by Chancellor Angela Merkel, Bulletin der Bundesregierung, No. 127–1 of 17 December 2009, p. 7 ff.

[38] For discussion of the goals of Irish climate change policy, see page 7 of the 2007 Strategy and page 2 of the 2000 Strategy.

Australian Government has established through legislation a market based Renewable Energy Target (RET) of 20% by 2020. The government has also put in place several funding initiatives to support renewable energy and clean energy technology. The Australian Government has also established the Global Carbon Capture and Storage Institute to strengthen international cooperation to develop this technology.

In Argentina, a group of measures and programs that lead to the mitigation of GHG emissions have been carried out or are being developed. Some of them have been implemented for coping with this main objective while others, primarily for economic or social development goals, also contribute to the GHG mitigation process. The Argentine Office of the Clean Development Mechanism evaluates and authorizes the projects to be presented to the CDM. To facilitate the mitigation project generation in a context of financial restrictions, the Government established the Argentine Carbon Fund (ACF) by the decree 1070/05 in September 2005.

As far as Japan is concerned, one characteristic is that the national regime is entirely based on the Kyoto Protocol. Thus, it does not go beyond the targets set by the protocol nor does it fall too short of what is demanded by the Protocol. The national programs reflect the limitations found in the Protocol itself. The Japanese government introduced in 2004 a system for mandatory calculating, reporting, and disclosing of GHG emissions. In 2005, the system was integrated into the Kyoto Protocol Target Achievement Plan, and then in the Climate Change Policy Act. The system requires large-scale GHG emitters, mostly business entities, emitting 3,000 or more t-CO_2 of GHGs and energy users using 1,500 kl or more of crude-oil-equivalent of energy to annually report their GHG emissions amounts. However, the Japanese official GHG emissions reduction regime basically depends on voluntary measures on the principle of "simultaneous pursuit of environmental protection, economic development and competitiveness of the domestic industry". Japan's strategy for reducing GHG emissions is highly dependent on such voluntary measures of major economic players as mentioned above.

11.2.3 Part III: Essence of Climate Law

11.2.3.1 Is There a Need for Climate Law?

In this part a more theoretical or academic about the essence of the new legal area of "climate law" will be discussed. Global warming and climate change refer to atmospheric and ecological processes which occur with or without human impact. Legislators may protect populations against predictable disasters and changes but it cannot influence the changes all over. Environmental law which often is considered as the main basis for climate approaches is used to operate with the relation between nature and the role of human activities but not to change natural ecosystems at least not at a large scale. The impact of greenhouse gases is also not dangerous for life or something that should be treated as a "pollutant". Therefore traditional environmental strategies do not reach the core of climate problems, the "climate". Additional elements are required. These elements are a combination of social planning policies and economic instruments.

The reporters were asked how they estimated the position or the need of climate law. Especially it seems interesting to see if there are other reasons guiding the understanding than those arising from international political commitments. It occurs that most states have adopted the concept of climate change but they still are reluctant to see climate law as something more than just a system of prescribed economic elements. Some others may have a more idealistic approach and see that there should be more precaution and more far reaching commitments in favor of future generations (sustainable development). It seems that one problem with the not so successful result of the Copenhagen conference in 2009 was that there was not a common view about a common goal and of the necessity to reach it. As mentioned in the US report, already the legal definition of "climate" causes problems for understanding what the regulatory system should deal with ("climate is not weather").

As cited in the US report, "Climate is not the same thing as weather. Weather is the minute-by-minute variable condition of the atmosphere on a local scale. Climate is a conceptual description of an area's average weather conditions and the extent to which those conditions vary over long time intervals."

In Germany, 'climate change mitigation by law' is from a legal system standpoint studied with increasing interest and intensity.[39] It is often recognized as a

[39] Martin Winkler, Klimaschutzrecht, 2005; Klaus F. Gärditz, "Schwerpunktbereich – Einführung in das Klimaschutzrecht," Juristische Schulung (2008), 324; Thorsten Müller and Helmuth Schulze-Fielitz, "Auf dem Weg zu einem Klimaschutzrecht," in *Europäisches Klimaschutzrecht,* ed. idem (Nomos, Baden-Baden), 9, particularly p. 15.

legislative field (climate change law) in its own right. It appears appropriate to define climate change law as "the sum of legal standards designed to protect the climate against anthropogenic effects".[40] Climate change law is also a cross-sectoral area which has been integrated in a complex of regulatory contexts and therefore it is often hard to determine the content of this field of law. The same of course applies to environmental law and energy law which both already have a rather stable position.

For Belgium climate change law is academically based on both environmental principles (precautionary principle, polluter pays principle, integration principle) and on economic concerns (use of flexible instruments, emission trading, use of other economic and voluntary instruments). The level of ambition is clearly guided by economic concerns.

In Japan, while enacting Climate Change Law Policy Law, the drafters and legislators took a position to keep a balance between the environmental protection and the development of the national economy. Given the great emphasis placed on the private businesses' voluntary programs, namely the Keidanren's Voluntary Action Plan for the Environment, and given the fact that the private business accounts for the majority of GHG emissions in Japan, the official environmental policy of Japan keeps to certain limits by avoiding to impose any strict mandatory measures to reduce GHG emissions. Exceeding such limits is considered to affect the vitality of the domestic businesses and the national economy by imposing excessive costs. According to the reporter, climate law should establish a set of mandatory rules to lead business entities into environmentally reasonable operations on one hand and to create certain economic conditions to reward those that take initiatives in pursuing GHG reducing ways of running business on the other.

In Norway, climate change is basically perceived as an environmental problem. The Ministry of the Environment is the coordinating ministry for climate change issues, and the main executive body is the Climate and Pollution Agency under this ministry. As a cross-sectoral issue, however, it engages – and requires measures – in most sectors. Many ministries are involved in formulating and executing climate policy. It has also important economic consequences, and the development of climate policy and law is to a great extent a matter also for the Ministry of Finance and the government as whole.

11.2.3.2 Environment and/or Economy

Not all countries address climate law as an environmental issue. Australia has chosen to adopt largely market based measures, in the form of an ETS, to mitigate climate change. Environmental principles are not reflected in the proposed climate scheme. There is no statement of the principles of ESD (Ecologically sustainable development) in the objects of the proposed legislation, as is now common place with environmental legislation in Australia. A decision has also been made to exclude environmental considerations (other than those related to carbon sequestration) from reforestation projects which may opt-in to the proposed scheme. The interaction of existing environmental impact assessment procedures and the emissions trading scheme is currently under review.

It seems that the political balance between "ecology" and "economy" tends to create more practical or sectoral instruments. Instead of proclaiming overwhelming principles of sustainability and biodiversity market instruments especially in the energy or agricultural sector get increasing support. In the energy sector it has become popular to speak of green or renewable energy. But it occurs that sometimes these solutions are in their enforcement not as ecological as they are supposed to be.

The reporters were also asked if there are any environmental conditions in relation to the adoption of Kyoto measures. Here most countries have chosen a formal or minimal position, especially in the Member States of the EU which have to adopt the emission trading scheme. In some cases granting of emission allowances may be connected to environmental permits which again allow for prescribing further measures. This applies especially for best available technology (BAT) and best environmental practice (BEP) which are not essential parts of international climate law. Permits may also depend on national climate change strategies. In Belgium, the National Climate Commission proposes yearly to the different authorities selected activities and priority countries with the aim of ensuring a geographical spread of project activities. Those activities should contribute to sustainable development aims of developing countries.

[40] Klaus F. Gärditz (footnote 31), 324.

11.2.4 Part IV: Structures of International (and EC Community) Climate Law

11.2.4.1 European Legal Basis

The European Union has enacted legislation in the framework of international climate commitments. The Kyoto mechanisms play a central part in the methodology of regulations. The Directive on an emission trading scheme (ETS) is mandatory for the Member States (Directive 2003/87/EC, which entered into force on 25 October 2003).[41] The states are also as parties directly under the obligations of the Kyoto regime.

The Directive has been amended and reviewed by Directive 2009/29/EC of the European Parliament and of the Council of 23 April 2009 amending Directive 2003/87/EC so as to improve and extend the greenhouse gas emission allowance trading scheme of the Community. This Directive was adopted with the objective to introduce a range of changes designed to strengthen, expand and improve the operations of the scheme for the period after 2012. Another Directive included aviation in the ETS scheme (Directive 2008/101/EC of the European Parliament and of the Council of 19 November 2008 amending Directive 2003/87/EC so as to include aviation activities in the scheme for greenhouse gas emission allowance trading within the Community).

In addition to emission trading other Kyoto mechanisms were covered be Community law by adopting the so-called "Linking Directive" (Directive 2004/101/EC of the European Parliament and of the Council of 27 October 2004 amending Directive 2003/87/EC establishing a scheme for greenhouse gas emission allowance trading within the Community, in respect of the Kyoto Protocol's project mechanisms). The aim is to link the emission trading scheme with other flexible mechanisms of the Kyoto Protocol, i.e. clean development mechanisms (CDM) and joint implementation (JI). This directive allows emissions credits generated by Kyoto project-based mechanisms (through JI and CDM) to be used to meet EU ETS obligations.

Finally worthwhile mentioning is the Directive 2009/28/EC of the European Parliament and of the Council of 23 April 2009 on the promotion of the use of energy from renewable sources and amending and subsequently repealing Directives 2001/77/EC and 2003/30/EC OJ L 140/16. See art 27(1) of this Directive.

The EU has established a package that should lead to 20% reduction of greenhouse gas emissions in 2020 compared to 1990. That binding commitment is divided into (1) the European greenhouse gas emissions trading system that covers a large part of industrial installations and (2) emission reduction targets for Member States concerning emissions not covered by the EU ETS (the so-called Effort sharing decision).[42] The latter approach, which covers approximately 60% greenhouse gases within the EU,[43] is less binding for the Member States as they may develop national policies for meeting the required targets including emissions trading by the countries themselves. As stated by the Dutch reporter, the design of a national accountability mechanism to ensure compliance with those EU-targets, the distribution of the burden among the responsible sectors, and the decision-making by the national government to use international emissions trading are core topics in this regard.

In Belgium, the competences for the implementation of these international and supranational obligations are partially a competence of the federal government and partially of the regions. A Co-operation Agreement[44] was elaborated between federal and regional governments (the Federal State and the Flemish, Walloon and Brussels Capital Regions of 2002). For the purposes of the Kyoto Protocol a National Climate Commission was established.

In Germany, the Constitution (Art. 1) is interpreted as assigning the state a responsibility to provide protection against risks arising from negative impacts on the environment: "Human dignity shall be inviolable. To respect and protect it shall be the duty of all state authorities." From these guarantees, a state obligation

[41] Directive 2003/87/EC of the European Parliament and the Council of 13 October 2003 establishing a scheme for greenhouse gas emission allowance trading within the Community and amending Council Directive 96/61/EC (IPPC).

[42] For effort sharing see Decision No 406/2009/EC of the European Parliament and of the Council of 23 April 2009 on the effort of Member States to reduce their greenhouse gas emissions to meet the Community's greenhouse gas emission reduction commitments up to 2020, OJ L 140/136. See also the Burden sharing decision (Council Decision 2002/358/EC, OJ L 130/1).

[43] European Commission, Questions and Answers on the Decision on effort sharing, MEMO/08/797, Brussels, 17 December 2008 (Question 1).

[44] Internal treaty approved by federal and regional parliaments.

is set to secure an "ecological minimum existence". However, in contrast to the EU Treaty, the German Basic Law assigns no general legislative powers to the Federal Government in respect of environment protection. Rules on climate change mitigation can in part be covered by the legislative area of "air pollution control", but must also be covered by the "law relating to economic affairs".[45]

11.2.4.2 Non-EU States

States outside the EU have arrangements if their own to fulfill international commitments. For Australia it is reported that in terms of supranational or international commitments which may be decisive for Australia's legal (and political) structure, the Commonwealth parliament has power under the Australian Constitution to implement the terms of international treaties which Australia has ratified as part of Australia's domestic law. The federal government has proposed an ETS – the Carbon Pollution Reduction Scheme (the CPRS) – as the mechanism through which Australia would meet its quantified GHG emission limitation or reduction commitments under Annex B to the Kyoto Protocol over the Protocol's first commitment period (2008–2012)(see question 32). The CPRS is designed to reduce Australia's GHG emissions, and its main objectives are to give effect to Australia's obligations under the UNFCCC and the Kyoto Protocol and to support the development of an effective global response to climate change. Emissions reduction targets under the CPRS are clearly joined to the content and ambitions of a global climate change agreement.

Argentina has public administration for the management of Climate Change policy. The Secretary of Environment and Sustainable Development (SAyDS) was appointed as the authority for the enforcement of the law 24295 by which the Republic of Argentina has ratified the UNFCCC.

International political aspects are also relevant for climate strategies as is reported for Israel. In the agreement between Israel and the Hashemite Kingdom of Jordan, Section 19 defines the general principles for cooperation in the use of energy. These principles include cooperation in the development of solar energy. This cooperation has already found fruit in the cooperative venture for solar energy in the Gulf of Aqaba and Eilat. In addition, further agreements ought to be signed between the two countries, once these agreements have been ratified by both sides. Regarding the Palestinian Authority, the agreement has not defined clearly the rights and responsibilities over energy uses. Part of the agreement, however, is Section 15, which makes a determination about gas and fuel containers. This section requires the Palestinian Authority to build and site gas and fuel containers in such a fashion as to not cause a negative effect on the environment or safety factors in Israel or Israeli settlements. The section requires the Palestinians to use standards for the protection of the environment that have been developed in the United States, Britain, or Israel.

11.2.5 Part V: Structure and Instruments of Energy and Climate Policies

11.2.5.1 Climate Policies and Energy Regimes

As it is obvious that energy issues are vital for the reduction of GHG emissions, climate policies highly concentrate on energy objectives. There are three main categories of instruments for reaching climate friendly energy objectives. First, developing the use of traditional energy sources technically in order to cut down GHG emissions, secondly energy saving measures concerning all modes of energy and third, the development of "new" energy sources which are supposed to be economically and ecologically friendly. Here the term "renewable" energy has been developed.

In addition to these methods, also passive instruments are relevant, e.g. storage of GHG in the soil or in the seabed.[46] Looking at the map, national and regional climate strategies are based somewhat differently on this composition of instruments. The following models are reported.

The Australian states have the power to adopt energy or climate strategies – so, for example, New South Wales has implements the NSW Greenhouse

[45] See *SRU*, Der Umweltschutz in der Föderalismusreform, Stellungnahme Nr. 10, Februar 2006, p. 5; Hans-Joachim Koch and Susan Krohn, "Umweltschutz in schlechter Verfassung," *Natur und Recht* (2006)28: 673 (676f).

[46] Directive 2009/31/EC of the European Parliament and of the Council of 23 April 2009 on the geological storage of carbon dioxide and amending Council Directive 85/337/EEC, European Parliament and Council Directives 2000/60/EC, 2001/80/EC, 2004/35/EC, 2006/12/EC, 2008/1/EC and Regulation (EC) No 1013/2006.

Gas Reduction Scheme (GGAS) and Queensland has implemented the Queensland Gas Scheme (New South Wales and Queensland are Australian states). The NSW GGAS is a baseline and credit emissions trading scheme focused on reducing greenhouse gas emissions associated with the production and use of electricity; the Queensland Gas Scheme is designed to encourage the development of Queensland's gas industry and to reduce greenhouse gas emissions from the Queensland electricity sector.[47]

States without national energy sources concentrate on measures of sustainability and national safety. Belgium's overall energy policy objectives have concentrated on security of supply based on diversification of geographical sources and fuels, liberalization of the electricity and gas market, energy efficiency, transparent and competitive energy pricing, and environmental protection. More recently, the Federal Plan for Sustainable Development (2004–2008) defined the key strategies in the field of energy policy related to climate change and more intensive use of clean energy.

The Czech Republic government is reported to continue fostering intense contacts with the nuclear industry. The Czech Republic also focuses on energy efficiency and supports a rapid switch towards the use of renewable sources, although it does suggest that (given current technology) renewable energy would not be able to deliver more than 20% of the Czech consumption by 2030. Therefore, its version relies on increased use of natural gas, most probably to be imported from Russia, in the interim. The scenario would prevent the Czech Republic from having to build new nuclear reactors and from extending coal mining activities beyond the territorial limits.

The Finnish government has adopted a climate and energy strategy. It contains to some extent detailed policies and measures which could be adopted up to the year 2020. It also contains certain visions for policies up to 2050. It is not legally binding per se, nor does it contain specific proposals for policies and measures in the form of, for example, legal proposals. Furthermore a special "Government foresight report on climate and energy policy" is being prepared and should be introduced to parliament in the fall of 2009. The foresight report is to outline long-term climate and energy policies and propose measures for action. In comparison to the climate and energy strategy, the foresight report will focus stronger the period after 2020 and up to 2050.

In Germany, it seems that climate strategies are mainly part of land use planning. According to the report "climate protection requirements" must be considered continuously in urban planning according to the Federal Building Code (Baugesetzbuch). Municipalities can and should make a level-specific, municipal contribution to climate change mitigation. This is also expressly recognized in judgments passed by the Federal Administrative Court. For example, under Section 9 (1) No. 23b of the Building Code areas may be designated in which "in the construction of buildings, certain building measures must be implemented to allow the use of renewable energy and particularly solar energy". Under Section 11 (1) No. 4 BauGB, municipalities may agree "the use of district networks and combined heat and power plants and solar energy facilities to provide heat, cooling and electricity supply".

The situation is similar in Ireland where planning and development is a local competence but in addition it has been national policy that has brought about the most significant changes in this area. The Minister for the Environment and Local Government has increased building regulations and efficiency standards, required that buildings which are offered for sale or lease should have a Building Energy Rating ("BER") certificate and exempted small installations of certain renewable energy technologies (wind turbines, solar panels and ground heat pump systems) from the requirement to obtain planning permission. In Ireland, sustainability is, according to the reporter, at the heart of the Government's energy policy objectives. The challenge of creating a sustainable energy future for Ireland is being met through a range of strategies, targets and actions to deliver environmentally sustainable energy supply and use. For this purpose the Government has adopted a White Paper on energy policy.

In Japan and some other states regions and municipalities are legally obliged to have their own action plans. Furthermore, in Japan, each prefecture or municipality has the power to adopt its own ordinances with various sanctions including criminal penalties. While an action plan serves as a guideline for policy-making, ordinances are the major tools for the local governments to implement their own policies effectively.

[47] See Hodgkinson (ed.), "Ch. 6: State and Territory-based Law and Policy" in *Australian Climate Change Law and Policy* (Chatswood: LexisNexis Butterworths, 2009).

In Argentina, the Secretary of Energy (SE) has established a Program of Rational Use of Energy in the year 2004 to encourage electric power savings. Besides, the SE developed the Project of Energy Efficiency with the funding support of the GEF and the participation of the power distributing companies. It is estimated that toward the year 2015, the Project would permit the reduction of 2,400 MW in the electricity demand and a savings of 1,700,000 Toe per year. The accumulated reduction of CO_2 emissions in the 10-year period (2006–2015) is estimated at 28,000,000 ton.

Regional activities within states may support or replace state actions. As reported earlier, the United States to a large extent acts on regional initiatives which, nevertheless, lack legal validity. The support of those initiatives adds pressure on official bodies to enforce legal rules or to adopt legal principles as well. To some extent the situation seems to be comparable in Australia. Here, in the framework of the UNFCCC and Kyoto regime both formal and informal forums present their views to the Commonwealth regarding Australia's position and policies in relation to international climate change processes (Council of Australian Governments, COAG). As the report claims, the Commonwealth Government states that "[m]anaging energy use is a critical issue Australian companies and individuals face in the years ahead, as the world responds to the challenges of climate change, energy security and economic competitiveness. The Australian Government has introduced a series of programs aimed at managing energy use and driving large-scale uptake of clean energy technologies … [These] energy programs and initiatives … represent an important part of the Australian Government's energy strategy."

11.2.5.2 Features on National Legislation

Looking at the content of national legislation on climate change mitigation there are differences both in terms of relation to environmental law and in the choice of legal and market instruments. Most of the EU Member States have transposed the ETS into national detailed law as the Directive requires. Other elements of climate policies or only to a minor extent been regulated by Community Law. There are also attempts to create a legal cover for climate change: the United Kingdom has adopted a "Climate Change Act" that contains provisions for mitigation and adaptation. For Germany it has been mentioned that building law and land use planning are decisive for the content of climate strategies. In addition environmental licensing is connected to climate regimes.

The national reports give detailed information about the legislation which has been adopted for the transposition of the main sources of climate law. EC law of course requires a formal transposition of the directives which mostly leads to the adoption of laws on emission trading schemes. In some countries specific "climate change laws" are projected, others tend to connect the climate change ruling with the legislation on environmental protection. This is in EU states due to the fact that the Directive on Integrated Pollution and Prevention Control (IPPC) is loosely linked to the emission trading scheme. This is the case for instance for the Netherlands. Some countries have adopted specific "carbon" legislation (Ireland). In other countries where national strategies for energy and climate are development, an implementing legislation is foreseen (e.g. Finland).

According to the German Baugesetzbuch a facility designed to use wind energy and hydropower may be approved under a simplified procedure as a development project conducted in the undesignated outlying area.[48] This applies also to a large extent to facilities designed for the use of biomass-generated energy. Also the Federal Immission Control Act (BundesImmissionsschutzgesetz) includes provisions on industrial facilities both about the requirement to use available technology in taking precautionary measures to prevent harmful impacts on the environment (Section 5 (1), first sentence, No. 2) and about the obligation to use energy economically and efficiently (Section 5 (1), first sentence, No. 4 BImSchG). However, these obligations are suspended for all facilities covered by the Emissions Trading Scheme as soon as CO_2 emissions are involved. In such instances, the law relates to industrial facility approval and licensing ranks behind the economic instrument of emissions trading which then comes into play.[49]

[48] For an in-depth view see Hans-Joachim Koch/Reinhard Hendler (footnote 49), § 25, Rn.79.

[49] See Hans-Joachim Koch and Annette Wienecke, "Klimaschutz durch Emissionshandel – Das europäische und deutsche Anlagengenehmigungsrecht als Ordnungsrahmen," *Deutsches Verwaltungsblatt* (2001) 14: 1085; Eckard Rehbinder and Michael Schmalholz, "Handel mit Emissionsrechten für Treibhausgase in der Europäischen Union," *Umwelt Und Planungsrecht* (2002) 22:1.

In Japan, the recent significant fluctuations in oil prices have particularly influenced the national energy policy, and the official programs stress the needs for the stabilization of the oil supply and demand structure. The impact of energy consumption on the global environment is the second concern. The Whitepaper on Energy, 2006, compiled by the Agency for Natural Resources and Energy under the Ministry of Economy, Trade and Industry, stresses the needs for simultaneously solving the energy supply issue and the environmental problems. The Basic Act on Energy Policy (2002) defines the three basic policy categories: the securing of the stable supply of energy, the environmental suitability, and the utilization of market mechanisms. – The Metropolitan (Prefectural) Government of Tokyo adopted in 2008 an ordinance to require all large-scale business operators to reduce their GHG emissions; the ordinance also introduced an emissions trading scheme to be implemented in 2010. Tokyo has been acting within the scope of the authority legally given to a prefectural government though the Metropolitan government engages in its own international activities. The only emissions trading mechanism in operation is Japan's Voluntary Emissions Trading Scheme (JVETS) that deals only with CO_2.

In Italy, a system of green certificates has been introduced in Italy by Decree.[50] This system is reported as an "Implementation of Directive 96/92 on the liberalization of the electricity market", which favors a policy of encouragement of renewable energy that is combined with the creation of a market for electricity.

In Israel, the major thrust of government legislation in the last several years has been twofold. The government has encouraged competition in the production of energy, while it is requiring energy conservation.[51] All large energy users are now required to prepare a study showing measures to conserve energy. The study is to be updated once a year. In addition, factories with large energy requirements must appoint an employee to be responsible for promoting the efficient use of energy. This employee prevents energy waste, supervises maintenance procedures, measures energy use and types of fuel, and trains personnel in energy conservation. The most ambitious piece of legislation in the field of energy was published in 1996, titled the Energy Enterprise Law.

In the Netherlands, the Environmental Management Act comprises a range of important regulatory tools, but in addition a range of other acts is relevant, notably in the field of energy law. The applicable legislation needs to be amended since the European Directive on renewable energy has to be implemented before 5 December 2010. Currently, access to the grid is a major problem: the government has proposed to adopt an act to give better access to renewable energy.[52] In order to advance the establishment of works in view of combating the economic crisis, the government has proposed a "Crisis and Restoration Act", which aims at relaxing substantive and procedural requirements for major construction activities like highways but also energy projects (like windmills and geological storage of carbon). This legislative proposal has been adopted – after much discussion about its usefulness – by the Dutch Parliament. Just before the adoption, members of Parliament (the Senate) requested to leave the geological storage of carbon dioxide out of the scope of this project, but that has not been supported by the majority.

11.2.5.3 Energy Policies and the Position of Renewable Energy

Use of Renewable Energy Sources

There are at least two main issues involved in the approach. First, countries with the possibility to favor the use of available natural resources may adopt priorities for different sources. In the future "energy mix", i.e. a rational combination of renewable energy sources (wind, water, solar energy, geothermal and biomass) will play an increasing role in the context of an environmentally friendly energy supply and the management of the infrastructure. Secondly, states may set requirements for the origin of sources of electricity and support the market for renewable sources ("green electricity").

In Germany, the renewable energy strategies have a central position in the mitigation of GHG emissions. Renewable energy resources are also seen as 'infinite'.

[50] Decree 16 March 1999 no. 79, Bersani Decree.

[51] Sources of Energy (Undertaking a Study to Find the Potential for Energy Conservation) Regulation, K.T. 5763 p. 1099 and Energy Sources (Supervision of Efficient Use of Energy) Regulation, K.T. 5764 p. 10.

[52] Wijziging van de Gaswet en de Elektriciteitswet 1998, tot versterking van de werking van de gasmarkt, verbetering van de voorzieningszekerheid en houdende regels met betrekking tot de voorrang voor duurzame elektriciteit.

The reporter emphasizes that this notion is ambivalent. First, the generation of biomass often conflicts with other uses of agricultural land and secondly in the production of renewable resources the interest of preserving nature and the landscape as well as nature conservation provisions must be taken into account.

Looking at the social and market situation, there is no common structure in the described aspects. The percentage of renewable sources in national electricity production seems to be rather modest, but still somewhat increasing. Numbers of growth were reported from Ireland. Here renewable primary energy grew by 12% in 2007, and the growth in the period 1990–2007 was 182% (6.3% per annum on average). At the same time renewable energy accounted for 2.9% of total primary energy requirement (TPER) in 2007.

Development plans are most concrete concerning wind and solar energy. Water energy would be rather efficient and technically easy to create but the opposition is often based on environmental concerns. The obstacles are both technical and economic by nature – in addition to the view that for instance nuclear energy would bring stability for industry and the households. Despite the reality some states have adopted a proactive position and strive to support renewal energy by law or at least by national strategies. The national reports are quite informative.

In Belgium the market share of the different energy sources in primary energy consumption in 2003 was as follows: petroleum and petroleum products: 41.4%; natural gas: 24.7%; nuclear energy: 21.2%; solid fuels: 10.6%; renewable fuels: 1.1%; other: 1.0%. The main renewable energy sources used in Belgium are biomass and renewable recovery fuels. Renewable energy represents only a small share of primary energy generation in Belgium.

The Belgian Federal Act on the operation of the electricity market of 1999 contains different articles on public service obligations, the market for green certificates for electricity produced from renewable energy and the construction of off-shore wind farms along the Belgian coast. A new market mechanism has been set up, consisting in a system of 'green certificates' (GC). These are delivered to the 'green' producer. In addition, procedures guaranteeing priority access to the network are implemented for renewable electricity or electricity from high quality CHP. Electricity suppliers are obliged to buy a minimum volume of 'green' electricity (i.e. made from renewable energy resources: wind, hydro, solar, biomass, cogeneration).

In Germany a successful regulatory instrument was introduced with the Renewable Energy Sources Act (EEG 2009). Germany has long played a pioneering role in the promotion of renewable energy, particularly wind energy. The aim of the later on amended act is to generate 30% of electricity supply from renewable energy resources by 2020. The underlying regulatory notion was implemented under the Stromeinspeisungsgesetz (law on feeding electricity from renewable resources into the public grid 1990). At the core there are two fundamental obligations for electricity grid operators: they must, first, give priority to feeding, transmitting and distributing energy generated by renewable resources. In return they, second, pay a guaranteed price designed to promote use of renewable energy, which is not yet market-ready.[53] The EU Court of Justice has classified this instrument as compliant with EU law. It does not involve unlawful state subsidies, because no state funding is involved. Regulatory requirements play a significant role in climate change mitigation also in the building sector. The Energy Saving Ordinance (EnEV 65, last amendment in 2009) deserves a special mention in this regard.

For the Czech Republic a rather reluctant position is reported due to its role as producer of hard coal. The state has one of the lowest energy import dependencies in the European Union, mainly due to its domestically produced solid fuels. Imports are limited to natural gas and oil from Russia. Still, the share of renewable energy sources has also been increasing, but below the EU average. An act on the promotion of electricity produced from renewable energy sources, which implemented the EU Directive 2001/77/EC, entered into effect on 1 August 2005. Key feature is preferential connection to the grid. There is an obligation for operators of the regional grid systems and the transmission system operator to purchase all electricity from renewable sources.

In Finland, the use of renewable energy sources forms a significant part of the national energy mix (about 25% of total energy consumption in 2006). A bulk of renewable energy production consists of the

[53] BGBl I 1990, p. 2633; last amended by law enacted 24 April 1998: BGBl I 1998, p. 730. On 1 April 2000 the Renewable Energy Sources Act (EEG 2000) dated 29 March 2000: BGB1 I 2000, p. 305 replaced the Stromeinspeisungsgesetz.

use of wood and similar biomass, such as for example residues in the lumber, pulp and paper industries. Currently there are plans of introducing a feed in tariff for electricity generated from some renewable energy sources. However, some contradictory incentives can also be found since for example the use of peat is also being subsidized in a similar manner.

The Irish Sustainable Energy Act 2002 creates Sustainable Energy Ireland (SEI), which has amongst its functions (a) to promote and assist environmentally and economically sustainable production, supply and use of energy and (b) to promote and assist energy efficiency and renewable sources of energy.

In the United States, every state had by 2006 adopted measures for climate change, and a number of cities have GHG-reduction targets.[54] As of August 2009, 23 states had announced GHG emissions targets, often expressed as a reduction of emissions to the level (or below the level) of a prior year State measures include more than 250 types of policy and regulatory actions. Some focus directly on GHGs and climate; others focus on energy, transportation, agriculture, land use, waste management, and construction.[55] Some states have climate change commissions to examine consequences of climate change and recommend policies; others have GHG mitigation action plans or broader climate action plans. A majority of states require or encourage major sources to report GHG emissions, often through the Climate Registry, a nonprofit North American collaboration that sets standards for identifying, calculating, verifying, and reporting GHG emissions. Some states have economy-wide emissions targets, while others have GHG standards for electric power or vehicles. A few states have standards for appliance efficiency that are more stringent than federal standards.

California has adopted solutions which are different from the other states of the US. As the reporter describes, California has enacted a comprehensive program to mitigate climate change. The state emits more GHGs than most nations and may suffer significant adverse effects from climate change, The Global Warming Solutions Act of 2006 recognized global warmings threat to the "economic well-being, public health, natural resources, and the environment of California," and therefore authorized legal mechanisms to reduce GHG emissions. Under AB 32, the California Air Resources Board (CARB) has authority to "adopt rules and regulations…to achieve the maximum technologically feasible and cost-effective greenhouse gas emission reductions." The law requires reduction of California GHG emissions to 1990 levels by 2020, with continued reductions thereafter. It requires mandatory reporting and verification of GHG emissions, as well as use of planning, regulations, and market mechanisms to achieve maximum reductions of GHGs.

In Argentina a national plan for wind power is linked to the development of the national wind energy industry: it foresees the installation of 300 MW of power in a first phase in various wind farms with an investment of the order of U$S 300 million. An act in 2006 regulates and promotes the production and use of biofuels. From the year 2010 on, it will be obligatory to add biofuels to all the liquid fuels used in transportation.

In Australia the use of renewable energy sources in Australia is limited. From 1 January 2010 the Commonwealth's RET commits Australia to increase it electricity from renewable energy sources by an additional 45,000 GWh per year by 2020; at least 20% of Australia's electricity needs will be met by renewable sources by that date. The RET 'places an obligation on energy retailers to purchase a certain proportion of their energy from renewable sources in the form of renewable energy certificates'.[56]

In Japan, the RPS (Renewable Portfolio Standard) program obliges power companies to supply certain amounts of electric power generated by renewable energy to consumers. It has not been quite successful so far because the deployment targets were set at such low levels that all power companies fulfilled the targets in excess, resulting in slow market activities for renewable energy.

The system is enforced under the New Energy Use Special Measures Act. The statute's stated purpose is

[54] E.g., US Conference of Mayors, Climate Protection Agreement, www.usmayors.org/climate protection/agreement.htm, joined by 1,011 mayors (last visited Oct. 22, 2009).

[55] Strategies include, e.g., efficiencies in energy, transportation, and land use, conservation of energy, efficiencies in agriculture and forestry, waste reduction and recycling, improvement in industry processes. See 42 U.S.C. § 6833(a), (b) (requiring states to review residential and commercial building codes and determine whether they should adopt specified energy codes for buildings).

[56] Shannon, Green and Thompson, 'Commonwealth Policy and Legislation' in Climate Change Law and Policy in Australia, LexisNexis, 2009 at [5–205].

"to take necessary measures relating to the use of new energy by electricity retailers in order to enhance the stability of energy supply, thereby contributing to environmental conservation and furthering the sound development of the national economy."

Incentives and Taxes

The reporters were asked about economic or other economic instruments for the use of renewal energy or for the mitigation of GHG emissions. Taxes may function as an incentive or as a burden.

The energy tax constitutes the most common steering element on the market; it favors environmentally friendly solutions and burdens others. Energy taxes are usually not ear-marked. In Finland there are constitutional reasons. In Japan the energy tax is imposed on the sales of petroleum, coal and electricity in Japan. The purpose of spending the tax is not specified except for the Power-Sources Development Promotion Tax imposed on the sales of electricity. The government spends Power-Sources Tax mainly for improving various conditions for power generation facilities: for example, communities surrounding nuclear power plants receive subsidies for accepting such "high-risk" facilities. The energy tax rate is relatively low in Japan.

In different regions of Belgium there is a support scheme for ecological investments, including investments in renewable energy and on the federal level there is 13.5% tax abatement for RES investments for corporation tax purposes. Similar is reported for some other countries as well.

Also tariff-based incentives exist (Czech Republic). In Australia where electricity needs to be met by renewable sources by 2020, financial support is given to accelerate the installation of renewable energy technologies. The purpose of the Act No 180/2005 on the promotion of electricity produced from renewable energy sources is to support the use of renewable sources of energy, specifically wind, solar and geothermal energy; hydropower; soil, air and biomass energy; landfill gas, sewer gas, and biogas.

In Germany car manufacturers who fail to meet the prescribed emission targets will in future pay a penalty (95 € for each gram emitted in excess of the threshold).[57] Japan may impose an obligation on electricity retailers to use a certain amount of electricity from new energy by declaring an order. It is a sanction-based program with criminal penalties.

Green or ecological certificates on techniques and products are a largely adopted marketing instrument.

11.2.5.4 Instruments of Mitigating CO_2 Emissions

Kyoto Related Mechanisms

The European Union has under the Kyoto regime adopted regional legislation on the reduction of CO_2 emissions. The emission trading scheme (ETS) is based on Directive 2003/87/EC.[58] As mentioned above, Directive 2008/101/EC extends the ETS to aviation activities in the scheme for greenhouse gas emission allowance trading within the Community from 2 February 2010 onwards. Further measures of harmonization are numerous.[59]

National reports present the national legislation of the Member States transposing the directives and related provisions. Other states may have corresponding regimes based on Kyoto or otherwise. All over, one relevant question is how seriously states are taking their commitments set under the international regimes including national emission limits; another how likely it is states will reach that goal. All reported states seem to have a political intention to do so as they have ratified or approved to follow the international target.

On the other hand, national reports show that the legislation on ETS is largely complicated and that the transparency and reviewability of the decision-making falls short. Traditional legal principles are at stake when dealing with the justification of the allocation

[57] Regulation (EC) No. 443/2009 of the European Parliament and the Council of 23 April 2009 on setting emission performance standards for new passenger cars as part of the Community's integrated approach to reduce CO_2 emissions from light-duty vehicles.

[58] Directive 2003/87/EC of the European Parliament and of the Council of 13 October 2003 establishing a scheme for greenhouse gas emission allowance trading within the Community and amending Council Directive 96/61/EC, amended by Directive 2004/101/EC of the European Parliament and of the Council of 27 October 2004 amending Directive 2003/87/EC establishing a scheme for greenhouse gas emission allowance trading within the Community.

[59] See e.g. Commission Regulation (EC) No 2216/2004 of 21 December 2004 for a standardized and secured system of registries pursuant to Directive 2003/87/EC of the European Parliament and of the Council, amended by Commission Regulation (EC) No 916/2007 of 31 July 2007 and Commission Regulation (EC) No 994/2008 of 8 October 2008.

and validity of trading allowances which, in the end, represent both property values and conditions for economic activities. In the Netherlands, the national climate legislation will be largely amended in 2010 or shortly there after in order to implement the EU climate and energy package that provided new rules with regard to emissions trading, renewable energy, and the geological storage of CO_2. One of the concerns is the transparency and structure of the national climate legislation.

In addition to the European Union other regional market organizations are relevant from a climate point of view. Argentina represents the MERCOSUR, Australia is a member of the Asia-Pacific Economic Organization (APEC) and the Pacific Islands Forum. Most of the reported countries are also members of the OECD (Organization for Economic Cooperation and Development) and other organizations with certain climate competences.

As reported for Australia, the country has a quantified GHG emission limitation or reduction commitment under Annex B to the Kyoto Protocol is 108% of its 1990 emissions over the Protocol's first commitment period (2008–2012). A national report states Australia ratified the Kyoto Protocol to the UNFCCC, agreeing to limit the annual carbon pollution to 108% of 1990 levels during the period 2008–2012. Without action by Australian governments, businesses and households, our carbon pollution would have risen to 124% of 1990 levels during the period 2008–2012.[60] Emissions projections released in August 2009 showed that Australia is on track to meet its Kyoto target, with emissions expected to reach on average 583 Mt CO_2-e per annum over the Kyoto period, which is 107% of 1990 levels.

According to the report, Japan is committed to reduce its GHG emissions by 6% from the level of the base year (1990) in the first commitment period. However, the GHG emissions in Japan have been increasing; the emissions amounted to 1,374 million t-CO_2 in 2007, an increase by 9.0% from the Kyoto Protocol base year (National Greenhouse Gas Inventory of Japan). – The basic strategy rests on carbon stocking through forest management and some market-based means of the Kyoto mechanisms. As for the domestic GHG emissions, the government stresses the significance of nuclear power generation as a non-GHG-emitting power technology although the environmental NGO's and other concerned citizens are opposed to the dependence on nuclear power generation for electricity supply. – As a result of the general elections held in August 2009, the new government led by the Democratic Party has started to campaign for a new direction. Prime Minister Hatoyama upholds a policy that seeks to reduce GHG emissions by 25% over 1990 levels by 2020. The previous government led by the Liberal Democratic Party set the 2020 goal at a 15% reduction from the 2005 levels, which meant only an 8% reduction from 1990. The new government policy may be based on the political ambition to create a clear image of difference from the former regime, on a genuine will to address the global environmental concern, or on both. It is too early to evaluate the content and nature of the new policy direction.

Within the European Union the use of instruments are similar or comparable transpositions of the EU strategies and regulations. For instance, the European Union and Germany have launched an energy efficiency offensive in all 'key sectors'. In the German policy key sectors involved in energy efficiency policy are: (1) boosting competition in energy efficiency in the course of the liberalization of the energy market; (2) promotion of energy efficiency in residential buildings; (3) efficiency requirements for energy-using appliances and equipment; (4) creating the conditions to increase energy efficiency in vehicles; and (5) promoting energy efficiency in industrial facilities.

For most EU Member States it is reported that the measures required, including the "EU bubble" of the Kyoto mechanisms and the burden share agreement are transposed at least to a minimum and that future policies will follow as soon as international commitments are reached. However, some countries see themselves as ambitious forerunners and try to reach further steps than the formal minimum set in international contexts. Mostly this attitude leads to the enlargement of the categories of sources in the Kyoto quota regime. The reporters largely explain that this trend is not common in their states.

Strategies and Sinks

Additional efforts occur in order to give strategies more efficiency than just a market system for economic business. Especially the national development of

[60] http://www.climatechange.gov.au/~/media/publications/international/dl-international-brochure-series.ashx.

climate-related energy policies in terms of subsidized renewal energies varies depending also on the structure and availability of these sources. In other countries sinks may play a role in the calculation of practical energy solutions. It seems also that some countries may use sinks basically as a political argument for profiting in international negotiations. This is a problem not only in terms of reaching consensus on caps but also sink calculations would treat states very differently both in setting targets and in emission trading. But it is difficult to point at players in this game – it is more important to find a reasonable solution for the role of sinks in the Kyoto process. Many countries, e.g. Italy, describe how reforestation and vegetation has been used strategically to influence the total emissions of GHG. There the national plan in order to set the maximum emission levels, takes into account the national potential maximum size of carbon that can be obtained through afforestation, reforestation, forest management , management of agricultural soils and pastures, revegetation.[61] According to the report, the whole amount is estimated on the assumption of fully using the potential for absorption of such activities. It also takes into account further reduction measures in individual sectors and additional carbon credits obtained through projects of joint implementation and clean development Mechanisms.

In other EU countries the situation is similar. For Finland the moment predictions seem to indicate that there would be a net increase in sinks during the period of 2008–2012. Also Ireland benefits from afforestation sinks and is in the process of developing policies.

Outside the EU sinks seem to have a high political status in some countries. Japan has two thirds of the national land covered by forest which makes the country heavily dependent on the carbon sink program. Of the 6% pledged reduction target, 3.8% is to be achieved through forest sink activities. In 2006, the carbon sequestrated by forest management in Japan was estimated to be 37.2 million t-CO_2, or 3.0% of the GHG emissions in the base year, 1990. According to the reporter, in order to achieve the official goal, trees must be cultivated on additional 200,000 ha or the total of 550,000 ha of forest land every year, according to the Forestry Agency under the Ministry of Agriculture, Forestry and Fishery. A national campaign has been in place since 2007. The goal of such campaign is to manage 3.3 million hectares of forest land in 6 years.

In Australia, the forestry sub-sector, under Kyoto accounting rules, covers new forests established by direct human action on land not forested in 1990. No forestry sinks are included in the 1990 baseline, and only afforestation and reforestation occurring since 1 January 1990 is credited. Australian forestry removals were 20.5 Mt CO_2-e in 2008 under Kyoto Protocol. Removals over the 2008–2012 period with the application of the Kyoto Protocol harvest sub-rule 8 are projected to also be 20.5 Mt CO_2-e per annum, and 5.1 Mt CO_2-e in 2020.[62] But it occurs that with emissions expected to reach on average 583 Mt CO_2-e per annum over the Kyoto period – 107% of 1990 levels – Australia is on line to meet its Kyoto Protocol target. – In 2010 the Australian Government noted that the land sector – agriculture and forestry – has an important role to play in reducing concentrations of greenhouse gases in the atmosphere. For Australia, emissions from natural events can overwhelm our national accounts. For example, greenhouse gas emissions from the January 2003 bushfires represented more than one-third of Australia's total emissions for that year. Because of the risk these events pose to meeting our emissions targets, Australia has not taken on voluntary accounting commitments for the land sector.

Enlargement of Kyoto Obligations

The discussion on enlarging the ETS to other than Kyoto substances and activities has met political interest especially in the Netherlands and Germany. The Dutch reporter takes up the fact that both directive 2003/87/EC and directive 1996/96/EC set limitations for actions. The directives state that emissions limit values shall not be prescribed for direct carbon emissions from installations covered by the EU ETS. This qualifies as a rule of total harmonization.[63]

[61] See for CIPE n. 123 del 19 dicembre 2002, G.U. n. 68 del 3.3.2003.

[62] Department of Climate Change, 'Tracking to Kyoto and 2020: Australia's Greenhouse Emissions Trends 1990 to 2008–2012 and 2020' at http://www.climatechange.gov.au/government/~/media/publications/projections/tracking-to-kyoto-and-2020.ashx, p 48.

[63] See about the role of art. 176 EC Treaty (now article 193 TFEU) in view of total harmonization Jan H. Jans, Hans H.B. Vedder, *European Environmental Law*, 3rd ed. (Groningen: Europa Law Publishing, 2008), 107. See also the recent interesting opinion of AG Kokott in case 378/08.

The EU Treaty should not on the other hand prevent Member States from adopting necessary more stringent measures, as long as they are compatible with the EC basic rules.[64] As a conclusion the report seems to support the wish of some Member States, like the UK, to move beyond the climate ambition of the EU. In view of article 193 TFEU Member States should be able to adopt further going commitments for the EU ETS installations like coal fired power plants. Currently, power installations covered by the EU ETS will most likely not be confronted with emission limitations with respect to the direct emissions of carbon dioxide.

In Germany, with the amendments to the Combined Heat and Power Act (KWPG) in 2008 and 2009, the percentage share of high-efficiency CHP plants in electricity and heat generation (primary energy use over 90%) will increase from 12% to 25%.[65] District heat networks will also be expanded. In the buildings sector, the Energy Saving Ordinance (EnEV) was amended, with the requirements for restricting primary energy use and transmission heat loss being significantly tightened. The Heat Cost Ordinance (HeizkostenV) was also amended to foster energy-saving behavior among tenants of rented premises. – In Finland some studies have been made as for the application of a quota or trading scheme as for certain polluting discharges in the Baltic Sea area.

Policies and National Measures on the Use of Climate Mechanisms (Mandatory and Voluntary)

Due to the multifaceted structure of climate strategies and legislation, the way of meeting global and regional goals often opens approaches, either new climate-oriented or embedded ones. In order to reach balanced and efficient tools, programmatic evaluations and strategies are required. These may present themselves as inventive or bureaucratic, the area is covered by often random models. Often states satisfy with adding climate change as a goal of laws on nature conservation and pollution control. Climate change also appears to be a largely accepted ground for collecting additional fees and taxes from all actors, and consumers who in the end pay the bill. In fact, it seems that there has been no real discussion about who should really pay. Payments are not optional since strategies cover all areas of economy and living. On the other hand, climate change also leads to value transfers because economical resources are used not only as burden but also as incentives and subsidies for others.

Argentina has a fiscal policy of subsidies and tax benefits for planted forests, which in addition to the promotion of the industry, contributes to its development in an environmentally sustainable way. This policy has led during the last years to the increment of the carbon stored in the commercial plantations. The network of national parks and other protected areas in the wooded regions totals 2,260,000 ha, and there is wide number of proposals of conservation programs that would considerably expand that surface. This network, and their eventual enlargement, will contribute to limit deforestation and eventually to generate net flows of carbon removal.

In Australia, individual Australians and Australian businesses were able since 2009 to open accounts in the Australian National Registry of Emissions Units, thus enabling them to participate in the global carbon market by trading Kyoto units using the Registry. Simultaneously also on Commonwealth established Australia's National Authority for the Clean Development Mechanism (CDM) and Joint Implementation (JI). The objective is to access the cost-effective abatement opportunities that exist internationally.[66] Carbon credits generated by CDM and JI projects can be traded on international carbon markets. Under the proposed Australian ETS, from 1 July 2011, liable entities will be able to use eligible credits generated from CDM and JI projects for compliance.

In addition to the ETS, EU Member States have additional economic incentives. Germany has developed a set of economic instruments aiming especially at energy efficiency and energy saving projects. Since the energy demand is increasing at the same time, new energy sources must developed and for this purpose economic incentives may be used to support the use of renewable energy sources. Similar approaches are found in the Dutch climate strategies. The challenge to overcome local resistance against windmill

[64] Jans and Vedder take a contrary position, see p. 108–109.

[65] See the instructive overview by Franz Reimer, "Ansätze zur Erhöhung der Energieeffizienz im Europarecht – eine kritische Bestandsaufnahme," in *Europäisches Klimaschutzrecht*, ed. Schulze-Fielitz and Müller (Baden-Baden: Nomos, 2009), 147.

[66] http://www.climatechange.gov.au/minister/wong/2009/media-releases/September/mr20090930.aspx.

parks and storage of CO_2 is common for most Member States as well states around the world. Local authorities may not necessarily act in favor of national energy strategies.

11.2.5.5 Emission Trading Scheme

Legislative Basis

Emission trading is one of the mechanisms under Kyoto and also an optional instrument for the management of emission rights in general. The national models may due to different origin have variable legal and economic structures. The reporters were first asked whether there is a legislation regulating emission trading and what the political basis has been. For the EU Member States the regular model is the transposition of the ETS of the EU but since this system allows for more stringent (broader) applications the legislative structures are not uniform. According to EU law ETS applies to carbon dioxide emissions from a number of high energy industries, including the production and processing of ferrous metals, the mineral industry, pulp and paper plants and aviation. Today, Member States are under the obligation to transpose the ETS as far as it applies to GHGs under the scheme. Later on the EU ETS will include perflourocarbons and nitrous oxide and thus cover the production of aluminum, non-ferrous metals and various types of chemicals. In the reports national ETS laws are presented.

Outside the EU, the US Energy Policy Act of 1992 is a broad statute that outlined a number of energy strategies and programs to reduce harmful emissions, responded to the UNFCCC. Addressing global climate change specifically, the Energy Policy Act established a Director of Climate Protection in the Department of Energy, required a national inventory of aggregate GHG emissions, called for guidelines for voluntary reporting of GHG emissions and reductions, and authorized a Global Climate Change Response Fund to help mitigate and adapt to world climate change. The US submits annual GHG inventory reports to the Convention of the Parties under the UNFCCC. In 2008, US officials announced a new national goal, applying incentives to stop growth of GHG emissions by 2025. The President renewed his commitment in September 2009 remarks to the UN Climate Change Summit, promising that the US would fight climate change by "investing in renewable energy and promoting greater efficiency and slashing our emissions to reach the targets we set for 2020 and our long-term goals for 2050".

As of February 2010, Australia does not have a national emission trading law. The 11 Bills which make up the Government's proposed CPRS legislative package were first introduced into the Commonwealth Parliament in 2009 and voted down by the Senate later on. Same was repeated with the same result. For a third time the proposed legislation was introduced and then subsequently passed by the House on 11 February 2010. Debate is now adjourned until May 2010. The proposed CPRS, the center piece of the Government's domestic climate change mitigation strategy, adopts a market-based cap and trade approach to put a price on carbon. As with any cap-and-trade system, the CPRS contains several core features. It places a cap on Australia's long-term carbon emissions levels, creates a mechanism to set annual scheme caps designed to achieve the long-term cap, provides for the allocation of tradable permits (Australian emission reduction units) up to the annual scheme cap, identifies entities liable under the scheme and requires those entities to surrender permits for each ton of carbon dioxide equivalent they emit each year and finally establishes an enforcement mechanism to ensure compliance.

Actors and Their Functions

Since the emission trading system is basically regulated by its objective, not by its mode of enforcement, the choices in this respect vary from state to state. The procedure of granting emission allowances is to some extent under legal control because actors must be treated equally and without disturbance on the economic market. The national reports give detailed information about adopted legislative measures. What is common, especially under the EU rulings, is the adoption of a national allocation plan for emission trading. This plan has a primary function due to its role as creating substantial emission rights. After that the market rules very much depend on the demand of new emission allowances and the values set for the exchange. In some cases it may be, in the long run, more profitable to a company to take measures for reducing emissions than to acquire expensive allowances. This choice again may depend on the national climate policy and its incentives for new technologies or energy sources. A stringent climate strategy may lead to a market with a low demand of allowances. If the market is supranational countries with a high demand may then neglect climate-based improvements and instead focus on getting additional allowance at a reasonable cost.

Here energy policies come in and of course also the use of other Kyoto mechanisms (JI, CDM), which basically is an option of the actors themselves. The two following structures concerning national allocation plans and the procedure for distributing allowances to operators are common for most reported Member States. Annex III of the EU Emissions Trading Directive[67] lists the criteria to be considered in the development of the National Allocation Plan. The EU Commission also issued guidelines.[68] Germany has adopted as its main objective the substitution of the carbon-containing fossil fuels coal, mineral oil and gas through the use of renewable energy. This has led to specific regulations on electricity feeding which has been mentioned above.[69]

In Belgium, the National Allocation Plan is elaborated by the National Climate Commission. It consists of the coordination and integration of four partial allocation plans, elaborated by the three regional governments and the federal government, each for the installations that fall under their competence. After adaptation in accordance with the remarks put forward by the European Commission, the initial allocation of allowances to the installations covered by the scheme is done by the federal and regional governments, each for the installations under their competence and registered in the National Registry kept by the Federal Public Service for the Environment. All transactions done by operators of installations which fall under the scheme will be registered in the National Registry.

In Ireland, operators in industries falling under the EU ETS are granted emissions credits by the Irish government. The allocation of these emissions credits is based on national allocation plan ("NAP") which is drawn up by the Environmental Protection Agency and approved by the European Commission. For the first 8 years of the scheme over 90% of these allowances are to be granted for free. On April 30 of each year, an operator must surrender sufficient allowances to cover the verified emissions it has produced or pay a penalty which is now €100 per ton. Unused allowances can be sold to other operators and under the Kyoto flexible mechanisms. The Emissions Trading Registry (ETR) for Ireland is managed by the Environmental Protection Agency.

In the Czech Republic, a publicly accessible allowance trading register is set up. The register is administered by the electricity market operator for an agreed fee. In Finland, allocation of allowances is governed by the Emissions Trading Act and the National Allocation Plan thereto. During the 2005–2007 and 2008–2012 periods allowances are allocated free of charge to installations in accordance with the Finnish National Allocation Plan and the Commission decision pertaining to it. The market is operated by private exchanges. Over the counter deals are also concluded. In Italy, since April 2007, a "Platform of exchange" is operating. The "Platform" is managed by the Energy Market Administrator (Gestore del Mercato Elettrico, GME), which used to operate with the market for green certificates and white certificates. The exchange of allowances can occur either on a bilateral basis (trade OTC, Over the Counter) or through the mechanisms of a Stock Exchange. The reporter claims that before establishing the platform "small" operators, such as small and medium enterprises experienced significant problems in finding missing shares necessary to cover their emissions both because of the cost and the objective difficulties in operating in foreign markets.

Position of Foreign Companies as Buyers of Allowances on the Stock Market

Since climate strategies are based on global and regional arrangements, nationally adopted mechanisms should function over state borders. Protectionism in the framework of the Kyoto mechanisms is not tolerated but on the other hand states have different positions in terms of their obligations and rights. Also, regional mechanisms, as for instance the EU ETS, have the intention to enforce the fulfillment of the burden of the EU as a whole. Emission trading is primarily a tool for these states to balance their national allocation schemes. Operators and other actors are therefore in principle entitled to buy and sell their allowances over state borders. These states may on the other at the same time profit from the two other Kyoto mechanisms (JI and CDM) and fulfill their obligations outside the EU. The EU ETS does not as such set market restrictions for the interchange of allocated allowances.

---

[67] Directive 2003/87/EC.

[68] COM(2003) 830 and COM(2005)703 see http://www.epa.ie/whatwedo/climate/etscheme/naps/.

[69] Stromeinspeisungsgesetz (law on feeding electricity from renewable resources into the public grid) and the Renewable Energy Sources Act (EEG) of 2008.

For Belgium is reported that only operators of installations subject to Directive 2003/97/EC which are established in Belgium can receive initial allowances from the competent authorities in application of the National Allocation Plan. There is a reserve for new entrants, but these allowances can only be allocated when operations are started in Belgium. In Finland, a registry account holder is allowed to buy allowances. The initial allocation of allowances has taken place in accordance with the Finnish National Allocation Plan.

In Ireland, any legal person may apply for a permit (allowance). This presumably includes foreign companies, although as the regulations are only effective within the territory of the state, these are unlikely to need permits. Foreign companies may also apply for an account on the ETR. Article 12 of the Regulations allows the transfer of allowances between persons within the European Community.

External Connections of the Emission-Trading Scheme and the Link to Energy Policies

Energy production is one of the major sources of GHG emissions. Therefore ETS affects this sector essentially. As states are autonomous concerning the choice of energy sources and various reasons may restrain from renewing the use of energy policies, the ETS does not necessarily lead to the adoption of sound technical solutions. Anyway, the reports show that there is a slow move towards modernizing GHG installations and that also the two other Kyoto mechanisms invite to invest in new energy choices. So far, some countries have already a rather detailed legislation for the electricity sector (Germany, Belgium and other EU countries). In many countries projects and programs have been adopted generally in order to reduce GHG emissions (US, Italy). Since CDM and JI projects are run abroad the role of international finance institutions (World Bank) may be important for the realization of installations and their technologies. For Italy it is reported that a Carbon Fund has been established; its purpose is to support the purchase of emission credits from "projects which will provide global environmental benefits while promoting the spread of modern technology and clean energy in developing countries and countries with economies in transition".

As far as the German legislation is concerned, the regulatory core of the Renewable Energies Heat Act (EEWärmeG) comprises the statutory obligation to cover a percentage of heat demand from renewable energy sources. The percentage involved depends on the type of energy used and ranges from 15% for solar energy to 50% for biofuel.[70] However, the obligation to meet heat demand using renewables may be replaced by other measures, however. This applies, for example, if at least 50% of heat demand is met from high-performance CHP plants. Also, it is permissible to substitute the use of renewable energy by meeting a greater percentage than that prescribed with high energy-efficiency in buildings.[71] This means that building owners must exceed the EnEV requirements by 15%. The aim of these and other provisions is to prevent the rise of the financial burden a reasonable level when these climate change instruments are used. Around half of the energy used in Germany goes to supplying heat and for refrigeration. The plan is presently that the share of renewable sources in heat supply will be increased from the current 6.6–14% in 2020.

The Position of ETS Allowances in Property and Tax Law

The picture of allowances as property and their legal treatment from this point is diffuse. It seems that some states have not clarified their position legally since allowances are treated rather as random bonuses or administratively granted rights (Ireland). Other countries have adopted clear taxation provisions for the distribution of allowances. This is the case in the Czech Republic; here, the Act of Value Added Tax No. 235/2004 Coll. applies when greenhouse gas emissions are transferred to another operator (the basic rate of the tax is 19%).

The Belgian reporter presents a case where the Constitutional Court ruled that the initial free distribution of allowances to operators of installations subject to the ETS for a period of 3 or 5 years does not entail that the operator becomes owner of those allowances and that he can use them as he wishes.[72] – As far as the VAT is concerned, the transfer of greenhouse gas emission allowances under Article 12 of Directive 2003/87/EC,

[70] Section 15 EEWärmeG.

[71] An annual deposit of 500 million euros is available up to 2012 to promote energy efficiency in buildings.

[72] Judgment No. 92/2006 of 7 June 2006 on the Walloon Regional Act to implement Directive 2003/87/EC.

is a taxable provision of services falling within the scope of Article 9(2) (e) of Directive 77/388/EEC. This is in accordance with the guidance provided by the European Commission.

Relation to Environmental Permit and Environmental Impact Systems

The UNFCCC and the Kyoto Protocol are neutral towards the national choice of legislative and administrative structures. The EU provisions on ETS do not require that there should be a connection between ETS and environmental decision-making. However, even under EU law most operations and activities under ETS may not run the activity without environmental permits and often also environmental impact assessment. The EU regulatory system exposes the result that an activity which, as far as the GHG emissions are concerned, is under the ETS regime, does not need an environmental permit for these emissions. In other words, the interpretation is that no conditions can be set on GHGs in an environmental licensing procedure. This approach indicates that there is no participation required on this issue in the permit procedure.

Installations involving major GHG emissions are from an environmental under both international and EC obligations. Internationally installations dealing with waste and chemicals are mostly obliged to apply for a national permit. Many operations are under the obligation to run an environmental impact assessment. Within the EU especially the Directive on integrated pollution control (IPPC, 96/61/EC with later amendments) sets the obligation to apply for a permit. The authority has to respect the requirement of best available technology (BAT) and to take into account existing emission limits. Many Member States go further than the EU requires but in the legislation of these states one mostly finds explicit transposition of this and other relevant directives.

There are administrative obstacles for handling ETS allowances and environmental licensing in the same procedure for various reasons. But since both "lines" are essential for running operations there must be at least a coordination of the procedures. As mentioned before, ETS installations are not supposed to get strained by additional GHG emission limits in the environmental procedure. In Belgium for instance, applications to the competent regional authority for an environmental permit, required for an ETS-installation, must include a description of (a) the installation and its activities including the technology used; (b) the raw and auxiliary materials, the use of which is likely to lead to emissions of gases listed in Annex I of Directive 2003/87/EC; (c) the sources of emissions of those gases from the installation; and (d) the measures planned to monitor and report emissions in accordance with the guidelines adopted pursuant to Article 14 of said Directive. For Finland, participation in the ETS excludes such installations from restrictions in the environmental permit as for the particular greenhouse gas emissions regarding which the installation is subject to the emissions trading scheme. However, if the particular emissions cause significant local pollution, such emissions are subject to being regulated in the environmental permit regardless of participation in the emissions trading scheme.

11.2.6 Adaptation Strategies to Global Warming

11.2.6.1 General Approach to Adaptation Strategies

Mitigation has been in the core of political actions in the area of climate law. Later on and especially since the adoption of the Bali Action Plan in 2008 mitigation measures seem not to be a satisfactory response to threats caused by already visible impacts of climate change on both human and social as well as natural media. The GHGs will persist and even increase for a long time in the atmosphere. Mitigation may eventually slow down the trend but not sufficiently to prevent remarkable losses to societies. Therefore adaptation becomes more and more vital. States need national action programs to ensure a safe future for their population. Legal key areas to address are flood control, drought, land use planning, forestry and housing.

The national reports present largely risks and changes estimated to follow from the increasing climate change. The predicted effects are not only global warming and related problems for human environment and nature. Regionally and periodically also low temperatures and snow may occur increasingly. All in all the modes of changes are characterized by unpredictability and increasing force. However, many states recognizing those threats seem not to be well prepared to adapt their conditions to meet the challenges ahead. For some populated developing countries the necessary measures would also be economically or socially harsh to enforce. Somewhat ironically global changes would mostly affect areas which are mostly populated and traditionally used by mankind, namely shores and river areas. Also natural conditions for species and consequently for activities, as well as forestry and agriculture would regionally change and affect economic life. Biodiversity would suffer losses and drought would lead to the need for intensified social programs.

On the other hand, some states and regions have developed programs and strategies for adaptation management. The basis for these activities shows similar basic patterns. First, research and investigation is necessary for collecting data about risks and possibilities, secondly programs and measures are required for the implementation of necessary political and legal measures. The latter part may be difficult because regular land use and property rights structures could be affected more than normal restrictions would allow for. One has to recall that global warming with all its effects is not an area of legislation where states would act freely. Instead they have to take responsibility for the wealth of future generations. In this work all citizens and institutions have their role and responsibility. Equitable share of burden between states and individuals is here an important principle, as also is the need of political precaution.

According to the IPCC's Fourth Assessment Report,[73] climate change is a real phenomenon and it is uncertain whether the policy objective of limiting global warming to 2°C compared to pre-industrial levels can still be achieved. In view of this situation, it is necessary to complement mitigation strategies with focused strategies towards adapting to the effects of climate change.

The European Union has realized the need of a political approach in the matter. The Commission published a white paper in 2009 entitled Adapting to Climate Change[74] and a working document to the white book entitled Adapting to Climate Change: The Challenge for European Agriculture and Rural Areas.[75] The white paper refers to all policy areas in order to assess Europe's awareness of the impacts of climate change, the working paper focuses more specifically on agriculture. This is partly due to the fact that the Common Agricultural Policy (CAP) comprises nature conservation figures as a pillar of agriculture. National investments should focus on environmental infrastructure, energy and resource efficiency and innovations. Balancing global warming with nature-based measures is also a soft part of adaptation strategies. The working paper is also an innovative approach towards mitigating the effects of global warming on the natural resources vital for survival and development. The EU approach is a concern of all its Member States within the next years when actions must be taken.

The reporters were first asked to present their views how seriously global warming and the need of adaptation was taken in their nations. Some reports did not touch this part, presuming either that this would have required specific studies beyond the previous part of the questionnaire or because the state in question had not taken manifested steps in the matter yet. Some reporters again have given quite detailed information about programs, strategies and measures in the area of adaptation. Some countries again have a restrictive approach in the sense that they consider stringent emission limits having a major role in the adaptation process as well: prevention includes the objective of adaptation. This may be rational in regional terms but surely not sufficient for mitigating global changes.

Global warming is regionally a threat all around the world. Argentina is reported as potentially vulnerable to Climatic Change, as a high percentage of its exports are agricultural commodities and manufactures of agricultural origin. In addition, the country relies on hydro-power for an important share of its electricity generation. Accordingly, various studies were carried out to characterize the impacts of current climate variability and of the climate changes that may take place in a time horizon of 10–40 years. For Argentina a great numbers of effects are reported but the adaptation is sectorally rather limited. Here adaptation has been developed especially in the farm sector. Though, this adaptation was in general successful from the short-time economic point of view, it is however causing environmental damages that according to climate projections would become devastating during the next decades. This adaptation consists of the expansion of the agriculture boundary toward the west and north of

[73] IPCC (Intergovernmental Panel on Climate Change, UN World Climate Council, 2007): Fourth Assessment Report (AR4) on Climate Change.

[74] EU Commission white paper of 1 April 2009, Adapting to Climate Change: Towards a European Framework for Action, COM(2009) 147 final.

[75] Commission staff working document accompanying the white paper: Adapting to Climate Change of 1 April 2009, SEC(2009) 388 final.

the traditional agricultural zone. It was motivated by both commercial and technological changes, but was enabled by the positive precipitation trends that occurred in those zones. This autonomous adaptation already requires public attention to minimize its negative impacts.

In Australia political awareness (and/or acceptance) of the need to adapt to the impacts of climate change is reported to vary between and within political parties in Australia. However, the Commonwealth government recently released its latest position paper on climate change adaptation in Australia, which sets out a vision for adapting to climate change in Australia and the practical steps that will need to be taken to achieve that vision. The position paper follows on from National Climate Change Adaptation Framework which was agreed by COAG (which includes representatives from each of the six Australian State and two Territory governments, and the Commonwealth government). – According to the position paper, the Commonwealth and COAG will work together to develop a national adaptation agenda (Adapting to Climate Change in Australia).[76]

Australia is also cooperating in international strategies. Australia has committed to invest AUD 150 million from 2008 to 2011 to meet adaptation needs in vulnerable countries in the Asia Pacific region through the International Climate Change Adaptation Initiative (ICCAI), which focuses primarily on two of Australia's closest neighbors, the Pacific Island countries and East Timor. In addition to investing through the ICCAI, Australia will contribute through programs such as the Pacific Climate Change Science Program, which is aimed at developing an effective and comprehensive policy development and planning knowledge base.[77]

The United States has a tradition of adaptation to natural changes. Though society has long adapted to climate and other environmental changes, adaptation to climate change in this century will be more difficult than in past eras because, as says the reporter, "society won't be adapting to a new steady state but rather to a rapidly moving target" with considerable uncertainty in the process. As the US Climate Action Report of 2006 indicated, "the ultimate goal of adaptation is to develop resilient societies and economies that have the knowledge and capacity to address both the challenges and the opportunities presented by changing climate conditions". According to the report, decision makers have experience with short-term (e.g., annual) climate variations, but long-term global warming raises new challenges.

The Federal German Government adopted the German Strategy for Adaptation to Climate Change on 17 December 2008. Like the European Commission's approach, Germany's strategy focuses primarily on creating further conditions to support a targeted adaptation strategy which will later be backed statutory instruments. In this way, research needs will be highlighted, monitoring models discussed for individual fields of action, and relevant legal regimes such as spatial planning, Länder-level planning, laws on nature conservation and protection of waterbodies, and agricultural law will be assessed with regard to their ability to absorb climate change adaptation provisions and, from an institutional perspective, provisions will be made such as the establishment of an 'inter-ministerial working group on climate change adaptation'. According to the reporter Professor Koch there are no legal details available at this time.

The Dutch Scientific Council for Government Policy advised in 2006 the national government to pay substantially more attention to adaptation in the Netherlands (such governmental investments benefit the Dutch people directly) instead of conducting mitigation efforts.[78] The Council on Housing, Spatial Planning and the Environment, argues that the government should take a leading role with respect to dealing with climate change effects, especially since citizens have hardly any knowledge or awareness about risks from changing weather patterns. Given these observations, the Dutch government has started in November 2007 a "national adaptation strategy" in order to make the Netherlands "climate proof". The focus of this strategy goes to spatial planning policies in order to make them fit for dealing with climatic change. Besides safeguarding the dikes, the core of the general policy

[76] http://www.climatechange.gov.au/publications/adaptation/position-paper.aspx.

[77] Engaging our Pacific Neighbours on Climate Change: Australia's Approach, Commonwealth of Australia, 2009 (at http://www.climatechange.gov.au/government/~/media/publications/international/engaging-pacific-neighbours.ashx).

[78] WRR, Klimaatstrategie – tussen ambitie en realisme, rapporten aan de regering nr. 47, 8 juni 2006, see http://www.wrr.nl.

in the Netherlands is to give water more space.[79] In the meantime, specific legislation has been proposed in order to support the adaptation policy. In early 2010 the Dutch government submitted to the Dutch Parliament a legislative proposal for a Delta Act (Deltawet waterveiligheid en zoetwatervoorziening).[80] The proposed Act aims to protect specifically against flooding and to protect the availability of freshwater. The proposed act entails a Delta-Program, a Delta-Committee, a Delta-commissioner (who has to manage the implementation of the Delta-Program) and a Delta-Fund. However, the procedure for the adoption of this legislative proposal has been suspended after the fall of the government in early 2010. Only after the elections in early June, with a new Second Chamber and a new government, the deliberations shall be resumed. In anticipation of the Delta Act some institutional steps have nevertheless already been made, like the appointment of the Delta-commissioner and the Delta-committee: both took office from 1 February 2010.

In Finland, the preparation of the Adaptation Strategy in Finland, coordinated by the Ministry of Agriculture and Forestry, started already in 2003 after an initiative of the Finnish Parliament.[81] This strategy was completed in 2005, and it is, supposedly, the first adaptation strategy in the world. The strategy defines the impacts of climate change in Finland and measures needed in the following sectors: agriculture and food production, forestry, fisheries, reindeer husbandry, game management, water resources, biodiversity, industry, energy, transport, land use and communities, building, health, tourism and recreation, and insurance. The detailed evaluation of the impacts and the definition of measures are integrated into the operations of various administrative sectors.

11.2.6.2 Land Use, National and Regional Strategies and Programs

In most of the Argentine territory and in regions of neighboring countries there were remarkable climatic trends during the last three or four decades, very likely related to the global warming trend. These climate changes have produced important impacts that required adaptation responses, which in some cases were already taken, but in others are still pending. In Argentina the projected changes for the period 2020/2040 were analyzed utilizing results from numerical experiments carried out at the Center for Ocean Atmospheric Research (CIMA) with a high resolution climatic model and from various GCM outputs. According to the climate scenarios projected by these models, global warming would create new vulnerabilities and enhance most current ones. Similarly, an increase in water stress is expected in most of the north and part of the west of the country. This would affect agriculture and, in some zones, might compromise the supply of drinking water.

Each of the changes and impacts will require adaptation measurements that according to some pilot studies would need important funds. However, it cannot be overlooked here the circumstance, until now quite special of Argentina, that due to the significant climate changes already occurring, an important autonomous adaptation has been developed, especially in the farm sector. Though, this adaptation was in general successful from the short-time economic point of view, it is however causing environmental damages that according to climate projections would become devastating during the next decades. This adaptation consists of the expansion of the agriculture boundary toward the west and north of the traditional agricultural zone. It was motivated by both commercial and technological changes, but was enabled by the positive precipitation trends that occurred in those zones. This autonomous adaptation already requires public attention to minimize its negative impacts.

In Australia, planning law and land use regimes are predominantly managed by state and local governments. As such, there has historically been little consistency in approaches to planning regimes and land use management across jurisdictions. Generally, however, local government planning schemes are consistent across jurisdictions in relation to dealing with climate change impacts. The National Sea Change Taskforce, which was set up in 2004 comprising local governments from each Australian State, released a report in July 2008 which highlighted the fact that very few local planning schemes include specific provisions dealing with climate change-related risks (see Planning for Climate Change: Leading Practice Principles and Models for Sea Change Communities in Coastal Australia, July 2008).

[79] VROM, The Netherlands' Report on demonstrable progress under article 3.2 of the Kyoto Protocol, December 2005.

[80] Deltawet waterveiligheid en zoetwatervoorziening, Second Chamber 2009–2010, dossier 32 304.

[81] Evaluation of the Implementation of Finland's National Strategy for Adaptation to Climate Change 2009. Ministry of Agriculture and Forestry 4a/2009, p. 3 and 6.

Land use planning is in most reported states the regular instrument for adaptation, for instance for appointing resettlement and escape areas. In some systems the need to adapt land use to climate change has been recognized as an objective, mostly in relation to sustainability. The national climate strategies include classifications of areas with different functions and requirements, so e.g. in the Finnish report. Long term planning is a way of dealing with changing scenarios. In the Netherlands, in addition to the proposed Delta Program, a recently adopted "Crisis and Restoration Act" is to a limited extent relevant for adaptation measures (for example with regard to strengthening of the coast).

The Irish Department of the Environment is working actively with local authorities to develop climate change strategies and some have already been prepared.[82] Other authorities have included adaptation strategies in their development plans, including actions relating to flooding, water supply, coastal management, and drainage. The protection and exploitation of natural resources, through agriculture, fisheries, forestry, maintenance of biological diversity, does not get the same level of attention, and there is not a great deal of concrete policy on adapting transport infrastructure.

The Italian National Action Programme to Combat Drought and Desertification, approved by the Inter-Ministerial Committee for Economic Planning in 1999, provides a set of actions to reduce the vulnerability due to desertification and to adapt to climate changes. The Plan entrusted the Regions and Watershed Authorities with the responsibility to implement specific agronomic, civil and social measures and to adopt supporting information, training and research programs in the following overriding sectors: (1) soil protection, (2) sustainable management of water resources, (3) reduction of environmental impact from productive activities and (4) land restoration. The National Committee started some pilot project in the five most affected regions of which the report gives examples.

[82] Dublin City Council's strategy is available at http://www.dublincity.ie/YourCouncil/CouncilPublications/Documents/Climate_Change_Strategy_as_adopted_by_City_Council_in_May_2008_.doc.

11.2.6.3 Allocation of Costs for Adaptation

Looking at the variety of cost recovery models, the most feasible solution would be to cover costs with fees and insurance. Ear-marked taxes would be difficult due to the diffuse structure of climatic effects. Some examples will be mentioned here.

In Australia the dominant approach of the Australian government currently is to provide direct funding for discrete programs by way of grants. In Belgium, at the federal level, recent legislative changes[83] introduced cover against flooding and other natural hazards in household fire insurance policies. Unlike the previous situation, the cover against natural disasters is not provided by state funds, except when the global cost exceeds a threshold linked to the turnover of the insurance companies. While the new laws are not primarily targeted at adaptation to climate change, they may possibly have a dissuasive effect on residential construction in areas where the risk of flooding is higher, in particular if this results in higher insurance premiums. In Finland no special fees are considered for covering the costs of adaptation to climate change. Under the regime of flood control the political discussion about the appropriate cost model is going on. The regime would especially affect shore constructions. Budget funding is still available. The State Budget for 2010 includes an additional appropriation amounting to about 11 million euros to be used as agricultural environmental aids for challenges concerning climate change, renewable energy and water management, biodiversity, as well as connected innovations. Italy has decided to set by law different incentives for covering adaptation costs in the sector of energy saving.

11.2.6.4 Role of Specified Policies: Policies on Water Management, Agriculture and Traffic

Waters and forests are ecologically related to the atmospheric system especially as they act as sinks. Waters, especially floods, on the other hand, are regionally a serious consequence of global warming, as in other areas the loss of forests due to erosion and forest fires. Therefore adaptation measures must be used targeted to relevant sectors and problems. For the European Union, one should here mention Directive 2007/60/EC

[83] Acts of 21 May 2003 and 7 September 2005.

of the European Parliament and of the Council of 23 October 2007 on the assessment and management of flood risks. Internationally to remember are a number of water-related conventions; for water management are relevant the Convention on the Protection and Use of Transboundary Watercourses and International Lakes (1996) and the Convention on the Protection and Use of Transboundary Watercourses and International Lakes (1992), including the Protocol on Water and Health of 1992.

The reporter for Australia gives a large and comprehensive presentation of the national water management system, based on the inception of national water reform policy in 1994. This policy includes two interrelated themes, namely (1) the transition to a new water access rights regime centered on proprietary 'water access entitlements' that are tradable in regulated water markets; and (2) the establishment of statutory water resources planning to secure environmental sustainability and to provide the foundation for the proprietary access entitlements. European readers recognize that there is in the objectives a similarity with the water framework policy of the EU as it was established in 2000.

The Australian model operates at the local or area management level. Environmentally sustainable levels of consumptive use of a water resource mean not only limiting of the grant of new access licenses in a fully allocated resource, but also reconceptualising water access authorisations as entitlements that are subject to ongoing definition in accordance with the terms of a water plan. There are now two basic forms of water access rights: landholder rights (including native title rights) and access rights held under a specific grant of authority in the form of a license or access entitlement. The volumes of water taken in exercise of landholder rights are generally small and used for the purposes of watering stock and domestic or indigenous cultural uses. All larger extractions of water for commercial or public water supply purposes require a specific grant of authority (typically called a water license) from the relevant State government. When answering to the question how well the national system is equipped to meet climate change, the reporter concludes that there is still a need to take climate change better into account in water management as a key theme.

In the United States, a number of sectors are reported to be affected by climate change and likely to require adaptive measures. These include water resources (water supply), ecosystems (biodiversity and condition), public health, coastal areas, transportation infrastructure and operations, energy (changes in demand, infrastructure), and agriculture. Though predictions indicate that the US can adapt successfully to climate change (at least at the lower end of projected warming), some sectors or regions and especially the ecosystem are likely to suffer losses. The report explains that moreover adaptation promises will be expensive. For example, an October 2009 report estimated that through 2050, US drinking water and wastewater utilities will spend from \$448 to \$944 billion to adapt infrastructure and operations to the changing climate.

In October 2009, the US Government Accountability Office (GAO) published a study of adaptation based on information provided by agencies that participate in the US Climate Change Research Project. The GAO reported that policy makers view adaptation as a risk management strategy intended to reduce vulnerability to unavoidable climate change. Noting that no coordinated national approach to adaptation exists, GAO identified a number of ad hoc federal activities that foster adaptation. The GAO recommended development of a national strategic plan for adaptation that builds on existing planning efforts, defines federal priorities for adaptation, identifies (and makes available) resources to implement the plan, makes clear the "roles, responsibilities, and working relationships among federal, state, and local governments," and identifies ways to consider climate change in government decisions. Another recent recommendation for adaptation had similar elements: a federal adaptation plan, federal agency strategic plans, and amendment of NEPA regulations to require consideration of climate change. Only about ten states have adaptation plans in place or in progress, and others expect to enact them. Vulnerable coastal states (Florida, California, Oregon, Washington, and Alaska) are among those with adaptation strategies. In August 2009, for example, California released a draft Climate Adaptation Strategy.

In the US also sectoral working groups (agriculture, water management, public health, and four others) provided expertise, making recommendations for both short-term and long-term strategies. Some counties and cities, including New York City, have also begun to formalize adaptation plans and implement adaptive measures. In addition, some plans implement adaptive responses to particular impacts, like drought or higher sea levels. Non-governmental organizations provide assistance to communities in assessing vulnerability and drafting adaptation plans.

The Dutch government conducted a legislative project to harmonize and integrate its environmental and spatial permit regimes, which has led to a new General Ambient Law Act ("Wet algemene bepalingen omgevingsrecht"). This would indeed mean that two central acts will be present: the Environmental Management Act and the General Ambient Law Act. Besides that, other acts will stay relevant, like the integrated Water Act which deals with all water-related issues among which water quality, and a separate Soil Protection Act. There is yet no initiative at the side of the government to systemize or codify the climate related rules into one Climate Act or into one chapter to the Environmental Management Act. According to the proposal the Climate Act should set emission budgets and would make governmental authorities responsible for complying with them. There is however not (yet) enough political support for adopting such an act, let alone an Act that would go beyond EU obligations. On the contrary, there is an overall resistance against adopting further going legally binding measures compared to what international and European law asks for (no "national headings" to European law).

Another sector is agriculture due to its diffuse GHG emissions. In Germany, agriculture contributes an annual 13% CO_2-equivalents to greenhouse gas emissions. These involve methane emissions from livestock management, nitrous oxide and CO_2 emissions from crop-growing, and CO_2 emissions from land use changes, not least from plowing grassland. However, the Federal German Government's Integrated Energy and Climate Programme, adopted in Meseberg in 2007, does not recognize this as a strategic challenge. The reporter also reminds that worldwide there is no adequate instrumentation of emission reduction targets for agriculture.

Australia's Farming Future is an initiative which provides $130 million of Commonwealth funding over 4 years for primary industries with the aim of assisting primary producers to adapt and respond to climate change. There are five key programs which cover funding for research projects and on-farm demonstration activities; skills and strategy development; financial assistance for primary producers who are experiencing financial difficultly as a result of climate change impacts on their farms; financial assessments, professional advice and training, transitional income support; and community networks and capacity building.

For Belgium it is reported that as far as agriculture is concerned, a slow but significant reduction in organic carbon content of most agricultural soils has been observed. Although this is mainly a consequence of intensive farming, increased temperatures also contribute to the decomposition of organic matter in soil. This may affect the availability of water to plants and the fertility of soils, thus contributing to a reduction of yields. Recent progress in agricultural policy promoting better recycling of organic matter in soils, as well as more efficient use of mineral fertilizers, are helping to mitigate this problem.

In Scotland, one of the requirements of the Climate Change (Scotland) Act 2009 is the production of a land use strategy. This must set out objectives for sustainable land use that contribute to achieving the emission reduction targets set in the Act, the objectives set out in the adaptation program[84] and sustainable development. At the same time, the Scottish Forestry Strategy already includes tackling climate change as a major objective. The EU Common Agricultural Policy plays a dominant role in shaping agricultural support and it continues to be revised away from direct support for production to meet a wider range of goals. According to the report, in Scotland the move away from a herd of specific schemes run by different bodies to the integrated Rural Development Programme allows land use issues to be dealt with in a more holistic way.

Production of goods is a sector of concern as well. The European Communities and the United States in December 2007 proposes to give priority in the WTO negotiations to climate –friendly goods and to services linked to addressing climate change. These climate-friendly products comprise about one third of the environmental goods already identified by a group of delegations. Sustainable and organic food production is important economic areas with impact on the GHG emission level. The protection and support of quality products and regional typicality is regionally an important feature e.g. in the Mediterranean area. Shortage of water and environmental restrictions favor the development of biotechnology and energy saving practices. Weather will cause additional stress on cultivations.

[84] As required by 2009 Act, s.53.

In Italy studies are launched to develop varieties of wheat and of other species that best adapt to climate change (the RIADE Project).[85] A lengthening of the growing period of about 10–15 days per each °C of rise in yearly average temperature and a consequent shortening of cold winter periods are expected. In terms of crop production, the outcomes of the PESETA project show that the change foreseen for 2020 and 2080 would result in a yield decrease from 1.9% to about 22.4% in the Southern Europe regions, caused primarily by likely reduction of the growing season, by extreme events more frequently during the production cycle phases, as for example strong precipitations during sowing dates, heat waves during the flowering period and longer dry spells.

11.2.6.5 Use of Nature Conservation Measures to Update Effects of Global Warming

Nature conservation and the protection of species habitats are largely covered by international conventions and by EU law.[86] Also biodiversity is a novelty introduced in the famous Convention in Rio de Janeiro in 1992. All these rulings are valid also when global warming with all its effects starts to occur. On the other hand the measures of protection and obligations of states are related to human activities, not to changes of the nature itself. Therefore these arrangements are not satisfactory models for the maintenance of life under global warming. On the other hand, nature always changes for different reasons and mostly recovers afterwards. Human societies should perhaps not interfere too much. In some countries also the intrusion of harmful alien species (immigrant species) is expected. State policies may, however, adopt conservation measures where the additional impact of global warming is taken into account (e.g. Arctic and marine environment). As noted in most reports, all measures must be founded on more detailed research and information. The situation therefore fosters research.

For Australia, its rich biodiversity is particularly vulnerable in a rapidly changing climate. According to a Commonwealth government report (2009), the "effects of climate change are already discernible at the genetic, species and ecosystem levels in many parts of the continent and coastal seas." The report notes that about 85% of Australia's terrestrial mammals, 91% of flowering plants, and 90% of reptiles and frogs are found nowhere else in the world. More than 50% of the world's marsupial species occur only in Australia. So there is much to lose if global temperatures rise outside of the 1.5–2.0°C range and there are corresponding increases in the level of extinction rates.

In Italy, the reduction in the number of stable plant species in 2100, compared to 1990, might range between 20% and 40% in Northern Italy and Apennines, 60–80% in the Mediterranean area, 4,060% in Southern Italy. The increased aridity observed in Central-Southern Italy makes the Italian forests more vulnerable to biotic and abiotic disturbances reducing their resistance and resilience. An oak deterioration, mainly associated to a 20-year-long water stress, is observed. It is an alarming data considering that oaks account for the 26.5% of national forests. Besides, an average of 55,000 ha of woodlands is more or less seriously damaged by fires every year.

The reports give lists of measures which are supposed to be suitable for the maintenance of life in endangered surroundings or harsh conditions. Those are (1) increased creation of protected areas, (2) establishment of buffer zones, (3) targeting of mitigating measures to especially sensitive sites, (4) use of financial guidance and (5) generally strengthening of political commitment and precaution. The German Advisory Council on the Environment focuses on nature conservation and climate change conditions for the development of a suitable policy; arguing from mitigation standpoint, has called in particular for more stringent statutory provisions to preserve and protect permanent grassland. In addition, the task should be both for nature conservation and agriculture to preserve and enhance carbon sinks. Also the Finnish strategy lists key points including measures as (1) taking valuable habitats into consideration in the management and use of forests, (2) conservation of valuable traditional farmland biotopes, (3) control and prevention of the spread of invasive alien species, and (4) reconstructing and restoring wetlands and mires.

In Ireland, the Rural Environment Protection Scheme 4, for the period 2007–2013 will take into account climate change issues. There is also state

[85] Lenticchia Lens esculentum (culinaria), various types of broad beans (Vicia faba major, Vicia faba minor), Lupines (Lupinus albus e Lupinus angustifolius), barley (Hordeum vulgare), chick peas (Cicer arietinum), artichoke (Cynara scolymus), Brassica (Brassica carinata) and Carthamus (Carthamus tinctorius).

[86] EU Bird and Habitat Directives 79/409/EC and 92/43/EC.

support for the reduction of nitrate use (the EU Nitrates Directive) a Bioenergy Scheme to support the planting of miscanthus and willow and a Biomass Harvesting Scheme to encourage the use of wood fuel. A policy to encourage the use of carbon sequestration and forest sinks is to be developed.[87]

In the Czech Republic the high concentrations of tropospheric ozone currently contribute to the damage to forest tree stands. The adopted measures have an effect both in reduction of emissions of carbon dioxide, methane and nitrous oxide (in agriculture) and in increasing the level of sinks for carbon dioxide through absorption (in forest management). In the adopted National Program, the sector of the Ministry of Agriculture pledged to implement measures related to afforestation of unused agricultural areas, maintenance of permanent grasslands, and use and introduction of new land use technologies and cultivation methods. Support is given for the afforestation of unused agricultural areas and agricultural land unsuitable for agrosystems.

11.2.6.6 Targeted Measures of Adaptation

Climate change may affect regions and environmental media unequally. National strategies are therefore not effective enough for all cases. Floods and erosion are naturally related to certain nature bases. The EU Directive 2007/60/EC on the assessment and management of floods obliges states to take the impacts of climate change into account in the management of flood risks. According to the Directive Member States shall first make a preliminary flood risk assessment before the end of 2011. On the basis of the assessment states have to identify and to map the areas where potentially significant flood risks exist or might be considered likely to occur by the end of 2013.

All Member States may not yet have transposed the requirements of the Directive. Some states already had existing provisions on flood abatement. So for instance, in the Walloon Region of Belgium a new flood prevention plan was approved in 2003 (PLUIES plan). This global plan aims to improve knowledge of the risk of flooding, reduce and decelerate the run-off of water on slopes, improve the management of rivers, decrease vulnerability of zones liable to flooding, and improve crisis management. SETHY is responsible for real-time monitoring of watercourses, hydrology studies, coordination and flood alert. Its work is based on a network of stations measuring the level of watercourses and amounts of rain. Rules banning the construction of buildings in areas prone to flooding have been imposed. In the Flemish Region the Decree of 2003 on integrated water management aims, inter alia, to give once more sufficient space to water systems and to reduce the risk of flooding.

In the Czech Republic the State Environmental Policy 2004–2010 defines the protection of waters and protection against floods as one of the priority areas. The adaptation measures are proposed in the T.G. Masaryk Water Research Institute. The proposals are result of analyses and comparison of changes in water management and the capacities of water sources with the current conception of developmental policy, with the state water management structure and with the state of the environment in the Czech Republic. The water management sector is clearly most sensitive to climate change under the conditions in the Czech Republic. Adaptation measures for this sector are concerned mainly with implementation of measures leading to an increase in the water retention properties of the landscape, restoration of individual systems, reduction of affecting of water quality by contamination and the safety of water works against overflowing.

In Finland the mean temperature in Finland will, without mitigation measures, rise 4–5°C in winter and 2–3°C in summer, with a precipitation increase of 20–30% according to regional climate models (e.g. RCAO[88]).[89] There are more than 60 flood-prone areas in Finland. The dam safety measures in Finnish legislation are mainly for the prevention of dam accidents and for the effective reduction of hazards. The new Dam Safety Act (2009) aims at securing safety of dam building, management and use, and reducing the risks and damages of dam accident. The Exceptional Flood Damage Compensation Act (1995) provides aid, financed from the State Budget resources, to be granted

[87] Climate Change Strategy 2007, 31–32.

[88] The Rossby Centre Atmosphere-Ocean model RCAO.

[89] As a particularly Finnish characteristic in future flooding events includes land uplift due to postglacial rebound, whereby channel gradients will decrease significantly, as uneven land uplift will change relative elevations. The highest predicted land uplift rate, i.e. up to 90 cm/100a, along the coastal areas of Western Finland will also affect estuary formations in combination with erosion –transportation –sedimentation processes.

for flood damage done to buildings, private roads and more.

In Italy, a special legislation for the protection of Venice (1984) has as its main goal in the defense of the inhabitants of the lagoon and of the city of Venice from high water occurrence. The solution identified as optimal strategy includes a combined framework of works that would allow the temporary closure of three inlets, through mobile devices in conjunction with the supports of rising local banks. This system of works for the tide regulation is able to withstand a height difference between sea and lagoon also of 2 m. The MO.SE (Experimental Electromechanical Module) was used to perform a series of tests on a full-scale prototype of a cofferdam and was a kind of "test laboratory" totally autonomous, situated in a remote area of the lagoon.[90]

11.2.6.7 Resettlement Programs

Global warming may affect directly both individuals and populations. Therefore responsible societies have to prepare for protecting threatened settlement and cultivated areas. Hereby law and especially conditions related to human rights and constitutional provisions may cause obstacles. People are supposed to have the right to choose home and living, and precautionary measures to interfere in those rights on the basis of calculations leads to problems in terms of legal competence and financial responsibility. If there is no imminent threat the normal solution is land use planning whereby people may participate when for instance settlement areas are transferred, limited or otherwise protected especially against floods. If a disaster already occurred, people concerned usually range under the rules of management of accidents and natural catastrophes. The problem for most reported states is that the scenarios for the future are vague for making precise planning decision.

Under the German Federal Environmental Appeals Act (section 2), a class action is permissible or justified only if a breach of environmental law encroaches third parties' individual rights. The reporter criticizes this ruling for being narrow in the sense that a so-called representative action is intended to be used where there is no individually actionable case. This would be the case when discussing the proper content of 'objective' law.

In Ireland, local authorities have the power to consider adaptation initiatives in relation to their development plans. The Planning and Development Act 2000 empowers planning authorities to provide, in their development plans, that development in areas at risk of flooding may be regulated, restricted or controlled. If development is proposed in a flood-risk area, the risk of flooding can be carefully evaluated and planning permission refused, if necessary.

The issue concerning participation in matters related to global warming may require a broader approach than just the opinion of local planning authorities. Since the content of climate strategies is not based on secure scientific knowledge and also the choice of appropriate instruments is apt to discussion, participation should eventually include interested groups and organizations. In the US and to some extent in Germany class actions or the citizen's right to appeal without having legal standing are available.

11.2.6.8 Preservation of Threatened Natural and Cultural Habitats: Science Supporting Law?

Natural destruction of sites which represent historical and cultural elements of mankind is unavoidable. Traditional instruments worldwide make efforts to protect and maintain both constructions and features of the landscape as well as habitats for endangered species. Global warming increases the need of precaution as far as protecting programs and measures are concerned. Even big cities may disappear and the sea takes over or vanishing forests lead to destructive erosion. Thus, global warming is a threat to mankind and human societies but it also may have a vital impact on ecosystems and habitats. The need of mitigation and adaptation is obvious because the global communities have committed themselves to maintain and to promote biological biodiversity. In addition, these goals are not without importance for the welfare of human life as well. The nature policies mainly focus at conservation strategies. Partly this is rational because nature as a concept implies that human measures should not interfere and if necessary only in order to support natural conditions. Does global warming require a different approach? This was a voluntary question to the reporters. Another topic in the same direction is the need of

[90] The MOSE is designed according to a precautionary policy to deal with an increase in the sea up to 60 cm, then higher than the latest estimates reported in the 4th IPCC report, which indicated an increase in the sea level, over the next 100 years, between 18 and 59 cm.

protection of cultural sites against disasters caused by climate change.

In a global context, biodiversity, sustainable development and climate change mitigation are interrelated, all having their methodological basis in the declarations at the UNCED Conference in Rio de Janeiro in 1992. The combination of these three elements has the shape of a triptych where three tableaux indicating different milieus altogether highlight a universal idea. Therefore it is not surprising that on the road of Bali and Copenhagen not only hard strategies for emission control but also concerns about the future development of natural processes have been evoked. Under the UNFCCC regime a report in this direction was elaborated in 2009. In this report "Biodiversity and Climate Change: A CBD Contribution to the Copenhagen Climate Agreement" the role of biodiversity in climate change adaptation and the links between biodiversity conservation and sustainable use in terms of climate change mitigation were analyzed.

As far as the position of cultural sites is concerned, the UNESCO holds an important role in evaluating threats and in creating appropriate strategies. In this sense, UNESCO's World Heritage Centre has in 2006 appointed a representative working group of experts. Its objective is to review the nature and scale of the risks which climate change among other factors may cause to sites under World Heritage protection. If necessary, strategies should be adopted and states concerned should get assistance for the maintenance of the sites. In general, the UNESCO has adopted strategies in terms of both mitigation and action in case of emergency.[91]

National approaches to the topics have been reported as well. In some countries the prognosticated changes in temperature remarkably. For instance in Ireland, temperatures are likely to rise by 1.25–1.5° as a result of climate change. This will have obvious impacts on rainfall, leading to an increased likelihood of both river flooding and drought. Winters and summers will be warmer. Sea levels are likely to rise, which is likely to cause serious difficulties for our major cities, most of which are coastal. Still, the overall ecological impact will probably be neutral or even positive.

Two reports by the Commonwealth which deal with the assessment of climate change impacts on Australia's World Heritage Areas and on Australia's National Reserve System. The reports were commissioned so that the results could inform management plans and government policy on World Heritage and National Reserve Systems and climate change adaptation plans into the future.[92]

[91]Climate and World Heritage. http://whc.unesco.org/en/climatechange. 27.10.2009 and UNESCO: Disasters Preparedness and Mitigation, UNESCO's role, 2007: http://unescdoc.unesco.org/images/0015/001504/150435/e.pdf. 27.10.2009.

[92]http://www.environment.gov.au/heritage/publications/climatechange/pubs/worldheritage-climatechange.pdf; http://www.climatechange.gov.au/~/media/publications/adaptation/nrs-report.ashx.

The Regulation of Private Equity, Hedge Funds and State Funds[1]

12

Eddy Wymeersch

12.1 Introduction

During the recent financial crisis, some types of collective investments have been the subject of criticism due to the destabilizing role – real or presumed – that they may have played in the economic and financial systems. The money market funds appeared not to offer the safe investment they purported to do, shaking investors' confidence and leading to massive divestment and withdrawals that urged the need for public intervention. The hedge funds created a similar scare, as their leverage might have created risks for the financial institutions that financed them, triggering massive disposals of their portfolios in case of urgent liquidity need, even engulfing their financiers and prime brokers. The case of the private equity funds is different as their impact on financial stability was mainly linked to the leverage of their investment. Often heard, rather populist, criticism related to their conduct on the markets – from their massive trading, their short selling, and their high frequency trading, to excessive build up of leverage or predatory activism as shareholders. The political world and the media called for more transparency, more regulation, and more control of their activities.[2] These developments lay at the basis of the present wave of regulation of their activity. Strikingly, concerns address mainly the issues of financial stability and systemic risk, less concerns of investor protection or market conduct. Another wave of uneasiness addressed the "sovereign wealth funds" that were feared to menace the economic sovereignty in some states.

A common denominator between these different groups of collective investment schemes is their potential impact on the larger equilibria in the developed economies, leading to concerns about financial stability, systemic risk, predatory market conduct and creation of economic disequilibria. However, the issues confronting each of these three groups are quite different and therefore they will be dealt with in three different parts.

12.1.1 Part 1. The "Hedge Funds"

12.1.1.1 Definition and Scope

Up to now, there has been no generally accepted definition of a "hedge fund". The wide variety of legal structures in which they operate, the diversity of investment strategies and the diversity and versatility of asset types they have invested in, makes any precise definition

[1] III.A.1, La réglementation des fonds spéculatifs.

E. Wymeersch (✉)
Professor, University of Ghent, Ghent, Belgium
e-mail: Eddy.wymeersch@ugent.be

[2] See § 31 of the Progress Report on the Actions to promote Financial Regulatory reform issued by the US Chair of the Pittsburgh G-20 Summit, 25 September 2009, stating "Hedge funds or their managers will be registered and will be required to disclose appropriate information on an ongoing basis to supervisors or regulators, including on leverage, necessary for assessment of the systemic risks they pose individually or collectively. Where appropriate registration should be subject to a minimum size. They will be subject to oversight to ensure that they have adequate risk management."

K.B. Brown and D.V. Snyder (eds.), *General Reports of the XVIIIth Congress of the International Academy of Comparative Law/Rapports Généraux du XVIIIème Congrès de l'Académie Internationale de Droit Comparé*, DOI 10.1007/978-94-007-2354-2_12, © Springer Science+Business Media B.V. 2012

very difficult and imprecise. The term "hedge fund" refers generally to pools of assets, usually securities that are managed by a professional manager using innovative investment strategies, but normally not registered as a traditional investment undertaking. Most hedge funds have only a limited number of investors, usually wealthy individuals or institutional investors, who are supposed to be able to take care of themselves. The relationship with investors is mostly a contractual one, adapting to the specific needs of the investors. The management contract typically provides for a management fee on the basis of the assets managed, and another fee on the value increase of the fund (usually 2% and 20%). Managers frequently hold a large stake in the fund, aligning their interests with the investors'. All these differences have resulted in international statements referring to hedge funds by enumerating their most frequently found characteristics.[3] International Organization of Securities Commissions (IOSCO) used this approach in defining hedge funds as all those investment schemes displaying a combination of some of the following characteristics:

- borrowing and leverage restrictions, which are typically included in collective investment schemes-related regulation, are not applied, and many (but not all) hedge funds use high levels of leverage;
- significant performance fees (often in the form of a percentage of profits) are paid to the manager in addition to an annual management fee;
- investors are typically permitted to redeem their interests periodically, e.g., quarterly, semi-annually or annually;
- often, significant 'own' funds are invested by the manager;
- derivatives are used, often for speculative purposes, and there is an ability to short sell securities; and more diverse risks or complex underlying products are involved.

The designation of hedge funds is also very diverse and often confusing. Hedging refers to covering one's risk, but that is not always the case for the funds that are viewed here. Most funds use leverage, whether in their assets (derivatives) or in their balance sheet (usually loans from prime brokers). But here again, not all funds use leverage. Sometimes these funds are designated as "speculative" funds,[4] which is a confusing designation, as all investments are based on some form or another of speculation. The investment strategies followed by these funds are different from the long-only strategy of the traditional investment funds: there is an indefinite variation of investment strategies, among which the "long-short" or the "constant return" strategy are frequently found. But these are only examples: the managers determine freely the strategies they will pursue, and some funds may specialize in commodities speculations. Others engage in activist actions, while leveraged trading, short selling or concentrated investing is left to the choice of managers and investors.

The designation of hedge funds in national regulations is equally confusing, and reference is made to the national reports to convince the reader of the diversity, whereby differences in substance further contribute to the confusion. Moreover, apart from hedge funds, some sources also view under similar terminology the private equity funds and even the sovereign wealth funds. Even the topics as identified for the present comparative law conference testify to the lack of clarity: it originally was termed, "La réglementation des fonds spéculatifs/The regulation of private equity, hedge funds and state funds," whereby apart from the difference between the two languages, a more precise title was proposed in the English version. It is the latter that will be followed in the present general report.

This lack of clarity as to the scope has led to difficulties in national legislation defining the ambit of their laws. Different techniques have been used, going from submitting hedge funds in principle to investment fund regulation, but exempting them as being restricted to sophisticated investors, thereby avoiding the need for a precise definition. In several cases, the funds have been exempted but not the asset managers that run them; this is the approach followed in the US, the UK and in the EU directive. The directive would apply to fund managers to the extent that they manage Alternative Investment Undertakings, being collective portfolios to which a number of investors have contributed with a view to developing a defined investment policy for their own benefit. As this definition is very far-reaching, some entities have to be excluded: traditional investment funds or UCITS, pension funds, international institutions and central banks, and governments and local authorities including social security and pension funds supported by them or securitization SPVs have all been exempted. Interesting is the exemption for international group

[3] See *International Organization of Securities Commissions* IOSCO, Hedge Fund Oversight, Final report, June 2009, § 5.

[4] This terminology is used in Italy.

entities such as cash pooling schemes. But one cannot conclude that this definition gives a very clear image of the scope of the directive and also of the activities not covered.[5]

12.1.1.2 Overview of the Present State of Regulation of Hedge Funds in a Selection of Legal Systems

In several jurisdictions, hedge funds are subject to the general regime applicable to investment funds, and hence have to be registered under that heading.[6] However, if the fund is distributed to retail investors, additional requirements would apply. This is the case in *Australia*, where in case of retail distribution the fund has to appoint non-executive directors, adopt a compliance plan, have valuation procedures, and publish a disclosure statement that is subject to ASIC[7] supervision. A comparable scheme is found in *Brazil* with respect to Brazil domiciled funds: they have to be registered, are subject to rules on conflicts of interest and risk controls, and adopt a charter to comply with legal provisions of the law. Foreign funds offered to Brazilian investors must be registered with the securities commission[8] and can only be sold through authorized brokers. Initiatives are being considered inter alia about valuation methods for the funds' assets. *Canada* distinguishes between offerings with a full prospectus, in which case the fund can be offered to the public, while the fund will have to publish regular financial statements and the offerings without a prospectus that can only be addressed to a defined class of more sophisticated investors.[9] All fund managers must be registered and are subject to the usual rules on minimum capital, proficiency and experience, but stiffer rules are reported to be under consideration. The distributors generally have to be registered; however, in some provinces, some unregulated dealers are still accepted, it is proposed to subject them to a uniform regime.

At the opposite end of the spectrum there are those states that do not directly regulate hedge funds, although they may have approached the phenomenon from another angle.

In the *United States*, federal regulation applicable to hedge funds derives from several bodies of law: the Securities Act of 1933 for the public issue of securities; the Investment Company Act of 1940 for the definition of the fund, the Securities Exchange Act of 1934 for defining the distribution, and finally the regulations of the Commodities Futures Trading Commission (CFTC) as to whether the fund qualifies as a "commodity pool". In all these cases the law defines the limits within which the regulation would not be applicable, and most hedge funds function outside the boundaries of regulatory oversight. Aside from federal regulation, some states apply their so-called blue-sky laws to hedge funds.

According to Regulation D under the Securities Act, offers to "accredited investors" without general public solicitation or intention to resell are exempted from the Act.[10]

The fund itself would qualify under the Investment Company Act unless it has less than 100 investors that are at the moment of investment "qualified purchasers". The conditions are more demanding than those used for defining "accredited investors".[11]

The distribution of hedge fund shares would take place through registered broker-dealers: that requirement does not apply to certain persons that perform substantial functions in the fund, or when it only involves sales to institutional investors and other financial institutions. The offer by non-US brokers is allowed for limited business activity, provided the foreign firm is "chaperoned" by a US broker-dealer. As a consequence, only institutional investors can be solicited.

The Investment Advisors Act calls for registration of managers of hedge funds with more than 15 clients, a fund being calculated as one client. The Act allows fund managers to be exempted from the prohibition to

[5] The EP report proposed to exempt credit institutions and insurance companies managing their internal AIF: see Committee on Economic and Monetary Affairs Draft report by Mr. Gauzès on the proposal for a directive of the European Parliament and of the Council on Alternative Investment Fund Managers and amending Directives 2004/39/EC and 2009/…/EC (COM(2009) 0207 – C7-0040/2009 – 2009/0064(COD)).

[6] This overview is partly based on the IOSCO survey, Hedge Fund Oversight, Consultation Report, March 2009, annex 5. For more details, also on the country reports, see: P. Astleford and D. Frase (eds.), Hedge Funds and the Law, Sweet and Maxwell, 2010.

[7] ASIC is Australian Securities and Investments Commission.

[8] CVM or Comissao de Valores Mobiliarios, Brazil.

[9] E.g., investment for more than cdn $ 150 000.

[10] The regulation contains a detailed list of categories of "accredited investors", inter alia persons with income in excess of $ 200.000 and $ 1 m net worth. But the limitation to 100 investors does not apply.

[11] Individuals with at least $ 5 m in investments, or companies and trusts with $ 5 m in investments.

receive any portion of the profits from the fund with respect to the funds invested by "qualified clients".[12]

The CFTC regime applies to "commodity pools" if the fund deals in futures or commodities. Registration will be avoided under the exemption for "sophisticated" investors, essentially the qualified purchasers under the Securities Act.

In the *United Kingdom*, the hedge funds as such are not supervised, but the managers located in the UK are subject to UK rules on the basis of MiFID and FSA rules. Hence the capital requirements directive is applicable to the management firm, along with the FSA rules on conduct of business. Some hedge funds are traded on regulated markets and subject to the disclosure rules applicable to listed companies. Indirectly, the FSA also obtains information from the banks that act as prime brokers or offer other financial services, or from institutional investors under FSA oversight. The FSA has been monitoring hedge fund activity for some time, closely overseeing the activity of the 40 largest funds, representing about half the market.

The *German* system is based on the difference between the so-called single hedge funds that can only be offered privately, and Funds of Hedge Funds (FoHF) that can also be offered to the public. For both types a prospectus is needed, which is more elaborate for a FoHF. This regime includes the public offer of foreign FoHF originating from jurisdictions with equivalent regulation and supervision, provided there is an agreement between competent supervisors for the exchange of information. The management is in the hands of a capital investment company[13] to be licensed by Bafin. In addition, German law allows more flexibility with respect to regulated "special funds" that are exclusively addressed to legal persons, e.g. institutional investors.

The *Italian* regime is based on the regulation of the asset management company by the Banca d'Italia, which regulates the structure and the activities of the fund. Hedge funds may only be offered to a maximum of 200 investors who contribute at least €0.5 million to the fund. Hence hedge funds are not regulated directly, but indirectly by the central bank.

The *Spanish* regime is also based on the distinction between single hedge funds, which can only be offered to qualified investors at a minimum investment of +€ 50.000 to at least 25 participants. Funds of hedge funds may be freely distributed to the public, provided they have at least 100 investors. The funds are managed by a management company that is registered with the CNMV. The marketing and sale of these funds in Spain is subject to the prior authorization of the CNMV, triggering a certain number of obligations. Hence actual practice is very concerned about avoiding the moment that distribution could be considered "marketing" to the public.

According to *French* law, the contract-based funds enjoy wide freedom in their investment policy, in the calculation of NAV and lock-up periods, and they may freely be constituted by a management company that is licensed. Access is restricted to qualified and wealthy investors. French regular investment funds may invest up to 10% in other assets i.e. hedge funds and foreign funds. This limit does not apply to the so-called ARIA funds, in which access is restricted except for the funds that offer a guarantee for the capital subscribed. These restrictions take account of the volume of the initial subscription or the criteria for defining professional investors.[14] The management of these funds is subject to the same rules as those applicable to the main group of UCITS management companies. Foreign hedge funds cannot be distributed in France except with the authorization of the AMF, which is granted on the basis of a finding of an equivalent disclosure regime and the existence of an agreement for the exchange of information. Here too there are discussions of what "marketing" really means, but it certainly does not allow for a private placement regime.

As *Luxembourg* and *Ireland* house a large part of the investment funds in the EU, it is useful to give a short overview of their regulatory regime. Different from the UK, where most hedge funds are managed in London but domiciled in low tax jurisdictions, Luxembourg and Ireland have introduced legislation that allow hedge funds to establish their domicile in their jurisdictions.

According to the *Luxembourg* legislation, a hedge fund may be constituted under the 2007 law relating to

[12] This refers to clients with $ 1.5 m invested.

[13] Kapitalanlagegesellschaft according to Investment Gesetz 2003 and Investmentaktiengesellschaftgesetz allowing entrepreneurs to associate investors to the common venture. See http://www.gesetze-im-internet.de/bundesrecht/invg/gesamt.pdf.

[14] On the basis of the three-pronged threshold: € 20 m balance sheet, € 40 m turnover and equity of € 20 m or more.

investment funds not placed with the public. The funds can take the form of common funds, sicavs or Specialized Investment Funds (SIF). In each case net assets of € 1,250 m are required. "Specialized Investment Funds" are subject to flexible rules, *e.g.*, 30% investment in securities of the same type from the same issuer. The SIF can be offered to "well informed investors" being, apart from institutional investors, persons with €125.000 in the fund or assessed so by the bank with respect to their experience and knowledge. The law requires the appointment of a Luxembourg central administration agent and a depositary, a Luxembourg financial institution or one established in Luxembourg from another Member state. Assets have to be valued at fair value as defined in the fund's charter. When proceeding to a public offering, a prospectus will be required as approved by the CSSF.

Traditional investment funds can also develop investment strategies followed by hedge funds, such as 130/30 strategies, or may borrow in some cases up to 400% of net assets. Funds of Funds may invest up to 20% in unregulated funds, but subfunds of an umbrella fund are treated as separate funds.[15]

The *Irish*[16] regulatory regime is based on a distinction between UCITS – that can be offered for sale throughout the European Union, and non-UCITS, that can only be offered abroad if the local regulation allows it, often on the basis of a private placement. Exceptionally non-UCITS funds can be offered to retail investors: this applies especially to Funds of Hedge Funds that can be entirely invested in a diversified range of unregulated funds. Hedge funds or private equity funds would normally choose one of the other non-UCITS forms, i.e. the Professional Investment Funds, or the Qualifying Investor Funds, in the latter case a formula for which the investment and borrowing requirements are relaxed. Both types are addressed to institutional investors or high net worth individuals.[17] Funds must appoint as custodian either an Irish credit institution or a branch or subsidiary of an EU credit institution established in Ireland. The management should be entrusted to a management company, licensed by the Irish supervisor, or qualifying for recognition under the EU MiFID regime.[18] Irish hedge funds often are listed on the Irish stock exchange.

Most other countries have only a limited number of hedge funds established on their territory. Some have, others have not enacted elaborate regulation. A sampling follows.

In *Belgium*, the existing UCITS regulation and its investment restrictions prevent creation of hedge funds in this form. Tax and disclosure obligations would prevent the use of the common corporate form. Hence there are practically no hedge funds on the market.

In *Denmark*, hedge funds and private equity funds are limited to the sphere of private investment: if investors from the public are solicited, the entire securities regulatory system would apply. However, there are two types of "association" that can call on the public for investing in SME and hedge funds activities,[19] but these two are strictly regulated and supervised and would not meet the expectations of the usual hedge fund or private equity manager. Their managers have to be licensed by the Danish supervisor.

In *Poland,* although there are a certain number of hedge funds active on the market, and certain companies act as private equity funds, there is no regulation applicable to these funds.

Under *Greek* law, there is no regulation for hedge funds or private equity funds, although venture capital firms have been the subject of regulation. There also is a market in venture capital firms, often subsidiaries of a bank.

The *Swiss* regime does not impose legal requirements to hedge funds, and foreign funds are freely offered to qualified or professional investors. Swiss-based fund managers of Swiss funds need to be registered, while managers of non-Swiss funds are merely registered under anti-money-laundering rules.

In *Croatia*, the general regime governing investment funds is generally applicable to hedge funds and private equity funds, both being open-ended funds with redistribution restricted to private offerings. This applies to the general rules on the structure of the funds, the role of the depository, valuation, etc. Entry into

[15] See M. Seimetz, Luxembourg Hedge Funds, Astleford & Frase, nt. 6, 12–041 e.s.

[16] For further details, see: D. O'Sullivan, Hedge Funds in Ireland, in: Astleford & Frase, nt. 6 12–074.

[17] The thresholds are €1.250.000 assets and € 250.000 for an initial investment. For institutions, a minimum of assets under management of € 25 m is required.

[18] On the board of which at least two Irish, mostly non-executive directors have been appointed.

[19] Called the SME association and the Hedge Association, the latter being entitled to invest in a wider range of assets.

these funds is restricted to qualifying investors, i.e., institutional investors and wealthy individuals. The requirements are significantly higher for investing in a venture capital fund. Investors are mainly insurance companies and pension funds, which can invest part of their assets in investment funds. Management companies must be appointed and are regulated by the securities supervisor Hanfa.

In *Japan*, investment managers that manage funds open to public investment have to be registered with the Japanese FSA. If the fund only targets qualified financial investors, no such registration is needed, but the manager has to be notified to JFSA.

Taiwan law provides for limited use of local hedge funds by institutional and financial investors and retail investors (up to 35 persons). The range of investments is negatively defined in the regulation, and would exclude all securities for which there may be a danger of a conflict of interest, but in other cases the supervisor can step forward and forbid any investment type. Moreover, remunerations are restricted, and in the absence of the limited partnership form, there are only contractual funds. As a consequence, hedge funds are mainly constituted abroad especially Korean funds that act as hedge funds. Investment in Taiwanese assets by off shore funds is closely monitored by the Investment Commission, but these funds may also be restricted as to trading activities (e.g. shorting). Offshore funds must appoint a local agent and an approved custodian.

12.1.1.3 Some Characteristics of the Legal Regime

The regulation of hedge funds can be divided in two periods. Before the financial crisis, most jurisdictions – with some exceptions[20] – had not adopted specific regulations addressing hedge funds. The applicable regulation if any derived from the application of existing rules that had mainly been conceived to deal with asset management activities in general,[21] or with investment funds in particular. So in France and Spain, and to a certain extent in the US as well, regulation is deeply linked to the existing regulation on common investment funds. All national reports mentioned, however, that asset managers were generally regulated, irrespective of their activity in the hedge fund field. Moreover, several states took a more liberal attitude with respect to funds of hedge funds, for which they adopted specific regulations.

This first type of regulation essentially addressed investor protection concerns, whether by excluding retail investors, insuring sufficient disclosure, warning about risks, or requiring organizational measures within the fund or asset manager. Rare were the concerns that have dominated the debate since the crisis, essentially focusing on systemic risk issues. This difference in approach explains why the "private offering" exemption and similar rules on distribution or on scope have now become less central to the regulators' concerns. They are focusing more on matters of risk management, fair valuation, ethical conduct, appropriate remuneration, and reporting to the supervisors. In that respect there is real change in the regulatory philosophy.

At the moment of writing, the main approach to regulation consists of exempting the solicitation of investors or the issuance of securities from the existing regulation.[22] Hedge funds were considered investment instruments only accessible to wealthy investors or at a later date to larger institutional investors. This leads to the paradox that in many jurisdictions, hedge fund regulation is essentially non-regulation, but this statement is to be nuanced as the asset managers are regulated. As mentioned above, some limited form of indirect supervision – especially through the prime brokers and the asset managers – is being exercised. This feature also explains why several of the country reports declare that no regulation has been in force, but there are elaborate exemption rules. A short overview of these, trying to identify their common features, is therefore useful.

(a) Hedge funds may be offered to investors

The permissive attitude toward hedge funds is not found in all jurisdictions. Some allow hedge funds, like other collective investment schemes, but they take into account the additional risks and therefore may impose tighter rules on the organization of the fund and may promulgate rules to insure adequate disclosure to investors. This is the scheme

[20] Most regulations define the conditions according to which hedge funds would not be regulated. Even today, no jurisdictions address hedge funds as such.

[21] Reference is to be made to the provisions of the Investment Company Act in the US, and the Investment Advisers Act, and the UCITS legislation in the EU.

[22] See, e.g., Switzerland, Belgium.

followed in Australia for the Managed Investment Scheme, where apart from organizational rules, a Product Disclosure Statement comparable to a prospectus must be issued. In Canada, hedge funds can be offered through a prospectus offering, where additional requirements apply to the dealers who sell the securities. The Brazilian regime does not distinguish hedge funds from other funds: it only imposes some stricter requirements on the former, e.g., with respect to disclosure (initial and continuous), risk control, and conflicts of interest.

(b) Express prohibition to create or to offer hedge funds

There are few if any jurisdictions that have adopted an outright prohibition to create or offer hedge funds. Most systems allow acquisition of hedge funds by institutional, professional or sophisticated investors, and funds can be freely created outside the regulated zone. Also, if these funds would be offered to the public, the regulation of the public offering of securities would apply. This is the regime applicable to foreign hedge funds, offered in Belgium: according to the directive, no prospectus is required for offers for individual amounts above € 50.000.[23]

(c) Exempting hedge funds

The most widely used technique for dealing with hedge funds has been the private offering exemption, allowing funds that in principle would be subject to the investment fund regulation to be exempted provided that they are not offered to the public at large. There are several ways to define the private character of such funds: usually a number of investors is mentioned, or the minimum entry investment establishes a floor. In several states, "qualified" or professional investors may be solicited. In others the number of investors per fund is limited.

A brief overview will give an insight into the diversity.

In the US, the involvement of less than 100 investors[24] was followed, later extended to "qualified purchasers", being individuals or institutional investors with a substantial amount of money.[25] In Canada, offerings without a prospectus can only be made to accredited investors who meet a net income or financial assets test, or make a minimum initial purchase for Can $ 150.000. In the UK, individual investors can only access hedge funds through a "qualified investor scheme". In Spain, the individual investment had to be at least € 50.000, and was limited to qualified or professional investors with a minimum of 25 persons involved.[26] The French system is also linked to a minimum investment ($125.000) and to the wealth of the investor.[27] In Italy, a minimum initial investment of € 500.000 is required.[28] The German system relies on the intermediary bank: private placements – whether to individual or professionals investors – are exempted but only banks are allowed to offer them. Finally, Switzerland and Japan rely on the intervention of authorized intermediaries; in Switzerland with a check by the supervisor on the prospectus for completeness and consistency.

(d) Funds of Hedge Funds

The restrictive attitude toward offering hedge funds to the public is relaxed for the offering of funds of hedge funds, as these insure wide risk spreading.

In the jurisdictions where FoHF may be offered to the public, these criteria are relaxed, whether by allowing free access – Germany, Spain – [29] or as is the case in France, down to a minimum investment of €10.000.[30] The same is planned in Italy. In Spain, FoHF can be offered provided the investor – other

[23] Another exception relates to the sale of hedge funds in private portfolios managed on a discretionary basis.

[24] The calculation basis excludes foreign and non-resident alien investors.

[25] In the US, different regimes apply under the Investment Company Act and the Securities Exchange Act. The former follows a cap on the number of investors involved (100 or less), the second uses the private placement exception, standing here for individuals with a minimum income of $200.000 or $1 million net worth; or $5 million assets for institutional investors. In these cases a prospectus must be published.

[26] See Machuca and Menendez, in: Astleford & Frase, nt. 6, 12–166.

[27] See French Report.

[28] And there may not be more than 200 investors per fund.

[29] See in Germany, at least for domestic FoHF; for foreign FoHF, a notification to Bafin and a cooperation agreement with the home supervisor is needed. A full prospectus is required.

[30] For whether wealthy investors or investors with experience in the financial sector.

than qualified investors – [31] acknowledges that he is aware of the risks in investing in the FoHF. In the UK, FoHF are accessible through the listing regime. In Belgium, the requirement of a full capital guarantee effectively prevents these funds from being distributed.

(e) Indirect regulation

The distribution or activity of hedge funds is often regulated indirectly, by addressing their financiers – the so-called prime brokers, viewed under banking regulations – or their distributors, or more importantly, their portfolio managers. In most jurisdictions, acting as a portfolio manager for any type of portfolio is subject to licensing and hence more or less strict regulation as well as ongoing supervision.[32] This is especially useful as managers often act for funds legally located abroad.[33] Often these requirements are stricter than for managers of investment funds in general due to the additional risks in their portfolio. This may seem paradoxical at first, as the investors in these funds would normally be able to fend for themselves better than the common fund investor, but financial stability objectives may justify supervision in these cases.

(f) Professional or industry regulation

The hedge fund industry has also taken some initiatives to develop voluntary codes relating to the activities of the fund managers. Several initiatives and statements should be mentioned, such as the Hedge Funds Standards Board (UK) that produced Hedge Fund Standards[34] on a wide range of organizational issues. The President's Working Group Private-Sector Committees released Best Practices for Hedge Fund Participants on April 15, 2008,[35] while the Alternative Investment Management Association has adopted a Guide to Sound Practices for Hedge Fund Administrators. The Managed Fund Association (MFA) has also been active in this field. Most of these voluntary instruments contain interesting ideas and have been used in formulating, inter alia, IOSCO's position.

(g) Contractual regulation

That most hedge funds are not regulated does not mean that no rules are applicable. In the absence of state regulation, parties to the fund will have developed elaborate rules on information, remuneration, organization, risk management, valuation, etc: these are governed by the contract between the investor and fund manager. Up to now, financial regulation does not intervene.[36] The information provided to their participants – whether in the form of voluntary prospectuses or other documents – would in some jurisdictions be subject to the rules prohibiting deceptive, misleading or fraudulent information.[37] In addition, most managers are registered as "asset managers" or "investment advisers", and under that heading they are subject to more or less elaborate rules: e.g., the MiFID rules in the EU, the Investment Advisors Act in the US. In the UK, where many asset managers of offshore hedge funds are located, they have to be registered with the FSA.[38] Moreover, in some jurisdictions, asset managers have subjected themselves to a voluntary code, and investment contracts will sometimes make reference to these standards or codes.[39]

Some national reports mention that the rules of general company law may impose certain provisions on hedge funds; however, most of the time these are not applicable to limited partnerships.

[31] According to a specific regulatory regime, see Machuca and Menendez, in: Astleford & Frase, nt. 6, 12–166.

[32] See for example Switzerland, where managers are subject to licensing and qualification conditions, and have to present a prospectus to the supervisor.

[33] See the UK where the asset manager regime applies with a close follow-up of about 40 major hedge fund managers. Most of the funds managed from the UK are located in tax friendly jurisdictions.

[34] See www.hfsb.org/?page=10915; compare the rules of the Swiss Funds Association: https://www.sfa.ch/self-regulation/selbstregulierungmusterdok. Danish funds may also subscribe to the Danish Venture Capital Association.

[35] http://www.ustreas.gov/press/releases/hp927.htm.

[36] To be mentioned however is the Swiss proposal according to which the new provisions on remuneration in financial institutions would have been applicable: the scope of the final regulation was considerably reduced, thereby excluding hedge fund managers: see Finam Circular 2010/1: Minimum standards for remuneration schemes of financial institutions http://www.finma.ch/f/regulierung/Documents/finma-rs-2010-01-f.pdf.

[37] E.g., in the US where rule 10B-5 would apply.

[38] See D. Frase, Hedge funds in the UK, nt. 5, at 12–004.

[39] See in the UK, the Hedge Funds Standards Board Code, with 57 signatory funds. See HFSB, www.hfsb.org/?section=11400. The IOSCO report, nt.2 raised the question of effectiveness: § 17.

The absence of the last-mentioned legal form has been mentioned as a handicap.[40] If hedge fund shares are traded on a regulated market, the disclosure, accounting, criteria for admission and so on would then become applicable.

To be mentioned is the regime for combating money laundering: this usually is applicable to funds and managers. In Switzerland, a license on the basis of AML-CTF is needed for resident managers of foreign funds.

(h) Alternative approaches

In some states, funds similar to hedge funds or private equity funds have been organized by the law. This is the case in Denmark and in Belgium. They are subject to rules similar to those applied to regular investment funds, but they have some more freedom in their investment and risk objectives. In the Belgian case, an "institutional" fund, aimed exclusively at institutional investors, can be created with a non-UCITS status, with free investment policies, no mandatory prospectus disclosure, nor publication of the net asset value. Also supervision is not exercised by the securities supervisor.

Recently, a certain number of hedge fund strategies have been proposed under the form of exchange traded funds (ETFs), opening up their distribution to all investors acquiring the funds on the open market. However, these funds will be managed by asset managers that are registered and overseen by the market supervisors.

(i) "Linked" or "substitute" products

In some states, investments in hedge funds may not be directly offered to the public, but a practice has developed to offer them indirectly through other products that are financially equivalent, but legally different. They may be differently regulated and may therefore not offer the same guarantees in terms of investor protection.[41] This is the case with "notes" or "certificates", which are debt instruments outside the scope of the general public offering laws, the capital of which is often "guaranteed" but the return linked to the return of a hedge fund or a portfolio of hedge funds. In some states, hedge funds have been offered under the formula of unit linked insurance products, or similar financial instruments, for which the rules on disclosure and distribution are considerably different from those applied in the investment fund sector.[42] Other techniques like regrouping small investors to reach the minimum floor of, e.g., € 50.000, was mentioned in the Spanish report. In the EU, the Commission intends to investigate this subject inter alia on the basis of a report to be submitted by the three financial supervisory committees.[43]

(j) Tax regulation

The hedge fund activity is deeply connected to the applicable tax regime, both at the portfolio and at the manager's level. Tax neutrality for the fund is pursued by domiciling funds in tax neutral jurisdictions e.g.in the Caribbean. The fund participants will then be taxed according to the regime applicable to them: exchange of information among tax authorities is here of the essence. At the level of the asset managers, a favorable tax regime helps to explain their location in cities like London. Changes in that regime may cause the managers to relocate. In the US, the report illustrates the complexity of the issues involved and mentions that managers changed to a partnership formula; as partners are taxed directly, double taxation can be avoided.

In the Belgian case, double taxation prevents fund creation outside the regulated area, i.e., as UCITS or as "institutional funds".

(k) Specialist funds

In some states, regulation has been developed aimed at creating specialist funds with a view to contributing to the financing of local industry or commerce, often of the SME type. Examples of these are found in Belgium, Denmark, or Taiwan. Germany has a significant number of specialist funds, addressed to institutional investors and enjoying a lighter regime.

[40] See Taiwan report.

[41] In Belgium, Germany, Denmark, e.g., see the EU Commission's statement on the Packaged Retail Investment Products, or "prips": for the latest update, see: ec.europa.eu/internal_market/finservices-retail/docs/investment_products/20091215_prips_en.pdf.

[42] Especially on suitability and conflicts of interest, including fee disclosure.

[43] Communication from the Commission on Packaged Retail Investment Products, COM(2009) 204 final, 30.4.2009, ec.europa.eu/internal_market/finservices-retail/docs/investment_products/29042009_communication_en.pdf.

12.1.1.4 Objectives of the Regulation of Hedge Funds

Hedge funds have remained unregulated for a long time; due to the composition of their membership, it was generally believed that there was no need for any regulation.[44] However, even before the recent financial crisis, attention was drawn to the possible systemic consequences of the collapse of a major hedge fund when Long Term Capital Management had to be rescued in 1998.[45] Although the idea was rejected for a long time by US regulators, it is now accepted that direct oversight of hedge fund managers is needed for financial stability.[46] Before, prudential supervisors relied on the information obtained from the prime brokers, but this does not allow aggregation of data from several prime brokers. Both in the US and in Europe, regulation is being developed to take account of this objective, especially by requesting hedge fund managers – and not individual hedge funds – to report to the supervisors about the positions they have taken. Whether this approach applies to all hedge fund managers – see the European regulation – or only to the most significant ones – more so in the UK and in the US approach – is a matter of a difference of opinion. This concern exceeds however the mere systemic issues: hedge funds should be well organized, respect integrity rules especially on business conduct and conflicts of interest, offer adequate guarantees in terms of management and organization, while the contagion effect should be minimized by requiring appropriate risk management systems allowing for monitoring counterparty risk. All these instruments serve both systemic risk detection and avoidance and financial stability.

The second objective for which hedge funds may need to be regulated concerns the offer or distribution of their securities or rights to the public at large and is a negative form of investor protection. Most jurisdictions have up to now restricted the distribution of hedge funds, especially for retail risk reasons, to the more sophisticated and institutional investors; at the same time they did not hold the existing rules relating to investment funds or investment management applicable. In several states there was an outright prohibition on offering hedge funds to retail investors. In other jurisdictions, hedge funds are lawfully offered to the public, and with more regulation becoming applicable it seems likely that investments in hedge funds will become accessible to a wider audience, provided certain conditions are met. One also sees some hedge funds adopting the legal form of UCITS, thereby availing themselves of the flexibility offered by the 3rd UCITS directive allowing for the use of derivatives in their portfolios: these funds are beneficiaries of the European passport, according to which the fund can be distributed all over Europe without any additional requirement (they are colloquially referred to as "newcits"). As mentioned, investor protection through distribution requirements becomes even more ineffective through the use of listed hedge funds, under the form of managed exchange traded funds.

Moreover, several jurisdictions allow the distribution of Funds of Hedge Funds (FoHF), even to the public at large. Some hedge fund investments come wrapped under other forms such as assurance products or bank issued certificates. The applicable rules are then considerably different, raising the question whether investors can be protected differently depending on the legal wrapper under which the investment is presented.[47]

Outside the realm of domestic regulation is the activity of investors acquiring hedge funds abroad, or where the fund is acquired locally but without solicitation of or offering to the investor. But this exemption for the "act of investing" is not necessarily extended to asset management services: asset managers may be subject to regulation and supervision in their jurisdiction of establishment with respect to the management of funds established outside their home jurisdictions.[48]

[44] This position was repeatedly voiced by several representatives of the Wharton School. This was still the case in February 2007, in a report of President's Working Group on Financial Markets, chaired by Treasury Secretary Henry M. Paulson, urged vigilance but concluded that new regulations are not needed (www.nytimes.com/2007/02/23/business/23hedge.html?_r=1&pagewanted=2). The Securities and Exchange Commission in 2004 tried to require them to register with the agency and make limited disclosures about their activities. But a federal appeals court ruled that the Commission did not have that authority: Ph. Goldstein v. SEC, 23 June 2006.

[45] See on this case: the US report.

[46] See e.g. statement by Lord Myners, .UK. Must Fix Hedge-Fund Oversight, Nov 10, 2009, online.wsj.com/article/SB125778995639339045.html. In the US, initiatives came mainly from Congress (Paul Kanjorski, Barney Frank).

[47] This subject is mentioned in several reports, and is sometimes referred to as relating to "substitute products", or "prips", (prepackaged retain investment products). See nt. 38.

[48] This is the case in the UK, but not in France.

The registration of hedge funds will also become necessary from a market integrity point of view. Recent cases have alleged that insider trading has been going on within insider rings constituted by hedge fund managers. Market manipulation cases are likely to have occurred.[49] Although these objectives can efficiently be pursued on the basis of the existing rules on market abuse, covering both insider trading and market manipulation, it would be helpful if the funds and their managers and staff would be readily identifiable, and could appropriately be sanctioned in case of violation.

In some jurisdictions hedge funds have been heavily criticized for their role as activist investors. Some high profile cases have led to public outcry as some funds have triggered – or attempted to trigger – major changes in listed companies, leading some to claim that their "excessive" conduct has to be curbed.[50] Sometimes there has been some confusion with the role of private equity funds, which after having invested in companies have massively increased the latter's leverage, sometimes threatening their survival. The now adopted EU AIFM directive contains some provisions in this respect.

12.1.1.5 Private Law Aspects

Hedge funds are organized in different ways: frequently they are legal persons set up in a jurisdiction with minimum formalities and little or no taxation. The fund is managed out of jurisdictions with advanced financial markets such as the US or the UK. Also depositaries and support functions will be located or managed out of the latter jurisdictions. Originally many funds were constituted as limited partnerships with the managers as active partners,[51] while investors as limited partners will limit their risk to their contribution. This organizational type is mentioned in some jurisdictions, e.g. in Switzerland.[52] These funds may organize the management of the portfolio within the fund, where the board of directors will be directly in charge of the management, usually with a professional manager as an advisor, or they may outsource the management and the administration to a professional asset manager. As mentioned above, "open ended companies" or "sicavs" are also used.

Purely contractual funds are frequently used especially for their tax neutrality. In the regulation they usually are unmentioned, except from the angle of the obligations of the asset manager. In France, this type of fund is subject to more severe requirements if it wants to address itself to "outside" investors.[53] The trust form should also be mentioned as used in the UK and other countries whose laws have adopted the use of the trust for business purposes.

The relationship between the fund and the members are essentially of a contractual nature. This means that relations are the result of individual negotiations, and often present considerable individual differences. To be mentioned are the clauses relating to the information to members, the valuation rules, to the fee due to managers, but also the conditions relating to repayment, especially the lock up rules, side pockets, reimbursement in kind, the duration of the fund (often limited to a certain number of years), etc. Generally these are left to the parties' negotiations,[54] except that the law may impose disclosure duties to ensure parties are well informed and if needed, warned.[55] Disclosure acts as a surrogate to substantive regulation: parties have to determine for themselves to what obligations they want to be bound. Interesting is the French technique, according to which the investor, along with receiving the prospectus, has to state in writing that he is informed that the investment is only addressed to certain, more sophisticated investors. This warning also applies to the due diligence investors are expected to undertake

[49] See the Galleon case in the US, involving an insider ring. In Oct 2011, the fund's CEO has been sentence to 11 years in jail. See for other cases: E. Allen, Hedge funds and related entities as defendants, in Astleford & D. Frase (eds) nt. 6, 7–041 e.s.

[50] Among these one can mention the dismantling of ABNAmro Bank and the attempts to urge Deutsche Börse to adapt its business plan. The opposition has been virulent in Germany – see the speech by Müntefering, referring to "the swarms of locusts": see Gumpel, P., The day of the Locust, Time, May 15, 2005, www.time.com/time/magazine/article/0,9171,1061439,00.html, and the French report.

[51] Held to unlimited liability, although this partner is often a limited liability entity.

[52] Where the Kommanditgesellschaft would constitute an adequate vehicle for a fund with only a few members.

[53] The minimum initial contribution to a contractual fund would be € 250.000, indicating that this type of fund is only addressed to professional or institutional investors.

[54] Spain is stricter in regulating these relations, dealing inter alia with organization and risk control measures, the relations with prime brokers, and the collateralization rules.

[55] This is the case in France, and in support of the regulatory obligations in Spain as well.

before entering into a fund. This especially applies to larger investors, but constitutes a handicap for smaller members, such as some pension funds or foundations that are unable to engage in expensive investigations. Hence hedge fund activity may affect investor confidence.

The regulation on hedge funds may also be applied to so-called private pools of capital, irrespective of their legal structure. This may extend to undivided assets, whether or not held in segregated accounts. The designation of applicable regulation would then mainly be based on the location of the managers and apply to all asset management activities.

12.1.1.6 Regulation of Hedge Funds or of Hedge Funds Managers

There are several techniques to approach hedge funds. Several national jurisdictions regulate the funds in much the same way as they regulate other investment funds.[56] This is the most effective approach in terms of investor protection and will be found in those states that allow funds to be publicly distributed, directly or as FoHF. Indeed in some jurisdictions the funds are a variety of the traditional investment funds, with however some derogatory rules. In some states, this has been refined by creating special fund types, related to the basic investment fund type: this is e.g. the case in France, in which case specific types have been developed for dealing with Funds of Hedge Funds,[57] where the common UCITS type constitutes the basic pattern amended to take account of the additional investor protection needs. The situation in Spain is similar, but more elaborate.

The other approach is primarily not to deal with the funds, individually, but with the managers of the funds, what allows the regulation to make abstraction of the different legal structures in which the portfolios are managed, including the managed accounts that do not correspond to the notion of a fund. Indeed, it is necessary to look at the aggregate position of all portfolios managed by the same managers, if one wants to have information about the systemic risk involved, or the possibility of contagion to other financial institutions. It is therefore no surprise that the UK, US, and the new regulations in the EU follow this aggregate approach, as these are more oriented toward the systemic issues. A certain number of provisions formulated as applicable to the manager will, however, affect the individual funds: risk management requirements, valuation rules or provisions on depositaries have "third-party effect".

Another indirect approach that has been followed for some time and that was considered sufficient for dealing with hedge funds, is some form of indirect supervision, through their prime brokers: as these are subject to banking regulation, the prudential supervisors have addressed these banks not only to inform them about the position and evolution of risks within their clients, the hedge funds, but also looking at the same time at their relations with the funds and the latters' risk assessment, e.g. for dealing with collateral. Indirectly these requirements will have affected the funds' functioning. However, this approach does not allow aggregating the information per manager, as there may be several prime brokers active for the same management firm.

12.1.1.7 The Future Regulation of Hedge Funds

The general absence of regulation is likely to be modified after the crisis. The crisis has considerably awakened the politicians, the public authorities and the media to the role of hedge funds in their economies.[58] Although it is recognized that hedge funds have not constituted a significant systemic risk,[59] it was considered that regulation is needed to take account of their potential impact on systemic developments, both from the angle of their financing through the banking system, as well as with respect to the effect of their trading activity on the markets.[60] Financial stability institutions[61]

[56] This is the case in Spain, France, Denmark and Taiwan.

[57] So-called ARIA; see also the FCIMT, which trades positions in the marché à terme.

[58] See above on the objectives of regulation.

[59] See IOSCO report, nt. 2: "However, the activities of hedge funds may have amplified the consequences of the crisis. This occurred, for instance, because of the need for hedge funds (along with many other market participants) to quickly unwind positions because of liquidity restrictions in meeting margin calls or significant requests for redemption by investors."

[60] See art. 2(a) of the proposed regulation on the ESRB defining "financial institution" as "any undertaking whose main business is to take deposits, grant credits, provide insurance services or other financial services to its clients or members or engage in financial investment or trading activities on its own account."

[61] The Central banks, and in Europe the European Systemic Risk Board. See Regulation 1092/ 2010 of 24 November 2010 on European Union macro-prudential oversight of the financial system and establishing a European Systemic Risk Board, OJEC 15 12 2010, L 331/1.

have stepped into the debate, asking for more and timely information.[62] Therefore states will require hedge funds to report to the financial supervisors and, according to some proposals, to restrict their leverage, to restrict their managers' remuneration, require a minimum capital, and so on. The oversight of hedge funds was expressly mentioned in the G 20 April 2009[63] statements[64] and is included in the mandate of the European systemic risk board.[65] This presupposes registration, whether on a fund's basis, or more likely on the basis of the fund manager's basis.[66]

Technical scrutiny of hedge funds was started by IOSCO several years ago.[67] In November 2007, a report was published dealing with issues surrounding the valuation of hedge fund portfolios.[68] In June 2009, IOSCO published its report on hedge fund oversight and formulated six high-level principles on the regulation and supervision of hedge funds. These principles will be mentioned in the appropriate sections of this report.

Over time the regulation in the European Union member states has developed from a total exclusion of hedge funds or private equity funds from the benefit of the UCITS directive, essentially by restricting the mutual recognition or "passporting" regime to funds organized in conformity with the UCITS directive, to a more liberal attitude allowing UCITS to engage in a wide range of activities that are normally undertaken by hedge funds – especially in the derivative sector – and even private equity funds. As a consequence one sees more and more previously excluded funds taking on the legal form of a UCITS and benefiting from the passporting regime, allowing the funds even to be offered to retail investors: they are sometimes called "newcits".[69] In some respects the UCITS regime does not give full freedom: borrowing is not allowed for UCITS,[70] investments may only be made in "transferable securities" but with the use of derivatives as allowed by the directive,[71] the restrictions for other assets is easily circumvented, provided the assets are liquid. The limitation to 10% OTC securities may also be a handicap, e.g., in the private equity sphere. Redemption is obligatory for UCITS and must be offered within 14 days. These and some other differences will avoid these funds being entirely absorbed by the UCITS regime. Some fear that this evolution may endanger the reputation of the "UCITS brand".

12.1.1.7.1 The International Initiatives

As a consequence of the financial crisis, several proposals have been discussed and some adopted, to introduce comprehensive regulation addressed to "hedge funds", "highly leveraged institutions", "private pools of capital" or comparable forms of collective investment. These proposals have first been formulated at the international level by the "Financial Stability

[62] See Hedge Funds and Their Implications for Financial Stability by T. Garbaravicius and F. Dierick, ECB, Occasional paper Series, nr. 34, August 2005.

[63] —"hedge funds or their managers will be registered and will be required to disclose appropriate information on an ongoing basis to supervisors or regulators, including on their leverage, necessary for assessment of the systemic risks that they pose individually or collectively. Where appropriate, registration should be subject to a minimum size. They will be subject to oversight to ensure that they have adequate risk management. We ask the FSB [Financial Stability Board] to develop mechanisms for cooperation and information sharing between relevant authorities in order to ensure that effective oversight is maintained where a fund is located in a different jurisdiction from the manager."

[64] The G-20 Action Plan states: "Private sector bodies that have already developed best practices for private pools of capital and/or hedge funds should bring forward proposals for a set of unified best practices. Finance Ministers should assess the adequacy of these proposals, drawing upon the analysis of regulators, the expanded FSF, and other relevant bodies." See Declaration Summit on Financial Markets and the World Economy, Action Plan to Implement Principles of Reform, G-20, 15 November 2008, available at http://www.g20.org/Documents/g20_summit_declaration.pdf.

[65] ESRB, see nt. 60.

[66] The latter would allow aggregation of data relating to all funds managed by the same firm; however, it excludes self managed funds.

[67] See IOSCO Regulatory and Investor Protection Issues Arising from the Participation by Retail Investors in (Funds-of) Hedge Funds – Final Report, Report of the Technical Committee of IOSCO, February 2003, p. 4, available at https://www.iosco.org/library/pubdocs/pdf/IOSCOPD142.pdf, and The Regulatory Environment For Hedge Funds, A Survey And Comparison – Final Report, Report of the Technical Committee of IOSCO, November 2006, available at https://www.iosco.org/library/pubdocs/pdf/IOSCOPD226.pdf.

[68] See IOSCO Principles for the valuation of hedge fund portfolios, November 2007.

[69] See PWC, Future Newcits Regulation? www.pwc.com/gx/en/asset-management/assets/newcits-regulation-0310.pdf.

[70] Leverage. See art. 83 of Directive 2009/65 of 13 July 2009, OJEC 17 November 2009, L 302/32.

[71] Directive art. 50(1)(9) of the Ucits directive, 17 July 2009, 2009/65 OJ. L. 302/66 of 17 November 2009 allows UCITS to invest in derivatives but the amount should be less than the total net value of the portfolio.

Forum", now Financial Stability Board, and by IOSCO. Support of the G 20 has been important. They have received further regulatory support in the EU directive on Alternative Investment Fund Management (AIFM), or in the Dodd Frank Act after its adoption by the US Congress.

Technical attention to hedge funds was started by IOSCO several years ago.[72] The FSF published in 2002 a Report on Highly Leveraged Institutions.[73] In November 2007, an IOSCO report was published dealing with issues relating to the valuation of hedge fund portfolios.[74] In June 2009, IOSCO published its Final Report on "Hedge Fund Oversight", in which it formulated six high-level principles on the regulation and supervision of hedge funds. These will constitute the international standard to be applied in all IOSCO member jurisdictions, in practice worldwide. The statement aims at dealing with both systemic issues and investor protection matters. For some matters, it refers to the cross sectoral aspects, referring to the Basel Committee. It draws attention to the global dimension of the hedge fund activity, the hedge fund industry being very mobile. It may suffice to reprint here the said six high-level principles that are likely to be guiding the future national or regulation regulations.

1. Hedge funds and/or hedge fund managers/advisers should be subject to mandatory registration.
2. Hedge fund managers / advisers which are required to register should also be subject to appropriate ongoing regulatory requirements relating to:
   (a) Organizational and operational standards; inter alia stress testing, protection of client's interest by segregation, designation of independent custodian and depositories and offering protection to client's assets;
   (b) Conflicts of interest and other conduct of business rules; strong independent compliance function;
   (c) Disclosure to investors; and
   (d) Prudential regulation.
3. Prime Brokers and banks which provide funding to hedge funds should be subject to mandatory registration/regulation and supervision. They should have in place appropriate risk management systems and controls to monitor their counterparty credit risk exposures to hedge funds.
4. Hedge fund managers/advisers and prime brokers should provide to the relevant regulator information for systemic risk purposes (including the identification, analysis and mitigation of systemic risks).
5. Regulators should encourage and take account of the development, implementation and convergence of industry good practices, where appropriate.
6. Regulators should have the authority to co-operate and share information, where appropriate, with each other, in order to facilitate efficient and effective oversight of globally active managers/advisers and/or funds and to help identify systemic risks, market integrity and other risks arising from the activities or exposures of hedge funds with a view to mitigating such risks across borders. Recently IOSCO has published "Elements of International Regulatory Standards on Funds of Hedge Funds Related Issues Based on Best Market Practice".[75]

12.1.1.7.2 The European AIFM Directive

In the EU, a directive on Alternative Investment Fund Management has been adopted: the final vote was cast by the EU parliament on the 22nd of September 2010.[76] The final text is expected early 2011, and therefore the present analysis will be based on the agreement between Parliament and the Council of Ministers. It contains a comprehensive and elaborate regime dealing with the managers of hedge funds, of private equity funds, and of other types of collective investment. The directive deals essentially with the management companies of these funds, and only indirectly with the funds themselves. To the extent that it introduces considerable substantive provisions for both the fund manager and indirectly the fund, the European approach is likely to be more interventionist than the comparable US regulation, raising issues of regulatory competition and arbitrage.

There remains considerable insecurity as to the legal regime currently applicable: the directive will enter into force 21 days after its publication, but national regulators have to implement it within 2 years. During this period numerous secondary legislative and regulatory acts will have to be adopted, the content of

[72] See nt. 67.

[73] Report of the Working Group on Highly Leveraged Institutions, see for the text Annex II of the IOSCO Documents PD288.pdf.

[74] See IOSCO Principles for the valuation of hedge fund portfolios, November 2007.

[75] IOSCO September 2009.

[76] Directive 2011/61 of 8 June 2011, OJEC, L.174/1 of 1 July 2011.

which is largely undetermined. For non EU-AIFM, the legal regime will only be determined after the Commission has adopted a certain number of secondary acts[77] what should normally intervene before the 2 year period has come to an end. This relatively long delay may incite non-EU operators to adopt an EU status and enjoy the privileges of the directive for their AIF that have been constituted according to EU law.

12.1.1.7.3 The US Debate

In the US, the 2010 Dodd Frank Wall Street Reform and Consumer Protection Act has modified a limited number of provisions relating to hedge funds, mainly approaching the matter from the angle of Registered Investment Advisers. The requirement to register with the SEC has been extended to advisors with more than $ 100 m under management, whereby the smaller advisors – between $ 25 and $100 m – can register with the state in which they are located. All large funds would therefore need to register, opening the SEC's right to examine the books or make inspections. Interesting is their obligation to appoint a compliance officer and develop a code of ethics. Very large funds that may create systemic risks will be held to additional reporting obligations.

Important are the exemptions to the registration rule: venture capital funds, small business investment companies, private equity fund advisers (less than 150 m in the US[78]), and family offices do not have to register with the SEC, but some obligations, e.g., on record keeping, will apply. Also, the SEC can inspect private funds. Future work will be undertaken to define these notions, like family offices.

Non-US advisors also have to register with the SEC unless they have no place of business in the US, manage less than $ 25 m. for US clients, have fewer than 15 US clients and do not hold themselves out as investment advisors in the US.

If trading in the OTC derivative market, the question will arise regarding their qualification as a "major swap participant" and their obligation to clear through a CCP.

It seems striking that the US approach mainly deals with changing the perimeter of the regulation, by subjecting a larger population to the already existing requirements, but does not fundamentally change the obligations imposed to hedge funds and their managers. These may however result from other parts of the regulatory system, such as the rules relating to OTC derivative trading. Further work has been planned about the custody rules, securities lending, short selling, and arbitrage. It will take several months if not years before more clarity about the applicable regulatory regime will have been attained.

12.1.2 Part 2. Private Equity Funds

To a certain extent, the issues flowing from the activity of private equity funds overlap those relating to hedge funds, especially in their relation to investee or portfolio companies, but the structure of private equity funds, their modus operandi and their transactions are usually substantially different.

12.1.2.1 Typology and Structure

As is the case for hedge funds, there is no standard definition of private equity funds, except that these normally are pools of non-public capital, aimed at financing investee companies by acquiring considerable stakes in these companies, often at the 100% level of ownership[79] and with a view of turning them around during a limited period of time after which the investees will be returned to the market, or sold in a private transaction. Most funds are not accessible to the public, even less publicly listed, and the investees are usually privately held firms or publicly traded firms that have been taken private. Usually one distinguishes several classes of PEF, starting with venture capital funds, specializing in start up investees, growth capital and buyout funds that usually aim at acquiring full control. But this classification is not a legal one and mixed forms are frequent.

12.1.2.2 Regulating Private Equity Funds

There has been an intense debate about the need for regulating private equity funds, sometimes confounding

[77] Art 63 (1) 3rd para.

[78] The definition of "accredited investor" with $ 100 m in assets has been strengthened by excluding his primary residence from the calculation.

[79] Thereby putting an end to the disclosure obligations: see the Danish report for the case of a failed 100% takeover whereby the disclosure duties to the market were maintained.

private equity with hedge funds.[80] Arguments are based on their opaqueness, both in structure and in operations. They are accused of being destructive of the long-term perspectives of the firms in which they invest. The high level of leverage and of remuneration of the funds and their managers are mentioned as creating too heavy burdens, weakening their investees and leading eventually to the latter's demise.

Private equity funds may create significant risk in the financial system, making use of considerable leverage to finance their investments with a view of maximizing their return from the investee firms. However, in case of a market squeeze and reduced ability to find adequate market financing, private equity funds have been obliged to offload some of their portfolios (in so-called "crowded trades"), at the same time straining the financial institutions that had promised the leverage or subscribed their bonds (relations to the banking system, whether as financier or as underwriter of debt securities). As both aspects might result in triggering systemic developments, this explains why the European directive include funds engaging in private equity in the mandate of the authorities in charge of monitoring financial stability. An April 2007 study by the ECB concluded that the exposure of the banks to the private equity sector in relation to the banks' own funds buffer was at that time relatively mild in relation to the banks' own funds. It drew attention, however, to rapidly increasing leverage, resulting in large LBO debt concentrations, with a caveat for the underwriting risks of banks for the unsold stock of private equity debt, and for the secondary market for LBO debt trading.[81] Some of these fears have materialized in the subsequent financial crisis. But it also showed that private equity funds, like hedge funds, are important sources of financing in the economy.

Most of the legal aspects in the national reports relate to the action of the private equity funds in connection with their investee companies. Some of these issues – e.g., their action as activist investors – are common with the hedge funds, but different in the sense that private equity investors usually strive for fully acquiring the investees and remain invested at least over the medium term. Moreover, they usually play an active role in the management of their investees, aiming at repayment of their investment with a view of reimbursing the leverage needed for financing the investment. This financing scheme has raised eyebrows in some jurisdictions as, depending on its conditions, it may be analyzed as "financial assistance" that before 2006 was strictly prohibited under the Second company directive.[82] Conflicts of interest between the investee, its directors and the private equity funds should also be mentioned, as these may be detrimental to the public investors at the moment of going private.

Another series of company law issues are related to the activist policy pursued by some of these funds. Some national reports refer to the danger of destabilizing the management by allowing investors' activism.[83] Apart from the general rules dealing with takeover bids – such as the mandatory bid rules, introduced by the takeover bid directive[84]– several company law provisions play an important role, such as the right to call a general meeting (often at 5%, in some cases at 1%) the right of the AGM to dismiss directors "ad nutum", by a simple majority vote of the shareholders present. In several jurisdictions, the board of directors cannot, independently from any shareholder vote, dispose of substantial assets of the company.[85] The law contains a certain number of protections for the companies and their management against involuntary takeovers, among which one can mention the right to know their

[80] See, by way of example, the Rasmussen and Lehne reports in the European parliament: Rasmussen Report, European Parliament 2007/2238(INI) of 18.4.2008 and Parliaments' motion: (http://www.europarl.europa.eu/sides/getDoc.do?pubRef=-//EP//NONSGML+REPORT+A6-2008-0338+0+DOC+PDF+V0//EN) and Lehne report (www.europarl.europa.eu/sides/getDoc.do?pubRef=-//EP//NONSGML+REPORT+A6-2008-0296+0+DOC+PDF+V0//EN) and the motion adopted.

[81] Large banks and private equity sponsored leveraged buyouts in the EU, April 2007 www.ecb.eu/pub/pdf/other/largebanksandprivateequity200704en.pdf.

[82] Art. 23 of the 2nd Company Law directive forbade any form of financial assistance. It has been changed in 2006, allowing financial assistance under certain conditions. See Wymeersch, Article 23 of the second company law directive: the prohibition on financial assistance to acquire shares of the company, Festschrift für U. Drobnig, Mohr Siebeck, Tübingen, 1998, 725–48.

[83] See the French report.

[84] Art. 5, Takeover Directive, of 21 April 2004, OJ L 142, 30.4.2004, 12–23.

[85] Comp. the German Holzmüller case BGH – Federal Court of Justice February 25, 1982, (BGH – Federal Court of Justice, BGHZ 83, 122 ("Holzmüller")) and the decisions of the Dutch Hoge Raad of 13 July 2007 ("La Salle") whereby the first decided that it was legally required to submit significant disposals of assets to the decision of the general meeting, and the second decided this to be in the remit of the board.

shareholders,[86] disproportional or double voting rights,[87] and several other takeover protections.

Private equity funds and hedge funds have been accused of destroying the firms in which they invest, by overloading them with debt, extracting the net value, laying off personnel, selling assets or divisions, and ultimately selling the remainder of the firm to another equity investor, or to the market. This is the caricature of the debate that has been carried on in the European media, and in some political statements that refer to the "locusts" (an expression used by a German politician) or to "predatory capitalism".[88] Additional concerns relate to issues like foreign dominance, referring to the debate about sovereign wealth funds. The debate was picked up in the European Parliament, inter alia in the Rasmussen Report, where the following ideas were put forward, many of which were later introduced in the AIFM proposed directive.

- Mandatory capital requirements for all financial institutions;
- Aligning reward packages with longer term outcomes, to reflect losses as well as profits;
- Full transparency of high level executives' and senior managers' remuneration systems;
- Disclosure of leverage/debt exposure, source and amount of funds raised, and identification of shareholders (above a certain level) for all investment products (and therefore including hedge funds and private equity) to investors and public authorities;
- Extending the Directive obliging employees to be informed and consulted during takeovers to include leveraged buy-outs;
- Measures to "avoid unreasonable asset stripping in target companies";
- Action to avoid excessive debt caused by leveraged buy-outs, so that "the level of leverage is sustainable both for the private equity fund/firm and for the target company";
- Employees or staff representatives of pension funds to be informed on how their pensions are invested and the associated risks.

From the national reports it appears that while this debate is quite active in some jurisdictions, it is nonexistent in most others.[89] So e.g. do the Danish and to a lesser extent the Swiss and French reports refer to the – largely past – negative political discussion,[90] but refer to subsequent reports especially dealing with the consequences on employment that may modify the first negative impressions. For their contribution to innovation and improving financial results of the investees, private equity funds have been considered positively. In the Netherlands the activist attitude of some of these funds – but also of other investors – have caused great concern.[91] Several of the national reports draw attention to the effects of the activity of these funds on the legal position of the investee companies.

The national reports frequently mention the need for the investee to know exactly who its shareholders are, and what are their intentions with the acquisition of a block of shares.[92] Several reports draw attention to the weakness of the rules on disclosure of significant holdings, as laid down in the Transparency directive, especially with respect to the cases of hidden ownership due to the use of derivatives, such as contracts for difference, or equity swaps. The general rules on declaration of significant holdings do not yield a sufficiently granular picture of the ownership of the target company, are not always fully respected, do not always yield the identity of the beneficial owner, and have raised difficult questions about concerted action.[93] Serious often highly publicized conflicts and surprise maneuvering by funds, along with fears of foreign takeovers have put both hedge funds and private equity funds in a negative light. It would seem however that

[86] See the French system of the "titres au porteur identifiables".

[87] See about these the Control enhancing mechanisms, see Report on "Proportionality between ownership and control in EU listed companies", ec.europa.eu/internal_market/company/docs/shareholders/study/final_report_en.pdf. See the French system whereby shareholders can form an association to protect their interest.

[88] Expression used inter alia by Frans Timmermans, Dutch junior minister.

[89] See also in the Spanish and Italian Reports.

[90] See the Danish report referring to "The Danish discussion" and the Rasmussen report Hedge Fund and private Equity, nt. 93. This report also refers to voluntary codes such as a Guide for responsible ownership and good corporate governance.

[91] However, there may be confusion as to whether they were due to the activity of hedge funds, rather than of private equity investors.

[92] The latter point is especially mentioned in the French report, although the obligation exists in similar terms in the takeover regulation of other jurisdictions. See also the Spanish report referring to the regulation. (p. 16).

[93] See about these points the Swiss report.

private equity funds adopt less of a conflicting or "activist" strategy, as they usually will have to rely on the management to develop a longer term relationship, than hedge funds that are usually adopting a more "short term" approach.

12.1.2.3 The AIFM Directive

The AIFM directive is fully applicable to private equity funds although these are not separately addressed. Certain provisions, however, relate more clearly to the activity of private equity funds.[94] That means that the funds' management company has to be authorized and will become subject to supervision according to the general rules applicable to all AIFM. Apart from the prudential requirements (essentially minimum capital, leverage ratio), the widely framed provisions on conflicts of interest and on conduct of business call for special attention. The rules on remuneration also apply even to fully privately owned funds. Risk management calls for special attention: it includes inter alia provisions on holding or on securitising investee securities or liabilities.[95] The rules on valuation and on the depository are also applicable, which may lead to specific issues, as these provisions may not fit well for holdings in non-listed entities.[96]

Only a few provisions of the directive deal more specifically with private equity funds: these are the provisions that deal with the notification disclosure of the holdings in non-listed entities.[97] In case of acquisitions of listed companies, the general financial disclosure obligations will apply (on the basis of the Transparency directive for substantial holdings). If applicable – i.e. on crossing the 30% or one third threshold – the rules on mandatory bids will also come into play. On acquisition of control, more specific special disclosures will become mandatory, especially with regard to the intentions of the AIFM as to the future business of the investee and the repercussions on employment.

Upon the acquisition of control in privately held companies – at more than 50%[98] – the AIFM will notify the investee, its shareholders and its employee representatives about the control acquisition, the level of control, its policy on managing conflicts of interest, its communication policy toward employees and the intentions of the AIFM as to the future business of the investee and the repercussions on employment. The supervisors and the shareholders of the AIF will also have to be informed, especially viewing the effects on the debt ratio. Finally the AIF annual report will contain an overview of the different businesses it has invested in. Information on the investee policies has been dropped. It is expected that these disclosures would allow supervisors and stakeholders to monitor the situation of the AIFM's activities.

Under the heading "asset stripping", the directive prohibits certain distributions by the investee for the first 2 years after acquisition: it relates to any form of distribution; whether under the form of dividends, share buy-backs, capital reduction, or the like. While reacquisition profits or reserves are viewed, current profits can be distributed or used otherwise.

The proposed directive was strongly opposed by the venture capital sector,[99] which objected most strenuously to the provisions on the depository[100] and the valuator.[101] Those provisions have nevertheless been maintained in the final text.[102]

12.1.3 Part 3. Sovereign Wealth Funds (SWFs)

Although the subject of the SWFs is substantially different from the two previously analyzed types of collective investment, there are a number of common points that deserve attention. The organization of the SWF, their investment practices and the procedures for investment in other jurisdictions will not be analyzed. The report will focus on the recently developed guidelines for SWFs, and on the most politically active

[94] Indirectly, art.26–30 focus more clearly on PEF, by addressing AIFM acquiring control of non-listed companies and assets.

[95] Including the retention by the originator of at least 5%: art 17. The rule will apply to all AIFM. The rules have to be further detailed in Commission secondary legislation.

[96] See for criticism: European venture capital association, or Alternative Investment Management Association.

[97] Art 26, also excluding SPVs for holding real estate.

[98] At the 50% + level: art 26(5).

[99] www.evca.eu/uploadedFiles/News1/News_Items/LPsurvey AIFMDventure_15_03_10.pdf.

[100] www.evca.eu/BTF/300909_Depositary_FINAL.pdf.

[101] www.evca.eu/BTF/Independent_Valuator_300909.pdf.

[102] See Gauzès Report, nt. 4.

issues, that of the restrictions to investment in mostly Western economies.

SWFs[103] play a considerable role in the financial system, with total assets of about 3,7 trillion, invested whether in significant stakes in their home area, or mostly minority stakes in foreign companies. During the crisis they intervened in some of the bank rescue operations, e.g. in UBS (Singapore Fund). Due to the crisis, they also become important investors in government bonds issued by states that had to come to the rescue of their banks. According to recent information, about 20% of their assets consist of government bonds, likely to increase significantly as a consequence of the financing needs of states (for an annual gross amount of $15 trillion, as far as OECD states are concerned)

12.1.3.1 Definition and Code of Conduct for SWF

The definition of foreign wealth funds has been widely discussed. It is now well defined in an international agreement, adopted in 2008 with the assistance of the IMF, "the Generally Accepted Principles and Practices (GAPP)", formulated by the International Working Group on Sovereign Wealth Funds.[104]

This agreement, the so-called "Santiago principles" define a SWF:

> Sovereign wealth funds (SWFs) are special purpose investment funds or arrangements that are owned by the general government. Created by the general government for macroeconomic purposes, SWFs hold, manage, or administer assets to achieve financial objectives, and employ a set of investment strategies that include investing in foreign financial assets. SWFs have diverse legal, institutional, and governance structures. They are a heterogeneous group, comprising fiscal stabilization funds, savings funds, reserve investment corporations, development funds, and pension reserve funds without explicit pension liabilities.

The Santiago principles were formulated after initial concern about the action of some SWF and government-related companies. They aim to improve understanding of the action of the SWF by creating transparency about their structure, providing for sound governance and adequate controls, risk management and accountability. They also call for members to ensure that investments will be made on the basis of economic and financial returns and return-related consideration, implicitly rejecting political investments. Finally they state that the maintenance of the free flow of capital, and of an open and stable investment climate will be a goal. Recipient countries from their side should maintain clear and non-discriminatory policies toward SWF.

In 2009 an International Forum of Sovereign Wealth Funds was established. It will inter alia look into the application of the Principles, the investment and risk management practices of the SWF and the developments in the investment environment and the recipient country relationships.

These initiatives have resulted in a more objective debate about the role of the SWF. However, implementation of the principles remains voluntary; compliance may be the crucial test.

Several national reporters have mentioned the creation or existence of a SWF in their jurisdiction.[105]

12.1.3.2 The Protective Measures

In the past the role of the SWF has mainly received attention from the point of view of supervision of their investment in activities that were considered strategic or essential in the host states. The attitude of the states toward this issue is however very diverse.

Some states have not adopted any rules in this respect.

This is also the case with the European Union: the issue has been debated without resulting in any legislative or other initiative. Rather, Commissioner McCreevy underlined in a December 2007 speech[106] that Europe has no interest in erecting barriers to investment and that the investment of the SWF should be seen as a financial opportunity. He further referred to the Treaty according to which measures for national security could be taken, while in the financial sector, capital movement may be restricted – by a unanimous vote, however – and that the "fit and proper" test, applicable

[103] The main SWF are the funds from the UAE (Abu Dhabi), Norway, Saudi Arabia, China (2 investment funds) Singapore, Kuwait, Russia, China (social security funds), and Hong Kong: D. Oakley and Gillian Tett, Sovereign Wealth Funds, courted in debt sales, FT, 25 March 2010.

[104] The members of which are: Australia, Azerbaijan, Bahrain, Botswana, Canada, Chile, China, Equatorial Guinea, Iran, Ireland, South Korea, Kuwait, Libya, Mexico, New Zealand, Norway, Qatar, Russia, Singapore, Timor-Leste, Trinidad & Tobago, the United Arab Emirates, and the United States.

[105] See the Greek report, the Taiwan report.

[106] Speech 4 December 2007, europa.eu/rapid/pressReleasesAction.do?reference=SPEECH/07/787&format=HTML&aged=0&language=EN&guiLanguage=en

to financial institutions, may be used for a similar purpose. The Commission formulated its official position in 2008 based on transparency and governance.[107] Also, the rules on freedom of capital transfers, the merger control regulation[108] but also the limits traced by the ECJ in the field of "golden shares"[109] allow Member states to take appropriate measures to protect legitimate interests other than competition or merger control interests. Public security, plurality of the media and prudential rules are considered "legitimate interests".

Some other jurisdictions had some limited restrictions on investments: these were sometimes dealt with under the heading of competition law, e.g. in the UK, where golden shares may be linked to ownership restrictions for other parties.

Provisions with respect to the investment activities of SWF have been introduced in several states and most of the time they are not explicitly addressed to SWF.

Several approaches should be mentioned:

- many jurisdictions have no regulation at all: this is the case in Belgium, Switzerland, and Denmark;
- some jurisdictions have introduced a procedure, requiring all foreign direct investment to be notified: Italy and France;
- in Italy, SWFs may qualify as "investment companies" and hence will be subject to general or specific disclosure obligations;
- other states have listed the sectors where foreign investment is subject to government decisions for considerations relating to public order, national security, but also more widely:
  - Taiwan requires an approval for all foreign investment, and prohibits certain categories on the basis of concerns of public order, national security and good customs and practices.
  - France requires an authorization for investments in certain industry sectors involving public order, public authority, national defense, and research, production of trade of armament, munitions, and explosives.
  - The US has a complex regime limiting or restricting foreign investment, or imposing specific disclosures: this applies to a wide range of activities such as banking, communications, transportation, natural resources, energy, agriculture and defense.[110] Formal authorization procedures apply to transportation, communications, and natural resources and energy. The implications of foreign investment on national security are analyzed by the CFIUS, the "Committee for Foreign Investment in the US". The American report indicates that while a limited number of requests have been refused, many were voluntarily withdrawn. Financial investments exceeding 10% of total ownership are subject to scrutiny, and conditions may be imposed that result in reducing the foreign investor's influence on the functioning of the investee company.
  - Some other jurisdictions practice some limited restrictions on investments: these were sometimes dealt with under the heading of competition law, e.g. in the UK, where golden shares may be linked to ownership restrictions for other parties.
  - Reference should also be made to the private law techniques, although these are not specifically addressed to foreign investors. The use of private law is also mentioned in the Swiss report.
  - Informal mechanisms have been used, consisting, e.g., in political pressure, formulation of a counterbid by national firms, mobilizing local (especially institutional) shareholders.

[107] A common European approach to Sovereign Wealth Funds, 27.2.2008 COM(2008) 115 final.

[108] Council Regulation (EC) No 139/2004 of 20 January 2004 on the control of concentrations between undertakings (the EC Merger Regulation).

[109] In the golden shares ECJ cases of 4 June 2002, the court took a restrictive attitude as to the compatibility of "golden shares" with the freedom of capital movement that can only be allowed for "overriding reasons of general interest", see ECJ, 4 June 2002, C.367/98 (Portugal: general financial interest is not an adequate justification); C 483/99 (France: general right of refusal for direct and indirect investment is not compatible) but C. 503/99 (golden shares acceptable for safeguarding energy supply); more recent cases (e.g. Netherlands, 28 Sept. 06 C 282/04 and C 283/04 restrictions extending beyond the needs of maintaining postal service) (C 463/04 Federconsumatori) have maintained this line. See also the Volkswagen case (C 112–05 Germany no showing of protection of minority shareholders as a legitimate interest).

[110] See for a detailed overview, Government Accountability Office (GAO), Sovereign Wealth Fund Laws Limiting Foreign Investment Affect Certain U.S. Assets, May 2009/www.gao.gov/new.items/d09608.pdf.

12.2 Conclusion

The regulation of the three types of investment vehicles reveals a wealth of issues and questions. They differ depending on the type of fund considered. The common denominator seems to be the effect of these investment funds on the investee companies. This issue is translated in different terms: for hedge funds it is more prominently their role as activist investors that comes to the forefront, while for private equity funds, it is their continuous relationship to the investee and the development, or nondevelopment, of the latter that receives most attention. In legal terms, the first item belongs to the overall field of company law and corporate governance, and the second relates to corporate finance, conflicts of interest and social relations. The sovereign wealth funds raise mainly political issues of sovereignty and possible abuse of economic influence: answers have been formulated at the political level, in an international conduct of business code, and in public interventions monitoring foreign investment.

Hedge funds and private equity funds have been the subjects of a significant regulatory effort, the implementation of which is still going on at the moment of writing. Some of the general features of these reforms have been mentioned. They will also affect the national reports. It will be interesting to verify in a couple of years how much has been changed, and whether these new regulations have effectively strengthened our financial system.

12.3 Contributions to the General Report

National Reporters

Belgium: Philippe Malherbe, Université Catholique de Louvain

Croatia: Edita Culinovic Herc, Faculty of Law Rijeka

Denmark: Simon Krogh, FOCOFIMA, University of Copenhagen

France: Alain Couret, Ecole de droit, Paris I – Panthéon – Sorbonne

Greece: Christos S. Chrissanthis, Faculty of Law, University of Athens

Hungary: Endre Gerenczy, Institut des Sciences Juridiques de ASH

Italy: Raffaele Lener, University of Rome, Tor Vergata, University Luiss

Poland: Mariola Lemonnier, Université de Warmia et Mazury, Olsztun

Spain: Reyes Pala, Faculty of Law University of Zaragoza

Switzerland: Myriam Senn, University of St Gallen

Taiwan: Ching-Ping Shao, College of Law, National Chung Cheng University

United Kingdom: Henry McVea, University of Bristol

United States: Henry Ordower, Saint Louis University School of Law

13 Corporate Governance[1]

Klaus J. Hopt

13.1 Introduction

Corporate governance as a concept and as a problem area was first discussed in the United States; later, the European discussion began first in the United Kingdom. From there corporate governance began its victorious run through all the modern industrial states, including Australia, China, and Japan. Contributions and research projects on the topic abound all over the world.[2] Since 1995 a European Corporate Governance Network in Brussels, now the European Corporate Governance Institute in Luxemburg,[3] has been carrying out its interdisciplinary work, gathering under its roof academics and practitioners, lawyers and economists, researchers and regulators. Their common aim is to better understand corporate governance and to improve it. In the meantime, corporate governance institutes and research groups have been formed in many countries and universities, including Harvard, Oxford, Cambridge, Hamburg, and many others. The topic is of particular concern in practice, too, especially for the stock exchanges, listed corporations, banks and financial institutions, industrial associations, regulators, and parliaments of many countries. During the last two decades in many of these countries, corporate and capital market law reforms have taken place or are under way with the express or implicit aim of improving corporate governance or special parts of it.

In a nutshell, the problem of corporate governance is contained in a sentence from Adam Smith's *An Inquiry into the Nature and Causes of the Wealth of Nations* of 1776:

> The directors of such companies, however, being the managers rather of other people's money than of their own, it cannot well be expected, that they should watch over it with the same anxious vigilance with which the partners in a private copartnery frequently watch over their own. . . . Negligence and profusion, therefore, must always prevail, more or less, in the management of the affairs of such a company.[4]

This problem, in modern language called the principal-agent conflict between the shareholders and the managers, has been a challenge for corporate law and legislators since the beginning of the modern corporation in the early nineteenth century. Efforts to balance this conflict have continued ever since with rather

[1] III.A.2, Le Gouvernement d'entreprises.

[2] A list of selected literature on corporate governance in general and in various countries can be found in K. J. Hopt, H. Kanda, M.J. Roe, E. Wymeersch, S. Prigge, eds., *Comparative Corporate Governance – The State of the Art and Emerging Research* (Oxford, 1998), 1201–10; K. J. Hopt, E. Wymeersch, H. Kanda, H. Baum, eds., *Corporate Governance in Context – Corporations, States, and Markets in Europe, Japan, and the US* (Oxford, 2005), 731–42; P. Hommelhoff, K. J. Hopt, and A. V. Werder, eds., *Handbuch Corporate Governance*, 2d ed. (Cologne, 2009), 931–52 (organized for 10 topics by P. C. Leyens).

[3] ECGI, see www.ecgi.org/ with comprehensive information and two working paper series "Law Series" and "Financial Series"; SSRN Corporate Governance Network (CGN), see www.ssrn.com/cgn.

[4] Book 5, Ch. 1.3.1.2, 5th ed. London 1789.

K.J. Hopt (✉)
Max Planck Institute for Comparative and International Private Law, Hamburg, Germany
email: hopt@mpipriv.de

K.B. Brown and D.V. Snyder (eds.), *General Reports of the XVIIIth Congress of the International Academy of Comparative Law/Rapports Généraux du XVIIIème Congrès de l'Académie Internationale de Droit Comparé*, DOI 10.1007/978-94-007-2354-2_13, © Springer Science+Business Media B.V. 2012

limited success, as the constant law reform – sometimes exhaustive new codifications, sometimes piecemeal reform acts – to the present day amply illustrates.[5] The history of corporate governance[6] is also a history of crises and scandals. Cases like Enron, WorldCom, Parmalat, and others in nearly every country stand as testimonies.[7] The financial crisis since 2007/2008 has added further illustrative examples of problem cases, governance and systemic failures, and reform experiments, though one has to keep in mind that the actual causal relevance of corporate governance failures to the coming about of the financial crisis is much debated. On the microlevel the same is true for the relevance of corporate governance for firm performance.[8]

A general problem around the world is certainly the difficult principal-agent relationship between the managers and the shareholders. This explains why board reform has come up as a major corporate governance problem in nearly every country. Yet a closer look at the corporate laws of the various countries and the scandals and crises therein reveals that two other relevant principal-agent conflicts can exist: first, depending on the different shareholder structures in various countries, between the controlling shareholders and their fellow shareholders; and, in a broader sense, between the shareholders as a group and various non-shareholders such as bondholders, labor, other creditors, and even the state.[9] More generally, the observation that all countries have experienced and still experience crises and scandals of corporate governance may obscure the fact that the problems are not necessarily the same; adequate answers and reforms are even less uniform. While legislators and regulators often tend simply to imitate responses given in other countries in the rather vague hope that this will also benefit their country, it is more likely the characteristic feature of the corporate governance system of each country that explains its unique crises and scandals. Reform proposals in particular go astray if one does not understand how the particular combination of economic, legal, and social determinants of corporate governance functions in each country. Only a functional comparative approach will help to better understand the similarities and differences of the corporate governance systems and to draw certain more general conclusions. Such an approach presupposes good information on the corporate governance feature of not just a small handful of more or less arbitrarily selected countries, but rather of a relatively large number of countries, and among them countries from different continents, legal families, cultures, and traditions. Such broad and various information will help to aid our understanding of the different systems and their path dependencies, develop best practices, and bring about meaningful reform on the basis of comparative experience.

Against this background, the International Academy of Comparative Law's decision to deal with corporate governance in a session at its 18th International Congress on Comparative Law in Washington 2010 and its commission of a general report on the problem opens up a great opportunity for research. The following report is based on 32 country reports; each contains a description of the corporate governance of the respective country following an introduction and a questionnaire filled out by the general reporter.[10] The focus of the reports is on internal corporate governance, with the first two above-mentioned principal-agent conflicts and the major actors involved, i.e., the board, the shareholders, labor, the auditors, and the supervisors and courts as enforcers.[11]

[5]Examples of codifications are the Australian Corporation Act 2001, the UK Companies Act 2006 and the plans of the "grosse Aktienrechtsreform" in Switzerland, 27CH 2. Germany stands as an example for piecemeal reforms with 68 reforms of the Stock Corporation Act 1965. For France 10RF 1; for Australia 2 Austr 1 et s. (Country reports are cited with the number of the report, an abbreviation of the country and the page number, f.ex. 31UK 1.)

[6]P. Frentrop, A History of Corporate Governance, 1602–2002, Amsterdam 2002/2003.

[7]J. C. Coffee, Gatekeepers, Oxford 2006; J. Armour and J. A. McCahery, eds., *After Enron, Improving Corporate Law and Modernising Securities Regulation in Europe and the US*, (Oxford/Portland 2006).

[8]Cf. f.ex. S. Bhagat and B. Bolton, "Corporate Governance and Firm Performance," *Journal of Corporate Finance* 14 (2008): 257. As to the problems of corporate governance indices cf. K. J. Hopt, "American Corporate Governance Indices as Seen from a European Perspective", *University of Pennsylvania Law Review PENNumbra* 158 (2009): 27.

[9]R. Kraakman, J. Armour, P. Davies, L. Enriques, H. Hansmann, G. Hertig, K. J. Hopt, H. Kanda and E. Rock, *The Anatomy of Corporate Law, A Comparative and Functional Approach*, 2d ed. (Oxford: Oxford University Press, 2009), 35 et s.

[10]An alphabetical list of the country reports is reprinted as the Annex.

[11]In the light of the various national reports this article does not follow completely the division of the questionnaire.

13.2 Corporate Governance: Concepts and General Problems

13.2.1 Concepts of Corporate Governance

13.2.1.1 Various Concepts and Definitions

The term "corporate governance" is relatively new; in most jurisdictions it is not a legal term and its definition is ambiguous. For the purposes of this comparative work, the broad definition of the Cadbury Commission of 1992 that stands at the beginning of the modern corporate governance movement[12] is best suited: corporate governance is "the system by which companies are directed and controlled."[13] Direction and control are the two cornerstones of a corporate governance system.

More specifically, shareholder or stakeholder orientation characterizes the system. The classic shareholder-oriented approach prevails in the United States and in economic theory. Many European countries such as Germany and the United Kingdom have a stakeholder approach instead, characterized in its strong form in the former by labor codetermination in the board. In its weaker form, corporate law mandates that the board act in the interest of the enterprise as a whole, whatever that means.[14]

The prevailing shareholder constituency of a country is also of considerable relevance.[15] Examples include the typical prevalence of public companies with dispersed shareholdings with "separation of ownership and control" (Berle-Means corporations),[16] as traditionally found in the United States, in Great Britain, and less well known in the Netherlands,[17] or the existence of many blockholdings, family corporations, and groups of companies, as found in many continental European countries. In addition, the presence of institutional shareholders, private equity, and hedge funds is of relevance.[18] Accordingly, the prevailing principal-agent conflicts differ: between the shareholders and the board or between the controlling shareholder and the minority shareholders. A third principal-agent conflict exists between the shareholders and other stakeholders.

13.2.1.2 Internal and External Corporate Governance

Corporate governance is focused on the internal balance of powers within a corporation. The main questions of this internal balance – sometimes called internal in contrast to external corporate governance – concern the board (unitary board or two-tier board), the shareholders (controlling and minority shareholders), labor (especially if there is boardroom codetermination), and of course the audit system. The audit system consists of the audit committee of the board and the auditors of the company (see 13.3.1.1). In some countries, internal auditors work as organs of the corporation; however, in most countries today the auditors are external professionals. These external auditors are in a hybrid situation between internal and external corporate governance because they are involved in the company's financial reporting but must be independent.

Forces from outside the corporation exercise a disciplining influence on the management as well, in particular the various markets such as takeovers and the market of corporate control,[19] but to a lesser degree also the product and services markets and the increasingly international market for corporate directors. Transparency of corporate affairs and disclosure (to the shareholders, supervisors if any, and the general public) are also such external forces. External corporate governance by takeover regulation and more generally disclosure and transparency are huge research fields of their own and cannot be treated in this report.[20]

[12] A. Cadbury, Report of the Committee on the Financial Aspects of Corporate Governance, London, December 1992; Combined Code, see infra note 34. For the US cf. American Law Institute, Principles of Corporate Governance, Philadelphia 1994.

[13] Cadbury Report, supra note 12, para 2.5.

[14] See section 76 of the German Stock Corporation Act and an endless amount of doctrinal controversy on this question. See infra 13.3.1.1.

[15] As to the patterns of corporate ownership F. Barca and M. Becht, eds., *The Control of Corporate Europe* (Oxford: Oxford University Press, 2001); Kraakman et al., Anatomy of Corporate Law, supra note 9, p. 29 et s., 305 et s.

[16] A. A. Berle and G. C. Means, *The Modern Corporation and Private Property* (New York 1932) (Brunswick 1991).

[17] 21Neth 5, 19 et s.: The country with the lowest degree of ownership concentration in Europe.

[18] See infra 13.3.2.2.

[19] In many countries, the codes as well as the discussions on corporate governance focus on internal corporate governance, takeovers being treated as a separate field.

[20] Takeovers in particular have already been the topic of a general report for the International Academy of Comparative Law, Kozyris, ed. Corporate Takeovers Through the Public Markets, The Hague 1996. For most recent analyses and literature cf. Kraakman et al., *Anatomy of Corporate Law*, supra note 9, ch. 8: Control Transactions, p. 225–73, and ch. 9.2.1: Mandatory disclosure, p. 277–89.

13.2.1.3 Economic and Societal Environment

The economic, societal, and cultural environment leads to path-dependent developments in corporate governance systems.[21] The corporate census shows huge differences in the various countries as to the number of stock corporations and their listings. Other well-known examples are the attitude of a country toward disclosure and transparency (traditionally more open in the United States, the United Kingdom, and possibly Sweden, but much less so in continental European countries); preference given to shareholder value or more to stakeholder concerns (as mentioned before, the United States and Germany being the main examples); and market orientation, or rather an alliance between industry and banks (such as the disappearing "Rhenish capitalism" in Germany), i.e., the so-called outsider/insider systems, which of course are never pure. More recently some players have gained considerable momentum, though to a very different degree in the various countries: institutional investors (very much so in the United Kingdom, somewhat less in the United States, much less in continental European countries), hedge funds, private equity, and foreign investors (among the latter most recently foreign state funds). This has created fears and defense movements and even increased protectionism in many countries.[22] Free trade or protectionism is relevant for corporate governance because of the more or less strong effects of competition from abroad and the reaction to it in the various countries. Most recently protectionism has gained additional momentum as a consequence of the financial crisis. According to some observers, even more general political forces and coalitions can explain differences in corporate governance systems.[23]

13.2.1.4 Specific (Corporate) Governance

The focus of this report is on corporate governance in general, i.e., on the governance of corporations, and above all of listed corporations. More recently, however, specific forms of corporate governance have also gained attention, such as the corporate governance of various company forms, family enterprises,[24] of public enterprises,[25] and of nonprofit organizations and foundations.[26] In the current financial markets crisis, the corporate governance of banks and financial intermediaries has received particular attention.[27] However, our topic is already so broad that these specific corporate governance forms cannot be treated here in more detail. If there is much discussion on one of these in a given country, some additional remarks may be made.

13.2.2 Corporate Governance in the Shadow of the Law

13.2.2.1 Corporate and Stock Exchange Law Versus Corporate Governance by Stock Exchange Self-regulation

Traditionally, corporate governance in most countries has been the turf of corporate and stock exchange law, both mandatory and fall-back rules.[28] In addition to formal law, self-regulation has long been a characteristic of the stock exchanges, even in those countries

[21] C. J. Milhaupt and K. Pistor, Law & Capitalism, Chicago/London 2008.

[22] K. J. Hopt, "Obstacles to corporate restructuring: observations from a European and German perspective," in M. Tison, H. de Wulf and R. Steenot, eds., Perspectives in Company Law and Financial Regulation. Essays in Honour of Eddy Wymeersch (Cambridge, 2009), p. 373. But one must also see that a fully liberal approach to foreign investment may lead to the economy being controlled by foreign investors, cf. for Hungary, 14Hung 5.

[23] M. J. Roe, Strong Managers, Weak Owners, The Political Roots of American Corporate Finance, Princeton 1994; idem, Political Determinants of Corporate Governance, Oxford 2003.

[24] For Switzerland 27CH 26; for Belgium B 28 et s.

[25] For Germany J. Schürnbrand, Public Corporate Governance Kodex für öffentliche Unternehmen, Zeitschrift für Wirtschaftsrecht (ZIP) 2010, 1105; for Switzerland 27CH 26. A special case involves the former socialist countries, where in the course of privatization the state has retained control of major blocks. For the grave lack of corporate governance in such (close or limited liability) corporations, see f.ex. 14Hung 19.

[26] F. ex. Swiss NPO Code and Swiss Foundation Code, 27CH 26; K. J. Hopt and T. von Hippel (eds.) Comparative Corporate Governance of Non-Profit Organizations, Cambridge 2010.

[27] P. Mülbert, "Corporate Governance of Banks," *European Business Organization Law Review* (EBOR) 10 (2009): 411; K. J. Hopt, "Corporate Governance von Banken," in *Entwicklungslinien im Bank- und Kapitalmarktrecht*, ed. M. Habersack et al. (Cologne: Festschrift für Gerd Nobbe, 2009), 853; 12Germ 7; 10RF 27.

[28] As to these laws, see the national reports. Cf. also K. J. Hopt, "Comparative Company Law" in *The Oxford Handbook of Comparative Law*, ed. M. Reimann, R. Zimmermann (Oxford: Oxford University Press, 2006), 1161 with further references.

where the stock exchanges were and still are public law institutions (this is the case in Germany, for example, though there was always a tension between self-regulation and state regulation).[29] This kind of self-regulation was always geared toward both having an institution and procedures that were attractive for traders, but also having rules which protected shareholders and other investors who otherwise might shy away from securities and securities trading. The interests of those who run the stock exchange – originally the merchants, but today most stock exchanges are firms with their own shareholders – were of course usually better taken care of.

But with the rise of the corporate governance movement, national stock exchanges that competed with each other – no longer nationally only but increasingly internationally as well – began to require the observance of good corporate governance as a listing condition. This was the case, for example, of the London Stock Exchange and the Combined Code of Corporate Governance.[30] The exchanges then provide for some enforcement as well, sometimes rather hesitantly only by recommendations to individual companies or a public announcement as in Japan,[31] but in the meantime in most countries, including for example Australia,[32] by a "comply-or-disclose" or "comply-or-explain" principle. Delisting is a threat in extremis but would hurt the shareholders and remains theoretical. Of course, such exchange requirements cannot extend beyond the reach of the stock exchange itself, i.e., cannot extend to non-listed companies. It is important to stress this because in some countries stock exchange listing remains an exception, or is at least much less frequent than in other countries; this is even true within the European Union if one compares the United Kingdom on the one side and Germany on the other. Sometimes the exchange itself practices additional self-restraint, as for example in the United Kingdom, where the Combined Code was applicable only to listed companies on the Main Market of the London Stock Exchange that were incorporated in the United Kingdom.[33]

13.2.2.2 Existence and Content of Corporate Governance Codes

More recently corporate governance in the form of soft law in its various forms has gained ground. Prominent examples are the host of corporate governance codes; non-binding recommendations of various sources such as chambers of commerce, business and banking associations, and international committees; best practice standards; and other forms of self-regulation and market discipline. Today most countries have corporate governance codes. These codes are not law and do not have binding force. The prototype and international model for these codes was and is the UK Corporate Governance Code that goes back to the Combined Code of the Cadbury Committee 1992.[34] In the meantime there has been a whole wave of corporate governance codes, and today practically all relevant countries have one or sometimes even more than one code.[35] Some of these codes stem from stock exchanges, some from business organizations,[36] others from special

[29]K. J. Hopt, *Der Kapitalanlegerschutz im Recht der Banken* (Munich: Beck, 1975), 152 et s.

[30]31UK 2.

[31]Tokyo Stock Exchange, but the corporate governance rules are under review and the independence requirement for directors and statutory auditors is expected to come, 17Jap 5.

[32]2Austr 3.

[33]From June 2010 on this has been extended also to overseas listed companies (OLCs) and to UK-incorporated subsidiaries of OLCs. See Financial Reporting Council, 2009 Review of the Combined Code: Final Report, December 2009; 31UK 2. On the Combined Code see note 34.

[34]The Combined Code on Corporate Governance stems from the Cadbury Committee, supra note 12, and is today promulgated by the non-governmental Financial Reporting Council, 31UK 2. See www.frc.org.uk/corporate/combinedcode.cfm. It is now renamed: Financial Reporting Council, The UK Corporate Governance Code, June 2010, http://www.frc.org.uk/documents/pagemanager/Corporate_Governance/UK%20Corp%20Gov%20Code%20June%202010.pdf. Cf. A. Cadbury, *Corporate Governance and Chairmanship: A Personal View* (Oxford: Oxford University Press, 2002).

[35]See the Weil, Gotshal & Manges Study for the European Commission, Comparative Study of Corporate Governance Codes Relevant to the European Union and Its Member States, Brussels, January 2002. An index of all corporate governance codes can be found on the ECGI website, supra note 3, under codes & principles. Cf. also European Corporate Governance in company law and codes, Report of the High Level Group of Company Law Experts, Rivista delle società 2005, 534.

[36]For example, the French AFEP/MEDEF, The Corporate Governance of Listed Companies, October 2003, consolidated with two recommendations on remuneration in 2008, and the Hellebuyck Report as of 2009, 10RF 2 et s. For Switzerland economiesuisse, 27CH 3.

governmental or similar public committees,[37] some from the supervisory agency,[38] and a few from academics and practitioners. Usually these codes are addressed only to listed corporations. But there are also specific corporate governance codes for family enterprises or for enterprises in which the state or other public bodies hold an important block of shares. Sometimes particular sectors of the economy such as banking or even individual corporations like formerly the Deutsche Bank AG have issued special corporate governance codes or similar recommendations.

The content of these corporate governance codes varies considerably. Some are very sophisticated. The UK Code, for example, contains high-level Main Principles, mid-level Supporting Principles, and low-level Provisions in a comprehensive way.[39] Others are shorter and much less explicit and demanding. This depends on the tradition and possibilities of the individual country and its institutions of having and credibly supporting self-regulation. In the City of London, of course, this is much more self-evident for all participants than in a federal state with diverse economic centers and participants, as traditionally in Germany. In Germany and some other countries the Corporate Governance Code is meant also to inform (foreign) investors on German corporate governance, whether resulting from actual formal law or from good corporate governance practice as recommended in the code.[40] In general, the corporate governance codes primarily regulate the board and its committees, or in the case of a two-tier board, both boards and the relationship between them. But there are also rules on the rights of the shareholders and on the auditors.[41] All of these corporate governance codes contain rules concerning internal corporate governance, in particular the board. Rules of external corporate governance, especially concerning takeovers, have traditionally developed as separate rules both in law and under self-regulation. The prime example is the Takeover Code of the Takeover Panel in the United Kingdom, which was formerly fully self-regulatory, but following the EU Takeover Directive now has legislative backing under the Companies Act 2006.[42] As between corporate law and takeover (legal and self-) regulation, this can lead to mutual neglect and even inconsistent rules and recommendations.

The rate of observance of these codes is different – high in the UK and Germany, for example, but less so in other countries[43] – but a clear link between the observance and the stock price of the corporation has not yet been empirically established.[44] In any case, the relevance of the codes for focusing the attention of the practice on good corporate governance and for research and academic debate is high.

13.2.2.3 Administration and Enforcement of the Codes

The administration and enforcement of the corporate governance codes differ considerably. In some countries there are no permanent code commissions or similar bodies, with the result that the code remains a mere recommendation; it is not enforced other than by peer pressure and self-interest and it is not regularly adapted to new needs and insights. Even then a mild form of disclosure is provided for in the countries of the European Union where the mandatory corporate governance statement must indicate whether the corporation is subject to a corporate governance code and, if so, to which one.[45]

[37] For Germany Deutscher Corporate Governance Kodex, latest revision in June 2010; comments by H.-M. Ringleb, T. Kremer, M. Lutter and A. v. Werder, *Kommentar zum Deutschen Corporate Governance Kodex*, 4th ed. (Munich: Beck, 2010).

[38] Argentina, 1Arg 6.

[39] 31UK 2.

[40] 12Germ 2; similarly the Best Practices for Warsaw Stock Exchange, 22Pol 4. This implies a clear separation between both parts. A further regulatory technique of the German Code is the distinction between formal recommendations (with disclosure, see infra 13.2.2.3) and mere suggestions (completely voluntary and without disclosure).

[41] See, for example, the German Corporate Governance Code, supra note 37, parts 2 and 7.

[42] 31UK 21.

[43] In Germany for 2009, the DAX-listed corporations complied with 96.3 (all listed companies: 85.8) percent of the recommendations and 85.4 (63.5) percent of the suggestions, A. v. Werder and T. Talaulicar, Kodexreport 2010: Die Akzeptanz der Empfehlungen und Anregungen des Deutschen Corporate Governance Kodex, Der Betrieb (Düsseldorf: Handelsblatt, 2010), 853. Cf. also for Spain 26Spain 23 et s. But in Denmark according to a 2009 study more than 50% of the companies did not comply with more than five of the recommendations of the Code, 8Denm 3.

[44] 12Germ 3 with references.

[45] Art. 46a of the European Directive 2006/46/EC of 14 June 2006 L 224/1 (modifying the 4th and 7th directives on annual accounts and consolidated accounts).

Stock exchanges may require more, namely asking listed companies in their listing conditions to observe the code, as in the United Kingdom and other countries.[46] This is not incompatible with the recent EU reform, according to which the listing decision as such is taken away from the stock exchanges and given to a special listing authority (an example is the UK Listing Authority, which since 2000 has been the Financial Services Authority (FSA)).[47] If observance of the code is a condition for listing, this leaves the corporation and its directors no choice but to agree if they want the corporation to be listed. Some observers have commented that in such a case, the observance of the code is no longer really voluntary except for non-listed companies.

In other countries, special corporate governance commissions are in charge of issuing, administering, and enforcing the code. Enforcement then can be simply self-regulatory, i.e., basically by peer pressure alone or through disclosure, usually on a "comply-or-disclose" basis. In some countries – such as the Netherlands, Germany, Austria, Denmark, Portugal, and Spain[48] – this disclosure (not the code and its content as such) is supported by law, for example by a provision in the stock corporation act that listed companies must "comply or disclose" or "comply or explain." This is an interesting technique that lies between self-regulation and regulation by law or self-regulation in the "shadow of the law." The extent to which non-observance must be explained varies considerably. Some codes do not detail what "explain" means; others distinguish between the main principles and the lower-level principles of the code.[49] Experience shows that such a legal disclosure rule may lead to thorny legal problems, not only as far as the reach and the content of the rule is concerned, but also the responsibility for such disclosure and legal consequences of non disclosure.[50] In some countries the courts attach legal consequences to false or omitted disclosure (provided that the corporation has declared that it complies with the code). An example is the voidability of a shareholder resolution on ratification of the management board's action.[51] False or non-disclosure is also a violation of a director's duty that carries legal consequences (critique by the shareholders, measures taken by a supervisory agency or the stock exchange, and possibly even personal liability).[52]

A further variation concerns the extent to which the corporate governance disclosure must be verified or even audited. As seen before, the comply-or-explain disclosure declaration is usually issued by the board as a whole. Yet if the company is obliged or chooses to publish information concerning its being subject to a corporate governance code or its observance or non-observance of such a code, and if this declaration is part of its annual accounts, this declaration is also subject to the annual audit. This is why most companies prefer to issue a separate declaration as an annex to the annual management report that is not subject to the auditing requirement.[53]

13.2.2.4 Code Reform

Parallel to the extensive corporate and stock exchange law reforms,[54] there has been a wave of corporate governance code enactments and reforms all over the world[55] since 1992 when the Combined Code was promulgated in the United Kingdom. If the administration and further development of such corporate governance codes is up to a special corporate governance commission, there is an inherent pressure on the commission by the financial press, the investing public, and even the legislators to come up with new rules every year, a phenomenon that

[46] F. ex. Poland, 22Pol 4. As to the role of the stock exchanges in corporate governance, see supra 13.2.2.

[47] 31UK 2 et s. The new UK governement intends to transfer the supervisory competences to the Bank of England.

[48] Since 2004 in the Netherlands, 21Neth 4; Sec. 161 of the German Stock Corporation Act; similarly for Austria 3A 1; 8Denm 3; 23Port 2; 26Spain 21.

[49] UK Listing Rule 9.8.6. 31UK 2.

[50] M. Lutter in Ringleb et al., supra note 37, nos. 1631 et s.; cf. Belgian case law when the code has been incorporated in the by-laws of the corporation, 4B 30.

[51] For Germany, see Federal Court of Last Instance (Bundesgerichtshof), 16.2.02009, case Kirch/Deutsche Bank, BGHZ 180, 9 (19 et s.); 29.9.2009, case Axel Springer, Zeitschrift für Wirtschaftsrecht (ZIP) 2009, 2051 (2054 no.18 et s. concerning nondisclosure of a conflict of interest).

[52] M. Lutter in Ringleb et al., supra note 37, no. 1634 with further references as to the controversy. Cf. also affirmatively for Poland 22Pol 5 et s.

[53] Member State option under the Directive of 14 June 2006 supra note 45.

[54] Supra note 5.

[55] Supra note 35.

can be observed in Germany[56] and which is certainly not healthy. In the United Kingdom this movement is rightly slower and leads to much better reform preparation. A new edition of the Combined Code, now the UK Corporate Governance Code, was elaborated by the Financial Reporting Council and became applicable on 1 June 2010; it contains many new requirements for the chairman and the non-executive directors and for ensuring an appropriate balance between the independence and the firm-specific knowledge of directors.[57] This corresponds to different methods and traditions of law reform. This thorough preparation of the UK Companies Act may be a model for other countries.

13.3 The Board and the Shareholders as the Two Key Actors in Corporate Governance

13.3.1 The Board(s)

13.3.1.1 Structure

Two-Tier and One-Tier Boards and the Option Between Both

(1) The most prominent structural characteristic of the board is whether it is a one-tier or a two-tier board. The members of the one-tier board and of the supervisory board are elected by the shareholders,[58] while the members of the management board are usually elected by the supervisory board. The two-tier board – a separated management and supervisory board[59] – is mandatory in the Netherlands (with the first listed company in the world, the VOC of 1602, since 1619),[60] Germany, Austria, Portugal, Poland, China, and some other countries;[61] in some countries, such as Switzerland, it is mandatory for bank and insurance corporations.[62] Historically, the supervisory board dates back to the second half of the nineteenth century, when the state withdrew its supervisory role from public companies and had to be replaced by another control mechanism.[63] The separation between management and control in the countries with two-tier boards is legally prescribed and buttressed by mandatory incompatibility rules, but de facto the supervisory board has rarely restrained itself to mere control; instead, it has also traditionally taken over an advisory function. In practice, the division between the tasks of the management board and the supervisory board varies according to business sector, size of the corporation, tradition, and in particular the presence of strong leaders on one board or the other. Sometimes the chairman of the management board, alone or together with the chairman of the supervisory board, selects the members of the supervisory board without much ado (though formally they have to be elected by the shareholders). Sometimes the chairman of the supervisory board is the leading figure on whose benevolence the chairman of the management board depends and who picks the

[56] The German legislators have repeatedly stepped in with legislation when the Corporate Governance Commission did not go far enough or did not act quickly enough. The three prominent examples are mandatory individual disclosure of remuneration of board members (2005); mandatory agreement of a 10% deductible if the corporation takes out a D & O policy for the board member (2009); and general prohibition of the direct change-over of a management board member into the supervisory board (2009). In June 2010 the minister of justice threatened that a board member quota regime for women will be mandated by law if the boards hesitate too long.

[57] See supra note 34; 31UK 8 et s.

[58] In practice, the (one-tier) board may have "subtle powers of influence over its own composition," 2Austr 14; the same is true for the supervisory board. The Finnish Corporate Governance Code recommends the election of all directors by the shareholders, even if the corporation has opted for the two-tier board system, 9Fin 15.

[59] Cf. K. J. Hopt and P. C. Leyens, "Board Models in Europe," *European Company and Financial Law Review* (ECFR) (2004): 135.

[60] E. Gepken-Jager, "Verenigde Oost-Indische Compagnie (VOC)/ The Dutch East India Company," in *VOC 1602–2002, 400 Years of Company Law*, ed. E. Gepken-Jager, G. van Solinge and L. Timmerman (Deventer: Kluwer Legal Publishers, 2005), 41 at 56 et s.: Committee of Nine; 21Neth 6.

[61] For Portugal 23Port 5. For Poland 22Pol 10. In China for stock corporations as well as for limited liability companies, 6China 4. Cf. also for Taiwan 29Taiw 4 et s.

[62] K.J. Hopt, "Erwartungen an den Verwaltungsrat in Aktiengesellschaften und Banken – Bemerkungen aus deutscher und europäischer Sicht," *Schweizerische Zeitschrift für Wirtschafts- und Finanzmarktrecht* (SZW/RSDA) (2008): 235 at 237 et s.; 12Germ 8 et s.; 27CH 26.

[63] K.J. Hopt, "The German Two-Tier Board: Experience, Theories, Reforms," in *Comparative Corporate Governance*, ed. K. J. Hopt et al., supra note 2, p. 227 at 230 et s. Cf. J. Lieder, *Der Aufsichtsrat im Wandel der Zeit* (Jena: JWV, Jenaer Wissenschaftliche Verlagsgesellschaft, 2006).

other supervisory members and proposes them to the shareholders. One reason for the strict maintenance of the two-tier board in Germany is the politically cemented quasi-parity labor codetermination,[64] which would hardly be tolerable for the shareholders in a one-tier board.

(2) Internationally, the far prevailing board structure is the one-tier board. It is the system of choice in the United States, the United Kingdom, Switzerland, and other countries.[65] The emergence of the one-tier board has historical reasons, too, such as the relative prominence of entrepreneurial ownership in Great Britain that carved out a lesser role for the state or other institutions to oversee management.[66] Later, the fact that the United Kingdom resisted all attempts to institute labor codetermination on the board may have helped to keep the one-tier system as the "virtually unanimous feature of UK public company governance structures."[67] The one-tier board is also the only board structure considered in the recommendations of the Combined Code viz. the UK Corporate Governance Code, though the statutory company law itself does not prescribe the structure of the board. The one-tier board unites the management and control functions that are separated in the two-tier system. Yet two recent developments in the one-tier system countries, in particular in the United Kingdom, qualify this observation: the movements toward independent directors and toward division of leadership. Both phenomena, which will be treated in more detail,[68] lead to a certain functional convergence between the one-tier and the two-tier systems.

While practitioners and academics of a given country usually hasten to declare that their board system is the best, there is no theoretical – let alone empirical – proof that one of the two systems is better than the other. Both systems have their roots in historical development, are path-dependent, and have advantages and disadvantages. The one-tier system may function better in the environment of the United Kingdom, especially if the recent developments mentioned above and the better flow of information between executive and non-executive directors in the same board[69] are taken into consideration. It is also cheaper and may therefore be better for smaller companies. This is also the reason why countries with two-tier board such as Germany do not make the second board mandatory for the limited liability company (GmbH) unless the conditions for labor codetermination apply.

(3) On the other hand, large international companies may prefer to separate management and control and to delegate the latter to a separate supervisory board. This is indeed what happened in France, where a choice between the two systems has been allowed since 1966.[70] While the overwhelming majority of corporations sticks to the old one-tier system (typically with the *président directeur général*, PDG),[71] around 20% of the mostly large and internationally active corporations of the CAC-40 companies have chosen the two-tier system (*directoire et conseil de surveillance*).[72] Similarly, in the Netherlands where there is a choice for non-codetermined corporations between the traditional two-tier and the one-tier board, only one of the larger listed corporations has adopted the one-tier board, namely Unilever N.V.[73] Giving shareholders a choice between two or even more board structures instead of prescribing one structure by law for all corporations therefore seems the best choice. The shareholders know better than the legislators what is best for them, and they also bear the risk in a competitive environment if they

[64] See infra 13.3.1.5.

[65] In the Nordic countries, the one-tier system prevails, cf. 28Swed 1, 20Norw 7, though besides the board of directors (*bestyrelse*) the executive management (direktion) is prescribed as a mandatory company organ, 8Denm 5, cf. also 20Norw7.

[66] 31UK 5.

[67] 31UK 5.

[68] See infra 13.3.1.1, Size and Composition of Board.

[69] This is the main advantage of the one-tier system as seen by P. Davies, "Board Structure in the UK and Germany: Convergence or Continuing Divergence?" *International and Comparative Corporate Law Journal* 2 (2000): 435 at 448 et s., 455.

[70] 10RF 4 et s.

[71] Usually corporations stick to what they are used to, in one-tier board countries like Belgium, 4B 4, as well as in two-tier board states, cf. Portugal 23Port 6; Croatia, 7Croat 6, and Hungary, 14Hung 6. For Japan see 17Jap 10: 97,7 of the Tokyo Stock Exchange listed corporations stick to the traditional system of a board with an additional internal auditors board, only 2.3% have chosen the committee structure.

[72] M. Cozian, A. Viandier and F. Deboissy, *Droit des Sociétés*, 22e éd. (Paris: LexisNexis Litec, 2009), 306 no 646.

[73] 21Neth 6.

choose the second-best option. France, the Netherlands, Belgium, Luxembourg, Finland, and most recently Denmark and some non-European countries[74] allow the choice; some, including Italy and Portugal, even provide a choice among more than two models;[75] and in the European Union the founders of a European Company can choose between the one-tier and the two-tier form, both being offered and regulated in the Statute of the European Company.[76] Apart from escaping the inflexible German labor codetermination, this may be an additional reasons for choosing the form of the European Company.[77]

Size and Composition of the Board, in Particular the Non-executive Directors (NEDs) and the Independent Directors

(1) In most countries, the stock corporation act contains many provisions on the board; for example, these may concern the size and the composition, the minimum and maximum number of seats, the duration of office,[78] the possibility of a staggered board, diversity and the controversial gender quota,[79] and others. Only very few countries, apart from certain states in the United States, have cumulative voting;[80] in Italy[81] there is a mandatory representation of minority shareholders in the board whether two-tier or only one-tier. The supervisory board of large German companies must have 20 seats (21 seats in the coal and steel sector), half of which must be filled by labor;[82] the term of office for management board members is up to 5 years with the possibility of reelection. In other countries, such as the UK, there are no or very few statutory prescriptions for the structure of the board, though the listing requirements of the stock exchange and/or the corporate governance codes usually require or recommend many details.[83] In the UK, in practice boards usually have between 10 and 15 members with a small majority of non-executives;[84] in Japan the average number of directors of all TSE-listed corporations is 8.68;[85] in Australia the average is seven for the

[74] France with two models to choose from, see note 70; Serbia followed the French example, 24Serb 8; the Netherlands with legislative proposal to widen the choice, 21Neth 6; Belgium "comité de direction" since 2002 by the law named "Corporate Governance," 4B 4; New Danish Companies Act No 470 of 12 June 2009, 8Denm 1, 4 et s.; Denmark as well as Luxembourg were motivated by the SE model, 18Lux 8; 11Georgia 3; Poland is expected to introduce two options, 22Pol 10.

[75] 16I 3, 6 et s.; Portugal since 2006 23Port 5.

[76] SE Statute of 8.10.2001, OJEC L 294/1 Art. 38, 39 et s. (dualistic), 43 et s. (monistic), 46 et s. (common rules for both types).

[77] Ernst & Young, Study on the operation and the impacts of the Statute for a European Company (SE), Final report (for the European Commission), 29.10.2009, ch. 3, 2.2 (p. 246 et s.).

[78] In the United States the usual term is 1 year, but the shareholders can opt for a staggered board with up to 3-year terms, Model Bus. Corp. Act Ann. § 8.06, 4th ed. 2008. In Finland it is also 1 year, staggered boards are permissible, but regarded as against good corporate governance, 9Fin 15 et s. In Norway it is 2 years, 20Norw 11, staggered boards seem problematic, but permissible; in Japan it is 2 years, but for executive officers only 1 year, 17Jap 11; in Australia 3 years, 2Austr 15; in the Netherlands and Portugal 4 years, 21Neth 7; 23Port 7. In some countries such as Germany and Austria the term of office can legally be and is usually 5 years and is renewable, 12Germ 8, 3A 6, but without a staggered board. In Belgium and Greece 6 years, 4B 5, 13Greece 11. In the UK the usual period was 3 years of office on a one-third staggered basis (Combined Code Provision A.7.1). But the formula in the UK Corporate Governance Code is now in B.7.1: All directors of FTSE 350 companies should be subject to annual election by shareholders.

[79] Since 2003 with reforms in 2004 and 2006, Norway has had a mandatory diversity quota (at least 40% for both genders) on the boards, with dissolution as the ultimate sanction, 20Norw 10. The Finnish Corporate Governance Code recommends that both genders be represented on the board, but without a minimum amount, 9Fin 15. In Germany the Corporate Governance Code Para. 5.1.2, 5.4.1 (as of June 2010) recommends appropriate representation of women and concrete targets to be set by the corporation, cf. also 12Germ 8. The UK Corporate Governance Code 2010, B 2 Supporting Principles, recommends "due regard for the benefits of diversity on the board, including gender". In Australia the Corporations and Markets Advisory Committee (CAMAC) supported increased diversity, but rejected mandatory quotas, CAMAC, Diversity of Board, Report 2009, disclosure additions are expected, 2Austr 14; similarly the Spanish Unified Code in one of its most controversial recommendations, 26Spain 13. According to the Dutch Parliament a 30% quota for women, to be enforced by a comply-or-explain provision in the stock corporation act, is currently under discussion, 21Neth 7.

[80] F.ex. California, Kraakman et al., supra note 9, p. 90 et s. For Portugal at the request of 10% (one board member), 10–20% (special election, but not more than a third), 23Port 6 et s. For Poland at the request of a 20% shareholder, 22Pol 20; cf. also Serbia 24Serb 8 et s.

[81] 16I 2, 7.

[82] As to labor codetermination see infra 13.3.1.5.

[83] 31UK 5. Between one and five regular members in Finland, unless otherwise stated in the articles of association, 9Fin 14.

[84] 31 UK 6.

[85] 17Jap 11.

Top 300 and nine for the Top 50;[86] and the Netherlands averages from three to nine, larger supervisory boards being rare.[87] Though it is well established in economics, group theory, and international practice that smaller groups function better, vested interests in Germany have up to now prevented the overdue reform. This inflexibility with respect to overly large boards is one of the main reasons for the success of the European Company in countries with codetermined boards.[88]

(2) Independent directors – as distinguished from mere non-executive directors (in English jargon NEDs) and outside directors (not working full time for the corporation, as commonly in Germany and Japan[89]) – have long been considered an important corporate governance mechanism in the United States, and some major public corporations had them well before they were required by stock exchange listing rules.[90] The scandals that led to the Sarbanes-Oxley legislation of 2002[91] stirred up increased attention and reform proposals for independent directors. While state corporate law in general does not require independent directors, under the listing rules of the New York Stock Exchange a majority of the directors of listed corporations[92] must now be independent, and the three key committees (audit, compensation, and nomination or corporate governance committees) must be composed exclusively of independent directors.[93] The Dutch Corporate Governance Code goes even further to recommend that all but one member of the supervisory board and its committees must be independent.[94] In the United Kingdom and other countries the independent directors are a more recent phenomenon, but their number is quickly increasing.[95] Traditionally the board has consisted of executives with some members who had a more consultative role. Even in countries with a separate supervisory board, non-executive members were not required to really be independent and very seldom were. In Great Britain the role of non-executive members on corporate governance had already been strengthened by the Cadbury recommendations, but it was not until 2003 that the Higgs Committee, under the influence of the Enron scandal, asked for majority-independent boards in the Combined Code.[96] Under the Combined Code, at least half of the board of British listed companies, excluding the chairman, should comprise non-executive independent directors, though for listed companies below FTSE 350 level only two independent non-executive board members are required.[97] The French Corporate Governance Code recommends that independent directors should account for half the members of the board in widely held corporations and without controlling shareholders, in others at least a third, and in the audit committee (*comité des comptes*) two-thirds without a corporate officer.[98] The European Commission recommendation of 2005 asks for a sufficient number of independent directors "to ensure that any material conflict of interest involving directors will be properly dealt with,"[99] but concerns only the three above-mentioned board committees and recommends a majority of independent directors in them. Even that would be difficult to prescribe for German codetermined corporations because the difficult balance (codetermination at parity in the supervisory boards of major corporations) would be tipped in favor of labor. Some countries go further:

[86] 2Austr 10.

[87] 21Neth 7.

[88] See infra 13.3.1.5.

[89] 17Jap 14. But reform is under way, see supra note 31.

[90] D. Higgs, *Review of the Role and Effectiveness of Non-Executive Directors*, Final Report, London 2003; J. N. Gordon, "The Rise of Independent Directors in the United States, 1950–2005: Of Shareholder Value and Stock Market Prices," *Stanford Law Review* 59 (2007):1465.

[91] Sarbanes-Oxley Act of 2002, PubLNo 107–204, 116 Stat 745.

[92] There is an exception for corporations with a 50% or more controlling shareholder. 32USAI no.51.

[93] E.g., NYSE, Listed Company Manual § 303A.02, 04, 05. 06 (2004).

[94] 21Neth 10.

[95] In Australia in the Top 100 corporations 64.5% of all directors are independent, 2Austr 11. According to the ASC Corporate Governance Recommendation 2.2 the chair should be an independent director, 2 Austr 16.

[96] 31UK 6.

[97] 31UK 5. Now the UK Corporate Governance Code B.1.2.

[98] 10RF 7, 18.

[99] European Commission Recommendation of 15.2.2005 on the role of non-executive or supervisory directors of listed companies and on the committees of the (supervisory) board, OJEU L 52/51, section II no. 4.

for example, the UK Corporate Governance Code expects that the audit committees of the FTSE 350 companies will be comprised entirely of independent directors and that at least one member of the committee possess recent and relevant financial expertise.[100]

While having independent directors seems a general trend, two cautionary remarks are necessary. First, the fact that independent directors are required is of relatively little relevance by itself; what is decisive are the criteria for independence and who determines[101] whether a non-executive director should be considered independent.[102] Second, the effectiveness of having independent directors has not yet been empirically established.

(3) It has been observed since the very beginning of the independent director movement and has been established in practical experience since then that there is a quid pro quo of directors' independence and firm-specific knowledge. Therefore, and in particular under the impression of the financial crisis, more efforts have been made to have both in the board: independence and firm-specific knowledge. This can be done by recommending or requiring that the members collectively have particular knowledge. This is especially important for the audit committee, whose members should, collectively, "have a recent and relevant background in and experience of finance and accounting for listed companies appropriate to the company's activities."[103] For all members a tailored induction program should be installed[104] and the particular competences of the individual director relevant to his service on the board should be disclosed.[105] The new UK Corporate Governance Code provision establishes the principle of the board's and the board committees' effectiveness with an "appropriate balance of skills, experience, independence and knowledge of the company to enable them to discharge their respective duties and responsibilities effectively."[106] The Walker Review of corporate governance in banks and other financial institutions went even further, but the Financial Reporting Council did not take this up for corporations in general.[107]

13.3.1.2 Tasks, in Particular the Shareholder- or the Stakeholder-Oriented Approach

The Shareholder-Oriented Approach

The classic shareholder-oriented approach prevails in the United States[108] and, at least judging from the UK Corporate Governance Code,[109] which is exclusively focused on the protection of shareholders from management, de facto also in Great Britain.[110]

Contrary to what is often believed, in particular since the financial crisis, this does not imply that labor interests are not well taken care of since it is in the self-interest of the corporation and the management to keep good relationships with labor and the trade unions. But even more important, labor interests can and are better and more precisely taken care of by labor law provisions and work council requirements. This is also true for other stakeholder interests and "non-company law," such as environmental and tax law. In Great Britain this is the traditional approach of "profit-making with the law."[111]

The Stakeholder-Oriented Approach

In many countries this view is considered too narrow, as has long been held in Germany and Austria, but also in the Nordic countries and in the Netherlands. There the corporation law provides that the management board has to steer the company in the interest of the enterprise as a whole.[112] Since the company law reform of 2006 this is also expressly laid down in the United Kingdom, though at least in the takeover con-

[100] Principle C.3.1 of the UK Corporate Governance Code, 31UK 20. As to the relevance of the requirement of financial expertise for liability, see 31UK 20 et s.

[101] See infra 13.3.1.2.

[102] See infra 13.3.1.2.

[103] EU Recommendation of 15.2.2005, supra note 99, no. 11.2.

[104] Idem no. 11.3. In Germany in 2010 a movement for better and continuous education of board members has been started by the German Share Institute (Deutsches Aktieninstitut, DAI), Frankfurt.

[105] EU Recommendation of 15.2.2005, supra note 99 no. 11.4.

[106] The UK Corporate Governance Code Principle B.1.

[107] 31UK 8.

[108] 32USAI 3 n. 13.

[109] See supra note 34.

[110] 31UK 2.

[111] 31UK 15.

[112] 12Germ 14; 3A 6 et s.; 20Norw 13 et s. For the Netherlands Supreme Court 13 July 2007, OR 2007, 178, 21Neth 8. Cf. for Australia 2Austr 6 et s.

text the ultimate decision on the bid rests with the shareholders.[113] This amounts to and is called the "enlightened shareholder value" principle.[114]

The evaluation of the stakeholder-oriented approach is mixed. While it might be said that such a legal duty helps labor, it is doubtful whether a legal duty really adds to the obvious interest of the corporation and the management to maintain good labor relations and to avoid strikes. The true effect of such a rule might only be larger discretion of the board to act, which in turn makes it more difficult to hold the board accountable. Labor then seems only to benefit from such a clause if the interest of management and the interest of labor coincide.[115] This is different if the legal obligation to manage the corporation in the interest of the enterprise as a whole is complemented by a boardroom codetermination.[116]

The discussion on which approach is preferable is old. While the traditional legal approach in most countries and the perspective of economics is shareholder-oriented, sociological theory and political science tend more toward stakeholder orientation. A paradigmatic example for these fundamentally different approaches is the evaluation of and political approach to labor codetermination in corporate boards.[117] Though in the view of this general reporter, and in particular under the economic perspective, the shareholder primacy norm is the better regulatory response, it must be conceded that increasing social inequalities and social unrest, as heightened by the financial crisis and more generally by globalization with a shift of wealth from the old industrial countries to the BRIC countries, put pressure on the legitimacy of this approach.[118] This also shows in the rise of the corporate social responsibility[119] movement, which has gained momentum alongside corporate governance.

13.3.1.3 Functioning, in Particular the Work of the Board Committees

Management and Control

As described before, management and control are two functions that are complementary and, at least in financial institutions or even major corporations, may need a certain separation. This separation can be legally prescribed, as in two-tier board countries, but may just be good practice as in one-tier board countries with clear separate functions of the executive and the non-executive and independent directors. Even if there is such a separation, the role of the supervisory board or the independent directors in the one-tier board will most often not just be one of controlling the management, but also of advising. In a number of instances, when their consent to important management decisions is legally required, this may even involve taking a joint responsibility with management. In some countries the very system is geared toward such co-steering of the corporation, as in Germany's Rhenish capitalism where banks and major competitors held directorship in the supervisory board, a system that is slowly disintegrating.[120]

In order to fulfill the control function, the directors must above all have the necessary qualifications and spend appropriate time on this task. The corporate laws have usually been silent on this, but the corporate governance codes – and, in the aftermath of the financial crisis, legal rules as well – have become more precise, first for banks and other financial institutions, then also for board committees and boards more generally. The Walker Review of corporate governance in the UK recommends for banks and other financial institutions (BOFI) that a majority of non-executive directors (NEDs) should be expected to bring materially relevant financial expertise, though there is still need for diversity, and that for several NEDs, "a minimum

[113]This is indeed a "conceptual ambiguity of the UK's regulatory response to the 'shareholder v stakeholder' issue when assessed on the whole," 31UK 30.

[114]P. L. Davies, in *Gower and Davies, Principles of Modern Company Law*, 8th ed. (London: Sweet & Maxwell, 2008), 16–25 et s.: no balancing of interest, but the "members' interests are paramount." Similarly for Finland 9Fin 3.

[115]Kraakman et al., *Anatomy of Corporate Law*, supra note 9, p. 266.

[116]See infra 13.3.1.5.

[117]See infra 13.3.1.5.

[118]Cf. 31UK 30 et s., calling for "a more rigorous examination of the conceptual and empirical bases of th(e) assumption" of the a priori link between shareholder value maximization and social welfare.

[119]Cf. A. Johnston, *EC Regulation of Corporate Governance* (Cambridge: Cambridge University Press, 2009), 356 et s. on the European Commission's approach; O. de Schutter, "Corporate Social Responsibility European Style," *European Law Journal* 14 (2008):203; 31Austr 52 et s.

[120]Cf. R. Elsas and J. P. Krahnen, "Universal Banks and Relationships with Firms," in *The German Financial System*, ed. J. P. Krahnen and /R. H. Schmidt (Oxford: Oxford University Press, 2004), ch. 7, p. 197 et s.

expected time commitment of 30–36 days in a major bank" is needed.[121] The Financial Services Authority should check this by interviews.[122] While the Financial Reporting Council did not extend this for corporations in general, the new UK Corporate Governance Code still contains an explicit statement of the respective governance responsibilities of the chairman and the non-executive directors, the latter having a role in challenging and developing strategy.[123] Under EU law there must be specific knowledge both in the audit committee and in the remuneration committee.[124]

Committee Work, Role of the Chairman, Lead Director, Evaluation

(1) Board committees can play an important role for the work of the board and therefore are contemplated under most corporate laws.[125] As generally agreed, at least three board committees are important for good corporate governance: the audit committee, the nominating committee, and the compensation committee. These three functions are key and therefore have to be taken care of by committees of the board that prepare them thoroughly and, as the requirement of independent directors in these committees shows,[126] without conflict of interest. The audit committee has been made mandatory in listed companies by the European Directive of 17 May 2006.[127] For small and medium corporations the establishment of such committees may be too costly and burdensome; for such cases these committees are optional and the whole board must step in.[128] Jurisdictions differ as to whether board committees may have delegated decision-making powers instead of the whole board. This is strictly forbidden in France,[129] for example, and, as far as directors' remuneration is concerned, most recently in Germany.[130]

(2) The role of the chairman of the board, though very important, is often not addressed by corporate statutes; however, sometimes special duties and legal rights of the chairman are spelled out. In practice, chairman-oriented boards as well as collegially working boards are found. This depends partly on law and tradition, as the role of the CEO in France shows; partly it depends on the individual corporations, sometimes with fine distinctions like large German banks that distinguish between the mere "speaker" of the board and the actual chairman. General statements on which type of board does better in practice are hard to make on more than just anecdotal knowledge. But as spectacular failures in various countries show, it is dangerous if the CEO – who in many legal orders such as France[131] and Japan[132] also chairs the board – is a person with an exaggerated ego that is not balanced by his or her colleagues in the board.

In two-tier board countries, the role of the chairman of the supervisory board is crucial, too. He or she is the real junction between the management and control sides, usually working closely with the CEO and occupying a place that is nearer to the corporate information. Responsible for keeping the necessary flow of corporate information to the supervisory board, the chair – sometimes together with the CEO – is also very often the one who picks new members of the supervisory board, even those who are to be considered independent.[133]

[121] The Walker Review, A review of corporate governance in UK banks and other financial industry entities, Final recommendations, London, 26.11.2009, at 14, 45 (Recommendation 3); 31UK 8

[122] Idem at 15, 51 (Recommendation 5); 31UK 8.

[123] The UK Corporate Governance Principle A.4.

[124] European Commission Recommendation of 15.2.2005, supra note 99, section III 11.2 (audit committee); European Commission Recommendation of 30.4.2009 … as regards the regime for remuneration of directors of listed companies, OJEU L 120/28, section III 7.1: "At least one of the members of the remuneration committee should have knowledge of and experience in the field of remuneration policy."

[125] E.g. Del.Code Ann. Tit. 8, § 141c (West 2009); 12Germ 13.

[126] See this section.

[127] Directive 2006/43/EC of 17 May 2006 on statutory audits of annual accounts and consolidated accounts …, OJEU L 157/87.

[128] European Recommendation of 15.2.2005, supra note 99, section 7.2.

[129] 10RF 7.

[130] Section 107 subsection 3 of the German Stock Corporation Act as amended by law of 31 July 2009, as a popular measure of the legislators in the aftermath of the financial crisis. In countries with labor codetermination this weakens the role of the chairman of the supervisory board and strengthens labor.

[131] Cozian/Viandier/Deboissy, supra note 72, nos 502 et s., 528: the old title of P-DG (*président directeur général*) has been retained by French practice, the new legal title is président du conseil d'administration. Since 2001 it is legally possible to divide the two functions of president and director general. The choice is made by the board (*conseil d'administration*).

[132] 17Jap 13: 79,9 percent of all TSE-listed corporations.

[133] See infra this section.

The financial crisis has led to even higher expectations on the chairman. The Walker Review in the UK recommends that the chairman of a bank or other financial institution dedicate "a substantial proportion of his or her time, probably around two-thirds"[134] to the task. While the Financial Reporting Council did not extend this for corporations in general, still the new UK Corporate Governance Code contains an explicit statement of the respective governance responsibilities of the chairman (and the non-executive directors).[135]

(3) In the United Kingdom a unique system of divided leadership responsibilities has evolved. This is different even from the United States, though the situation there is changing. This development is due to the institutional investors who are the most important players in the UK, much more so than in any other country, including the United States.[136] They were the ones who in their own interest put the companies under pressure to divide the roles of the CEO and the chairman of the board. Later the Combined Code provided for the separation between the CEO, who should be responsible for day-to-day management, and the chairman of the board, whose role is leading and coordinating the board meetings with the aim of fostering constructive dissent and not only rubber-stamping the views of the management.[137] This function of the chairman is even better fulfilled if he or she is independent. Even if both roles are separated, independence is also endangered if – as was common practice in the UK, Germany, and other countries – the former CEO or chairman of the management board switches over into the chair of the board or supervisory board immediately after the end of his or her term or after having given up his position for other reasons. The Combined Code and the new UK Corporate Governance Code hold this to be incompatible with good corporate governance and insist on "clear division of responsibilities at the head of the company", "(n)o one individual should have unfettered powers of decision".[138] While current practice is still different in many countries such as France,[139] a similar development has taken place in other countries. A recent German reform set an end to the traditional practice of the chairman of the management board immediately taking up the chairmanship in the supervisory board and prescribed a 2-year waiting period for members of the management board unless the general assembly of the shareholders, upon a motion of shareholders with more than 25% of the voting rights, permits this.[140] Because of the low attendance ratio, this quorum will usually be reached only if there is a controlling shareholder or major blockholders. Yet whether such a mandatory and inflexible rule is really beneficial is open to doubt, since in some occasions the experience and qualification may be more relevant for the corporation than actual independence.

The United Kingdom has developed this principle further by installing a third leadership figure or "point of authority" on the board.[141] The function of this so-called senior independent director is

> to provide a sounding board for the chairman and to serve as an intermediary for the other directors when necessary. . . . Led by the senior independent director, the non-executive directors should meet without the chairman present at least annually to appraise the chairman's performance. . . .[142]

While this system could already be found among British public companies prior to the 1990s, today nearly all FTSE 350 boards have adopted it.[143] Other countries such as Switzerland[144] have followed the concept of "lead director."

(4) Evaluation of the performance of the board (including the supervisory board) has become part of good board corporate governance. Many corporations have taken up this practice by themselves. According to the European Recommendation of

---

[134] Walker Review, supra note 121, p. 15 (Recommendation 7).

[135] The UK Corporate Governance Code 2010, Principle A.3 and A.4; 31UK 9.

[136] Davies, supra note 114, p. 426 (15–12); Kraakmann et al., *Anatomy of Corporate Law*, supra note 9, p. 83, 108.

[137] 31UK 7.

[138] The UK Corporate Governance Code 2010, A.2.

[139] 10RF 7/8.

[140] Section 100 subsection 2 sentence 1 no. 4 of the Stock Corporation Act as amended by law of 31.7.2009, 12Germ 12.

[141] 31UK 6 et s.

[142] UK Corporate Governance Code 2010 A.4.1 and A.4.2; formerly Combined Code Provision A.3.3; 31UK 7. See also for the USA 32USAI after n. 152: "The independent board must meet in executive session without the inside directors."

[143] 31UK 7.

[144] 27CH 9.

2005, this evaluation should be carried out every year and

> should encompass an assessment of its (the board's) membership, organisation and operation as a group, an evaluation of the competence and effectiveness of each board member and of the board committees, and an assessment of how well the board has performed against any performance objectives which have been set.[145]

Even then the practice varies considerably as to how the evaluation is carried out, whether it is done within the board itself, or whether professional outside advice is taken.[146] The tendency to the latter is clear and may already be a best standard.

Independent Directors: Definition, Role, and Performance

The definitions of the meaning of independence[147] and the competence to judge this vary considerably. In the EU, independence is defined as being "free of any business, family or other relationship, with the company, its controlling shareholder or the management of either, that creates a conflict of interest such as to impair his judgement," but the recommendation goes on in giving far-reaching though non-binding criteria concerning threats to directors' independence.[148] A similar list of criteria is contained in the UK Corporate Governance Code,[149] the NYSE Listing Company Manual,[150] and the codes of other countries.[151]

While in the United States the independence criteria set up in the listing conditions must be complied with,[152] in many other countries the final determination of what constitutes independence remains fundamentally an issue for the (supervisory) board itself to determine. This is the case not only under the European recommendation of 2005,[153] but also in Great Britain where the board should determine whether each director is independent in character and judgment. The above-mentioned criteria are then only non-binding guidelines for the board that is told about circumstances which may threaten the independence of a particular director under the comply-or-explain principle.[154]

The high expectations set on independent directors have only partially been fulfilled.[155] Independent directors seem to have had an impact on replacing executive directors, but actually this was often mainly due to pressures from institutional investors.[156] More recently independent directors have not been able to prevent huge scandals, e.g., in Enron where the board was composed of a majority of qualified independent directors. Among the factors that reduce the impact of independent directors is foremost the fact that they are usually picked or proposed by the CEO or executive directors who have professional or personal relationships with them that do not fall under the above-mentioned criteria.[157] Unless they are professional non-executive directors, they are working part time and, while being independent, may not have the necessary know-how, either of the business sector or the actual corporation. Furthermore, the flow of information to them is often suboptimal, in particular in the case of supervisory boards.[158] To a certain degree this is the consequence of their role. In the Enron case, prominent, well-qualified independent directors

[145] EU Recommendation of 15.2.2005, supra note 99, No. 8.

[146] The UK Code of Corporate Governance recommends annual evaluation of the board, the committees and individual directors and external facilitation for the FTSE 350 companies' boards at least every 3 years, B.6 and B.6.2. Similarly for France, 10RF 8; for Belgium every 2 or 3 years at a minimum, 4B 6 et s. In the Netherlands there is a growing practice for boards to have external evaluation at least once every 3–4 years, 21Neth 9.

[147] As to the requirement to have independent directors, see supra 13.3.1.1.

[148] EU Recommendation of 15.2.2005, supra note 99, no. 13.1. Some EU accession countries followed in a nearly identical way, f. ex. Hungary, 14Hung 9.

[149] UK Corporate Governance Code 2010 B.1.1; Combined Code Provision A.3.1.

[150] NYSE Listed Company Manuals § 303A.02(b) (2004).

[151] F.ex. Belgian Code, 4B 7 et s.; Comisión Nacional de Valores (CNV) Rules in Argentina, 1Arg 16.

[152] NYSE Listed Company Manual § 303A.02; 31UK 6; but 31USAI n. 51.

[153] European Recommendation of 15.2.2005, supra note 99, no. 13.2.

[154] 31UK 6 speaks of "default" regulatory independence criteria.

[155] F.ex. Davies, supra note 114, p. 409 (no. 14–33).

[156] Examples from the U.S. in the early 1990s included General Motors, Kodak, American Express, Sears, Westinghouse, and IBM, 31USAI n 54; as to the financial institutions in the USA see Roe, Strong Managers Weak Owners, supra note 23, p. 267 et s.

[157] This is usually not articulated but is actually the case. Cf. for Poland 2Pol 11 et s.

[158] P. C. Leyens, *Information des Aufsichtsrats* (Tübingen: Mohr Siebeck, 2006), 156 et s.

learned of the existence and extent of special purpose vehicles only from the financial press after the scandal had broken. The corporate insiders kept control of such relevant information. It is also said that independent directors may have fewer incentives to monitor than other directors because their pay is less and – more recently – without stock options. In the end, group-think plays an important role. As always, it requires courage to stand up with questions and voice criticism against the mainstream.

Risk Management and Early Detection of Difficulties

Corporate law has traditionally refrained from telling management in detail what to do. This has included internal control systems[159] and risk management, which remained the domain of business administration and auditing. Though risk management in general has long been part of the board's duty of care, the corporate governance codes and more recently corporate laws have spelled it out as a concern for the board, the audit committee, and the auditors who have to report on what is done in this respect.[160] Legal protection of whistleblowers was installed in the United States by the Sarbanes-Oxley Act and since then has become rather popular in other countries as well.[161]

In the wake of the financial crisis there has been dramatically increased attention on risk management by regulators, legislators, and academia. While their focus for the moment is still on banks and other financial institutions – in particular, of course, the so-called systemic ones – these requirements tend to spill over to general corporate law.[162] However, norms that may make good sense for state-supervised branches and branches with particular risks and even systemic risks, if they are extended to corporations in general, may not only be unnecessarily burdensome but outright paralyzing.[163]

13.3.1.4 Rights, Duties, and Liabilities

The rights, duties, and liabilities of the directors are traditionally the domain of corporate law. While the corporate governance movement has led to emphasizing this area and to stiffening the requirements, this is not the place to describe this in more detail. Some quick observations must do.

Duty of Loyalty, Regulation of Conflicts of Interest

The duty of loyalty and particularly the rules concerning conflicts of interest of directors have long received a great deal of attention in the United States,[164] the United Kingdom,[165] and Australia,[166] but only much more recently in continental European countries such as Germany, Italy, France, and Switzerland.[167] Yet while conflict of interest may not have been regulated there as such, in most of these countries there are corporate law provisions or case law that deal with specific instances of conflict of interest, such as competition with the corporation, self-dealing, or use of corporate opportunity.[168] These different developments are due to general differences between case law and statutory law, varying enforcement patterns, and economic and cultural path dependencies. Yet today, both in law and

[159] In Japan the Osaka District Court for the first time held directors responsible for keeping an appropriate internal control system, Daiwa Bank Case decision of 20.9.2000; similarly under the Financial Instruments and Exchange Act, 17Jap 15.

[160] For Germany section 91 subsection 2 of the Stock Corporation Act since 1998, 12Germ 9 et s. The UK Corporate Governance Code 2010 C.2 mentions expressly the board's responsibility for sound risk management and internal control systems. In Switzerland expressly since 2008, 27CH 8, 10; Australia since 2003, revised in 2007 by the ASX corporate governance principles, 2Austr 18. For the Netherlands under the Corporate Governance Code , 21Neth 10.

[161] In Switzerland legislation is still pending, 27CH 10.

[162] See f.ex. section 302 of the Sarbanes-Oxley Act (supra note 91), 15 U.S.C. § 7241; 32USAI 37 n. 150.

[163] 31UK 8; D. Weber-Rey, "Ausstrahlungen des Aufsichtsrechts (insbesondere für Banken und Versicherungen) auf das Aktienrecht – oder die Infiltration von Regelungssätzen," *Zeitschrift für Unternehmens- und Gesellschaftsrecht* (ZGR) 39, no. 2–3 (2010): 543.

[164] 32USAII 3 et s.

[165] Davies, supra note 114, p. 557–574 (nos. 16–63 et s.).

[166] With additional provisions for public corporations, 2Austr 19 et s.

[167] For Germany K. J. Hopt, "Die Haftung von Vorstand und Aufsichtsrat – Zugleich ein Beitrag zur corporate governance-Debatte," in Festschrift für Mestmäcker, ed. U. Immenga, W. Möschel and D. Reuter (Baden-Baden: Nomos, 1996), 909 at p. 917, 921 et s.; for Italy16I 12 et s.; for France 10RF 9, but there are special rules, for example, for transactions between board members and the corporation; as to Switzerland 27CH 10.

[168] See K. J. Hopt, "Trusteeship and Conflicts of Interest in Corporate, Banking, and Agency Law: Toward Common Legal Principles for Intermediaries in the Modern Service-Oriented Society," in *Reforming Company and Takeover Law in Europe*, ed. G. Ferrarini, K. J. Hopt, J. Winter and E. Wymeersch (Oxford: Oxford University Press, 2004), 51. For Japan see 17Jap 16 et s.

practice, a trend can be observed internationally to be more conscious of and more strict with duty-of-loyalty violations and conflict-of-interest situations. As a general rule, directors are in a conflict of interest if they have a financial interest that might reasonably be expected to influence their judgment.[169] But a bright line test beyond this formula is difficult to find, as the varying American case law shows. The practice of obtaining disinterested directors' approval for acting in conflict-of-interest situations and for accepting compensation usually shields the actors from court interference.[170] A clear influence of American law, of American and British institutional investors, and more generally of globalization can be observed in this context.[171]

Business Judgment Rule, Standard of Care

In contrast to the duty of loyalty, the duty of care has been at the forefront in continental European countries. The standard of care is still general negligence. In some countries like the United States, this standard can be lowered by shareholder resolution, but not for breaches of the duty of loyalty and acts not in good faith.[172] More recently the duty of care has lost some of its relevance under the influence of the business judgment rule. Typically this rule is first introduced by the courts – as in Switzerland[173] and Japan[174] – and only later, following the American example, was it enacted by the legislators in Germany,[175] Portugal,[176] Australia,[177] and other countries.[178] The business judgment rule gives the board a broad discretion and safe haven from liability, provided the board has fully observed its duty of information. In effect, this amounts to a standard of gross negligence. The business judgment rule is certainly no excuse for not following legal requirements. This is particularly true when the corporation gets into a crisis, as with a special rule like the British wrongful trading[179] or the French *action en responsabilité pour insuffisance d'actif.*[180]

Remuneration, Stock Options, Other Incentives

The remuneration of directors and "pay without performance"[181] has become a primary topic in the United States, in Great Britain, and more recently, before and after the financial crisis,[182] in many other European and non-European countries as well, such as Germany, France, Italy, Switzerland, and Australia.[183] Traditionally such remuneration rules have been coined in rather general terms, such as requiring that the remuneration be adequate. Today these rules have become more and more detailed in substance. Regarding disclosure, the traditional rule of disclosing just the total board remuneration of perhaps the five top-earning directors has given way to individual disclosure stating the total remuneration of each director. The effect of this reform has been sobering, not to say counterproductive. While it stirred up some jealous discussions in the general assemblies, the overall effect was a general increase in remuneration since lower-earning directors pushed to be paid like everyone else. In Europe, the Recommendation of 2004 deals with remuneration policy, the remuneration of individual directors, and share-based remuneration; in response to the crisis, two Recommendations were added in 2009.[184]

Traditional accounting standards have tolerated the common practice of mentioning outstanding share

[169] Model Bus. Corp. Act § 8.60(1).

[170] 32USAII 5.

[171] As to institutional investors see infra 13.3.2.2. Cf. more generally K. J. Hopt, "Company Law Modernization: Transatlantic Perspectives," *Rivista delle società* 51 (2006): 906–34.

[172] Section 102(b)(7) of the Delaware General Corporation Law.

[173] 27CH 11, but there is no clear standard. Similarly in Norway, 20Norw 17, 21.

[174] 17Jap 15 et s.

[175] 12 Germ 19.

[176] 23Port 21.

[177] Since 2000, 2Austr 21 et s. with critique and reform proposals.

[178] For Denmark 8Denm 8; for Serbia 24Serb 18 et s.

[179] Section 214 of the Insolvency Act, see Davies, supra note 114, p. 217 et s. (9–7 et s.). For a comparative evaluation of the rule, see infra this section, Liability in Crisis Situations.

[180] Formerly action *en comblement du passif*, Cozian et al., supra note 72, nos. 298 et s. A similar action exists in Belgium. As to evaluation see supra note 179.

[181] L. Bebchuk and J. Fried, *Pay without Performance* (Cambridge, MA/London: Harvard University Press, 2004).

[182] See Walker Review, supra note 121.

[183] In Germany since 2005, 12Germ 15 et s. As to France 10RF 1 et s., 10 et s. As to Italy 16I 15; in Switzerland a far-reaching citizens' initiative with the aim to fully empower the shareholders is under way to be voted in 2010 ("Abzocker-Initiative"), 27CH 11 et s. For Australia 2Austr 26 et s. As to Japan 17Jap 18 et seq.

[184] European Commission Recommendation of 14.12.2004, OJEU 29.12.2004 L 385/55. As to the 2009 Recommendations, see infra notes 189 and 194.

options in a mere note on the balance sheet. Only more recently have first the IAS/IFRS and then the U.S. GAAP made it a requirement to treat stock options as a cost. This diminishes the distributable profit and thereby is thought to activate shareholders. But pricing these stock options is difficult and the balance sheet effect is usually small and hardly relevant for setting dividends.

While the issue of stock options has long been subject to shareholder approval because of its watering-down effect on the old shares, the United Kingdom first came up with the "say on pay," i.e., a rule that the shareholders have a say on remuneration policy, though not binding and not as to individual contracts. Others have followed – for example, the Netherlands[185] and Australia,[186] and, albeit with little success, the European Commission in its 2004 Recommendation.[187] There are also plans to introduce such a rule in the United States in the pending financial regulation.[188] The financial crisis has led to more rules on remuneration, some badly needed for doing away with perverse incentives in financial institutions, and some generally for corporations, as in the EU,[189] the UK and Germany.[190] The general thrust of the latter rules is to balance the non-variable and variable components of the remuneration, to define performance criteria in view of long-term value creation, to defer a major part of the variable component for a certain period of time, to have contractual arrangements permitting the reclamation of variable components under certain circumstances, and to limit termination payments.[191] Remuneration of non-executive or supervisory directors should not include share options.[192] While the legislators and rulemakers should not interfere with the details of remuneration, the situation is different and interference is legitimate for the sake of the taxpayers if upper limits are set by the state as a condition for helping banks and corporations on the verge of bankruptcy,[193] and if the remuneration rules limit or take away perverse incentives, especially in systemically relevant institutions of the financial sector.[194] But there is an unfounded and unfortunate tendency, not restricted to remuneration rules, of regulation spilling over from the regulated financial sector to general corporate law.[195]

Liability, in Particular in Crisis Situations

Liability of directors is a venerable topic of corporate law and need not be treated here but for two quick remarks. First, in many countries liability of board members is only toward the corporation,[196] with the consequence that the (supervisory) board is in charge of enforcing the claim of the corporation. Unless forced by law,[197] the (supervisory) board will generally be reluctant to do this. In other countries the shareholders and sometimes also creditors and investors have direct claims against the director who violated his duties. This makes a crucial difference.[198] Liability under capital market law rules tends to be toward investors, i.e., third parties. In some countries like the U.S., securities regulation even contains strict liability rules for persons and certain categories of wrong information.[199]

---

[185] 21Neth 20.

[186] 2Austr 28. Also 20Norw 19.

[187] European Commission Staff Working Document, Report on the application by Member States of the EU of the Commission Recommendation on directors' remuneration, Brusssels 13.07.2007, SEC(2007) 1022. But see for Italy 16I 15 et s.: remuneration is established by the ordinary shareholder meeting.

[188] 32USAI 40 n. 160.

[189] European Commission Recommendation of 30 April 2009 (complementing the Recommendations of 14.12.2004 and 15.2.2005), OJEU L 120/28.

[190] The UK Corporate Governance Code Section D and Schedule A; Section 87 of the German Stock Corporation Act as of 31.7.2009.

[191] Commission Recommendation of 30 April 2009, supra note 189, no. 3.1–3.5.

[192] Commission Recommendation of 30 April 2009, supra note 189, no. 4.4. The UK Corporate Governance Code D.1.3 with details.

[193] Germany Commerzbank 500.000 Euro.

[194] See European Commission Recommendation of 30 April 2009 on remuneration policies in the financial services sector, OJEU L 120/22.

[195] 10RF 2. More generally see 13.3.1.3.

[196] Unless a shareholder has suffered damage "directly" beyond the damages to the corporation (reflexive damage); for Italy see 16I 11.

[197] As to Germany see the ARAG case, infra note 203.

[198] Cf. K.J. Hopt and H.-C. Voigt, eds., *Prospekt- und Kapitalmarktinformationshaftung – Recht und Reform in der Europäischen Union, der Schweiz und den USA* (Tübingen: Mohr Siebeck, 2005); for the UK P. Davies, *Davies Review of Issuer Liability*, Final Report, London June 2007. As the controversial discussion in Italy 16I 11.

[199] In the USA section 11(a) Securities Act 1933 for issuers; 17Jap 21 et s.; in Portugal for issuers and offerors, K. J. Hopt and H.-C. Voigt, supra note 198, p. 83.

More generally, it can be observed that the various jurisdictions differ not so much in their actual regulation of liability of directors but in their enforcement. While there is rich case law in the United States and in France, for example, there have traditionally been very few actual liability court cases in Germany,[200] Switzerland,[201] and Japan, though under the influence of the big scandals and the financial crisis this is changing.[202] In the landmark case *ARAG*, the German federal court of last instance held that in general the supervisory board has a duty to bring suit against the management board directors who violated their duties and damaged the corporation.[203]

Second, there are special liability provisions for directors in case of a crisis situation. In such situations the board of directors may have a duty to inform and convene the general assembly and/or to file for bankruptcy and become liable if this is not done in time. The various jurisdictions – for example, the United Kingdom, France, Belgium, Germany, and Australia[204] – have found different solutions as to how quickly the directors have to react in such situations and to what degree and how long they have discretion to look for rescue. The most timely and highly controversial policy question is how to balance the company's and general public's interest in trying to rescue the corporation on the one side and the interest of the creditors not to suffer from delayed bankruptcy on the other. British wrongful trading – i.e., giving the directors broad discretion, but with the risk of liability if rescue does not come about – is a challenging idea, but it seems not to really bite in practice.

13.3.1.5 Codetermination on the Board

In many European countries there is mandatory labor codetermination, usually at a parity of one-third. Germany is unusual among non-Communist countries because it goes much further by mandating even shareholder and labor members at parity on the supervisory board.[205] France has recently and cautiously followed this trend by giving labor, under certain circumstances, only two seats on the board.[206] In some countries, labor codetermination goes together with a mandatory large board size, for example in Germany[207] with 20 seats in companies with a workforce of at least 2000 and 21 seats in large coal and steel companies. The Netherlands have reduced their special paritary codetermination system but have kept a strong influence of the working force (structure regime).[208] If this regime applies, the mandatory non-executive or supervisory board appoints, suspends, and dismisses the executive directors, while the general meeting of shareholders appoints the supervisory directors but can only reject candidates who must be nominated by the supervisory board in accordance with a certain profile. As to the composition of the supervisory board, the works council has an enhanced right of recommendation with respect to one-third of the members of the supervisory board.

Shareholders are usually not very fond of labor codetermination because it diminishes the lots for their

[200] Cf. for Germany Hopt, supra note 167.

[201] It is different there for auditor liability cases, 27CH 12, 18 et s.

[202] In Germany the financial crisis has led to many damages suits against former directors who had been fired; for Japan 17Jap 19; see also for Norway 20Norw 21 et s.

[203] German Bundesgerichtshof, decision of 21.4.1997, BGHZ 135, 244 (ARAG Garmenbeck).

[204] For wrongful trading and similar actions in France and Belgium see supra note 180. Cf. the comparative report of the Forum Europaeum Group Law, Corporate Group Law for Europe, European Business Organization Law Review (EBOR) I (2000) 165–264 at 245–257, on the UK, France, Belgium, and Germany. For the Netherlands with case law 21Neth 13. Australia has been said to arguably be the strictest in the world, 2Austr 20, 53 et s. In Hungary only since 2006, no case law, 14Hung 11. See also 8Denm 8 only case law; 18Lux 13 with case law; 15 Ireland 11; 17Jap 20.

[205] Cf. C. Windbichler, "Cheers and Boos for Employee Involvement: Co-Determination as Corporate Governance Conundrum," *European Business Organization Law Review* (EBOR) 6 (2005): 50.

[206] For France since 2002, provided employees own more than 3% of the capital, Art. L. 432–6 Labor code; 10RF 18. For Sweden 28Swed 5, appointment not by the employees, but by the unions under collective agreements. For Norway 20Norw 8 et s. For Finland 9Fin 19 et s.: codetermination results from labor law, not corporate law. For Denmark 8Denm 10. The UK has always resisted introducing labor codetermination, though it was suggested at a certain point by the Bullock report, 31UK 15/16. In Japan mandatory codetermination does not exist, though there is discussion of introducing some of it, 17Jap 28, but in fact directors are very often former top employees of the corporation, so labor interests do play an important role in Japanese corporations.

[207] 12Germ 27 et s.

[208] 21Neth 25 et s., also as to further, still pending legislation. There is an exemption to the structure regime for companies with a majority of the workforce of the company or the group being outside the Netherlands. As a result most large listed companies are exempted.

own candidates and seriously weakens their role in the decision-making of the (supervisory) board. Therefore, labor codetermination is introduced very rarely on a merely voluntary basis, apart from certain state-owned or state-influenced enterprises and enterprises that are in difficulties, rescue situations, or other special conditions. Economists hold this fact as an argument against codetermination in principle, because if codetermination were beneficial for the enterprise, shareholders would have adopted it without it being mandated by law.[209] Since labor codetermination in Germany and a number of other states is mandatory by law independent of the legal form of limited liability companies and even in groups of companies, corporations have no recourse but to live with it and to some degree come to terms with it. This does not mean that they would choose codetermination to begin with, if there were a choice. Now just such a choice has been opened up in the European Union by the possibility of becoming a European Company subject to a more flexible, consensus-based labor codetermination system.[210] The best example is the Allianz Corporation, the largest German insurance corporation, that changed its legal form to a European Company and thereby was able to reduce its board from 20 to 12 members, while voluntarily keeping the paritary labor codetermination on the board.[211]

Of course, labor codetermination is a strong means of corporate governance if the latter is conceived not only as shareholder-oriented but also stakeholder-oriented,[212] the workers of the company being the most obvious creditors among the stakeholders. Under a more shareholder-oriented concept of corporate governance, the experiences with labor codetermination are mixed. In theory, the labor representatives on the board serve as an additional check on management, not only as far as labor interests are concerned, but more generally as to too much risk-taking and other activities that are potentially disadvantageous to the enterprise and therefore to the jobs. Yet experience shows that labor codetermination has not prevented major frauds and scandals, though the shareholder-elected representatives also did not do better. As far as external corporate governance is concerned, the interests of management in defending the corporation – not only against possible raiders, but more generally against hostile takeovers – are often paralleled by labor interests in keeping the jobs. Actually, labor codetermination is sometimes considered to be one of the many structural obstacles to the development of a lively takeover market. Most recently in some countries – for example, Germany – the decision-making on the remuneration of directors has been taken away from the remuneration committees and mandatorily given to the plenum of the board.[213] The expectation with this step was to install a serious brake on excessive remuneration. Yet labor seems to be not really interested in whether there are higher or lower remunerations to directors, as the Mannesmann case[214] illustrates. Instead, the natural interest is in having more general influence in the board and maybe using the remuneration issue as a leverage. On the other side, it is also true that labor codetermination may bring problems between labor and capital to the attention of the board at a very early stage, which may also be good for the shareholders and more generally may enhance cooperation between capital and labor and thereby improve productivity. On yet another side, such corporate governance effects come at a price since the corporate governance activities and possibilities of the shareholder side are correspondingly weakened and the decision-making process is more costly and slow. In the end, this is an empirical question that still has to be answered.[215]

[209] As to the highly controversial economic and political pros and cons of labor codetermination, see K. Pistor, "Corporate Governance durch Mitbestimmung und Arbeitsmärkte," in Hommelhoff et al., supra note 2, p. 231; Windbichler, supra note 205; K. J. Hopt, "Labor Representation on Corporate Boards: Impacts and Problems for Corporate Governance and Economic Integration in Europe," in *International Review of Law and Economics* 14 (1994): 203.

[210] Council Directive 2001/86/EC of 8.10.2001 supplementing the Statute for a European company with regard to the involvement of employees, OJEC L 294/22. There is a clear relative success of the SE in member states with extensive employee participation, Ernst & Young-Study for the European Commission, supra note 77, p. 243 et s.

[211] Empirical data covering most of the European members states on the SE can be found in Ernst & Young-Study for the European Commission, supra note 77.

[212] Supra 13.3.1.2.

[213] See supra note 140.

[214] Milhaupt/Pistor, supra note 21, p. 69 et s.

[215] As to empirical research so far, see most recently the report by K. Pistor, "Corporate Governance durch Mitbestimmung und Arbeitsmärkte," in: Hommelhoff et al., supra note 2, p. 231 at 245 et s.

13.3.2 The Shareholders

13.3.2.1 Fiduciary Duties of Controlling Shareholders and Group Law (Konzernrecht)

In widely held corporations without blockholders, the shareholders as principals are protected against the board as their agent by the classical instrument of company law, i.e., duties and liabilities of the directors.[216] The corporate governance movement with its emphasis on the corporate board has been treated in part 13.3 of this article. These duties and liabilities also exist and are relevant in corporations with a controlling shareholder or several blockholders, and usually the stock corporation acts of the various countries do not have different rules for the boards of widely held corporations and others. In practice, however, the real principal-agent problem in non-widely held corporations is not between the shareholders and the board, but between minority shareholders and the controlling or blockholding shareholders.[217] Here corporate law can intervene in two ways: either by imposing general or specific fiduciary duties on the agent-shareholder[218] and/or by mandating rules of the game between the controlling and controlled members of a group, i.e., parent and direct and indirect subsidiaries. The first approach is the one chosen by some countries without a formal group law (such as France[219]) when they try to prevent tunneling by controlling shareholders; others (such as the U.S.,[220] Italy,[221] and Switzerland[222]) shy away from imposing a fiduciary duty on the controlling shareholders, let alone on non-controlling shareholders.

The protagonist of the second approach is Germany, which has an extensively codified group law (*Konzernrecht*) of stock corporations, besides also acknowledging fiduciary duties of the controlling shareholders and duties between shareholders more generally.[223] A few countries have followed the German example, including Portugal, Brazil, and Croatia. Others like Italy[224] have recently enacted their own group laws. Details are beyond the scope of this report, but they can be found in the various corporate laws.[225]

13.3.2.2 Shareholder Rights, Minority Protection, Institutional Investors

Shareholders Rights and Minority Protection

Every country with a corporate law gives special rights to shareholders and has more or less detailed minority protection rules in its stock corporation acts. The details of these minority protection rules vary considerably.[226] Some harmonization has been brought about by the European Shareholder Rights Directive of 11 July 2007[227] with the aim of "strengthening shareholders' rights." In non-EU countries, similar discussion

[216] Supra 13.3.1.4.

[217] See supra text before note 9 with references.

[218] F.ex. 9Fin 18: fiduciary duty of the controlling shareholders towards the company and its other shareholders; 23Port 24; de facto also in the Netherlands, not restricted to the controlling shareholder, 21Neth 15 et s. with case law. Controversial in Poland, 22Pol 12 et s., 18. In countries as Japan, 17Jap 24, where such a fiduciary duty of the controlling shareholder is not (yet) recognized, particular situations may be caught under the duty of loyalty or the doctrine of the de facto director may help for limited cases.

[219] *Abus de majorité* under case law is a widely used remedy, 10RF 16; P.-H. Conac, L. Enriques and M. Gelter, "Constraining Dominant Shareholders' Self-Dealing: The Legal Framework in France, Germany, and Italy," *European Company and Financial Law Review* (ECFR) (2007): 491.

[220] Exceptions exist if the shareholders are in a position to use their influence over the board – for example, in transactions between them and the corporation – and according to some courts in close corporations; then a fairness test applies, but approval by a negotiating committee of independent directors or a majority of the minority shareholders may turn the burden of proof. For case law, see 32USAII 5 et s.

[221] Only in case of *abuso della maggioranza*, 16I 17.

[222] 27CH 13, though tunneling is illegal. Similarly Denmark 8Denm 8 et s.; Norway 20Norw 22; Argentina, 1Arg 24 et s.

[223] For Europe K. J. Hopt, "Konzernrecht: Die europäische Perspektive," *Zeitschrift für das gesamte Handelsrecht und Wirtschaftsrecht* 171 (2007): 199.

[224] Important parts of the Italian group law are disclosure, holding company liability to minority shareholders, and creditors in case of abuse of power, Art. 2497 of the Civil Code, 16I 8; Conac et al., supra note 219, p. 504 et s.

[225] For a functional comparative analysis of group law, see Kraakman et al., *Anatomy of Corporate Law*, supra note 9, p. 153 et s. on related-party transactions.

[226] Kraakman et al., *Anatomy of Corporate Law*, supra note 9, p. 89 et s., 275 et s; 32USAI 20 et s.

[227] European Directive of 11 July 2007 on the Exercise of Certain Rights of Shareholders in Listed Companies, OJEU L 184/17.

and legislation is going on, particularly and very controversially in the United States.[228] Again, details can be found in the various corporate laws; furthermore, minority protection was previously treated by the XVIth Congress of the International Academy of Comparative Law in Brisbane in 2002 with Evanghelos Perakis as general reporter.[229] So it suffices here to make some short remarks on the rational apathy of the shareholders and the relevance of institutional shareholders for corporate governance.

Shareholder codecision rights must be exercised in order to be effective. Yet experience shows that the attendance rate in the general assemblies can be very low. In Germany in major public corporations the attendance rate is occasionally as low as 30%, with the consequence of ad hoc majorities and a virtual impossibility to reach qualified majorities of all shareholders. This is true even though under German law the banks may vote as a proxy for those shareholders whose shares they have in deposit and who have authorized them to vote.[230] The "absent owner" phenomenon appears not only in corporations with a dispersed shareholdership, but as far as the minority shareholders are concerned also in controlled corporations. This can also be seen in China,[231] where the state is the majority shareholder in many corporations that were formerly mostly state-owned. The attendance rate in some other countries is much higher; in the United Kingdom, for example, attendance in the FTSE 100 firms is regularly as high as 70–80%, but upon closer inspection this proves to be due to institutional shareholdership.[232]

Even apart from codecision rights and their exercise when attending the general assembly, institutional shareholders can exercise a considerable influence on the corporation, the board, and corporate governance. The rise of the institutional investors has been described at length elsewhere.[233] There are still considerable differences between the United States and Great Britain on the one side and most continental European countries on the other. Institutional investors have long been important in the United States[234] and in the United Kingdom, partly because of the lack of a state-provided old age and social security system, thus driving the population into becoming shareholders and investors. In the UK, the country where institutional shareholding is most predominant, institutional shareholders – i.e., mainly occupational pension funds and insurance companies as well as mutual funds – constitute about three-quarters of the overall market capitalization.[235] In other countries, for example Germany, institutional shareholding is slowly but steadily in advance.

Traditionally these institutional shareholders have followed the Wall Street rule, i.e., they sold when they were not satisfied with a corporation. But more recently there has also been a certain development of institutional shareholders in voting at the general assembly and thereby engaging in internal corporate governance.[236] This is partly so because selling blocks, even if they most often do not go beyond 3–5%, influences the stock price negatively. Furthermore, there has been a lot of pressure on institutional investors to actively vote, and corporate governance codes such as the Combined Code in the UK[237] and institutional shareholders' self-regulatory instruments have supported this.[238] As a result, the attendance rate in general assemblies in some countries has moved up and there is also a clear increase in voting by institutional shareholders. In the UK and in the Netherlands, the press has given wide coverage to cases in which the general assembly

[228] 32USAI 24, 40 n. 162.

[229] E. Perakis, ed., *Rights of Minority Shareholders, General and National Reports* (Brussels: Bruylant, 2004).

[230] So-called bank depository vote, 12Germ 24 et s.

[231] 6China 19 et s. with the consequence that local officers who are dependent on local government instead of higher government levels decide in different ways, cf. D. C. Clarke, Corporate Governance in China: Dilemmas of Reform and the Institutional Environment, unpublished manuscript 2006, p. 73.

[232] 31UK 10. For French CAC 40 corporations the figures of 2008 are 68.3%, 10RF 16.

[233] Cf. T. Baums, R. M. Buxbaum and K. J. Hopt, eds., *Institutional Investors and Corporate Governance* (Berlin, New York: W. de Gruyter, 1994).

[234] 32USAI 5 n. 17.

[235] 31UK 13.

[236] The classic article is by B. S. Black, "Agents Watching Agents: The Promise of Institutional Investor Voice," *University of California, Los Angeles Law Review* 39 (1992): 911.

[237] 31UK 13. See now the UK Corporate Governance Code 2010, supra note 34.

[238] 31UK 13, 11 n. 40.

with active institutional shareholders voted down remuneration proposals of the board.[239] In some countries, the codes impose on institutional investors the duty to disclose and explain their voting behavior.[240]

The voting behavior of hedge funds is somewhat different.[241] Their "offensive" shareholder activism has led to considerable repercussions. In the Netherlands, ABN AMRO, at the instigation of the hedge fund TCI, was taken over and dismantled by a consortium of three, including another Dutch bank, Fortis, which later had to be bailed out by the Dutch government.[242] In Germany, hedge funds, led by TCI too, drove out the management and the supervisory board of the Deutsche Börse in 2005.[243] But all this is still sporadic.

In sum, institutional shareholders – and to a lesser degree and more ad hoc, the hedge funds – have gained considerable influence on the corporations and potentially also on their corporate governance. But they do more via external corporate governance over the market than by internal corporate governance. Even in Great Britain, the country with the highest rate and influence of institutional shareholders, it seems that the orthodox institutional shareholders have continued to be "defensive" and reluctant to take the costly route of internal monitoring of corporations.[244] A more general change in the trend of shareholder (in)activism overall in British public corporations cannot yet be observed.[245] In other countries, increased shareholder activism remains even more the exception.[246]

In many countries for example in the USA, Germany, France, the Netherlands and Argentina shareholder associations play an important role for shareholder protection and for corporate governance in general.[247] In others like Switzerland such organizations do not exist.[248]

13.4 Conclusions and Theses

1. *Corporate governance* is the *system by which companies are directed and controlled.* This system depends heavily on the prevailing shareholder structure of a country (dispersed as in the United States and Great Britain or blockholdings). The principal-agent conflict is then either between the shareholders and the board or between the minority and the controlling shareholder. Protection of labor is usually not the task of corporate law. Internal corporate governance works within the corporation; external corporate governance works via takeovers and other market forces. For banks and other sectors there are specific forms of corporate governance.
2. Corporate governance in the shadow of the law, i.e., soft law, has traditionally played a major role at the stock exchanges. Since *Cadbury* in 1992, the *corporate governance code movement* has swept from the United Kingdom all over the world. These codes usually concentrate on the board and internal corporate governance, including auditing. Enforcement is often by a "comply-or-disclose/explain" provision that is sometimes bolstered by law.

[239] See 31UK 13 with further cases. For the Netherlands Philips, VastNed Retail, Corporate Express and Royal Dutch Shell, 21Neth 20.

[240] 4B 19.

[241] For the UK J. Armour and B. Cheffins, "The Rise and Fall (?) of Shareholder Activism by Hedge Funds," ECGI Law Working Paper No. 136/2009; 31UK 14 n. 42. For the USA M. Kahan and E. Rock, "Hedge Funds in Corporate Governance and Corporate Control," *University of Pennsylvania Law Review* 155 (2007): 1021.

[242] 21Neth 19.

[243] J. Faber, "Institutionelle Investoren (einschließlich Hedgefonds und Private Equity)," in Hommelhoff et al., supra note 2, p. 218 at 228 et s.

[244] 31UK 13; 32USAI 6 n 21.

[245] 31UK 14: "instances of offensive shareholder activism in the UK to date have tended to be relatively sporadic and isolated" and "targeted (and heavily publicised) … against individual companies".

[246] See for France 10RF 17. For the Netherlands 21Neth 19 et s. Cf. 8Denm 9 et s.; 20Norw 27. For Australia see 2Austr 34 et s. In Japan, too, institutional investors start to play a certain but still very limited role, 17Jap 26. As to a slow rise of the institutional investors in China 6China 22; for Taiwan 29Taiw11.

[247] Schutzvereinigung für Wertpapierbesitz in Germany, 12Germ 45; Association de défense des actionnaires minoritaires (ADAM) since the early 1990s in France, 10RF 26; VEB and Eumedion in the Netherlands, 21Neth 49; 1Arg 43.

[248] 27CH 15: basically unknown.

3. The *board* is a prime actor in corporate governance. Most countries have a one-tier board structure; some divide the management board from the supervisory board. Neither of the two systems is inherently better. Modern corporate laws, therefore, let the corporations choose. Smaller boards are more effective than bigger boards. The boards are composed of executive and non-executive – preferably independent – directors. As to the overall task of the board, it is controversial whether shareholder or stakeholder orientation is preferable.
4. Corporate governance reform concentrates on the *good functioning of the board.* Having separate committees for auditing, nomination, and remuneration is recommended. The role of the chairman of the (supervisory) board is key. More recently this role has been matched by a lead director. Regular evaluation of the board and its members, preferably helped by outside experts, is on the advance. Regarding organization, internal control systems and risk management have gained momentum.
5. The *rights, duties, and liabilities of the directors* are traditionally a domain of corporate law. More recently there has been a focus on the duty of loyalty and conflicts of interest. The standard of the duty of care varies. In any case, the business judgment rule opens a safe haven provided there has been appropriate information. Most attention is given today to remuneration. The slogan is "pay without performance;" the task is doing away with perverse incentives, in particular in financial institutions. Liability is an important incentive, especially for crisis situations, but it is not a panacea.
6. *Shareholder protection* is the major concern of corporate governance. In blockholder systems this protection is not so much from the board but from the controlling shareholder. The latter can be done either by imposing fiduciary duties on the controlling shareholder or by enacting specific rules for corporate groups as in Germany (*Konzernrecht*). Individual shareholders or minorities can also be given rights to protect themselves. Apart from financial rights there are rights of information (disclosure), codecision (voice), and withdrawal (exit). Yet there is the old phenomenon of the rational apathy of shareholders. It remains to be seen whether the rise of institutional investors and shareholder activism will bring more than an ephemeral change.
7. Corporate governance is also concerned with stakeholder interests, especially with *labor.* Many European corporate governance systems are characterized by labor codetermination on the board. Germany goes particularly far by having codetermination at parity. The evaluation of this is highly controversial, and in the end it is an empirical question. Other means of protecting labor include information rights and codecision on labor issues.
8. Corporate governance needs the help of *gatekeepers such as auditors* and other professionals. Most important is mandatory auditing by external auditors. The auditors' tasks and the accompanying expectations have been constantly increasing, resulting in the so-called expectation gap. Auditors can fulfill their task of confidence-building only if they are independent. The extent of auditors' liability is highly controversial.
9. Corporate governance rules are only as good as their enforcement. Corporate governance actors need some kind of *supervision.* This can be done by capital market authorities as they exist today in most countries, the stock exchanges, or self-regulatory bodies. Each of these ways have advantages and disadvantages. The right mix is difficult and path dependent.
10. The role of the courts in corporate governance can be very different. Some countries try to keep the courts out or to bring them in only as the last means. In other countries, nearly every contested corporate governance question ends up in the courts. Procedural law is fundamentally different in various countries, as are the styles of the courts. In the end, a comparative view of corporate governance shows a great deal of convergence, but many path-dependent differences still remain.

Annex: List of Country Reports

(all on file with the author of this article)

1Arg	Argentina: Professor Raúl Aníbal Etcheverry, Rafael Mariano Manóvil (Buenos Aires)
2Austr	Australia: Professor Jennifer Hill (Sydney)
3A	Austria: Professor Susanne Kalss (Vienna)
4B	Belgium: Alexia Autenne, Gilles Collard, Ariane Alexandre (Louvain-La-Neuve/Liège)
5Brazil	Brazil: Dr. Nelson Eizirik, Ana Carolina Weber (Rio de Janeiro)
6China	People's Republic of China: Professor Liu Junhai (Beijing), Dr. Knut Benjamin Pißler (Hamburg)
7Croat	Croatia: Ass't. Professor Dionis Juric (Rijeka)
8Denm	Denmark: Professor Jan Schans Christensen (Copenhagen)
9Fin	Finland: Professor Jukka Mähönen (Turku)
10RF	France: Professor Pierre-Henri Conac (Luxembourg)
11Georgia	Georgia: Professor Lado Chanturia, Dr. George Jugeli (Tbilisi/Bremen)
12Germ	Germany: Professor Hanno Merkt (Freiburg)
13Greece	Greece: Dr. Konstantinos N. Kyriakakis (Athens)
14Hung	Hungary: Péter J. Nikolicza (Budapest)
15Ire	Ireland: Professor Irene Lynch Fannon (Cork)
16It	Italy: Professor Francesco Denozza (Milan), Professor Paolo Montalenti (Torino)
17Jap	Japan: Professor Nobuo Nakamura (Tokyo)
18Lux	Luxembourg: Isabelle Corbisier, Professor Pierre-Henri Conac (Luxembourg)
19Macau	Macau: Professor Augusto Teixeira Garcia (Macau)
20Norw	Norway: Assoc. Professor Beate Sjafjell (Oslo)
21Neth	The Netherlands: Professor Jaap Winter, Jaron van Bekkum, Steven Hijink, Michael Schouten (Amsterdam)
22Pol	Poland: Professor Stanislaw Soltysinski (Warsaw)
23Port	Portugal: Professor Jorge Manuel Coutinho de Abreu (Coimbra)
24Serb	Serbia: Professor Mirko Vasiljevic (Belgrade)
25SKor	South Korea: Professor Young Shim (Seoul)
26Spain	Spain: Professor José Antonio García-Cruces Gonzáles, Professor Ignacio Moralejo-Menéndez (Saragossa)
27CH	Switzerland: Professor Peter V. Kunz (Bern)
28Swed	Sweden: Magdalena Giertz, Professor Carl Hemström (Uppsala)
29Taiw	Taiwan: Wen-Yeu Wang, Wang-Ruu Tseng (Taipei)
30Turk	Turkey: Dr. Asli E. Gürbüz Usluel (Ankara)
31UK	United Kingdom: Dr. Marc Moore (London)
32USAI	United States: Professor Arthur R. Pinto (New York)
32USAII	United States: Frank A. Gevurtz (Sacramento)

Financial Leasing and Its Unification by UNIDROIT[1]

14

Herbert Kronke

14.1 Introduction

In the history of the Academy and its International Congress of Comparative Law, this is in all likelihood the first time that one of its topics is not phrased as the program of an inquiry into the differences and similarities of a certain area of the law in a number of jurisdictions. Rather, the Academy's executive has tasked the national reporters and the general reporter with analyzing the achievements of an intergovernmental organization pursuant to that organization's mandate of harmonizing the law in an area that its member states' governments[2] have identified as one where harmonization was particularly desirable. Indeed, investing part of the exceedingly limited resources of the International Institute for the Unification of Private Law (UNIDROIT) over more than two decades in work on various instruments designed, *inter alia,* to promote standards for both modern sophisticated asset-based financing and basic leasing transactions shows remarkable determination – or missionary zeal – in particular if one takes into consideration that other intergovernmental organizations,[3] during overlapping periods of time, have also carried out substantial and related work.

An interesting feature of this section's reports is the change of perspective: while we are used to taking a comparative law study as basis and point of departure for any work aimed at modernizing commercial law in an internationally co-ordinated and harmonizing fashion, to this writer's knowledge there has so far never been an effort to look systematically into the harmonizing effect – both conscious and unconscious, intended and *de facto* – of transnational commercial law[4] instruments in domestic law. With respect to the method employed as well as the findings, it should be noted that not always will it be possible to establish a clear link of causation between the state of the law in a given jurisdiction and its having been the subject of studies and/or intergovernmental discussion, negotiation and, eventually, adoption of an international instrument. This is particularly true of the earliest and the most recent of the documents we will examine, i.e. the 1988 Ottawa Convention and the 2008 Model Law.

Taking all that into account this General Report – as well as a number of the National Reports on which it is

[1]III.A.3, Le credit-bail financier et son unification par UNIDROIT.

[2]At the time of writing, there are 63 Member States: Argentina, Australia, Austria, Belgium, Bolivia, Brazil, Bulgaria, Canada, Chile, China, Colombia, Croatia, Cuba, Cyprus, Czech Republic, Denmark, Egypt, Estonia, Finland, France, Germany, Greece, Holy See, Hungary, India, Indonesia, Iran, Iraq, Ireland, Israel, Italy, Japan, Latvia, Lithuania, Luxembourg, Malta, Mexico, The Netherlands, Nicaragua, Nigeria, Norway, Pakistan, Paraguay, Poland, Portugal, Republic of Korea, Republic of Serbia, Romania, Russian Federation, San Marino, Saudi Arabia, Slovakia, Slovenia, South Africa, Spain, Sweden, Switzerland, Tunisia, Turkey, United Kingdom of Great Britain and Northern Ireland, United States of America, Uruguay, and Venezuela.

[3]*See infra* 14.8.

[4]For an extensive discussion of this concept, see Roy Goode, Herbert Kronke, Ewan McKendrick, Transnational Commercial Law. Text, Cases, and Materials (2007), 1.37–1.67.

H. Kronke (✉)
Institute for Comparative Law, Conflict of Laws and International Business Law, Heidelberg University, Heidelberg, Germany, Former-Secretary-General, UNIDROIT, Rome, Italy
e-mail: Kronke@ipr.uni-heidelberg.de

K.B. Brown and D.V. Snyder (eds.), *General Reports of the XVIIIth Congress of the International Academy of Comparative Law/Rapports Généraux du XVIIIème Congrès de l'Académie Internationale de Droit Comparé*, DOI 10.1007/978-94-007-2354-2_14, © Springer Science+Business Media B.V. 2012

based – while complying with the Academy's instruction to focus on work carried out by UNIDROIT, will attempt to provide an analysis of the state of the law of financial leasing as it has developed since the mid-1980s both domestically and at the level of transnational commercial law instruments.

14.2 Relevant UNIDROIT Instruments

To date, five instruments on leasing have been elaborated under the auspices of UNIDROIT[5]: The UNIDROIT Convention on International Financial Leasing (Ottawa, 28 May 1988); the Convention on International Interests in Mobile Equipment (Cape Town, 16 November 2001); the Protocol to the Convention on International Interests in Mobile Equipment on Matters Specific to Aircraft Equipment (Cape Town, 16 November 2001); the Protocol to the Convention on International Interests in Mobile Equipment on Matters Specific to Railway Rolling Stock (Luxembourg, 23 February 2007); the Model Law on Leasing (Rome, 13 November 2008).

A third industry-specific protocol to the Cape Town Convention, the draft Protocol on Matters Specific to Space Assets, is still being negotiated and is expected to be adopted in 2011 or 2012.

While there is a certain logic in the history and sequence of the instruments, the underlying policies and strategic objectives pursued by member state governments were – and are – varying, as will be shown in more detail below. Consequently, even basic features, such as definitions and the respective scope of application, are not necessarily and entirely consistent. Rather, each instrument reflects its own policies, as cast by negotiating governments, industry as well as other private-sector stakeholders and advisers at the time when that particular step was made.

Turning to the statistics reflecting governments' involvement in the elaboration of the various instruments, there is a clear increase in tangible interest. Whereas roughly a third of the (then existing) states on which reports were submitted did not participate in the diplomatic conference for the adoption of the 1988 Ottawa Convention, almost all of them were represented in 2001 in Cape Town and/or in 2007 in Luxembourg as well as at (at least) one of the sessions of any of the three bodies involved in the preparation and adoption of the 2008 Model Law.[6]

14.3 National Reports

At the time of the congress, of 21 national reports that had been announced through the national committees 14 had been submitted[7] and 2 more were envisaged to be submitted subsequently.[8] Two national reports (for Canada and the United States of America) cover what modern private-law treaties define as 'multi-unit states', i.e. states within which two or more territorial units of that state, or both the state and one or more of its territorial units, have their own rules of law in respect of any of the issues falling within the substantive scope of the instrument. Article 52(1) of the Cape Town Convention and Article XXIX of the Aircraft Protocol refer to 'territorial units (of a Contracting State) in which different systems of law are applicable in relation to matters dealt with in this Convention'. This provision was specifically drafted with a view to encompassing also the People's Republic of China and its Special Administrative Regions.[9] Under Article XXIX, the Government of the People's Republic of China lodged a declaration that 'unless otherwise notified by the Government of the People's Republic of China, the

[5] All instruments, including *travaux préparatoires*, continually updated information of their respective status, commentary, bibliography etc. are accessible at www.unidroit.org.

[6] Initially the advisory board, followed by two sessions of a committee of governmental experts, and, for the instrument's adoption a joint session of the General Assembly and the committee of governmental experts.

[7] Belgium, Canada (common-law provinces), China, Croatia, France, Greece, Netherlands, Norway, Peru, Poland, Portugal, Slovenia, Turkey, United States of America. In addition, statistics and other illustrative material on certain developments in Latin America as a region were provided.

[8] Italy and Canada (Quebec). There was, moreover, hope that a report on Germany could be submitted. Some National Reports had been published at the time of the congress in collections under the auspices of the national committees. All reports (including this general report) will be published in the Uniform Law Review/Revue de droit uniforme 2011.

[9] Comments on (1) "Designated Entry Points" Article (2) "Territorial Units" Article Presented by China, DCME Doc No 27, 24/10/01, in Diplomatic Conference to Adopt a Mobile Equipment and an Aircraft Protocol. Acts and Proceedings 172 (2006).

Convention and the Protocol shall not apply to the Hong Kong Special Administrative Region and the Macão Special Administrative Region'. Also, the national report does not cover those territorial units.

The general reporter had circulated a rather detailed questionnaire[9a], but national reporters were free to either answer the questions and comment on issues raised or to submit a classic learned article. Some chose the former, others opted for the latter format; others still invented hybrid forms of reporting. As regards the questionnaire, a number of questions may have been relevant for a limited number of jurisdictions and were addressed only by a small number of national reporters. On the other hand, not all national reporters included all relevant UNIDROIT instruments in their analysis. In both instances the present writer took the liberty of filling gaps and leaving white spots according to otherwise available – or unavailable – sources. Finally, it will not escape the sharp observer's attention that the general report in rare instances 'overrules' a national report where insider knowledge gained during the general reporter's time at UNIDROIT is more precise. For example, a national reporter may not be aware of his or her government's actual involvement in the negotiation of one of the relevant instruments and his or her respective inaccurate information therefore needed to be rectified.

14.4 Basic Notions and Distinctions

14.4.1 Finance Lease

The law of 12 out of 15 countries[10] on which reports were received draws a distinction between 'true lease' or 'operating lease' on the one hand and 'finance lease' on the other hand. In the case of an operating lease the lessor (owner of the asset) contracts with the lessee granting possession for a specified period of time; the lessee acquires no property interest in the asset other than a right of possession and a right of use. This type of transaction is generally used where the lessee's objective is to have a right of use in relatively new equipment without incurring the expense of the full purchase price, and where the lessor's calculation is to have its own investment in the purchase price plus amortization plus profit margin covered by the aggregate rental payments, frequently paid for a number of lease periods by a number of lessees.

A 'finance lease', on the other hand, is according to this widely adopted categorization a tri-partite relationship between the lessor and the lessee, who are the parties to a lease contract, and the lessor and the supplier, who are the parties to a sales contract. Chronologically and functionally, the tri-partite relationship evolves in four stages: (1) the lessee selects the supplier (manufacturer or distributor of the goods) and the equipment according to its requirements. (2) the lessee thereafter enters into a lease contract with the lessor (a specialized leasing company or other financial institution) for that piece of equipment from that supplier. (3) the lessor enters into a sales contract with the supplier, acquiring the asset selected by the lessee. (4) the supplier delivers the equipment to the lessee. Typically, the lease term is equal – or almost equal – to the (assumed) useful economic life, and the lessor does not normally expect the return of the property. At this point it is important to note that, for the purposes of categorizing the type of transaction, in certain jurisdictions the lessee's end-of-lease term options and/or obligations are critical.

Canada, where the courts refuse to adopt any bright-line test favoring instead a 'substance test' by looking at the totality of the circumstances, is a particularly clear illustration. If the lessee has an *obligation* to purchase the leased property at the end of the lease period this is taken as a strong indication that it is a security lease. In the same vein, if there is an *option* to purchase the leased property at the end of the lease period and if the option is to be exercised at less than fair market value at the time – in other words, an incentive offered only to the lessee and not to other market participants – this can be taken as the lessee 'building equity' (an exquisite metaphor) in the asset, and therefore this speaks in favor of a security lease.

French law as well as other continental European systems and Chinese law take the 'true lease' (*louage, location, bail; Miete* in German; *huur* in Dutch, etc.), as provided for in the great nineteenth century civil codes, firmly as the point of departure and nucleus of any leasing transaction. A 'finance lease' (*crédit-bail*) where other elements such as the lessor's mandate to enter into a contract with the supplier and the supply contract are grouped around that nucleus is, according

[9a]www.ipr.uni-heidelberg.de/cms/content/kronke/questionnaire.pdf

[10]This noun – rather than 'jurisdiction' – is deliberately employed with a view to including multi-unit states.

to French law, characterized by an end-of-term obligation incumbent on the lessor: the mandatory unilateral undertaking to sell at the end of the lease period to the lessee. Moreover, since the aggregate value of the rentals includes more than the value of the right of use, namely part of the amortization and the lessor's profit margin, French law and its civilian/continental siblings do recognize that the *crédit-bail*'s essential function is that of a financing transaction rather than a mere grant of possession and a right of use for a period of time.

The national report for the United States highlights the importance of even the slightest variations of terminology and, at the same time, the efforts that parties to a transaction may invest in arranging it so as to be a (true) lease for one purpose but not for another. Commercial law, tax law and accounting rules seem to be developing in opposite directions. A 'finance lease', a term of art, is a true lease (!) in which the lessor and the supplier are separate and only the supplier, not the lessor, has responsibility to the lessee for conformity (quality, absence of defects, performance, etc.) of the goods.[11] In this connection, the national report emphasizes that, 'financing lease' and 'financial lease' are – unlike 'finance lease' – *not* terms of art in commercial law, that they are broader and that both the legislative history of the Bankruptcy Reform Act of 1978 and subsequent case law suggest that they refer to a 'disguised security interest, as opposed to a true lease'. The reporter recommends avoiding the term 'financing lease' for commercial law purposes altogether while conceding that it cannot be avoided when discussing U.S. accounting rules.

It follows that another distinction has to be made, and that is between a true lease (including a finance lease) and a security interest. Section 1-203 of the U.C.C. defines the true lease by establishing that a 'transaction in the form of a lease' is not a true lease but a disguised security interest if (a) it is not subject to termination by the lessee and (b) at least one of four listed situations is present. These are (i) that the original term of the lease equals or exceeds the remaining economic life of the asset, (ii) that the lessee is bound to renew for the remaining economic life or to become the owner of the asset, (iii) that the lessee may renew for the remaining economic life for no or a nominal additional payment, and (iv) that the lessee may become the owner at the end of the lease term for no or a nominal additional payment. However, the courts have held that, even if none of these four criteria is met, the transaction may be characterized as a disguised security interest if the lessor has no reasonable expectation of a meaningful residual value in the goods.

Apart from the fact that using the terms 'finance lease' and 'financial lease' interchangeably has become common in particular in transnational commercial law instruments,[12] whereas greater precision is required with respect to jurisdictions such as France and the United States, this brief discussion of the most basic notions permits three statements. Firstly, the distinction between true leases and finance leases as well as the criteria for drawing the line between them are almost universally accepted. Secondly, it is generally accepted that certain types of finance lease serve similar functions as secured transactions. Thirdly, the degree to which the finance lease's roots in the true (or simple, or traditional) lease entails the applicability of common-law or legislative rules governing true leases varies. Canadian law seems to be least inclined to follow tradition and most determined to adopt a functional approach.

14.4.2 Commercial Transactions

Starting in the early 1970s, courts, legislators and legal writers increasingly paid attention to the phenomenon of structural imbalances that typically characterized contracts between large corporations and other businesses and less knowledgeable, less informed individuals with inferior bargaining power (the 'weaker party'). Legal systems throughout Western Europe and North America responded in different ways, one being the development of special rules ('consumer contract law') designed to remedy certain undesirable consequences of those imbalances. Businesses that contracted with consumers were required to provide more, and more detailed, information about goods and services they offered, consumers were given specific rights to terminate contracts, demand replacement of nonconforming goods, or claim damages if those duties had not been complied with, etc. For this reason

[11] U.C.C. § 2A-103(1)(g).

[12] Obviously, what may appear as sloppy drafting is irrelevant for legal systems in all non-English-speaking countries.

and in view of the international instruments tending to address only commercial transactions, the general reporter's questionnaire inquired whether legislation or judge-made law in the relevant jurisdiction distinguished between commercial/professional leasing transactions and consumer transactions. It appears from the national reports that this distinction is actually made in the vast majorities of legal systems. In all Member States of the EC/EU the Directives 87/102/EEC and 2008/48/EC have been implemented which leads to a special regimen at least for the purposes of those instruments. Only the report for the People's Republic of China states that – except for the purposes of standard-terms scrutiny – no such distinction is made. It has to be borne in mind that until 1999, when the new and unitary Contract Law, which does regulate financial leasing as a distinct type of lease, entered into force, Chinese contract law distinguished according to the social and economic status of the contracting partners[13] and that the legislator in all likelihood rated the uniformity achieved higher than any considerations labeled as 'consumer protection'. Moreover, the use of financing leases as a means to provide credit to consumers is (or has until recently been) probably not as economically relevant as in other jurisdictions.

14.5 The 1988 Ottawa Convention

14.5.1 Scope

The Ottawa Convention applies, as its title indicates, only to *international* transactions. The internationality requirement and the relevant connecting factors[14] are set forth in Article 3. According to Article 3(1) the Convention applies when the lessor and the lessee have their places of business in different states and (a) those states and the state in which the supplier has its place of business are "Contracting States" or, (b) both the supply agreement and the leasing agreement are governed by the law of a Contracting State. Quite in line with the general policy pursued by many governments at the time, both alternatives lead to an exceedingly modest scope of application. This is particularly obvious with respect to alternative (b): for the provision to apply the court seised must, firstly, be the court of a Contracting State and, secondly, the forum's conflict-of-laws rules – with their full range of conceivable connecting factors – must point to the law of a Contracting State not only with respect to one but two different agreements.

14.5.2 Objectives of the Convention and Position Under National Legal Systems

The Convention has five key objectives[15]: the recognition of the typical tri-partite relationship (*supra* 14.4.1), Article 1(1); to transfer responsibility for nonconforming equipment from the lessor to the supplier; to restrict the lessor's liability to third parties; to safeguard the lessor's property interest in the event of the lessee's insolvency; and to ensure the effectiveness of provisions for certain default remedies of the lessor, such as accelerated payment, liquidated damages, etc.

[13]The Contract Law of the People's Republic of China was adopted at the Second Session of the Ninth National People's Congress on March 15, 1999. Lease contracts are regulated in arts. 212–36, financial leases in arts. 237–50. On the state prior to 1999 and the reform process, see Herbert Kronke, "Der Gesetzgeber als Rechtsvergleicher, Aspekte der chinesischen Vertragsrechtsreform," in *Festschrift für Ulrich Drobnig zum siebzigsten Geburtstag*, ed. Jürgen Basedow, Hein Kötz, Ernst-Joachim Mestmäcker (Tübingen: Mohr Siebeck, 1998), 579.

[14]*See generally* Herbert Kronke, "Internationality and Connecting Factors in Conflict of Laws and Transnational Commercial Law," in *Convergence and Divergence in Private International Law – Liber Amicorum Kurt Siehr*, ed. Katharina Boele-Woelki, Talia Einhorn, Daniel Girsberger and Symeon Symeonides (2010), 57.

[15]For an overview, see Ronald Cuming, "Legal Regulation of International Financial Leasing: The 1988 Ottawa Convention," *Arizona Journal of International and Comparative Law* 7 (1989): 39; Carsten Dageförde, *Internationales Finanzierungsleasing* (1992); Franco Ferrari, General principles and international uniform commercial law conventions: A study of the 1980 Vienna Sales Convention and the 1988 Unidroit Conventions," *Unif. L. Rev.* 451 (1997); Daniel Girsberger, "Leasing," in *Handbuch Internationales Wirtschaftsrecht*, ed. Herbert Kronke, Werner Melis and Anton Schnyder (Köln: O. Schmidt, 2005), 757–68; Martin Stanford, "Explanatory Report to the Preliminary Draft Uniform Rules in International Financial Leasing," *Rev. dr. unif.* 76 (1984).

14.5.2.1 Shifting Responsibility from Lessor to Supplier

Under a traditional lease the lessee has rights against the lessor, but the standard terms of a finance lease usually make it clear that the equipment is selected by the lessee, who exercises its own skill and judgement, and that the lessor has no responsibility for nonconformity of the equipment and is entitled, under so-called 'hell or high water' clauses, to be paid the agreed rent come what may. Two techniques have evolved to deal with this problem. In the first, the lessor agrees to make claims against the supplier on the lessee's behalf as well as, or as an alternative to, its own claims. The problem here is that the lessor can recover only for its own loss, and its exclusion of liability and right to payment of rent in any event usually means that it suffers no loss. In the second, the lessor agrees to assign to the lessee any claim it may have against the supplier. Again, however, the lessee, claiming in right of the lessor, can recover only for the lessor's loss, which is usually zero. Articles 8, 10, 11 and 12 of the Convention, first, give the lessee direct rights against the supplier and, second, remove liability from the lessor, though not completely. Apart from a warranty of quiet possession (Article 8(2)) the lessee has no other claim against the lessor except to the extent to which the breach results from the act or omission of the lessor, Article 12(5).

As a logical concomitant of the special features of a finance lease the vast majority of national legal systems examined for this session recognizes the tri-partite relationship. A minority, however, insists on basing its analysis on the two separate contracts (supply contract and lease). Consequently, this latter group does not normally contemplate a transfer of responsibility for nonconformity to the supplier but provides in a traditional fashion for claims of the lessee against the lessor.

14.5.2.2 Liability to Third Parties

It follows from the special features of a finance lease that the lessor shall not, in its capacity as lessor, be liable to third parties for death, personal injury or damage to property caused by the equipment, Article 8(1)(b). This principle does not govern any liability of the lessor in any other capacity, for example as owner, Article 8(1)(c). Ownership of movables as such does not usually attract liability in national legal systems. In the case of motor vehicles, it is usually the 'operator' who is liable in tort or under some special regime. But these cases fall typically in the category of 'operating lease' (see *supra* 14.4.1). A prominent case of owner liability derives from the 1969 Brussels International Convention on Civil Liability for Oil Pollution which establishes liability of the owner of a vessel for oil pollution.

The position under the Ottawa Convention would appear to be shared by a majority of States on which reports were received.

14.5.2.3 Protection Against Lessee's Insolvency

Article 7 provides that the lessor's real rights are valid against the lessee's trustee in bankruptcy (more recent instruments use the neutral term 'insolvency administrator') and creditors, including creditors who have obtained an attachment or execution. By 'real rights' is meant rights *in rem,* or proprietary rights, as opposed to purely personal rights, or obligations. In many systems even a lessor who is not the owner but who holds under a head lease or a conditional sale agreement is considered to have real rights in the equipment in the sense of rights available against third persons generally, not only against its own lessor or conditional seller. Article 7 is designed to prevent the leased asset from being treated as part of the insolvent lessee's estate so as to be available to its general creditors. However, under Article 7(2) any public notice requirements prescribed by the applicable law (see Article 7(3)) as a condition of validity against the insolvency administrator and general creditors must be satisfied.

At least the basic rule enshrined in Article 7(1) appears to enjoy unanimous support in the national legal systems that form subject of a report to the session.

14.5.2.4 Default Remedies of the Lessor

Article 13 confers on the lessor a set of basic default remedies of the kind given by national laws. The lessor is entitled to recover unpaid rentals with interest and, in the case of substantial default, may require accelerated payment of the value of the future rentals or alternatively terminate the leasing agreement and recover such damages as will place it in the position in which it would have been if the lessee had performed the agreement in accordance with the terms. Article 13(3) validates a provision in the agreement for liquidated damages, which is enforceable unless it would result in damages substantially in excess of what is necessary to put the lessor in the position in which it would have been if the contract had been properly performed.

Nine out of fourteen reporting national laws are in conformity with the general approach taken by Article 13 subject, however, to a number of general limits (on agreed penalties) and qualifications.

14.5.3 Results: Evaluation of the Ottawa Convention

14.5.3.1 Formal Results

Viewed purely in terms of the number of ratifications the Convention, despite its merits in overcoming the problems created by the tripartite relationship of lessor, lessee and supplier, has not become one of the – exceedingly few – success stories of transnational commercial law. It has so far attracted only ten ratifications, and only two of the reporting states (France and Italy) are among the Contracting States. Moreover, for important categories of high-value mobile equipment it has been – or, in the case of future protocols, will most likely be – superseded by the 2001 Cape Town Convention. The low level of adoption may reflect the point made in the Explanatory Report of the draft Convention that one of the major facts to emerge from preparatory research was the narrow scope of application (*supra* 14.5.1) and that truly cross-border leasing transactions are still relatively rare occurrences.[16]

14.5.3.2 Informal Results

However, the Convention has had a significant impact on domestic developments that are, according to submitted national reports, occasionally reflected in the *travaux préparatoires* to domestic legislation as well as case law. In this respect the reader is referred in particular to the Italian national report, which provides rich evidence for the Italian courts' habit to either apply the Convention to domestic cases by analogy or in any event to acknowledge its persuasive authority. Furthermore, there is anecdotal evidence gleaned from inquiries on the part of international law firms with the UNIDROIT Secretariat that the Convention may serve as a template for the documentation in truly tri-partite cross-border transactions. Lastly, the Convention is the model adopted by those engaged in running projects for the International Finance Corporation for the building up of leasing industries in developing countries, and it forms the basis of the work on the Model Law (*infra* 14.7) that commenced 15 years later.

14.6 The 2001 Cape Town Convention and Its Protocols

The 1988 Ottawa Convention is essentially an instrument aimed at the harmonization of contract law. Article 7, the provision dealing with the protection of the lessor's real rights in the lessee's insolvency, is, however, an early harbinger of the ever-increasing importance of property in international transactions. The idea of building on the leasing convention to provide an international regime for security interests (in the broadest possible sense of the term) in high-value mobile equipment was first mooted by the Canadian President of the Ottawa Diplomatic Conference, T B Smith, QC, and later promoted by the Canadian Government. The rationale for such a regime was that a security interest in such equipment that had been created validly and that was enforceable in one jurisdiction might be unprotected or less efficacious when the equipment moved to another jurisdiction, so that creditors, conditional sellers and lessors could not be confident of the validity and ready enforceability of their interests outside their own jurisdiction. This uncertainty either inhibited asset-based financing or made it significantly more expensive. The ordinary – and universal – conflict-of-laws rule, namely that property rights were governed by the *lex rei sitae* (or *lex situs*) was unsuited to dealings in equipment having no fixed situs but moving routinely across national frontiers. Moreover, there was the problem of wide differences in the substantive laws of different States, some of which were considerably less favorable to non-possessory security interests.

14.6.1 Scope

The Cape Town Convention did not follow earlier instruments (concerning vessels and aircraft) in their approach of providing for the recognition of an interest

[16]Explanatory Report on the Draft Convention on International Financial Leasing, in Diplomatic Conference for the Adoption of the Draft Unidroit Conventions on International Factoring and International Financial Leasing. Acts and Proceedings, I, 27 no. 3 (1991).

created under the law of one jurisdiction in all other Contracting States. Rather, the 'international interest' under the Convention is a property interest deriving its force from the Convention, not from national law. It is an artificial concept encompassing the position of (i) a seller under reservation of title; (ii) a chargee under a security agreement; and (iii), relevant for our purposes here, the lessor under a leasing agreement, Article 2(2).

Another significant break with tradition, and a bold step forward, is that there is no 'internationality' requirement, the only – but obviously functional – delimitation being the connecting factor that the debtor is situated in a Contracting State, Article 3. Again, a change that met immediate approval on the part of both negotiating Governments and industry: situations involving property in aircraft, railway rolling-stock, space assets and the like are by definition at least potentially transborder situations.

14.6.2 Key Features and Position Under Domestic Law Prior to Ratification or Accession

Prior to the adoption of the Convention and its equipment-specific Protocols all but two (Canada, United States) of the jurisdictions that are the subject of national reports characterized the 'security giver's' legal position along the lines of traditional concepts (owner, chargee, lessor) rather than based on their economic function and a 'substance test'. Apart from re-conceptualizing three technically distinct legal positions functionally as a uniform and genuinely international property right, the 'international interest' (*supra* 14.6.1), there are four key features of the Cape Town instruments.

14.6.2.1 Registration

The Convention (Articles 16–28), the Aircraft Protocol (Articles XVII–XX) and the Rail Protocol (Articles XII–XVII) provide for registration in an international registry (one for each category of mobile equipment under its respective Protocol). Registration is not a prerequisite for the creation of the international interest (see Article 7). However, upon registration the international interest is accorded priority over purely national interests (whether registered or not) and over subsequently registered and unregistered interests (Article 29). Moreover, in insolvency proceedings against the debtor an international interest is effective if prior to the commencement of the insolvency proceedings that interest was registered in conformity with the Convention (Article 30).

The registration system is asset-based, not debtor-based. An entry is made against an asset that is uniquely identifiable, e.g. an airframe through a manufacturer's serial number. In line with the design of a uniform property right (subject to distinguishing for the purposes of available remedies, see Articles 8 and 10), the registration system covers interests of charges, of conditional sellers as well as *interests of lessors*. Prior to adopting and implementing the Convention, the latter were not registrable outside Canada, the United States and New Zealand. More generally, it is to be emphasized that registration in the international registry goes far beyond the ones provided for in certain national systems, such as Croatia, where the transactions are registered but where leasing contracts on the one hand and charges and title reservations on the other hand are registered in separate registries reflecting the law's non-functional but conceptual approach.

As a consequence of the international registry's being a fully electronic automated system (without legally trained staff) operating 24 h a day and 7 days a week no transaction documentation is examined or even submitted, and the Registrar is under no duty to enquire whether a consent to registration under Article 20 has in fact been given or is valid (Article 18(2)). In other words, the Convention opted for the legal technique of 'notice filing'. Essentially the function of an entry is to warn third parties, who, for example, contemplate extending credit to a potential borrower against security in an asset to verify whether an interest entered into the registry actually exists.

14.6.2.2 Equipment-Specific Remedies

Secondly, the decision in favor of a two-instrument approach (the Convention containing the general part, i.e. provisions applicable to all categories of equipment, and each protocol addressing the specifics of each category and the needs of financing practice in that industry) enabled the protocols to provide for additional equipment-specific remedies to the basic default remedies under Articles 8–15 of the Convention.

The most prominent, and for that industry critical, example is the irrevocable de-registration and export request authorization issued by a debtor in accordance with a template annexed to the Aircraft Protocol,

Article XIII. The authorization is a necessary prerequisite for the creditor's effective exercise of any of the remedies provided for under the Convention where taking control of the aircraft depends on the ability to legally remove it from the debtor's country of residence and the State of registration of the aircraft under the Chicago Convention.

14.6.2.3 Enhanced Creditor Rights in Lessee's Insolvency

The acid test of a security interest is its efficacy in the debtor's insolvency, and as the Convention characterizes a finance lease functionally as a security interest, this focuses our analysis on the lessor's rights in the lessee's insolvency. As mentioned, under Article 30 an international interest registered prior to the commencement of the insolvency proceedings is effective – that is, enforceable against the insolvency administrator and creditors – except so far as it is subject to avoidance under rules of insolvency law relating to preferences and transfers in fraud of creditors. Article XI of the Aircraft Protocol (see also Article IX of the Rail Protocol with a modified approach that takes the rail industry's specific level of development and its practices into account[17]), which applies only in a Contracting State that has made a declaration to that effect, goes further. Alternative A, the so-called 'hard option', which a Contracting State may select by declaration, provides that on the occurrence of an insolvency-related event the insolvency administrator must either cure all defaults and agree to perform all future obligations within a specified waiting period, or give up possession of the aircraft object. This provision is based on the US Bankruptcy Code and leaves the court no discretion to impose a stay. Alternative B, the so-called 'soft option', requires the insolvency administrator, at the request of the creditor (i.e. the lessor), to give notice within the time specified in the Contracting State's declaration whether it will cure all defaults and agree to perform all future obligations or give the creditor an opportunity to take possession of the aircraft object. Upon the insolvency administrator's failure to give such notice or to honor its undertaking to give possession the court may permit the creditor to take possession. A contracting State may also choose not to make any declaration under Article XI. In that event its own insolvency law will continue to apply.

Of the 40 Contracting States (including the EU) 24 have made a declaration opting for either of the alternatives, and only one of those, Mexico, has chosen Alternative B.

14.6.2.4 Party Autonomy Regarding Governing Law

Provided that a Contracting State has made a declaration to this effect, under Article VIII of the Aircraft Protocol and Article VI of the Rail Protocol the parties to an agreement (i.e. a security agreement, a title reservation agreement, or a leasing agreement, cf. Article 1(a) of the Convention) may freely agree on the law which is to govern their contractual rights, wholly or in part. Given the persistent reluctance of a great number of legal systems to grant unlimited party autonomy in conflicts rules on contracts the fact that Articles VIII and VI respectively do so in the immediate vicinity of property law (some even within the boundaries of property law *strictu sensu*) certainly is a qualitative leap ahead.

Of the 40 Contracting States no fewer than 28 from all four corners of the world (among them the reporting states of China and the United States) and of all legal traditions have made that leap. Moreover, all Member States of the European Union, among them Ireland, Luxembourg and Malta, who are also Contracting States, as well as Belgium, France, Greece, Italy, Poland, Portugal and Slovenia, jurisdictions on whom national reports were submitted, would make that declaration since it is in accordance with Article 3 of EC Regulation 593/2008.

14.6.3 Methods Employed

A comparative law study is carried out as a matter of course in all major harmonization projects undertaken by any of the relevant intergovernmental organizations.[18] In the Cape Town context, however, that study was only a first step. Following a survey of the existing

[17]Convention on International Interests in Mobile Equipment and Luxembourg Protocol Thereto on Matters Specific to Railway Rolling Stock. Official Commentary by Professor Sir Roy Goode CBE, QC, as approved for distribution by the UNIDROIT Governing Council pursuant to Resolution No. 4 adopted by the Luxembourg Diplomatic Conference (2008) Article IX, Comment 5.27, 5.37–5.41.

[18]For an overview, see Roy Goode, Herbert Kronke, Ewan McKendrick, *supra* note 3, 4.33–4.48, 6.10–6.12.

legal environment two leading applied economists were tasked with an economic impact assessment study aimed at identifying the salient features of a secured-credit financing instrument capable of producing the benefit which in law reform projects is so often promised but rarely ever measurable. The economic impact assessment study did actually quantify potential benefits – that is savings on interest certain legal features were capable of achieving – and these targets then served as a starting point for what is now called the 'commercial approach' to commercial law reform.[19]

Indeed, the Cape Town Convention is probably still the best example of an instrument aimed at reaching a predetermined economic objective and where Contracting States stand to gain from making the right choices. The objective is lower credit cost, and it is pursued by way of providing for predictable, measurable, risk-reducing creditor rights in default and insolvency situations. The goal was not to compromise between pre-existing solutions under the law of negotiating states but instead to provide rules that, according to the economists' assessment, would yield the maximum benefit due to maximum predictability of the outcome upon default. Therefore, the Convention and the Protocols offer a menu of options on certain key issues such as the insolvency regime mentioned above. As we have seen, the clear majority has made the right choice, i.e. has opted for a 'hard' (and economically beneficial) rather than a 'soft' (and economically neutral or detrimental) solution.

14.6.4 Results: Evaluation of the Cape Town Convention

14.6.4.1 Formal Results

With 40 Contracting States (including the European Union as a Regional Economic Integration Organisation, cf. Article 48 Cape Town Convention, Article XXVII Aircraft Protocol, Article XXII Rail Protocol) at the time of writing and, according to industry sources, an estimated 80–85% of all secured-credit transactions (mainly finance leasing) for aircraft worldwide covered by the Convention, it is fair to state that the Convention so far has registered a phenomenal success. Of the countries on which national reports were submitted China and the United States are Contracting States.

14.6.4.2 Informal Results

Over and above the foregoing, the Cape Town Convention and Protocols had and continue to have a significant impact on domestic developments in states preparing for ratification or accession. In certain cases the impact extends beyond the Convention's substantive scope, i.e. high-value mobile equipment, as legislators come to appreciate features, such as the design of certain default remedies or the registration system. Moreover, for the first time in the history of transnational commercial law we have tangible evidence for the impact the instruments have on contract practice. This is made possible by leading practitioners'[20] decision to share their experience with other stakeholders and to publish relevant documentation.[21]

14.7 The 2008 Model Law on Leasing

14.7.1 Historical Background, Scope, and Principal Features

While a model law on leasing could have been the natural follow-up to the 1988 Ottawa Convention,[22] the limited resources of the UNIDROIT Secretariat and important member states' governments were thought to be needed with a higher degree of urgency for the work on what was to become the 2001 Cape Town

[19]See Jeffrey Wool, "Rethinking the Notion of Uniformity in the Drafting of International Commercial Law: A Preliminary Proposal for the Development of a Policy-Based Unification Model," *Uniform Law Review* 46 (1997); idem, "Economic Analysis and Harmonised Modernisation of Private Law," *Uniform Law Review* 389 (2003); Herbert Kronke, "The Takeover Directive and the 'Commercial Approach' to Harmonisation of Private Law," in Private and Commercial Law in a European and Global Context – Festschrift für Norbert Horn ed. Klaus Peter Berger, Georg Borges, Harald Herrmann, Andreas Schlüter & Ulrich Wackerbarth (Berlin: De Gruyter Recht, 2006), 445.

[20]The Legal Advisory Panel of the Aviation Working Group – AWG.

[21]See The Uniform Law Foundation (ed.), Contract Practices Under the Cape Town Convention, Cape Town Paper Series, Volume I, Cwmbran (2004); idem, Advanced Contract and Opinion Practices Under the Cape Town Convention, Cape Town Paper Series, Volume 2, Oxford and Portland, Oregon (2008).

[22]For an early analysis by one of the pioneers and fathers of work on leasing at UNIDROIT, see Ronald Cuming, "Model Rules for Lease Financing: A Possible Complement to the UNIDROIT Convention on International Financial Leasing," *Uniform Law Review* 371 (1998).

Convention. It was only in late 2005 that work on the Model Law commenced, starting with three sessions of an advisory board made up primarily of UNIDROIT correspondents and involving, firstly, experts working for the International Finance Corporation (I.F.C.) on commercial law reform in developing countries and transition economies and, secondly, relevant industry associations from a variety of geographic regions.[23] The composition of the Advisory Board and the committee of governmental experts, as well as the history of the formulating stages, reflect the understanding that this instrument was primarily aimed at developing countries and their small and medium-size businesses.[24]

With respect to its substantive scope of application, it is important to note that the Model Law not only contemplates financial leases but any lease, Article 2. On the other hand, the Model Law does not apply to a lease that functions as a security right, Article 3(1), nor to a lease or a supply agreement for large aircraft equipment unless the lessor, the lessee and the supplier have otherwise agreed, Article 3(2). This exclusion removes a potential source of conflict between the Model Law and the Cape Town Convention and the Aircraft Protocol.

Conversely, the provisions of the Model Law cover the full range of relevant issues, as addressed in items D(10) to (23) and E(10) to (23) of the questionnaire circulated to national reporters (*supra* 14.3) except insofar as issues of general contract law are not taken up by the Model Law; in this respect its users are referred to the UNIDROIT Principles of International Commercial Contracts, or they can rely on their domestic law. The Model Law provisions' content reflects the basic features of the 1988 Ottawa Convention and develops details on the basis of state-of-the-art comparative analysis and benchmark contract practice.

14.7.2 Results: Evaluation of the Model Law

Model laws as one type of the by-now large variety of facultative instruments[25] are usually easier to negotiate than binding treaties, but their implementation at the domestic level is exceedingly difficult to monitor. The model-law technique has been very successful in some instances, where legislators were keen to benefit in the international arena from the "hi-fi factor" (as in the case of the 1985 UNCITRAL Model Law on Arbitration). But where no such incentive exists, the absence of a depositary and fellow-signatories, who take an interest in their peers' handling of the negotiated template, makes a sufficiently reliable feed-back from users a rare occurrence. Taking this into consideration, with respect to leasing we are in an above-average situation. Reference to the (draft) Model Law is or has been made in current domestic reform discussions in four of the states on which national reports were submitted. Moreover, recent reports from the UNIDROIT Secretariat indicate that the following States have implemented the Model Law or that implementation is underway: Afghanistan, Jordan, Latvia, Palestinian National Authority, Tanzania, and Yemen.

14.8 Work of Other Intergovernmental Organizations and Cooperation Among Organizations

14.8.1 Scope of Inquiry

All national reporters were invited to indicate whether and, if so, to what extent their governments had participated in related work on secured-credit transactions and functional equivalents carried out within the framework of other intergovernmental organizations, such as the Organization of American States (OAS), the United Nations Commission on International Trade Law (UNCITRAL), the European Bank for Reconstruction and Development (EBRD), or other regional development banks. Only a limited number of national reporters answered the relevant questions in section D of the questionnaire.

The Secretariats of the Organization of American States and of UNCITRAL very generously either provided answers to the questions raised or submitted general comments on the topic and the instruments adopted by their respective organizations as well as on the coordination of governments' work in the three organizations and cooperation among them.

[23] For details, see Official Commentary to the UNIDROIT Model Law on Leasing, UNIDROIT 2010 – Study LIXA Doc. 24, *Uniform Law Review* (2010): 548–609.

[24] See, in particular, the first, second, fourth and eighth recitals of the Preamble.

[25] On the available types of instrument, see Roy Goode, Herbert Kronke and Ewan McKendrick, *supra* note 3, 5.07–5.16.

14.8.2 OAS Model Law and Model Regulations

The Organization of American States adopted the 2002 Model Inter-American Law on Secured Transactions and the 2009 Model Registry Regulations.[26] Mindful of the need for close coordination in all attempts to provide a consistent legal framework for asset-based, nonpossessory secured credit financing, UNIDROIT and the OAS Secretariat for Legal Affairs participated as observers in each other's work. The OAS, like UNIDROIT, places emphasis on a 'substance test' that should be used to examine the relationship between the parties to determine whether a transaction is a (true) lease or a security device. Secondly, the OAS Model Law, like the Cape Town instruments, recognizes that systems in which the law of leasing and the law of secured transactions compete against each other in the manner in which they provide (or do not provide) notice to third parties, are inherently inefficient, as they produce legal uncertainty concerning the applicable rules and the effect they have on priority. The OAS Model Law creates a uniform system for all nonpossessory interests in movable property by way of a single registry and priority system. Whereas the provisions relating to creation, priority and enforcement testify to the existence of a common core of benchmark principles, the design of the registration system under the Model Regulations reflect important differences not least due to the comprehensive scope of the Model Law as opposed to the narrow class of high-value mobile equipment contemplated by the Cape Town instruments.

While a number of OAS Member States have made use of the Model Law, a first assessment of the experience with law reform efforts based on the instrument points to as yet insufficient implementation.[27] Mexico being the only country that has ratified the Cape Town Convention and adopted the OAS Model Law it would appear worthwhile to closely monitor implementation and application of both instruments in that country.

14.8.3 UNCITRAL Legislative Guide

The UNCITRAL Legislative Guide on Secured Transactions, adopted on 14 December 2007, may be considered as an educational exercise for policy makers engaged in designing a system of secured-transactions law for their countries.[28] The document identifies and discusses substantive issues and problem areas as well as options for solutions and offers recommendations.

The Guide does not deal with security interests in high-value mobile equipment as covered by the Cape Town instruments. The notion of 'security right' (preferred to 'security interest') includes all types of right created by agreement to secure payment or other performance of an obligation, regardless of the apparent form of the transaction or the language used by the parties. It thus includes financial-lease rights if they function as an 'acquisition security right'. Security rights have to be registered in a notice-based public registry for third-party and priority effects.

As this is the first legislative guide developed in intergovernmental negotiations, the international law-reform community will be watching closely whether and, if so, how legislators will make use of both the exceedingly rich materials discussed and the recommendations. Viewed from the perspective of the Academy's query, i.e. the results of UNIDROIT's three decades of work on the unification and modernization of the law of financial leasing, it may be stated that the guide is a high quality complementary tool for legislators called upon to make informed choices at the intersection of the law of leases and secured financing.

14.9 Conclusions

Although the limited number of national reports submitted as well as the degree of detail provided in some of them call for caution in formulating results, it would appear safe to conclude that the law of financial leasing has advanced significantly since UNIDROIT took up work on this topic 35 years ago.

[26] The Model Law is reproduced in *Uniform Law Review* 262 (2002) with an introduction by Boris Kozolchyk and John Wilson, *The Organization of American States: The New Model Law on Secured Transactions* at 69; most recently, see John Wilson, "Model Registry Regulations under the Model Inter-American Law on Secured Transactions," *Uniform Law Review* 515 (2010).

[27] For a recent evaluation, see Alejandro Garro, "The OAS-sponsored Model Law on Secured Transactions: Gestation and Implementation," *Uniform Law Review* 391 (2010).

[28] For an overview, see Spiros Bazinas, "The Work of UNCITRAL on Security Interests," *Uniform Law Review* 315 (2010).

As mentioned *supra* 14.1, in many instances it will (outside the Cape Town context) not be possible to find hard evidence that certain choices made at the intergovernmental level have had identifiable effects domestically. However, this note of caution is not confined to this specific area of the law but reflects a more general experience in the process of harmonization of commercial law.

Finally, law reformers should take comfort from the finding that it was not a great design, such as a comprehensive instrument (be it a convention, be it a model law) that brought about the measure of harmonization achieved. It was incremental progress by sector, including trial-and-error approaches, especially in the early stages. Patience on the part of all involved, coupled with steadily increasing realism, is bearing fruit.

15 Insurance Contract Law Between Business Law and Consumer Protection[1]

Helmut Heiss

15.1 Preliminary Remarks

15.1.1 The Legal Systems Represented in the General Report

The present General Report draws upon 18 *national* reports. The country reports are from: Australia, Austria, Belgium, Brazil, the Czech Republic, Denmark, Finland, France, Germany, Greece, Italy, Japan, Norway, Portugal, Taiwan, United Kingdom, the United States and Venezuela.

The national reports do not restrict themselves to information regarding developments within a particular country but also describe, at least occasionally, legal trends in the *region* to which these countries belong. For instance, the national reporters were not only asked to discuss the economic significance of commercial insurance and consumer insurance in their countries, but also the commercial relevance of these types of insurance in the regions to which the countries reported on belong. Within the regional *legal* developments, the intensive harmonization efforts made by the *European Union* are of particular relevance. The General Report therefore refers to both *existing* European insurance law (the "*acquis communautaire*")[2] and the "Principles of European Insurance Contract Law (PEICL)", the recently published results of a scholarly project to establish a European insurance contract law.[3]

There are, moreover, also sporadic references to national legal systems which are *not* represented by the national reports. This applies, for example, to Swiss and Swedish law.

15.1.2 The Global Representativeness of the General Report

Using the 18 national reports, it is possible to cover the various regions of the world in which insurance is of particularly great importance. To some extent, this is almost comprehensive; however, it will in part only provide examples. There will, moreover, remain "unchartered territory" on the global map of insurance laws as drawn by this General Report.

By arranging the national reports according to regional factors and/or along the traditional lines of classification for *legal families* of the world[4], the following situation may be depicted: *Europe* is especially vigorously represented. This is clearly the case with regard to the law of the European *Union*. It also applies to an equivalent extent to the *continental* European legal traditions. With Germany, Austria and individual references to the legal situation in Switzerland, the

[1] III.A.4, Le droit des contrats d'assurance entre le droit des affaires et la protection des consommateurs.

[2] See, for example, Mönnich in Beckmann and Matusche-Beckmann (eds), *Versicherungsrechts-Handbuch* (2009) § 2.

[3] J Basedow, J Birds, MA Clarke, H Cousy and H Heiss (eds), *Principles of European Insurance Contract Law (PEICL)* (Sellier 2009).

[4] See, for example, Zweigert and Kötz, *Einführung in die Rechtsvergleichung* (3rd edn, 1996) 62f.

H. Heiss (✉)
Chair of Private, Comparative and Private International Law, University of Zurich, Zurich, Switzerland
e-mail: helmut.heiss@rwi.uzh.ch

K.B. Brown and D.V. Snyder (eds.), *General Reports of the XVIIIth Congress of the International Academy of Comparative Law/Rapports Généraux du XVIIIème Congrès de l'Académie Internationale de Droit Comparé*,
DOI 10.1007/978-94-007-2354-2_15, © Springer Science+Business Media B.V. 2012

Germanic legal systems have been dealt with *comprehensively*. Furthermore, Greece can be referred to in the context of the Germanic legal systems, as it tends to follow the German example especially where insurance contract law is concerned[5]. Represented in a similarly strong way are the *Roman legal systems*, since national reports from Belgium, France, Italy and Portugal have been written. The *Nordic legal systems* are also represented fairly well by Denmark, Finland and Norway. The same is, however, not true of *Central and Eastern European countries*, to which attention should be paid with regard to insurance law as in this respect they are still in a period of legal transformation. An individual national report, which must therefore be treated as a mere example of these systems, comes from the Czech Republic. Beyond continental Europe, the *common law* legal tradition is represented well since Australian law, which is very progressive with regard to insurance law, can drawn upon in addition to English and American law. As far as the *Asian* legal systems are concerned, Japan and Taiwan are two nations with highly developed market economies. These countries are only capable of representing a *section* of the living law in Asia. No conclusions can be drawn from this General Report for other countries, in particular the developing and emerging markets. Despite it being one of the largest regional insurance markets[6], *South/Latin America* is only represented by Brazil and Venezuela. As, however, the socio-economic conditions are likely to be similar among some of the other South American countries, it should be possible to extrapolate, albeit with caution, the findings made in Brazil and Venezuela. Systems of *religious law*, especially the laws of the Arab states, are without any representation. The same is true of the countries south of the Sahara, i.e. of *sub-Saharan Africa* in its entirety. The Arab states and sub-Saharan Africa both have distinct socio-economic characteristics. The findings of the General Report can, therefore, not simply be transferred to the countries in these regions. These regions – unfortunately – constitute the unchartered territory on the map drawn here.

[5]See, in general, Zweigert and Kötz, 154f.

[6]Brazil, Priscila Mathias Fichtner, Tomaz Tavares de Lyra and Marcela Levy, para 8.

15.1.3 Representativeness of the Report in Relation to Various Insurance Sectors

The title of the General Report suggests that modern insurance contract law roams somewhere *between* business law and consumer protection. This of course requires insurance contracts to, in theory, be available equally well as either commercial transactions or consumer transactions.

This is, however, clearly not the case for *reinsurance*. As an insurance contract concluded by two insurance companies, it can only ever be described as a b2b transaction, never as a b2c transaction. While it is indeed true that risks attached to reinsurance are part commercial and part consumer risks, such that the distribution of these risks on the direct insurance market is reflected on the reinsurance market, this by no means corresponds proportionately to the premium income received in the direct insurance market because the *quota share* for reinsurance can vary considerably depending on the individual branch of insurance concerned. Particularly for reinsurance of life assurance, which contains a savings element, the quota share is marginal as the accumulated savings do not need to be reinsured. Be that as it may, reinsurance will be *excluded* from the scope of this report as a necessary commercial transaction which can never be classified as a consumer transaction.

In contrast, the *direct* insurance sectors may, in principle, either be b2b or b2c transactions. Yet, distinctions must also be made in this regard. Some risks typically constitute the subject-matter of commercial insurance. To be counted among these are, in particular, insurance of transport vehicles (comprehensive or hull insurance), of goods in transit (cargo insurance) and of third party liability arising from transport (third party transport insurance), i.e. *marine* and *inland transportation insurance*. Despite the fact that transport insurance can also be concluded as a consumer transaction, e.g. as small craft insurance,[7] consumer contracts ultimately do not carry considerable weight in this sector. Conversely, there are insurance sectors

[7]Australian Insurance Contract Act 1984, s. 9 excludes marine insurance from its scope of application, 9A makes clear that this exception does not apply to small craft insurances which are "consumer marine insurances" while for instance; see McNaughton, Australia, para 39.

which generally only deal with *consumer risks*, such as *life assurance* and *private medical insurance*. Of course, such insurance is often taken out by an employer on behalf of his/her employees in the manner of a collective insurance contract. Consequently, the contract is concluded with a *businessperson* rather than with a consumer[8]. Yet, even in this situation, the underlying risks are of a private, not a commercial nature and the corresponding purpose of the insurance contract relates to the private sphere of the employee rather than business sphere of the employer. At the same time, the insured employees very frequently make the premiums payments to the employer and become an insured only after having opted for the insurance. In doing so, they, functionally speaking, equate to policyholders. For instance, they also require as much advice and information when deciding upon whether to sign up for the collective insurance as an insured as do individual policyholders in these sectors[9]. It is also striking that the employer, as the organizer of the collective insurance, to a certain extent undertakes both the sales and administrative tasks of an insurer. This distances him/her from the formal role as a policyholder and draws him/her closer to being an insurance intermediary. All of this creates considerable problems in relation to consumer protection and allows collective insurance concluded by employers to be examined critically through the lens of consumer protection law. In contrast, it would amount to an oversimplification of reality if one were to classify collective insurance taken out by an employer as a genuine commercial transaction.

Standing truly *between* business law and consumer protection, in contrast, are the common sectors of *property* and *liability insurance*. These can typically be taken out as part of a business transaction for commercial or professional purposes or, however, as consumer transactions for private purposes. In these sectors, the bipolarity of modern insurance contract law dealt with in this General Report must therefore primarily be noted.

However, the differentiation of transport insurance, life assurance and health insurance, as well as property and liability insurance described here does not justify excluding transport insurance, nor life and health insurance from the scope of this General Report. Life and health insurance are subject to the *general principles* of insurance contract law and are therefore exposed to the bipolarity of business law and consumer protection in the same way as other risks. This also applies to inland transportation insurance, which is frequently governed by general principles of national insurance contract law, such that elements of consumer law may also have an effect on these principles in inland transportation insurance. With regard to marine insurance, this only applies to a *lesser extent*. As it is often governed by special laws, the developments in general insurance law can only have an indirect impact.

15.2 Economic Aspects

15.2.1 General Remarks

The economic importance of insurance business as a whole as well as of individual sectors can be determined using various *parameters*. In addition to premium income, the volume of the insurance services provided and the profitability of individual sectors are also relevant indicators. However, as far as the *macroeconomic* impact of insurance and its individual sectors are concerned, the premium income appears to be the key point of reference. It is therefore this parameter on which the General Report will focus.

At this point, reinsurance will also continue to be excluded. The reason can be found in the economic context that reinsurance is only ever concluded between insurance companies and never as a consumer transaction.

Similar to the legal classification of sectors, as shown above, the economic categorization by insurers/associations of insurance companies of the volume of premiums in the individual insurance sectors does not follow the pattern of separating commercial/business risks on the one hand from consumer risks on the other. A distinction is also made here between life assurance, which very predominantly epitomizes a consumer transaction, and non-life insurance, which, in some sectors, chiefly covers commercial risks, but which combines commercial and consumer risks without distinction in many of the other sectors. Consequently, it is *not* possible to compare precisely the premium income from consumer transactions with that from

[8] Belgium, Herman Cousy, para 20; UK, David Hertzell, para 1.10.

[9] Portugal, Maria José Rangel de Mesquita, paras 46, 53f.

commercial risks. Nevertheless, the data cited in the national reports clearly demonstrate discernible trends, which moreover turn out to be quite uniform at the international level.

15.2.2 Economic Data in an Overall as well as a Differentiated View

When the premium volume is viewed in its *entirety* (excluding reinsurance, however), it becomes clear that *consumer* transactions currently *prevail*[10]. This picture emerges in particular by including *life* assurance into the overall view[11]. It should of course be pointed out that life assurance premiums are mostly characterized by the fact that they, in addition to containing a minor share of the risk, incorporate a fairly lofty savings element. The consequential cash value purpose of life assurance, for its own part, creates special requirements for protecting consumers, for example when calculating the surrender value on termination of the insurance policy prior to maturity or where the policyholder's share of the insurer's return on capital at expiration of the contract are concerned. With the exception of these consumer protection issues, which relate particularly to life assurance, the cash value function of life assurance does not represent a hazardous transaction for an insurer. It therefore becomes immediately clear that the accumulation of capital must be fully financed by each individual policyholder, which naturally means that the premium for the cash value life assurance must be especially high. This is a predominant reason why the premium income in typical consumer insurance sectors is much higher than in sectors of commercial insurance.

Taking this into consideration, it would make sense to make distinctions in the overall view and, subsequently, to examine *non-life* insurance by itself. Again, however, the overall economic picture shows that consumer transactions, measured according to their premium income, are at least balanced in comparison to commercial insurance[12]. The costs involved in protecting private funds are thus commensurate with the expense of protecting commercial assets. It becomes clear from this that, even when life assurance is excluded, considerable economic importance is attributed to consumer risks. Having taken this economic fact into account, it is unsurprising that consumer protection has also become increasingly more significant from a legal perspective.

15.3 Academic Perception

The economic data has revealed that nowadays consumer transactions are of the same importance as commercial insurance. The fact that insurance law is perceived by the law and legal academics as a part of commercial or general private law signals a similar trend. Where an insurance contract, viewed from its historic origins, is considered to be a commercial transaction and it will be researched and taught academically as a part of commercial law[13]. In its purest form, this is now only the case in a few countries, for example in Greece[14], Japan[15] and Taiwan[16]. Other countries are instead showing a tendency towards moving insurance law away from commercial law, either into general private law or, however, to establish it as a quasi-independent discipline. Belgian law, for example, which had initially placed insurance contracts definitively within commercial law, is displaying a tendency of allowing the discipline to become independent[17]. The same is true of Portugal where this development has been linked to the new codification of

[10]According to the following reports: Czech Republic, Josef Fiala and Marketa Selucka, para 3; Finland, Jaana Norio-Timonen, para 9; France, Sophie Gaudemet, para 10; Germany, Christian Armbrüster, para 1; Greece, Alexandra E. Douga, paras 1f; Italy, Diana Cerini, Giovanni Comandé, Maria Gagliardi and Onofrio Troiano, para 1; Japan, Yoshiro Yamano, para 1; Taiwan, Yu-Ting Lin, para 1; UK, David Hertzell, para 2; USA, Jeffrey E. Thomas, para 9; see also the figures presented by de Mesquita, Portugal, Appendix A.

[11]Denmark, Ivan Sørensen, para 1; Belgium, Herman Cousy, paras 18f; and Selucka, Czech Republic, Josef Fiala and Marketa Selucka, para 2; Finland, Jaana Norio-Timonen, para 1; Sophie Gaudemet, France, para 13; Germany, Christian Armbrüster, para 1; Italy, Diana Cerini, Giovanni Comandé, Maria Gagliardi and Onofrio Troiano, para 1; Taiwan, Yu-Ting Lin, para 3; USA, Jeffrey E. Thomas, paras 4, 7; see also the figures given by Fichtner, de Lyra, Levy, Brazil, Appendices A and B.

[12]Denmark, Ivan Sørensen, para 1; Finland, Jaana Norio-Timonen, para 3; Greece, Alexandra E. Douga, para 2; Italy, Diana Cerini, Giovanni Comandé, Maria Gagliardi and Onofrio Troiano, para 1; Japan, Yoshiro Yamano, para 1; Taiwan, Yu-Ting Lin, paras 1 to 3; see also the figures given by Schauer, Austria, paras 1f.

[13]Australia, Anne Naughton, para 13.

[14]Greece, Alexandra E. Douga, para 6.

[15]Japan, Yoshiro Yamano, para 8.

[16]Taiwan, Yu-Ting Lin, para 8.

[17]Belgium, Herman Cousy, paras 22f. Same for Venezuela, Baumeister, Venezuela, para 8.

insurance contract law in a self-contained piece of legislation[18]. In other countries, such as France and Germany, the fact that insurance law is being researched and taught independently of other disciplines is also likely to be due, at least in part, to the insurance contract laws having been codified in their own acts[19]. Since these acts were codified in the first half of the twentieth century (in 1908 in Germany, in 1930[20] in France,) this process is now complete in both countries. A similar development appears to have taken place in Brazil, which has not led insurance law from being a part of commercial law to being a single discipline, but rather into general private law. Here, too, academics have astonishingly adhered to the decision of the legislature to codify insurance law as a part of the new Civil Code of 2002; the former had previously been modified to the benefit of consumers by the Consumer Protection Act in 1999[21]. The same is true of the Czech Republic where, in accordance with legislation on the matter, insurance law is to a large extent assigned to private law[22]. Likewise, the situation in Denmark[23] and Finland,[24] where insurance law is deemed to belong to general private law, despite there being separate codifications in both countries. In Austria[25] and Italy[26], this matter has yet to be settled. Both general private law and commercial law lawyers are among the Austrian academics actively researching and teaching insurance law. In Italy, no answer has been provided to this issue because it is unlikely that the provisions in the new separate codification can be classified exclusively under either general private law or commercial law[27]. A natural assumption is that, following the independent codification, there are also signs here of a development towards a separate discipline, which is to be positioned between general private and commercial law. No clear classification is provided among the common law jurisdictions. While insurance law tends to be assigned to commercial law in Australia[28], it is simply regarded as a part of contract law, which subsumes both general and commercial contract law, in England[29] and the USA[30]. The Australian position may be influenced by the fact that insurance law is currently a "neglected area of scholarship"[31] and the leading texts on the subject are published by legal practitioners.

Being able to identify a trend using this information is most likely among the codified legal systems, where academic scholars predominantly imitate the approach codified by their national legislatures. This in turn, and this makes sense, is oriented towards the importance of insurance in commercial and private customer business. As private customer business has relatively gained significance, insurance law has detached from general commercial law and is developing itself, for the most part, into a separate discipline, although at times also within general private law. In this respect, law-making and legal research emulates business developments, albeit with a certain time delay.

15.4 Procedural Aspects

15.4.1 General Remarks

Before dealing with the possible distinctions between consumer insurance and commercial insurance in substantive law, procedural aspects with a view to insurance law in practice will be addressed. The considerations are based on the idea that the *mode* of application and enforcement of the law is ultimately dependent on which *proceedings* there are in place and on the type of *institution* by which the cases will be heard and decided. It is therefore possible to assume that special *commercial courts* will, on the one hand, have a higher degree of specialization and expert knowledge of insurance law; in their mentality, on the

[18] Portugal, Maria José Rangel de Mesquita, paras 7f.

[19] France, Sophie Gaudemet, para 17; Germany, Christian Armbrüster, para 8.

[20] The first independent insurance legislation in France was the law on land insurance of 1930 which was finally integrated into the Insurance Code in 1976 together with the law on marine insurance and the law on insurance activities, France, Sophie Gaudemet, paras 16f.

[21] Brazil, Priscila Mathias Fichtner, Tomaz Tavares de Lyra and Marcela Levy, paras 12f.

[22] Czech Republic, Josef Fiala and Marketa Selucka, para 10.

[23] Denmark, Ivan Sørensen, para 3.

[24] Finland, Jaana Norio-Timonen, para 6.

[25] Austria, Martin Schauer, paras 8f.

[26] Italy, Diana Cerini, Giovanni Comandé, Maria Gagliardi and Onofrio Troiano, paras 4f.

[27] Italy, Diana Cerini, Giovanni Comandé, Maria Gagliardi and Onofrio Troiano, para 7.

[28] Australia, Anne Naughton, paras 13f.

[29] UK, David Hertzell, para 7.

[30] USA, Jeffrey E. Thomas, paras 10f.

[31] Australia, Anne Naughton, para 16.

other hand, they are more likely to concentrate on the smooth running of commercial matters than to be concerned with protecting the consumer as the weaker contracting party. *General courts* hearing insurance cases may instead not provide the same degree of specialization and at the same time lack a commercial or consumer-oriented mentality. In contrast, special *consumer courts* and institutions offering modes of *alternative dispute resolution* specifically to consumer policyholders may provide a high degree of specialization and knowledge in insurance law combined with a strong consumer mentality.

15.4.2 Insurance Disputes and State Courts

Yet, the findings in the national reports illustrate that actions concerning insurance matters are generally heard before *general courts* of law[32]. General civil law judges, consequently, decide on actions concerning insurance law without having any special competency in commercial or consumer law or being specially guided by particular considerations of commercial or consumer law. There are, however, separate courts or senates in numerous countries which deal with the law of commercial insurance[33], in particular of *marine insurance*[34]. To the extent that the competence of the commercial court depends on the branch of insurance involved in the particular case, it can be presumed that specific case law is created in these branches. However, the Austrian[35] and Belgian[36] legal systems also demonstrate the opposite phenomenon. In these two countries, there are special commercial courts hearing cases of commercial insurance as well as consumer insurance[37]. Due to the character of the insurer as a merchant, an insurance contract is considered a commercial transaction and, thus, dealt with by a commercial court even if the policyholder is a consumer. In this respect, commercial and consumer insurance benefit from the "specialist knowledge" of such commercial law judges. However, despite the lack of empirical evidence on this point, it seems doubtful that these judges have the "consumer law orientation" required for modern situations.

15.4.3 Arbitration of Commercial Insurance Disputes

This clearly applies all the more to the observation made in many of the national reports that commercial insurance contracts often contain *arbitration clauses.*[38] These lead to a private dispute resolution mechanism, which is based on the principle of party autonomy and is frequently managed by *insurance experts* which may but do not have to be legal experts. Most of the decisions reached by these arbitral tribunals are not published, which prevents a body of case law from being developed. Thus, commercial insurances subject to arbitration live in a world of their own if looked upon from a procedural point of view.

15.4.4 Alternative Resolution of Consumer Disputes

Where insurance matters are within the competence of general courts, legal actions concerning commercial insurance are often distinguished from those relating to consumer insurance by the value of the claim in dispute. Whereas the high value of claims in commercial matters often justifies incurring the costs of proceedings in a court of law, such costs quite frequently prevent consumer disputes being brought to court. This leads to deficiencies in the legal protection offered by the court

[32]Australia, Anne Naughton, para 17; Czech Republic, Josef Fiala and Marketa Selucka, para 13, 14; Finland, Jaana Norio-Timonen, paras 10, 11; in principle also Armbrüster, Germany, paras 12f; Greece, Alexandra E. Douga, paras 9f; Italy, Diana Cerini, Giovanni Comandé, Maria Gagliardi and Onofrio Troiano, paras 16f; Japan, Yoshiro Yamano, paras 11f; Norway, Kaja de Vibe Malling, paras 10f; Portugal, Maria José Rangel de Mesquita, paras 15f, 20f.; Taiwan, Yu-Ting Lin, paras 11f; USA, Jeffrey E. Thomas, para 13.

[33]For example, in France, insurance disputes fall within the competence of commercial courts when both parties to the contract are merchants and within the competence of general civil courts in any other case (eg in case of disputes concerning mutual insurance), France, Sophie Gaudemet, paras 47f; see also Sørensen, Denmark, para 6.

[34]Portugal, Maria José Rangel de Mesquita, para 18; Venezuela, Alberto Baumeister Toledo, para 8.

[35]Austria, Martin Schauer, para 14.

[36]Belgium, Herman Cousy, paras 29f.

[37]The same was true for Venezuela until recently; for economical reasons they had to cancel this special competence and now all insurance matters, except marine insurance, are heard before general civil courts, Venezuela, Alberto Baumeister Toledo, para 11.

[38]See Cerini, Comandé, Gagliardi and Troiano, Italy, para 15; Norway, Kaja de Vibe Malling, para 11; Portugal, Maria José Rangel de Mesquita, para 21; UK, David Hertzell, para 10.

system for consumer issues. It is therefore unsurprising that efforts are being made to introduce special *small claims procedures* into the judicial system. The European Union has made *FINNET*, a cross-border out-of-court complaint scheme, available especially for financial services[39]. In the Australian and Brazilian court systems, there are *separate procedures* for small claims[40]; in Brazil, these are particular proceedings specifically for actions brought by consumers[41]. The institution of the *justice of the peace* seems to fulfill a similar function in Portugal[42]. Yet, most countries treat small consumer claims and commercial claims alike.

Most reporting countries use *alternative dispute resolution* (ADR) in order to overcome consumer problems[43]. Though most mechanisms of alternative dispute resolution do not restrict access to private end-consumers, with some exceptions such as, for instance, the German Insurance Ombudsman[44] or also pursuant to Directive 2002/65/EC (Distance Marketing Directive)[45] and Directive 2002/92/EC (Insurance Mediation Directive,)[46] such mechanisms play a vital role in consumer insurance and less a role in commercial insurance. A typical example of such mechanisms is *ombudsmen*, who may be special insurance ombudsmen, consumer ombudsmen or ombudsmen concerned with issues relating to financial services[47] or general consumer ombudsmen[48]. The importance of such alternative dispute resolution mechanisms is underlined by the fact that Article 1:302 of the Principles of European Insurance Contract Law (PEICL) refers in this respect to the existing national systems of alternative dispute resolution, which will also have effect where the PEICL are applicable even though the PEICL themselves do not provide for a separate system of alternative dispute resolution.

The significance of these ombudsmen in the individual reporting countries continues to vary considerably. This is true, first, with regard to the number of cases. While, for example, reports from England show that consumer claims are to all intents and purposes dealt with exclusively by the Financial Ombudsman Service[49], the same cannot be said of the proceedings before the German Insurance Ombudsman[50]. Second, the authority of the ombudsmen also differs to a large extent from country to country. They do not always have the authority to make decisions[51] and even where they do, the quality of these decisions is characterized by whether or not they are binding on insurance companies[52]. Third, the amount the claim in dispute is worth varies enormously. In Australia, for example, a

[39]http://ec.europa.eu/internal_market/fin-net/index_en.htm.

[40]Australia, Anne Naughton, paras 20f; Brazil, Priscila Mathias Fichtner, Tomaz Tavares de Lyra and Marcela Levy, paras 27f.

[41]Brazil, Priscila Mathias Fichtner, Tomaz Tavares de Lyra and Marcela Levy, para 27.

[42]Portugal, Maria José Rangel de Mesquita, para 17.

[43]Australia, Anne Naughton, paras 17f; Austria, Martin Schauer, paras 16f; Belgium, Herman Cousy, paras 36f; Brazil, Priscila Mathias Fichtner, Tomaz Tavares de Lyra and Marcela Levy, para 30; Denmark, Ivan Sørensen, para 7; Finland, Jaana Norio-Timonen, paras 11f; France, Sophie Gaudemet, paras 51f; Germany, Christian Armbrüster, paras 14f; Greece, Alexandra E. Douga, paras 18f; Italy, Diana Cerini, Giovanni Comandé, Maria Gagliardi and Onofrio Troiano, paras 17f; Japan, Yoshiro Yamano, para 12; Norway, Kaja de Vibe Malling, paras 13f; Portugal, Maria José Rangel de Mesquita, paras 21f; Taiwan, Yu-Ting Lin, paras 12f; Hertzell, UK, David Hertzell, para 11; the situation is different in Venezuela where alternative dispute resolution mechanisms for consumer disputes play no practical role, Venezuela, Alberto Baumeister Toledo, paras 16f.

[44]Germany, Christian Armbrüster, paras 14f.

[45]Directive 2002/65/EC of the European Parliament and of the Council of 23 September 2002 concerning the distance marketing of consumer financial services and amending Council Directive 90/619/EEC and Directives 97/7/EC and 98/27/EC [2002] OJ L271/16.

[46]Directive 2002/92/EC of the European Parliament and of the Council of 9 December 2002 on insurance mediation [2003] OJ L9/3.

[47]Australia, Anne Naughton, paras 20f; UK, David Hertzell, para 11.

[48]In France, a distinctive ombudsmen (médiateur) is competent depending on whether the dispute arises between a private person and an insurance company (médiateur FFSA) or a private person and a mutual (médiateur GEMA), France, Sophie Gaudemet, para 51; Greece, Alexandra E. Douga, para 18; Norway, Kaja de Vibe Malling, para 13.

[49]UK, David Hertzell, para 11.

[50]Germany, Christian Armbrüster, paras 14f.

[51]With regard to the different competences of an ombudsman office, see: Australia, Anne Naughton, para 29; Austria, Martin Schauer, para 18; Belgium, Herman Cousy, paras 43f; France, Sophie Gaudemet, para 53; Christian Armbrüster, Germany, paras 14f; Greece, Alexandra E. Douga, paras 18f; Norway Kaja de Vibe Malling, paras 14f; Portugal, Maria José Rangel de Mesquita, para 24; UK, David Hertzell, para 11. In Switzerland, the Insurance Ombudsman deals with the entire range of issues relating to private insurance, including claims of third parties. The Swiss Insurance Ombudsman does not however act as a judge or arbitrator nor does it take, impose or enforce any decisions (for details see: http://www.ombudsman-assurance.ch/index.html).

[52]This may depend on the individual case, see Armbrüster, Germany, para 15; Greece, Alexandra E. Douga, para 20; Taiwan, Yu-Ting Lin, para 13; In France, the opinion of the médiateur in a case between a private person and a mutual is binding on the mutual, France, Sophie Gaudemet, para 53.

matter concerning insurance amounting up to 500,000 Australian dollars may be heard by the Financial Ombudsman Service[53], whereas the German Ombudsman is limited to hearing disputes worth up to 80,000 euros and its decisions will only be binding on the insurer in disputes worth up to 5,000 euros[54]. Fourth, the respective institutions have traditions of varying length and consequently different degrees of experience[55].

In any event, the more the hurdles of the court system induce consumers to turn to alternative dispute resolution mechanisms, the more established becomes a separate *consumer case law*, as for example can undoubtedly be seen in England[56]. In addition, the more the bodies responsible for alternative dispute resolution *publish* the reports of their cases, the more generally binding the precedents will become, until they are consolidated as "*soft* case law" or even as general insurance *codes of conduct* as known, for instance, in England[57] and Australia[58]. Since the main importance of mediation by ombudsmen lies in the consumer field, a corresponding orientation towards consumer protection is inherent in the decisions or recommendations of the ombudsmen. This holds true despite the fact that most of the existing national ombudsmen institutions are, in principle, also accessible to small businesses.

15.4.5 Collective (Consumer) Law Enforcement: Pre-emptive Actions and Class Actions

In addition to the individual legal protection provided by alternative dispute resolution mechanisms, special importance is attached to the *collective* mechanisms of legal protection precisely for consumer issues. In this regard, however, it is generally *pre-emptive* legal protection, rather than the enforcement of individual claims which are concerned. The latter can be made as a *class action*, although this is only common in a few countries[59]. Even there, this form of action does not appear to be of much practical importance, except in the USA[60]. The American national report evinces that the disputes which are the subject of class actions are frequently consumer cases[61]. It is, however, not possible to foresee whether this type of legal protection will ever become available on a considerable scale outside of the USA. The German legislature has, for example, not introduced a class action in insurance matters but authorized interest groups to *represent* the claimant and thus to finance the individual claim before court[62]. This does not reduce the costs of consumer claims but takes away the preventive burden of such costs from the individual consumer. In this way, actions based on claims which are also of significance for other consumers may be sustained and relevant case law will be created.

Of greatest significance is, on the other hand, the pre-emptive legal protection provided by so called *injunctions*. They predominantly serve, albeit often not solely, the enforcement of consumer interests. Such actions are in part only available for issues concerning consumers, a concept which underlies, for instance, Directive 2009/22/EC (Injunctions Directive,)[63] the Brazilian Consumer Protection Law[64] and the Japanese Consumer Contract Act[65]. Where such restrictions are not in place, applications for injunctions are made particularly often by consumer protection associations, leading consumers to be the main field of focus[66]. With regard to the relevance of injunctions in insurance matters, the national reports demonstrate that applications

[53] Australia, Anne Naughton, para 30.

[54] Germany, Christian Armbrüster, para 15.

[55] The institution of an insurance ombudsman is still very young in some countries; see for example: Australia, Anne Naughton, para 20; Austria, Martin Schauer, para 18; Greece, Alexandra E. Douga, para 18; Portugal, Maria José Rangel de Mesquita, para 24.

[56] UK, David Hertzell, para 11.

[57] UK, David Hertzell, para 11.

[58] Australia, Anne Naughton, para 32 (even though a direct influence of the FOS decisions is not mentioned, the FOS is charged with monitoring compliance with the Code of Conduct).

[59] USA, Jeffrey E. Thomas, para 14; Finland introduced a class action for consumers in 2007, but it has never been used, see Norio-Timonen, Finland, para 14; for a possible future class action in Belgium and Italy, see Cousy, Belgium, para 55; Italy, Diana Cerini, Giovanni Comandé, Maria Gagliardi and Onofrio Troiano, para 21.

[60] USA, Jeffrey E. Thomas, para 14.

[61] USA, Jeffrey E. Thomas, para 14.

[62] Germany, Christian Armbrüster, para 18; in France, the French Consumer Code also authorizes interest groups which have been mandated by at least two consumers to bring an action against unfair contract terms, France, Sophie Gaudemet, paras 56f.

[63] Directive 2009/22/EC of the European Parliament and of the Council of 23 April 2009 on injunctions for the protection of consumers' interests [2009] OJ L110/30.

[64] Brazil, Priscila Mathias Fichtner, Tomaz Tavares de Lyra and Marcela Levy, paras 31f.

[65] Japan, para 13.

[66] See for example Armbrüster, Germany, para 17 (*Verbandsklage*); Austria, Martin Schauer, para 20.

against *unfair terms* in general policy conditions in particular are concerned[67]. Consequently, these applications are of acute importance for the *entire market* with regard to the drafting of contracts and designing of products by the insurer. As, for example, the numerous applications for injunctions made in Germany in the field of life assurance evidence, such instruments can have dramatic effects[68]. For this reason, the Principles of European Insurance Contract Law (PEICL) make a reference in their Art 1:301 to Directive 2009/22/EC (Injunctions Directive)[69] and make injunctions available for any infringement of the PEICL.

15.4.6 The Role of Insurance Supervision

Insurance supervision is, in contrast, orientated at safeguarding the interests of the insured as part of the collective whole, without distinguishing fundamentally between consumers and businesses[70]. There are only few special supervisory rules for consumer transactions, for example those contained in the English ICOBS[71]. Similarly in Australia, the Securities and Investment Commission Act 2001 contains rules which are weighted according to the value of the transaction, leading to the emergence of consumer protection law albeit not formally enacted as such[72]. In Belgium, too, the financial regulatory authority will in future be able to examine the integrity of advertising for investment business and compliance with the so-called MiFID Directive on an individual basis. It is envisaged that the corresponding rules will also be applied to insurance companies[73]. Furthermore, in spite of the absence of a formal distinction between consumer and business insurance, numerous systems tend to shift the *main focus of supervision* to branches which are typically associated with *consumer* contracts[74]. Nevertheless, the purpose of the supervisory board remains to protect the insured persons as a whole rather than to guard their individual interests. This may nevertheless be of great significance to individual consumers especially when supervisory authorities approve general policy conditions, as appears to be the case in Japan[75]. Within the EU, however, legal requirements for an ex ante approval of general policy conditions have almost completely been abolished[76].

With regard to the *individual* complaints made to supervisory authorities, the national report on American law emphasizes that state supervision plays hardly any role in enforcing individual consumer claims[77].

[67] Belgium, Herman Cousy, para 70; Czech Republic, Josef Fiala and Marketa Selucka, para 25; Germany, Christian Armbrüster, para 22.

[68] Germany, Christian Armbrüster, para 22.

[69] Directive 2009/22/EC of the European Parliament and of the Council of 23 April 2009 on injunctions for the protection of consumers' interests [2009] OJ L110/30.

[70] Australia, Anne Naughton, para 32; Brazil, Priscila Mathias Fichtner, Tomaz Tavares de Lyra and Marcela Levy, para 34; Czech Republic, Josef Fiala and Marketa Selucka, para 17; Finland, Jaana Norio-Timonen, para 15; Japan, Yoshiro Yamano, para 14; Norway, Kaja de Vibe Malling, paras 25f; Portugal, Maria José Rangel de Mesquita, paras 31f. In Switzerland, the Swiss Financial Market Supervisory Authority (FINMA) supervises private insurers engaged in accident and health insurance; mandatory basic health insurance and the Swiss Accident Insurance Fund (SUVA) are primarily supervised by the Swiss Federal Office of Public Health (FOPH). Key matters of consumer protection are dealt with by the Ombudsman of Private Insurance and SUVA, the Ombudsman for Health Insurance, or the Swiss National Guarantee Fund in respect of mandatory motor vehicle liability insurance. For details see: http://www.finma.ch/e/Pages/default.aspx.

[71] UK, David Hertzell, para 13.

[72] Australia, Anne Naughton, para 37.

[73] Belgium, Herman Cousy, para 58.

[74] Belgium, Herman Cousy, para 89; Finland, Jaana Norio-Timonen, para 14; Germany, Christian Armbrüster, para 24; Greece, Alexandra E. Douga, para 23; Italy, Diana Cerini, Giovanni Comandé, Maria Gagliardi and Onofrio Troiano, para 22; Portugal, Maria José Rangel de Mesquita, para 32.

[75] Japan, Yoshiro Yamano, para 27. In theory, the same seems to be the case in Venezuela, Baumeister, Venezuela, para 29. One of the key objectives of the Swiss FINMA is also to protect insured persons against abusive contractual conditions and disadvantages resulting from unequal treatment that is not legally or actuarially justifiable.

[76] Arts 181 and 182 of Directive 2009/138/EC of the European Parliament and of the Council of 25 November 2009 on the taking avoid-up and pursuit of the business of Insurance and Reinsurance (Solvency II) [2009] OJ L335/1.

[77] Australia, Anne Naughton, para 41; Austria, Martin Schauer, para 23; Belgium, Herman Cousy, para 61; Czech Republic, Josef Fiala and Marketa Selucka, paras 18f; Finland, Jaana Norio-Timonen, para 17; France, Sophie Gaudemet, para 16; Germany, Christian Armbrüster, para 26; Greece, Alexandra E. Douga, para 24; Italy, Diana Cerini, Giovanni Comandé, Maria Gagliardi and Onofrio Troiano, para 23; Japan, Yoshiro Yamano, para 15; Norway, Kaja de Vibe Malling, para 28; Portugal, Maria José Rangel de Mesquita, para 33; Taiwan, Yu-Ting Lin, para 15; Venezuela, Alberto Baumeister Toledo, para 19; insurance contract law is still governed in the Civil and/or Commercial Code in Brazil, Priscila Mathias Fichtner, Tomaz Tavares de Lyra and Marcela Levy para 35; or is still uncodified and functions as a mixture of legislation and court decisions in the UK: UK, David Hertzell, para 14. For obvious reasons, there is no uniformity in insurance contract law regulation in the USA: Thomas, USA, para 19. USA, Jeffrey E. Thomas, para 18. The situation is different in France where the Autorité de Contròle des Assurances et des Mutuelles also inspects insurance contracts upon individual complaints.

Regulatory law, thus, also confirms the particular need for alternative dispute resolution methods for consumer insurance.

15.5 Legislation

15.5.1 Insurance Contract Law in General Does Not Differentiate between Consumer and Commercial Insurance

The legislation concerning insurance matters presents, at least at first glance, a fairly clear overall picture. In virtually all of the national reports, insurance contract law today constitutes the subject of *special legislation*. The insurance contract is therefore essentially no longer governed in a general civil code nor in a commercial code, but rather in an insurance contract act[78]. An exception was formed by Japanese law which traditionally had regulated insurance in its Commercial Code. This exception has, however, been abolished by the entry into force of the Japanese Insurance Act on 1st April 2010[79].

This also applies to marine insurance as long as it is regulated in a separate piece of legislation, such as the Marine Insurance Acts as found in the common law jurisdictions of England[80] and Australia[81]. However, in several countries, marine insurance is regulated within a commercial code[82] and, therefore, more integrated into general commercial law.

In general, *no distinction* is made by the insurance contract acts between consumer and commercial insurance contracts[83]. Where insurance contracts are divided at all, this is done by privileging the typically commercial risks of marine insurance using a separate special law, which is usually characterized by a fairly inclusive principle of freedom to contract[84]. These findings can ultimately also even be projected on to the special case of Brazil, where, although the law of insurance contracts has been incorporated into and is governed by the Civil Code, no distinction is made between consumer and commercial insurance; marine insurance law is moreover dealt with separately in the Commercial Code[85].

A well known exception is presented by *Swedish* law. A separate consumer insurance act was enacted in 1980[86], which has now been absorbed into the new Insurance Contract Act of 2005, in which however consumer insurance is governed in special sections[87].

Special developments also appear to be taking place in *English* and *Scottish* law. In 2009, the Law Commission and the Scottish Law Commission published a report and a draft bill,[88] which deal with the policyholder's pre-contractual duties to disclose information specifically in relation to consumer insurance. The national report on the UK, however, indicates that the Law Commissions are in the process of drafting proposals for business insurance as well and, thus, consumer insurance legislation as proposed may only be an intermediate step towards a comprehensive regulation[89]. If, however, the draft bill is implemented, English insurance contract law will be divided by the respective legislation, at least in respect of pre-contractual disclosure duties, into a general insurance contract law which will remain based on case law, a marine insurance law which is codified in the Marine Insurance Act and a consumer insurance

[78] France, Sophie Gaudemet, para 57.

[79] Japan, Yoshiro Yamano, para 15.

[80] UK, David Hertzell, para 14.

[81] Australia, Anne Naughton, para 42.

[82] Austria, Martin Schauer, para 25; until 2008 Germany, Christian Armbrüster, para 9; Japan, Yoshiro Yamano, para 16.

[83] Australia, Anne Naughton, para 42; Austria, Martin Schauer, para 27; Belgium, Herman Cousy, para 62; Brazil, Priscila Mathias Fichtner, Tomaz Tavares de Lyra and Marcela Levy para 41; Czech Republic, Josef Fiala and Marketa Selucka, para 22; France, Sophie Gaudemet, para 1; Germany, Christian Armbrüster, para 29; Italy, Diana Cerini, Giovanni Comandé, Maria Gagliardi and Onofrio Troiano, paras 25f; Japan, Yoshiro Yamano, paras 16f; Norway, Kaja de Vibe Malling, para 35; Portugal, Maria José Rangel de Mesquita, para 35; Taiwan, Yu-Ting Lin, paras 16f; USA, Jeffrey E. Thomas, para 21; Venezuela, Alberto Baumeister Toledo, para 20. Some distinctions are made in other countries, Finland, Jaana Norio-Timonen, para 19; Greece, Alexandra E. Douga, para 26.

[84] Greece, Alexandra E. Douga, paras 24-29; Italy, Diana Cerini, Giovanni Comandé, Maria Gagliardi and Onofrio Troiano, para 4; UK, David Hertzell, para 7; Venezuela, Alberto Baumeister Toledo, para 19.

[85] Brazil, Priscila Mathias Fichtner, Tomaz Tavares de Lyra and Marcela Levy para 35.

[86] A translation of the 1980 Act ('CIA 1980') can be found in A Neal and A Victorin (eds), *Law and the Weaker Party: an Anglo-Swedish Comparative Study* (Professional Books, Abingdon, 1983), Vol III, 113.

[87] *Försäkringsavtalslag* (SFS 2005:104), Swedish text can be found at: http://www.notisum.se/rnp/sls/lag/20050104.htm.

[88] Law Commission and Scottish Law Commission, *Consumer Insurance Law: Pre-Contract Disclosure and Misrepresentation* (Law Com No 319, Scot Law Com No 219, 2009).

[89] UK, David Hertzell, para 15.

law providing special rules for consumers. As a result, the statutory law will to a certain degree reflect the situation which has already been reported in case law given the special rulings on consumer law by the Financial Ombudsman Service. In fact, existing English law already bears a tendency to treat consumer insurances differently. While English common law generally does not distinguish between consumers and policyholders carrying on a business, the special function of the Financial Ombudsman Service in matters relating to consumers and the use of the former Statement of General Insurance Practice 1986, despite this having been withdrawn in 2005, lead to a separate body of consumer insurance case law.[90] Moreover, under supervisory law, the "Insurance: Conduct of Business Sourcebook (ICOBS)" has been provided which safeguards the protection of both private policyholders and those carrying on a business; consumer-related issues are consistently dealt with specifically[91].

Tendencies towards a system of consumer protection in insurance contract law can also be identified in *Greek law*. In Greece, there is a series of basically mandatory provisions which can however expressly be made optional where the policyholder takes out insurance for a business purpose. This limits the mandatory character of these provisions, which are in no small number, to the field of consumer protection[92].

There are further *exceptions* to the general approach where *specific provisions* are limited in scope to consumer insurance. In France, without being systematical, consumer protection in insurance contract law is becoming stronger through the introduction of specific legislation and court activity[93]. Recently, some specific provisions to protect consumers in the context of insurance contracts were introduced into the Insurance Code[94] and two provisions of the Consumer Code are specifically concerning insurance contracts[95]. Furthermore, the provisions of the Insurance Code are generally applied by the courts taking into account the quality of the insured in the specific situations and some provisions of the Consumer Code are also applied by extension to insurance contracts[96]. In Australian law, there is one single provision which limits the scope of the policyholder's pre-contractual duty to disclose information with a view to consumer transactions[97]. Yet, even this rule does not directly hinge on the policyholder being a private end-consumer, but rather merely has a de facto impact on these contracts. Similarly in Austrian law, one lone provision is cited which is concerned with the duration of the insurance contract and was passed especially for consumer transactions[98]. The situation is also very similar in German law, where s. 214 of the Insurance Contract Act (VVG) has established an out-of-court complaint mechanism specifically for consumers[99]. There are also two provisions in the draft version of the new Swiss Insurance Contract Act that specifically concern consumer protection.[100] Finally, American law illustrates that special consumer protection can, at least rudimentarily, also be developed by case law. Thus, while the doctrine of reasonable expectations is not sharply limited to the area of consumer transactions, this is where it actually has an impact. Such rules can probably only be regarded as *exceptions which validate the rule* that policyholder protection extends to entrepreneurs in small and medium-sized businesses[101].

To sum up these reports altogether, it is at the most possible to state that general insurance contract law and consumer insurance contract law are drifting apart in Swedish law, to a much lesser degree in French law and maybe in future English statutory law.

---

[90] See supra 15.4.4.

[91] UK, David Hertzell, para 13.

[92] Greece, Alexandra E. Douga, paras 25f.

[93] Gaudemet, France, para 38.

[94] Insurance Code Art. L.112-2-1 (distance marketing), L.112-9 (doorstep selling), L. 113-15-1 (renewal of the contract), Gaudemet, France, paras 33-36.

[95] Consumer Code Art. L. 122-11-2 and L. 312-9, Gaudemet, France, para 37.

[96] Gaudemet, France, paras 28 and 39-45.

[97] Australia, Anne Naughton, para 44.

[98] Austria, Martin Schauer, para 27.

[99] Germany, Christian Armbrüster, para 33.

[100] Art. 5 of the E-VVG guarantees a minimum three-week binding period of the insurer's offer towards a consumer and Art. 104 of the E-VVG deals with the protection of consumer claims in the area of transport insurance. For the German text of the draft version of the Swiss Insurance Contract Act, see: http://www.efd.admin.ch/dokumentation/gesetzgebung/00571/01345/index.html.

[101] USA, Jeffrey E. Thomas, para 25.

15.5.2 General Consumer Law Applicable to Insurance Contracts

The situation is different when the question is not answered from the basis of insurance law, but rather from national *consumer protection law*, irrespective of whether it is provided for in national consumer codes as, for instance, in Austria[102], France[103], Japan[104] and Taiwan[105], or single consumer laws covering general issues such as the judicial control of contract terms under the Norwegian Formation of Contract Act (FCA) s. 37[106], or by several provisions in the general civil code, such as the German Civil Code[107]. Namely, to the extent that general consumer protection law is even applicable to insurance contracts, consumer protection laws supplement national insurance contract laws. In doing so, consumer insurance contract law is being created, which might perhaps often not be perceived as such. In this way, general consumer law does, for all intents and purposes, have a considerable impact on consumer insurance contracts. For instance, an application of the rules on judicial control of terms in consumer contracts to general policy conditions may bring product standards on national markets to a certain minimum level which will supplement the standards provided for by mandatory provisions of insurance contract law.

In principle, this analysis also applies to the existing *acquis communautaire*. Directive 1993/13/EEC (Unfair Contract Terms Directive,)[108] which is limited in scope to consumer contracts, also covers insurance. This is also the case for Directive 2002/65/EC (Distance Marketing Directive)[109] and Directive 2009/22/EC (Injunctions Directive)[110]. These directives especially strengthen European policyholder protection for consumer contracts. Ultimately, however, it is for a national legislature to decide whether those directives create consumer insurance law in a formal sense or not. While national legislatures are bound to enforce the consumer protection granted by the directives, they have the option to expand the subjective scope of protection to non-consumers such as small and medium-sized enterprises. For example, the German legislature has decided to expand the protection provided by both Directive 1993/13/EEC (Unfair Terms Directive)[111] as well as Directive 2002/65/EC (Distance Marketing Directive) to policyholders who take out insurance for business purposes[112]. Austria also applies the rules on unfair contract terms in favor of entrepreneurs[113], whereas the rules on the distance marketing of financial services remain restricted in scope to consumer contracts.[114] The same applies in France, where article L.112-2-1 of Insurance Code protects policyholders in distance marketing only insofar as they act without any direct relation with business purposes.[115]

Finally, it is interesting to observe, as the Italian national report does, that judicial control of general policy conditions which is restricted to consumer insurance contracts may ultimately also influence business insurance. At least in branches of insurance in which insurers apply the same general policy conditions to consumer insurance as well as to business insurance, a clause which is judged as unfair will disappear from the general conditions of the insurer with respect to consumer as well as business insurance[116].

15.5.3 "Consumerism" in the Insurance Contract Acts

As has been shown, legislation on insurance contracts is not usually concerned with developing separate consumer protection rules. Thus, insurance contract law

[102] Austria, Martin Schauer, para 28.

[103] France, Sophie Gaudemet, paras 21 and 39-45.

[104] Japan, Yoshiro Yamano, para 17.

[105] Taiwan, Yu-Ting Lin, para 19.

[106] Norway, Kaja de Vibe Malling, para 29.

[107] Germany, Christian Armbrüster, para 29.

[108] Council Directive 93/13/EEC of 5 April 1993 on unfair terms in consumer contracts [1993] OJ L95/29.

[109] Directive 2002/65/EC of the European Parliament and of the Council of 23 September 2002 concerning the distance marketing of consumer financial services and amending Council Directive 90/619/EEC and Directives 97/7/EC and 98/27/EC [2002] OJ L271/16.

[110] Directive 2009/22/EC of the European Parliament and of the Council of 23 April 2009 on injunctions for the protection of consumers' interests [2009] OJ L110/30.

[111] In view of unfair terms, consumer protection is enhanced to a certain extent by s. 310 (3) German Civil Code.

[112] Germany, Christian Armbrüster, paras 46f.

[113] Austria, Martin Schauer, para 52.

[114] See s. 1(1) of the Law on the Distance Selling of Financial Services.

[115] France, Sophie Gaudemet, para 33.

[116] Italy, Diana Cerini, Giovanni Comandé, Maria Gagliardi and Onofrio Troiano, para 36.

does not change into consumer law in a *formal* sense. Instead, recent insurance contract acts or reforms of such acts increasingly protect the policyholder, consumers as well as small and medium-sized enterprises. Thus, if one looks at *substance* rather than formal criteria, national insurance contract acts absorb typical *instruments*[117] of consumer protection and apply a *philosophy* of protecting the weaker party which mirrors the philosophy of consumer protection. In this way, "consumer" protection is noticeably developing into a *lodestar* for legislation in insurance matters internationally. Protection of the weaker contracting party, which is ultimately the goal of all consumer law in a broad sense, forms the fundamental basis of modern codifications of insurance law. This has been clearly expressed by the Australian legislature[118], and does not apply any the less to, for instance, the new German Insurance Contract Act which came into force in 2008[119].

In this regard, the general remarks made by *Herman Cousy*, which were by no means exclusively referring to Belgium, have been validated, according to which the modern codifications ultimately exhibit a *schizophrenic* character[120]. On the basis of his comments, three stages of development can, rather rudimentarily, be described. (1) The creation of insurance contract acts which are based on the conventional general policy conditions of insurance companies and turn insurance practice into their contents. In doing so, primary attention is not paid to protecting consumers, but quite on the contrary to protecting insurers and possibly the "community of insured people" which serves as a rather fictitious figure to justify harsh rules against insured persons. Hence, the codifications are particularly concerned with balancing out the risks among the "community" of the insured both fairly and mathematically correctly. This includes efforts by the legislatures to prevent fraudulent claims being brought against the insurer. (2) These codifications already contained rules *mitigating* the harsh results of insurance practice in favor of the policyholder or the insured, as the case may be. Periods of grace in cases of late payments of premium or requirements of fault and causation for an insurer to be freed from performance due to breach of warranties are just two examples which should be mentioned. (3) A genuine *consumer-protection-orientated thinking* first appeared in insurance contract law with the development of consumerism at the end of the 1950s. The more recent legislative acts have assimilated this idea and now also protect the policyholder, for example, from the effects of an *information asymmetry*. These legislative developments oriented towards consumer protection really do give the codifications a schizophrenic character as they protect both the insurer and the "community" of the insured from unwarranted claims by individual customers, whilst at the same time wishing to safeguard the claims of individuals and their enforcement in equal measure.

In practice, this entire development has been documented by the interaction between the *general policy conditions* and the insurance contract law codifications. The legislative rules, and this also includes in particular the legislation on marine insurance, which do not have a mandatory character are regularly and almost completely displaced by the contractual agreements and hence by an insurer's general policy conditions[121]. Predominantly only provisions which contain mandatory principles are of utmost relevance. This leads to the more modern laws entrusting the general policy conditions of the companies with the development of insurance *products*, whilst they restrict themselves to setting the *compulsory boundaries* of the companies' de facto power to regulate[122]. This approach also serves as the basis for the Principles of European Insurance Contract Law[123]. Therefore, while provisions protecting the insurer which are predominantly not mandatory in favor of the insurer lose their relevance in the living insurance law, protective rules which are mandatory in favor of the policyholder form the major, or at least the most relevant, part of modern insurance contract acts.

[117] As to those instruments, see infra 15.7.1.

[118] Australia, Anne Naughton, para 37.

[119] Germany, Christian Armbrüster, para 29. *Versicherungsrecht in Europa - Kernperspektiven am Ende des 20. Jahrhunderts*

[120] Belgium, Herman Cousy, para 16.

[121] See the historical explanation given by F Reichert-Facilides, 'Gesetzgebung in Versicherungssachen: Stand und Ausblick' in F Reichert-Facilides and AK Schnyder (eds), *Versicherungsrecht in Europa - Kernperspektiven am Ende des 20. Jahrhunderts* (2000) 1 (3); see also Austria, Martin Schauer, para 25.

[122] Reichert-Facilides (n 138) 6f considering the protection of the policyholder as the weaker party; see Austria, Martin Schauer, para 56.

[123] See Article 1:103 PEICL (Mandatory Character).

In *conclusion*, it can be stated: in their wording, the insurance contract acts display no or only very few tendencies towards consumer protection law. Their contents, however, are increasingly being filled with ideas from consumer protection law. At the same time, rules which incorporate such ideas regularly represent mandatory statutory law, which plays a crucial role in legal practice, while the importance of non-mandatory laws is reduced due to their displacement by the general policy conditions.

15.6 "Consumer" and "Commercial" Risks

As with consumer contract law in general, the question regarding the *demarcation* between consumer risks and commercial risks must be posed in relation to consumer insurance contract law. Whereas, in general consumer protection law, this issue turns out to be principally a technical legal problem concerning the definition of the consumer, it represents the main fundamental problem in insurance contract law of protecting the weaker contracting party. Since traditional systems of insurance contract law admit, in addition to the private end-consumers, small and medium-sized enterprises into the scope of protection, the issue is of key importance for the subjective scope of protection provided to the weaker party.

For the *European Union* region, there are certain specifications contained in primary as well as in secondary European private international law. The European Court of Justice, for example, in its judgment of 4th December 1986, Case 205/84 (*Commission v Germany*)[124], recognized protecting policyholders as being a national *general interest*, which can justify restrictions to fundamental freedoms (especially the freedoms of establishment[125] and to provide services)[126] in the European Union. In that case, the European Court of Justice, unlike in decisions concerning other legal areas, not only referred to consumer protection, but also used the wider expression of "protection of the policyholder". This broad protective approach is also reflected in secondary private international European law. Thus, the insurance law provisions in Regulation (EC) 44/2001 (Brussels I)[127] and Regulation (EC) 593/2008 (Rome I)[128], which are to a very large extent of a mandatory nature, not only protect the consumer but also every policyholder. It is merely so-called *large risks* that are not subject to such broadly mandatory provisions. With regard to the substantive *acquis communautaire*, the same is true of the few protective provisions favoring the policyholder in its contract law. When establishing duties of disclosure to the benefit of the policyholder, Art 36 of Directive 2002/83/EC (Life Assurance Consolidation Directive)[129], for example, does not differentiate between private end-consumers and policyholders carrying on a business. Pursuant to Art 12(4) of Directive 2002/92/EC (Insurance Mediation Directive)[130], such duties are only excluded in respect of large risk policyholders. This approach has also been adopted for the model law contained in the Principles of European Insurance Contract Law (PEICL), according to whose Art 1:103 para 1 only a few, exhaustively listed provisions are absolutely mandatory. In accordance with Art 1:103 para 2 of the PEICL, the rest of the rules are only mandatory when any derogation is to the benefit of the policyholder. Where, however, large risk insurance is concerned, the policyholder is not protected under Art 1:103 para 2 and there is freedom of contract in this regard.

On the whole, the delineation between *large risk* insurance and *mass risk* insurance, which also encompasses the risks of small and medium-sized enterprises, turns out to be vital when viewed from the perspective of European Union law. A line is drawn by European law between large risks and mass risks in Art 13 para

[124] Case 205/84 *Commission of the European Communities v Federal Republic of Germany* [1986] ECR 3755.

[125] Ibid, para 54.

[126] Ibid, para 27.

[127] Council Regulation (EC) No 44/2001 of 22 December 2000 on jurisdiction and the recognition and enforcement of judgments in civil and commercial matters [2001] OJ L12/1.

[128] Regulation (EC) No 593/2008 of the European Parliament and of the Council of 17 June 2008 on the law applicable to contractual obligations (Rome I) [2008] OJ L177/6.

[129] Art. 36 of the Directive 2002/83/EC of the European Parliament and of the Council of 5 November 2002 concerning life assurance [2002] OJ L345/1 to be replaced by Art. 185 of the Directive 2009/138/EC of the European Parliament and of the Council of 25 November 2009 on the taking-up and pursuit of the business of Insurance and Reinsurance (Solvency II) [2009] OJ L335/1.

[130] Directive 2002/92/EC of the European Parliament and of the Council of 9 December 2002 on insurance mediation [2003] OJ L9/3.

27 of Directive 2009/138/EC,[131] using a technical legal definition, which naturally also contains arbitrary elements. This reads:

"(27) *'large risks' means:*

(a) *risks classified under classes 4, 5, 6, 7, 11 and 12 in Part A of Annex I*[132]*;*

(b) *risks classified under classes 14 and 15 in Part A of Annex I*[133] *where the policy-holder is engaged professionally in an industrial or commercial activity or in one of the liberal professions, and the risks relate to such activity;*

(c) *risks classified under classes 3, 8, 9, 10, 13 and 16 in Part A of Annex I*[134] *in so far as the policy-holder exceeds the limits of at least two of the following criteria:*

  (i) *a balance-sheet total: of EUR 6,2 million;*

  (ii) *a net turnover, within the meaning of Fourth Council Directive 78/660/EEC of 25 July 1978 based on Article 54(3)(g) of the Treaty on the annual accounts of certain types of companies ([1978] OJ L222/11), of EUR 12,8 million;*

  (iii) *an average number of 250 employees during the financial year*

If the policyholder belongs to a group of undertakings for which consolidated accounts within the meaning of Directive 83/349/EEC are drawn up, the criteria set out in point (c) of the first subparagraph shall be applied on the basis of the consolidated accounts.

As in European Community law, the dual terms "commercial insurance" and "consumer insurance" have not become established in the national insurance contract legal systems, either. To a degree, Swedish law constitutes an exception.[135] In contrast, the national reports document that, in general, the legal systems do not distinguish between private policyholders and the policyholders who carry on a business, and that, by virtue of mandatory law, the subjective scope of protection goes beyond the narrow field of consumer protection.[136] In cases where there are rules which specifically protect private end-consumers, these represent exceptional provisions.[137]

This situation raises the question of which limits there are to policyholder protection if it is not confined to consumers in the usual way. A look at the national reports shows that to date only a handful of countries have adopted into insurance contract law the technical distinction, found in European law, between *large* and *mass risks*. Germany[138], in particular, but also the France[139] Czech Republic[140] should be pointed out. Norway and Portugal are pursuing similar approaches[141]. American law demonstrates that case law also leads to similar distinctions, namely when large insurance customers are excluded from the protective elements of common law by the "sophisticated insured" doctrine[142]. A tendency towards confining policyholder protection to mass risks can also be identified in the laws of Belgium and Denmark[143]. Belgian law, as a matter of principle, protects every policyholder, but restricts certain protective rules to so-called contracts covering mass risks. This indirectly leads to insurance of large

---

[131] Directive 2009/138/EC of the European Parliament and of the Council of 25 November 2009 on the taking-up and pursuit of the business of Insurance and Reinsurance (Solvency II) [2009] OJ L335/1.

[132] The specified risks are:

4. Railway rolling stock
5. Aircraft
6. Ships (sea, lake and river and canal vessels)
7. Goods in transit (including merchandise, baggage, and all other goods)

...

11. Aircraft liability
12. Liability for ships (sea, lake and river and canal vessels)...
16. Miscellaneous financial loss

[133] The specified risks are:

14. Credit
15. Suretyship

[134] The specified risks are:

8. Fire and natural forces
9. Other damage to property

...

13. General liability

...

16. Miscellaneous financial loss

[135] See supra 15.5.1.

[136] See supra 15.5.1.

[137] See supra 15.5.1.

[138] Germany, Christian Armbrüster, para 30.

[139] France, Sophie Gaudemet, paras 23-27.

[140] Czech Republic, Josef Fiala and Marketa Selucka, para 23.

[141] Norway, Kaja de Vibe Malling, para 35; Portugal, Maria José Rangel de Mesquita, para 36.

[142] USA, Jeffrey E. Thomas, para 24.

[143] Belgium, Herman Cousy, paras 62f.

risks being excluded[144]. *Another approach* is taken by Finnish law, which protects the policyholder if he/she is a consumer or an undertaking which can be compared to a consumer. This delineation of the subjective scope of policyholder protection is likely to be considerably narrower than by confining protection to mass risks[145]. A third, rather *traditional approach* is taken by Austria[146] and Japan[147]. With regard to the scope of protection, these legal systems do not distinguish between large and mass risks, but rather exclude typical commercial risks, in particular those associated with transport insurance, from the scope of application of the insurance contract act or at least from the mandatory nature of its provisions[148].

15.7 Substantive Aspects

15.7.1 "Consumer Rights" in Insurance Contract Law

It has been observed in this Report that with a view to the topic of consumer protection insurance contract law is a rather *monolithic* branch of law which does not traditionally differentiate between consumer and types of commercial contracts. In contrast, some types of commercial insurance, such as reinsurance and frequently marine insurance, are regulated by their own legislation and establish something close to a *commercial* insurance contract law.

However, in *substance* consumer law has penetrated insurance contract law to a considerable extent. This development has mainly taken place in two ways: Consumerism from the 1950s onward has led to the creation of *consumer protection laws* which apply to insurance contracts and create consumer insurance law, even though they do not contain insurance contract law strictu sensu[149]. Consumerism has also led legislature to amend national insurance contract acts by implanting *instruments of consumer protection* even though the personal scope of application of these acts extends to entrepreneurs[150]. In substance, therefore, we can observe that insurance contract acts are increasingly gaining the characteristics of a consumer protection law.

A typical example of a substantive consumer rule which heavily influences the living law of insurance even though it is not part of insurance contract law strictu sensu is the protection afforded against *unfair contract terms*[151]. Insurance is a mass business by nature which can only be run with the help of general policy conditions. Obviously, any judicial control of general contract terms will be of strong influence on general policy conditions. General policy conditions describe the cover afforded by the insurer and, thus, control of general conditions may directly influence the insurance products as offered in a particular market. In this respect, general rules on judicial control of unfair terms have a much more significant effect on insurance contracts than on other branches of law. The lively and quite contradictory debate we find on the issue whether Directive 1993/13/EEC (Unfair Terms Directive) allows judicial control of exclusion clauses evidences the impact of such control on insurance contracts. And the national reports, especially on German and Belgian law, show that judicial control of insurance contract terms within proceedings for injunctions for the protection of consumers' interests have had considerable influence on the insurance markets[152] and mutuals.[153]

Typical examples of consumer rules penetrating the insurance contract acts are rights of the policyholder to withdraw (*cooling off* period)[154], to obtain *information* and *advice* from the insurer, agent and/or

[144] Belgium, Herman Cousy, paras 62f.

[145] Finland, Jaana Norio-Timonen, paras 22f.

[146] Austria, Martin Schauer, paras 36f.

[147] Japan, Yoshiro Yamano, paras 20f.

[148] Austria, Martin Schauer, para 38; Japan, Yoshiro Yamano, para 20.

[149] Australia, Anne Naughton, paras 50f; Belgium, Herman Cousy, paras 67f; Brazil, Priscila Mathias Fichtner, Tomaz Tavares de Lyra and Marcela Levy, para 52; France, Sophie Gaudemet, para 37; Portugal, Maria José Rangel de Mesquita, para 69.

[150] Finland, Jaana Norio-Timonen, paras 24f; Taiwan, Yu-Ting Lin, para 22.

[151] Australia, Anne Naughton, para 46.

[152] Germany, Christian Armbrüster, paras 46f.

[153] France, Sophie Gaudemet, para 57.

[154] Czech Republic, Josef Fiala and Marketa Selucka, para 28; Germany, Christian Armbrüster, para 40; Greece, Alexandra E. Douga, para 35; Italy, Diana Cerini, Giovanni Comandé, Maria Gagliardi and Onofrio Troiano, para 41; Japan, Yoshiro Yamano, para 24; Taiwan, Yu-Ting Lin, para 23; UK, David Hertzell, para 19.

broker[155] and to obtain contractual *documents* in time and in writing[156]. Australia even accepts an implied warranty of fitness for purpose whenever a specific purpose of the requested insurance product has been communicated to the insurer.[157] Special protection in the context of *enforcement of claims* of policyholders is to be mentioned as well, most notably the US model Unfair Claims Practices Act[158] as well as the remedies under US tort law granting policyholders a right to economic damages as well as compensatory damages for emotional distress and punitive damages[159]. In Europe, "consumer" rights were granted to policyholders to a large extent when transposing EU directives into national law. Mention shall be made of just one example: Article 35 of Directive 2002/83/EC (Life Assurance Consolidation Directive) grants policyholders a cooling off period[160], and Article 36 of the same Directive grants policyholders rights to information both pre-contractually as well as post-contractually[161]. Some national laws have even broadened the scope of such consumer rights when amending their insurance contract acts. A striking example is the new German Insurance Contract Act 2008, which grants a general cooling off period in its s. 8, a general right of the policyholder to obtain information in s. 7 and to obtain advice in s. 6 as well as corresponding rights against insurance intermediaries in s. 60–63. The Principles of European Insurance Contract Law (PEICL) follow a similar pattern: General rights to obtain information and advice are afforded in Articles 2:201–2:203, a cooling off period is granted by Article 2:303, abusive clauses in insurance contracts are specifically dealt with in Article 2:304 and Article 1:301 allows qualified entities to sue for injunctions in case of any violation of the PEICL by an insurer.

15.7.2 "Consumer Philosophy" in Recent Legislation on Insurance

It has also been observed that consumer policy strongly influences the philosophy of modern insurance contract law reform. As far as the new German Insurance Contract Act 2008 is concerned, consumer protection has even been identified as a *lodestar* of the overall law reform project[162]. This shift in perspective is very well demonstrated by the development of pre-contractual information duties in insurance law over the last 200 years.

It is mentioned in one of the leading textbooks on English insurance law by *M. Clarke* that from about 1800 on English courts have used the principle of *good faith* to establish a duty of disclosure on the prospective policyholder concerning all material information affecting the risk. This duty would be necessary to *protect the insurer* against the policyholder who has the advantage of holding information which may possibly cause an adverse risk selection by the insurer.[163] In contrast, even though the principle of good faith is a reciprocal duty owed not only by the insured to the insurer but also by the insurer to the insured and the insurer enjoys the advantage of information concerning the scope of cover, the insurer is not put under a general obligation to point out to a prospective policyholder that the cover offered does not adequately meet the needs of the customer.[164] A similar position was taken by the national codifications of insurance contract law which were enacted in the first half of the twentieth century. For instance, the old German Insurance Contract Act of 1908 specifically regulated the duty of disclosure of a prospective policyholder but did not establish a duty of the insurer to

[155] Czech Republic, Josef Fiala and Marketa Selucka, para 29; Germany, Christian Armbrüster, para 42; Greece, Alexandra E. Douga, para 33; Italy, Diana Cerini, Giovanni Comandé, Maria Gagliardi and Onofrio Troiano, para 42; Japan, Yoshiro Yamano, para 25; Taiwan, Yu-Ting Lin, para 23; UK, David Hertzell, para 20.

[156] Australia, Anne Naughton, para 52.

[157] Armbrüster, Germany, para 41; Douga, Greece, para 34; Cerini, Comandé, Gagliardi and Troiano, Italy, para 42.

[158] USA, Jeffrey E. Thomas, para 29.

[159] USA, Jeffrey E. Thomas, para 30.

[160] Art. 35 of Directive 2002/83/EC of the European Parliament and of the Council of 5 November 2002 concerning life assurance [2002] OJ L345/1 to be replaced by Art. 186 of the Directive 2009/138/EC of the European Parliament and of the Council of 25 November 2009 on the taking-up and pursuit of the business of Insurance and Reinsurance (Solvency II) [2009] OJ L335/1.

[161] Art. 36 of Directive 2002/83/EC of the European Parliament and of the Council of 5 November 2002 concerning life assurance [2002] OJ L345/1 to be replaced by Art. 185 of the Directive 2009/138/EC of the European Parliament and of the Council of 25 November 2009 on the taking-up and pursuit of the business of Insurance and Reinsurance (Solvency II) [2009] OJ L335/1.

[162] See E Lorenz, 'Reform des Versicherungsvertragsrechts in Deutschland. Grundsätze und Schwerpunkte', Versicherungsrundschau (VR) 2005, 265–274.

[163] See Malcolm A. Clarke, *The Law of Insurance Contracts* (6th edn, 2009) 23-1A.

[164] In detail Clarke 23-1B.

inform or advise a customer[165]. Duties of advice have been established only to a certain degree in German case law and only based on the general principle of good faith ("Treu und Glauben") followed by the Civil Code, in particular by s. 242 of the Civil Code.[166] Consumerism has led to a significant *change in perspective*. As the Law Commission points out in its Report on Consumer Insurance Law of December 2009, the Financial Ombudsman Service (FOS) refuses to allow insurers to avoid a consumer policy for non-disclosure where no question has been asked. The draft Bill of the Law Commission wants to give statutory effect to the FOS approach.[167] This "questionnaire approach" is also taken, for instance, by the new German Insurance Contract Act 2008, s. 19, the Swiss Insurance Contract Act 1908, s. 4, as amended, the Finnish Insurance Contracts Act 1994, s. 22, the Spanish Insurance Contract Act 1980, s. 10 and the Principles of European Insurance Contract Law (PEICL), Article 2:101 para 1. Overall there is a clear tendency to restrict the duty of disclosure of a prospective policyholder. At the same time, recent legislation has increasingly introduced duties of the insurer to provide the prospective policyholder with pre-contractual information and partly even with advice[168]. Within Europe this process is stimulated by EU directives on insurance law and/or consumer law[169]. There is a clear shift in perspective: While protection of the insurer and/or the fictitious "community of the insured persons" against adverse risk selection is lowered significantly, protection of the individual policyholder against an adverse selection of the insurance product is significantly increased.

15.8 Summary

1. In its *origins*, insurance emerges from *commercial* activity. This fact is contrasted by current economic parameters assigning a significant, if not dominant position to non-commercial/consumer insurance in the insurance markets. Indeed, statistics show that premium income of insurers in non-commercial/consumer insurance *outweighs or even gets ahead* of the premium income in commercial insurance when reinsurance is left aside. This significant rise of consumer insurance also changes the legal perspective: Insurance can no longer be characterized as a solely or even just predominantly commercial transaction.
2. Academic teaching of and scholarly works on insurance contract law increasingly seem to follow this pattern: they tend to treat insurance law as a *subject of general private law* rather than commercial law (only).
3. While certain branches of insurance such as reinsurance and marine insurance remain parts of commercial law, insurance contract law in general covers *both business as well as consumer insurance*. This reflects the development of insurance from a commercial product to a product relevant and partly even essential to most aspects of human life.
4. Consumerism, though also of considerable influence in the insurance sector, has so far *not* led to a development of a significant body of "consumer insurance law". Leaving aside the example of Swedish law, national insurance contract laws as well as EU insurance law apply to business insurance just as to consumer insurance. One of the major reasons seems to be the fact that small and medium sized enterprises are in just as weak a position towards the insurer as are consumers.
5. Insurance contract laws therefore usually do not provide a demarcation between business and consumer insurance. If a distinction is drawn at all, it is mainly between "large" risks including re-insurance, marine insurance and certain industrial insurances and "mass" risks including consumer insurances and insurances of small and medium sized enterprises.

[165] Gesetz über den Versicherungsvertrag vom 30. Mai 1908 (RGBl. page 263).

[166] See, for example, Marlow in Beckmann and Matusche-Beckmann (eds), *Versicherungsrechts-Handbuch* (2009), § 13, para 77.

[167] See Law Com No 319/Scot Law Com No 219. p. 38 at 4.6.

[168] Austria, Martin Schauer, para 41; Czech Republic, Josef Fiala and Marketa Selucka, para 27; Germany, Christian Armbrüster, para 37; Cerini, Comandé, Gagliardi and Troiano, Italy, para 42; Norway, Kaja de Vibe Malling, para 64; Portugal, Maria José Rangel de Mesquita, paras 45f; but there is no legal obligation on the insurer to give advice in the UK, Hertzell, UK, para 18.

[169] See for insurance: Articles 183 to 186 of the Directive 2009/138/EC of the European Parliament and of the Council of 25 November 2009 on the taking-up and pursuit of the business of Insurance and Reinsurance (Solvency II) [2009] OJ L335/1; with regard to the directives on consumer law, see Articles 3 to 5 of the Directive 2002/65/EC of the European Parliament and of the Council of 23 September 2002 concerning the distance marketing of consumer financial services and amending Council Directive 90/619/EEC and Directives 97/7/EC and 98/27/EC [2002] OJ L271/16, which also applies to insurance.

6. Consumer law is, nevertheless, of influence on insurance law through various channels. *First, procedural* differences allow specific consumer insurance law to emerge to a certain extent. In several jurisdictions, re-insurance and large risk insurance both live in a separate procedural world of private arbitration. Matters of general insurance including business insurance are usually heard by general civil courts. Small claims, such as many consumer claims, are quite frequently ill suited for costly and long lasting proceedings in state courts. Therefore, mechanisms of alternative dispute resolution, particularly Ombudsmen proceedings, have been introduced. In some countries, the decisions of the Ombudsman are published and form a separate body of insurance case law which is predominantly relevant only for consumer insurance.
7. *Secondly, general consumer contract law* often also applies to insurance contracts and, thus, amends to a certain degree general insurance contract law in the specific context of consumer insurance. Such influence can be highly significant as demonstrated by the examples of Directive 1993/13/EEC (Unfair Contract Terms Directive) and Directive 2009/22/EC (Injunctions Directive).
8. Even though legislation in matters of insurance contract law has not created a significant body of consumer insurance acts, consumerism has, *thirdly*, significantly influenced the *philosophy* and *contents of insurance contracts acts*. Instruments of protection, typical for consumer law, such as cooling off periods, rights to information, advice and documentation of the contract in writing, have been introduced into insurance contracts acts in more recent amendments. Modern insurance contract law legislation though not consumer law legislation in a formal sense follows the protective approach of consumer law.

The Balance of Copyright* 16

Reto M. Hilty and Sylvie Nérisson

16.1 Introduction

The balance to be achieved in copyright law traditionally can be described as follows. Whose liberties should be given priority? Those of creators or those of the rest of society? In other words, how is the balance to be achieved between the interests of copyright holders and those of the users of works? The reality principle actually dictates a broadening of the circle of players, so as to refine the naming of stakeholders: creators and artistic performers, investors and professional users (employers, publishers and producers, distributors), end-users, creative and amateur users, etc. Nevertheless, one has to bear in mind firstly that every creator, by creating, uses what he has learnt and experimented with thanks to works of former creators; secondly that copyright policies actually have to enhance scientific progress and the spreading of culture.

The achievement of a balance in copyright law proceeds mainly through tailoring the scope of protection. It appears in the lawmaking process *a priori* by designing the protection and answering the question of which works and which uses are protected[1] (meaning which use of which object requires right-owner consent) and for how long[2]. Lawmakers adjust the balance also *a posteriori*. After the settlement of protection principles, copyright acts remove certain uses from the scope of protection.[3] Thereby, they grant realms of freedom,[4] the so-called limitations and exceptions to the copyright – in other words and from the point of view of users, user rights.[5]

As in many areas of law, digitization and the Internet have shifted benchmarks in copyright law. In the early stage of copyright policies, a fundamental (and obvious) distinction was laid between "public" and "private." Only the public uses, meaning those intended to reach a public, were protected. Nowadays, as a matter of fact, a simple e-mail can reach more addressees than a theater in the eighteenth century. Furthermore, technical protection measures make it possible to control and numerate every use. This puts the essence of copyright into question. How far does this shift in balance provoked by new technological possibilities make it necessary for lawmakers to grant new rights, and to

* III.B.1 La mise en balance du droit d'auteur. National reports received from **Argentina**, D. Lipszyc and P. Wegbrait; **Australia**, A. Christie and J. Liddicoat; **Belgium**, B. Vanbrabant and A. Strowel; **Brazil**, A. Rocha de Souza; **Canada**, Y. Gendreau; **China**, L. Xiuqin; **Croatia**, I. Gliha; **Cyprus**, T. Sinodinou; **Denmark**, J. Schosvo; **Egypt**, A.H. Al-Saghir and H.A. Raslan; **France**, C. Alleaume; **Germany**, T. Dreier and L. Specht; **Greece**, D. Kallinikou; **Hungary**, P. Mezei; **India**, V.C. Vivekanandan; **Israel**, G. Pessach; **Italy**, S. Sica and V. D'Antonio; **Japan**, R. Kojima; **Lithuania**, V. Mizaras; **Macau**, R.J. Neuwirth and L. Min; **Norway**, O.A. Rognstad; **Poland**, J. Bleszynski; **Portugal**, D.M.L. Moura Vicente; **Spain**, R. Xalabarder; **Taiwan**, C.-H. Hsu; **UK**, J. Griffiths; **USA**, P. Maggs.

R.M. Hilty (✉) • S. Nérisson
Max Planck Institute for Intellectual Property, Competition and Tax Law, Munich, Germany
e-mail: hilty@ip.mpg.de; sylvie.nerisson@ip.mpg.de

[1] See questions 1 and 2a.

[2] See questions 1b.

[3] See questions 2c, 2d, 2e.

[4] On the way lawmakers handle this issue, see question 3.

[5] See answers to questions regarding user rights free of charge, subject to compensation and mandatory licenses, 2c, 2d, and 2e, and under Question 6.

K.B. Brown and D.V. Snyder (eds.), *General Reports of the XVIIIth Congress of the International Academy of Comparative Law/Rapports Généraux du XVIIIème Congrès de l'Académie Internationale de Droit Comparé*, DOI 10.1007/978-94-007-2354-2_16, © Springer Science+Business Media B.V. 2012

which right holders? To put it in a nutshell: since the 1990s by revolutionizing the way in which copyright-protected works are dealt with, new technologies have induced changes which have confronted copyright law – and the trade of related products (mainly industries of entertainment, news and scientific publications) – with profound challenges. The obvious balance underlying copyright law, which was till then implicit, has since become disruptive in international law.

The balance first appeared in the TRIPS Agreement of 1994:

> The protection and enforcement of intellectual property rights should contribute to the promotion of technological innovation and to the transfer and dissemination of technology, to the mutual advantage of producers and users of technological knowledge and in a manner conducive to social and economic welfare, and to a balance of rights and obligations.[6]

It concerned the whole intellectual property spectrum and applies to all WTO members, therefore, to the 27 countries concerned by this report.[7]

Moving closer to our issue, the WIPO treaty of 1996 regarding copyright (WCT) reveals that the balance was already achieved in the Berne Convention (1886). Furthermore it directly refers to the balance between creators and copyright owners on the one hand, and the users of works on the other. It thus recognizes "the need to maintain a balance between the rights of authors and the larger public interest, particularly education, research and access to information, as reflected in the Berne Convention."[8] This provision applies to 22 of the countries observed in this paper[9]; whereas, the Berne Convention has been implemented in all countries.

Moreover, regarding the law applicable to 14 countries considered in this report, the European Directive on the harmonization of certain aspects of copyright and related rights in the information society (InfoSoc Directive)[10] of 2001 states:

> A fair balance of rights and interests between the different categories of right holders, as well as between the different categories of right holders and users of protected subject-matter must be safeguarded. The existing exceptions and limitations to the rights as set out by the Member States have to be reassessed in the light of the new electronic environment.[11]

In addition, the balance to be achieved regarding the dealing with copyright-protected works can also be assisted by external measures. Copyright law does not exist in isolation. Fundamental rights like the freedom of speech and expression and the right to be informed can help, especially when the application of copyright rules appears as a hurdle against the dissemination of works. Besides this, more trade-related areas of law interact with copyright law. The most well-known and actually closest to copyright law is antitrust law, since it shares the goal of defending individuals against conglomerates. General principles of contract and civil law also govern the relations between license contracting parties.[12]

1. To what extent does national law differentiate in terms of the effects of copyright law: (a) according

[6] Art. 7 of the Agreement on Trade-Related Aspects of Intellectual Property Rights (TRIPS) adopted in Marrakesh, Agreement Establishing the World Trade Organization, Annex 1, (1994).

[7] In the absence of explicit references, articles (Art.) and sections (Sec.) quoted in this report refer in following countries to following acts: **Argentina**: Copyright Act No. 11.723 1933; **Australia**: Copyright Act 1968 (Cth); **Belgium**: loi du 30 juin 1994 relative *au droit d'auteur et aux droits voisins*; **Brazil**: Copyright Act (Law 9.610 1998); **Canada**: Copyright Act, L.R.C. 1985, ch. C-42; **China**: Copyright Act (adopted in 1990, revised in 2001); **Croatia**: Copyright and Related Rights Act of October 1st 2003; **Cyprus**: Copyright Law 59/1976; **Denmark**: *Lovbekendtgoerelse* (Consolidated Act) No. 587/20.6.2008 *om ophavsret*; **Egypt**: Intellectual Property Law No. 82/2002 (EIPL); **France**: *Code de la propriété intellectuelle* 1992; **Germany**: German Copyright Act of September 9, 1965; **Greece**: Copyright Law (Law 2121/1993); **Hungary**: Copyright Act LXXVI of 1999; **India**: Copyright Act, 1957; **Israel**: Copyright Act, 2007; **Italy**: Law for the Protection of Copyright and Neighbouring Rights 1941; Japan: Copyright Act, Act No. 48 of May 6, 1970; **Lithuania**: Law of the Republic of Lithuania on Copyright and Related Rights 1999; **Macau**: Author's Rights and Neighbouring Right Act 1999; **Norway**: *Lov om opphavsrett til åndsverk*, May 12, 1961; **Poland**: Act of February 4, 1994 on Copyright and Neighbouring Rights; **Portugal**: Code of Copyright and Related Rights, last amended by Law No. 16/2008, of April 1, 2008; **Spain**: *Texto Refundido de la Ley de Propiedad Intelectual* (Royal Legislative Decree 1/1996 of April 12), **Taiwan**: Copyright Act last amended on February 10, 2010; **UK**: Copyright Designs & Patents Act 1988; **USA**: title 17 of the *United States Code,* Copyright Act of 1976.

[8] Preamble of WCT, December 20, 1996.

[9] **Brazil**, **Egypt**, **India**, **Macao**, **Norway** and **Taiwan** are not contracting parties. **Canada** and **Israel** are signatories, but the WIPO treaties are not in force yet. **Canada** will probably begin parliamentary work this year.

[10] Directive 2001/29/EC of the European Parliament and of the Council of May 22, 2001 on the harmonization of certain aspects of Copyright and related rights in the information society, *OJ* L 167, June 22, 2001 p. 10.

[11] Heading 31 of the InfoSoc Directive.

[12] On the interaction of these legal areas in copyright law, see answers to Question 12.

to the various work categories[13]; (b) according to factual aspects, e.g. different markets,[14] competitive conditions,[15] other factual aspects; and (c) according to other criteria?[16]

Most reporters point out that the copyright of their country does not theoretically distinguish in terms of the effects of copyright law and, however, list exceptions to the principle. The dogma of the blind approach, probably related to considerations issued from the *unité de l'art* principle and supported by the condemnation of artistic or political censorship, yields to the need for adaptation to multifaceted reality which possibly establishes a differentiated approach.

1a. Differentiation according to the work categories

All countries in our project distinguish copyright and neighboring rights. This distinction corresponds to different kinds of objects; the former protect creation, and the latter protect the achievement of acts related to creation, such as performances, the production of cinematographic and audiovisual works, sound recordings and the broadcasting of protected works. The differences regard mainly the scope of granted rights. For instance, moral rights in respect of copyrighted works are significantly stronger, and the protection term of neighboring rights is mostly shorter.

Except for this basic distinction, the leading principle is to confer the same scope of protection to all works, as long as they fulfill the conditions of being copyrighted. Each jurisdiction, however, provides for exceptions to this principle. The most recurrent exception to this one-size-fits-all approach occurs concerning computer programs. Twenty-five reports mention special treatment for software.[17]

A recurrent point among the reports is the exclusion of specific kinds of works from the scope of protection, such as official publications,[18] expressions of folklore,[19] news information,[20] standards, facts and daily news items underlying announcements released in the printed press,[21] ideas, procedures, processes, systems, methods of operation, concepts, principles, discoveries or mere data.[22]

One also has to note that the definition of some peculiar copyrights and of most users' rights expressly focus on specific categories of works due to the nature of the works and of the uses at stake. It is obviously the case of specific

[13] For instance: special provisions for cinematographic works, computer programs, etc.

[14] For instance: different treatment of literary works according to whether they are works of fiction or academic works.

[15] For instance: no possibility of substitution of a work marketed by only one of the right holders.

[16] For instance: Art. 2 para. 2 Berne Convention (BC).

[17] **Argentina** (special provisions for the vesting of rights: presumption they vest in the employer of the persons hired for the making of the program), **Australia** Art. 47b et seq., (only concerning some particular user rights, reserved to users of software), **Belgium** (specific Act), **Brazil** (specific Act, shorter protection, specific provisions for the ownership of the work in case of employment contract), **China** (specific Act but mentioned among the copyrighted work in the Copyright Act, specific provision for the rental right), **Croatia** Art. 17/6, 108 et seq., **Cyprus** Art. 7B, **Denmark** Arts. 36 and 37, **Egypt** Art. 147, **France** (Art. L. 122-6), **Germany** Sec. 69 et seq., **Greece** Art. 2 para. 3 and 45A, **Hungary** Arts. 58–60A, **Israel** Sec. 45 (no moral right), Italy Art. 64bis–64^quarter^, **Japan** Art. 47-2, **Lithuania** Art. 10 para. 1, **Macau** Sec. X Arts. 166–169, **Norway** Sec. 39h and 39i, **Poland** Arts. 74–77, **Portugal** Art. 36 and a specific act, **Spain** Act 16/1993, **Taiwan** Art. 59, **UK** Sec. 50A–C, **USA** Secs. 109 and 117.

[18] **Belgium** Art. 8 Sec. 1 para. 2 and Sec. 2 (mentions also any public speech delivered in political assemblies), **Brazil** Art. 8, **Croatia** Art. 8, **Germany** Sec. 5, **Greece** Art. 2 para. 5, **Hungary** Art. 1 paras. 4–5, **Lithuania** (which views as belonging to this category also: their official translations, official State symbols and insignia the protection whereof is regulated by other laws, officially registered drafts of legal acts, and folklore works), **Macau** Art. 6 para. 1 and para. 2 (in the same category: texts of treaties, laws and regulations and those of reports or decisions by authorities of any kind, and translations thereof), **Portugal** Art. 7 and 8. **French** law, on the opposite, urges works of State employee do not receive any derogatory treatment Art. L. 111-1.

[19] **Croatia** Art. 8.2, **Greece** Art. 2 para. 5, **Cyprus** traditional folk dances were excluded from copyright protection on the basis of case law (Supreme Court of Cyprus, *Gregoris K. Ashiotis v. The Attorney General of the Republic and others*, (1967) 1 C.L.R. 83) because they are considered as the common heritage of the Cypriot nation.

[20] **Croatia** Art. 8 para. 2, **Greece** Art. 2 para. 5, **Japan** Art. 10 para. 2, **Lithuania**, **Macau** Art. 5 (in the same category: texts presented and speeches given to assemblies or other collegiate, political and administrative bodies, or in public debates, on topics of common interest; political speeches).

[21] **Hungary** Art. 1 paras. 4–5.

[22] **Croatia** Art. 8 para. 2, **Cyprus** Art. 3 para. 3, **Italy:** Court of cassation, February 13, 1987, no. 1558, **Lithuania**, **Macau** Art. 1 para. 2, **USA** Art. 102(b) Leading cases on the line between protection of ideas and non-protection of expression are: *Baker v. Selden,* (1879), *101 U.S. 99* (accounting system not protected) and *Nichols v. Universal Pictures Corp.,* (1930) 45F.2d 119 (2d Cir.) (plot scheme similar to Romeo and Juliet not protected).

provisions for publishing contracts (*contrat d'édition*) only regarding texts and pictures[23] and for performing contracts only affecting dramatic and musical works.[24] Specific licensing rules also are foreseen for audiovisual works[25] and other categories.[26] Thereby, lawmakers have paid attention to a mix of considerations regarding the single nature of some categories of works and the economic conditions of their exploitation. It is typically the case of the resale royalty (*droit de suite*), that only regards works whose market value mainly relies on the original copy, such as works of (fine) art[27] including photographs.[28] The rights of exhibition and of presentation are, in some countries, only provided for concerning similar categories of works.[29] This last consideration depends on the need for adaptation of general rules to the specific nature of the works in question. This aim leads also to the fact that reporters evoke in their statements that the right to perform does not apply to artistic works or to typographical arrangements[30]; the right of distribution only applies to cinematographic work[31]; authors of typefaces do not have the right to be identified as such[32]; in two countries, this right does not exist either with respect of computer programs,[33] authors of which also do not have any right to object to the derogatory treatment of a work.[34] Reporters also notice here that among the differentiations of the protection depending on the categories of works, authors of the literary and musical parts of a cinematographic work may use their work separately.[35] Similarly, provisions addressing translation only concern written works and necessarily regard mostly foreign works that are therefore submitted to a specific treatment since their translation into a national language is protected by a narrower scope of protection in order to promote this use.[36]

The reasons for the specific design of the scope of protection depending on categories of works are always mixed. One can however list, apart from the specific treatment relying on the nature of the works, some differentiations provided because of economic reasons. Therefore, the rental right may be provided only for cinematographic work,[37] sound recordings[38] and computer software[39]; and the private copy exception/right may require a remuneration only for certain kinds of works.[40] Exclusive rights are limited for computer programs.[41] Similarly, some countries do not provide

[23] **Belgium, Germany** German Act on Publishing (*Verlagsgesetz*) of 1901 (it concerns in Germany also musical works, which is to be explained by the date of this act, stemming from the era before the commercial development of phonograms, as musical works were mostly spread through book notes).

[24] **Belgium, Italy** Arts. 33–37 (near dramatic and musical works, one finds in that category the choreographic works and pantomimes).

[25] **France** Art. L. 121-5, **Germany** Sec. 88 et seq., **Greece** Art. 34, **Italy** Arts. 44–50, **Poland** Art. 70, Spain Art. 87.

[26] See in **Italy**: beside the cases already listed, collective works, magazines and newspapers (Arts. 38–43), works broadcast (Arts. 51–60), works recorded on mechanical devices (Arts. 61–64), software (Art. 64bis–64^quarter^), databases (Art. 64^quinquies^–64^sexies^). The Spanish law also distinguishes between works of collaboration, collective woks and composite works.

[27] **Cyprus, Germany** Sec. 26, **Hungary** Art. 70, **Italy** Art. 145 para. 1, Art. 14ter Berne Convention.

[28] **Cyprus, Germany, Hungary** Art. 70, **Italy** Art. 145 para. 1.

[29] The right of exhibition is only provided for works of fine art and photographic works (**Canada, China, Hungary**), architectural and applied art works (**Hungary** Art. 69), the right of presentation is only available for a work of the fine arts (**China**), a photographic work (**China**), a cinematographic work (**China**).

[30] **UK**.

[31] **Japan** Art. 26.

[32] **UK** Sec. 79 para. 2.

[33] **Israel** Sec. 45, **UK** Sec. 77.

[34] **Israel** Sec. 45, **UK** Sec. 81 para. 2.

[35] **Portugal, Spain**.

[36] **Egypt** Art. 148 expressly allowed for developing countries by the Annex to the Berne Convention Arts. I, II.

[37] **China, Egypt, India.**

[38] **Canada, India**.

[39] **Canada, China, Egypt, India**.

[40] In countries where private copying is compensated, sound recordings are the objects most often charged (for which a remuneration is foreseen and thereby the works used for the sound recording, like musical scores and texts). Apart from sound recordings, audiovisual and written works may also be concerned. See answers to Question 10.

[41] **USA** Sec. 117.

broadcasts and typographical arrangements for moral and rental rights[42] or grant them a shorter term of protection.[43] On the other hand, the first-sale doctrine can be excluded for cinematographic films[44] and sound recordings.[45] The specific provision most recurring is the fact that the author of a sound recording cannot prohibit it from public performance or covering but may only make a claim for remuneration.

1b. Differentiations according to factual aspects such as different market, competitive competition.

Most reporters answered that their jurisdiction does not, in principle, distinguish according to any market or competitive consideration; although, they mentioned some provisions bound to such concerns.

There are, however, situations where market and competitive considerations underlie specific rules. The Norwegian reporter evokes here the exhaustion-of-rights doctrine[46] commanded by the EEA.

Courts in Australia have recently indicated that when assessing whether a "substantial part" of the copyrighted work has been reproduced for the purposes of infringement,[47] this assessment may include considerations of broader "interests" being protected by copyright.[48] The High Court has indicated that such interests may include commercial and competition-based considerations such as industry standards and the market to which the work belongs (which might include whether or not the work/subject-matter is substitutable).[49]

Furthermore, the Spanish report mentions the specific provisions ruling the licensing of rights to audiovisual works and films. The scope of the transfer presumption regarding the exploitation rights in favor of film producers is broader in respect of audiovisual works[50] than in respect of cinematographic films (that is, an audiovisual work initially intended for exploitation in theaters).[51]

In many cases, limitations/exceptions/users' rights do differentiate according to the use made of copyrighted works in different markets. It is the point of privileges in favor of uses for educational or scientific purposes, or within the frame of such institutions.

The reporters did not analyze this feature as a market or competitive consideration, except for the German ones. One can indeed consider certain uses, which otherwise might form a market, have been exempted from copyright's exclusive rights (but not necessarily of the payment of a levy/fee), so far as the education and the scientific research do constitute a parallel market, being privileged in order to promote the transmission of knowledge and culture.

Some uses are allowed without authorization only when there is no commercial offer to acquire the work in question. Such figures appear in European countries essentially for online uses, since the InfoSoc Directive permits it.[52] Belgian law also provides a similar requirement for libraries, archives, educational institutions or museums to be allowed to make works available on dedicated terminals.[53]

1c. Other factual aspects

Creation circumstances as such matter the most when the creator is employed and creates the work in the course of duties.[54] For

[42] **UK**.

[43] **Canada**.

[44] **India**.

[45] **India**.

[46] **Norway** Sec. 19.

[47] **Australia** Sec. 14 para. 1.

[48] **Australia** *Desktop Marketing Ltd v Telstra Corporation Ltd* (2002) 55 IPR 1, 107; *IceTV Pty Ltd v Nine Network Australia Pty Ltd* (2009) 80 IPR 451, 491.

[49] **Australia** *IceTV Pty Ltd v Nine Network Australia Pty Ltd* (2002) 55 iPR 1, at 490–491.

[50] **Spain** Art. 86.

[51] **Spain** Art. 88 para. 1 *in fine*.

[52] See Art. 6 para. 4 al. 4 of the InfoSoc Directive, stating the scope of the user rights can be reduced in respect of works made available online when there is a commercial offer to access to those works. It has been implemented in **Belgium** Arts. 23bis al. 3 and 79bis Sec. 3, **Germany** Sec. 53a, and **Greece** Art. 22 *in fine*.

[53] **Belgium** Art. 22 para. 1 9°.

[54] **China** Art. 21, **Cyprus** Art. 11 para. 1b (private employment, commissioned works and works ordered for advertising), **Greece** Art. 8, **Hungary** Art. 63, **Macau** Art. 12 para.1, 13 para. 1, 164 para. 1.

example, the copyrights vest in the employer and the term of duration is, in certain countries, shorter.[55] Where the employer is the State (or the Crown)[56] or a newspaper[57] this leads to some more specific provisions.

Independent of labor contracts, where the creator was not isolated is also considered by copyright acts. When the work was created by a collective under the leadership of a single person (be it a natural person or a legal entity, on the initiative and under the direction and organization of which the work has been done), the rights vest in that person. Such a situation is exceptional in *droit d'auteur* countries, since it can lead to the original right vesting in a legal entity.[58] As such, in China collective works enjoy a shorter period of protection.[59] French law distinguishes three cases of plural works, stating different regimes.[60] Collective works are the exceptional case, in which ownership originally vests in a legal entity. In case of collaborative works, meaning when several creators participate in the process of creation without a subordination relationship, copyright vests in all co-authors,[61] requiring the consent of all for exercising the copyright. Lastly, concerning derivative works, the Copyright Act states the copyright vests in the creator of the new work, requiring that he/she respects the original author's rights.[62]

Disclosure circumstances also participate in tailoring the scope of protection. The anonymity, that is to say the fact the author is unknown, impacts the method of calculation of the duration of protection, or on the person in which the rights vest.[63] It is obviously a way to deal with the uncertainty regarding the regular running point of the term protection.

Fixation expressly required for copyright protection in countries from the common law tradition[64] and in China.[65] Otherwise jurisdictions only require an "outward manifestation of the work"[66] and fixation in a material carrier is only required in peculiar cases such as works of choreography or mime.[67]

The recognition of copyrights is exempted from registration, deposit or any other formalities.[68] It is required by the Berne Convention.[69] That is why USA partly abandoned the registration requirement as a condition of copyright protection under Chap. 5 of the Copyright Act.[70] Yet, registration remains a precondition to suit for United States works, and a

[55] **Brazil**, **China**.

[56] **Canada** Art. 12, **Israel** Secs. 38–42 (shorter duration, 50 years after the making instead of 70 pma), **UK** Secs. 163–167.

[57] **France** Art. L. 132-35, **Portugal** Art. 173 para. 2.

[58] **France** Art. L. 113-5, **Lithuania** Art. 1 para. 1, **Macau** Art. 16 para. 1 and 162 para. 1.

[59] **China.**

[60] **France** Art. L. 113-2.

[61] **France** Art. L. 113-3.

[62] **France** Art. L. 113-4.

[63] See **Cyprus** Art. 11 para. 5: in the case of an unpublished work where the identity of the author is unknown, but where there are reasons supporting the view that he or she is a citizen of the Republic the copyright subsisting by virtue of the Law 59/1976 shall be deemed to vest in the Minister of Education; and **Macau** Art. 12 para. 3, where the name of the intellectual creator is not mentioned, it is presumed that the economic rights have been assigned to the entity for which the work was made. Regarding the protection term, see answers under Question 5.

[64] **Australia** Sec. 22 para. 1, **Canada** expressly required by Art. 2 only for computer programs, choreographic works or mime although the case law established it for every kind of work, see *Canadian Admiral Corp. v. Rediffusion Inc.* (1954) Ex. C.R. 382, **Cyprus** Art. 3 para. 2a, **Egypt** lectures, speeches, sermons and any other oral works must be recorded in order to be protected Art. 140 para. 4, **Israel** Sec. 4 para. a, **UK** Sec. 3 para. 2, **US** Federal law (with the exception of Sec. 1101 on "unauthorized fixation" of performances) protects only fixed works. In the **USA**, unfixed works, such as ad lib public lectures, are protected, but only by state law. For a critical analysis of the issue, see Y. Gendreau, "The criterion of fixation in Copyright law", (1994) 159 *R.I.D.A.* January 1994, p. 111.

[65] The work shall be "capable of being reproduced in a tangible form." A limit to this rapprochement to US law is that oral works are protected.

[66] **Macau** Art. 1 para. 3, **Poland** Art. 1, **Portugal** Art. 1 para. 1 and 2.

[67] **Macau** Art. 2 para. 1d.

[68] **Macau** Art. 10, **Poland** Art. 1 Sec. 4, **USA** Art. 102a.

[69] **BC** Art. 5 para. 2.

[70] On this matter, see Ginsburg, Jane C., "The US Experience with Copyright Formalities: A Love/Hate Relationship". *Columbia Public Law Research Paper* no. 10-225; *Columbia Journal of Law & the Arts* 33, no. 4 (2010).

precondition to recovery of statutory damages for all works. Furthermore, registers regarding copyright works still exist for specific categories of works.[71]

Following the chronology of the life of a copyrighted work, we now come to the usage circumstances impacting the scope of protection. Some of the reporters mentioned here that acts of non-public communication are not covered by copyright at all,[72] and vice versa private use is free.[73] Also, when a work is permanently situated in a public place or in premises open to the public,[74] limitations and exceptions are granted and give broader liberties regarding the allowed use made of it. When cable and satellite television signal suppliers deliver remote signal to unserved households, those suppliers are privileged.[75] Finally, the coexistence of copyright protection and of that of industrial design leads some jurisdictions to exclude the industrial use from the scope of copyright.[76]

2. **Which of the following legal instruments are used by national copyright law[77] in order to achieve a "balance" of interests and to what extent are they used: (a) specific preconditions or thresholds allowing a work's protection only if it surpasses a particular degree of creativity; (b) period of protection; (c) specific user rights, free of charge, granted by the law in favor of third parties[78]; (d) specific user rights granted by the law in favor of third parties subject to the payment of a remuneration to the right holder(s)[79]; (e) obligations to conclude a contract established by law to grant a third party specific user rights in return for payment of a fee (mandatory license)[80]; (f) rules on misuse?**

2a. **Do specific preconditions or thresholds allow for a work's protection only if it surpasses a particular degree of creativity used by national copyright law in order to achieve a "balance" of interests, and to what extent are they used?**

Only seven reporters expressly state that the preconditions or threshold for being protected are used by national copyright law in order to achieve a balance,[81] but all reports mention the originality requirement as the core condition for works to be protected.[82] Actually the Belgian reporters urge neither creativity nor originality as a protection requirement, but the *mise en forme* requirement (in other words the protection of expression and not of ideas) is. The French report points out that lawmakers and judges balance the interests at stake, but this cannot be reduced to the originality concern. The Brazilian report expressly rejects the idea of a threshold of creativity as achieving a balance. The Japanese reporter states that some case law did balance the creativity thresholds as regards works with a functional nature,[83] thus showing a preference for the protection of functional works to apply an objective

[71] RCPA for films in **France**, *Urheberrolle* for anonymous works in **Germany**, **Macau** Publication Information Department for newspaper titles (Art. 163 para. 1), *Registro de la Propiedad Intelectual* in **Spain** Art. 145.3.

[72] **Germany** Sec. 53 et seq., see also Sec. 15 para. 2.

[73] **Brazil.**

[74] **Brazil** Art. 48, **China** (any use but not foreseen by the Regulation on Information networks) Art. 22(10), **Croatia** Art. 91, **Egypt** (only reproduction), **Europe** (reproduction and making available) InfoSoc Directive Art. 5 para. 3h, **Germany** Sec. 59, **Greece** Art. 26, **Hungary** Art. 68 para. 1, **Israel** Sec. 23, **Japan** Art. 46, **Lithuania, Macau** Art. 61j, **Poland** Art. 33 point 1, **Portugal** Art. 75 para. 2q, **Spain** Art. 35 para. 2, **Taiwan** Art. 58, **UK** Art. 62 (but not if the copied work is two dimensional).

[75] **USA** Sec. 119 (The term "unserved household", with respect to a particular television network, means a household that cannot receive, through the use of a conventional, stationary, out-door rooftop receiving antenna, an over-the-air signal of a primary network station affiliated with that network of Grade B intensity as defined by the Federal Communications Commission under section 73.683(a) of title 47 of the Code of Federal Regulations, as in effect on January 1, 1999).

[76] **Brazil** Art. 8 para. 7, **Japan**.

[77] For the rules *outside* copyright law see Question 12.

[78] For instance: Art. 10 para. 1 Berne Convention (permission to quote from a work).

[79] For instance: Art. 7 para. 3 WCT (right of rental of copies of works embodied in phonograms).

[80] For instance: Art. 13 para. 1 Berne Convention (authorization of sound recording of musical works).

[81] **Belgium, Canada, China, France, Italy, Macau, Portugal.**

[82] See for further developments the answer to question 6.

[83] See J. Boyle, *The Public Domain: Enclosing the Commons of the Mind* (Yale University Press 2008) at 165 and S. Teramoto, "*Copyrightability and Scope of Protection for Works of Utilitarian Nature under Japanese Law*", 1997 *IIC* 51.

creativity requirement[84] to the subjective creativity.[85] The latter is used as the criterion for artistic and literary works.[86]

2b. Are periods of protection used by national copyright law in order to achieve a "balance" of interests, and to what extent are they used?

Term of protection is only rarely expressly described by national reporters as achieving a balance.[87] The Brazilian report expressly rejects this idea since period of protection depends in Brazil on the person in which the right is vested, which is, according to him, not related to a balance of interest. In case of corporate ownership – film producers, publishers of unknown author's works – the protection span extends 70 years from the publication, whereas in the case of personal ownership of the creator, it extends 70 years *post mortem auctoris* (pma).

Differently, the Belgian report states the duration is unique (70 years pma), without any shorter time span. The sole exception to the principle of 70 years pma in Belgium is foreseen to let the duration run not from the death of the author but from the creation or the publication of anonymous works, in cases of works published under a pseudonym and of works published after the death of the author.[88] Ultimately, the time span varies in 24 countries.[89]

<u>Preliminary remarks regarding user rights</u>
One should explain the quotation marks around "user rights." The wording "user rights" allows almost everybody agree on a certain discomfort by the use of this wording. The term "user rights" is expressly rejected by Argentina, Belgium, Croatia, Denmark, Germany, Greece, Italy, Norway, Portugal, Spain, and Taiwan, and it is only admitted by the Cypriot and UK reporters in respect of provisions concerning computer programs and databases. The French report urges such a conception, as the one of "free-of-charge *statutory license*", is unfamiliar to French lawmakers. The Japanese report states that the current situation in Japan forces one to speak of exceptions rather than about rights, at least until a reform.

This reluctance regarding the acknowledgement of user rights is not surprising from France, since it is *the* traditional country of *authors'* rights. On the other hand, it appears strange, or very symptomatic of the author-centered conception of the European, continental tradition of copyright, when one considers the Belgian situation where all limitations and exceptions are binding, meaning the permitted acts granted by statutes may not be contracted out.[90]

Instead of user rights, the following terms are preferred and mainly used by the following countries: "limitations" (Brazil, Croatia, Denmark, Germany, Greece, Italy, Lithuania, Portugal, and Taiwan); "exceptions" (Argentina, Belgium, Canada, China, Cyprus, France, Italy, Poland, and the UK); "fair use" (China, India, Israel ("fair use defence"), and Macau); "fair dealing" (Australia, Canada, Cyprus, and India); "privilege" (Croatia, Germany, and the USA); "liberties" (Cyprus and the UK); "permitted use" (Israel and Poland); "permitted act" (UK); "limits" (Spain).

2c. Whether user rights free of charge are used by national copyright law in order to achieve a "balance" of interests and to what extent are they used?

Again, only eight reporters expressly state "user rights," free of charge, help achieve a balance.[91] The Israeli report appears to subscribe to this point of view as well. The Greek report does not expressly describe the limitations as a balancing tools but points out that the limitations on economic rights are justified

[84] Focusing the "room for choice".

[85] Focusing the "effluent of personality".

[86] **Japan** About this subjective creativity see Judgment of the Tokyo High Court on February 19, 1987, *Hanrei Jiho* No. 1225, p. 111 (case on expectancy table on an outcome of the election) and Judgment of the Tokyo District Court on October 11, 1972, *Hanrei Taimuzu* No.289, p. 377 (*Confess of Minsei* case).

[87] **China**, **Germany**, **Italy**, **Macau**, **Portugal**, **Taiwan**.

[88] **Belgium** Art. 2.

[89] **Argentina**, **Australia**, **Brazil**, **Canada**, **China**, **Croatia**, **Cyprus**, **Denmark**, **Egypt**, **Germany**, **Hungary**, **Italy**, **India**, **Israel**, **Italy**, **Japan**, **Lithuania**, **Macau**, **Norway**, **Poland**, **Portugal**, **Spain**, **Taiwan**, **USA**.

[90] See Question 9.

[91] **Belgium**, **China**, **France**, **Germany**, **Italy**, **Japan**, **Macau**, **USA**. Actually, according to the **French** reporter, authorizations for users to use Copyright protected works *almost always* achieve a balance. And the **US** reporter held this opinion actually only regarding privileges for reproduction by libraries and archives.

on the grounds of social policy and aim at the protection of society as a whole since the free dissemination of works meets society's need for information, assists scientific progress, and meets various educational and cultural needs.

Regarding the free-of-charge limitation/exception, the German reporters state: "the respective interests of the public in using the work are believed to outbalance the interests of the right holders in exclusively exploiting the work." Contrary to the two other kinds of user rights that we present below, the *free* uses are considered so important that right owners may not hinder them, nor require a financial compensation.

2d. Are user rights subject to the payment of a remuneration to the right holders used by national copyright law in order to achieve a "balance" of interests and to what extent are they used?

First, it is noteworthy that Brazil and the UK do not have any license conceded by the State in return for payment of a fee or a royalty. Brazilian copyright law only knows user rights free of charge on the one hand and the copyright owner's scope of protection on the other hand – the latter left to the freedom of right holders. Differently, UK law always recurs to mandatory licenses when it comes to granting users the possibility to undertake specific acts, provided the right holders are remunerated. This specificity of the UK system relies on the systematic distinction between user rights in return for a remuneration right and mandatory licenses. Considering the former occurs when the fee amount is fixed by law or by the executive, and the latter when the rate is left in the first instance to be negotiated between the parties, one can only regard it as obvious that the British liberalism always prefers to give a chance to contractual freedom. This system is not so precise in *droit d'auteur* countries. Thus, we will see private copying is considered in France and Germany as a remuneration right, and not as a mandatory license, although the rate is fixed in France by an administrative commission and has been fixed by the Parliament for 20 years in Germany. On the contrary, in accordance with the British system and with the lineage with the UK, Canada only knows a single remuneration right in respect of the private copying.

Only four reports expressly state that remuneration rights help achieve a balance of interests.[92] Besides those four general answers concerning remuneration rights, the French report points out the public lending fee is a wonderful mirror of the balancing of copyright. It was a new copyright prerogative implemented in France. In order to consider the general interest mission undertaken by public libraries, this prerogative has not been enshrined as an exclusive right but as a remuneration right. It is actually not paid by libraries but half by the State and half by books suppliers.

2e. Are mandatory licenses – obligation to conclude a contract established by law to grant a third party specific user rights in return for payment of a fee – used by national copyright law in order to achieve a "balance" of interests and to what extent are they used?

Regarding mandatory licenses, the UK and Canada appear isolated by using mandatory licenses first and as a matter of course when it comes for the lawmaker to deter right holders from hindering access to or the use of protected works. On the contrary, other countries resort to mandatory licenses only in incidental or residual cases, and prefer remuneration rights. One cannot summarize this difference with *copyright* countries on the one hand and *droit d'auteur* countries on the other, because Australia and the US only have residual cases of mandatory licenses and nevertheless cannot be considered as *droit d'auteur* countries.

Ignoring remuneration rights schemes (defined by the British reporter as a right to use a work subject to the payment of a license fee, the rate of which is fixed by law) UK law resorts to mandatory licenses in miscellaneous cases. In those cases the copyright owner is obliged to conclude a contract with a user, but under those provisions the rate is left in the first instance to be negotiated between the parties ("compulsory licenses" or "mandatory licenses"). Under

[92] **Belgium**, **China**, **Italy** and **Macau**.

United Kingdom copyright law, these are generally described as "uses as of right" and are subject to a "reasonable royalty". In Canada, a mandatory license is an exception which allows a use only with the payment of royalties to the relevant collecting societies.

2f. Are copyright rules on misuse used by national copyright law in order to achieve a "balance" of interests and to what extent are they used?

Generally copyright law does not contain any specific rules on misuse. Most reports refer to general principles of civil law (Israel, Lithuania and Spain), some to competition law (France and Japan).[93]

Actually, the only jurisdiction expressly mentioning "abuse" is the French law, as regards the exercise of moral rights by the heirs of the creator. And international law deserves to be mentioned here since Arts. 8, 48(1) and 53(1) of the TRIPS Agreement foresee indemnification for and condemnation of the abuse of IP rights. But as a matter of fact, other jurisdictions provide for similar provisions in respect of moral rights after the author's death.[94]

3. Are user rights regulated abstractly, concretely, or by means of a combination of the two?

The main issue of the distinction relies on the fact that abstract regulations are considered to be non-exhaustive whereas concrete enumerations of specific cases are mostly closed lists.[95] As a matter of fact, a general clause allows more adaptability and interpretational freedom for judges[96] than a list of peculiar situations. In this respect it is important to bear in mind: *droit d'auteur* countries traditionally provide only exceptions for users, meaning the privilege scopes to be interpreted are narrow.[97] Yet continental European countries have implemented in one way or another the three-step test, leading one then to speak of a combination.

Twenty reporters have analyzed the ruling of the user rights foreseen by their law as concrete,[98] seven as a combination.[99] Only the Taiwanese reporter sees the user rights remunerated by a fee as regulated solely abstractly. Apart from this exception, a purely abstract regulation of the user right is nowhere to be found. Noteworthy is that the famous American *fair use* is heavily bordered and actually limited by concrete requirements, even if it is broader than the similar Canadian *fair dealing*. The line between purely concrete regulations and combining regulations corresponds exactly to the *copyright/droit d'auteur* border.

Before presenting the abstract ruling of the three-step test, it makes sense to mention *the* common point ignoring any frontier: the permitted uses of computer programs are exhaustively enumerated everywhere (which certainly relies on international law requirements implementation).

4. The three-step test

Since the 1967 Stockholm conference, the Berne Convention states:

> It shall be a matter for legislation in the countries of the Union to permit the reproduction of literary and artistic works in certain special cases, provided that such reproduction does not conflict with a normal exploitation of the work and does not unreasonably prejudice the legitimate interests of the author.[100]

Article 13 of the TRIPS Agreement took up this point, actually extending it to any exploitations protected by the Agreement (the Berne Convention only applied this test to eventual permission by national lawmakers to *reproduce*) and referring to the legitimate interests of *right holders* instead of those of the *author* evoked in the Berne Convention. The WIPO Agreements of 1996 took up the wording

---

[93] One should, however, mention here Art. 70.5 of the **Canadian** Copyright Act since it belongs to the copyright-specific provisions. This special provision foresees the enforcement of competition law considerations against agreements between a collective society and a user, if the Competition Commissioner considers the agreement contrary to the public interest.

[94] See the details in the answers to Question 6.

[95] Although, German case law opened the list of exceptions, see for example BGH GRUR 2002, 963 – *Elektronischer Pressespiegel*.

[96] That is the reason why the **Japanese** reporter relates the ongoing debate in Japan on the issue of introducing a standard rule in this matter. **Egyptian** reporters also mention the debate regarding the implementation of a provision similar to the three-step test so as to provide for a flexible rule.

[97] **Spanish** law is here an exception since several limits are interpreted broadly.

[98] **Argentina**, **Australia** (regarding remunerated user rights and the mandatory license), **Belgium**, **Brazil**, **China**, **Croatia**, **Denmark**, **Egypt**, **Germany**, **Greece**, **Hungary**, **Italy**, **Japan**, **Lithuania**, **Macau**, **Norway**, **Poland**, **Portugal**, **UK**.

[99] **Australia** (only regarding user rights free of charge), **Cyprus** (fair dealing clause + list), **India**, **Israel** (beside an enumeration of free-of-charge user rights, the Israeli Copyright Act contains a fair use defense clause and a provision allowing the judge to decide as to the appropriate sanction), **Israel**, **Spain**, **Taiwan**, **USA**.

[100] BC Art. 9.2.

of the TRIPS Agreement (Art. 10 WCT), thereby extending it to phonograms (Art. 16 WPPT). The last big step on the international level has been its implementation into Art. 5.5 of the EU InfoSoc Directive (with its broad scope and the reference to right holders rather than authors), where the possible "exceptions and limitations" exhaustively listed shall respect the three steps.

Has the three-step test been explicitly implemented in national law (legislation)?

Most countries did not expressly implement the three-step test.[101] Yet its enactment in the TRIPS Agreement makes it binding on every country observed in this report. Ten legislations took up the three-step test as a general interpretation principle.[102] In order to be exact, one should specify, the French, Hungarian, Portuguese and Spanish reporters add that the implementation in their countries "omitted" the first step; the implementation in Poland and Macau is similar. The Hungarian reporter regards this "omission" as a consistent consideration of the fact that the first step intends to bind lawmakers and not judges.

Beside the consistent first-step omission, some countries have implemented it in their own way. Thus, the Spanish implementation followed the order given by the database and computer programs directives and not the order which is to be found in Art. 5.5 of the InfoSoc Directive. Furthermore, the Hungarian provision implementing the three-step test contains a second sentence: "Furthermore, use is allowed and can occur without remuneration if it fulfills the requirements of decency and its goal is not inconsistent with the purpose of free use."[103] This sentence makes the interpretation of the given use by courts even stricter and narrower, though these requirements are not directly mentioned in the three-step test.

In Belgium, this issue has been widely discussed. The Belgian Copyright Act did not implement the three-step test as such; however, some provisions do repeat the second "step", meaning the requirement to comply with the normal exploitation of the work.[104] Some of these provisions also require the examination of the third step involving the absence of prejudice of legitimate interests of right holders.

Did it play a role in the determination of the legal standards?

Twelve reporters state that the three-step test was considered in the course of the determination of their national legal standards.[105] Brazil should actually be added to those countries, since the currently applicable legal standards were not influenced by the three-step test, but the current discussion preparing the upcoming copyright reform does consider the three-step test, as do the discussions around it.

In the UK, the consideration of the three-step test led to the restriction of two permitted acts. On the contrary, despite the consideration the three-step test received there, the US reporter states domestic politics led to the three-step test being ignored, most notably in Sec. 110 para. 5 of the Copyright Act, which violates the test as embodied in Sec. 13 TRIPS, and gave rise to the famous WTO Dispute 160, requested by the European Communities.

---

[101] **Argentina**, **Australia**, **Belgium**, **Canada**, **Cyprus**, **Egypt**, **Germany**, **India**, **Israel**, **Japan**, **Norway**, **Taiwan**, **UK**, **USA**.

[102] **China** Art. 21, **Croatia** Art. 80, **France** Art. L. 122-5 9° para. 4, **Greece** Art. 28C, **Hungary** Art. 33 para. 2, **Italy** (also in several provisions, but as a general principle:) Art. 71^{nonies}, **Lithuania** Art. 19 para. 3 and 58, **Macau** Art. 62, **Poland** Art. 35, **Portugal** Art. 75 para. 4 and 81b, **Spain** Art. 40bis (and 100 para. 7 sooner implemented for computer programs). **Australian** law did not implement the three-step test as a general clause leading the interpretation of limitations and exceptions. Yet, one provision on permitted acts for libraries or archives, educational institutions and disabled persons repeats the three steps and expressly refers to their meaning in Art. 13 of the TRIPS Agreements, see Sec. 200AB.

[103] **Hungary** Art. 33 para. 2.

[104] See the exceptions for reprography for private purposes, for reproduction and communication within a closed network for teaching or scientific research purposes, for reproduction and communication of databases for public security purposes or for judicial or administrative proceedings, for the preservation of cultural and scientific patrimony and in favor of handicapped persons.

[105] **Belgium**, **Canada** ("possibly"), **Cyprus, Germany**, **Greece**, **Israel** (the three-step test has not been mentioned in the explanatory notes of the new law, but several public officials of the Ministry of Justice evoked it during conferences and discussions dealing with the new law, stating for example the fair use defense of the new Copyright Act is in accordance with the three-step test), **Norway, Poland, Portugal, Taiwan, UK, USA**.

The Croatian reporter urges as follows:

> the role of the "three-step test" in the Croatian law is not to enable the user to use the work outside of the list of limitations, but as a control mechanism if the provided limitation leads to a conflict with a normal exploitation of the work and unreasonably prejudices the legitimate interests of the author.

The same line of thought is found in the Chinese report. The Chinese reporter urges the restricting effect of the three-step test in relation to already existing permitted uses. "The three-step test is regarded in China as an additional condition to apply the limitations and exceptions to copyrights explicitly enumerated in the Copyright act, instead of an independent ground to justify an unauthorized use".

Is it directly applied by judicial practice?

Most reports answer in the negative[106]; although, eleven reporters relate case law in which judges expressly referred to the three-step test.[107] It is noteworthy that the French Supreme Court (Cour de cassation) did so before its explicit implementation. It then went with the current application in the UK, referring to international law since the three-step test has not been expressly implemented there.[108]

Several decisions of the tribunal civil de Bruxelles relied on the three-step test in order to state the narrow interpretation of limitations and exceptions,[109] and the Constitutional Court of Belgium definitely applied the "normal exploitation step" of the three-step test to censure a provision allowing the reproduction of an entire music score for purposes of teaching.[110] The French Supreme Court used the three-step test in order to reduce the scope of the private copy exception.[111] And the Hungarian Copyright Board directly applied the three-step test, and used it to decide against a file-sharing system.[112]

Is the "Declaration ..." well known, and ultimately which role did it play?[113]

The Declaration did not play any salient role in either legislation or the courts. Nevertheless, it comes with debates regarding the role the three-step test should play,[114] and it seems unknown only in very few countries.[115] The Chinese reporter points out the three-step test did not gain the attention of scholars in China at all; although, it has been expressly implemented in the Copyright Act.

5. **If categories of works are distinguished according to Question 1, to what extent do the legal instruments in Questions 2a–f differentiate according to these categories?**

Consideration of work categories in respect of preconditions or thresholds allowing a work's protection only if it surpasses a particular degree of creativity

Differences in approach between the common law *copyright* tradition and the civil law *droit d'auteur* tradition are clear here. As a matter of principle, continental European countries do not distinguish among works in respect of the conditions for works to be protected, outside of special cases regarding recent and technological or informational works such as computer programs and databases. On the contrary, even if the originality requirement is the same for all works, in common law countries (Australia, Canada, India, and the UK) eligibility conditions depend on the work categories in which the object at stake can fit. Thus, the fixation requirement can lead to the

[106] **Argentina**, **Australia**, **Belgium**, **Brazil**, **Croatia**, **Cyprus**, **Egypt**, **Israel**, **Japan**, **Lithuania**, **Norway**, **Portugal**, **USA**.

[107] **Belgium**, **Canada** (only a recent decision of the Copyright Board), **China**, **Germany**, **France**, **Italy** (only in respect of private copy disputes), **Norway** (actually only by the Remuneration Commission), **Poland** (direct application of the national implementation), **Spain**, **Taiwan**, **UK**.

[108] Only very occasionally as a general background principle favoring the claimant in cases concerning the application of the "fair dealing" exceptions. See *Hyde Park Residence Ltd v Yelland* (2001) Ch 143 (CA) and *Fraser-Woodward v BBC* (2005) FSR 762.

[109] **Belgium**, see among others the judgement of February 13, 2007, *A&M*, 2007, p. 107.

[110] **Belgium**, Decision 29/09 of the Belgian Constitutional Court.

[111] **France** Cass. Civ. 1, February 28, 2006, *IIC* 2006 760.

[112] **Hungarian** Copyright Board 07/08/1.

[113] Geiger, Griffiths and Hilty, Towards a Balanced Interpretation of the "Three-Step Test", (2008), EIPR 2008, 489, IIC 2008, 707: www.ip.mpg.de/files/pdf2/declaration_three_step_test_final_englishl.pdf.

[114] See for instance in **Brazil** and **Spain**.

[115] **Argentina**, **Australia**, **Egypt**, **India**, **Israel**, **Poland**, **Taiwan**.

exclusion of some work categories from copyright protection.

Beside this theoretical distinction, it appears in all reports that the functional feature of works is actually considered in respect of the appreciation of reproduction rights infringement.

It appears especially in Australian law:

> where infringement of works and subject matter is determined by whether a "substantial part" of the work/subject matter has been taken (sec. 14 para. 1). Whether a literary work is of fact or fiction will influence how much of the creation can be taken before infringement occurs. The Australian High Court has held that facts, especially those limited to their expression, involve minimal creative effort and therefore are of "thin" subsistence.[116] As such, for infringement to have taken place in regards to a work of non-fiction, particularly tables of data, a larger proportion of the literary work must be taken.

The consideration of the functional nature of a work also occurs, although not that expressly, in *droit d'auteur* countries. The functional feature is actually not expressly considered in civil-law countries, but the specific provisions regarding databases and computer programs is considered by the French reporter as an implicit consequence of their industrial nature. Yet an important difference has to be pointed out, since the need for protection of these specific objects actually leads to a stronger protection of these works. For example, computer programs do not need to prove originality for being protected under French copyright law but must show some "personalized effort,"[117] and most countries reduce the scope of permitted use of these works, first of all the private copy. The Japanese reporter confirms the connection of computer programs with functional works, stating compilations and databases are regarded as copyrighted works with a functional nature. But this attention paid to computer programs, databases and DRM lies on specific legal clauses, mostly required by international law.

Beside these implicit considerations of the functional characteristics of works categories in the legal provisions, the way judges view the originality condition also concerns the functional features of works inside works categories, or, more precisely, without consideration of the works categories in *droit d'auteur* countries, and regarding the Australian requirements to fit in the category of artistic works of craftsmanship. Facing functional constraints and a very narrow scope of design choice for the author, copyright protection does not occur.[118] In this vein, Chinese copyright also refuses to protect the expression of technical ideas.[119] In short, the functional character of a creation leads to a restriction of the scope of protection.[120]

Finally, the consideration of the functional feature of a work can also bear the requirement for both quantity and quality, as in *common law countries*, or of a substantive creativity, as in Germany.[121] Thus, the Australian substantiality requirement[122] is near to the German *Schöpfungshöhe* requirement, relying on the originality requirement.

Period of protection

The Belgian and Croatian reports relate no distinction among works beside the necessary consideration of the lack of an initiation of

[116] *IceTV Pty Ltd v Nine Network Australia Pty Ltd* (see note 49), at 463.

[117] Cour de cassation., ass. plén., March 7, 1986, *Pachot*, *JCP E*, 1986, II, 14713 et 14737bis, note Mousseron, Tessier and Vivant; *D.*, 1986, 405, concl. Cabanes et note Exelmans.

[118] **Japan**. For a call of **Danish** scholars in this sense, see Schovsbo and Rosenmeier, *Immaterialret* (2008), 63.

See also, subsequently, an Australian case refusing copyright protection to a "mold" for the hull of a boat, which cannot qualify as "artistic craftsmanship" as it is limited by functional constraints and aesthetic considerations form only a minor aspect of the work, *Burge v Swarbrick* (2007) 72 IPR 235, 256.

[119] **China** *Qian Wang*, Textbook on Intellectual Property Law (Chinese People's University Press, 2007), 49–50.

[120] **Australia** *Burge v Swarbrick* (2007) 72 IPR 235, 256, **Belgium**, **Japan**, **Portugal** see judgment of December 16, 2008, case no. 8864/2008-5, available at http://www.dgsi.pt, **Taiwan** (but only in the literature of scholars).

[121] And in **Brazil**, where the creativity requirement is actually expressly required by the Copyright Act only for two kinds of works: derived and transformed works, **Brazil** Art. 7 caput XI, and anthologies, compilations, dictionaries and databases, **Brazil** Art. 7 caput XIII.

[122] **Australia** Sec. 14 para.1, and *IceTV Pty Ltd v Nine Network Australia Pty Ltd* (see note 49), at 458–9.

the period of protection when considering anonymous works, which are mentioned by most reports for having a specific protection time span.[123] The specificity lies in the fact the duration lasts from the publication date rather than the author's death. In Argentina, further, the term is then shorter.[124] It can be considered as an enhancement for authors to disclose their identity.

But regarding the categories of works, the industrial or functional feature is the characteristic most regarded. Thus, for cinematographic and audiovisual works, the start of the period of protection is, in some countries, rather than the death of the author(s) for "regular" works, the public communication[125] or the completion of the work provided the work has never been published.[126] In other words, the time span is shorter,[127] or the protection is counted in a genuine way.[128] On the contrary, the fact some protected objects require more investment than a pencil and a paper sheet, leads to a longer period of protection for cinematographic works. In this regard, Japanese law the best example, clearly stating cinematographic works get an additional 20 years of protection.[129] In *droit d'auteur* countries the protection term begins with the public communication of the work only for neighboring rights.[130] Although, copyright does not last longer as a matter of principle, lawmakers chose the latest time period possible, the last death among the co-authors,[131] which corresponds to the general principle assessing the duration in respect of works created by several co-authors.

In some countries, photographic works,[132] works of applied art,[133] software[134] and databases[135] also receive specific and shorter time span protection. Regarding such works being on the boundary between artistic expressions and industrial exploitation, noteworthy is also the situation of *artistic works exploited by an industrial process,* in the UK.

The usual period of protection (governed by provisions implementing the Term Directive) is effectively reduced to 25 years from the end of the year in which marketing of the articles in question takes place. This alteration is effected by CDPA 1988, Sec. 52, which permits the making of otherwise infringing articles after the expiry of that 25 year period (i.e., copyright is not entirely suppressed, but it becomes possible to make and market such articles without infringing copyright). This provision was designed to minimise the extent to which copyright can be relied upon to extend the effective protection of industrial designs beyond the duration of registered design protection.

[123] **Argentina**, **Belgium** Art. 2, **Brazil**, **Canada, Croatia**, **Cyprus** Art. 11 para. 5, **Denmark**, **France** (L. 123-3), **Lithuania**, **Macau** Art. 23 para. 1, **Norway** Sec. 41 para. 1, (3rd sentence), **Poland** Art. 36, **USA** Chap. 3.

[124] The protection thereof lasts 50 years instead of 70 years.

[125] **Australia** Sec. 94, **Brazil**, **Canada** Art. 11.1 (only for cinematographic work not having a dramatic character), **China**, **Taiwan** Art. 34 I, **Macau** Art. 106.

[126] **China**.

[127] **Argentina**: 50 years, but running from the death of the last collaborators among: the producer, the script author, the director, and for musical films, the composer of the soundtrack.

[128] **Japan** Art. 54 (70 years from the creation of the work instead of 50 years following the 50 year period following the making public of the work).

[129] **Japan** Art. 54.

[130] **Italy** Art. 78[ter], **Lithuania** Art. 59 para. 4.

[131] Those co-authors are the principal director, the author of the screenplay, the author of the dialogue, the art director, and the director of photography and the composer of music, **France**, **Lithuania** Art. 35 para. 4, **Portugal** Art. 34.

[132] The duration runs from the public communication in **Argentina**, **Brazil**, **China**, **India**, **Italy**, **Norway** (for the producers of the photographic picture) Sec. 43a, **Taiwan** Art. 34 I; or from the completion of the work, **Canada** Art. 10.1 (for photographs of which the owner is a corporation), **China** (provided the work has never been published), **Macau** Art. 155. More discriminating, the term can be much shorter, **Argentina** 20 years instead of 70 years, running from the first publication, *idem* in **Italy** Art. 92, **Macau** 25 years Art. 155, **Taiwan**. A similar differentiation was removed in Germany in 1985. In **Spain**, "mere photographs", meaning those not fulfilling the originality requirement, are protected 25 years from the making of the photograph, Art. 128.

[133] **China** (since implementation of the International Copyright Convention only for foreign works), **Egypt** Art. 164 (25 years after publication), **Macau** (actually also covering works of architecture and of graphic arts) Art. 148.

[134] Software only enjoys 50-year protection in **Brazil** (instead of 70 years for "regular" works), and the protection period runs from publication in **Brazil**, in **Portugal** in case of copyright originally vesting in a person other than the creator of the work Art. 36-2, and in **Taiwan**, but only if the author of the computer program is not an individual person Arts. 30 and 33.

[135] **Denmark**, **Portugal**, **Lithuania** Art. 64 para. 1 and 2, **Norway**.

In the same vein, stage sets are protected in Italy for only 5 years from their first publication or communication to the public.[136]

Objects protected by neighboring rights have also been mentioned by reporters for having a specific regulation ruling the period of protection.[137]

Some national reporters also related the fact that the rights originally vesting in persons other than the creator lead to a specific protection term. That is the case for works made for hire[138] when the rights vest in a corporate body,[139] for works of which the first owner is the State (when created by State employee),[140] or other public organizations such as provinces, communities, academies or public cultural organizations, or to entities of a non-profit character.[141]

On the extreme opposite, the US situation of moral rights in a visual work deserves to be mentioned; they are limited to the life of the author.[142] The delicate balance between the protection of the relation between the author and his or her work on the one hand, and the general interest for easy access to works on the other, is also very specific in respect of anthologies in Greece, where the use of works in anthologies can only be forbidden by the author during his life[143]; in respect of translations in Egypt, where authors can forbid use only 3 years from the publication[144]; and for communications and memoranda published by academies and other public cultural organizations in Italy, where "the term is reduced to 2 years, after which the author wholly recovers his right to the unrestricted disposal of his writings."[145]

User rights and mandatory licenses

Most reports mention computer programs and databases because they are not covered by most exceptions and limitations,[146] or have their own.[147] Furthermore, their specificity is underlined by the fact that in European countries and in those belonging to the *droit d'auteur* tradition, the "exceptions and limitations" granted in their respect actually are the only "user rights", meaning right holders may not restrict these liberties by contract. On the contrary, US law provides extra rights to owners and users of computer programs, yet allows right holders to restrict these rights by contract.[148]

Apart from fine distinctions, the copyright laws of all countries (except one, Macao) devote special provisions to the exceptions

[136] **Italy** Art. 86.

[137] The **Chinese** and **German** reporters mentioned it generally; for *sound recordings and performances*, see also **Australia** Sec. 93; **China** 50 years from the first fixation; **Cyprus**, 50 years from public communication or in default from recording Art. 3 para. 1b and Art. 10c for performers; **Denmark**, **Hungary** Art. 84 para. 2; **Israel** Art. 41 instead of 70 years *pma*, it is 50 years from the date of making the works; **Italy** 50 years running from the first publication or public communication instead of 70 years pma, Art. 75 for phonographic producers, Art. 78[ter] for producers of cinematographic or audio-visual works, Art. 79 for radio and television broadcasting companies, and Art. 85 for performers; **Lithuania** Art. 59 para. 1 for performers and Art. 59 para. 2 for producers; **Macau** Art. 182 (the rights of performers lapse 50 years after the performance) and 188 (the rights of producers of phonograms and videograms shall lapse 50 years after fixation); **Norway** Sec. 42 for performers, Sec. 45 for producers; **Taiwan** Art. 34I running from the public release of the work; **UK** 50 years instead of 70. For broadcasts, see **Australia** 50 years from the broadcast Sec. 95, **China** 50 years from the first transmission, **Cyprus** 50 years from publication and in default the date of the broadcast instead of 70 years pma, **Denmark**, **Hungary**, **Italy** like in Cyprus Art. 79, **Lithuania** Art. 59 para. 3, **Macau** 20 years from the broadcast Art. 192, **Norway** Sec. 45a, **UK** 50 years instead of 70. For typographical arrangement, see **Australia** 25 years running the publication of the edition Sec. 96, **China** (10 years running from the first publication), **UK** 25 years instead of 70.

[138] **Macau** Art. 22, **USA** Chap. 3.

[139] **Brazil**, **Macau** (actually collective works and works created for others) Art. 22 para. 3, **Taiwan** Art. 33, **Poland** Art. 36.

[140] **Canada** Art. 5 para. 1, **Israel** Art. 42 instead of 70 years pma, it is 50 years from the date of making the works.

[141] **Italy** Art. 29 (20 years from the first publication).

[142] **USA**, Sec. 106A. *Eldred v. Ashcroft*, (2003), 537 U.S. 186 (2003) held that this period of protection did not violate the Constitutional provision providing that copyright protection could last only for a limited time.

[143] **Greece** Art. 20 para. 2.

[144] **Egypt** Art. 148.

[145] **Italy** Art. 29.

[146] For example in **Spain**, the private copying limitation expressly excludes databases and computer programs, see Art. 31 para. 2.

[147] Urged by the **Egyptian**, **Hungarian**, **Lithuanian**, **Portuguese** and **Spanish** reporters. Although parody, reporting of news, personal use in the family circle, and use in the course of teaching exception apply to databases works in **Belgium**, see Art. 22[bis] para. 1(2).

[148] **USA** Sec. 117.

and limitations on computer programs,[149] and most of them to databases.[150]

In addition, in most countries architectural works also receive special treatment in respect of user rights. For example, they can freely be reproduced when they are permanently located in public spaces.[151] In addition, the specific nature of architectural works, when they in fact are constructions, also leads some countries to provide specific rights for users such as the right to reproduce the work by adding to it, renovating it, or implementing changes required by security.[152]

Finally, one should mention the specific status of musical scores, which are for the most part excluded from the field of user rights.[153]

6. **Provisions and case law considering the creativity threshold (2a), user rights free of charge (2c), user rights with a fee (2d), mandatory licenses (2e), specific copyright misuse regulation (2f)**

Creativity threshold

Most reports state that their copyright law does not distinguish among categories of works (beside the core distinction between works protected by the copyright and subject matter protected by neighboring rights – considering here the creation, we only regard works). As regards the preconditions or thresholds allowing a work's protection only if it surpasses a particular degree of creativity, jurisdictions of the *droit d'auteur* tradition state the idea/expression dichotomy as the only general limitation,[154] and jurisdictions of the common-law tradition, beyond this fundamental dichotomy, require the fixation of the expression to be protected (or works to have a material form[155]). Therefore, the sole requirements for the works to be protected are to be expressed (and shaped or designed[156]) and *original*.[157] Actually some countries apply the threshold of originality although their copyright acts do not expressly require it,[158] and use the term "individual",[159] "personal"[160] or

[149] **Australia** Sec. 47 B et seq., **Belgium** Art. 6 of the Computer Programs Act of June 30, 1994, **Brazil** Law 9.605 of 1998, **Canada** Art. 30.6, **China** Art. 16 et seq. of the regulation on the computer software protection, **Croatia** Art. 108 et seq., **Cyprus** Art. 7B para. 4 et seq., **Denmark**, **Egypt**, **France** Art. L. 122-6-1, **Germany** Sec. 69d–e, **Greece** Arts. 42–44, **Israel** Sec. 24a et seq., **Italy** Art. 64[bis] et seq., **India, Japan** Art. 47-2, **Lithuania** Arts. 30–32, **Norway** Sec. 39, **Poland** Art. 74 et seq., **Portugal** Art. 6 of the decree-law 252/94, **Spain** Art. 100, **UK** Sec. 296A, **USA** Sec. 117.

[150] **Belgium** Art. 22[bis] Sec. 1 para. 5, **Croatia** Art. 97 and 151, **Cyprus** Art. 7C para. 2a and 7C para. 3b, **France** Art. L. 432-3, **Germany** Secs. 55a and 87c, **Hungary** Art. 33, **Italy** Art. 64[quinquies–sexies], **Lithuania** Arts. 30–32, **Portugal** Art. 10 of the Decree Law 122/2000, **Spain** Art. 34, **UK** Sec. 296B.

[151] **Brazil** Art. 48, **China** (any use but not foreseen by the Regulation on Information Networks) Art. 22 para. 10, **Croatia** Art. 91, **Egypt** (only reproduction), **Europe** (reproduction and making available) InfoSoc Directive Art. 5 para. 3h, **Germany** Sec. 59, **Greece** Art. 26, **Hungary** Art. 68 para. 1, **Israel** Sec. 23, **Japan** Art. 46, **Lithuania, Macau** Art. 61 j, **Poland** Art. 33 point 1, **Portugal** Art. 75 para. 2q, **Taiwan** Art. 58, **UK** Art. 62 (but not if the copied work is two-dimensional).

[152] **Croatia**, **Lithuania**, **USA**.

[153] See for example **Croatia** Arts. 32 and 82, **Cyprus** Art. 7 para. 2p, **France** L. 122-10, **Lithuania** Art. 23 para. 1(1) and 3.

[154] Mostly implicit in copyright acts (except in **Macau** Art. 1, **Poland**, Art. 1 Sec. 2) and in the Berne Convention. It is however in the TRIPS Agreement, Art. 9.2.

[155] **Australia** Sec. 14 para. 1, **Canada** *Canadian Admiral Corp. v. Rediffusion Inc.* [1954] Ex. C.R. 382, **Israel**, **UK** Sec. 3 para. 2.

[156] "*mis en forme*", in **France** and **Belgium**.

[157] **Argentina**, **Belgium**, **Canada** Art. 5 para. 1, **Croatia** in respect of clothing model, see Supreme Court – VSRH II Rev-2/94,1 September 1994, Gliha, I., *Autorsko pravo – sudska praksa* (Copyright law – Court's Case-Law) o.c., 1996, Dec. 13, **Cyprus** Art. 3 para. 2 and see for the case law acknowledgement of the idea/expression dichotomy Supreme Court of Cyprus, *Sokratous v. Gruppo: Editoriale Fabbri – Bompiani and "Gnosi"* publications, 1997, **Denmark**, **Egypt** Art. 138 para.2, **Greece** Art. 2 para. 1, **France** (in the literature but neither in the Copyright Act nor in the case law), **Hungary** Art. 1 para. 3, **India**, **Israel** Sec. 4(a), **Italia** Art. 1, **Lithuania** Art. 4 para. 1 and Art. 2 para. 19, **Macau** Art. 1 para. 4 and 2, **Norway**, **Portugal** Art. 1, **Taiwan** Art. 31, for the requirement of being expressed and Art. 2 for the originality, **UK** Art. 1 para. 1 a (for literary, dramatic, musical or artistic works), **USA** Art. 102a and the *Feist* decision stating: "the sine qua non of Copyright is originality", and **international law**: Art. 9.1 of the TRIPS Agreement.

[158] **France**.

[159] **Belgium**, **Croatia** Art. 5, **Germany** Art. 2, **Hungary** Art. 1 para. 3, **Poland** Art. 1.

[160] **Belgium** C. of Cass., February 24, 1995, *Pas.*, 1995, I, 211 and Rec. Cass., 1995, p. 318, comment M. Buydens; C. of Cass., December 10, 1998, *Pas.*, I, 516, **Cyprus** Art. 3 para. 2b, **France**, **Italy**, **Lithuania** similar to the French doctrine, Lithuanian legal literature explains that originality manifestsitself in the expression of the author's personality in the work, S.A. Vileita. *Lietuvos autorių teisių ir gretutinių teisių komentaras* [Commentary on the Law on Copyright and Neighbouring Rights] (Vilnius, 2000), 33.

"creative".[161] A condition is more or less explicitly contained in this definition of originality: the requirement for the work to be intellectual, meaning the creation of a human being,[162] which excludes creation by "machines",[163] and the original vesting of copyright in a corporate entity, except in the case of collective works. In most EU Member States, the definition of the creativity threshold as it appears in the European *acquis communautaire*,[164] does not correspond to the general originality requirement but is stated for specific works of which the creativity raises specific issues, such as computer programs or photographs.[165] Apparently nearer to the common-law criterion, the Portuguese report defines originality as the requirement for the subject matter to *be the product of a creative effort by their authors*.[166] One should mention here that Belgian case law also uses the criterion of effort in order to establish the individual feature of a work, but it is then only an instrument to indicate the personality reflection criterion.[167] This proximity to common law copyright tradition is confirmed in the Portuguese report, urging that creations must *pertain to the literary, scientific or artistic fields*.[168] Also Italy has a kind of maverick approach among the *droit d'auteur* countries. The Italian Copyright Act requires for a work to be protected by copyright that it proves a low degree of creativity,[169] and is objectified or externalized,[170] which is almost "classical" since it corresponds to the originality and exteriorization requirements; but further on, the work shall be new (novelty requirement). Lastly the object should be affiliated to art or culture (meaning it fits in one of the ten categories listed in the Copyright Act).[171]

Japanese law apparently does not use the term originality, and refers to "creativity,"[172] but follows the very low threshold of *droit d'auteur* countries, using as a criterion the fact that the copyrighted works are considered as an "effluent of personality", therefore using a "subjective creativity."[173] Article 2 para. 1 item 1 of the Japanese Copyright Act provides a definition of "copyrighted works" as follows: "'work' means a production in which thoughts or sentiments are expressed in a

[161] **Brazil** Art. 7 caput XI (for derived and transformed works) and XIII (for anthologies, compilations, dictionaries, databases), **Poland** Art. 1, **Lithuania** Art. 4. para. 1, **Macau** Art. 1 para. 4.

[162] **Germany**, **Portugal**.

[163] **Hungary**, **Portugal** Art. 1. Cf. the originality requirement in **Canada** that implies the work should not be the result of only mechanical treatment, *CCH Canadian Ltd. v Law Society of Upper Canada*, (see note 102), at p. 356.

[164] See Art. 6 of the Directive 2006/116/EC of the European Parliament and of the Council of December 12, 2006 on the term of protection of copyright and certain related rights, "author's own intellectual creation".

[165] See for example in **Belgium**, Art. 2 para. 5 for photographic works, Art. 20bis para. 1 on databases and Art. 2 of the Belgian Computer Program Act (*Loi du 30 juin 1994 transposant en droit belge la directive européenne du 14 mai 1991 concernant la protection juridique des programmes d'ordinateur, M.B.*, July 27, 1994).

[166] This condition is implicit in several provisions of the Copyright Code (such as Art. 2, which defines original works) and has been recognized by the Lisbon Court of Appeal, according to which the creative nature of a work "depends upon the fact that such a work is not the copy of another work (minimum requisite), that it is not the result of the mere application of pre-established criteria, notably of technical nature, from which true choices or options of the author are absent, and that it expresses a result that is not obvious or trivial, and hence may be distinguished from other works and recognized in it its individuality as a work", see the judgment of December 16, 2008, case no. 8864/2008-5, available at http://www.dgsi.pt.

[167] Court of Appeal Brussels (9e ch.), February 1, 2002, *A.J.T.*, 2001-02, p. 748.

[168] **Portugal** Art. 1.

[169] **Italy** Cass. no. 425/2005, Cass. no. 5089/2004, Cass. no. 13937/1999 and Cass. no. 908/1995.

[170] **Italian** Court of cassation, February 13, 1987, no. 1558.

[171] Meaning it should fit in one of these categories: 1. literary works, 2. musical works, 3. choreographic or pantomimic works, 4. sculpture, picture and design, 5. architectural works, 6. cinematographic works, 7. photographic work, 8. software, 9. database and 10. industrial design (Art. 2).

[172] **Japan** Art. 2 para. 1 item 1.

[173] Some **Japanese** case law mentions that a sufficient level of creativity is satisfied if the work embodies "some kind of personality" (Judgment of the Tokyo High Court on February 19, 1987), *Hanrei Jiho* No. 1225, p. 111 (Case on expectancy table on an outcome of the election) or is "not an imitation of others" (Judgment of the Tokyo District Court on October 11, 1972), *Hanrei Taimuzu* No. 289, p. 377 (*Confess of Minsei* case).

creative way and which falls within the literary, scientific, artistic or musical domain."[174]

Other considerations do not matter in *droit d'auteur* countries: there is not another formal requirement on the form of expression, disclosure, publication, communication or purpose, merit, use, or economic exploitation.[175] This disregard for the merit of creators is also to be found in Australia,[176] but it concerns the literary merit and is therefore probably to be understood as a qualitative appreciation, which is obviously to be avoided, since it would bring about the danger of censorship. In any case, the core difference between copyright countries and *droit d'auteur* countries relies on the consideration of labor by the former and not by the latter.

As a matter of fact, originality is also a requirement for *works* to be protected in common-law tradition countries, but it covers a broader scope than in the *droit d'auteur* conception. The originality requirement in common law countries includes "sweat of the brow", in other words in Australia the efforts of the author,[177] or in the UK a *sufficient degree of "labor and skill."*[178] US case law has required originality since the nineteenth century[179] and stated again what the required originality means in the *Feist Decision* in 1991: "that the work was independently created (as opposed to copied from other works), and that it possesses at least some minimal degree of creativity."[180] However, a decision of the early twentieth century "held that the required degree was low."[181] The Canadian Copyright Act requires originality. It deserves to be mentioned that "creativity" appeared in the British Copyright Act in relation to databases[182] following Directive 96/9/EC, and this requirement is assumed to have the value of a standard also for computer programs and photographs.

India "shows a departure from this requirement of labor, judgment or skill, by adopting a midway between English 'sweat of the brow' and the US 'modicum of creativity' approach."[183] The Israeli Supreme Court stated the investment of efforts, resources and skills in the production of an intangible work does not suffice for a work to be protected by copyright,[184] and moved with this decision to a more US-oriented approach as adopted in the *Feist* decision,[185] requiring a minimum of creativity.[186] Cypriot case law does not refer to the efforts but defines the requirement to be protected similarly to the US *Feist* decision. Yet, the Cypriot Supreme Court interpreted the legal requirement of originality that states a work shall be a personal, intellectual creation[187] of the author by grounding on the case law of other Commonwealth countries,[188] "But

[174] Concerning the details about "copyrighted works" under **Japanese** law, see Hisayoshi Yokoyama, Works, available at http://www.tomeika.jur.kyushu-u.ac.jp/ip/index.html (Last visited on October 18, 2010).

[175] **France** Art. L. 112-1, **Hungary**, **Macau** Art. 1 para. 1 and Art. 1 para. 3, **Spain**.

[176] *IceTV Pty Ltd v Nine Network Australia Pty Ltd* (2009) 83 ALJR 585, 595.

[177] **Australia**, **Macau** Art. 1 para. 4.

[178] **UK** for recent application, see the decision of the Court of Appeal in *Sawkins v Hyperion* [2005] WLR 3281 (CA).

[179] See the *Trademark cases* 100 U.S. 82 (1879).

[180] **Taiwan** also uses this definition of originality.

[181] **USA** *Bleistein v. Donaldson Lithographing Co.* 188 U.S. 239 (1903).

[182] **UK** Sec. 3A para. 2.

[183] So the **Indian** reporter, referring to *Eastern Book Co v. D. B. Modak* [(2008) 1 SCC 1].

[184] **Israel** see, C.A. 513/89 *Interlego A/S v. Exin-Line Bros. S.A.*, 48(4) P.D. 133 (1991).

[185] *Feist Publications, Inc. v. Rural Telephone Service Company* (1991) 499 US 340 (1991) (**USA**).

[186] That is why in a recent decision, the Tel Aviv District Court rejected the protection for a mere live television broadcast of a sporting event since it does not amount to an original creative work, see *The Football Association Premier League, Ltd. v. Ploni*, Tak-District 08(3) 2514 (2008). Waiting for the decision of the Supreme Court in this case, the reporter urges it is questionable whether this decision reflects the law in **Israel** since other judgments are satisfied with a minimum amount of skill, labor and judgment, see *Kimron v. Shanks*, C.A. 2811/93, 54 P.D. (3) 817.

[187] **Cyprus** Art. 3 para. 2b.

[188] **Cyprus**: Supreme Court of Cyprus in the *Sokratous v. Gruppo Editoriale Fabbri – Bompiani and "Gnosi" publications* decision (1997), referring to the famous UK decision *University of London Press Ltd. v. University Tutorial Press Ltd* (1916, 2 Ch. 601) andto the decisions *Macmillan & Co. Ltd. v. Cooper (K. & J.)* (1923, L.R. 51 Ind. App. 109, 93 L.J.P.C. 113, 40 T.L.R. 186), *British Broadcasting Co. v. Wireless League Gazette Publishing Co* (1926) Ch. 433 and *Wham-O Manufacturing Co. v. Lincoln Industries Ltd*, (1985, R.P.C. 127, New Zeeland Court of Appeal).

the Act does not require that the expression must be in an original or novel form, but that the work must not be copied from another work – that it should originate from the author."[189]

User rights free of charge

The ground for free-of-charge user rights granted by the law in favor of third parties (meaning a third party to any license contract) lies in the need for granting access to the public or to some specific users; a need that overrides the regular economic rights of copyright holders.

Beside specific cases brought about by practical issues (such as incidental uses), the Israeli Act provides for a definition of fair use summing up concerns dealt with by the regulations at stake in all reports: "purposes such as: private study, research, criticism, review, journalistic reporting, quotation, or instruction and examination by an educational institution".[190]

The fairy tale of the "fair use" clauses in the UK, USA and parent countries needs to be refined. Australia, Canada, Cyprus, India, Israel, Taiwan, the UK and USA indeed know "fair use" or "fair dealing" provisions.[191] Their specificity lies essentially in the fact that they allow "uses" (and not specifically reproduction or performance, etc.). Furthermore, thanks to their abstract writings, they offer the possibility for judges to go beyond the specific cases lawmakers could have had in mind when enacting the statute.

The first aspect of the general interest considered by lawmakers for authorizing use of copyright protected work free of charge is the expression and information freedom. Thus, every country allows quotation and fair use for reporting or reviewing, criticism and parody. Actually, most countries do not expressly authorize parody and caricature.[192]

The balance in respect of quotation is mostly found by requiring the reproduction to be "*short*" or "*not longer than the extent necessary to the purpose,*" the quoted work has been lawfully published, and as far as possible source and attribution are mentioned in the quoting work. Furthermore, quotation or reviewing requires the quoting work to be independent and self-sufficient – more consistent than a mere compilation. Regarding the relation between the quoted and the quoting work, two Chinese cases provide an interesting example of the balance at stake. They concern fair use of music in a popular TV series and on a website. The length of the "quotations" did not matter. The whole issue actually rests on whether the substantial part of a work is reproduced or not. In both cases, uses reproducing in the first case "a part of the song which substantially reflects the original creation and personality of the authors,"[193] and in the second case "the climax part of the song," even for only 23 s,[194] go beyond fair use and constitute an infringement of the plaintiff's right.

Here the Argentinean law deserves a special mention since the provision allowing quotation for educational or scientific purposes, comments, criticism and report not only refers to the necessary extent but adds a concrete quantity of the allowed reproduction.[195] Still in South America, the Brazilian law also contains a very specific provision related to the expression freedom: transformative use is allowed as such, provided the work is used only partially.[196]

[189] So *University of London Press Ltd. v. University Tutorial Press Ltd* (1916, 2 Ch. 601) quoted by the **Cypriot** report.

[190] **Israel** Sec. 19.

[191] **Australia** Sec. 40 et seq. and 103 et seq., **Canada** Art. 29, **Cyprus** Art. 7 para. 2, **India** Sec. 52, **Israel** Sec. 19, **Taiwan** Sec. 65, **UK** Sec. 30 of the CDPA and 137 of the Broadcasting Act 1996 and **USA** Sec. 107.

[192] Parody and caricature, or any use of work thanks to humor, are only mentioned by the **Australian**, **Belgian**, **Brazilian**, **Canadian**, **Croatian**, **French**, **Japanese**, **Lithuanian**, and **Spanish** reports.

[193] **China** *Years with Enthusiastic Passion* Case (2004) Beijing Higher People's Courts, Civil Affair Division, no. 627.

[194] **China** Case *Wine of 9th September*, (2007) Wuhan, Intermediate People's Court, Intellectual Property Division, no. 179.

[195] Maximum 1000 words for written works or eight bars for musical scores, **Argentina** Art. 10.

[196] Visual art works can be fully reproduced, **Brazil** Art. 46 VIII.

Quotation is authorized as such, but the "right to" reproduce for reporting or criticizing is abstractly authorized only in a few countries, mostly common-law countries.[197] Beside such general privilege, the fair use or fair dealing provisions for reporting or reviewing, reproduction and communication of published articles on current topics,[198] press review,[199] reproduction and communication of works in the context of reporting on or advertising for current art exhibitions or public sales,[200] and reproduction and communication of public speeches[201] (speeches in political or judicial assemblies, addresses, sermons, academic lectures) each receives a single provision.

The second area where the general interest takes precedence over the interest of right holders is research and education.

Here again, the dichotomy appears between common-law countries which generally state a fair dealing provision for purposes of research and study, as well as for teaching,[202] and other countries which list very specific cases devoted to education and research. In order to present an outline of these situations, we will first mention the collective then the individual uses.

The most often recurring exception is for uses in the classroom,[203] educational institutions[204] and during examinations,[205] for teaching purposes,[206] or for critical, scientific or educational lectures.[207] School broadcasts also occur and receive an exception provided the school does not conserve the copies over a certain period.[208] Specific provisions for

[197] It is noteworthy, also **Brazil** and **Portugal** provide for such a general clause.

[198] **Germany** Sec. 50.

[199] **Cyprus** Art. 7 para. 2f, **France** Art. L. 122-5 para. 3 b, **Germany** Sec. 49, **Italy** Art. 65, **Hungary** Art. 36 para. 2, **Israel** Sec. 19, **Macau** Art. 61b, **Poland** Art. 26, **Portugal** Art. 75 para. 2c.

[200] **Belgium** Art. 22 para. 1 12°, **Croatia** Art. 93, **Denmark** Sec. 24, **Europe** InfoSoc Directive Art. 5 para. 3j, **France** Art. L. 122-5 para. 3d, **Germany** Sec. 58, **Greece** Art. 28, **Japan** Art. 47, **Lithuania** Art. 24, **Norway** Sec. 24, **Poland** Art. 33 point 2, **Portugal** Art. 75 para. 2 l.

[201] **Argentina** Art. 27, **Belgium** Art. 8 Sec. 1 al. 2 and Sec. 2, **Brazil** Art. 46 para . Ib, **Canada** Art. 32.2 para. 1c and e, **China** Art. 22 para. 5 for fair use exception to copyright and Art. 6(4) of the Regulation on the Protection for the Right of Communication via Information Network, adopted on May 10, 2006, effective since July 1, 2006, **Cyprus** Art. 7 para. 2n, **Denmark** Sec. 26, **Egypt**, **France** Art. L. 122-5 para. 3c, **Germany** Sec. 45 and 48, **Greece** Art. 25 para. 1b and para. 2, **Hungary** Art. 36 para. 1 and Art. 41, **Italy** Art. 66, **Japan** Art. 40, **Lithuania** Art. 24, **Macau** Arts. 6 and 61a, **Norway** Sec. 26, **Poland** Art. 25, **Portugal** Art. 75 para. 2b, **Spain** Art. 31bis para. 1 and Art. 33 para. 2, **Portugal**, **Taiwan** Arts. 50 and 62. And especially for judicial proceedings: **Australia** Sec. 43, **Belgium** Art. 8 Sec. 1 al. 2 and Sec. 2, **Brazil** Art. 46 VII, **China** Art. 22 para. 7 for fair use exception to copyright and Art. 6 (6) of the Regulation on the Protection for the Right of Communication via Information Network, adopted on May 10, 2006, effective since July 1, 2006, **Croatia** Art. 87, **Cyprus** Art. 7 para. 2m, **Denmark** Sec. 26, **Egypt**, **Germany** Sec. 45, **Greece** Art. 24, **Hungary** Art. 41 para. 2, **Israel** Sec. 20, **Italy** Art. 67, **Japan** Arts. 40 and 42, **Lithuania** Art. 27, **Macau** Art. 61L, **Poland** Art. 33, **Portugal** Art. 75 para. 2n, **Taiwan** Arts. 45 and 62.

[202] See for example **Australia** Sec. 40 and 103C, **Cyprus** Art. 7 para. 2, **Israel** Sec. 17, **USA** Sec. 107.

[203] **China** Art. 22 para. 6 for the fair use exception to copyright and Art. 6 para. 5 of the Regulation on the Protection for the Right of Communication via Information Network, adopted on May 10, 2006, effective since July 1, 2006, **Japan** Art. 35, **Taiwan** Art. 46. Especially for visual works, **Hungary** Art. 68 para. 2. Outside of the very broad scope of the quotation exception, **Spanish** law also foresees an exception for teaching in the classroom, explicitly referring to "teachers of officially regulated education", Art. 32 para. 2.

[204] **Canada** Art. 29.5, **Croatia** Art. 88, **Greece** Art. 21 (only concerns short written works – articles from newspaper or periodical, short extracts of a work or parts of a short works – or lawfully published works of fine arts), **Japan** Art. 35, **Macau** Art. 61e, **Poland** Art. 27. See, only for reproduction, and provided it affects only short extracts of written or visual works, **Lithuania** Art. 22 para. 1(1).

[205] **Belgium** Art. 22 para. 1 7°, **Israel** Sec. 19, **Norway** Sec. 13a, **Taiwan** Art. 54. Greek law restricts the scope of the permitted use to articles lawfully published in a newspaper or periodical, short extracts of a work or parts of a short work or a lawfully published work of a work of fine art, **Greece** Art. 21. Furthermore, Japanese law requires for this permitted use that the institution operates on a non-profit basis, see **Japan** Art. 36.

[206] **Cyprus** Art. 7 para. 2q, **Lithuania** Art. 22 para. 1(1).

[207] See the very narrow permitted use in **Canada,** Art. 29.4, allowing manual reproduction of a work in order to display it. See also the Nordic exception, which explicitly refers to works of art and of a descriptive nature in critical and scientific presentation, **Denmark** Sec. 23, **Norway** Sec. 23 para. 1. Hungary also foresees a specific limitation (although broader here than in the Nordic countries) for works of visual art, see **Hungary** Art. 68 para. 1.

[208] **Cyprus** Art. 7 para. 2e, **Germany** Sec. 47, **Norway** Sec. 13.

reproduction in school textbooks are also found.[209] Those liberties for schools and educational institutions are limited to short extracts or short works, and mostly reserved for institutions involved in non-profit purposes.

At the boundary between collective and individual use, UK law offers an illustration of the balance at stake regarding free uses where the access should be granted but the investment of publishers enhanced. UK copyright law allows reprographic copying of passages from published works, provided it is done by or on behalf of educational establishments, and only as long as no licenses are available regarding the works in question.[210]

Regarding individual use for research and study, the exception and limitations sometimes overlap the principle of free private use. Yet, since private use is not necessarily free of charge, the redundancy is only an impression. The guiding thread of this chapter still points out that several countries provide for a general principle authorizing users to use works as long as it serves only their personal study or research.[211] A particular provision recurs in most countries, especially European countries since this provision belongs to the catalog of the InfoSoc Directive: communication by public libraries, educational institutions and archives (provided they do not work for direct or indirect commercial advantage) is allowed when done through dedicated terminals on the premises of the mentioned locations for the purpose of research or private study, to individual members of the public, and provided the works thereby communicated are contained in the collections of the communicating institution.[212] A supplementary requirement sometimes occurs: works concerned should not be subject to purchase or licensing terms, or at least not at a reasonable price. Canadian law is more restrictive here for this communication to be free of charge, since it also provides that it only concerns works of which the copy possessed by the institution cannot be viewed, handled or listened to because of conservation concerns.[213]

Cultural preservation is also an issue taken into account by lawmakers. Therefore, public libraries, museums and archives which do not seek direct or indirect advantage are allowed to reproduce works for cultural and scientific heritage, in other words, in order to maintain their collection and thereby the availability of works.[214] These provisions are very limited, permitting on the one hand conservation, but

[209] **Australia** Sec. 44, **Greece** Arts. 20 and 21, **Japan** Art. 33, **Macau** Art. 61g, **Poland** Art. 29 para. 2. **Canadian** Art. 30 is very narrow, as far as it grants the free use: The exceptions only cover short passages from published literary works in which copyright subsists and are not themselves published for the use of educational institutions. And, in addition to the necessary acknowledgement of the source and the author, one publisher may not proceed so in respect of more than two passages from works by the same author within 5 years.

[210] **UK** Sec. 36.

[211] See for example **Canada** Art. 29, **Israel** Sec. 19, **USA** Sec. 110 but also **China** Art. 22 para. 1 of the Copyright Act and Art. 6 of the Regulation on the Protection for the Right of Communication via Information Networks, and **Poland** Art. 27.

[212] **Belgium** Art. 22 para. 1 9°, **Europe** InfoSoc Directive Art. 5 para. 3n, **France** Art. L. 122-5 para. 8 of *Code de la Propriété intellectuelle* and Art. 132-4 *du Code du Patrimoine*, **Hungary** Art. 38 para. 5, **Italy** Art. 71ter, **Portugal** Art. 75 para. 2o, **Lithuania** Art. 22 para. 1(3), **Norway** Sec. 16, **Poland** Art. 28, **Portugal** Art. 75 para. 2o. NB: **Spanish** law foresees a fair compensation for this use, see **Spain** Arts. 19 and 37 para. 2.

[213] **Canada** Art. 30.1.

[214] Reproduction for preservation of the cultural and scientific patrimony, (only phonograms and videograms in **Italy**), made by publicly accessible libraries, museums or archives (**China** Art. 22 para. 8 for the fair use exception to the reproduction right, **Greece** Art. 22, **Italy** Art. 69 para. 2, **Japan** Art. 31, **Lithuania** Art. 23, **Spain** Art. 37 para. 1, **Taiwan** Art. 48) which further are not for direct or indirect economic or commercial advantage (**Belgium** Art. 22, Sec. 1 8° (NB: in this provision the unique foreseen access right is the access by the author, provided he pays a fair remuneration of the services done by the institution for the conservation), **Croatia** Art. 87 (for public archive), **Denmark** Sec. 16, **Europe** InfoSoc Directive Art. 5 para. 2c, **Greece** Art. 22, **Israel** Sec. 30c), or for display (**China** Art. 22 para. 8 for the fair use exception to reproduction rights). The Italian Act only allows on this matter photocopying (**Italy** Art. 68 para. 2), **Lithuania** excludes the making available on information networks (**Lithuania** Art. 23), **Canadian** and **Greek** laws further require that an additional copy of the work at stake cannot be obtained on the market promptly and on reasonable terms (**Canada** Art. 30.1 para. 2, **Greece** Art. 22). And in **Canada** this exception requires from the institutions concerned that the original they own in their permanent collection is rare or unpublished, and deteriorating, damaged or lost or at risk of deterioration or becoming damaged or lost (**Canada** Art. 30.1).

granting on the other it does not prejudice the commercial exploitation of works. Thus the Italian Act only provides for such an exception only for photocopying[215]; Lithuania excludes the making available on information networks[216]; Canadian and Greek laws require that an additional copy of the work at stake cannot be obtained in the market promptly and on reasonable terms[217]; and in Canada, this exception further requires from the institutions concerned that the original they own in their permanent collection is rare or unpublished, or at risk of deterioration or becoming damaged or lost.[218] Similar provisions allow broadcasting enterprises,[219] or film archives[220] to reproduce and keep copies. In Israel, recordings have a special clause allowing their reproduction for archival purposes.[221] The US Copyright Act allows the Librarian of Congress to make exceptions to digital rights protection schemes,[222] as Canadian law foresees specific provisions for the Canadian Librarian and the Archivist of Canada.[223]

Education, expression and information freedom are not the only considerations which give rise to a limitation of the scope of protection. Enhancement of an indiscriminate access to works, a smooth secondary exploitation of works and the consideration of a world of uses "parallel" to commercial markets are also considered by limitations and exceptions, or user rights, free of charge. Avoiding discrimination regarding access to works forms the basis of the free reproduction or adaptation in favor of disabled users,[224] or hospitals and prisons. Allowing temporary[225] and incidental[226] reproduction permits professional users to exploit works and to compensate or apply for agreement only for uses having an independent economic value.

Regarding private uses, the recurring distinction among common-law tradition countries and *droit d'auteur* countries quite disappears since the only common-law country providing for a general liberty for private use is

[215] **Italy** Art. 68 para. 2.

[216] **Lithuania** Art. 23.

[217] **Canada** Art. 30.1 para. 2, **Greece** Art. 22.

[218] **Canada** Art. 30.1.

[219] **Cyprus** Art. 7 para. 2k *in fine*, **Macau** Art. 132 para. 4.

[220] **Greece** Art. 23.

[221] **Israel** Sec. 25c.

[222] **USA** Sec. 1201, the reporter states this section is of dubious constitutionality, because the Librarian of Congress is part of the Legislative branch of government, which normally can legislate only by a majority vote of both houses of Congress.

[223] **Canada** Library and Archives of Canada Act Art. 30.5.

[224] **Argentina** Art. 36, **Brazil** Art. 46 para. Id, **Canada** Art. 32, **China** Art. 22(12) for the fair use exception to copyright and Art. 6 para. 8 of the Regulation on the Protection for the Right of Communication via Information Networks, adopted on May 10, 2006, effective since July 1, 2006, **France** L. 122-5 para. 7, **Lithuania** Art. 22 para. 1(2), **Macau** Art. 65, **Portugal** Art. 75 para. 2I, **Spain** Art. 31[bis] para. 2.

[225] Regarding temporary or incidental reproduction: **Australia** Sec. 43A and B, **Belgium** Art. 21 Sec. 3, **Croatia** Art. 81, **Cyprus** Art. 7 para. 5, **Denmark** Sec. 11a, **Egypt** see H.A. El Saghir, Suppl. 53 (Egypt) *in International Encyclopaedia of Laws* 61 (R. Blanpain & M. Colucci eds., Kluwer Law International 2009), **Europe** InfoSoc Directive Art. 5 para. 1, **France** Art. L. 122-5 para. 6, **Germany** Sec. 44a, **Greece** Art. 28B, **Hungary** Art. 5 para. 1, **Israel** Sec. 26, **Italy** Art. 68[bis], **Lithuania** Art. 29, **Macao** Art. 56i, **Norway** Sec. 11a, **Poland** Art. 23-1, **Portugal** Art. 71 para. 1, **Spain** Art. 31 para. 1, **UK** Sec. 31. Regarding ephemeral recording: ephemeral recordings made by broadcasters: **Belgium** Art. 22 para. 1 10°, **Canada** Art. 30.9, **Croatia** Art. 83, **Cyprus** Art. 7 para. 2k, **Denmark** Sec. 31, **Europe** InfoSoc Directive 5(2)d, **Egypt** see H.A. El Saghir, Suppl. 53 (Egypt) in *International Encyclopaedia of Laws* 61 (R. Blanpain & M. Colucci eds., Kluwer Law International 2009), **Germany** Sec. 55, **Israel** Sec. 25, **Japan** Art. 44, **Lithuania** Art. 29, **Macau** Art. 132 para. 1, **Norway** Sec. 31, **USA** Sec. 112 (according to US law, ephemeral recordings are not all free of charge, but the ones caused by the five time zones (six in the summer) are free of charge) and by programming undertaking, **Canada** Art. 30.8.

[226] Incidental inclusion of a work or other subject matter in other material (**Canada** Art. 30.7, **Europe** InfoSoc Directive Art. 5 para. 3 I, **Israel** Sec. 22, **Portugal** Art. 75 para. 2r), under following supplementary conditions in the following countries: the work at stake shall be in a public place (**Belgium** Art. 22 para. 1 2°, **Cyprus** Art. 7 para. 2b), it shall be in course of reporting (**Germany** Sec. 50, **Greece** Art. 25 para. 1a, **Italy** Art. 65 para. 2, **Spain** Art. 35 para. 1, **Taiwan** Art. 49) or insignificant (**Germany** Sec. 57); in Cyprus it concerns only artistic works (**Cyprus** Art. 7 para. 2d); in Hungary it covers expressly television broadcasts and expressly exempts from the requirement of giving the source (**Hungary** Art. 36 para. 3); it is otherwise defined in Australia: exceptions for public displays of artistic works that are included in broadcasts or films (**Australia** Secs. 65–73).

India.[227] The general principle is the freedom of private use of works for the personal use of the copyist.[228] Here, Norwegian law deserves a specific mention since its law states a similar liberty for users, even if it grants right holders compensation for this. It should although be considered free of charge because the compensation of those uses is paid via the State budget.[229] Yet, for the most part the scope of this privilege free of charge is very limited. Greece limits it to reproduction carried out without a technical device; in Italy, the involvement of a machine is possible provided it is by a means of reproduction unsuitable for marketing; the limit in Lithuania is "one copy;" in France all private reproductions done with the aid of a machine and a blank carrier are allowed but are not free of charge, and, be it via the general prescription of the three-step test or via an express provision regarding private use,[230] it shall not hamper the normal exploitation of the work. And when not accompanied by several and severe limitations, the permission for private use is strictly delimited and dispersed in several provisions.[231]

Concluding remarks about user rights free of charge

Several reporters point out those exemptions reflect the overriding of social interests by the uses at stake, meaning the individual interests of right holders shall then be suspended. But such a need for thorough description of the permitted uses shows the imbalance and the extent to which prohibition is the rule and freedom the exception.

The questionable influence of international law becomes obvious when observing that several copyright acts of civil law countries, despite the fact that their tradition generally commands synthetic texts, use subheadings extending far beyond the first letters of the alphabet. On the other hand, although judicial precedents are very important in the US for the application of the fair use clause, regarding the specific user right stated in US Secs. 109–122, judicial practice has played a rather small role because those provisions are extremely detailed and leave little room for court interpretation.[232]

At the end of the day, international and domestic lawmakers seem engaged in a race to the longest list of exceptions, although actually limiting the scope of permitted uses. And considering the general principle of restrictive interpretation, the soft provisions do not help users. Several keywords, such as "appropriate", "to the extent necessary to the purpose", "fair use/dealing/practice", "within reasonable limit", "reasonable terms", "acceptable means", "special artistic value", "low quality", "normal exploitation", "legitimate interest", "public interest" appear in most definitions of said user rights/exceptions/limitations. It is to be read as latitude given to the judge in order to appreciate the extent of the allowance. The counterpart of this flexibility is the lack of juridical certainty, which is detrimental to all stakeholders.

Finally, regarding the role played by case law in respect of exceptions and limitations, most reports relate rare cases. However, in several other countries, exceptions and limitations (or user rights) disputes are plentiful.[233] In fact, the services Google Inc. offers are again and again the object of innovative decisions or at

[227] **India** Sec. 52 para. 1a (we have already seen, however, that most copyright countries provide for fair use or fair dealing for private research and study).

[228] **Brazil** Art. 46 para. II, **China** Art. 22 para. 1, **Denmark** Sec. 12, **Egypt, Greece** Art. 18, **Italy** Art. 68, **Japan** Art. 30 (free of charge only for writings), **Lithuania** Art. 20 para. 1, **Macau** Art. 60, **Poland** Art. 23 (and 33 concerning the limit to this free use as regards architectural works), **Taiwan** Art. 51. The **French** reporter mentions in this context Art. L. 122-5 para. 2, although it seems to be in contradiction with Art. L. 311-1 et seq., which he mentions later in his report.

[229] **Norway** Sec. 12.

[230] See **Belgian** and **Egyptian** law.

[231] See for example **Australian** law devoting five different provisions to different situations of private use of specific works (Secs. 43C, 47J, 109A, 110AA and 111).

[232] Consider that the **US** provision in respect of the exemptions for bars and restaurants provides for the exact superficies of concerned establishments: "3,750 gross square feet of space (excluding space used for customer parking and for no other purpose)".

[233] Most significantly in **Belgium**, **France** and **Germany**, also in the **US**. Ad hoc commissions such as the Canadian Copyright Board mostly deal with similar issues.

least of innovative questions.[234] Thus in Belgium, an action engaged against Google news led the Brussels Civil Court to state: the automatic (via googlebots machine) indexation of newspaper articles cannot be covered by the quotation exception, which requires the inclusion in an independent text for purposes of criticism, debate, review, teaching or scientific research, complying with the fair usages of the sector and is restricted to the extent deemed necessary for this use.[235] The benefit of the review exception was of no help to Google either, since the underlying aim of this freedom is the need for the news press to be able to quickly report and react to news provided the use of copyrighted works is only a part of a comment or of a report that should remain the primary element in the derived work. Lastly, the Brussels Civil Court answered in Google's defense relying on the lack of expressed opposition from the publishers against the use Google undertook as the copyright system does not rely on a right to oppose uses, but on the requirement of prior consent of right owners. Along this line, developing a business model grounded on an opt-out model is risky in countries where copyright is being enforced.

User rights subject to the payment of a remuneration

On this matter, differences already mentioned between *droit d'auteur* and copyright traditions occur once again; however, the common-law countries cannot be considered as a block. US law has only a few cases in which the law-maker prevents right holders from freely exercising their exclusive right although granting remuneration and thereby only foresees user rights subject to the payment of remuneration. On the contrary, UK law only knows mandatory licenses and no remuneration right, which is to be considered as a way to let the contractual freedom play as far as possible. Australian law, along another line, foresees only few user rights free of charge, recurs in numerous cases to remuneration rights, but is reluctant to mandatory license providing only one, in respect of the manufacture of a record of musical works that have been previously embodied in a sound recording.

The Germany-specific authorization reserved to public libraries to reproduce and supply on request copies of copyrighted works in their collections is in this vein.[236] Spanish law on the other hand allows libraries (like museums and archives) to reproduce works of their collection for research purposes without fee; whereas, the use of reproduction devices is available to the public at the location. It remains doubtful however whether copies produced by libraries on behalf of researchers may be made available online.[237] German law presents a good example of the adjustment made possible by remuneration completing user rights with the provision related to school broadcast. Reproduction and representation in the context of the teaching activities of a school is a user right free of charge, but in case the school keeps the recording over a year, this use becomes subject to a remuneration.[238]

The cultural discussion is also seen again here. Where other countries authorize public libraries, scientific institutions and non-commercial documentation centers to reproduce works of their collections for conservation under complex and extensive requirements, Macanese law authorizes it generally, under the requirements that the work has been legally published, that the reproduction is not otherwise available to the public, and that right holders will be remunerated.[239] In this vein, seeking to grant continuous access to works, while at the same time considering right holders' interests, the right to lend is reserved to public libraries and foreseen by

[234] See in **France** and the **USA** regarding Google Book Search, in **France** and **Germany** on the thumbnails used in Google Pictures, in **Belgium** on Google News.

[235] **Belgium** Google vs. Copiepresse, February 13, 2007, A&M, 2007, p. 107.

[236] **Germany** Sec. 53a.

[237] **Spain** Art. 37.

[238] **Germany** Sec. 47.

[239] **Macau** Art. 61d.

copyright law as a remuneration right.[240] Serving both the need for preventing exploitation hurdles and granting remuneration to right holders, one should mention gratis live performances and those in the context of religious services in Germany, where payment of a fee is required except when carried out in an educational or social-welfare context or when no participant is either paid or has been paid.[241]

Countries in which no free-of-charge user rights are provided for disabled users, actually authorize uses for their benefit against the payment of a fee.[242] Along the same line, some countries distinguish press review and press clipping, where only the latter is subject to a payment.[243]

Consideration of privacy and of the weak feasibility of any control in such an area explains the fact why lawmakers authorized the private copy. But the quantity concerned, and the economic interests of right holders supposedly endangered by this parallel consumption has driven lawmakers to authorize private copying, and at the same time to establish a way to compensate right holders.[244] In this respect, several common-law countries are to be distinguished, since they do not recognize such a general privilege.[245] Reprography (which has a broader scope than the private copy, since it covers professional and collective uses) is also regulated by a remuneration right in several countries, mainly in the EU.[246]

In addition, economic considerations and the enhancement of the dissemination of works are also grounds for granting remuneration rights instead of exclusive rights. The rental right has been mentioned by a few countries,[247] but this concerns, firstly, secondary uses, mainly the broadcasting of recordings, their communication to the public,[248] and the license for musical works which have already been recorded in phonograms in countries where this issue is not regulated by a mandatory license.[249] Noteworthy is that ephemeral recording mostly free of charge is subject to a remuneration in the USA.[250] Lastly Macanese law allows the reproduction of photographs under similar conditions as press review.[251] To put it in a nutshell, remuneration rights help achieve a balance when the legislature considers it would be unfair to give right holders the opportunity to hinder

[240] **Belgium** Art. 23, **Croatia** Art. 33, **France** Art. L. 133-1 et seq., **Germany** Sec. 27 (where it actually is more a consequence of the exhaustion right than of a remuneration right), **Lithuania** Art. 16 para. 3, **Spain** Arts. 19 and 37 para. 2.

[241] **Germany** Art. 52.

[242] **Australia** Part VB division 3 and Sec. 47 A, **Germany** Sec. 45a and **Japan** Art. 33-2.

[243] **Germany** Sec. 49. **Spanish** law also has a similar distinction following the implementation of the InfoSoc Directive, see Art. 32 para. 1.

[244] **Belgium** Art. 22, Sec. 1 4°, **Canada** Arts. 79–88 (only for musical works), **Croatia** Arts. 32 and 82, **Cyprus** Art. 7 para. 2o, **Denmark** Secs. 12 and 39–46, **France** Art. L. 311-1 et seq., **Germany** Sec. 53 et seq., **Greece** Art. 18, **Hungary** Art. 35, **Italy** Arts. 68.3 and 71[sexies] et seq., **Japan** Art. 30, **Lithuania** Art. 20 para. 6, **Norway** Sec. 12, **Portugal** Arts. 75 para. 2a, and 76 para. 1b, **Spain** Art. 31 para. 2.

[245] See **Canada**, **UK** and **USA**.

[246] **Belgium** Art. 22 para. 1 4°, **Canada** Art. 30.3 (for reprography made by educational institution or a library, archive or museum), **Croatia** Arts. 32 and 82, **Cyprus** Art. 7 para. 2p, **France** L. 122-10, **Germany** Sec. 53, **Lithuania** Art. 23 para. 1(1) et 3. NB: this is also the case in Spain thanks to a collective license scheme, without any limitation of the exclusive right.

[247] **Germany** Sec. 27 para. 1, **Lithuania** Art. 11 para. 4 and Art. 15 para. 4 for authors and Art. 53 para. 4 et 5 for performers, **Taiwan** Art. 38 para. 5 (Taiwanese law actually provides this right without requiring right holders' agreement only for education institutions and non-profit establishments). The rental right follows a similar regime in **Spain**, although the Spanish report presents it under *mandatory licenses*, see Art. 90 para. 2.

[248] Regarding broadcasting **Australia** Sec. 47, **Cyprus** Art. 10C para. 2, **Lithuania** Art. 55, **Macau** Art. 130, and 137, **USA** Secs. 117 and 119; regarding communication to the public in different ways **Australia** Secs. 70, 108, and 135ZZK, **Cyprus** Art. 10C para. 2, **Lithuania** Art. 55, **Macau** Art. 130, **USA** Secs. 111, 114 and 116. Mixing both ideas, reproduction for the purpose of including a work in a television broadcast requires in **Australia** only remuneration, Sec. 70. Finally the specific **Italian** provision for reproduction of broadcasts made by hospitals, prisons or institutions helping youth and impaired people, provided those institutions do not act for commercial advantage.

[249] **Cyprus** Art. 7 para. 2h, **Macau** Art. 125(1), **USA** Sec. 115. The cable retransmission in **Canada** is also governed by a remuneration right, Art. 31.

[250] **USA** Sec. 112.

[251] **Macau** Art. 152.

the dissemination of works, and at the same time tries to ensure them a revenue income.[252]

Mandatory licenses

Chinese, Croatian and Polish laws do not know the term mandatory license. Israel does not distinguish the figures of remuneration rights and mandatory licenses. On the contrary, as already mentioned, UK law only provides for mandatory licenses, since in cases of user rights not free of charge, it is always left to the party to fix the fee amounts.

The educational purpose supports only two cases, which are to be found in Belgium and Canada. In Belgium, reproduction of deceased authors' works for teaching or scientific purposes in anthologies requires only a payment and is designed as a mandatory license.[253] Along a line similar to that applied in Germany for school broadcasts, Canadian schools may copy and perform broadcasts, but after a certain term they have to pay fees if they keep the reproduction. They may keep news programs or a news commentary programs for 1 year and other kinds of programs for 30 days. Afterwards, they are obliged to pay a fee.[254] In addition, concerning uses covered in other countries by remuneration rights, Canadian law governs reprography[255] and UK law public lending[256] thanks to mandatory licenses.

The cases most concerned by mandatory license are the license for phonograms allowing "covering" musical works having already been embodied in a commercial phonogram,[257] and the cable retransmission.[258] Inclusion of sound recordings in broadcasts is also governed in this way in the UK[259] and Japan.[260]

UK law governs two very specific licenses via mandatory licenses: broadcast schedules[261] and performing licenses regarding the play "Peter Pan" by JM Barrie.[262] German law also uses mandatory licenses for the highly specific case of licensing standing orders or company rules and regulation.[263] Hungary and Japan handle the orphan works issue according to a similar method,[264] followed by Macau although only regarding related rights.[265]

Finally, on the boundary between copyright law and competition law, UK copyright law provides courts the possibility to order license, to modify licensing conditions or to cancel licenses when they infringe domestic competition laws.[266] Cypriot copyright law invests an ad hoc authority to impose mandatory licenses to collecting societies when these impose unreasonable terms in their relation to users.[267] In this respect, US antitrust consent decrees requiring music rights organizations to grants licenses could be mentioned, as could Secs. 12 and 13 of the German Copyright Administration Law, preventing collective management societies from refusing to conclude contracts with users. In respect of collective management,

[252] The US situation of derivative works in the context of restored works is a demonstrative example, **USA** Secs. 104A para. 3 and 111.

[253] **Belgium** Art. 21 para. 2.

[254] **Canada** Art. 29.6 for news programs, and Art. 29.7 for other programs.

[255] **Canada** Art. 30.3.

[256] **UK** Sec. 66.

[257] **Australia** Sec. 55, **Germany** Sec. 42a, **Hungary** Art. 19, **Israel** Sec. 32, **Japan** Art. 69, **Taiwan** Art. 69. The latter requires 6 months after the release of the first recording; Hungary also covers the making of multimedia works and the compilation for databases.

[258] **Cyprus** Art. 10B, **France** Art. L. 132-20-1, **Germany** Sec. 87 para. 5, **UK** Sec. 74 para. 4. NB: **Spanish** law foresees here a "limit" (meaning a user right) free of charge (Art. 36). "No compulsory licences on broadcasting are envisaged in the Spanish Copyright Law". Furthermore, although *compulsory licenses are not generally used within Spanish copyright tradition,* Art. 20 para. 4 foresees a mandatory license via a CMO for cable distribution when the retransmissions of broadcasts are undertaken by a third broadcasting company.

[259] **UK** Sec. 135 A–G.

[260] **Japan** Art. 68.

[261] **UK** Sec. 176 and sch. 17.

[262] **UK** Sec. 301 and Sch. 6. Even though the exploitation rights expired, each performance of this play grants remuneration to the Trustees of the Hospital for Sick Children, Great Ormond Street, London.

[263] **Germany** Sec. 5 para. 3.

[264] **Hungary** Art. 57 A–C, **Japan** Art. 67.

[265] **Macau** Art. 175.

[266] **UK** Sec. 144.

[267] **Cyprus** Art. 15.

but regarding the other contractual relation collective societies have, the Polish report refers to provisions vesting copyright collective management societies with the right to provide collective management based on statutory representation.[268]

Rules on misuse

Croatian and German reporters point out the provisions as to the coexistence of technical protection measures (TPMs) and exception, limitations or user rights and how these can be related to misuse considerations.[269] As a matter of fact, copyright acts protect TPMs but limit the liberty of copyright owners to reduce the permitted acts.[270]

French copyright law appears to be the only one expressly aiming at abuse, and precisely at the "manifest abuse in the exercise or non-exercise of the economic rights by the deceased author's representatives". In such an event, someone willing to use such works should call for the court that may order *any appropriate measure*.[271] This is a temperament of the omnipotence the *droit moral* gives to the author, in order to protect the intimate relationship the author has with his/her works. After the author's death, this omnipotence loses its *raison d'être.* Argentinean, Macanese, Portuguese and Spanish copyright laws contain similar provisions foreseeing mandatory licenses for the eventuality of abuse undertaken by an author's heir(s) in respect of the republication of works, especially when out of print and concerning posthumous publications.[272]

Other types of misuse mentioned by reporters also involve moral rights. In Lithuania, the right to claim authorship only occurs when the mention of the author is possible. Therefore, the misuse of this authorship right is avoided. In the same manner, the Lithuanian copyright law states that the moral rights of an author of a computer program or of a database may not be used in a manner that unreasonably prejudices the rights of a holder of rights on the subject matter.[273] Along the same line, but dealing with the moral right of integrity, Israeli law states its enforceability only if the requirement constitutes a "reasonable act in the circumstances of the case".[274] Staying in Israel, we eventually return to economic rights: Israeli copyright law expressly states that judges may or may not pursue when facing an injunction relief.[275] This possibility to decide according to equity more than only according to legal texts opens the possibility to punish misuses.

Considering the "special artistic value" of a cinematographic work, the Greek Minister of Culture in accordance with the opinion of the Cinematography Advisory Council, can permit the reproduction of the work at stake for purpose of preserving it in the National Cinematographic Archive.[276] Macanese copyright law knows a broader provision on the conservation of works of cultural value since the administration may institute adequate measures to grant the authenticity or integrity of works when they come to be threatened, after the right holders of the works have failed to protect the work.[277]

7. Have certain legal instruments according to Questions 2a–f only been introduced in the course of time or have they been repealed and if so, why?

All members of the European Union amended their exceptions and limitations provisions after the InfoSoc Directive. It has led to new exceptions,

[268] **Poland** Arts. 21 and 70.

[269] **Croatia** Art. 98, **Europe** Art. 6 para. 4 InfoSoc Directive, **Germany** Sec. 95b.

[270] See answers to Question 9.

[271] **France Art.** L. 122-9.

[272] **Argentina** Art. 6: if heirs do not publish, republish, or allow translation 10 years pma, a third party may apply for it before the court; **Macau** Art. 38: similar provision, 25 years pma, and for works out of print, and 59 for posthumous works. **Portugal** Art. 70 para. 3: posthumous works may be published by third parties if the heirs of the author do not provide for it within 25 years pma. **Spain** Art. 40: if the work remains undisclosed after the death of the author, heirs are entitled to decide as to its publication for as long as the work remains protected, but any person holding a legitimate interest may request the adoption of any judicial measure to impose release.

[273] **Lithuania** Art. 14 para. 3.

[274] **Israel** Sec. 50.

[275] **Israel** Sec. 53.

[276] **Greece** Art. 23.

[277] **Macau** Art. 44.

like those in favor of disabled persons or in respect of temporary reproduction.[278] Yet the overall result definitely looks like a general restriction of the scope of user rights, above all since the list of exceptions in this directive is closed[279] and because of the right-holder friendly interpretation made of the three-step test, as the above-mentioned renaming of the Italian chapter "*utilizzazioni libere*" to "*eccezioni e limitazioni*" in 2003 attests.

This Directive implemented the WIPO treaties of 1996, which are still being implemented in countries like Canada, or are to be implement in Israel or Brazil. The most salient feature of this implementation is the protection of TPMs.

Back to Europe, the database and computer programs directives had a huge impact, which is visible in the fact that the wording of provisions granting their protection and user rights in this respect are quite similar in all EU Member States. The rental and lending right directive reduced the scope of libraries' allowance to lend works without restriction as stated by the Hungarian and UK reports. The protection term directive also extended the monopoly, even in Germany which had the longest term. Interestingly, in Poland, between the Copyright Law of 1926 and the recent implementation of this longer term, the tendency was to reduce copyright duration.

Outside Europe too, international law let the realm of monopoly extend. For example, the only influence of international law referred to by the Australian report is the protection term extension due to the free trade agreement with the USA, which entered into force on January 1st 2005. The USA inserted a minimal *droit moral* and copyright protection of architectural works in order to be able to adhere the Berne Convention. China "drastically" reduced the breadth of its fair use rules before acceding to the WTO.

8. **Are there rules that restrict the scope of user rights according to Questions 2c–e, in particular: by laying down specific preconditions for the applicability of individual user rights,[280] by laying down abstract preconditions for the applicability of individual user rights?[281]**

All copyright laws contain both specific and abstract preconditions for the applicability of individual user rights.

Among the specific preconditions most recurring are private or personal use,[282] teaching and research purposes,[283] and non-commercial or non-profit uses.[284] Furthermore, a fair acknowledgement of the author and source of the work used is required; "fair" meaning the acknowledgement is only required when it is reasonably feasible.[285]

Abstract preconditions apply in all countries taken into account in this report, at least a fair use provision in common-law countries or the three-step test. The most often recurring abstract preconditions are the consideration of the legitimate interests of copyright holders and the limit to the extent justified by the purpose.

9. **Are there rules to protect the existence of user rights according to Questions 2c–e? In particular: What kinds of binding rules are there to prohibit the undermining of statutory user rights? How is the relationship between TPMs (technical protection measures)/DRM (digital rights management) and statutory user rights regulated? Is there a decision (explicit or**

---

[278] Expressly pointed out by the **Greek** report.

[279] See recital 32 of the Directive.

[280] For instance: only non-commercial use, only use for educational and research purposes, etc.

[281] For instance: preconditions of the kind contained in the three-step test.

[282] See for example: **Australia** Secs. 47F, 47J, 109A, 110A and 111, **Cyprus** Art. 7 para. 2aa, **Italy** Arts. 68, 71bis, 71$^{sexies–octies}$, **Portugal** Art. 75 para. 2a, **Spain** Art. 31 para. 2 and ex Art. 34 para. 2a.

[283] See for example: **Australia** Secs. 40, 103C, 135E, 135F, 135ZMD, 135ZP, **Cyprus** Art. 7 para. 2aa, 7 para. 2e, Art. 7 para. 2r, **Germany**, **Hungary** Arts. 34 para. 2, Art. 35 para. 4 and para. 5, **Spain** Art. 32 para. 1, 21 para. 2, 34 para. 2b (and only for research, silent about teaching) Art. 37 para. 1 and 37 para. 3.

[284] See for example: **Belgium** (the requirement not to prejudice the normal exploitation of the work arises in four exceptions), **China** Art. 22 para. 7 and Art. 22 para. 9, **Cyprus** Art. 7 para. 2j and 7 para. 2o, **Germany**, **Hungary** Art. 35 para. 6, Art. 38 para. 1, Art. 41 para. 1, **Spain** Art. 31 para. 2, Art. 31bis para. 2, Art. 32 para. 2, Art. 34 para. 2b, Art. 37 para. 1, Art. 37 para. 2 and Art. 38, **USA** (in the fair use clause).

[285] **Australia** Secs. 40 and 103C, **Croatia** Arts. 85, 89, 90, 91, 93, **Cyprus** Art. 7 para. 2aa, **France** Arts. L. 122-6-1 et seq. and L. 342-3, **Germany** Sec. 63, **Italy**, **Japan** Art. 48 and 60, **Poland** Art. 34, **Taiwan** Art. 64, **Spain** Art. 32 para. 1, 32 para. 2, 33 para. 1, and 32 para. 2b, **UK**.

implicit) on the extent to which exclusivity rules to the benefit of the right holder or access possibilities in favor of third parties should enjoy priority in the event of doubt?

The undermining of statutory user rights is twofold: by contract and by TPMs.

Regarding the contractual undermining of user rights, four reports state that their national copyright law protects as a matter of general principle all *exceptions and limitations* against contractual provisions, therefore contractual provisions limiting the legally permitted scope are null and void.[286] Otherwise, numerous countries actually only protect user rights in respect of computer programs and databases,[287] or in respect of single specific "user rights".[288] But most copyright laws considered in this report do not provide for any regulation of this issue, actually considering that *privileges,* or the *exceptions and limitations,* or *privileges* only apply when licensing terms do not govern the issues,[289] thereby leaving this field to be governed by the *private economy.*[290]

The danger of shifting the balance achieved by lawmakers, or by making the law an empty shell is a well-known concern. A report by the Australian Copyright Law Review Committee in 2002 describes how statutory user rights can be undermined in practice by contractual provisions and states that the legal effect of these provisions is uncertain.[291] This report recommends amending the Copyright Act 1968, but in vain.

The Canadian Supreme Court took notice of the question and expressly acknowledged the user right feature of what is mostly called exceptions:

> Procedurally, a defendant is required to prove that his or her dealing with a work has been fair; however, the fair dealing exception is perhaps more properly understood as an integral part of the Copyright Act than simply a defense. Any act falling within the fair dealing exception will not be an infringement of copyright. The fair dealing exception, like other exceptions in the Copyright Act, is a user's right. In order to maintain the proper balance between the rights of a Copyright owner and users' interests, it must not be interpreted restrictively.[292]

This invitation to reject a narrow interpretation of "exception" and to broadly interpret "user rights" followed another decision which recommended a few years earlier a more general approach:

> The proper balance among these [promoting the public interest in the encouragement and dissemination of works of the arts and intellect and obtaining a just reward for the creator (or, more accurately, to prevent someone other than the creator from appropriating whatever benefits may be generated)] and other public policy objectives lies not only in recognizing the creator's rights but in giving due weight to their limited nature. In crassly economic terms it would be as inefficient to over compensate artists and authors for the right of reproduction as it would be self-defeating to under compensate them. Once an authorized copy of a work is sold to a member of the public, it is generally for the purchaser, not the author, to determine what happens to it. / Excessive control by holders of copyrights and other forms of intellectual property may unduly limit the ability of the public domain to incorporate and embellish creative innovation in the long-term interests of society as a whole, or create practical obstacles to proper utilization.[293]

Regarding TPMs, most jurisdictions consider the possible conflict arising between user rights and the protection allowing TPMs to operate on protected contents (six country reports state that their copyright law does not provide any rule on this conflict[294]). The difference occurring here is

---

[286] **Belgium** Art. 23bis, **Poland**, **Portugal** Art. 75 para. 5, **Taiwan**.

[287] **Australia**, **Croatia** Arts. 97, 110, 111 and 151, **Cyprus**, **France**, **Germany** Sec. 69g para. 2 et 3, Secs. 69e and 87e, BGH February 24, 2000, *GRUR* 2000, p. 866, **Italy** Art. 64quarter and 64sexies para. 3, **Spain** Art. 34 para. 1 and Art. 100 para. 2, **UK**.

[288] See **UK** Sec. 36 para. 4 of the CDPA 1988 and 137 of the Broadcasting act.

[289] **Argentina**, **Australia**, **Canada**, **China**, **Croatian**, **Egypt**, **Hungary**, **Israel**, **Italy**, **Japan**, M. Kato (et.), *Zadankai: Chosakukenho 100 Nen to Kongo no Kadai* [Round-table discussion: 100 year's Copyright legislation and future tasks], *Juristo* no. 1160 (1999), pp. 26 (a remark by M. Kato), **Lithuania**, **Macao**, **US**.

[290] So the **German** reporter.

[291] **Australia** Copyright Law Review Committee, *Copyright and Contract*, Executive Report (2002) 2.11.

[292] **Canadian** Supreme Court, *CCH Canadian Ltd.* v. *Law Society of Upper Canada*, (see note 102) at point 48.

[293] **Canadian** Supreme Court, *Théberge v. Galerie d'Art du Petit Champlain inc.*, [2002] 2 S.C.R. 336, 2002 SCC 34, at point 30.

[294] **Argentina**, **Brazil**, **Egypt**, **India**, **Israel**, **Poland**.

obvious among countries providing for some ruling on this issue. EU Member States follow the regulation of Art. 6 para. 4 of the InfoSoc Directive, allowing legitimate users of listed exceptions to apply for means allowing them to access works in these specific cases[295] and requiring that the amount of fees compensating user rights takes into account the limitations due to TPMs. Other countries in the world providing the priority for certain user rights before TPMs offer an easier way for users: the prohibition of TPM circumvention does not apply to the enumerated rights or exceptions.[296] US case law seems to distinguish among cases in which TPMs are employed to prevent piracy and those in which TPMs are employed in an attempt to suppress competition in areas unrelated to copyright; the former should be resolved in favor of right holders, the latter in favor of third parties.[297]

10.

10a. How is the amount of the fee determined for cases covered by Question 2d and for cases covered by Question 2e separately and in the event of conflict?[298]

Fees related to statutory and mandatory licenses are basically determined by contract.[299] State organs only intervene in case of conflict or to determine a ceiling[300] or minimum rate.[301]

In Germany and Spain the contractual determination of fees follows a legally prescribed process, relying upon collective management societies.[302] For the rest, the statute law,[303] an administrative ad hoc commission,[304] an administrative institution,[305] or ministers[306] determine the amount of fees, whereas several countries provide for such an administrative

[295] **Belgium** Art. 79, **Croatia** Art. 98 paras. 2 and 3, **Cyprus** Art. 14B para. 3, **France** Arts. L. 331-5 para. 4, 331-6 and 342-3-1, **Germany** Sec. 95b, **Greece** Art. 66A para. 5, **Italy** Art. 77[quinquies], **Lithuania** Art. 75 para. 4, **Portugal** Art. 221, **Spain** Arts. 160–162, **UK** Secs. 296–296ZF. **Belgian**, **Portuguese** and **Spanish** laws broadened the scope to private uses, although **Belgian** law actually still awaits an executive decree for this possibility to be enforceable, and **Spanish** law makes only non-digital, private copies enforceable. **Croatian** provisions foresee several possibilities for proceedings, whereas other countries refer to an ad hoc commission acting as a mediator to help users in case right holders do not supply the necessary means. **Spanish** law requires the application for the means allowing enjoyment of the limitation to be filed before ordinary courts.

[296] **Australia** Part V subdivision 2A, **China** Art. 12 of the Internet regulation, **Taiwan** Art. 80[bis], **USA** Sec. 1201: only for specific cases detailed in this section, and regarding classes of copyrighted works about which the Librarian of the Congress has stated in a rulemaking.

[297] **USA** *Lexmark International, Inc. v. Static Control Components, Inc.*, 387F.3d 522 (6th Cir. 2004) (Maker of printers and printer cartridges could not use copyright to prevent competition in the sale of replacement printer cartridges). *Chamberlain v. Skylink*, 381F.3d 1178 (Fed. Cir. 2004) (Maker of garage door openers and remote controls could not use Copyright to prevent competition in the sale of remote controls).

[298] For instance: public authorities, general or special courts, etc.

[299] *All remuneration rights* in **China** and **Italy**, also in **Portugal** (except for covering of musical works already embodied in aphonograms). Being determined case by case: see for example for pedagogical use in **France** Art. L. 122-5 para. 3e (this should have come into effect on January 1, 2009. By December 2009, two contracts have been concluded, actually concerning only films and musical works), **Croatia**, **Germany** and **Taiwan**; for *reprography*, **Croatia**, **France** and **Germany** (in **Spain** also, but reprography is not subject to any user rights); for *public lending right*, **Croatia**, **Germany**, **Lithuania** and **Portugal;** for private copy in **Croatia** and **Germany**; for *broadcasting and communication to the public of phonograms* in **Germany** and **Lithuania**; for school broadcasting in **Germany**; for use of protected works for *examinations* in **Japan**; for manufacturing "*cover versions sound recording*" in **Israel** Sec. 32; *all cases of mandatory licenses* in **UK** and **USA**; publication of a work after the author's death or after 10 years without any action of heirs or right holders; mandatory license for anthologies of deceased authors in **Belgium**.

[300] For example **Hungary** for the reprography, Art. 21 para. 4.

[301] In **Belgium** for the private copy, see arrêté royal of March 28, 1996.

[302] See the **German** Copyright Administration Act and **Spain** Art. 157.

[303] *Private (and analogue) copying: **Spain** Art. 25. *Private (and digital) copying: **Spain** Art. 25 para. 6 and Order PRE/1743/2008 of June 18, *BOE* 148. *Public lending fee: **France** Art. L. 133-3, **Lithuania** government resolution no. 905 of August 14, 2007. *Reprography in **Greece** and **Portugal** (private copy law no. 62/98 of September 1, 1998, last amended in 2004).

[304] *Private copy: **France** Art. L. 311-5, **Lithuania** Art. 20 para. 5 and government resolution no. 997 of September 19, 2007, **Israel** Sec. 3B–F Copyright Ordinance as they remain in effect pursuant to Sec. 69 of the Copyright Act. *Reprography: **Lithuania** government resolution n° 181 of February 6, 2002. *Reproduction in school books: **Japan** Art. 71, etc.

[305] **India** for all remuneration rights.

[306] Private copy **Poland** Art. 20 para. 1, **Cyprus**.

ruling only as a default rate.[307] Most countries institute special arbitration boards for conflict cases.[308]

10b. Are there particular procedural rules for statutory and mandatory licenses or for misuse rules, e.g., concerning the distribution of the burden of proof, provisional measures, other aspects?

Most reports refer to regular proceedings. The Lithuanian and Polish reports relate special provisions facilitating the obtaining of information from the opposing parties.[309] In Canada,[310] Germany[311] and Lithuania, collective management organizations (CMOs) are required to publish their tariffs, and these are specifically controlled. CMOs enjoy in Germany (under requirements) and in Poland the presumption to be entitled to act in judicial proceedings.[312] In addition, German copyright administration law provides several provisions on proceeding before the arbitration board.

The Italian report notes the possibility of a pecuniary penalty fixed in principle as double the work's value[313]; Canadian law foresees a similar possibility but determines a ceiling at five times the amount of the levy determined by the tariffs of the CMO.[314]

Finally, the Croatian report points out that in case of a user objecting to tariffs, the burden of proof lies on him, and he has to pay the amount according to the tariffs until a court passes a decision.

10c. How is the fee paid to the right holders by the party entitled to use?

Both kinds of remuneration rights are for the most part paid via the agency of CMOs.[315]

Debtors are the legitimate users paying the fees to CMOs.[316] When the end user is difficult to reach, debtors are mostly intermediaries who may then charge end users. Thus, a reprography fee is paid by the reprography service providers,[317] and the private copy fee by manufacturers and importers of the blank carriers enabling the private copy.[318] The Greek report is the only one that mentions photocopy paper among blank carriers. Some countries also add a charge on recording equipment for sound and audiovisual works.[319]

Israel and Norway present a very specific situation since private copy fees actually are not paid by end users but by the State.[320]

307 Mandatory license for covers of musical works already embodied in phonograms, **Australia** Sec. 55. *Private copy **Poland** Art. 20 para. 1.

308 **Australia** a copyright tribunal decides upon equitable remuneration or the appropriate royalty in respect of the mandatory license for sound recording Sec. 55; **China** (the commission is then the national Copyright Administration Department or the price administration department); **Cyprus** Art. 10C para. 2 and Art. 15 ("competent authority" means the authority consisting of not more than five persons appointed by the Minister from amongst persons having experience in and knowledge of matters of copyright, at least three of which are not members of the public service); **Germany** (Arbitration Board, at the German Patent and Trademark office) Sec. 14 et seq. *Urheberrechtswahrnehmungsgesetz*; **India** (Copyright Board); **Lithuania** (Council of Copyright and Neighbouring Rights) Art. 72 para. 4; **Spain** Art. 158 (Intellectual Property Commission); **Taiwan** a Copyright Examination and Mediation Committee intervenes especially in respect of statutory license for pedagogical use in Taiwan, in any case to examine the rate and in case of conflict; **UK** Copyright Tribunal; **USA** Copyright Board and the court supervising the antitrust consent decrees.

309 **Lithuania** Art. 80, **Poland** Art. 47 and especially for collective management societies Art. 105.

310 **Canada** Art. 83 para. 1.

311 **Germany** Secs. 12–13 of the German Copyright Administration Act (*Urheberrechtswahrnehmungsgesetz*).

312 **Germany** Sec. 13 *Urheberrechtswahrnehmungsgesetz*, **Poland** Art. 105.

313 **Italy** Arts. 71^{septies} and 174bis.

314 **Canada** Art. 88 para. 2.

315 With some exceptions, see for example the case of press-clipping compensation in Spain, about which the Spanish reporter notices: "Since the law does not require collective management, it is unlikely that this compensation becomes a reality".

316 For example broadcasters for broadcasting fees **Lithuania**, **UK**.

317 For example **France**, **Croatia**, **Poland**.

318 **Belgium** Art. 55, **Croatia** Art. 32, **France** Art. L. 311-4, **Germany** Sec. 54, **Greece, Hungary, Israel, Lithuania** Art. 10 para. 5, **Poland** Art. 20 para. 1, **Spain**.

319 **Belgium** Art. 55, **Croatia** Art. 32, **Germany** Sec. 54, **Spain** Art. 25.

320 **Israel** Sec. 3B–F Copyright Ordinance as they remain in effect pursuant to Sec. 69 of the Copyright Act, **Norway** Sec. 12.

Similarly, genuine public lending fees are paid in France: half by the State[321] and half by the books suppliers.[322]

In the USA, the legal intermediary for mandatory licenses is not a CMO but the Copyright office.[323]

10d. Does national law contain rules that regulate the distribution of fees between the various categories of right holders?[324] If so, which? If not, how are such distributions determined?

Most reports do not relate any provision regarding these questions. The distribution rules are then settled by contract, between the different right holders or within the CMOs.[325]

Chinese law requires CMOs to fairly distribute the collected sums. Lithuanian law further states that distribution of collected fees shall be as proportional as possible to the actual use of the work and subject matter, and in Hungary the Copyright Act only requires the distribution of public lending remuneration to be equitable.[326] Thus, the distribution of remuneration for the rental of audiovisual works is regulated by the responsible Lithuanian CMO.[327] German law refers to the internal proceedings within collective management societies. According to the German Copyright Management Act,[328] disbursements made by CMO (thus regarding all remuneration rights) have to be based on a fixed disbursement scheme thereby preventing arbitrary payments.[329] Furthermore this Act allows CMOs to favor "culturally important works" and to allocate a part of the revenues to social funds benefitting to their members.[330] Portuguese law has similar provisions regarding the obligation for collective management societies to determine the share in their by-laws.[331]

Yet some jurisdictions state exact shares for some of the remuneration rights. Private copy fees for sound recordings shall be distributed as follows: 50% for authors, 25% for performers, 25% for producers in France (Art. L. 311–7), Poland (Art. 20 para. 2), and Spain (Royal Decree 1434/1992); 40% for authors, 30% for performers, 30% for producers in Lithuania (Art. 21 of the government resolution no. 1106); 33% each for the three groups in Israel. Private copy fees for recordings of audiovisual works shall be distributed as follows: one third for authors, one third for performers, one third for producers in Israel, France (Art. L. 311-7), and Spain; 35% for authors, 25% for artistic performers and 40% for producers of videograms in Poland (Art. 20 para. 2). Private copy fees for other works privately reproduced on digital carriers shall be distributed on equal shares to authors and publishers in France (Art. L. 311–7). Spanish law further foresees private copying fees for books, and assimilated publications (not including newspapers) shall be distributed as follows: 55% for authors and 45% for editors (Art. 36 Royal Decree 1434/1992).

Remuneration for broadcasting and communication to the public of phonograms must be distributed in equal shares among performers and producers in Lithuania, whereas Greece foresees 55% for the intellectual creators, 25% for performers and 20% for producers[332]; and Hungary 45% for authors, performers 30%, producers 25%.[333] Hungarian law also states regarding movies: 22% for filmmakers, 16% for scriptwriters, 20% for composers and lyricists, 25% for performers, 4% for fine artists, applied artists and photog-

[321] In **Lithuania**, the State pays the whole fees.

[322] **France** L. 133-3.

[323] **USA**.

[324] For instance: between the creators/performers and the producers; between the different creators involved in a production, etc.

[325] Expressly: **Egypt, UK, USA**.

[326] **Hungary** Art. 23/A para. 1.

[327] Distribution as follows: 40% for the principal director, 24% for screenplay author and dialogue author together, 15% for the operator, 12% for the music composer, and 9% for the painter .

[328] *Urheberrechtswahrnehmungsgesetz* of Septermber 9, 1965.

[329] **Germany** Sec. 7 *Urheberrechtswahrnehmungsgesetz*.

[330] **Germany** Secs. 7 and 8 *Urheberrechtswahrnehmungsgesetz*.

[331] **Portugal** Art. 5 para. 2e.

[332] **Greece** Art. 18.

[333] **Hungary** Art. 21 para. 4.

raphers, 13% for producers, unless the parties agree otherwise.[334]

In Lithuania, distribution of the public lending fee is regulated by a government resolution,[335] the amounts of which depend on the kind of work. It is noteworthy that the distribution occurs between authors and translators. Publishers are not involved. Along the same lines, Spanish statute law makes it clear that the compensation for public lending is set only in favor of authors,[336] excluding any other right owners such as publishers, performers or producers. Differently, in France a public lending fee shall be, for at least half of it, distributed in equal shares to authors and publishers.[337] The other part of the collected sums (maximum half of the amount) shall be allocated to the complementary pensions of writers and translators insured in France (Art. L. 133–4).

11. **Does national law contain general rules based on a differentiation between different categories of right holders,[338] in particular binding rules on contractual relationships between different categories of right holders (copyright contract),[339] differences with respect of the scope of statutory user rights, or others?**

A few reporters do not find any such distinction in their jurisdictions.[340]

Most reports relate specific provisions regarding moral rights vesting only in the creator and restraining their transferability,[341] their assignability,[342] or their waivability.[343] In countries of civil law tradition, remuneration rights also are generally unwaivable, not granting creators control over their work but their participation in the benefits made thanks to their works.[344]

Apart from provisions protecting the weakness of creators, and therefore commanding a restrictive interpretation of the transferee rights,[345] or to defend authors where the contract freedom could lead to unfair results,[346] provisions mentioned by reporters regarding distinctions among right holders are those provided in order to defend the interests of investors[347] such as employers[348] and audiovisual producers.

It is also noteworthy that the Spanish report mentions the distinction made between assignees of exclusive license and those of non-exclusive license: only the former may sub-license.[349]

Finally, one should point out that some lawmakers use the time as a tool allowing a rebalancing, as it clearly appears in the Canadian reversionary right,[350] or by the possibility that the license can be terminated by any party respecting

[334] **Hungary** Art. 20 para. 5.

[335] **Lithuania** government resolution no. 905.

[336] **Spain** Art. 132.

[337] **France** Art. L. 133-4.

[338] For instance: original right holders who are creators on the one hand and right holders who have acquired the copyright subsequently on the other (derivative right holders).

[339] For instance: non-transferability of certain rights, e.g. moral rights.

[340] **Hungary**, **India**, **Macau**, **UK**.

[341] **Canada** Art. 13.1 para. 2, **Portugal** Art. 42, **USA** Sec. 106A.

[342] **Australia** Sec. 195AN para. 3and 248N.

[343] **Egypt** Art. 145, **Israel** Sec. 45(b), **Italy** Art. 23, **Macau** Art. 41, **Spain** Art. 14 for authors and Art. 113 for performers, **Taiwan** Art. 21. Regarding only the revocation right, **Croatia** Art. 50.

[344] For instance *Rental and public lending right for example: **Belgium** Art. 24, **Croatia** Arts. 33, 115 and 126, **Cyprus** Art 12 para. 2, **Lithuania** Art. 11 para. 4 and Art. 15 para. 4 for authors and Art. 53 para. 4 et 5 for performers, **Spain** Art. 90 para. 2 (for rental right); * *droit de suite*, **Croatia** Art. 37, **Cyprus** Art. 12 para. 3; * private use **Belgium** Art. 55; *Reprography **Croatia** Art. 32, **Poland** Art. 18 para. 3; *Remuneration rights granted to co-authors of an audiovisual work, **Spain** Art. 90 para. 4 and para. 5; *Right of performers to receive a supplementary remuneration for the broadcasting of their performance **Macau** Art. 179 para. 5. See also the **German** general prohibition (Sec. 63a) allowing transfer in advance only to collective management societies.

[345] **Egypt**, **France** Art. L. 131-3, **Lithuania**, **Poland** Art. 41 para. 2, **Taiwan** Art. 36, **Spain** Arts. 43, 51, 69 for creators, and 75 for performers, see also **Spanish** case law of the Supreme Court October 29, 1999 *Isla Beach* Westlaw.ES RJ1999/ 8167 and October 29, 1999, *Saminar* Westlaw.ES RJ1999/8165.

[346] **Belgium** Art. 26 para. 2 and **Portugal** Arts. 83–106 in respect of publishers. **Belgium** Art. 32 para. 2 in respect of performance contract, **USA** Sec. 101 in respect of the employer.

[347] **Canada** Art. 13.

[348] **Portugal** Arts. 13–14, **Spain** Arts. 51 for "regular" works, 97 para. 4. for computer programs, and 110 for performances.

[349] **Spain** Arts. 48–49.

[350] **Canada** Art. 14.

a period then set by statute law should the license not provide such term.[351]

12. **Which of the following legal instruments or mechanisms are used in national law outside copyright in order to achieve a "balance of interests": (a) fundamental rights, (b) competition law, (c) contract law, (d) general rules on misuse, (e) consumer protection law, (f) media law, (g) other?**

Outside of internal limitations and exceptions to the copyright owners' power or specific rights granted to users, copyright law is also subject to external limitations stemming from the need for conciliation with other rights and interests defended by legal areas other than IP. In this respect, fundamental rights and competition law are the areas most often pointed out by reporters.

Fundamental rights

Six reports answer clearly that fundamental rights help to achieve a balance within or against copyright law.[352] The Australian, Hungarian and Japanese reports point out, on the contrary, that fundamental rights are not applied in copyright cases.[353]

Several reports point out that copyright enjoys constitutional protection in their countries.[354] For the most part copyright law finds its foundation among fundamental rights in the right to private property (which already implies a balance eventually leading to expropriation in favor of the general interest), but also in the right to human dignity, freedom of expression or the freedom of art and science. Indeed, those rights can support and ground some copyright prerogatives (such as the moral right relying on personal rights, or an individual's right to develop his or her own personality[355]), but can also require the scope of copyright protection to fall back on.

Belgian, German and Israeli case law, as well as the Canadian and Spanish reports, state that copyright law as such already achieves a balance[356] thanks to the limitations it contains or the fair uses it allows, but also thanks to the idea/expression dichotomy.[357] In addition, Italian judges also find a constitutional foundation for the right to obtain remuneration for exploitation of a work.[358] However, constitutional judges use the fundamental right of freedom of speech, or of freedom of the arts, or the enhancement of development of culture and progress in science to ground or to extend the scope of user rights.[359] In France, the first attempt of lawmakers to implement the termination of an internet connection as punishment for copyright infringement has been hollowed out by the Constitutional Council considering it would undermine the fundamental right to internet access, which is protected as part of the communication freedom.[360]

[351] **Lithuania** Art. 40 para. 2 setting a 1-year period. See also the Spanish law, setting several periods depending on the kind of contract, **Spain** Art. 69.

[352] **Belgium**, **Germany**, **India**, **Israel**, **Italy**, **Portugal.** See on eventual collisions from a Portuguese point of view: J. de Oliveira Ascensão, "Sociedade da informação e liberdade de expressão", *in Direito da Sociedade da Informação,* vol. VII, Coimbra, 2008, pp. 51 et seq.; A. Libório Dias Pereira, *Direitos de Autor e Liberdade de Informação,* Coimbra, 2008, pp. 169 et seq. and *Droit d'auteur et liberté d'expression. Regards francophones, d'Europe et d'ailleurs*, sous la direction d'A. Strowel et Fr. Tulkens, Brussels, Larcier, 2006.

[353] It is noteworthy those fundamental rights do not explicitly exist in **Australian** law, and that the debate about the relevancy of such an intervention of fundamental rights regarding copyright law is ongoing in **Japan**.

[354] **Brazil**, **Croatia**, **Cyprus**, **France**, **Germany**, **Greece**, **Israel**, **Lithuania**, **Poland**, and the **USA**.

[355] **Germany**, and the **Israeli** decision: CA 2790/93 *Eisenman v. Qimron*, 54(3) P.D. 817 (2000).

[356] **Belgium** Court of cassation, September 25, 2003, *Pas.*, 2003, I, 1471, Arr. Cass. 2003, p. 1733, concl. G. Bresseleers, **Germany**, **Canada**, **Spain**.

[357] **Israeli** Supreme Court P.L.A. 2687/92 *Geva v. Walt Disney Company*, 48(1) P.D. 251 (1993).

[358] **Italy** Const. Court no. 108/1995.

[359] **Cyprus** (no related case, but the right to use a work for purposes of caricature, parody or pastiche is considered relying only on the freedom of communication, since the copyright law does not guarantee this liberty), **Germany** *Heiner Müller case* BVerfG, no. 1 BvR 825/98, June 28, 2000, **Italy** Const. Court no. 108/1995, **USA** *"Copyright cannot legally be used to suppress criticism"*.

[360] **France** Const. Court, decision no. 2009-580DC, June 10, 2009, point 12, the decision is available in English: http://www.conseil-constitutionnel.fr/conseil-constitutionnel/root/bank_mm/anglais/2009_580dc.pdf. "In the current state of communication means and given the generalized development of public online communication services and the importance of the latter for the participation in democracy and the expression of ideas and opinions, this right implies freedom to access such services."

Lastly, the Chinese reporter mentions such a possibility in Chinese law, but sounds skeptical regarding the chances of success of the eventual process: "Fundamental rights such as the freedom of speech under China's Constitutional Law might be helpful for users in the most desperate cases, but the chance is remote."

Competition law

Competition law is regarded as a means of achieving a balance in copyright cases in ten countries,[361] only as a possible means in Cyprus, Greece, Egypt and Spain, and considered for such a role only in extreme cases in the USA.[362] This latter position is the method retained by European judges when they condemned the refusal to license in respect of informative or functional works.[363]

Canadian and UK copyright laws includes references to competition law.[364] Spanish provisions regarding computer program protection do as well.[365] Yet the Canadian reporter urges the difficult application of competition law principles to copyright cases; whereas, the UK reporter relates several cases where competition law played a role in the solution of conflicts.[366] Vice versa, Chinese anti-monopoly law provides for specific consideration of IP rights, commanding to intervene in intellectual property cases only when facing abuse.[367] The Australian Trade Practices Act contains similar provisions, which state a limitation of the application of the Act at stake, and specify that the prohibitions only apply to licensing, assignment and ownership of copyright in scenarios of misuse of market power and resale price maintenance.[368]

The Italian reporters considered unfair competition law in this context and point out several cases in which the prohibition of professionally incorrect competition acts have helped resolve copyright cases.[369]

Contract law

Nine countries consider contract law as a legal instrument contributing to the balance in copyright law, be it the prohibition of immoral contracts, of disturbing the public order,[370] or infringing good faith.[371] In Brazil it could be the case, but there is no salient case law thus far. The US reporter urges as follows, a mitigated position:

> Contracts are used by commercial software copyright owners to achieve an imbalance of interests strongly in favour of the copyright owners. On the other hand contracts are extensively and successfully used by proponents of open source and public licenses to ensure that derivative works will also be available to the public.

In the UK, "British contract doctrines have been employed to secure the interests authors (against subsequent owners of copyright interests), but are not generally employed to secure the balance of interests between users (or the public more generally) and copyright owners."

[361] **Belgium, France, Germany, India, Israel, Japan, Lithuania** (without judicial practice yet), **Poland, Portugal, Taiwan, UK. Italy** should also be mentioned here, but reporters consider unfair competition, whereas other reporters mostly considered antitrust law.

[362] See the *Microsoft* case http://www.justice.gov/atr/cases/ms_index.htm (Last visited on October 18, 2010).

[363] *IMS* case, Case C-481/01, *IMS Health GmbH & Co. OHG v. NDC Health GmbH & Co. KG*, 2004 O.J. (C3) 16 (April 29, 2004). This case is similar to the case mentioned by the French reporter, regarding a database, Cass. Com. December 4, 2001, Bulletin 2001 IV no. 193 p. 185. See also ECJ Cases C-241/91 and C-242/91 – *Magill*; CFI Case T-201/04 – *Microsoft*. The tie-in sale also was an issue in Japan.

[364] **Canada** Art. 70-5, **UK** Sec. 144.

[365] **Spain** Art. 100 para. 4 and para. 5, and Art. 104.

[366] See, for example, **Israel** *Attheraces Ltd v British Horseracing Board Ltd* [2007] ECC 7 (CA) and *Murphy v Media Protection Services Ltd* [2008] FSR 33 and *Football Association Premier League Ltd v QC Leisure* [2008] FSR 22.

[367] **China** Art. 55 of the China Antimonopoly Law.

[368] **Australia** Trade Practice Act 1974 (Cth), Sec. 46, 46A, 48 and 51 para. 3.

[369] See **Italian** cases: Cass. No. 5346/1993, Trib Milan September 28, 1976 or Trib Genoa June 19, 1993 Trib. Turin November 24, 1994 and Trib. Genoa December 3, 1997.

[370] The **Japanese** reporter mentions the public order in respect of mass market licenses (especially regarding computer programs such as shrink wrap license and clickwrap licenses) R. Kojima, "Information Transactions in a Digital Environment: From the Perspective of Intellectual Property Law", 12 *Intellectual Property Law and Policy Journal* 185 (2006), available at http://www.juris.hokudai.ac.jp/coe/pressinfo/journal/vol_11/11_8.pdf (Last visited on October 18, 2010).

[371] **Croatia, Egypt, Germany, Japan, Lithuania, Macao, Poland, Portugal, Taiwan, UK.**

On the very opposite end of the scale, in Israeli and Italian laws, contract law does not intervene in copyright cases.

In China, contract law contains a provision specifically dedicated to cases involving technology: When a computer software licensing contract is suspected of monopolizing and impeding technological progress, the licensee may claim for invalidation of the contract.[372]

In Australia, implied licenses will be read into a contract where it is necessary not to undermine accrued rights. This means that

> [t]he engagement for reward of a person to produce material of a nature which is capable of being the subject of copyright implies a permission, or consent, or licence in the person giving the engagement to use the material in the manner and for the purpose in which and for which it was contemplated between the parties that it would be used at the time of the engagement.[373]

In applying this principle, the High Court has suggested that a government authority to which conveyance plans had been submitted would be permitted to make internal reproductions and "back-up" copies of the plans without remunerating the author.[374]

General rules on misuse

Although all countries acknowledge such rules, only few report cases affecting copyright.[375]

The Brazilian and Israeli Supreme Courts mentioned the option of applying the general misuse doctrine in the context of copyright law,[376] but it has not yet explicitly been applied.

In Belgium, the misuse doctrine concerns economic and moral rights. Thus, it has been used by judges to restrict the demands of the plaintiff,[377] or to order that the transfer of the ownership of DAT tapes containing a work also transfers the right to adapt and use the work, except if the transferee communicates in due time his or her will to retain the copyrights at stake. In the latter case, the right holders complained 4 years after the transfer.[378]

In Greece, the Supreme Court decided according to the general principle of abuse of rights to refuse an author the right to oppose exploitation after he failed to invoke, following a long period of time, the invalidity of a convention as it was not written. Therefore, the defendant was right to believe the author would not exercise his right.[379] The balance of interest was expressly referred to in another case implying the general principle of the abuse of rights. The right of integrity to an architectural work was exercised by the author contrary to the right of the owner of the building. The court balanced the interests at stake and *sacrificed the integrity of the work.*[380] Reference to the balance of interests and abuse of rights in the case of architectural works occurred several times.[381] The abuse of moral rights also led a Greek court to order the exploitation of a song where one of the co-authors refused consent, ruling that the authors or heirs obviously exceed the limits imposed by good faith or morality by refusing their consent.[382]

[372] See the Art. 328 of the **Chinese** Contract Law.

[373] **Australia**, *Beck v Montana Constructions Pty Ltd* [1964-5] NSWR 229, 23 approved of by the High Court in *Copyright Agency Ltd v New South Wales* (2008) 233 CLR 279, 304.

[374] **Australia** *Copyright Agency Ltd v New South Wales* (2008) 233 CLR 279, 306.

[375] **Belgium**, **Brazil**, **Germany**, **Greece**, **Israel, UK**. Yet, in Brazil and Israel cases reported mention the possibility to apply general rules on misuse to copyright cases, but did not use it.

[376] **Brazilian** Court case, in 1977, RE 75.889, available at http://redir.stf.jus.br/paginador/paginador.jsp?docTP=AC&docID=171495&pgI=1&pgF=100000 (last visited on October 18, 2010), **Israel** *ACUM v. Galei* (P.L.A. 6142/02 *ACUM Ltd v. Galei Zahal Radio Station*, 57(2) P.D. 625 (2003)).

[377] **Belgium** Civil Tribunal Brussels, January 5, 1996, *I.R.-D.I.* 1996, p. 97.

[378] **Belgium** Tribunal 1st instance Brussels, March 9, 2005 *Ing.-conseils* 2006, p. 135.

[379] **Greek** Court of cassation, 1009/2007.

[380] **Greece** Multimember Court of First instance of Athens 2028/2003.

[381] **Greece** see also One-member Court of First Instance of Athens, 276/2001, and Multimember court of first instance of Thessaloniki 13300/2004, see also One-member Court of First Instance of Athens, 276/2001, and Multimember Court of First Instance of Thessaloniki 13300/2004.

[382] **Greece** One-member Court of First Instance of Athens 36247/1999.

In Germany,

> the general provision on misuse of the law (§ 242 of the German Civil Code; Bürgerliches Gesetzbuch, BGB) applies. In a recent case, e.g., a court of appeal has denied injunctive relief on the grounds of abusive behavior of the right holder.[383] Also, an abuse of the exclusive rights will be found if the refusal is made in circumstances in which the right holder would have to grant a mandatory license.[384]

In the UK, there is a general judge-made principle preventing or restricting the enforcement of copyright on the grounds of public interest. The application of this rule in the sphere of copyright is explicitly preserved by the CDPA 1988,[385] but its scope is contested.[386] Nevertheless, it is certain that the principle is of narrow application and will only rarely be applied.

Consumer protection law

No case has been reported, but the Chinese, Cypriot, German, Greek, Polish, Portuguese, Taiwanese and UK reports mention that provisions protecting consumers could be used in order to help achieve a balance.

The Belgian reporters, however, state that consumer groups played an important role during parliamentary debates regarding copyright and are the initiators of complaints before courts involving exceptions and limitations, especially to have user rights recognized in the digital and online sectors, although in vain.[387] Lastly, the Spanish reporter mentions that consumer protection is not foreign to some of the limitations contained in the copyright law, especially those in respect of computer programs and databases.[388]

Media law

Most provisions mentioned here actually are copyright provisions which have already been addressed and which are contained in special acts, in particular broadcasting, cable distribution or journalist-specific acts.

The Israeli Communications Act 1982 obliges multi-channel television broadcasters to – simultaneously – carry the broadcasts of certain "off-air" Israeli broadcasts, which are free to the general public.[389] Regarding such broadcasts, the multi-channel television broadcasters are exempted from paying royalties to copyright owners of the materials that were simultaneously rebroadcasted.[390]

German must-carry rules oblige the operators of analogue cable networks to carry certain programs as defined by law in order to guarantee that customers have access to a certain number of programs which are considered to be of importance in view of safeguarding free access to information (*Grundversorgung*). Must-carry rules are not part of federal but of state legislation; hence, they vary from state to state.

British broadcasting acts contain several provisions, which we have presented here dealing with user rights such as the fair dealing for reporting events[391] or mandatory licenses like those relating to broadcasting schedules.[392]

Another regulation concerning copyright can be found in the Law on the German National Library (*Gesetz über die Deutsche Nationalbibliothek*, DNBG), namely its Secs. 13 and 14, which oblige authors to hand over copies of their media works – such as musical or literary works – to the national library. This enables third parties to participate in the works' use and therefore supports a proper balance of interests.

[383] Court of Appeal Jena, *MMR* 2008, 408 [413] – *Thumbnails*.

[384] **German** Federal Supreme Court (BGH) *NJW-RR* 2009, 1047 [1049]: for reasons of competition law.

[385] UK **Sec. 171 para. 3.**

[386] UK **cf.** Hyde Park Residence Ltd v Yelland **[2001] Ch 143 (CA);** Ashdown v Telegraph Group Ltd **[2002] Ch 149 (CA).**

[387] **Belgium** *Test achats v. EMI* case, Brussels, September 9, 2005, *A&M* 2005, p. 301. It also was the case in **France** regarding the leading case re private copy vs. DRM on DVD, *Stéphane P. and UFC – Que Choisir v. Universal Pictures Vidéo France*, Court of cassation February 28, 2006.

[388] **Spain** Art. 34 para. 1, 100 para. 5 and para. 6.

[389] Art. 6 para. 49 (4) of the **Israeli** Communications Act, 1982.

[390] Art. 6 para. 49(1)(A) *ibid.*

[391] **UK** Sec. 137 Broadcasting Act 1996.

[392] **UK** Sec. 176 and sch. 17 Broadcasting Act 1990 and the must carry provision for cable retransmission Sec. 73 para. 4 and 138, and sch. 9 Broadcasting Act 1996.

16.2 Conclusion

The lack of differentiation among protected works and uses may lead to some overprotection, impeding uses that lie in the public interest. The "one-size-fits-all" approach indeed only serves the interests of commercial users since the preconditions or thresholds to enter into protection are quite low, be it in common law systems or in those of civil law. One must for example be concerned that the upcoming reform of copyright law in Brazil will follow the international law standards in restraining the free private use and compensating it, without granting any right to use for end users. In this regard, the general reluctance of reporters to use the phrase "user rights" (except in Canada, where the Supreme Court expressly recognized it) can only feed this fear. Along the same line, the lack of common definitions of "user rights", opposed to the relative harmonization of economic rights, and the extreme scarcity of acknowledgement of misuse of copyright as such also appears as symptoms of the unbalance. Moreover, the disparity between the defense of right holders and that of end users is also revealed by the strong majority of reporters considering the ruling of user rights as concrete, in other words as a closed list of specific cases, whereas the exclusivity rights are mostly abstractly ruled. Much worse, user rights are mostly simple presumptions, easily circumvented by contract. Also the interpretation that judges have made of the three-step test shows this unbalance: it always goes in favor of copyright holders except in cases mentioned by the Chinese and Spanish reporters. At the end of the day, the balance appears to be most effectively achieved by recourse to other branches of law, especially fundamental rights, competition and contract law. But except in the case of contract law, one can hardly be comforted by such assessment, since fundamental rights and competition law only can help users if they sue rights holders, which results in huge costs and offers a solution far after the use was desired.

Consequently one must hope that lawmakers will concentrate their efforts (also) in the implementation of Art. 7 and 8 of the TRIPS Agreement, fostering the balancing of rights and obligations to the mutual advantage of producers and users, and urging the need for preventing the potential abuse of IP rights.

17 Jurisdiction and Applicable Law in Matters of Intellectual Property*

Toshiyuki Kono

17.1 Introduction

One of the main events that accelerated the development of private international law of intellectual property was the Hague Judgments project initiated in early 1990 by the US at the Hague Conference on Private International Law. The initial goal of this initiative was to adopt an international convention which would harmonize rules on international jurisdiction and the recognition and enforcement of foreign judgments. However, after more than a decade of intense negotiations, the project unfortunately failed because some of the major negotiating parties – mainly the US and the EU – did not manage to find compromise on the underlying concepts. One of the principal reasons for such disagreements was also related to the problems concerning international jurisdiction in IP and Internet-related disputes.[1]

In order to save the Hague negotiations, several legal scholars (Rochelle C. Dreyfuss, Jane Ginsburg and François Dessemontet) created a special working group with an objective to draft more detailed framework regarding court jurisdiction in IP matters. At the outset such draft proposal was intended to be put forward to the Hague Conference. However, as it became obvious that the project to conclude the Hague judgments convention will fail, the Dreyfuss-Ginsburg initiative was further pursued under the auspices of the American Law Institute. As a result the ALI Principles on Intellectual Property[2] were adopted in 2007 at the meeting of the ALI General Assembly. The ALI Principles provide for a comprehensive set of rules concerning various issues on international jurisdiction, applicable law and the recognition of judgments in IP disputes. One of the focal objectives of the ALI Principles was to restrict possible jurisdictional grounds in cross-border IP disputes and to facilitate coordination and consolidation of the proceedings.[3]

The adoption of the ALI Principles was a milestone in trying to harmonize the settlement of multi-state IP disputes. However, the ALI Principles is not the only initiative in the field: a number of reform steps were taken in other continents too. In Europe, the Brussels/Lugano regime is in the process of review;[4] while

* III.B.1, La competence et la loi applicable en matiere de la propriete intellectuelle.

[1] *See e.g.* R. Dreyfuss, "An Alert to the Intellectual Property Bar: The Hague Judgments Convention," *University of Illinois Law Review* (2001): 421; A. F. Lowenfeld, L. J. Silberman, eds. *The Hague Convention on Jurisdiction and Judgments* (Huntington: Juris, 2001).

T. Kono (✉)
Faculty of Law, Kyushu University, Fukuoka, Japan
e-mail: glyndebourne@gmail.com

[2] The American Law Institute, *Intellectual Property: Principles Governing Jurisdiction, Choice-of-law and Judgments in Transnational Disputes* (Philadelphia: ALI Publishers, 2008).

[3] R. Dreyfuss, "The American Law Institute Project on Intellectual Property: Principles Governing Jurisdiction, Choice-of-law and Judgments in Transnational Disputes," in *Intellectual Property and Private International Law*, ed. S. Leible and A. Ohly (Tübingen: Mohr Siebeck, 2009), 15–30.

[4] Green Paper on the Review of the Council Regulation (EC) No. 44/2001 on Jurisdiction and the Recognition and Enforcement of Judgments in Civil and Commercial Matters (21.4.2009), COM(2009) 175 final.

K.B. Brown and D.V. Snyder (eds.), *General Reports of the XVIIIth Congress of the International Academy of Comparative Law/Rapports Généraux du XVIIIème Congrès de l'Académie Internationale de Droit Comparé*, DOI 10.1007/978-94-007-2354-2_17, © Springer Science+Business Media B.V. 2012

choice-of-law issues were harmonized by the Rome I[5] and Rome II[6] Regulations. In addition, the proposal of regulating private international law issues of IP rights at the EU level has been further elaborated in the CLIP Principles.[7] Similar changes have been taking place in Asian countries too. New private international law statutes were adopted in S. Korea, Japan and Taiwan; the discussion concerning the settlement of multi-state IP disputes has received increasing attention. Notably, similar principles to those drafted by the ALI and CLIP were drafted in Korea (so called "Korean Principles") and Japan.[8]

This General Report was drafted on the basis of national reports from 21 different countries.[9]

17.2 The Principle of Territoriality of IP Rights

The principle of territoriality has been the source of many controversies often arising in disputes concerning cross-border enforcement of IP rights. In the field of private international law, the principle of territoriality denotes the territorial boundaries of state jurisdiction. Namely, territoriality of state jurisdiction has been understood that states have full competence to regulate legal matters domestically by adopting legal statutes and establishing institutions which function to assure the enforcement of these statutes. Over centuries many theories have been developed putting forward novel arguments in what circumstances state courts should exercise international jurisdiction over cases with a foreign element as well as trying to find justifications why laws of other countries should be applied.

Slightly different understanding of the territoriality principle has evolved in the field of IP. The first examples of exclusive IP rights could be traced back to the middle ages when sovereigns and princes granted exclusive monopoly rights on an individual basis.[10] However, as the time passed, such royal concessions became more institutionalized when special statutes establishing a system of grant of IP rights were adopted. At the mid-nineteenth century, most Western countries had their own domestic statutes dealing with IP rights. Yet, differences among domestic legislation often resulted in situations where creators were not equally protected in third countries. This inadequacy was one of the reasons for the proliferation of bilateral agreements among states the purpose of which was to assure mutual protection of creators in other contracting states.[11] By the end of the nineteenth century these bilateral agreements gradually transformed into multilateral agreements for the protection of IP rights (namely, 1883 Paris Convention for the Protection of Industrial Property and 1886 Berne Convention for the Protection of Literary and Artistic Works).

Both Paris and Berne Conventions rest upon several legal principles which shape the international protection of IP rights. The principle of national treatment requires countries to give the same legal protection for nationals of any other state of the Union as the protection granted to their own nationals.[12] One of the ideas behind the

[5] Regulation (EC) No 593/2009 of the European Parliament and of the Council of 17 June 2008 on the law applicable to contractual obligations (Rome I), (2008) *OJ* L 177/6.

[6] Regulation (EC) No 864/2007 of the European Parliament and of the Council of 11 July 2007 on the law applicable to non-contractual obligations (Rome II), (2007) *OJ* L 199/40.

[7] The Third Draft of the CLIP Principles is available at http://cl-ip.eu/ (last visited 20 October 2010).

[8] In Japan two working groups have been working on Private international law aspects of IP. The so called "Transparency Principles" have been finalized in 2010 and "Waseda Principles" should be completed by the end of 2010. For a comparative study concerning ALI, CLIP and Transparency proposals *see* J. Basedow, T. Kono, A. Metzger, eds., *Intellectual Property in the Global Arena – Jurisdiction, Applicable Law, and the Recognition of Judgments in Europe, Japan and the US*, (Tübingen: Mohr Siebeck, 2010).

[9] Austria (Prof. Thomas Petz), Belgium (Marie-Christine Janssens), Canada (Joost Blom), Croatia (Ivana Kunda), France (Marie Elodie Ancel), Germany (Axel Metzger), Greece (Anastasia Grammaticaki-Alexiou and Tatiana Synodinou), Hungary (Tattay Levente), India (Vandana Singh), Italy (Nerina Boschiero and Benedetta Ubertazzi), Japan (Dai Yokomizo), the Netherlands (Dick van Engelen), Portugal (Alexandre Dias Pereira), Slovenia (Damjan Možina), Spain (Pedro A. de Miguel Asensio), South Korea (Gyooho Lee), Sweden (Ulf Maunsbach), Switzerland (Amélie Charbon and Iris Sidler), Taiwan (Ming-Yan Shieh), United Kingdom (Christopher Wadlow), and the United States (Howard B. Abrams).

[10] J. Basedow, "Foundations of Private International Law in Intellectual Property," in J. Basedow, et al., *supra* note 8, p. 7; F. Dessemontet, "The ALI Principles: Intellectual Property in Transborder Litigation" in J. Basedow, et al., *supra* note 8, p. 32.

[11] J. Ginsburg, "The Private International Law of Copyright in an Era of Technological Change," *Recueil des Cours* 273 (1998): 260.

[12] The principle of national treatment is entrenched in Art. 2 of the Paris Convention.

Paris and Berne Conventions is territoriality. The general understanding is that protection in a particular state could be granted if certain requirements posited in the laws of that state are fulfilled. In the case of copyrights or related rights, the Berne Convention established minimum standards of protection and requires that the protection must not depend upon the compliance with any additional formalities. Article 5(1) of the Berne Convention provides that authors of the works protected under the Convention shall enjoy protection in other states of the Union that the country of origin the rights granted by the laws of other states as well as rights granted under by the Berne Convention. Further, Article 5(2) stipulates that the enjoyment and exercise of rights shall be independent from the existence of the protection in the country of origin of the work. Similar ideas could be also found in the Paris treaty, which, with regard to patents, states that the application for a patent in one country is independent from the patents obtained for the same invention in another country of the Paris Union. One more reflection of territoriality could be found in Article 5(2) of the Berne Convention according to which the term of protection as well as the means of redress of the author shall be governed by the law of the country where the protection is sought (so called *lex loci protectionis* principle).

Both notions of territoriality as known in private international law and intellectual property are closely intertwined with the sovereignty concept. In particular, sovereign states aim to implement certain economic, cultural, or foreign-relations policies. These policy considerations often shape the level of protection of IP rights or the exercise of international jurisdiction of domestic courts. Nonetheless, three changes in the second half of the 20th century contributed to the decline of the importance of the sovereignty and territoriality principles. First, regional and international economic integration shifted the regulation from national to supranational level. Hence, many, yet not all issues pertaining to IP rights have been harmonized by regional and international acts.[13] The second challenge is the development of the Internet. Third, the circle of stakeholders has dramatically shifted: differently from the nineteenth century landscape, the role of states has demised while a number of new players have emerged (e.g. multinational corporations, intermediaries etc.). Accordingly, sovereign interests of states have been supplanted by the greater emphasis put on the market and interests of private parties. The discussion about the role of the territoriality principle has been intense since the emergence of the Internet and global exercise of IP rights.

17.3 International Jurisdiction in IP Disputes

17.3.1 Personal Jurisdiction

The first issue that the court dealing with an international dispute has to decide is whether it has jurisdiction to hear the case. Only if jurisdiction over a dispute is asserted, the court can decide upon the merits. Since the subject of the current project was related to the intersection of IP and private international law, one of the initial issues which had to be clarified was related to the "general" jurisdiction of domestic courts. By and large, most of the jurisdictions have developed principles that courts would have international jurisdiction to adjudicate the case if the defendant is domiciled or resident in the forum state. Although the jurisdiction based upon defendant's domicile appears to be a firmly established principle, national reporters were asked to elaborate the modes of application of it in disputes involving domestic and foreign IP rights.

The principles of asserting international jurisdiction in the US were developed by the courts. In one of the landmark judgments *International Shoe Co.* v. *Washington*, the US Supreme Court decided that *in personam* jurisdiction may be asserted if the defendant had sufficient minimum contacts with the forum and such exercise of jurisdiction does not offend traditional notions of fair play and substantial justice.[14] Such contacts must result from some deliberate conduct of the non-resident defendant who has to purposively avail himself to the benefits and protection of the forum law.[15] In Canada, the determination of whether a Canadian court has international jurisdiction depends on rules which determine the court's jurisdiction

[13] *E.g.* Patent Cooperation Treaty; WIPO Performances and Phonograms Treaty (1996); WIPO Copyright Treaty (1996); or Agreement on Trade-Related Aspects of Intellectual Property Rights (TRIPS).

[14] 326 US 310 (1945) at 316.

[15] *World-Wide Volkswagen Corp.* v. *Woodson*, 444 US 286 (1980).

(so called "jurisdiction *simpliciter*"). Legal sources governing jurisdiction *simpliciter* differ according to the province; however, the laws of all provinces require the existence of *in personam* jurisdiction. This requirement is by and large satisfied if the party resides in the province. The laws of Canadian provinces also establish that Canadian courts have *in personam* jurisdiction if a party submits itself to the jurisdiction of a court. In addition to general jurisdiction requirements, the doctrine of *forum non conveniens* plays an important in both North American countries. As regards disputes pertaining to IP rights, national reporters indicated that Canadian and US courts would exercise their adjudicative authority if they have *in personam* jurisdiction and subject-matter jurisdiction. Subject-matter jurisdiction would usually mean that Canadian and US courts are not competent to hear disputes concerning the validity and infringement of foreign IP rights. This will be dealt with in 17.3.2.

Within the European Union matters related to international jurisdiction of the Member State courts are governed by the Brussels I Regulation.[16] The general principle is entrenched in Article 2 of the Regulation and provides that persons who are domiciled in a Member State shall be sued in the courts of that Member State. This principle applies regardless of the nationality of the parties and even in those cases where the plaintiff is not resident in the EU.[17] The underlying rationale of *forum domicilii* rule is to make it easier for a defendant to defend himself.[18] The question whether a natural person is resident in EU should be determined according to domestic rules of the forum (Art. 59). As regards legal entities, Article 60(1) provides that a company or other legal person or association of natural persons is domiciled at the place where it has its (a) statutory seat; (b) central administration; or (c) principal place of business. If the defendant is not domiciled in EU, the court seized has to apply its domestic jurisdiction rules. The rule pursuant to which the courts of the defendant's domicile have jurisdiction could be derogated from only in situations prescribed by the Regulation itself (Arts. 5–31). Such clear-cut jurisdiction framework was established with the objective to facilitate free circulation of judgments within the EU. In addition, Article 5(5) of the Brussels I Regulation establishes a special ground of jurisdiction and stipulates that in disputes arising out of the operations of a branch, agency or other establishment, a person domiciled in a Member State may be sued in another Member State in which the branch, the agency of other establishment is situated. In one of its early judgments, the ECJ clarified that for the purposes of establishing international jurisdiction over the parent body at the place of its branch, agency or establishment, such branch, agency or establishment should be subject to direction and control of the parent body.[19]

In cross-border IP litigation, it is necessary to determine the relationship of different grounds of jurisdiction and whether the territorial nature of IP rights does not prevent the court of the country where the defendant is domiciled to hear the dispute which might be related to foreign IP rights. Most of the EU reports noted that the principle of the defendant's domicile (*actor sequitur forum rei*) equally applies with regard to actions concerning IP rights. Therefore, the court of the country where the defendant is domiciled can assert jurisdiction over actions involving claims related not only to infringements of domestic IP rights but also claims concerning foreign IP rights (e.g. when IP infringing acts occurred in another Member State or in a non-EU state). This approach also appears to be well-established practice by domestic courts of many EU Member States. Hence, in cases where foreign IP rights are infringed by acts committed abroad, the Brussels/Lugano regime allows to sue the defendant (alleged infringer of IP rights) before courts of an EU Member State if the defendant has his domicile there. Many national reporters noted that in many cases related to the Internet, courts of the state where the defendant has his domicile should be competent to hear the dispute. Courts of the country where the defendant is domiciled

[16] The Brussels I Regulation came into force on 1 March 2002 and replaced the 1968 Brussels Convention. International jurisdiction of the EEA states (Iceland, Norway, and Switzerland) is governed by the 2007 Lugano Convention which based on the same principles as Brussels I Regulation.

[17] ECJ, Case C-412/98 *Group Josi Reinsurance Comp* v. *UGIC* [2000] *ECR* I-5925, para. 61.

[18] ECJ, Case C-26/91 *Handte* v. *Traitements Mécano-chimiques des Surfaces* [1992] *ECR* I-3967, para. 14.

[19] ECJ, Case 14/76 *A. De Bloos, SPRL* v. *Société en commandite par actions Bouyer* [1976] *ECR* 1497, paras. 20 and 21; ECJ, Case 139/80 *Blanckaert and Willems PVBA* v. *Luise Trost* [1981] *ECR* 819, para. 9.

are competent also to hear disputes concerning unitary Community IP rights.[20] The jurisdiction of the court in IP-related cases based upon Article 2 covers all kinds of IP disputes, except disputes related to the registration or validity of foreign registered IP rights.[21] From the national reports it may be also concluded that, within the EU, courts whose jurisdiction is based upon the defendant's domicile can also order cross-border injunctions in IP infringement cases.

The Brussels/Lugano regime does not apply to disputes where the defendant is not resident in any of the Member States. In such cases, domestic courts of EU and EEA States must decide whether they are competent to exercise international jurisdiction according domestic jurisdiction rules of the forum (Art. 4 of the Regulation). Some EU Member States (the Netherlands, Spain) have aligned their domestic jurisdiction rules to the Brussels/Lugano regime. However, not all EU countries follow principles similar to those laid down in the Brussels/Lugano instruments. This means that each court would determine whether it has international jurisdiction according to domestic rules and established precedents.[22] In so far as courts' competence to decide over the damage claims is concerned, the legal situation would again be less clear in cases involving defendants non-domiciled in any EU Member State. However, many national reports noted that courts would have unlimited jurisdiction to decide over the damage sustained in the forum state given that prescribed due process requirements (e.g. service of the defendant) are met.

In Japan, the case law until recently played an important role because the Code of Civil Procedure did not contain any rules on international jurisdiction. In one of its landmark decisions, the *Malaysia Airlines* case, the Supreme Court decided that Japanese courts should have international jurisdiction if one of the venues is established according to the domestic territorial rules.[23] Further, in order to prevent situations where courts exercise exorbitant jurisdiction, Japanese law contains a "special circumstances test": in deciding whether international jurisdiction should be asserted, the court should take into consideration such principles as fairness between the parties, expediency and appropriateness of adjudication of the dispute.[24] Actions could be also brought against agencies and branches of foreign corporations if the claims are related to their activities.[25] These Principles are now entrenched in Articles 3-2, 3-3 and 3-9 of the Code of Civil Procedure of Japan (adopted in 2011). Similar rules exist also in Korean Law. With regard to multi-state IP disputes, Japanese and Korean court practice is more similar to the European approach because international jurisdiction over the dispute can be asserted even in those cases where the IP rights involved are granted in a foreign country.

From the overview of represented legal systems, it could be concluded that courts would by and large assert international jurisdiction if there is a close connection between the dispute and the forum. Yet, in the case of multi-state IP disputes, the problem which arises is that IP rights could exist in several countries. This means that in many cases there will be a discrepancy of the location of the owner of IP rights and the location of IP rights at stake. Such discrepancy will be "default" situation especially in copyright-related disputes. Here, the major differences between the different legal systems become obvious: courts of continental European or Asian (Korean, Japanese) countries would assert international jurisdiction if the defendant has his domicile in the forum country; the mere fact that IP rights at stake are granted in a foreign country would not be relevant at the jurisdiction stage. Courts of common-law countries (Canada, US and UK courts in disputes to which the Brussels/Lugano regime does not apply) would hear the action only if they have both jurisdiction *in personam* and subject-matter jurisdiction. This mandatory requirement of subject-matter jurisdiction

[20] Article 97 of the Council Regulation (EC) No. 207/2009 of 26 February 2009 on the Community trade mark (codified version), *OJ* L 79/1 (24.3.2009); Art. 82 and 83(1) of the Council Regulation (EC) No. 6/2002 of 12 December 2001 on Community Designs, *OJ* L 3/1 (5.1.2002); and Art. 101 of the Council Regulation (EC) No. 2100/94 of 27 July 1994 on Community plant variety rights, *OJ* L 227/1 (1.9.1994).

[21] Disputes where the registration or validity of foreign registered IP right arises even as a preliminary question fall under the exclusive jurisdiction of the granting state; see further discussion in Sect. 17.3.2 *infra*.

[22] The standards of asserting international jurisdiction thus differ from country to country. For instance, UK courts would assert jurisdiction if the claim could be validly served to the defendant.

[23] Supreme Court of Japan, Judgment of 16 October 1981, *Minshû* Vol. 35, No. 7, p. 1224 ("*Malaysia Airlines*" case).

[24] Supreme Court of Japan, Judgment of 11 November 1997, *Minshû* Vol. 51, No. 10, p. 4055 ("*Family*" case); Art. 2(2) of the KOPILA.

[25] Article 12 of the Korean Civil Procedure Act; Art. 5(v) of the Code of Civil Procedure of Japan.

in practice means that in Canada and US (as well as other common law jurisdictions) most IP disputes are adjudicated on a territorial basis which means that courts are not able to exercise jurisdiction if the action involves IP-related claims over which they do not have subject-matter jurisdiction.

17.3.2 Subject-Matter Jurisdiction

Due to certain economic or political considerations, countries may find that some kinds of legal disputes should be adjudicated exclusively by their own domestic courts. In the area of IP, registration, existence or other matters often are considered to fall under the exclusive competence of the granting country. For a long time, such issues which require the participation of administrative agencies have been considered to be within the sovereign powers of a given state.[26] Although the underlying idea is the same, different terminology has been used to describe this phenomenon (i.e. "subject-matter jurisdiction", "exclusive jurisdiction", "justiciability"). The national reporters were asked to explain the peculiarities of application of exclusive jurisdiction rules in IP disputes in their countries.

Since both Canada and United States are federal countries, one of the first questions for the courts to determine is whether a dispute is subject to federal courts or courts of a particular state/province. In the US, federal courts have subject-matter jurisdiction over cases "arising under" the Copyright or the Patent Act.[27] However, disputes concerning contractual arrangements regarding IP rights (e.g. transfer of the ownership of a patent or copyright) are not considered as falling under the subject-matter jurisdiction of federal courts. With regard to possibility of bringing an action concerning foreign IP rights, the leading US case-law takes a rather territorial approach: a US court could exercise subject-matter jurisdiction over a dispute involving foreign IP rights if such rights were infringed in the US and grant remedies only for acts of infringement which occur in the US.[28]

In Canada, courts have not yet had any opportunity to decide whether they would assert jurisdiction over disputes concerning validity or infringement of foreign IP rights. However, since Canadian private international law has to a large extent developed on the basis of English law, it is very likely that Canadian courts would take into consideration the jurisprudence of other Commonwealth jurisdictions. In this regard, the Canadian Report referred to the 2009 decision of the English Court of Appeals in the case *Lucasfilm Ltd.* v. *Ainsworth*[29], where the question of subject-matter jurisdiction was at the heart of the dispute. In particular, the Court of Appeals found that English courts were barred from hearing claims for the infringement of the US copyrights. In addition, even though the alleged infringer was domiciled in England, the subject-matter jurisdiction rules rendered claims for the infringement of foreign IP rights non-justiciable. As regards the question of ownership of IP rights, the leading US judgment was handed in the *Itar-Tass* case, where the court found that the law of the nation with the most substantial relationship should be applied to determine the ownership; however, the court did not hesitate to exercise jurisdiction and decide the case.[30]

In the EU, Article 22(4) of the Brussels I Regulation provides for exclusive grounds of jurisdiction according to which proceedings concerning registration or validity of registered IP rights can be brought only before the courts of the country where the right in question was registered. Notably, Article 22(4) confers exclusive jurisdiction on the basis of the substance of the dispute (i.e. the (in)validity of the patent right) and does not depend on other factors such as the characteristics of the parties. Further, exclusive jurisdiction rules apply regardless of how IP rights were registered or deposited. However, Article 22(4) does not apply if the dispute is concerned with the registration or validity of an IP right which is registered in a third country. Exclusive jurisdiction rules are of a mandatory nature: any court of a Member State shall declare of its own motion that it has no jurisdiction if the claim is principally concerned

[26] *See e.g. Potter* v. *Broken Hill Ltd.*, (1906) 3 CLR 479.

[27] 28 U.S.C. § 1338(a) 2006 where it is also provided that cases involving trademarks could be either brought before federal or state courts.

[28] *Subafilms Ltd.* v. *MGM-Pathe Communications Co.*, 24F.3d 1088 (9th Cir. 1994), *cert. denied sub nom.*, *Subafilms Ltd.* v. *United Artists Corp.*, 513 U.S. 1001 (1994); but see *Update Art, Inc.* v. *Modiin Publishing, Ltd.*, 843F.2d 67 (2d Cir. 1988).

[29] (2008) EWHC 1878 (Ch). But see (2010) FSR 10 and the decision of the Supreme Court (2011) UKSC 39.

[30] *Itar-Tass Russian News Agency* v. *Russian Kurier Inc.*, 153F.3d 82, 90 (2d Cir. 1998).

with a matter over which the courts of another Member State have exclusive jurisdiction by virtue of Article 22.

The material scope of exclusive jurisdiction rules was clarified in the ECJ jurisprudence. In the *Goderbauer* case, the ECJ decided that the definition of "proceedings concerned with the registration and validity" of patents or other registered IP rights does not cover claims related with initial ownership in general, or attribution of ownership in case of employee inventions.[31] For a long time, there was no consent among the courts of different EU Member States whether exclusive jurisdiction rules extend to cross-border IP disputes where one of the parties challenges the validity of foreign IP rights. The ECJ put an end to the discussion of different practice of domestic courts by its ruling in the *GAT* v. *LuK* case.[32] The dispute arose between two German companies "GAT" and "LuK" who were competitors in the car manufacturing industry. GAT was supplying certain vehicle parts to another manufacturer (Ford) which allegedly infringed two patents owned by LuK in France. The alleged infringer (GAT) brought a suit for declaration of non-infringement to District Court of Düsseldorf and argued that patents which LuK had in France were either void or invalid. The ECJ decided that exclusive jurisdiction rules shall come into play in every situation where the issue of validity is at stake. Therefore, it does not matter whether the validity question is part of the main claim or is raised as a plea in objection. Consequently, exclusive jurisdiction rules would be undermined if the question of (in)validity of a patent was decided by any other court than the court of the granting country.[33] The ECJ judgment was harshly criticized mainly on the grounds that the Court did not take into account efficiency considerations of adjudicating multi-state IP disputes.[34] Further, it was argued that the *GAT* v. *LuK* decision opened the gates for the alleged infringer to delay the proceedings by raising an invalidity defence.

In Asia, the situation differs from country to country. For instance, Indian courts would in principle reach the same conclusions as courts of other common law countries and exercise jurisdiction only over disputes concerning Indian IP rights. In Korea, issues of registration and validity of foreign IP rights have to be adjudicated by the courts of the granting country. In Japan, a path-breaking judgment was handed down by the Tokyo District Court in 2003 (the so-called "*Coral Sand*" case[35]), where the validity of a foreign patent in a patent infringement dispute was at stake. The Court found that the question of infringement is inseparable from the validity of a right and that such a decision on the validity had effects only between the parties of the dispute (yet, it should be noted that both parties in that case were Japanese corporations). Article 3-5(iii) of the CCP (adopted in 2011) posits that actions related to the existence and effects of IP rights (as they are defined in Article 2(2) of the Intellectual Property Basic Act), which are subject to registration, shall be subject to the exclusive jurisdiction of Japanese courts if such IP rights are to be registered in Japan. The drafters of the new Code of Civil Procedure discussed the two following situations. Firstly, cases in which an action the object of which is the validity of a foreign registered IP right is brought before a Japanese court when the defendant is domiciled in Japan. Secondly, situations where the validity of a foreign registered IP right is challenged as a defence. However, no particular solution had been reached and it is yet not clear how these provisions will be applied in practice.

The closer analysis of the represented legal systems shows that the adjudication of multi-state IP disputes is often constrained by subject-matter jurisdiction requirement or a narrow interpretation of exclusive jurisdiction rules. One notable difference between the common law jurisdictions and continental European countries deserves attention. According to the Canadian and American reports, the subject-matter jurisdiction requirement would practically pre-empt the courts from hearing any claims concerning infringement or validity of foreign IP rights. Jurisdiction could be asserted only with regard to some incidental issues

[31] ECJ, Case 288/82 *Ferdinand Duijnstee* v. *Lodewijk Goderbauer*, [1983] *ECR* 3663, paras. 26–28.

[32] ECJ, Case C-4/03 *Gesellschaft für Antriebstechnik mbH & Co. KG (GAT)* v. *Lamellen und Kupplungsbau Beteiligungs KG (LuK)* [2006] *ECR* I-6509.

[33] *Ibid.*, paras. 25–26.

[34] A. Kur, "A Farewell to Cross-Border Injunctions? The ECJ Decisions GAT v. LuK and Roche Nederland v. Primus Goldenberg" 7 *IIC* (2006), p. 850 *et seq.*; P. Torremans, "The Way Forward for Cross-Border Intellectual Property Litigation: Why GAT Cannot be the Answer," in *Intellectual Property and Private International Law,* ed. S. Leible and A. Ohly, 194 (Tübingen: Mohr Siebeck, 2009).

[35] Tokyo District Court, Judgment of 16 October 2003, *Hanrei Jihô* No. 1874, p. 23.

such as ownership of foreign IP rights. Under the European Brussels/Lugano regime, disputes concerning non-registered IP rights (such as copyrights, neighboring rights) do not fall under the exclusive jurisdiction rules and thus could be adjudicated by any courts which have jurisdiction pursuant to one of the provisions of the Brussels/Lugano instruments. Exclusive jurisdiction rules as they were interpreted by the ECJ in the *GAT* case would apply only with regard to registered IP rights. In the background of such legal environment, a number of legislative proposals put forward various possibilities of how to facilitate resolution of multi-state IP disputes and overcome limitations related to subject-matter/exclusive jurisdiction requirements.[36] One of the possible solutions to the problem was firstly established in the 2001 Proposal for Hague Judgments Convention. Namely, it was proposed in Article 12 that decisions over such issues as the grant, registration, validity, abandonment or revocation of patent or mark should have *inter partes* effects.[37] If any initiatives concerning adjudication of multi-state IP disputes are pursued in the future, the starting point should be the 2001 Draft of the Hague Judgments Convention.

17.3.3 Jurisdiction over IP Infringement Disputes

National legal systems establish possibilities to bring actions not only on the basis of the defendant's domicile, but also on other grounds of jurisdiction. One of the special grounds of jurisdiction is the place of the infringement. In the light of the territorial nature of IP rights it has been long argued that infringements of IP rights could only occur in the country where the infringing acts were committed. However, the emergence of digital technologies changed significantly traditional notions of the place of infringement as a ground of jurisdiction: the damage caused by a single tortuous act may arise in multiple states. The national reporters were asked to address numerous questions concerning the exercise of international jurisdiction over IP infringement disputes.

In Canada and the US, jurisdiction in IP infringement disputes could be exercised if a court has both (1) *in personam* jurisdiction[38] and (2) subject-matter jurisdiction. By and large, courts would have *in personam* jurisdiction if the defendant was resident in the forum state or if the defendant submitted himself to the jurisdiction of the court seized. In both countries, the defendant may challenge the jurisdiction of the court seized by claiming that a court of a foreign country is *forum conveniens*. As it was shown above, such jurisdictional framework in practice means that courts would hear only claims related to the infringement of IP rights in the forum state.[39] Besides, the subject-matter jurisdiction requirement would bar Canadian and American courts from hearing disputes over the validity and infringements of foreign IP rights. With regard to the scope of court's authority to award damages, a Canadian court could decide on damages sustained also in foreign countries, if the defendant has his residence in Canada. However, if the jurisdiction of a Canadian court was based on the *situs* of the tort (i.e. tort in Canada), the court could decide only on damages which occurred in that particular jurisdiction. In order to succeed, the plaintiff would have to convince the court that there is a real and substantial connection between the local forum and those claims. The situation would be similar in the US.[40]

The primary legal source determining international jurisdiction of EU Member State courts in cross-border IP infringement cases is the Brussels I Regulation and the Lugano Convention. Pursuant to Article 5(3), the defendant who is resident in a Member State may be also sued before the courts of the place where the harmful event occurred or may occur. The expression "place where the harmful event occurred" is understood as covering both the place where the damage occurred and the place of the event giving rise to it. Consequently, the defendant may be sued, at the option of the plaintiff, either in courts of the country where the damage occurred or in courts of the country where the harmful

[36] §§ 211–214 of the ALI Principles; Art. 2:401 and 2:402 of the CLIP Principles; Art. 103 of the Transparency Principles; Art. 10 of the Korean Principles.

[37] Available at http://www.hcch.net/index_en.php?act=publications.details&pid=3499&dtid=35 (last visited 20 October 2010).

[38] In Canada it is known as "jurisdiction *simpliciter*".

[39] *See e.g. Voda* v. *Cordis Corp.*, 476 F.3d 887 (Fed. Cir. 2007); *Subafilms Ltd.* v. *MGM-Pathe Communications Co.*, *supra* note 28.

[40] *See e.g. Sheldon* v. *Metro Goldwyn Pictures Corp.*, 106 F.2d 45, 52 (1939), *aff'd*, 309 U.S. 390 (1940).

event occurred.[41] In case *Marinari*, the ECJ ruled that the "place where the harmful event occurred" should mean only the place of direct damage.[42] Besides, Article 5(3) has been interpreted autonomously[43] as covering all actions which seek to establish the liability of the defendant except actions related to "contract" within the meaning of Article 5(1) of the Brussels I Regulation.[44]

The scope of the court's jurisdiction was clarified in the *Shevill* case. A UK national Fiona Shevill brought a defamation action in the UK against a French publisher of a newspaper who published an article stating that Ms. Shevill together with other plaintiffs was taking part in a money laundering network. The ECJ ruled that courts of the country where the publisher is established and where the event giving rise to the damage occurred shall have jurisdiction to award damages for all the harm caused by the defamation.[45] Courts of other countries where the damage occurred could exercise jurisdiction only with regard to the damage sustained in that country.[46] The *Shevill* case concerned jurisdiction over claim for damages arising from defamation, therefore, even though some national reports referred to domestic case law where the same approach was established, it remains controversial whether it could be applied to multi-state IP infringement actions. Similar uncertainty concerning the application of Article 5(3) exists also with regard to jurisdiction over ubiquitous infringements. Meanwhile, it is expected that some guidance will be given by the ECJ which will have to hand down judgment in one pending case.[47]

According to Japanese and Korean law, actions for an infringement of IP rights may be brought in the place of the infringement.[48] More precisely, courts in Korea and Japan would generally assert international jurisdiction if the event giving rise to the damage or the results occur in the forum country. In Japan, this approach taken by the courts was changed by newly adopted Code of Civil Procedure. Namely, Article 3-3(viii) of the CCP (2011) provides that Japanese courts shall have jurisdiction over actions concerning unlawful acts if such acts occurred in Japan. However, this rule shall not apply with regard to infringing acts undertaken abroad, the effects of which occurred in Japan, if it could not have been generally foreseen that the effects of such acts would occur in Japan.

Comparative analysis of the laws of different jurisdictions highlighted rather different approaches of adjudication of IP infringement actions. The territorially limited approach of American and Canadian courts stands in contrast with more flexible regime according to the Brussels/Lugano regime and the laws of the represented Asian countries. Yet, in all countries the issue of jurisdiction over ubiquitous infringements remains nebulous; however, some practical proposals have been laid in the legislative proposals.[49] Besides these legislative proposals, the results achieved at the negotiations to draft the Hague Judgments Convention could be a solid starting point if further harmonisation initiatives on a multilateral level are pursued.

17.3.4 Parallel Proceedings in IP Disputes

The existence of different grounds of jurisdiction in international IP cases means that the plaintiff will have a possibility to choose the country of litigation. This may result not only in the situation where the defendant is sued before an improper forum, but also cases where the same or similar disputes are litigated before the courts of different countries. For example, the plaintiff may bring an infringement action before a court of country A and the defendant may file a suit in a court of country B seeking a declaration of non-liability. The laws of different countries often contain special legal mechanisms in order to prevent such multiplication of the proceedings. Parallel proceedings is one of the difficult problems of cross-border adjudication of IP disputes as well. Strict territoriality principle might pose significant limitations according to which

[41] ECJ, Case C-21/76 *Handelskwekerij G. J. Bier BV* v. *Mines de potasse d'Alsace SA* (1976) ECR 1735, paras. 24–25.

[42] ECJ, Case C-364/93 *Antonio Marinari* v. *Lloyds Bank plc and Zubaidi Trading Company* [1995] *ECR* I-2709, paras 14–15; ECJ, Case C-220/88 *Dumez France SA and Tracoba SARL* v. *Hessische Landesbank and others* [1990] *ECR* I-49, para. 20.

[43] ECJ, Case 189/87 *Kalfelis* v. *Bankhaus Schröder* [1988] *ECR* 5565, paras. 15 and 16.

[44] *Ibid.*, paras. 17 and 19.

[45] ECJ, Case C-68/93 *Shevill* [1995] *ECR* I-415, para. 24.

[46] *Ibid.*, paras. 29–30.

[47] *See* in particular pending ECJ Case C-509/09.

[48] *See e.g.* Art. 5(ix) of the Japanese Code of Civil Procedure.

[49] *See inter alia* § 204 of the ALI Principles; Art. 2:202 of the CLIP Principles; Art. 11 of the Korean Principles and Art. 105 of the Transparency Proposal.

IP-related disputes can be adjudicated only before the courts of the country where IP rights were created. However, in jurisdictions where a more flexible interpretation concerning the adjudication of disputes related to foreign IP rights is adopted, the likeliness of parallel proceedings is higher. The national reports provided for a thorough overview of how courts deal with parallel proceedings in IP disputes.

The question of international parallel proceedings under the Canadian and the US law is subject to several considerations. Namely, the situation of international parallel proceedings would occur if the dispute is pending before Canadian or American courts and courts of another country. In order to decide upon the merits, Canadian and US courts would have to establish *in personam* and subject-matter jurisdiction. Only then Canadian or US courts would investigate how to deal with the issue of parallel proceedings. The Canadian Report noted that the question of parallel proceedings is an important element of the *forum non conveniens* doctrine. Accordingly, Canadian courts would try to undertake a general evaluation whether Canadian courts or the court of a country seized is a more appropriate forum to hear the dispute. In cases where it appears that both Canadian and foreign courts are more or less in an equal position to adjudicate the dispute, Canadian courts may decline jurisdiction if the foreign court was the court first seized or if the foreign court was first to assert jurisdiction over the dispute. The question of parallel proceedings in the area of IP should be understood in the light of the limitations posed by the subject-matter jurisdiction requirement which bars Canadian and American courts from asserting jurisdiction over actions concerning infringements of foreign IP rights. Hence, in most cases the court would not defer to foreign parallel proceedings unless such proceedings involve the question of ownership of rights.[50] In addition, the Canadian report noted that in the case where the proprietor of foreign IP rights seeks to sue the alleged infringer who is located in Canada, Canadian courts would not issue anti-suit injunctions preventing the alleged infringer from seeking declaration of non-liability.

In Europe, the Brussels I Regulation establishes two cornerstone rules related to the coordination of parallel proceedings. Firstly, Article 27 deals with parallel proceedings which arise between the same parties and are based upon the same cause of action. Secondly, Article 28 covers related Actions which are pending before courts of several Member States. More particularly, Article 27 posits the first-in-time principle: if the proceedings have the same cause of action and are between the same parties, any court other than the court first seized shall of its own motion stay the proceedings until the jurisdiction of the court first seized is established. Further, if the court first seized decides to hear the case, any other court later seized shall decline jurisdiction in favour of the court first seized (Art. 27(2)). The Brussels I Regulation *expressis verbis* indicates that the court second seized has no discretion and must stay the proceedings. Thus, Article 27 is designed to preclude the possibility of a situation where a judgment given in a particular case is not recognized on the basis of its irreconcilability with a judgment given in proceedings between the same parties in the State in which recognition is sought.[51] According to the ECJ, Article 27 does not provide for any other requirements than the sameness of the parties and the sameness of the cause of action.[52] According to the ECJ, Article 27 should interpreted broadly so as to cover various situations where cases having the same cause of action are pending before courts of different courts and might end in conflicting decisions.[53] For instance, in the *Tatry* case the ECJ ruled that an action for a declaration that the plaintiff is not liable and an action commenced subsequently whereby the plaintiff in the first action is sued for compensation of damages had the same object.[54] Besides, according to the ECJ judgment in the case *Gubisch*,[55] the requirement of the "sameness of the parties" applies regardless of the procedural position of each of the parties in the two actions.

In the area of cross-border IP disputes, strict interpretation of the duty of the court second seized to stay the proceedings facilitated the development of

[50] *Itar-Tass Russian News Agency* v. *Russian Kurier Inc.*, 153 F.3d 82 (2d Cir. 1998).

[51] ECJ, Case 144/86, *Gubisch Machinenfabrik* v. *Palumbo* [1987] *ECR* 4861, para. 8.

[52] *Ibid.*, para. 14.

[53] ECJ, Case C-351/89, *Overseas Union Insurance et al.* v. *New Hampshire Insurance Company* [1991] *ECR* I-3317, paras. 12–17.

[54] ECJ, Case C-406/92, *The Tatry* v. *Maciej Rataj* [1994] *ECR* I-5439, para. 44.

[55] ECJ, Case 144/86, *Gubisch Machinenfabrik* v. *Palumbo* [1987] *ECR* 4861, para. 13.

specific litigation strategies. Namely, the alleged infringer of IP rights in one Member State could launch an action for a negative declaration seeking the establishment of the fact that certain acts do not constitute IP infringement or that particular IP rights are not valid. The abusive character of such actions could be often inferred from the fact that the action is brought before a court of a state which hardly bears any relationship with the dispute or is known for lengthy court proceedings. The procedural advantages for the person who brings an action for a negative declaratory judgment are related to the mandatory stay of the proceedings of the court subsequently seized by the plaintiff. Accordingly, such actions were ironically called "torpedoes".

In this regard, in the case *Gasser*, the ECJ once again confirmed that the *lis pendens* rule established in Article 21 of the Brussels Convention does not cease to apply if the suit is instituted before a court of a country where proceedings are known to be excessively long or even if it obvious that the court seized has no jurisdiction over the merits.[56] In another case the ECJ held that the court second seized may only stay the proceedings and cannot *sua sponte* examine the jurisdiction of the court first seized.[57] Yet answers provided in national reports highlighted different approaches taken by domestic courts concerning the adjudication of cross-border IP disputes. Due to the territorial nature of IP rights, different opinions still exist with regard to the notion of the "same cause of action" and whether Article 27 of the Regulation should be equally applied to registered and non-registered IP rights. In order to resolve some of the controversies, Sect. 7 of the CLIP Principles provides for a more comprehensive legal framework containing significant corrections and improvements of the established legal practice concerning the application of Articles 27–30 of the Brussels I Regulation.

The courts of represented Asian countries did not have many opportunities to develop a more comprehensive framework concerning international parallel proceedings. In India, subject-matter jurisdiction requirement also plays a significant role before Indian courts who generally assert jurisdiction only with regard to claims concerning Indian IP rights and therefore would not defer to foreign proceedings. According to the Civil Procedure Law of Taiwan, Taiwanese courts would stay the proceedings if the same dispute had been prior initiated before a court of another state and the following two requirements are satisfied: firstly, it is possible that the foreign judgment on the action can be recognized in the Republic of China; and, secondly, it is not substantially inconvenient for the defendant to participate in the proceedings. However, as regards IP disputes, the situation is rather less certain: a Taiwanese court would not stay the proceedings if the defendant in Taiwanese proceedings had filed a suit in a foreign state challenging the validity of IP rights which were not registered in that state.

In Japan, Article 142 of the Code of Civil Procedure prohibits the parties from instituting parallel proceedings. Since this provision was originally meant to deal only with domestic situations, several different theories on how it should be applied to international parallel proceedings were proposed. Some scholars argued that proceedings pending in a foreign state should be viewed as an element of the special circumstances test; others argued that Japanese courts should decline jurisdiction if the prior action brought before a foreign court could be recognized in Japan; the proponents of the third approach suggested treating international parallel litigation as an issue of the standing of the suit. All these approaches received some support in the court practice; yet, there is no single prevailing approach. However, the Japanese Report noted that Japanese courts would usually take into consideration the fact that proceedings were instituted before a foreign court. There are no special black-letter rules in the new Code of Civil Procedure (2011). Therefore, issues concerning parallel proceedings may fall under Article 3–9 which confers discretion upon Japanese courts to dismiss an action if there are special circumstances. The Transparency Principles establish the first-in-time rule which is supplemented by some alternative provisions (Art. 201). It is also worth noting that, in order to facilitate effective dispute resolution, the Transparency Principles also allow the court to communicate directly or request information from the court in which parallel proceedings are pending (Art. 201(4)).

The analysis of the national reports concerning international parallel proceedings highlighted different approaches. Courts of common law countries in most cases would not defer to foreign proceedings. In Europe, although the Brussels/Lugano regime contains uniform rules to tackle parallel proceedings giving

[56] ECJ, Case C-116/02, *Gasser* v. *MISAT* [2003] *ECR* I-14693, paras. 71–73.

[57] ECJ, Case C-159/02, *Turner* v. *Grovit* [2004] *ECR* I-3565, para. 31.

priority to the action at the court first seized, differences still exist with regard to proceedings pending before courts of third states. Approaches also differ in the represented countries of Asia. In addition, answers provided by national reporters illustrated that, on one hand, absence of clear rules concerning international parallel proceedings might be a source of uncertainty; yet, on the other hand, the existence of clear-cut rules might lead to rigidity and possible avenues for abuse and forum shopping. In the light of such considerations, the cross-border enforcement of IP rights could be fostered if a "middle approach" could be established. Namely, the 2001 Draft of the Hague Convention could serve as the basis for further improvements, while IP related aspects of parallel proceedings could be elaborated according to the academic proposals (e.g. ALI Principles etc.).

17.3.5 Consolidation of Proceedings

Consolidation of cross-border IP disputes became one of the most debated topics in recent years. High costs of country-by-country litigation has been often described as an Achilles heel, whereas consolidation of proceedings could be one of the most promising measures to create an efficient cross-border IP litigation system.[58] Yet in practice, national courts still take a restrictive approach with regard to multi-state IP disputes. The national reporters were asked to explain possibilities of consolidating claims or proceedings under their domestic laws; in addition, several questions related to actions concerning multiple IP rights in several states or actions against multiple defendants were raised in the hypothetical case.

In Canada and the US, the consolidation of claims is possible if the court has both *in personam* and subject-matter jurisdiction. One of the recent US decisions handed down in *Voda* v. *Cordis* case[59] could be an example. In *Voda*, the action was brought before an American court for the infringement of US and foreign patents. The plaintiff argued that allegedly infringing products were manufactured in the US and sold in foreign countries. The plaintiffs argued that the court is competent to hear an action pursuant to Section 1337 of the Judicial Code which establishes supplemental grounds of jurisdiction. However, upon appeal, Federal Circuit court found that based on the "considerations of comity, judicial economy, convenience, fairness, and other exceptional circumstances" there were compelling reasons to decline jurisdiction under § 1367(c). The judgment in the *Voda* v. *Cordis* case reaffirmed the previous US court practice.[60] In effect, claims concerning infringements of foreign IP rights could not be adjudicated before common law courts.[61]

In Europe, although the Brussels I Regulation does not contain any specific rules for the consolidation of proceedings, there are some provisions which allow the plaintiff to sue several defendants before a single court. In particular, pursuant to Article 6(1), a person domiciled in an EU Member State who is one of a number of defendants, may also be sued in the courts of the place where any of them is domiciled. In order to maintain the predictability of the application of the Brussels/Lugano regime, Article 6 has been interpreted narrowly[62] as requiring the establishment of a connection between the actions against multiple defendants.[63] The connection between actions should be such so as the risk of irreconcilable judgments resulting from separate proceedings could be avoided.[64]

Nonetheless, the application of Article 6(1) by the domestic courts was not uniform. English courts were reluctant to join claims against multiple parties if claims were related to foreign IP rights.[65] The courts of

[58] P. Torremans, "The Way Forward for Cross-Border Intellectual Property Litigation: Why GAT Cannot be the Answer," in *Intellectual Property and Private International Law* ed. S. Leible and A. Ohly, 207 (Tübingen: Mohr Siebeck 2009); A. Kur, "A Farewell to Cross-Border Injunctions? The ECJ Decisions GAT v. LuK and Roche Nederland v. Primus Goldenberg" 7 *IIC* (2006): 854–855.

[59] *Voda* v. *Cordis Corp.*, 476 F.3d 887 (Fed. Cir. 2007).

[60] *See e.g. Mars Inc.* v. *Kabushiki-Kaisha Nippon Conlux*, 24 F.3d 1368 (Fed. Cir. 1994); *Ideal Instruments, Inc.* v. *Rivard Instruments, Inc.*, 434 F. Supp. 2d 598 (N.D. Ia. 2006).

[61] The same result would be reached also by Indian courts.

[62] ECJ, Case 189/87 *Kalfelis* v. *Bankhaus Schröder* [1988] *ECR* 5565, para. 8; ECJ, Case C-51/97 *Réunion européenne* [1998] *ECR* I-6511, paras. 46 and 47.

[63] Report on the Convention on jurisdiction and the enforcement of judgments in civil and commercial matters ["Jenard Report"], *OJ* C 59, 1979, p. 49.

[64] ECJ, Case 189/87 *Kalfelis* v. *Bankhaus Schröder* [1988] *ECR* 5565, para. 8.

[65] *See e.g. Coin Controls Limited* v. *Suzo International Limited et al.*, (1997) *Ch* 33; *Fort Dodge Animal Health Limited et al.* v. *Akzo Nobel N.V.*, (1998) *I.L.Pr.* 732, esp. paras. 21–22 (per Lord Woolf).

continental European countries took a more liberal approach and allowed the consolidation of actions related to infringements of national bundle patents granted in accordance to the European Patent Convention. For instance, in one of its landmark decisions in *Expandable Grafts* v. *Boston Scientific* case, the Hague Court of Appeals upheld the claim of the proprietor of a bundle of European Patents to bring an action against several companies belonging to the same corporate group given that such companies are selling identical products in different national markets based on a joint business plan. The Hague Court of Appeals held that such joint claims could be brought only before the courts of the domicile of the head office which is in charge of the business operations in question or from whom the business plan originated (so called "spider in the web" doctrine).

The differences of interpretation were eliminated by the European Court of Justice. The judgment in the case *Roche Nederland* granted on the same day as *GAT* v. *LuK* followed the same strictly territorial approach to cross-border adjudication of IP disputes. In *Roche*, two American proprietors of European bundle patents brought an action in the Netherlands and sought to enjoin eight other companies that belonged to the same corporate group and were allegedly engaged in common infringing activities. The ECJ ruled that Article 6(1) must be interpreted as meaning that it does not apply in European patent infringement proceedings involving a number of companies established in various Member States concerning acts committed in one or more of those States even where those companies, which belong to the same group, may have acted in an identical or similar manner in accordance with a common policy elaborated by one of them.[66] The ECJ found that there is no risk of irreconcilable judgments in European patent infringement proceedings because even if patents are granted according to the EPC, patent rights remain independent and enforcement of these rights has to be pursued before the courts of each granting state.[67] The ECJ judgment was criticized on numerous grounds, in particular, for failing to uphold Dutch court practice which "has laid a solid foundation for a balanced and pragmatic solution"[68] and for not taking into consideration the interests of the business community. The combined effects of the ECJ judgments in cases *Roche Nederland* and *GAT* is that cross-border IP litigation, at least in so far as registered IP rights are concerned, has to be conducted before courts of each country for which protection is sought.[69]

The notion of "joinder of claims" is known in both Korean and Japanese law. Although statutory law does not provide for a clear-cut answer as to joinder of claims, the court practice of both countries generally favours the need to protect the interests of the defendant. Hence, international jurisdiction over multiple claims should be asserted if the defendant (or multiple defendants) is not unreasonably forced to appear before a court seized and procedural defence rights are not undermined.[70] Moreover, there should be a close connection between the claims.[71] Hence, the courts of Korea and Japan would take into consideration all relevant facts of the case. The court practice with regard to joinder of claims in multi-state IP disputes is scarce, from a purely theoretical point of view, it is likely that Japanese or Korean courts would assert jurisdiction over claims if the court has jurisdiction over one of these claims. Nevertheless, it remains rather unlikely that such close connection could be affirmed in cases where parallel IP rights are infringed by persons who act independently in different foreign countries. Only where disputes arise out of contracts for the transfer of IP rights and the obligations have to be performed in Japan or Korea respectively, courts of these countries would consider whether the joinder of claims is possible.

As in other matters related to the adjudication of multi-state IP disputes, joinder of actions is often affected by the need to balance the interests of the

[66] ECJ, Case C-539/03 *Roche Nederland BV and Others* v. *Frederick Primus and Milton Goldenberg* [2006] *ECR* I-6535, para. 41.

[67] *Ibid.*, paras. 25 and 27–28.

[68] A. Kur, "A Farewell to Cross-Border Injunctions? The ECJ Decisions in *GAT v. LuK* and *Roche Nederland v. Primus and Goldenberg*", *IIC* (2006) 850.

[69] Yet, the decision of the Hague Court of Appeals of 23 August 2007 might serve as an example that spider-in-the-web doctrine was not completely eliminated by the ECJ and could still find its way in multi-state infringement disputes of Community IP rights.

[70] Supreme Court of the Republic of Korea, Judgment of 26 September 2003, Case No. 2003 Da29555; Tokyo District Court, Judgment of 5 February 1997, *Hanrei Taimuzu* No. 936, p. 242.

[71] Supreme Court of Japan, Judgment of 28 April 1998, *Minshû*, Vol. 52, No. 3, p. 853; Supreme Court of Japan, Judgment of 8 June 2001, *Minshû*, Vol. 55, No. 4, p. 727 ("*Ultraman*" case); Art. 3–6 of the new CCP (2011).

litigants and at the same time consider the territorial nature of IP rights. As a result, courts are rather reluctant to enjoin actions with multiple claims, even more so if such claims are raised against foreign defendants or if IP rights at stake were granted in foreign states. The answers received from various countries illustrated that disputes concerning IP rights to a large extent still have to be adjudicated on a country-by-country basis. Yet, in order to improve the multi-state IP dispute settlement regime the first step should be the adoption of a more flexible and efficient approach to the joinder of claims. The second step could be the introduction of an adjudication system which allows consolidation and coordination of proceedings. Some academic proposals which have been made with regard to multi-state IP disputes[72] and other matters (e.g. international insolvency disputes) could serve as a source of inspiration.

17.3.6 Jurisdiction to Grant Injunctions

One of the most controversial questions in international IP litigation concerns jurisdiction to issue provisional and protective measures. In multi-state IP litigation, the availability of provisional or protective measures plays a crucial role because right-holders are firstly interested to stop allegedly infringing activities and only then raise claims for the compensation of damages. Thus, Article 50 of the TRIPS Agreement provides that national judicial authorities shall have the authority to order prompt and effective provisional measures. The following sections review the answers submitted by the national reporters concerning the jurisdiction to order provisional and protective measures as well as the territorial reach of such measures in IP disputes.

In Canada and the US, injunctive orders can be issued if courts have personal and subject-matter jurisdiction over the dispute. As regards injunctions in IP cases, Canadian and US courts would have jurisdiction to issue orders concerning activities of the alleged infringer who has his personal residence in the forum State. In such cases, the legal effects of a court order could extend also to defendant's activities in foreign states. However, as a practical matter, subject-matter jurisdiction would bar Canadian and US courts from issuing such measures with extra-territorial effects. Besides, Canadian and US courts might request the party seeking an injunction to provide a security for the compensation to the defendant in case the claim for injunction appears to be invalid. Similarly, in India which is also common law country, courts could order injunctions only with regard to infringements affecting Indian IP rights. In cases concerning injunctions to cease copyright infringements, the plaintiff must prove, firstly, that the alleged infringer undertakes certain factual business activities in India and, secondly, provide sufficient evidence proving the fact of copyright infringement.

In the European Union, the Brussels I Regulation creates a two-tier jurisdiction regime for granting provisional and protective measures. Provisional measures can be granted by courts which have international jurisdiction over the substance of the case. In addition to that, an application for provisional or protective measures may be made to courts of another Member State (Art. 31). In the latter case, the availability of provisional and protective measures will be usually decided according to the domestic law; the question of whether such measure could have cross-border effects would depend on the enforceability in a third country. Such seemingly broad jurisdiction was narrowed by the ECJ who introduced two additional requirements for granting provisional and protective measures. Firstly, a real connecting link between the subject-matter of the measures sought and the territorial jurisdiction of the forum state should exist.[73] Secondly, provisional measures should help to preserve factual or legal situation so as to safeguard rights the recognition of which is otherwise sought from the court having jurisdiction over the merits of the case.[74]

The question concerning jurisdiction to order provisional and protective measures in IP disputes is complex because of the principle of territoriality of IP rights and the double-faced nature of Article 31. Some of the EU national reporters indicated that courts would issue provisional and protective measures if they had

[72] *See e.g.* Chapter Three of the ALI Principles and Arts. 2:701–2:206 of the CLIP Principles.

[73] ECJ, Case C-391/95, *Van Uden Maritime* v. *Kommanditgesellschaft in Firma Deco-Line and others* [1998] *ECR* I-7091, para. 40.

[74] *See e.g.*, ECJ, Case C-261/90 *Reichert and Kockler* [1992] *ECR* I-2149, para. 34; and ECJ, Case C-104/03, *St. Paul Diary* v. *Unibel* [2005] *ECR* I-3481, para. 13.

jurisdiction over the merits of the case according to the Brussels/Lugano regime. As it was noted previously, the mere fact that IP rights involved are foreign IP rights does not *per se* mean that the EU Member State court has to decline jurisdiction. The scope of jurisdiction, that is whether the court could issue provisional or protective measures which would have cross-border effects, would depend on the ground upon which the court exercised its jurisdiction. Hence, a court of a Member State could issue provisional and protective measures with cross-border effects if the defendant was domiciled in the forum state (Art. 2). Yet, if a court exercises jurisdiction on any other ground than defendant's domicile, it would only issue provisional or protective measures that have effects in the forum state. The CLIP Principles proposed certain clarifications regarding provisional and protective measures. Article 2:501(1) *inter alia* states that courts having jurisdiction over the substance of the case may also issue provisional and protective measures. In addition to that, courts of a country where the measure is to be enforced or the country for which protection is sought shall have jurisdiction to issue provisional and protective measures. However, the exclusion of such measures from the recognition and enforcement regime (Art. 4:301(1)) means that their legal effects would be limited to the forum state.

Taiwanese and Korean national reports noted that courts in these countries would generally issue provisional measures with cross-border effects only if they have jurisdiction over the main dispute. Further, before granting cross-border measures, the courts may consider whether such interim measures would be recognized and enforced in a foreign country concerned. Taiwanese and Korean courts have also discretion of requiring the party who seeks issuance of provisional measures to provide a guarantee.

In Japan the prevailing approach is that in cases where Japanese courts have jurisdiction over the merits of the dispute, or if rights that should be preserved or the subject of the dispute is located in Japan, courts can assert international jurisdiction and issue provisional and protective measures. In deciding whether to order provisional or protective measures, Japanese courts will take into account whether there are special circumstances which would prevent Japanese courts from issuing provisional or protective measures. Yet, the possibility of granting provisional measures is rather controversial issue in disputes involving foreign IP rights. Namely, in the *Card Reader* case,[75] the Supreme Court of Japan refused to issue provisional measures ordering the defendant to cease activities which contributed to the infringement of the US patent. The Supreme Court decided that issuing an injunction order in accordance with the US Patent Law would run counter with the principle of territoriality and therefore contravene the public policy of Japan. Nevertheless, the Japanese report noted that mere fact that the rights for which protection is sought are foreign IP rights does not negatively affect the existence of international jurisdiction of Japanese courts although it remains unclear whether such measures could have extra-territorial effects. Further, Japanese courts may require granting a guarantee in order to safeguard the interests of the defendant.

The answers received from the represented countries confirmed that much further discussion is necessary with regard to jurisdiction to grant injunctions and other provisional and protective measures. In particular, it is necessary to investigate the implications of the principle of territoriality and the scope of the courts to grant provisional measures in multi-state IP infringement cases. This is particularly significant concerning jurisdiction to grant provisional and protective measures in cases over ubiquitous infringements. The solid basis for future work could be the 2001 draft of the Hague Judgments Convention (Art. 13) together with subsequent legislative proposals concerning cross-border enforcement of IP rights.

17.3.7 Choice-of-Court Clauses in IP Disputes

Choice-of-court agreements play an important role in international litigation. Prorogation or derogation clauses are often included in international commercial contracts and thus contribute to the legal certainty and foreseeability. In practice, however, different interests of the parties mean that agreements on jurisdiction will seldom be reached after the dispute arose. Nonetheless, from an academic point of view, choice-of-court

[75] Supreme Court of Japan, Judgment of 26 September 2002, *Minshû* Vol. 56, No. 7, p. 1551.

agreements might be an "elegant"[76] and efficient way to avoid the application of complex jurisdictional rules and fragmentation of litigation.

Choice-of-court agreements would be generally enforced by Canadian and American courts unless it is obvious that the litigation is absolutely unconnected to the forum or the litigation appears unjustified. Contractual choice-of-court clauses concerning foreign IP rights would also be honoured; yet, limitations posed by the subject-matter jurisdiction would mean that American and Canadian courts would not enforce choice-of-court agreements concerning infringement of foreign IP rights. A similar approach would be also taken in other common law jurisdictions (e.g. India).

Choice-of-court agreements would be generally enforceable in the represented Asian countries (Taiwan, Korean and Japan) if the dispute is sufficiently connected to the forum and regardless of whether the dispute involves foreign IP rights or not. Yet, the situation in these three Asian countries is not crystal clear as regards the effects of choice-of-court agreements with regard to IP-related matters which might fall under the exclusive jurisdiction rules of other states. In order to solve many of the ambiguities, specific legislative proposals have been made.[77]

In Europe, parties are free to make a choice-of-court agreement with regard to any legal relationship (Art. 23 of the Brussels I Regulation / Revised Lugano Convention). Choice-of-court agreements are deemed to be exclusive unless the parties agree otherwise. The Brussels I Regulation does not require any specific connection between the dispute and the forum state; for a choice-of-court agreement to be enforceable, at least one of the parties has to be resident in the Member State. Choice-of-court agreements conferring jurisdiction upon court of a Member State are enforceable even if both parties reside in the same Member State. Conversely, in cases where neither of the parties is resident in a Member State, courts of other Member states shall have no jurisdiction unless the court chosen has declined its jurisdiction (Art. 23(3)). In cases where none of the parties is resident in a Member State, the effectiveness of choice-of-court clauses is determined under the domestic law of the court seized. Parties' freedom to enter into choice-of-court agreements is limited by the mandatory nature of exclusive jurisdiction rules from which the parties cannot escape. Additional limitations are established with regard to jurisdiction over consumer contracts (Art. 17) and individual employment contracts (Art. 21). Such limitations of party autonomy are imposed with an objective to assure the protection of the weaker party (consumer or the employee).[78] According to the established practice of the ECJ, the Brussels I Regulation does not provide courts other than designated by the parties with the possibility to control the grounds of jurisdiction of a court chosen by the agreement.[79] Nevertheless, courts can declare null and void choice-of-court agreements which are considered unfair. Similarly, the court can also decline jurisdiction of its own motion if it becomes clear that such choice-of-court agreement is an unfair standard term.

As regards choice-of-court agreements in IP disputes, the distinction is drawn between contractual and non-contractual disputes. In the case of contractual disputes (e.g. disputes concerning the performance of obligations), choice-of-court agreements would be enforced if at least one of the parties is resident in a Member State. Choice-of-court agreements would be also enforceable if the dispute concerns foreign IP rights. According to the ECJ, in determining whether the choice-of-court agreement is effective, only those requirements which are provided in Article 23 of the Brussels I Regulation could be taken into consideration[80]; hence arguments related to the territorial nature of IP rights at stake should be considered as a matter of substantive law and do not affect determination of international jurisdiction. According to the prevailing opinion, the court designated in a license contract could also hear infringement claims. However, one of the side-effects of the ECJ judgment in the *GAT* v. *LuK* case is that the choice-of-court agreement would become practically ineffective if the proceedings were

[76] A. Metzger, "Jurisdiction in Cases Related to IP Infringements on the Internet. Brussels-I-Regulation, ALI Principles and Max Planck Proposals," in *Intellectual Property and Private International Law,* ed. S. Leible and A. Ohly (Tübingen: Mohr Siebeck, 2009), 266.

[77] *See inter alia* Art. 107 of the Transparency Principles and Art. 37 of the Korean Principles.

[78] Recitals 13 and 14 of the Preamble of the Brussels I Regulation.

[79] ECJ, Case C-281/02 *Owusu* [2005] *ECR* I-1383, paras. 37–40.

[80] ECJ, Case C-159/97 *Transporti Castelletti Spedizioni Internazionali SpA* v. *Hugo Trumpy SpA* [1999] *ECR* I-1597, para. 52.

concerned with the patent infringement and the validity of the patent was challenged by the defendant.

It is expected that more certainty will be brought by the Hague Choice-of-Court Convention which was adopted on 30 June 2005.[81] Similarly to the 1958 New York Convention on Recognition and Enforcement of Foreign Arbitral Awards, the 2005 Hague Convention constitutes a great leap forward in creating a comprehensive legal framework ensuring the effectiveness of exclusive choice-of-court agreements. The future of the 2005 Hague Choice-of-Court Convention seems to be much promising since at the time of writing of the present Report, the United States and European Union signed the Convention and Mexico ratified it.[82] IP matters posed significant hurdles in the drafting of the Hague Judgments Convention and were to large extent resolved in the 2005 Hague Choice-of-Court Convention.

According to Article 3 of the Convention, "exclusive choice-of-court agreements" are agreements concluded in writing or any other alternative means and designating one or more court of a Contracting State to decide disputes which have arisen or may arise in connection with a particular legal relationship. Choice-of-court agreements are deemed to be exclusive unless the parties have expressly agreed otherwise. While formal validity requirements are harmonized in the Convention itself, substantial validity of a choice-of-court agreement (e.g. fraud, mistake, misrepresentation, duress or lack of capacity) was left to the law of the forum.[83] The Hague Convention also entrenches the so called "separability" principle according to which the validity of a choice-of-court clause is independent from other terms of a contract. In the same vein, the validity of a choice-of-court clause cannot be challenged on a mere basis that the contract is invalid (Art. 3(d)). Article 5 of the Convention entrenches another cornerstone rule that the court designated in a choice-of-court agreement shall have jurisdiction over the dispute and shall not decline jurisdiction on the sole ground that a court of another Contracting State is competent to decide the dispute. Any other court of another Contracting State is obliged to suspend or dismiss the proceedings to which an exclusive choice-of-court agreement applies except where the choice-of-court agreement is null and void, giving effect to choice-of-court agreement would result in a manifest injustice, the court designated in the choice-of-court clause decides not to hear the case or if there are other exceptional reasons beyond the control of the parties (Art. 6). Recognition and enforcement issues are governed in Articles 8–15 of the Convention. A general principle is that a judgment given by a court of a Contracting State designated in a choice-of-court clause shall be recognized by courts of other Contracting states. A judgment can be recognized only if it is effective in the country of origin. Moreover, recognizing courts cannot review the merits of judgments handed down by a court designated by the parties (*révision au fond* is prohibited, Art. 8). The recognition or enforcement may be refused only if there are certain legal grounds provided in Article 9 of the Convention: namely, if the agreement was null and void, a party lacked capacity to conclude the agreement, the judgment was obtained by fraud or if the recognition or enforcement would be against public policy of the requested state or inconsistent with another judgment.

The final approach towards IP matters could be best understood from the material scope (application *ratione materiae*) of the Convention. The Hague Choice-of-court Convention excludes a number of matters from its scope. The Convention shall not apply *inter alia* to choice-of-court agreements pertaining to the validity and infringement of IP rights other than copyrights and related rights (Art. 2(2)(n)), except where infringement proceedings are brought for a breach of a contract between the parties relating to such rights, or could have been brought for breach of that contract (Art. 2(2)(o)). Hence, two issues should be clarified. Firstly, the Convention makes a distinction between copyrights and related rights and other (registered) IP rights (e.g. patents, trademarks, designs). Such distinction is made mainly on the ground that existence of copyrights and related rights does not depend on registration. The Hague Choice-of-Court Convention does not apply to choice-of-court agreements concerning disputes over registration and validity of (registered) IP rights mainly because in many legal systems such disputes fall under exclusive

[81] *Available at* http://www.hcch.net/upload/conventions/txt37en.pdf (visited on 20 October 2010).

[82] Status of the 2005 Hague Choice-of-court Convention is *availableat*http://www.hcch.net/index_en.php?act=conventions.status&cid=98 (visited on 20 October 2010).

[83] *See* Hartley / Dogauchi Report, available at http://www.hcch.net/upload/expl37e.pdf (visited on 20 October 2010), paras. 125–126.

jurisdiction of the granting country. Nevertheless, the Convention would still apply to choice-of-court agreements concerning disputes where validity of a registered IP right is challenged as a defence (e.g. in dispute for payment of royalties, where the licensee raises a claim that the licensed IP right is invalid[84]). In such cases the court can decide upon the validity of the IP right as a preliminary matter; however, such decisions would not be subject to recognition under the Convention. Secondly, the Convention does not apply to choice-of-court agreements which designate a competent court to hear IP infringement disputes unless such a dispute arises from a pre-existing relationship. An example of such pre-existing legal relationship could be a licensing contract and infringement proceedings related to it. According to the Official Commentary IP "infringement actions are covered, even if brought in tort, provided they could have been brought in contract".[85] It should be noted that copyright-related disputes are fully covered by the Convention (including infringement disputes and disputes where the court should decide upon the validity, Art. 2(2)(o)).

17.4 Applicable Law

17.4.1 Applicable Law to Initial Title

One of the primary questions which arise in IP disputes is related to the initial ownership of IP: in contractual as well as in non-contractual cases the judge has to determine whether a party who claims protection is actually entitled to such protection. Besides, in multi-state disputes the question of initial ownership may often arise as a preliminary issue. The growth of cross-border exploitation of IP rights means that in the course of contract negotiations issues related to ownership of IP will be subject to due diligence before the conclusion of the contract. Therefore, there is a need for more foreseeability of the national and international legal framework concerning the issues pertaining to the initial ownership. The national reporters were asked to elaborate how the following questions are dealt with under their domestic legal systems: whether there are any domestic choice-of-law rules dealing with the ownership of IP rights; how ownership issues are solved with regard to IP objects created on the basis of employment or other contractual agreements; and how the legal provisions of the represented State would be applied to works in the digital environment.

The general principles concerning the initial title to IP rights are similar according to the laws of the US and Canada. The prevailing approach in both Canada and the US is that the issue of ownership to non-registered rights should be determined according to the law of the State which has the most significant relationship with the works origin. In one of the leading cases *Russian News Agency* v. *Russian Kurier Inc.*[86] the US court did not hesitate to apply Russian law to proceedings concerning copyright infringement. In so far as initial title to registered IP rights is concerned, the law of the country of registration should be applied. These principles do not apply in cases where the work or invention is created by an employee; the exploitation of the work as well as the question of who – the employer or the employee – is entitled to apply for a patent can be agreed by the parties. The parties' agreement on the applicable law may be implicit or explicit; the question of who will have the right to apply for a patent would be considered as an issue of a contract. Yet, in the absence of choice, the court would apply the law of the country which has the closest and most real connection to the contract. The question of the remuneration for the employee would depend on how the claims are characterized. In particular, the court may look to the contractual agreement between the parties. If the claim for damages was made on the basis of the employer's breach of obligations not to misuse the information, the claim would be determined by the law of the country which governs the obligation. If the claim for the compensation was characterized as the one of unjust enrichment, the employee's claim would arise out of the breach of contractual obligation and the law governing the obligation would also apply to the claims for the compensation.

In Europe, such matters as initial ownership, registration, existence, validity, content, duration, transferability and effects are governed neither by the Rome I nor the Rome II Regulation. Therefore, the applicable law to these issues will have to be determined according

[84] T. Hartley / M. Dogauchi Report, para. 37, available at http://www.hcch.net/upload/expl37e.pdf (last visited 20 October 2010).

[85] *Ibid.*, para. 39.

[86] 153 F.3d 82 (2d Cir. 1998).

to the choice-of-law provisions of the forum country. In the absence of any harmonizing acts, domestic legal regimes differ to some extent. In some European countries, private international law statutes contain specific choice-of-law provisions dealing with IP issues. For instance, Article 54 of the Italian PIL Statute entrenches a special rule on rights related to intangible assets and provides that rights related to intangible assets shall be governed by the law of the State in which they are exploited. This rule has been interpreted as pointing to the law of the protecting country (*lex loci protectionis*). The *lex loci protectionis* principle determines the existence and creation of the right, the scope, validity, attributes, duration, infringement and remedies. For instance, Article 10.4 of the Spanish Civil Code contains a choice-of-law provision mandating the application of the law of the protecting country. Article 93 § 1 of the Belgian Code of Private International Law (CPIL) establishes a rule that all issues related to initial copyright ownership should be governed by the law of the country for which protection is sought. The majority opinion in Germany supports the application of the *lex loci protectionis* principle to determine the question of initial ownership. The *lex loci protectionis* in case of registered rights leads to the application of the law of the country of registration. In case of non-registered IP rights the majority approach – which was also followed by the German Federal Supreme Court (*Bundesgerichtshof*) – is that the law of the country for which protection is sought should be applied.

Besides, the national reports also discussed further alternatives to the *lex loci protectionis* principle. In particular, it was argued that initial ownership to copyright works could be also determined by the law of the country of origin (*lex originis*). According to this conflicts rule, the law of the place where the IP asset was created has to be applied. The advantage of the *lex originis* rule is that it would result in the application of the law of a single country and therefore better suits authors and entertainment industries. In addition it was argued that the *lex originis* rule leads to more predictability especially in cases related to the Internet. The French Report referred to the judgment of the Paris Court of Appeals in the *Le Chant du Monde* case[87] where the *lex originis* principle was applied.

In so far as initial title to works created in the course of employment or other kind of contractual relationship, two separate issues have been distinguished: namely, the question of who actually was the author of the work/invention and who is entitled to obtain rights in the work. Most of the European reports noted that the issue of initial ownership to IP assets created on the basis of pre-existing relationship constitutes an exception to the general principles determining initial ownership. Further, if the work is created on the basis of a pre-existing contractual relationship, the question of initial title should be determined by the law governing the contract. This means that the principle of party autonomy would be applied. If the work/invention is created on the basis of employment contract, Article 8 of the Rome I Regulation together with the limitations posed by the public policy exception would determine the governing law. National reporters noted that in so far as copyright works created on the basis of employment contracts are concerned, agreements between the parties would not affect such issues as moral rights which are not assignable. Further, it should be noted that Article 60(1) of the European Patent Convention stipulates that, if the inventor is an employee, the right to the European patent shall be determined in accordance with the law of the State in which the employee is mainly employed. If the State in which the employee is mainly employed cannot be determined, the law to be applied shall be that of the State in which the employer has his place of business to which the employee is attached. Various questions related to the initial ownership and other related issues pertaining to IP rights have been further elaborated in Part 3 of the CLIP Principles.

The issue of initial ownership in the Republic of Korea is addressed in Article 24 of Private International Law Act which refers to the law of the State where protection is sought. Similarly, to determine the initial owner of copyright works and other IP rights Japanese courts applied the principle of *lex loci protectionis* even though it is not established in the Private International Law Act of 2006 ("*Tsûsoku hô*"). One of the leading cases concerning the exploitation of inventions created in the course of employment relations is the so called *Hitachi* case.[88] The dispute arose between

[87] *See e.g.*, Paris Court of Appeal, Judgment of 16 February 2007, *Prop. intel.* July 2007, p. 338.

[88] Supreme Court of Japan, Judgment of 17 October 2006, *Minshû*, Vol. 60, No. 8, p. 2853 ("*Hitachi*" case).

the Hitachi Corporation and its employee Mr. Yonezawa who created three inventions concerning the transfer of data to optical discs. Yonezawa signed an agreement whereby rights to obtain patents were assigned to Hitachi. This contract did not explicitly deal with the territorial scope of the transferred rights. Later Hitachi filed patent applications in Japan and a number of foreign countries. Hitachi made huge profits from the commercialization of the patented inventions and Yonezawa filed a lawsuit requesting the court to order the payment of reasonable compensation. The Supreme Court accepted that the Japanese Patent Act does not deal with initial ownership issues regarding foreign patent applications and held (although in *orbiter dicta*) that this issue should be considered according to the law of each country where the patent application is made. With regard to the claim for reasonable compensation, the Supreme Court held that the statutory duty of compensation established in Article 35 of the Japanese Patent Act applies also with regard to foreign patents based upon the same invention. National reporters indicated that the prevailing opinion in Japan and Korea is that parties are not allowed to agree upon such issues as initial ownership; instead, the law of each country of protection should be applied to determine the initial owner. This approach was also followed in the Transparency Principles (Art. 305) and the Korean Principles (Art. 24).

Information provided by the national reporters confirmed that the determination of the initial owner of IP objects in most countries is made according to the principle of *lex loci protectionis*. This is especially true in the case of registered IP rights whose owner is usually determined according to the law of the registering country. The opinions differ however with regard to initial ownership of copyrights: in some countries the *lex loci protectionis* principle is applied, whereas the law in other countries supports the application of the law of the country where the work was first published.

Further differences among the law applicable to initial title could be seen in the area of IP objects created on the basis of a contractual relationship. Although the laws of many countries would allow parties to agree who should be entitled to be the rightholder of IP rights, the laws of Asian countries are more territoriality-oriented which means that party autonomy would have a very limited role, if any. In the light of these considerations, one of the fields where the laws of various countries are not established is initial ownership of works in the digital environment. The ALI Principles and other academic proposals have put forward various possible regulatory regimes which could bring more clarity in terms of the existing laws.

17.4.2 Applicable Law to Infringements of IP Rights

National reporters were asked to address one of the most controversial issues related to the applicable law to infringements of IP rights. Although the traditional approach was to consider IP rights as firmly based on the principle of territoriality, the emergence of the Internet and various digital technologies provoked new debates concerning the suitability of the principle of territoriality to multi-state infringements of IP rights. The following sections offer a brief overview of choice-of-law rules dealing with IP infringements followed by the courts of different represented countries.

The adjudication of multi-state IP disputes before the US and Canadian courts largely depends on the court's powers to hear claims related to foreign IP rights. It was already noted before, that the need to establish both *in personam* and subject-matter jurisdiction resulted in the situation where Canadian and American courts could hear only actions related to infringements which occurred in the forum country.[89] Accordingly, choice-of-law issues would seldom arise, and the *lex fori* would be applied. Canadian and US courts have taken a strict approach with regard to the application of domestic IP statutes to cross-border patent infringing activities. For instance, in *Beloit Canada Ltd.* v. *Valmet-Dominion Inc.*[90] the question was whether Canadian patent was infringed by the manufacturing of components of a patented press machine which were exported and assembled abroad. The Federal Court of Appeal (Canada) held that the mere selling of the components of a patented invention even if the seller is aware that such components may be used for latter infringement of the Canadian patent is not an infringement as such. The US Supreme Court has also

[89] *See e.g. Subafilms, Ltd. v. MGM-Pathe Communications Co.*, 24 F.3d 1088 (9th Cir. 1994); also *Curb* v. *MCA Records, Inc.*, 898 F. Supp. 586 (M.D. Tenn. 1995).

[90] [1997] 3 F.C. 497 (C.A.).

adopted the same reasoning and emphasized the presumption against territoriality of the U.S.C.[91]

Limitations resulting from the subject-matter jurisdiction requirement affect also the court's authority with regard to infringements occurring in the digital environment. As a result, Canadian and the US courts would have international jurisdiction only over infringements of IP rights which are protected by the forum country. Thus, the law of the forum would be applied. Nevertheless, the American report referred to several court decisions which might probably serve as a possible solution to the adjudication of ubiquitous infringement disputes. In *Sheldon* v. *Metro Goldwyn Pictures Corp.*[92] a number of copies of the pictures were made in the US and later sent to foreign countries for exhibition. Since the infringement occurred in the US and in foreign countries, the US court took into consideration foreign infringements in assessing the damages.[93] A more elaborate proposal was made in the ALI Principles where parties are allowed to make an agreement on the applicable law (§ 302). In the case of an ubiquitous infringement, the court would be allowed to choose the law of the State or States with close connection to the dispute (§ 321).

In Europe, the law governing non-contractual obligations is determined according to the Rome II Regulation[94] which came into force on 11 January 2009. It supersedes domestic choice-of-law provisions and establishes the universality principle which mandates the application of any law regardless of whether or not it is the law of a Member State (Art. 3). The general choice-of-law rule is that non-contractual obligations arising out of delict or tort should be governed by the law of the country where the damage occurs (*lex loci damni*, Art. 4(1)). The place where damage occurs is to be understood only as the place of direct damage. However, if both parties have their habitual residence in the same State when damage occurs, the law of that State should be applied (Art. 4(2)). In addition, these choice-of-law rules may be avoided if from the circumstances of the case it is clear that the tort/delict is manifestly more closely connected with another country. In this case, the law of that country which is manifestly more closely connected with the dispute shall be applied (Art. 4(3)).

Article 8 of the Rome II Regulation contains a special choice-of-law rule for IP infringements. The regulation of IP matters within the EU affected the structure of Article 8: paragraph (1) deals with infringements of national IP rights; and paragraph (2) addresses infringements of unitary Community IP rights. In addition, there is a special provision stipulating that parties cannot make agreements on the choice-of-law with regard to non-contractual obligations arising from infringements of IP rights (Art. 8(3)). Article 8(1) is based on the "universally acknowledged principle"[95] of the *lex loci protectionis* according to which "non-contractual obligations arising out of infringements of IP rights are governed by the law of the country for which protection is claimed". It should be noted that Article 8(1) of the Rome II Regulation refers to "the law of the country *for which* the protection is claimed" (emphasis added). This terminology slightly differs from Art. 5(2) of the Berne Convention[96] and reflects Article 5(3) of the Brussels I Regulation according to which courts of EU Member States have international jurisdiction over IP infringement claims even if infringing acts affect foreign IP rights. The scope of the applicable law is determined in Article 15. This provision *inter alia* stipulates that the law applicable to non-contractual obligations governs also the basis and extent of liability, including persons who may be held liable for acts performed by them.

The practical effects of the Rome II Regulation were criticized on the basis that it adopts the territorial *lex loci protectionis* approach which leads to the "mosaic" application of the laws of every country for which the protection is sought. It has been argued that especially in the case of ubiquitous infringements of IP rights this would cause much burden to the courts. Further, the Rome II Regulation has been criticized

[91] *See Microsoft Corp.* v. *AT&T* Corp., 500 U.S. 437 (2007).

[92] *Sheldon* v. *Metro Goldwyn Pictures Corp.*, 106 F.2d 45, 52 (1939), *aff'd*, 309 U.S. 390 (1940).

[93] *See also Update Art, Inc.* v. *Modiin Publishing, Ltd.*, 843 F.2d 67 (2d Cir. 1988).

[94] Regulation (EC) No 864/2007 of the European Parliament and of the Council of 11 July 2007 on the law applicable to non-contractual obligations (Rome II), [2007] *OJ* L 199/40.

[95] Recital 26 of the Rome II Regulation.

[96] Article 5(2) of the Berne Convention inter alia provides that "the extent of protection, as well as the means of redress afforded to the author to protect his rights, shall be governed exclusively by the laws of the country *where* protection is claimed" (emphasis added).

because it explicitly prohibits the parties to choose the law governing IP infringements (Art. 8(3)).

As regards represented Asian countries, the principle of the protecting country is to be firmly established. Article 24 of the Korean Private International Act stipulates that infringements of IP rights should be governed by the *lex protectionis*.[97] The Japanese PIL Act of 2006 ("*Tsûsoku hô*") does not contain any special rules for IP matters; however, the *lex protectionis* principle is firmly established in the case law.[98] The question which law should govern ubiquitous infringements remains controversial. In order to remedy the situation, the Korean and the Transparency Principles provided for some proposals. Namely, the Korean Proposal follows the ALI Principles, whereas the Transparency Principles support the market-oriented approach.[99]

From the answers provided in the national reports, several remarkable conclusions could be drawn. On the one hand, as regards the court practice, it should be noted that the strict territoriality principle appeared to be followed in most jurisdictions. In common law countries the questions of applicable law to infringements of IP rights do not even arise because of the limitations resulting from the subject-matter jurisdiction. Mainly because of peculiarities of asserting international jurisdiction over claims involving foreign IP rights, Canadian and US laws do not provide for a choice-of-law regime concerning the law governing infringements of IP rights. In European countries, even though courts are able to hear actions concerning infringements of foreign IP rights, the possibility of the application of the foreign *lex loci protectionis* in fact could be only possible in cases concerning non-registered IP rights. On the other hand, various legislative proposals contain more specific conflicts rules for multi-state infringements of IP rights. Albeit the principle of *lex loci protectionis* is maintained with regard to registered IP rights, the parties are allowed to agree on the law governing damages. In addition, legislative proposals establish specific provisions to solve the problem of applicable law to ubiquitous infringements. Yet it remains to be seen whether and to what extent the legislative proposals could affect the established practice of domestic courts.

17.4.3 Applicable Law to Contracts for the Transfer of IP Rights

A number of applicable law questions arise in disputes concerning transfer of IP rights. In practice some problems might arise because the law governing contractual obligations between the parties may be different from the law governing proprietary issues (e.g. transferability etc.). Although party autonomy is a generally established principle, the applicable law to international contracts for the transfer of IP rights may be also problematic because of differences in national economic policies of particular countries. Further, often contracts for the transfer of IP rights are complex and involve numerous mutual obligations. Therefore, it might be especially difficult to determine the governing law in the absence of choice. The national reporters were asked to elaborate on these issues in their reports.

In Canada, both Canadian common law as well as the Civil Code of Quebec allows the parties to choose the proper governing law of their contractual obligations. The proper law governs most of the issues related to the validity and operation of the contract. In the absence of choice, conflicts rules of Canadian common law provide that contractual obligations are governed by the law that has the closest and most real connection to the contract. The Civil Code of Quebec follows the so called "closest connection" doctrine according to which in the absence of choice the contract is governed by the law of the country in which the party who is to perform the obligation which is characteristic of the act is resident or has its business establishment. As for IP-related contracts, Canadian courts would distinguish the law applicable to contractual obligations and the law which governs issues related to IP rights themselves. Hence, in transfer of rights agreements Canadian courts would also try to determine the law governing the waiver of moral rights. The law chosen by the parties would only determine whether parties were bound by the agreement and the interpretation of

[97] The principle of *lex protectionis* is also established in the case law; *see e.g.* Seoul Central District Court, Judgment of 30 August 2006, Case No. 2006Gahap53066 (concerning trademarks).

[98] Supreme Court of Japan, Judgment of 26 September 2002, *Minshû* Vol. 56, No. 7, p. 1551 ("*Card Reader*" case).

[99] *See* Art. 302 of the Transparency Principles which *inter alia* provides that "[i]ntellectual property infringements where the alleged infringement act is "ubiquitous" shall be governed by the law of the place where the results of the exploitation of intellectual property are or to be maximized".

the agreement but would not affect such issues as transferability or waivability of IP rights. It should be noted, that the jurisdiction of Canadian courts would be limited only with regard to claims concerning Canadian IP rights. Accordingly, parties could enforce only those claims which are related to Canadian IP rights.

In the United States, choice-of-law rules for contracts are established in the Restatement (Second) of Conflict of Laws. Yet, it is generally accepted that parties are allowed to choose the governing law. Further, in the absence of choice, § 188 of the Restatement (Second) posits that the contract is governed by the "local law of the state which has the most significant relationship". In determining which State has the most significant relationship the court should take into account "(a) the place of contracting; (b) the place of negotiation of the contract; (c) the place of performance; (d) the location of the subject-matter of the contract; and (e) the domicil, residence, nationality, place of incorporation and place of business of the parties" (§ 188(2)). Insofar as contracts for the transfer of IP rights are concerned, the ALI Principles clarify that parties may not choose the law that will govern the validity and maintenance of registered rights, the existence, attributes and duration of rights, notwithstanding whether they are registered or not, and formal requirements for recording assignments and licenses (§ 302). In the absence of choice or in cases where a party agreement on the governing law is invalid, the agreement pertaining to the transfer of title and grants of license is governed by the law of the country of the State which has the closest connection to the contract. § 315(2) establishes that the contract is presumed to be most closely connected to the State in which the assignor or the licensor resided at the time of the execution of the contract. However, the ALI Principles remain silent on the strength of the presumption and in what circumstances this presumption could be rebutted.

In Europe, a novel regime for the determination of the applicable law was established by the Rome I Regulation[100] which is in force since 17 December 2009. Choice-of-law rules provided for in the Regulation apply also to contracts for the transfer of IP rights. Article 3 enshrined the cornerstone principle of freedom of choice. The law chosen by the parties does not necessarily have to be connected to the contract or the domicile or nationality of the parties. Besides, the Rome I Regulation allows to choose a non-State body of law or an international convention.[101] Hence, parties may incorporate a reference to such instruments as the UNIDROIT Principles of International Commercial Contracts or the ALI Principles on Intellectual Property. The freedom of choice is limited with regard to consumer or individual employment contracts which are subject to special provisions of the Regulation (Arts. 6 and 8). Parties' choice-of-law is also subject to the public policy exception and the application of overriding mandatory rules (Art. 9).

One of the most remarkable modifications introduced by the Rome I Regulation is related to the determination of the applicable law in the absence of choice. More precisely, Article 4 introduced a newly designed methodology which aims to increase predictability of the outcome of litigation; assure legal certainty and foreseeability of the application of choice-of-law rules within the European judicial area.[102] Such modifications represent the European legislator's response to the differences in application of the closest connection test and the relationship between presumptions stipulated in Article 4 of the Rome Convention. Article 4 of the Rome I Regulation establishes a four-step cascade of conflict rules. Firstly, Article 4(1) provides clear-cut conflict rules for particular types of contracts (contracts of sale, provision of services, rights *in rem* in immovable property or tenancy, franchise and distribution as well as sale of goods by auction or contracts concluded within a multilateral system). Secondly, where a contract is not covered by Article 4(1), or where the elements of a contract are covered by more than one conflicts rule provided in paragraph one, the applicable law should be determined according to the characteristic performance rule. Namely, characteristic performance means that the contract shall be governed by the law of the place where the party required to effect the characteristic performance of the contract has his domicile (Art. 4(2)). Thirdly, Article 4(3) states that where it is clear from all the circumstances of the case that the contract is manifestly more closely connected with a country other than indicated in paragraphs 1 and 2, the law of that country shall apply.

[100] Regulation (EC) No 593/2009 of the European Parliament and of the Council of 17 June 2008 on the law applicable to contractual obligations (Rome I), (2008) *OJ* L 177/6.

[101] Recital 13 of the Rome I Regulation.

[102] *See* Recitals 6 and 16 of the Rome I Regulation.

Fourthly, where the law applicable cannot be determined pursuant to paragraphs 1 or 2 of Article 4, the contract shall be governed by the law of the country with which it is most closely connected.

The principle of freedom of choice equally applies to contractual aspects of IP transfer agreements. However, matters related to the transferred IP rights themselves (transferability etc.) are governed by the *lex loci protectionis*. The Rome I Regulation was criticized on the ground that it did not provide for a clear-cut solution to determine the law applicable to contracts for the transfer of IP rights. In particular, the application of general choice-of-law rules provided for in Article 4 to IP contracts is problematic because contracts for the transfer of IP rights do not fit in any categories of contracts for which "default" choice-of-law rules are provided in Article 4(1). Indeed, Art. 4(1) establishes special choice-of-law provisions for franchise and distribution contract according to which the law of the place where the franchisee/distributor has habitual residence should be applied. Nevertheless, the transfer of IP rights usually is one of constitutive parts of the contract. Therefore, choice-of-law rules for franchise and distribution contracts could not be applied to other kinds of contracts for the transfer of IP rights.

Applicable law to contracts not covered by default choice-of-law rules of Article 4(1) should be determined according to the characteristic performance doctrine (Art. 4(2)). This would mean that the contract for the transfer of IP rights should be governed by the law of the state where the party who is to perform the characteristic obligation has its habitual residence. However, again, as regards transfer of IP rights, there is no uniformity of opinions concerning which party is performing the characteristic obligation. As for such contracts which consist of a bundle of rights and obligations, the characteristic performance of the contract should be determined having regard to its centre of gravity.[103] Yet, the notion of the "centre of gravity" remains unclear and has to be interpreted on a case-by-case basis. In order to solve this ambiguity, the CLIP Principles neither follow the characteristic performance doctrine, nor aim to identify one of the parties who is presumed to have performed characteristic obligations. Instead, the CLIP Principles provide for two different groups of factors which might show the closest connection of the contract with the State where the transferor/licensor or transferee/licensee has his habitual residence at the time of the conclusion of the contract (Art. 3:502).

In Japan and Korea, the law governing contracts for the transfer of IP rights could be chosen by the parties. In the absence of choice, the closest connection doctrine would be applied to determine the law governing contractual obligations of the parties.[104] However, parties are not allowed to choose the governing law to such issues as transferability of rights. In both countries issues pertaining to IP rights themselves are governed by the *lex protectionis*. Korean courts would consider such choice-of-law clauses with regard to proprietary issues of IP rights as contrary to public policy of Korea and to that extent would refuse to enforce a choice-of-law clause. Hence, the question of transferability of IP rights would have to be decided by the law of the protecting country.

From the reports received a few comparative remarks deserve attention. Firstly, in most countries, there are no specific choice-of-law provisions dealing with contracts for the transfer of IP rights. The practical outcome is that courts of different countries apply different methodologies to deal with applicable law issues. Secondly, approaches also differ with regard to the determination of the law governing the contract in the absence of choice. Thirdly, differences could be also seen even among the recent legislative proposals concerning private international law aspects of IP rights. Accordingly, in so far as contracts for the transfer of IP rights are concerned, one could see that there is the need for a more elaborate discussion, especially as regards the determination of the law governing the contract in the absence of choice by the parties.

17.4.4 Other Choice-of-Law Issues: Securities of IP Rights

In the last few decades IP rights have become one of the valuable assets of companies. One of the possible ways of exploitation of IP rights is to use them as a collateral in financing transactions. It is established business practice to use portfolios of IP rights together with other corporate assets as a collateral.

[103] Recital 19 of the Rome I Regulation.

[104] *See* Art. 8 of the Japanese PIL Act (2006).

Such exploitation of IP rights generally falls under the domestic regulations on secured transactions. International financing contracts are usually very complex and a number of particular problems may arise. For instance, the IP licensor (original payee) may securitize his rights of payment under an IP contract whereby a third party (e.g. securitization vehicle or a factor) obtains the right to be paid. One problem could arise if the original payee (IP licensor) who securitized his right to a third party becomes bankrupt. The question then arises whether a third party is still entitled to the payments from the payor (i.e. IP licensee) or whether the creditors of the original payee should be entitled to the payments. Issues related to effectiveness against third parties and priority of rights become even more complicated in cross-border transactions. The national reporters were asked to explain whether and how taking security of IP rights is addressed within the choice-of-law framework of their countries.

National reporters indicated that in most countries IP rights can be used as a collateral. This is usually established in statutes dealing with particular IP rights and sometimes also provided in special acts dealing with security rights. Even if there are no special statutory provisions which clearly stipulate that IP rights could be used as a collateral, this is still possible in business practice. Although initially, registered IP rights such as patents had been used as a collateral, gradually any kind of IP rights became an object of secured transactions. In practice, different due diligence procedures are undertaken with regard to registered and non-registered rights mainly because there is no registry containing information about the status of non-registered IP rights. Further, as regards non-registered IP rights, securities could be created only with regard to economic rights.

In common law jurisdictions of Canada, the validity, perfection, and the effects of perfection would typically be governed by the law, including the conflict of laws rules, of the jurisdiction in which the debtor is located at the time when the security interest attaches. Issues of priority would be governed by the *lex fori*. In Quebec, which is a civil law jurisdiction, the law of the grantor of security would govern the validity of the security as well as publication and its effects (Art. 3105 of the Civil Code of Quebec). In the US, secured transactions are governed in the Uniform Commercial Code. Article 9 of the UCC provides for a comprehensive legal framework which equally applies also to securities of IP rights. According to Article 9-301(1) of the UCC, the perfection, the effects of perfection or nonperfection, and the priority of a security interest in collateral is governed by the law of the place where the debtor (i.e. the person assigning the right to payment) is located. Similar approach was followed also in the 2001 UN Convention on Assignments of Receivables in International Trade[105] which *inter alia* stipulates that the law of the State in which the assignor is located governs the priority of the right of an assignee in the assigned receivable over the right of a competing claimant (Art. 22).

In the EU, the Rome I Regulation also deals with the applicable law to voluntary assignment. The concept of assignment includes outright transfers of claims, transfers of claims by way of security and pledges or other security rights over claims (Art. 14(3)). According to Article 14(1), the relationship between assignor and the assignee shall be governed by the law that applies to the contract between the assignor and assignee under the Rome I Regulation. Hence, the governing law can be chosen by the parties (Art. 3). In the absence of choice such contract for the assignment of IP rights should be considered as a contract for the sale of goods.[106] Therefore, the law where the seller (assignor) has his habitual residence should be applied. A number of European national reports indicated that the principle of *lex loci protectionis* would be applied to the creation, effectiveness against third parties, priority and the enforcement of these security rights over IP.[107] The law of the protecting state should be also applied according to the European Patent Convention (Art. 74) as well as the ALI Principles (§ 317) and the Transparency Principles (Art. 308). The application of the *lex loci protectionis* principle to the creation of securities in IP rights has been subject to criticism because it would require compliance with the requirements of a valid creation of security interests in every state concerned. In particular, the application of the law of the country of protection

[105] Available at http://www.uncitral.org/pdf/english/texts/payments/receivables/ctc-assignment-convention-e.pdf (last visited on 20 October 2010).

[106] ECJ, Case C-533/07, *Falco Privatstiftung and Thomas Rabitsch* v. *Gisela Weller-Lindhorst* [2009] *ECR* I-3327.

[107] *E.g.* Croatia, Italy (Art. 54 of the Italian PIL Act), Portugal, or Spain (Art. 10.4 of the Civil Code). The same approach is also taken in Japan, Korea (Art. 24 of the Private International Act).

does not fit the needs of financial markets where bundles (portfolios) of IP rights are used as a single collateral.

A notable project concerning secured transactions was undertaken under the auspices of the United Nations Commission on International Trade Law (UNCITRAL). At the UNCITRAL the work on secured credit law was initiated in 2000 and in 2001 the Working Group IV (Security Interests) was entrusted with a task of developing an efficient legal regime for security interests in goods involved in a commercial activity. The studies conducted over 12 sessions epitomized in the preparation of the Legislative Guide on Secured Transactions which was adopted on 14 December 2007.[108] The Legislative Guide deals with a number of substantial law issues including the creation of a security right, effectiveness against third parties, registration, priority and enforcement. The need to deal particularly IP problems in creation and enforcing of security rights, the UNCITRAL prepared a "Supplement on Security Rights in Intellectual Property" which was adopted on 29 June 2010.[109] According to the Recommendation No. 208 of the Legislative Guide (2007), the law applicable to the creation, effectiveness against third parties and priority of a security right in an intangible asset is the law of the State in which the grantor is located. In addition to that, Recommendation No. 248 set up in the Supplement on Security Rights in IP further stipulates that the law applicable to the creation, effectiveness against third parties and priority of a security right in IP is the law of the State in which the IP is protected. Besides, according to Lit. (c) of the same recommendation, the law applicable to the enforcement of a security right in intellectual property is the law of the State in which the grantor is located. In the light of these proposals made by the UNCITRAL, three alternative provisions were included in the Third Draft of the CLIP Principles (Art. 3:508). The issues concerning creation of securities over IP rights will be an intensively debated topic in the second decade of the millennium. Acknowledging the great leap forward in the area concerning security rights in IP, proposals made by the UNCITRAL concerning choice-of-law issues should be thoroughly reviewed jointly by lawyers from both fields of IP and private international law.

17.5 Recognition and Enforcement of Judgments in IP-Related Disputes

The final issue which might arise in multi-state IP disputes is related to the recognition and enforcement of foreign judgments. In the US there is no federal statute dealing with the recognition and enforcement of foreign judgments. Yet, although the law differs from state to state, the US report indicated that a foreign judgment would generally be recognized if the defendant was adequately served; if a foreign judgement was rendered by a fair and impartial tribunal[110]; and if the law or public policy of the US is not undermined.[111] According to the Canadian common law, foreign judgments can be recognized and enforced if the following three requirements are met. Firstly, the judgment debtor must have residence in the state where the judgment was handed down. Secondly, there should be a submission of the judgment debtor to the courts of the originating country. Thirdly, there should be a real and substantive connection between the defendant or subject-matter of the dispute and the originating state.[112] As regards the enforcement of foreign judgments, Canadian law established various alternatives which could be chosen by the plaintiff according to the particular circumstances of the enforcement. Canadian courts would usually recognize monetary judgments; other judgments had not been recognized in Canada. However, the adoption of Enforcement of Canadian Judgments and Decrees Act opened the gates to the recognition of "decrees" other than orders for monetary payments.

Recognition of judgments in IP disputes rendered by foreign courts would be subject not only to general conditions for recognition established in Canadian or US law but also to subject-matter jurisdiction

[108] *Available at* http://www.uncitral.org/pdf/english/texts/security-lg/e/09-82670_Ebook-Guide_09-04-10English.pdf (last visited 20 October 2010).

[109] *Available at* http://www.uncitral.org/pdf/english/texts/security-lg/e/Final.Draft.15_July.2010.clean.pdf (last visited 20 October 2010).

[110] *Bank Melli Iran* v. *Pahlavi*, 58 F.3d 1406 (1995).

[111] *Chromalloy Aeroservices* v. *Arab Republic of Egypt*, 939 F. Supp. 907 (D.D.C. 1996); *La Ligue Contre Le Racisme et, L'Antisemitisme* v. *Yahoo! Inc.*, 547 U.S. 1163 (2006).

[112] The latter ground was established by the Supreme Court of Canada in the case *Morguard Investments Ltd.* v. *De Savoye*, (1990) 3 S.C.R. 1077, 76 D.L.R. (4th) 256.

considerations. While personal jurisdiction requirements could be easily established, courts would hardly find the existence of subject-matter jurisdiction of the foreign court in such dispute. In practice this would mean that foreign judgments over matters which fall under the subject-matter jurisdiction of Canadian or US courts would not be recognized. Nevertheless, the Canadian report indicated one recent case in a contractual dispute where a foreign judgment concerning the ownership of a Canadian patent was recognized and enforced in Canada.[113]

Within the EU, one of the underlying objectives of the Brussels/Lugano regime is to facilitate efficient and rapid recognition of judgments rendered in other Member States. In addition to provisions of jurisdiction, the Brussels I Regulation establishes special rules on jurisdiction and enforcement of judgments. Article 33(1) provides that judgments rendered in an EU Member State are recognized in the other Member State without any special proceedings being required: the declaration that the judgment is enforceable should be issued after purely formal checks of the documents leaving only the possibility to raise issues based on the rights of defense.[114] Article 34 establishes four grounds when judgments shall not be recognized: (1) the recognition would be manifestly contrary to public policy if the State where the recognition is sought; (2) in cases where the judgment was rendered in default, the defendant was not served with the document which instituted the proceedings unless the defendant failed to commence the proceedings to challenge the judgment when it was possible to do so; (3) if the foreign judgment is irreconcilable with a judgment rendered in a dispute between the same parties by a court of a Member State where the recognition is sought; or (4) if the foreign judgment is irreconcilable with a judgment given in another Member State. In addition, the judgment cannot be recognized if it was issued in breach of other jurisdiction rules of the Brussels Regulation (Art. 35).

The recognizing court is not allowed to review the jurisdiction of the court whose judgment is submitted for the recognition (Art. 35(3)).[115] In the same vein, the Brussels I Regulation strictly forbids the recognizing court to the review the substance of the judgment the recognition of which is sought (Art. 36). The judgment shall be declared enforceable immediately upon the completion of formalities provided in Article 53 of the Regulation. The judgment debtor is not allowed to make any submissions at this stage (Art. 41). The Regulation further requires that the judgment debtor is notified about the decision of enforceability of the foreign judgment. However, the decision on the enforceability may be appealed by any of the parties to the competent court within 1 month of service thereof or within 2 months if the judgment debtor is resident in a country other than the country where the recognition is sought. In practice it is enough to present the recognizing court the original judgment.

With regard to IP matters, foreign judgments which were rendered in breach of jurisdiction rules established in the Regulation are not subject to recognition. This would be especially the case if a court of a Member State decided the case in breach of exclusive jurisdiction rules. The ECJ judgment in the case *Duijnstee*[116] is worth another look: in this case the Court decided that exclusive jurisdiction rule applied with regard to IP infringement and validity matters and does not cover disputes between the parties over the determination of who is entitled to an existing IP right created on the basis of a previously existing contractual relationship.[117] Hence, foreign court judgments ordering the revocation of IP rights registered in another Member State cannot be recognized because of the infringement of exclusive jurisdiction provisions.

In Japan, foreign judgments can be recognized according to Article 118 of the Code of Civil Procedure. The enforcement of foreign judgments is governed *inter alia* by Article 24 of the Code on Civil Enforcement. In order to be recognized, a judgment of a foreign court has to be final and satisfy four additional requirements provided in Article 118: (1) the foreign court should have international jurisdiction over the dispute from the Japanese point of view; (2) the defendant should be appropriately served; (3) the content of the judgment and the court proceedings should not be contrary to Japanese public policy; and (4) there

[113] *Pro Swing Inc.* v. *Elta Golf Inc.*, (2006) 2 S.C.R. 612, 2006 SCC 52.

[114] See Recitals 17 and 18 of the Brussels I Regulation.

[115] ECJ, Case C-7-98 *Krombach* [2000] *ECR* I-1956, para. 29.

[116] ECJ, Case 288/82 *Ferdinand Duijnstee* v. *Lodewijk Goderbauer*, [1983] *ECR* 3663.

[117] *Ibid.*

should be reciprocity in the area of recognition of judgments between the rendering State and Japan. Japanese law is not clear whether foreign judgments granted in *ex parte* proceedings as well as interim and provisional measures can be recognized and enforced in Japan, albeit scholars strongly support that the general recognition requirements of Article 118 CCP should be applied. With regard to foreign judgments in IP cases, the Japanese Report noted that general requirements of recognition and enforcement would be applied; however, Japanese courts would be reluctant to recognize foreign judgments which were rendered in breach of exclusive jurisdiction rules of Japanese courts.

In the light of answers provided in the national reports several important conclusions could be made. Firstly, the law of every represented country contains established mechanisms for the recognition and enforcement of foreign judgments. Yet, the recognition and enforcement is still to a large extent viewed from viewpoint of the recognizing country. This leads to the second consideration which is particularly relevant to IP matters. Namely, exclusive jurisdiction over particular IP issues also is reflected at the stage where a foreign judgment has to be recognized: if the judgment was rendered in breach of exclusive jurisdiction rules of the state where the recognition is sought (even though the rendering court finds itself competent to decide the case), such judgment is not likely to be recognized. The Canadian Report referred to the ruling in the *Pro Swing* case[118] dealing with the recognition of foreign judgments related to IP ownership; nevertheless, the practical effects of this judgment in IP matters will be of rather limited importance.

17.6 Conclusions

The intersection of two areas of law – intellectual property and private international law – was analyzed from the angle of peculiarities of adjudication of multistate IP disputes. A number of issues mainly concerning the international jurisdiction, the applicable law and recognition of foreign judgments were addressed. The comparative study showed that the territorial nature of IP rights has largely contributed to current legal framework of adjudication of IP disputes. In common law states courts can decide the case if they have both *in personam* and subject-matter jurisdiction. In effect, this means that only infringement claims concerning IP rights which are protected in the forum state could be brought before the court. Accordingly, such jurisdictional regime also is reflected at the choice-of-law level: the law of the state which has the most significant relationship has to be applied. In the case of infringement the governing law will in most cases be the law of the forum which will most likely coincide with the law of the state for which protection is sought.

In the European Union, the territoriality principle had similar implications to the adjudication of IP-related disputes. The Brussels/Lugano regime aims to facilitate free movement of judgments. The ECJ had interpreted jurisdiction rules rather strictly giving priority to legal certainty and foreseeability of results. In terms of jurisdiction, the fact that claims are related to foreign IP rights does not prevent a Member State court from hearing the case. However, at least as registered IP rights are concerned, country-by-country adjudication of IP infringement disputes is inescapable if the question of validity is a part of the main claim or is raised as a plea in objection. Due to territoriality of IP rights, there are little possibilities of bringing multiple actions concerning IP rights protected in several states or actions against multiple defendants. Meanwhile, it remains controversial to what extent territoriality principle affects the adjudication of disputes concerning non-registered IP rights. Yet, at the time of writing of the report, EU jurisdiction rules were in the midst of a reform process where the CLIP Proposal is expected to contribute to the clarification of jurisdiction matters IP cases. Further, as regards the choice-of-law, some issues were harmonized by the adoption of the Rome I and Rome II Regulations. Nonetheless, some applicable law issues, especially related to initial ownership, multi-state infringements as well as law governing contracts for the transfer of IP rights need further elaboration.

In Asian countries (Republic of Korea, Taiwan and Japan), the courts tend to assert jurisdiction taking into consideration the connection between the dispute and the forum state. The mere issue that rights at stake are foreign IP rights does not negatively affect the exercise of international jurisdiction over the dispute. Although courts would strictly enforce exclusive jurisdiction rules, some recent judgments (e.g. *Coral Sand* case) suggest that the laws are in the process of constant development too. As for the choice-of-law in IP disputes, the

[118] *See supra* note 113.

principle of *lex loci protectionis* would determine the applicable law to proprietary aspects of IP rights while remaining aspects would be determined by the general choice-of-law rules. In all three represented Asian countries legislative proposals concerning private international law aspects of IP rights have been drafted and are expected to shape the further development of this field of law in the near future.

Generally, it may be observed that the cross-border enforcement of IP rights is subject to limitations posed by the subject-matter / exclusive jurisdiction requirements. The jurisdictional regimes reflect long-standing domestic legal cultures and established legal principles. Yet, in order to create a more efficient cross-border adjudication environment, certain flexibility is inevitable. One of the feasible developments that could be introduced into this area of law is the possibility of rendering decisions with *inter partes* effects over issues which had been traditionally viewed as falling within the sovereign domain of the states. In this regard, the 2001 Draft of the Hague Judgments Convention could serve as a solid basis for future discussions. A number of jurisdiction and applicable law questions arising in disputes related to digital technologies still urge for further elaboration. The national reports illustrated that court practice has been facing many challenges in applying traditional concepts to cross-border IP disputes and that a wide gap remains between legal practice and the academic proposals (ALI, CLIP, Transparency and other proposals). Therefore, the discussion between lawyers from both fields of IP and private international law as well as between academics and practitioners should continue. It is hoped that these academic proposals will stimulate the functioning of legal institutions and contribute to the development of more efficient mechanisms in the area of adjudication of multi-state IP disputes.

18 The Prohibition of Age Discrimination in Labor Relations[1]

Monika Schlachter

18.1 Introduction

The relevance of "age discrimination" as a topic increased significantly in the last decade, primarily in countries with an aging population.[2] How to define "countries with an aging population" can certainly be measured in absolute terms: Where the increase in age groups above 45 is much higher than in all other groups with a distinct increase especially in the age group over 65, the population is supposed to be aging.[3] But age discrimination is not only confined to such societies. Whether or not the number of elderly in a given population is felt to be "too high" is obviously dependent on the economic status of the society. An increasing percentage of elderly people in poor states may give rise to negative attitudes towards seniors much earlier than in more affluent societies. As is reported from sub-Saharan Africa, the combination of rising longevity, civil war and HIV/AIDS may outweigh high fertility rates, resulting in an age structure like an aging nation.[4] Combined with low tax returns, available resources for social security, health care and pensions are scarce in such states, leaving elderly people dependent on family members at a time in which family structures tend to erode for multiple reasons.

Greater sensitivity to unfair treatment of the elderly in employment matters may also be strengthened in times of economic crisis. The demographic shift with all its potentially problematic economic consequences is still not a global phenomenon and is most visible in societies with a declining birth-rate over several decades. Young societies and their economies do not experience as many difficulties with diminishing labor market participation rates of the elderly. Not only are there enough young people to replace any senior willing to leave employment, additionally the fact of being eligible for a pension may be a relief from a harsh and physically demanding professional life. The possibility of actually leaving the labor market nevertheless depends on the economic situation of the workers concerned: If they have neither property nor a sufficient pension, they will have to stay on working no matter how bad the conditions offered.

As the economic implications of age discrimination may not be equally distributed among countries, the human rights-aspect of anti-discrimination legislation on the other hand may very well be. Age as well as

[1] III.C., L'interdiction de la discrimination à cause de l'âge dans les relations du travail.

[2] Compare: Report on Canada: A. Introduction; Hessel, Roger, "Aktives Altern in einer alternden Gesellschaft: Weiterbildung in jedem Alter," *Europäische Zeitschrift für Berufsbildung* 45 (2008/3): 157; IAB (Institut für Arbeitsmarkt- und Berufsforschung) Kurzbericht 16/2009; Fujimoto, Makoto, "Employment of Older People After the Amendment of the Act Concerning Stabilization of Employment of Older Persons," *Japan Labour Review* 5 (2008): 59, reference 1.

[3] Sargeant, Malcolm, "Age Discrimination," in *The Law on Age Discrimination in the EU* ed. Sargeant, M., 5 (Alphen aan den Rijn: Kluwer Law International, 2008), chapter 1.

[4] See: M'Nhongo, Tavengwa, *Age Discrimination in Africa, International Federation on Ageing Conference* (Copenhagen, 2006), Seminar 1.

M. Schlachter (✉)
Institute for Labor Law and Industrial Relations
in the European Community, University of Trier,
Trier, Germany
e-mail: schlachter@iaaeg.de

K.B. Brown and D.V. Snyder (eds.), *General Reports of the XVIIIth Congress of the International Academy of Comparative Law/Rapports Généraux du XVIIIème Congrès de l'Académie Internationale de Droit Comparé*,
DOI 10.1007/978-94-007-2354-2_18, © Springer Science+Business Media B.V. 2012

other personality aspects, e.g. religious or political belief or sexual orientation, have become more of a "suspicious motive" to base decisions in employment matters on. Thus, in most jurisdictions the list of forbidden grounds for differentiations in employment nowadays includes the notion of age. Whether this includes only persons of a certain age onwards or at least in principle all age groups equally differs among countries. Nevertheless, the attempt of reaching a full picture of prohibiting age discrimination in labor relations has to include both aspects: The economic and the human rights arguments.

18.1.1 The Economic Perspective on Prohibition of Age Discrimination

The demographic factor,[5] brought about by a combination of greater longevity (=more seniors) and lower fertility (=fewer children), is taken into account by the economic perspective on the prohibition of age discrimination: Where fewer young people enter the labor force, it is more efficient to give all of them, including the uneducated ones, a better training, as well as caring for an ongoing employability of elderly employees. In order to meet an increasing demand despite shrinking supplies, rejecting applicants or workers who do not entirely fit a job description might no longer remain an option. In developed countries, the notion of an aging society leads to the prediction that, in the year 2050, 33% of the population will be over 60 years of age.

Even before the economy runs short of qualified employees, publicly funded social security systems become underfinanced as less and less labor force participants contribute while the number of beneficiaries increases. Estimations in the US are that in 2050 for 100 people active in the workforce there will be 45 people receiving public pensions. Age-related spending will lead to increased costs not only for pensions, but also for health care and long-term care. Privately financed occupational pension schemes also offer no durable protection in a situation of economic crisis. Age-related costs for health care and long-term care will be increasing not only due to the greater longevity of beneficiaries but also due to the progress of modern medicine. Increasing the participation in the labor force of anyone capable of work is a tool for combating financial problems due to the demographic shift.

Encouraging diversity in the workforce may also be one of the tools to strengthen competitiveness of undertakings while allocating the best available person to a workplace without any prejudice or pre-occupation. When governments try to advance labor market participation rates, it is first and foremost to influence retirement habits by increasing the age at which a person will be entitled to a full pension. This aims at the decision of elderly employees to remain members of the workforce. Whether they in fact are able to stay in employment depends not only on their own decision. If older workers indeed are not quite fit to work, or are only perceived to be less fit, they might be made redundant whether or not they prefer to stay on working. In that case it would become highly unfair to hand all the detriments of unemployment plus a later retirement age to elderly employees. If only for the reason of fairness, governments need to prepare measures to allow the elderly to actually stay employed as long as they are fit and prepared to work.

18.1.2 The Human Rights Aspect of Age Discrimination

When it comes to non-economic reasons for prohibiting age discrimination, naturally the right of all people to equality before the law and to protection against all forms of discrimination is the principle to look at. This speaks for extending the reach of protective legislation not only to the elderly but to any age group as stereotyping easily affects young workers, too.[6] They tend to be seen as less reliable, more inclined to take days off, less committed to work than to their social life and less responsible. This may not be as fundamental as negative stereotypes associated with older age, but they nevertheless become detrimental to prospects on the labor market. A human-rights approach would disapprove all stereotyping.

[5] Meenan, Helen, "Age Discrimination on the EU and the Framework Directive," in *The Law on Age Discrimination in the EU,* ed. Sargeant, M. 11 (Alphen aan den Rijn: Kluwer Law International, 2008), chapter 2.

[6] For an example from Japan, see: Sakuraba, Ryoko, "The Amendment of the Employment Measure Act: Japanese Anti-Age Discrimination Law," *Japan Labour Review* 6 (2009); 56, 60, 65.

But the International Human Rights instruments quoted regularly in this context do not explicitly refer to age as a prohibited ground for differentiation. The Universal Declaration of Human Rights, the United Nations Convention on the Elimination of all Forms of Discrimination against Women, the United Nations' Conventions on Civil and Political Rights and on Economic, Social and Cultural Rights or the European Convention for the Protection of Human Rights and Fundamental Freedoms do not specifically mention "age." Some documents allow for the inclusion of age by implication as they create an open-ended list of grounds by referring to any "other status" to be protected from discrimination. Age as a personal characteristic beyond the individual's control is deemed to deserve such special protection. In a labor market set up under a merit-principle, employment opportunities and career chances should be distributed accordingly. Therefore, excluding some members of society from labor market participation chances due to a fact mostly unrelated to performance would be judged both undesirable and unfair.

On the other hand, arguing from a freedom of contract approach, the freedom to choose with whom to deal is essential for free markets. In the US, Friedman[7] even went so far as to finding a similarity "in principle" between prohibiting discrimination and the Nazi regime's so called Nuremberg laws prohibiting marriages between Jewish and non-Jewish Germans for racial reasons. From a German perspective, this comparison certainly is unacceptable, as the Constitution (art. 1 para. 1 of the Basic Law) values human dignity above other human rights exactly because of the experience of systematic, state enforced discrimination against Jews and many other minorities which ended in all crimes against humanity, including mass murder. The human rights aspect of anti-discrimination legislation is far from being obvious and acknowledged by everyone, though. Opponents often describe such legislation as a populist play to the sentiment of voters, to the effect that it only promotes "political correctness" instead of social welfare. In order to see the bigger picture and to better understand what kind of legislation is needed to reach a better labor market participation rate for elderly employees, it seems necessary to understand why there is discrimination.

[7]Friedman, Milton, *Capitalism and Freedom* (Chicago: University of Chicago Press, 1962), 113.

18.1.3 Reasons to Discriminate

The main reasons for discriminatory behavior discussed among economists are the following: Taste for discrimination (people discriminate against a group because they dislike the group as such[8]); statistical discrimination (people discriminate against a group because they suppose that group members, on average, are worse as party to a contract than other members of society[9]); discrimination for diminishing competition (people discriminate against a group to gain benefits from warding off competition[10]). Especially when looking at age discrimination, the explanatory value of those approaches differs extremely.

Taste-based discrimination on the one hand might be able to describe why a landlord refuses to lease his property to a person of different ethnicity because he prefers living next to his or her kind of people. Assuming that, in comparison, the landlord does not like to associate with a certain age group seems far from convincing. There might be exceptions to this, as discrimination for the reason of disliking elderly people can root in a wide spread belief that the elderly can be considered dangerous like in the report from some African countries[11] where elderly women are supposed to practice witchcraft. Apart from these special circumstances, age as such will not draw as much disregard as other "suspect grounds" for discrimination like ethnicity, religious belief or sexual orientation. It is frequently found that elderly people are regarded as competition that needs to be abandoned if younger workers are to obtain career positions or labor contracts at all. Albeit comparable, this is not identical to disliking elderly persons because of their age. However, we will turn to the implications of the competition-problem below.

Without even trying to judge the explanatory merits of the taste-based economic approach in general, it does not seem very helpful for explaining age discrimination. This is certainly related to the fact that age as

[8]Becker, Garry S., *The Economics of Discrimination*, 2nd ed. (Chicago: University of Chicago Press, 1973).

[9]Phelps, Edmund S., "The Statistical Theory of Racism and Sexism," *American Economic Review* 62 (1972): 659.

[10]Richard Allen Epstein, *Forbidden Grounds* (Cambridge: Harvard University Press, 1992) 91.

[11]See: M'Nhongo, Tavengwa, *Age Discrimination in Africa, International Federation on Ageing Conference* (Copenhagen, 2006), Seminar 1.

a reason for discrimination is a very special ground, not easily compared to other criteria. This ground does not readily allow for sorting people into certain groups, as it constantly changes over time: One who is an inexperienced youngster now will move on to become a member of the age group in high demand, whereas members of that group see themselves threatened by the prospect of getting too old to meet expectations. Unlike race, ethnic origin, gender, sexual orientation or even religious belief, all members of society will (save an early death) live through all emanations of age, i.e. the life cycles. With the prospect of one day becoming a member of another group it is much more difficult to build a strong group identity, even if the very young and the very old members of society might behave differently as the clash of generations sometimes indicates.[12] But decision making in the labor market cannot be explained that way: Everyone must envision themselves as getting old one day, so the idea of simply disliking elderly people merely for their age is rather strange.

Statistical discrimination, on the other hand, seems to predict discrimination on the labor market much better.[13] Under this theory, discrimination is used as a means to achieve certain useful ends, such as avoiding loss or making a profit. So if a person has a certain characteristic or disposition that can cause extra costs, the other party to a prospective contract would consider that person a bad choice. If it is hard to observe whether a person indeed has such a characteristic, future partners to a contract will search for an apparent indicator allowing to presume the existence or non-existence of such disposition.[14] The presumption then is, that certain apparent characteristics such as age are positively correlated with other dispositions, hard or even impossible to detect, which make for costly risks. For example, an employer deciding which employees should receive costly special training will be eager to keep the well-trained personnel employed for at least a certain amount of time after completing the courses. Further, gender (as female employees more often stay home with children than males do) or age (as older employees more often choose early retirement than younger workers do) may be seen as signs for employees' inclination to quit their job by the employer. If being of an older age statistically correlates with low level of education,[15] laying off or refusing to hire workers above 40 years of age is not primarily due to their chronological age. Whether or not this presumption is true or false for a specific person is obviously not important.

On the other hand, not training women or elderly employees may lead to the exclusion of valuable workers who remain in their given employment relationship. It may not even be necessary to avoid losses as undertakings could conclude training contracts binding workers to a predetermined future length of service giving the employer enough time to recover costs. But as long as the employer presumes that the indicators work well enough statistically, discriminating will be cheaper on average and easier applied. For that reason, statistical attributes may very well work for explaining age discrimination given the many negative stereotypes associated with a higher age:[16] Technology-averse, outdated knowledge and not interested in further education or re-training, more formal and less flexible attitudes, frequent absenteeism due to bad health, diminished physical and mental capacity or operating effectiveness.

Discrimination to exclude competition may also offer insights into why disadvantageous treatment of elderly workers is common place. This occurs when members of the majority systematically agree to deal with one group on less favorable terms and exclude them from certain profitable activity.[17] Through this all members of such a cartel could earn monopoly rents from members of the excluded group. This explains the persistence of systematic discrimination in societies where a political system creates and stabilizes the

---

[12] Hoffman, Eileen B., "Working Effectively Across the Generations," *Perspectives on Work (Magazine of LERA)* 13, no. 2 (winter 2010): 29.

[13] Engert, Andreas, "Allied by Surprise? The Economic Case for an Anti-discrimination Statute," *German Law Journal* 4 (2003): p. 685 et sequ.

[14] O'Cinneide, Colm, *Age Discrimination and European Law* (Luxembourg: Office for Official Publications of the European Communities, 2005), 5, 10, 14.

[15] Report on Macao, reference 6, indicating that in Macao 62% of employed persons had an education below junior school level (age dependent).

[16] Wood, Geoffrey/Wilkinson, Adrian/Harcourt, Mark, "Age Discrimination and Working Life: Perspectives and Contestations – A Review of the Contemporary Literature," *International Journal of Management Reviews* 10, no. 4 (2008): 425.

[17] Darity, William, "The Functionality of Market-Based Discrimination," *International Journal of Social Economics* 28 (2008): 980.

existence of such a cartel through targeted violence or political unrest. Ultimately this is not sufficient as a comprehensive explanation for labor market discrimination, because some questions remain: Is it possible to describe elderly employees as a minority? Not only are their numbers increasing but also the fact that everyone expects to enter this group one day would normally disallow an "us versus them"-cartel. On the other hand, there are common justifications for ending labor relationships with elderly employees to "give way to the younger generation." The idea of furthering the labor market participation of young people after completion of their training or stabilizing career advancement of the middle aged generation at the expense of older employees is wide spread. Here, a coalition of interests between employers seeking to avoid additional costs for elderly workers and younger employees/job-seekers hoping to attract a better position for themselves could well foster a cartel against elderly workers. If such a cartel works in any given society, government intervention may be necessary to end it.

18.1.4 Anti-discrimination Legislation?

Trying to explain or understand reasons why it might be rational to discriminate on the basis of age does not count for an excuse. Not all "rational" decisions are justified, maximizing one's own benefits may be efficient but nonetheless illegal. The fundamental right to equal treatment, enshrined in human dignity as one of the central elements of law, can claim superiority over many efficiency standards.[18] When comparing different national solutions it is sensible to consider which solution is suitable as best practice.

Firstly, the notion of statistical discrimination makes it very clear that legislation should not go unaccompanied: As long as decision makers are poorly informed about current knowledge on the productivity of elderly employees, their general level of fitness, their health status and so forth, they might act on prejudice rather than on actual statistical correlation between two parameters. Additionally, information on the consequences of the demographic shift, especially for small and medium sized undertakings or a notoriously underpaying public sector, may support a better decision making process. Even if older workers have a shorter working life ahead of them over which employers could amortize the costs of training in new technologies, staff turnover rates for older workers are lower than for younger ones. On a closer look, evaluating older workers as more costly than younger ones may not hold true for all fields of employment. The natural response to error-based decisions is to provide better information from reliable third parties. Anti-discrimination legislation will not suffice in this perspective. It may serve as a very indirect and unnecessarily complicated way for government to spread information that not all people of a certain age are utterly unsuitable labor contract partners.

But then again, there are some positive correlations between age as an apparent factor and additional costs of a prospective employee. Insofar as statistical discrimination really works as an effective screening tool for sorting out higher risks, legal intervention must show exactly which targets to address. All of this might often be quite possible in age discrimination: While being a person of a certain age is an immutable characteristic, it is next to impossible to evade every age based judgement on employability. Even if it is forbidden by law to include questions for specific age-related information in the recruiting process, at some point the employer will find out the true age of an employee. So if the employer relies on age as a proxy for higher costs he will still be able to adjust the perceived risk by ending the contractual relationship early.

However, it may be argued that this outcome is not always useful: Some age-related costs are just as immutable as reaching a certain age. On the other hand, whether their knowledge is outdated, their job-specific skills are lacking, or their ability to work in teams of mixed age groups is low are aspects which employees may influence through their own efforts. Only a few features such as bodily strength, optimal eye-sight or quickness of reaction are related to age without much influence of the person concerned. These parameters are a necessary precondition for employment only in very limited fields. For other occupations the fact of not being given the chance to prove one's employability after a certain age actually induces workers not to put in any extra effort to maintain or

[18] O'Cinneide, Colm, *Age Discrimination and European Law* (Luxembourg: Office for Official Publications of the European Communities, 2005), 11.

even strengthen their existing capabilities.[19] For these workers, it does not seem to pay to invest in employability as they are not given the chance to remain in a meaningful employment relationship. Such a loss of interest is quite rational, but it nevertheless constitutes an unnecessary loss of potentially productive human resources. Especially in aging societies where not enough young people and immigrants stand ready to replace the leaving workers, this threat will be felt sooner rather than later. Under those circumstances, age discrimination is not only unfair but ineffective.

This insight implicates that legislation banning age discrimination should work best in fields where elderly employees have a considerable influence on the existence of costly characteristics or dispositions. In that case, giving elderly employees the possibility of remaining in employment for longer years will benefit all parties concerned, including state social security systems. On the other hand, banning age discrimination in fields where there is a close correlation between an employee's age and higher costs of employment will probably meet so much resistance from the employer's side that law enforcement will become very costly for society. Thus, said kind of legislation may not prove very effective.

Discrimination to exclude competition, on the other hand, may not be overcome save for special legislation. If older workers face more intense discrimination because they are in such a weak position that they are perceived to be obedient, they will bear a disproportionate share of globalization-induced changes. As undertakings may want to compete by cutting costs and furthering flexibility they may actually need a sector of low wages and numerical flexibility next to a high-commitment and high-productivity core workforce. In the decision of whom to assign into the low cost-group, age may work as a widely accepted screening mechanism: Dominant, younger workers may agree to protect their own superior labor market position. In a general climate of employment insecurity, younger workers may claim that state run pension systems unacceptably burden the economically active population, and that older workers nearer to "normal" retirement age should go first. Given the fact that in many societies older people are among the poorest population groups, they are easily ready to accept lower wages and insecure working conditions in unskilled or semi-skilled jobs after being made redundant because they need the money for basic living expenses or increasing health-related expenses. So in a situation where interests of employers and younger employees meet in singling out older workers for bearing the biggest part of the burden of lower employment standards in a changing economy, this association of interests may in fact function as a cartel to the detriment of the elderly. To change this, the legislator will have to step in.

To find out to what extent legislators nowadays act to combat age discrimination, a questionnaire was sent out to 27 National Reporters who indicated their willingness to describe their respective country's state of age discrimination in labor relations.[20] In Sect. 18.2 we will discuss the results.

18.2 Prohibiting Age Discrimination in Labor Relations

18.2.1 Statutory Instruments Addressing Age Discrimination and Alternative Means of Protection

In many countries the instrument of choice for combating age discrimination is statutory law. As for the human rights aspect of anti-discrimination legislation, some special protection may also be enshrined in the constitution or specific Human Rights Acts or is provided for by international instruments[21] ratified by the respective country. In that case providing for protection against age discrimination may become an obligation for governments. Such constitutionally or internationally set norms provide for standards to measure national rules and regulations which the legislator is obliged to respect.[22]

Where regulations governing labor relations are customarily not enacted in statutes but bargained for by means of collective bargaining, both sides of industry

[19] Sargeant, Malcolm, United Kingdom, in *The Law on Age Discrimination in the EU,* ed. Sargeant, M. 213 (Alphen aan den Rijn: Kluwer Law International2008), chapter 10.

[20] Of the resulting National Reports 23 are published below.

[21] Report on Macao, following reference 11; Report on Argentina, question 1; Report on Uruguay, question 1; Report on Poland, question 1; Report on Czechia, question 1.

[22] For a different perception compare: Report of New Zealand, reference 3.

may be responsible for barring discrimination in employment.[23]

18.2.1.1 Constitutional Protection

Protection of basic human rights and freedoms regularly guarantees a right to equality and/or proscription of discrimination.[24] If equality rights expressly include proscribed grounds for discrimination, such criteria might be on an open ended list or limited to enumerated reasons.[25] Nevertheless it is conceivable that the degree of protection provided by such clauses does not primarily depend on such technicalities but on the willingness of the courts responsible for interpreting constitutional rights to recognize a narrower or a wider standard.

One of the core questions in this respect is whether the constitutional clause is merely prohibiting discrimination, or promoting a concept of "substantive equality," thereby authorizing the state to forward positive measures benefiting formerly disadvantaged groups.[26] If so, the law itself or the judicial interpretation thereof will have to create standards, what type of distinction between groups is discriminatory and therefore forbidden or ameliorative in purpose and therefore justifiable.

18.2.1.2 Ordinary Statutory Protection of Equality Rights

The prohibition of discrimination or unfair treatment is mostly enacted through regular legislative procedures.[27] Because of the distinct human rights aspect of anti-discrimination legislation it nevertheless may be considered to be of special nature as it creates public policy in matters of general concern. The Canadian Supreme Court[28] therefore declared such statutes to be quasi-constitutional in nature to the effect that they can only be altered or amended to a limited extent. Therefore, exceptions to its provisions can only be created by clear legislative pronouncement. Such an approach would not only disallow administrative actions diminishing equality rights but also set boundaries to collective agreements.

Enactment of anti-discrimination law either creates a uniform code aimed at tackling discrimination in employment (or beyond, by including several civil law contracts)[29] on all forbidden grounds[30] or dedicate a separate statute to any one such ground.[31] The latter approach is represented by the US as it created different statutes for each protected category next to Title VII of the Civil Rights Act which includes five protected categories at once. Once a state deals exclusively with one protected category, parliament can focus on the special circumstances related to such ground.[32] This might count as an advantage of a single-ground statute. On the other hand, there are down sides, too. As statutes are of different origin in time, a more recent law might provide up-to-date answers to questions not prevalent earlier on but now relevant for more than just one category. Therefore, the existence of different solutions in different statutes is not an obvious indicator for solutions meant to accommodate just the one category of forbidden grounds. So the question remains whether or not it is for the courts to interpret these special statutes in a "unified" way, which is in the light of or consistent with other anti-discrimination legislation.

18.2.1.3 Statutory Protection in Employment Law

Besides specific anti-discrimination legislation focussing on the human rights aspect of protection against age discrimination, general employment laws may provide special conditions for recruiting or terminating a labor contract[33] as well as forbidding discriminatory

[23] Report on Portugal, reference 13; Rapport de la Belgique, reference 6, 7.

[24] Report on Macao, reference 9; Report on Japan, chapter C.II.; Report on Ireland, question 1; Report on Romania, question 1; Rapport de la Belgique, chapter A.I.; Report on Slovenia, question1; Report on Italy, question 1; Report on Poland, question 1.

[25] Report on Canada, chapter B.; Report on Japan, chapter C.II.; Report on Argentina, question 1; Report on Venezuela, question 1; Report on Norway, question 1; Report on Portugal, question 1; Report on Croatia, question 1.

[26] Report on Canada, chapter B., reference 15.

[27] Report on the US, reference 1–6; Report on Australia, question 1; Report on Argentina, question 1; Report on the Netherlands, question 1; Report on Ireland, question 1; Report on Norway, question 1; Report on Slovenia, question 1.

[28] Report on Canada, chapter C., reference 32.

[29] Report on Ireland, question 1; Report on Romania, question 1; Report on Portugal, question 4.

[30] Report on Macao, reference 10–11; Report on Romania, question 1; Report on Portugal, question 1; Report on Italy, question 1; Report on Sweden, question 1; Report on Poland, question 1; Report on Croatia, question 1.

[31] Report on the Netherlands, question 1.

[32] Report on the US, prior to reference 8; Report on Australia, question 1.

[33] Report on Japan, chapter J.I.3.

or unfair treatment.[34] Correspondingly, the level of protection provided here will not depend directly on the kind of statute that realizes it. The legislative norms will nevertheless be different. On the one hand, an act on employment relations will regulate employment contracts through all phases of their existence, incidents of discrimination being just one of several aspects. An act on specific terms of labor relations (e.g.: remuneration, holidays, parental leave) will focus on particular problems in employment. This may lead to different consequences: Either tackling the discrimination aspect only regarding some terms of a contract[35] while omitting the rest, or a duplication of protective measures under employment as well as under human rights statutes. So duplication of protection in one specific area (like dismissal protection) will raise questions concerning a potential claimant's obligation to elect under which procedure to pursue a complaint.[36]

18.2.1.4 Collective Agreements

Collective agreements have to be taken into consideration as additional – or alternative – sources of protection against discrimination. When enacting age discrimination statutes, legislators often include a clause that collective agreements governing employment conditions must not contain discriminatory clauses.[37] This amounts to an obligation to omit age discrimination in sub-statutory norm-setting. Additionally, collective agreements can easily promote anti-discrimination clauses by providing for specific obligations to make workplaces more age-friendly. It should not pose a problem from the viewpoint of legislators once collective bargaining partners are also legally competent to further elderly worker's employability by setting up specific training programs or the like. Nevertheless, the realization of said plans depends on certain factual preconditions not automatically existent in most countries.

18.2.2 Protected Age Groups

Age discrimination occurs when a person of a particular age is treated unfavorably "because of" his or her age. This treatment may happen due to the actual age of the person concerned or due to characteristics associated with the age (truly or falsely).[38] When defining which age groups to protect one must rely on the chronological age status.

Age discrimination seems to be prevalent concerning older workers. From what age onwards persons are counted as "older workers" differs between countries. Whether the relevant legislation/alternative protecting measures include elderly people in general or only up to the point where they reach an upper age limit depends on the existence of a mandatory retirement age. If there is wide consensus in society that at some age employees should leave employment, they are normally not entitled to protection after reaching the age in question.[39]

Age discrimination may also affect younger workers after completing their training or school/university education. The transition between apprenticeship or professional training and becoming a regular member of the workforce can be difficult at times so that there might be special regulations with specific standards for inexperienced workers.[40]

Finally, special measures protecting minors from working at all or under "normal" working conditions may also be considered as a measure of special preference for a certain age group.

18.2.2.1 Lower Age Limits

The scope of protection against age discrimination can depend on the technical decision of the scope of application of special statutes: The **lower age limit** can be either set by law explicitly, like in the US, where only employees of at least 40 years of age are protected against age discrimination.[41] Such a provision does not render a distinction based on age suspicious as long as the workers affected by the measure are not hindered by their age to find alternative employment.

The US Supreme Court even went further by relying on legislative history exemplifying that the protection given by statute is intentionally limited to older workers as opposed to younger ones.[42] This limits the

[34] Report on New Zealand, reference 4; Report on Australia, question 1; Report on the Netherlands, question 1.

[35] Report on Japan, chapter J.I.2.

[36] Report on New Zealand, reference 6.

[37] Report on Australia, question 1.

[38] Report on Australia, introduction.

[39] Report on Argentina, question 17; Report on Norway, question 1, 18; Report on Portugal, question 17.

[40] Report on Japan, chapter B.I., reference 4; Report on Portugal, question 2; Report on Poland, question 2.

[41] Report on the US, reference 71.

[42] Report on the US, reference 215–218.

available protection even among the protected category itself; therefore it is not unlawful to prefer older workers in the protected category over younger workers in that category – only the reverse type of preference is forbidden.

If there is no explicit threshold enacted, the lower age limit for age discrimination protection will depend on an implicit scope of application of the relevant statute. In Canada, human rights legislation protects citizens of the "age of majority,"[43] so that it depends on the distinct concept of majority whether or not protection against age discrimination is available.[44]

Other concepts prefer a lower age limit independent from the age of majority, e.g. New Zealand providing statutory protection against discrimination from the age of 16 onwards.[45] Working minors are protected under the different standards of special legislation on underaged workers.[46] Such employment protection legislation will set a minimum age below which young people are not allowed to work at all, which is normally set by the duration of compulsory education. Children of school age should attend school or be on vacation instead of working. However, there also are exemptions to this rule.[47] The main problem of the approach is not primarily the fact that minors are allowed to work under certain circumstances. Under the age-discrimination approach problems arise concerning working conditions. If age discrimination legislation is simply not applicable to minors, minimum wages can be easily set differently than those of adults without the necessity to justify such a measure following the test applicable to cases of detrimental treatment.[48] If anti-discrimination statutes do not specify any certain age group as their scope of application at all, this would allow for an overall protection[49] with special conditions applying for minors additionally.

18.2.2.2 Upper Age Limit

The existence of an **upper age limit** of protection against age discrimination depends primarily on the existence of mandatory retirement rules. A mandatory retirement age has to be distinguished from a pensionable age at which employees legally are entitled to draw a state pension. An entitlement will not necessarily as such influence the existence or termination of an employment relationship,[50] as states could leave it to the employee whether to apply for a pension. Sometimes, employees may even decide to draw pension entitlements partly while continuing to work.[51] Many countries nevertheless will make the entitlement to social security benefits dependent on ending the labor relationship or, the other way round, create a mandatory retirement age at which the labor contract terminates while social security benefits are provided for.

Prior to enacting age discrimination prohibitions, mandatory retirement was wide spread and commonly seen as legitimate.[52] This dates back to the beginning of social security legislation when the normal retirement age was set at an age that was close to or even higher than average life expectancy.[53] Under such conditions mandatory retirement was a benefit rather than detrimental and for dangerous or hazardous occupations or workers carrying out heavy, physically demanding work this still holds true today.[54] Many employees would actually prefer early retirement from other types of work, too. However, this leaves two options, either a lower retirement age or facilitation of the preconditions for early pension entitlement in countries with a younger population.[55] In aging countries, though, the approach meanwhile became different.

[43] Report on Canada, chapter C.II., reference 53.

[44] Report on Canada, chapter D.

[45] Report on New Zealand, reference 7.

[46] Report on Macao, reference 13; Report on Japan, chapter B. II.4.; Report on Argentina, question 3; Report on Ireland, question 2; Report on Romania, question 2; Report on Norway, question 3; Report on Portugal, question 2; Rapport de la Belgique, chapter A.VI.; Report on Slovenia, question 2, 3; Report on Italy, question 1, 9; Report on Czechia, question 5.

[47] Report on Canada, chapter D., reference 88; Report on Portugal, question 2; Report on Italy, question 15.

[48] Report on Canada, chapter D., reference 89; for a comparable problem concerning discrimination of students: Report on Norway, question 20.

[49] Report on the Netherlands, question 2; Report on Norway, question 2.

[50] Report on Czechia, question 18.

[51] Report on Sweden, question 18.

[52] Report on Japan, chapter J.II.; Report on Venezuela, question 18; Report on the Netherlands, question 18; Report on Norway, question 4, 18.

[53] Report on the US, following reference 35. Report on Croatia, question 18.

[54] Report on Croatia, question 18.

[55] Report on Uruguay, question 2.

Given the change in health status and longevity in the population and the decrease of manual labor in most developed economies, mandatory retirement became a matter of concern with respect to age discrimination legislation nowadays.[56] Several reasons for keeping it are common among states, such as promoting a system of labor force renewal, refraining from demeaning performance tests among elderly workers or even the workforce in general,[57] and furthering a proper mix of experienced older staff and newly trained younger personnel whose technical knowledge is up-to-date. Additionally, mandatory retirement is deemed justified as being the result of an implicit bargain according to which workers earn less when starting their career and earn more the longer they stay employed; this "proceeding through the ranks" has to finish at a certain point in time in order to allow employers a proper calculation and co-workers to be promoted to better ranks.

Following this argumentation courts were mostly rather reluctant to interpret anti-discrimination legislation as disallowing mandatory retirement clauses.[58] To decide whether they are to be abolished is seen as the parliament's prerogative. As a consequence there are states like the US and New Zealand that explicitly outlaw mandatory retirement[59] or most Canadian jurisdictions[60] repealing the upper limits on age protected by their human rights codes. Under those circumstances, age as such is no longer a factor justifying the termination of an employment relationship[61] no matter whether or not this was previously agreed upon in an individual or collective agreement. Making mandatory retirement a discriminatory practice is subject to the employer's right to terminate the labor contract for reasons that are regularly accepted. Additionally, some exceptions may be set out, especially for high risk occupations like airline pilots, firefighters, or members of the armed forces. The US allows an exception for "executive or high policymaking positions," provided that the employee is at least 65 years of age and has for a 2-year period immediately before retirement been entitled to an annual retirement benefit of at least 44,000 $. Australia also allows for a selected group of professions with compulsory retirement,[62] a prominent example (enacted in the Constitution) being federal judges.

Where mandatory retirement clauses are not outlawed by parliament, they continue to exist, be it in statutes[63] or in collective agreements[64]. The simplest way of putting mandatory retirement is that a given employment contract is terminated on the worker reaching the set age.[65] A different approach for reaching the same result would mean not automatically terminating the employment relationship upon the worker's reaching retirement age, but rather asking that person to submit a request for receiving a pension first. Once the employee refuses such request to retire, though, they lose dismissal protection so that the employer can easily end the employment relationship on his own initiative.[66] In Portugal, for example, the contract of employment of a person above the normal retirement age is automatically converted into a fixed-term contract for the period of 6 months in case the worker does not choose to retire,[67] so that then the employer faces no difficulty ending the employment relationship with the worker.

By legal standards, the fact that mandatory retirement allows for a burden to be imposed upon a group of employees defined by age cannot be contested.[68] So the infringement of equality rights through such clauses will not be too controversial as such,[69] transferring the question of legality to the justification analysis by the courts.

In any case, maintaining a mandatory retirement age does not normally prohibit workers above such age to be employed, either with another employer or with the one they had worked for earlier.[70] They just have no contractual rights from their original contract to remain

[56] Report on Ireland, question 2.

[57] Report on the Netherlands, question 18.

[58] Report on Canada, chapter B., reference 18, 21–23.

[59] Report on the US, reference 88; Report on New Zealand, reference 8; Report on Australia, question 18.

[60] Report on Canada, chapter C.II., reference 59–61.

[61] Report on Slovenia, question 18.

[62] Report on Australia, reference 7.

[63] Report on Canada, chapter C.II., reference 63; Report on Japan, chapter E.II; Report on Portugal, question 18 (public administration); Report on Poland, question 18; Report on Croatia, question 18.

[64] Report on Norway, question 18.

[65] Report on Italy, question 18 (for the public sector).

[66] Report on Romania, question 18; Report on Norway, question 18.

[67] Report on Portugal, question 18.

[68] Compare: European Court of Justice, March 5, 2009, C-388/07 (Age Concern England).

[69] For a different approach: Report on Japan, chapter E.I.

[70] Report on Italy, question 18 (private sector).

in employment because such contract ceases to exist. So it is up to the employer to decide whether or not he wants to maintain the contractual relationship[71] and for the worker to agree or disagree upon the offer. Some countries explicitly mention that employing workers older than the pensionable age falls outside the scope of dismissal protection,[72] or that employing them only on the basis of fixed term contract is not considered age discrimination.[73] Sometimes, even employees continuing their former labor relationship with all the previous contractual duties simply earn a wage many percentage points lower than before.[74]

18.2.3 Protected Contractual Relationships

18.2.3.1 Labor Relations

Age discrimination legislation is relevant to and primarily applied to labor contracts.[75] So far as the provided protection is laid down in labor law statutes they regulate circumstances within an established[76] or soon to be established contractual relationship involving an employer and a worker. The coverage depends on the existence of a labor relationship, excluding non-workers, but including everyone providing dependent work. There may be exceptions from this: States exempt public administration employees from age discrimination provisions or people under vocational training contracts or in marital or family relationships.[77]

As the differentiation between employees and independent contractors is not always easy, legislation might decide to protect not only people working under a contract for service; a more human rights-orientated approach therefore would tend to have a wider scope of application of anti-discrimination legislation, for example including discrimination in partnerships[78], against contract-workers[79], in education in general, in accommodation or provision of goods and services.[80] Due to the difficulties of precisely differentiating between a labor contract and a near-employment relationship and due to the similarity of discriminatory decisions possible in both contexts, the statutory protection might be comparable for everyone providing work.[81] As this would overstep the concept of employment protection legislation, a decision to extend the scope of protective regulations will not be left to the courts in many countries but rather remain in the legislator's responsibility.[82]

18.2.3.2 Non-labor Contracts

The EU provides an example for such a decision by extending the scope of application of the Equal Treatment Framework Directive to the conditions of access to self-employment and occupation.[83] But, there is no prohibition of age discrimination in working conditions or in terminating the contract.[84] For terms and conditions of providing services the contractual freedom of the parties is given more weight in comparison to an employment relationship.

In most surveyed countries protection against age discrimination applies not only to workers already employed but also during the recruitment process as such.[85] So applicants are included, as the selection

[71]Report on Sweden, question 18.

[72]Report on the Netherlands, question 18.

[73]Report on Ireland, question 1; Report on Romania, question 3.

[74]For a survey conducted by the Japan Institute for Labour Policy and Training see: Fujimoto, Makoto, "Employment of older people after the ammendment of the Act concerning stabilization of employment of older persons," *Japan Labour Review* 5 (2008):59, 85 f.

[75]Report on the US, reference 3; Report on New Zealand, reference 13; Report on Japan, chapter B.II.1.; Report on Argentina, question 5; Report on Uruguay, question 5; Report on the Netherlands, question 4; Report on Ireland, question 5; Report on the Netherlands, question 4; Report on Romania, question 5; Rapport de la Belgique, chapter A.II.1.; Report on Slovenia, question 4; Report on Czechia, question 4.

[76]Report on New Zealand, reference 13.

[77]Report on Macao, reference 16.

[78]Report on New Zealand, reference 14, 63; Report on Ireland, question 5.

[79]Report on New Zealand, reference 59; Report on Ireland, question 5.

[80]Report on Australia, question 4; Report on Ireland, question 5; Report on Sweden, question 4.

[81]Report on Ireland, question 5; Report on Portugal, question 5; Report on Croatia, question 5.

[82]Report on Australia, question 5; Report in Argentina, question 5.

[83]Directive 2000/78/EC, art. 3 para. 1(a); Report on the Netherlands, question 4, 5; Report on Norway, question 4 (no Member State to the EU); Report on Slovenia, question 4; Report on Italy, question 4, 5; Report on Sweden, question 4, 5; Report on Poland, question 4, 5; Report on Czechia, question 5.

[84]For a more inclusive concept see Report on Australia, question 5.

[85]Report on Canada, chapter C.II., before reference 49; Report on New Zealand, reference 18; Report on Japan, chapter B.II.3.; Report on Portugal, question 1; Report on Coratia, question 4.

process tends to be especially prone to discriminatory incidents. From a technical standpoint, though, employment law would not be applicable without a specific declaration to include it, as the employment relationship has not even begun by then.[86] Furthermore, in near-employment relationships the decision to hire contractors or not may be influenced by discrimination. Normally, the customer of a service provider or independent contractor would not be included as addressee of employment related provisions.[87] The scope of applicability will usually refer to employers or labor market related organizations who are not allowed to discriminate: Consumers as mere recipients of a service provided cannot be included in such a notion. As long as the anti-discrimination legislation aims at protecting dependent employment it will not reach beyond the labor contract.

18.2.3.3 (Occupational) Pension Schemes

Discriminating decisions can also concern the post-contractual period of receiving pension benefits. As entitlement hereto is a consequence of the former labor relationship, depending on length of service and the remuneration earned, in several countries it is within the scope of protection. The EU draws a distinction between payments made by state social security of social protection schemes on the one hand and occupational pension schemes on the other: While the former is explicitly excluded from the scope of the relevant Directive,[88] the latter has always been included into the concept of "pay" under a labor contract and is therefore covered. The underlying reason for exempting state run schemes is not a very distinct concept of discrimination excluding social security, but merely the European Union's lack of competency to legislate in that field.

While the application of anti-discrimination legislation on occupational pension schemes may be acknowledged in several legal systems, there also are exemptions.[89] Providing for or requiring contributions to such a scheme can reasonably rely on age if this is done on the basis of satisfactory statistical data or actuarial advice.[90] Next to those general prerequisites are specific clauses on an age eligible for benefits provided or a threshold for maximum age for the application to join such schemes.[91] These exemptions are provided for when age discrimination legislation is introduced to a legal system with many viable decisions based on age. If occupational pension schemes are made available by employers without statutory obligations, they will only continue to be offered if employers are not deterred through far reaching legislative restrictions. On the other hand, having occupational pension schemes available on fair, non-discriminatory terms becomes even more necessary the more emphasis is put on the so-called "third pillar" of pensions. The necessary policy balance between those two goals reflects why such schemes come under anti-discrimination legislation in the first place and at the same time why there are frequent exceptions attached to it.

18.2.4 Types of Forbidden Discrimination

Which measure constitutes a discrimination can be defined differently. In the longest serving statute, the ADEA in the US, the scope of protection is specified by the notion of "unlawful practices" directed against elderly employees by employers, employment agencies or labor organizations.[92] The type of practice regarded as unlawful for an employer is described specifically,[93] including hiring, refusing to hire, discharging a person, discriminating in terms and conditions of employment or compensation or depriving individuals of employment opportunities. When exemplifying a "detriment" to a claimant, the focus frequently is on whether he or she has been treated less favorably then other employees of essentially similar qualifications, experience or skill under similar circumstances. Claimants need to compare themselves to other suitable comparators to convince the court that they have been treated detrimentally at all.[94] The next step would

[86] Report on Argentina, question 4.

[87] Report on Canada, chapter C.II., following reference 64; Report on Australia, question 5; Report on Macao, reference 17; Report on Norway, question 5.

[88] Directive 2000/78/EC, art. 3 para 3.

[89] Report on Australia, question 4; Report on Ireland, question 4; Report on Croatia, question 8; Report on Greece, question 4.

[90] Report on New Zealand, reference 22; Report on Ireland, question 4; Report on Greece, question 4.

[91] Report on Japan, chapter H.

[92] Report on the US, reference 72–74.

[93] Compare also Report on New Zealand, reference 72.

[94] Report on New Zealand, reference 80; Report on Australia, question 6.

be to establish the fact that the action was taken "because of" the claimants' age. The types of discrimination a claimant could base a discrimination-suit on are not always statutorily defined. In this respect, the EU may be seen as one example where a statutory definition of the types of discrimination covered is available;[95] this may not be the case in other jurisdictions.

18.2.4.1 Directly Age-related Discrimination

Understandably, the subject of a prohibition of age discrimination would address detrimental distinctions made relating immediately to a person's age. The common pivot of direct discrimination may be age as the immediate reason for different treatment because the treatment relates to the notion of age itself. Indirect discrimination, on the other hand, will appear as a neutral action, not linked to age as such, but in effect favoring or disfavoring one or more age groups compared to others. Details nevertheless vary considerably:

In the US, types of discrimination were developed as judicial theories of proof.[96] The three types frequently debated in recent years rely on disparate treatment, disparate impact, and retaliation.

Once the focus shifts to statutory definitions, the notions of discrimination include the "direct/indirect" differentiation,[97] others, for example, rely on the absence of an intention to discriminate.[98]

Among such types, intentional discrimination certainly is the act disregarded the most and yet, at the same time, extremely complicated to prove. Unless decision makers act on prohibited grounds without even trying to cover it up, it is next to impossible to prove the intention governing any measure or decision. Therefore, several statutes forgo the requirement of intent but rely on the objective fact that a person has been treated less favorably than a suitable comparator on a forbidden ground.[99] In the US, the disparate treatment theory seems to apply a standard, asking the claimant to establish a prima facie case that the questionable act would not have treated him adversely even if he or she were not a member of the protected group. At the same time, the intention to discriminate a protected group seems to be a necessary precondition.[100] In New Zealand, on the other hand, direct discrimination includes conduct that is immediately apparent as being discriminatory,[101] i.e. the act "obviously" contravenes a prohibition. This backs the consequence that no lawful decision may be based on any criteria from the list of forbidden grounds. This, though, may be too extensive: The intention to discriminate may very well be present in a case where a measure explicitly targets one age group. However, it is not necessarily present.

Some states pay special attention to specific employment situations: Canada prohibits "systemic discrimination"[102] which is characterized by the attitudes of decision makers in the labor relationship who accept stereotyped visions of the skills or the "proper role" for a protected group leading to the firmly held conviction that the group is incapable of doing a particular job. So even if decisions discriminate unintentionally as decision makers are convinced their world view is accurate, it is not necessary to retreat to the concept of indirect discrimination here.

18.2.4.2 Indirectly Age-related Discrimination

In addition to simply prohibiting the use of suspect criteria in decision making, most countries under survey[103] prohibit some kind of adverse effect discrimination[104] (indirect discrimination). This type occurs

[95]Directive 2000/78/EC, art. 2; Report on the Netherlands, question 6; Report on Ireland, question 6; Report on Romania, question 6; Report on Portugal, question 6; Rapport de la Belgique, chapter A.III.; Report on Slovenia, question 6; Report on Italy, question 6; Report on Sweden, question 6; Report on Poland, question 6; Report on Czechia, question 6.

[96]Report on the US, reference 232–234; Report on Uruguay, question 6.

[97]Report on Australia, question 6; Report on Argentina, question 6.

[98]Report on Canada, chapter C.I.

[99]Directive 2000/78/EC, art. 2 para. 1 for Europe; Report on Australia, question 6.

[100]Report on the US, reference 233.

[101]Report on New Zealand, reference 73.

[102]Report on Canada, chapter C.I., reference 35.

[103]No such approach is applied in Macao and Japan: Report on Macao, previous to reference 20; Report on Japan, chapter B. II.2.

[104]Report on the US, reference 235 showing that it took some time before such disparate impact theory was acknowledged also under the ADEA. Report on New Zealand, reference 74; Report on Australia, question 6; Report on Ireland, question 6, Report on Portugal, question 6; Report on Canada, chapter C.I., reference 37; Report on New Zealand, reference 77; Report on the Netherlands, question 6; Report on Ireland, question 6.

when a practice is neutral at first sight but nevertheless has a negative impact on a group identified by suspect criteria.[105] In Australia, the concept of indirect discrimination does not focus on a "neutral" criteria but on the fact that an action caused disadvantage through imposing "unreasonable conditions or requirements" that are especially difficult to meet for members of a certain age group.[106] In effect, such preconditions or requirements will also be "neutral on their face." Here, too, the problem is proving the facts. As the concept aims at "neutral" labor practices it will easily cover situations where the disadvantaged group is composed totally homogenous regarding a known criterion: if a certain rule in employment relationships leads to benefits only for workers under the age of 40, or affects negatively only workers over the age of 55, the causal link between age and benefit or age and detriment can be convincingly established. But whenever such an outcome does not 100% refer to a particular age group, the causal link will be hard to prove.

Concepts for this vary considerably among countries. In the US, the Supreme Court referred to the textual differences between anti-discrimination statutes to show that a disparate effects theory in age discrimination is available, but of a much narrower scope than in other statutes.[107] Whenever the defendant can demonstrate that the detrimental effect is based on "reasonable factors other than age" even regularly prohibited acts would be permitted. The employer only has to show a business justification for the decision negatively affecting elderly workers, which would not have to satisfy the strict standards for other forbidden grounds.

Under any legal system, indirect discrimination is closely linked to the justification available to an employer against whom a prima facie case of indirect discrimination has been established. There may be different standards of justification available in direct or indirect discrimination situations,[108] or there may be a single standard for justifying both types.[109] The EU, while in principle following the unified approach, nevertheless pays special attention to the sometimes shaky proof of causation in cases of indirect discrimination: For this concept, an additional possibility to justify adverse effects of an employment measure on protected groups is available which, if satisfied, totally exempts the taken measure from the notion of discrimination. If the practice concerned is justified by a legitimate aim and the means of achieving it are appropriate and necessary,[110] the practice will not be deemed discriminatory even if it only affects negatively employees belonging to a protected group.

18.2.4.3 Harassment

Many countries also include the prohibition of age-based harassment in their anti-discrimination legislation.[111] The gist of the notion of harassment is unwanted conduct with regard to age, with the effect or purpose of creating an intimidating, humiliating or offensive working environment. The harasser may not only be the employer but co-worker, even customer or any other business contact of the employer. If harassing acts are caused not by parties to the labor contract but by third parties, the employer's liability is stated only in some countries.[112] If the discriminatory act is committed by a co-worker or customer it certainly falls outside the contractual employer-employee relationship. But this does not necessarily save the employer from liability for discrimination. Once the employer fails to take reasonable steps to protect the employee, or does not realize preventive measures like information or awareness raising campaigns, or does not properly investigate the improper conduct, it may amount to liability on the part of the employer.[113]

While for practical reasons the concept of "harassment as discrimination" is wide spread[114] (discrimination against elderly workers will often be associated

[105] Report on Canada, chapter C.I, reference 37; Report on New Zealand, reference 77; Report on the Netherlands, question 6; Report on Ireland, question 6.

[106] Report on Australia, question 6.

[107] Report on the US, reference 254.

[108] Report on Canada, chapter C.I., reference 39; Report on the Netherlands, question 6.

[109] Report on Canada, chapter C.I., reference 43.

[110] Directive 2000/78/EC, art. 2 para. 2 (b) (i).

[111] Report on the US, reference 78; Report on New Zealand, reference 49–53; Report on the Netherlands, question 7; Report on Ireland, question 7; Report on Romania, question 7; Report on Norway, question 7; Rapport de la Belgique, chapter A.IV.; Report on Slovenia, question 7; Report on Italy, question 7; Report on Sweden, question 7; Report on Poland, question 7; Report on Croatia, question 7; Report on Greece, question 7.

[112] Report on Ireland, question 7.

[113] Report on New Zealand, reference 38, 39.

[114] Compare: Report on Portugal, question 7; no such approach is applied in Macao: Report on Macao, previous to reference 19.

with a hostile working environment), from a theoretical view point harassment may not regularly be a problem of violating the equality principle but rather of violating human dignity. Whereas such conduct may be seen as a differential treatment adverse to the members of a protected group and therefore as a form of discrimination,[115] in practice the difference of treatment as such is not the point of concern here. Even if an employer would harass all age groups equally, this type of behavior violates any employee's human dignity and is therefore unacceptable.[116]

18.2.4.4 Further Types of Age-related Detrimental Treatment

The EU also includes the **instruction to discriminate** against a member of a protected group in the notion of discrimination.[117] This creates additional protection only in situations where instructions by an employer or supervisor are not attributable to the employer anyway. It is very likely that an instruction to discriminate is of relevance only if the instructed person refuses to obey the order and does in fact not discriminate against the victim but may be sanctioned for disobeying instructions.

Ireland introduced the prohibition of **discrimination by association,**[118] meaning that the person discriminated against is not a member of a protected group but associates with a person who is. A comparable concept, though narrower in its scope of application, was applied also by the European Court of Justice[119] when the court protected a mother against indirect disability discrimination because caring for her disabled child gave reason to termination of her employment contract.

Belgium mentions the case of **publicly announcing** the non-suitability of members of a protected group for certain types of jobs,[120] which relates to direct discrimination independent from the availability of an actual job offer at the time of announcement. This also relates to a decision handed down by the ECJ[121] where it was argued that such a public announcement works as a deterrent to future applicants who may be discouraged from participating in any recruiting process with the company.

The US explicitly includes **retaliation** in the unlawful employer practices.[122] This prohibits adverse action against an employee for protected conduct such as opposition to an unlawful employment practice or the participation in an investigation or proceeding. In the EU, the approach to that type of unlawful action differs slightly. The relevant Directive prohibits "victimization"[123] aiming at protecting employees specifically against adverse treatment because of legal proceedings connected to the equal treatment-principle. The legislator in this situation considers the employee's action as a way of enforcement of the equal treatment standard in employment that has to be protected to guarantee more effective law enforcement.

Moreover, there may be explicit prohibition of "**multiple discrimination,**" established when a worker is treated less favorably for more than one reason.[124] This approach acknowledges that discrimination tends to affect mostly workers in an already weak position who find it difficult to change their place of work. Discrimination of elderly employees for example might hit hardest people whose higher age goes along with disability/illness or being female.

18.2.5 Exemptions or Justifications

18.2.5.1 General or Specific Exemptions from Anti-discrimination Legislation

In employment relationships many advantages or disadvantages have customarily been distributed along age lines (or have at least been associated with length of service as a criterion closely linked to age), yet it is impossible that the prohibition of age discrimination simply outlaws the use of "age" as a criterion for differentiation under all circumstances. One solution to

[115] Report on Canada, chapter C.II., reference 50; Report on the US, reference 78.

[116] Report on Japan, chapter G.

[117] Directive 2000/78/EC art. 2 para. 4; Report on Slovenia, question 6; Report on Poland, question 6; Report on Ireland, question 6.

[118] Report on Ireland, question 6.

[119] European Court of Justice, July 17, 2008, C-303/06 (Coleman).

[120] Rapport de la Belgique, reference 15.

[121] European Court of Justice, July 10, 2008, C-54/07 (Feryn).

[122] Report on the US, reference 234.

[123] Directive 2000/78/EC, art. 11; Report on New Zealand, reference 38, 39.

[124] Report on Italy, question 6.

such a problem narrows the scope of application of the respective statutes, specifically exempting certain branches/professions from the prohibition. For example, in some states regulations explicitly allow the exemption of the armed forces[125] from the prohibition of age discrimination. Other exemptions relate to work performed outside the home territory where the laws of the host state demand a certain age group to perform specific tasks,[126] or to domestic work in a private household.[127] Some statutes exclude "practices of religious institutions,"[128] others exclude civil servants working for national or local governments.[129] Greece allows collective bargaining partners and even employers – seemingly without any restrictions[130] – to create additional exemptions as they think fit.

More general concepts of exemptions use an approach comparable to that of international treaties allowing member states to enact measures which, in a democratic society, are necessary for public security, public order, the prevention of crime, for protection of health or of the rights and freedoms of others.[131] Such general exemptions can be invoked once a measure, although deliberately discriminating against members of a protected group, does this to further a high ranking common good as enlisted. This could be, for example, an early retirement scheme for police, fire fighters or pilots[132] in order to protect the employees from negative effects of physically and mentally demanding work, and third parties from potentially hazardous consequences resulting from any possible age related shortcoming of the concerned employee.

18.2.5.2 Preferential Treatment

Depending on the concept, preferential treatment of a protected group can also be construed as an exemption from prohibiting age discrimination: Measures benefiting one age group over others may be seen as discrimination, so that preferential treatment needs special admission by law. From a different viewpoint, substantive equality needs special treatment for disadvantaged groups[133] to allow for equality of chances. Here, preferential treatment would not discriminate by itself but be a measure for rectifying post discrimination. For such measures a specific legal basis may nevertheless be required, but then different treatment generally needs a legal basis for the sake of clarity. It is considered as a means of providing equality, not as an exemption from prohibiting discrimination.

Examples for such preferential treatment are workplace programs permitting employees facing retirement to reduce work schedules, or phased retirement programs, benefitting older workers over younger ones. Other examples are senior card discounts, youth welfare services or employment programs promoting the employment interests of particular age groups[134] or providing longer notice periods of termination for elder employees.[135]

The scope of exceptions for certain preferences depends on varying preconditions. Mostly an age related act (or omission) must have been done in good faith serving a purpose of assisting or advancing members of a protected group who need such assistance to arrive at an equal level as other citizens. This perspective's pivotal question is whether rules of preference are restricted to people who themselves have been disadvantaged before or whether it is enough to be a member of a protected group generally perceived to need assistance.[136]

[125] Directive 2000/78/EC, art. 3 para. 4 for the European Union; Report on Ireland, question 8; Report on Norway, question 18; Report on Italy, question 4; Report on Sweden, question 4; Report on Poland, question 8; Report on Czechia, question 15; Report on Greece, question 8.

[126] Report on New Zealand, reference 97.

[127] Report on New Zealand, reference 99; Report on Australia, question 9 (construed as a justification).

[128] Report on Australia, question 8.

[129] Report on Japan, chapter B.II.1.; Report on Uruguay, question 9; Report on Sweden, question 8, 4, Report on Czechia, question 15.

[130] Report on Greece, question 8.

[131] Report on Italy, question 4.

[132] Report on the Netherlands, question 17; Report on Norway, question 18.

[133] Report on Canada, chapter B., reference 15; Report on New Zealand, reference 9; Report on Australia, question 9; Report on the Netherlands, question 8; Report on Ireland, question 3; Report on Romania, question 8; Report on Portugal, question 8; Rapport de la Belgique, chapter A.V.3; Report on Slovenia, question 3; Report on Poland, question 8; Report on Croatia, question 3, question 8.

[134] Report on Australia, question 8; Report on Japan, chapter B. II.4.; Report on the Netherlands, question 8; Report on Romania, question 2; Report on Italy, question 15.

[135] Report on Australia, question 9.

[136] Report on New Zealand, reference 12; Report on Australia, question 8.

18.2.5.3 Justification

In principle, distinctions which result in detriments to a protected group are prohibited unless they are justifiable. Reasons for justifying distinctions based on age can either be specifically listed in the relevant statute or be formulated in general terms. Specific justifications normally relate to commonly accepted grounds. One of those grounds could be the recognition of "experience" as a suitable element in the determination of wages.[137] This approach was taken on by the European Court of Justice[138] allowing Member States of the European Union the determination of wages according to experience and expertise of an employee. As this "length of service" criterion is inextricably linked to age its ability to justify distinctions based on age is disputable.[139] However, given that this distinction enjoys a certain level of acceptance among workers and employers alike, legislators and courts tend to accept it nevertheless.

The European Union features more of the mentioned specific justifications of differences of treatment on grounds of age.[140] They relate to special labor market policies targeted at promoting employment for certain groups of workers overrepresented in unemployment statistics (young workers and the elderly[141]). These provisions allow offers with less favorable terms and conditions of employment, including lower rates of pay, to improve labor market participation rates through "cheaper" work. Whether this kind of labor market policy is judged as beneficial to groups facing specific problems of finding a job or as detrimental due to its unfavorable conditions of employment[142] is left to the legislator to decide upon. Australia specifically states a provision allowing the setting of lower "youth wages" for people under 21 years of age,[143] whereas Japan allows for special wage cuts for the elderly[144] when changing from age-based to performance-based wages. Romania allows employers to conclude special fixed term contracts with employees if they reach retirement age in the 5 years following the hiring.[145] Portugal affords tax breaks or temporary exemption from social security contributions for employers recruiting young people seeking a first job or elderly workers above the age of 55.[146]

Some distinctions such as fixing a minimum age or seniority or professional experience for access to employment or specific employment conditions[147] will be included as justifications because employers may wish to maintain them.[148]

Other such grounds are the fixing of a maximum age for recruitment, which may also be justifiable if based on the need for a reasonable period of employment before retirement. The admission to occupational social security schemes or the entitlement to retirement or invalidity benefits may depend on age criteria in actuarial calculations fixing different admission ages for specific categories of workers.[149]

Adding a ground for justification related to third parties' preferences remains highly debatable: While it is partly seen as legitimate to accept one's customers' or co-workers' views regarding the (un-)suitability of specific age groups in some countries, others oppose this view.[150] Such specific age-related grounds for justification tend to have one point in common: They tend to reflect on the highly controversial debate on the suitability of prohibiting different treatment because of age. More often than not this leads to the conclusion that it should be considerably easier[151] to justify age discrimination than differences due to other protected grounds.

Providing for a justification standard that takes peculiarities of age-related aspects into concern may include the application of general standards of justification

[137] Report on Canada, chapter C.IV., reference 83; Report on Japan, chapter C.I.; Report on Portugal, question 16.

[138] European Court of Justice, October 3, 2006, C-17/05 (Cadman).

[139] Report on Japan, chapter C.II.; Report on the Netherlands, question 6.

[140] Directive 2000/78/EC, art. 6.

[141] Report on Portugal, question 3; Report on Italy, question 9.

[142] Report on Portugal, question 15, 16; Report on Italy, question 15.

[143] Report on Australia, question 9.

[144] Report on Japan, chapter C.IV.

[145] Report on Romania, question 3, 8.

[146] Report on Portugal, question 3, 9.

[147] Report on Ireland, question 8; Report on Croatia, question 9; Report on Greece, question 9.

[148] Report on Japan, question 8.

[149] Report on Portugal, question 3; Report on Italy, question 9.

[150] Rapport de la Belgique, reference 21.

[151] Report on the US, reference 255; Report on the Netherlands, question 6; Report on Ireland, question 9; Report on Norway, question 8; Report on Italy, question 9.

which are more lenient or allow for broad policy-considerations when applying a proportionality test. A general concept used in anti-discrimination legislation relies on genuine occupational requirements, which have to be applied in good faith[152] ("bona fide occupational requirements/qualifications").[153] This justification of age discrimination relates to the fact that there may be objectively age-related differences among workers and that it is nevertheless legitimate for an employer to maintain certain requirements that are necessary to carry out the work, even if these requirements disadvantage some age groups. How this standard is applied in practice depends on the respective concept and cannot be compared easily. Statutes regularly put emphasis on the condition that differentiating requirements may only be used if the employer pursues a legitimate objective and they are applied proportionately.

Those wider concepts come closest to defences to a claim of age discrimination. Prima facie cases of unlawful employer practice can be counterbalanced by establishing a defence. In the US, the most prominent defence, that age is a "bona fide occupational qualification"[154] is only available under the disparate treatment theory. Another defence, according to which the suspect differentiation is based on "reasonable factors other than age"[155] is also available under the disparate impact theory. The non-statutory defence acknowledged by the courts, that an employer based his action on "business necessity" is also available only under the disparate impact theory.[156] Another defence allows an employer to discharge or discipline workers "for good cause"[157] even if that results in an age specific outcome. If one reason for such measure is "good cause," others are not considered. Finally, the US statute allows for agreements in which older workers can waive their statutory protection, if such waiver is "knowing" and "voluntary."[158] Such a possibility puts much emphasis on the freedom of the contracting parties but would not be admitted under a human rights-approach to anti-discrimination legislation.

18.2.6 Legal Consequences of Violating the Prohibition of Age Discrimination

The effectiveness of prohibiting discrimination will in many ways depend on the consequences attached to a violation of that provision. Will there be a sanction working as a deterrent to employers, like criminal[159] or administrative[160] sanctions overseen by public prosecution? Or will it be left to the individual victim of such discrimination seeking relief through a court? In case of civil action, are damages calculated in a way that actually gives potential claimants an incentive to sue or is the attainable gain of initiating legal procedure not worth the effort?

The person entitled to bring a cause of action will always be the one personally aggrieved by discriminatory action. As there can be several reasons for such a person to be reluctant to take action, legal consequences of violating anti-discrimination legislation may be avoided. Therefore, several countries follow a wider approach also allowing third parties to complain, e.g. unions/industrial associations[161], a labor inspector[162], an ombudsman or special interest groups.[163] Sweden even provides a prerogative for unions to take action when discrimination occurs in employment-cases; the individual worker is entitled to act only after the

[152] Directive 2000/78/EC, art. 4 para. 1, for the European Union; Report on Ireland, question 8, Report on Romania, question 9, Report on Norway, question 8; Report on Portugal, question 8, Rapport de la Belgique, chapter A.V.1.; Report on Slovenia, question 9, Report on Italy, question 9; Report on Poland, question 8.

[153] Report on Canada, chapter C.I., reference 39; Report on the US, reference 80; Report on New Zealand, reference 100; Report on Australia, question 9; Report on Macao, previous to reference 19; Report on Croatia, question 8.

[154] Report on the US, reference 80.

[155] Report on the US, reference 81.

[156] Report on the US, reference 87.

[157] Report on the US, reference 86.

[158] Report on the US, reference 90–92.

[159] Report on Australia, question 10; Report on Macao, reference 23; Report on Romania, question 10; Rapport de la Belgique, chapter A.VII.2; Report on Slovenia, question 10; Report on Poland, question 10; Report on Croatia, question 12.

[160] Report on Portugal, question 10; Report on Slovenia, question 10; Report on Czechia, question 10; Report on Greece, question 10.

[161] Report on the Netherlands, question 14; Report on Norway, question 10; Report on Portugal, question 10; Report on Sweden, question 10; Report on Autralia, question 10.

[162] Report on Autralia, question 10.

[163] Report on Argentina, question 10; Report on the Netherlands, question 10; Report on Sweden, question 10; Report on Croatia, question 10.

union and the ombudsman decline to do so.[164] New Zealand's Human Rights Act follows the most liberal approach by allowing any natural or legal person to complain of discrimination,[165] once they have an interest greater than the general public's.

If the alleged violation has been established, legal consequences vary: Frequently the authority responsible for enforcement of the relevant legal statute will try to settle, mediate or conciliate a charge of age discrimination whenever possible.[166] If this attempt remains unsuccessful and discrimination has been established in court, statutory remedies are available that may include: Declaring a discriminatory act to be null and void;[167] giving an injunction to repeat such act; providing for damages[168] (in the US: neither compensatory nor punitive damages)[169], reinstatement,[170] promotion, back pay (compensating lost pay from the time of the alleged violation until the violation is determined) and front pay (compensating lost pay from the determination of a violation until the claimant finds comparable employment), compensation for injury to feelings and humiliation,[171] and other remedies aiming at returning claimants to the condition in which they would have been but for the age discrimination.[172]

Whether the court has the power to order a defendant undertaking to hire an unsuccessful applicant or not varies considerably. This legal consequence may either be seen as giving the claimant what he would have been entitled to were it not for his age, or as an infringement of the freedom of contracts-principle.[173] Comparable doubts may arise when dealing with discriminatory termination of a contract: Will the consequences of establishing such breach of law be that the employment relationship is continued[174] or will the employee concerned only be given some indemnification for loss of employment?

Before a court or tribunal, court costs, attorneys' fees and expert witness' fees can be awarded.[175] The deciding body might also declare that the defendant has committed an infringement of anti-discrimination legislation and restrain them from continuing or repeating such breach.[176]

If provisions of a statute are discriminatory, such clauses may also be declared void, though regularly only if procedure before a superior or Constitutional Court is followed.[177] If discriminatory regulations are part of a collective agreement, EU Directives explicitly render them not binding in nature. I.e. an employer would not be obliged to implement a discriminatory regulation in a collective agreement otherwise binding him. On the other hand, the risk of misjudging the existence of such an exemption will probably prevent him from applying the measure in question.

18.2.7 Burden of Proof in Discrimination Cases

The burden of proof is decisive for the effectiveness of enforcing anti-discrimination provisions through individual claims. Whether potential claimants can hope for winning their case in court will influence their willingness to take on such procedure. What is necessary to win the case is hugely important to make individual court cases an enforcement mechanism of choice.

In countries under survey it is accepted that in discrimination suits the burden of proof lies primarily

[164] Report on Sweden, question 10.

[165] Report on New Zealand, reference 121.

[166] Report on New Zealand, following reference 121; Report Australia, question 10; Report on the Netherlands, question 12, 13.

[167] Report on the Netherlands, question 10; Report on Portugal, question 10; Rapport de la Belgique, chapter A.VII.1.a); Report on Slovenia, question 10 (= termination of the contract); Report on Italy, question 10.

[168] Rapport de la Belgique, chapter A.VII.1.a); Report on Poland, question 10; Report on Croatia, question 10.

[169] Report on the US, reference 99.

[170] Rapport de la Belgique, chapter A.VII.1.a); Report on Slovenia, question 10; Report on Italy, question 10; Report on Uruguay, question 10; Report on Portugal, question 10.

[171] Report on Uruguay, question 10; Report on Portugal, question 10.

[172] Report on Romania, question 10, Report on Norway, question 10.

[173] Report on Japan, chapter B.III.2.a); Report on the Netherlands, question 15; Rapport de la Belgique, chapter B.I.

[174] Report on the Netherlands, question 12; Report on Ireland, question 10; Report on Italy, question 10; Report on Poland, question 10; Report on Greece, question 17.

[175] Report on Argentina, question 10.

[176] Report on Uruguay, question 10; Report on Portugal, question 10.

[177] Report on Poland, question 10.

with the plaintiff.[178] But many legal systems agree that this burden on the plaintiff is to be facilitated. In principle, claimants have to establish a prima facie case of discrimination, by establishing that the alleged (discriminatory) actions have really occurred and that they at least indicate the existence of a discrimination "because of" a suspect criterion. But at some stage the burden of proof shifts to the defendant to justify the discriminatory practice, rule or standard. Once the elements defining such indications have been established, the defendant's answer needs to be a justification of or a defence against the claimant's case of discrimination. If the defendant fails to prove such elements, age discrimination is established. The shifting of the burden of proof is not available in cases before a criminal court.[179] What exactly the parties have to prove varies in detail, depending on the relevant underlying concept of discrimination.

If discriminatory intent or purpose is not expressly shown by the decision maker, the claimant, as a starting point, has to present serious indicators allowing for the conclusion that a detrimental differentiation based on age has occurred.[180] Afterwards it is up to the defendant to prove that no discrimination exists.

Canadian courts show a case of slowly developing a standard of proof in practice.[181] Originally in cases of intentional discrimination the defendant had to prove a subjective element (the questionable standard was imposed in good faith and not designed to undermine the legislative objectives) and an objective element (the standard is necessary to the efficient performance of the work and does not place an unreasonable burden on the workers concerned), whereas in adverse effects discrimination, the subjective element was not required. Instead the defendant had to establish that there is a rational connection between the job and the questionable standard, and that the defendant cannot further accommodate the claimant without incurring undue hardship.[182]

As the two standards obviously place rather different burdens on the defendant, problems arise as soon as the demarcation line between the two concepts of discrimination is not obvious. Thus, if tribunals and courts characterize the relevant type of discrimination differently, the outcome will vary accordingly. As a very practical solution, the Canadian Courts opted to impose a unified standard for the burden of proof applicable to all forms of discrimination:[183] The defendant employer has to prove on the balance of probabilities standard that the questionable measure was adopted for a purpose rationally connected to job performance, that the defendant imposed such measure in good faith, believed that it was necessary to fulfill that job-related purpose, and that the standard was necessary to accomplish that job-related purpose. Therewith the elements of proof concerning both types of discrimination have been combined so that the burden on the defendant no longer depends on how the tribunal characterizes the discrimination. However, proving the necessity of the questionable standard is more demanding for all types of discrimination and this has become the faltering point for defendants. In order to meet that requirement it must be demonstrated that it is impossible to accommodate employees of the protected group without imposing undue hardship to employers. This seems to be a rather tough requirement even though the courts emphasize that the employer does not need to demonstrate that it was literally "impossible" to integrate employees not meeting the standard.[184]

As a rule, a defence against a prima facie case of discrimination in many countries will only be successful once the fairness, reasonableness and job-relatedness of a questionable standard is shown and the court or tribunal is satisfied that the defendants' standard is not asking more than what is necessary to fulfill the contract. In many systems, this amounts to a proportionality test: If there is a less discriminatory alternative available, not even an objectively job-related standard may be imposed (due to its discriminatory consequences).

[178] Report on New Zealand, reference 128, 129; Report on Australia, question 11; Report on Macao, reference 25; Report on Japan, chapter B.III.2.a).; Report on Argentina, question 11; Report on Uruguay, question 11; Report on Venezuela, question 11; Report on Romania, question 11; Report on Norway, question 11; Report on Portugal, question 11; Report on Sweden, question 11.

[179] Rapport de la Belgique, chapter A.VIII.1.

[180] Report on Argentina, question 11; Report on Ireland, question 11; Report on Italy, question 11.

[181] Report on Canada, reference 39.

[182] Report on Canada, reference 40.

[183] Report on Canada, reference 42.

[184] Report on Canada, reference 45.

In the US on the other hand, the burden of proof in discrimination cases is far from representing a unified system. Under the disparate treatment standard,[185] the claimant must establish a prima facie case of discrimination. Then the burden of persuasion shifts to the defendant who has to articulate legitimate reasons for the contested action, and finally the claimant has to prove discrimination by showing that the reason offered by the defendant is unbelievable. Ultimately, the burden of proof therefore remains with the claimant. Moreover, the Supreme Court introduced another proof scheme[186] according to which the claimant must establish an unlawful employment practice through direct evidence that the forbidden grounds was at least one motivating factor for the employer's action even though other factors might also have been relevant. This standard was lately rejected for age discrimination cases by the Supreme Court,[187] so that the claimant has to prove by a preponderance of the evidence that age was the "but-for" cause of the employer's action. Apart from clearly being a rather harsh proof scheme, this very detailed approach is so distinct that it is not comparable to the more general, unified system referred to above.

Other jurisdictions are still more reluctant to ease the burden of proof in discrimination cases. In New Zealand, the concept of sharing the burden of proof between the complaining and the defending party to anti-discrimination cases has not been widely elaborated. A successful claim therefore more or less depends on establishing a link between a claim of discrimination and a claim of unjustified dismissal or other unjustified disadvantages in the labor relationship.[188] Only under such preconditions will the burden of justifying such an action fall largely on the employer. In Australia, a comparable effect will result from applying different concepts in the Age Discrimination Act and the relevant labor legislation: While the discrimination legislation in principle lays the burden of proof on the claimant, with some alleviations especially for indirect discrimination, labor statutes ask the employer to prove that adverse acts or cases were not taken for prohibited reasons, or a dismissal was not based on such grounds.[189] Macao in its legal system does not acknowledge any shift of the burden of proof at all,[190] but instead the Labor Inspection Bureau and Public Prosecutors may be called upon to find out the facts of case.[191]

18.2.8 Enforcing Mechanisms

Apart from individual claims in court or a tribunal[192] there are several alternative enforcement measures for anti-discrimination legislation. Under certain cultural preconditions, alternative means may even become the only accepted form of rights enforcement: Macao reports not a single case of age discrimination before courts or any other competent state bodies.[193] Governments mostly set up **agencies** with varying competencies. Some provide best-practice examples for undertakings how to avoid discrimination, and/or legal advice for persons believing they had been discriminated against. Others work as mediation/conciliation services furthering quicker and cheaper solutions to a conflict than a court could. Others may take over individual claims and bring them to court, be it in the claimant's name or at least with the claimant's consent or on the agency's own behalf.

Enforcement can also be achieved through **NGOs** working for the elderly[194] or through unions protecting their member's rights[195] or benefits from collective agreements. Normally the NGO can only act on behalf of an employee once they have been delegated by her or him.

18.2.8.1 Statutory Agencies

The involvement of statutory agencies in the enforcement procedure is for the benefit of the implementation and administration of the relevant anti-discrimination legislation. To promote public confidence in impartiality

---

[185] Report on the US, reference 261.

[186] Report on the US, reference 263.

[187] Report on the US, reference 274.

[188] Report on New Zealand, reference 132.

[189] Report on Australia, question 11.

[190] Report on Macao, reference 26.

[191] Report on Macao, reference 26, 27.

[192] Report on Ireland, question 12 and 20; Report on Italy, question 12.

[193] Report on Macao, final page.

[194] Report on Romania, question 14; Report on Poland, question 14; Report on Croatia, question 14; Report on Greece, question 14.

[195] Report on Sweden, question 14; Report on Czechia, question 14.

in most countries statutory agencies have to be independent of government influence:[196] If agencies conduct complaint procedures, the state or state agencies as employers participate in the process as respondents. On the other hand, once countries exempt their public administration employees totally from being covered from anti-discrimination legislation, a conflict of interest for an agency will not be apparent even if such agency is not independent from State authorities.[197] Statutory agencies may have additional functions: Most of them fulfill educational or preventive purposes through programs designed to prevent breaches of legislation and issuing interpretative guidelines for the relevant law.[198] Agencies can also investigate and mediate complaints of individuals or groups claiming to be aggrieved by a violation of anti-discrimination legislation. In the US, it is possible for the agency to file a charge on behalf of a person in order to protect the aggrieved person's identity.[199] Sometimes the agency can initiate a complaint on its own,[200] although often public interest groups/NGOs are not given standing to complain. There may even be involvement of third parties, but generally the agency has to seek consent of the individual affected by the alleged misconduct.

Any person claiming to be aggrieved has to show a written complaint to an agency serving compliance purposes to launch an investigation.[201] If this results in a prima facie finding of discrimination, the next step is to try to reach settlement through mediation[202] which, if not successful, will then be followed by a formal hearing by a board or tribunal.[203] Sometimes, the agency itself acts as a kind of tribunal by giving a reasoned opinion on the merits of the case.[204] Unsuccessful conciliation attempts will allow the aggrieved person to sue if an age discrimination law suit can be filed with (civil or labor) courts. If, on the other hand, a successful mediation, conciliation or settlement is reached the parties are blocked from filing suit unless the terms of the agreement are not honored.

The procedure with an agency, as long as no expenses are incurred by the complainant,[205] can be attractive to both parties as usually it is far quicker than a court procedure. On the other hand, countries may as well provide for a special procedure in discrimination court-cases aiming at simple and quick procedures and a far reaching provisional judgement system instead.[206] The finding of a tribunal would also be open for judicial review or some other form of appeal,[207] so that even a "quick" solution may take some time until completion.

Some countries establish a civil cause of action for breach of anti-discrimination legislation in addition to agency proceedings. If both paths exist, it is not always the claimant's choice whether to file a lawsuit in a court or a complaint with the agency. In the US, age discrimination cases must be filed with the agency first and only 60 days later the discriminated person can file suit.[208] This guarantees the agency exclusive competence for 2 months, and only if the claimant is not satisfied with the process taken on during that time can he consider a lawsuit. In case the agency decides to close the files, the aggrieved person still has the right to sue for 90 days after receiving notice from the agency. Under other systems, statutes will leave the choice to the claimant whether to take their case to either the agency or to the relevant court.[209] The decision will then depend on the relief sought as the agency will not be vested with providing all the remedies that can be awarded by a court.[210]

---

[196] Report on New Zealand following reference 140; Report on the Netherlands, question 12; Report on Ireland, question 13; Report on Norway, question 13.

[197] Report on Macao, previous to reference 29; Report on Japan, chapter E.III.3.a).

[198] Report on Canada, chapter C.III.; Report on Australia, question 13; Report on Argentina, question 13; Report on Ireland, question 13; Report on Romania, question 13; Rapport de la Belgique, chapter A.IX.; Report on Slovenia, question 13; Report on Sweden, question 13 ("Equality Ombudsman"); Report on Croatia, question 13.

[199] Report on the US, reference 95.

[200] Report on Canada, reference 70; Report on the Netherlands, question 13; Report on Sweden, question 13.

[201] Report on the US, reference 97.

[202] Report on the US, reference 97.

[203] Report on Canada, reference 73.

[204] Report on the Netherlands, question 13; Report on Romania, question 10; Report on Norway, question 12.

[205] Report on the Netherlands, question 12; Report on Norway, question 12; Report on Slovenia, question 13.

[206] Report on Italy, question 12.

[207] Report on Canada, chapter C.III.; Report on Norway, question 12.

[208] Comparable: Report on Australia, question 13.

[209] Report on Norway, question 12.

[210] Report on Norway, question 12.

18.2.8.2 Arbitration

Special employment related institutions such as arbitrators may also be competent to hear discrimination complaints in their field.[211] In some countries the availability of such procedures may depend on a union being present at the workplace. Arbitration is attractive to employees if the procedures are simple and quick and the unions involved in the process are effective enough to protect their members' interests. If such prerequisites are not granted, compulsory arbitration will bar employees from their statutory rights to file charges with the agency and/or a competent court.[212] Without union involvement that is, the statutory standard of protection must not be replaced by an agreement to arbitrate workplace disputes through an informal procedure, in case an individual employee signs an arbitration agreement.[213]

18.2.8.3 Supervision

Implementing supervision on collective agreements[214] or other collective instruments whether or not they contain discriminatory elements is a distinct approach followed by some states. The labor administration responsible for conducting a substantial analysis of the content of collective instruments refers them to court to nullify the provisions that are discriminatory. While such an approach highlights the importance of non-discrimination provisions it could nevertheless be considered as interfering with the autonomy of collective bargaining.

18.2.9 Involvement of Collective Bargaining Partners

The role of collective bargaining is of special significance when safeguarding against age discrimination. Can collective agreements provide for (additional) protection? Are they able to deviate from existing standards of protection, for example to secure jobs?

It is undisputed that collective bargaining in principle is legally suitable to promote additional measures of protection for the elderly. Whether or not collective agreements in fact contain such clauses depends on the union's bargaining power in a country and/or the sense of urgency in reacting to problems of the demographic shift on both sides of industry. In Germany, for example, a collective agreement for the chemical industry[215] from 2008 requires every business in that branch to conduct a demographic analysis of their respective workforce. Depending on the outcome of the survey, businesses are obliged to develop measures for restructuring and redeveloping workplaces and organizational structures[216] to accommodate elderly workers, including personnel re-training measures.

If collective bargaining indeed succeeds in providing additional protection against age discrimination, there will be no reason for legal concern. If, on the other hand, collective bargaining is used for furthering flexibility through deviation from statutory norms, problems of competency may very well arise. Where anti-discrimination law has the status of (quasi-) constitutional legislation it cannot be altered, amended, or repealed unless the legislator expressively states otherwise.[217] Especially the development of additional exemptions from protective standards are legislative prerogatives in most countries not open to employers, social partners, or other players in the field.[218]

A different approach allows unions to conclude bargaining agreements which subjects all age discrimination claims exclusively to arbitration, thereby barring all procedures from the competent agency or courts and the remedies available in such procedure.[219] Whether unions in principle are competent to bargain for arbitration on behalf of their members is only the starting point of discussion here. Later the decision has to be taken whether the state allows collective agreements to deviate from all kinds of statutes or if it exempts particular protected rights. If emphasis is given to the human rights-aspect of anti-discrimination legislation, collective bargaining rights of unions will be balanced against protection of individual rights.

---

[211] Report on Canada, reference 77.

[212] Report on the US, reference 117.

[213] Report on the US, reference 299.

[214] Report on Portugal, question 13.

[215] For a brief description of that collective agreement see the chemical union's journal: IGBCE kompakt (Februar 2009), p. 9–11.

[216] Compare: ILO Recommendation No. 162 concerning older employees (1964).

[217] Report on Canada, reference 32.

[218] Report on Canada, chapter C.II.

[219] Report on the US, reference 109.

This may be especially problematic in situations, where statutory law does not specifically regulate the consequences for the labor relationship when retirement age is reached.[220] If collective agreements provide for an automatic termination of a contract when the worker reaches retirement age and therefore would be entitled to claim pension statutorily, it may also add to employers' abilities to change conditions of employment: bargaining partners could be allowed to deviate from statutory provisions giving the employer a wider latitude, e.g. in setting selection criteria for deciding who they would like to keep as employees beyond the low contractual retirement age.[221]

Unions can be involved in the enforcement process filing anti-discrimination suits on behalf of their members[222] including class actions.[223] This may help to protect the aggrieved individual from retaliation by providing anonymity or by simply providing assistance,[224] depending on the statute. Another way of making use of unions' or other special interest groups' specific knowledge in this domain is giving them the right to complain on their own behalf once they take an interest greater than the general public's. Under the system of Macao, that allows no unions,[225] representatives of workers' associations only may take part in a complaint alongside the claimant in actions regarding collective interests.[226] Under certain circumstances the involvement of unions in the process of preventing age discrimination will not only depend on the legal system allowing this. Sometimes, unions simply see no urgent necessity to act in this field.[227] But whenever age discrimination is a point of major concern for labor organizations, the process of termination of employment and its consequences especially for elderly workers will call for attention. So unions (or works councils if provided for) will become engaged in collective redundancy or company restructuring procedures promoting special conditions for older workers.[228]

18.2.10 Effects on the Labor Relationship

As shown in the introductory remarks, anti-discrimination legislation is widely criticized by economists and representatives of employers for its presumed hazardous consequences on the labor market. The consequences for an effective recruitment process, for equitable working conditions, for the possibility of termination of employment with workers no longer meeting the demands, and for a regular retirement process are considered to be especially adverse. In this chapter typical situations are shown which gave rise to concern with regard to the prohibition of age discrimination.

18.2.10.1 The Recruitment Process

As discrimination in the **personnel selection** process is not only widespread but also has especially detrimental consequences to a victim's rights, countries tend to be strict on that point. The formulation of employment offers or advertisement has to be strictly neutral[229] without indication of any preference or limitation based on age, unless the situation is covered by a statutory exemption or justification. If there is an exception,[230] other protective measures are applied trying to compensate for it: An employer's stated preference can constitute evidence for discriminatory intent. Where preference statements are not admitted, such a prohibition is not only aimed at employers but also employment agencies[231] or entities that may be involved in the selection process (such as labor organizations). Exceptions to such a rule are rare: The Netherlands report on a special agency, actively enforcing the labor market participation of unemployed people by acting as intermediaries between employers and job seekers.

[220] Report on Italy, question 17.

[221] Report on Japan, Chapter E.II.

[222] Report on Australia, question 14; Report on the Netherlands, question 14; Report on Norway, question 14; Rapport de la Belgique, chapter A.VII.1.b).

[223] Report on Norway, question 14; Report on Italy, question 14.

[224] Report on Venezuela, question 14; Report on Portugal, question 10.

[225] Report on Macao, previous to reference 34.

[226] Report on Macao, reference 34.

[227] Report on Uruguay, question 14.

[228] Report on the Netherlands, question 14; Report on Sweden, question 3.

[229] Report on the US, reference 79; Report on New Zealand, reference 151, 152; Report on Australia, question 15; Report on Japan, chapter B.II.3.; Report on Ireland, question 15; Report on Portugal, question 15, Rapport de la Belgique, chapter B.I.; Report on Poland, question 15.

[230] Report on Sweden, question 15.

[231] Report on Australia, question 15; Report on Japan, chapter B.II.3.

Such an agency is allowed to set age limits in job advertisements to give (temporarily) priority to certain age groups.[232]

The request for **application files** as well as guidelines for selection and job interviews have to be conducted in a manner avoiding all indicators for discriminatory intent.[233] This may result in forbidding questions regarding an applicant's age or date of birth or even a picture. There may also be considerations on the transparency of the selection process, establishing selection criteria and rules for interviews.[234]

In order to further everyone's equal access to any opportunity of employment, statutes can make sure that vacancies have to be publicly advertised.[235] Unsuccessful applicants must be notified of the fact that they were not selected soon after the contract of employment with the selected worker has been concluded. Sometimes, such applicants can demand information on the qualifications of the person selected.[236]

18.2.10.2 The Working Conditions

Working conditions tend to be less influenced by statutes prohibiting age discrimination. The use of age or age related criteria such as length of service[237] is widely accepted here and therefore the likelihood of additional exemptions, justification grounds or statutory defences under the different legal concepts is rather high.

In principle, the composition of **remuneration** depending directly on age is no longer acceptable in most countries[238] with the notable exception of special youth wages,[239] or special rates for first entry jobs aiming at stabilizing young peoples' labor participation rate. Regular wage increases according to age, i.e. wages proceeding through age, is met with suspicion within merits-based wage systems.[240] But this does not mean that age cannot be a factor for wage determination, especially because length of service as a closely age-related criterion is still widely used. Seniority related bonuses are especially common.[241]

Whether there are other types of **preferences** especially for older workers depends on the statutory concept of discrimination. Once "positive action" compensating for specific difficulties of a protected group is accepted, items as additional days of vacation for the elderly,[242] the possibility to demand shorter working hours[243] or protection of contractual remuneration despite age-related job transfer can be included. If such positive action is regarded discriminatory, privileges for older workers cannot be found.[244] There may also be restrictions on the competence of the employer to order older employees to work overtime.[245] This does not prevent them from working overtime but only once they have consented. Special preferences for young workers,[246] on the other hand, are commonly limited to minors protected by statutes restricting working time, overtime work, or night shifts, or adding several days of paid leave for such age groups.

18.2.10.3 Termination of Employment

As the ending of an employment relationship is rather prone to age-based decision making, a narrow approach in this respect would be expected. But here countries do not provide a homogenous trend.

Whereas special **dismissal protection** with regard to old age or length of service is acceptable for many

[232] Report on the Netherlands, question 15.

[233] Report on Ireland, question 15; Report on Slovenia, question 15.

[234] Report on Ireland, question 15.

[235] Report on Slovenia, question 15.

[236] Report on Sweden, question 15.

[237] Report on Uruguay, question 16; Report on Venezuela, question 16; Report on the Netherlands, question 16; Report on Ireland, question 16; Report on Portugal, question 16; Rapport de la Belgique, chapter B.II.; Report on Poland, question 16; Report on Czechia, question 16; Report on Greece, question 16.

[238] Report on New Zealand, following reference 153; Report on Australia, question 16.

[239] Report on New Zealand, reference 153; Report on Australia, question 16.

[240] For difficulties in this respect: Report on Japan, chapter C.I.; Report on Italy, question 16.

[241] Report on Japan, chapter C.I.; Report on Argentina, question 16; Report on Uruguay, question 16; Report on Ireland, question 8; Report on Norway, question 16; Report on Portugal, question 16; Report on Slovenia, question 16; Report on Italy, question 16; Report on Poland, question 16.

[242] Report on Japan, chapter C.III.; Report on Uruguay, question 16; Report on Venezuela, question 16; Report on Romania, question 16 (public service only); Report on Norway, question 3; Report on Portugal, question 16 (public service); Report on Slovenia, question 16; Report on Poland, question 16.

[243] Report on Portugal, question 16 (concept of pre-retirement).

[244] Report on New Zealand, reference 155.

[245] Report on Slovenia, question 16.

[246] Report on Romania, question 16; Report on Slovenia, question 16.

countries,[247] this does not necessarily amount to a huge impact on employers' selection processes: A loss of capability would still count as a valid reason for terminating a contract, even if age-dependent.[248]

In several countries, dismissing elderly workers will not be more complicated but more expensive than in the case of dismissal of their younger counterparts.[249] Some countries provide for a statutory notice period increasing with age,[250] thus enabling elderly workers to maintain their employment relationship for longer periods. This protection would even hold when applying a "last-in-first-out" principle when selecting workers for dismissal due to economic reasons.[251] But such safeguard is often counterbalanced by some sort of protection of the employer's interest in maintaining younger employees as well.[252]

Sweden for example principally provides for a statute according to which redundancy lists have to be drawn up which have to give preference to age and length of service.[253] At the same time collective bargaining is allowed to derogate from statutory requirements and draw up different requirements[254] which may not even have to be disclosed to employees. In some countries laying off employees to avoid vesting of pension benefits or to save on their (higher) levels of compensation is permitted,[255] whereas dismissing older workers in preference for hiring younger ones is not.[256] Employers may offer incentives to induce employees to leave before they reach retirement age, but selection criteria need to avoid discrimination.

Voluntary **early retirement** schemes can be supported by state policy, providing for favorable tax breaks or supported income for an employee leaving early.[257] While such policy has been popular among countries earlier on,[258] by now most states' policies aim at increasing the labor market participation rate of older workers. Tools for reaching such goals include[259] reducing pension rates for early retirement, increasing the pensionable age for becoming eligible to public pensions[260] or actively supporting the participation of elderly workers through special programs. But early retirement incentives may also be provided directly by undertakings,[261] which will be more likely once older workers earn age-related (higher) wages. Once governments have decided to prevent early retirement they may introduce additional taxes for employers trying to induce workers to retire.[262]

Another way of terminating an employment relationship with elderly workers would be the conclusions of **fixed-term contracts** with the concerned age group.[263] Specific regulation on fix term contracts for elderly employees would only be of interest in a legal system which principally requires a legitimate ground to implement a fixed-term contract. Once legislatures have restrictions in place they may decide to allow for exemptions in case the employee concerned is counted among the elderly.

The single most disputed question in the context of terminating employment relationships concerns the **mandatory retirement** of an employee. While such a statutory regulation clearly amounts to a prohibited discrimination in some states, open only to very narrow exceptions,[264] many other countries still allow it.[265]

[247] Report on Australia, question 17; Report on Slovenia, question 17; Report on Portugal, question 2.

[248] Report on New Zealand, reference 156; Report on Australia, question 17; Report on Uruguay, question 17; Report on Ireland, question 17; Report on Norway, question 17; Report on Sweden, question 17; Report on Poland, question 17.

[249] Report on Uruguay, question 17; Report on Venezuela, question 16; Report on the Netherlands, question 17; Report on Portugal, question 17.

[250] Report on the Netherlands, question 17; Report on Portugal, question 17; Rapport de la Belgique, chapter B.II.; Report on Slovenia, question 17; Report on Poland, question 17; Report on Norway, question 17; Report on Czechia, question 17.

[251] Report on Norway, question 17; Report on Czechia, question 17.

[252] Report on the Netherlands, question 17.

[253] Report on Sweden, question 3.

[254] Report on Sweden, question 17.

[255] Report on the US, reference 298; Report on Japan, chapter D.I.2.

[256] Report on Australia, question 3.

[257] Report on Australia, question 19; Report on Venezuela, question 3; Report on Norway, question 19, 18; Report on Poland, question 19.

[258] Report on Sweden, question 19; Report on Australia, question 20.

[259] Report on Australia, question 20.

[260] Report on Japan, chapter E.I.

[261] Report on Japan, chapter F; Report on Argentina, question 19; Report on Uruguay, question 19.

[262] Report on the Netherlands, question 17; Report on Poland, question 20.

[263] Report on Portugal, question 17, question 9; Report on Sweden, question 17.

[264] Report on the US, reference 89; Report on New Zealand, reference 162, 163; Report on Australia, question 18.

[265] Report on Japan, chapter E; Report on Argentina, question 17, 18; Report on the Netherlands, question 17; Report on Ireland, question 18; Rapport de la Belgique, chapter B.IV.; Report on Croatia, question 17, 18.

Statutes and courts[266] interpreting those exceptions struggle to define preconditions that must be met for mandatory retirement to be lawfully imposed. If there is no statutory regulation, the question arises whether other rules may set a mandatory retirement age. If collective agreements implement a policy, its effectiveness depends on who will be bound by the agreement.

If individual labor contracts implement it,[267] consequences depend on the way such rules are construed: Will such a clause re-define the contract as a fixed-term contract ceasing to exist once the employee reaches the age agreed upon? Or will the employer nevertheless have to take action to terminate the contract,[268] in which case the employee could at least seek judicial control? Another way to spell out the said outcome would be to allow reaching pensionable age as one objective justification for dismissal,[269] so that an employer faces no problems or additional costs when terminating the contract of an employee entitled to a state pension.[270]

18.3 Conclusion

When individuals or groups are treated differently on grounds of age it is often based on generalized assumptions or on the fact that competing age groups presume they have to gain advantage from stereotyping or excluding other groups. Whenever individuals are subject to detrimental treatment as a result of demeaning stereotypes, it results in denying them equality of treatment and personal respect. Thereby, the groups concerned are prevented from fully participating in the labor market. Then again, certain age-based distinctions may be designed to protect particular age groups, especially under-aged workers, or people working under especially dangerous or hazardous working conditions.

The use of age as a representative for other characteristics may serve economic objective but nevertheless is questionable from a human rights-based point of view. As discussed above in the introduction, economic efficiency does not always demand the use of such representatives, as the denial of employment opportunities and rights to older and younger age groups may deliver inept results not only in cases where individual assessment of applicants/workers is available at low costs. The same holds true in situations where setting disincentives to excluded groups due to negative stereotypes results in producing the negative attitudes they are meant to combat. So states will have to give all due consideration on how to proceed regarding prevention and prohibition of discrimination. Simply putting a general prohibition of all age-based distinctions in place is neither sufficient nor appropriate. Likewise the continuous use of age-related criteria, habitually used to date, cannot be allowed.

Thought has to be given to what constitutes direct and indirect discrimination, whether appropriate comparators need to be identified for this purpose, and what kind of practices will allow for a presumption of existence of age bias in a decision. As the country reports indicate, not only do details vary considerably, but also fundamental approaches. The necessary implementation measures are not converging either, nor are the decisions on union involvement or the participation of NGOs or statutory agencies.

Counting by the numbers, the country survey produced the following results:

- Age discrimination in most countries is prohibited by statute. Several states additionally provide for protective clauses in their constitution or specific international instruments combating discrimination. However, the source of protection provided did not have visible influence on the quantity or quality of the protection.
- Protected age groups are defined differently:
  Some statutes define their scope of application by referring to the lower and upper age of persons protected, others simply prohibit any discrimination based on "age" without specification. Underaged workers will normally be given special protection aiming at protecting minors during years of compulsory education and apprenticeship under specific statutes. Whether or not anti-discrimination legislation is applicable additionally will nevertheless have an impact on the standard of justification of differential treatment, especially in the context of minimum wages.

As for elderly workers approaching retirement, the main topic certainly is the existence of a mandatory retirement age, set by law, collective agreement or an employer's decision. While some states judge

[266] Report on Poland, question 17.

[267] Report on Ireland, question 18; Report on Norway, question 17.

[268] Report on Uruguay, question 18.

[269] Report on the Netherlands, question 18.

[270] Report on the Netherlands, question 18.

the existence of an automatic termination of employment simply by reaching a predetermined age as a discriminatory practice, many others still allow it. Whether such generosity would apply across the board as a general exemption from the equal treatment-provision or would have to be justified depending on the circumstances of the segment of the labor market concerned, is not met with unanimity.

- Protected contractual relationships are commonly contracts of employment, including the pre-contractual situation of application. Some states broaden such concept by providing protection also to (some or all kinds of) independent contractors, or employee-like self employed workers. Others include training and education, membership in professional organizations or specific civil law obligations. Private occupational pension schemes may also be included, whereas Public Social Security pensions are not.
- In most cases, forbidden discrimination includes a directly and an indirectly age related differentiation. Most countries additionally prohibit harassment, sometimes only by implication or by providing for protection against infringement of dignity.
- Exemptions from the prohibition of age discrimination are widespread. The means of achieving this objective are obviously dependent on the doctrine of the relevant statutes: Some states define a narrow scope of application of the prohibited clause itself, others provide for far reaching exemptions, others implement generous tools of justification. Common ground is established by focusing on protection for the young ("first job") or the elderly workers (approaching retirement). Especially people working with dangerous, physically demanding or safety-related professions like members of the army, fire fighters, police and pilots are often excluded under broad terms. Whether public service should be exempted as such is not unanimously agreed, though.

Countries tend to explicitly allow "positive measures" aiming at special advantages for previously disadvantaged groups, even though preconditions can vary strongly. In some cases, specific forms of advantageous differentiations are admitted; in other cases, especially differences according to the relevant person's age are easier justifiable than in case of other personal characteristics. Justification requirements for this purpose tend to be either interpreted broadly or are applied more leniently than would be the case for other grounds for discrimination.

- Enforcing mechanisms come in all possible forms: Individual enforcement in court is mostly available, even though in some countries only if a competent union or (in others) a competent statutory agency has not taken up a complaint. Some countries provide for conciliation/adjudication measures first, others make them mandatory. Some states allow class actions, most others do not. Some allow unions to step in independently, protecting the anonymity of members who so wish, most have the explicit consent of the worker concerned as a precondition. Some allow the participation of NGOs, many are rather reluctant in this regard. Some countries provide enforcement through labor inspectorates or even public attorneys/prosecutors.
- If a discrimination claim is brought to court, the overwhelming majority of the examined countries agrees that some alleviation to the "normal" burden of proof standard applies. Details vary considerably, taking into account the rather complex differences in litigation procedures. Common ground seems to be that claimants to an anti-discrimination action need to establish some facts for a prima facie case of detrimental acts showing that they were disadvantaged "because of" their age, before the burden shifts to the employer.
- The legal consequences of an established violation of anti-discrimination provisions include almost anything one can imagine: Criminal sanctions, administrative fees, civil law instruments of remedy. Most countries provide some form of damages, compensation for humiliation or injury to feelings and the declaration that the discriminatory act be void. Some countries provide for reinstatement or promotion whereas others explicitly protect the employers' freedom of contract in selecting personnel. It is heavily disputed whether damages should include lost pay for a future period until claimants find a comparable job. Opinions are also divided as to whether court costs, attorney's or expert witness' fees may be awarded.

The broad variety of solutions provided for can be easily seen in the National Reports on questions 15–18 regarding the consequences of anti-discrimination legislation for the application/employee selection phase, the terms and conditions of employment, the termination of employment contracts and the retirement phase. It does not come as a surprise that undeniably every phase of an employment contract is influenced by the prohibition of age discrimination. The extent of the influence and the various means to apply it depend so much on the technicalities of the respective legal system that there are very different solutions provided.

The Law Applicable on the Continental Shelf and in the Exclusive Economic Zone[1]

19

Moira L. McConnell

19.1 Introduction

As an initial observation, I note that this topic presents a challenge for comparative law scholars.[2] As one scholar suggested in correspondence about the questionnaire for this Session, the topic is, arguably, simply a question of implementation of public international law rather than domestic (and comparative) law as such. This view points to a problem of disciplinary boundaries and the potential overlap between comparative law and international law[3] and the emerging regional law scholarship.[4] I mention this at the beginning of my General Report because that tension is apparent in both the National Reports[5] and the questionnaire prepared for this Session. Are we simply looking at the question of jurisdictional claims and national implementation of the law of the sea, as codified in the 1982 *United Nations Convention on Law of the Sea*[6] (LOSC) or the predecessor 1958 Conventions[7] and/or customary international law for countries that have not ratified the 1982 Convention?[8] If this is the case, particularly in the context of codification and the inevitable tendency to uniformity under the LOSC, is this Session concerned only with descriptive reports of spatial claims and the extent of implementation of these public

[1]II.D., Le droit applicable sur le plateau continental et dans la zone économique exclusive.

[2]National reports were submitted by the following: Belgium (Eduard (Eddy) Somers, Frank Maes); Canada (Denis Roy); Germany (Wolfgang Wurmnest); Italy (Tullio Treves, Irini Papanicolopulu); Japan (Souichirou Kozuka, Hideyuki Nakamura); Netherlands (Christiaan P. Verwer); Norway (Tore Henriksen); Peru (José Antonio Saavedra Calderón, Angel Horna); Poland (Maria Dragun-Gertner, Dorota Pyć, Zuzanna Peplowska); Portugal (Luís de Lima Pinheiro); Slovenia (Petra Ferk); USA (Rachael E. Salcido), and Venezuela (Angelina Jaffé). This General Report benefited from comments at the Session from the reporters for Poland, Belgium, Japan, USA, and Portugal and from the Chair, Dr. Jürgen Basedow.

[3]See, for example, the *International and Comparative Law Quarterly* (Cambridge University Press/British Institute of International and Comparative Law) or even more recently, a journal *Transnational Legal Theory* (Hart Publishing, Oxford) <http://www.hartjournals.co.uk/tlt/index.html>. It was interesting to see that this issue was also the subject of debate at the opening plenary of the 18th Congress on "The Role of Comparative Law in Courts and International Tribunals" and at the Session on "International Law in Domestic Systems". As Craig Scott, the Convening Editor, notes in "Introducing Transnational Legal Theory" in Volume 1, March 2010:

> *Transnational Legal Theory*'s mandate includes theoretical work that explores fresh (or revived) understandings of both international law and comparative law 'beyond the state' (and the interstate). In particular, we seek works that explore the interfaces, intersections and mutual embeddedness of public international law, private international law and comparative law, in terms of whether and how such inter-relationships are reshaping and blending these sub-disciplines in directions that are in important respects 'transnational' in nature.

[4]Especially in the European Union (EU) context.

[5]See, for example, the National Report by Dr. Wurmnest (Germany).

[6]ILM 1261 (1982). Online: <http://www. un.org/depts./los>.

[7] *Convention on the Continental Shelf*, 29 April 1958, 499 U.N.T.S. 311; *Convention on the High Seas*, 29 April 1958, 450 U.N.T.S. 82.

[8]See the National Reports by Professor Salcido (United States of America (USA)) and Professor Jaffé (Venezuela).

M.L. McConnell (✉)
Schulich School of Law, Marine & Environmental Law Institute, Dalhousie University, Halifax, NS, Canada
e-mail: moira.mcconnell@dal.ca

K.B. Brown and D.V. Snyder (eds.), *General Reports of the XVIIIth Congress of the International Academy of Comparative Law/Rapports Généraux du XVIIIème Congrès de l'Académie Internationale de Droit Comparé*,
DOI 10.1007/978-94-007-2354-2_19, © Springer Science+Business Media B.V. 2012

international law obligations and rights as "the law" applicable to these areas?

Certainly, recent events such as the environmental disaster and the loss of life from the accident in the offshore oil exploitation in the Gulf of Mexico[9] and, before that, the shipping-related spills near the coasts of Europe[10] or Australia[11] and elsewhere[12] have generated significant interest in questions such as who regulates? to what standards? and, ultimately, who has responsibility and liability for activities in these wider ocean areas near coastlines? In fact these incidents, as well as the development of technology to allow for more activities in and near coastal waters, have been the catalyst for the developments in the law of the sea and the related international regulatory regime under the auspices of the International Maritime Organization (IMO), largely because activities such as shipping are often inherently transnational or global in their operations and not only cross jurisdictions but are also a point where multiple jurisdictions intersect. Despite an increasingly elaborate and articulated regime at the international level there are, however, some areas of tension. The resulting challenges to the international regime arise from national responses to such incidents, particularly in connection with the question of navigational rights of foreign flag ships navigating through the Territorial Sea and Exclusive Economic Zone (EEZ) of another State.[13]

However disturbing and interesting these high profile events and their potential impact on the international legal regime is, the focus and concerns of this General Report are somewhat different. The questionnaire prepared for this Session reflected the view that the topic, "the law applicable on the continental shelf and in the exclusive economic zone," provides an opportunity to engage in a broad consideration, on a comparative basis, of the extent and nature of coastal States' juridical "occupation" of the extended areas of ocean and submerged land (i.e., the continental shelf). It suggested that this field of study might consider, and indeed it is difficult to avoid, the implications for the international regime and questions of implementation of conventional law or the development of customary law. However, it should also include an examination of the extent to which coastal States have "occupied" this new spatial frontier in their domestic law in the various spheres of concern. Of course this consideration must necessarily be viewed against the backdrop of the unique legal nature of these extended spaces and the troubling problem of articulating the basis of claims to jurisdiction, particularly in connection with the EEZ. At the same time the inquiry should heed the caution voiced by Bernard Oxman in his 2006 essay "The Territorial Temptation: A Siren Song at Sea"[14] where he argues that:

> … in fact the law of the land and the law of the sea developed in very different ways. If the history of the international law of the land can be characterized by

[9] For example, at the end of April 2010, the "Deep Water Horizon" deep sea offshore oil drilling unit spill/leak in the Gulf of Mexico that involved the death of a number of rig workers and that is having a major impact on the coast of the USA, as well as resulting in multiple investigations and a burgeoning number of law suits and other claims. As noted by Professor Salcido (USA) in her comments to the Congress Session, crisis often drives the development of law and reforms.

[10] In 2002, the *Prestige* sought and was denied a place of refuge. Ultimately it sank and began to leak oil approximately 250 km off Spain and polluted much of the coastline.

[11] On 5 April 2010, the grounding of the coal carrier *Shen Neng 1* caused a fuel oil and possible coal spill on the Great Barrier Reef.

[12] The early-1990s oil spill from the *Exxon Valdez* in Alaskan waters promoted the push in IMO to "double hull" tankers. The *Amoco Cadiz* incident in 1976 near the coast of France is often heralded as the turning point with respect to MARPOL 73/78 and related instruments.

[13] See, for example, the reference to the European Court of Justice regarding the validity of an EC Directive 2005/35 on ship-source pollution and penalties for infringements and its decision in Case 308/06: The Queen on the application of *INTERTANKO, INTERCARGO, The Greek Shipping Cooperation Committee, Lloyd's Register, The International Salvage Union* v. *The Secretary of State for Transport*. Judgment. At <http://eur-lex.europa.eu> Court of Justice of the European Communities (Grand Chamber), June 3, 2008. The Court was asked to consider the following questions:

- Whether the EU can impose criminal liability for discharges from foreign-flag ships on the high seas or in the Exclusive Economic Zone independently of MARPOL, thereby limiting MARPOL defences;
- Whether the standard of criminal liability for discharges resulting from "serious negligence" breaches the right of Innocent passage";
- Whether the EU can legislate for discharges in territorial seas otherwise than in accordance with MARPOL, again limiting MARPOL defences and expanding parties who might be liable;
- Whether the standard of liability in the European Union directive of "serious negligence" satisfies the requirement of legal certainty.

[14] *Centennial Essays*, 100 *AJIL* (2006), 830–51, at 830.

> the progressive triumph of the territorial temptation, the history of the international law of the sea can be characterized by the obverse; namely, the progressive triumph of Grotius's thesis of *mare liberum* and its concomitant prohibition on claims of territorial sovereignty.…That triumph reflected not only the transitory nature of human activity at sea, but a rational conclusion that the interests of states in unrestricted access to the rest of the world outweighed their interests in restricting the access of others at sea.

This General Report, and the National Reports on which it is based, cannot, and do not, pretend to provide a definitive answer to the question implicitly posed in the title of the Session, as rhetorically posed by Dr. Wurmnest (Germany) – is this a "law free zone?" The answer in these National Reports is clear: it is not "law free". In fact, as Professor Dragun-Gertner (Poland) observed in her comments during the Session, the space for unique or diverse domestic legislation in the EEZ is, if anything, increasingly smaller because of the growth in overlapping international and regional regulatory regimes.[15] However, the question of what is the applicable law and the basis for that law, particularly in connection with private law matters (e.g., contracts, property rights, torts), remains uncertain, and even undeveloped in many countries. The reasons for this vary but may include the fact that the range of activities in these areas still remains relatively narrow and primarily concerned with living and non-living resource exploitation and navigation. In addition the public nature of the space poses difficulties in some cases for developing individual legal rights. Thus there has been little need, and in indeed barriers, to develop the law. It may also be, as has been pointed out elsewhere that the "… classical manifestations of jurisdiction [territoriality, nationality and universality] are not followed in the law of the sea, where jurisdiction is attributed to States in their maritime context, i.e., either as flag States, coastal States and/or port States."[16] While the law of the sea framework could also be understood as flowing from the "classical" basis it is also evident that the question of applicable law will depend on a range of factors.

The topic of this Session has preoccupied many scholars and formed the basis of nearly as many books and careful surveys on the nature of the EEZ and the continental shelf and the allocation of rights and responsibilities in these spaces, including the important general review in 1989 by Barbara Kwiatkowsa, *The 200 mile Exclusive Economic Zone in the New Law of the Sea*,[17] and more recently Maria Gavouneli, *Functional Jurisdiction in the Law of the Sea*,[18] or the more sector specific analysis such as that by Eric Jaap Molenaar, *Coastal State Jurisdiction Over Vessel-Source Pollution*,[19] to name but a few.

This General Report and the related National Reports can only purport to offer a "snapshot" of the current situation in a limited number of countries and legal systems combined with observations on some common themes and difficulties. Before moving to consider these snapshots of the contemporary situation it is useful to briefly review the legal background to the EEZ and the continental shelf.

19.2 Background: The EEZ and the Continental Shelf

It will be recalled that the term and the concept of the "Exclusive Economic Zone", as a description of coastal State use and legislative and management rights (with responsibilities) within a spatial area out to 200 nautical miles (NM) from shore was adopted in 1982 under the LOSC. It will also be recalled that the earlier Conventions, which were adopted in 1958, the

[15] She made this observation in connection with the interaction between the LOSC, IMO Conventions, the various UNEP and other UN Conventions, the Helsinki Convention (1992 *Convention on the Protection of the Marine Environment of the Baltic Sea Area*) and the various EU Directives.

[16] Erik Franckx, "Book review of Maria Gavouneli, *Functional Jurisdiction in the Law of the Sea,* Vol. 62, Publications on Ocean Development (Leiden: Martinus Nijhoff, 2007)," in *Ocean Yearbook,* vol. 23 eds. Coffen-Smout, S., Chircop, A., McConnell, M. (Leiden: Brill, 2009), 532. Of course these terms are simply descriptions of particular kinds of interest and legal roles since most States that have a maritime interest assume all three roles to varying degrees. Interestingly, under the ILO's *Maritime Labour Convention, 2006* (NIF but expected 2012/2013) an additional "maritime" interest, that of labour-supplying responsibilities, is emerging, particularly in connection with regulation of seafarer recruitment and placement services and social security protection.

[17] Dordrecht/Boston/London: Martinus Nijhoff Publishers: 1989.

[18] Maria Gavouneli, *Functional Jurisdiction in the Law of the Sea,* vol. 62, Publications on Ocean Development (Leiden: Martinus Nijhoff, 2007).

[19] *International Law and Policy Series,* vol. 51 (The Hague: Kluwer, 1998).

water column beyond the Territorial Sea was considered as high seas,[20] while the continental shelf was considered as a prolongation of the coastal State's land.

The development of the legal concept of an extended area, described as a "zone" – which in its very nomenclature reflects the increasingly dominant "planning" approach to the treatment of spatial areas where there may be conflicting users and claims,[21] was described by Satya N. Nandan[22] as follows:

> The concept of the exclusive economic zone is one of the most important pillars of the 1982 Convention on the Law of the Sea. *The regime of the exclusive economic zone is perhaps the most complex and multifaceted in the whole Convention.* The accommodation of diverse issues contributed substantially to the acceptance of the concept and to the Convention as a whole. The 1982 Convention on the Law of the Sea is often referred to as a package. The metaphor is derived from a decision made during the Third United Nations Conference on the Law of the Sea that the Convention would be adopted *in toto,* as a "package deal". No single issue would be adopted until all issues were settled. This decision provided an essential mechanism for reconciling the varied interests of the states participating in the Conference. If a state's interests in one issue were not fully satisfied, it could look at the whole package and find other issues where its interests were more fully represented, thereby mitigating the effects of the first. *Thus, the Convention became an elaborately-constructed document built on trade-offs, large and small. The larger package consists of: a twelve-nautical-mile territorial sea; an exclusive economic zone of up to 200 nautical miles in which coastal states have preeminent economic rights and which obviates the need for a territorial sea of 200 nautical miles claimed by some states; extension of the continental shelf regime to the margin, with revenue-sharing obligations beyond the exclusive economic zone*; a regime for transit passage through straits used for international navigation and for archipelagic sea-lanes passage; guaranteed access to and from the sea for land-locked states; a regime for the administration and development of the common heritage resources of the international sea-bed area; protection and preservation of the marine environment; and adequate mechanisms for settlement of disputes concerning the interpretation and application of the provisions of the Convention. *Within this larger package are many smaller packages of which the exclusive economic zone is one of the most interesting examples. The provisions contained in articles 55 and 75 reflect an array of interests: the sovereign rights of coastal states to manage the zone in good faith; the regard for the economic interests of third states; regulation of certain activities in the zone, such as marine scientific research, protection and preservation of the marine environment, and the establishment and use of artificial islands, installations and structures; freedom of navigation and overflight; the freedom to lay submarine cables and pipelines; military and strategic uses of the zone; and the issue of residual rights in the zone.* (emphasis added)

Article 55 to which Nandan refers is the first Article in Part V, *Exclusive Economic Zone*, of the LOSC. It provides:

> *Article 55*
>
> *Specific legal regime of the exclusive economic zone*
>
> The exclusive economic zone is an area beyond and adjacent to the territorial sea, subject to the specific legal regime established in this Part, under which the rights and jurisdiction of the coastal State and the rights and freedoms of other States are governed by the relevant provisions of this Convention.

Articles 56–75 outline the various rights, jurisdiction, and responsibilities of the coastal State in this zone beyond its Territorial Sea[23] (maximum of 12 NM) and deals with specific activities, primarily in

[20] Article 1, *Convention on the High Seas*, *supra* note 7.

[21] The term itself implies a more abstract notion, clearly a legal construct, differing from "territory". See: Moira L. McConnell, "Conflict Prevention and Management: Designing Effective Dispute Resolution Strategies for Aquaculture Siting and Operations," in *Aquaculture Law and Policy: Towards Principled Access and Operations,* ed. VanderZwaag, D., and Chao, G. (London/New York: Routledge Press, 2006), 171–206 and sources discussed therein at footnote 21.

[22] S. N. Nandan, "The Exclusive Economic Zone: A Historical Perspective," in *Essays in Memory of Jean Carroz* (Rome: FAO, 1987). Available at: <http://www.fao.org/docrep/s5280T/s5280t0p.htm>. Jean Carroz is quoted in Nandan's paper as stating, in 1981, that:

> Since the seventeenth century, when the development of seaborne trade and the emergence of powerful maritime nations led to a shift from the notion of closed seas claimed by a few countries to the concept of open seas, the two basic principles of the law of the sea have been that a narrow strip of coastal waters should be under the exclusive sovereignty of the coastal state and that the high seas beyond should be freely accessible to all. These principles were originally intended to satisfy and reconcile the requirements of national security with freedom of trade and navigation. But they were applied to all activities in both areas and ipso facto defined the legal framework within which fishing activities were carried on. At the Conference on the Law of the Sea, there was only limited support for maintaining the status quo…

[23] Article 2 of LOSC extends coastal State sovereignty from land and internal waters out to an adjacent belt of sea, the territorial sea, and to the seabed and subsoil and airspace above it, to a maximum of 12 NM from a State's baselines.

the water superjacent to the seabed and subsoil out to 200NM. Specifically, Article 56 provides that:

> *Rights, jurisdiction and duties of the coastal State in the exclusive economic zone*
>
> 1. In the exclusive economic zone, the coastal State has:
>   (a) *sovereign rights* for the purpose of exploring and exploiting, conserving and managing the natural resources, whether living or non-living, of the waters superjacent to the seabed and of the seabed and its subsoil, and with regard to other activities for the economic exploitation and exploration of the zone, such as the production of energy from the water, currents and winds;
>   (b) *jurisdiction* as provided for in the relevant provisions of this Convention with regard to:
>   (i) the establishment and use of artificial islands, installations and structures;
>   (ii) marine scientific research;
>   (iii) the protection and preservation of the marine environment;
>   (c) other rights and duties provided for in this Convention.
> 2. In exercising its rights and performing its duties under this Convention in the exclusive economic zone, the coastal State shall have due regard to the rights and duties of other States and shall act in a manner compatible with the provisions of this Convention.
> 3. The rights set out in this article with respect to the seabed and subsoil shall be exercised in accordance with Part VI. (emphasis added)

Paragraph 3 references Part VI, *Continental Shelf*, and in so doing incorporates Articles 76–85, as applicable. Key amongst these is Article 77 which provides:

> *Rights of the coastal State over the continental shelf*
>
> 1. *The coastal State exercises over the continental shelf sovereign rights* for the purpose of exploring it and exploiting its natural resources.
> 2. *The rights referred to in paragraph 1 are exclusive* in the sense that if the coastal State does not explore the continental shelf or exploit its natural resources, no one may undertake these activities without the express consent of the coastal State.
> 3. The *rights of the coastal State over the continental shelf do not* depend on occupation, effective or notional, or on any express proclamation.
> 4. The natural resources referred to in this Part consist of the mineral and other non-living resources of the seabed and subsoil together with living organisms belonging to sedentary species, that is to say, organisms which, at the harvestable stage, either are immobile on or under the seabed or are unable to move except in constant physical contact with the seabed or the subsoil. (emphasis added)

Article 81 further clarifies that the coastal State has the exclusive right to authorize and regulate drilling on the continental shelf for all purposes. Article 78 makes it clear, however, that these rights do not affect the legal status of the superjacent waters or airspace above the waters.

Both Parts V and VI also preserve certain pre-existing "high seas freedoms" that can be exercised by other States in the EEZ and on the continental shelf. Notably in the EEZ, Article 58, expressly references freedom of navigation and overflight and laying of submarine cables and pipes and incorporates other provisions from Part VII, *High seas*, in Articles 88–115 if not incompatible with Part V. A State operating (e.g., flag State with a ship navigating) in another State's EEZ is to comply with laws adopted under Article V and other applicable international law adopted by the coastal State. Similarly, in Part VI, Article 79 expressly preserves the right of other States to lay submarine cables and pipes on the continental shelf, subject to a right of the coastal State to regulate for specific purposes. It should be noted that under Article 60, coastal States have the exclusive right to construct and authorize the construction of artificial island installations and have exclusive jurisdiction over these with respect to customs, fiscal, health, safety, and immigration law and regulation. Article 73 sets out coastal States' rights regarding enforcement of law and regulation in the EEZ in connection with its "sovereign rights to explore, exploit, conserve and manage the *living resources* in the exclusive economic zone" (emphasis added). Despite this seemingly comprehensive catalogue of activities, Article 59 envisages activities where jurisdiction is not allocated and leaves it to be determined on a case by case basis[24]:

> *Basis for the resolution of conflicts regarding the attribution of rights and jurisdiction in the exclusive economic zone*
>
> In cases where this Convention *does not attribute rights or jurisdiction to the coastal State or to other States within the exclusive economic zone*, and a conflict arises between the interests of the coastal State and any other State or States, the conflict should be resolved on the basis of equity and in the light of all the relevant

[24] It has been argued that this provision may be the basis for the "creeping jurisdiction" by coastal States: See: Niquole Esters, "Impacts of Language: Creeping Jurisdiction and its Challenges to the Equal Implementation of the Law of the Sea Convention", in Difficulties in Implementing the Provisions of UNCLOS, Conference paper for the 2008, HO/IAG Advisory Board on the Law of the Sea Conference. Online<http:www.gmat.unsw.edu.au/ablos/ABLOS08Folder/Session5-Paper1-Esters.pdf>.

> circumstances, taking into account the respective importance of the interests involved to the parties as well as to the international community as a whole. (emphasis added)

Finally, it must be recalled that within the potential 188 NM of an EEZ beyond the 12 NM Territorial Sea, there is also the possibility that a State can declare a "contiguous zone" of an additional 12 NM beyond its Territorial Sea where it can apply certain national legislation.[25] There are also a number of other provisions in the Convention involving regulatory rights and responsibilities in the EEZ in connection with Part XII, *Protection and Preservation of the Marine Environment,* and Part XIII, *Marine Scientific Research.*

For the purposes of this General Report, whether or not a State has ratified LOSC, the main point to take from this resume of the LOSC provisions is that coastal States have significant regulatory ambit in these areas if their legislation is tied to natural resource or other economic activities or protection and preservation of the marine environment subject to the specific freedoms or rights identified. While it was at one point, particularly before the 1982 LOSC entered into force, of some interest to question whether the law relating the EEZ was customary international law or debate the legal nature of the EEZ, given the number of countries that have ratified the LOSC,[26] it is now clear that a spatial claim out to 200 NM, if geographically possible, is not contested. For the most part, the jurisdictional allocations as set out in LOSC are generally observed (even if they are not yet customary international law). However, especially since the early 1990s, there have been challenges posed to these allocations by countries that, although party to the LOSC, have proposed extensions of jurisdiction, based on concepts such "mar presencial"[27] or "stewardship",[28] to areas adjacent to the EEZ or have attempted to impose national laws in excess of international standards on foreign-flagged ships navigating in the EEZ. [29]

---

[25]LOSC, Article 33, *Contiguous Zone*, provides

1. In a zone contiguous to its territorial sea, described as the contiguous zone, the coastal State may exercise the control necessary to: (a) prevent infringement of its customs, fiscal, immigration or sanitary laws and regulations within its territory or territorial sea; (b) punish infringement of the above laws and regulations committed within its territory or territorial sea.
2. The contiguous zone may not extend beyond 24 nautical miles from the baselines from which the breadth of the territorial sea is measured.

[26]As of 20 September 2011, 162 States are party to the LOSC, online: <http://www.un.org/dept/los reference_files/status2010.pdf>. Or, even if they have not ratified the Convention, they have adopted extended maritime claims either before its adoption or after 1982. As of 2010, on a very "rough count", 135 States, had claims for either a 200 NM EEZ or Exclusive Fisheries Zone or some other zone, or had extended claims delimited by agreement with other opposite or adjacent States. See: published summary table of claims in 31 July 2010, online: <http://www.un.org/Depts/los/LEGISLATIONANDTREATIES/PDFFILES/table_summary_of_claims.pdf>.

As noted in the National Reports by Mag. Petra Ferk (Slovenia) and by Drs. Treves and Papanicolopulu (Italy) the countries bordering the Mediterranean have some difficulty in making such claims because of proximity; however, some States are claiming ecological protection or similarly named zones beyond the Territorial Sea, e.g., France, Solvenia, Italy. However, these countries have also adopted a regional convention-based regime, the Barcelona Convention (1976 *Convention for the Protection of The Mediterranean Sea Against Pollution),* a system to address environmental protection concerns. See Discussion in: *Seminar on the legal aspects of the Barcelona Convention and its Protocols*, online: <http://www.mepielan.gr/int-sem-02-en.html>.

[27]The concept of "mar presencial" (Presential sea) was initially proposed by Chile as a solution for the problem of straddling stocks. See: Christopher C. Joyner and Peter N. De Cola, "Chile's Presential Sea Proposal: Implications for Straddling Stocks and the International Law of Fisheries", in *24 Ocean Development & International Law*, 99 (1993); Thomas A. Clingan Jr., "Mar Presencial (the Presential sea): Deja Vu all over again? – A Response to Francisco Orrego Vicuna", in 24 *Ocean Development & International Law*, 93 (1993).

[28]A concept that has been discussed in Canada, in connection with concerns about overfishing of the straddling stocks adjacent to Canada's EEZ in the Atlantic.

[29]For example. the European Directive, *supra* note 13. Or, as noted by Charlotte Briede and Phillip Saunders in "Challenges To The UNCLOS Regime: National Legislation Which Is Incompatible With International Law" (citations removed):

> In another example of a coastal State regulation which may extend beyond the confines of MARPOL (and thus of UNCLOS), the Canadian government in 2005 responded to a perceived problem with seabird oiling caused by oily bilge water dumping by amending the *Migratory Birds Convention Act (MBCA).* The amended Act, which applies in the EEZ, makes it an offence for any person or vessel to "deposit a substance that is harmful to migratory birds, or permit such a substance to be deposited, in waters or an area frequented by migratory birds…" (see s. 5.1(1)).

It is well known that increasingly wider areas of offshore jurisdiction, albeit on varying bases and using varying terminology (for example, territorial sea, exclusive fisheries zone), were already claimed by a number of States well before the development of the EEZ concept in the 1970s in connection with the negotiation of LOSC. In fact, coastal State claims over marine resources in areas of various breadth beyond the, then accepted, Territorial Sea in relation to coastal fisheries and the continental shelf were established in the 1940s.[30] As noted by Churchill and Lowe,[31] it is customary to regard the Proclamations by President Truman of the USA in 1945 as the first clear assertion of the idea that the continental shelf belongs to the coastal State on the basis that:

> [T]he exercise of jurisdiction over the natural resources of the subsoil and sea bed of the continental shelf by the contiguous nation is reasonable and just, since the effectiveness of measures to utilize or conserve these resources would be contingent upon cooperation and protection from the shore, since the continental shelf may be regarded as an extension of the land-mass of the coastal nation and thus naturally appurtenant to it [].

This claim and its rationale (which came to be known as the "continental shelf doctrine") was followed in the late 1940s with 200 NM claims regarding extended marine areas (then described as a "patrimonial sea") made in Proclamations and Declarations issued by Chile and Peru and others.[32] The efforts to codify the law of the sea in 1958 with the Geneva Conventions adopted at UNCLOS I and later in 1982 in the LOSC at UNCLOS III, were, in part, the result of concerns about "creeping" coastal State jurisdiction and potential conflicts with States exercising traditional navigational and other rights in these areas.[33]

> MARPOL-compliant discharges, such as permissible levels of oily bilge water, would be protected by a separate provision exempting "authorized" discharges under the *Canada Shipping Act 2001*, which applies MARPOL standards. However, the broad language of the prohibition, which would apply to substances other than oil, comes up against the requirement under UNCLOS that such measures must be made pursuant to an internationally accepted standard, and there is no indication of what international rule or standard this provision is implementing.

Conference paper for the 2008, HO/IAG Advisory Board on the Law of the Sea Conference: Difficulties In Implementing The Provisions Of UNCLOS, online <http:www.gmat.unsw.edu.au/ablos/ABLOS08Folder/Session5-Paper2-Briede.pdf>

[30]R. R. Churchill and A. V. Lowe, *The Law of the Sea,* 3rd ed. (Manchester: JURIS Publishing/Manchester University Press, 1999), 143. They note that there was an earlier treaty in 1942, entered into by the United Kingdom on behalf of Trinidad, with respect to the Gulf of Paria: Great Britain – Venezuela, Treaty relating to the Submarine Areas of the Gulf of Paria, Caracas, 26 February 1942, 205 LNTS 121. President Truman of the United States issued two proclamations in 1945, *Policy of the United States with Respect to the Natural Resources of the Subsoil and Sea Bed of the Continental Shelf* and *Policy of the United States with Respect to Coastal Fisheries in Certain Areas of the High Seas.*

[31]Churchill & Lowe, *id.*

[32]Santiago Declaration 1952, and see also examples in Churchill & Lowe, *supra* note 32 at 160, note 2. Oxman, *supra* note 14 comments at 831–32:

> The mid-twentieth century was also a watershed for the international law of the sea, but of a very different sort. At the same time that the territorial temptation ran up against increasingly important legal constraints on land—often in response to the values of facilitation of trade, communication, and cooperation, which had traditionally informed the law of the sea—the obverse again occurred at sea. The territorial temptation thrust seaward with a speed and geographic scope that would be the envy of the most ambitious conquerors in human history. The effective start of this process—President Truman's claim to the continental shelf in 1945[]—was so quickly accepted and emulated by other coastal states []that the emergence of the regime of the continental shelf, in derogation of the principle of *mare liberum*,[ ] has been cited as an example of instant customary law.[ ] The Truman Proclamation unleashed a quarter-century of territorial and quasi-territorial claims to the high seas so vast that, at the dawn of the Third United Nations Conference on the Law of the Sea, the leader of the Canadian delegation, Ambassador J. Alan Beesley, could quip that he comes to bury Grotius, not to praise him.

[33]The adoption of the EEZ can also, perhaps, be viewed as an example of "creeping" coastal State jurisdiction or property rights claims challenging the management problems posed by freedom of the seas "commons"/high seas regime. Certainly the recognition of extended legal jurisdiction for coastal States must be understood as a necessary accompaniment to the technological developments that increasingly permit the use or occupation of ocean space and submerged lands for a variety of purposes (e.g., communications, resource development, and wind and tidal energy). At the same time, some of the traditional high seas navigational and other user rights and freedoms of other States (most notably "freedom of navigation") are also preserved in the EEZ that is described in LOSC. Recently, however, there have been attempts by coastal States to exercise greater control in this zone vis-à-vis maritime transport and other users, largely on the basis of a need to provide protection to coastal interests and resources. As explained by Eric Franckx in his interesting study ("The 200-Mile Limit: Between Creeping Jurisdiction and Creeping Common Heritage? – Some Law of the Sea Considerations from Professor Louis Sohn's Former

As mentioned earlier, in the infancy of the development of the EEZ there was also some debate about whether its legal nature was really that of the high seas with some limitations on freedoms or the territorial sea with some incursions on sovereignty. This question was extensively analyzed by Kwiatkowska[34] in her examination of the arguments for the residual High Sea character of the EEZ versus the *sui generis* character. The more contemporary view is, perhaps, best captured by Churchill and Lowe who argue that neither the residual High Sea character nor the Territorial Sea character was accepted. They suggest that: "[i]nstead, the EEZ must be regarded as a separate functional zone of *sui generis* character situated between the territorial and high sea."[35] Of course this view still leaves open the question of the continental shelf which is claimed on what are, essentially, traditional notions of territory.

Thus under LOSC there appears to be two distinct legal bases for claims. The first is the "classical" continental shelf doctrine, which is set out in the 1958 *Convention on the Continental Shelf*, and retained in Part VI of LOSC, and the second is the modern basis for the EEZ in Part V of LOSC. The result is that under LOSC the maximum (EEZ)/minimum (CS) breadth is 200 NM, however the continental shelf exists *ipso facto* while the EEZ must be claimed. As noted in the oft cited judgment of Judge Oda (in dissent) in the 1982 *Case concerning the Continental Shelf* (Tunisia/ Libyan Arab Jamahiriya)[36]:

> 120. It is widely recognized that the concept of the exclusive economic zone has become irresistible, and the way seems paved towards the institution of a régime for it under international law, incorporating a uniform limit of 200 miles. Throughout the history of international law, scarcely any other major concept has ever stood on the threshold of acceptance within such a short period. Even apart from the provisions of the 1981 draft convention, the Court need have few qualms in acknowledging the general concept of the exclusive economic zone as having entered the realm of customary international law. Yet I cannot but point out two problems in this respect: first, quite apart from the treaty-making process, the sui generis régime of the exclusive economic zone is going to require much more careful examination before the rules so far adumbrated may be viewed as susceptible of adoption into existing international law; secondly, the relation of the zone to the continental shelf remains profoundly ambiguous, particularly where such "interface" issues as the exploitation of ocean-floor minerals are concerned.

Despite the aspirations of the 1970s regarding a new international economic order[37] and the potential wealth generated by the exercise of exclusive economic rights in this area, there has been relatively little development and use of these areas other than in connection with fisheries and offshore oil and gas exploitation. Even this has been problematic, with significant management failures on the part of coastal States and

LL.M. Student", *The George Washington International Law Review*, 39(3) (2007): 467–98) of this phenomenon outside 200 NM (citation removed):

> Creeping can be carried out either by the coastal State, in which case the widely used term "creeping jurisdiction" is normally relied upon, or by the international community, a process referred to by the term "creeping common heritage." Creeping jurisdiction can further be subdivided into creeping "qualitatively inside the 200-mile limit and spatially beyond that limit."

See concerns voiced by Oxman, *supra* note 14.

[34] See Kwiatkowsa, *supra* note 14 at pages 230–235.

[35] Churchill & Lowe, *supra* note 30 at pp. 160–161.

[36] *ICJ Reports* (1982) 222–34, paras. 108–130. Online at <http://www.icj-cij.org/docket/index.php?p1=3&p2=3&code=lm&case=68&k=a8>.

[37] Churchill & Lowe, *supra* note 30, explain that the concept of the EEZ, which eventually "effectively merged" with the South American concept of the "patrimonial sea", was first put forward at UNCLOS III by Kenya in 1971. They point out,

> The EEZ is a reflection of the aspiration of the developing countries for economic development and their desire to gain greater control over the economic resources off their coasts, particularly fish stocks, which in many cases were largely exploited by the distant-water fleets of developed States.

The authors conclude (at page 179), however, that the establishment of the EEZ/EFZ led to some redistribution of fishery resources from distant-water fleet flag States to the coastal State and that with respect to resources other than fish, in the case of offshore oil and gas, "the introduction of the EEZ effected no redistribution…. Overall, therefore it is likely that the introduction of the EEZ concept has not produced as much material gain for the developing countries as its original proponents suggest." It should be noted that in 1999 the potential value of genetic resources or other mineral resources such polymetallic sulfides was not well developed; however, the conclusions are likely to remain much the same. I note the absence of National Reports from the countries most involved in the development of the EEZ concept is unfortunate. A similar problem and gap was identified at the 10th IACL Congress in 1978 by the General Reporter, Kenneth Simmonds (Great Britain), on the topic, "International Law and the New International Economic Order."

increasing pressure to "globalize" regulation of fisheries in the EEZ through regional organizations.[38]

However, with growing demands for alternative forms of energy, particularly wind energy and other forms of marine renewable energy, and more research into more diverse resources and activities such as bio-prospecting for genetic resources, there is now a need to provide for regulation and operation of these activities and also to support the commercial aspects of economic development, including, for example, matters such as property rights to secure credit for investors and employment law to govern the situation of workers.

There are some parallel trends that must also be considered. In 1992, a decade after the adoption of LOSC, the international community also began to adopt an eco-systemic world view and an integrated management based approach to addressing the relationship between human activities – particularly economic activities – and the natural environment. In connection with ocean and resources, this has generated the development of integrated ocean action plans or strategies and/or policies together with a related legal framework to govern activities in these areas. These ocean governance policies also serve to align the institutions that regulate ocean and seabed uses, usually on a sectoral basis. The national policies have also evolved in different ways and reflect differing themes over time, for example, in some countries, "healthy oceans" is now a unifying theme. For example, a relatively recent project (2007)[39] by the Intergovernmental Oceanographic Commission (IOC) of the United Nations Educational, Scientific and Cultural Organization (UNESCO) reflects the current interest in comparative studies of this new generation of approaches to ocean space governance.

19.3 The National Reports: Illustrative Studies of the National Treatment of the EEZ and Continental Shelf

As mentioned above, this General Report and the National Reports on which it is based, can do no more than provide a snapshot of the contemporary situation regarding the extent of a coastal State's legal occupation of these two areas, to the extent that they are distinguishable.

19.3.1 General Information

The questionnaire for this Session asked some basic background[40] questions relating to ratification of the LOSC and prior Conventions. Of the National Reports

[38]See the 1995 *Agreement for the Implementation of the Provisions of the United Nations Convention on the Law of the Sea of 10 December 1982 Relating to the Conservation and Management of Straddling Fish Stocks and Highly Migratory Fish Stocks,* online: <http://www.un.org//depts/los/convention_agreements/texts/fish_stocks_agreement/CONF164_37.htm>, and the "compatibility principle":

Article 7

Compatibility of conservation and management measures

1. Without prejudice to the sovereign rights of coastal States for the purpose of exploring and exploiting, conserving and managing the living marine resources within areas under national jurisdiction as provided for in the Convention, and the right of all States for their nationals to engage in fishing on the high seas in accordance with the Convention…
2. *Conservation and management measures established for the high seas and those adopted for areas under national jurisdiction shall be compatible in order to ensure conservation and management of the straddling fish stocks and highly migratory fish stocks in their entirety. To this end, coastal States and States fishing on the high seas have a duty to cooperate for the purpose of achieving compatible* measures in respect *of such stocks. In determining compatible conservation and management measures, States shall: …* (emphasis added)

[39]See: IOC Technical Series, 75. Law of the Sea Dossier 1: Intergovernmental Oceanographic Commission. *National Ocean Policy. The Basic Texts from: Australia, Brazil, Canada, China, Colombia, Japan, Norway, Portugal, Russian Federation, United States of America (*Paris, UNESCO, 2007). Online: <http://ioc3.unesco.org/abelos/index.php?option=com_content&task=view&id=55&Itemid=62>. This study comprises a collection of national ocean policies, including the legislation, much of which establishes the legal framework for the EEZ or similar zones underpinning these policies.

[40]Specific questions to consider in relation to national legislation, case law or other policies and practices:

General/Descriptive

1. Is your country a party to the 1982 United Nations Convention on the Law of the Sea?
2. Is or was your country party to the 1958 Convention on the Continental Shelf?
3. Did your country adopt legislation to implement the 1958 Convention (if a party)? Was this legislation amended after 1982?
4. Has your country adopted national legislation with respect to its maritime boundaries?

received, three States[41] are not party to the 1982 LOSC, but do claim an extended jurisdictional zone out to 200 NM. The point of interest was whether all States claimed areas beyond the Territorial Sea and, if so, what name was used and what form did national law take to cover this area.[42] In line with the point mentioned above regarding ocean polices, the specific interest was whether an "Oceans Act" or some other form of unifying legislation or policy had been adopted and/or whether there was spatial management policy or law in this area. The National Reports indicate that some countries[43] have adopted an integrating "Oceans Act." Drs. Kozuka and Nakamura note with respect to Japan:

> … a substantial shift in the Japanese law more than a decade after the ratification of LOSC. The *Basic Act on Ocean Policy* …, enacted in 2007, acknowledged the importance of becoming "a new ocean-oriented nation striving for harmony between the peaceful and positive development and exploitation of the oceans and the conservation of the marine environment."

However, many do not follow this approach although a number of countries in Europe, largely as a result of EU regionalism, have adopted marine spatial planning approaches.[44] Although not in the EU, it is notable that Norway is gradually adopting a spatial planning approach.[45]

Others noted significant fragmentation and sectoral management and legislation, despite efforts at integration.[46] In her report on the USA Professor Salcido explains that:

> The United States has a multitude of overlapping and untidy laws "on the books" applicable to the EEZ. It has leadership capacity, and it has the public's interest in the resources in mind. To date, however, these elements have failed to yield an effective legal framework for ocean management.

Similarly Professor Dragun-Gertner, Dr. Pyć and Zuzanna Peplowska note in their report on Poland that:

> Applicable national legislation is partially specific for maritime activities and partially of a general nature. A dual approach to maritime areas management of Poland consists of both the sectoral approach (e.g., fishing, shipping, marine spatial planning) and the integrated approach

---

5. How wide is the territorial sea? If jurisdiction over any area of water or seabed beyond the territorial sea is claimed, what is the name and size of that area and what is the nature of the claim?
6. Has your country claimed an extended continental shelf? If so, what national legislation relates to that claim?

[41] Peru, USA, Venezuela.

[42] For example as noted earlier, *supra* note 26, Drs. Treves and Papanicolopulu, National Reporters for Italy, point out that in 2006 Italy adopted "ecological protection zones":

> In 2006, Italy passed framework legislation for the creation of "ecological protection zones", to be established by Presidential Decree, wherein it will exercise part of the rights attributed to the coastal State by international law of the sea within its exclusive economic zone." No ecological protection zone has yet been established on the basis of this law. The reason seems to be the wish of Italy to negotiate the external boundaries of these areas before formally establishing them. It may be noted that Italian legislation refers to "zones" in the plural. However, these zones should not be confused with marine protected areas: the former are in fact maritime zones which can be established along portions of the entire coastline, while the latter are specific areas protected because of their special biological characteristics. The use of the plural is probably due to the intention of Italy not to establish an entire zone at once, but to begin along those coasts where environmental threats require urgent action. It is expected that the first ecological protection zone, encompassing the northern Tyrrhenian Sea, will be established during 2010.

See also National Report for Slovenia by Mag. Ferk, *supra* note 28.

[43] In addition to Japan, Canada and the USA have enacted "Oceans" Acts.

[44] As noted by Drs. Maes and Somers in their National Report for Belgium:

> The legislative framework in Belgium has shaped marine spatial planning (MSP) into a continuous process.

See also the Reports from the other EU countries.

[45] Dr. Henriksen (Norway) explains that

> There is a gradual spatial approach in newer legislation pertaining to the maritime areas.
>
> The 2009 *Nature Management Act*, aimed at preserving diversity of biology, landscapes, and geology, is also applicable to the maritime zones of Norway. The Act includes more specific objectives to protect the diversity of habitats and ecosystems, and is applicable across sectoral legislation. It reflects the ecosystem approach, requiring a more spatial approach in the management of natural resources and the environment. One of the measures under the Act is marine protected areas (MPAs). This measure is not applicable to the EEZ or the continental shelf as measures adopted under MPAs arguably may impede on the rights of other states under the law of the sea. The *Planning Act* has recently been amended to be made applicable in maritime areas (one nautical mile from the baselines), including internal waters and a minor part of the territorial sea. Spatial planning and a more holistic approach to management in the maritime areas are mainly regulated through government policy. The ecosystem-based approach is a central element in Norwegian ocean's policy ….

[46] See the National Report for Japan.

(e.g., environmental protection, nature conservation, general principles of coastal and marine spatial planning, as well as construction permits). The problem with the good practice of managing space of the marine environment is that it is done on a single-sector basis, mainly without a plan-based approach and with little or no consideration of objectives from other conflicting uses or conservation requirements. The lack of an integrated approach that pays attention to the heterogenic characteristics of marine space leads to conflicts among users, and between human uses and the natural environment.

In general, boundary making and continental shelf claims especially where extended claims might exist was reported as a preoccupation[47] even for countries that have not ratified the LOSC.[48] As noted by Dr. Jaffé in connection with Venezuela:

> Venezuela was an active participant in the development and creation of the 1982 United Nations Convention of the Law of the Sea (UNCLOS). However, as article 309 explicitly forbids the possibility of making reservations to any article or part of the Convention, Venezuela was one of the four States that voted against it.
>
> Venezuela's main objections concern article 15, which refers to the delimitation of territorial waters; article 121, which establishes distinctions between different categories of islands; and the part referring to the creation of the International Tribunal on the Law of the Sea. The underlying concern is a pending delimitation problem with the Republic of Colombia in the Gulf of Venezuela.

However, as Dr. Roy (Canada) explains, Canada is one of the relatively few countries that will be able to claim a continental shelf extending beyond 200 NM.

19.3.2 National Law and Practice

The purpose of this section of the General Report is not to reproduce or even attempt to summarize the National Reports, many[49] of which are published elsewhere, but rather to highlight some points that are of special interest. The questionnaire for this Session asked whether legislation had been adopted with respect to specific resource management and regulation in these areas and related jurisdictional questions, as well as inviting observations and reflections by the National Reporters.[50] One point that appears common is that the EEZ and the continental shelf, irrespective of the continental shelf doctrine, is not[51] regarded as "territory" and requires an express extension to also apply national public law in areas beyond the Territorial Sea.[52] For example, as explained by Dr. Wurmnest (Germany) regarding the situation in Germany:

> Therefore the legislature must (directly or implicitly) state in each law it passes in the realm of public law,

---

[47] See e.g., Dr. Roy, (Canada); Dr. Henriksen (Norway).

[48] See the National Reports for the USA and Venezuela.

[49] See *inter alia*: *Ocean Yearbook*, Vol. 25, eds. S. Coffen-Smout, A. Chircop, M. L. McConnell (Leiden: Brill, 2011)

[50] Sectoral Resource Management

7. Has legislation been adopted with respect to specific resource management and regulation? More specifically has it been adopted or changed with respect to
   - energy (wind or other sources of ocean energy)
   - mineral resources
   - genetic resources
   - fisheries
   - aquaculture
   - maritime transport
   - communication
   - scientific research
8. How are investment and the need for financial security(ies) addressed? How, if at all, has the private sector addressed this issue (contracts? loans/credit?) Has there been any case law in connection with investments?
9. How is the area as a "work space" (labor/employment law) regulated? How is it addressed, if it is, in private sector employment relationships e.g., contracts, collective bargaining arrangements?
10. Has any preventative action taken place, e.g., creation of marine protected areas? If so, was this in connection with the LOSC or MARPOL?

Enforcement of Jurisdiction

11. Does your country enforce legislation/rights in these areas and, if so, how does it do so?
12. Are national courts given jurisdiction in these areas? If so, in what form is this granted? Has it ever been exercised?
13. What institutions or agencies are responsible for enforcement of jurisdiction in these areas?

Reflection

Please include a brief reflection on what you perceive to be the interests of your country and private sector actors in connection with this topic and what you see as the main issues in the future.

[51] But see: Dr. Luís de Lima Pinheiro (Portugal) where this does not appear to be the case.

[52] See Dr. Wurmnest (Germany) Although not specifically addressed in Dr. Roy's National Report for Canada, it is noted that the *Oceans Act* "(1996, S.C., c.31) adopts an approach to addressing this issue by generally extending legislative and court jurisdiction to the EEZ and continental shelf "…as if the places referred to … formed part of the territory of Canada.…" (e.g., s.20 (2) s.21 (31)).

> whether this law (or parts of it) shall cover activities on the German continental shelf or in the EEZ claimed by Germany. As matters relating to the EEZ and the continental shelf are often seen as "side issues" of legislation relating to specific fields, for example legislation covering environmental protection or spatial planning, the Federation has not enacted a comprehensive "maritime code", but has passed or amended various (public law) statutes and regulations in order to cover activities in the waters beyond Germany's territorial sea. (notes removed)

A similar conclusion and doubt as to the application of legislation adopted by the Netherlands was expressed by Dr. Verwer who points out that:

> The *Water Management Act* essentially went into effect on 1 January 1997. Its purpose is to protect waterworks owned by the Kingdom of the Netherlands against damage of any kind and to promote an efficient and safe use of these waterworks. Although the intention is clearly to make the *Water Management Act* applicable to the EEZ, (regulated by Act of November 15, 2000 which went into effect on 6 December 2000) one might conclude the method to achieve this result is not effective. In article 1, paragraph 2, the definition of waterworks has been extended to the EEZ as well. *This deserves critical consideration; I propose that applicability beyond the boundaries of the territorial waters can only exist by means of an explicit article in the Act stating its applicability. Here the only mention is of extension of a definition to cover the EEZ as well, which is quite different from the explicit statement of applicability outside of the territorial waters.* The Act's explicit statement that it is not applicable to extractive activities in the EEZ, leading to the contrary rationale that the Act is applicable to the EEZ regarding all other aspects, does not convince me. This exemption of applicability to the EEZ is caused by the fact that the *Extraction Act* has its own system for licensing and supervision by authorities. (emphasis added)

In that context it is interesting to note that Dr. Verwer (The Netherlands) points out, by contrast, in connection with (presumably) Dutch workers on the EEZ:

> Apart from the applicability of the acts and regulations presented above, I would like to draw attention to certain other aspects in Dutch legislation applicable in the EEZ. Article 2, paragraph 3 of the Industrial Disability Insurance Order (Besluit uitbreiding en beperking kring verzekerden WAZ) states that *workers in the EEZ are not considered to be working abroad. Therefore they have the full benefit of the national social security system as far as disability insurance is concerned. This means that a part of the Dutch social security system has extraterritorial applicability.* This is not the only example. Article 12, paragraph 3 of the Extension and Limitation Circle Insured People National Insurance Order 1999 (Besluit uitbreiding en beperking verzekerden volksverzekeringen 1999) contains the same extension concerning national insurance in favor of workers in the EEZ (notes removed, emphasis added).

Other countries such as Belgium have adopted legislation explicitly directed to the EEZ and/or the continental shelf. Drs. Maes and Somers (Belgium) explain:

> The focus of the 1999 EEZ Act is on exercising sovereign rights for the purpose of exploring and exploiting natural resources, as well as conservation, protection, and management of these living and non-living natural resources, whether on the subsoil, the seabed, or in superjacent waters. The Act enables further legislation regarding other economic activities, such as production of energy from the water, currents, and winds (see supra offshore wind energy) (article 4).

The majority of the National Reports are concerned with what may be regarded as the application of reasonably well developed (even if fragmented) public law. Most did not address the private law aspects in great detail. However Dr. Wurmnest in his report on Germany provides a thoughtful and lengthy exposition of potential private law questions in the context of both the application of general principles on the conflict of laws and the application of EU treaty law on the conflict of laws:

> Thus far, this report has highlighted public law provisions applicable to the EEZ and the continental shelf. The increased number and intensity of activities taking place outside territorial waters have also generated a variety of legal problems falling in the realm of private law. German private law applies to offshore activities on the continental shelf or in the German EEZ if envisaged by the rules of private international law. For certain areas of law, most notably contract and tort law, these rules were recently "communitarized" by enacting the so called Rome I and Rome II Regulations. Other matters are still governed by the German conflict rules laid down in the Introductory Act to the Civil Code (EGBGB). None of the aforementioned statutes comprises a special conflict rule for activities on the continental shelf or in the EEZ. Therefore existing general rules must be adapted to fit into the maritime context. Due to space constraints, the following overview is limited to three examples of private disputes: ship collisions, selected labor law disputes arising from employment contracts that are performed in the EEZ, and property rights related to objects located on the continental shelf or in the EEZ.

Similarly, also in the EU context, Dr. Luís de Lima Pinheiro,[53] in the National Report for Portugal, considers questions of private law but focuses more on the question of which court would have jurisdiction, describing the situation as follows:

> Regarding jurisdiction for private law claims, the jurisdiction rules in tort matters shall be taken into account. In tort matters, the rules of the Brussels I Regulation (EC Regulation no 44/2001) are applicable where the defendant is domiciled in a Member State (Article 4(1)). A person domiciled in a Member State may be sued in the courts of that Member State (Article 2(1)) and in the courts of the place where the harmful event occurred or may occur (Article 5(3)). For this purpose the exclusive economic zone and the continental shelf are parts of the coastal state. The Brussels I Regulation does not affect the conventions to which the Member States are parties and which, in relation to particular matters, govern jurisdiction (Article 71(1)). .... Outside the scope of application of the Brussels I Regulation and of the aforementioned Brussels Convention, the jurisdiction in tort matters is defined by internal rules. The general jurisdiction rule is contained in Article 65 of the Code of Civil Procedure. Article 65(1)(b) refers to the rules of territorial jurisdiction. According to these rules, the court of the place where the harmful event occurred has jurisdiction in tort matters (Article 74(2)). .... Article 65(1)(c) allows the jurisdiction of the Portuguese courts where any of the facts that form the cause of action occurs in Portuguese territory. This paragraph has been abrogated by the Lei no 52/2008, of 28 August, but it is doubtful whether this abrogation has any effect before 1 September 2010 (Article 187 of the referred Lei). It seems sustainable that for the purpose of all these internal jurisdiction rules the exclusive economic zone and the continental shelf may be considered part of the Portuguese territory. The reporter has no notice that this jurisdiction has been exercised.

Questions of property law are, however, more complex. As Professor Salcido (USA), also points out, there is, increasingly, an interest, even an "agitation" as she describes it, in the USA, regarding the lack of developed property law for the EEZ and continental shelf and the problems posed by these demands in the context of what is seen as public resources:

> B. Agitation for Property Rights in the OCS and EEZ
>
> As the previous sections have indicated, new developments on the OCS [outer continental shelf] and in the EEZ have required assessing existing legal tools. Among the multiple policy prescriptions suggested, many call for increased reliance on property rights. Yet concern about awarding exclusive rights to public resources, even within a limited time frame, accompanies all new authorizations of EEZ and OCS uses.
>
> By proclaiming a 200-mile EEZ, the United States does not claim exclusive ownership of the seabed and subsoil or of the water column above. While it has not been tested, the issue of property rights on the OCS and in the EEZ is unclear and only recently is being explored by scholars. Gail Osherenko puts it thus:
>
>> [T]he 1982 Convention does not clarify whether the extension of sovereign rights over the EEZ includes property rights ... Commentators and scholars have expounded at length on the extension of authority under the 1982 Convention, as well as the constraints on coastal state authority. But they have not explored the nature of property rights, if any, that coastal states may claim as a result of declaring an EEZ.
>
> ...
>
> The question of property rights is pertinent today because investors in EEZ development have agitated for maximum financial security. In general, the federal government has provided security to investors in OCS and EEZ developments through permits, leases, easements, licenses, and right-of-ways. OCSLA property rights have been the subject of interpretation in U.S. courts, exposing the limited nature of the rights conveyed by OCSLA leases. A lease under OCSLA does not convey title. Nonetheless, it is a vested property interest which allows one granted such interest recourse to the government to stand behind an assertion of the rights granted.
>
> U.S. courts also seek to address issues of security regarding offshore development by contract law, or by alternative legal analyses such as application of the Sovereign Acts Doctrine or the Unmistakably Doctrine. For example, an agency must compensate for a breach of

---

[53] In his comments to the Session at the XVIIIth Congress, Dr Pinheiro made proposals, essentially agreeing with points made by Dr Wurmnest, on the question of which law would likely apply, at least in the EU context (Rome Treaty). In his view it was important to try to present some suggestions as to the likely application of law in order to help provide certainty. He provided suggestions with respect to contract, tort and property claims. In his opinion the following could be seen as likely scenarios:

1. Contracts: The choice of law under the contract would prevail followed by location of the object (if a contract regarding an immovable) and if a contract is for employment then it would be the place where the work is located subject to the overriding provisions regarding the law most favorable to protect the workers.
2. With respect to torts it is likely to be the general principle of "where the damage occurs." However, in the case of "internal torts"on ships, that would be the law of the flag state, while in the case of "external torts" it would be the coastal state.
3. In connection with property claims it would be the most recognizable law and distinctions might be drawn between, for example, chattels on rigs and other claims.

> its regulatory contract even if the breach is compelled by an act of Congress. In *Mobil Oil Exploration & Producing Southeast, Inc. v. United States*, the Supreme Court granted restitution to plaintiffs whose oil and gas "lease contracts" were breached by delay and subsequent revision of the process for approving exploration and production plans and obtaining drilling permits.
>
> Thus, there are a variety of ways to ensure reliability and security of tenure for offshore developers vis-à-vis the U.S. government which has not required resolution of the exact nature, if any, of the property rights of the United States in the EEZ. Remedies arising from contract law and other principles of restitution serve as security for investors. Yet each step taken toward increasing security in offshore developments is accompanied by criticism regarding the abdication of government responsibilities toward quintessentially public resources. In the following section this critique is evaluated through discussion of a public trust in EEZ resources.

In connection with use of contractual arrangements for projects located in the EEZ it is of interest to note the situation in Poland that is described by Professor Dragun-Gertner, Dr. Pyć and Zuzanna Peplowaka in their National Report:

> The Contract for Use is in fact a lease contract. By definition, all Polish sea areas within the territorial sea and internal sea waters are the property of the State and cannot be sold, therefore the lease is given for a limited period. The contract contains the amount of the annual rent, the calculation of which is defined by law. Stipulations of the *Erecting and Use Permit* are an integral part of the Contract. Of course the Contract cannot be drawn for sea areas located in the EEZ, since by international law, though their use is controlled by the coastal State, they are not a part of its territory.

19.4 Observations and Conclusions

The foregoing discussion has highlighted some points of interest with respect to "the law applicable on the continental shelf and in the EEZ". The following observations can be made:

- Despite the codification and development of the international regime, the "applicable law" still remains uncertain, fragmented and in general undeveloped or certainly misunderstood, particularly with respect to application of private law.
- At the same time, the EEZ and continental shelf are clearly not "law free zones."
- Regionalism is having a significant impact on the law applicable in these areas, and also creating additional uncertainty even while seeking to create a further level of harmonization in approach among countries that are part of the European Union. The situation is complex in these countries with the various allocations of competencies in these areas.
- The law is also more complex in countries where there is a division of legislative jurisdiction between levels of governments in a State (for example, in federations).
- Significant attention has been paid to domestic law (which in turn reflects regional pressures) in connection with regulation of living resources (i.e., fish) in the EEZ and to spatial claims, especially in connection with establishing the outer limits of the continental shelf if it extends beyond the EEZ or is contested, even for states that are not party to the LOSC.
- Although the terminology differs, States have advocated and pursued various spatial planning efforts to develop integrated management and ocean policy conceptual approaches. However, in many cases, the law remains sectoral in focus.
- Relatively little attention has been paid to private law questions. There are clearly some problems and uncertainty in connection with, for example, mobile offshore drilling rigs, in connection with the question of the applicability of, for example, labor standards or jurisdiction to hear cases in the event of an incident or determining the applicable law.

The proposition can be advanced that the applicable law on the continental shelf and in the EEZ will *probably* be the law of the proximate coastal State (subject to internal or regional division of authority) except for the specific exceptions under the LOSC and other international law pertaining to flag state responsibility for events on board ships and aircraft when navigating through or flying over these areas. However, the extent to which national law does apply is not certain unless the State has expressly extended its law to apply outside its territory to these areas. The question of the application of private law in these two areas appears more complex and, as yet, relatively undeveloped. However, it is likely that the general principles of private international law that would apply in the case of conflict of law for contracts, torts and property law (for chattels) would be equally applicable, with the EEZ and continental shelf being considered as the territory of the relevant coastal State for this purpose.

The Protection of Foreign Investment[1]

20

Wenhua Shan

20.1 Introduction

The law of foreign investment is at a crossroad, in the wake of a dramatic surge of investment treaty arbitration cases (Chart 20.1) and an unprecedented global financial crisis leading to sharp decrease in global investment flows (Chart 20.2). Scholars and government officials from both developed and developing worlds have been debating whether and to what extent the previously neo-liberalist approach represented by liberal BITs should be reformed to fit the new reality of the current world. This study presents an updated account of the *status quo* of the legal protection of foreign investment in the world, on the basis of a comparative study of reports on the subject from 22 representative jurisdictions, taking into account other relevant recent studies such as those conducted by the UNCTAD and OECD.

The main purpose of this report is to identify major differences, similarities and trends in the law of foreign investment protection in different jurisdictions, and make suggestions for future actions to be taken at global and/or jurisdictional levels. The surveyed laws cover both domestic law and applicable international treaties. Whenever possible, it also investigates how they have been implemented and interpreted in practice.

This report is primarily based on 20 original jurisdictional reports[2] produced by leading scholars from the corresponding jurisdictions, including Argentina, Australia, Canada, China, Croatia, Czech Republic, Ethiopia, France, Germany, Greece, Italy, Japan, South Korea, Macau, Peru, Portugal, Russia, Singapore, Slovenia, Turkey, UK and USA. They cover all of the five continents, and three major categories of economies namely developed, developing and the transition economies. They not only include seven of the top ten foreign direct investment (FDI) recipients in the world, but also eight of the top ten capital exporting countries (Chart 20.3). Six of the reported economies are also among the top ten signatories of BITs up to end 2008 (Chart 20.4). It can therefore be said that, to a considerable extent, this study illustrates the *status quo* of legal protection of foreign investment in the world.

As do the jurisdictional reports, this general report follows the questionnaire designed by the general reporter for this study. It intends to cover the most important aspects concerning the protection of foreign investment, ranging from admission regimes to post-admission standards of treatment, from protection against expropriation and guarantee of free transfer to settlement of investment disputes. It starts with a

[1] IV.A.1, La protection des investissements étrangers.

W. Shan (✉)
College of Humanities and Social Sciences, Xi'an Jiaotong University, Xi'an, China
e-mail: shan@mail.xjtu.edu.cn

[2] The commonly used term is "national report". However, the term "jurisdictional report" is used here as it is more appropriate to also cover the report of Macau, which is not a "National Report".

K.B. Brown and D.V. Snyder (eds.), *General Reports of the XVIIIth Congress of the International Academy of Comparative Law/Rapports Généraux du XVIIIème Congrès de l'Académie Internationale de Droit Comparé*, DOI 10.1007/978-94-007-2354-2_20, © Springer Science+Business Media B.V. 2012

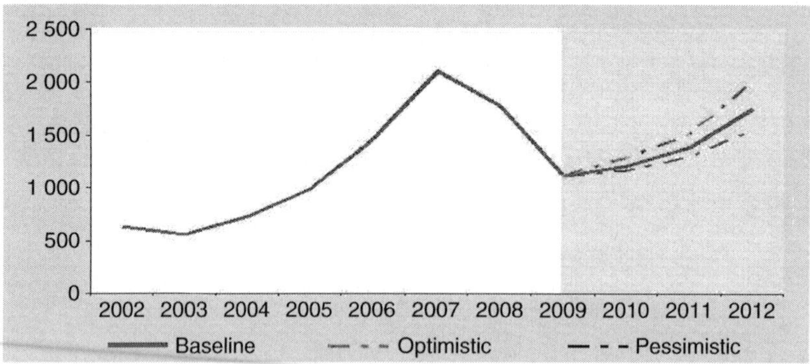

Chart 20.1 Global FDI Flows 2002–2009 with predictions for 2010–2012 (US$ Billion) (Source: UNCTAD, *World Investment Report 2010*)

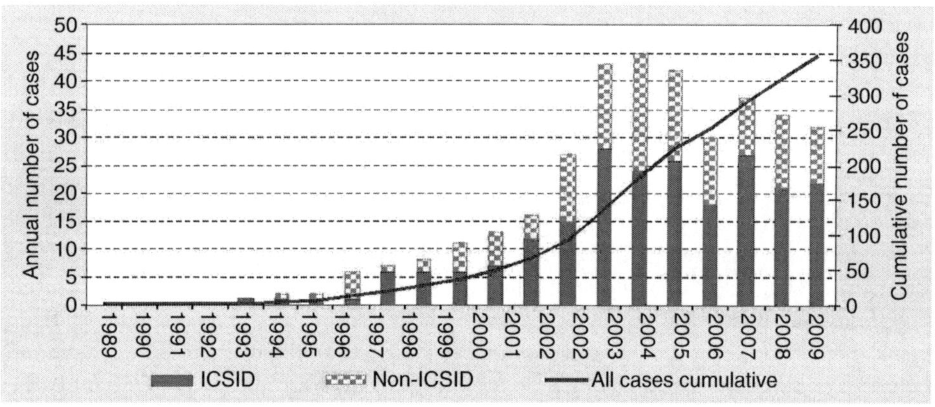

Chart 20.2 Known investment treaty arbitration cases (Cumulative and new cases) 1989–2009 (Source: UNCTAD, *World Investment Report 2010*)

comparison of the overall legal framework for foreign investment and concludes with an outlook at the future regime on international investment.

The study has identified three main themes of recent development in foreign investment protection, namely "harmonisation", "balancing" and "socialisation". It concludes that the paradigm of international investment law has been shifted from "North-South Divide" to "Private-Public Debate", and that the future development of international investment law will most likely lead to a multilateral investment agreement (MIA) effectuating a "balanced liberal" investment regime.

20.2 Legal Framework Governing Foreign Investment

To compare foreign investment laws and treaties it is important to understand how they fit together and interact with each other. In other words, it is important first of all to establish the general legal framework that governs foreign investment in a given jurisdiction including both domestic and international laws. The relationship between domestic and international laws should also be discussed to ascertain any hierarchy between them. The issue of transparency is also addressed, as a subject of growing importance.

Top 20 FDI Importers and Exporters 2008-2009 (Billion US$)

	2009	2008
United States	129.9	324.6
China	95.0	108.3
France	59.6	62.3
Hong Kong, China	48.4	59.6
United Kingdom	45.7	91.5
Russian Federation	38.7	75.5
Germany	35.6	24.4
Saudi Arabia	35.5	38.2
India	34.6	40.4
Belgium	33.8	110.0
Italy	30.5	17.0
Luxembourg	27.3	9.3
Netherlands	26.9	
Brazil	25.9	45.1
British Virgin Islands	25.3	44.6
Ireland	25.0	
Australia	22.6	46.7
Canada	18.7	55.3
Singapore	16.8	10.9
Spain	15.0	73.3

	2009	2008
United States	248.1	330.5
France	147.2	161.1
Japan	74.7	128.0
Germany	62.7	134.6
Hong Kong, China	52.3	50.6
China	48.0	52.2
Russian Federation	46.1	56.1
Italy	43.9	43.8
Canada	38.8	80.8
Norway	34.2	29.5
Sweden	30.3	27.8
British Virgin Islands	26.5	39.2
Ireland	20.8	13.5
United Kingdom	18.5	161.1
Australia	18.4	32.8
Netherlands	17.8	20.1
Spain	16.3	74.9
Denmark	15.8	13.9
Switzerland	15.5	51.1
Luxembourg	15.0	16.6

Source: UNCTAD: World Investment Report 2010

Chart 20.3 Top 20 FDI importers and exporters 2008–2009 (Billion US$) (Source: UNCTAD: World Investment Report 2010)

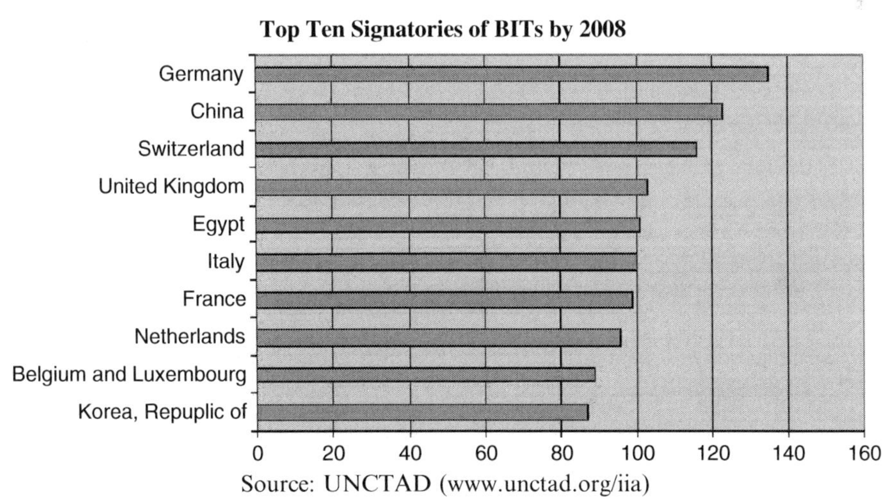

Chart 20.4 Top ten signatories of BITs by 2008 (Source: UNCTAD (www.unctad.org/iia))

20.2.1 The Legal Framework

20.2.1.1 Domestic Laws and Regulations

Protection of foreign investors and investments is often provided in the constitutions[3] of the host economy. Many of the constitutions stipulate that foreign investments and investors are protected in the same way as native investments and investors (national treatment).[4] Also, they tend to provide protection of property, as well as guarantees against impairment of contractual rights.[5]

Protection of foreign investments can also be found in other forms of domestic law than the constitution, such as the laws, regulations and administrative decrees. As Table 20.1 demonstrates, 11 of the 22 jurisdictions have special laws regulating foreign investment, whilst others do not. Australia, Canada, China, Russia and Turkey are among these having special foreign investment laws. In Australia Foreign Acquisitions and Takeovers Act 1975 (the FATA) and its implementing regulations have been promulgated to regulate foreign acquisition and takeovers of Australian companies.[6] In Canada the law governing foreign direct investment activities is the Investment Canada Act.[7] Foreign investment in China is primarily governed by Sino-Foreign Equity Joint Venture Law, Sino-Foreign Contractual Joint Venture Law and the Wholly Foreign Owned Enterprises Law.[8] In Russia, the two basic laws governing foreign investment are the Federal Law on Foreign Investment in the Russian Federation and the Federal Law on Investment Activity in the Russian Federation.[9] In Turkey, foreign direct investment is governed by the Foreign Direct Investment Law.[10] (Table 20.1) It can be seen that not only developing states have adopted special regimes for foreign investment; developed states such as Australia, Canada and Greece have taken the same course of action. There seems to be no clear-cut distinction between developed and developing states in this regard.

20.2.1.2 Applicable International Treaties

So far there is no comprehensive agreement on a global scale on foreign investment, a sharp contrast to the area of international trade where the World Trade Organisation (WTO) Agreements provide the general legal framework for world trade regulation. There are nevertheless some specialised multilateral investment treaties, such as ICSID Convention, MIGA Convention, which focus on certain aspects of investment protection. The *General Agreement on Trade in Service* (GATS) and the *Trade Related Investment Measures Agreements* (TRIPS) under the regime of WTO, and New York Convention are also very important for protection of foreign investments. Among the 22 jurisdictions, 20 are WTO members (excluding Ethiopia, Russia and Slovenia); 17 ratified the ICSID Convention (except Canada, Ethiopia and Macau); 21 are parties to the New York Convention (excluding Ethiopia and Macau); 22 are MIGA member states (excluding Macau). In other words, these multilateral agreements are playing important roles in regulating and facilitating foreign investment in these jurisdictions, as they do in the rest of the world. (Table 20.1)

However, the most important instrument for investment protection continues to be bilateral investment treaties (BITs).[11] It is unsurprising that all the 22 jurisdictions have concluded BITs, together the number has reach 1,355 (Table 20.1). Six of them are

[3] In the case of Macau, the "Constitution" is the Basic Law of Macau Special Administrative Region of the People's Republic of China.

[4] For example, the Peruvian Constitution states that "National and foreign investments are subject to the same terms." The United States Constitution prohibits state and local governmentsfrom discriminating against resident aliens, except in the case of the exercise of political rights or employment as a public officer. See Article 63 of the Peruvian Constitution; US Report, Section on "General standard of treatment of foreign investment and investors".

[5] The Charter of Fundamental Rights and Freedoms of Czech Republic, for example, guarantees the right to property for everyone including foreign investors. On the other hand, the "Contracts Clause" in US Constitution prohibits the state or local government from impairing the obligation of contracts. See the Czech Report, Section 1 (on the Framework and hierarchy of foreign investment laws and treaties); US Report, Section on "Investment Contracts" (citing Article 1 Section 10 of the US Constitution).

[6] Australia Report, Section 1.

[7] Canada Report, Section 1.

[8] China Report, Section 1.

[9] Russia Report, Section 1.

[10] Turkey Report, Section 1.

[11] According to the statistics of UNCTAD, the total number of BITs rose to 2,750 at the end of 2009. See UNCTAD, World Investment Report 2010, at 81.

Table 20.1 Legal framework

		International treaties		International treaties vs. domestic law			Transparency	
Jurisdiction	**Special FI Law**	*BITs*	*Multilateral Agreements*	*Transformation*	*Incorporation*	*Partial Incorporation*	*Public Access*	*Public consultation*
Argentina	√ (Foreign Investment Law, law 21382 of 1976)	59	ICSID, New York Convention, MIGA, WTO		√		√ (Official Gazette, Congress's website)	√ (public hearings and comments)
Australia	√ [Foreign Acquisitions and Takeovers Act 1975 (Cth) (the FATA)]	23	ICSID, New York Convention, MIGA, WTO	√			√ (Australasian Legal Information Institute)	√ (Parliamentary committee system at federal and state levels)
Canada	√ (Investment Canada Act)	28	New York Convention, MIGA, WTO, NAFTA	√		(Customary IL automatically incorporated)	√ (Access to Information Act, Privacy Act, Official Gazette)	√ (public hearing, consultation, and Parliamentary committee system at federal and state levels)
China	√ (EJCL, CJVL, WFEL, etc)	130	ICSID, New York Convention, MIGA, WTO, FTAs	√			√ (State Council Gazettes, Official Websites)	√ (public hearing, expert consultation and congress discussions)
Croatia	×	59	ICSID, New York Convention, MIGA, WTO		√		√ (Official Gazette)	√
Czech Republic		83	ICSID, New York Convention, MIGA, WTO, and the ECT		√		√ (Law on free access to information)	/
Ethiopia	√ (Investment Proclamation, *etc.*)	30	MIGA, COMESA, IGAD		√		√ (National Gazette, EIA website)	/
France		102	ICSID, New York Convention, MIGA, WTO, and the ECT			EU law has direct effect.	√	√
Germany		139	ICSID, New York Convention, MIGA, WTO, ECT	√		(customary law and general principles of public international law)	√ (Official Gazette)	√ (public hearings, expert consultation, etc.)
Greece	√ (Legislative Decree 2687/1953)	44	ICSID, New York Convention, MIGA, WTO, ECT	√		EU law has direct effect	√ (Government Gazette (Efimerida tis Kyvrniseos)	/

(continued)

Table 20.1 (continued)

Jurisdiction	Special FI Law	International treaties		International treaties vs. domestic law			Transparency	
		BITs	*Multilateral Agreements*	*Transformation*	*Incorporation*	*Partial Incorporation*	*Public Access*	*Public consultation*
Italy		95	ICSID, New York Convention, MIGA, WTO, ECT	√		EU law has direct effect	√ (the national Official Journal etc)	√
Japan		16	ICSID, New York Convention, MIGA, WTO, ECT			√ (Self-executing treaties directly applicable)	√ (government's website)	√
South Korea	√ (Foreign Investment Promotion Act)	94	ICSID, New York Convention, MIGA, WTO		√		√ (Official Gazette, internet)	√
Macau		2	/			√ (direct effect depends on the treaty itself)	√ (Official Bulletin)	√
Peru	√ (Legislative Decree No 662 and Decree No 757)	29	WTO, ICSID, MIGA, New York Conventions, WTO,		√		√ (official gazette)	/
Portugal		51	ICSID, New York Convention, MIGA, WTO, ECT		√		√ (publication as a condition for validity)	√
Russia	√ (*The Law on Investment Activity* and *the Law on Foreign Investments)*	67	ICSID, New York Convention, MIGA		√		√ (Official Gazette, internet)	√
Singapore		41	ICSID, New York Convention, MIGA, WTO		√		√ (Government Gazette and database)	
Slovenia	√ (Promotion of Foreign Direct Investment and Internationalisation of Enterprises Act)	38	ICSID, New York Convention, MIGA, WTO, ECT		√		√ (Official Gazette, internet)	√
Turkey	√ *(Foreign Direct Investment Law)*	80	ICSID, New York Convention, MIGA,WTO		√		√ (Official Gazette and internet)	√
UK		105	ICSID, New York Convention, MIGA, WTO, and the ECT	√		EU law has direct effect.	√ (Official Gazette and internet)	√ (a comprehensive system)
USA		40	ICSID, New York Convention, MIGA, WTO,			√ (self-executive directly applicable)	/	/
Total	**11**	**1355**		**7**	**11**	**3**		

among the top ten signatories of the world.[12] Germany is leading the league table, followed by China (Second), UK (Fourth), France (Seventh) and South Korea (Tenth).[13] Other international investment-related agreements ("other IIAs" as termed by the UNCTAD reports), such as free trade agreements (FTAs), have gained significance in investment protection.[14] For example, Canada, China, France, Germany, UK, US and Korea have all concluded at least one new IIAs between November 2009 and May 2010.[15] It should nevertheless be noted that such IIAs tend to focus on investment liberalisation and investment promotion, rather than providing a full set of investment protection provisions typically found in BITs.[16] They therefore tend to be complimentary to rather than substitutes for BITs.

20.2.2 The Relationship Between International Treaties and Domestic Laws

To establish the legal framework for foreign investment protection, it is necessary to investigate the relations between domestic and international norms existing within the framework. Without indulging in a lengthy discussion on relevant theories, suffice it to remind that there are different theories on such relationship, including *dualism*, *monism* and 'a third approach, being somewhat a modification of the dualist position'.[17] Another classification is between "transformation" or "incorporation" approaches. In practice, it is not always so easy to classify a jurisdiction as falling squarely within one of categories. Whilst the dualist theory may still represent the legal reality of the world, the Kelsenian monist theory seems to have been gaining ground with international law making more and more significant inroads into domestic legal systems.[18] In this regard international investment law provides a significant example, as it is increasingly impacting domestic law and policy makings.

Most of the 22 jurisdictions have some express rules on the relationship between international law and domestic law in their constitutions, except China, Japan and the UK which does not have a written constitution as such. With respect to the hierarchy between international treaties and domestic laws, most of the constitutions recognize the supremacy of the constitution. In general, the legal hierarchy goes from higher to lower as follows: the Constitution, international treaties, and national laws.[19] However, there are exceptions and complications. The Supreme Court of Japan, for instance, considers that certain types of treaties such as the peace treaties and treaties modifying territories are superior to the Constitution.[20] The Constitution of Argentina gives primacy of integration and human rights treaties over other treaties.[21] Under the Peruvian laws, the hierarchy of international treaties depends on the status of the legal entity approving the treaties.[22] Consequently, the hierarchy of the laws goes from higher to lower as follows: Constitution, international treaties approved by congress, national law, international treaties approved by the President.[23]

In cases of conflict between international treaties and domestic laws, most States provide that international treaties shall prevail. However, in US a treaty has the same status as a federal law, and a subsequently enacted federal law can supersede a treaty for domestic purposes, even though the treaty may still be binding as a matter of international law. The same applies to Germany where international treaties are conceived as federal statutes within the domestic hierarchy. International treaties may be abrogated or amended by subsequent

[12] See UNCTAD/WEB/DLAE/IA/2009/8, Recent Developments in International Investment Agreements (2008-June 2009), IIA MONITOR No.3 (2009), available at:
http://www.unctad.org/en/docs/webdiaeia20098_en.pdf.

[13] Id.

[14] UNCTAD statistics show that by the end of 2009, 2,894 double taxation treaties (DTTs) and 295 other IIAs have been concluded, making the total number of IIAs reaching 5,939. See UNCTAD, World Investment Report 2010, at 81.

[15] UNCTAD and OECD, Third Report on G20 Investment Measures (Geneva and Paris, 14 June 2010), at p 7.

[16] It is however noted that most of Canada's FTAs (e.g., NAFTA and FTA with Chile, Jordan but not EFTA and the Costa Rica FTA) include investment chapters that are just like Canada's BITs.

[17] See e.g., Malcolm N. Shaw, *International Law*, 5th ed. (Cambridge: Cambridge University Press, 2003), 121–124.

[18] A Cassese, *International Law*, 2nd ed. (Oxford: Oxford University Press, 2005), 216–217.

[19] In Argentina, for instance, treaties prevail over internal laws, but not provisions of the Federal Constitution. See Argentina Report, Section 1.

[20] Japan Report, Section 1.

[21] Argentina Report, Section 1.

[22] Peru Report, Section 1.

[23] Id.

federal statutes, even though it might trigger international responsibility from an international law perspective. German constitution nevertheless requires subsequent statutes being interpreted and applied in utmost conformity with previous international treaties, unless the legislator's intention to deviate from a previous treaty is explicit and unquestionable.

As Table 20.1 shows, many jurisdictions do not recognize "direct effect" of international treaties within the domestic legal system. Thus in states such as UK, Germany, China, Australia, Canada and Greece, foreign investors cannot directly invoke international treaties before local courts.[24] However, international law may still play a significant indirect role in domestic courts of these jurisdictions. In Australia, for example, the highest court confirmed in the *Toeh* case that: "Apart from influencing the construction of a statue or subordinate legislation, an international convention may play a part in the development by the courts of the common law. The provisions of an international convention to which Australia is a party, especially one which declares universal fundamental rights, may be used by the courts as a legitimate guide in developing the common law."[25]

In US and Japan, whether an international treaty can be directly invoked depends on the nature of the particular case. Only "self-executing" treaties can be directly invoked whilst others can not.[26] To some extent Czech Republic and Slovenia seem to have adopted the same line.[27] Some jurisdictions such as Germany, however, accept direct application of customary international law and general principles of international law.[28] Canada also admits the automatic incorporation of customary international law into its domestic laws, but this does not apply to the extent that it conflicts with existing Canadian laws or common laws.[29]

In other jurisdictions, however, international treaties automatically become part of the domestic law. Thus a treaty ratified by the federal Parliament of Ethiopia automatically becomes an enforceable law as the same as other domestic legislation. Courts of appropriate jurisdictions are therefore empowered to apply the law should the need arises. Accordingly, foreign investors are able to rely on these laws either before domestic or international tribunals.[30] The same applies to Peru and South Korea. Moreover, in EU Member States such as UK, Germany, France, Italy, Greece and Slovenia, the EU Law can be directly invoked by EU investors before domestic courts, as established by the European Court of Justice (ECJ) in the *Van Gend* case.[31]

A unique problem for the EU Member States is the overlap between the BITs the have signed and the EC law. Traditionally the Member States enjoy the power to enter into BITs, whilst the EU also has certain powers over foreign investment, e.g., on monetary transfer. Such overlap of competence has led to some cases before European courts[32] and international arbitration tribunals.[33] In the European court cases, the supremacy of EC law was upheld and the relevant Member States were ordered to modify their BITs to comply with the EC law requirements.[34] In some

[24] See relative Section of the Jurisdictional Reports respectively.

[25] *Minister for Immigration and Ethnic Affairs v Teoh* (1995) 183 CLR 273 per Mason CJ and Deane J at 288. Citing *Mabo v Queensland (No 2)* (1992) 175 CLR 1, 42 per Brennan J (with whom Mason CJ and McHugh agreed); *Dietrich v The Queen* (1992) 177 CLR 292, 321 per Brennan J, 360 per Toohey J; *Jago v District Court of New South Wales* (1988) 12 NSWLR 558, 569 per Kirby P.

[26] See Section 1 of the US and Japan Reports.

[27] See Section 1 of the Czech and Slovenia Reports.

[28] See Germany Report, Section 2.

[29] A very similar position is taken in the UK; see e.g. Trendtex Trading Corporation v Central Bank of Nigeria [1977] QB 529.

[30] See e.g. *Salini Costrutorri S.p.A and Italstrade S.p.A v. The Federal Republic of Ethiopia*, Addis Ababa Water and Sewerage Authority (Award regarding the suspension of proceedings and jurisdiction), ICC, Case No. 10623/AER/ACS (December 7, 2001), also available at http://www.asil.org/ilib0616.cfm#j2 (accessed September 17, 2009). See Section 1 of the Ethiopia Report.

[31] See *Case 26/62, Van Gend en Loss v Nederlanse Administratie der Belsatingen*, ECR1(1963).

[32] In 2004, the European Commission filed cases against Austria, Finland, Sweden and Denmark before the European Court of Justice (ECJ), alleging that some of their pre-accession BITs with non-EU countries may be in conflict with the EC Law. According to the Commission, the BITs signed between these four Member States and non-EU states do not include exceptions allowing for possibility of EU controls on capital flows in exceptional circumstances.

[33] See, for instance, Eastern Sugar BV (Netherlands) v The Czech Republic (*Eastern Sugar v Czech*), SCC No. 088/2004. the Award is available at: http://ita.law.uvic.ca/documents/EasternSugar.pdf.

[34] In March 2009, the ECJ held that Austria and Sweden were both in breach of Article 307 of the EC Law as regards their failure to revise BITs with certain non-EU countries. On 19 November 2009, in Commission v Finland (Case C 118/07), the ECJ held that Finland also failed to take the appropriate steps to eliminate incompatibilities with EC Law with regard to transfer of capital contained in the BITs at issue. See PLC Arbitration, ECJ finds Finland's BITs breach article 307 of the EC Treaty, available at: http://arbitration.practicallaw.com/1-500-8076.

investment treaty arbitration cases, several EU Member States were ordered to honor BIT commitments, notwithstanding the conflicting EC law requirements.[35] The inclusion of "foreign direct investment" (FDI) in the Common Commercial Policy under the 2009 Treaty of Lisbon might not have completely cured the problem. At least portfolio investment is not yet brought under the express exclusive competence of the Union. It is therefore only a halfway towards a complete "common investment competence".[36] Recently, the EU has launched an investment package, which comprises two documents: a policy paper entitled "Towards a comprehensive European international investment policy", and a proposal for a Regulation that would establish transitional arrangements regarding BITs concluded by EU member states third states before the Lisbon Treaty.[37] It is intended that to provide legal security for European and foreign investors, without hampering the EU's ability to negotiate new investment treaties at EU level. Whether or not it will succeed remains to be seen.

20.2.2.1 Hierarchy in Domestic Laws and Regulations

Generally speaking, the hierarchy goes from higher to lower as follows: the Constitution, national law and local law.[38] At national law level, formal laws prevail over administrative regulations, which in turn prevail over ministerial orders. It shall however be noted that in small countries such as Singapore there is no hierarch of domestic laws because all domestic legislation is national legislation due to its size.[39]

[35] See e.g. *Eastern Sugar v Czech*, *supra* footnote 33.

[36] Further details and analysis can be found in e.g., Wenhua Shan and Sheng Zhang, "*The Lisbon treaty: A Halfway towards a Common Investment Policy of the EU,*" European Journal of Int'l Law, no. 4, 2010.

[37] The two documents can be found at: http://trade.ec.europa.eu/doclib/docs/2010/July/tradoc_146308.pdf (last visited on July 10, 2010).

[38] It is noted that under federal structure such as that in Canada, the provincial governments have exclusive (or shared) jurisdiction over many matters relevant to commercial regulation, such as environmental protection. See Canada Report for further details.

[39] See e.g., Singapore Report, Section 3.

20.2.2.2 Transparency

Almost all the 22 jurisdictions[40] have reported certain mechanisms to ensure transparency of foreign investment law and policies. This requirement is stipulated in domestic laws and/or international treaties. Article 52 of the Czech Constitution, for example, provides that the publication is required as a condition for its validity.[41] Canada has issued many acts concerning access to public information, including the federal *Access to Information Act* and *Privacy Act*.[42] On the other hand, the Sino-New Zealand FTA[43] and the Sino-Australia BIT[44] are examples of BITs that contain transparency provisions.[45] North American Free Trade Agreement (NAFTA) also requires the member states to ensure that all laws, regulations, procedures and administrative rulings of general application are published promptly or made available to interested persons.[46] In practice, the relative laws and regulations are published in the official *gazette*, and could also be accessed online. In Australia, there is a designated

[40] Some Jurisdictional Reports, such as the US and Peru Reports, did not provide complete information on this.

[41] Czech Report, Section 1.

[42] Canada Report, Section 1.

[43] According to this FTA, Committee of Investment established by Contracting Parties will consider to develop procedures that can enhance the transparency of non-confirming measures.

[44] Article 6 'transparency of laws' of Sino-Australia BIT provides that:

> Each Contracting Party shall, with a view to promoting the understanding of its laws and policies that pertain to or affect investments in its territory of nationals of the other Contracting Party:
> (a) make such laws and policies public and readily accessible;
> (b) if requested, provide copies of specified laws and policies to the other Contracting Party; and
> (c) if requested, consult with the other Contracting Party with a view to explaining specified laws and policies.

[45] China Report, Section 1.

[46] Article 1802 'publication' of NAFTA provides that,

> Each Party shall ensure that its laws, regulations, procedures and administrative rulings of general application respecting any matter covered by this Agreement are promptly published or otherwise made available in such a manner as to enable interested persons and Parties to become acquainted with them.
>
> To the extent possible, each Party shall: publish in advance any such measure that it proposes to adopt; andprovide interested persons and Parties a reasonable opportunity to comment on such proposed measures.

organization, namely the Australian Legal Information Institute, which provides free and comprehensive online access to Australian legal materials.[47] In Argentina, all congressional debates are published and the general public can readily access them[48]. In Singapore, online database is provided by the Ministry of Trade and Industry.[49]

In addition, some jurisdictions provide for public consultation procedures in relation to foreign investment laws and regulations. In Japan, comments from the public have to be sought when an administrative organ intends to lay down an administrative order.[50] Chinese law also requires that opinions from relevant organs, organizations and citizens be solicited when drafting administrative regulations.[51] The solicitation of opinions may be conducted in such forms as meetings, seminars and public hearings. In Argentina, a public hearing is required before any change of tariffs or other substantial changes can be implemented by the Controlling Bodies in the system of privatized public services. Non-governmental organizations (NGOs) and the general public can participate in such hearing to discuss any amendment to the system of tariffs or any procedures that may affect consumers.[52] Similar hearings are required when there are important changes in federal environmental matters affecting regulated industries. Such mechanism helps to alert the public and the investors of any regulatory changes that may adversely affect their interests.[53] In Italy, a number of general principles are provided in local statutes with regard to access to the documents of the procedure, right to participate and submit (written) observations, the duty to motivate and decision of the public administration, the duty to adopt a final decision when the procedure is obligatorily initiated upon request of an interested party.[54] An impact assessment may also be carried out to assess the potential effexts of any administrative or regulatory act on foreign investment.[55]

[47] Australia Report, Section 1.

[48] Argentina Report, Section 1.

[49] Singapore Report, Section 3.

[50] Japan Report, Section 1.

[51] Article 58 of Chinese Law on Legislation 2000.

[52] Argentina Report, Section 1.

[53] Id.

[54] Italy Report, Section 1.

[55] Id.

20.3 General Standards of Treatment

The general standards of treatment determines the general status of foreign investment in a given host state. They are often stipulated in a separate provision in investment treaties. Other common BIT provisions, such as expropriation and compensation, monetary transfer, subrogation, also set forth standards of treatment but on more confined albeit important issues. As Table 20.2 shows, on the one hand, the most common general standards of treatment under international investment treaties are non-discrimination treatment including national treatment and MFN treatment, and fair and equitable treatment, complimented by international minimum/law standard and constant protection and security. On the other hand, domestic law tends to focus on the implementation of (or the deviation from) national treatment.

20.3.1 Standards of Treatment Under International Treaties

Under international treaties, some general standards of treatment have been established. The most common standards of treatment under investment treaties are don-discrimination treatment including national treatment and most-favoured-nation treatment, fair and equitable treatment. In some cases investment treaties also require international law/minimum treatment and constant protection and security. Such standards are nevertheless subject to variations in detail and may also be interpreted in different ways by arbitration tribunals. The following discusses the three most common standards.

20.3.1.1 Non-discrimination Treatment

The non-discrimination principle is one of the fundamental principles underpinning international investment treaties. Its most common manifestations are the most-favored-nation (MFN) clause and the national treatment (NT) clause.[56] Lorz noted in his German report that the two standards appeared to be central to

[56] Norah Gallagher and Wenhua Shan, *Chinese Investment Treaties: Policy and Practice* (Oxford: Oxford University Press, 2009), 139.

Table 20.2 Standards of treatment

Jurisdiction	Treatment under international treaties						Treatment under domestic law	
	Fair and Equitable Treatment	*National treatment*	*MFN Treatment*	*International law/minimum standard*	*Constant protection and security*	*Other Standards*	*National Treatment*	*Other Standards*
Argentina	√	√	√	√	√	/	√	/
Australia	√	√	√	√	√	transparency	√	/
Canada	√	√ (+admission)	√ (+admission)	√	√	Transparency, Limitations on performance requirements, nationality requirements for senior officers.	√ (on property interests under the Citizenship Act)	/
China	√	√ (recent treaties)	√	√	√	/	√	/
Croatia	√	√	√	√	√	/	√	region and industry-specific incentives
Czech Republic	√	√	√	√	√	/	√	/
Ethiopia	√	√	√	√	√		/	/
France	√	√	√	√	√	/	√	/
Germany	√	√	√	√	√	/	√	/
Greece	√	√	√	√	√	/	√	/
Italy	√	√	√	√	/	/	√	/
Japan	√	√ (+admission)	√ (+admission)	√	√		√	/
South Korea	√	√	√	√	√	/	√	/
Macau	√	√	√	√	√		√	/
Peru	√	√	√	√	√		√	/
Portugal	√	√	√	√	√	/	√	Preferential treatment (PIN)
Russia	√	√	√	√	√	/	√	/
Singapore	√	√ (some)	√	√	√	/	√	/
Slovenia	√	√	√	√	√	/	√	/
Turkey	√	√	√	√	√	/	√	/
UK	√	√	√	√	√	Reasonable treatment	√	/
USA	√	√ (+admission)	√ (+admission)	√	√	/	√	/
Total	**22**	**22 (3+ admission)**	**22(3+admission)**	**22**	**21**	/	**21**	/

German BIT policy and have been characterized as '*sine qua non conditions*' for the conclusion of an investment treaty by Germany.[57] Indeed, they are standards that have now been accepted by all of the 22 Jurisdictions. (Table 20.2)

20.3.1.2 MFN Treatment

The MFN standard of treatment is the most commonly adopted standard in international investment treaties. Under such a standard, the relevant parties undertake to treat each other in a manner that is at least as favorable as they treat third parties. The purpose of this standard therefore is to create a level playing field among different foreign states by prohibiting discrimination on the basis of different foreign nationalities.[58] The MFN treatment in most of the BITs and FTAs is restricted to the post-establishment phase of an investment. However, in the recent BIT practice by US, Canada and Japan, this treatment is extended to cover the establishment stage of foreign investment.[59]

The most controversial question concerning MFN treatment is whether it would cover dispute-resolution provisions. On the one hand, the MFN clause has been used to effectively bypass purely procedural matters, such as the requirement of a period before submission to international arbitration.[60] On the other hand, it may be relied on to broaden the tribunal's jurisdiction.[61] To avoid such extension, a good practice is to include an express provision precluding the MFN applying to dispute resolution. The Japan-Peru BIT and the Japan-Switzerland EPA explicitly exclude clauses on dispute settlement form the scope of the MFN.[62] According to the Czech National Report, the Czech doctrine and practice share the view that MFN applies only to substantive law provisions of the BIT and not to the arbitration clause.[63] The investment chapter in the Sino-New Zealand FTA also clarifies that 'for great certainty, the obligation in this Article does not encompass a requirement to extend to investors of the other Party resolution procedures other than those set out in this chapter.'[64]

In most of the BITs and FTAs there are also some general exceptions to the MFN clause. These exceptions include regional economic integration, taxation treaties and frontier trade. Several of the most recent Chinese BITs contain a 'grandfather clause' exempting existing non-conforming measures or changes thereto from the reach of the MFN clause.[65] The Canadian New Model BIT has contained GATT-like general exceptions allowing parties to take measures necessary to (a) protect human, animal, or plant life or health; (b) ensure compliance with laws and regulation that are not inconsistent with the provisions of the Agreement and (c) to conserve living or non-living exhaustible natural resources.[66] These general exceptions, of course, apply to the MFN treatment.

---

[57] Germany Report, Section 2.

[58] Gallagher and Shan, *supra* footnote 52, at 140.

[59] Article 2.2 of the Japan-Republic of Korea BIT provides that 'Each Contracting Party shall in its territory accord to investors of the other Contracting Party and to their investments treatment no less favorable than the treatment it accords in like circumstances to investors of any third country and to their investments (hereinafter referred to as 'most-favored-nation treatment') with respect to investment and business activities.' Article 2.1 of this BIT provides that 'investment and business activities' refer to 'the establishment, acquisition, expansion, operation, management, maintenance, use, enjoyment, and sale or other disposal of investments.' Article 4 'most-favored-nation treatment' of the US Model BIT 2004 provides that 'Each Party shall accord to investors of the other Party treatment no less favorable than it accords, in like circumstances, to investors of any non-Party with respect to the establishment, acquisition, expansion, management, conduct, operation, and sale or other disposition of investments in its territory.' Article 4 of the Canada Model BIT 2004 has almost the same stipulation with that of the USA.

[60] Such as the case *Emilio Agustín Maffezini v. Kingdom of Spain* (ICSID Case No. ARB/97/7).

[61] Such as the case *RosInvest Co UK Ltd v Russian Federation*, Jurisdiction award, SCC Case No V079/2005, 5 October 2007 (became public in 2008).

[62] Japan Report, Section 2.

[63] Czech Report, Section 2.

[64] China Report, Section 2.

[65] Such as Article 3.3 of the Sino-Czech Republic BIT provides that the obligation to ensure MFN treatment to investors shall not apply in respect of the People's Republic of China to:

(a) *Any existing non-confirming measures maintained within its territory;*

(b) *The continuation of any non-confirming measure referred to in subparagraph* (a);

(c) *An amendment to any non-confirming measure referred to in subparagraph* (a) *to the extent that the amendment does not increase the non-conformity of the measure, as it existed immediately before the amendment, with those obligations.*

China nevertheless undertakes to take all appropriate steps in order to progressively remove the non-confirming measures. See China Report, Id.

[66] Canada Model BIT 2004, Article 10. See Canada Report, Section 2.

20.3.1.3 National Treatment

National treatment (NT) standard is the other main standard that underpins the principle of non-discrimination under investment treaties.[67] The purpose of this clause is to oblige a host state to make no negative differentiation between foreign and national investors.[68] However, the NT clause is not as common as the MFN clause in the BITs. In China's more than 120 BITs, for example, less than half of them have an NT provision. However, given that all the Chinese BITs contain a MFN clause, the investors and investments covered by a BIT without an NT clause may be entitled to NT by virtue of the MFN clause.[69] In most BITs, including these concluded by EU Member States, China, Russia and the Latin American States, the NT clause only applies to the post-establishment phase.[70] This is contrasted to the BIT practice of US, Canada and Japan, which tend to have NT clause to cover both market access and pre-establishment rights.[71] Likewise, not every Singaporean BIT has a NT clause.[72]

In most BITs the NT obligation is subject to qualifications and exceptions. The UK-USSR BIT for instance provides for a national treatment 'to the extent possible' and 'in accordance with its laws and regulations'.[73] The UK-Papua New Guinea BIT provides that 'special incentives granted by one contracting Party only to its nationals in order to stimulate the creation of local industries are considered compatible with this Article provided they do not substantially impair the investments and activities of nationals and companies of the other Contracting Party in connection with an investment.'[74] NAFTA also provides exceptions from the NT obligations for measures relating to the allocation of government procurement and subsidies and grants.[75] In the Canadian New Model BIT, the above-mentioned general exceptions also apply to the NT clause.[76] In Chinese investment treaties, six different approaches of NT provision can be identified, and most of them are subject to certain exceptions.[77]

20.3.1.4 Fair and Equitable Treatment

Fair and equitable treatment (FET) is an absolute standard of treatment, whilst the MFN and NT are relative standards of treatment. FET has been a most commonly used standard of treatment under BITs, (Table 20.2) and is the most frequently invoked standard in investment disputes.[78] This is because in BITs there is normally no further definition for this standard. Most BITs, including those signed by UK,[79] Germany, and China, typically simply prescribe fair and equitable treatment without any further explanation.[80] NAFTA Article 1105, however, links the FET standard with the standard required under of general international law. It reads,

> Each Party shall accord to investments of investors of another Party treatment in accordance with international law, including fair and equitable treatment and full protection and security.

However, this did not seem to have provided sufficient clarity. A few earlier arbitration cases have led to unwanted interpretation of this provision by the tribunals. As a result, in 2001 the Free Trade Commission (FTC) of NAFTA adopted an official interpretation. It stipulates that the FET standard reflects the customary international law minimum standard and does not

---

[67] Gallagher and Shan, *supra* footnote 52, at 157.

[68] Rudolf Dolzer and Christoph Schreuer, *Principles of International Investment Law* (Oxford: Oxford University Press, 2008), 178.

[69] Gallagher and Shan, *supra* footnote 52, at 157.

[70] See Section 2 of these respective Jurisdictional Reports.

[71] See Section 2 of these respective Jurisdictional Reports.

[72] Singapore Report, Section 3.

[73] UK Report, Section 2.

[74] Id.

[75] Article 1108.7 provides that,

> Articles 1102 (national treatment), 1103 (most-favored-nation treatment) and 1107 do not apply to:
> (a) procurement by a Party or a state enterprise; or
> (b) subsidies or grants provided by a Party or a state enterprise, including government supported loans, guarantees and insurance.

[76] Canada Report, Section 2.

[77] Gallagher and Shan, *supra* footnote 52, at 166–171.

[78] Dolzer and Schreuer, *supra* footnote 64, at 119.

[79] In some cases concerning the UK BITs with other states, such as the *Biwater Gauff Ltd v Tanzania* and *the National Gird PLC v Argentina*, both the tribunals took the view that fair and equitable treatment is an autonomous treatment standard, which is different from customary international law. See Section 2 of the UK Report.

[80] See Section 2 of the UK, Germany and China Reports respectively.

require treatment in addition to or beyond that which is required by the customary international law minimum standard. Also, the determination that there has been a breach of another provision of the NAFTA, or of a separate international agreement, does not establish that there has been a breach of fair and equitable treatment. The interpretation has been followed by the US and Canada in their subsequent BIT practice and their Model BITs.

Recent BIT practice has witnessed a wider acceptance of the FTC's interpretation of FET beyond North America. Article 3(1) of the UK-Mexico BIT, for example, provides that: "Investments of investors of each Contracting Party shall at all times be accorded treatment in accordance with customary international law, including fair and equitable treatment … in the territory of the other contracting party."[81] Article 5 'Minimum Standard of Treatment' further defines the standard of treatment as follows:

1. Each Contracting Party shall accord to investments of investors of the other Contracting Party treatment in accordance with international law, including fair and equitable treatment and full protection and security.
2. For greater certainty, this Article prescribes the international law minimum standard of treatment of aliens as the minimum standard of treatment to be afforded to investments of investors of the other Contracting Party. The concepts of "fair and equitable treatment" and "full protection and security" do not require treatment in addition to or beyond that which is required by the international law minimum standard of treatment of aliens as evidence of State practice and opinio juris. A determination that there has been a breach of another provision of this Agreement, or of a separate international agreement, does not establish that there has been a breach of this Article.

Clearly this is almost the same as the NAFTA and FTC language, except the addition of "as evidence of State practice and *opinio juris*" as a qualification on international law minimum standard. This addition seems to suggest an equation between customary international law standard and international law minimum standard.

Some recent Japanese BITs and Economic Partnership Agreements (EPAs) also include notes similar to the FTC interpretation.[82] For instance, the Japan-Brunei EPA notes that FET "do[es] not require treatment in addition to or beyond that which is required by customary international law minimum standard of treatment of aliens.[83](Art. 59)" Also, some BITs/EPAs note that "a determination that there has been a breach of another provision of this Agreement, or of a separate international agreement, does not establish that there has been a breach of this Article." (with slight difference of the terms: Japan-Mexico EPA (Art. 60 Note), Japan-Philippines EPA (Art. 91 Note), Japan-Thailand EPA (Art. 95 Note) and Japan-Laos BIT (Art. 5(1) Note 1)).[84] Further, some EPAs add further clarifications. For example, the Japan-Peru EPA stipulates that "'[f]air and equitable treatment' includes the obligation of the Contracting Party not to deny justice in criminal, civil, or administrative adjudicatory proceedings in accordance with the principle of due process of law. Each Contracting Party shall accord to investors of the other Contracting Party, non-discriminatory treatment with regard to access to the courts of justice and administrative tribunals and agencies of the former Contracting Party in pursuit and in defence of rights of such investors" (Art. 5(2) Note).[85]

According to the Peruvian report, fair and equitable treatment must be understood as the protection of legitimate expectations, good faith, transparency, consistency, and non-discrimination. Moreover, the Peru-Japan BIT stipulates that FET standard includes the obligation of "due process of law".[86]

Another approach can be found in some Russian and Chinese BITs, which link the FET standard with the MFN and NT standards. For instance, Article 3 of the Sino-Qatar BIT reads:

1. Investments and activities associated with investments of investors of either Contracting Party shall be accorded fair and equitable treatment and shall enjoy protection in the territory of the other Contracting Party.
2. The treatment and protection referred to in Paragraph 1 of this Article shall not be less favorable than that accorded to investments and activities associated with such investments of investors of a third State.

[81] UK Report, Section 2.

[82] Japan Report, Section 2.

[83] Id.

[84] Id.

[85] Id.

[86] Peru Report, Section 2.

This linkage helps in providing at least further criteria for the assessment of the FET standard. Thus the fair and equitable standard not only provides a fixed reference point, a definite standard that will not vary according to external considerations, because its content turns on what is fair and reasonable in the circumstances. It also prevent discrimination against the beneficiary of the standard, where discrimination would amount to unfairness or inequity in the circumstances.[87] However, such further criteria, namely the MFN and NT standards, are serving as merely minimum requirements for the FET standard. How much higher the FET standard may lie above them is still an open question.

20.3.2 Standards of Treatment under Domestic Law

It is common in the 22 jurisdictions that foreign investors and investments are accorded national treatment under domestic laws (Table 20.2). Such treatment is often affirmed in the national Constitution. The United States Constitution, for example, prohibits state and local governments from discriminating against resident aliens.[88] However, the concept of national treatment seems to vary among the 22 jurisdictions. Under Argentine law, the state does not give foreigners greater rights than those enjoyed by its citizens.[89] This could be regarded as a demonstration of the Calvo Doctrine.[90] In Portugal, particularly complex investments with high national interest may be granted with a special status with advantages for the investor-Special Projects of National Interest (PIN).[91] In China, foreign investors used to enjoy 'superior' national treatment in some respects; while in other respects may be subject to 'inferior' national treatment. However, such superior or inferior treatment has been significantly decreased as China's rapid economic growth coupled with continuous reform and opening-up to the outside world.[92]

[87] UNCTAD, Fair and Equitable Treatment, UNCTAD Series on issues in international investment agreements, UNCTAD/ITE/IIT/11(Vol. III)

[88] US Report, Section 2.

[89] Argentina Report, Section 2.

[90] See Wenhua Shan, "Is Calvo Dead?" *American Journal of Comparative Law* 55, no. 1 (2007): 123–164.

[91] Portugal Report, Section 2.

[92] China Report, Section 2.

Deviation from the national treatment is also possible under domestic laws of some jurisdictions. Thus in Russia restrictive measures may be adopted against foreign investments by the federal law, for the protection of the constitutional system, morals, health, rights, and lawful interests of others, national defense and state securities. Other exceptions to the NT relates to admission and ownership of property, which will be discussed in detail below.

To summarise, the general standards of treatment for foreign investment under international treaties have been largely standardized. This can be seen from the fact that almost all BITs have included such common standards as FET, MFN and NT standards. However, variations remain in different states. Thus the NT standard applies to both admission and operation stages of foreign investment under investment treaties signed by US, Canada and Japan, whilst it applies to only operation stage under investment treaties by other jurisdictions. Moreover, China has long been reluctant in accepting this standard due to its planned economy legacy. It is now implementing the standard in more recent BITs but still subject it to significant reservations. Under domestic laws of these jurisdictions, NT is generally upheld but also subject to variations in its implementation. Thus in Latin American States such as Argentina it is emphasized that foreign investors should not be granted better treatment than domestic investors. In contrast, preferential treatment can be granted to foreign investors in states such as Portugal or Croatia if they invest in PIN projects, or in certain regions or industries. For reason mentioned above, China was not able to implement the NT standard but had to offer foreign investors a combination of both "superior" and "inferior"-national treatments.

20.4 Admission and Entry Requirements

20.4.1 The Admission Regime and Areas Open to Foreign Investment

The first step in any foreign investment process is the admission, or entry, or establishment of the investment. Unless there are overriding treaty obligations, the host state has the discretion in deciding whether and on what conditions a foreign investment project may be accepted in its territory.[93] In most investment treaties, BITs or otherwise, states do not undertake any substantial obligation with regard to investment admission. Thus BITs concluded by European countries (such as UK, Germany, France, Italy, Czech Republic, and Slovenia), China and Australia have affirmed such right of the host state concerning admission.[94] A typical clause provides that each contracting state shall in its territory promote as far as possible investments by investors of the other Contracting State and admit such investments in accordance with its legislation.[95] This type of admission clause exposes the host state no obligation to revise it domestic laws of admission after the ratification of the BIT.[96]

However, the US, Canada and Japan take a different approach.[97] The BITs negotiated by these States, to some extent, impose market access obligations. Under these BITs, a right of admission is established on the basis of national treatment and most favored nation treatment (Chart 20.2).[98] The US Model BIT (2004), for example, provides in its Article 3.1 (National Treatment) that,

> Each Party shall accord to investors of the other Party treatment no less favorable than that it accords, in like circumstances, to its own investors with respect to establishment, acquisition, expansion, management, conduct, operation, and sale or other disposition of investments in its territory.

Likewise, Article 4.1 of the US Model BIT (Most-Favored-Nation Treatment) reads:

> Each Party shall accord to investors of the other Party treatment no less favorable than that it accords, in like circumstances, to investors of any non-Party with respect to the establishment, acquisition, expansion, management, conduct, operation, and sale or other disposition of investments in its territory.

The extension of MFN and NT obligation to cover "establishment, acquisition, expansion" of foreign investment clearly imposes obligation regarding investment admission. On the other hand, exceptions are also provided in the Model BIT in a 'negative-list approach' listing the sectors, sub-sectors and activities to which the non-discrimination treatments do not apply.

Under domestic laws of these jurisdictions, investment admission regime is generally liberal but varied. Most of the 20 jurisdictions (such as Argentina, Australia, Czech Republic, Germany, Italy, Japan, Macau, Peru, Portugal, Singapore, Slovenia, UK and USA) do not attach special conditions other than those required for domestic investors. In other words, national treatment on admission is generally upheld.[99] Other jurisdictions have either special registration/notification or approval/authorization requirements as the general admission regime. Thus in Canada, France, Italy, Russia, Singapore, South Korea and Turkey, a registration system for foreign investments is in place.[100] China, on the other hand, is a representative of an authorization system by which every foreign investment projects is subject to governmental approval/authorization.[101] Ethiopia and Greece seem to also follow this approach. (Chart 20.3)

On the whole, it can be seen that again there is no clear gap in the level of liberalization in admission regime: Some developing and transition economies (such as Argentina, Czech Republic, Peru, Portugal and Slovenia) are implementing the most liberal regime imposing no additional requirement fore foreign investment admission, whilst a few developed economies (such as Greece, Canada and France) are actually practicing less liberal admission mechanism requiring notification and authorization for foreign investment.[102] There is no longer any clear sign of "north-south divide". States regulate investment admission wherever

[93] Dolzer and Schreuer, *supra* footnote 64, at 79–80.

[94] See the Admission Section of the Jurisdictional Reports respectively.

[95] Article 2.1 of the German Model BIT (2005).

[96] Dolzer and Schreuer, *supra* footnote 64, at 81.

[97] Section 3 of the US, Canada and Japan Reports respectively.

[98] Id.

[99] Some of these jurisdictions nevertheless have registration or approval requirements for foreign investment in some sectors or industries. For example, registration or authorization is required for foreign investment in few economic areas. See Chart 20.3 and US Report for further details.

[100] Some of them require approval/authorization for some foreign investment projects. Thus in Canada, review and approval required for large, cultural and national security investments. See Chart 20.3 and Canada Report for further details.

[101] China requires that every foreign investment project be approved by the relevant authorities. It is pointed out that foreign investment projects as a rule are either approved by various development and reform authorities or the authorities in charge of commerce, while contract of foreign investment projects and articles of association are approved by development and reform authorities.

[102] See Section 3 of the Jurisdictional Reports of these jurisdictions respectively.

they deem necessary, regardless of their level of economic development.

With regard to the specific areas open for foreign investment, no state grants unlimited access.[103] A 'negative-list' approach is favored by most of the 22 jurisdictions. (Chart 20.3) In the US, for example, ownership is only limited to American citizens and corporations in some sensitive industries, or the magnitude of foreign holdings is limited. These industries cover airlines, telecommunication and others deemed to affect national security. Meanwhile, political reaction to certain proposed foreign investments may also have an adverse effect on the prospects for the investment.[104] In Italy, special authorizations are needed if foreign investors want to invest in areas such as civil flights.[105] In Peru, restrictions of foreign investments can be found in areas such as radio and television, commercial airline transportation and marine merchant activities.[106] In Japan, investments in certain areas, such as those in defense industry, agriculture, forestry, mining, infrastructure and telecommunication industries, are required to be notified in advance to the competent ministries. The ministries may order foreign investors to change or discontinue their investments, if the investments are considered to impair national security, to disturb the maintenance of public order, to hinder the protection of public safety or to bring significant adverse effect to the smooth management of the Japanese economy.[107] Also, only Japanese nationals are qualified to hold mining rights or radio license.[108] German Foreign Trade and Payments Act also empowers the government to control or restrict investments and trade for reasons of foreign policy and national security.[109] In Portugal, private enterprise is not allowed in certain areas of activity, including rail transport in the public interest, communications by mail, the exploitation of seaports, collect, treat and distribute water for public consumption.[110] Although the UK does not require authorization for foreign investments admission, the government retains some statutory powers to block acquisitions of companies by foreign investors in certain circumstances.[111] For instance, it could prohibit the change of control of an important manufacturing undertaking, on the ground of national interests.[112] It also can refer a merger to the Office of Fair Trading on the grounds that the merger raises issues of public interest, including national security and the stability of the financial system.[113] Finally, it may regulate the control of certain privatized companies through the insertion of certain clauses such as those limiting the ability of any individual or corporation to control a certain percentage of shares.[114]

An obvious trend in this respect is that the monitoring of Sovereign Wealth Funds (SWFs) is becoming more and more important. In Australia, all proposed investments by foreign governments and their agencies are subject to notification and screening requirements, irrespective of their size of the proposal.[115] In 2007, the Minister of Industry of Canada issued guidelines regarding the approach to be taken to reviewing acquisitions by state-owned enterprises (SOEs) to determine if the net benefit test is met.[116] The guidelines indicate that the Minister will examine whether the SOE adheres to Canadian standards of corporate governance and to Canadian laws and practices. This trend demonstrates a growing concern of some states to SWFs investments.

20.4.2 Competition Policy and Antitrust Law

Most of the 22 jurisdictions monitor foreign investments by virtue of competition policy and antitrust law, which take the form of either a special legislation or provisions within a more general legislation

[103] Dolzer and Schreuer, at 81.

[104] US Report, Section 3.

[105] Italy Report, Section 3.

[106] Peru Report, Section 3.

[107] Japan Report, Section 3.

[108] Id.

[109] Germany Report, Section 2.

[110] Portugal Report, Section 3.

[111] UK Report, Section 3.

[112] Id.

[113] Id.

[114] Further details see the respective Jurisdictional reports.

[115] While some other foreign investment proposals are subject to notification and vetting requirements in the condition that they are above a certain prescribed value. See the Australia Report, Section 3.

[116] The guidelines can be accessed on the Investment Canada web site http://www.ic.gc.ca/eic/site/ica-licnsf/eng/lk00064.html#state-owned. See the Canada Report, Section 3.

such as the Enterprise Law, Commercial Law or Trade Law.

In USA, an investment or acquisition may trigger an antitrust review, if its effect would be to create a monopoly or a restraint on trade.[117] Japan maintains an Act on Prohibition of Private Monopolization and Maintenance of Fair Trade to monitor investments which may substantially restrain competition.[118] Within the EU, some member states have promulgated their own competition or antitrust law,[119] though they should be in conformity with the EU Law, which has established a Community mechanism in this area. China's Anti-monopoly Law was passed in 2007, which also applies to foreign invested enterprises.[120] The main piece of federal legislation protecting competition in Canada is the Competition Act, the Act contains provisions relating to anti-competitive behavior including agreements among competitors to fix prices, and abusive behavior by a dominant firm that reduces competition.[121]

20.5 Investment Contracts

Investment contracts are often used when conducting international investment. In a broader sense, they include all kinds of contracts for making a foreign investment, such as various joint venture contracts between private parties. In a narrow sense, they only refer to state contracts, in which the host state government is a party. The dual role of the host government in such contracts, namely a contracting party and a regulatory authority, has led to significant complications and controversies. As a result, they are often subject to more strict rules than normal commercial contracts. For instance, they are often subject to local law and local jurisdiction whilst in normal commercial contracts party autonomy in those aspects is usually guaranteed.

None of the 22 jurisdictions has maintained a strict requirement on the form of investment contracts (Table 20.3). In practice, the most common forms of such contracts seem to include Private-Public-Partnership (PPP), Built-Operate-Transfer (BOT), economic development contracts, concession agreements and licensing, and joint venture contracts. PPP is most common in Australia, Canada, Greece and Slovenia.[122] In France, investment contracts include BOT contract, joint-venture contract and contract for explorations of natural resources.[123] In Italy, investment contracts may take such forms as BOT, sponsoring contracts, leasing, outsourcing and urban concessions.[124] In USA, investment contracts are sometimes used by a state or local government or its subsidiary economic development agency to encourage business to locate in a particular city or region by offering the investor a special benefit or concession.[125] In Peru, the Constitution provides for a 'law contracts' regime by which the State provide guarantees and grant securities that cannot even be modified by law. This kind of contract can be modified only if the State and the other party agree to do so.[126]

As a matter of practice, state contracts tend to be governed by domestic laws and are subject to jurisdiction of local courts. However, only a minority of the 20 jurisdictions maintain explicit local law and local jurisdiction requirements as a matter of law. (Table 20.4) Thus in Argentina, all contracts between the government and Argentine companies controlled by foreign investors are subject to Argentina internal laws and shall be submitted to Argentina courts.[127] Article 126 of the Chinese Contract Law also provides that '[F]or contracts fulfilled in the territory of the People's Republic of China on Chinese-foreign equity joint ventures, on Chinese-foreign contractual joint ventures and on Chinese-foreign cooperation in exploring and exploiting natural resources, the laws of the People's Republic of China shall apply.'[128] In Australia, if the contract is for the purchase of interests in real estate,

[117] US Report, Section 3.

[118] Japan Report, Section 3.

[119] Germany, for example, has its *German Law Against Restraints on Competition.*

[120] China Report, Section 3.

[121] Canada Report, Section 3.

[122] See Section 4 of the Jurisdictional Reports of Australia, Canada and Slovenia, and Section 3 of the Greece Reports.

[123] France Report, Section 4.

[124] Italy Report, Section 4.

[125] The incentives can include assistance in acquiring suitable parcels of land for the enterprise, provision of infrastructure development, and tax incentives. However, the Economic development can contain performance requirements, such as local employee requirement. See US Report, Section 4.

[126] Peru Report, Section 4.

[127] Argentina Report, Section 4.

[128] China Report, Section 4.

Table 20.3 Admission and Entry

	Admission regime			**Areas of investment**	
Jurisdiction	*No special formality*	*Registration/ notification*	*Approval/authorisation*	*Negative list*	*Positive list*
Argentina	√		"national interest" investments	√ (Selective/restrictive for investments in certain types of industry and its specific location, particularly in mining, forestry, and the automobile industry.)	
Australia	√		Notification and approval required for defined investments	√ (defined by FATA and its regulations, including large, sensitive, and urban land projects)	
Canada		√	Review and approval required for large, cultural and national security investments	√ (National security investments. Also ownership restrictions in sensitive industries as required by relevant laws.)	
China			√	√ (All are "Permitted" FI projects unless they fall within the "encouraged", "prohibited" or "restricted" categories stipulated in the Investment Catalogue.)	
Croatia	/	/	Approval required in certain sectors such as banking, insurance, energy, etc.	√	/
Czech Republic	√ (registering in the Commercial Register for a Trade License)			√ (Only few areas reserved to protect state interest and individuals.)	
Ethiopia			√ (licensing)	√ (By Proclamation 280/2002 and Council Regulation 84/2003)	
France		□ (1.a statistical registration with the Banque de France so as to make out the French balance of payments; or 2. a registration with the French minister of economy and finances for the finances department;) and		√ (Some specific strategic areas, listed in article R.153-2 of the French Monetary and Financial Code. A prior authorization from the minister of economy and finance required for such investment.)	
Germany	√	Registration of certain monetary transactions with the German Central Bank (*Deutsche Bundesbank*) for the sake of statistical reports.	Acquisitions of 25% or more of a German enterprise by a foreign undertaking are now subject to scrutiny.	/	/

(continued)

Table 20.3 (continued)

	Admission regime			Areas of investment	
Jurisdiction	*No special formality*	*Registration/ notification*	*Approval/authorisation*	*Negative list*	*Positive list*
Greece	/	/	√ (Approval required by Greek foreign investment law Legislative Decree 2687/1953.)	/	/
Italy	√	√	Exceptional, only for particular protection purposes such as the field of civil flights.	√ (there might be intense controls by national authorities, particularly in regulated industries)	/
Japan	√		Exceptional, only for investments likely to impair national security, public order, public safety or to bring significant adverse effect to the smooth management of the Japanese economy.	√ (Areas specified in the Public Notice of the Prime Minister's Office, etc)	
South Korea		√ (Notification at Invest KOREA (KOTRA), etc.)		/	
Macau	√			/	/
Peru	√ (Registration with PROINVERSION) (national treatment)			√ (Only few restrictions in fields such as radio and television, commercial airline transportation and marine merchant activities.)	
Portugal	√ (National treatment)			/	/
Russia		√	The authorization regime was enacted only for entities that have strategic importance for ensuring the country's defense capacity and state security.	√ (The Federal Law of April 29, 2008 N.57-FZ enumerates 42 kinds of activity.)	
Singapore		√ (registration pursuant to the Business Registration Act)		√ (business which is unlawful or prejudicial to public welfare or national security is not allowed)	
Slovenia	√ (Generally national treatment.)	some forms of foreign investments are subject to registration	some business activities need authorisation	√	
Turkey		√		/	/
UK	√		Exceptional	√ (As stipulated by law such as Industry Act 1975, Enterprise Act 2002.)	
USA	√	Registration required for investment in agricultural land	Exceptional	√ (Industries such as airlines, telecommunication, and other industries deemed to affect national security.)	
Total	**12**	**7**	**3**	**16**	**0**

Table 20.4 Investment contracts under domestic law

	Forms required		Domestic law requirement		Domestic jurisdiction requirement	
Jurisdiction	*yes*	*no*	*yes*	*no*	*yes*	*no*
Argentina		√ (BOT)	√		√	
Australia		√ (PPP)	Real estate contracts	√		√
Canada		√	Real estate contracts	√		√
China		√ (BOT)	√		√	
Croatia		√		√	/	/
Czech Republic		√		√		√
Ethiopia		√		√		√
France		√ (BOT)		√		√
Germany	/	/	/	/	./	/
Greece		√ (PPP)	√			√
Italy		√		√		√
Japan		√	√		√	
South Korea		√	/	/	/	/
Macau		√ (concession agreement or licensing)	√		√	
Peru		√ (law contract)	√		/	/
Portugal		√		√		√
Russia	/	/	/	/	/	/
Singapore		√		√		√
Slovenia		√ (PPP)	√ (Public-Private Partnership Act 2006)			√
Turkey		√ (BOT)	/	/		√
UK		√		√		√
USA		√ (economic development contracts)	√			√
Total		**20**	**8**	**10**	**4**	**13**

the governing law is the law of Australia.[129] In Japan, although there is no specific provision on the governing law in investment contracts, these contracts will usually be governed by Japanese law according to the Act on General Rule for Application of Laws, and it will usually be the Japanese courts that have jurisdiction over such disputes.[130] Here again there seems to be no clear gap between developed and developing states in the way they treat investment contracts. There are developed states such as Japan, Greece, Portugal and US that are imposing local law requirement, whilst most reported developing states do not have such a requirement.

An additional aspect that should be noted here is the 'umbrella clause', which can be found in more than half of the BITs. It typically goes like follows:

> Each contracting party State shall observe any other obligation it has assumed with regard to investments in its territory by investors of the other Contracting State.

This clause has been put into BIT practice by most states, including UK, France, Australia, Argentina, Greek, Germany, US, China, Japan and South Korea.[131] The exact legal effect of such a clause is still subject to vigorous debate due to inconsistent arbitral interpretation.[132] However, at least some of the relevant

[129] Australia Report, Section 4.

[130] Japan Report, Section 4.

[131] OECD Working Papers on International Investment, Interpretation of the Umbrella Clause in Investment Agreements, October 2006, available at: http://www.oecd.org/dataoecd/3/20/37579220.pdf.

[132] Id. See also Dolzer and Schreuer, *supra* footnote 64, at 152.

arbitration awards have confirmed that it may elevate the disputes arising out of investment contracts subject to domestic court and domestic law, to the international level and be reviewed by an international tribunal applying international law. It can therefore be concluded that freedom of contracts is generally upheld in domestic laws, whilst investment treaties tend to offer further protection on foreign investors' contractual rights.

20.6 Performance Requirements

Performance requirements refer to measures adopted by the host state requiring foreign investors to fulfill certain requirements as a condition of either investment approval, or as a condition for the enjoyment of certain advantages. Since some of such requirements have the effect of distorting international trade and/or investment, efforts have been made to regulate such measures. At global level, the WTO Agreement on Trade-Related Investment Measures (TRIMs) is an agreement regulating certain performance requirements. As noted above, 17 out of the 20 jurisdictions are members of the WTO, so most of them are subject to obligations set forth by the TRIMs Agreement. Similar regulation can also be found in some EPAs and/or BITs. Some of Japan's EPAs, such as the Japan-Brunei EPA, Japan-Malaysia EPA and the Japan-Switzerland EPA, incorporate TRIMs' prohibitions of performance requirements by reference.[133] Article 8 of the US Model BIT 2004, for example, also prohibits certain categories of performance requirements. In addition, some performance requirements are found in domestic laws, either as conditions for authorization or as conditions for investment incentives.

20.6.1 Performance Requirements as Conditions for Authorization

Most performance requirements as a condition for authorization are industry-specific, whilst others are more general by nature. In Peru, for instance, performance requirements are reserved when investment is related to hygiene and industrial security, environmental conservation and health.[134] In Japan, a Japanese ship may be possessed by a foreign company on the condition that all of its representatives are Japanese nationals.[135] In France, according to French Monetary and Financial Code, foreign investors might be required to have the ability to guarantee the security of the supply, to preserve the durability of its activity, and to execute its contractual obligations arising from public procurements or contracts relating to public security, national defense or research interests, production or business of arms, munitions, gunpowder or explosive substances.[136] In Argentina, performance requirements are required as conditions of approval of investments in some industries, such as the automobile industry. Such requirements include capital investment requirement and export commitment requirement.[137] In Australia, specifications regarding the time for completion of development activities or environmental requirements are examples of conditions which may be imposed when approving a particular foreign investment project.[138] According to the *Investment Canada Act*, performance requirements may be imposed as conditions for approval of an investment.[139] In Ethiopia, foreign investors are encouraged to transfer technology to the local partner.[140]

It should be noted that some performance requirements are performed after the admission of an investment has been authorized. According to Article 54 of the Slovenian Companies Act 2006, all companies and sole traders must keep the books of account and make year-end accounts once a year in accordance with the Slovenian Accounting Standards or the International Financial Reporting Standards, unless otherwise stipulated by the law.[141] There are also financial reporting and auditing requirements in respect of all enterprises doing business in Macau, which apply to foreign investments.[142]

[133] Japan Report, Section 5.

[134] Peru Report, Section 5.

[135] Japan Report, Section 5.

[136] France Report, Section 5.

[137] Argentina Report, Section 5.

[138] Canada Report, Section 5.

[139] Where an investment is subject to review under the *Investment Canada Act*, the investor's plans regarding employment, resource processing, domestic content, exports, and technology development or transfer and the other factors relevant under the *Investment Canada Act* are examined by Investment Canada. See Canada Report, Section 5.

[140] Ethiopia Report, Section 5.

[141] Slovenia Report, Section 5.

[142] Macau Report, Section 5.

20.6.2 Performance Requirements as Conditions for Incentives

In most circumstances, performance requirements are imposed as non-mandatory conditions for enjoyment of certain incentives. Such requirements exist in almost all of the 20 jurisdictions.

In US, the economic development agreements signed between state or local development agencies and foreign investors may contain some kinds of performance requirements such as the requirement of creation of jobs in the local market.[143] The "new generation" BITs/EPAs of Japan normally permit certain performance requirements only in exchange for certain advantages conferred by the host State. Such performance requirements include: technology transfer, location of headquarters, achieving research and development within the host State and destination of export.[144] In Portugal, the creation of local employment, the obligation to transfer technology and other requirements may be part of the requirements for the granting of certain benefits or advantages to the investor concerned.[145] There are also performance requirements in Czech Republic, as a requirement to enjoy some tax incentives, such as technology transfer requirement and local employment requirement, local content requirement.[146] In Greece, performance requirements are imposed as conditions for incentives. These include tax exceptions, grants and subsidized loans to stimulate regional development, job creation, competitiveness, industrial restructuring, environmental protection and energy saving.[147]

20.7 Tax Regime and Incentives

20.7.1 General Tax Regime

Most of the domestic legislations in the 22 jurisdictions uphold the principle of equality of treatment. Article 51 of the Croatian Constitution for instance states that everyone needs to participate in the defrayment of public expenses in accordance with his or her economic capabilities and that the system of taxation shall be based on the principles of equality and equity.[148]

---

[143] US Report, Section 4.

[144] Article 4 of the Japan-Vietnam BIT, for example, reads as follows:

1. Neither Contracting Party shall impose or enforce, as a condition for investment activities in its Area of an investor of the other Contracting Party, any of the following requirements:
   (a) to export a given level or percentage of goods or services;
   (b) to achieve a given level or percentage of domestic content;
   (c) to purchase, use or accord a preference to goods produced or services provided in its Area, or to purchase goods or services from natural or legal persons or any other entity in its Area;
   (d) to relate the volume or value of imports to the volume or value of exports or to the amount of foreign exchange inflows associated with investments of that investor;
   (e) to restrict sales of goods or services in its Area that investments of that investor produces or provides by relating such sales to the volume or value of its exports or foreign exchange earnings;
   (f) to appoint, as executives, managers or members of boards of directors, individuals of any particular nationality;
   (g) to transfer technology, a production process or other proprietary knowledge to a natural or legal person or any other entity in its Area, except when the requirement(i) is imposed or enforced by a court, administrative tribunal or competition authority to remedy an alleged violation of competition laws; or (ii) concerns the transfer of intellectual property rights which is undertaken in a manner not inconsistent with the Agreement on Trade-Related Aspects of Intellectual Property Rights, Annex 1 C of the Marrakesh Agreement Establishing the World Trade Organization;
   (h) to locate the headquarters of that investor for a specific region or the world market in its Area;
   (i) to achieve a given level or value of research and development in its Area; or
   (j) to supply one or more of the goods that the investor produces or the services that the investor provides to a specific region or the world market, exclusively from the Area of the former Contracting Party.
2. The provisions of paragraph 1 above do not preclude either Contracting Party from conditioning the receipt or continued receipt of an advantage, in connection with investment activities in its Area of an investor of the other Contracting Party, on compliance with any of the requirements set forth in paragraph 1 (f) through (j) above.

See Section 5 of the Japan Report.

[145] Portugal Report, Section 5.

[146] Czech Report, Section 5.

[147] Greece Report, Section 3.

[148] Croatia Report, Section 5.

20.7.2 Special Tax Regimes for Foreign Investors?

Many states, particularly the developing states, often adopt special tax regimes to attract foreign investment, usually in the form of tax reduction or exemption. Some reduction and exemption may apply to all foreign investment, but others which constitute the majority of them target certain industries or regions. In Ethiopia, for example, foreign investors enjoy income tax exemption for up to 5 years provided that they are able to export at the required level. Further income tax exemptions are provided for investors engaged in least developed regions of the country such as the Somali, Afar and Gambella regional states.[149] Such incentives can also be regarded as performance requirements.

Croatia has issued a series of laws to regulate the performance of business activities in respective areas, and they also include tax relief and exemptions. The laws include: Reconstruction and Development of the Town of Vukovar Act, Areas of Special State Concern Act, Hill and Mountain Areas Act, Free Zones Act and Investment Promotion Act.[150] According to these laws, taxpayers that do business in the given areas can enjoy tax relief and exemptions.[151] In order to improve living conditions and development of certain Peruvian regions, Peru also provides for tax incentives to investment in areas such as the Amazonian region and certain high Andean territories.[152]

Free trade zones in Slovenia are regulated by the *Act on Special Economic Zones* 1998.[153] Currently there are only two special economic zones in Slovenia – the Koper economic zone, which is located in the port of Koper on the Slovenian Adriatic coastline; and the other is the Maribor. A company operating in a special economic zone may claim tax concessions.[154]

As mentioned above, in some jurisdictions tax reduction and exemption may be granted to foreign investments in certain industries. They exist in both developed and developing countries. In Canada, for example, the use of tax measures as instruments to encourage investment in Canada can be traced back to early 1970s, when Canada introduced tax credits measure and the Accelerated Capital Cost Allowance to encourage investments in manufacturing, processing and primary industries, such as agriculture, food processing, and forest products.[155] More recently, the government has implemented a number of tax incentive programmes to attract foreign investments in sectors such as research and development (R&D), natural resources and film production.[156] Most of these incentives are available only to foreign investors that have established a corporation in Canada in order to be qualified as a resident under Canadian tax law.[157] In Peru, there are advantageous tax and labour regimes applicable to investments made in certain industries such as agricultural and aquacultural industries.[158] In Greece, a more favorable treatment was offered by a special legislation to the shipping industry.[159] Under the Law on Encouragement of Tourism, Turkey also uses tax incentives to promote the development of tourism.[160]

20.7.3 Double Taxation Treaties (DTTs)

A potential significant problem for international investors the problem of double taxation. To a large extent, the problem of double taxation is solved through international treaties. All the 20 jurisdictions have concluded

[149] See Section 6 of the Ethiopia Report. In China, tax incentives used to be a major tool to attract foreign investment. Tax incentives are provided in the *EJV Tax Law* 1980 and the *Foreign Enterprise Income Tax Law* 1981. Furthermore, local governments were authorized to provide more tax incentives in *FIEs Income Tax Law* 1991. However, with the improvement of the investment environment in China, the tax incentives are removed by large. In 2007, *Enterprise Income Tax Law* was issued, repealed the abovementioned two laws. Article 4 of this Law provides that 'the rate of enterprise income tax shall be 25%'. This law constitutes a fundamental step for China to build a neutral investment regime without differentiating domestic investors and foreign investors through unify tax burden. See Section 6 of the China Report.

[150] Croatia Report, Section 5.

[151] Id.

[152] Peru Report, Section 6.

[153] Slovenia Report, Section 6.

[154] Id.

[155] Canada Report, Section 6.

[156] Id.

[157] Id.

[158] Peru Report, Section 6.

[159] Greece Report, Section 3.

[160] Turkey Report, Section 6.

double taxation treaties. However, the number of these DTTs in each jurisdiction varies. Among them China has the most DTTs with a number of 90, whilst Macau only has only two.[161] The double taxation issue is also addressed in domestic law. The UK, for example, provides unilateral tax credit relief under certain circumstances.[162] To a certain extent Peruvian law allows companies registered in Peru to deduct from their gross revenue income tax paid abroad.

20.7.4 Other Incentives

Apart from the various tax incentives, some jurisdictions have taken a number of other incentives to attract foreign investments. In Macau, the government provides support to private companies in the form of interest subsidies to their bank loans. There are also employment subsidies and export diversification incentives available.[163] The European Union also plays a great role in providing incentives to foreign investment. It provides incentives for investments through the European Social Fund as well as the European Regional Development Fund. In Germany, there are not only "investment incentives" aiming at covering investment costs, but also "operational incentives" supporting investors after their investment has been realized by subsidizing operating costs. Such incentive may be in the form of for example cash incentives, interest-reduced public loans, or public guarantees.[164]

In addition to tax incentives, the Canadian federal government offers a number of assistance programmes to stimulate economic activities, which apply to foreign investment.[165] Under these programmes, financial support, technical assistance, loan guarantees, equity financing, and advisory assistance are provided.[166] The Peruvian Investment Law provides four basic types of incentives: (a) capital aids in the form of cash grant; (b) leasing subsidy, which covers partial payment by the State of the installments relating to a lease which has been entered into for the use of new mechanical and other equipment; (c) tax-free reserves; and (d) subsidies for the expenses of wages relating to the employment created by the investment.[167]

20.8 Property Rights, Expropriation and Compensation

Security of investment is the most fundamental concern to any foreign investors. The protection of property right, particularly in case of expropriation, is therefore the most important aspect in foreign investment law. Such protection is typically offered by domestic laws, but more importantly, by international treaties.

20.8.1 General Protection of Property Rights

Protection of property rights is offered by domestic law in almost all of the 22 jurisdictions, which tend to guarantee national treatment. (Table 20.5) Often, right to property of foreigners (and nationals) is provided by the Constitution as a fundamental right. The property of foreign investors is thus guaranteed at the highest level of the domestic legal system. Article 13 of the Chinese Constitution 2004, for example, stipulates that "[T]he State protects the right of citizens to own lawfully earned income, savings, houses and other lawful property". The Canadian Constitution, however, does not contain express provision on the protection of property rights. In the UK, there is no written constitution, but property protection is covered by the Human Rights Act 1998.

20.8.2 Protection of Intellectual Property Rights (IPRs)

With respect to the protection of intellectual property rights, the domestic laws of many jurisdictions, including China, US, Peru, Japan, Germany, France, Italy, Singapore and Argentina, provide the protection of

[161] One is signed with China and the other with Portugal.

[162] *Income and Corporation Taxes Act* 1988s 790. See Section 6 of the UK report.

[163] Macau Report, Section 6.

[164] Germany Report, Section 2.

[165] Canada Report, Section 6.

[166] Id.

[167] Peru Report, Section 6.

Table 20.5 Property and expropriation

	Protection of property		**Conditions for expropriation**				**Standards for compensation**	
Jurisdiction	*National treatment*	*Other standards*	*Public purpose*	*Non-discrimination*	*Due process of law*	*Compensation*	*Hull formula*	*Other standards*
Argentina	√		√	√	√	√		lost profit excluded
Australia	√		√	√	√	√	√	
Canada	√	BITs offer higher treatment	√	√	√	√	√	'special economic advantage' might be added
China	√	Higer treatment under BITs	√	√	√	√		"appropriate compensation" but not materially different from Hull formula
Croatia	√		√	/	/	√	/	Fair market value
Czech Republic	√		√	√	√	√	√	
Ethiopia	/	/	√	√	√	√	√	
France	√		√	√	√	√	/	Fair compensation under domestic law
Germany	√		√	√	√	√	√	Reasonable compensation under domestic law
Greece	/	/	√	√	√	√	√	
Italy	√		√	√	√	√	/	/
Japan	√		√	√	√	√	√	
South Korea	/	/	/	/	/	/	/	/
Macau	√		√	√	√	√		Due compensation
Peru	√		√	√	√	√	√	
Portugal	√		√	/	/	√	/	Just compensation under domestic law
Russia	/	/	/	/	/	/	/	/
Singapore	√	/	√	√	√	√		Compensation shall be valued prior to expropriation.
Slovenia	√ (reciprocal)		√	√	√	√	√	Just compensation
Turkey	√		√	√	√	√	/	Full and prompt compensation
UK	√		√	√	√	√	√	"Appropriate compensation" under ECHR
USA	√		√	√	√	√	√	"just compensation"
Total	**18**		**20**	**18**	**18**	**20**	**11**	

IPRs regardless of the nationality of the beneficiary.[168] The BITs and EPA concluded by most of the jurisdictions contain a clause explicitly including intellectual property rights in the definition of investments.

[168] See the relative Section of the Jurisdictional Reports of these Jurisdictions respectively.

20.8.3 Right to Expropriate

It is recognized by customary international law that a state enjoys the right to expropriate property of foreign investors located within its territory.[169] Such sovereign

[169] Dolzer and Schreuer, *supra* footnote 64, at 89.

right is sometimes ensured in the constitution of some states. Article 29 of the Japanese Constitution for instance explicitly provides that private property may be expropriated.[170] Article 13 of the China's 2004 Constitution stipulates that: "[T]he state may, for the public interest, expropriate or take over private property of citizens for public use, and pay compensation in the accordance with law".[171] Pursuant to Article 17 of the Argentina's Constitution, expropriation is permitted when conducted in the public interest and under the conditions provided by law.[172] Article 42 of the Italian Constitution provides that in cases defined by the law, and provided compensation is paid to the owner, property can be expropriated for reasons of general interest.[173] According to the local statute in Singapore, the government may acquire land for either any public purpose or any residential, commercial or industrial purposes.[174]

The right to expropriate by host states is also affirmed by international treaty law. Almost every BIT contains an article on expropriation. Whilst it typically details the conditions and standards of compensation for expropriation, it implicitly affirms the host state's right to expropriate alien's property.

20.8.4 Definition of Expropriation

Direct expropriation or outright nationalization of an asset is generally easier to define as there is a physical taking by the states of the relevant assets.[175] However, indirect expropriation or measures equivalent to expropriation are much more difficult to define.

Argentina is one of the few states that have defined direct and indirect expropriation in its domestic law.[176] According to its domestic laws and regulations, direct expropriation is resorted to when the Government as guarantor of public interest needs certain property in order to satisfy a general and collective community interest and therefore has to take or use property owned by a person. Indirect or irregular expropriation takes place when (i) there is a law declaring the public interest of certain goods and the State takes it without previous compensation; (ii) when the good declared to be of public interest by law cannot be disposed of in normal conditions and (iii) when the State imposes an unlawful restriction upon private property. In all these cases, the affected owner may take the matter to court in which a judge may declare whether indirect expropriation actually has taken place.[177] It is therefore clear that the irregular/indirect expropriation under Argentine domestic law differs from indirect or creeping expropriation as understood in international law. Under international law, indirect expropriation deals with State measures which substantially deprive investors of their private property. These kinds of measures do not generally qualify as expropriation under Argentine domestic law. Rather, the deprived owner should seek compensation through the broader concept of state responsibility.[178]

In Germany, Article 14(3) of the Basic Law set forth specific criteria for the constitutionality of an expropriation. According to this article, four elements should be fulfilled: every expropriation must be based on a statutory law passed by the legislation; the intent of an expropriation should be to promote a common good or further national welfare; expropriations need to meet the principle of proportionality; expropriations should be executed in exchange for a reasonable compensation.[179] In France, four conditions[180] must be met to qualify as an indirect expropriation, and the foreign investor will have to prove each and every of the four criteria in case of an indirect expropriation.[181]

---

[170] Japan Report, Section 7.

[171] China Report, Section 7.

[172] Argentina Report, Section 7.

[173] Italy Report, Section 7.

[174] Singapore Report, Section 2.

[175] Gallagher and Shan, *supra* footnote 52, at 257.

[176] Argentina Report, Section 7.

[177] Id.

[178] Id.

[179] Germany Report, Section 2.

[180] According to Section 7 of the France Report, the four conditions include: (1) The possession must be irregular and must have arisen at the occasion of an ordinary and regular operation (such as an operation of public work) or must have become irregular when the transfer of property was later declared void; (2) The possession must be maintained by the public authority for reasons of public necessity; (3) The beneficiary of the indirect expropriation must not provoke direct expropriation or agree with the owner of the property to pay it/him an periodical indemnity for the occupation of the property; (4) The owner of the property must ask the judge of the French civil court of justice: the Tribunal de Grande Instance to declare the transfer of property and to fix the amount of the indemnity which must be accompanied by a dispossession indemnity.

[181] Id.

Although an expropriation clause can be found in every BIT, most of them do not contain a definition of the concept of indirect expropriation. However, some BITs do attempt to give a definition to this concept. Article 5 of the Slovenia-Kuwait BIT provides that for the purposes of the agreement, the term "expropriation" includes also interferences or regulative measures, which have a *de facto* expropriatory effect, because of which the investor is dispossessed of his property rights, control or substantial benefits related to his investment; or his investment is deprived of its economic value or suffers substantial damage. Examples of these interferences include the freezing or blockage of the investment, introduction of arbitrary or disproportionate taxes, forced sale of the whole investment or its part, and other comparable measures.[182]

Some recent BITs include what may be called "public welfare or exceptions" to ensure that public welfare/interest measures by the host state are not caught by the expropriation clause. Thus the US Model BIT 2004 stipulates that:

> (b) Except in rare circumstances, non-discriminatory regulatory actions by a Party that are designed and applied to protect legitimate public welfare objectives, such as public health, safety, and the environment, do not constitute indirect expropriations.[183]

Similar provision can be found in Article 17 of the Japan-Uzbekistan BIT, which states that,

> Nothing in this Agreement [...] shall be construed to prevent a Contracting Party from adopting or enforcing measures:
>
> (a) necessary to protect human, animal or plant life or health;
> (b) necessary to protect public morals or to maintain public order.

An explanatory note was added to this provision: "The public order exception may be invoked only where a genuine and sufficiently serious threat is posed to one of the fundamental interests of society." This should help to avoid abuse of this exception.[184]

The FTAs signed between Australia and other States, such as the Australia-United States Free Trade Agreement (AUSFTA) and the Australia – New Zealand Free Trade Area (AANZFTA), include an Annex on Expropriation to clarify the parties' mutual understanding on the constitution of expropriation. The Annexes make clear that an action or a series of actions by a government cannot constitute an expropriation unless "it interferes with a tangible or intangible property right or property interest in an investment".

20.8.5 Conditions of Expropriation

Conditions of expropriation are provided in both domestic laws and international treaties. However, the latter is more comprehensive than the former. According the American domestic laws, the usual standard is that expropriations can only be undertaken for public purposes and that the compensation should be 'prompt, adequate and effective.' Article 70 of the Peruvian Constitution grants the necessity guarantees required in case of expropriation. Only for national security or public purposes, declared by law and accompanied with cash payment of the appraised value can expropriations be legally justified. The Japanese Constitution also provides that '[P]rivate property may be taken for public use upon just compensation.' Accordingly, public purpose and compensation are the two key elements enshrined in domestic laws and regulations.

In most BITs/FTAs, four conditions are required to qualify for a lawful expropriation: (1) for a public purpose; (2) on a non-discriminatory basis; (3) in accordance with due process of law; (4) upon payment of prompt, adequate and effective compensation. However, this formula has not always been closely followed. Chinese investment treaties, for example, although generally follow the prototype in requiring the four substantive requirements, they do not expressly accept the "prompt, adequate and effective" standard of compensation.[185] This is because China has traditionally supported the developing states' position that in case of expropriation, it is "appropriate compensation", rather than the "Hull Formula" of "promote, adequate and effective" compensation, that is required.[186] They nevertheless accept the common methods of valuation, such as 'market value' or 'fair

[182] Slovenia Report, Section 7.

[183] US Model BIT 2004, Annex B (Expropriation) point 4 (b).

[184] Japan Report, Section 7.

[185] China Report, Section 7.

[186] Id.

market value' or 'genuine value' of the taken assets.[187] Acceptance of these concepts, particularly the concept of "market value" suggests that the actual standard of compensation available under Chinese BITs do not materially differ from BIT practice of the rest of the world. (Table 20.5)

It can be observed that international investment treaties tend to attach more stringent conditions on the exercise of the right of expropriation than what is required under domestic laws. Thus two more conditions are added, namely the due process of law and non-discrimination requirements. One might argue that since most states tend to guarantee the two aspects either in their constitution or other forms of laws, they are implicitly included as conditions of expropriation. However, the explicit inclusion of them in investment treaties suggests that such assumption might not always be valid-otherwise there should be no such need as to explicitly incorporate them in the treaties. Thus the treaty standard here is clearer, and in some cases perhaps higher, than domestic law standard.

20.8.6 Compensation for Expropriation

As indicated above, the most widely used standard of compensation under investment treaties seems to be the so-called 'Hull Formula' requiring that they "promote, adequate and effective" compensation. However, there are states that persistently reject to include the formula in their BITs. China is an example. So far no Chinese BIT has explicitly accepted the three term formula, even though, as mentioned above, the actual standard of compensation provided under Chinese BITs might not be materially different from the Hull formula requirements.

Under domestic laws, terms used for the standard of compensation vary. US and Japan tend to use 'just compensation' in their domestic laws, whilst France often uses 'fair compensation'.[188] Other terms such as "full and just compensation" (Argentina), "appropriate compensation" (China), "reasonable compensation" (Germany), "due compensation" (Macau) are also used. Whilst "just compensation" is often interpreted to mean the same as "Hull formula" in the US, this interpretation is certainly not the uniform interpretation accepted in all other states. The European Court of Human Rights has held that 'Article 1 does not … guarantee a right to full compensation in all circumstances, since legitimate objectives of "public interest" may call for less than reimbursement of the full market value.'[189] Although Argentina adopts "full and just compensation" as the standard of compensation, it excludes any loss of future profit from its calculation (Table 20.5).[190] To summarize, whilst the standard of compensation is largely standardized under investment treaties, varied terms are used under domestic laws. Again the treaty standard appears clearer, and perhaps in some cases higher, than the domestic law standards.

Most BITs do not have express provisions on the valuation methods for compensation. Many BITs/FTAs simply provide that compensation should be paid without delay, and the compensation should be equivalent to the fair market value of the expropriated investment immediately before the expropriation took place. They also provide that the compensation should not reflect any change in value as a result of the intended expropriation becoming publicly known. In addition, most BITs stipulate that interests from the date of expropriation to the date of payment should be included in the compensation. Finally, some BITs, such as the Sino-Germany BIT, emphasize that the MFN principle applies to the expropriation provisions.[191]

20.9 Monetary Transfer

20.9.1 Transferable Assets

Most investors expect to be able to transfer any profits made from their investment back to their home states. Such expectation is protected under most BITs. Article

[187] Id.

[188] See Section 7 of the Jurisdictional Reports of these Jurisdictions respectively.

[189] *Holy Monasteries v Greece* (Judgment of 9 December 1994) (1995) 20 EHRR 1, para 71.

[190] Argentina Report, Section 7.

[191] Article 4 (3) of the Sino-Germany BIT, for example, reads:

> Investors of either Contracting Party shall enjoy most-favoured-nation treatment in the territory of the other Contracting Party in respect of the matters provided for in this Article.

8(2) of the UK-Mexico BIT, for example, sets out a much more detailed list of transfers coved by the provision of transfer:

(a) Profits, dividends, interests, capital gains, royalty payments, management fees, technical assistance and other fees and amounts derived from the investment;
(b) Proceeds from the sale of all or any part of the investment, or from the partial or complete liquidation of the investment;
(c) Payments arising from compensation from expropriation;
(d) Payments pursuant to the application of provisions relating to the settlement of disputes;
(e) Payments arising from the compensation and losses under Article 6 of this Agreement.

Likewise, most China's BITs also include such an open-definition, and provide that the list is non-exhaustive.[192]

20.9.2 Restrictions to Transfer

The transfer or repatriation of funds provision in BITs is at the heart of the object and the purpose of an investment treaty.[193] Most jurisdictions thus guarantee free transfer with only few exceptions/restrictions. The UK Model BIT, for instance, prescribes that the contracting parties shall guarantee the unrestricted transfer of any investment which falls within the treaty regime and any returns on such investments. The Model BIT does not include any general exceptions.[194] In USA, there are no restrictions on the transfer of money to or from the US through the usual banking channels.[195] There are no restrictions in Macau on the transfer of investment assets.[196]

However, restrictions do exist. They can be summarized as follows:

- Situations of exceptional of balance of payment difficulties. For instance the UK-Singapore BIT provides that the monetary transfer should be subject to 'the right of each Contracting Party in exceptional financial or economic circumstances to exercise equitably and good faith powers conferred by laws'.[197] Article 59 of the European Community Treaty states that in case of exceptional circumstances for which transfer of assets from or to foreign countries cause or threaten to cause serious difficulties for the functioning of the economic and monetary union, the institutions of the European Union can take protective measures for a period not exceeding 6 months.
- Anti-money laundering and anti-terrorism. Transport of cash in excess of $10,000 across the borders is subject to reporting in US in order to prevent money laundering.[198] Australia also has an extensive asset freezing regime as part of its anti-terrorism and anti-money laundering exercise. The federal government of Canada has also strengthened its anti-money laundering regime to deal with terrorism and money laundering that threaten the security of the state.[199]
- Registration or report. In Germany, there is an obligation to register certain monetary transactions with the German Central Bank for the sake of statistical reports.[200] Australia also requires that the export from, or import to, Australia of any currency in excess of A$ 10,000 in value must be reported to the Australian Financial Transaction Reports and Analysis Centre.[201]

In recent BIT practice, the exceptions to monetary transfer have become more sophisticated. Again, the UK-Mexico BIT is a example in point. Its Article 8(3) contains a broader list of exceptions which allows a Contracting Party to prevent a transfer in cases of:

(a) bankruptcy, insolvency, or the protection of rights of creditors;
(b) issuing, trading or dealing in securities;
(c) criminal or administrative violations;
(d) reports of transfers of currency or other monetary instruments;
(e) ensuring the satisfaction of judgments in adjudicatory proceedings.

Among the 20 jurisdictions, Argentina and Ethiopia seem to have a more restrictive regime on monetary transfer. Since early 2002 the Central Bank of Argentina

[192] China Report, Section 8.
[193] See Gallagher and Shan, *supra* footnote 52, at 175.
[194] UK Report, Section 8.
[195] US Report, Section 8.
[196] Macau Report, Section 8.
[197] UK Report, Section 8.
[198] US Report, Section 8.
[199] Canada Report, Section 8.
[200] Germany Report, Section 2.
[201] Australia Report, Section 8.

has tightened its control over foreign currency exchange transactions in an effort to mitigate the volatility of foreign currency exchange rates against the Argentine peso as a consequence of the current international financial crisis.[202] Monetary transactions require authorization in accordance with foreign exchange regulations. Prior registration is required, and exchange transaction must be documented in an exchange contract to be executed with authorized foreign exchange entity.[203] Moreover, all foreign currency transfers into Argentina have to be translated into local currency.[204] In Ethiopia, payments and transfers are subject to a stringent supervision and control by the National Bank of Ethiopia (NBE), which enjoys a monopoly over all sorts of foreign currency transactions. Foreign investors are entitled to open and operate a foreign currency account in Ethiopia, although not more than $ 50, 000. There is a full set of regulations concerning the exchange currency rates.[205]

20.9.3 Currency Exchange

Most of the States provide that the currency exchange should use ‘freely convertible currency’ or ‘freely usable currency’. The UK Model BIT additionally guarantees the right to have the transfer made in the currency in which the capital was originally invested.[206] In Argentina, the exchange transaction must be executed by the authorized foreign exchange entity. And the operator will convert the foreign currency into local currency, then change it into the desired currency, and finally make the transfer.[207] In Ethiopia, currency exchange rates are determined and fully regulated by the National Bank of Ethiopia.[208]

20.10 Dispute Settlement

The greatest breakthrough in the area of international investment law is the creation of an investor-state dispute settlement mechanism enabling foreign investors to sue the host government. Most of the 20 jurisdictions have been involved in investor-state disputes. According to the statistics of the UNCTAD, Argentina leads the table of known investment treaty claims (as defendant) with 51 cases. The Czech Republic ranked the third with 16 cases. Both the US and Canada have 14 cases each. Turkey and Russia have the same number of 8. Slovenia and Germany have two cases. UK, Portugal, France and Croatia all have been involved in one case, while China, Italy and Singapore have not been exposed to any international arbitration cases.[209]

20.10.1 Domestic Jurisdiction

By default, all foreign investment disputes are subject to the jurisdiction of the domestic courts and tribunals of the host state, unless there is any overriding international law arrangement. As can be seen in Table 20.6, none of the 22 jurisdictions has established special rules or mechanism for the settlement of foreign investment disputes. Rather, such disputes are subject to the general rules and mechanism of dispute settlement, available in the host jurisdiction. In other words, national treatment is guaranteed in this regard.

In some jurisdictions, exhaustion of local remedies is required as a condition to submit investment disputes to international arbitration. According to the US Report, for example, the US requires that a foreign investor must exhaust available local remedies before turning to international arbitration.[210] Article 10 of the Germany-Argentina BIT also provides that an investor-state dispute must be submitted to the national courts of the host State first.[211] Older generation Chinese BITs (before 1997) reserve all foreign investment disputes other than those concerning the amount of compensation to be submitted to local courts.[212] Since 1998, China embarked on a new generation of BITs allowing all foreign investment disputes to be submitted to international arbitration including ICSID

[202] Argentina Report, Section 8.

[203] Id.

[204] Id.

[205] Ethiopia Report, Section 8.

[206] UK Report, Section 8.

[207] Argentina Report, Section 8.

[208] Ethiopia Report, Section 8.

[209] UNCTAD, Latest Developments in Investor-State Dispute Settlement, IIA ISSUES NOTE No.1 (2010), p.13.

[210] US Report, Section 9.

[211] Argentina Report, Section 9.

[212] China Report, Section 9.

Table 20.6 Dispute settlement

	National jurisdiction		**ICSID Arbitration**		**Non-ICSID arbitration**		**National control**	
Jurisdiction	*Special rules*	*General rules*	*ICSID membership*	*ICSID reservations*	*UNCITRAL*	*Others (pls specify)*	*On ICSID arbitration*	*On other arbitrations*
Argentina	×	√	√	×	√	√ (MIGA, ICC)	√ (constitution-ality)	√
Australia	×	√	√	×	√	/		√
Canada	×	√		×	√	√ (ICSID Additional Facility)		√
China	×	√	√	(notifica-tion)	√	√ (ICC, ICSID Additional Facility)		√
Croatia	×	√	√	×	√	√ (MIGA, ICC)	/	√
Czech Republic	×	√	√	×	√	√ (ICC)	/	/
Ethiopia	×	√	×	×	√	√ (MIGA, ICC)	/	/
France	×	√	√	×	√	√ (ICC)	/	/
Germany	×	√	√	×	/	/		√
Greece	×	√	√	×	√	/	/	/
Italy	×	√	√	×	√	√ (MIGA, ICC)		
Japan	×	√	√	×	√	√	√ (constitution-ality)	
South Korea	/	/	√	/	/	/	/	/
Macau	×	√	√	(notification)	/	/		√
Peru	×	√	√	×	/	/	/	√
Portugal	×	√	√	/	/	/	/	/
Russia	/	/	√	/	/	/	/	/
Singapore	×	√	√	×	√	√ (ICC)		
Slovenia	×	√	√	×	√	√		√
Turkey	×	√	√	×	/	/	/	√
UK	×	√	√	×	√	√ (PCA)	(Registration)	√
USA	×	√	√	×	√	√		√
Total	**× (20)**	**√ (20)**	**√ (20)**	**× (17)**	**√ (15)**	**√ (12)**	**√ (2)**	**√ (13)**

arbitration.[213] China nevertheless requires resort to local administrative review before submission to international arbitration. Another technique to uphold national jurisdiction is through the so-called 'fork-in-the-road' clause, which aims to preclude an investor from commencing international arbitration after having chosen local remedies.[214]

It is noted that without a 'fork-in-the-road' clause and the 'exhaustion of local remedy' requirements, it

[213] Id.

[214] It is noted that some investment agreements, such as NAFTA and other Canadian agreements, require the investor to waive claims for financial relief in other for a as a condition of making an investor-state claim.

is likely to have parallel proceedings and conflicts. The duplication of international and domestic proceedings is an unresolved problem to date. This makes the state run the risk of multiple liability, and the authority and efficacy of both judicial systems. The international and the national dispute settlement mechanisms will be severely damaged if conflicting decisions are rendered on the same foreign investment case.[215]

20.10.2 International Arbitration

The charm of international investment law lies in its state-investor arbitration system though it is not provided in every investment treaty.[216] International investment arbitration cases have been on rapid surge in the first decade of the new century, with the ICSID playing a prominent role.[217] Among the 22 jurisdictions, 20 are members to ICSID. Canada, Ethiopia and Macau are the few exceptions (Table 20.6). Of the 20 Member States, only China made a notification when ratified the ICSID Convention, allowing only dispute concerning compensation on expropriation to be submitted to ICSID. However, this notification was effectively changed in 1998 when the Sino-Barbados BIT was concluded to provide that any investment dispute may be submitted to the ICSID, or ad hoc arbitration under the UNICITRAL Arbitration Rules.

The earlier BITs concluded by some States only provide for the ICSID arbitration. Most UK BIT concluded before February 1982 for example contained a dispute settlement clause that allowed an investor to submit a dispute only to ICSID conciliation or arbitration.[218] Earlier Japanese BITs also did not mention other arbitration mechanism than the ICSID.[219] However, other arbitration mechanisms are becoming more and more common in BITs and FTAs. They include ICSID Additional Facility, the UNCITRAL Arbitration, the ICC arbitration and *ad hoc* arbitration. MIGA arbitration mechanism is also recently used in some cases against Argentina (Table 20.6).[220]

For non-ICSID arbitration, the New York Convention is of vital importance in guaranteeing enforcement. Most of the 20 jurisdictions are members to the New York Convention. Article V of the 'New York Convention' sets forth the grounds upon which a state might refuse the recognition and enforcement of the arbitration awards.[221] In addition, there tend to be

[215] Germany Report, Section 3.

[216] However, not every BIT contains a state-investor dispute resolution clause. The Germany-Somali BIT, for example, does not contain the consent to investor-state arbitration. See Section 2 of Germany Report.

[217] According to the Statistics of UNCTAD, of the total 357 known disputes until the end of 2008, 225 were filed with the International Centre for Settlement of Investment Disputes (ICSID) or under the ICSID Additional Facility, 91 under the United Nations Commission on International Trade Law (UNCITRAL) rules, 19 with the Stockholm Chamber of Commerce, eight were administered by the Permanent Court of Arbitration in the Hague, five with the International Chamber of Commerce (ICC) and four are ad hoc cases. One further case was filed with the Cairo Regional Centre for International Commercial Arbitration. In four cases the applicable rules are unknown so far. See UNCTAD, Latest Developments in Investor-State Dispute Settlement, IIA ISSUES NOTE No.1 (2010), p.2.

[218] UK Report, Section 9.

[219] Japan Report, Section 9.

[220] In 2006, MIGA was actively seeking to solve three pending claims involving issues of expropriation between Argentina and the Kyrgyz Republic. At that time MIGA was also closely monitoring and actively working to resolve the problems of eight other disputes relating to investments guaranteed by the agency in Argentina, Guatemala, the Kyrgyz Republic, Mauritania, Nicaragua, Senegal, and Venezuela. Four of these involve issues related to expropriation; three involve breach of contract; and two involve transfer convertibility issues, see the Argentine National Report.

[221] The Article reads:

1. Recognition and enforcement of the award may be refused, at the request of the party against whom it is invoked, only if that party furnishes to the competent authority where the recognition and enforcement is sought, proof that:
   (a) The parties to the agreement referred to in article II were, under the law applicable to them, under some incapacity, or the said agreement is not valid under the law to which the parties have subjected it or, failing any indication thereon, under the law of the country where the award was made; or
   (b) The party against whom the award is invoked was not given proper notice of the appointment of the arbitrator or of the arbitration proceedings or was otherwise unable to present his case; or
   (c) The award deals with a difference not contemplated by or not falling within the terms of the submission to arbitration, or it contains decisions on matters beyond the scope of the submission to arbitration, provided that, if the decisions on matters submitted to arbitration can be separated from those not so submitted, that part of the award which contains decisions on matters submitted to arbitration may be recognized and enforced; or
   (d) The composition of the arbitral authority or the arbitral procedure was not in accordance with the agreement of the parties, or, failing such agreement, was not in accordance with the law of the country where the arbitration took place; or

detailed rules in each jurisdiction setting forth certain domestic control mechanisms on international arbitration. In UK, for instance, an arbitral award may be challenged on the ground that the tribunal did not have substantive jurisdiction.[222] Also, an arbitration award may be challenged on the basis of serious irregularity affecting the tribunal, the proceedings, or the award. In this respect, it is also necessary to show that the serious irregularity has caused or will cause a substantial injustice to the applicants. Japan's Arbitration Act sets forth two conditions of arbitrability: an arbitrable dispute must be a "civil dispute" that "may be resolved by settlement between the parties."[223]

For ICSID arbitration, the situation is rather different. According to Article 26 of the ICSID Convention, ICSID arbitral awards will be automatically recognized and enforced without control in most of the cases. However, the solution provided in the ICSID Convention was severely criticized by some Argentine scholars who consider it to be unconstitutional.[224] However, although the Argentine Government has declared that it would subject ICSID awards to the review of local courts, it is yet to happen in practice.[225] ICSID arbitration awards may also be subject to constitutionality review in Japan. (Table 20.6) The UK maintains a registration requirement for ICSID awards to be enforced in the country.[226]

In short, national treatment is commonly guaranteed under domestic laws with regard to the resolution of foreign investment disputes. Under treaty law, international state-investor arbitration is provided in almost all investment treaties, in some states subject to restrictions on the scope of disputes that may be submitted. Most of the reported jurisdictions have accepted ICSID jurisdiction. Decisions rendered out of ICSID arbitration may nevertheless be subject to constitutionality review in some states such as Argentina and Japan.

20.11 FDI Statistics, Policies and Authorities

Recent decades has seen significant rise in outward and inward flows of investment in most of the 20 jurisdictions. This is at least partly due to the improvement of foreign investment environment and the liberal approaches taken by these jurisdictions. FDI is playing a more and more significant role in economic development. The only exception seems to be Argentina. FDI in Argentina can be divided into two periods. The first, from 1990 to 2001, indicates strong foreign and local investment due to free trade and open market policies and the whim of foreign exchange controls. The second period started with the national crisis that reached its critical point between December 2001 and January 2002 and is demonstrative of constant capital flight from Argentina.[227]

All the economic groupings, including developed countries, developing countries and the Commonwealth of Independent States, suffered losses when the financial crisis exploded in 2008. However, it is noted that whilst FDI inflows fell in developed countries in developing and transition economies they actually continued to increase.[228] According to the World Investment Report 2010, "FDI inflows plum- meted in 2009 in all three major groupings – developed, developing and transition economies … After 6 years of uninterrupted growth, FDI flows to developing countries declined by 24% in 2009."[229] However, it also predicts that "The recovery of FDI in- flows in 2010 – if modest in global terms – is expected to be stronger in developing countries than in developed ones."[230]

(e) The award has not yet become binding, on the parties, or has been set aside or suspended by a competent authority of the country in which, or under the law of which, that award was made.

2. Recognition and enforcement of an arbitral award may also be refused if the competent authority in the country where recognition and enforcement is sought finds that:
   (a) The subject matter of the difference is not capable of settlement by arbitration under the law of that country; or
   (b) The recognition or enforcement of the award would be contrary to the public policy of that country.

See Article V of the New York Convention.

[222] UK Report, Section 9.

[223] Japan Report, Section 9.

[224] Argentina Report, Section 9.

[225] Id.

[226] UK Report, Section 9.

[227] Argentina Report, Section 10.

[228] UNCTAD, World Investment Report 2009, Transnational Corporations, Agricultural Production and Development, available at: http://www.unctad.org/templates/webflyer.asp?docid=11904&intItemID=1397.

[229] World Investment Report 2010, p.3.

[230] Ibid.

In order to attract FDI, some states have taken measures to promote investments. Portugal for example has established some institutions to promote investments. These institutions include the Agency for Investment and Foreign Trade (AICEP), the Institute of Support to Small and Medium Industrial Enterprises (IAPMEI) and the Instituto de Turismo de Portugal.[231] In contrast, some jurisdictions have tightened up the foreign investment review procedures. For instance, the Investment Canada Act was amended in 2009, introducing a process for national security reviews.[232] The federal Cabinet acting on a recommendation of the Minister can require such a review where deemed necessary regardless the size of the transaction.[233]

20.12 Trends in Foreign Investment Laws

It is difficult to identify the trends of development in foreign investment law out of reports from 22 distinctive jurisdictions covering such wide range of issues. It is however a "must" for a general report. Nevertheless it seems that three trends of the law of foreign investment protection have emerged, namely "harmonization", "balancing" and "socialization".

20.12.1 "Harmonization"

The first and perhaps also the most significant finding is that the legal principles of foreign investment protection in different jurisdictions have been, by and large, harmonized. This is largely due to the proliferation of BITs and other investment treaties such as FTAs and EPAs. Since such instruments have adopted largely the same or at least similar language on some of the core aspects (such as standards of treatment, expropriation and compensation, freedom of transfer and international arbitration to resolve investment disputes), the general principles or norms of foreign investment protection in different jurisdictions has been by and large "harmonized". Obviously different variations exist and in some cases such variations are material. For example, US, Canada and Japan tend to extend national treatment obligations to the stage of investment admission, whilst other BITs normally leave investment admission to the complete discretion of the host state authorities. Another example is perhaps China's long resistance to the national treatment standard, which has not been a problem to most other jurisdictions. Such variations, however, have not prevented those jurisdictions from consenting to the core principles of investment protection in the form of international treaties.

Understandably the languages adopted in the domestic laws of different jurisdictions are less unified. Yet they also seem to uphold the same or similar principles, such as national treatment to foreign investors. Even in the area of investment admission, which is traditionally left to the discretion of the host states, there is now significant convergence between developed and developing states, as observed above. This further confirms that the past two decades of investment liberalization has indeed resulted in a generally level playing field for foreign investment, in the forms of both international treaties and domestic laws.

However, it should be pointed out that the harmonization of core principles is not the end of the story. Rather harmonization is still an ongoing process. This is because whilst the principles are harmonized, the detailed meanings of such principles are subject to the often varied implementations and interpretations by domestic authorities of different jurisdictions and different international arbitration tribunals. For instance, whilst the NT standard is equally upheld in different jurisdictions, as observed above, different jurisdictions actually have different understandings on the standard. The same applies to the standard of compensation for expropriation where a number of different terms are used under domestic laws of different states. To make it worse, international arbitration tribunals often offer varied interpretations of such principles. The aforementioned diverse interpretations by different arbitration tribunals on the principles of FET, MFN and umbrella clause are telling examples in point. The harmonization process therefore still has a long way to go to build up a more solid consensus in international investment protection. As discussed below, much effort has been made in recent investment treaties to clarify the meanings of some of the core principles with a view to preventing too far-fetching interpretations. Also, domestic laws are to be further harmonized as the more and more liberalization measures continue to be adopted by states in recent years, as demonstrated in Chart 20.5. Hence harmonization of foreign

[231] Portugal Report, Section 10.

[232] Canada Report, Section 10.

[233] Id.

Chart 20.5 National investment policy changes 1992–2009 (Source: UNCTAD, *World Investment Report 2010*)

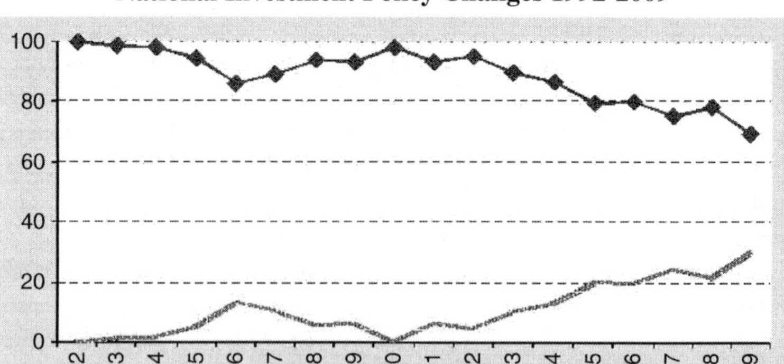

Source: UNCTAD, *World Investment Report 2010*

investment laws is not a done business, but an ongoing process and a current trend of development.

20.12.2 "Balancing"

Second, there seems to be an emerging trend among states to pursue an investment regime that is more "balanced" in the rights and obligations of the host state and the foreign investors, revising the previously "one-sided" regime committed to unfettered investment protection and liberalization. Thus as noted above, the FTC of the NAFTA parties has adopted interpretations on such core principles as FET and expropriation, with a view to preserving necessary regulatory powers of host states, which have been incorporated into the new model BITs of both US and Canada, as well as BITs concluded by some other states. This is confirmed by the recently released World Investment Report 2010 (WIR 2010), which has noted that many of the recent ones demonstrate governments' effort to "seek to formulate agreements more precisely, paying greater attention to ensuring that the treaty language reflects their domestic policy objectives, reaffirming and strengthening States' right to regulate in the public interest, and trying to enhance the legitimacy of the ISDS processes."[234] In particular, it has noted five broad developments in these IIAs, namely the clarification of the scope of the treaty; the introduction of general and security exceptions that allow more room for regulation by host states; the clarification of the scope and meaning of specific obligations; the addition of environmental clauses and the inclusion of corporate social responsibility clauses.[235] Among them, three developments are directly targeting at increasing the policy space of the host state, whilst the other two (the clarifications of relevant scope and terms) indirectly have the same effect. The balancing trend is thus highly visible in investment treaty practice, which seems to have also had an impact on investment arbitration practice, as more and more tribunals have opted for a "balanced" approach of treaty interpretation.[236]

The balancing trend is also evident in domestic legal changes. As Chart 20.5 shows, although states continue to adopt more favorable than restrictive

[234] UNCTAD, World Investment Report 2010, at 87.

[235] UNCTAD, World Investment Report 2010, at 87–88.

[236] In the *Noble Ventures inc. v Romania*, for instance, the tribunal pointed out that "it is not permissible, as is too often done regarding BITs, to interpret clauses exclusively in favor of investors." Also, the El Paso decision on jurisdiction is noted for its "balanced interpretation". The relevant sentence goes as follows:

> The tribunal considers that a balanced interpretation is needed, taking into account both State sovereignty and State responsibility to create an adapted and evolutionary framework for the development of economic activities, and the necessity to protect foreign investment and its continuing flows.

See *Noble Ventures, Inc. v. Romania*, ICSID Case No. ARB/01/11, Award, 12 October 2005, at § 52; *El Paso Energy International Company v. The Argentine Republic*, ICSID Case No. ARB/03/15, Decision on Jurisdiction, 27 April 2006, at para 70.

Table 20.7 Three Generations of International Investment Regimes: a Comparison

Generation	Principal feature	Primary need served
First generation (1945–1970)	Nationalisation	Political need
Second generation (1980–1990)	Liberalisation	Economic need
Third generation (2000–)	Balancing/ socialisation	Social need

measures on foreign investment, the portion of restrictive regulatory changes has been increase rapidly in recent years with an annual 3% increase since 2000. In 2009, restrictive changes reach 30% of the total changes. (Chart 20.5) If this trend is to continue, within 8 years time the world will see more restrictive measures adopted than favorable ones. By then there should be a better chance to strike a balanced investment regime in states around the world.

From a historical perspective, the current balancing trend can be viewed as a necessary balance between the generally nationalistic trend on foreign investment experienced in 1960 and 1970s, and the liberalist trend commenced in late 1980s. (Table 20.7) Both trends have had their historical values: the nationalistic campaign helped the nation-building process of numerous states emerged in the decolonization process whilst the liberalistic movement contributed to the economic development of those states as well as other ones. However, as a legal system, both of the nationalist and the liberalist regimes were biased towards only one side and failed to strike a balance between the rights and obligations of the host states and foreign investors. A balanced investment regime will, hopefully, be a more sustainable regime.

20.12.3 "Socialization"

Last but not least, the "social dimensions" of the investment regime have been increasingly stressed. There are two sides of the coin. On the one side, more and more model and real BITs have expressly carved out regulations in the areas of key social concern such as health, safety, environment as exceptions to the expropriation rules or the treaty regime in general. For example, the US Model BIT 2004 excludes "non-discriminatory regulatory actions by a Party that are designed and applied to protect legitimate public welfare objectives, such as public health, safety, and the environment" from the scope of "indirect expropriations."[237] The Canadian Model BIT contains similar provisions in Annex B.13(1), in addition to the "general exceptions" provided in Article 10 relating to health and the protection of environment. Another example can be found in Article 17 of the Japan-Uzbekistan BIT. On the other side, some recent investment treaties have started to emphasize social responsibilities of foreign investors. For instance, attempt has been made in the 2007 Norwegian Model BIT draft to include a "best effort" provision promoting "corporate social responsibility."[238] Such efforts, including both sides of the coin, actually serve to improve the balance of the investment regime, by affirming the host state's right on the one hand and promoting the social obligations of foreign investors on the other.

The trend of "socialization" also fits well in the above historical analysis. The nationalist approach before 1980s was used mainly to serve the "political" need of the time, namely to solidly establish the newly emerged states by exercising their newly found sovereign power to nationalize foreign investments that controlled their economy. The liberalist approach prevalent in 1990s served primarily the "economic" needs of the time when almost every state around the world were committed to economic construction after their state sovereignty has been solidly established. The current "socialization" campaign adds to the dialogue a third dimension, the "social" dimension of the investment regime. In so doing it aims to establish an investment regime in which the political, economic and social rights and interests of all stake holders (including not only host states, foreign investors and home states, but

[237] US Model BIT 2004, Annex B on Expropriation, point 4 (b).

[238] The article reads as follows,

> ARTICLE [32] CORPORATE SOCIAL RESPONSIBILITY
> The Parties agree to encourage investors to conduct their investment activities in compliance with the OECD Guidelines for Multinational Enterprises and to participate in the United Nations Global Compact.

See Norway Model BIT draft 2007, Article 32. The draft, however, has been shelved by the government in 2009. See Damon Vis-Dunbar, Norway shelves its draft model bilateral investment treaty, Investment Treaty News, 8 June 2009, available at http://www.investmenttreatynews.org/cms/news/archive/2009/06/08/norway-shelves-its-proposed-model-bilateral-investment-treaty.aspx (last visit on July 19, 2010).

also other parties such as local and indeed foreign citizens who might have an direct or indirect interest in the regime) are equally respected, promoted and protected (Table 20.7).

20.13 General Conclusions

Without repeating the specific findings out of this comparative study, several general conclusions might be drawn.

20.13.1 The Need of Comparative Studies Based on In-depth Country-Specific Studies

The importance of comparative study based on in-depth country-specific studies should be stressed. International investment law is at crossroad and demand in-depth studies. Existing studies tend to be general studies on the subject as a whole. Yet with the MFN provisions found in almost every investment treaties, one could not really obtain a thorough understanding of the applicable international and domestic rules to any given case, without in-depth comprehensive country-specific studies. Comparative studies on the basis of such country-specific studies could serve invaluable guides to governmental officials, legal professionals and academics alike. This study is a first attempt towards this direction.

20.13.2 The Change of Paradigm: From "North-South Divide" to "Private-Public Debate"

The study confirms that the primary tension or theme or paradigm of international investment law is shifting from "north-south divide" to "private-public debate", as the gap between developed and developing states on investment protection has been significantly closed whilst the remaining theme of reform and controversy is focused on the balance of rights and obligations of private investors on the one hand and host government on the other.[239] Thus not only developing states have adopted special laws to deal with foreign investment, developed states such as Canada, Australia and Greece also do the same. In the traditionally domestic law area of investment admission, many developing states have adopted a complete national treatment approach whilst a few developed states are implementing special regimes scrutinizing foreign investment. Hence there is no more clear-cut distinction between the approaches adopted in developed and developing states toward foreign investment under domestic laws. Under international treaties, the general standards of treatment of foreign investment are largely harmonized. Although they are still subject to different interpretations such differences in interpretation do not appear to show a "north-south divide". On the contrary, the debate is now being shifted to the conflicting rights and interests of host states and foreign investors, which is essentially a "private-public debate".

Indeed, the three trends identified above all help to confirm that this shift is indeed taking place. "Harmonization" helps to close the gap between the developed and developing states in investment regime, whilst both "balancing" and "socialization" aim at redressing the balance of rights and interests of the two primary parties of the investment regime, namely the host states and the foreign investors.

Many factors might have contributed to this shift. The most fundamental factor is that "private-public" tension is actually the basic tension underlying the international investment regimes. On the surface, however, the most significant factor is perhaps the change of roles, or the understanding of the roles, of both the developed and developing states in international investment regime. Facing considerable number of investment claims, many developed states have now realized that as large recipients of investment they could also be "bitten" by the liberal investment regime they established. They therefore have an equally important interest to protect the rights of the host state in investment treaties, much as their interest in protecting their investment abroad. On the other hand, some previously pure capital importing states, such as China, have become noticeable capital exporters.[240] This change of

[239] For further discussion on the shift of focus, see Wenhua Shan, "From "North-South Divide" to "Private-Public Debate"," 27, no. 3, p. 631. *Northwestern Journal of International Law and Business* (2007).

[240] According to UNCTAD, China ranked 13th in the world FDI supplier league table, with an increase of 132% in the year of 2008. This does not take into account FDI outflow from Hong Kong, which itself ranked in 10th place in the world. Much of such outward investment from Hong Kong is believed to be ultimately originated from mainland China. See World Investment Report 2009: Overview (UNCTAD, 2009), at 6.

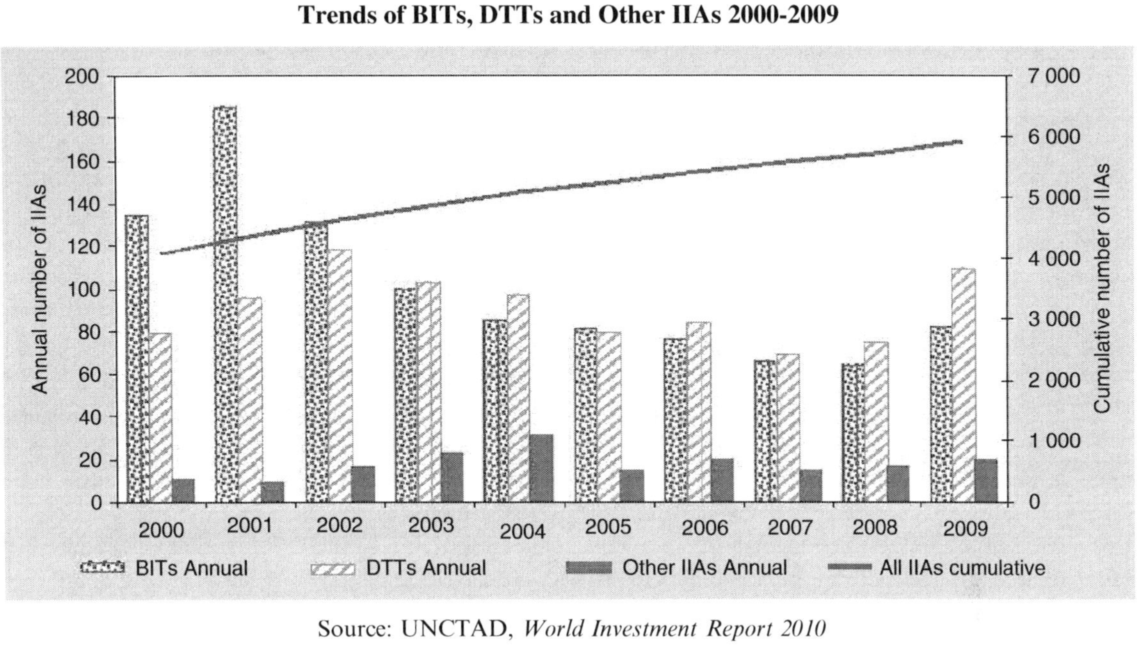

Trends of BITs, DTTs and Other IIAs 2000-2009

Source: UNCTAD, *World Investment Report 2010*

Chart 20.6 Trends of BITs, DTTs and other IIAs 2000–2009 (Source: UNCTAD, *World Investment Report 2010*)

role helps push them to abandon their previously conservative approach and to accept a more liberal international investment regime. Increasingly the two trends, namely the conservative trend of developed states and the liberalist trends of developing states are converging with each other and, as a result, the previous "north-south divide" is giving way to the currently "private-public debate".

20.13.3 Future Investment Regime: Liberalist or Protectionist?

It is believed that states will continue to liberalize their investment regime, but will also try to balance the regime by asserting or when necessary strengthening the regulatory power of the state. In other words, a "balanced liberal regime" might be the outcome of the development. On the one hand, investment liberalization will continue to be pursued by states, given the increasing interdependence of states resulting from the irreversible globalization process. Therefore, new domestic measure will continue to be adopted by states to open their markets, facilitate investment entry and operation. Meanwhile BITs and other IIAs will also increase to provide protection and promotion of international investment. On the other hand, however, states will also be more and more ready to exercise their sovereign rights to regulate foreign investments making sure that the host state benefits from the investment. Accordingly they will be more and more assertive in retaining their regulatory discretion when negotiating or re-negotiating BITs or other IIAs. Surge of investment arbitration cases and global financial crisis might have significantly contributed to this process.

Both trends can be clearly seen from the data on national regulatory changes recorded by the UNCTAD. On the one hand, the vast majority of regulatory changes continue to be in favor of foreign investors. For example, in 2009, 102 regulatory changes were adopted in the world, in which 71 changes were favorable to investors. On the other hand, as mentioned above, restrictive legal changes have increased very rapidly particularly since beginning of the twenty-first century.

The same can also be seen from the most recent developments in investment treaty practice. As Chart 20.6 demonstrates, on the one hand, states are carrying on entering into international investment treaties promoting and protecting foreign investments. On the other hand, as mentioned above, states are revising or renegotiating their real and model investment treaties with a view to preserve their necessary power to regulate foreign investment. It can therefore be argued that the current dual trends of liberalization and balancing will carry on until a "balanced liberal" investment regime is finally achieved.

20.13.4 Towards a Multilateral Investment Agreement?

The current state of international treaty network for investment protection is commonly and vividly described as a "spaghetti bowl". It can be anticipated that, in the years to come, with more BITs being concluded, the bowl will become larger and larger. But the question is whether such expansion would eventually lead to a multilateral investment agreement, or merely a larger "spaghetti bowl"?

It is believed that a multilateral investment agreement (MIA) is a desirable outcome and will be achieved eventually. It is desirable first because it can bring uniformity in the substantive and procedural rules of foreign investment in the world. As observed above, international investment rules have now been harmonized with a set of core obligations being established in the network of BITs. However, beyond that core, there are numerous variations, some of which are rather significant such as the North American preference for concrete obligations on investment admission and complete abandonment of dispute resolution provisions in some BITs. A MIA will establish universal rules of foreign investment, which will build a level playing field for foreign investors around the globe. Second, a MIA would also be more cost-efficient in that it could save the resources invested in the negotiation and implementation of the large number of BITs. Third, as the WTO regime demonstrates, less developed states, particularly the least developed states, would be better off by relying on a multilateral system. Finally, a MIA would be more comprehensive in coverage so that important player current left out of the BRIT system might be attracted to the MIA system because the loss would be too big to afford.

The possibility of a MIA has been increased thanks to the following factors. First, the global financial crisis has passed its worst stage and is on the way to a full recovery, which promises a better economic foundation for a multilateral regime on investment. Second, as demonstrated by the G20 declarations, leaders from the major economies in the world are mindful of the harm of investment protectionism and are committed to investment liberalization. This provides a sound political and institutional foundation for a global pact on investment. Third, international BIT practices have been continuously harmonized. One recent example is the wider acceptance of the FTC interpretation on the meaning of FET standards by states beyond North America. So the legal foundation for such a MIA is becoming more and more solid. Obviously there are still many legal disagreements on which compromises are needed. But it is clear that with the proliferation of BITs and the continuous liberalization of domestic investment regimes, the world is technically much more prepared for a MIA than say 20 years ago. Fourth, some major players particularly the EU and OECD have announced plans to draft their new model BITs, which could serve as step stones toward a global MIA.[241] Finally, since the EU is a major advocate for a MIA, its newly acquired exclusive competence on FDI matters will certainly increase the momentum for the potential MIA.

To achieve such a MIA, three main aspects merit thorough consideration. First, the forum needs to be carefully selected, be it the WTO, OECD, UNCTAD or the World Bank. Second, the interested parties particularly the main stakeholders must have a chance to fully participate in the negotiations. A MAI-type of "closed-door" negotiation excluding the majority of

[241] In a recent conference held in Washington in March 2010, Angel Gurría, the OECD Secretary-General, said that OECD was considering the feasibility of a non-binding "Model Investment Treaty" to avoid an escalation of investment restrictions. See Angel Gurría, The global economy and the global investment agenda – an OECD perspective, available at: http://www.oecd.org/document/0/0,3343,en_2649_34529562_44775040_1_1_1_1,00.html.

the world will not work. Third, again, various interests must be carefully balanced, particularly the interests of the foreign investors on the one hand and the host government on the other. A one-sided agreement will not be accepted by the world.[242]

Certainly there are details that need to work out. But in a globalizing world with international investment serving as life blood, there is every reason to be optimistic about the prospect of a MIA. It might not be too far away![243]

[242] For further details of these considerations, see Wenhua Shan, *The Legal Framework of EU-China Investment Relations: A Critical Appraisal* (Oxford: Hart Publishing, 2005), 270–276.

[243] It is interesting to see that the newly published World Investment Report 2010 seems to share the same view, when it notes that development in IIAs in 2009 indicate that "the landscape of the IIA system is consolidating in different respects", "from a rapid expansion of IIAs at the bilateral level to a more integrated, inclusive and elaborate approach." UNCTAD, World Investment Report 2010, at 83–85.

21 International Law in Domestic Systems*

Dinah Shelton

21.1 Introduction

Rapporteurs for 25 countries submitted national reports on the topic of international law in domestic systems. Despite invitations sent to rapporteurs from under-represented regions of the world, no reports issued from Africa or from a country basing its legal system on Islamic law. The geographic distribution is thus heavily weighted towards Europe: nine reports were prepared for Western European countries,[1] while an additional seven came from Central and Eastern Europe.[2] The other eight reports were divided between three from Latin America,[3] two from North America,[4] three from the Asia/Pacific region,[5] and a report submitted from Israel. The analysis that follows, therefore, may not reflect the situation pertaining in the other 85% the world, although there are some reasons to think that the trends perceived here can be generalized.[6]

Several elements stand out in assessing the national reports as a whole. The first is the marked impact that changes in the international legal system have had on constitutions adopted or amended since World War II. The influential changes, reflected in constitutional law and practice, include the growth and proliferation of global and regional institutions, including courts and other tribunals with the power to adopt binding decisions, the development of international human rights and international criminal law, and the increasing use of informal agreements like memoranda of understanding and other executive instruments negotiated and concluded independently of the classic, formal treaty-making practice. Declarations, codes of conduct, and other normative instruments adopted by international organizations and conferences – commonly described as "soft law" – appear to have some impact in domestic legal systems, in particular in interpreting constitutional and statutory provisions. Domestic courts are also adopting the international doctrine of peremptory norms or *jus cogens*.[7] In sum, the growing complexity and content of international law-making finds an echo in domestic legal systems, in practice even in those countries where the constitutions have not been formally amended.

A second related set of events also appears to have had a significant impact on the place of international law in domestic legal systems. Those countries that have experienced dictatorships or foreign occupation reveal greater receptivity to international law, often

* IV.A.2, Le droit international en droit interne.

[1] Austria, France, Germany, Greece, Italy, Luxembourg, the Netherlands, Portugal and the United Kingdom.

[2] Bulgaria, Czech Republic, Hungary, Poland, the Russian Federation, Serbia, and Slovakia.

[3] Argentina, Uruguay and Venezuela.

[4] Canada and the United States.

[5] Australia, Japan, and New Zealand.

[6] See e.g. P.F. Gonidec, "The Relationship of international Law and National Law in Africa," 10 *African Journal of International and Comparative Law* 244–247 (1998); T. Maluwa, "The Incorporation of International Law and its Interpretation in Municipal Legal Systems in Africa: An Explanatory Survey," 23 *South African Yearbook of International Law* 45 (1998).

[7] France appears to be an exception. According to its national report, the government maintains its consistent opposition to the concept of *jus cogens*.

D. Shelton (✉)
George Washington University Law School, Washington, DC, USA
e-mail: dshelton@law.gwu.edu

K.B. Brown and D.V. Snyder (eds.), *General Reports of the XVIIIth Congress of the International Academy of Comparative Law/Rapports Généraux du XVIIIème Congrès de l'Académie Internationale de Droit Comparé*, DOI 10.1007/978-94-007-2354-2_21, © Springer Science+Business Media B.V. 2012

incorporating or referring to specific international texts in their post-repression constitutions. The failures of the domestic legal order seemingly have inspired in these countries a turn towards an international "safety net." This is evident not only in the new constitutions of Central and Eastern Europe,[8] but also in those of Argentina and, from an earlier period, Spain and Portugal. In addition, a small state like Luxembourg, which owes its creation to a series of treaties, and has been dependent on international cooperation for its economic well-being and even its sovereignty, shows similar deference to international law, giving it primacy in the domestic system. Countries that have not had such experiences, like the United States – which also has the oldest written Constitution among the reporting states – appear less likely to adhere to international agreements or to incorporate customary international law into its judicial decisions. France, also, has shown a certain reticence in regard to international engagements.

Thirdly, while the literature on the relationship between international law and domestic legal systems has traditionally classified the latter as monist or dualist,[9] the 25 national reports suggest it is rare to find a system that is entirely one or the other. As Emmannuel Decaux stated in his report on 'monist' France, the direct application of a treaty properly incorporated into the domestic system is by no means automatic. This is also true of other so-called "monist" states. Among the "dualist" states, there are similarities between the countries whose systems are based on common law traditions, but it may be useful as well to regroup systems according to whether or not the country has a single written constitution, a series of constitutional texts, or no constitution; when the constitution was written, if there is one; and whether or not the country adheres to the European Union or other law-making entity.

In general, the place of international law in the domestic legal system depends on the source of the international law in question: whether it is a treaty, customary international law, a general principle of law, or derives from the decision of an international organization. In some countries international treaties are of constitutional rank, but with many provisos.[10] Other systems place treaties above legislation but under the national constitutions, e.g. Bulgaria, France, Germany, Greece, and Portugal, while other states separate out human rights treaties for enhanced status (the Czech Republic, Russia, Slovakia, Venezuela).[11] In general, approval by the legislative branch has increasingly become a precondition for the internal effect of treaties, as there has been a gradual extension of the categories of treaties subject to such approval.[12] France has perhaps evolved the furthest from its tradition of a strong executive towards greater legislative and judicial involvement in the role of international law in the domestic system.

Entry into the European Union (EU) has complicated the situation for European states.[13] Member states must now implement and apply the legal norms

[8] See generally, E. Stein, "International Law in Internal Law: Toward Internalization of Central-Eastern European Constitutions?" 88 *American Journal of International Law* 427 (1994). Similarly, but with respect to the issue of post-totalitarian constitutions, see A. Cassese, "Modern Constitutions and International Law", *Recueil des Cours de l'Academie de la Haye* 192-III (1985), 331–474, and especially at 351 et cf.

[9] See, e.g. M. Kumm, Towards a Constitutional Theory of the Relationship between National and International Law International Law Part I and II, National Courts and the Arguments from Democracy, 1–2, www.law.nyu.edu/clppt/program2003/readings/kumm1and2.pdf; L. Wildhaber, *Treaty-Making Power and the Constitution* (Basel, 1971), 152–153.

[10] See *Doorwerking internationaal recht in de Nederlandse rechtsorde* (Governmental note on the effect of international law in the Netherlands legal order), *Parliamentary documents* 2007–2008, 29861 No. 19, 3.

[11] C. Economides, "The Elaboration of Model Clauses on the Relationship between International and Domestic Law", (The European Commission for Democracy Through Law, Council of Europe, 1994), 91–113, 101–2; L. Erades, *Interactions between International and Municipal Law* (The Hague: T.M.C. Asser Institute, 1993).

[12] The Constitution of the Netherlands, like that of many other countries, sets some conditions for the internal effect of a treaty, such as Parliamentary approval and official publication. Art. 91 of the Constitution provides:

> 1. The Kingdom shall not be bound by treaties, nor shall such treaties be denounced without the prior approval of the States General. The cases in which approval is not required shall be specified by Act of Parliament.
>
> 2. The manner in which approval shall be granted shall be laid down by Act of Parliament, which may provide for the possibility of tacit approval.
>
> 3. Any provisions of a treaty that conflict with the Constitution or which lead to conflicts with it may be approved by the Houses of the States General only if at least two-thirds of the votes cast are in favor.

[13] The Rome Treaty created a supra-national system, which differs from regular international law. Regarding EC and EU, after the Lisbon Treaty (the Treaty on the Functioning of the EU, TFEU) it has all become EU law.

issued by EU institutions and also the international commitments undertaken at the regional level. Some member states leave it to the courts to find a solution. Italy's Constitutional Court has given a special status to the European Community treaties through a particular interpretation of Article 11 of the Constitution.[14] In contrast, constitutional amendments may be required and enacted to ensure that the provisions of treaties governing the European Union and the rules issued by its institutions apply directly as national law, as provided by European Union law.[15] Beyond the legislative parameters of the EU, the jurisprudence of the European Court of Justice (as well as that of the European Court of Human Rights) has added a new dimension to the interaction of domestic and international law within Europe.

21.2 The Legal Systems

Half a dozen reports came from legal systems based on British common law; many of them have relatively long-standing constitutions or constitutional traditions that are difficult to change in practice. Their legal framework largely pre-dates the creation of international organizations and multilateral treaties. Perhaps because of this, the constitutions contain few references to international law. Although the United Kingdom has no written constitution, the constitutions of common law countries sometimes comprise both written and unwritten elements.[16] In Canada there are two references to international law,[17] the more significant of which relates to the development of international criminal law. The provision incorporates the principle of *nullem crimen sine lege* into the Canadian Charter of Rights and Freedoms[18] and mentions specifically offenses under international law, encompassing both treaty and customary international law. Australia's 1901 Constitution, which remains almost completely as it was when enacted,[19] contains a single reference to treaties, providing that the High Court has original jurisdiction of any matter arising under a treaty.[20] The word "international" does not appear at all in Australia's federal constitution.

Aotearoa/New Zealand, which has no codified constitution,[21] has an 'international' treaty as its foundational document. The Treaty of Waitangi/Te Tiriti o Waitangi[22] is described as being close to a written

[14] See: Constitutional Court, *Frontini*, Decision No. 183 of 18 December 1973. Article 11 was drafted to permit Italy to join the United Nations. It affirms that "Italy rejects war as an instrument of aggression against the freedoms of others peoples and as a means for settling international controversies; it agrees, on conditions of equality with other States, to those restraints on sovereignty which are necessary to a legal system grounded upon peace and justice between Nations; it promotes and encourages international organizations having such ends in view."

[15] This is the case with Portugal and the Slovak Republic. Article 7(2) of the Slovak Constitution provides: The Slovak Republic may, by an international treaty, which was ratified and promulgated in the way laid down by a law, or on the basis of such treaty, transfer the exercise of a part of its powers to the European Communities and the European Union. Legally binding acts of the European Communities and of the European Union shall have precedence over laws of the Slovak Republic. The transposition of legally binding acts which require implementation shall be realized through a law or a regulation of the Government according to Article 120 Paragraph 2.

[16] In Canada, in addition to the federal constitution, various enactments of the British Imperial Parliament, Royal Proclamations and Letters Patent; and enactments of the Canadian Parliament as well as provincial legislation provide sources of constitutional law, to which common law constitutional principles must be added. With two notable exceptions Canada's written constitution makes no reference to international agreements or treaties. The report explains that Canada's written constitution is virtually silent with respect to international law and foreign relations because at confederation the conduct of foreign affairs continued to be carried out by the British government.

[17] The first reference, to implementation of Imperial Treaties, plays little role today.

[18] Part I of the Constitution Act 1982.

[19] It has had few amendments, the last being enacted in 1977.

[20] Section 51, Constitution of Australia ("in all matters – (i) arising under any treaty; ... the High Court shall have original jurisdiction."

[21] If New Zealand has a constitution, then according to this traditional approach, it can be regarded as a single sentence; 'Parliament can do anything'. F. Ridley, "A Dangerous Case of the Emperor's New Clothes", 41 *Parliamentary Affairs* (1988), 340.

[22] See M.S.R. Palmer, *The Treaty of Waitangi in New Zealand's Law and Constitution* (Wellington: Victoria University Press, 2005). The Treaty was signed between Maori Iwi (tribes) and Hapu (sub-tribes) and the British Crown on 6th February 1840, a date now celebrated in New Zealand as Waitangi Day, a national holiday. The signing of the Treaty/te Tiriti is surrounded by controversy caused not least by the fact that the Teo Reo Maori version (signed by the Maori signatories) differs in significant parts from the English language version. In particular, the English version ceded "sovereignty" to the British Crown in return for the recognition of the Maori population as British subjects. The Te Reo Maori version made no such reference to sovereignty, instead using the term kawanatanga (a transliteration of governership).

constitution today,[23] acquiring additional legal status through statutory references and judicial decisions referring to its principles. Scholars have traditionally described New Zealand as having a 'dualist' approach to international treaties and a 'monist' approach to international custom.[24] Practice suggests a system somewhere between the two,[25] influenced by the growth of international norms, particularly in the field of human rights.[26]

Unlike the preceding common law countries, the United States legal system has functioned for over two centuries under essentially the same single written constitutional text,[27] yet there remains uncertainty about many issues concerning the role of international law in the domestic legal system. The U.S. Constitution leaves important issues unresolved and answers have been slow to come because the Supreme Court issues opinions annually in fewer than 100 cases, ones that it generally selects to hear.[28] U.S. courts have articulated a range of doctrines[29] that channel questions of ultimate constitutional power away from the judiciary and toward the political branches of government. Even when courts do take up such questions, they apply the principle that cases should be decided on the narrowest possible grounds.

Israel has no formal, written constitution. The *Knesset* (parliament) was originally elected in 1949 as a Constituent Assembly, but decided the following year to focus on passing a number of basic laws which, in time, would become Israel's formal constitution. Accordingly, the *Knesset* has enacted laws concerning basic civil rights,[30] as well as Basic Laws that define the respective roles of the *Knesset*, the Government, the Judiciary and the President. The Basic Laws do not address the relationship between international law and domestic law.

Written constitutions on the continent are often terse about the place of international law in the domestic legal system. The Constitution of the Netherlands, for example, simply provides in Art. 90: "The Government shall promote the development of the international legal order."[31] Other general constitutional provisions make reference to the principles and norms of international law or international obligations,[32] such as the constitutions of Portugal[33] and Slovakia.[34] The Constitution of the Russian Federation,

[23] R. Cooke, "Introduction", (1990) 14 NZLUR 1.

[24] See, e.g. *The Laws of New Zealand: International Law*, LexisNexis, Section 4–111.

[25] See, e.g. Joseph, "Parliament, the courts, and the collaborative enterprise." *King's College Law Journal* 15, no. 2 (Summer 2004), 321–345.

[26] See e.g., *R v Pora* (2001) 2 NZLR (CA) and *Simpson v A-G (Baigent's Case)* (1994) 3 NZLR 667 (CA).

[27] The U.S. Constitution has been amended 17 times after ratification of the Bill of Rights. None of these amendments specifically relates to international or comparative law. Overwhelmingly, these amendments relate to purely domestic law matters; many concern extending the suffrage.

[28] Nearly all matters before the U.S. Supreme Court arrive there by writ of *certiorari*; only in rare instances is the Court required to consider a case.

[29] E.g., legal doctrines relating to standing, ripeness, abstention, political questions, and acts of state.

[30] I.e., Basic Law: Human Dignity and Liberty and Basic Law: Freedom of Occupation.

[31] Subsection 2 of Chapter 5 'Legislation and Administration', entitled '*Miscellaneous Provisions*'.

[32] Examples include the Czech Constitution Article 1, Section 2, which provides: "The Czech Republic respects the obligations arising to it from international law." Similarly, Art. 7(1) of the Hungarian Constitution (1989 amendment) provides: "The legal system of the Republic of Hungary accepts the generally recognized principles of international law, and shall harmonize the country's domestic law with the obligations assumed under international law." Article 7 is silent about the possible solution of conflicts between international law and national law and about the problem of self-executing norms. In the case-law of the Constitutional Court, the notion of 'general principles of international law,' as it appears in the Constitution, seems to refer to customary international law and international *jus cogens.* See 53/1993 (X. 13.) AB határozat, (CC decision), (ABH, 1993), 323, 329.

[33] The 1976 Constitution of the Republic of Portugal in Article 8 is explicit that " The rules and principles of general or ordinary international law are an integral part of Portuguese law." (para. 1). Paragraph 2 adds that rules provided for in international conventions duly ratified or approved, following their official publication, apply in national law as long as they remain internationally binding with respect to the Portuguese State. Other paragraphs concern the rules and decisions of international organizations.

[34] Article 1, para. 2 of the Constitution of the Slovak Republic provides that the Republic acknowledges and adheres to general rules of international law, international treaties by which it is bound, and its other international obligations. Other post-communist constitutions contain similar provisions. See, e.g. Serbian Constitution, Article 16: "The foreign policy of the Republic of Serbia shall be based on generally accepted principles and rules of international law." See generally, E. Stein, "International Law in Internal Law: Toward Internalization of Central-Eastern European Constitutions?" 88 *American Journal of International Law* 427 (1994). Similarly, but with respect to the issue of post-totalitarian constitutions, see A. Cassese, "Modern Constitutions and International Law", *Recueil des Cours de l'Academie de la Haye* 192-III (1985), 331–474, and especially beginning at p. 351.

part 4 Article 15, broadly provides that the universally-recognized principles and norms of international law and international treaties of the Russian Federation shall be a component part of its legal system. Other Russian Constitutional provisions refer to treaties and/or customary international law.[35]

21.3 Treaties

In all countries today, there is some form of democratic participation in the process of making treaties part of domestic law. In one group of states, the head of state or government concludes treaties which then must be approved by all or part of the legislature prior to ratification. Among states that require pre-ratification approval are Argentina, where the Executive makes treaties which are approved or rejected by the Congress, and Japan, where the Cabinet concludes treaties, but the Diet (both houses) must approve.[36] The United States also requires consent to treaty ratification, but limits this to the upper chamber, the Senate.[37] In Germany, the legislature has a perogative to authorize the executive to conclude an international treaty[38] while Article 154 of the Venezuelan Constitution also generally requires an act of Parliament before the President of the Republic ratifies an international treaty. In Russia, the President of the Russian Federation signs international treaties and agreements, but Article 106(2) of the Constitution stipulates that federal laws on ratification and denunciation of international treaties of the Russian Federation shall be considered by the Council of the Federation. Luxembourg's constitution provides in Article 37 that the Grand Duke concludes treaties but they have no domestic effect until being approved by law and published. Treaties that involve a transfer of governmental powers to international institutions require a super-majority. In Hungary, administrative agencies as well as the legislature may play a role in the conclusion of treaties.[39] The head of state ratifies the treaty, but consent of the Parliament is needed for treaties of particular importance as listed in the Constitution.[40] In Israel, the Attorney General issued guidelines in 1984 concerning the ratification of treaties[41] which provide that every treaty which requires implementing legislation must be ratified by the Government.[42]

---

[35] Under Article 62 (part 1–3) of the Constitution of the Russian Federation international treaties may regulate dual citizenship. Part 2 Article 63 of the Constitution of the Russian Federation specifies that extradition shall be carried out on the basis of federal law or the international treaty of the Russian Federation. Part 2 Article 67 provides that the Russian Federation shall possess sovereign rights and exercise jurisdiction on the continental shelf and in the exclusive economic zone of the Russian Federation according to the rules established by federal law and the norms of international law. Article 69 guarantees the rights of the indigenous minority peoples according to the universally-recognized principles and norms of international law and international treaties of the Russian Federation. Article 79 provides that the Russian Federation may participate in interstate associations and transfer to them part of its powers according to international treaties and agreements, if this does not involve the limitation of the rights and freedoms of man and citizen and does not contradict the principles of the constitutional system of the Russian Federation.

[36] If they are divided or the House of Councilors fails to take a decision within 30 days, the House of Representatives' decision controls.

[37] Approval requires a two-thirds majority vote of the Senate. However, in practice, the judicial doctrine of self-executing treaties has brought the House of Representatives into the process in many instances where implementing legislation is deemed necessary.

[38] "Treaties that regulate the political relations of the Federation or relate to subjects of federal legislation require the consent or participation, in the form of a federal statute, of the bodies competent in any specific case for such federal legislation." Article 59 para. 21st sentence GG. The authorization of the German legislature under Art. 59(2) of the GG (Basic Law) is given in the form of a federal law (which later becomes the implementing legislation).

[39] According to the authors of the national report, Hungarian Act L of 2005 on Procedures relating to International Agreements refers to "treaty preparation" which has a broader meaning than negotiation of treaties. It includes adopting Hungarian policy, elaborating the concept and the draft of the treaty, communicating to the other party/parties the intention to conclude a treaty, transmitting the draft or the concept, as well as negotiating the text. The minister which has authority according to the subject of the treaty decides in agreement with the Foreign Minister about the preparation of the treaty taking into consideration the principles determined by the Parliament and the government. Government authorization is needed for adopting the final text of the treaty.

[40] The Parliament must approve treaties which affect, inter alia, the content or scope of fundamental rights and obligations, contains provisions contrary to an existing domestic act, or which regulates directly other matters falling within the competence of the Parliament. Act L of 2005 Art. 7.

[41] Attorney General Guidelines 64.000A – International Conventions: Ratification Process (1.1.1984).

[42] The Minister of Foreign Affairs and the Minister of Defense may jointly decide to deviate from this procedure on the grounds of urgency or secrecy. In that case, the Government alone will ratify the treaty. The Government may also decide that a certain treaty, because of its importance, should be first approved by the *Knesset* prior to its ratification by the Government, as was done in the case of the Camp David Accords and the Peace Agreement with Egypt.

A second group of states, mostly following British tradition, does not require prior approval, but insists on post-ratification incorporation by legislation for the treaty to have domestic effect. In Australia, where there is no express constitutional provision on the modes of entering into international agreements, common law and custom vests the executive branch with exclusive power to conclude treaties. Parliamentary approval is unnecessary to make the treaty legally binding or to validate the ratification. In New Zealand, as well, foreign affairs are a perogative power exercised by the New Zealand Crown[43] and there are no formal constitutional limits to its actions. The legislature has no formal role in treaty ratification or acceptance, although in practice, a limited consultative role for Parliament has developed in recent years in relation to multilateral treaties.[44] Attempts to increase Parliamentary involvement in international affairs have largely failed.

In some countries both pre-ratification approval and subsequent incorporation are required. Somewhat surprisingly, the requirement of domestic incorporation does not necessarily mean that the judiciary will view the provisions in the treaty as directly applicable or self-executing even with the implementing law. In a few instances, where the constitution is silent on the issue, courts still determine the place of binding treaties in the domestic legal hierarchy.

Some constitutions, especially of countries within the European Union, establish different procedures for different types of treaties. In Slovakia[45] and the Czech Republic, for example, the ratification of a treaty transferring governmental powers to an international body requires a special procedure for approval.[46] The Greek Constitution similarly provides for approval by higher majorities for certain types of treaties.[47] Austrian law establishes three types of approval[48] while Polish law distinguishes four modes of ratification, two of which concern international organizations or institutions.[49] While these treaties require approval by a

[43] These are powers originally held by the monarch that have not been legislated for by Parliament. They have been inherited by the New Zealand executive.

[44] New Zealand Parliamentary Standing Orders 387–390 – as amended in 1998.

[45] The Slovak Republic's Constitution, Art. 7(4), designates the categories of treaties for which approval of the national Council is required prior to ratification. These are: international treaties on human rights and fundamental freedoms, international political treaties, international treaties of a military character, international treaties from which a membership of the Slovak Republic in international organizations arises, international economic treaties of a general character, international treaties for whose exercise a law is necessary and international treaties which directly confer rights or impose duties on natural persons or legal persons. As in some other states, the Constitutional Court may be requested to decide on the conformity of a treaty with the constitution, prior to ratification, at the request of the President of the Republic or the Government. If it finds that the treaty is contrary to the constitution or constitutional law, it cannot be ratified.

[46] Article 39, Section 4.

[47] The Greek Constitution requires approval by a super-majority when government functions or powers provided in the Constitution are to be recognized and ceded by treaty to an international organization. In that case a three-fifths majority is required (Article 28 par.2). In other instances, "Greece shall freely proceed by law passed by an absolute majority of the total number of Members of Parliament to limit the exercise of national sovereignty, insofar as this is dictated by an important national interest, does not infringe upon the rights of man and the foundations of democratic government and is effected on the basis of the principles of equality and under the condition of reciprocity."

[48] In Austria, the Federal President concludes international agreements upon suggestion of the government and countersignature of the Federal Chancellor or competent minister (Art. 65(1) and 67, Federal Constitution) after the Federal Parliament approves of those that fall into the four categories which require legislative approval according to Article 50 of Austria's Federal Constitution: (1) political agreements that concern, for example, the existence of the State, its territorial integrity and independence; (2) agreements that contain provisions which modify or contradict existing law; (3) agreements that have no basis in existing law; and (4) agreements modifying the treaty foundations of the European Union. Treaties that have been approved by the National Council must also be approved by the other chamber, the Federal Council, if they regulate subject matters falling within the sphere of state competences or if they modify the treaty foundations of the European Union. For other treaties, the Constitution grants the Federal Council a veto, which may be overridden by the National Council. The third type of agreement, the executive agreement, is discussed later.

[49] Article 90 of the Constitution reads:

1. "The Republic of Poland may, by virtue of international agreements, delegate to an international organization or international institution the competence of organs of State authority in relation to certain matters.

2. A statute, granting consent for ratification of an international agreement referred to in para. 1, shall be passed by the Sejm by a two-thirds majority vote in the presence of at least half of the statutory number of Deputies, and by the Senate by a two-thirds majority vote in the presence of at least half of the statutory number of Senators.

3. Granting of consent for ratification of such agreement may also be passed by a nationwide referendum in accordance with the provisions of Article 125.

4. Any resolution in respect of the choice of procedure for granting consent to ratification shall be taken by the Sejm by an absolute majority vote taken in the presence of at least half of the statutory number of Deputies."

super-majority, other categories of treaties also have to be ratified with prior consent granted by statute (i.e. by both Chambers of the Parliament).[50]

21.3.1 Domestic Incorporation

Many countries automatically incorporate ratified treaties into domestic law. This is the case in Greece,[51] Bulgaria,[52] and Serbia,[53] In Serbia, as in several other countries, separate constitutional provisions govern specific subject matter, in particular human rights and the status of minorities.[54] In addition, some Serbian constitutional provisions on human rights were taken verbatim from international human rights treaties, notably the ICCPR and ECHR and the Constitution provides that obligations arising from such treaties may not be subject to referendum. Venezuela's Constitution Article 23 also gives special treatment to human rights treaties, granting them direct and immediate application by courts and public offices.

So-called dualist countries require legislation to transform treaties into domestic law.[55] Going further, some constitutions, like those of Hungary[56] and

[50] They are enumerated in Article 89 para. 1: "Ratification of an international agreement by the Republic of Poland, as well as renunciation thereof, shall require prior consent granted by statute – if such agreement concerns:

1. peace, alliances, political or military treaties;
2. freedoms, rights or obligations of citizens, as specified in the Constitution;
3. the Republic of Poland's membership in an international organization;
4. considerable financial responsibilities imposed on the State;
5. matters regulated by statute or those in respect of which the Constitution requires the form of a statute."

See also the Bulgarian Constitution, Art. 85, par. 3 and Art.149, par.1, 4 in connection with Art 5, par. 4, and Article 85. (1) The Bulgarian National Assembly ratifies or denounces with a law international treaties that:

1. Are of a political or military nature;
2. Concern the participation of the Republic of Bulgaria in international organizations;
3. Call for corrections to the borders of the Republic of Bulgaria;
4. Contain financial commitments by the state;
5. Stipulate the participation of the state in any arbitration or court settlement of international disputes;
6. Concern basic human rights;
7. Affect the action of a law or require new legislation for their implementation;
8. Specifically require ratification.

[51] According to the Greek Constitution, Article 28 par. 1, "... international conventions as of the time they are ratified by statute and become operative according to their respective conditions, shall be an integral part of domestic Greek law and shall prevail over any contrary provision of the law. The rules of international law and of international conventions shall be applicable to aliens only under the condition of reciprocity."

[52] E. Tanchev, *International and European Legal Standards Concerning Principles of Democratic Elections*, p. 8. A judicial interpretation of the relevant constitutional provisions holds that the Constitution has situated treaties second only to the Constitution itself, above national legislation.

[53] The Serbian Constitution, Article 16, provides ratified international treaties are an integral part of the legal system of the Republic of Serbia and directly applicable, but they must be in conformity with the Constitution.

[54] Article 18, entitled, Human and Minority Rights and Freedoms, Direct Application of Human Rights, provides:

"Human and minority rights guaranteed by the Constitution shall be directly applicable.

This Constitution guarantees and makes directly applicable those human and minority rights which are guaranteed by the generally accepted rules of international law, ratified international treaties and the law. Enjoyment of rights and freedoms may be further regulated by the law only if the Constitution explicitly provides so or if it is necessary due to the nature of the right, provided that the law in no way impairs the guaranteed right.

Provisions on human and minority rights shall be interpreted so as to promote the values of a democratic society and in accordance with international human and minority standards as well as practice of international institutions monitoring their enforcement."

Article 22 guarantees the right of petition to international institutions, while 75(1) refers to guarantees for national minorities under treaties. Treaty rights of aliens are guaranteed under Article 17. The Constitution of the Russian Federation, Article 46(3) also provides that everyone shall have the right to appeal, according to international treaties of the Russian Federation, to international bodies for the protection of human rights and freedoms, if all the existing internal state means of legal protection have been exhausted.

[55] In the Italian legal system, like treaties are incorporated by means of the laws of ratification and must be consistent with the Constitution. After the 2001 constitutional reform, the new Art. 117, para. 1, reads: "Legislative powers shall be vested in the State and the Regions in compliance with the Constitution and with the constraints deriving from EU-legislation and international obligations." The Italian Constitutional Court clarified the meaning of this provision in its Decisions Nos. 348 and 349 of 24 October 2007.

[56] According to Hungarian scholars, Article 7(1) is essentially dualist in character. Cf., Németh, János, "Az európai integráció és a magyar Alkotmány [European integration and the Hungarian Constitution]," in *Nemzetközi jog az új alkotmányban* [International law in the new constitution] ed. Bragyova András (1997), 107.

Poland[57] provide for pre-ratification constitutional review of the conformity of a proposed treaty to the Constitution.[58] Poland also provides review through preliminary questions submitted by the courts[59] or by a constitutional complaint.[60] The review may concern the substantial and formal (procedural) conformity to the Constitution, but it may also include reviewing the constitutionality of the Parliamentary act granting the consent for ratification.[61]

A few federal states, like Austria, require consent to an international agreement by component states or provinces if the agreement affects them.[62] Other federal states, including Australia[63] and the United States, consider external affairs among the exclusive subject areas in the control of the national government. In Russian, too, international relations and international treaties are under the authority of the Russian Federation.

Treaties to which the U.K. is a party do not automatically become part of U.K. law. They become part of the domestic law only when their contents are enacted into law by Parliament.[64] The one notable exception to this general principle is treaties concluded by the institutions of the EU with non-EU states. These treaties have been held, as a matter of European Community law, to be directly enforceable within the member states.[65] Treaties that have not been incorporated into British law nonetheless exert a certain influence over the courts. This was the case regarding the European Convention on Human Rights prior to the enactment of the Human Rights Act 1998. It was said to have exerted "a persuasive and pervasive influence on judicial decision-making . . ., affecting the interpretation of ambiguous statutory provisions, guiding the exercise of discretions, bearing on the development of the common law."[66] In New Zealand, too, a treaty must be implemented in domestic law if it is to be part of New Zealand law.[67] Yet, there are also significant numbers of regulations ("executive legislation") which implement specific technical bilateral agreements, such as double taxation agreements.[68] In addition, human rights treaties, and at times the jurisprudence of international bodies, may be implemented in New Zealand law through the medium of the domestic courts.

The national reports indicate that domestic legal systems increasingly recognize a distinction between formal treaties that require ratification and less formal

[57] Article 133 of the Constitution allows the President to request such a ruling from the Constitutional Court. In case of a negative ruling, the Constitution must be amended or the agreement must be either renegotiated or abandoned.

[58] In Hungary the Constitutional Court has competence to carry out an *ex ante* review of the constitutionality of provisions of an international treaty and if the Constitutional Court finds a problem, the treaty cannot be ratified until the unconstitutionality is repaired. Articles 1(1), 36 of the Act on the Constitutional Court.

[59] E.g. Article 193 allows any court to refer a question of law to the Constitutional Court as to the conformity of a normative act to the Constitution, ratified international agreement or statute, if the answer to such question is necessary to enable it to give judgment.

[60] Article 79 para. 1 of the Constitution reads: "In accordance with principles specified by statute, everyone whose constitutional freedoms or rights have been infringed, shall have the right to appeal to the Constitutional Tribunal for its judgment on the conformity to the Constitution of a statute or another normative act upon which basis a court or organ of public administration has made a final decision on his freedoms or rights or on his obligations specified in the Constitution."

[61] Until 2010 there were only three cases of constitutional review of treaties. In 2000 the Constitutional Court rejected the complaint on the ground that the treaty had been executed (judgment of 24 October 2000, SK 31/99), see *point 2.3*. The Court allowed the control in two other cases: the judgment of 11 May 2005 (K 18/05) on the EU Accession Treaty (brought under Article 191); the judgment of 18 December 2007, SK 54/05, on Article 32 of the Protocol No. 4 to the Europe Agreement (constitutional complaint).

[62] Austrian Federal Constitution, Art. 3(2) requires that a constituent state consents to a treaty changing its borders. Note that the Senate advice and consent requirement in the U.S. is deemed to protect the rights of the component states.

[63] The High Court has clarified that when Australia becomes a signatory to a treaty, the Commonwealth Parliament has all necessary powers to pass implementing legislation. *Commonwealth v Tasmania* ("Tasmanian Dams case") [1983] HCA 21; (1983) 158 CLR 1 (1 July 1983); *Pulyukhovich v Commonwealth* ("War Crimes Act case) [1991] HCA 32; (1991) 172 CLR 501 (14 August 1991); *XYZ v Commonwealth* [2006] HCA 25; (2006) 227 ALR 495; (2006) 80 ALJR 1036 (13 June 2006).

[64] See *Maclaine Watson & Co. Ltd. v. Department of Trade and Industry*, (1990) 2 A.C. 418, speech of Lord Oliver at 500; and *British Airways v. Laker Airways* (1985) AC 58.

[65] See *Bresciani Case*, (1976) E.C.R. 129; and *Kupferberg Case*, (1982) E.C.R. 3641.

[66] *R. v. Lyons*, H.L., (2003) 1 A.C. 976, (2002) UKHL 44, (2002) 3 W.L.R. 1562; (2002) 4 All E.R. 1028, speech of Lord Bingham, para 13. See also, for example, *Attorney General v. Guardian Newspapers Ltd* (No. 2) (1990) 1 AC 109, speech of Lord Goff, at 283.

[67] This classic dualist approach was most clearly stated in *Attn-Gen Ontario v Attn-Gen Canada* (1912) AC571 (PC).

[68] For example SR 1972/244 (Australia), SR 1980/112 (Germany). See Law Commission, 1996 above, nt 19, p116.

agreements, often of a political or administrative nature, that can be approved through a simplified process or implemented by the executive without legislative involvement.[69] Some constitutions expressly recognize the existence of such agreements. Other constitutions are silent on the issue, with the result that as the practice has increased, courts have had to affirm or deny the constitutionality of such agreements and their place in the legal system. Today, executive or administrative agreements largely outnumber formal ratified treaties, reflecting the growth in international administrative and regulatory practice.[70] In fact, only Serbia seems not to follow the modern practice of executive or administrative agreements, but requires all international agreements to be formally ratified.[71] In some instances, the practice of concluding executive or administrative agreements has grown up without a clear constitutional mandate. This leaves issues about the legal status of such agreements somewhat uncertain.

The courts in the United States have long affirmed that the Article II advice-and-consent process is not the exclusive route by which the U.S. can enter into binding international agreements. Congressional-executive agreements became an increasingly important part of the landscape more than a century ago[72] and today, there is a proliferation of so-called "sole-executive agreements."[73] Controversy remains over how far the President can enter into binding international agreements without formal approval by one or both houses of Congress and about the extent to which the political branches experiment with new procedures for entering into international agreements. Status of forces agreements, weapons sales, and claims settlements have been concluded on the sole authority of the president, sometimes triggering heated political debate.

21.3.2 The Law of Treaties

The Vienna Convention on the Law of Treaties (VCLT), although adhered to by just 58% of UN member states,[74] is considered in large part to codify the customary rules on the conclusion and interpretation of treaties. Both the political branches and courts of many states thus use the VCLT when issues related to a treaty arise, including the preliminary question of distinguishing a binding treaty from a non-binding instrument or political commitment. Constitutions generally do not define the term "treaty" and it has been left up to the courts in most instances to identify treaties and determine the rules by which to interpret them.[75] The Italian domestic courts interpret treaties on the basis of Articles 31 and 32 of the Vienna Convention on the Law of Treaties.[76]

[69] For examples, Article 87, para. 8, of the Italian Constitution specifies that the President of the Republic "ratifies international treaties which have, where required, been authorised by the Houses." Article 80 indicates that authorization by law is required for the ratification of international treaties "which are of a political nature, or which call for arbitration or legal settlements, or which entail changes to the national territory or financial burdens or changes to legislation." Article 89 provides for further governmental control on the President's power of ratification by requiring the proposing minister – usually the President of the Council of Ministers –, to countersign, assuming the political responsibility, the act of ratification for it to be valid. Argentina, Austria, Germany, Poland, the United States and Venezuela also recognized have simplified procedures or recognize executive agreements.

[70] See D. Shelton, ed., *Commitment and Compliance: The Role of Non-Binding Norms in the International Legal System* (Oxford: Oxford University Press, 2000).

[71] In Serbia, all binding agreements must be ratified. Thus, the Dayton Peace Agreement signed between the Bosnia and Herzegovina, Croatia and FR Yugoslavia, which marked the end of war in the territory of Bosnia, entered into force on the day of its signature on December 14, 1995 according to its Article 11. According to international treaty rules, no ratification was required for this Agreement to be binding and applicable. However, the Constitution requires ratification and publication, and the treaty was ratified by the Yugoslav parliament in December 2002. Act on Ratification of the General Framework Agreement for Peace in Bosnia and Herzegovina, *Official Gazette of FR Yugoslavia – International Treaties*, no. 12/2002.

[72] *See*, e.g., *B. Altman & Co. v. United States*, 224 U.S. 583, 601 (1912) (recognizing congressional-executive agreements).

[73] Although not mentioned in the Constitution, the power of the President to enter into sole-executive agreements in at least some contexts has been validated by the Supreme Court. *See*, e.g., *Dames & Moore v. Regan*, 453 U.S. 654, 679–80, 686 (1981) (recognizing presidential authority to conclude sole executive agreements to end the Iranian hostage crisis); *United States v. Pink*, 315 U.S. 203, 229.

[74] As of May 16, 2010, the VCLT had 111 states parties among the 192 UN member states.

[75] Argentina is not a party to the VCLT but utilizes it in determining what is a treaty. Dotti, Miguel A., Fallows: 321:1226, Supreme Court of Argentina. Poland, Russia and Venezuela do the same.

[76] See, e.g., *Corte di Cassazione* (Judgment No. 9321 of 16 December 1987); *Corte di Cassazione* (Judgment No. 7950 of 21 July 1995). The *Corte di Cassazione* (Judgment No. 6100 of 13 July 1987) has underlined that treaties codifying "general

Most legal systems accept that treaty interpretation is a legal matter to be determined by the courts. The courts of the United States are unusual in deferring to the political branches to decide issues of treaty interpretation,[77] but this deference is not without limits. As with statutory interpretation, the analysis focuses on the precise words used in the treaty, even more than the treaty's overriding object and purpose.[78] If the text is deemed to be unambiguous, courts in the U.S. may dispense with any analysis of extra-textual sources or do so in only a cursory fashion. Second, the views of the executive branch receive less deference when they conflict with those of Congress, as expressed either in implementing legislation or RUDs.[79] Third, the views of the executive branch may receive less deference if those views have changed significantly with changes in presidential administration.

The legal systems of France and Luxembourg reveal a certain tension between the role of the courts as interpreters of the law and the role of the Minister of Foreign Affairs who should be consulted to obtain the view of the government about the interpretation of clauses in a treaty.[80] In Britain, in contrast, once a treaty has become incorporated into domestic law, it is the task of the courts to interpret that treaty and there appear to be no instances in which courts have deferred to executive interpretations, although there can be, and sometimes are, statutory instructions to the courts as to interpretation, made part of the law at incorporation.[81] The courts are bound to follow any such statutory commands.

Other courts use the rules of interpretation contained in the VCLT, although they do not always cite to its articles in their judgments and opinions.[82] Almost no cases are reported of courts considering matters of reservations, although some of them have the power to determine whether a statement is or is not a reservation.

21.3.3 Self-execution and Direct Applicability

Courts utilize different terminology when they decide whether or not to enforce a treaty provision invoked by one of the parties to a case. U.S. courts as well as those of Japan and several other countries refer to the doctrine of "self-executing" treaties, while European courts tend to discuss "direct applicability" or "direct effect." In all these instances, however, the courts are examining the question of whether the treaty provision in question is capable of judicial enforcement or whether an intervening domestic legal act is required.[83]

---

customary laws" must be interpreted in the light of these international customary rules and, if necessary, the international customary rules shall be used to fill in any gap in the treaty provisions. However, in its Judgment No. 3610 of 24 May 1988, the *Corte di Cassazione* affirmed that when two interpretations of the same provision of an international treaty are possible, one in pursuance of and the other against the Italian Constitution, the first interpretation must be preferred by the court.

[77] United States courts have long accorded deference to the executive branch's views as to the meaning of a treaty to which the United States is a party. *See* e.g., *Medellin v. Texas*, 128 S. Ct. 1346 (2008); *Medellin v. Dretke*, 544 U.S. 660 (2005); *Chan v. Korean Air Lines, Ltd.*, 490 U.S. 122 (1989); *United States v. Stuart*, 489 U.S. 353 (1989); see generally Scott Sullivan, "Rethinking Treaty Interpretation", 89 *Tex. L. Rev.* 777, 789 (2008) (describing contemporary treaty interpretation as involving "near-total deference.")

[78] *See Medellin v. Texas, supra; United States v. Alvarez-Machain*, 504 U.S. 655 (1992); *Sumitomo Shoji America v. Avagliano*, 457 U.S. 176, 180 (1982) ("The clear import of treaty language controls unless "application of the words of the treaty according to their obvious meaning effects a result inconsistent with the intent or expectations of its signatories") *quoting Maximov v. United States*, 373 U.S. 49, 54 (1963). American courts rarely make reference to the Vienna Convention's rules on treaty interpretation.

[79] Reservations, understandings, and declarations.

[80] However, according to the President of the Cour de cassation, the court applies the ECHR extensively directly – cf. Guy Canivet, "The Use of Comparative Law before the French Private Law Courts," in Canivet et al. eds., *Comparative Law before the Courts* (BIICL 2005) 181, 189 f.

[81] See, for example, the Carriage by Air Act 1961, sec. 4A, concerning interpretation of terms in the Warsaw Convention of 1929.

[82] In Japan, the Courts apply the general rules of treaty interpretation and have cited Articles 31 and 32 of the VCLT. There is no particular deference accorded the views of the government, except as concerns the issue of the constitutionality of a treaty or concerning whether a statement is a reservation or an interpretive declaration. The Tokushima District Court, in its judgment on March 15, 1996 in a case claiming State compensation for a prisoner who was obstructed in efforts to see his counsel concerning a civil suit by prison guards (*Hanrei Jihō*, vol.1597, p.115), reproduced the provisions of Article 31, paragraph 3 (a), (b), (c) in detail in examining the relevance of the jurisprudence of the European Court of Human Rights on Article 6, paragraph 1 of the European Convention of Human Rights for the purpose of interpretation of Article 14, paragraph 1 of the ICCPR.

[83] Even dualist countries where treaties must be incorporated into domestic law face this issue. The exception seems to be Israel,

Almost no constitutions specifically refer to this issue; Article 91(1) of the Polish Constitution is rare in requiring explicitly not only that the treaty should be ratified and promulgated but also that the norm should be suitable for direct application. Today, in the majority of cases the courts more or less repeat the formula of Article 91(1).[84] According to the Constitutional Court, a treaty norm can be applied directly if it contains all normative elements essential for its judicial application (a norm has to be complete).[85] One factor is the intention of the parties to a treaty and its terms (the way the rights or obligations are formulated). The second is the constitutional regulation on incorporation of international law into domestic legal order. Slovakia's constitution provides direction to the courts in a different manner, apparently making all human rights treaties self-executing by Article 128 of the Constitution.

For other countries, the doctrine of self-executing treaties or direct applicability has developed as a matter of judicial doctrine, rooted in notions of separation of powers. Most courts look for expressions of the intent of the parties and to whether or not the agreement creates specific rights in private parties and whether the provisions of the treaty are capable of being applied directly. The factors utilized by national courts on these issues are strikingly similar,[86] relying on the language of the treaty and an assessment of whether or not the provision can be applied directly within the functions of the judiciary. While the courts often refer to the intent of the parties, the decisive criterion is whether or not the provision is sufficiently precise to be capable of judicial enforcement.[87] Some courts have referred to the second test as one of the "self-sufficiency" of the provision.[88] In some instances, the political branches may indicate during the approval process that a treaty requires implementing legislation.

The Netherlands is typical: the criteria mix international and domestic law and the outcome does not entirely depend on the intention of the States parties.[89]

---

where it has been accepted that treaties are not automatically accepted into domestic law but need to be implemented by primary legislation, or by secondary legislation if such implementation was previously authorized in principle by primary legislation. Non-implemented treaties are not devoid of any legal effect, though, since the courts have adopted a rule of interpretation and a rule of presumption which ensure, to the extent possible, the compatibility of Israeli domestic law with Israel's international commitments. The incorporation doctrine and practice means there is very limited scope for the notion of self-executing treaties in Israel. See National Report of Israel, pp. 17–21.

[84] The concept of self-executing treaties had become well established in Polish judicial practice long before the 1997 Constitution entered into force. In the judgment of 21 November 2003 (I CK 323/02) the Supreme Court referred to the conditions of direct applicability in the following manner: "The so-called formal condition is that the treaty must be duly ratified and published in the Journal of Laws. The substantive condition requires the completeness of the treaty provision that enables its operation without any additional implementation".

[85] The Court added that such a view is confirmed by Article 91 para. 1 of the Constitution stipulating that an international agreement shall be applied directly, unless its application depends on the enactment of a statute.

[86] In the Czech Republic, as in most other states, a ratified treaty is regarded as self executing if the rights and obligations stipulated therein are sufficiently specific that such a treaty can be applied in the legal order without any further legislative specification in a separate act. In Greece, similarly, international agreements have a "self-executing" character if their provisions have sufficiency and fullness and either attribute or recognize rights of private persons, capable to support legal actions before tribunals, or prescribe obligations of the executive which private persons can invoke before tribunals. See, e.g., the international convention signed under the auspices of the United Nations in Ramsar of Iran (1973) for the protection of wildlife reserves of international interest. The disregard of the obligations imposed on the contracting parties legitimized the legal interest of injured physical persons to have recourse before tribunals. Supreme Court, 2343/1987. "Non-self-executing" treaties are those international conventions which do not produce direct legal effects in the internal legal order, either because their application requires the promulgation of supplementary measures in the internal field, or because their purpose is not the recognition or the attribution of rights capable of being pursued by judicial procedures.

[87] Cf. Administrative Court, Collection No. 5819 F, October 21, 1983; Supreme Court, Decision No. 7Ob1/86, February 20, 1986.

[88] *Ann. dr. lux.* 5 (1995) 307. See the discussion in the National Report, p. 10.

[89] The leading Supreme Court judgment considered that it was not relevant whether the

> "States parties intended to recognize the direct effect of Art. 6 para. 4 of the European Social Charter, since neither from the text nor from its travaux préparatoires could it be inferred that such effect had been excluded. In those circumstances, according to Netherlands law, only the contents of the provision are decisive: does it oblige the Netherlands legislator to make rules of a certain content or import or is that provision of such a nature that it can be applied as objective law right away." Supreme Court *HR* 30 May 1986 (NS/FNV), *NJ* 1986, 688 § 3.2.

Domestic courts have examined:[90] the way in which the engagements of the States parties to a treaty have been couched, including whether implementation is gradual and whether the conduct required is 'positive' or 'negative';[91] whether the provision is suitable to be applied by the courts; whether it sufficiently concrete; and whether the provision is binding on the State in its relations to other States only.

Even where treaties are not self-executing or directly applicable they may have persuasive effect in interpreting domestic law. In New Zealand[92] it is now settled that such international agreements can be an aid to statutory interpretation. However, the extent of the relevance of an individual treaty to an individual statute or administrative decision varies according to judicial interpretation of that treaty and the domestic context. This makes the application of international treaties in New Zealand extremely difficult to predict.

The Serbian Constitution[93] empowers courts to apply treaties without demanding any implementing legislation. Direct applicability of treaties has been consistently accepted by the courts.[94] In one case, the Supreme Court of Serbia stressed the direct applicability of the European Convention on Human Rights and its Protocols, as envisaged by the Constitution.[95] The Constitutional Court has struck down certain provisions of the Act on Pensions and Disability Allowances as contrary to a International Covenant on Economic, Social and Cultural Rights thereby granting direct applicability to a treaty which is not generally assumed to be self-executing or of direct applicability.[96] Although the Serbian Constitution and courts deem all ratified treaties to be self-executing, specific provisions may be found not self-executing because they explicitly demand the adoption of national legislation.[97]

U.S. law in this area is in the process of change. In *Sanchez-Llamas v. Oregon*,[98] a majority of the Supreme Court referred to what it characterized as "a long-established presumption that treaties and other international agreements do not create judicially enforceable individual rights." Writing in dissent, Justice Breyer restated the test articulated by the Court in 1884: a treaty is directly applicable federal law "whenever its provisions prescribe a rule of law by which the rights of the private citizen or subject may be determined" and "when such rights are of a nature to be enforced in a court of justice."[99] Further, the dissent in *Sanchez-Llamas* referred to a string of cases from 1886 to 1961

[90] See generally Fleuren *op.cit.*

[91] With respect to the International Covenant on Economic, Social and Cultural Rights (*ICESCR*), the courts – with a few exceptions – have not considered its provisions as self-executing. The Government, when submitting the treaty for parliamentary approval, observed that most of its provisions would not be directly applicable. In support of that view it pointed to Art. 2 para. 1 where the State "undertakes to take steps [..] to the maximum of its available resources, with a view to achieving progressively the full realization of the rights concerned in the present Covenant".

[92] See Geiringer C, "Tavita and All That: Confronting the Confusion Surrounding Unincorporated Treaties and Administrative Law", 21 NZULR 66, 2004.

[93] Article 16(2) of the Serbian Constitution provides that "[g] enerally accepted rules of international law and ratified international treaties shall be an integral part of the legal system of the Republic of Serbia and directly applicable."

[94] Commercial Court in Belgrade, Decision no. Pž. 480/2000 of February 10, 2000.

[95] Supreme Court of Serbia, Judgment no. Už. 74/2004 of September 6, 2004. Published in: Bilten sudske prakse Vrhovnog suda Srbije, no. 2/2004 , at 111.

[96] The Constitutional Court found that restrictions imposed by the Law on Pensions and Disability Allowances were contrary to Article 3, 6(1), 11 of the ICESCR.

[97] High Commercial Court, Decision no. Pž. 9881/2005 of November 11, 2005. In those cases which dealt with the Agreement on Succession Issues after it entered into force, petitions for establishment of property rights on the date of succession, December 31, 1990, were denied due to the wording of Annex G to the Agreement on Succession Issues. The issue before domestic courts was whether the Agreement, read as a whole, purported to restore property rights itself or only after some other national measures are undertaken. Domestic courts opted for the latter option offering the following reasoning: "According to Articles 4 and 7 of the Annex G to the Agreement on Succession Issues, it is clear that the intent of parties to this Agreement was to conclude bilateral agreements in order to set forth procedures for handling these requests and to establish special commissions for these procedures and implementation of the Agreement so that natural and legal persons may have their petitions for establishment of property rights heard. Only after this procedure, as to be envisaged by a bilateral agreement, and if their petitions are denied, the courts will be entitled to hear these cases. Therefore, any judicial determination on these issues is conditioned upon the preliminary proceeding before these commissions in the procedure to be set forth in the bilateral agreements of successor states, which is, for this Court, a preliminary procedural issue." See also High Commercial Court, Decision no. Pž. 255/2006 of January 24, 2006; High Commercial Court, Decision no. Pž. 6178/2006 of October 30, 2006.

[98] 548 U.S. 331 (2006).

[99] 548 U.S. at 373 *quoting Head Money Cases*, 112 U.S. 580, 598–99 (1884).

in which the court had found similar treaty provisions to be enforceable in domestic judicial proceedings. When read in conjunction with the Court's 2008 opinion in the *Medellin* case, *Sanchez-Llamas* creates the clear impression that fewer treaties will be found to be self-executing in the United States in the foreseeable future.

21.4 Custom

National constitutions rarely use the term customary international law or custom. It is much more common for the phrase "general principles and norms of international law" to appear. Some older constitutions refer to the "law of nations." Article 98 of the Japanese Constitution, for example, states that "the established laws of nations" shall be faithfully observed.

Most continental European constitutions refer to "rules" or "norms" or "principles" of international law. Austria's Federal Constitution, Article 9(1) provides that "generally recognized rules of international law form part of federal law." Similarly, Germany's Article 25 GG provides: "The general rules of public international law are an integral part of federal law. They take precedence over statutes and directly create rights and duties for the inhabitants of the federal territory." The Greek Constitution also refers to "generally recognised rules of international law"[100] and elsewhere to a "generally accepted rule of international law." The position of customary international law is defined in Article 28 par.1 which states that "The generally recognized rules of international law…shall be an integral part of domestic Greek law and shall prevail over any contrary provision of the law"[101] The Constitution of the Russian Federation similarly provides that the universally-recognized principles and norms of international law shall be a component part of its legal system.[102] Hungary includes and seems to require application of generally recognized principles of international law as part of domestic law,[103] but there has been a heated debate on the topic.[104] In contrast, the 1997 Polish Constitution, Article 9, declares generally that "the Republic of Poland shall respect international law binding on it." Judges[105] invoke this provision in

[100] Article 2 par.2 prescribes that "Greece, adhering to the generally recognised rules of international law, pursues the strengthening of peace and of justice, and the fostering of friendly relations between peoples and states."

[101] It must be noted, however, that "The rules of international law and of international conventions shall be applicable to aliens only under the condition of reciprocity"

[102] Unlike the term treaty, the phrase 'universally recognized principles and norms of international law' is not defined in Russian legislation. The Presidium of the Supreme Court of the Russian Federation addressed the constitutional provision in Decision of 31 October 1995 № 8. It held that universally recognized principles and norms of international law shall be set directly in international documents. In a separate Presidium Decision of the Supreme Court of the Russian Federation of 10 October 2004 № 5 "universally recognized principles of international law" were defined as fundamental imperative norms, departure from which is inadmissible while "universally recognized norms of international law" are standards of conduct, accepted and applicable as legally binding by international community of states.

[103] See Bragyova, András, "A magyar jogrendszer és a nemzetközi jog kapcsolatának alkotmányos rendezése" [The constitutional organization of the connection between the Hungarian legal system and International law], in *Nemzetközi jog az új Alkotmányban* [International law in the new Constitution] ed. Bragyova, András (Budapest: Közgazdasági és Jogi Könyvkiadó MTA Állam- és Jogtudományi Intézete, 1997), 16. Zagrebelsky, op. cit. n. 6, at p. 120.

[104] See Bodnár, László, "A nemzetközi jog magyar jogrendszerbeli helyének alkotmányos szabályozásáról" [On the constitutional regulation of the place of International law in the Hungarian legal system], in *Alkotmány és jogtudomány. Tanulmányok* [Constitution and Jurisprudence, Studies] (Szeged, 1996) p. 23. Compare Sulyok, Gábor: A nemzetközi jog és a magyar jog viszonya, Korreferátum Molnár Tamás A nemzetközi jog és a magyar jogrendszer viszonya 1985–2005 cím előadásához [The relationship between international law and Hungarian law, reflections to the presentation held by Tamás Molnár on The relationship between international law and Hungarian legal order] In A magyar jogrendszer átalakulása, 1985/1990–2005:II. Kötet [Transforming Hungarian legal system], szerk. Jakab András – Takács Péter [ed. Jakab, András and Takács, Péter], Gondolat: Eötvös Loránd Tudományegyetem Állam- és Jogtudományi Kar, Budapest, 2007, p. 947.

[105] The finding of the Court conforms to the opinion of the scholars who have participated in the drafting of the Constitution. E.g. R. Szafarz wrote in 1997 that Article 9 "expresses the principle of (…) Polish legal order in respect to the norms of international law and establishes a presumption of automatic, even if only indirect, incorporation of those norms into that order." (Międzynarodowy porządek prawny i jego odbicie w polskim prawie konstytucyjnym [International Legal Order and Its Reflection in the Polish Constitutional Law], (in:) M. Kruk ed., Prawo międzynarodowe i wspólnotowe w wewnętrznym porządku prawnym [International Law and Community Law in the Domestic Legal Order], Warszawa 1997, p. 19.

reference to customary law and the decisions of international organs or organisations.[106]

Despite the paucity of constitutional provisions on customary international law, judges refer to custom and generally have the power to take judicial notice of its existence. They do not often do so, however, unless one of the parties has presented a legal argument based on custom. The cases in which customary international law most commonly arises concern sovereign or diplomatic immunity,[107] treaty law, and law of the sea. Legal systems differ over the extent to which courts defer to the views of the executive branch on the content of custom. The place of custom varies, but many systems, like that of France, privilege written law and are cautious about "spontaneous" or diffuse law derived from practice as opposed to clear expressions of intent.

In Argentina[108] and Japan, judges will take judicial notice of customary law and have applied it in cases involving sovereign, diplomatic and consular immunity, the political offense exception to extradition, immigration, and principles of armed conflict. In Austria, courts have to apply it, unless it is so insufficient in precision that it has to be deemed non-self-executing. As with other countries, many of the cases concern immunity of States or international organizations and their organs.[109] The Supreme Court has also pronounced on customary norms concerning territorial sovereignty, state succession, extraterritorial jurisdiction, and the principle *pacta sunt servanda*.

Canada adheres to the system of British common law where customary international law that does not conflict with legislation automatically forms part of the common law and has direct legal effect in courts without the need for incorporation.[110] Lower court decisions have been more explicit in supporting the adoption of customary international law,[111] while the Supreme Court's most recent pronouncement *obiter dicta*[112] has been read to support numerous different theories on customary international law.[113] Judicial notice is to be taken of customary international law[114] and the courts do not defer to the executive or legislative branches with respect to the existence or content of customary international law, but courts will give effect to clear statutory language even if it contradicts the international norm.[115] The primary subject matter in which customary international law has been invoked or applied by Canadian courts include sovereign or diplomatic immunities, maritime zones, self-determination and state succession, international criminal law, human rights, environmental law and state jurisdiction.[116] Like Canada, New Zealand's constitutional framework recognizes the principles of customary international law as part of the common law of New Zealand[117] but there is not much

[106] The confirmation of the legal effects of Article 9 is found in the judgment of the Constitutional Court of 11 May 2005 (K 18/05) on the EU Accession Treaty of 2003. The Court declared that "Article 9 expresses an assumption of the Constitution that, on the territory of Poland, a binding effect should be given not only to the acts (norms) enacted by national legislature, but also to the acts (norms) created outside the framework of national law-making authorities. The Constitution accepts that the Polish legal system consists of multiple components/elements."

[107] On immunities, see R. van Alebeek, *The Immunity of States and their Officials in International Criminal Law and International Human Rights Law* (OUP, Oxford 2008); Arthur Watts, *The Legal position in International law of Heads of states, head of Governments, and Foreign Ministers*, in *Recueil des cours* 1994-III, Vol. 247 (Martinus Nijhoff, 1995); Hazel Fox, *The Law of State Immunity* (Oxford, 2005).

[108] D. Rufino Basavilbaso c. Ministro Plenipotenciario de Chile, Dr. Diego Barros Arana, Fallos: 19:108.

[109] In 1950, the Supreme Court found that customary international law had shifted from a rule providing absolute immunity to a more restrictive practice. Supreme Court, Collection No. SZ23/143, May 10, 1950, translated in ILR 77, 155.

[110] *Reference re Powers of Ottawa (City) and Rockcliffe Part*, (1943) S.C.R. 208; *Reference re Newfoundland Continental Shelf*, (1984) 1 S.C.R. 86; *In re Secession of Quebec*, (1998) 2 S.C.R. 217.

[111] See, e.g. *Jose Pereira E Hijos S.A.v. Canada (Attorney General)*, (1997) 2 F.C. 84 at para. 20 (T.D.); *Bouzari v. Islamic Republic of Iran* (2004), 71 O.R. (3d) 675 at para. 65 (C.A.); and other cases cited in the National Report of Canada, pt. 1, p. 21–22.

[112] *R. v. Hape*, [2007] 2 S.C.R. 292.

[113] National Report of Canada, p. t, pp. 22–23.

[114] *The Ship "North" v. The King* (1906) 37 S.C.R. 385. See National Report of Canada, pt. 1, pp. 26–27.

[115] The legislature has also on occasion called upon the courts to apply customary international law. See Crimes against Humanity and War Crimes Act, ss. 4(3) and 6(3)–(4) defining genocide, crimes against humanity and war crimes with reference to their definitions in customary international law.

[116] National Report of Canada, p. 1, p. 27.

[117] The classic embodiment of this approach is found in works of the English jurist, Blackstone, who describe the relationship in simple terms; 'the law of nations…is here adopted in its full extent by the common law, and is held to be part of the law of the land' Blackstone's Commentaries on the Laws of England, Book 4, Chap. 5, *Of Offences Against the Law of Nations*.

application of it[118] outside the field of sovereign immunity.[119]

German courts tend to apply customary international law in practice, at least if the parties to the case rely on it. Such application is facilitated by a special procedure provided by Article 100 para. 2 GG. "If, in the course of litigation, doubt exists whether a rule of public international law is an integral part of federal law and whether such rule directly creates rights and duties for the individual (Article 25), the Court shall obtain a decision from the Federal Constitutional Court." This so-called norm verification procedure allows any German Court, when confronted with a norm of universal customary law to refer questions of interpretation to the Federal Constitutional Court.[120] After having obtained a decision from the Federal Constitutional Court, the original court will apply the norm of customary law in order to decide the outcome of the case. In general, judges take judicial notice of customary international law. The most important part of customary international law that has been verified by the Federal Constitutional Court concerns the rules of state immunity.

Greek courts have applied the indisputable rules of international law, general principles and customary rules, since 1896 in the jurisprudence[121] in order to clarify legal facts which might affect disputes between parties. The courts have jurisdiction to investigate the elements to determine the existence of a rule of customary law.[122] The courts may investigate the existence and the content of a rule of international customary law.[123] Furthermore, the Special Highest Court is competent to qualify an asserted rule of international law as generally accepted, in cases where this rule has been questioned by courts.[124] Most cases involving customary international law have concerned the immunity of diplomatic agents,[125] state immunity;[126] and state succession.[127]

In Israel, customary international law is "part of the law of the land", whether codified in treaties or not. According to Israeli courts, "[a] rule of international law ... has to be proven by adequate evidence from which it may be deduced that the State has recognized the rule and acted upon it, or that the nature of the rule, or the fact that it is recognized by many states and is widespread, necessarily give rise to the assumption, that no civilized state will ignore it."[128] In a recent case, the Supreme Court held that "[t]he burden to prove the existence of a custom with the characteristics and status ascribed in Article 38 of the Statute of the International Court of Justice, falls upon the party which pleads its existence."[129] Customary international law has been applied primarily in international humanitarian law matters and cases concerning sovereign immunity from jurisdiction and execution (prior to the enactment of the Foreign States Immunity Law, 5769–2008), as well as diplomatic and consular relations. Finally, in almost every case concerning basic human rights (as well as animal rights), the courts check whether customary international law rules have developed.

118 The notable exception to this is Treasa Dunworth's work; T Dunworth, *Hidden Anxieties: Customary International Law in New Zealand*, (2004) 2 NZPIL 67–84.

119 Dunworth id., at 69.

120 For a practical example see Press Release No. 97/2003 of 13 November 2003 – Extradition to the United States of America, http://bundesverfassungsgericht.de/en/press/bvg97-03en.html/

121 Supreme Court, 14/1896.

122 Appeal Court of Athens, 6384/1989: "...the 135/1971 international convention of the International Labour Organization has not been promulgated by law and, therefore, it cannot be applied for the reason that it does not establish generally accepted rules since it has received ratifications only by nine states among the 150 member states of the International Labour Organization."

123 Supreme Court, 11/2000: "...the state immunity on civil matters does not cover actions of state organs, illegal according to international law (war crimes), but the relevant to this matter Convention of the Council of Europe on state immunity (1972), despite the fact that it has not been put into force, codifies rules of international customary law."

124 48/1991: "...in the case of a convention between the United States and Greece establishing taxation waivers, the longstanding abstention of the Greek Treasury from tax claims does not constitute a legal commitment based on generally accepted rules of the general international law."

125 Supreme Court 14/1896: "...the immunity derived from the general custom between states and its recognition is generally accepted."

126 Supreme Court 11/2000.

127 Military Court of Athens 1463/1993: "...the not yet in force 1978 Vienna Convention on state succession has codified the customarily valid rule on the continuity of conventional obligations."

128 *Shimshon* v. *Attorney General*, (1951) 4 PD 143, at pp. 145–146.

129 *Abu 'Aita* v. *Commander of the Judea and Samaria Region*, 37(2) P.D. 197 (1983), at 241.

International customary law is automatically incorporated into domestic law in Italy.[130] Also included are peremptory rules of international law (*jus cogens*),[131] thus providing domestic courts with the opportunity to interpret and apply such norms to give judgment in a case pending before them. All domestic courts have the competence to verify the existence or the content of international customary rules and the changes that their automatic incorporation produces in the Italian legal system. International customary law has been invoked on the matters' of: custom surveillance at sea,[132] diplomatic agent immunity from civil jurisdiction of the receiving State,[133] *ne bis in idem*,[134] the obligation of a State not to require foreign citizens to serve in the army,[135] state immunity from civil jurisdiction,[136] and immunity of state officials from foreign criminal jurisdiction.[137]

In Luxembourg, in the absence of a constitutional provision, the courts have themselves considered the possibility of applying customary law and have concluded that it is possible under certain conditions: there must be a norm of customary law; the norm must be of direct applicability; and the norm will be determined by the judge without reference to legislative or executive views. There is no need that the norm be proven as a fact, since the issue is one of law. The most recent case in which the issue arose concerned the claimed possibility to prosecute Augusto Pinochet for crimes against humanity. The Luxembourg court found no rule of customary international law on universal jurisdiction.[138]

The direct application of international customary law is well grounded in Polish case law, on diplomatic[139] and state immunities.[140] The prevailing opinion of the scholars is that customary law is automatically incorporated into the Polish legal order, based on Article 9 of the Constitution. Specific statutory references can be found as well.[141] The Court has not deferred to the government or legislature on the existence or content of customary international law in respect to State immunity.

21.5 Other Sources of International Law

Few constitutions, apart from those of EU member states, contain references to other sources of international law, whether declarations and other acts of international organizations or the decisions of international tribunals. There is nothing in the Japanese and Austrian[142] constitutions and the Israeli Basic Laws. Argentina is one of the few to contain specific references[143] to the Universal Declaration of Human Rights and the American Declaration on the Rights and Duties of Man. Most references to so-called "soft law" (declarations and resolutions of international organizations) thus occur in judicial decisions.

[130] Art. 10, para. 1, Const. expressly establishes that: "The Italian legal system conforms to the generally recognised rules of international law". This amounts to a "special" method of implementation of international customary law not requiring legislation by the Parliament or the Government in order to implement international law – the method is usually used to incorporate treaties or binding acts adopted by international organizations that are not considered to be self-executing.

[131] See *Corte di Cassazione* (Supreme Court), *Corte di Cassazione, Ferrini v. Federal Republic of Germany*, Judgement No. 5044 of 11 Mar. 2004, Orders Nos. 14200–14212 of 29 May 2008, *Lozano*, Judgment No. 31171 of 24 July 2008; *Criminal Proceedings against Josef Max Milde,* Judgment No. 1072 of 13 January 2009.

[132] See Constitutional Court, Judgment No. 67 of 1961.

[133] See Constitutional Court, Judgment No. 135 of 1963.

[134] See Constitutional Court, Judgment Nos. 48 of 1967 and 69 of 1976.

[135] See Constitutional Court, Judgment No. 131 of 2001.

[136] *Corte di Cassazione*, *Ferrini*, Judgment No. 5044 of 2004, Orders Nos. 14200–14212 of 2008, *Milde,* Judgment No. 1072 of 2009.

[137] See, *Lozano*, Judgment No. 31171 of 2008.

[138] Cour d'appel 11 février 1999, *Ann. dr. lux.* 10 (2000) 363, 369–370.

[139] Orzecznictwo Sądów Polskich, 1926-V, nr 342.

[140] Orzecznictwo Sądów Polskich, 1926-V, nr 418.

[141] E.g. the provisions of Criminal Procedure Code or Civil Procedure Code refer to jurisdictional immunities of diplomats (Article 1111 para. 1), the Law on Excise Duties of 2004 (Article 25 para. 1), the Law on Local Taxes or Duties of 1991 (Article 13 para. 2) and the Road Traffic Law of 1997 (Article 77 para. 3) – concern the taxes or duties exemptions for diplomats.

[142] The Constitutional Court of Austria deems a decision of an international organization to become domestic law after it is published in the Federal Law Gazette, while the Administrative Court seems to require implementing legislation.

[143] Article 75(22) of the Constitution.

21.5.1 Resolutions or Decisions of International Organizations

Austrian courts occasionally interpret laws using non-binding texts such as recommendations of the Council of Europe. Canadian courts have referred to numerous sources of international human rights law, including declarations and judicial or quasi-judicial decisions of international tribunals, as well as treaties and custom, finding them all to be relevant and persuasive sources for interpreting the Canadian Charter of Rights.[144] Canada's courts have on occasion made reference to the significance of resolutions, declarations or the decisions of international tribunals. In particular the Supreme Court of Canada has suggested some deference to decisions of the ICTY and the ICTR when interpreting domestic criminal law on crimes against humanity.[145] Some members of the Supreme Court have also noted the utility and relevance of the teachings of publicists.[146] The Supreme Court has also found persuasive non-binding sources like model laws, but carefully distinguishes them from binding treaties.[147] Canadian courts generally have called for consideration of judgments of international tribunals and other sources of human rights law to interpret the Canadian Charter of Rights and Freedoms.

German courts consider non-binding declarative texts as soft law and it may play a role in the interpretation of legally binding acts such as treaties. In addition, such declarative texts may be used in order to illustrate societal developments which have indirect effects on the evolution of legal concepts. However, there is no systematic use of such sources in the jurisprudence of German courts. Similarly, non-binding declarative texts are regarded by the Greek national courts as a guidance material to interpret the relevant domestic law. The Polish courts use non-binding sources including documents of the United Nations and of the Council of Europe,[148] unratified treaties,[149] and declarations.[150]

Israeli courts have referred to a variety of soft law texts, including those setting standards for treatment of prisoners.[151] The National Labor Court considered ILO texts as both authoritative and relevant[152] in a claim brought by a woman who was the victim of forced labor and human trafficking. The Supreme Court has cited as authoritative and relevant the Guidelines of the

[144] National Report of Canada, pt. 2, pp. 2–7.

[145] National Report of Canada, part 1, quoting *Mugesera v. Canada* (Minister of Citizenship and Immigration), [2005] 2 S.C.R. 100 at para. 126.

[146] Id., p. 7, quoting *R. v. Finta*, (1994) 1 S.C.R. 701, per La Forest J dissenting on another point.

[147] Id. pp. 1 7–8.

[148] Constitutional Court judgment of 30 September 2008 (K 44/07) referring to the UN global strategy on counter-terrorism of 8 September 2006, Security Council resolutions, in particular resolution 1267 (1999) and its successor resolutions, resolutions 1373 (2001) and 1540 (2004), Plan of Action, Secretary General report of 2006 "Uniting against terrorism: recommendations for a global counter-terrorism strategy" (A/60/825), the European Convention on Human Rights of 1950, the European Convention on the Suppression of Terrorism of 1977, amended by the Protocol of 2003, Council of Europe Convention on the Prevention of Terrorism of 2005, resolutions and declarations of the Committee of Ministers and the Parliamentary Assembly, e.g. Guidelines on Human Rights and the Fight against Terrorism of 2002, Opinion of the European Commission for Democracy through Law (Venice Commission) on the Protection of Human Rights in Emergency Situations of 2006 etc.

[149] In the judgment of 23 April 2008 (SK 16/07) on the freedom of expression and medical ethics the Constitutional Court interpreted Polish law in the light of the Council of Europe Convention on Human Rights and Biomedicine of 1997, signed but not ratified by Poland and a non-binding document of the World Medical Association – the International Code of Medical Ethics and the numerous judgments if the European Court of Human Rights

[150] In the judgment of 18 December 2007 (SK 54/05) to establish the content of the right to good administration the Constitutional Court drew inspirations from the provisions of the non-binding documents – Article 17 I 20 of the Code of Good Administration of the EU Parliament of 2001 and Article 41 of the Charter of Fundamental Rights of the European Union (judgment para. 2.6). In the judgment of 1 July 2008 (K 23/07) the Constitutional Court found support i.a in the Universal Declaration on Human Rights to prove that on the ground of the Constitution nobody can be forced to assemble or to be the member of a trade union (negative assembly right).

[151] In determining the appropriate Israeli standard, the Supreme Court considered as both authoritative and relevant the UN Economic and Social Council Standard Minimum Rules on the Treatment of Prisoners, 1955 (Sect. 10 and 19), as well as the UN Center for Human Rights Basic Principles for the Treatment of Prisoners, 1990 (Arts. 1, 5). The Supreme Court further considered the European Prison Rules, 1987 (Rules 15, 24), as well as legislation in European countries and the US. HCJ 4634/04 *Physicians for Human Rights – Israel* v. *Minister of Public Security and Commissioner of the Prisons Service*, tak-Supreme 2007(1), 1999.

[152] Labor Appeal (National) 480/05 *Eli Ben-Ami* v. *plonit* tak-National 2008(3), 6.

Committee of Ministers of the Council of Europe on Human Rights and the Fight against Terrorism.[153] Finally, Israeli Courts have cited, on occasion, decisions of the ICJ, decisions of the International Criminal Tribunal for Yugoslavia, the European Court of Justice, and, especially, numerous decisions of the European Court of Human Rights.[154] None of these decisions were held binding, but the Supreme Court considered them very seriously and gave weight to their interpretation of international norms.[155]

Italian domestic courts consider non-binding declarative texts as political recommendations from international institutions to Member States. Sometimes, domestic courts make reference to these texts in order to verify the *opinio juris* among States and consequently demonstrate the existence or establish the content of an international customary rule. Italian courts do not apply or enforce any decision or recommendation of a non judicial treaty body, considering such a decision not-legally binding.[156] At most, such "soft law" decisions or recommendations are taken into consideration to confirm an interpretation of binding international rules or of national rules.[157]

Japanese courts do not use soft law to interpret domestic laws, but do use it to interpret treaty provisions, including reference to the Standard Minimum Rules for the Treatment of Prisoners and other GA resolutions on the treatment of detainees. In Argentina, reports of the HRC and the IACHR are considered relevant in interpreting domestic law. The same is true in the Netherlands, where non-binding declarative texts like the Universal Declaration of Human Rights[158] and the UN and European standards for the treatment of prisoners are relevant and often authoritative for the courts. They can also become legally binding if enhanced by later developments.

The Russian Federation recognizes as legally binding the decisions of European Court of Human Rights in relation to the Russian Federation. In jurisprudence, the place of decisions of the European Court of Human Rights in the legal system is debated. Some jurists consider that decisions of European Court of Human Rights are a source of Russian law, while others criticize this view. Recommendations of international organizations are not considered to be legally binding, but recommendations of Conferences or Meetings of treaty parties may be considered as a subsidiary source of interpretation or application of international treaties by courts. The Constitutional Court of the Russian Federation has referred in its decisions to documents of the Conference on Security and Cooperation in Europe.[159]

In Serbia, the Constitution, Article 18(3), calls for the implementation of international jurisprudence related to international human rights.[160] In Serbian domestic courts, there are few examples of courts using non-binding international texts as the tool of interpretation. Among other national and international legal sources, courts have relied on the 1948 UN Universal Declaration on Human Rights.[161] Lastly, a District Court (Criminal Chamber) found that the length of the criminal proceeding in one case breached the standard of "reasonable time" guaranteed by Article 6(1) of the European Convention on Human Rights.[162] In devising a remedy for the human rights violation, the court relied, inter alia, on the Council of Europe Committee of Ministers' Recommendation on the Improvement of Domestic Remedies.[163]

[153] HCJ 3239/02 *Mar'ab* v. *Military Commander of Judea and Samaria*, tak-Supreme 2003(1), 937.

[154] HCJ 7052/03 *Adallah* v. *Minister of the Interior,* tak-Supreme 2006(2), 1754.

[155] National Report, pp. 42–47.

[156] See, e.g. *Corte di Cassazione*, Judgments Nos. 6030 and 6031 of 29 May 1993, relating to the applicability of the Universal Declaration of Human Rights in the national legal order.

[157] See, e.g. Constitutional Court Decision No. 45 13 January 2005.

[158] HR 28 November 1950, *NJ* 1951, 137 (Tilburg).

[159] E.g., the Helsinki Final Act 1975, Concluding Document of the Vienna meeting 1986, the Document of the Copenhagen Meeting of the Conference on the Human Dimension of the Conference on Security and Co-operation in Europe 1990.

[160] "Provisions on human and minority rights shall be interpreted so as to promote the values of a democratic society and in accordance with international human and minority standards as well as practice of international institutions monitoring their enforcement." According to the opinion of the Venice Commission, this provision enables the introduction of international case law into the Serbian Constitutional system: "From a European perspective this means that above all the case law of the European Court of Human Rights is of highest significance for the interpretation of fundamental rights in the Constitution of Serbia." Id., at 8, para. 26.

[161] *District Public Prosecutor v. Nikolic*, Case No. Kž. I 1594/02, Supreme Court of Serbia, February 24, 2003, 128 ILR 691 (2006).

[162] District Court in Subotica (Criminal Section), Judgment no. Kž. 266/05 of August 15, 2005.

[163] Recommendation of the Committee of Ministers to Member States on the Improvement of Domestic Remedies, REC (2004)6.

In the U.S., declarative texts in the field of international law can serve as evidence of the formation of customary international law. Many U.S. cases take this approach, particularly as to international human rights law. Courts tend, however, not to give the text, standing alone, any legal effect within the U.S. legal system, including when asked to use them to interpret U.S. statutes that incorporate or make reference to international law.[164] For example, in citing the United Nations' Standard Minimum Rules for the Treatment of Prisoners, the Supreme Court listed the document among many in a string-cite to "modern legislation" deemed to codify a "common-law view" obliging the state to provide medical treatment to prisoners unable to care for themselves.[165] Fewer than two dozen reported cases cite to the U.N. prison treatment rules, and the most recent instance was in 1988.[166] Some texts have achieved considerable influence. A search shows 265 citations to the Universal Declaration of Human Rights,[167] in decisions at all levels of the federal court system. However, the Supreme Court made clear in its 2004 decision in *Sosa* that although the UDHR may enjoy "moral authority," it enjoys "little utility" in determining binding norms of international law, for the reason that "the Declaration does not of its own force impose obligations as a matter of international law."[168] In short nonbinding, declarative instruments amount to an extremely soft version of what international lawyers call "soft law."

The Constitution of Venezuela, Article 31, refers to the measures to be taken by Venezuela in order to enforce "decisions adopted by international organs created by international treaties to hear petitions for protection, or complaints for violation of human rights." The last part of Article 153 provides that norms adopted within the framework of the Latin American and Caribbean integration treaties shall be deemed to be part of the Venezuelan legal order, and of direct and preferential application vis-à-vis domestic legislation. Article 217 mentions "international usages" in respect of the determination of the opportunity to publish in the Official Gazette the act of Parliament authorizing the ratification of an international treaty by the President of the Republic. Non-binding declarative texts are considered to have persuasive authority, relevant in interpreting and applying domestic law, subject to strict conformity with the Constitution.

As for international jurisprudence, Argentina has accepted the jurisdiction of the Inter-American Court of Human Rights, but the government is charged with compliance and not the courts. In one case, the Supreme Court refused to give effect to part of a judgment that it found it was contrary to the Constitution.[169] Similarly, the Constitutional Chamber of the Venezuelan Supreme Court of Justice[170] denied enforcement of a ruling rendered by the Inter-American Court of Human Rights on August 5 2008 against the Republic of Venezuela, claiming that such ruling violated the Venezuelan constitutional order.

Within Europe, Article 46 of the European Convention on Human Rights makes judgments of the European Court against a state binding on it. This has resulted in several new laws in European states. In Austria, in criminal cases, the law now allows for the reopening of proceedings in some instances.[171] The Czech Constitution[172] now provides that the Constitutional Court can decide on "[…] measures necessary for executing a decision of an International

[164] *See,* e.g., *Natural Res. Def. Council v. EPA*, 464 F.3d 1, 8–9 (D.C. Cir. 2006) (holding that consensus decisions by state parties to the Montreal Protocol reached after treaty ratification are "not law" within the meaning of the Clean Air Act and thus not enforceable in U.S. courts); *Flores v. S. Peru Copper Corp.*, 414 F.3d 233, 263 (2d Cir. 2003) (finding Rio Declaration not legally binding and therefore not the basis for a human rights suit under the Alien Tort Claims Act).

[165] *Estelle v. Gamble*, 429 U.S. 97, 103–04 & n.8 (1976).

[166] *Carmichael v. United Technologies Corp.*, 835 F.2d 109, 113 n.6 (5th Cir. 1988). Cited in the same list were two other instruments with similar status, the U.N. Code of Conduct for Law Enforcement Officials (1979) and the U.N. Principles of Medical Ethics (1982).

[167] G.A. Res. 217A (III), U.N. Doc. A/810 (1948) [hereinafter UDHR]. The number is based on a Oct. 14, 2009, search of the allfeds database.

[168] *See Konar v. Illinois*, 327 Fed.Appx. 638, 640(7th Cir. 2009) (in divorce and custody matter, declining to apply either the UDHR or the Vienna Declaration and Programme of Action, U.N. Doc A/ CONF.157/23 (July 12,1993), reasoning that both are "non-binding declarations that provide no private rights of action").

[169] Cantos, Fallos: 326–2: 2968, Supreme Court of Argentina.

[170] December 18, 2008, Corte Primera de lo Contencioso case.

[171] This is also the case in the Netherlands. The Code of Criminal Procedure in Art. 957 para. 1 sub 3 provides for reopening of the contested proceedings.

[172] Article 87, Section 1, Letter i.

Tribunal that is binding for the Czech Republic, if it cannot be executed in any other way,[...]" The Constitutional Court has also addressed some of the opinions of the ICCPR's Human Rights Committee, refusing to apply the Committee's conclusions, although it took cognizance of them. Under the constitution, the Constitutional Court is not entitled to apply and enforce decisions of the bodies that do not fall under the legislative definition of an international court under Article 87, Section 1 of the Constitution.

The German Federal Constitutional Court decided in 2004[173] that all provisions of the German legal order have to be construed in accordance with the ECHR so as to avoid any conflict. However, there is a limit to the admissibility of such an interpretation of national law. If the provisions of the Basic Law clearly and unambiguously deviate from the ECHR as interpreted by the European Court of Human Rights, if a conflict therefore cannot avoided, the constitution outranks the ECHR. In addition, all German authorities are bound by a judgment in a case to which Germany is a party. This means that administrative authorities and courts must take into account the decisions as part of the interpretation of the relevant German law. If they fail in doing so it is the ultimate responsibility of the Federal Constitutional Court to remove violations of the Convention by voiding the judgments of lower courts.

In Hungary, Act L of 2005, Art. 13(4), provides that the compulsory decisions of international courts and other organizations relating to interpretation of agreements must be enacted and promulgated in *Magyar Közlöny*. It has not been determined how and in what form the binding decisions of the UN Security Council should be enacted in Hungarian legal system.[174] Security Council resolutions are promulgated mostly in Government Decrees, but in one case in the form of government resolution. It also occurs that resolutions which suspend or terminate former resolutions are referred to only in a Foreign Ministry guide – the text of the resolution is not even published.[175] The same uncertainty applies to NATO decisions.[176]

The Netherlands Constitution places in juxtaposition the provisions of both treaties and decisions of international organizations "which may be binding on all persons by virtue of their contents." The Supreme Court turned down the argument advanced by a taxpayer that the Universal Declaration of Human Rights qualified as 'a decision of an international institution'; it found that the United Nations General Assembly from which the Declaration originates has no power to issue decisions that are binding on the Netherlands.[177] With respect to judgments of the European Court of Human Rights, the binding force or *erga omnes* effect of the latter has been explained as some sort of '*incorporation*': the case law of the ECrtHR being construed as an authoritative interpretation of the ECHR and, therefore, entailing the same binding force as has been attributed to the Convention itself. The courts have extended this reasoning to the views of the UN Human Rights Committee supervising the Covenant on Civil and Political Rights and other international bodies supervising the interpretation and application of human rights, though formally non-binding.[178]

There are several examples when the Serbian courts have been asked to apply or enforce decisions of international courts and recommendations of the UN treaty-based bodies for protection of human rights. The legal framework of Serbia enables application of international decisions both for the purpose of interpretation of international treaties applicable for the particular case as well as for the enforcement of an international decision which is directly related to the case at hand, provided that the remedy requested by the international decision can be awarded by the domestic court. The case law on this matter is quite scarce[179] and strictly

[173] Federal German Constitutional Court, Press Office, Press release no.92/2004 of 19. October 2004 – On the consideration of the decisions of the European Court of Human Rights by domestic institutions, in particular German courts, http://www.bundesverfassungsgericht.de/en/press/bvg04-092en.html.

[174] Originally Act L of 2005 would have ruled on this matter: it would have amended Act I of 1956 on the Promulgation of the Charter of the United Nations, and these resolutions would have to be promulgated in Magyar Közlöny. (The parliament has not accepted the proposal.)

[175] Csuhány Péter: Gondolatok a nemzetközi jog és a belső jog viszonyáról, Állam- és Jogtudomány, 2005, 267.

[176] Molnár, *supra* n.104, 943.

[177] HR 7 November 1984, *NJ* 1985, 247.

[178] Occasionally, Netherlands courts also refer to General Comments of the Committee supervising the ICESCR; an example albeit negative is: *Centrale Raad van Beroep* (Central Appeals Tribunal: Supreme court in matters of social security) 11 October 2007 (*LJN* BB 5687).

[179] In one case, the Supreme Court of Serbia denied the request for damages of the legal person for the alleged breach of its reputation on the ground that there is no legal basis in domestic

applies international treaty law.[180] However, Article 422(10) of the Civil Procedure Act introduces the possibility of re-opening a case if "after the final decision had been handed down before the domestic court, the European Court for Human Rights reached contrary conclusion in a decision in the same or similar matter against Serbia." Similarly, Article 428(2) of the Criminal Procedure Act provides for a remedy against the final judgment in criminal matters and re-opening of the criminal proceeding.[181] There are examples when Serbian domestic courts were asked to enforce international decisions of treaty bodies other than the European Court, including a case before the U.N. Committee against Torture (CAT).[182] It seems that the national courts implemented the international decision in the way they saw compatible with their jurisdiction, awarding damages instead of the specific performance required by the international decision.

Outside of Europe, the approach to international tribunals is similarly mixed. In Canada, courts have rejected enforcement of the decisions of human rights treaty bodies. The Canadian Supreme Court considered one matter, *Ahani*[183] in which the UN Human Rights Committee had issued interim measures, calling upon Canada to suspend deportation until the full consideration of the applicant's case. This was refused. In the second matter, *Suresh*,[184] which was heard by the Ontario Court of Appeal, the petitioner sought and was denied[185] an injunction to suspend the deportation order on the basis of the Human Rights Committee interim measure of protection, and thus "preserve an effective remedy in international law."[186] In the first case, the majority held that Anahi's position must be rejected because it "would convert a non-binding request in a Protocol [i.e. interim measure], which has never been part of Canadian law, into a binding obligation enforceable in Canada by a Canadian court, and more, into a constitutional principle of fundamental justice."[187] Concerning the nature of the international interim measure of protection from the Human Rights Committee, the Court found it evident that neither the Committee's final views nor its interim measures requests are binding or enforceable in international law, based on the wording of the Protocol and the Committee's Rule 86, from the Committee's own pronouncements, from the opinions of recognized international law scholars and from caselaw. It noted that the Committee itself has said that its "decisions" are not binding.[188] In concluding on this issue, Laskin J.A. for

law to grant damages for this cause of action. Though the claimant relied on the case law of the European Court of Human Rights in order to prove that reputation of legal and natural persons have been equally recognized and protected by the European Convention on Human Rights, the Supreme Court went into analysis of several ECHR cases but refused to apply their rationale mostly because of the temporal limitation on the application of the European Convention. Supreme Court of Serbia, Judgment no. Prev. 265/2007 of June 10, 2008.

[180] Supreme Court of Serbia, Judgments nos. Rev. 971/2007(1) and Rev. 971/2007(2) of September 6, 2007.

[181] These provisions are also in line with the *Recommendation of the Committee of Ministers of the Council of Europe 2000 (2) on the re-examination or reopening of certain cases at domestic level following judgments of the European Court of Human Rights*, adopted by the Committee of Ministers on 19 January 2000 at the 694th meeting of the Ministers' Deputies, available at: https://wcd.coe.int/ViewDoc.jsp?id=334147&BackColorInternet=B9BDEE&BackColorIntranet=FFCD4F&BackColorLogged=FFC679.

[182] U.N. Comm. Against Torture, Comm. No. 113/1998, *Ristić v. Yugoslavia*, U.N. Doc. CAT/C/26/D/113/1998 (2001), (May 11, 2001).

[183] *Ahani v. Canada (Attorney General)*, (2002) 58 or (3d) 107 (CA).

[184] *Suresh v. Canada (Minister of Citizenship and Immigration)*, Supreme court of Canada) (2003) SCR 3.

[185] See, generally on the case, Joanna Harrington, "Punting Terrorist, Assassins and Other Undesirables: Canada, the Human Rights Committee and Requests for Interim Measures of Protection," 48 *McGill Law Journal* 55 (2002).

[186] *Ahani v. Canada (Attorney General)*, *supra* note 183, para. 29.

[187] *Ahani v. Canada (Attorney General)*, *supra* note 183, at para. 33.

[188] "It is useful to note that the Committee is neither a court nor a body with a quasi-judicial mandate, like the organs created under another international Human Rights instrument, the European Convention on Human Rights (i.e., The European Commission of Human Rights and the European Court of Human Rights). Still, the Committee applies the provisions of the Covenant and of the Optional Protocol in a judicial spirit and, performs functions similar to those of the European Commission of Human Rights, in as much as the consideration of applications from individuals is concerned. Its decisions on the merits (of a communication) are, in principle, comparable to the reports of the European Commission, non-binding recommendations. The two systems differ, however, in that the Optional Protocol does not provide explicitly for friendly settlement between the parties, and, more importantly, in that the Committee has no power to hand down binding decisions as does the European Court of Human Rights. States parties to the Optional Protocol fendeaf to observe the Committee's views, but in case of non-compliance the Optional Protocol does not provide for an enforcement mechanism or for sanctions." "Introduction", *Selected Decisions of the Human Rights Committee under the Optional Protocol*, Vol. 2 (1990), at p. 1.

the majority held that, while the *Optional Protocol* gives a right to individuals to seek the Human Rights Committee's views, Canada may reject them and, more importantly, it "reserved the right to enforce its own laws before the Committee gave its views."[189]

Japanese courts have not been asked to enforce an international decision. As for views under the Optional Protocol, general comments and final observations, many cases have sought to use them, but the number of decisions referring to them remains relatively small. The courts are divided, with some denying any juridical weight to views of international treaty bodies but instead considering them as non-binding statements of opinion. The HRC has criticized Japan on this point in its concluding observations to the 4th report of the State.

In the United States, the *Medellín* case[190] centered on a request for the Supreme Court to give direct domestic effect to a ruling of the International Court of Justice. The matter concerned a foreign national sentenced to death without having been informed of his treaty-based right to contact his consulate. The issue was whether he was entitled to further "review and reconsideration" after the claim had been denied by a state court and rejected based on a failure to comply with state procedural rules.[191] The Supreme Court affirmed the ruling of the lower court and declined to follow the course of action suggested by the ICJ. Figuring prominently in the Supreme Court's analysis was the wording of Article 94 of the U.N. Charter, by which UN member states "undertake[] to comply with" ICJ decisions.[192] That formulation, according to a majority of the justices, evidences that ICJ judgments were not intended to be directly applicable in the legal systems of UN member states. Thus a 5–4 majority held that Article 94 constituted a promise to take action in the future rather than a duty to accord the ICJ judgment immediate domestic effect. The ramifications of the *Medellín* decision remain uncertain, but most commentators regard *Medellín* as a retreat from international law. International courts have emphasized that a state may breach international law through the acts of any of its organs, including the judiciary. For many years prior to *Medellín*, similarly worded treaty provisions had been construed as self-executing; in terms of textualism, *Medellín* seems to have raised the bar. Moreover, in a related case, the Court held that, as a matter of U.S. federalism, a litigant's failure to comply with the procedural rules of state courts in the U.S. could result in that litigant's inability to gain the benefits of even those treaties that are self-executing.[193]

21.6 Federal Systems

Three main issues concerning international law arise in federal systems. The first is the extent to which, if at all, foreign affairs matters, including the conclusion of treaties, are reserved exclusively for the national government. The second issue is the place of international law in the law of the component parts of the federal system, including the problem of "federalizing" local matters through exercise of the treaty-making power. Finally, there may be adoption of international law by local authorities in regulating local matters. It is in respect to the first issue that federal systems differ the least. In all federal states, foreign affairs, including issues of international law, are generally considered matters for the national government. Thus, Argentina's constitution, Article 31, establishes the supremacy of federal law, including international law, over the law of the provinces. Argentine state bodies must ensure the primacy of treaties over contrary domestic law, pursuant to the hierarchy established in Article 31 of the Constitution.[194]

In Austria, however, under some limited authority, constituent states may negotiate specific international

---

See also See Burgers and Danelius, *The United Nations Convention against Torture: A Handbook on the Convention against Torture and Other Cruel, Inhuman or Degrading Treatment or Punishment* (1998), at p. 9. See also Ghandhi, *The Human Rights Committee and the Right of Individual Communication: Law and Practice*; Duxbury, "Saving Lives in the International Court of Justice: The Use of Provisional Measures to Protect Human Rights", (2000) 31 *California Western International Law Journal* 141;

[189] *Ahani.*, at para. 42.

[190] *Medellín v. Texas*, 128 S. Ct. 1346 (2008).

[191] *Id.* at 1352 (discussing *Case Concerning Avena and Other Mexican Nationals* (Mex.v.U.S.), 2004 I.C.J. 12 (interpreting Vienna Convention on Consular Relations, Art. 36(1)(b), Apr. 24, 1963, [1970] 21 U.S.T. 77, T.I.A.S. No. 6820), in challenge brought by Medellín and 50 other Mexican nationals awaiting execution in the United States).

[192] U.N. CHARTER, Art. 94(1)), *quoted in Medellín*, 128 S. Ct. at 1354.

[193] *See Sanchez-Llamas v. Oregon*, 548 U.S. 331 (2006).

[194] *Cafés Law Virginia S.A.*, Fallos: 317–3:1282, Supreme Court of Argentina.

agreements according to Article 16(1) of the Federal Constitution. The power to do so was added to the constitution in 1988 to strengthen the role of the constituent states in foreign policy matters.[195] This limited treaty-making power of states has not been used to date. In addition to the mandate granted by Article 16, Article 10(3) requires that constituent states be given occasion to comment on treaties which require implementing measures by them and treaties which touch on their autonomous sphere of competence. If a joint position is taken, the federal government is bound by the statement of the states except in a case of compelling foreign policy. Italy and Germany[196] also delegate some limited foreign relations powers to component units.

In contrast to the previous examples, the U.S. Constitution expressly deals with the extent to which international law is a realm reserved for federal rather than state authority. The Supremacy Clause of Article VI subordinates the laws of the component states to the nation's treaty obligations.[197] Second, under Article I treaty-making is, with rare exceptions, an exclusively federal activity. The component states of the Union do not enter into treaties of their own with foreign countries. Rather, the role of state officials in treaty formation is quite limited, even when the proposed treaty will have a large impact on particular states.[198] Yet States of the U.S. have entered into agreements among themselves and with foreign countries as far back as the eighteenth century.[199] The number of wholly domestic interstate compacts grew exponentially in the twentieth century.[200] During this period, the trend was to move beyond traditional litigated boundary disputes to creating governing mechanisms in such areas as interstate ground transportation infrastructure[201] and information sharing.[202] Recently, this form of Congressionally-approved agreement has assumed international importance. In 2001, eight states bordering the Great Lakes[203] entered into the Great Lakes-St. Lawrence River Basin Water Resources Compact, the main purpose of which is to govern the withdrawal of water from the Great Lakes Basin. In 2008, this domestic interstate compact served as the basis for a nonbinding companion agreement with two Canadian provinces, Ontario and Quebec.[204] In the future, should disputes arise among the parties to these compacts, potentially complicated issues may surface with respect to how the nonbinding international agreement will interact with the binding interstate compact.

In federal states, tensions may arise when treaties extend into matters previously regulated at the state and local level. In Australia, the courts have held that for implementing legislation to be valid on the basis of the external affairs power of the federal government, the legislation must be enacted to fulfill obligations assumed under the treaty. If the treaty expresses political aspirations and not binding obligations, the external affairs power will not be sufficient grounds to override the rights of the states.[205] The Australian

---

[195] The authority added by Article 16(1) is narrowly drawn; it allows constituent states to negotiate agreements only on subject matters within their own sphere of competence and only with States bordering Austria and their respective constituent states. There are also specified procedures that must be followed, including obtaining the consent of the federal government before the treaty is concluded by the Federal President on behalf of the state. Moreover, the treaty must be terminated if the Federal Government so requests due to a predominant federal interest. National Report of Austria, p. 8.

[196] "Relations with foreign states shall be conducted by the Federation."

[197] U.S. Const., Art. VI[3]:

> This Constitution, and the Laws of the United States which shall be made in Pursuance thereof; and all Treaties made, or which shall be made, under the Authority of the United States, shall be the supreme Law of the Land; and the Judges in every State shall be bound thereby, any Thing in the Constitution or Laws of any State to the Contrary notwithstanding.

[198] U.S. Const., Article I, § 10. The safeguards of federalism in this realm are political rather than juridical. Each state sends two senators to the U.S. Senate, the body that gives "advice and consent" on proposed treaties, and each state sends a delegation to the House of Representatives, which often enacts implementing legislation in order to carry out treaty obligations.

[199] *See,* e.g., Virginia-Maryland Compact of 1785 (governing fishing and navigation rights in the Potomac River, the Pocomoke River, and the Chesapeake Bay)

[200] *See* Caroline N. Broun et al., *The Evolving Use and the Changing Role of Interstate Compacts: A Practitioner's Guide 4 (2006).*

[201] Washington Metropolitan Area Transit Regulation Compact (1981).

[202] Driver License Compact (1960).

[203] Illinois, Indiana, Michigan, Minnesota, Ohio, Pennsylvania, New York, and Wisconsin.

[204] Great Lakes-St. Lawrence River Basin Water Resources Agreement (2005).

[205] See *Victoria v. Commonwealth* (Industrial Relations Act Case) (1996) 187 CLR 416.

federal government may also work with state and territorial governments to ensure uniform application of treaties through state legislation.

Finally, in many federal systems, like those of Austria, Australia, Russia, and the United States, the component states may provide more extensive guarantees than those provided under federal law. In Australia, while the national constitution does not contain a bill of rights, the Australian Capital Territory has incorporated international human rights law into its local legal system through the Human Rights Act 2004 (ACT). It provides that the term human rights as defined in the act "is not exhaustive of the rights an individual may have under domestic or international law." It makes specific reference to "rights under the ICCPR not listed in this Act" and elsewhere notes that the primary source for the Act was the ICCPR. Section 31 provides that international law, including the judgments of foreign and international courts and tribunals, relevant to a human right, may be considered in interpreting the right.

21.7 Indirect Application: Using International Law to Inform Domestic Law

The courts of many states have adopted a presumption that domestic law is intended to conform to international law. Australia,[206] Canada, and the United States, in particular, have a doctrine of statutory interpretation that laws will, so far as possible, be interpreted by the courts to conform to treaty obligations, but Australian law seems to suggest that a treaty should be used only to resolve ambiguities in the law. British courts presume, when interpreting legislation (or statutory instruments or orders in council), that the British Parliament did not intend to legislate in violation of Britain's international obligations.[207] It has also been held that there is a presumption that Parliament would not intend for any power to be conferred by statute which could be exercised in a manner contrary to the U.K.'s treaty obligations.[208] This general presumption is rebuttable and it has been rebutted on several occasions.[209] Regarding the European Convention on Human Rights specifically, there is a statutory instruction to British courts to interpret statutes and subordinate legislation, "[s]o far as it is possible to do so," in a manner compatible with the European Convention.[210] If it should not prove "possible" for courts to interpret legislation compatibly with the Convention, then the courts must enforce British law rather than European Convention law. When that occurs, the courts will issue a declaration of incompatibility, which will activate a sort of fast-track procedure for alteration of the legislation by the Parliament, so as to instate compatibility between British law and European Convention law.[211] As of June 2009, 17 of these had been issued in final form. Treaties, as well as customary international law, can be used to develop the common law.[212]

As a matter of statutory construction, the presumption of conformity has not proven to be particularly controversial. Debate has arisen, however, over the use of international norms to interpret and apply the provisions of national constitutions. The Israeli courts (and the parties who argue before them) do turn quite often to international law to substantiate their constitutional rights.[213] In contrast, both the United States Supreme Court and the Australian High Court have split over the role of international law in interpreting the respective national Constitutions. In a 2004 case, an Australian justice concluded that requiring the constitution to be read consistently with the rules of international law would make those rules part of the Constitution,

[206] *Polites v. Commonwealth* (1945) 70 CLR 60 (10 April 1945 at 69; *Chu Kheng Lim v. Minister for Immigration, Local Government & Ethnic Affairs*, (1992) HCA 64; (1992) 176 CLR 1 (8 December 1992).

[207] See, to this effect, *Mortensen v. Peters* (1906) 8 F 93; *Collco Dealings Ltd. v. IRC*, (1962) A.C. 1; *Salomon v. Customs* and *Excise Commissioners*, (1967) 2 Q.B. 116; *Post Office v. Estuary Radio Ltd.*, (1968) 2 Q.B. 740; *Post Office v. Estuary Radio Ltd.*, (1968) 2 Q.B. 740; *Garland v. British Rail Engineering Ltd* (1983) 2 AC 751; R v. Lyons, H.L., (2002) UKHL 44; (2003) 1 A.C. 976; (2002) 3 W.L.R. 1562; (2002) 4 All E.R. 1028; and *A (FC) v. Secretary of State for the Home Department*, House of Lords, (2005) UKHL 71.

[208] See *R. v. Secretary of State for the Home Department, Ex parte Venables*, House of Lords, (1997) 3 W.L.R. 23(1998) A.C. 407, speech of Lord Bingham, at 499.

[209] See, e.g. *Mortensen v. Peters* (1906) 8 F 93; and *Collco Dealings Ltd. v. IRC,* (1962) A.C. 1.

[210] Human Rights Act 1998, sec. 3.

[211] Human Rights Act 1998, sec. 4.

[212] *Mabo v. State of Queensland* (No. 2), (1992) 175 CLR 1 (3 June 1992); *Minister for Immigration and Ethnic Affairs v. Teoh*, (1995) 183 CLR 273 at 288.

[213] National Report of Israel, pp. 36–38.

contrary to the amendment process set forth in the Constitution.[214] Justice Kirby disagreed, finding a presumption that the Constitution is not intended to violate international law. In his view separating constitutional law from the "dynamic impact of international law is neither possible nor desirable today." Therefore, national courts have a duty "to interpret their constitutional texts in a way that is generally harmonious with the basic principles of international law, including as that law states human rights and fundamental freedoms."

Canadian courts use human rights obligations when construing the fundamental guarantees of the Canadian Charter of Rights and Freedoms.[215] As early as 1989, the Supreme Court held that the Charter "should generally be presumed to provide protection at least as great as that afforded by similar provisions in international human rights documents which Canada has ratified."[216] Later case law endorsed the use of all the various sources of international human rights law as relevant for interpreting the Charter's provisions and suggested a presumption of conformity, even in one case seeming to require a conforming interpretation unless the express wording of the Charter provision makes compliance impossible.[217] Later cases continue to fluctuate in the use of international law to interpret the Charter.

In the Netherlands, international law guarantees for human rights have had and still have an enormous impact on domestic case law. This is particularly so for the civil and political rights laid down in the ECHR and the International Covenant on Civil and Political Rights *(ICCPR)*. Most of them are considered to be self-executing. Through 'incorporation' the judiciary takes due account of the interpretation by the ECrtHR and the UN Committee on Human Rights, and the Committee on the Elimination of All Forms of Racial Discrimination.[218] Some treaties, such as the European Social Charter and the International Covenant on Economic, Social and Cultural Rights, are less influential. A special problem is posed by the internationally guaranteed principle of equality and non-discrimination. That has been enshrined in numerous treaties, including the Treaties, Regulations and Directives of the EC. Disputes about social fundamental issues linked with discrimination may be of such a political caliber if not 'explosiveness' that the judiciary tends 'to pass the buck' to the legislature and, in doing so, in fact declines to apply the self-executing non-discrimination principle.

Austrian courts refer to treaties in interpreting or applying domestic law, including constitutional matters. In one case[219] interpreting Article 7 of the ECHR and Article 4 of Protocol No. 7, the court referred to comparable provisions in the American Convention on Human Rights, finding its provisions relevant to interpreting the ECHR.[220] In contrast, Italian courts do not make reference to treaties to which Italy is not a party in interpreting domestic law, including constitutional matters. In Greece, the courts apply the international conventions promulgated by law[221] or published in the Official Journal by Presidential Decree or Ministerial Decision. However, there are some exceptions: (1) the application of an international convention which has not been promulgated is acceptable if a reference to it is made by an internal act, legislative or administrative;[222] (2) the application of a non-promulgated by law convention is possible if this is provided in a private agreement as the applicable law agreed by the parties (Article 25 of the civil code);[223] the application of a provision of a non-promulgated convention is acceptable if this provision is considered as reflecting customary international law.[224]

There are also many examples of the indirect application of treaties in Polish practice, that is to say, application for the purposes of interpretation of domestic law.[225] A judgment of 11 January 1995 of the Supreme

[214] *Al-Kateb v. Godwin* (2004) 208 ALR 124 at 140–4, 168–9.

[215] National Report of Canada, pt 1, 43–51.

[216] *Slaight Communications Inc. v. Davidson*, [1989] 1 S.C.R. 283. Commentators refer to this as the "minimum content presumption." Ibid. at n. 236.

[217] National Report of Canada, pt 1, p. 48.

[218] HR 15 June 1976, *NJ* 1976, 551.

[219] Constitutional Court, Decision No. B559/08, July 2, 2009.

[220] American Convention on Human Rights, November 22, 1969, 1144 UNTS 123.

[221] Articles 28 par.1 and 36 par.2 of the Constitution.

[222] Supreme Court, 450/1996.

[223] First Instance Court of Athens, 9934/1983.

[224] Supreme Court (in plenary), 11/2000.

[225] See e.g. the decision of the Supreme Administrative Court of 3 September 1997 (III RN 38/97) in which the Court interpreted the Code of Administrative Procedure in the light of Article 6 ECHR finding that whenever there were serious doubts regarding the admissibility of a recourse, the Court should proceed on the merits since the purpose of the Code seen in the light of

Court should be highlighted in that regard since it formulated a general guideline concerning the application of the European Convention of Human Rights.[226] The Polish courts sometimes refer to treaties to which Poland is not a party in interpreting or applying domestic law, including constitutional matters. They use it as an additional argument to prove the existence of international standards in the area in question. For example they have invoked the Revised Charter of Social Rights or the Council of Europe Convention for the Protection of Human Rights and Dignity of the Human Being with regard to the Application of Biology and Medicine: Convention on Human Rights and Biomedicine of 1997.[227] Similarly, in a very few instances Serbian courts applied international treaties which were not binding upon Serbia to illustrate the content of certain international human rights[228] or as additional argument to support the conclusion reached on other grounds.[229] The practice is not common, however.

Japanese courts undertake "indirect application" of international law, i.e. the use of international law for the purpose of affirming and supporting the interpretation of domestic law, is reportedly favored and more easily accepted by the courts than is direct application of international law.[230] The courts have developed case law concerning "indirect application" of the International Convention on the Elimination of All Forms of Racial Discrimination (ICERD), which the Diet has not taken any legislative measures to

Article 6 of the Convention is to allow the citizen to fulfill its right to be heard by an independent tribunal; judgment of the same court of 4 February 1997 (III RN 59/96), interpreting the statute of the Supreme Administrative Court in such a way as to provide for judicial control of an administrative refusal to send a pensioner for spa treatment; decision of the Supreme Court of 11 January 1995 (III ARN 75/94), in which the Court held that the decision to reject a plea for exemption from court costs should be especially carefully assessed in order to exclude barring the individual from access to justice; similarly, the Supreme Administrative Court judgment of 5 December 2001 (II SA 155/01) concerning a journalist's access to official documents; judgment of 13 November 1997 (I CKN 710/97) of the Supreme Court in which the Court interpreted the Unfair Competition Law of 1993 in the light of Article 8 of the Paris Convention of 1883 on industrial property protection as revised by the 1967 Stockholm Act. In the judgment of 17 November 2004 the Supreme Administrative Court held that the concept of pattern, model or sample in the Customs Code of 1997 "has to be understood in the context of Article II of the International Convention to Facilitate the Importation of Commercial Samples and Advertising Materials of 1952 (…) using in that regard the criterion of "negligible value"". In the judgment of 22 November 2007 the Supreme Court interpreted Polish Transport Law of 1984 in conformity with the Convention on the Contract for the International Carriage of Goods by Road (CMR) of 1956, and to interpret the provisions of the said Convention the Court referred to the relevant judgments of French, Austrian and German courts.

[226] The statement was later repeated in many other judgments: "Since the accession of Poland to the Council of Europe, the case law of the European Court of Human Rights in Strasbourg should be applied as an essential source of interpretation of the provisions of the Polish domestic law." III ARN 75/94.

[227] E.g. the judgment of the Constitutional Court of 23 April 2008 (SK 16/07) on the freedom of expression and medical ethics.

[228] Belgrade District Court granted a prohibitory injunction to stop the distribution of the information contained in a newspaper article. In its reasoning the court rejected arguments of respondents based on the ICCPR and ECHR relying on national security and proper administration of justice. The court noted that ECHR at that time was not in force for Serbia: "Despite the fact that the European Convention was not ratified by the State Union of Serbia and Montenegro, the Court still decided to take into consideration its provisions. (…) Therefore, apart from the restrictions based on national security and public order, which have been laid down in the Act on Public Information, the European Convention also envisages the possibility to restrict freedoms in order to maintain the authority and impartiality of the judiciary." – *Public Prosecutor v. Magazine "Svedok"*, Belgrade District Court, Judgment of 6 June 2003 in: 127 International Law Reports 315, 319.

[229] High Commercial Court, Decision no. Pž. 4039/2004 of September 15, 2004. The issue before the court was the recognition of the foreign non-judicial decision. In reaching its conclusion that under certain circumstances foreign non-judicial decisions may be equated with judicial decisions, the court relied, inter alia, on international instruments which were not binding upon Serbia and Montenegro.

[230] See, e.g. the March 27, 1997 judgment of the Sapporo District Court in the so-called *Nibudani Dam Case* involving the claim for annulment of a project of dam construction on a site worshiped as a sacred place by the Ainu, the indigenous people in Japan. *Hanrei Jihō*, vol.1598, p.33, *Hanrei Taimuzu*, vol.938, p.75 (holding the authorization of the project by the authorities illegal as exceeding the authorities' scope of discretionary power given by the Land Expropriation Law). The Court noted that the Japanese government had recognized the Ainu people as a "minority" protected by ICCPR Article 27 during the examination of State report by the Human Rights Committee in 1991. Affirming that the Ainu people's right to enjoy its culture is guaranteed by Article 27, the Court stated that "in light of the object of the enactment of Article 27 of the Covenant, the restriction [of the right] must be limited to the minimum extent necessary", and concluded that the authorization of the project by the authorities was illegal.

implement.[231] In one case, the Sapporo District Court, conceding that the ICERD, as well as Article 14 of the Constitution on the equality before law and the ICCPR, do not directly regulate the relationship between private parties, affirmed that they could be a standard of reference in interpreting provisions of private law.[232] On appeal, the Sapporo High Court took the same position.[233] The Supreme Court has also come to take such an attitude recently on the issue of the rights of the child.[234] The Court pointed to the International Covenant on Civil and Political Rights and the Convention on the Rights of the Child in its judgment. At the same time, courts in Japan tend to decline using international law to interpret constitutional provisions. In particular they have rejected arguments based on human rights treaties, assuming that the Constitution is as protective of human rights as the treaty cited. The Supreme Court recently, however, did take provisions of a human rights treaty into account in interpreting the Constitution.

In a set of cases invalidating certain forms of capital punishment, some members of the United States Supreme Court referred to the near global consensus against capital punishment for minors and for the mentally retarded.[235] Other members of the Court criticized any reliance on international sources such as the United Nations Convention on the Rights of the Child and the International Covenant on Civil and Political Rights.[236] In a case closely followed around the country regarding race-conscious college admissions policies, a concurring opinion found support for such programs in the International Convention on the Elimination of All Forms of Racial Discrimination.[237] In an equally controversial case grappling with the constitutionality of state laws criminalizing homosexual sodomy, Justice Anthony Kennedy referred to the jurisprudence of the European Court of Human Rights.[238] Despite lengthy opinions in these cases and numerous pointed dissents and concurrences, there is at present no closure on this set of issues. The Senate Judiciary Committee now commonly asks judicial nominees for their views on the appropriate use of foreign law and international law in constitutional interpretation.[239] In addition, members of the Supreme Court have addressed this issue in their extrajudicial writings, in their speeches,

---

[231] In a case concerning the rejection of a foreign client by a jewelry shop, in which a Brazilian woman window-shopping in a jewelry shop was ousted by a shop clerk, the Court said: "the International Convention on the Elimination of All Forms of Racial Discrimination … requires State parties to take legislative or other measures against discriminatory acts by individuals and groups. … If we premise the view of the Ministry of Foreign Affairs that this Convention does not require any legislative measures, it is understood that substantive provisions of the Convention operate as an interpretative element of tort, in a case, such as the present one, concerning a claim for compensation based on an unlawful act against an individual". The Shizuoka District Court, in its judgment on October 12, 1999 (*Hanrei Jihō*, vol. 1718, p.92, *Hanrei Taimuzu*, vol.1045, p.216), ordered the owner of the shop to pay compensation to the plaintiff, by applying Article 709 of the Civil Code on tort interpreted in light of the Convention.

[232] The definition of "racial discrimination" and the requirement of prohibition of private discrimination in the ICERD played an essential role in the Court's judgment. November 11, 2002, *Hanrei Jihō*, vol.1806, p.84, *Hanrei Taimuzu*, vol.1150, p.185.

[233] September 16, 2004, unreported.

[234] In a case filed by children born to unmarried Japanese men and Philippine women, children who were recognized by their father after birth, the Grand Chamber of the Supreme Court held the provision of the Nationality Law requiring the marriage of parents as a condition of obtaining Japanese nationality unconstitutional (Article 14 on the equality before the law), confirming the Japanese nationality of all ten plaintiffs. *Hanrei Jihō*, vol.2002, p.3, *Hanrei Taimuzu*, vol.1267, p. 92.

[235] *See Roper v. Simmons*, 543 U.S. 555 (2003); *Atkins v. Virginia*, 536 U.S. 304, 316 n.21 (2002) (referring to practices in other countries in concluding that execution of mentally retarded persons violates the Eighth Amendment); *Thompson v. Oklahoma*, 487 U.S. 815, 830–31 & n.34 (1988) (Stevens, J.) (plurality opinion) (invalidating state practice of executing defendants under 16 years of age and referring to "other nations that share our Anglo-American heritage" and citing treaties signed but not ratified by the U.S.).

[236] *See Roper v. Simmons*, 543 U.S. 555, 624 (Scalia, J., dissenting) ("[T]he basic premise of the Court's argument-that American law should conform to the laws of the rest of the world-ought to be rejected out of hand.").

[237] *See Grutter v. Bollinger*, 539 U.S. 306, 344 (2003) (Ginsburg, J., concurring).

[238] *See Lawrence v. Texas*, 539 U.S. 558, 572–73 (2003).

[239] Justices Roberts and Alito assured the committee that they saw no role for foreign law in interpreting the U.S. Constitution. *See U.S. Senate Judiciary Committee Holds a Hearing on the Nomination of Judge Samuel Alito to the U.S. Supreme Court*, Jan. 12, 2006, Westlaw, allnewsplus database; *Transcript: Day Three of the Roberts Confirmation Hearings (Morning Session: Sens. Brownback and Coburn)*, WASHINGTONPOST.COM, Sept. 14, 2005, *available at* 2005 WLNR 14639466 (remarks of Sen. Tom Coburn (R-OK)); *Transcript: Day Two of the Roberts Confirmation Hearings; (Part III: Sens. Kyl and Kohl)*. WASHINGTONPOST.COM, Sept. 13, 2005, available at 2005 WLNR 14576513.

and even in television programs addressed to the general public.[240]

21.8 Hierarchy

As the following review indicates, the idea of peremptory norms that override all other legal sources, international and national, is growing in acceptance, but remains controversial. Apart from that issue, the main distinction on this topic is between those states that place international treaties and/or custom at a constitutional rank and those that place it below the constitution. In addition, those states that place international law below the constitution may be divided into those that give it supremacy over statutory law and those that do not.

Serbia's Constitution is one of the few that has a specific article entitled "hierarchy of national and international legal norms" (Article 194) which provides that the Constitution is the highest legal act in Republic of Serbia, with which all laws and other general legal acts enacted in the Republic of Serbia must be in conformity.[241] Statutes and other general legal acts must not be contrary to ratified international treaties and generally accepted rules of international law. This hierarchy of legal norms is further confirmed by Article 167 of the Constitution which defines the jurisdiction of the Constitutional Court of Serbia, since this provision gives power to the Constitutional Court to decide on the conformity of statutes and other pieces of legislation with the Constitution, ratified treaties and generally accepted rules of international law, as well as on the conformity of ratified international treaties with the Constitution. In case of non-conformity of the national legislation with treaties, Constitutional Court will strike down the inconsistent domestic statute, in part or in whole.[242]

21.8.1 Jus Cogens

In Argentina, jus cogens has been recognized in reference to crimes against humanity, to give effect to an extradition without regard to the normally applicable statute of limitations. In the interpretation of the Hungarian Constitutional Court certain jus cogens norms have priority over Constitution as well through authorization based on constitutional regulations. Austrian courts have referred to the doctrine of jus cogens but it has not been the basis of a decision thus far. It appears that the Supreme Court understands that UN Security Council resolutions based on Chapter VII of the UN Charter have a higher status in international law, but that certain human rights have the status of jus cogens and prevail even over binding UN Security Council resolutions.[243]

Canadian courts have given limited recognition to the doctrine of jus cogens but little if any domestic legal consequence has resulted from the characterization of a norm as jus cogens.[244] German courts have recognized the existence of jus cogens under international law, but they are very much aware of the stringent requirements for the verification of jus cogens. Very few norms of jus cogens have therefore been

[240] *See* Ruth Bader Ginsburg, *Looking Beyond Our Borders: The Value of a Comparative Perspective in Constitutional Adjudication*, 22 Yale L. & Pol'y Rev. 329 (2004); Stephen Breyer, *Constitutionalism, Privatization, and Globalization: Changing Relationships among European Constitutional Courts*, 21 Cardozo L. Rev. 1045 (2000). *See also* the exchange of views between Justices Breyer and Scalia on January 13, 2005 at a debate at the American University's Washington College of Law, *available at* http://www.freerepublic.com/focus/news/1352357/posts.

[241] Similar but still different wording of the same rule is to be found in Articles 194 and 16 of the Constitution. Different wording of what seems to be the same intent of the legislator was criticized in this particular instance by the Venice Commission: "Finally, rules similar to Article 16 appear, in a different wording, in Article 194. Such repetitions, especially if not identical, are undesirable since they risk opening delicate issues of interpretation." – European Commission for Democracy through Law (Venice Commission), Opinion on the Constitution of Serbia, adopted by the Commission on its 70th plenary session, Opinion No. 405/2006, CDL-AD(2007)004, Strasbourg, 19 March 2007, p. 6, para. 19, available at: http://www.venice.coe.int/docs/2007/CDL-AD(2007)004-e.pdf.

[242] For example, in a series of cases involving the conflict between the Insurance Act and several bilateral treaties on social security, where the two provided for different and mutually exclusive solutions, domestic courts routinely gave preference to bilateral treaties. The courts found that "in case of conflict between the treaty and domestic legislation, the treaty shall be applied".See, High Commercial Court in Belgrade, Decision no. Pž. 333/2001 of January 26, 2001; High Commercial Court in Belgrade, Decision no. Pž. 7768/2001 February 8, 2001; High Commercial Court in Belgrade, Decision no. Pž. 4212/2001 July 13, 2001.

[243] National Report of Austria, pp. 49–50.

[244] National Report of Canada, pt. 1, pp. 40–41.

recognised and even fewer have been deemed to have an effect on the outcome of specific cases.[245]

In Italy, in the *Ferrini* case, the *Corte di Cassazione* held that Germany is not entitled to sovereign immunity for serious violations of human rights carried out by German occupying forces during World War II.[246] In order to exclude the applicability of the traditional regime of foreign state immunity with regard to international crimes, the Court refers to the principle of primacy of jus cogens rules. The Court seems to agree that the formal supremacy of jus cogens gives it prevalence over all other non-peremptory rules of international law, among which there is the international customary rule concerning foreign state immunity. The *Corte di Cassazione* affirmed its approach to the question of the immunity from civil jurisdiction in relation to gross violations of human rights committed by German military forces in Italy during World War II in its 13 Orders of 2008.[247] All the Orders are formulated in substantial similar terms.[248]

Japanese courts have not recognized jus cogens, indeed, one court denied its existence, but at the same time it recognized that no legal system could give effect to illegal agreements that conflict with "public order and good morals" in international law.

The Israeli courts have recognized jus cogens norms.[249] In addition to the prohibitions of genocide, crimes against humanity, and torture, a court held that the prohibition of corrupt practices and money laundering is now part of international jus cogens.[250] Russian courts and other public authorities also acknowledge the doctrine of jus cogens and the courts apply such norms in accordance with Article 53 of the Vienna Convention on the Law of Treaties 1969. The United States has also recognized the doctrine of jus cogens, but the cases have not given it the "trumping" value that theory suggests it should have. The national courts in the Czech Republic similarly and theoretically accept jus cogens, via the practice of the European Court of Human Rights. British courts have recognised torture as a violation of a jus cogens norm.[251] Finally, in Venezuela, although the doctrine of jus cogens is recognized by commentators, no cases have been reported applying it by Venezuelan courts

21.8.2 Treaties

The status of treaties in domestic systems varies considerably, with the Constitution of Japan being the only one that does not specify the status of a treaty in domestic law.[252] In many continental systems, treaties (either all or specific categories of treaties) have constitutional rank.[253] A second group of states, including France,[254] takes an intermediary position, placing treaties below the constitution, but above other domestic law. Thirdly, some states (generally those with common law systems) rank treaties as equivalent to legislation, meaning that the later in time prevails in case of

[245] See: *Federal Republic of Germany v. Giovanni Mantelli and Others*, Preliminary Order on Jurisdiction, No. 14201/2008, ILDC 1037 (It 2008), May 29, 2008.

[246] See *Corte di Cassazione*, *Ferrini*, Judgement No. 5044 of 2004.

[247] See *Corte di Cassazione*, Orders Nos. 14200–14212 of 2008.

[248] In all these cases, the Court dismisses jurisdictional immunity of foreign States in relation to claims by individuals as victims of gross violations of human rights, driving Germany to bring an action before the International Court of Justice complaining that Italy, by the conduct of its courts, has violated the principle of sovereign immunity (International Court of Justice, *Jurisdictional Immunities of the State (Germany v. Italy)*).

[249] See, e.g. Criminal Appeal 336/61 *Adolph Eichmann v. The Attorney General*, 16 PD 2033 (1962); HCJ 5100/94 *Public Committee against Torture in Israel* et al. v. *Government of Israel* et al., 53(4) PD 817 (1999). The judgment is excerpted in English in 30 *Israel Yearbook on Human Rights* 352 (2000).

[250] Originating Summons (Jerusalem) 2212/03 *Nissan Albert Gad* v. *David Siman-Tov*, tak-District 2004(1), 623.

[251] See *R. v. Bow Street Metropolitan Stipendiary Magistrate, Ex Parte Pinochet Ugarte* (No. 3), House of Lords, [1999] 2 W.L.R. 827[2000] 1 A.C. 147, Lord Browne Wilkinson, at 198; Lord Hope, at 244–45, 247; Lord Hutton, at 261; and Lord Millett, at 275; R. *(Binyan Mohamed) v. Secretary of State for Foreign and Commonwealth Affairs*, Queen's Bench Division Divisional Court, [2008] EWHC 2048 (Admin), paras. 170–76; and *A (FC) v. Secretary of State for the Home Department*, House of Lords, [2005] UKHL 71, speech of Lord Bingham, para. 33.

[252] Article 98 of the Constitution provides, without further elaboration in the text, that the Constitution is the supreme law of the land and that "The treaties concluded by Japan … shall be faithfully observed."

[253] The Russian Federation Constitution provides that if an international treaty of the Russian Federation establishes other rules than those envisaged by law, the rules of the international agreement shall be applied.

[254] Article 55 of the 1958 Constitution provides: "Les traités ou accords régulièrement ratifiés ou approuvés ont, dès leur publication, une autorité supérieure à celle des lois, sous réserve, pour chaque accord ou traité, de son application par l'autre partie." This domestic hierarchy was recognized by the Cour de cassation, in the judgment *Jacques Vabre* of 1975 and by the Conseil d'État, with the *Nicolo* judgment of 1989.

conflict. Courts, however, generally have adopted a presumption that the legislature intends to conform domestic law to international obligations and will attempt to reconcile the two if possible.[255]

In Argentina and Venezuela, special status is given to human rights treaties. The Argentine Constitution mentions a number of human rights treaties, giving them constitutional status; they cannot be repealed by the legislature.[256] Similarly, the 1999 Venezuelan Constitution, Article 23, grants human right treaties constitutional hierarchy to the extent that those treaties contain provisions more favorable than domestic legislation. Austria and Italy require a parliamentary supermajority to give treaties the same status as constitutional provisions.

Other states that give treaties a rank above domestic legislation include the Czech Republic[257] and the Slovak Republic, whose constitution provides that specific categories of treaties have superior status: international treaties on human rights and fundamental freedoms and international treaties for whose exercise a law is not necessary and international treaties which directly confer rights or impose duties on natural persons or legal persons. However, Article 154c provides that human rights treaties adopted prior to July 1, 2001 have this status only if the rights are of greater scope than those provided in the constitution.

In Canada, like Australia, treaties must be legislatively implemented and thus have the same rank as other domestic legislation, but the presumption that domestic law should be implemented in conformity with international legal obligations in practice gives treaties a slightly higher status. Nonetheless clear legislative language will override treaty provisions where the two cannot be reconciled.

The situation in the Russian Federation is based on part 4 Article 15 of the Constitution according to which a ratified treaty has primacy over federal law. The Presidium of the Supreme Court[258] has indicated that not every international treaty of the Russian Federation has a priority over federal laws but only those that are ratified and published.[259]

21.8.3 Custom

Many countries lack a clear rule on the place of custom in the domestic legal order. Like many other constitutions, the Netherlands Constitution is silent on customary international law.[260] There are, however, some specific statutory provisions recognizing custom as a source of law that prevails over all other domestic legal norms. In other instances, customary international law is being recognized as a source of international law that could and should be applied by the courts[261] taking priority over domestic *delegated* legislation only.[262] In doctrine it is held that international law binding on the Netherlands and not mentioned in the Constitution enjoys priority. However, so far that has not been borne out by practice. Conflicts between Community law and other international legal obligations may occur.[263]

---

[255] Canada's domestic implementing legislation sometimes explicitly provides that interpretation of legislation should be consistent with the relevant international agreement. See e.g., North American Free Trade Implementation Act, S.C. 1993, c. 44, s. 3.

[256] *Monges, Amalia c. Universidad de Buenos Aires*, Fallos: 319:3148, Supreme Court of Argentina.

[257] Art, 95 sec 1, adds that "The Judge is obliged to follow the Law and the Treaty while rendering judgment, which constitutes part of the legal order; he is entitled to analyze whether another legal enactment runs counter to the Law or such Treaty.

[258] In Decision of 31 October 1995 № 8 and Decision of 10 October № 5.

[259] Under the law on treaties, provisions of officially published international treaties of the Russian Federation which do not require municipal action to be applicable shall operate directly Part 3 Article 5 Federal Law of 15 July 1995 № 101-ФЗ on International Treaties of the Russian Federation.

[260] See L. Erades, "International Law and the Netherlands Legal Order", in *International Law in the Netherlands, ed.* H.F. van Panhuys et al. (Alphen a.d. Rijn etc. 1980), 3: 388.

[261] District Court of Rotterdam 8 January 1979 *NJ* 1979,113 (Stichting Reinwater et al. MDPA) where the court considered: "this law [i.e. the law prevailing in the Netherlands] includes the unwritten rules of international law; Dutch courts are not only empowered, but even obliged to apply unwritten international law where appropriate", *NYIL* XI (1980), 329.

[262] So Governmental note *op.cit.* (*supra* note 1), 5.

[263] This was the case in the *Barber* judgment of the Court of Justice (CoJ) Court of Justice E.C., Case of 17 May 1990 C—262/88 (Barber); it was followed by a 'view' of the UN Committee on Human Rights in a case concerning the Netherlands. View of 26 July 1999 Communication nr. 768/1997 (*Vos v. the Netherlands*). The legal dispute revolved around the date as from which a distinction based on sex with regard to pensions was to be illegitimate. The Government endorsed the point of view of the EC CoJ and a similar judgment of the *Centrale Raad van Beroep* (Central Appeals Tribunal: Supreme Court in matters of social security, Decision of 26 November 1998, *RSV* 1999, 92) and reacted by stating that it was unable to share the 'view' "for compelling reasons of legal certainty".

Whether or not customary international law overrides inconsistent common law precedent in Canada is unclear, but it does yield to inconsistent statutory language.[264] As is the case with courts in the United States, Canadian courts have developed and entrenched an interpretive doctrine that presumes legislative intent to conform domestic law to international law, whether the source is a treaty or customary law.[265] As a consequence, courts must interpret domestic law in conformity with international legal obligations where possible. Domestic legislation continues to prevail when it cannot be reconciled with international law.

Customary international law has the force of constitutional law in Italy and any domestic law in conflict with the international law thus indirectly violates the Italian Constitution and can be repealed by the Constitutional Court. When an international customary law conflicts with a constitutional principle, the Constitution prevails over the observance of international customary law.[266] If a rule of international customary law conflicts with an inalienable human right, it cannot be implemented in the Italian legal system.[267]

The Portuguese Constitution does not clearly indicate hierarchy. Authors, almost unanimously, ascribe a superior value to general or ordinary international law, but as for its hierarchical position in relation to the constitution, opinions are divided: for some, the former (or, at the very least, a part thereof) must yield to the Fundamental Law, for others, on the contrary, general international law has a superior or constitutional value. The Portuguese Constitution considers that the rules and principles of general or ordinary international law comprise an integral part of Portuguese law (Article 8, paragraph 1) and some interpret this to mean the primacy of that type of international law in relation to domestic law.

The issue of the hierarchy of customary international law has not been addressed by Venezuelan courts. According to the Supreme Court of Justice international law must conform to the Constitution, otherwise it will not be enforceable in Venezuela.[268] It is common that Venezuelan courts resort to international law to interpret constitutional provisions. However, the Supreme Court considers that it is the exclusive and only interpreter of the Constitution, and therefore it is not bound by any such rule of international law.[269]

21.9 Conclusion

The relationship between international law and domestic legal systems is increasingly complex, reflecting the growing complexity of the international legal system itself. With the growth of international organizations, emergence of the European Union, and the proliferation of international courts, domestic legal systems have adapted in various ways to accommodate the new realities. Some of the adaptations are in tension with each other. There is a growing democratic participation in the treaty-making and approving process, but also a recognition of the existence and need for informal or executive agreements that do not follow the normal treaty-making procedures. Given the continuing evolution in this regard, any conclusion about the incorporation of international law into domestic legal systems remains uncertain and fraught with difficulties.

[264] National Report of Canada, pt. 1, 28–31.

[265] Ibid pp. 32–33.

[266] In Decision No. 73 of 23 March 2001, in *obiter dictum*, the Constitutional Court stated that "fundamental principles of constitutional order" and "inalienable rights of the human being" are a limit to the automatic incorporation of international customary law into the Italian legal order. In the *Russel* case (Decision No. 48 of 18 June 1979), the Constitutional Court deals with a potential conflict between customary international law and the fundamental principles of the Constitution but held that "the claimed contrast is only apparent and can be solved applying the *lex specialis* principle.

[267] See Constitutional Court, Judgements No. 15 of 29 January 1996, No. 73 of 22 March 2001. The *Corte di Cassazione* seems to share the same point, holding that "… Article 10, paragraph 1, of the Constitution affirms that the Italian legal order must conform to the generally recognised rules of international law […]. However, even those scholars maintaining that customary rules incorporated by means of Article 10 enjoy a constitutional status […] recognise that they must respect the basic principles of our legal order, which cannot be derogated from or modified. Fundamental human rights are among the constitutional principles which cannot be derogated from by generally recognised rules of international law." See *Corte di Cassazione*, *Milde*, Judgment No. 1072 of 2009.

[268] Constitutional Chamber of the Supreme Court of Justice, decisions of July 15, 2003, Rafael Chavero case; October 17, 2008, Article 258 of the Constitution case; December 18, 2008, Corte Primera de lo Contencioso case; and February 11, 2009, Articles 1 and 151 of the Constitution case.

[269] Constitutional Chamber of the Supreme Court of Justice, decision of July 15, 2003, Rafael Chavero case.

The current lack of clarity is unlikely to be resolved any time soon. Indeed, the recourse to "soft law" instruments and the power of international tribunals to pronounce judgments or make decisions on international legal issues raises problems for many legal systems, whose constitutions delimit the structure and powers of the domestic judiciary, providing legal certainty by indicating the highest tribunal to determine with finality the resolution of a dispute. The place of decisions of international tribunals in the domestic order remains controversial and uncertain.

In many systems, although the existing legal framework may seem favorable to the application of international law in its various forms, a number of problems prevent the comprehensive application of international law. There are far more binding international instruments than cases in which these instruments could have been effectively applied. Courts are still not well trained for the application of international law and very rarely proceed *ex officio* to apply it. In many cases, the parties provide inadequate legal arguments based on international treaties. In addition, some courts demonstrate a pronounced and unwarranted deference to the political branches on matters of international law. The view that international law is not "real law" still seems to resonate in many courtrooms, despite the constitutional provisions and legislation that calls for the application of international treaties and custom. The gulf between the paper and the practice seems to be narrowing, however, as the various legal systems of the world grapple with an increasing number of transboundary, regional and global issues.

List of National Rapporteurs

Argentina	Hortensia D.T. Gutierrez Posse, Buenos Aires University Law School
	Professor Frida M. Armas-Pfirter, Austral University Law School.
Austria	Elisabeth Handl-Petz, Federal Chancellery of Austria
Australia	Alice de Jonge, Monash University Law School
Bulgaria	E. Tanchev, Constitutional Court of Bulgaria
Canada	John H. Currie, Faculty of Law, University of Ottawa
	Professor Stéphane Beaulac, Faculté de droit, Université de Montréal
Czech Republic	Alexander J. Bělohlávek, Ph.D., Dipl. Ing. (oec), Dr. h.c.
France	Emmanuel Decaux, University of Paris
Germany	Privatdozent Dr. Hans-Peter Folz, University of Augsburg
Greece	Angelos Yokaris, Law School, University of Athens
Hungary	Nora Chronowski, Faculty of Law, University of Pécs
	Ildikó Ernszt, Faculty of Law, Károli Gáspár University
	Tímea Drinóczi, Faculty of Law, University of Pécs
Israel	Talia Einhorn, Tel-Aviv University Faculty of Management
Italy	Giuseppe Cataldi, University of Naples
Japan	Hae Bong Shin, Aoyama Gakuin University, Tokyo
Luxembourg	Patrick Kinsch, University of Luxembourg
Netherlands	Evert A. Alkema, Faculty of Law, Leiden University
New Zealand	W. John Hopkins, University of Canterbury Law School
Poland	Anna Wyrozumska, Faculty of Law & Administration, University of Lodz
Portugal	Francisco Antonio de Macedo Lucas Ferreira de Almeida
Russian Federation	Yu.A Tikhomirov, Institute of Legislation & Comparative Law
Serbia	Sanja Djajic, University of Novi Sad School of Law
Slovakia	Dagmar Lantajova, Trnava UniversityLaw Faculty
United Kingdom	Stephen Neff, School of Law, University of Edinburgh
United States	Paul Dubinsky, Wayne State University Law School
Uruguay	Jose Mario Gamio
Venezuela	Eugenio Hernández-Bretón, Dean, School of Law and Political Sciences, Universidad Monteávila (Caracas)

Les Électeurs Étrangers[1]

22

Jacques Robert

L'étranger ne semble bénéficier un peu partout d'aucun préjugé apparemment favorable. Le terme lui-même n'a qu'un contenu « négatif ».

L'étranger - pour nous – c'est celui qui n'a pas notre nationalité. Par extension, c'est celui qui n'appartient pas à un groupe donné. Ne dit-on pas d'un corps étranger qu'il est une chose ne faisant pas partie de l'organisme, qui se trouve en quelque sorte contre-nature dans celui-ci ?

On avance volontiers, dans la France profonde, qu'une jeune fille s'est mariée avec un « étranger » quand elle épouse quelqu'un de la commune voisine !... Et un proverbe arabe ne conseille-t-il point de se marier avec quelqu'un de sa tribu, de son village, si possible de son immeuble, voire – encore mieux – de son pallier ?

Et pourtant, nous sommes tous des étrangers... de quelqu'un. Dès que nous franchissons nos frontières, nous voila considérés par nos voisins comme des étrangers.

De ce fait même, nous devrions nous intéresser à la situation qui est faite à l'étranger chez nous pour pouvoir prétendre être aussi bien traités nous-mêmes chez les autres. On considérera que ce problème est récurrent et que rares sont les solutions retenues qui donnent satisfaction.

Il est vrai que cette question de la présence sur le territoire de tout État d'une minorité étrangère se trouve au centre de nombreuses interrogations politiques, économiques et sociales.

On frise la politique, pour ne pas dire la polémique à tout instant. Car l'étranger, par nature, véhicule un nombre de préjugés, de fantasmes, de frayeurs qui grippent le tissu social avant que de le déchirer.

Il convient donc de faire attention, quand on étudie ce tout complexe, délicat, passionnel, de garder à tout prix son objectivité pour ne point troubler la recherche de solutions équilibrées par des a priori excessifs et douteux.

À ce titre, le rapporteur général, signataire de ce texte, tient à remercier et féliciter les différents rapporteurs des textes qui lui sont parvenus pour l'impartialité et la modération de leurs écrits[*].

S'ils ont émis d'utiles comparaisons, ce n'est jamais pour juger certains propos ou en condamner d'autres. Chaque pays a adopté le système de son choix en raison de motivations tenant à son histoire, au nombre de sa population, à sa psychologie, à l'importance des étrangers sur son sol, à la structure de son État...

C'est assez dire que nous serons ici obligés, pour opérer une synthèse à l'échelle du monde, de catégoriser les diverses situations pour présenter un tableau sinon exhaustif, du moins assez significatif.

Pour ne point répondre – une à une (ce qui serait fastidieux) à chacune des questions que je me suis permis de poser à l'ensemble des rapporteurs nationaux, je proposerai ici de traiter successivement les trois points fondamentaux de notre sujet : I. Quels étrangers ? II. Quelles élections ? III. Dans quel but ?

I – Les grandes déclarations de droit international n'ont guère été prolixes sur le sort – spécifique ou non – à réserver à ces hommes qui ont, un jour, décidé de se fixer dans un pays autre que le leur. Elles ne mentionnent pas directement les étrangers, ne parlant que des citoyens, n'abordant notre problème que sous l'angle de la discrimination interdite.

La première, la Déclaration des droits de l'homme de 1789, dans son article 6, stipule, au titre de la souveraineté de la loi, que celle-ci est l'expression de la volonté générale et que tous les « *citoyens* » ont droit de

[1] IV.B.1, Foreign Voters.

J. Robert (✉)
Centre for Comparative Law, Paris, France

Honorary President, University of the Pantheon, Paris, France

Former Member, Constitutional Council, Paris, France
e-mail: cfdc@legiscompare.org

K.B. Brown and D.V. Snyder (eds.), *General Reports of the XVIIIth Congress of the International Academy of Comparative Law/Rapports Généraux du XVIIIème Congrès de l'Académie Internationale de Droit Comparé*, DOI 10.1007/978-94-007-2354-2_22, © Springer Science+Business Media B.V. 2012

concourir personnellement ou par leurs représentants à sa formation. Elle ajoute qu'elle doit être la même pour tous. Tous les *citoyens* étant égaux à ses yeux, ils sont également admissibles à toutes dignités, places et emplois publics, selon leur capacité et sans autre distinction que celle de leurs vertus et de leurs talents.

Après quoi, aux articles suivants, il est question de l'*homme* en général auquel il est reconnu certains droits protecteurs de sa personne physique. Mais s'agissant de la liberté de communication des pensées et des opinions qui est un droit de l'homme, la Déclaration restreint aux seuls citoyens le droit de parler, d'écrire, d'imprimer librement....

Le terme d'étranger n'est employé nulle part. Il ne s'agit que de l'homme et du citoyen. Et le droit de vote n'y est jamais évoqué.

Il n'étonnera point que la Déclaration universelle des droits de l'homme du 10 décembre 1948 ait, comme celle de 1789, choisi de rester dans une même généralité d'expression. Intéressant l'humanité tout entière, elle utilise les termes de «*personne*» et «*d'individu*», de «*nul*» et de «*tous*», d'*êtres humains*, ou de «*chacun*» ...

Mais elle se fait plus accueillante en disposant, dans son article 1er, que tous les *êtres humains* naissent libres et égaux en dignité et en droits et, à l'article 3, que chacun peut se prévaloir de tous les droits et libertés proclamés par elle, sans distinction aucune, notamment de *race*, de *couleur*, de sexe, de langue, de religion, d'opinion politique ou de tout autre opinion, d'*origine nationale* ou sociale.

La Déclaration de 1948 assure donc bien qu'aucune discrimination ne doit être tolérée entre les êtres humains et que tous doivent jouir des mêmes droits mais ces derniers contiennent-ils le vote ? Aucune précision n'est apportée sur ce point.

Pas davantage ne trouve-t-on mention de ce droit dans la Convention européenne des droits de l'homme de 1950 qui utilise – notons-le – une terminologie différente (mais peut-on en tirer une conséquence quelconque ?) en disposant que la jouissance des droits et libertés qu'elle reconnaît doit être assurée à *toute personne* sans distinction aucune, fondée notamment... «sur *l'origine nationale* ou sociale, *l'appartenance à une minorité nationale*...».

L'appartenance à une minorité nationale vise sans ambiguïté l'étranger qui ne se trouve pas dans son propre pays mais dans un autre où, avec d'autres comme lui, il constitue un groupe juridiquement spécifique. Mais trois réserves semblent devoir être apportées à cette interprétation ouverte de la reconnaissance des mêmes droits à tous. La première est que les mêmes membres de ces communautés minoritaires doivent être les «nationaux» d'un autre pays ; la seconde est que rien ne permet d'affirmer que le droit de vote soit un droit fondamental ; la troisième se trouve dans le fait que chaque État est libre d'adopter à son choix la définition de l'étranger, comme il est libre, en fonction des impératifs de l'ordre public, de prendre toute mesure contre lui, qui – par définition – ne s'appliquerait point au «national».

Et pourtant, la même Convention européenne dispose dans son article 21 alinéa 2 que «*toute personne* a le droit de prendre part à la direction des affaires publiques de son pays, soit directement, soit par l'intermédiaire de *représentants librement élus*, voire d'accéder, dans des conditions d'égalité, aux fonctions politiques de son pays». Quand, par ailleurs, le même article 21 dans son alinéa 3 déclare sans ambages que la volonté du peuple, fondement de l'autorité des pouvoirs publics s'exprime par des élections honnêtes qui doivent avoir lieu, périodiquement, *au suffrage universel égal*, on peut se demander légitimement si – du moins dans des pays européens le droit de vote ne devrait pas être reconnu, de manière générale, à toute personne vivant sur le territoire de l'État européen en cause, pour toutes les votations quelle que soit leur nature ?

Alors, pourquoi ne point l'avoir dit clairement ?

Sans doute, à la fin du second conflit mondial qui avait opposé avec férocité la plupart des grandes puissances et où les nations et les peuples, dans leur totalité, avaient affreusement souffert, hommes, femmes et enfants, les plaies n'étaient point suffisamment cicatrisées pour que puisse être accepté que de tous récents ou d'anciens ennemis résidâssent les uns chez les autres et puissent être autorisés à voter dans leur pays de résidence. Il fallait attendre. Les repentances ne fleurissaient point, comme les pardons. L'Europe était dans les limbes et personne ne parlait de «mondialisation».

Et puis surtout, l'immigration, faible, ne posait aucun problème aigu. Les femmes allaient à peine se voir reconnaître le droit de vote. Pourquoi, en plus, les étrangers ? Certains n'hésiteraient pas à avancer que c'était déjà un beau cadeau que l'on faisait en les accueillant...

Est-ce une coïncidence ou l'évolution de notre monde qui ont conduit les textes les plus récents à se pencher plus directement sur le problème des étrangers par le biais plus commode de la « citoyenneté » ?

La Charte des droits fondamentaux de l'Union européenne du 7 décembre 2000 contient plusieurs et importantes dispositions concernant la *nationalité* et la *citoyenneté*.

À l'article 2 de cette Charte, il est posé comme un impératif que *toute discrimination fondée sur la nationalité est interdite.* Cet article 2 figure dans le chapitre III consacré à l'égalité. Il signifie – sans discussion possible – qu'il n'y a point – au plan de l'égalité – à souffrir la moindre différence entre les nationaux et les non-nationaux. Donc si les premiers ont le droit de vote, les seconds doivent l'avoir aussi. Comme hommes et femmes peuvent légitimement bénéficier des mêmes droits. Des exceptions, certes, peuvent être prévues par les législations nationales mais elles ne seront admises que si elles sont imposées par des circonstances urgentes, proportionnées au danger et justifiées par une exacte proportionnalité.

Le chapitre V, en entier, est consacré à *la citoyenneté*. Deux articles visent directement celle-ci.

À l'article 39, est accordé à tout citoyen ou citoyenne de l'Union le droit de vote ou d'éligibilité aux élections au Parlement européen dans l'État membre où il ou elle réside, dans les mêmes conditions que les ressortissants de cet État.

Ces deux articles accordent donc à tous les citoyens de l'Union, c'est-à-dire à tout ressortissant d'un pays de l'Union qui jouit, chez lui, de ses droits politiques, le droit, non seulement de voter ou d'être candidat au Parlement européen dans l'État où il réside mais de voter ou d'être candidat aux élections municipales de cet État.

La notion d'étranger recouvre ainsi plusieurs catégories et chaque État peut vouloir ou non – puisque cela est de sa compétence – privilégier (ou non) telle ou telle catégorie.

1. L'étranger est d'abord celui qui, ayant une autre nationalité que celle de son pays de résidence souhaiterait (mais combien sont-ils ?) s'installer lui et sa famille dans son pays d'accueil, définitivement.
2. Celui qui vient en France avec une autre nationalité mais qui ne souhaite s'y installer durablement.
3. Celui qui se trouve en situation irrégulière dans son pays d'accueil.
4. Celui qui est installé, dans son pays d'accueil, et qui souhaite pouvoir voter, non pas dans ce pays d'accueil mais aux élections de son pays d'origine.
5. Des individus venus de pays ou l'on parle la langue de leur pays d'accueil et qui préfèrent faire leur vie dans ce pays plutôt que dans leur pays d'origine.
6. Celui qui est né dans un pays ex-colonisé et qui, au moment de l'indépendance de ce pays, a souhaité, rentré sur le territoire de l'ex-colonisateur, refaire sa vie dans ce dernier.

Nous pourrions, bien évidemment, allonger la liste de ces cas, mais notre propos n'est pas de traiter de l'immigration en général ni des modalités du droit d'asile en particulier, ni de l'extradition. Il est de faire prendre conscience des nombreux et immenses problèmes que pose cette délicate question de la présence – de plus en plus nombreuse, dans une grande quantité de pays, de personnes de nationalité étrangère qui, sans rompre totalement avec leur pays d'origine par une demande de naturalisation dans leur pays d'accueil, veulent y faire leur vie ou y rester un temps important. Doit-on les considérer comme des « ressortissants » à part, dotés d'un statut spécifique ou – au bout d'un certain temps (et lequel ?) les faire participer à la vie politique d'un pays dont ils partagent depuis longtemps la vie quotidienne ? Mais à toutes les élections ?

II. – Nombreux sont les pays qui, encore aujourd'hui, ne veulent point entendre parler d'une reconnaissance quelconque, à toute élection, d'un droit de vote à des personnes qui n'ont pas la nationalité du pays dans lequel elles souhaiteraient voter puisqu'elles y résident. Ici droit de vote et citoyenneté se rejoignent. On ne jouit pas du premier sans posséder la seconde. Si les étrangers veulent voter, qu'ils acquièrent la nationalité du pays qu'ils ont choisi pour y vivre. C'est une position logique. Mais répond-t-elle au vœu profond des intéressés ?

On connaît en général dans chaque pays le pourcentage des étrangers par rapport à la population globale. Mais a-t-on fait des sondages sérieux sur le nombre exact des étrangers qui désirent vraiment voter dans le pays où ils résident mais dont ils ne sont pas les nationaux ? Nous retrouverons ce problème plus loin.

Aussi la question du vote des étrangers semble se centrer sur les seules élections locales dans les pays où il s'agit d'une préoccupation récurrente. Et encore plus particulièrement sur les étrangers dont, dans un pays, le nombre est significatif.

Mais la question du nombre peut justifier des raisonnements et des conséquences contradictoires. Si leur nombre est faible, pourquoi nourrir une inquiétude quelconque et ne pas leur accorder le droit de voter dans la région où ils habitent, où ils travaillent, où ils ont mis leurs enfants à l'école ? L'influence de leur bulletin de vote sera négligeable, mais peut-être leur satisfaction grande. Pourquoi, de plus, continuer à nourrir un débat aussi passionné ? Mais si, précisément, l'influence de leur vote est négligeable, quel intérêt trouveraient-ils à demander à l'exercer ?

En revanche, si leur nombre est important, notamment dans les circonscriptions où ils sont regroupés, et où ils peuvent avoir une influence dans les résultats du scrutin, l'État concerné peut vouloir éviter – pour ménager les craintes de son opinion publique – une trop grande pression d'une minorité étrangère.

De là, la division qui s'opère un peu partout entre les élections locales et les élections nationales se comprend aisément. Les premières ne servent qu'à choisir les personnes destinées à gérer les affaires locales, donc les plus proches des gens et de leurs conditions matérielles d'existence. Les secondes consistent à désigner des gouvernants qui décideront, au niveau national, de la politique générale du pays. On peut aisément comprendre que la participation des étrangers aux élections locales soit assez naturelle dès lors qu'ils sont intéressés – ni plus ni moins que les nationaux – à la bonne tenue de la cité où ils vivent. Il est en revanche plus difficile d'admettre que des individus qui n'ont ni notre passé, ni notre culture, ni souvent l'usage courant de notre langue et que ne relient au pays dans lequel ils veulent voter que le fait qu'ils y résident depuis plus ou moins longtemps puissent, par leur vote à des élections nationales, influer sur la politique globale du pays d'accueil. C'est peut-être ici qu'il convient de signaler la différence entre les étrangers et les « intégrés » car c'est au sujet de ces derniers que de nombreux nationaux manifestent un fort sectarisme.

L'étranger – on l'a vu plus haut- est celui qui ne possède pas la nationalité du pays où il réside. Cela permet de le distinguer des nationaux par naissance ou par acquisition, c'est-à-dire par naturalisation, par mariage ou par déclaration à leur majorité. S'agissant des immigrés, le Haut-Conseil français à l'intégration a recommandé il y a quelques années la définition suivante : « Est immigré toute personne née étrangère à l'étranger et venue s'installer en France ». Or l'opinion confond souvent les deux catégories et les ajoutant, s'effraie de constater leur grande importance numérique et l'impact qu'aurait sur la détermination de la politique nationale la masse de leurs bulletins dans les urnes au niveau des élections générales.

Aussi fait-on aujourd'hui de plus en plus la distinction entre les *élections locales* et les *élections nationales* ? Il faudrait évoquer en outre d'autres élections ou consultations : *le référendum, l'élection de Président de la République, les élections européennes.*

Faire la différence entre les uns et les autres pour bien identifier celles qui sont nationales et celles qui sont locales, celles qui influent sur la politique du pays et celles qui n'intéressent que la gestion territoriale.

Si l'élection du Président de la République au suffrage universel est bien, en France, une élection nationale, qu'en est-il dans certains États fédéraux, des référendums dont de nombreux ne sont organisés que par canton (Suisse) ?

À l'évidence, on voit progresser à l'heure actuelle le soutien d'opinions publiques nationales au vote des étrangers. Et 66 pays dans le monde pratiquent aujourd'hui, sous une forme ou sous une autre, le vote des étrangers. Mais pour ceux qui exigent une certaine durée de résidence dans l'État d'accueil, le nombre d'années varie de 3 ou 5 à 10 ou 15.

La France se propose – seulement aujourd'hui – d'envisager l'attribution aux étrangers du droit de vote pour les élections locales mais la question reste encoure ouverte de l'éligibilité à certaines fonctions exécutives locales.

Beaucoup pensent cependant que ceux qui souhaitent exercer les droits politiques dans le pays où ils résident devraient faire preuve, sans équivoque, de leur attachement à ce pays en passant par la procédure de la naturalisation. On devrait également exiger d'eux l'accomplissement du service militaire. Mais dans les pays – la majorité aujourd'hui – où il a été aboli, les convoquerait-on à un « service civil » si du moins il est organisé ?

Certains iront même jusqu'à dénoncer une rupture d'égalité entre étrangers et nationaux au détriment de ces derniers du fait même que – privilège suprême ! – les étrangers pourront exercer leur droit de vote dans deux pays : celui qui les a accueillis et celui d'où ils viennent.

D'aucuns s'inquièteront que, même si on ne leur accorde que le droit de vote à l'occasion d'élections locales, il faudra – dans certains pays – une modification de la constitution. Et après ? Ne l'a-t-on pas déjà en France modifiée une vingtaine de fois ?

On dit aussi que les inspirations des puissances ex-coloniales viennent de leur passé de domination mais l'Allemagne, qui n'a pas cette histoire, est tout aussi fermée que la France sur ce sujet.

On fait enfin de cette question politique, un drapeau de discorde entre la droite et la gauche mais il existe bien d'autres pays où le sujet a été l'objet de calculs politiques évidents et contradictoires et a pourtant abouti.

III – On aura compris que, derrière un sujet qui peut paraître mineur et que l'on grossit sans doute trop se dissimulent des questions juridiquement et politiquement fondamentales. C'est au fond la conception même de la société politique qui se trouve au centre du débat.

Quelle société chaque État veut-il bâtir ? Aucune ne saurait avoir la même réponse. Car celle-ci tient à de nombreux critères que tous ne partagent pas. D'ailleurs a-t-on les mêmes définitions du *peuple* et de la *nation* ?

Si la nation retient comme ciment la nationalité, qui compose exactement le peuple ? Quand on déclare solennellement que le peuple est souverain qui englobe-t-on dans le terme de *peuple* ? Tous ceux qui vivent sur un territoire minutieusement délimité quelle que soit la durée de leur implantation ou ceux là seuls qui bénéficient de la nationalité de l'État qui les régit ou qui sont implantés depuis plusieurs années ?

On peut leur accorder à tous – sans discussion – la jouissance des libertés publiques dont l'égalité doit être totale. Mais de là à les faire participer à la prise des décisions qui intéressent l'ensemble, donc la vie politique du pays ?

On admet pourtant que l'État d'accueil s'il se veut démocratique doit permettre à chacun, citoyen national ou ressortissant, de librement exercer son culte et de respecter ses croyances et traditions (si, bien sûr, elles ne portent pas atteinte à l'ordre public) ; faut-il, pour autant, qu'il aille plus loin et invite tous ceux qui résident sur son territoire à participer à la vie politique par un droit de vote largement entendu ?

C'est précisément à ce point du débat que se situe la gravité du choix.

Veut-on considérer que l'objectif de tout État est d'assimiler les « étrangers » pour en faire – par étapes – des citoyens à part entière ? Ou ne préfère-t-on pas plutôt penser qu'accueillir un étranger ne signifie pas nécessairement son *assimilation* à plus ou moins longue échéance ?

Après tout, pourquoi ne pas admettre que des communautés étrangères puissent vivre paisiblement sur un autre sol que le leur, appartiennent toujours à leur pays de départ et donc participent à la vie politique de ce dernier dont ils restent les nationaux ? Sait-on en effet s'ils resteront toujours dans le pays qui les a accueillis et ne retourneront jamais, un jour, dans le pays où ils sont nés et dont – pour beaucoup – ils ont conservé la citoyenneté ? C'est alors que l'on invoque les dangers du *communautarisme*. Ne pas courir le risque que se constituent au sein d'États unitaires des petites – ou grandes – communautés étrangères refermées sur elles-mêmes et constituant des minorités agissantes, voire agressives, en quelque sorte des États dans l'État ?

Que ces minorités soient quantitativement faibles ou nombreuses, le mythe de l'invasion planera toujours sur certains peuples. Qu'à l'époque de la mondialisation on ferme hermétiquement ses frontières n'apparaît guère envisageable. Mais qu'au moins, on n'admette point dans les centres du pouvoir des gens que l'on ne connaît guère, qui ne parlent point toujours notre langue et dont on se méfie. Le nombre de ces étrangers ne fait rien à l'affaire.

Le Japon, qui commerce dans le monde entier dans les conditions et avec les succès que l'on saut mais qui n'a jamais dans sa longue histoire connu d'occupation étrangère, développe encore de nos jours une instinctive méfiance de l'étranger, de l'autre… Dans les chemins de fer de l'archipel la présence d'un étranger suscite la surprise, l'étonnement. Les enfants vous dévisagent ; leurs parents vous regardent avec curiosité ; les vieillards se demandent ce que vous venez bien faire dans leur pays. Et si – par hasard – vous parlez le japonais, la crainte devient panique. Pourquoi avoir pris la peine d'apprendre une langue fort difficile si ce n'est pour entrer dans l'intimité étroite du pays ? De là à développer le fantasme de l'espionnage… Comment – dans ce climat équivoque qui trouble tous les rapports, du moins dans un premier temps - envisager sans maintes réticences la participation à la vie politique du pays de ces « corps étrangers » qu'il est si difficile de comprendre !

D'autres nations qui se sont historiquement constituées par des apports successifs et cosmopolites de populations venues de toutes les parties du monde, seront plus souvent ouvertes aux mélanges des races et au rapprochement des ethnies. Comment dans ce tissu constitué de morceaux épars et de civilisations sans âge, opérer une discrimination entre les statuts des uns et des autres ? Il y aura un vote noir (chèrement acquis), un vote hispanophone, francophone… Ici les communautarismes ne choquent pas. La richesse américaine se nourrit de cette cohabitation dans le creuset d'une harmonieuse fusion.

De nombreux États qui se préoccupent – eux – de concilier envers et contre tout la traditionnelle souveraineté nationale avec l'idée démocratique et l'autonomie locale adopteront des formules moyennes (France).

On ne permettra aux étrangers que de voter aux élections locales et non aux votations nationales (Argentine) ; les étrangers pourront être élus mais pas à des fonctions exécutives (Grèce). Certaines législations nationales exigent la *réciprocité.* D'autres, voulant rompre le lien entre nationalité et droit de vote, ouvriront le vote aux étrangers qui résident un certain temps dans le pays (inscrits, par exemple, depuis 3 ans, comme habitant le pays et domiciliés dans la commune où ils votent).

Certains statuts privilégiés seront accordés par les législations nationales pour renforcer une communauté géographique. Ainsi les « Nordiques » pourront voter dans un autre pays nordique que le leur s'ils y sont domiciliés à une date fixée.

En Europe, les ressortissants européens pourront facilement voter dans un des pays de la communauté quelqu'il soit, notamment pour l'élection au Parlement européen.

Les affinités historiques ou culturelles joueront également pour faciliter les votes. Par exemple dans la zone hispanophone (Espagne, Amérique latine). On notera la particularité de certains États fédéraux. En Suisse, par exemple, rien n'empêche les cantons d'être plus généreux que l'État fédéral. Dans la mesure où des cantons accordent le droit de vote des étranger à leur niveau, ceux-ci peuvent participer à l'élection d'une des Chambres du Parlement fédéral (le Conseil des États). Le droit fédéral ne s'y oppose pas.

On terminera par une interrogation qui laisse encore l'observateur perplexe.

Ce vote qui nous pose à tous d'innombrables problèmes, les étrangers le demandent-ils vraiment ?

On n'a guère d'informations précises dans les pays où il est déjà organisé. Sinon quelques constatations d'ordre général. Les étrangers ne votent guère partout en masse (3,7% sur l'ensemble de la Norvège !). Et l'exercice de leur droit varie avec la durée du séjour dans le pays, l'âge et le niveau de revenu et de formation… Curieusement, leur abstentionnisme s'explique par leur participation, plus active, à la vie politique de leur propre pays.

À cet égard, il faut se féliciter que d'une manière générale, ces élections concernant le pays d'origine soient organisées convenablement dans le pays d'accueil. Ces élections doivent évidemment se dérouler conformément au droit du territoire mais les modes de scrutin et les procédures du vote appartiennent au pays d'origine.

Un dernier point : les étrangers présentent-ils des listes « à eux », composées uniquement de leurs candidats ? En général, les étrangers se répartissent dans les listes communes. Dans un État comme la France où l'opinion admet, dans sa majorité, que les étrangers – réguliers – puissent voter aux seules élections locales (qui ne touchent point à la souveraineté nationale) il serait, à notre avis, fort dangereux que se généralise un jour la constitution de « listes d'étrangers » qui serait contraire à notre tradition d'une France républicaine et indivisible.

Professeur Jacques ROBERT
Président honoraire de l'Université Panthéon-Assas
Ancien membre du Conseil constitutionnel

Annexe 1: Liste des rapports nationaux

Allemagne: Prof. Dr. Lothar Michael, Professur für öffentliches Recht Düsseldorf

Argentine: Alberto Dalla Via, Buenos Aires

Danemark: Professor Eva Ersboll, The Danish Institute for Human Rights

Espagne: Amelia Pascual Medrano, Prof. Titular Derecho constitucional, Universidad de La Rioja

Grèce: Ms. Theodora Antoniou, Assistant Professor, Faculty of Law, University of Athens

Hongrie: Halász Iván, Senior research fellow (MTA-JTI), Budapest

Japon: Mr. Atsushi Kondo, Professor, Meijo University, Faculty of Law Nagoya

Norvège: Dr. juris Eivind Smith, Department of Public and International Law, Oslo

Portugal: Vital Martins Moreira, Coimbra

Royaume-Uni: Dr Paul James Cardwell, School of Law, University of Sheffield

Slovénie: Prof. Dr. Bojan Bugarič, Faculty of Law, University of Ljubljana
Suisse: Thierry Tanquerel, Professeur à l'Université de Genève
Taiwan: Chao-Chun Frederick Lin, National Taipei University Department of Law
Uruguay: Dr. Ruben Correa Freitas, LLD Professor of Constitutional Law

Annexe 2: Questionnaire

1. *Définition*
   (a) Qu'est-ce – d'après vous – qu'un « étranger » ?
   (b) Quel droit s'applique à lui ? Celui de son pays d'origine ou celui de son pays d'accueil ?
2. *Principes*
   (a) Dès lors qu'il n'a pas la nationalité du pays dans lequel il vit, peut-il participer à une élection quelle qu'elle soit ? L'accès aux urnes doit-il être réservé aux seuls citoyens ?
   (b) Une certaine présence dans le pays – et de quelle durée ?- vous parait-elle nécessaire pour l'admettre à voter ?
   (c) Peut-on faire des distinctions parmi les élections entre celles qui concernent la vie locale et celles qui, au niveau national, peuvent influer sur l'expression de la souveraineté nationale ?
   (d) Un étranger en situation irrégulière depuis plus de 10 ans et qui, malgré tout, installé dans le pays d'accueil, y vit et y travaille avec sa famille peut-il être éloigné délibérément de tout bureau de vote ? Ne doit-on pas régulariser son cas ?
   (e) Peut-on opérer une différence entre les étrangers selon le pays d'où ils viennent ? Peut-on, sans risquer de tomber sous le coup de discriminations interdites, permettre le vote à certains étrangers et pas à d'autres ?
   (f) Certaines grandes puissances ont eu jadis ce que l'on appelait un « Empire colonial » et se sont nécessairement créées entre elles et lui des affinités qui n'ont point disparu. Chaque État est-il habilité à organiser des traitements électoraux différents selon que l'on appartient ou non à ces zones naguère sous son contrôle ?
3. *Procédure*
   (a) Combien y a-t-il d'étrangers vivant dans votre pays ? Combien ont acquis votre nationalité ?
   (b) Leur participation à certains votes, si elle se trouve autorisée, est-elle massive ? Ou l'abstentionnisme apparaît-il inquiétant ? Et pourquoi ?
   (c) Y a-t-il des listes de candidats composées entièrement d'étrangers ?
   (d) Votre législation recommande-t-elle, ou non, la présence d'étrangers sur les listes de candidats ?
   (e) Les étrangers, non nationaux, qui ne sont pas autorisés à voter dans leur pays d'accueil votent-ils sur place pour les élections qui se déroulent dans leur propre pays ? Dans leurs consulats ? Par correspondance ou par procuration ?
   (f) Peuvent-ils mener, dans leur pays de résidence, des campagnes électorales publiques concernant les élections qui se déroulent dans leur pays d'origine ?
   (g) Peut-on exercer une fonction exécutive locale (maire, président de conseil général ou régional) et être étranger ?
   (h) L'existence, dans votre pays, de communautés étrangères importantes, ne pousse-t-elle pas au « communautarisme »? Quel est votre sentiment ?

Constitutional Courts as Positive Legislators[1]

23

Allan R. Brewer-Carías

23.1 Preliminary Remarks

23.1.1 The Subordination of Constitutional Courts to the Constitution

In all democratic countries, Constitutional Courts[2] have the same role of interpreting and applying the Constitution in order to preserve its supremacy testing the constitutionality or conventionality of statutes,[3] and in order to assure the prevalence of the democratic principle and of fundamental rights they even have the role of adapting the Constitution when changes and time imposes such task.

And this is true in all systems of constitutional judicial review, where a progressive convergence of principles and solutions has been consolidated over the past decades,[4] being nowadays very difficult even to draw in a clear way the classical distinction between the concentrated and the diffuse systems of judicial review[5] so commonly used during many decades.[6]

---

[1] IV.B.2, Les cours constitutionnelles en tant que législateurs positifs. The text of this Report has been published in: Allan R. Brewer-Carías, *Constitutional Courts as Positive Legislators*, Cambridge University Press, 2011, pp. 889–923.

[2] For the purpose of the *General Report*, due to the variety of solutions, I have used the expression "constitutional court" in a general sense, as referring to any court acting as constitutional judge.

[3] For the purpose of the *General Report*, I have used the expression "control of constitutionality" as comprising not only judicial review of statutes regarding their conformity with the Constitution, but also comprising "control of conventionality" in the sense of their conformity with International Conventions, particularly on matters of Human Rights, as is the case, for instance, in The Netherlands, in the U.K., in France and in many Latin American countries; as well as their conformity with "Constitutional Conventions," called by John Bell, the *British National Reporter*, as "constitutional review." See in general Ernesto Rey Cantor, *El control de convencionalidad de las leyes y derechos humanos* (Mexico: Ed. Porrúa, 2008); Juan Carlos Hitters, "Control de constitucionalidad y control de convencionalidad. Comparación (Criterios fijados por la Corte Interamericana de Derechos Humanos)," in *Estudios Constitucionales*, Año 7, no. 2 (Santiago de Chile, 2009), 109–28.

[4] See Lucio Pegoraro, "Clasificaciones y modelos de justicia constitucional en la dinámica de los ordenamientos," in *Revista Iberoamericana de Derecho Procesal Constitucional*, no. 2 (Mexico: Instituto Iberoamericano de Derecho Procesal Constitucional, Editorial Porrúa, 2004) 131 ff.; Alfonse Celotto, "La justicia constitucional en el mundo: formas y modalidades," in *Revista Iberoamericana de Derecho Procesal Constitucional,* no. 1 (Mexico: Instituto Iberoamericano de Derecho Procesal Constitucional, Editorial Porrúa, 2004), 3 ff.

[5] See for example, Francisco Fernández Segado, "La justicia constitucional ante el siglo XXI," in *La progresiva convergencia de los sistemas americano y europeo-kelseniano* (Bologna: Librería Bonomo Editrice, 2003), 40 ff.; Francisco Fernández Segado, "La obsolecencia de la bipolaridad 'modelo Americano-modelo europeo-kelseniano' como criterio analítico del control de constitucionalidad y la búsqueda de una nueva tipología explicativa," in his book *La Justicia Constitucional: Una visión de derecho comparado* ed. I. Tomo (Madrid: Dykinson, 2009), 129–220; Guillaume Tusseau, *Contre les "modèles" de justice constitutionnelle: essai de critique métodologique* (Bononia University Press, Edition bilingue: français-italien, 2009); Guillaume Tusseau, "Regard critique sur les outils méthodologique du comparatisme. L'example des modèles de justice constitutionnelle," in *IUSTEL, Revista General de Derecho Público Comparado,* no. 4(Madrid: enero 2009), 1–34.

[6] See Mauro Cappelletti, *Judicial Review in Contemporary World* (Indianapolis: Bobbs-Merrill, 1971), 45; Mauro Cappellettiy and J.C. Adams, "Judicial Review of Legislation: European

A.R. Brewer-Carías (✉)
Central University of Venezuela, Caracas, Venezuela
e-mail: allan@brewercarias.com

K.B. Brown and D.V. Snyder (eds.), *General Reports of the XVIIIth Congress of the International Academy of Comparative Law/Rapports Généraux du XVIIIème Congrès de l'Académie Internationale de Droit Comparé*,
DOI 10.1007/978-94-007-2354-2_23,

In all the systems, the basic principle that can be identified is that Constitutional Courts, when accomplishing their roles, must always be subordinated to the Constitution, not being allowed to invade the field of the legislator or of the constituent power, The contrary would be, as asserted by Sandra Morelli the *Colombian National Reporter*, to develop an "irresponsible judicial totalitarianism,"[7] which of course is a chapter of the pathology of judicial review.

That is to say, Constitutional Courts can assist the legislators in the accomplishment of their functions, but they cannot substitute the Legislators and enact legislation, nor they have any discretionary political basis in order to create legal norms or provisions that could not be deducted from the Constitution itself.

It is in this sense that it is then possible to affirm as a general principle, that Constitutional Courts, still are considered to be – as Hans Kelsen used to say – "Negative Legislators"[8] or that they are not "Positive Legislators" in the sense that, as affirmed by Richard Kay and Laurence Claus, *the American National Reporters*, they are not able to consider, propound or create *ex novo* pieces of legislation "of their own conception," or to introduce "reforms" on statutes conceived by other legislative actors.[9]

23.1.2 New Role of Constitutional Courts and the Question of Acting as Positive Legislators

This continues to be the general principle in comparative law, notwithstanding the fact that during the past decades the role of Constitutional courts has dramatically changed, due to the fact that their role is not limited to declare the unconstitutionality of statutes or to annul or not to annul a statute on the grounds of its unconstitutionality.

In all systems, new approaches have been developed, for instance, based on the principle of conservation of statutes, due to their presumption of constitutionality, empowering Constitutional Courts not to annul or declared them unconstitutional (even though being contrary to the Constitution), but to interpret them according to the Constitution or in harmony with the Constitution. This has allowed the Courts to avoid creating any legislative vacuum, and in some cases, to fill permanently or temporarily the vacuums that could be originated by the nullity.

In addition, nowadays is more frequent to see Constitutional Courts, instead of dealing with existing statutes, to deal with the absence of statutes or with absolute or relative omissions or abstention incurred by the Legislator. By controlling these omissions, Constitutional Courts in many cases have assume the role of legislative assistant or auxiliaries, creating

Antecedents and Adaptations", Harvard Law Review 79(6, April 1966):, 1207; Mauro Cappelletti, "El control judicial de la constitucionalidad de las leyes en el derecho comparado," in *Revista de la Facultad de Derecho de México*, no. 61, 1966, 28; Allan R. Brewer-Carías, *Judicial Review in Comparative Law* (Cambridge: Cambridge University Press, 1989); Allan R. Brewer-Carías, *Étutes de droit pubic comparé* (Bruxelles: Bruilant, 2000), 653 ff. Regarding the distinction, it can be said that the only aspect of it that nowadays remains is the one referred to the organ of control, in the sense that in the diffuse system of judicial review all courts are constitutional judges without the need for their powers to be expressly established in the Constitution; whether that in the concentrated system, it is the Constitution the one that must expressly establish the Constitutional Jurisdiction, assigning to a single Constitutional Court, Constitutional Tribunal or Constitutional Council, or to the existing Supreme or High Court or Tribunal of Justice, the power to control the constitutionality of statutes and to annul them.

[7] See Sandra Morelli, *La Corte Constitucional: un papel por definir* (Bruxelles: Academia Colombiana de Jurisprudencia, 2002); and "*The Colombian Constitutional Court: From Institutional Leadership, to Conceptual Audacity,*" Colombian National Report, XVIII International Congress of Comparative Law, Washington, July, 2010, 3. See also, Allan R. Brewer-Carías, "*Quis Custodiet Ipsos Custodes*: De la interpretación constitucional a la inconstitucionalidad de la interpretación," in *VIII Congreso Nacional de derecho Constitucional, Perú*, Fondo Editorial 2005, Colegio de Abogados de Arequipa,Arequipa, Septiembre 2005, 463–89, and in *Revista de Derecho Público*, no. 105 (Caracas: Editorial Jurídica Venezolana, 2006), 7–27; *Crónica sobre la "In" Justicia Constitucional. La Sala Constitucional y el autoritarismo en Venezuela* (Caracas: Editorial Jurídica Venezolana, 2007); and *Reforma Constitucional y Fraude a la Constitución* (Caracas: Academia de Ciencias Políticas y Sociales, 2009).

[8] See Hans. Kelsen, "La garantie juridictionnelle de la constitution (La Justice constitutionnelle)," in *Revue du droit public et de la science politique en France et a l'ètranger* (Paris: Librairie Général de Droit et the Jurisprudence, 1928), 197–257; Hans Kelsen, *La garantía jurisdiccional de la Constitución (La justicia constitucional)* (Mexico: Universidad Nacional Autónoma de México, 2001).

[9] See Laurence Claus and Richard S. Kay, "*Constitutional Courts as 'Positive Legislators' in the United States,*" U.S. National Report, XVIII International Congress of Comparative Law Washington, July 2010, 3, 5.

norms they normally deduct from the Constitution; and even, in some cases, substituting the Legislator, by assuming an open role of "Positive Legislators," issuing temporary or provisional rules to be applied on specific matters pending the enactment of legislation.

One of the main tools to trigger this new role of Constitutional Courts, has been the principles of progressiveness and of the prevalence of human rights,[10] as has occurred in many cases with the rediscovery of the right to equality and non discrimination. In these cases, in the interest of the protection of citizens' rights and guaranties, there have been no doubts in accepting the legitimacy of Constitutional Courts' activism interfering with the Legislative functions, applying constitutional principles and values.

In these matters, the main discussion today is directed, not to reject these legislative activities by the courts, but to determine the extent and limits of Constitutional Courts decisions, and the degree of interference allowed regarding Legislative functions, as expressed by Francisco Fernandez Segado, the *Spanish National Reporter*, in order to avoid "transforming the guardian of the Constitution into sovereign."[11]

My analysis of this topic in comparative law,[12] has allowed me to identify four main trends regarding the relations of the Constitutional Courts not only with the Legislator, but also with the "Constitutional Legislator," that can be considered as expressions of their activities acting as been positive legislators. These are:

First, the role of Constitutional Courts interfering with the Constituent Power, enacting constitutional rules and even mutating the Constitution;

Second, the role of Constitutional Courts interfering with existing legislation, assuming the task of being assistants to the Legislator, complementing statutes, adding to them new provisions, and also determining the temporal effects of legislation;

Third, the role of Constitutional Courts interfering with the absence of Legislation due to absolute and relative legislative omissions, acting in some cases as Provisional Legislators; and

Fourth, the role of Constitutional Courts as Legislators on matters of judicial review.

23.2 First Trend: Constitutional Courts Interfering with the Constituent Power

The first trend that comparative law shows us is the role of Constitutional Courts, interfering with the "Constitutional Legislator", that is with the Constituent Power, in some cases enacting constitutional rules, for instance, when resolving constitutional disputes between State organs; when exercising constitutional control over constitutional provisions or over constitutional amendments; and when mutating in a legitimate way the Constitutions by means of adapting their provisions to current times, giving them concrete meaning.

23.2.1 Constitutional Courts Resolving Constitutional Federal Disputes and Enacting Constitutional Rules

The first case refers to the Constitutional Courts interfering with the Constituent power, when they resolve constitutional conflicts or disputes between State organs, which is a common role in Federal States, as has been highlighted by Konrad Lachmayer, the *Austrian National Reporter*, referring to the Austrian Constitutional Court, saying that it has acted as a "positive legislator," "enacting constitutional law" when exercising positive powers regarding the division of competences between the Federation and the "*Länder*," having the final say

[10] See Pedro Nikken, *La protección internacional de los derechos humanos: su desarrollo progresivo* (Madrid: Instituto Interamericano de Derechos Humanos, Ed. Civitas, 1987); Mónica Pinto, "El principio *pro homine*. Criterio hermenéutico y pautas para la regulación de los derechos humanos," in *La aplicación de los tratados sobre derechos Humanos por los tribunales locales* (Buenos Aires: Centro de Estudios Legales y Sociales, 1997), 163.

[11] See Francisco Fernández Segado, "Algunas reflexiones generales en torno a los efectos de las sentencias de inconstitucionalidad y a la relatividad de ciertas fórmulas esterotipadas vinculadas a ellas," in *Anuario Iberoamericano de Justicia Constitucional*, no. 12 (Madrid: Centro de Estudios Políticos y Constitucionales, 2008), 161.

[12] For the preparation of the *General Report* I received 36 **National Reports** from 31 counties: 19 from Europe (including 6 from Eastern Europe), 10 from the American Continent (3 from North America, 5 from South America, and 2 from Central America); 1 from Asia, and 1 from Australia. The **National Reports** are listed in the *Appendix* of this article.

on the matter.[13] It has also been the case in the United States, where the Supreme Court has been progressively determining the powers of the federal government regarding the states, based on "commerce clause," being difficult nowadays to imagine anything that Congress could not regulate.[14] By means of these case law on matters related to the federal State, the Supreme Court's decisions, without doubt, eventually have enacted constitutional rules; although in some cases, they have distorted the constitutional frame of power distribution, as has been the case in Venezuela.[15]

23.2.2 Constitutional Courts Exercising Judicial Review on Constitutional Provisions

The second way in which Constitutional Courts can participate in the enactment of constitutional rules is when they are empowered to review the Constitution itself, as is also the case in Austria, where the Constitutional Court is empowered to confront the Constitution with its own basic principles, like the principle of democracy, the federal state, the *Rechtsstaat*, separation of powers and the general system of human rights.[16]

23.2.3 Constitutional Courts Exercising Judicial Review Constitutional Reforms and Amendments

The third way Constitutional Courts interfere with the Constituent Power, is when they are empowered to review constitutional amendments, as is the case of Colombia, Ecuador and Bolivia, although limited to its procedural aspects.[17]

In other countries, discussions have been developed regarding the powers of Constitutional Courts to exercise judicial review powers on the merits of constitutional reforms or amendments, for instance, regarding the unchangeable constitutional clauses (*cláusulas pétreas*) expressly defined in the Constitutions. The basic principle here is that in such cases, the courts' powers derive from the supremacy of those constitutional clauses. In such cases, in order not to confront the will of the people and not to substitute the constituent power, the control must be exercised before the reform has been enacted through popular vote, when this is the case.[18]

Nonetheless, even in the absence of constitutional authorization, there are cases in which Constitutional Courts have exercise judicial review regarding constitutional amendments. It was the case, a few months ago, in Colombia where the Constitutional Court (February 26, 2010) annulled a Law convening a referendum for the purpose of approving a reform of an article of the Constitution directed to allow the reelection for a third period of the President of the Republic, by considering that such reform contained "substantial violations of the democratic principle," introducing

[13] See Konrad Lachmayer, "*Constitutional Courts as 'Positive Legislators,'*" Austrian National Report, XVIII International Congress of Comparative Law, Washington, July, 2010, 1–2.

[14] See Erwin Chemerinsky, *Constitutional Law. Principles and Policies* (New York: Aspen Publishers, 2006), 259–60.

[15] Decision of the Constitutional Chamber no. 565 of April 15, 2008, Case: Procurador General de la República, *Interpretación del artículo 164.10 de la Constitución de 1999*, available at http://www.tsj.gov.ve/decisio-nes/scon/Abril/565-150408-07-1108.htm. See the comments in Allan R. Brewer-Carías, "La ilegitima mutación de la Constitución y la legitimidad de la jurisdicción constitucional: la "reforma" de la forma federal del Estado en Venezuela mediante interpretación constitucional," in *Memoria del X Congreso Iberoamericano de Derecho Constitucional,* tomo. 1 (Lima: Instituto Iberoamericano de Derecho Constitucional, Asociación Peruana de Derecho Constitucional, Instituto de Investigaciones Jurídicas-UNAM and Maestría en Derecho Constitucional-PUCP, IDEMSA, 2009), 29–51.

[16] Decision of the Constitutional Court, VfSlg 16.327/2001. See in Konrad Lachmayer, "*Constitutional Courts as 'Positive Legislators,'*" Austrian National Report, XVIII International Congress of Comparative Law, Washington, July, 2010, 6 (footnote 20).

[17] See the references in Allan R. Brewer-Carías, *Reforma Constitucional y Fraude a la Constitución. Venezuela 1999–2009* (Caracas: Academia de Ciencias Políticas y Sociales, 2009), 78 ff.

[18] See Allan R. Brewer-Carías, *Reforma Constitucional y Fraude a la Constitución. Venezuela 1999–2009* (Caracas: Academia de Ciencias Políticas y Sociales, 2009), 78 ff.; and "La reforma constitucional en América Latina y el control de constitucionalidad," in *Reforma de la Constitución y control de constitucionalidad. Congreso Internacional, Pontificia Universidad Javeriana, Bogotá Colombia, junio 14 al 17 de 2005* (Bogotá: Pontificia Universidad Javeriana, Facultad de Ciencias Jurídicas, 2005), 108–59.

reforms implying the "substitution or subrogation of the Constitution."[19]

In other cases, like in India, it has been the Supreme Court the one that has imposed "implied" limits on the power of Parliament to amend the Constitution, excluding basic features or basic structure of the Constitution,[20] like for instance, the scope of judicial review powers,[21] the Supreme Court being converted, as said by Surya Deva, in the *Indian National Report*, "as probably the most powerful court in any democracy."[22]

23.2.4 The Role of Constitutional Courts Adapting the Constitution on Matters of Fundamental Rights

The fourth case Constitutional Courts interfering with the Constituent Power, is when they assume the role of adapting constitutional provisions by means of their interpretation, particularly on matters of fundamental rights. In these cases, as said by Laurence Claus and Richard S. Kay, the *U.S. National Reporters*, Constitutional, Courts "engage in positive constitutional lawmaking" particularly when the rule they "formulate, creates 'affirmative' public duties."[23]

This role of Constitutional Courts has been the result of a "discovering" process of fundamental rights not expressly enlisted in the Constitutions, enlarging the scope of its provisions in order to maintain the Constitution "alive."[24] Referring to the U.S. Supreme Court role in the elaboration of constitutional principles and values, as mentioned by Laurence Claus and Richard S. Kay, "provides perhaps the most salient example of positive lawmaking in the course of American constitutional adjudication."[25] It was the case, for instance beginning *Brown v. Board of Education of Topeka*, 347 U.S. 483 (1954), when the Supreme Courts interpreted the "equal protection" clause of the Fourteenth Amendment in order to expound the nature of equality; or when having argued about the constitutional guarantee of "due process" (Amendments V and XIV), or the open clause of Amendment IX, in order to construct the sense of "liberty." This process has converted the Court, they have said, in "the most powerful sitting [constitutional] lawmaker in the nation."[26]

The same has happened in France, where the Constitution does not have at all a declaration of fundamental rights, the role of the Constitutional Council during the past decades has been precisely of mutating the Constitution, enlarging the *bloc de constitutionnalité*, by giving constitutional rank, through the Preamble of the 1958 Constitution, to the Preamble of 1946 Constitution, and eventually to the 1789 Declaration of Rights of Man and Citizens.[27]

This role of Constitutional Courts adapting the Constitution in order to guaranty fundamental rights can be nowadays considered as a main trend in comparative law, which can be identified in many countries with different systems of judicial review, as is the case

[19] The Decision, in September 2010, have not been published. See the Communiqué of the texto f the decision published by the Constitutional Court, no. 9 of February 26, 2010, available at www.corteconstitucional.com. See the comments in Sandra Morelli, "*The Colombian Constitutional Court: From Institutional Leadership, to Conceptual Audacity*," Colombian National Report, XVIII International Congress of Comparative Law, Washington, July, 2010, 13–6.

[20] Case *Kesvananda Bharti v State of Kerala*, Supreme Court of India, in Surya Deva, "*Constitutional Courts as 'Positive Legislators: The Indian Experience,*" Indian National Report, XVIII International Congress of Comparative Law, Washington, July, 2010, 5–6.

[21] Cases *Waman Rao v Union of India* AIR 1981 SC 271; *S P Sampath Kumar v Union of India* AIR 1987 SC 386; and *L Chandra Kumar v Union of India* AIR 1997 SC 1125, in *Idem*, 6 (footnote 41).

[22] *Idem*, 6.

[23] See Laurence Claus and Richard S. Kay, "*Constitutional Courts as 'Positive Legislators' in the United States,*" U.S. National Report, XVIII International Congress of Comparative Law, Washington, July 2010, 6.

[24] See Mauro Cappelletti, "El formidable problema del control judicial y la contribución del análisis comparado," in *Revista de estudios políticos*, 13 (Madrid, 1980), 78; "The Mighty Problem of Judicial Review and the Contribution of Comparative Analysis," *Southern California Law Review* (1980): 409.

[25] See in Laurence Claus and Richard S. Kay, "*Constitutional Courts as 'Positive Legislators' in the United States,*" U.S. National Report, XVIII International Congress of Comparative Law, Washington, July, 2010, 12–13.

[26] *Idem*, 20.

[27] See Louis Favoreu, "Le principe de Constitutionalité. Essai de definition d'apres la jurisprudence du Conseil Constitutionnel", *Recueil d'étude en Hommage a Charles Eisenman*, Paris 1977, 34. See also in comparative law, Francisco Zúñiga Urbina, *Control de Constitucionalidad y sentencia*, no. 34 (Santiago de Chile: Cuadernos del Tribnal Constitucional, 2006), 46–68.

of Switzerland, Germany, Portugal, Austria, Poland, Croatia, Greece, and India, where Constitutional Courts have introduced important changes in the Constitution, expanding the scope of fundamental rights.[28]

23.2.5 The Mutation of the Constitution on Institutional Matters

On the other hand, on matters different to fundamental rights is also possible to find legitimate constitutional mutations made by Constitutional Courts referred to other key constitutional matters related to the organization and functioning of the State. The German Federal Constitutional Tribunal, for instance, in the case *AWACS-Urteil* of July 12, 1994,[29] ruled on the deployment in time of peace, of missions of German Armed Forces to foreign countries, detailing a substitute legislation (provisional measures) ordering the Legislator and the Executive to proceed according to it, imposing the formal participation of the Legislator.

The Constitutional Court of Austria, has even created new constitutional framework to be followed by Parliament in areas not expressly provided in the Constitution, like the privatization process, imposing rules to all State authorities.[30]

The Council of State of Greece has also imposed limits on matters of privatization excluding for instance police powers.[31] The Constitutional Court of the Slovak Republic, has reshaped the constitutional provisions regarding the position and authority of the President of the Republic within the general organization of the State, being the Court considered by Ján Svák and Lucia Bertisová, the *Slovak National Reporters* as "the direct creator of the constitutional system of the Slovak Republic."[32]

Finally, the Supreme Court of Canada, through the very important instrument of the "reference judgments" has created and declared constitutional rules, for instance, governing important constitutional processes as the patriation of Canada's constitution from the United Kingdom (*Patriation Reference,* 1981)[33]; and the possible secession of Quebec from Canada (*Quebec Secession Reference*, 1998),[34] laying down as mentioned by Kent Roach, the *Canadian National Reporter*, some basic rules to guide constitutional change and to advert potential constitutional crises.

In these matters, unfortunately, there are also examples of Constitutional Courts mutating the Constitution but

[28]See Tobias Jaag, "*Constitutional Courts as 'Positive Legislators:' Switzerland,*" Swiss National Report, XVIII International Congress of Comparative Law, Washington, July 2010, 11; I. Härtel, "*Constitutional Courts as Positive Legislators,*" German National Report, XVIII International Congress of Comparative Law, Washington, July 2010, 12; Marek Safjan, , "*The Constitutional Courts as a Positive Legislator,*" Polish National Report, XVIII International Congress of Comparative Law, Washington, July 2010, 9; Sanja Barić and Petar Bačić, "*Constitutional Courts as positive legislators. National Report: Croatia,*" Croatian National Report, XVIII International Congress of Comparative Law, Washington, July 2010, 23 ss; Julia Iliopoulos-Strangas and Stylianos-Ioannis G. Koutna, "*Constitutional Courts as Positive Legislators. Greek National Report,*" XVIII International Congress of Comparative Law, Washington, July 2010, 14; Joaquim de Sousa Ribeiro and Esperança Mealha, "*The Constitutional Courts as a Positive Legislator,*" Portuguese National Report, XVIII International Congress of Comparative Law, Washington, July 2010, 9–10; Surya Deva, "*Constitutional Courts as 'Positive Legislators: The Indian Experience,*" Indian National Report, XVIII International Congress of Comparative Law, Washington, July 2010, 4.

[29]Cases: BVferG, July 12, 1994, BVeffGE 90, 585–603, in Christian Behrendt, *Le judge constitutionnel, un législateur-cadre positif. Un analyse comparative en droit francais, belge et allemande* (Bruxelles: Bruylant, 2006), 352–6.

[30]Cases: "Austro Control" VfSlg 14.473/1996; "Bundeswertpapieraufsicht" (Federal Bond Authority) VfSlg 16.400/2001; "E-Control" VfSlg 16.995/2003; "Zivildienst-GmbH" (Compulsory community service Ltd), VfSlg 17.341/2004, in Konrad Lachmayer, "*Constitutional Courts as 'Positive Legislators'*" Austrian National Report, XVIII International Congress of Comparative Law, Washington, July, 2010, 11 (footnote 31).

[31] Decision of the Council of State no. 1934/1998, *ToS* 1998, 598 (602–3), in Julia Iliopoulos-StrangasyStylianos-Ioannis G. Koutna, "*Constitutional Courts as Positive Legislators,*" Greek National Report, XVIII International Congress of Comparative Law, Washington, July, 2010, 16 (footnote 125).

[32] Decision no. I. ÚS 39/93, in Ján Svák and Lucia Berdisová, "*Constitutional Court of the Slovak Republic as Positive Legislator via Application and Interpretation of the Constitution,*" Slovak National Report, XVIII International Congress of Comparative Law, Washington, July, 2010, 4.

[33] Decision (1981) 1 S.C.R. 753, in Kent Roach, "*Constitutional Courts as Positive Legislators:* Canada Country Report", XVIII International Congress of Comparative Law, Washington, July, 2010, 9.

[34] Decision (1998) 2 S.C.R. 217, in Kent Roach, "*Constitutional Courts as Positive Legislators:* Canada Country Report", XVIII International Congress of Comparative Law, Washington, July, 2010, 9.

with the purpose of destroying the democratic principle, as happened in Venezuela with the Constitutional Chamber implementing a rejected 2007 constitutional reform by mean of constitutional interpretation.[35]

23.3 Second Trend: Constitutional Courts Interfering with the Existing Legislation

The most important and common role of Constitutional Courts is developed regarding existing legislation, not only declaring their unconstitutionality but interpreting statutes in conformity to or in harmony with the Constitution, giving directives or guidelines to the Legislator.

23.3.1 Constitutional Courts Complementing Legislative Functions Interpreting Statutes in Harmony with the Constitution

This role of Constitutional Courts has resulted from the surpassing of the classical binomial: *unconstitutionality/invalidity-nullity* that conformed the initial activity of Constitutional Courts as "Negative Legislators,"[36] having Constitutional Courts, on the contrary, progressively assumed a more active role interpreting the Constitution, and the statutes in order not only to annul or not to apply them when unconstitutional, but to preserve the Legislator actions and the statutes it has enacted, interpreting them in harmony with the Constitution[37]; molding these Constitutional Courts as important constitutional institutions in order to assist and cooperate with the legislator in its legislative functions.

These sort of interpretative decisions have been widely used by the Constitutional Court in Italy, Spain, France and Hungary,[38] where in many cases they have decided not to annul the challenged law, and instead have ruled modifying its meaning by establishing a new content, making the law constitutional as it result from the constitutional interpretation.[39]

In all these cases, the interference of Constitutional Courts with existing legislation has followed two main courses of action: first, complementing legislative functions as provisional Legislators or by adding rules to existing Legislation through interpretative decisions; and second, interfering with the temporal effects of existing legislation.

---

[35] See the comment son some Cases in Allan R. Brewer-Carías, "El juez constitucional al servicio del autoritarismo y la ilegítima mutación de la Constitución: el caso de la Sala Constitucional del Tribunal Supremo de Justicia de Venezuela (1999–2009)," in *Revista de Administración Pública*, no. 180 (Madrid, 2009), 383–418; "El Juez Constitucional vs. La alternabilidad republicana (La reelección continua e indefinida)," in *Revista de Derecho Público*, no. 117 (enero-marzo 209) (Caracas, 2009), 205–11; "La ilegítima mutación de la constitución por el juez constitucional: la inconstitucional ampliación y modificación de su propia competencia en materia de control de constitucionalidad," in *Libro Homenaje a Josefina Calcaño de Temeltas* (Caracas: Fundación de Estudios de Derecho Administrativo (FUNEDA), 2009), 319–62; "La ilegitima mutación de la Constitución y la legitimidad de la jurisdicción constitucional: la "reforma" de la forma federal del Estado en Venezuela mediante interpretación constitucional," in *Memoria del X Congreso Iberoamericano de Derecho Constitucional* (Lima: Instituto Iberoamericano de Derecho Constitucional, Asociación Peruana de Derecho Constitucional, Instituto de Investigaciones Jurídicas-UNAM and Maestría en Derecho Constitucional-PUCP, IDEMSA, 2009), 1: 29–51.

[36] See F. Fernández Segado, *"El Tribunal Constitucional como Legislador Positivo,"* Spanish National Report, XVIII International Congress of Comparative Law, Washington, July, 2010, 8 ff.

[37] Case Ashwander v. TVA, 297 U.S. 288, 346–8 (1936), Supreme Court of the United States (Justice Brandeis). The principle was formulated for the first time in the Case Crowell v. Benson, 285 U.S. 22, 62 (1932). See "Notes. Supreme Court Interpretation of Statutes to avoid constitutional decision," in *Columbia Law Review*, 53, no. 5, New York, May 1953, 633–51.

[38] See Gianpaolo Parodi, *"The Italian Constitutional Court as 'Positive Legislator,'"* Italian National Report, XVIII International Congress of Comparative Law, Washington, July, 2010, 3; Francisco Fernández Segado, *"El Tribunal Constitucional como Legislador Positivo,"* Spanish National Report, XVIII International Congress of Comparative Law, Washington, July, 2010, 34; Bertrand Mathieu, *"Le Conseil constitutionnel 'législateur positif. Ou la question des interventions du juge constitutionnel français dans l'exercise de la fonction legislative,"* French National Report, XVIII International Congress of Comparative Law, Washington, July, 2010, 13; Lóránt Csink, Józef Petrétei and Péter Tilk, *"Constitutional Court as Positive Legislator. Hungarian National Report,"* XVIII International Congress of Comparative Law, Washington, July, 2010, 4.

[39] See Francisco Javier Díaz Revorio, *Las sentencias interpretativas del Tribunal Constitucional* (Valladolid: Lex Nova, 2001), 59 ss; and in José Julio Fernández Rodríguez, *La justicia constitucional europea ante el Siglo XXI* (Madrid: Tecnos, 2007), 129 ff.

23.3.2 Constitutional Courts Complementing the Legislator by "Adding" to the Existent Legislative Provision New Rules When Giving It a New Meaning

Regarding the process of interpreting statutes in harmony with the Constitution, when testing their unconstitutionality, Constitutional Courts, in order to avoid their invalidation, have frequently create new legislative rules, in some occasions altering the meaning of the particular provision, and adding to its wording what is considered to be lacking.

These are the so-called "additive decisions" that have been extensively issued by the Italian Constitutional, as explained by Gianpaolo Parodi, the *Italian National Reporter*, through decisions in which although leaving unaltered the text of the provision that is declared unconstitutional, the Court have "transformed its normative meaning, at times reducing, at others extending the sphere of application, not without introducing a new norm into the legal system," or "creating" new norms.[40] These additive decisions have also been applied for instance in Germany by the Federal Constitutional Court and in Peru by the Constitutional Tribunal.

These additive decision have been regularly applied in cases related to the protection the right to equality and non discrimination, seeking to eliminate the differences established in the law. This is the case in Spain, where the Constitutional Tribunal for instance, has extended to "sons and brothers," the benefit of Social Security pensions granted to "daughters and sisters;"[41] to those living in a marital de facto and stable way, the right of those married[42]; cases in which Francisco Fernandez Segado, the Spanish National Reporter, has said that is possible to consider the Spanish Constitutional Tribunal as a "real positive legislator."[43]

A similar situation can be found in Portugal, where the Constitutional Tribunal, for instance, has extended to the widower, the allowances assigned to the widow[44]; to the de facto unions, rights of married persons; and legal protection given to children of de facto unions, similar to the one given to legitimate children.[45]

In similar way, in South Africa, the Constitutional Court has extended to the same sex partner in a stable condition, some rights assigned to married couples.[46]

In Canada, the Ontario Court of Appeal to strike down a definition of marriage as a union of a man and a woman substituting it with the gender neutral concept of a union between persons, in order to allow same sex marriages. These decisions, as affirmed by the *Canadian National Reporter*, Kent Roach, "amount to judicial amendments or additions to legislation."[47]

A similar solution of additive decisions to enforce the right to equality and non discrimination can also be found in many similar cases in the Netherlands, in Peru, Costa Rica, Argentine, Poland, the Czech Republic and France,[48] where, in a particular case

[40] See Gianpaolo Parodi, "*The Italian Constitutional Court as 'Positive Legislator,'*" Italian National Report, XVIII International Congress of Comparative Law, Washington, July, 2010, 6.

[41] Decision STC 3/1993, January 14, 1993, in Francisco Javier Díaz Revorio, *Las sentencias interpretativas del Tribunal Constitucional* (Valladolid: Lex Nova, 2001), 177, 274; F. Fernández Segado, "*El Tribunal Constitucional como Legislador Positivo,*" Spanish National Report, XVIII International Congress of Comparative Law, Washington, July, 2010, 42.

[42] Decision STC 222/1992, December 11, 1992, in Francisco Javier Díaz Revorio, *Las sentencias interpretativas del Tribunal Constitucional* (Valladolid: Lex Nova, 2001), 181, 182, 275; F. Fernández Segado, "*El Tribunal Constitucional como Legislador Positivo,*" Spanish National Report, XVIII International Congress of Comparative Law, Washington, July, 2010, 41.

[43] See F. Fernández Segado, "*El Tribunal Constitucional como Legislador Positivo",* Spanish National Report, XVIII International Congress of Comparative Law, Washington, July, 2010, 48.

[44] Decision no. 449/87 del Tribunal Constitucional, in Joaquim de Sousa Ribeiro and Esperança Mealha, "*Constitutional Courts as 'Positive Legislators,'*" Portuguese National Report, International Congress of Comparative Law, Washington, July, 2010, 8.

[45] *Idem*, 9.

[46] See in Iván Escobar Fornos, "Las sentencias constitucionales y sus efectos en Nicaragua," in *Anuario Iberoamericano de Justicia Constitucional*, no. 12 (Madrid: Centro de Estudios Políticos y Constitucionales, 2008), 111–2.

[47] See Kent Roach, "*Constitutional Courts as Positive Legislator,*" Canadian National Report, XVIII International Congress of Comparative Law, Washington, Julio 2010, 7.

[48] See por ejemplo, Marek Safjan, "*The Constitutional Courts as a Positive Legislator,*" Polish National Report, XVIII International Congress of Comparative Law, Washington, Julio 2010, 13–4; Lóránt Csink, Józef Petrétei and Péter Tilk, "*Constitutional Court as Positive Legislator. Hungarian National Report,*" Hungarian National Report, XVIII International Congress of Comparative Law, Washington, Julio 2010, 5; Zdenek Kühn, "*Czech Constitutional Court as Positive Legislator,*" Czech National Report, XVIII International Congress of Comparative Law, Washington, Julio 2010, 9; J. Uzman T. Barkhuysen and M.L. van Emmerik, "*The Dutch*

regarding the right to respond on matters of TV Communications, as mentioned by Bertrand Mathieu, the French National Reporter, the Constitutional Council has substituted the will of the legislator.[49]

23.3.3 Constitutional Courts Complementing Legislative Functions by Interfering with the Temporal Effects of Legislation

The second role of Constitutional Courts interfering with existing legislation refers to the power of said Courts to determine the temporal effects of legislation. Decades ago, the matter of the temporal effects of the decisions issued by Constitutional Courts was one of the main aspects of the distinction between the diffuse and the concentrated system of judicial review. Nowadays, this distinctive element has completely disappeared, and a process of convergence can be found between all the systems, so the role of Constitutional Courts on matters of interfering with the temporal effects of legislation is common.

This can be seen, in comparative law, regarding three different situations: in postponing the effects of the Courts decisions; in extending retroactively or prospectively the effects of the Courts decisions and on reviving repealed legislation as a consequence of the constitutional control.

Supreme Court: A Reluctant Positive Legislator?", Dutch National Report, XVIII International Congress of Comparative Law, Washington, Julio 2010, 14; Fernán Altuve Febres, , "*El Juez Constitucional como legislador positivo en el Perú,*" Peruvian National Report, XVIII International Congress of Comparative Law, Washington, Julio 2010, 14–5; Rubén Herández Valle, "*Las Cortes Constituitonales como Legisladores positivos,*" Costa Rican National Report, XVIII International Congress of Comparative Law, Washington, Julio 2010, 38; Alejandra Rodríguez Galán and Alfredo Mauricio Vítolo, "*Constitutional Courts as "Positive Legislators,"* Argentinean National Report," XVIII International Congress of Comparative Law, Washington, Julio 2010, 17.

[49] See in Bertrand Mathieu, "*Le Conseil constitutionnel 'législateur positif. Ou la question des interventions du juge constitutionnel français dans l'exercise de la function legislative,*" French National Report, XVIII International Congress of Comparative Law, Washington, Julio 2010, 16.

23.3.3.1 The Power of the Constitutional Court to Determine in the Future When an Annulled Legislation Will Cease to Have Effects: The Postponement of the Effect of the Courts' Ruling

The first of the cases in which the Constitutional Courts interfere with the legislative function modulating the temporal effects of its decision declaring the unconstitutionality or nullity of a statute, is when the Court establishes a *vacatio sentenciae*, determining when an annulled legislation will cease to have effects in the future by postponing the beginning of the effects of its own decision and extending the application of the invalidated statute. This is the situation in Austria, Greece, Belgium, the Czech Republic, France, Croatia, Brazil, Poland and Peru[50] In Mexico, if it is true that in principle, the Court's decisions have general effects since the date of its publication, the Court can establish another date in order to avoid legislative vacuums, giving time to the Legislator to

[50] See Konrad Lachmayer, "*Constitutional Courts as 'Positive Legislators,'*" Austrian National Report, XVIII International Congress of Comparative Law, Washington, Julio 2010, 7; Julia Iliopoulos-Strangas and Stylianos-Ioannis G. Koutna, "*Constitutional Courts as Positive Legislators. Greek National Report,*" XVIII International Congress of Comparative Law, Washington, Julio 2010, 20; Christian Behrendt, *Le judge constitutionnel, un législateur-cadre positif. Un analyse comparative en droit francais, belge et allemande* (Bruxelles: Bruylant, 2006), 87, 230, 235, 286, 309; P. Popelier, "*L'activité du judge constitutional belge comme législateur,*" Belgium National Report, XVIII International Congress of Comparative Law, Washington, Julio 2010, 4–7; Zdenek Kühn, "*Czech Constitutional Court as Positive Legislator,*" Czech National Report, XVIII International Congress of Comparative Law, Washington, Julio 2010, 12; Sanja Barić and Petar Bačić, "*Constitutional Courts as positive legislators. National Report: Croatia,*" XVIII International Congress of Comparative Law, Washington, Julio 2010, ; Jairo Gilberto Schäfer and Vânia Hack de Almeida, "O controle de constitutionalidade no dereitto brasileiro e a possibilidade de modular os efeitos da decisão de inconstitutionalidade," in *Anuario Iberoamericano de Justicia Constitucional*, no. 12, 2008 (Madrid: Centro de Estudios Políticos y Constitucionales, 2008), 384; Domingo García Belaúnde and Gerardo Eto Cruz, "Efectos de las sentencias constitucionales en el Perú," in *Anuario Iberoamericano de Justicia Constitucional*, no. 12 (Madrid: Centro de Estudios Políticos y Constitucionales, 2008), 283–4.

enact a new legislation in substitution of the annulled one.[51]

The same solution is found in Germany, although without a clear provision and based in the Constitutional Tribunal Law provision that gives it the power to establish the way in which the execution of the decision will take place.[52]

Also, in Italy, although the Constitution establishes in a clear way that when the Constitutional Court declares the unconstitutionality of a statutory provision it ceases in its effects the following day after its publication (Article 136),[53] there are important decisions of the Constitutional Court of deferment of the effects in time of the declaration of unconstitutional provision.[54] The same has happened in Spain and Canada, in the absence of any legal rule on the matter, the Constitutional Courts have assumed the power to postpone the beginning of the effects of its nullity decisions[55]; and also in Argentina, having a diffuse system of judicial review.[56]

23.3.3.2 The Power of the Constitutional Court to Determine Since When an Annulled Legislation Will Have Ceased to Have Had Effects: The Retroactive or Non Retroactive Effects of Its Own Decisions

Another aspect regarding the temporal effects of the Constitutional Courts decisions, refers to their retroactive or non retroactive effects, in which a process of convergence has occurred between all systems of judicial review, where is not possible now to find rigid solutions.

The Possibility of Limiting the Retroactive Ex Tunc Effects Regarding Declarative Decisions

The classic approach to these matters was that as a matter of principle, in a diffuse system of judicial review, the judicial review decisions were considered to be declarative ones, with *ex tunc*, *ab initio* and retroactive effects. This was the traditional principle for instance in the United States, assigning the U.S., the Supreme Court decisions' retroactive effects, particularly in criminal matters.[57] Nonetheless, the principle has been progressively relaxed, due to its possible negative or unjust effects regarding the effects already produced by the unconstitutional statute; so the former "absolute rule," has been abandoned, recognizing its authority to give or to deny retroactive effects to its ruling on constitutional issues. The same solution has been followed in Argentina,[58] and in the Netherlands, regarding the control of "conventionality" of statutes.[59]

The same relaxation of the principle has occurred in countries with a concentrated system of judicial review

[51] See "Tesis jurisprudencial" P./J 11/2001, in SJFG, Tomo XIV, Sept. 2001, 1008, in *Las sentencias de los Tribunales Constitucionales* ed. Héctor Fix Zamudio and Eduardo Ferrer Mac Gregor (México: Porrúa), 69; and in "Las sentencias de los tribunales constitucionales en el ordenamiento mexicano," in *Anuario Iberoamericano de Justicia Constitucional*, no. 12 (Madrid: Centro de Estudios Políticos y Constitucionales, 2008), 247–8.

[52] Case BVferG, May 22, 1963 (Electoral Circuits), in Christian Behrendt, *Le judge constitutionnel, un législateur-cadre positif. Un analyse comparative en droit francais, belge et allemande* (Bruxelles: Bruylant, 2006), 299–300. Case BVferG, November 7, 2006 (Impuesto sucesoral), in I. Härtel, "*Constitutional Courts as Positive Legislators,*" German National Report, International Congress of Comparative Law, Washington, July, 2010, 7.

[53] The non approved constitutional reform draft seek to authorize the Constitutional Tribunal to postpone up to one year the effects of its nullity decisions. See Francisco Javier Díaz Revorio, *Las sentencias interpretativas del Tribunal Constitucional* (Valladolid: Lex Nova, 2001), 125 (footnote 166).

[54] Decision nos. 370/2003; 13 and 423/2004 (on matter of education), in Gianpaolo Parodi, "*The Italian Constitutional Court as 'Positive Legislator,*'" Italian National Report, XVIII International Congress of Comparative Law, Washington, Julio 2010, 13.

[55] Case *Manitoba Language Reference* [1985] 1 S.C.R. 721, in Kent Roach, "*Constitutional Courts as Positive Legislator,*" Canadian National Report, XVIII International Congress of Comparative Law, Washington Julio 2010, 7 (footnote 8).

[56] Case *Rosza*, *Jurisprudencia Argentina*, 2007-III-414, in Néstor P. Sagües, "Los efectos de las sentencias constitucionales en el derecho argentino," in *Anuario Iberoamericano de Justicia Constitucional*, no. 12 (Madrid: Centro de Estudios Políticos y Constitucionales, 2008), 352.

[57] Case *Norton v. Selby County*, 118 US 425 (1886), 442. See the critic to this decision in J.A.C. Grant, "The Legal Effect of a Ruling that a Statute is Unconstitutional," in *Detroit College of Law Review* (1978), 2: 207.

[58] Case Itzcovich, *Jurispudencia Argentina* 2005-II-723, in Néstor P. Sagües, "Los efectos de las sentencias constitucionales en el derecho argentino," in *Anuario Iberoamericano de Justicia Constitucional*, no. 12 (Madrid: Centro de Estudios Políticos y Constitucionales, 2008), 351.

[59] Case *Boon v. Van Loon* de 27 de noviembre de 1981, *NJ* 1982/503, in J. Uzman T. Barkhuysen and M.L. van Emmerik, "*The Dutch Supreme Court: A Reluctant Positive Legislator?*" *Dutch National Report*, XVIII International Congress of Comparative Law, Washington Julio 2010, 42 (footnote 138).

where the same retroactive principle was adopted for decisions annulling statutes. It is the case of Germany, where although being the declarative effects of the Federal Constitutional Tribunal the applicable rule, in practice is uncommon to find decisions annulling statutes with purely *ex tunc* effects.[60] In Poland, and Brazil, the Constitutional Courts are authorizes to restrict the retroactive effects of their decisions and to give them *ex nunc, pro futuro* decisions.[61]

The Possibility of Giving Retroactive Effects to Ex Nunc Constitutive Decisions

On the other hand, in countries with concentrated systems of judicial review, although the initial principle following Kelsen's thoughts adopted in the 1920 Austrian Constitution was the constitutive effects of the Constitutional Courts decision annulling a statute, having in principle *ex-nunc, pro futuro* or prospective effects,[62] such principle has also been mitigated particularly in criminal cases, accepting the retroactive effects of the annulment decision. This general trend is today the common principle applied for instance in Spain, Peru, France, Croatia, Serbia, the Slovak Republic, Mexico and Bolivia.[63] In other countries like Venezuela, Brazil, Colombia and Costa Rica, the principle is that Constitutional Court is authorized to determine the temporal effects on its judicial review decisions, which according to the case, can have or not retroactive effects.[64]

23.3.4 The Power of Constitutional Courts to Revive Repealed Legislation

Finally, although as a matter of principle, also according to Hans Kelsen 1928 writings,[65] judicial review decisions declaring the nullity of a statutory provision adopted by a Constitutional Court, does not imply the revival of the former legislation that the annulled statute had repeal, the contrary principle has been the one adopted in Austria, and is the one applied in

[60] See Francisco Fernández Segado, "*El Tribunal Constitucional como Legislador Positivo,* Spanish National Report," XVIII International Congress of Comparative Law, Washington, July, 2010, 8, 14.

[61] See for instance, Marek Safjan, "*The Constitutional Courts as a Positive Legislator,*" Polish National Report, XVIII International Congress of Comparative Law, Washington, July, 2010, 5; Maria Fernanda Palma, "O Legislador negativo e o interprete da Constitucão," in *Anuario Iberoamericano de Justicia Constitucional*, no. 12 (Madrid: Centro de Estudios Políticos y Constitucionales, 2008), 174, 329; Francisco Fernández Segado, "Algunas reflexiones generales en torno a los efectos de las sentencias de inconstitucionalidad y a la relatividad de ciertas fórmulas esterotipadas vinculadas a ellas," in *Anuario Iberoamericano de Justicia Constitucional*, no. 12 (Madrid: Centro de Estudios Políticos y Constitucionales, 2008), 174; Iván Escovar Fornos, *Estudios Jurídicos*, ed. Tomo I (Managua: Hispamer, 2007), 493; Joaquim de Sousa Ribeiro and Esperança Mealha, "*Constitutional Courts as "Positive Legislators*," Portuguese National Report," XVIII International Congress of Comparative Law, Washington, July, 2010, 6; Thomas Bustamante and Evanlida de Godoi Bustamante, "*Constitutional Courts as "Negative Legislators:" The Brazilian Case,*" Brazil National Report, XVIII International Congress of Comparative Law, Washington, July, 2010, 26.

[62] See Konrad Lachemayer, "*Constitutional Courts as 'Positive Legislators,'*" *Austrian National Report*, XVIII International Congress of Comparative Law, Washington, July, 2010, 7–8.

[63] See for instance, Francisco Javier Díaz Revorio, Las *sentencias interpretativas del Tribunal Constitucional* (Valladolid: Ed. Lex Nova, 2001), 104–05; 126–27; Francisco Fernández Segado, "Algunas reflexiones generales en torno a los efectos de las sentencias de inconstitucionalidad y a la relatividad de ciertas fórmulas esterotipadas vinculadas a ellas," in *Anuario Iberoamericano de Justicia Constitucional*, no. 12 (Madrid: Centro de Estudios Políticos y Constitucionales, 2008), 192–94; Domingo García Belaúnde and Gerardo Eto Cruz, "Efectos de las sentencias constitucionales en el Perú," in *Anuario Iberoamericano de Justicia Constitucional*, no. 12 (Madrid: Centro de Estudios Políticos y Constitucionales, 2008), 281–2.

[64] See for instance, Allan R. Brewer-Carías, "Algunas consideraciones sobre el control jurisdiccional de la constitucionalidad de los actos estatales en el derecho venezolano," in *Revista de Administración Pública*, no. 76 (Madrid, 1975), 419–46; and in *Justicia Constitucional. Procesos y Procedimientos Constitucionales* (Mexico: Universidad Nacional Autónoma de México, 2007), 343 ff.; Jairo Gilberto Schäfer and Vânia Hack de Almeida, "O controle de constitucionalidade no dereito brasileiro e a possibilitade de modular os effeitos de decisão de inconstitucionalidade," in *Anuario Iberoamericano de Justicia Constitucional*, no. 12 (Madrid: Centro de Estudios Políticos y Constitucionales2008), 383–84; Héctor Fix Zamudio and Eduardo Ferrer Mac Gregor, *Las sentencias de los Tribunales Constitucionales* (Méxcio: Ed. Porrúa), 69; and "Las sentencias de los Tribunales Constitucionales en el ordenamiento mexicano," in *Anuario Iberoamericano de Justicia Constitucional*, no. 12 (Madrid: Centro de Estudios Políticos y Constitucionales, 2008), 248.

[65] See Hans Kelsen, *La garantía jurisdiccional de la Constitución (La justicia constitucional)* (Mexico: Universidad Nacional Autónoma de México, 2001), 84.

Portugal and Belgium.[66] In other countries like in Poland, Mexico and Costa Rica, it is for the Constitutional Courts to decide on the matter.[67]

23.4 Third Trend: Constitutional Courts Interfering with the Absence of Legislation or with Legislative Omissions

In contemporary world, one of the most important roles of Constitutional Courts is not to control the constitutionality of existing legislation, but the absence of such legislation, or the omissions the statutes contain, when the Legislator does not comply with its constitutional obligation to legislate on specific matters, or when the legislation has been issued in an incomplete or discriminatory way.

Two sorts of legislative omissions are generally distinguished: absolute and relative omissions, being both subjected to judicial review.[68]

23.4.1 Constitutional Courts Filling Absolute Legislative Omissions

Regarding judicial review over absolute legislative omissions, Constitutional Courts have carried out constitutional control through two judicial means: First, when deciding a direct action filed against the unconstitutional absolute omission of the Legislator; and second, when deciding a particular action or complaint for the protection of fundamental rights filed against an omission of the Legislator that in a particular case prevents the possibility of enjoying such right.

23.4.1.1 The Direct Action Against Absolute Legislative Omissions

The direct action in order to seek judicial review of unconstitutional absolute legislative omissions was first established in the 1974 Constitution of the former Yugoslavia, and 2 years later, was incorporated in the 1976 Constitution of Portugal, giving standing to sue to some high public officials.[69] The decisions of the Constitutional Tribunal in these could only inform the competent legislative organ of its findings conduct.[70]

A few years later, the direct action for judicial review of absolute unconstitutional legislative omissions was adopted in a few Latin American countries, in particular in Brazil (1988),[71] Costa Rica, Ecuador and Venezuela, where it has been used extensively. Nonetheless, the main difference regarding these countries is that in the case of Venezuela, the action is conceived as a popular action,[72] and Constitutional Chamber has been granted express powers to establish not only the unconstitutionality of the omission but the terms, and if necessary, the guidelines for the correction of the omission. Nonetheless, the Constitutional Chamber has enlarge its powers controlling the legislative omission regarding non-legislative acts, and in 2004, after the National Assembly fail to appoint the members of the National Electoral Council, the Chamber not only declared the unconstitutionality of the omission, but proceeded to appoint directly those high officials, usurping the Assembly's exclusive

[66] See for instance, Christian Behrendt, *Le judge constitutionnel, un législateur-cadre positif. Un analyse comparative en droit francais, belge et allemande* (Bruxelles: Bruylant, 2006), 280, 281; 436–37.

[67] See for instante, Héctor Fix Zamudio and Eduardo Ferrer Mac Gregor, *Las sentencias de los Tribunales Constitucionales* (Méxcio: Ed. Porrúa), 63–64, 74; and "Las sentencias de los Tribunales Constitucionales en el ordenamiento mexicano," in *Anuario Iberoamericano de Justicia Constitucional*, no. 12 (Madrid: Centro de Estudios Políticos y Constitucionales, 2008), 252.

See Iván Escovar Fornos, *Estudios Jurídicos*, ed. Tomo I (Managua: Hispamer, 2007), 513; and in "Las sentencias constitucionales y sus efectos en Nicaragua," in *Anuario Iberoamericano de Justicia Constitucional*, no. 12 (Madrid: Centro de Estudios Políticos y Constitucionales, 2008), 114.

[68] See José Julio Fernández Rodríguez, *La inconstitucionalidad por omisión. Teoría general. Derecho comparado. El caso español* (Madrid: Civitas, 1998), 33, 114 ff.

[69] See Jorge Campinos, "Brevísimas notas sobre a fiscalizacão da constitucionalidade des leis em Portugal," in Giorgo Lombardi (Coord.), *Constituzione e giustizia constitutionale nel diritto comparato* (Rímini: Maggioli, 1985); and *La Constitution portugaise de 1976 et sa garantie* (México: UNAM, Congreso sobre La Constitución y su Defensa, (mimeo), Agosto, 1982), 42.

[70] See in José Julio Fernández Rodríguez, *La inconstitucionalidad por omisión. Teoría general. Derecho comparado. El caso español* (Madrid: Civitas, 1998), 265–66.

[71] See for instance, Marcia Rodrigues Machado, "Inconstitutionalidade por omissão," in *Revista da Procuradoria Greal de São Paulo*, no. 30, 1988, 41 ff.

[72] See Allan R. Brewer-Carías and Víctor Hernández Mendible, *Ley Orgánica del Tribunal Supremo de Justicia* (Caracas: Editorial Jurídica Venezolana, 2010).

powers, assuring in this way the complete control of the Electoral branch of government by the National Executive.[73] A case, also, for the Chapter of the pathology of judicial review.

Also in Hungary, the Constitution grants the Constitutional Court to decide *ex officio* or at anyone's petition, upon the unconstitutionality of legislative omissions, being able to instruct the Legislator to fulfill its task within a specific deadline, and even defining the contents of the rules to be sanctioned.[74] This power has also been attributed in Croatia to the Constitutional Court, which can also proceed *ex officio*.[75]

23.4.1.2 The Protection of Fundamental Rights Against Absolute Legislative Omissions by Means of Actions or Complaints for Their Protection

The other mean commonly used for Constitutional Courts to exercise judicial review regarding unconstitutional legislative omissions are the specific actions of amparo[76] or of complaints for the protection of fundamental rights that can be filed against the harms or threats that such omissions can cause to such rights.

In this sense, it is the case in Germany, where the complaint for the constitutional protection of fundamental rights (*Verfassungsbeschwerde*),[77] has been used by the Federal Constitutional Tribunal as a mean for judicial review of absolute legislative omissions, applied, for instance in cases regarding rights of illegitimate children, imposing the application of the same conditions referred to the legitimate ones, exhorting the Legislator to reform the Civil Code in a giving specific term.[78]

In India, also, the Supreme Court has controlled the legislative omissions, ruling in cases of complaints for the protection of fundamental rights, like in the important case regarding ragging (bullying) menace at Universities, in which the Court not only urged the Legislator to enact the omitted legislation, but prescribed detailed steps to curb the practice, and outlined diverse modes of punishment that educational authorities may take. The Indian Supreme Court even directly appointed, in 2006, a Committee to suggest remedial measures; ordering in 2007, the implementation of its recommendations.[79]

In a similar orientation, and also through equitable remedies like the injunctions, the U.S. Supreme Court progressively developed the protection of fundamental rights filling the gap of legislative omissions, particularly using coercive and preventive remedies, as well as structural injunctions.[80] This was very important after the Supreme Court's decision in *Brown v. Board of Education* case 347 U.S. 483 (1954); 349 U.S. 294 (1955) declaring the dual school system discriminatory, allowing the courts to undertake the supervision over institutional State policies and practices in order

[73] See the commenst regarding Decisions no. 2073 of August 4, 2003 (Case: *Hermánn Escarrá Malaver y otros*) and no. 2341 of August 25, 2003 (Case: *Hermánn Escarrá M. y otros*), in Allan R. Brewer-Carías, "El secuestro del Poder Electoral y la confiscación del derecho a la participación política mediante el referendo revocatorio presidencial: Venezuela 2000–2004," in *Boletín Mexicano de Derecho Comparado*, no. 112 (México: Instituto de Investigaciones Jurídicas, Universidad Nacional Autónoma de México, enero-abril, 2005),11–73.

[74] See in Lóránt Csink, József Petrétei and Péter Tilk, "*Constitutional Court as Positive Legislator*," Hungarian National Report, XVIII International Congress of Comparative Law, Washington, July, 2010, 5–6.

[75] See Sanja Barić and Petar Bačić, "*Constitutional Courts as positive legislators*," Croatian National Report, XVIII International Congress of Comparative Law, Washington, July, 2010, 12–13.

[76] See in general in comparative law, Allan R. Brewer-Carías, *Constitutional Protection of Human Rights in Latin America. A Comparative Study of Amparo Proceeding* (New York: Cambridge University Press, 2009), 324 ff.

[77] See in general, Francsico Fernández Segado, "El control de las omisiones legislativas por el Bundesverfassungsgericht," in *Revista de Derecho*, no. 4 (Montevideo: Universidad Católica del Uruguay, Konrad Adenauer Stiftung, 2009), 137–86.

[78] Decision of the Federal Constitutional Tribunal No 26/1969 of January 29, 1969, in I. Härtel, "*Constitutional Courts as Positive Legislators*," German National Report, XVIII International Congress of Comparative Law, Washington, July, 2010, 19.

[79] Cases *Vishwa Jagriti Mission v Central Government* AIR 2001 SC 2793, and *University of Kerala v Council of Principals of Colleges of Kerala,* in Surya Deva, "*Constitutional Courts as 'Positive Legislators: The Indian Experience*," Indian National Report, XVIII International Congress of Comparative Law, Washington, July, 2010, 9 (footnote 58).

[80] See William Tabb and Elaine W. Shoben, *Remedies* (St. Paul: Thomson West, 2005), 13; Owen M. Fiss, *The Civil Rights Injunctions* (Bloomington, London: Indiana University Press, 1978), 4–5; Owen M. Fiss and Doug Rendelman, *Injunctions* (New York: The Foundation Press, 1984), 33–34; and Allan R. Brewer-Carías, *Constitutional Protection of Human Rights in Latin America* (New York: Cambridge University Press, 2009), 69 ff.

to prevent discrimination.[81] This injunction activism was later applied in other important cases of civil rights litigations involving electoral reappointments, mental hospitals, prisons, trade practices, and the environment. Also, deciding these equitable remedies for the protection of fundamental rights, the U.S. Supreme Court has also created complementary judicial legislation, for instance, regarding the conditions for lawful search and arrest in connection with investigation and prosecution of crime.

In Latin America, these complaints for the protection of legislative omissions have also been used.[82] It has been the case of the Brazilian *mandado de injunção*, as writ of injunction granted whenever the lack of regulatory provision makes the exercise of constitutional rights and freedoms, unfeasible. If these injunction the courts can given the Congress not only a term to repair its omission, but established the rules, some time by analogy, to be applied if the omission persist. As has occurred on matters of social security regime and strike Rights of public sectors employees.[83]

The same general approach of the Constitutional Court complementing the Legislator on matters of protection of fundamental rights deciding actions of amparo can be found in Argentina.[84] Also, in Colombia, deciding actions of *tutela*, in the case of massive violations of human rights regarding displaced persons, the Constitutional Court has created even ex officio, what it has called factual a "state of unconstitutionality" (*estado de cosas inconstitucionales*) used in order to substitute the ordinary judges, the Legislator and the Administration in the definition and coordination of public policies.[85]

In Canada, in a very similar way to the Latin American amparo proceeding for the protection of constitutional rights, according to the Charter the courts have the power to issue a wide variety of remedies including declarations and injunctions requiring the government to take positive actions to comply with the Constitution and to remedy the effects of past constitutional violations. These judicial powers have been widely used for instance enforcing protection on minority language in order to assure bilingualism obligations of the Provinces; on matters of criminal justice, due to the absence of legislative response to enact statutory standards for speedy trials and disclosure of evidence to the accused by the prosecutor; and on matters of extradition of person that could face death penalty in the requesting state.[86]

In a certain way, in the United Kingdom, although the basic principle is that the courts does not substitute itself for the legislature, it is also possible to identify important activity developed by the courts on matters of constitutional review regarding the protection of human rights, by issuing decisions with guidelines that supplement the jurisdiction of the legislator or the administration, as has occurred on matters related to sterilization of intellectually handicapped adults, and persons in a permanent vegetative state, providing rules for future application.[87]

Also in the Czech Republic the Constitutional Court has filled the gap derived from legislative omission on specific matters like the one related to rent rising in apartment houses, in which the Court considered that

[81] Case Missouri v. Jenkins, 515 U.S. 70 (1995), in Laurence Claus and Richard S. Kay, "*Constitutional Courts as 'Positive Legislators' in the United States,*" US National Report, XVIII, International Congress of Comparative Law, Washington, July, 2010, 31 (footnote 104).

[82] See Allan R. Brewer-Carías, *Constitutional Protection of Human Rights in Latin America* (New York: Cambridge University Press, 2009).

[83] See Thomas Bustamante and Evanlida de Godoi Bustamante, "*Constitutional Courts as "Negative Legislators:" The Brazilian Case,*" Brazil National Report, XVIII, International Congress of Comparative Law, Washington, July 2010, 19.

[84] See in Alejandra Rodríguez Galán and Alfredo Mauricio Vítolo, "*Constitutional Courts as "Positive Legislators,"* Argentinean National Report," XVIII, International Congress of Comparative Law, Washington, July, 2010, 17.

[85] See in Sandra Morelli, "*The Colombian Constitutional Court: from Institutional Leadership, to Conceptual Audacity,*" Colombian National Report, XVIII, International Congress of Comparative Law, Washington, July, 2010, 5.

[86] Cases: *Reference re Manitoba Language Rights* (1985) 1 S.C.R. 721; (1985) 2 S.C.R. 347; (1990) 3 S.C.R. 1417n; (1992) 1 S.C.R. 212; *R. v. Stinchcombe* (1991) 3 S.C.R. 326, in Kent Roach, "*Constitutional Courts as Positive Legislators: Canada Country Report*", XVIII, International Congress of Comparative Law, Washington, July 2010, 11–2.

[87] Cases *Re F (Mental Patient: Sterilisation)* (1990) 2 *AC 173; and Airedale NHS Trust v Bland,* in John Bell, "*Constitutional Courts as 'Positive Legislators': United Kingdom,*" British National Report, XVIII, International Congress of Comparative Law, Washington, July, 2010, 7.

"its role of protector of constitutionality, can not limit its function to the mere position of a 'negative' legislator."[88]

23.4.2 Constitutional Court Filling the Gap of Relative Legislative Omissions

In the case of judicial review regarding relative legislative omissions, when dealing with poor, deficient or inadequate legislative regulations affecting the enjoyment of fundamental rights, during the past decades, particularly in concentrated system of judicial review, Constitutional Courts have developed the technique of declaring the unconstitutionality of the insufficient provisions but without annulling them, sending instead to the Legislator, directives, guidelines and recommendations, and even orders, in order to seek for the correction of unconstitutional legislative omissions. In all these cases, the Constitutional Courts have developed a role of assisting and collaborating with the Legislator, particularly in order to protect the right to equality and non discrimination. These instruction or directives sent by Constitutional Courts to the Legislator are in some cases non binding recommendations; in other cases they have an obligatory character; and in others, they are conceived as provisional pieces of legislation.

23.4.2.1 Constitutional Courts Issuing Non Binding Directives to the Legislator

In general terms, regarding the non compulsory judicial recommendations, called in Italy, exhortative decisions, delegate decisions or *sentenze indiritzzo,*[89] the Constitutional Court declares the unconstitutionality of a provision but does not introduce the norm to be applied through interpretation leaving this task to the Legislator. In other cases the instruction directed to the legislator can have a conditional character regarding the judicial review power of the Constitutional Court, so that in Italy, through the so-called *doppia pronuncia* formula,[90] if the Legislator fails to execute the recommendations of the Court, in a second decision, the Court would declare the unconstitutionality of the impugned statute.

This sort of exhortative judicial review is also accepted in Germany, and is called "appellate decisions," where the Federal Constitutional Tribunal can issue "admonitions to the Legislator," containing legislative directives giving a term to enact the omitted provision.[91]

This same technique has been applied in France and Belgium, where the Constitutional Council and Court have also issued these directives addressed to the Legislator, which and even without normative direct effects, can establish a framework for the future legislative action.[92] A similar technique has been applied in Poland, called "signalizations," through which the Constitutional Tribunal directs the legislator's attention to problems of general nature[93]; and has also been applied in Serbia, the Czech Republic and Mexico.[94]

Also in countries with diffuse systems of judicial review, like Argentina, these exhortative rulings have also been issued by the Supreme Courts, in cases related to collective habeas corpus petition, exhorting the involved authorities to sanction new legal provisions

[88] Decision Pl. ÚS 8/02, *Rent Control II*, no. 528/2002 Sb. Of November 20, 2002; and Pl. ÚS 2/03, *Rent Control III*, no. 84/2003 Sb, of March 19, 2003, in Zdenek Kühn, "*Czech Constitutional Court as Positive Legislator,*" Czech National Report, XVIII, International Congress of Comparative Law, Washington, July 2010, 14 (footnote 58).

[89] See L. Pegoraro, *La Corte e il Parlamento. Sentenze-indirizzo e attivitá legislativa* (Padova: Cedam, 1987), 3 ff.; and Francisco Javier Díaz Revorio, Las *sentencias interpretativas del Tribunal Constitucional* (Valladolid: Ed. Lex Nova, 2001), 268.

[90] See Iván Escovar Fornos, *Estudios Jurídicos*, ed. Tomo I (Managua: Hispamer, 2007), 504.

[91] See Francisco Javier Díaz Revorio, *Las sentencias interpretativas del Tribunal Constitucional* (Valladolid: Ed. Lex Nova, 2001), 264; and Iván Escovar Fornos, *Estudios Jurídicos*, ed. Tomo I (Managua: Hispamer, 2007), 505.

[92] Decision BVerfG, de 19 de Julio de 1966, BVerfGE 20, 56 (114–115), in Christian Behrendt, *Le judge constitutionnel, un législateur-cadre positif. Un analyse comparative en droit francais, belge et allemande* (Bruxelles: Bruylant, 2006), 176–9, 185 ff.

[93] See for instance the "signalization" regarding tenents' protection of June 29, 2005, OTK ZU 2005/6A/77, in Marek Safjan, "*The Constitutional Courts as a Positive Legislator,*" *Polish National Report*, International Congress of Comparative Law, Washington, July, 2010, 16 (footnote 45).

[94] See por ejemplo, Héctor Fix Zamudio and Eduardo Ferrer Mac Gregor, "Las sentencias de los tribunales constitucionales en el ordenamiento mexicano," in *Anuario Iberoamericano de Justicia Constitucional*, no. 12 (Madrid: Centro de Estudios Políticos y Constitucionales, 2008), 252.

in order to take care, for instance, of the overcrowding and dreadful situation in the prisons system.[95] These powers have also been used in cases of judicial review of "conventionality" regarding the American Convention of Human Rights. A similar position has been adopted by the Supreme Court of the Netherlands giving its "expert advice" to the Legislator.[96]

23.4.2.2 Constitutional Courts Issuing Binding Orders and Directives to the Legislator

In many other cases of judicial review referred to relative legislative omissions, generally based on the violation of the right to non discrimination and to equality, Constitutional Courts, when declaring the unconstitutionality of a provision without annulling it, have progressively assumed a more positive role, issuing regarding the Legislator, not only directives, but orders or instructions, in order for it to reform or correct pieces of legislation in the sense indicated by the Court. This has transformed Constitutional Courts into some sort of auxiliary of the Legislator, imposing them certain tasks, and establishing a precise term for its performance.

This judicial review technique has been used in Germany, where the Federal Constitutional Tribunal, through injunctive decisions has issued orders to the Legislator on matters related of the regime of alimony, professional incompatibilities, reimbursement of electoral expenses in electoral campaigns, status concerning professors, abortion, and alternative civilian service, even indicating the Legislator what not to do that could aggravate the unconstitutional inequalities.[97] A similar sort of decision of the Constitutional Court can be found in Belgium, Austria and Croatia, and Colombia.[98]

In the case of France, due to the traditional a priori judicial review of legislation system exercised by the Constitutional Council, one of the most important means in order to assure the enforcement of the Council's decisions have been the directives called "*réserves d'interprétation*" or "*réserves d'application*" although directed to the administrative authorities that must issue the regulations of the law and to the judges that must apply the law.[99]

23.4.3 Constitutional Courts as Provisional Legislators

Finally, in many other cases facing relative legislative omissions, Constitutional Courts have not limited themselves to issue orders to the Legislator seeking the enactment of legislative provisions, but have assumed the direct role of being "provisional Legislators" by including in their decisions when declaring the unconstitutionality of statutes, provisional measures or regulations to be applied in the specific matter considered unconstitutional, until the Legislator sanctions the statute it is obliged to produce.[100] In these cases, the Court immediately stops the application of the unconstitutional provision, but in order to avoid the vacuum that a nullity can originate, temporarily establishes certain rules to be applied until the enactment of a new legislation. Constitutional Courts, in these cases, in some way act as "substitute legislators" although not in order to usurp its functions but in order to preserve its legislative freedom.[101]

[95] Case *Verbitsky*, CSIJ, Fallos. 328:1146, in Néstor P. Sagües, "Los efectos de las sentencias constitucionales en el derecho argentino," in *Anuario Iberoamericano de Justicia Constitucional*, no. 12 (Madrid: Centro de Estudios Políticos y Constitucionales, 2008), 340.

[96] Case *Harmonisation Act* de 1989, in *J.* Uzman T. Barkhuysen and M.L. van Emmerik, "*The Dutch Supreme Court: A Reluctant Positive Legislator?,*" Dutch National Report, XVIII, International Congress of Comparative Law, Washington, July 2010, 6.

[97] Decisions BVerfG, of July 14, 1981, BVerfGE 57, 381; BVerfG, of February 15, 1967, BVerfGE 21, 183; BVerfG, of March 9, 1976, BVerfGE 41, 414, in I. Härtel, "*Constitutional Courts as Positive Legislators,*" German National Report, XVIII, International Congress of Comparative Law, Washington, July, 2010, 9.; and Christian Behrendt, *Le judge constitutionnel, un législateur-cadre positif. Un analyse comparative en droit francais, belge et allemande* (Bruxelles: Bruylant, 2006), 259–88.

[98] See for instance, Mónica Liliana Ibagón, "Control jurisdiccional de las omisiones legislativas en Colombia," in *Instrumentos de tutela y justicia constitucional. Memoria del VII Congreso Iberoamericano de Derecho Constitucional*, ed. Juan Vega Gómez and Edgar Corzo Sosa (México: Universidad Nacional Autónoma de México, 2002), 322–23.

[99] See Bertrand Mathieu, "*Le Conseil constitutionnel 'législateur positif. Ou la question des interventions du juge constitutionnel français dans l'exercise de la function legislative,*" French National Report, XVIII International Congress of Comparative Law, Washington, July, 2010, 10.

[100] See Christian Behrendt, *Le judge constitutionnel, un législateur-cadre positif. Un analyse comparative en droit francais, belge et allemande* (Bruxelles: Bruylant, 2006), 333 ff.

[101] See Otto Bachof, "Nuevas reflexiones sobre la jurisdicción constitucional entre derecho y política," in *Boletín Mexicano de Derecho Comparado*, XIX, no. 57 (Mexico, 1986), 848–49.

This technique has been applied also in Germany by the Federal Constitutional Tribunal, assuming "an auxiliary legislative power," and acting as a "parliamentary reparation enterprise,"[102] on a matter like the one resolved in 1975, on the partial decriminalization of abortion. In the case, after declaring unconstitutional the provisions of the Criminal Code, the Tribunal considered that "in the interest of the clarity of law" it was suitable to establish "provisory regulation" that was to be applicable until the new provisions would be enacted by the "Legislator,"[103] and proceed to enact a very detailed "provisional legislation" on the matter that was applied for nearly 15 years, until 1992. In 1993, after the corresponding reform, the Federal Constitutional Tribunal issued a new decision considering it to be contrary to the Constitution,[104] and establishing once more in an extremely detailed way, as "real legislator," all the rules applicable to abortion in the country.

In Switzerland, the Supreme Court in various cases has also provided for rules in order to fill the gap due to legislative omissions concerning enforcement of constitutional rights, as has happened, for instance, regarding the proceedings concerning the detention of foreigners; the right of asylum; and the rules on expropriation.[105]

Also in India, the Supreme Court has assumed the role of provisional legislator, also on matters of protection of fundamental rights related to police arrest and detention, issuing notices to all state governments, establishing very detail "requirements to be followed in all cases of arrest or detention till legal provisions are made." In this case, even though the requirements were seemingly intended to be temporary, they have continued to be the main rules applicable on the matter.[106] The Supreme Court has also exercised the same powers protecting these rights of working women against sexual harassment at workplace, issuing "for the protection of these rights *to fill the legislative vacuum.*"[107]

Within these sort of judicial review decisions including provisional regulations by interpreting the Constitution, it is possible to mention the cases of "*súmula vinculante*" issued by the Federal Supreme Tribunal of Brazil, for instance, regarding the prohibition of nepotism in the Judiciary, and the demarcation of indigenous people land.[108]

Also in Venezuela it is possible to find cases in which the Constitutional Chamber of the Supreme Tribunal, in the absence of the corresponding statutes, has issued decisions containing legislation, when exercising what the Chamber has called its "normative jurisdiction," establishing complete regulations for instance regarding the *de facto* stable relations between men and women, and on matters of in vitro fertilization.[109]

[102] See Christian Behrendt, *Le judge constitutionnel, un législateur-cadre positif. Un analyse comparative en droit francais, belge et allemande* (Bruxelles: Bruylant, 2006), 341, footnotes 309 and 310.

[103] Decision BVerfG, of February 25, 1975, BVerfGE 39, 1 (68), in Christian Behrendt, *Le judge constitutionnel, un législateur-cadre positif. Un analyse comparative en droit francais, belge et allemande* (Bruxelles: Bruylant, 2006), 342 ff; and I. Härtel, "*Constitutional Courts as Positive Legislators,*" German National Report, XVIII International Congress of Comparative Law, Washington, July, 2010, 14.

[104] Decisions BVerfG, of March 25, 1993 (*Schwangerrschaftsabbruch II*), and BVerfGE 88, 203, de of February 25, 1975, in Christian Behrendt, *Le judge constitutionnel, un législateur-cadre positif. Un analyse comparative en droit francais, belge et allemande* (Bruxelles: Bruylant, 2006), 346–51.

[105] Decisions BGE 91 I 329 ff. (Sustantive expropriation); BGE 94 I 286 ff. (Taking Neighbors rights). See in Tobias Jaag, "*Constitutional Courts as 'Positive Legislators:' Switzerland,*" Swiss National Report, XVIII International Congress of Comparative Law, Washington, July, 2010, 16 (footnote 89).

[106] Case *D K Basu v State of West Bengal* (1997) 1 SCC 416, in Surya Deva, "*Constitutional Courts as 'Positive Legislators: The Indian Experience,*" Indian National Report, XVIII International Congress of Comparative Law, Washington, July, 2010, 6–7.

[107] Case *Vishaka v State of Rajasthan,* 1997 SC 3011, in Surya Deva, "*Constitutional Courts as 'Positive Legislators: The Indian Experience,*" *Indian National Report*, XVIII International Congress of Comparative Law, Washington, July, 2010, 8 (footnote 49).

[108] *Súmula vinculante* no. 13, STF, *DJ* 1°.set.2006, ADC 12 MC/DF, Rel. Min. Carlos Britto, and STF, *DJ* 25.set.2009, Pet 3388/RR, Rel. Min. Carlos Britto, in Luis Roberto Barroso et al. "Notas sobre a questão do Legislador Positivo" (*Brazil),* XVIII International Congress of Comparative Law, Washington, July, 2010, 33–37; 43–46.

[109] Decision no. 1682 of July 15, 2005, Case *Carmela Manpieri, Interpretación del artículo 77 de la Constitución*, available at http://www.tsj.gov.ve/decisiones/scon/Julio/1682-150705-04-3301.htm; and Decision no. 1456 of July 27, 2006, Case *Yamilex Núñez de Godoy,* available at http://www.tsj.gov.ve/decisiones/scon/Julio/1456-270706-05-1471.htm See Daniela Urosa Maggi, "*Cortes Constitucionales como 'Legisladores Positivos:' La experiencia venezolana,*" Venezuelan Nacional Report, XVIII International Congress of Comparative Law, Washington, July 2010, 19–20.

23.5 Fourth Trend: Constitutional Courts as Legislators on Matters of Judicial Review

Finally, the fourth trend that can be identified in comparative law regarding the role of Constitutional Courts as "positive legislators," is related to matters of legislation on judicial review, not only regarding the powers of the Court when exercising judicial review and the actions that can be filed before them, but regarding the rules of procedure applicable to the judicial review proceedings. This situation varies according to the system of judicial review adopted.

23.5.1 Constitutional Courts Creating Their Own Judicial Review Powers

23.5.1.1 The Judge-Made Law Regarding the Diffuse System of Judicial Review

In the diffuse or decentralized system of judicial review, being a power attributed to all courts which derives from the principle of the supremacy of the Constitution and the duty of the courts to discard statutes contrary to the Constitution, such power does not need to be expressly established in the Constitution. This was the main doctrine established by Chief Justice Marshall in *Marbury* v. *Madison* 1 Cranch 137 (1803). Consequently, in the U.S., due to this essential link between supremacy of the Constitution and judicial review, judicial review was a creation of the courts, as was also the case a few decades later in Norway, in Greece, and in Argentina,[110] where judicial review was also a creation of the respective Supreme of High Courts.

23.5.1.2 The Extension of Judicial Review Powers in Order to Assure the Protection of Fundamental Rights

Also in the same sense, and in particular regarding the protection of fundamental rights and liberties, Constitutional Courts in many Latin American countries, in their character of supreme interpreter of the Constitution have created in the absence of legislation, the action of amparo, as a special judicial mean for the protection of fundamental rights. This was also the case in Argentina in 1957, in Dominican Republic in 1999,[111] and in the Slovak Republic, where the Constitutional "created" a specific means of protection.[112]

In Venezuela, the Constitutional Chamber has admitted the direct amparo action for the protection of diffused and collective rights and interests established in the Constitution,[113] and in India, the Supreme Court has also expanded the action for the protection of fundamental rights for the protection of collective or diffused rights, called "public interest litigation" (PIL).[114]

23.5.2 The Need for the Express Provision in the Constitution of Judicial Review Powers of the Constitutional Jurisdiction and Its Deviation

Nonetheless, and specifically referring to the concentrated system of judicial review, the power to judge the control of constitutionality of legislative acts when reserved to a Supreme Court of Justice or to a Constitutional Court must be accomplished as expressly

[110] See Allan R. Brewer-Carías, *Judicial Review in Comparative Law* (Cambridge: Cambridge University Press, 1989).

[111] See Allan R. Brewer-Carías, *Constitutional Protection of Human Rights in Latin America* (New York: Cambridge University Press, 2010).

[112] Decision of the Constitutional Court no. III. ÚS 117/01, in Ján SvákyLucia Berdisová, "*Constitutional Court of the Slovak Republic as Positive Legislator via Application and Interpretation of the Constitution,*" *Slovak National Report*, XVIII International Congress of Comparative Law, Washington, July 2010, 9.

[113] Decisions no. 656 of June 30, 2000, Case *Dilia Parra Guillen (Peoples' Defender),* in http://www.tsj.gov.ve/decisiones/scon/Junio/656-300600-00-1728%20.htm; no. 1395 of November 21, 2000, Case *William Dávila* Case, in *Revista de Derecho Público*, no. 84 (Caracas: Editorial Jurídica Venezolana, 2000), 330; no. 1571 of August 22, 2001, Case *Asodeviprilara,* available at http://www.tsj.gov.ve/decisiones/scon/Agosto/1571-220801-01-1274%20.htm. See Daniela Urosa Maggi, "*Cortes Constitucionales como 'Legisladores Positivos:' La experiencia venezolana,*" Venezuelan National Report, XVIII International Congress of Comparative Law, Washington, July, 2010, 11–12.

[114] Cases *S P Gupta v Union of India* AIR 1982 SC 149; *PUDR v Union of India* AIR 1982 SC 1473; *Bandhua Mukti Morcha v Union of India* (1984) 3 SCC 161, in Surya Deva, "*Constitutional Courts as 'Positive Legislators: The Indian Experience*," Indian National Report, XVIII International Congress of Comparative Law, Washington, July, 2010, 2, 4–5.

provided in the Constitution; and cannot be developed by deduction through court's decisions.[115]

Notwithstanding, regarding their judicial review powers, in some cases, Constitutional Courts have extended or adapted them, as happened for instance, when applying the technique of declaring the unconstitutionality of statutes, but without annulling them, including the powers to extend the application of the unconstitutional statute for a term, and to issue directives to the legislator for him to legislate in harmony to the Constitution. This was a technique developed in Germany, as mentioned by Ines Härtel, the *German National Reporter*, "without statutory authorization, in fact *contra legem*"[116]; and in Spain, where the Constitutional Tribunal, has applied the technique in spite of the provision on the contrary contained in the Organic Law of the Constitutional.[117]

But in other cases, Constitutional Courts have created their own judicial review powers not established in the Constitution, as has been the case in Venezuela, where the Constitutional Chamber of the Supreme Tribunal has created as a new means of judicial review not envisaged in the Constitution, the so called "abstract recourse for constitutional interpretation,"[118] through which at the Attorney General requests, the Constitutional Chamber has distorted important constitutional provisions. It was the case, for instance, of the decisions adopted regarding the consultative and repeal referendums between 2002 and 2004, where the Chamber transformed the repeal referendum into a ratification referendum not established in the Constitution.[119] Any way, these are cases for the chapter of the pathology of judicial review.

23.5.3 Constitutional Courts Creating Procedural Rules on Judicial Review Processes

Finally, regarding Constitutional interfering upon the legislative functions, the process of creating rules of procedures for the exercise of their constitutional attributions, when not established in the legislation regulating their functions, must also be mentioned.

For such purpose, Constitutional Courts, as is the case of the Constitutional Tribunal of Peru, have claimed to have "procedural autonomy" having exercise their extended powers developing and complementing the procedural rules applicable in judicial review process not expressly regulated in the statutes.[120]

---

[115] See Allan R. Brewer-Carías, *Judicial Review in Comparative Law* (Cambridge: Cambridge University Press, 1989), 185 ff.; and Jorge Carpizo, *El Tribunal Consitucional y sus límites* (Lima: Grijley Ed, 2009), 41.

[116] See I. Härtel, "*Constitutional Courts as Positive Legislators,*" German National Report, XVIII International Congress of Comparative Law, Washington, July, 2010, 8; Francisco Fernández Segado, "Algunas reflexiones generales en torno a los efectos de las sentencias de inconstitucionalidad y a la relatividad de ciertas fórmulas esterotipadas vinculadas a ellas," in *Anuario Iberoamericano de Justicia Constitucional*, no. 12 (Madrid: Centro de Estudios Políticos y Constitucionales, 2008), 162.

[117] See F. Fernández Segado, "*El Tribunal Constitucional como Legislador Positivo,*" *Spanish National Report*, XVIII International Congress of Comparative Law, Washington, July, 2010, 6, 11.

[118] Decision no. 1077 of September 22, 2000, Case *Servio Tulio León,* in *Revista de Derecho Público*, no. 83 (Caracas: Editorial Jurídica Venezolana, 2000), 247 ff. See Allan R. Brewer-Carías, "Le Recours d'Interprétation Abstrait de la Constitution au Vénézuéla," in *Renouvau du droit constitutionnel. Mélanges en l'honneur de Louis Favoreu* (Paris, 2007), 61–70; and "La ilegítima mutación de la constitución por el juez constitucional: la inconstitucional ampliación y modificación de su propia competencia en materia de control de constitucionalidad," in *Libro Homenaje a Josefina Calcaño de Temeltas* (Caracas: Fundación de Estudios de Derecho Administrativo (FUNEDA), 2009), 319–62.

[119] The constitucional mutación occurred precisely for the purpose of preventing repealing the mandate of President Chávez in 2004. He was elected in August 2000 with 3,757,744 votes; being enough in order to repeal his mandate according to the Constitution, that the votes dor the revocation be more that such figure. The number of votes in favor od the repeal of the President cast in the August 15 2004 voting was 3,989,008, so the mandate was constitutionally repealed. Nonetheless, the national Electoral Council on August 27, 2004, due to the fact that the votes No for the revocation were 5.800.629, decided to "ratify" the Presdient in his post, until the end of his term in January 2007. See *El Nacional*, Caracas, August 28, 2004, pp. A-1yA-2. See the comments on this case in Allan R. Brewer-Carías, "La Sala Constitucional vs. El derecho ciudadano a la revocatoria de mandatos populares o de cómo un referendo revocatorio fue inconstitucionalmente convertido en un 'refrendo ratificatorio,'" in *Crónica sobre la "in" justicia constitucional. La Sala Constitucional y el autoritarismo en Venezuela*, Colección Instituto de Derecho Público, Universidad Central de Venezuela, no. 2 (Caracas: Editorial Jurídica Venezolana, 2007), 350 ff.

[120] Decisión of the Constitutional Tribunal, Exp. no. 0020-2005-AI/TC, FJ 2, in Francisco Eguiguren and Liliana Salomé, "*Función contra-mayoritaria de la Juridicción Constitucional, su legitimidad democrática y los conflictos entre el Tribunal Constitucional y el Legislador,*" Peruvian National Report, XVIII International Congress of Comparative Law, Washington, July, 2010, 14; and Fernán Altuve-Febres, "*El Juez Constitucional como legislador positivo en el Perú,*" *Peruvian National Report II*, XVIII International Congress of Comparative Law, Washington, July, 2010, 22–3.

In Germany, the same principle of procedural autonomy has been used (*Verfahrensautonomie*) to explain the powers developed by the Federal Constitutional Tribunal to complement procedural rules on judicial review process based on the interpretation of article 35 of the Law of the Federal Constitutional Tribunal related to the execution of its decision.

In other cases, judicial interference on legislative matters related to rules of procedures on matters of judicial review has been more intense, as in Colombia, where the Constitutional Court has assumed the exclusive competency to establish the effects of its own decisions.[121] And in Venezuela, the Constitutional Chamber of the Supreme Tribunal of Justice, has also invoked its "normative jurisdiction" in order to establish the procedural rules for judicial review when not regulated in statutes, in particular regarding the action for controlling absolute legislative omission,[122] and on matters of the habeas data, establishing detail procedural regulations "in order to fill the existing vacuum."[123]

[121] See Decision C-113/93, in Germán Alfonso López Daza, "*Le juge constitutionnel colombien, législateur-cadre positif: un gouvernement des juges Colombian National Report I,*" XVIII International Congress of Comparative Law, Washington, July, 2010, 9.

[122] Decision no. 1556 of July 9, 2002, Case *Alfonzo Albornoz y Gloria de Vicentini*, available at http://www.tsj.gov.ve/decisiones/scon/Julio/1556-090702-01-2337%20.htm. See Daniela Urosa Maggi, "*Cortes Constitucionales como 'Legisladores Positivos:' La experiencia venezolana,*" Venezuelan National Report, XVIII International Congress of Comparative Law, Washington, July, 2010, 10–1.

[123] Decision no 1511 of November 9, 2009, Case *Mercedes Josefina Ramírez, Acción de Habeas Dat,* available at http://www.tsj.gov.ve/decisiones/scon/Noviembre/1511-91109-2009-09-0369.html. See Allan R. Brewer-Carías, "El proceso constitucional de las acciones de habeas data en Venezuela: las sentencias de la Sala Constitucional como fuente del Derecho Procesal Constitucional" in Eduardo Andrés Velandia Canosa (Coordinador), *Homenaje al Maestro Héctor Fix Zamudio. Derecho Procesal Constitucional. Memorias del Primer Congreso Colombiano de Derecho Procesal Constitucional* Mayo 26, 27 and 28 de 2010, Bogotá 2010, 289–95; and Daniela Urosa Maggi, "*Cortes Constitucionales como 'Legisladores Positivos:' La experiencia venezolana,*" Venezuelan National Report, XVIII International Congress of Comparative Law, Washington, July, 2010, 13.

23.6 Final Remarks

The main conclusion that we can deduct from this comparative law study on "Constitutional Courts as Positive Legislators," is that in contemporary world, Constitutional Courts have progressively assumed roles that decades ago only corresponded to the Constituent power or to the Legislator, in some cases, discovering and deducting constitutional rules particularly on matters of human rights not expressively enshrined in the Constitution, and that could not even be considered to have been the intention of an ancient and original Constituent when sanctioning a Constitution conceived for other society.

In other cases, Constitutional Courts have progressively been performing legislative functions, complementing the Legislator in its role of lawmaker, in many cases, filling the gaps resulting from legislative omissions, or sending guidelines and order to the Legislator, and even issuing provisional legislation resulting from the exercise of their functions.

These common trends, found in different countries, and in all legal systems, are of course more numerous and important than the possible essential and exceptional differences that could exist. That is why, in these matters of judicial review, Constitutional Courts in many countries, in order to develop their own competencies and exercise their powers to control the constitutionality of statutes, to protect fundamental rights and to assure the supremacy of the Constitution, have progressively begun to study and analyze the similar work developed in other Courts and in other countries, enriching their ruling.

Consequently, it is possible to say that nowadays, perhaps with the exception of the United States Supreme Court, is common to find in Constitutional Courts' decisions, constant references to decisions issued on similar matters or cases by other Constitutional Courts, so it can be said that in general there is no aversion about using foreign law, to interpret, when applicable, the Constitution.

On the contrary, in the United States is possible to hear voices like those of Justice Sonia Sotomayor at her Senate confirmation hearings a few month ago, affirming that "American Law does not permit the use of foreign law or international law to interpret the Constitution" being this a "given" question regarding which "There is no debate."[124] On the contrary, on these matters, Justice Ruth Bader Ginsburg, has said that she: "frankly don't' understand all the brouhaha lately from Congress and even from some of my colleagues about referring to foreign law," explaining that the controversy was based in the misunderstanding that citing a foreign precedent means for the court to considers itself bound by foreign law as opposed to merely being influenced by such power as its reasoning holds. That is why she formulated the following question: "Why shouldn't we look to the wisdom of a judge from abroad with at least as much ease as we would read a law review article written by a professor?"[125]

And this is precisely what is now common in all Constitutional Jurisdiction all over the world, were Constitutional Courts commonly consider foreign law, when they have to decide on the same matter and based on the same principles. In such cases, in the same sense as of studying the matter according to authors' opinion and analysis in books and articles, they can also rely on courts' decisions from other countries, which can be very useful because they dealt not only with a theoretical proposition, but with a specific solution already applied by a court in the solution of a particular case. And it is here, precisely, where comparative law is a very important and useful tool

23.7 Appendix: National Reports

This General Report synthesizes information I received from the following National Reporter: **ARGENTINA I**: Alejandra Rodríguez Galán and Alfredo Mauricio Vítolo; **ARGENTINA II**: Néstor Pedro Sagües; **AUSTRALIA**: Cherryl Saunders; **AUSTRIA**: Konrad Lachmayer; **BELGIUM**: Patricia Popelier; **BRAZIL I**: Thomas Bustamante and Evanilda de Godoi Bustamante; **BRAZIL II**: Marcelo Figuereido; **BRAZIL III**: Luis Roberto Barroso, Thiago Magalhães and Felipe Drummond; **CANADA**: Kent Roach; **COLOMBIA I**: Germán Alfonso López Daza; **COLOMBIA II**: Sandra Morelli; **COSTA RICA**: Rubén Hernández Valle; **CROATIA**: Sanja Barić and Petar Bačić; **CZECH REPUBLIC**: Zdenek Kühn; **FRANCE**: Bertrand Mathieu, **GERMANY**: Ines Härtel; **GREECE**: lia Iliopoulos-Strangas and Stylianos-Ioannis G. Koutna; **HUNGARY**: Lóránt Csink, Józef Petrétei and Péter Tilk; **INDIA**: Surya Deva; **ITALY**: Giampaolo Parodi; **MEXICO**: Eduardo Ferrer Mac Gregor; **NETHERLANDS**: J. Uzman, T. Barkhuysen & M.L. Emmerik; **NICARAGUA**: Sergio J. Cuarezma Terán and Francisco Enríquez Cabistán; **NORWAY**: Eivind Smith; **PERU I**: Francisco Eguiguren and Liliana Salomé; **PERU II**: Fernán Altuve Febres; **POLAND**: Marek Safjan; **PORTUGAL**: Joaquim de Sousa Ribeiro and Esperança Mealha; **SERBIA**: Boško Tripković; **SLOVAKIA**: Ján Svák and Lucia Berdisová; **SPAIN**: Francisco Fernández Segado; **SWEDEN**: Joakim Nergelius; **SWITZERLAND**: Tobias Jaag; **UNITED KINGDOM**: John Bell; **UNITED STATES**: Laurence Claus and Richard S Kay; **VENEZUELA**: Daniela Urosa.

[124] See the comments of Justice Sonia Sotomayor, in the Senate confirmation Hearings on July 15, 2009, in "Sotomayor on the Issues," *The New York Times,* 16 de Julio de 2009, A18.

[125] See Adam Liptak, "Ginsburg Shares Views on Influence of Foreign Law on Her Court, and Vice Versa," in *The New York Times*, 12 de abril de 2009, 14.

Plurality of Political Opinion and the Concentration of the Media[1]

24

Allen P. Grunes and Maurice E. Stucke

24.1 Introduction

We received reports from ten countries in response to Professor Laurence Idot's questionnaire: Germany (Professor Dr. Matthias Cornils), Greece (Dr. iur. Athanasios D. Tsevas), Italy (Professor Vincenzo Zeno-Zencovich), Japan (Professor Keigo Komamura), EU/Luxembourg (Professor Mark D. Cole), Netherlands (Professor Wouter Hins), Portugal (Professor A.L. Dias Pereira), Switzerland (Professor Bertil Cottier), Taiwan (Professors Kuo-lien Hsieh and Jimmy Chia-shin Hsu), and the United States (Professor William B. Fisch). The Country Reporters responded to a series of questions, including:

i. How "media" is defined in their country and is this definition adequate given new media?
ii. What are the sources that guarantee plurality of media and what are the justifications for protecting plurality?
iii. What media-specific laws or regulations limit concentration?
iv. What other ways is plurality guaranteed by media-specific laws or regulations?
v. How do general competition laws apply to media and how are product markets defined?
vi. What is the relationship between regulatory control and competition law?
vii. Are there any recent significant cases?
viii. What are the trends and future challenges?

From the responses to the questions, it is possible to conceptualize the discussion as follows: One may think of a "U" shaped curve. At one end of the "U," there is a state media monopoly. Most if not all of the reported countries (other than the U.S.) began with state-controlled broadcasting, and have little or no interest in returning to that paradigm. At the other end of the "U" would be a dominant firm (or a few firms) controlling all of the major media outlets in a country. All the reported countries have competition laws and sector regulation that are intended to prevent the formation of such private concentrations of power. Between these two extremes, different countries are at different points on the curve.

Throughout the reports there is a widely shared concern that technological change is making both competition law and sector-specific regulation inadequate to ensure a desirable level of media pluralism. At present, there is no consensus on how to address this concern. Should competition law be more vigorously enforced in media transactions? Are new media-specific regulations needed to address new technologies? Or should government simply step out of the way? Even within governments there are differences of opinion, as illustrated by the controversy in the Netherlands at the end of 2009 over whether to extend that country's Temporary Act on Media Concentrations.[2]

[1] IV.C.1, La pluralité des opinions politiques et les concentrations des medias.

A.P. Grunes (✉)
Brownstein Hyatt Farber Schreck, Washington, DC, USA
e-mail: agrunes@bhfs.com

M.E. Stucke
University of Tennessee College of Law, Knoxville, TN, USA
e-mail: mstucke@utk.edu

[2] Netherlands Country Report at 1.

K.B. Brown and D.V. Snyder (eds.), *General Reports of the XVIIIth Congress of the International Academy of Comparative Law/Rapports Généraux du XVIIIème Congrès de l'Académie Internationale de Droit Comparé*,
DOI 10.1007/978-94-007-2354-2_24,

In this General Report, we first provide an overview of media, second, discuss some common themes in the Country Reports in terms of the importance of media and media pluralism, third, discuss the balance between public support and private ownership and the measures each provides to ensure pluralism, and finally discuss some of the future challenges.

24.2 Overview of Media

One preliminary question is how the term "media" is defined and whether this definition is adequate given the growth of new media. The term "media" includes many different forms of content and distribution: films, books, newspapers, periodicals, radio, broadcast television, cable television, satellite television, and content delivered over the Internet are all "media." And the number of media sources continues to grow, as evidenced by the growth of mobile Internet.

Most reported countries' legal regimes focus on newspapers, radio, and television, since these are and have been the most significant sources of news and information, and remain most important in opinion formation in their countries. They are also the focus of most of the existing regulation and litigation.

Newspapers are treated differently from broadcasting in most reported countries (*see, e.g.*, Germany[3]). Newspapers are less regulated, have fewer restrictions on editorial independence, and may have greater protection from censorship.[4] In the Netherlands, it was expressed this way: "the best press law is no press law."[5]

Broadcasting, both public and private, is subject to greater regulation. In general, publicly supported media is charged with providing content that is deemed important but that may be underserved by the market. Commercial media is regulated both by a sector-specific regulator and by competition law. In many reported countries, these regulations are being reconsidered in light of technological changes.

Data about how households with televisions access programming has been collected by the OECD. According to the OECD, out of 24 countries surveyed, in 2006–2007 terrestrial broadcasting was the dominant delivery method in 8 countries. Terrestrial networks were particularly important in Greece and Italy. Cable was the dominant technology in 15 countries with Switzerland, Belgium and the Netherlands having the most cable subscribers relative to other technologies. Direct broadcast satellite (DBS) was the dominant delivery method only in Austria but there were a total of 11 countries where the number of DBS subscribers outnumbered terrestrial broadcast viewers. The data included market shares based on three distribution methods: free-to-air, cable, and satellite. The OECD did not have sufficient data on television programming delivered over the Internet, although that is obviously an increasingly important fourth alternative in some countries.[6]

Regulation of the Internet is still highly controversial in most reported countries. On the one hand, the Internet is a complement to traditional media (*e.g.*, newspapers and television stations have websites). On the other hand, the Internet offers another distribution "pipe" that is an emerging competitor to traditional media. The Internet is also a disruptive technology, accelerating audience fragmentation and cutting into the advertising revenues of traditional media. In addition, certain issues that were less important in traditional media are much more important with respect to the Internet – *e.g.*, privacy, copyright and access.

There is a general concern that the focus on the "traditional" media may be missing part of the story, and attempts to fit new media within old media classifications may be unsatisfactory. As one author put it, "Technological convergence and changes brought by the Internet may require the concept of media to be redefined, in the sense that the Internet offers a single online digital medium as a complement, or as a substitute, to a variety of means of communication. Nonetheless, despite the migration to the Internet, media are still operating through the traditional channels."[7]

24.3 Importance of the Media and Media Pluralism

However media is defined, all the reported countries recognized the importance of media in informing citizens and serving as a check on government and private power. Freedom of the press and freedom of expression

[3] Germany Country Report at 1.

[4] Japan Country Report at 3–4; Greece Country Report at 2–3.

[5] Netherlands Country Report at 3.

[6] OECD Communications Outlook 2009 at 190, http://browse.oecdbookshop.org/oecd/pdfs/browseit/9309031E.PDF

[7] Portugal Country Report at 1.

(or speech) is constitutionally guaranteed in all of the reported countries. The principle of pluralism is also embedded in Article 11 of the Charter of Fundamental Rights of the European Union.

In Germany, the concept of "broadcasting freedom" has been viewed by the Constitutional Court as an "instrumental" freedom, serving the more fundamental goals of freedom of speech. These goals include an informed democracy and the lively discussion of a variety of views. Unlike the United States, where the First Amendment is viewed largely as protecting broadcasters against government interference, the German view of broadcasting freedom protects the interests of audiences in a wide range of programs and requires the government to ensure that broadcasting is not dominated by the state or by commercial interests. From this standpoint it is less important in Germany than in the U.S. to determine precisely who exercises free speech rights than to ensure that broadcasting institutions are composed and regulated to protect the exercise of free speech. Courts in other European countries, including France and Italy, have taken a similar approach.[8]

Although the reported countries have different historical approaches toward the media (and have had different forms of government in the past), several common themes emerged from the Country Reports.

First, the media help form public opinion, which is crucial for the sound development of democracy (*see, e.g.,* Germany,[9] Japan,[10] Portugal[11]). As the European Commission put it, "Ensuring media pluralism… implies all measures that ensure citizens' access to a wide variety of information, voices etc. in order to form their opinion without the undue influence of one dominant opinion forming power" (quoted in Greece[12]).

Second, media pluralism also can provide an important means of preserving language and cultural diversity (*see, e.g.,* Portugal[13]).

Third, media pluralism can act as a counterweight to political power. In Taiwan, the primary justification for media pluralism has been to dismantle the remnants of the past authoritarian government, which had controlled the media.[14]

Fourth, a robust media can increase political accountability and reduce corruption. Thus, for example, the World Bank found that corruption is lower in countries that have a free press.[15] In countries with media monopolies, the World Bank reported, "political, economic, and social outcomes are worse than in those where the media are competitive, in part because the former are less effective in improving institutional quality (governance)."[16] An independent and competitive media can also inform policy makers of the unintended social effects of their policies, and provide a voice to pressure the government for change.

24.4 Balance Between Public and Private Media

Although one common theme throughout the Country Reports is the importance of maintaining a sufficient diversity of viewpoints, the means to promote such diversity differed among the countries. All of the countries have a mix of publicly-owned or supported media and privately-owned commercial media. But the mix varies from country to country. Some countries (such as the Netherlands) rely more on the public broadcasting sector to provide the diversity of viewpoints than other countries (like the U.S.).

All of the reported countries have privately-owned media. Indeed, in most countries private media, and in particular commercial television, have grown significantly in the past two decades. Their growth represents a challenge to public media. Public broadcasting and commercial broadcasting are both competitors and complements. They are direct competitors for some types of programming, where both may be bidders. This has generated increasing protests from private broadcasters about improper state aid; the claim is that

[8] Eric Barendt, *Broadcasting Law: A Comparative Study* (1994), at 34 (citing cases). *See also* Germany Country Report at 6.

[9] Germany Country Report at 5.

[10] Japan Country Report at 9.

[11] Portugal Country Report at 2.

[12] Greece Country Report at 1.

[13] Portugal Country Report at 2.

[14] Taiwan Country Report at 2; *see also* Germany Country Report at 7.

[15] World Bank, World Development Report 2002: Building Institutions for Markets 19, 107 (2002), http://www-wds.worldbank.org/external/default/WDSContentServer/IW3P/IB/2001/10/05/000094946_01092204010635/Rendered/PDF/multi0page.pdf.

[16] World Bank, supra, at 188.

state support is distorting competition. They are also competitors in a looser sense, in that they must compete for viewers. Especially in those countries that have a robust public broadcasting tradition, fears have been raised that if public broadcasting is inadequately funded, or is overly regulated, it is at risk of becoming only a niche service relative to its commercial competition. In a recent speech, the Director General of the BBC noted that in France, the budget of the public broadcaster has been slashed, and in Germany and Japan, the public broadcasters are prohibited from significant activity on the Internet, "something which everyone recognizes may turn out to be a death sentence in the long run."[17]

24.4.1 Public Broadcasting and Pluralism

Public broadcasting (or public service broadcasting) has been described as a normative, not merely descriptive, concept. Among democracies, such as the reporting countries, public broadcasting typically has a number of features, including: (1) general geographical availability; (2) concern for national identity and culture; (3) independence from both the state and commercial interests; (4) impartiality of programs; (5) range and variety of programs; and (6) substantial financing by a general charge on users.[18]

Some of the stated goals of public broadcasting are to: compensate for inadequacy of commercial television and raise cultural and educational standards (Taiwan[19]); provide basic information about the society and differing views but not take a direct role in political debate (Japan[20]); present a complete and undistorted view of campaigns for election (Greece[21]); enhance international understanding, European integration, and social cohesion, and provide cultural contributions (Germany[22]).

As may be seen from these goals, public broadcasting is expected to provide a balance of programming, including programming that might not otherwise be provided commercially. Programs with a high cost (relative to the projected financial return) or a low audience share may not be aired in a commercial environment.[23] As one author put it, "competition does not always lead to pluralism."[24] As another author stated, "Commercial competition in the area of broadcasting, which aims at constantly higher viewing figures, is likely to lead to the predominance of intellectual currents and of contents which are attractive to the wider audience as well as to the ongoing assimilation of programs, while transmissions of interest to more narrow parts of the audience, such as transmissions of an informational or educational character and especially ambitious cultural transmissions will, as a rule, take second place, if they are not excluded…."[25]

The output of news, which is generally expensive, may be increased through state support. Under the Dutch Media Act, for example, as a condition to receiving state aid, periodicals must show that they are providing a substantial amount of news, analysis, comments and background information about current events.[26] In essence, the state is underwriting part of the cost of news.

Public broadcasting is usually funded through license fees or government appropriations. This funding can result in conflicts with private broadcasting when the public broadcaster competes directly for popular programming such as sports (Germany[27]). In Europe, public funding also must comply with limitations on state aid contained in Article 107 of the Lisbon Treaty.[28]

Public funding also creates certain risks. Public broadcasting needs to be protected from unnecessary state interference and manipulation. In Japan, the public broadcaster is assumed to be susceptible to political pressure, and such pressure has in fact occurred.[29] As one World Bank study found, media in countries with high levels of state ownership were much less free, as they transmit much less information to people in

[17] Mark Thompson, "Public Media in a Digital Age" (Oct. 5, 2010), available at http://www.bbc.co.uk/pressoffice/speeches/stories/thompson_naf.shtml.

[18] Barendt, *Broadcasting Law: A Comparative Study* at 52.

[19] Taiwan Country Report at 9.

[20] Japan Country Report at 19.

[21] Greece Country Report at 20–21.

[22] Germany Country Report at 17.

[23] Netherlands Country Report at 18.

[24] Taiwan Country Report at 15.

[25] Greece Country Report at 8.

[26] Netherlands Country Report at 7.

[27] Germany Country Report at 32.

[28] Portugal Country Report at 12.

[29] Japan Country Report at 16–18 (discussing *VAWW Net v. NHK* (2000)).

economic and political markets.[30] This was historically a concern in Taiwan,[31] and one still sees today governments censoring or manipulating news on public as well as private news broadcasts.[32]

Public broadcasting may be insulated from political pressure in several different ways: Legislatively, the broadcaster may be set up so that it is removed from direct political influence. Courts may also place limits on government interference. In the U.S., the Supreme Court has held that the government cannot constitutionally forbid public broadcasters from expressing editorial viewpoints, even though the government has a legitimate interest in limiting the use of government dollars for such purposes.[33] It appears crucial that the media have at least some real protection from government retaliation for editorial decisions.

A second complementary measure could be called "democratizing" public broadcasting. In Germany, for example, public broadcasters have an internal supervisory committee composed of various social groups, to ensure pluralism. All relevant parties must be represented on the committee.[34]

A third measure to minimize the incentive to bias public broadcasting is to promote competition with, and the economic freedom of, private media. The government may be less inclined to manipulate the news on a public broadcasting station that faces significant competition from many private independent news outlets. The private news outlets, which are not captured, have an incentive to publish the embargoed news story (and bolster their reputation).[35] This in turn can diminish the reputation of the public broadcaster, lead to reduced public support and, in democratic governments, lead to less funding for the public broadcaster.

24.4.2 Commercial Media and Pluralism

There are benefits and risks to private media ownership. Among the benefits of private media ownership are the benefits of competition generally. Competition among private entities for readers and advertisers may yield lower prices for media (lower subscription prices, lower advertising rates), better quality products (such as greater investment in investigative journalism), better services (such as providing important financial information quickly to news subscribers) and more innovation. Competition may also increase the number of points of view, and lessen media bias as media firms in more competitive markets have stronger incentives to reveal important information. With competitive media markets, there is also less need for day-to-day government regulation. Moreover, competition can lead to greater dispersal of economic and political power.

One concern over media markets is that market forces, if left unchecked, will yield concentrated media markets that will hinder pluralism and the marketplace of ideas. News collection and production of media content often involve high fixed costs. For example, the cost to publish the "first copy" of the N.Y. Times newspaper would be in the millions of U.S. dollars, given the costs of the news bureaus and journalists. This fixed cost can be absorbed with each additional copy of the newspaper being sold above marginal cost. (The increase in readership can also bring more advertising revenue.) Thus media mergers can be an attractive option to reduce these fixed costs or to spread them over a wider audience.

Media also has a different form of market failure. With many commodities, market failure manifests in higher prices. The consumer pays more. But market failure in the media may not manifest itself simply with higher prices. Increased concentration may lessen the competition among news providers and the quality of reporting. In highly concentrated media markets, private owners associated with the state or political parties – or protecting their business interests – can shape or control the dissemination of information. Increased media concentration may also increase the risk of self-censorship. Journalists and media watchdogs

[30] World Bank, supra, at 183–85.

[31] Taiwan Country Report at 4 (concern that governmental and partisan ownership caused partisan slanting of political opinion).

[32] One recent example is China's internal embargo of news on the Nobel Peace Prize to Liu Xiaobo, including blocking coverage on the cable news station CNN.

[33] United States Country Report at 30 no.75 (citing *FCC v. League of Women Voters of California*, 368 U.S. 364 (1984)); Lee Bollinger, *Uninhibited, Robust and Wide-Open* (2010) at 109–10. In the U.S., public broadcasting receives some financial support from the government, but it is largely funded by private donations.

[34] Germany Country Report at 4, 11.

[35] Matthew Gentzkow and Jesse M. Shapiro, "Competition & Truth in the Market for News," *Journal of Economic Perspectives* 22 (2008): 133–154.

in the U.S. have expressed concern about the rise of self-censorship and the loss of journalistic independence following the increasing media concentration. If the media is dependent upon government funding or a few major advertisers through overall industry concentration, the risk of self-censorship also increases.

Although concentrated media can be more easily captured by the government, economically powerful media companies can also serve as counterweight to concentrated political power. Resource rich corporations may be well positioned to invest in journalism, combat government censorship, and support freedom of speech. Smaller organizations may not be powerful enough to effectively monitor and check the authority of the state.[36] Given the high fixed costs involved in broadcasting, in particular, it can be dangerous to require too much fragmentation of the market under the name of enhancing pluralism. The result may be entrenchment of existing firms, prevention of mergers of any scale, and an inefficient market.[37]

24.4.3 Structural Limitations

Just as no reported country relies exclusively on state or private media, so too no reported country relies exclusively on a laissez-faire or central-planning approach to media regulation of private media firms. To prevent market failure and to promote the plurality of viewpoints in the media, most country participants reported media-specific regulations that impose some limits on private ownership of media. These are in addition to competition law measures.

The ownership regulations do not directly govern the behavior of the media firms (such as content), but seek to preserve a competitive market structure. The regulations may place limits on the absolute number of newspapers, television stations, or radio stations that one individual or corporation may own or control (Portugal,[38] Greece[39]). Or the government regulations may place limits on the total audience share or market share that one individual or corporation may own or control in a single medium (*see, e.g.*, Italy,[40] Taiwan,[41] U.S.[42]).

There are also cross-ownership rules, preventing for example a television station owner from owning a newspaper in the same community. These limits have been relaxed in recent years in a number of countries (*e.g.*, Netherlands,[43] Taiwan,[44] Italy[45]), although attempts to relax the limits have also been challenged (U.S.[46]).

Some countries have limits on the total audience share or "market" share (*e.g.*, Netherlands[47]) that can be owned across media. This is another sort of cross-ownership limit.

One issue is the extent to which these media restrictions are arbitrary. It does not appear from the Country Reports that media regulations are supported empirically.[48] Who can say, based on sound empirical data, whether a market share of 25% ensures diversity of opinion, while 35% does not? Plus there seems to be some history of evasion in some countries (*e.g.*, Taiwan[49]). Nonetheless, these ownership limits are generally oriented (and defended) as necessary to ensure pluralism. Moreover, in seeking to prevent undue concentration in media markets and preserve a competitive market structure, the structural limitations can be relatively less intrusive than attempts to regulate the behavior and content of media firms in concentrated industries.

24.4.4 Content-Based Limitations

In addition to structural ownership and cross-ownership rules, there are content-based rules. There is agreement among the Reported Countries, especially in

[36] Lee Bollinger, *Uninhibited, Robust and Wide-Open* (2010) at 109.

[37] Italy Country Report at 6, 8.

[38] Portugal Country Report at 3 (radio).

[39] Greece Country Report at 10 (newspapers).

[40] Italy Country Report at 3 (newspapers and broadcasting).

[41] Taiwan Country Report at 6 (cable television).

[42] United States Country Report at 40, 42, 44 (national broadcast television).

[43] Netherlands Country Report at 6.

[44] Taiwan Country Report at 5–6.

[45] Italy Country Report at 3, 4.

[46] United States Country Report at 44–49.

[47] Netherlands Country Report at 6. The "market share" is determined based on newspaper circulation, radio listening time, and television viewing time.

[48] Taiwan Country Report at 13–14; Italy Country Report at 3.

[49] Taiwan Country Report at 6.

broadcasting, to protect children from violent or sexually explicit content. This is generally justified because of the presence of televisions in most households, the difficulty of preventing children from having access to television, and the importance of television for opinion formation. But beyond that agreement about protecting children, the Country Reports reflect varying approaches to content regulation.

In the U.S., content-based rules are hard to justify under the protections afforded under the First Amendment of the U.S. Constitution.[50] Thus even a rule concerned with use of indecent speech was recently struck down by a federal appellate court. This is because in the U.S., freedom of speech is generally viewed as a restraint on the ability of the government to act. In many other countries, freedom of speech (or expression) is treated as a value which may sometimes compel the government to act: for example, to regulate broadcasting standards, to limit advertising in the interest of viewers and listeners, or to insure pluralism by preventing the formation of monopolies.[51]

Moreover, a number of countries require or incentivize broadcasters to air domestic programming. For example, in Portugal, broadcasters must include a certain percentage of European works and works in Portuguese.[52]

A number of countries provide for a right of reply (*e.g.*, Portugal,[53] Greece[54]). In the U.S., the Supreme Court limited this right to broadcast media and did not impose this obligation on newspapers. Then, during deregulation in the 1980s, the right was significantly curtailed even in broadcasting (U.S.[55]).

Generally, there appear from the Country Reports fewer restrictions on content for private broadcasters than public broadcasters (*see, e.g.*, Netherlands). However, in Portugal, the Press Act and the Television Act do not distinguish between the public and private sectors, and apply equally to both.[56] And in Greece, commercial broadcasters have obligations to present the full range of political opinions on all subjects of any political controversy.[57]

24.4.5 Role of Competition Policy to Protect Media's Plurality of Voices

Many countries now have competition authorities with the power to apply competition law to the media. Competition law comes into play in two primary ways: as a means of preventing abuse of a dominant position (monopolization), and as a means of preventing anticompetitive mergers. Courts in Italy, France and Germany have ruled that commercial broadcasting must be regulated by antitrust rules sufficiently stringent to safeguard plurality of opinion.[58]

Media markets, like other markets, tend to be defined in economic terms by competition law. Countries typically distinguish a free over-the-air broadcasting market (which is advertising-supported) from a subscription television market. Within advertising-supported media, different media (e.g., radio, television, newspapers) are often considered to be in separate economic markets: Portugal, for example, defines radio, broadcast, and outdoor advertising as separate markets.[59]

However, attempts have been made within competition law to account for the importance of media to opinion formation and to ensure diversity of opinion. Article 21(3) of the European Commission's Merger Regulation provides that member states may not apply their own national competition laws to mergers with a community dimension (i.e. those mergers that exceed certain aggregate sales thresholds and affect more than one member state). However, Article 21(4) expressly makes exception for "plurality of media," which is regarded under that Article as one of the legitimate interests that may be protected by a member state as long as such protection is compatible with the general principles and other provisions of community law.

In Germany, broadcasting and press mergers have a lower "minimum turnover" (annual revenue) requirement than other mergers, which allows the competition authority to intervene in mergers of medium-sized enterprises in these industries.[60] But one issue in Germany and other reported countries remains how,

[50] U.S. Country Report at 51.

[51] Greece Country Report at 4, 21.

[52] Portugal Country Report at 5.

[53] Portugal Country Report at 5.

[54] Greece Country Report at 6.

[55] United States Country Report at 18–27.

[56] Portugal Country Report at 3.

[57] Greece Country Report at 21.

[58] Barendt, *Broadcasting Law: A Comparative Study* at 127–28 (citing cases).

[59] Portugal Country Report at 13–14.

[60] Germany Country Report at 22.

and whether, competition agencies should take media pluralism or other non-economic concerns into account.[61] It has been suggested that such concerns are better left to other agencies besides the competition authorities.[62]

Generally, competition law remedies take the form of structural relief – i.e., mergers are blocked or divestitures are ordered.[63] However, in some cases, behavioral relief has been ordered. For example, in the Netherlands, the condition was placed on a merger that one of three television stations involved had to be a "news only" channel.[64]

Most countries appear to favor some coordination – either formal (Netherlands,[65] Italy[66]) or informal (U.S.[67]) – between the competition authority and the sector regulator. In Taiwan, the Fair Trade Commission is obligated to take into account the opinion of the National Communications Commission in cable television mergers.[68] A similar situation exists in Portugal, where the Media Regulatory Authority is able to issue a binding opinion in television mergers which are also being reviewed by the Competition Authority. The Media Regulatory Authority is able to block television mergers when there are well-grounded risks to freedom of expression and plurality of opinion. A similar provision exists in press mergers.[69]

[61] Germany Country Report at 21 (noting narrow market definition, and no market recognized yet for television viewers).

[62] Greece Country Report at 8–9 (arguing that if competition law were encumbered with the task of ensuring pluralism it would be deprived of its clarity and stringency).

[63] Germany Country Report at 23 (competition authority rejected behavioral remedy in a large media merger); U.S. Dep't of Justice, Antitrust Division, Antitrust Division Policy Guide on Merger Remedies 8 (Oct. 2004) (discussing why structural relief, which is "relatively clean and certain, and generally avoids costly government entanglement in the market," is preferred over conduct remedies), http://www.justice.gov/atr/public/guidelines/205108.htm#3a.

[64] Netherlands Country Report at 20.

[65] Netherlands Country Report at 14.

[66] Italy Country Report at 6–7 (protocol between the two agencies).

[67] United States Country Report at 8–9.

[68] Taiwan Country Report at 8.

[69] Portugal Country Report at 2, 4.

24.5 Trends and Future Challenges in Preserving the Plurality of the Media

A number of common trends appear in the Country Reports and the literature. Economic trends include the declining readership of printed newspapers (*see, e.g.*, Netherlands,[70] Italy[71]), decline in free over-the-air television viewership in many countries (*see, e.g.*, OECD[72]), the shift of advertising from traditional media to online services (*see, e.g.*, Italy[73]), and the convergence of services offered by cable companies and telecommunications companies (*see, e.g.*, OECD[74]). These industry trends are challenging private traditional media companies to develop new business models in order to remain viable.

The growth of new media has led to increasing audience fragmentation. With the increasing centrality of the Internet as a means of expression, there are concerns about whether the fragmentation of social discourse (the decline in a few commonly read or viewed media outlets) "will deprive societies of shared information and experiences, leaving us less able to discuss issues, less exposed to diverse viewpoints, and more inclined to connect primarily, or only, with those with whom we agree."[75] The danger to a democracy is no longer the historical concern of supply-driven bias (when the biased news coverage primarily originates with the media firms, and deviates from the news coverage that consumers prefer). Now the greater danger to a democracy is demand-driven bias (which is when consumers demand biased news coverage that comports with their pre-existing beliefs).[76] With greater fragmentation of news coverage on the Internet, and more coverage that caters specifically to certain ideological or political beliefs, the danger exists that people will only seek out on the Internet viewpoints that they

[70] Netherlands Country Report at 22.

[71] Italy Country Report at 4 (newspaper circulation less than 80 years ago when population was half current level and illiteracy was high).

[72] OECD Communications Outlook 2009 at 189.

[73] Italy Country Report at 9.

[74] OECD Communications Outlook 2009 at 193.

[75] Lee Bollinger, Uninhibited, Robust and Wide-Open (2010) at 119.

[76] Gentzkow and Shapiro, Market for News, supra, at 134, 144.

already agree with, making reasoned debate more difficult. There is some evidence, at least in the United States, that the multiplication of media choices is having this effect. "We found that people generally chose media messages that reinforced their own preexisting views," wrote the author of one study. "In general, they don't want their views to be challenged by seriously considering other viewpoints."[77]

The dynamic nature of media markets also poses difficulties for competition law. First, it is becoming harder to define relevant antitrust markets (Netherlands[78]). Market shares may be less meaningful in a rapidly changing industry. As the U.S. Supreme Court recognized in the *General Dynamics* case, "[e]vidence of past production does not, as a matter of logic, necessarily give a proper picture of a company's future ability to compete."[79] Only in examining "its structure, history and probable future" does one provide "the appropriate setting for judging the probable anticompetitive effect of [a] merger."[80] In making predictions about future market behavior, competition officials often look for answers by looking backwards.

Moreover, media-specific regulation based on a scarcity rationale is becoming more questionable (Japan[81]). Yet the scarcity rationale has been one factor underlying government intervention in the market, at least in some reported countries. This regulation also tends to be somewhat backward looking.

An alternative to regulation would be to increase the support for public media. But there does not appear to be much support to return to the days of a largely government-controlled media. Nor, in the current economic downturn, is there necessarily the money to increase the level of government support.

As previously noted, the traditional media remain the most important sources of news and information, and probably will be for the foreseeable future. Technological changes are driving competition law to allow greater concentration, while at the same time calling into question some of the underlying reasons to regulate electronic media. There is a concern that competition law, by itself, may not adequately protect pluralism (Taiwan[82]). At the same time, at least one reporter has questioned whether an excessive concern with pluralism may simply be a way to protect the economic and political interests of printed media groups and public broadcasters (Italy[83]).

There is therefore no consensus among the Country Reports that the growth of new media, and especially the Internet, is sufficient to prevent market failure in media markets. But there is also no consensus that there is, in fact, market failure. And perhaps most importantly, there is no consensus on how, and whether, the Internet should be regulated.

Going forward, to foster a competitive media, the Country Reports would appear to support some measures. One measure is for the government to remove onerous regulations that reduce the media's independence and increase the risk of supply-side media bias. Globally, some government licensing requirements extend beyond technical feasibility and impose restrictions on content. After the Korean government, for example, replaced the newspaper licensing requirements in 1987 with more liberal ones, "the number of newspapers grew from 6 to 17 in Seoul alone, and dozens more were launched" in other parts of Korea, providing more diverse coverage.[84] At the same time, requiring too much market fragmentation deprives the media of the benefits of scale economies (Italy[85]).

A second measure is in responding to global convergence. The Country Reports describe the challenge to maintain plurality in each country with the new technological convergence. Even if a country can maintain such plurality, there exists the danger that another country's laws may impair such plurality. The Internet and other improvements in communication technology have lowered the costs and speed in

[77] Study: Americans choose media messages that agree with their views, http://esciencenews.com/articles/2009/05/28/study.americans.choose.media.messages.agree.with.their.views (quoting Professor Silvia Knobloch-Westerwick).

[78] Netherlands Country Report at 22.

[79] United States v. General Dynamics Corp., 415 U.S. 486, 501 (1974).

[80] Ibid.

[81] Japan Country Report at 8.

[82] Taiwan Country Report at 15.

[83] Italy Country Report at 1.

[84] World Bank, supra, at 186.

[85] Italy Country Report at 2, 8; see also Joaquín Almunia, Vice President of the European Commission responsible for competition policy, Competition in Digital Media and the Internet, SPEECH/10/365, 7 July 2010, http://europa.eu/rapid/pressReleasesAction.do?reference=SPEECH/10/365&format=HTML&aged=0&language=EN&guiLanguage=en.

communicating around the world. But therein exists a new danger. Government censorship of the Internet (for example, Facebook's, Twitter's, and Google's recent experience in China), and the enforcement of libel laws for content delivered across borders via the Internet, could adversely affect freedom of the press in ways that could not be imagined a few years ago. Thus, governments may need to better coordinate to further reduce friction among them. Ultimately the heat from any friction will depend on the advancement of international mechanisms to secure the just, speedy and inexpensive resolution of any conflicts.

Are Human Rights Universal and Binding?[1]

25

Rainer Arnold

25.1 Universality of Human Rights

25.1.1 How to Define Universality?

It is difficult to define universality. It is a complex concept which incorporates geographic, cultural, historical and political dimensions.[2] As of now, there is no generally accepted notion of universality of human rights.

Universality of human rights can be understood as a *propensity* for *global acceptance* of human rights. This is a *territorial* or *outer dimension*.

One may identify, in this territorial dimension, a *vertical* and a *horizontal* acceptance of human rights.

A *vertical* acceptance of human rights takes place on three levels: national (local), regional and international. This cross-level perspective is important for universality in order to give a comprehensive insight into the interactions of these levels.

A *horizontal* dimension implies a tendency towards the acceptance of human rights in all the geographical parts of the world.

Universality also has an *inner dimension* which relates to the qualities of universality as such. Universality also touches on the questions: who is entitled to human rights, who has to respect human rights, what scope do human rights have,[3] are they functioning efficiently?

Distinction can be made between a substantive and functional aspects in this context:

The *substantive aspect* of this dimension includes:

(a) human rights are inherent to all human beings – *active aspect;*
(b) human rights must be protected against all encroachments (by public and private powers) – *passive aspect;*
(c) the basic values such as dignity, freedom and autonomy of an individual must be explicitly or implicitly protected – *objective aspect.*

The *functional aspect* of the aforementioned inner dimension of human rights embraces the following requirements:

1. Necessary limitations must respect a *principle of optimalization* of human rights.
2. Intervention by public power must be founded on law; it must be backed up by a legitimate reason, be necessary for the needs of a democratic society[4] and be the sole adequate means of achieving such a legitimate reason *(principle of proportionality).*
3. The *core (the very nature, the essence)* of human rights must not be affected.
4. *Efficient judicial protection* is indispensable.

We can therefore state that universality of human rights has (1) horizontal and vertical geographical

[1] IV.C.2, Les droits de l'homme, sont-ils universels et normatifs?

[2] Solomon Islands 2. Here and on references are given to the pages of the original national reports as submitted to the General Reporter and later made public on the website of the IACL prior to and during the IACL Congress of 2010.

[3] Poland 2.

[4] Canada 2; Hungary 14; Greece 19.

R. Arnold (✉)
Chair of Public Law, Jean Monnet Chair of EU Law, Faculty of Law, University of Regensburg, Germany
e-mail: rainer.arnold@jura.uni-regensburg.de

K.B. Brown and D.V. Snyder (eds.), *General Reports of the XVIIIth Congress of the International Academy of Comparative Law/Rapports Généraux du XVIIIème Congrès de l'Académie Internationale de Droit Comparé*, DOI 10.1007/978-94-007-2354-2_25, © Springer Science+Business Media B.V. 2012

dimensions as well as (2) an inner, quality-related dimension with substantive (matter-related) and functional (efficiency-related) aspects.[5]

25.1.2 The Human Rights Idea, the Political Transformation of this Idea into Normative Structures and the Gap Between a Normative Claim and Reality

Universalism of human rights is an *ideological concept* which presently constitutes a pillar of public awareness in the world despite the many reported and unreported human rights violations. Such public awareness results in manifold political initiatives to ameliorate the legal protection of human rights on all three levels (national, regional and international). Judicial activism in promoting effective protection of human rights also plays an important role in this cause.

Whilst the *idea* of universalism of human rights is widely shared, its *political* and *normative reality* bears serious shortcomings, in particular, with regard to the mechanisms of *control* and *sanctions* on the *international level*.[6]

25.1.3 Normative Claim and Normative Reality

Universalism of human rights can be considered from various perspectives.

Firstly, universalism of human rights can be understood as an *idea* or *concept*.

Secondly, it can be understood as a *normative reality* (normative requirement and normative fact[7]).

Universal human rights protection is an *ideological concept* deeply rooted in American history with impact on the formulation of the international key instruments,[8] the UN Charter and the Declaration of 1948. The universality formula was affirmed in the Vienna Declaration of the UN World Conference on human rights expressing the opinion of 171 states[9] – a quasi-universal opinion – that human rights derive from "dignity and worth inherent in the human person"[10] and are "universal, indivisible, interdependent and interrelated"[11] and must be treated by the international community "globally in a fair and equal manner, on the same footing, and with the same emphasis".[12]

This ideological concept has been transformed into *normative structures*, on the international level in particular in the form of the UN Covenants and specific human rights instruments, on the regional level with guarantee systems in America, Africa,[13] and – deemed as the most efficient and influential of them – the ECHR,[14] In the beginning of state constitutionalism national rights have developed autonomously, but have later received considerably reinforcing incentives from the human rights internationalization process. The autonomy of the national level still exists but is characterized, as one of the consequences of globalization, by a growing "internationalization" or, in EU Europe, with even more external impact, by a tendency towards "supranationalization" in the field of fundamental and human rights. The EU Charter, in force with the Lisbon Treaty since December 1, 2009, applies to a great extent also to state action in the frequent cases where national administration executes EU law. This also influences the remaining national field of action and promotes conceptual convergence.

Regional human rights stemming from the ECHR, which enjoys high authority for its elaborated jurisprudence and long human rights experience, are respected as convincing sources of inspiration both for national and supranational judges.

The influence of international law can be realized in various ways: through interpretation of internal laws in the light of international human rights, on the basis of a principle of "friendly attitude towards international law" or even of a *presumption* of the willingness of national organs to conform to international law or through filling up national discretionary power clauses with international law contents, etc.

In *monist systems* international law, including human rights, constitutes an integral part of the state

[5] See also Brazil 2 ("universalism of confluence").

[6] Great Britain 2.

[7] Slovakia 7.

[8] USA 2, 4.

[9] Germany 2.

[10] See Hungary 12; Japan 4.

[11] Ibid.

[12] Ibid.

[13] Democratic Republic of the Congo 3–4.

[14] Great Britain 6; Slovakia 6; Ukraine 6; Netherlands 15; Scotland 2; Taiwan 3; Norway 2.

order and prevails regularly over national ordinary laws,[15] a kind of highly effective impact of international law on the state level. Such impact is even stronger in the case of EU law which enjoys primacy over national ordinary and – in the opinion of the ECJ[16] – even constitutional law.

Thus, the human rights idea has become a legal reality in wide parts of the world. However, it does not fully satisfy the ideological claims, in particular, on the international level. State sovereignty, the coordination structure of mutual relations, the lack of a sufficient legal position of an individual in the state-related international community, deficient complaint, control and sanction mechanisms have created a rather weak human rights protection system. Neither the rudimentary elements of individual-related elements of the Optional Protocols to the human rights treaties can be regarded as adequate nor the modest beginnings of an evolving objective, *jus cogens* value order with *erga omnes* effect especially in the field of international human rights.

Thus, the normative reality does not correspond in many respects to the normative claim. In regard to the aforementioned three levels, it can be said that the more legally and socially integrated a system is (state, region) the higher the chances are for a legal claim to be approximated to the reality. The least integrated system, the international community, shows the most striking deficiencies of all the three levels in the human rights protection mechanisms.

25.1.4 Universality vs. Culturalism[17]

Are there limits to the idea of universal human rights? This question seems to be crucial in our context. It is a global problem which appears particularly significant in regions where "clashes of culture" are imminent. But also in countries with marked cultural diversity and distinct political decentralization, such as Canada, culture-related divergences in interpreting human rights texts are visible.[18] It should also be mentioned, quite generally, that any interpretation of normative texts in any country is interdependent with local and regional culture[19]; what is decisive is the readiness of the interpreter to objectivize her/his culture-shaped mindset and to duly respect the international obligations. Thus, the need for universality is satisfied and cultural particularity is observed to the extent that the universal documents explicitly or implicitly allow it.

We can roughly distinguish three approaches to the question of conflict of relativism v. universalism:

(a) *absolute relativism* – a rather seldom approach, which totally denies, for whatever conflicting cultural reasons, the universal, or at least quasi-universal, normative effect which results from the human rights treaties. This approach cannot be upheld.

(b) *relative (limited or moderate) universalism* which upholds the treaty-based human rights as such (or at least the core of it[20]), but allows consideration of particular cultural aspects when interpreting the – often vaguely formulated – human rights, when filling up a "margin of appreciation"[21] or, particular significant, when weighing human rights and public interests.[22] Collectivism could prevail over individualism in the judicial assessment process.[23]

With this approach a conciliation of the universality claim with cultural diversity could be reached. The core of a human right, however, must remain intangible. It remains doubtful whether, for example, "patriarchal attitudes" can be regarded compatible with a universal human rights claim for gender equality.[24]

(c) "Universality through culture" approach which confirms an inner link, not a contrast between both dimensions saying that cultural adaptation increases or even creates sociological acceptance of the normative prescription and therefore gives real efficiency to human rights.[25] This (rarely formulated) approach is not far from the first mentioned one and is subject to the same objections.

[15] Greece 3; Belgium 3.

[16] ECJ, Case 11/70, Rep. 1970, 1125.

[17] Netherlands 6.

[18] Canada 1.

[19] Ukraine 5, 8; Great Britain 3; Taiwan 2; Russia 9; Belgium 1.

[20] Netherlands 7, 21; Great Britain 3; Portugal 7; Ukraine 6; Slovakia 8; Solomon Islands 5.

[21] Netherlands 21; Slovakia 2.

[22] Belgium 7, Japan 5; Croatia 1–2.

[23] See Taiwan 3.

[24] Japan 12.

[25] See also Netherlands 8; Taiwan 2; Russia 9.

25.1.5 Human Rights and National Constitutional Law

Initially, fundamental and human rights were a purely internal matter, progeny of a long political and cultural evolution centered in the Anglo-American world[26] and in revolutionary France. The emancipation of an individual has become a predominant characteristic of the national legal orders and is an achievement of modern constitutionalism – a process in Europe with a far-reaching impact also on non-European countries and which started in its particularly significant phase after the Second World War. In three sub-phases[27] (the immediate post-war period with the influential anthropocentric model of the German *Grundgesetz*, the 1970s with the post-authoritarian constitutions in Spain, Portugal and Greece, and the last and most advancing period of the turn from the 1980s to the 1990s with the transformation of communist states to new democracies[28]) *individualization* has become the main feature of the new constitutionalism. It focuses on an efficient protection of the individual's rights, based on human dignity[29] (a rather undetermined concept undergoing various definition attempts[30]), with a comprehensive scope of protection covering explicitly or implicitly (that is by judge-made guaranties) all threats to freedom, and aims at its functional efficiency which consists, in particular, of in an adequate judicial control, the application of the principle of proportionality and the observance of the essence of a right even by the legislator. These are general characteristic elements of protection efficiency, which have already been referred to above in the context of the "functional universality" of international human rights.

The New Constitutionalism combines individual protection with a modern approach to rule of law: human rights are part of it[31]; it is, therefore, value-oriented with human dignity as a supreme value and basic for state and society. Legality is no longer the leading principle; it is complemented by constitutionality addressed to the legislator. Assuring the primacy of the Constitution with that of the individual rights is a task which today is often attributed to constitutional courts.

Human rights as part of fundamental rights, held by all,[32] not only by citizens (as is the case for political rights), have been developed in a country, in principle, autonomously, based on own tradition and legal culture. It should be noted that the states undergoing transformation commonly adopt models and inspiration in the field of human rights from either the experienced democratic constitutions or from international, in particular, regional human rights systems, in order to effectuate transition from authoritarian regimes or even dictatorships to pluralistic democracies.[33] The ECHR played an extraordinary role in this context, particularly in Central and Eastern Europe countries. This role can be seen in the process of reforming national constitutions or their redrafting. Later reference to the ECHR was also frequently made by the national constitutional courts, in particular, to the Strasbourg jurisprudence, in order to legitimize and confirm their own constitutional solutions using arguments from a highly respected European institution.[34] As constitutional courts regularly apply only constitutional law, except for the procedures where international law is relevant (such as the review of the compatibility of national legislation, as it is foreseen in some countries), references to the international level function as confirmation of their own solutions based on national law.

In some systems legislation is reviewed under international covenants and not under national constitutional law such as in the Netherlands (Article 120 of the Dutch Constitution).[35] This results in regional human rights, as embodied by the ECHR and interpreted by the Strasbourg Court, having a direct impact on the internal legal order while the impact of the own constitution being reduced.[36] Such a phenomenon also exists in other countries where the international treaties, in particular those on human rights, prevail over ordinary national law as it is, for example, in France under Article 55 of the Constitution.

[26] See USA 5–12.

[27] R. Arnold, "Die staatliche Verfassung im europäischen Kontext: Überlegungen zum heutigen Stand des Konstitutionalismus," in *La Constitution hier, aujourd'hui et demain*, Belgischer Senat, Heft 2 2006, 41–50.

[28] Armenia 1.

[29] Slovakia 8; Portugal 4.

[30] Great Britain 12.

[31] Taiwan 3; Germany 10.

[32] Italy 7–16.

[33] See Poland 4–14.

[34] See also Portugal 10, 16; Slovakia 4.

[35] Netherlands 25 ff.

[36] See also Netherlands 24.

Many of the Central Eastern Europe countries have assumed the monist model where by national law is superseded by the international treaty law.[37] It is significant that in some of these countries this primacy model was originally introduced to the human rights treaties and was later expanded to the international treaties as such. The international influences are even greater where an international treaty (e.g. the ECHR) has become part of the internal constitutional order as, for example, in Austria. A similar situation can be found in Switzerland where the ECHR has a rank of constitutional law: it is evident that Swiss legal thinking is adapting to a great extent to the Strasbourg solutions. In other countries, such as Spain, the international instruments, in particular the Convention, serve as means of interpretation of internal rights as embodied in the Constitution. Thus, the Constitution itself opens the door for international concepts with the intention of overcoming national legal isolation.

The power of the international order is so mighty that it is able to reform, from outside, deeply rooted traditional systems as, for example, in the United Kingdom. Sovereignty of Parliament, the supreme constitutional dogma in this country, has been seriously relativated both by the EU law (the famous *Factortame* case[38]) and the Strasbourg law which was introduced into the internal legal order about 10 years ago by the Human Rights Act. Functionally, the Human Rights Act mechanisms are destined to override Westminster legislation in case it is incompatible with the Strasbourg Convention. If a higher court states such incongruence, the Minister has to adapt the existing legislation to the Convention with prior or, in urgent cases, subsequent consent of the Parliament. Thus, Westminster legislation is no longer able to avoid being challenged by the courts. Although the courts cannot annul the incompatible laws, they can interrupt their application and launch the process of a reform. Besides the impact of the regional human rights instruments on British law it should be stated that European continental concepts are adopted by a system which for a long time guaranteed fundamental human rights by common law. In the words of Lord Denning, M.R: European law is "like an incoming tide. It flows into the estuaries and up the rivers. It cannot be held back".[39]

Even in Germany where the traditional dualist view restrains the full internal deployment of international law, a principle of 'open statehood'[40] has developed. Thus, internal legislation is interpreted in a way favourable to international and (as the Federal Constitutional Court recently said in the Lisbon Treaty decision) also to the European Union law. Primacy of Union law has long since been accepted also in the field of fundamental rights (with a certain evolution from *Solange I*[41] to *Solange II*[42]). The recent decisions of the Constitutional Court are not manifestly contrary to this position but try to ensure the remaining fundamentals of the national sovereignty. Thus, 'constitutional identity', as a core set of principles which cannot be destructed by Union law, have been declared sacrosanct under the protection of the Constitutional Court itself.[43] The external obligations are fully respected, but on the internal scale there is no primacy of international treaties over national law with regard to the traditional yet anachronistic dualism. This is also valid for the ECHR. The famous *Caroline von Monaco*[44] and *Görgülü*[45] cases illustrate the possibility of major divergences between the Karlsruhe and Strasbourg jurisprudences on human rights. It seemed more appropriate to have adapted the solution to the national Constitution than to the Convention because the normative context was found to be better elaborated under the former.

In conclusion it can be said that human rights expressed by national constitutions have developed autonomously but are found to be more and more under the influence of the international law experience.[46] In a regional integration system vertical and horizontal impacts and influences can be distinguished which are able to harmonize the human rights protection to a certain extent and favour universalism by doing so. The vertical impact results in the primacy of

[37] Poland 4 ('general incorporation').

[38] *R v Secretary of State for Transport (ex parte Factortame)* (1990) 2 /AC 85, (1991) 1/AC 603.

[39] *H.P. Bulmer Ltd v. J. Bollinger SA* (1974) Ch 401, at 418.

[40] Federal Constitutional Court (FCC), vol. 111, 317/318.

[41] FFC vol. 37, 271.

[42] FFC vol. 73, 339.

[43] FFC judgment of June 30, 2009 see: http://www.bundesverfassungsgericht.de/entscheidungen/es20090630_2bve000208en.html (English translation).

[44] FCC vol. 101, 361.

[45] FCC vol. 111, 307; see Germany 7.

[46] See also Hungary 3.

the European Union law over national ordinary and even constitutional law. This phenomenon seems to be unique in the European area. The impact originating from the ECHR is traditional in its forms; it is an international treaty with a binding force but not with primacy in the sense of the EU law. Functionally, however, the impact of the Strasbourg Convention goes significantly beyond and can be said to have a constitution-like character. The national constitutional concepts, in reverse, had their significant influence on the shaping and interpretation of the EU as well as the ECHR human rights.[47]

Horizontally, the ECHR exercised much influence on the EU legal thinking and will soon become a formal source of it. EU human rights are recognized by the Strasbourg Court as a high level protection system. The Strasbourg Court declared its trust in the EU human rights system and presumes the compatibility of the EU acts to this system (the *Bosphorus* case).[48] Therefore, it no longer reviews such acts under the ECHR except for in the cases of manifest violations. This means that Strasbourg confirms the equivalence of the EU human rights – a further step towards universalism through harmonization and mutual recognition.

25.2 Are Fundamental Rights Binding?

25.2.1 International and Regional Level

This question may be answered shorter than the question of universality as the two issues overlap in part.[49]

What is binding? From the view point of a lawyer, only normative texts are binding in so far as reference can be made to the traditional sources of law. It should be taken into consideration that also non-normative acts which can be called 'soft law' are able to create law: they can be an element of a developing common conviction which leads, if practice follows it, to customary law or constitutes general principles of law.

On the international and regional level the human rights guarantees are laid down by treaties which belong to the sources of law indicated by Article 38 of the Statute of the International Court of Justice. The binding character results from the principle of *pacta sunt servanda.*

It is true that the fully binding force can be relativated by the reservations (or declarations) made by some of the parties to the treaty.[50] The state practice shows numerous examples of such declarations reducing the binding force of the treaties. Under the Vienna Convention on the Law of Treaties such reservations can be made but must not affect the "objective and purpose of the treaty" (Article 19 of the Vienna Convention on the Law of Treaties, 1969). Reservations are particularly problematic in the field of human rights. If we look at Article 57 (1) of the ECHR, regional human rights treaty, reservations can only be made at the moment of ratification, not afterwards, and only if they are referred in an abstract way to national laws. Thus, the scope of reservations and equivalent declarations are limited.

On the international law front reservations to the international treaties on human rights can be made by the countries who want to uphold their own national solutions. Such reservations try to make the treaty protection compatible with internal, in particular, constitutional requirements and to gain acceptance instead of a possible refusal by that state.

Human rights have an inherent tendency to objectivize the values embodied by them[51] and to make them resistant against unfavourable modification by the treaty parties. The idea of *jus cogens* embraces human rights more and more.[52] It can be seen that an objective public order develops (on the international level and even with more consistency on the regional level), which is no longer dependent on the will of the contracting parties. This is also the reason of referring, sometimes, to such international law as 'constitutional'. The intention is to qualify these norms as basic, inalienable and with particularly binding force as it is known in a state.

[47] R. Arnold, "European Constitutional Law," in *The Process of Constitutionalisation of the EU and Related Issues*, ed. N. Šišková (Groningen: Europa Law Publishing, 2008), 41.

[48] No. 45036/98 (complaint), Neue Juristische Wochenschrift (NJW) 2006, 197.

[49] See also Ukraine 1, 2.

[50] See USA 25–26.

[51] See also Hungary 13.

[52] See Ukraine 1, 2; Portugal 7.

25.2.2 State Level

Human rights are regularly embodied in a state's constitution, which is the supreme law of the land. They share the binding force of the constitution which prevails over legislation and all other public acts. This binding force results from the hierarchy of norms and is regularly defended by the courts. In human rights matters the jurisdiction of the administrative courts, and, in so far as the legislator is concerned, constitutional courts also has an elaborated procedural system of guaranteeing their binding force. There are rare exceptions, as in Great Britain where a formal constitution does not exist; there, however, and it has already been pointed out, the ECHR, as a regional treaty, assures the binding force of human rights in the interior of the state as well.

In the well integrated system of a state, reservations, which are possible to a certain extent on the international level, cannot be made. Constitutional human rights have an all over binding effect. National constitutions are *per se* objective public orders, which do not allow individual exceptions. The principle of equality, which is reflected in the abstract character of legislation and constitution, cannot accept an exceptional exemption from binding rules.

The binding force of human rights is not hindered by the fact that in the many cases of conflicts between various human rights as well as human rights and public interests, weighing out of the conflicting values has to be effectuated. This means a concretization of conflicting principles which the human rights are. The aim of the human rights protection system is reached by an 'optimal' solution which realizes best the obligation of human rights in concrete cases. Of course, in this context it should be mentioned that human dignity (despite any problems arising in defining it[53]) cannot be weighed out against other constitutional values. It is the very basis of the values system, and affecting it would impair the human rights idea as such. So, dignity has a primary binding force.

The binding force of national human rights is not threatened by an integration system where national and multinational, especially supranational human rights co-exist. If one looks at the question of whether German or EU human rights should be applicable in EU-related cases to be administered by German authorities, the Federal Constitutional Court has renounced, in its *Solange II* decision of 1986, to apply national human rights and left this task to the supranational level. This is a substitution of a national protection by supranational which does not, abstractly, diminish the binding force resulting from human rights. In integration systems the instruments of the international level can by replaced by those of the supranational level given that the basic task of the individual's protection is adequately fulfilled.

A similar consideration can be made in the conflict of EU human rights with the rights of the Strasburg Convention. As already mentioned, the *Bosphorus* case allowed the non-application of conventional rights if it can be presumed that the EU actions conform to their own supranational human rights. No relativation of the Strasbourg Convention and its binding force can be stated here.

25.2.3 The Effects of Human Rights Soft Law

Whilst the Universal Declaration of 1948 was not normatively binding, its ideology was extremely influential and turned out to be a certain landmark in the further development of human rights even in legally binding forms.[54] We can state that the directive effects of normative prescriptions can be reached, to a certain extent, by 'soft law' (non-binding resolutions) which have the power to shape the peoples' conscience. In the field of human rights the most effective steps were done politically and not normatively, that is to say in the non binding 1776, 1789 and the 1948 Declarations. This holds as evidence that many non normative declarations, especially in the field of human rights, should not be underestimated as to their effects; they can even exceed the effects of a binding norm.

In a more advanced stage the threshold from not binding to binding, from formal declaration to normativity, can be crossed.

25.2.4 Human Rights and Rule of Law

Modern constitutionalism confirms the binding character of human rights by integrating it in a new concept of

[53] Great Britain 11, 12 ("equal moral worth"); Portugal 4; Ukraine 2; Slovakia 8.

[54] See USA 27–28.

rule of law, which is value-oriented, so that the constitutional guarantee of rule of law extends also to the guarantee of human rights; so, there exist a double normative basis: the rights as embodied in constitutional law and the rule of law as a normative concept. The binding character also reflects the judicial attitude of interpreting existing normative texts in a way which is favourable to an individual's protection using the principle of *effet utile*[55] in giving full effect to the written norm. Added to this, the judge has taken on the function of expressly completing the human rights protection by interpretation or law development. In this way the normative effect is extended to newly formulated rights. Besides these procedural techniques in interpretation, the growing willingness of national constitution makers to introduce specific action forms for defending human rights as an individual complaint ('Verfassungsbeschwerde' in Germany,[56] 'recurso de amparo' in Spain, the 'Individualanfechtung' in Austria and the many forms of individual complaints in the new democracies in Central and Eastern Europe) can clearly be stated. The judicial system has been individualized on the national level and, in part, on the regional levels whereas on the international level only small steps in this direction can be seen.[57] This corresponds, of course, to the vital lacking law subjectivity of an individual.

Human rights can be qualified as binding internationally, regionally and nationally in so far as they constitute a source of law. Also 'soft law' has its important political effects and can serve as a base for future normativity. Limitations of the binding effect can be stated particularly on the international level. On this level the gap between a normative claim and reality is significant. The strengthening of the human rights on the regional and, in particular, on national level has its positive incentives also for the international community.

National Reporters:

Armenian National Report	*Armen Harutyunyan*
Belgian National Report	*Matthias Storme*
Brazilian National Report	*Marcelo Figueiredo*
British National Report	*Steven Greer*
Canadian National Report	*Frédérique Sabourin*
Croatian National Report	*Siniša Rodin*
Democratic Republic of the Congo National Report	*Ghislain Mabanga*
German National Report	*Norman Weiß*
Greek National Report	*Michail Vrontakis*
Hungarian National Report	*Nóra Chronowski* *Tímea Drinóczi* *József Petrétei*
Italian National Report	*Alessandro Pace*
Japanese National Report	*Kohki Abe*
Norwegian National Report	*Njål Høstmælingen*
Polish National Report	*Ewa Łętowska*
Portuguese National Report	*Ana Maria Guerra Martins* *Miguel Prata Roque*
Russian National Report	*Daria Trenina* *Mark Entin*
Scottish National Report	*Jim Murdoch*
Slovak National Report	*Darina Macková*
Solomon Islands National Report	*Jennifer Corrin*
Taiwanese National Report	*Yean-Sen Teng*
Ukrainian National Report	*Alla Fedorova* *Olena Sviatun*
United States National Report	*Mortimer Sellers*

[55] See also Russia 2.

[56] Germany 9.

[57] See also Slovakia 8; Great Britain 6.

26 Les Partenariats Publics Privés[1]

Ou la seconde vie de Frank Lloyd Wright[2]

François Lichère

Les partenariats public-privé (ci-après « PPP ») apparaissent aujourd'hui comme un sujet incontournable de la littérature juridique de droit administratif. Le nombre de rapports nationaux envoyés pour le congrès de Washington, dix-huit en l'occurrence, pourrait à lui seul en témoigner.[3] Nul pays, parmi ceux étudiés dans le cadre du présent rapport général, n'en ignore l'acronyme, y compris ceux qui, à l'image de la Nouvelle-Zélande ou de l'Uruguay, ne connaissent d'aucune législation relative aux PPP, fût-elle partielle.

Cette dernière remarque peut nourrir une première réflexion : le phénomène juridique dépasse les frontières sans que le législateur s'en empare nécessairement, ni même parfois les juges. Il n'y a là rien d'étonnant s'agissant d'un instrument juridique qui prend la forme contractuelle : la liberté contractuelle peut très bien être à l'origine de nouveaux moyens juridiques qui se répandent sans que la loi n'ait à intervenir. L'exemple de l'Angleterre est à cet égard topique : le pays qui est parfois perçu comme étant à l'origine du concept de PPP, du moins sous sa forme moderne, ne connaît pas d'une législation qui lui est propre. D'autres pays, en revanche, ont institué des législations soit d'ensemble, soit plus ponctuelles ou sectorielles. Il y a là une première différence qui rend la comparaison non pas impossible, mais délicate.

La difficulté est accrue dans la mesure où le concept échappe à toute définition précise et communément admise. Cette absence de cohérence n'est guère surprenante dans un contexte de droit comparé, malgré l'existence de cadres supra nationaux : la présence d'un guide législatif sur les PPP issu de la Commission des Nations Unies pour le Droit du Commerce International (CNUDCI), en dépit de l'influence certaine de ce guide sur certains pays, n'a pas permis d'assoir une définition commune, faute de caractère contraignant et de diffusion généralisée.[4]

L'absence de cohérence est un peu plus surprenante dans un contexte d'harmonisation européenne, d'autant que le droit communautaire[5] s'intéresse aux contrats publics depuis le début des années 70 et a connu deux autres vagues de directives en 1989–1992 puis en

[1] IV.D., Public Private Partnerships.

[2] Architecte américain, 1867–1959; voir la conclusion du présent rapport

[3] Afrique du Sud, Angleterre, Allemagne, Argentine, Belgique, Canada, Etats-Unis, France, Grèce, Hongrie, Italie, Nouvelle-Zélande, Pologne, Portugal, Russie, Slovénie, Turquie, Uruguay. Il est à noter qu'au Canada, la législation sur les PPP relève de la compétence des provinces de sorte qu'il existe potentiellement 14 régimes légaux pour les PPP selon les niveaux (fédéral, provincial, territorial) mais seules 4 provinces et le niveau fédéral ont une structure administrative ou législative dédiée aux PPP. Aux Etats-Unis, il existe aussi des législations et/ou une *soft law* sur les PPP dans chaque Etat mais le rapport américain s'est – heureusement pour le rapporteur général – largement focalisé sur le niveau fédéral.

[4] Voir Commission des Nations Unies pour le droit commercial international (CNUDCI), projet de guide législatif sur les projets d'infrastructures à financement privé : Documents officiels de l'assemblée générale, 51ème session, suppl. no. 17 (A/51/17).

[5] Les expressions droit communautaire et droit européen seront utilisés indifféremment dans le présent rapport, sachant qu'elles visent toutes deux le droit issu de l'Union européenne.

F. Lichère (✉)
Department of Law, University of Aix-Marseille,
Marseille, France
e-mail: lichere.francois@orange.fr

K.B. Brown and D.V. Snyder (eds.), *General Reports of the XVIIIth Congress of the International Academy of Comparative Law/Rapports Généraux du XVIIIème Congrès de l'Académie Internationale de Droit Comparé*, DOI 10.1007/978-94-007-2354-2_26, © Springer Science+Business Media B.V. 2012

2004. Elle est toutefois explicable dans la mesure où la Commission européenne n'est pas convaincue de la nécessité d'une réglementation européenne s'agissant des PPP contractuels, même si sa position est différente pour les partenariats publics privés institutionnalisés (PPPI).[6]

Mais, en outre, l'absence de cohérence conceptuelle au plan international et européen se double d'une absence de cohérence à l'intérieur de bon nombre de pays étudiés. A quelques exceptions près, il n'existe pas de définition générale des PPP en droit positif et, quand elles existent, l'identification des contrats concernés ne va pas sans poser problème. Certains pays, comme la Belgique, réglementent les PPP sans nécessairement les définir de façon précise ; d'autres, à l'image de la France, ne définissent que certains PPP (cas des contrats de partenariat ou des partenariats sectoriels) et ne connaissent pas l'expression « partenariats public privé » en droit positif. Or, par ailleurs, les auteurs ne s'entendent guère sur le contenu à donner à la notion. On ne sera donc pas surpris d'apprendre que la partie relative au concept de PPP occupe une place importante dans le présent rapport, comme elle l'est dans la plupart des rapports nationaux.

Le présent rapport est basé sur le questionnaire qui a été envoyé aux rapporteurs nationaux. Ce dernier a proposé de répondre à 33 questions réparties en 4 thèmes (voir l'annexe du présent rapport). Ces thèmes répondent à une logique assez largement chronologique sur la façon dont peuvent se mettre en place des PPP : une fois le concept de PPP identifié, il convenait de se pencher sur la passation, puis l'exécution et enfin le contentieux des PPP. Le rapport général reprend donc cet ordre qui a, nous semble-t-il, l'avantage d'éviter les recoupements et redites, bref qui permet d'apporter un peu de cohérence dans l'étude d'une technique juridique qui en manque.

Cette présentation, qui pourrait apparaître comme excessivement descriptive au premier abord, est néanmoins sous-tendue par un fil conducteur : en quoi les PPP apparaissent-ils comme une nouveauté dans le paysage juridique d'un pays ? Autrement dit, y a-t-il une véritable spécificité des PPP au regard des contrats publics traditionnels que sont les marchés publics et les concessions voire par rapport à des formes de coopération institutionnelle entre personnes publiques et personnes privées déjà existantes ? On remarquera que la question précédente insiste surtout sur les PPP contractuels et place au second plan les PPP institutionnalisés, c'est-à-dire ceux qui se concrétisent par la création d'une personne morale associant personne publique et personne privée. C'est que cette dernière hypothèse semble plus rarement mise en œuvre et en tout cas n'est pas toujours comprise dans l'expression PPP.

Qu'elle qu'en soit la forme, contractuelle ou institutionnelle, il apparaît que dans la plupart des pays, si ce n'est dans tous, il est possible d'établir une distinction entre le phénomène et l'appellation : le phénomène aurait ainsi largement précédé la dénomination, du moins si l'on comprend l'expression PPP dans une acception large. D'où l'interrogation sur la nouveauté, réelle ou supposée, des PPP au regard des outils juridiques existants.

A côté de ce questionnement central, d'autres problématiques émergent : quel rôle jouent les considérations idéologiques dans l'émergence de cette technique juridique ? Qu'impliquent les PPP en termes de changements des pratiques administratives ? Quelles sont les conséquences sur les distinctions juridiques traditionnelles, à l'image de la distinction entre marchés publics et concessions ? Est-ce que les procédures de passation font l'objet d'adaptation pour tenir compte de la complexité induite par les PPP ? Est-ce que, et de quelle manière, l'évolution des besoins et des techniques est prise en compte au stade de l'exécution des PPP c'est-à-dire tout au long de leur existence ? Y-a-t-il des phénomènes de convergence entre les pays ? A titre subsidiaire, peut-on distinguer pays de *common law* et pays civilistes ? Telles sont les questions que pose également le développement des partenariats publics privés et auxquelles il sera tenté de répondre, de manière nécessairement incomplète dans le cadre restreint qui est le nôtre.

26.1 Concept de PPP

La lecture des rapports nationaux permet de se pencher sur les raisons qui peuvent expliquer l'émergence des PPP (I.2), après en avoir précisé les contours (I.1).

[6]Livre vert sur les partenariats public-privé et le droit communautaire des marchés publics et des concessions, COM/2004/0327 Final ; communication interprétative du 5 février 2008 concernant l'application du droit communautaire des marchés publics et des concessions aux partenariats public-privé institutionnalisés (PPPI).

26.1.1 Les contours de la notion de PPP

L'apparition de l'acronyme PPP est globalement assez récente, autour des années 1990–2000, avec toutefois l'exception de la Turquie où l'expression est apparue en 1984 avec une loi sur l'électricité. Mais lorsque l'on regarde non pas seulement le droit positif mais aussi l'ensemble des auteurs (ci-après « la doctrine »), les partenariats public-privé font généralement leur apparition dans la littérature juridique avant d'être éventuellement consacrés en droit positif.

Ce dernier cas est illustré par exemple par la Belgique (fin des années 1990) ou la Slovénie (loi de 2006).

Plusieurs rapports, à l'image du rapport américain, soulignent qu'en réalité le terme PPP n'est apparu qu'assez tard alors que le phénomène qu'il est censé décrire est bien antérieur.

Le rapport hongrois se penche, de manière assez inédite, sur les origines des PPP dans différentes littératures. Il prend ainsi soin de noter que dans la littérature hongroise, allemande et française, le pays d'origine – ou présenté comme tel – varie nettement. Ainsi la littérature hongroise attribue-t-elle – par erreur dit le rapport – l'origine des PPP à l'Angleterre, alors qu'un auteur français fait remonter l'origine des PPP à la Grèce antique – de manière anachronique dit encore le rapport hongrois – et qu'en réalité les PPP remonteraient aux années 1940 aux Etats-Unis.

Il parait difficile de donner raison ou tort au rapporteur hongrois sur ce point, tout simplement parce qu'il est difficile de s'entendre sur la définition et le contenu même de l'expression. Le rapport américain souligne lui-même que l'expression « PPP » est certes apparue bien avant les années 1990 mais alors avec d'autres significations (rénovation urbaine ou politiques publiques) que celle qu'on lui attribue généralement aux Etats-Unis aujourd'hui qui renvoie à la réalisation d'infrastructures. Dans son acception moderne, elle ne remonte qu'aux années 1990 et provient de l'Angleterre, ce que confirme le rapport anglais en faisant des contrats de *Private Finance Initiative* (PFI), lancés en 1992 par le chancelier de l'échiquier, les premiers PPP.

Il est clair en revanche que l'acronyme PPP a connu une diffusion internationale assez rapide, même sans modification du droit positif, comme l'illustre le rapport uruguayen qui indique que l'expression est apparue dans la littérature nationale en 2003 par référence à l'exemple canadien alors même que le législateur ne s'en est jamais emparé.

La question que l'on est naturellement amené à se poser est celle de la nouveauté par rapport à l'existant. Les définitions, qu'elles soient doctrinales ou légales, illustrent d'ailleurs la difficulté à démontrer la nouveauté de ces formes de coopération, en ce qu'elles sont plus ou moins précises et ont parfois du mal à clairement les différencier des concepts juridiques classiques, comme les marchés publics et les concessions.

Lorsqu'il n'existe pas une définition légale, la doctrine se penche alors sur le concept. Le rapport américain souligne, sur la base d'une définition donnée par le GAO en 1999, qu'il est difficile de définir de façon complète les PPP mais que l'on peut néanmoins les décrire comme entrainant une plus grande implication du secteur privé dans la confection d'un projet public que traditionnellement. Mais tous les auteurs américains ne s'accordent pas ensuite, surtout pour savoir si cela ne concerne que les infrastructures ou de manière plus générale tous les contrats de la commande publique. Le rapport allemand fait aussi état d'un consensus sur une conception assez générale, basée sur l'idée d'une participation d'une personne privée à l'exécution de missions publiques. Les autres rapports où il n'existe pas de définition légale mettent parfois l'accent sur le financement par le secteur privé de missions publiques, à l'image de la Hongrie.[7] En Uruguay, la doctrine s'appuie sur l'idée de risque, alors que le financement peut être privé ou public ou n'importe quelle combinaison des deux. Le cas anglais est un peu particulier : s'il n'existe pas une définition légale des PPP, il en existe une dans la *soft law*, issue du gouvernement britannique en 2000. Cette définition fait des contrats de *private finance initiative* (*PFI*) une sorte de PPP parmi d'autres, aux côtés d'une part de la privatisation des capitaux publics des entreprises publiques et d'autre part de la valorisation du patrimoine public opérée par des entreprises privées. Si le deuxième aspect peut correspondre à l'idée de partenariats public-privé institutionnalisés, ce troisième et dernier aspect de PPP est, des 18 rapports étudiés, totalement inédit. La définition des PPP a été toutefois revue en

[7]Selon une définition donnée par un auteur hongrois en 2001, "PPP is an investment form, when the public sector executes the obligatory public tasks with contributions by private capital investors."

2008 et cette troisième forme de PPP ne semble plus être incluse dans la définition.[8]

La plupart des autres pays connaissent d'une définition légale, i.e. opérée par une loi ou plus rarement par un texte de valeur infra-législative, bref par un texte de droit positif. Ceci dit, l'existence d'une définition légale ne clôt pas nécessairement les débats doctrinaux sur la notion. Il faut dire que les définitions légales ne sont pas toujours très précises, ni – on s'en doutera - uniformes d'un pays à l'autre. En Slovénie, pays membre de l'Union européenne, la définition légale est basée de manière originale sur les critères comptables mis en avant en 2004 par l'organisme européen Eurostat pour déterminer si un contrat de PPP doit entrer dans le calcul de la dette publique. La Slovénie, comme l'Italie, assimile par ailleurs les PPP institutionnalisés aux PPP. La Grèce donne une définition assez générale fondée sur l'idée de coopération.[9] Un projet de loi turc sur les PPP reste lui aussi assez général en évoquant un partage des risques. La loi québécoise (Canada) donne une définition précise, quoique assez ouverte en ce que le financement privé n'est pas nécessairement requis.[10] Une loi de la Colombie britannique (Canada) assimile PPP et concessions dans le domaine routier mais la définition administrative est plus large et d'ailleurs assez imprécise, simplement fondée sur la répartition des risques.[11] Au niveau fédéral, c'est davantage la longue durée et la responsabilisation du partenaire privé qui est mise en avant.[12] La définition légale des PPP en Pologne s'appuie sur l'idée d'un partage des tâches et des risques (loi de 2008). La définition légale italienne est encore plus précise puisqu'outre le partage des risques et de responsabilité elle intègre le financement partiel ou total par le partenaire,[13] à l'image de la France et du Portugal.[14] La législation de ces deux derniers pays ne fait pas allusion au partage des risques dans la définition des PPP mais en fait une clause obligatoire, ce qui revient à en faire un élément essentiel de la définition. De même, la définition sud-africaine, issue d'une loi de 1999 alors que l'expression n'est apparue dans la littérature qu'en 1998, ouvre plusieurs options mais dans tous les cas les risques doivent être assumés de façon « substantielle » par la partenaire privé.[15]

[8] HM Treasury, 2008, 18 : *"PPPs are arrangements typified by joint working between the public and private sectors. In their broadest sense they can cover all types of collaboration across the private-public sector interface involving collaborative working together and risk sharing to deliver policies, services and infrastructure"*.

[9] Law 3389/2005 (Article 1 par. 2) : " written commercial co-operation agreements for the performance of construction work and/or services ("Partnership Agreements"), between Public Entities within their sector of activity and bodies governed by private law ("Private Entities")". Mais l'article 16 de la loi précise les données en attribuant au partenaire une part significative des risques et la charge de financer en tout ou partie de l'ouvrage ou du service. La loi précise que les contrats concernés peuvent être des concessions ou des marchés publics de type PFI (private finance initiative).

[10] "Un contrat de partenariat public-privé est un contrat à long terme par lequel un organisme public associe une entreprise du secteur privé, avec ou sans financement de la part de celle-ci, à la conception, à la réalisation et à l'exploitation d'un ouvrage public. Un tel contrat peut avoir pour objet la prestation d'un service public."

[11] "A public-private partnership is a legally binding contract between government and business for the provision of assets and the delivery of services. The contract allocates responsibilities and business risks among the various partners."

[12] « une démarche à long terme, fondée sur le rendement, qui permet d'approvisionner des projets d'infrastructure publique avec l'aide du secteur privé. Ce modèle d'approvisionnement se démarque parce que le secteur privé assume une part importante de la responsabilité des livrables et du rendement de l'infrastructure, qu'il s'agisse de conception, de planification structurale et architecturale, ou d'entretien à long terme »

[13] "public-private contracts' are contracts which have as their object one or more services such as the design, construction, management or maintenance of a public work or a public utility, or the provision of a service, including in any case total or partial funding of such services by the private sector, in both normal and non-standard forms, with an allocation of risks in accordance with applicable Community requirements and guidelines"

[14] Pour le Portugal : « le contrat ou l'union de contrats par lesquels des entités privées, nominées partenaires privés, s'obligent, durablement, à exercer, pour un partenaire public, une activité visant la satisfaction d'un besoin collectif, assurant, intégralement ou partiellement, le financement et la responsabilité par l'investissement et la gestion de la dite activité ». En France en revanche, l'activité de service public ne peut être comprise dans la mission du partenaire.

[15] "a commercial transaction between an institution and a private party in terms of which the private party:

(a) performs an institutional function on behalf of the institution; and/or
(b) acquires the use of state property for its own commercial purposes; and
(c) assumes substantial financial, technical and operational risks in connection with the performance of the institutional function and/or use of state property; and
(d) receives a benefit for performing the institutional function or from utilising the state property, either by way of:
    (i) consideration to be paid by the institution which derives from a revenue fund or, where the institution is a national government business enterprise or a provincial

Enfin, la définition argentine, issue d'une loi de 2005, apparaît comme le summum de la précision.[16] La Russie quant à elle ne connaît légalement que des concessions.

Le concept de partenariats public privé institutionnalisés, d'origine communautaire, ne pose guère de problème en revanche dans la plupart des pays qui l'assimilent à des entreprises à capitaux public et privés. Il est néanmoins plus délicat à identifier dans le cas anglais dès que le rapport note qu'un *joint venture* ne dispose pas nécessairement de la personnalité juridique en Angleterre, de sorte que la distinction n'est pas tranchée entre PPP contractuels et PPP institutionnalisés, à l'image aussi de l'Afrique du Sud.

Certains pays affinent le concept de PPP en distinguant différentes sous-catégories à l'intérieur de la catégorie des PPP contractuels. On ne sera pas surpris d'apprendre que les Etats-Unis sont à l'origine de la déclinaison des PPP en différents acronymes anglais (pas moins de 18 selon le GAO dans un rapport de 1999)[17] et que cette déclinaison se retrouve peu ou prou dans d'autres pays de *common law*, comme l'Afrique du Sud.[18]

On le sera un peu plus de voir que ces modèles s'exportent, y compris dans des pays de tradition continentale ou civiliste. Le rapport belge fait ainsi référence aux DBFM («Design, Build, Finance, Maintain»), DBFO («Design, Build, Finance, Operate»), BOOT («Build, Own, Operate Transfer»). On peut s'interroger sur le fait de savoir si ces formules, ou du moins certaines d'entre elles, se démarquent réellement des différentes formes connues de concessions. Sans reprendre ces acronymes anglais, le rapport allemand fait état de toute une variété de PPP selon le degré d'implication du partenaire.

A propos des concessions, il est à noter que les conceptions en matière de concession peuvent varier d'un pays à l'autre, le Portugal envisageant 3 types de concession selon que le concessionnaire est rémunéré par l'usager ou par la personne publique, et, dans ce dernier cas, selon qu'il nourrit des rapports avec les usagers ou pas. En sens inverse, l'Afrique du Sud a une conception beaucoup plus restrictive de la concession puisque cela ne vise que les contrats par lesquels un opérateur exploite un ouvrage public déjà construit, ce qui correspond en droit français à l'«affermage».

On doit noter enfin que, s'agissant des législations relatives aux PPP, c'est-à-dire des sources du droit des PPP, toutes les solutions sont possibles :

- soit il n'existe ni législation, ni circulaires (guidelines) comme en Nouvelle-Zélande ou en Uruguay et, dans une certaine mesure en Russie qui ne connaît que d'une législation sur les concessions au niveau fédéral ;
- soit il n'existe que des circulaires comme en Angleterre (à l'exception d'un *Act* de 1994 mais qui répond à un problème très circonscrit – cf. infra) ;
- soit il existe des législations sectorielles, c'est-à-dire des lois qui interviennent pour favoriser le recours aux PPP dans certains secteurs, comme en Turquie ou encore en Belgique avec des lois relatives aux PPP dans les domaines scolaire, ferroviaire ou du logement social ;

government business enterprise, from the revenues of such institution; or

(ii) charges or fees to be collected by the private party from users or customers of a service provided to them; or

(iii) a combination of such consideration and such charges or fees.

[16] "Public-Private Partnership contracts are cooperation agreements between the Public and Private Sector by which the parties are bound with an aim to partner for the execution and development of public works and services or any other delegable activity, in accordance with the following principles: (a) Efficient performance and compliance with the State's duties; (b) Respect for the rights and interests of users of the public services and of the private entities which are engaged in the execution of the public ventures; (c) Non-delegability of the State's regulation duties and police power; (d) Tax liability in the execution and performance of the relevant contracts; (e) Transparency in decision-making and operation; (f) Economic sustainability of Public-Private Partnership projects; (g) Allocation of risks based on the management capacity of the contracting parties and best practices."

[17] (1) O&M: Operations and Maintenance (*concession*); (2) OMM: Operations, Maintenance & Management (wastewater treatment); (3) DB: Design Build; (4) DBM: Design-Build-Maintain; (5) DBO: Design-Build-Operate; (6) DBOM: Design-Build-Operate-Maintain; (7) DBFOM: Design-Build-Finance-Operate-Maintain (*concession*); (8) DBFOMT: Design-Build-Finance-Operate-Maintain-Transfer; (9) BOT: Build-Operate-Transfer also called greenfield PPP; (10) BOO: Build-Own-Operate; (11) BBO: Buy-Build-Operate; (12) Developer Finance; (13) EUL: Enhanced Use Leasing or Underutilized Asset (the Department of Veterans Affairs (VA)); (14) LDO or BDO: Lease-Develop-Operate (*affermage*) or Build-Develop-Operate (municipal transit facilities); (15) Lease/Purchase; (16) Sale/Leaseback; (17) Tax-Exempt Lease (used to finance a wide variety of capital assets, ranging from computers to telecommunication systems and municipal vehicle fleets); (18) Turnkey

[18] lease, management service, BOT, concessions

- soit il n'existe une législation que pour les PPP institutionnalisés comme en Argentine ;
- soit il existe des lois applicables à tous secteurs (cas de la majorité des pays) ; encore dans ce cas convient-il de distinguer les législations relativement complètes des législations qui sont venues simplement adapter à la marge la législation existante, comme le *PPP acceleration act* en Allemagne ;
- soit enfin il existe, comme dans le cas français, des lois à la fois sectorielles (prisons, commissariat de police, défense) et une loi générale postérieure qui n'a pas abrogé les législations sectorielles.

Le Canada, à lui seul, permet, semble-t-il, d'illustrer toutes ces options selon les provinces considérées.

Pour résumer la notion de PPP, il ressort de l'ensemble des rapports que, largement entendus, les PPP ne sont pas un phénomène nouveau puisqu'il existait depuis longtemps des formes de collaboration avec le secteur privé qui déjà attribuaient à ce dernier un rôle bien supérieur à celui de simple fournisseur ou constructeur comme dans le cadre d'un marché public classique, à l'image des contrats de concession. Mais la nouveauté vient de ce que certains de ces contrats voient la personne publique payer pour le service rendu alors que le partenaire a pris en charge le financement. La différence tient donc surtout à l'émergence de ces contrats avec paiement différé par la personne publique mais financement par le partenaire privé.

Comme l'indique le rapport hongrois,[19] on peut dire que les PPP sont une forme de rénovation des contrats de concession et de développement d'un mode spécial de marchés publics qui voient le partenaire financer en tout ou partie l'ouvrage ou le projet et jouer un rôle plus déterminant dans sa construction ou sa mise en place, voire dans sa conception. La difficulté tient à ce que, lorsqu'ils évoquent les PPP, une partie des auteurs englobe souvent des formes contractuelles anciennes, comme les concessions, et des formes contractuelles nouvelles qui se différencient en partie – mais en partie seulement – des marchés publics. La tentation est grande alors d'exclure les concessions du champ des PPP, à l'image du rapport argentin, tenu il est vrai par une définition légale assez restrictive.

On doit aussi mesurer la difficulté qu'il y a à apprécier la portée d'un concept né dans des pays de *common law* et fondé sur une approche financière lorsqu'il est transposé dans les pays de droit civil ou continental qui raisonnaient habituellement sur des schémas fondés sur le critère de la rémunération (publique ou privé), c'est-à-dire sur une approche économique. Dans l'approche financière, il importe moins de savoir qui paye au final l'ouvrage ou le service que de savoir qui porte le financement. De ce fait, les PPP vont surtout regrouper des contrats (ou éventuellement des sociétés à capitaux publics et privés) qui prennent en charge une activité publique en assurant son financement, la question de la rémunération finale passant au second plan. Il n'est pas surprenant que ce concept englobe alors des contrats de concessions et certains marchés publics dits complexes. La dichotomie entre marchés publics et concession ne résiste pas conceptuellement à cette approche financière. Mais comme cette dichotomie perdure en droit positif dans tous les pays de tradition civiliste et également en Grande-Bretagne du fait des directives communautaires marchés publics (ne serait-ce que pour la détermination des procédures de passation), le concept de PPP dans sa globalité a du mal à pénétrer le droit positif de ces pays. De fait, les PPP largement entendus regroupent ainsi au moins deux catégories de contrats dont le régime n'est pas uniforme. L'Union Européenne elle-même n'a pas souhaité adopter une législation propre aux PPP en raison de la prégnance de la dichotomie traditionnelle susévoquée.

Ce n'est que dans une acception restrictive, entendue comme n'incluant que les contrats dans lesquels la personne publique verse un loyer une fois l'ouvrage construit ou restructuré ou le service mis en place par le partenaire, qu'il y a vraie nouveauté au regard des marchés publics traditionnels, tout en se distinguant des concessions car le partenaire n'assume pas le risque économique de l'exploitation de l'ouvrage ou du service, même s'il assume d'autres risques.

26.1.2 Sur les raisons de l'émergence des PPP

Plusieurs rapports nationaux se sont penchés sur cette question sans que les réponses soient catégoriques. La première interrogation tient à l'influence de l'idéologie libérale dans l'émergence du phénomène

[19] Rapport hongrois : "The standpoint which interprets PPP as an improvement of concessions on the one hand, and as a special model of public procurement on the other is correct in general terms"

et sa promotion. Il n'est pas toujours très clair de savoir si les PPP sont une conséquence directe du regain, en particulier dans les pays occidentaux, des théories néo-libérales à compter des années 1980–1990.

Le rapport américain relève cette interrogation en notant que le développement des PPP dans les années 1990 correspond à l'idée d'un gouvernement agissant de manière efficiente et à moindre coût sous l'influence de la doctrine du *New Public Management*, même si le Président de l'époque était démocrate. Des autres rapports émerge ici ou là l'idée selon laquelle les PPP seraient d'une certaine façon une voie médiane entre une privatisation complète et les marchés publics classiques, à l'image du rapport belge qui situe les PPP dans une perspective historique, avec le modèle de la concession au XIXème siècle, puis celui de l'appropriation publique au milieu du XXème siècle, puis celui de la privatisation dans les années 1980 avant de voir l'émergence des PPP à compter des années 1990. Les PPP seraient donc un retour à un juste milieu entre interventionnisme et libéralisme tel que l'avait connu le XIXème siècle avec la concession, idée que l'on retrouve dans l'approche historique du rapport américain, même si alors ce n'est pas le modèle de la concession qui est aujourd'hui dominant mais celui du PPP/marchés public, i.e. d'un contrat avec paiement du partenaire par la personne publique et non par l'usager mais financement par le partenaire.

Le cas français, quoique non dénué d'ambigüité, va semble-t-il dans le sens de cette 3ème voie. Une commission parlementaire avait été constituée pour réfléchir à une réforme visant à encourager le recours aux PPP et regroupait plusieurs groupes parlementaires, y compris des représentants du parti socialiste. En outre, les contrats de partenariat ne confient pas au partenaire la charge de gérer une mission de service public. Néanmoins, certains parlementaires socialistes se sont déclarés ouvertement contre les PPP, au point d'attaquer devant le Conseil d'Etat l'ordonnance du 17 juin 2004 qui avait créé les contrats de partenariat.

Le rapport allemand contribue également à illustrer l'idée d'une voie médiane : même si les PPP sont parfois assimilés en Allemagne à une forme privatisation dans un sens large – comme en Angleterre – il s'agit alors simplement d'une privatisation « fonctionnelle » dans laquelle la personne publique garde la maîtrise de l'organisation du service, contrairement à la privatisation « substantielle » qui équivaut à un transfert au secteur privé (les deux se distinguant d'une privatisation « formelle », c'est-à-dire du passage d'un organisme de droit public sous le giron du droit privé).

Une idée semble néanmoins faire l'unanimité des rapports qui se sont penchés sur la question : les PPP apparaissent comme un outil indispensable pour faire face à la pénurie financière des collectivités publiques face au sous-équipement public. Le rapport polonais souligne clairement cette origine liée au manque de fonds publics, tout comme, entre autres rapports, le rapport allemand. Le cas anglais est également significatif car les PPP/PFI sont une réponse directe à ce sous-équipement dû en grande partie à la politique du précédent premier ministre, Margaret Thatcher. Le rapport canadien avance d'autres arguments pratiques: les PPP limitent l'endettement public, ils permettent des économies d'échelle grâce à l'expertise du secteur privé et ils font supporter la plupart des risques par le partenaire privé.

Enfin, on n'est peut-être pas en la matière à l'abri d'un certain phénomène de mode. Ainsi le Portugal a créé en 2003 une législation sur les PPP alors qu'il avait mis en place en 2002 une législation sur les contrats de « collaboration » qui pouvait paraître comme suffisante. La Hongrie a également adapté son cadre légal en 2003 pour favoriser l'usage des PPP avec un organisme en charge de leur promotion alors qu'il existait depuis 1992 une législation sur les PPP. Dans ce dernier cas, comme pour beaucoup de législations d'ailleurs, il est difficile de savoir la part qui relève de l'affichage – donner l'impression que la législation est, en quelque sorte, « PPP *friendly* » – des réelles avancées juridiques. Mais, en sens inverse, on ne doit pas négliger l'impact que peut avoir l'existence d'une législation, aussi ténue soit-elle, sur le développement des PPP. Le rapport néo-zélandais fait ainsi état des critiques adressées à l'égard de l'absence de législation car cela freinerait les investissements sur ce genre de contrats. Le rapport américain souligne aussi l'inconvénient qu'il peut y avoir pour certains des Etats américains à ne pas avoir adopté de législation sur les PPP. Toutefois, le rapport allemand, tout en soulignant l'émergence récente des PPP en pratique, fait écho à l'idée de certains auteurs selon laquelle la situation actuelle est finalement préférable pour favoriser le développement des PPP à une législation complète qui pourrait apporter des restrictions.

26.2 Passation des PPP

La passation concerne pour l'essentiel les modalités selon lesquelles le partenaire privé sera choisi. Mais les PPP soulèvent d'autres questions relatives à la passation plus largement entendue, au premier rang desquelles on trouve la question de savoir s'il s'agit d'un mode contractuel privilégié, neutre ou restreint.

26.2.1 Sur les restrictions et la priorité à l'usage des PPP

Les restrictions à l'usage des PPP sont un préalable à examiner et notamment la question de savoir quelle est l'étendue des missions qui peuvent être confiées au partenaire. Tous les pays connaissent d'une limite à l'externalisation d'activités publiques mais il est à noter que ces limites varient d'un pays à l'autre et peuvent, en outre, évoluer. En Nouvelle-Zélande, les prisons ne pouvaient faire l'objet d'externalisation de 2004 à 2009, alors qu'en France comme en Allemagne l'interdiction demeure, aux côtés d'autres missions de souveraineté. En Uruguay, c'est tout ce qui a trait à l'hygiène publique et à la consommation d'eau qui doit relever de l'Etat. Aux Etats-Unis, peu de choses ne sont pas délégables dès lors que le gouvernement ratifie ces délégations, sauf pour les fonctions inhérentes au gouvernement.[20] En Grèce, les fonctions régaliennes sont exclues (Défense, Police, Justice, exécution des condamnations pénales). En Turquie, les PPP ne sont pas prévus dans le domaine de la justice, de l'Education et des activités culturelles. En Slovénie, l'objet des PPP ne peut toucher de manière générale aux « matières administratives ».

Néanmoins, ces activités non susceptibles d'être déléguées ne sont généralement pas précisées par les textes relatifs aux PPP. Il ne s'agit donc pas de contraintes propres aux PPP mais de contraintes inhérentes à tout phénomène de contractualisation ou d'externalisation de l'action publique, même s'il est vrai que les PPP induisent une très forte externalisation. La Grande-Bretagne a toutefois assoupli ces restrictions en autorisant le transfert de certaines missions dites de souveraineté par le *deregulation and contracting out Act* de 1994 spécialement adopté pour favoriser le développement des contrats de PPP/PFI et l'Argentine a seulement exclu les missions de police et de réglementation dans la loi de 2005 sur les PPP.

Une fois que l'on est assuré d'être dans le champ des missions délégables, des différences existent également de manière notable pour ce qui est de la question de savoir si les PPP bénéficient ou non d'une priorité par rapport aux moyens contractuels classiques. Une très grande variété de solutions se fait jour. La majeure partie des pays ne donnent aucune priorité, même s'il faut en règle générale établir une évaluation préalable qui doit préciser les avantages et inconvénients d'un PPP comme en Angleterre ou encore au Portugal. D'autres donnent une « prime » aux PPP, à l'image de la Slovénie pour laquelle les marchés publics ne peuvent être choisis que s'il est prouvé que le PPP est moins efficace, ou de l'Italie, où l'inscription d'un principe de subsidiarité « horizontale » dans la Constitution, qui privilégie l'initiative individuelle sur l'initiative publique, favorise le recours aux PPP. Encore faut-il réaliser néanmoins une évaluation, en termes de coût et d'efficacité, du recours aux PPP. De même, en Colombie britannique (Canada), il existe aussi une prime aux PPP puisque ils devront être mis en œuvre au-delà de tout projet supérieur à 50 millions de dollars canadiens, à moins qu'il soit démontré qu'un procédé traditionnel est plus avantageux. En Alberta, c'est le même principe qui s'applique sauf que le seuil est porté à 100 millions de dollars. Au Québec et en Ontario, la formulation semble plus neutre – tout comme au niveau fédéral – puisque le PPP doit seulement être envisagé au-delà d'un certain seuil.

En France, ce sont plutôt des freins à l'usage des PPP qui prévalent : s'il est envisagé de recourir à un PPP, il faut non seulement réaliser une étude comparative préalable mais surtout prouver qu'il existe un

[20] OMB Circular A-76 :

(1) Binding the United States to take or not to take some action by contract, policy, regulation, authorization, order, or otherwise;

(2) Determining, protecting, and advancing economic, political, territorial, property, or other interests by military or diplomatic action, civil or criminal judicial proceedings, contract management, or otherwise;

(3) Significantly affecting the life, liberty, or property of private persons; or

(4) Exerting ultimate control over the acquisition, use, or disposition of United States property (real or personal, tangible or intangible), including establishing policies or procedures for the collection, control, or disbursement of appropriated and other federal funds.

motif d'intérêt général justifiant de recourir aux contrats de partenariat (urgence, complexité ou bilan favorable), ceci en raison d'une jurisprudence du Conseil constitutionnel qui a considéré que la généralisation de tels contrats porterait atteinte à l'égal accès à la commande publique, à la protection de la propriété publique et au bon usage des deniers publics. Seuls certains PPP sectoriels sont exclus de ces limitations.

On peut ranger dans la catégorie des freins à l'usage des PPP des solutions encore plus originales comme celle de la Hongrie qui limite l'utilisation des PPP à un pourcentage des ressources de l'Etat[21] ou celle de la Grèce qui limite les PPP/marchés publics à un montant de 200 millions d'euros.

26.2.2 Sur les procédures de passation

L'originalité dans la passation ne s'illustre guère quant aux procédures de passation *stricto sensu*, c'est-à-dire quant aux modalités de publicité et de mise en concurrence. La plupart des pays assimilent, sur ces plans, les PPP soit à des marchés publics, soit à des concessions.

Encore convient-il de nuancer le propos. Pour les PPP de type marchés publics, on note des différences avec les marchés publics classiques en pratique ou dans les textes dans le choix des procédures de passation. A cet égard, l'existence d'une harmonisation légale entre différents pays, comme c'est le cas en Europe en raison de la présence de la directive 2004/18 du 31 mars 2004, ne garantit nullement une application uniforme des procédures de passation des PPP.

Certains pays européens adoptent une approche souple de la passation des PPP/marchés publics en admettant que tous les PPP peuvent faire l'objet d'un dialogue compétitif, cette procédure permettant comme son nom l'indique de discuter de plusieurs aspects de la proposition des candidats, alors que dans les pays de l'Union européenne, la procédure de principe est la procédure ouverte ou restreinte (appels d'offres ouverts ou restreints) qui n'autorise aucun dialogue ou aucune négociation. Cela signifie que certains pays considèrent que tous les PPP sont nécessairement « complexes » au sens qu'en donne la directive 2004/18 du 31 mars 2004 (cas de la Slovénie). Toujours dans cette approche souple, on trouve même des rapports, comme le rapport belge et le rapport grec, qui font état de l'adoption, pour certains PPP, de la procédure négociée, procédure encore plus flexible que le dialogue compétitif, car les personnes publiques s'appuient alors sur un article de la directive 2004/18 qui autorise le recours à la procédure négociée avec publicité « lorsqu'il s'agit de travaux dont la nature et les circonstances incertaines ne permettent pas de fixer le prix global au préalable » ou alors « lorsque la nature des services est telle que les spécifications du marché ne peuvent pas être déterminées avec suffisamment de précision ».

D'autres pays européens, que l'on qualifiera d'intermédiaires, n'admettent la procédure négociée que pour les PPP inférieurs aux seuils d'application des directives marchés publics et, pour les autres, n'assimilent pas systématiquement PPP et complexité. En ce cas, le recours au dialogue compétitif, pour les PPP assimilables à des marchés publics, dépendra des circonstances ; à défaut, c'est la procédure d'appel d'offres qui s'imposera (cas de la France). Sans systématiser le recours au dialogue compétitif, la position officielle anglaise réside dans l'idée qu'il y a une présomption que la majorité des PPP seront éligibles à cette procédure. En revanche, les PPP assimilables à des concessions font l'objet d'une procédure négociée avec publicité.

Par ailleurs, la Slovénie adopte des procédures de passation différenciées entre les concessions d'une part et les PPP de type marchés publics et les PPPI d'autre part. C'est un des seuls pays à prévoir une procédure de passation pour les PPPI, avec l'Italie.

D'autres pays enfin adoptent une vision assez stricte: le Portugal soumet les PPP/concession à l'appel d'offres ouvert ou restreint ou à la négociation, au choix. En revanche, un PPP/marché public sera soumis seulement à l'appel d'offres ouvert ou restreint.

En dehors de l'Union européenne, la Turquie assimile les PPP aux concessions pour ce qui est de la procédure de passation et les Etats-Unis admettent que pour de tels contrats complexes, une procédure négociée est possible et la personne publique n'a pas à établir à l'avance les spécifications techniques du contrat. L'Afrique du Sud assimile tous les PPP à des marchés publics mais il y a alors une certaine adaptation des procédures en autorisant de manière plus large la négociation que pour les marchés publics et en prévoyant la passation en différentes phases.

[21] Rapport hongrois : "These covenants can be accepted by governmental decisions and it cannot exceed 3 % of the gross revenue of the state budget per year."

On voit néanmoins que la complexité de ces contrats questionne la pertinence des procédures de passation classiques. Même lorsque les PPP sont assimilés à des marchés publics, la plupart des pays cherchent à ouvrir le recours à une procédure plus flexible, ce qui peut se comprendre au vu des enjeux et de la durée généralement longue de ces contrats. Il paraît en effet peu adapté d'envisager de tels contrats aux objets multiples et qui s'inscrivent dans la durée sans entrer un minimum dans une discussion avec les candidats. Le Canada semble être d'ailleurs le seul pays à avoir poussé cette logique jusqu'au bout, puisque la procédure de passation est officiellement aménagée pour les PPP.

Il convient en effet de relever l'originalité du système canadien qui prévoit une étape préalable qui paraît, au premier abord, innovante et particulièrement adaptée à la complexité des PPP : il s'agit de l'appel d'intérêt.[22] Véritable étape exploratoire, elle permet, selon le rapport canadien, « de sonder l'intérêt et la capacité du secteur privé de participer à un éventuel projet réalisé en mode PPP, en permettant au secteur privé (partenaires éventuels et prêteurs) de se prononcer sur les différents aspects du partenariat envisagé: durée, structure de financement, nature de la relation entre les partenaires, principaux obstacles à la réussite du projet, répartition des risques commerciaux ». Bien sûr, cela n'empêche pas des candidats qui ne se seraient pas manifestés lors de cette étape exploratoire, de candidater au niveau de la deuxième étape, appelée étape de qualification, qui consiste en la sélection des candidats. Cette deuxième étape ne fige pas totalement d'ailleurs non plus le projet puisqu'il est admis que le gouvernement peut encore modifier les termes du futur contrat avant l'étape de l'appel de propositions et, par ailleurs, les candidats eux-mêmes peuvent suggérer des modifications lors de leur remise de proposition. Cet exemple montre qu'au moins dans un pays, il a été explicitement tenu compte, au stade de la passation, des particularités de ces contrats publics que sont les PPP. Ce mode de passation souple conduit néanmoins les rapporteurs canadiens à s'interroger sur sa compatibilité avec les exigences de réalisation d'une étude d'impact sur l'environnement suffisamment en amont. Le rapport américain fait écho à cette remarque en soulignant toutes les questions que soulèvent le fait de confier la réalisation du projet à une personne privée qui n'est pas toujours soumises aux mêmes obligations et, si elle l'est, n'est peut-être pas la mieux armée pour les mettre en œuvre (réglementations sur l'environnement pour la participation du public).

Il est à noter que si l'initiative d'un projet vient d'une personne privée, la plupart des pays n'exclue ni ne favorise l'entreprise à l'origine du projet, comme en Europe ou comme il est recommandé aux Etats-Unis, au nom du principe d'égalité. Seule l'Argentine donne en quelque sorte une prime à l'innovation privée en accordant une « priorité » à l'entreprise à l'origine du projet.

Hormis l'exemple canadien, la spécificité de la passation des PPP s'illustre en réalité surtout lorsque l'on sort des procédures de publicité et de mise en concurrence *stricto sensu* pour s'intéresser à tout ce qui entoure le processus de passation. Il en va ainsi des obligations d'évaluation préalable de l'intérêt de recourir à des PPP et de l'intervention d'organismes extérieurs. Il est souvent question en effet de faire appel à des organismes experts, généralement dépendants du gouvernement (notamment Slovénie, France, Grèce, Argentine, Canada et Angleterre où il en existe 4 dont 3 ont des liens forts avec le gouvernement), parfois indépendants (Allemagne). Il existe toutefois des contre exemples, comme la Pologne qui ne connait pas d'organismes experts ni d'évaluation préalable alors même que ce pays connaît d'une législation propre aux PPP ou encore la Turquie qui connaît d'un organisme expert mais pas d'obligations d'évaluation préalable.

Quand il existe des organismes experts, leur rôle varie néanmoins d'un pays à l'autre. Une partie de ces organismes a pour fonction, comme en Belgique flamande, aux Etats-Unis, en Allemagne ou en Angleterre (Task force), de faciliter le recours aux PPP. L'Afrique du sud lui attribue notamment le rôle d'établir des standards de contrats et de développer la formation des agents et, par ailleurs, d'assister les personnes publiques dans la passation et l'exécution des PPP. Elle en a tiré la conséquence que cet organisme ne peut procéder à la « faisabilité » du PPP pour un projet précis, le gouvernement faisant appel à des consultants privés, ce que l'on peut tout à fait comprendre dans un souci d'objectivité mais qui est loin d'être généralisé à l'ensemble des pays. Si cet aspect « promotion » des PPP n'est pas totalement absent des missions des organismes experts des autres pays, ces derniers ont plutôt un rôle d'évaluateur de l'intérêt de recourir à un PPP et d'assistance dans la passation et l'exécution

[22] aussi appelé appel de manifestation d'intérêt ou *Request for Expressions of Interest document*

comme par exemple en France ou en Grèce. Le Canada va plus loin en confiant, outre ce rôle d'évaluateur, la négociation, la signature et le suivi des contrats de PPP à un tel organisme, au niveau fédéral surtout et dans une moindre mesure au Québec également, ce qui consacre alors pleinement sa fonction d'expertise.

L'évaluation tend presque toujours à démontrer les avantages de la solution des PPP par rapport à des schémas classiques (ou l'inverse s'il existe une priorité pour les PPP). Certains rapports soulignent la difficulté, constatée par des organismes officiels ou par la doctrine, à établir de manière objective de tels avantages (cas de la Hongrie et de la France).

La prise en compte des effets induits par de tels contrats, et notamment de l'exclusion de fait de Petites et Moyennes Entreprises (PME), est plutôt peu fréquente. Les PPP sont en effet des projets d'une telle ampleur généralement que ces entreprises ne peuvent porter le projet, même en se regroupant. Rares sont les pays qui prévoient des dispositifs visant à s'assurer la présence de Petites et Moyennes Entreprises, à l'exception de la France. La France a prévu un mécanisme incitatif en faisant de la part du contrat réservé à des PME un critère de choix des offres, sans toutefois que soit prévue une pondération minimale. En Argentine s'applique une législation générale qui donne la priorité aux PME, tout comme s'applique aux Etats-Unis le *small business act* ou encore des *guidelines* en Angleterre en faveur des *small and medium sizes enterprises* mais toutes ces initiatives ne sont pas propres aux PPP. L'Afrique du sud ne connaît pas de mécanisme en faveur des PME mais applique une législation générale destinée à promouvoir la *black economy*.

De la même façon, les considérations tenant à la qualité architecturale sont rarement présentes, à l'exception de la France qui en fait un critère de choix obligatoire, ici encore sans pondération minimale, ou encore des *guidelines* anglaises. La protection du secret commercial est encore plus rarement prise en compte : hormis une disposition issue du droit communautaire concernant le dialogue compétitif, seules apparemment là encore des *guidelines* anglaises cherchent à prévenir concrètement tout risque de divulgation à cet égard.

Rares aussi sont les pays qui encadrent la passation des contrats passés par le partenaire. Le principe en général est celui de la liberté. La Slovénie prévoit un dispositif complet, de même que la Pologne, qui oblige le partenaire à respecter des règles de transparence quand il contracte avec des tiers. Les autres pays européens se contentent d'appliquer les directives marchés publics qui imposent de telles règles aux seuls concessionnaires de travaux publics ou aux organismes subventionnés à plus de 50 %, comme le rappelle par exemple le rapport portugais.

Enfin, en ce qui concerne la création des partenariats public privé institutionnalisés, la plus grande variété existe. Entre les pays qui l'interdisent (Grèce par exemple), ceux qui ne prévoient rien en droit positif (Angleterre), ou ceux qui ne le prévoient que pour certaines missions (cas de la France pour les collectivités locales) et ceux qui l'envisagent mais avec accord du Parlement (Uruguay), toutes les solutions imaginables peuvent se retrouver. Certains pays, on l'a vu, envisagent le choix du partenaire privé dans l'entreprise mixte après publicité et mise en concurrence mais c'est loin d'être la majorité des cas.

Au-delà de la diversité de situations s'agissant des restrictions à l'usage des PPP, l'existence de systèmes de priorité ou de freins au recours aux PPP, ainsi que l'exigence assez générale d'évaluation, montre en tout cas qu'en la matière les PPP se distinguent nettement des autres contrats publics traditionnels.

26.3 Exécution

On sera plus bref dans cette section, car la relative nouveauté des PPP, dans leur acception moderne et restrictive, celle des PPP/marchés publics, n'a pas encore permis de nourrir une expérience suffisante pour que le droit adapte éventuellement ses outils aux problématiques propres à ce genre de procédés. Il est donc difficile d'apprécier la nouveauté en la matière, sauf en ce qui concerne le partage des risques, dont il a déjà été question plus haut.

Il est possible au préalable de faire état de quelques retours d'expériences des PPP peu favorables voire négatifs, du moins dans les pays qui ont mis en place des PPP (dans leur acception moderne) en nombre conséquents depuis plus d'une dizaine d'années, c'est-à-dire pour l'essentiel l'Angleterre et les Etats-Unis. Ainsi, aux Etats-Unis, certains Etats comme le Texas ont décidé d'un moratoire sur les PPP et, par ailleurs, le rapport américain attire l'attention sur les effets pervers que l'enthousiasme pour les PPP peut avoir sur la concurrence (surcoûts liés à l'externalisation notamment), la protection de l'environnement (diminution de la qualité des études d'impact du fait de la rationalisation du processus quand un PPP est envisagé) et sur le développement de clauses de non concurrence (qui peuvent avoir l'effet pervers de ne pas moderniser, par exemple, un moyen de transport susceptible de concurrencer le partenaire privé). De même, l'externalisation de services inclut nécessairement que certaines fonctions d'autorité seront exercées par une entreprise privée qui n'est alors pas tenue d'appliquer toutes les règles protectrices pour les administrés, à l'image du *due process* et de l'*equal protection.* Ces préoccupations ne semblent pas encore avoir touché les autres pays, sans qu'il soit possible de savoir si cela tient à l'existence de garde-fous juridiques, à l'absence de pratiques problématiques (pour l'instant) ou encore au fait que la question ne se pose pas faute de ne pas transférer des missions sensibles (cas de la France puisqu'aucune mission de service public ne peut être confiée à un partenaire).

En Angleterre, la doctrine s'intéresse également aux questions de légitimité et d'*accountability*[23] des partenaires et par ailleurs différentes études font état d'une moindre attirance pour les PPP/PFI depuis quelque temps, liée notamment au fait que la rentabilité escomptée de ces contrats ne seraient pas au rendez-vous. Au Portugal, les premières années ont montré des difficultés d'exécution, avec des modifications importantes des contrats, allant parfois même jusqu'à changer la nature du contrat (adoption de péages dans le domaine routier par exemple). En France, les premiers ouvrages livrés en PPP (prisons) ont eu mauvaise presse en termes de qualité. En Allemagne, le retour d'expérience n'est pas encore très important mais il pourrait l'être car la loi impose une évaluation postérieure au PPP afin d'établir si les objectifs et gains annoncés dans l'évaluation préalable ont été atteints. Mais il est vrai qu'il est une tendance naturelle à ne parler que des trains qui arrivent en retard, et les rapports passent généralement sous silence les projets réalisés avec succès, à l'exception du rapport canadien. Il est néanmoins fait aussi allusion dans ce dernier à quelques difficultés d'application et à quelques litiges, qui en général ont conduit à donner raison aux partenaires, faute de clauses contractuelles suffisantes au bénéfice du cocontractant public et en l'absence des règles applicables sans textes aux contrats de l'administration, du moins en pratique, contrairement à ce qui existe en France en présence de contrats administratifs.[24]

On peut justement noter que les règles d'exécution peuvent dépendre du point de savoir si les contrats de PPP sont des contrats administratifs ou de droit privé, dans les pays où la notion de contrat administratif existe. Or, là encore, toutes les solutions sont présentes : soit les contrats de PPP sont de droit privé, comme tous les autres contrats publics (au sens de contrats passés par des personnes publiques), soit ils sont des contrats administratifs (comme en France), soit cela dépend du type de contrat. Ainsi, en Russie, seul le contrat de concession est un contrat administratif alors que les marchés publics sont des contrats qui relèvent du code civil et l'on retrouve à peu près la même dichotomie en Allemagne.

Pour le reste, on se bornera à envisager, dans la mesure du possible, les spécificités pour l'essentiel textuelles qui existent par rapport aux marchés publics classiques en ce qui concerne l'exécution des PPP, tout en essayant de vérifier si la distinction pays de *common law* / pays de droit continental a ici un sens. Seront tout d'abord examinés les sources des règles d'exécution, puis seront évoqués deux types de clauses afin d'illustrer la diversité des solutions, relatives à la propriété des ouvrages et à la fin des contrats, afin d'apprécier les divergences et convergences d'un pays à l'autre.

26.3.1 Sources des règles d'exécution

Concernant les sources des règles d'exécution, il existe soit des clauses obligatoires, c'est-à-dire des dispositions contractuelles imposées par des textes de droit positif, soit des modèles de contrats ou de clauses posés par des circulaires ou *guidelines*, soit les deux. Il ne semble pas que l'on puisse dresser ici une ligne nette entre pays de *common law* et pays civilistes.

La question de la référence à des modèles de contrat est très variable, même sur le continent européen. En Belgique, il est fait référence au cahier des charges des marchés de travaux, mais avec des dérogations, alors qu'en France, pays pourtant très attaché à ces cahiers

[23]Le terme n'a pas de véritable équivalent en français.

[24]Il existe bien un pouvoir discrétionnaire permettant des modifications des obligations contractuelles mais le coût de telles modifications est, selon le rapport canadien, très dissuasif.

des charges types en matière de marchés publics, aucun cahier des charges type n'est prévu.

En France comme en Grèce ou encore en Russie pour les contrats de concessions, il existe en revanche une liste de clauses obligatoires, à l'exemple du partage des risques. Le contenu de ces clauses n'est toutefois guère précisé en général dans la loi et laisse donc une certaine place à la liberté contractuelle. La question de la répartition des risques n'est par exemple pas du tout détaillée dans le cas français. Dans le cas grec, la loi ajoute néanmoins que certains risques relèvent de la personne publique.[25] C'est plutôt par l'intermédiaire de la *soft law* (circulaires ou guides) ou par la doctrine (comme en Allemagne) que les principes sont fixés, généralement fondés sur l'idée qu'il faut attribuer un risque à la partie la mieux à même de l'assumer.

Dans les pays de *common law*, on ne sera pas surpris d'apprendre qu'il n'existe pas de clauses obligatoires mais que des *guidelines* prévoient une certaine standardisation des clauses. C'est notamment le cas en Afrique du Sud[26] ou du Royaume-Uni. Aux Etats-Unis, la situation est intermédiaire avec la possibilité de déroger aux dispositions du Federal Agencies Regulation (F.A.R.) mais à condition de justifier ces dérogations. Les clauses standards américaines établissent la propriété des constructions ou la propriété intellectuelle, ou encore les possibilités de modification unilatérale du contrat à la demande du gouvernement et la manière de compenser financièrement le loyer en cas d'éventuelles défaillances. Au Canada, il est fait officiellement référence au *standardisation of PFI contract* de 2004 issu des *guidelines* anglaises. On retrouve donc les clauses de partage de bénéfice en cas de refinancement, les clauses de partage des risques et un recours accru à l'arbitrage. Un contrôle de la personne publique s'opère sur la fin des sous-contrats c'est-à-dire sur les contrats passés par le partenaire pour la réalisation du PPP. Le Québec présente aussi une intéressante illustration de l'adaptation d'un outil issu du *common law* dans une province régie par le droit civil. Le rapport souligne le caractère surabondant de certaines formules issus de ces *guidelines*, à l'image du devoir de prudence ou de diligence déjà prévu en droit civil des contrats. En revanche, de telles clauses types impliquent parfois une adaptation afin de ne pas tomber sous le coup d'une qualification qui, en droit civil québécois, revêt une autre signification (à l'instar du « partenariat de droit civil »).

L'Allemagne connaît aussi des clauses standards mais par secteur d'activité (transports par exemple), tout comme l'Angleterre (déchets, défense, éducation).

De manière intéressante, la France, dont la loi impose on l'a vu des clauses obligatoires, a combiné ce modèle de type plutôt continental avec des clauses types définies dans des guides. L'idée actuelle est d'aller vers ce qui existe en Allemagne et en Angleterre, c'est-à-dire de développer des standards par secteurs d'activités.

En Pologne, il n'existe pas de clauses obligatoires. Néanmoins, il y a une obligation de donner des informations relatives à l'exécution aux administrations centrales et il semble que ces informations devraient permettre de créer à terme un modèle type de PPP.

26.3.2 Questions de propriété

La question de la propriété des terrains et surtout des ouvrages construits par le partenaire fait elle aussi l'objet d'une très grande variété de solutions d'un pays à l'autre mais la variété existe aussi à l'intérieur de chaque pays généralement puisque la plupart des pays laisse une assez grande marge de manœuvre aux cocontractants pour ce qui est du sort des ouvrages et des terrains à l'issue des PPP. Il n'y a pas, ici encore,

[25] Voir le rapport Grec : "According to Articles 21, 23 and 24 of Law 3389/2005, the Public Entity is obliged to compensate the Private Entity in the case of delays caused by the intervention of public authorities when required, such as the Archaeology Service and Public Utilities, as well as in the case of delays in issuing acts of expropriation"

[26] Voir le rapport sud-africain : "The National Treasury's '*Standardised PPP Provisions*' (issued 11 March 2004 as National Treasury PPP Practice Note Number 01 of 2004) make provision for a number of clauses that are specific to PPPs. As noted, examples of clauses include those dealing with: insurance, relief events, compensation events and force majeure, unforseeable and discriminatory government conduct and variations, termination and step-in. Specific provision is made for 'assignment, subcontracting and changes in shareholding and control' in Part S of the document. An example is also given of a standard assignment clause. Provision is further made for 'methods of calculating, sharing and paying refinancing gains' in Part Q of the document. The National Treasury's '*PPP Manual*' and '*Standardised PPP Provisions*' stipulate that the parties to the contract should identify every risk that may be applicable to the particular contract. They should identify the impact of that risk occurring on the parties and on the contract, and identify possible methods to limit or mitigate the risk, including the cost of taking those measures. The parties should then negotiate and agree on who is the most appropriate party to bear the risk."

une claire distinction entre pays de *common law* qui laisseraient plus de libertés en la matière, et pays de droit civil.

Certes, la plupart des pays de *common law* illustrent cette liberté contractuelle.

Ainsi, au Canada, pays de *common law* en grande majorité, tous les modes opératoires se retrouvent, allant du cas dans lequel le secteur public conserve la propriété de l'infrastructure tout au long du contrat, jusqu'au cas où l'infrastructure demeurera la propriété du partenaire privé à l'échéance du contrat. Les 18 formules contractuelles américaines identifiées par le GAO en 1999 elles aussi permettent toute combinaison possible en termes de propriété. Mais cette liberté est à nuancer dans d'autres pays de *common law*.

En Angleterre, si la liberté contractuelle prévaut aussi, il est intéressant de noter que la position officielle a évolué, passant d'une situation où, sans être favorisée, la propriété privée à l'issue du contrat était très largement pratiquée, à une recommandation en 2008 visant à distinguer entre les contrats nécessitant un retour à la propriété publique en fin de contrat et les autres contrats. En Nouvelle-Zélande, l'ouvrage construit reste propriété du partenaire.

A l'inverse, la tradition civiliste (ou continentale[27]), ne conduit pas nécessairement à un encadrement de la liberté contractuelle. La France envisage toutes les solutions concernant le sort des biens à l'issue du contrat, même si en pratique les ouvrages construits reviendront souvent à la personne publique en fin de contrat si leur objet est conforme aux missions de la personne publique.

La question de la propriété des ouvrages pendant la durée du PPP connaît elle moins de diversité. Cela tient à la logique même du PPP (le financement privé) qui conduit à donner quelques garanties de stabilité au partenaire investisseur et ces garanties se traduisent en général par la propriété des ouvrages pendant la durée du contrat. Même dans les pays comme la France ou la Belgique qui connaissent traditionnellement d'un régime de précarité des occupations privatives sur le domaine public, les textes ont assoupli ce principe dans le cas des PPP. En Belgique comme en France, la spécificité des PPP est donc reconnue en ce que les biens construits sur le domaine public par le partenaire sont grevés de droits réels, c'est-à-dire que le partenaire bénéficie de tous les droits et obligations du propriétaire sur l'ouvrage construits pendant la durée du PPP. En France toutefois, le contrat peut en disposer autrement mais il ne semble pas qu'en pratique cette disposition soit très utilisée puisque, encore une fois, elle s'oppose à la logique du financement privé qui implique des droits réels sur l'ouvrage construits afin de pouvoir hypothéquer le bien et donc emprunter à des taux convenables.

Ces questions de propriété privée peuvent avoir un impact fiscal et, d'une certaine façon, handicaper le recours aux PPP. Ainsi, des pays comme l'Allemagne ou la France ont cherché à rendre neutre le dispositif fiscal lorsque les personnes publiques envisagent de recourir à un PPP en alignant les impôts dus dans le cadre d'un PPP sur ceux à acquitter en marchés publics classique pour tenir compte du fait que la propriété de l'ouvrage devra en principe revenir dans le giron public.

Dans d'autre cas, la propriété publique prédomine. Ainsi, en Italie, la propriété publique s'étend jusqu'à la propriété intellectuelle des ouvrages.

Au-delà de la question de la propriété des ouvrages, l'adaptation du régime juridique traditionnel pour prendre en compte les nécessités des PPP se traduit aussi en Belgique par le fait que l'on admet également les partenariats public privé institutionnalisés alors que jusque là les personnes publiques ne pouvaient prendre des participations au capital.

De toute évidence la propriété des ouvrages distingue les PPP des marchés publics classiques pour les rapprocher des concessions. On ne peut donc parler d'innovation en la matière.

26.3.3 Fin du contrat

Les dispositions là encore varient d'un pays à l'autre, et là encore les situations ne recoupent pas la dichotomie *common law*/droit continental. Cela tient principalement au fait que le droit continental n'est pas uniforme, partagé qu'il est entre les pays où les contrats publics (c'est-à-dire les contrats des personnes publiques) sont des contrats soumis au droit privé ou très exceptionnellement au droit public, et les pays, minoritaires, où les contrats publics sont très souvent des contrats administratifs qui dérogent au droit

[27]Expression préférable dans un contexte de droit administratif, en particulier dans le cas français s'agissant de contrats qui sont administratifs et donc non soumis aux règles du code civil.

civil. Mais les différences ici peuvent s'estomper – et s'estompent souvent – en raison de la possibilité reconnue explicitement ou implicitement par un droit national d'introduire des clauses qui permettent une adaptation du contrat à l'écoulement du temps, particulièrement bienvenue pour ces contrats de longue durée que sont les PPP. On doit noter toutefois que l'absence de telles clauses peut conduire à des situations contre productives, ainsi qu'il en a déjà été fait état à propos des Etats-Unis. Seuls les pays reconnaissant un pouvoir de modification ou de résiliation unilatérale sans clause garantissent nécessairement cette adaptation, mais au pris d'une atteinte à la force obligatoire des contrats.

De manière générale, comme on peut s'en douter, dans les pays de *common law*, seule la présence d'une clause en ce sens permet une résiliation unilatérale au profit des personnes publiques. En Afrique du Sud, ce sont les *guidelines* qui recommandent d'introduire des clauses de résiliation dans certains cas.[28]

En Angleterre, comme pour la question de la propriété des ouvrages en fin de contrat, la position officielle a évolué. Les *guidelines* recommandent désormais d'insérer les possibilités de résiliation unilatérale dans les clauses du contrat afin de donner de la souplesse à l'action publique.

La situation est toutefois inverse au Canada, puisque la résiliation unilatérale du contrat par le « client » est toujours possible en principe mais les clauses des PPP ont tendance à supprimer cette faculté, sauf pour les cas de « défaut » du partenaire. Il semble que le Canada privilégie ainsi la stabilité des relations contractuelles afin d'attirer les investisseurs privés.

Dans les pays de droit civil ou continental, la situation est très diverse.

En Pologne, il n'y a pas de dispositions particulières sur la fin du contrat donc ce sont les règles classiques qui s'appliquent, en l'occurrence les règles du code civil : sauf clauses contraires, il n'est pas possible de résilier unilatéralement.

En Italie, la résiliation unilatérale pour motif d'intérêt général n'est possible que rarement.

En Allemagne, c'est pour l'essentiel le code civil qui s'appliquera pour la majorité des PPP et il n'admet qu'exceptionnellement une résiliation unilatérale. Cependant, des clauses standardisées élargissent le spectre de la résiliation unilatérale.

En France, la plupart des PPP sont des contrats administratifs et en tant que tels, soumis au pouvoir de modification unilatérale ou de résiliation unilatérale de l'administration lequel est, dans ce pays, un principe général du droit qui existe donc sans texte dès lors que le contrat est qualifié d'administratif, ce qui est le cas des contrats de partenariat. Le contrat doit néanmoins prévoir les conséquences, notamment financières, de la mise en œuvre de ces pouvoirs.

Mais il est à relever une différence entre pays de *common law* et pays de droit civil : les premiers semblent recommander d'adapter les clauses aux cas des PPP par rapport aux autres contrats publics, alors que les seconds se bornent à appliquer les règles propres à l'ensemble des contrats publics.

26.4 Contrôles juridictionnels

Cette section fera également l'objet de développements moindres. Car, de manière générale, les contrôles juridictionnels sont très largement identiques à ceux qui existent pour les autres contrats publics. Il n'y a pas, en la matière, un début d'adaptation des règles applicables aux autres contrats publics pour le cas des PPP. De ce fait, la grande variété de situations existant d'un pays à l'autre en matière de contrats publics se retrouve en matière de PPP : entre les pays dont le contentieux des contrats publics relève pour l'essentiel des juridictions administratives, ou à l'inverse d'une juridiction judiciaire, ou des deux suivant que le litige est contractuel ou pas ou bien selon la nature du contrat ou encore

[28] "The National Treasury's '*Standardised PPP Provisions*' make provision in Part N for the termination of a PPP agreement before its expiry for any one of the following reasons:

- Institution Default
- Private Party Default
- Force Majeure or
- Corrupt Acts

It is expressly stated (in para 60.1.2) that the above reasons 'should be the only reasons for termination and the Institution should not be entitled to terminate the PPP Agreement for convenience even if it is of the view that it is better equipped to render the Services itself'. Insofar as damages or the payment of compensation is concerned, the '*Standardised PPP Provisions*' provide that – [t]he value of compensation payable to the Private Party on an early termination will vary depending on the reason for that termination. Where the termination is a result of Institution Default, the value of the compensation payable to the Private Party is usually greater than that payable in the event of Force Majeure termination or termination as a result of a Private Party Default. The compensation payable on Private Party Default should be substantially less than the compensation payment on termination for any other reason."

un contentieux qui voit l'intervention d'un organe spécialisé pour tout ou partie des PPP, toutes les solutions imaginables se retrouvent dans la réalité juridique. Loin de tendre à l'exhaustivité, on se bornera à faire état de quelques solutions nationales.

En Allemagne, la passation des PPP/marchés publics relève d'une juridiction spéciale alors que le contentieux de l'exécution dépendra de la nature du contrat, lequel est privé s'il s'agit d'un PPP assimilable à un marché public.

En Slovénie, les actions contentieuses sont partagées entre un juge administratif pour les concessions et un organisme spécial pour les PPP assimilables à des marchés publics alors qu'en Turquie seul le contentieux des concessions ne relève pas du juge judiciaire.

En Uruguay, une cour administrative est compétente pour certains actes administratifs unilatéraux.

En Pologne, tout le contentieux relève du juge judiciaire.

En Belgique, comme tout contrat public, le contentieux contractuel relève du juge civil mais le contentieux des actes détachables du contrat, dont ceux de la passation, relève du juge administratif.

En Hongrie, il existe un organisme administratif spécialisé pour les recours en matière de marchés publics qui se prononcera aussi sur les PPP/marchés publics.

En Angleterre, tous les contentieux contractuels relèvent du juge civil. Toutefois, les décisions prises dans le cadre de la passation des marchés publics relèven du *judicial review*.

Au Portugal tout comme en Argentine et en France, le juge compétent est en principe le juge administratif mais il est généralement évité par le biais de clauses compromissoires.

Au Canada, c'est le juge judiciaire qui est en principe compétent, mais il sera rarement saisi du fait du recours à l'arbitrage ou à d'autres modes alternatifs de règlements des différends. Une seule exception est à relever : il est recouru à une juridiction spécialisée pour la passation des marchés publics fédéraux, le tribunal canadien pour le commerce extérieur, mais qui n'est évidemment pas compétent que pour les questions de marchés publics.

C'est peut-être dans la place donnée aux modes alternatifs de règlement des litiges que peuvent se trouver les rares spécificités du contentieux des PPP par rapport au contentieux des autres contrats publics, et que l'on peut noter une certaine harmonie d'un pays à l'autre. Même la France autorise le recours à l'arbitrage pour les contrats de partenariat alors que le principe en matière de contrats publics – comme pour tout contentieux concernant des personnes publiques – reste l'interdiction de recours à l'arbitrage. La Grèce est allée même plus loin en imposant l'arbitrage, ce qui ne va pas sans poser des questions de constitutionnalité puisque la constitution grecque dispose que personne ne peut être privé contre sa volonté du droit au recours contre le juge normalement compétent.

26.5 Conclusion

L'étude du phénomène des partenariats publics privés nous a montré une grande diversité des approches entre les pays. A cet égard, une métaphore nous vient à l'esprit, tirée de l'œuvre de l'architecte américain Frank Lloyd Wright. Ce dernier prônait volontiers l'intégration de la maison dans son environnement (architecture « organique »), donc de tenir compte de la situation locale, tel un arbre (sa propre maison à Chicago, Oak Park, traversée par deux arbres), une rivière (la « river house ») ou un terrain rectangulaire (La « Robie » House à Chicago). La maison devait par ailleurs répondre à plusieurs fonctions (habitation/travail/loisir) et devait être susceptible d'évoluer face aux besoins changeants de ses habitants. Néanmoins, le style de cet architecte, quelque peu hétérogène (car il ne construisît pas que des « prairies house ») était le reflet de l'adaptation aux exigences de ses clients. L'architecture ainsi comprise, plus qu'un style, reflétait surtout une technique répondant à une certaine philosophie, même s'il ne s'agissait pas de s'inscrire dans une idéologie (contrairement par exemple à un Speer en Allemagne et, dans une moindre mesure et surtout dans un autre genre, au Corbusier en France). Mais cette technique architecturale assise sur une philosophie n'était point entièrement nouvelle, ne serait-ce que parce qu'elle était fondée sur des bases architecturales indépassables.

Les PPP apparaissent aussi comme une technique – juridique – répondant à une certaine philosophie pas si éloignée de celle de F. Lloyd Wright. La philosophie du PPP consiste en premier lieu en une plus grande collaboration des différents partenaires dans la conception et dans la réalisation du projet, sans qu'il soit possible de savoir si cette association répond à des exigences factuelles ou à des considérations idéologiques. La technique juridique permet de répondre à plusieurs fonctions (concevoir/construire/entretenir/financer) et doit permettre une adaptation de l'ouvrage tout au long de sa vie (modification des clauses, refinancement du partenaire, etc.). La nouveauté est réelle, pour qui sait regarder de suffisamment près et ne pas se contenter d'une vision d'ensemble,[29] que ce soit dans le partage des risques et responsabilités, dans le financement par le partenaire de rémunération à la performance ou dans les exigences d'évaluation préalable.

Cette technique s'adapte surtout aux exigences locales – géographiques ou humaines – de sorte qu'il est difficile d'y déceler un style unique. La grande diversité de mise en œuvre des PPP, que ce soit dans leur définition, leur passation, leur exécution ou leur contentieux, révèle ces adaptations « locales ».

On ne doit pas non plus négliger que cette technique, quoique nouvelle, n'échappe pas à une certaine forme de mode.

Bien que nouvelle, cette technique juridique reprend néanmoins les bases de toute technique juridique contractuelle publique, et ne saurait donc innover outre mesure. Il y a en la matière des données incontournables, que ce soit en termes de publicité et de mise en concurrence, de règles d'exécution ou de contentieux.

Mais la métaphore architecturale s'arrête là. Il y manque en effet un élément déterminant : nulle part l'on a pu identifier quel était le grand architecte à l'origine du développement des PPP. Il ne s'agit certainement pas d'un quelconque organisme international qui diffuserait un modèle, ni d'une entité régionale qui en aurait assuré la promotion au-delà de ses limites géographiques. Peut-être, simplement, faut-il voir dans l'expansion du phénomène des PPP une nouvelle illustration de la globalisation du droit qui échappe, à bien des égards, à toute emprise humaine.

Annexe: Questionnaire envoyé aux rapporteurs nationaux

Par François Lichère
Professeur agrégé de droit public, Université d'Aix-Marseille – France
Rapporteur Général de Droit administratif – Congrès de l'Académie Internationale de droit comparé 25 – 31 juillet 2010

1. Concept
   - Quand la notion de partenariat public-privé est-elle apparue pour la première fois dans la littérature juridique et avec quel sens ?
   - Existe-t-il une définition juridique (textuelle ou jurisprudentielle) des PPP dans votre pays ? Si oui, laquelle ? Sinon, existe-t-il une définition juridique de contrats qui s'apparentent à des PPP (à l'image des contrats de partenariat en France) ?
   - Existe-t-il une législation/réglementation spécifique à l'ensemble des partenariats publics-privés dans votre pays ? A défaut, existe-t-il une législation propre à certaines formes de PPP ? Pouvez-vous donner les sources textuelles ?
   - Du point de vue doctrinal, qu'entend-on généralement par PPP dans votre pays ? Y a-t-il plusieurs conceptions doctrinales des PPP et si oui quelles sont-elles ?
   - Existe-t-il une distinction entre PPP institutionnels (c'est-à-dire associant des personnes publiques et des personnes privées au sein d'une même entité) et PPP contractuels du point de vue doctrinal ou du droit positif ?
   - S'agissant des PPP institutionnels, existe-il une législation/réglementation propre à ces PPP institutionnels ? Si oui, sur quoi porte cette législation/réglementation et quel est son objet ? Existe-t-il une procédure de mise en concurrence concernant le choix du partenaire institutionnel ? Si oui, pouvez-vous décrire sommairement cette procédure ?
   - Comment la catégorie des PPP contractuels (ou de contrat de partenariat) s'est-elle intégrée aux catégories juridiques existantes ? S'agit-il d'une catégorie à part ? Si la réponse est négative, les PPP sont-ils assimilés à une ou plusieurs catégories existantes et lesquelles (marchés publics ? concession ? autre ?) ?
   - A l'intérieur des PPP contractuels, le droit ou la pratique distinguent-t-ils PPP de type concessif, c'est-à-dire avec paiement principalement par l'usager du service, et PPP de type non concessif, c'est-à-dire avec paiement par l'administration ?
   - En quoi les PPP contractuels présentent-ils des nouveautés par rapport aux contrats publics traditionnels ? Quels sont les particularités par

[29] Une maison de F. Lloyd Wright, n'est après tout, à une certaine distance, qu'une villa comme une autre.

rapport à des marchés publics ou des concessions classiques ? Quels sont les avantages et les inconvénients attendus des PPP par rapport à des contrats publics plus classiques ?

- Les PPP contractuels sont-ils plus considérés comme des contrats de financement (autrement dit avec comme objectif principal de trouver un financement) ou plutôt comme des contrats de travaux ou de service ? Du point de vue plus strictement juridique, les PPP contractuels sont-ils considérés comme des contrats de travaux ou des contrats de service ? Si vous n'avez pas de réponse en droit positif, quel est votre avis ? Est-ce que la réponse peut dépendre de chaque contrat ou est-ce que les PPP contractuels appartiennent selon vous nécessairement à l'une ou l'autre catégorie ?
- S'agissant des PPP contractuels, quelle est leur importance économique ? Disposez-vous de statistiques régulièrement mises à jour à cet égard ?

2. Attribution/Award
   - Existe-t-il des limites juridiques (constitutionnelles ou autres) au recours aux PPP ? Si oui, quelles sont-elles et sur quoi sont-elles fondées ?
   - Y a-t-il une obligation ou une recommandation d'évaluer ou de comparer les PPP avec d'autres montages avant de choisir le recours à un PPP ? Si oui, le PPP ne peut-il être choisi qu'après qu'il a été démontré qu'il s'agissait du meilleur contrat ?
   - Existe-t-il un (ou des) organisme(s) expert(s) qui assiste(nt) les personnes publiques pour la passation et/ou l'exécution des PPP ? Est-ce que le recours à cet organisme est obligatoire ? Est-il indépendant de l'Etat ? Comment est-il composé ? A-t-il des missions de formation aux PPP ?
   - Existe-t-il des modèles d'évaluation ? S'agit-il de modèles généraux ou par secteurs d'activité ? Sont-ils contraignants ?
   - Quelles sont les procédures de passation (publicité et mise en concurrence) pour choisir le partenaire ? Y a-t-il des spécificités par rapport au choix d'un cocontractant dans le cadre d'un marché public ? Ces procédures vous paraissent-elles adaptées à ce genre de contrats ?
   - Les procédures de passation ouvertes aux PPP vous paraissent-elles adaptées à ces contrats (en particulier si la négociation reste interdite) ?
   - Y a-t-il des garanties légales, au stade de la passation destinées à assurer une certaine présence des PME dans l'exécution des PPP ? Si oui lesquelles ?
   - Y a-t-il des garanties légales, au stade de la passation, destinées à assurer une certaine qualité architecturale ? Si oui lesquelles ?
   - Y a-t-il des garanties, au stade de la passation, quant à la protection du secret commercial des offres ?
   - Y a-t-il une obligation pour le partenaire de respecter des obligations de publicité et de mise en concurrence pour les contrats qu'il passe avec des tiers pour l'exécution du contrat de partenariat ?
3. Exécution/performance
   - Disposez-vous d'études dressant un bilan des expériences de PPP ? Si oui, pourriez-vous mettre en avant ce qu'il ressort en termes d'avantages et d'inconvénients par rapport à des montages plus classiques ?
   - Le droit positif (ou la soft law) de votre pays prévoient-ils des clauses obligatoires ou des clauses-types ? Si oui, quelles sont-elles ?
   - En pratique, quelles sont les clauses propres aux PPP que l'on retrouve le plus souvent ? Existe-t-il des clauses d'intéressement en cas de refinancement, des clauses de cessions de créances ?
   - Quel est le régime des biens de retour, c'est-à-dire des biens qui doivent revenir à la personne publique en fin de contrat ? Le partenaire est-il propriétaire des biens qu'il construit pendant la durée du contrat ?
   - Existe-t-il des modèles de répartition des risques entre personnes publiques et partenaires ? Quels sont les principes de répartition ? Quels sont les risques listés ?
   - Existe-t-il des règles de consolidations des contrats de PPP dans les comptes publics ? Si oui, quels sont les règles de consolidations (selon les types de risques – ex. Eurostat ou sur la base de critères de type risks and rewards ou sur la base de critères de contrôle – type IPSASB ou autres) ?
   - Y a-t-il un droit de regard du cocontractant public sur les contrats passés par le partenaire ?
   - Existe-t-il des possibilités de résiliation unilatérale des PPP contractuels ? Si oui, à l'initiative de qui (personne publique, partenaire ?) et pour

quels motifs (faute, motifs d'intérêt général, autres)? En cas de résiliation (unilatérale ou conventionnelle), les parties peuvent-elles fixer librement le montant de l'indemnisation ? Y a-t-il un plafonnement de l'indemnisation (forfait) ?

4. Recours contentieux/remedies
   - Les recours contentieux contre les PPP contractuels sont-ils fréquents ?
   - Existe-t-il des procédures ou des règles contentieuses particulières aux PPP par rapport aux autres contrats publics ?
   - Existe-t-il des procédures d'urgence antérieures à la signature du contrat ? Quelles sont les conditions de recours ?
   - Les contentieux des PPP (de la passation et de l'exécution) relèvent-ils d'un juge spécialisé ? Si oui lequel, pourquoi et quels sont ses autres domaines de compétences ?
   - Si les PPP sont soumis aux mêmes règles contentieuses que les autres contrats publics, y a-t-il des spécificités contentieuses par rapport aux contrats de droit privé ? Si oui, quelles sont-elles ?
   - Si la résiliation unilatérale est possible, faut-il la demander au juge ou peut-elle être prononcée d'office par une des parties ? L'autre partie peut-elle attaquer la décision de résiliation unilatérale ou seulement demander des dommages et intérêts ?
5. Si vous souhaitez attirer l'attention du rapporteur général sur des questions qui n'auraient pas été abordées dans ce questionnaire, vous pouvez le faire ci-dessous:

27 Regulation of Corporate Tax Avoidance[1]

Karen B. Brown

27.1 Introduction

Corporate tax avoidance presents a serious challenge to the effective administration of tax laws. Tax avoidance involves arrangement of a transaction in order to obtain a tax advantage, benefit, or reduction in a manner unintended by the tax law. It is an unacceptable manipulation of the law which is unlike legitimate tax mitigation. Mitigation involves use of the tax law to achieve anticipated tax advantages embedded in tax provisions. Tax avoidance is also to be distinguished from tax evasion. Evasion involves outright fraud, concealment, or misrepresentation in order to defeat application of the tax laws.[2]

Tax avoidance is an affront to tax administration when it violates core principles. Efficiency, fairness, and administrability support the effective administration of tax laws. Taxpayers engaging in tax avoidance transactions undermine the ability of the tax authority to predict the amount of revenue to be raised by a given tax provision. In addition, if the tax laws impact similarly situated taxpayers differently as a result of tax avoidance, fairness is sacrificed. Moreover, authorities expend significant resources in attempts to combat tax avoidance techniques. To the extent that tax avoidance transactions fail to enhance productivity or to marginally increase resources, increased costs of administration constitute a waste.

This report fulfills two goals.[3] It uses a number of measures to analyze and contrast the laws regulating corporate tax avoidance in more than 15 countries. It also considers whether a country's approach to combating tax avoidance is guided by the manner in which tax avoidance techniques assault core values supporting the system. The Appendix includes a chart that summarizes the major features of the tax avoidance law of the countries covered in this report.

27.2 Regulation of Tax Avoidance – In General

The divide between acceptable mitigation (tax planning) and unacceptable avoidance is variable and depends upon the foundational principles of a country's tax laws. In the U.S., maintaining a common law

[1] IV.E., L'évasion fiscale.

[2] The distinction between tax mitigation, avoidance, and evasion is detailed in Zoë Prebble and John Prebble, "Comparing the General Anti-Avoidance Rule of Income Tax Law with the Civil Law Doctrine of Abuse of Law," *Bulletin for International Taxation* (April, 2008):151–170. Electronic copy available at: http://ssrn.com/abstract=1605483.

K.B. Brown (✉)
George Washington University, Washington, DC, USA
e-mail: Karenbrown@law.gwu.edu

[3] This General Report synthesizes national reports prepared for the following countries: Austria (Sabine Kirchmayr); Australia (Maurice Cashmere); Canada (Carl MacArthur); China (Kevin Holmes); Croatia (Natasa Zunic Kovacevic); France (Daniel Gutmann); Germany (Ulrich Palm); Greece (Theodore Fortsakis); Hungary (Eva Erdos, Zoltan Nagy, Zoltan Varga); Italy (Carlo Garbarino); Japan (Keigo Fuchi); Netherlands (Raymond Luja); New Zealand (Zoë Prebble, John Prebble); Poland (Bogumil Brzezinski, Krzysztof Lasinksi-Sulecki); Russia (Zhuravleva Oxana); Slovenia (Nana Sumrada); Sweden (Mattias Dahlberg);Taiwan (Keh-Chang Gee, Yuan Chun (Martin) Lan); United Kingdom (Sandra Eden); United States (Tracy A. Kaye).

K.B. Brown and D.V. Snyder (eds.), *General Reports of the XVIIIth Congress of the International Academy of Comparative Law/Rapports Généraux du XVIIIème Congrès de l'Académie Internationale de Droit Comparé*, DOI 10.1007/978-94-007-2354-2_27, © Springer Science+Business Media B.V. 2012

tradition at the federal level, the judiciary ultimately holds responsibility for determining whether to deny expected tax benefits in a tax avoidance transaction. As discussed below, the U.S. legislature has enacted a form of a general anti-avoidance rule, codifying the economic substance doctrine, a common law device employed by courts to scrutinize various tax-minimizing schemes. Despite codification of a key anti-avoidance principle, federal courts nonetheless retain the power to determine whether a transaction that meets technical requirements of a statute fails to achieve the tax-reducing result sought by the taxpayer.

While generally, a taxpayer in the U.S. may organize its affairs so as to minimize the tax consequences of a deal,[4] Congress has taken the opportunity to curtail attempts to circumvent the expected application of a tax provision. One tool is to build into selected sections of the tax code itself statutory language restricting attempts to accomplish indirectly results prohibited by direct steps. These provisions, also known as targeted anti-avoidance rules, frequently deny tax benefits if the transaction is undertaken with the principal purpose of tax avoidance.

For example, one provision disallows any deduction, credit, or other tax benefit, if avoidance of income tax is the principal purpose of the acquisition of control of a corporation.[5] Another provision, attributes items of income, deduction, credit, and other allowances to the employee-owners of a professional corporation formed with the principal purpose of diverting tax liability from the owners.[6] Another more subtle provision, like the loss disallowance rule, which denies deduction of a loss sustained on direct sale of an asset to a related party, also disallows a loss on an indirect sale to a related party. Thus, the restructure of a transaction as a sale to an unrelated third party who immediately re-sells the asset to the intended related party would not achieve allowance of the loss because the statute itself negates losses on indirect sales as well.[7]

Administrative regulations also contain targeted anti-avoidance rules (TAARs). Those contained in the conduit financing rules under Regs. §188-1.3 were issued after the IRS lost several cases in which the courts refused to curtail treaty shopping by disregarding entities inserted into a transaction in order to reduce or eliminate U.S. tax liability. Partnership anti-abuse regulations limit the ability to organize a business as a partnership in order to reduce tax liability of partners in a manner inconsistent with the intent of the partnership provisions.[8]

When the statute and regulations are silent regarding the results of circuitous steps taken by taxpayers, the courts have filled a gap to determine when tax planning crosses the line into unacceptable tax avoidance. They have employed some version of a "substance over form" approach to defeat manipulation of enacted provisions by ingenious schemes. The usual trigger for such an analysis is the tax authority's contention that a particular deal constitutes an end-run around the statute. Courts resort to the "step transaction," "sham transaction," or "business purpose" common law doctrines to determine whether the tax benefits sought are obtained. This inquiry by the courts requires maintenance of a difficult balance between scrutiny of tax code compliance, a legitimate task, and enactment of supplemental tax law, which constitutes illegitimate assumption of authority in a legal system like that in the U.S. where the executive, legislature, and judiciary possess discrete powers and spheres of influence.[9]

In addition to the more general doctrines described above, courts have also applied an "economic substance" test. Primarily, this test applies to find tax avoidance when a taxpayer enters into a transaction with no realistic possibility of economic profit ("economic substance") and with no business purpose other than tax minimization.[10] Although generally both the absence of a profit motive and lack of business purpose are necessary to disallowance of tax benefits, some courts have found no tax avoidance when the transaction had either economic substance or a business purpose.

[4] *Gregory v. Helvering*, 293 U.S. 465 (1935).

[5] Internal Revenue Code (IRC) §269.

[6] IRC §269A.

[7] IRC §267(a)(1).

[8] While courts accord substantial authority to regulations issued under general or specific authority delegated by Congress, regulations may be challenged as beyond the IRS's interpretive power. See, e.g., *Mayo Foundation for Medical Education & Research v. U.S.*, 131 S. Ct. 704 (Jan. 11, 2011); *Mannella v. Comm'r*, 132 T.C. 196 (2010), *rev'd*, 631 F.3d 115 (3rd Cir. 2011); *Swallows Holding Ltd. v. Comm'r*, 126 T.C. 96 (2006), *vacated and remanded*, 515 F.3d 162 (2008).

[9] *Coltec Industries, Inc. v. U.S.*, 62 Fed. Cl. 716 (2004), *vacated and remanded*, 454 F.3d 1340 (Fed. Cir. 2006).

[10] Commentators often describe the inquiry into the existence of economic substance as an objective one, while the business purpose test is described as subjective.

While, as discussed below, the U.S. has chosen to codify the economic substance doctrine, in part, in order to dictate to courts the parameters of the tax avoidance inquiry, an alternative approach would emphasize the role of the courts in scrutinizing legislative intent. One well-regarded U.S. scholar argues that the economic substance doctrine is an ill-suited tax avoidance weapon. She finds it more appropriate to address the question whether "tax results are abusive" by leaving it to the courts to search for congressional intent. The ascertainment of congressional intent, she contends, offers a court the opportunity to balance the twin goals of an income tax statute – to measure income and to induce desired behavior. This is an enterprise more fruitful than the labeling of transactions as "tax shelters" and the subjective determination of the existence of economic substance.[11]

As described above, the U.S. courts have taken an "activist" approach to addressing tax avoidance techniques employed by taxpayers. The judiciary has employed a wide range of devices to shut-down taxpayer tax-minimizing schemes that are adjudged to run afoul of Congressional intent in enacting a particular statute. These judicial strategies are rarely condemned as an unauthorized exercise of legislative power.[12] The lee-way afforded courts to disregard manipulative business transactions may explain the relatively late adoption by Congress in 2010 of a general anti-avoidance rule ("GAAR"), in the limited and modest form described in Part II, below. Yet even U.S. courts have acknowledged the potential risks of a judicial activist approach that frustrates the expectations of businesses to organize transactions in a manner that technically complies with a statute (although in a manner not contemplated by the drafters) and mitigates the impact of corporate taxation.[13]

At a moment in history where countries are competing to attract and retain the corporate presence believed to bring production, investment in infrastructure, jobs, and revenue for government spending, strategies employed by jurisdictions to limit tax avoidance may result in flight to more tax-friendly locales.[14] Action by governments hoping to deter unacceptable subversion of tax laws necessarily involves a balancing of competing concerns. This involves assessment of the importance of the country's desire to ensure that taxpayers contribute their fair share of revenue under a tax code reflecting the jurisdiction's moral values and fiscal policy choices as well as the legitimacy of the interest of corporate citizens in the ability to rely on the literal contours of tax provisions to structure business arrangements that bring predictable consequences.

Reporters in all other countries indicate that their legislatures have employed varying strategies to address unacceptable techniques employed by taxpayers to minimize tax liability. While all of the reported countries use legal doctrine to foreclose attempts to use statutes in an unintended way, there is wide variation in practice. Perhaps because none of these countries has emulated the judicial activist approach in operation in the U.S., many countries adopted a GAAR well before the U.S.[15]

In all common law countries, in some circumstances, the courts have been accorded the authority to determine whether a business transaction meets the literal terms of a statute. If the terms are ambiguous or it appears that allowance of the tax benefits sought would defeat the legislative intent in enacting a provision, many would allow the courts to employ anti-avoidance doctrine in order to prevent abrogation of the statute. Because in most of the common law jurisdictions, other than the U.S., courts have acknowledged significant limitations on their interpretive authority, many of these countries have adopted a GAAR in an effort to furnish guidance. The law of these countries prior to enactment of a GAAR is discussed below.

Because many of the common law countries are former colonies, the anti-avoidance approach in the U.K. has had influence. While there were some indications that the U.K. courts were willing to take a more activist approach in anti-avoidance jurisprudence, there is a pronounced reluctance to deny tax benefits to transactions that fall literally within the terms of a statute merely because of the presence of artificial steps. In a line of cases beginning with the Ramsay case in

[11] Leandra Lederman, W(h)ither Economic Substance? 95 *Iowa Law Review* (2010): 389, 396–97.

[12] But see *Coltec Industries, Inc. v. U.S.*, 62 Fed. Cl. 716 (2004), *vacated and remanded,* 454 F. 3d 1340 (Fed. Cir. 2006).

[13] *ACM Partnership v. Comm'r.*, 157 F. 3d 231 (3rd Cir. 1998).

[14] See the report on the United Kingdom.

[15] All of the common law countries, except the UK, adopted a GAAR well before 2010, the year in which the U.S. codified the economic substance rule. The UK has not yet adopted a GAAR.

1982, the courts appeared to announce a new purposive approach permitting a disregard, as a matter of statutory construction, of the insertion of transactional steps taken lacking a commercial purpose. This approach seemed especially appropriate when circuitous steps were taken to obtain a pre-ordained result in defeat of a statute.

However, in 2004, in *Barclays Mercantile Business Finance Ltd*, the British courts eschewed the idea of a judicial anti-avoidance rule and indicated that the approach is primarily one of statutory construction. It appears to involve an inquiry into whether on a realistic view of the transaction at hand the statute intended to provide the tax benefits sought. Although the British case law does not provide detailed guidance concerning the extent to which a court will examine the policy underpinnings in order to determine whether a given scheme seeks to undermine it, Parliament has not attempted to provide further instruction to taxpayers in the form of a GAAR.

Although the British Parliament has not moved to enact a GAAR, it has taken steps to include TAARs in over 200 provisions. For example, one of the targeted rules works to deny capital loss relief if the main purpose of a transaction is to secure a tax advantage. In many of these provisions, the presence of a commercial purpose is determinative. When a TAAR is operative, the notes accompanying the legislation furnish a framework for application of the provision by the taxing authority. In the event the taxpayer and taxing authority do not reach agreement, the question whether a scheme is motivated by a business purpose will be decided by the court.

The anti-avoidance tradition in Canada traces its roots to the British *Duke of Westminster* case in which the court announced a strict interpretive approach. The Canadian courts have strictly construed the statutory language, finding generally that devices employed by taxpayers to avoid a given tax result are to be respected. A temporary shift to a modern view acknowledging the importance of the tax law as a tool of economic policy allowed the court in *Stubart Investments* to consider the object and spirit of legislation, in order to reach transactions intended to be covered by Parliament, even if they literally fell beyond statutory reach. The court in *Shell Canada Limited* found a role for a contextual and purposive approach, while noting that legal relationships must be respected.

Subsequent to *Stubart* some courts found a limitation on the purposive approach, determining that it only applied in the event of statutory ambiguity. Others, including *Canada Trustco Mortgage Co.* in 2005, recognized the dominant role of textual interpretation, but nonetheless authorized a search for ordinary meaning, context and legislative purpose in an effort to read a tax statute as a "harmonious whole." In general, however, the Canadian courts continue to apply a plain meaning/textual interpretation approach in order to afford taxpayers consistency and predictability.

As anti-avoidance doctrine developed in Canada, the courts rejected reliance upon a business purpose test or an economic substance test (termed a "reasonable expectation of profit") as a basis for disregarding a transaction for tax purposes. The enactment of a robust GAAR in 1988 is attributed to the reluctance of Canadian courts to take an activist approach.

Anti-avoidance law in two other important common law jurisdictions, Australia and New Zealand, has developed in conjunction with judicial interpretation of the application of the respective GAARs. These longstanding codifications have captured the direction of the jurisprudence and will be discussed below. The UK is the only common law country covered in this report that lacks a GAAR.

In most of the civil law countries, the "abuse of law" or "abuse of right" doctrine that targets circumvention of the law in general holds sway in tax law as well. In the tax law context, anti-abuse rules are founded on the principle that citizen-taxpayers must be treated equally. Such equality means that each must pay its fair share of tax in accordance with ability to pay. To allow some taxpayers to shoulder less than the appropriate share of the tax burden through aggressive tax planning runs counter to this general principle. This notion of equality may be based in the Constitution, as in the case of Germany, or simply upon core values embedded into a country's social and political structure, as in the case of the People's Republic of China.

In France, both the tax administration and the legislature have shifted from addressing tax avoidance by crafting a clear and precise juridical rule to reliance on the more general principles that are now reflected in its GAAR, which was most recently modified in 2009. The complexity and sophistication of taxpayer strategies to reduce taxes has caused the French authorities to broaden the anti-tax avoidance arsenal to find a mechanism to address artificial transactions manufactured solely to achieve tax minimization. The GAAR, which is the centerpiece of the French effort, is discussed below with the GAARs of the other civil law countries.

Greece, a civil law country, has not enacted a GAAR. Greek law is characterized by strict, literal interpretation of tax legislation by the administrative courts and Council of State. However, "substance over form" operates as a general principle of tax law, based presumably on the principle of equality among taxpayers according to ability to pay embodied in the Greek Constitution. Accordingly, Greece relies upon TAARs, focusing on particular types of tax avoidance, including the use of offshore companies.

Although the legislature in Poland enacted a GAAR in 2003, it was declared unconstitutional in 2005 because of a concern about condemning lawful behavior. An anti-avoidance rule, short of a GAAR, exists in article 199A of the General Law, which allows the tax authority to look beyond the literal terms of the statute to the intention of the parties when determining the tax consequences of a transaction. Polish law also contains TAARs relating to transfer pricing, thin capitalization, and mergers and other corporate reorganizations.

Taiwan has not enacted a GAAR. In 2010, it enacted article 12–1 of the Tax Collection Act which gives the tax authority the power to employ a substance over form approach when determining tax consequences of a transaction.

Russia has enacted no GAAR. However, a substance over form approach allows the courts to determine whether the facts and circumstances support the existence of a business purpose that would justify allowance of the expected tax benefits.

While there was debate in Japan in the 1950s concerning adoption of an economic substance test, it was never enacted. Accordingly, the courts employ an approach based on strict interpretation of the statute in order to determine whether a taxpayer achieves the desired tax-reducing result. However, Japan's Supreme Court has found that the lack of a proper business purpose justified defeat of a taxpayer's attempt to make use of an excess foreign tax credit by making a loan to a foreign branch.[16]

Although Japanese courts do not use the language of tax avoidance, as discussed above, they do consider the entire circumstances, including lack of a non-tax business purpose, in the decision-making process. In addition, the legislature has enacted two TAARs that govern certain transactions involving related parties. A transaction between a shareholder and related corporation is disregarded if the effect is an improper decrease of the corporation's income.

As a backstop to the GAAR, which is discussed below, Germany has enacted a number of TAARs. In contrast to a rule of general application, these are complex and are intended to address a narrowly prescribed set of circumstances. With the proliferation of clever anti-avoidance arrangements, the legislature's ability to combat unacceptable tax minimization is necessarily after-the-fact. The insertion of a targeted rule applicable to one type of transaction hampers the legislature's ability to systematically treat in a timely fashion a pervasive problem. Upon enactment of a targeted rule, a legislature is likely to uncover creative strategies that manage to circumvent taxation in a host of other not-yet-targeted areas. Perhaps for this reason, many countries, like Germany, with targeted anti-avoidance rules have nonetheless felt compelled to enact a GAAR.

Germany and other members of the European Union may not regulate tax avoidance if it infringes on community fundamental freedoms. To date the European Court of Justice ("ECJ") has found that national measures against tax avoidance do not violate these freedoms if the legislation covers artificial arrangements that do not reflect economic reality. However, legislation by member states that seek to prevent abusive transactions in areas covered by EU Directives, as in the case of Parent-Subsidiary, is handled by the ECJ on a case by case basis. While location of a subsidiary in a member state in order to take advantage of lower tax rates may not be penalized, allowance of a foreign tax credit in lieu of a participation exemption to foreign parents from member states has been found a valid mechanism to target anti-avoidance.

The progression of anti-avoidance jurisprudence has led to a third strategy for curtailing unacceptable exploitation of perceived loopholes in tax law, which consists of legislative enactment or codification of a general anti-avoidance rule. All but seven of the countries considered in this report have enacted varying types of GAARs. These will be considered in the next section.

[16] See the report on Japan.

27.3 General Anti-avoidance Rules (GAARs)

In recent years, codification of a general anti-avoidance rule has emerged as the anti-avoidance weapon of choice of many legislatures. The hallmark of a GAAR is that it provides to tax authorities and courts a set of parameters of broad application that aid in determining when a strategy for the reduction of tax crosses the line of acceptable tax planning and becomes unacceptable tax avoidance. While the existence of a GAAR does not obviate the need to interpret statutory language, it does signal the relevant considerations that support denying benefits to transactions that literally comply with the letter of the statute. Uniform application of anti-avoidance doctrine leads to a perception of fairness and taxpayer buy-in regarding the bona fides of the tax system. The four oldest GAARs in Australia, Canada, Germany, and New Zealand provide detailed guidance that applies widely.

After enacting previous GAARs which were viewed as unsuccessful, in 2008, Germany enacted a rule applicable to all taxpayers and to all taxes in the domestic or international sphere.[17] The statute applies when a taxpayer attempts to circumvent legislation by abusing legal options for tax planning. Abuse occurs where the taxpayer selects in appropriate legal options to obtain tax advantages unintended by law. If a transaction is covered, a court may determine tax consequences as if only appropriate steps were taken.[18] However, the presence of a sufficient nontax reason supporting the particular steps taken by the taxpayer, even if circuitous, renders the GAAR inapplicable.[19]

The most recent version of New Zealand's GAAR, embodied in its 2007 Income Tax Act, provides the example of one of the most detailed GAARs. It declares tax avoidance arrangements to be void and confers authority upon the Commissioner of the Inland Revenue to deny the tax advantage sought.[20] A tax avoidance arrangement includes any contract, agreement, plan or understanding (including all steps) by which the taxpayer:

1. directly or indirectly alters incidence of tax
2. directly or indirectly relieves any person from current or future tax liability, or,
3. directly or indirectly avoids, postpones, or reduces any current or future tax liability.

The Commissioner lacks the power to disallow any tax advantage if the arrangement does not have tax avoidance as its purpose or effect. However, if one of its (non-incidental) purposes or effects (whether or not attributed to standard business or family dealings) is tax avoidance, the tax benefit may be denied.

The New Zealand GAAR permits the Commissioner to determine tax consequences by reference to the true substance, giving effect to the "business reality" operative in absence of the arrangement. Because Inland Revenue's Adjudication Unit has authority to screen these cases at the administrative stage, fewer reach the courts and there is "relatively little tax litigation." However, the courts have reached opposite results for similar transactions, notably in situations in which professional individuals choose the corporate form in order to obtain lower tax rates.

The cases that end up in litigation tend to be the largest cases. While serious penalties result from disallowed tax avoidance schemes, where large sums are involved taxpayers may determine that the potential risks of disallowance are outweighed by the potential benefits. The New Zealand Supreme Court's recent application of the GAAR in a broader number of cases may restrict further taxpayer use of such a calculus.[21]

Although Australia has had a GAAR since 1879, the modern form has been in effect since 1981 without amendment. It accords the Commissioner of Revenue discretion to cancel any tax benefit arising out of a scheme and the authority to reconstruct the transaction in order to assess the tax where the dominant purpose is to obtain a tax benefit for any connected party.

A scheme is broadly defined to include any consensual or unilateral action and any inaction. The requisite dominant purpose may be discerned on the basis of a list of eight criteria. These include: the manner in which the scheme was carried out, the form and substance of the scheme, the income tax result but for the scheme, any change in the financial position of the taxpayer or any connected party, and the connection of the parties.

[17] See report on Germany.

[18] The GAAR does not apply to transactions covered by a TAAR. Such transactions are safe if they are not caught by the anti-avoidance rule contained in the TAAR.

[19] See report on Germany.

[20] See report on New Zealand. The first New Zealand GAAR was enacted in 1891 as part of the Land Tax.

[21] See report on New Zealand.

Canada's adoption of a GAAR followed a series of decisions in which the Supreme Court of Canada ("SCC") rejected use of a business purpose test and a reasonable expectation of profit test to assess tax transactions. While the SCC temporarily diverged from a "plain meaning" analysis in favor of a more modern "purposive" approach in which it looked beyond technical compliance (legal formalism) to scrutinize the contextual meaning of a statute, it ultimately returned to "textual interpretation," preferring "not to give too much weight to factors other than the clear requirements established by the words of a particular provision." This approach rested upon the court's desire not to erode the "consistency, predictability, and fairness" of the tax system.

Canada's Parliament enacted its GAAR in 1988. It allows redetermination of the tax consequences of a transaction in order to deny a tax benefit that would result, directly or indirectly, from that transaction or a series of transactions. The GAAR is applicable only if it may reasonably be considered that the avoidance transaction would result directly or indirectly in a misuse of the provisions of the Income Tax Act read as a whole. It targets only an "avoidance transaction," which is a transaction or series of transactions undertaken or arranged primarily for no bona fide purpose other than to obtain a tax benefit. Determination of the applicability of the GAAR rests with the courts.[22]

The Canadian GAAR affords authority to the courts to re-determine the consequences of an "avoidance transaction" in order to "deny a tax benefit that… would result, directly or indirectly, from that transaction or from a series of transactions that includes that transaction." An "avoidance transaction" is any transactions (or series) that "would result, directly or indirectly, in a tax benefit if it is undertaken or arranged primarily for no bona fide purpose other than to obtain a tax benefit". A tax benefit is any reduction, avoidance, deferral, or refund of tax whether under the Income Tax Act or any tax treaty. The GAAR may only be applied in the event of a direct or indirect misuse of the Act or any abuse of the Act "read as a whole."

While the Finance Minister determines whether to assess a tax under the GAAR, the court ultimately determines whether the GAAR applies. The Supreme Court of Canada views the GAAR as a means to balance support of taxpayer's right to certainty in planning affairs with a desire to maintain fairness for all taxpayers. Yet the taxpayer interest in certainty in planning would not cause the court to ignore the application of a tax statute to transactions clearly intended to be covered. The Supreme Court has rendered three decisions detailing application of the GAAR.

In implementing the GAAR, the Supreme Court employs a three-step analysis. The first two steps require determination of whether there has been a tax benefit (the taxpayer does not pay the maximum tax payable) and whether there is an avoidance transaction. The third requires the Court to limit its review to the relationship between the parties and the actual transactions taking place. The Court is not permitted to re-characterize the transaction by going beyond the legal substance and re-constituting it on the basis of its economic substance. Moreover, consistent with the Parliament's desire to preserve predictability and certainty in tax law, a lack of a business purpose is not fatal. Although existence of a non-tax or business purpose will remove a transaction from the ambit of the GAAR, there is no requirement of an independent business purpose because many Canadian tax benefits are conferred without regard to any such purpose.

The most difficult exercise in application of the Canadian GAAR is determination of the existence of an avoidance transaction. At this stage, the Court is required to engage in a textual, contextual, and purposive interpretation of the statute to discover whether the transaction frustrates legislative intent. Such a finding will occur:

> [W]here the result of the avoidance transaction (a) is an outcome that the provisions relied upon seek to prevent; (b) defeats the underlying rationale of the provisions relied on; or (c) circumvents certain provisions in a manner that frustrates the object, spirit or purpose of those provisions.[23]

Thus, the Court will look at the overall result of a series of transactions viewed as a whole. Here the

[22] See report on Canada. Although the courts ultimately determine applicability, the Minister of National Finance alone determines whether to assess a taxpayer under the GAAR. Taxpayers are not permitted to self-assess under the GAAR. A GAAR Committee, whose members represent the Department of Finance, the Department of Justice, and the Canada Revenue Agency, make a recommendation to the Minister on advisability of assessment.

[23] See the report on Canada.

interest in preserving taxpayer certainty must give way to the interest in preventing subversion of legislative intent.

The Canadian reporter notes that the Canadian GAAR "has had some degree of success in limiting the use of abusive tax avoidance transactions."[24] This includes situations not previously susceptible to challenge. However, because the Supreme Court remains divided in its interpretation of the GAAR, some aggressive transactions may escape the effects of the GAAR and a great deal of uncertainty may expose taxpayers seeking to arrange legitimate transactions to a level of uncertainty.

South Africa has had a GAAR since 1941. Most recently amended in 2008, the South African GAAR is viewed as a residual measure which may apply to situations covered by a specific anti-avoidance provision or as an alternative to any other. That GAAR gives the Commissioner of South African Revenue Service (SARS) the authority to reduce, eliminate or neutralize any tax benefit derived from an impermissible avoidance arrangement. The affected arrangements are those solely or mainly driven by tax considerations which lack commercial substance, possess abnormal features in the manner carried out, involve non-arm's length rights or obligations, or involve misuse or abuse of the provisions of the South African Income Tax Act.[25]

The People's Republic of China ("China") adopted a GAAR, effective in 2008. The rule of law in China is quite different than that in the other countries described in this report. There is no separation of powers and the law exists primarily as an instrument of the government. The Standing Committee of the National People's Council ("NPC") possesses the sole power, derived from the Constitution, to interpret the law. The courts, on the other hand, exist primarily to regulate procedural, but not substantive matters of tax law.

The Chinese GAAR is part of the corporate income tax law adopted in 2007. Article 47 of the Corporate Income Tax Law confers upon the State Administration of Taxation ("SAT"), the taxing authority, the power to re-characterize a business arrangement entered into without reasonable business purposes which result in reduction of taxable income or revenue. The accompanying regulations find a lack of a reasonable business purpose when the primary purpose of the arrangement is reducing, avoiding, or deferring payment of taxes. Transfer pricing, controlled foreign corporation, and thin capitalization arrangements are not covered by the GAAR because they are governed by separate targeted anti-avoidance rules. Numerous activities are covered by the GAAR, including treaty shopping, abuse of tax incentives, abuse of corporate organizational form, use of tax havens, and any business arrangement lacking a bona fide commercial purpose.

The substance over form approach sanctioned by the regulations requires consideration of the following factors:

- the form of the arrangement,
- the substance of the arrangement,
- the duration of the arrangement,
- the form of implementation,
- relationship of the steps taken to construct the arrangement,
- financial effects, and
- tax consequences.

The imprecision of the standard for the application of the GAAR, depending upon words like "reasonable," "business purpose," and "economic substance," has provided some cause for concern. Although the vague language may have an *in terrorem* effect on some business transactions, discouraging some legitimate ones, the legislation may also have the beneficent effect of encouraging more economically prudent arrangements that are not dependent upon tax reduction for profitability.

The GAAR appears to be aimed primarily at the use of conduit companies in international transactions. The use of special purpose vehicles by foreigners investing in China is under special scrutiny. In these arrangements, foreign investors hold investments in China through companies organized in tax haven or very-low-tax jurisdictions in order to take advantage of tax treaties that provide for reduced withholding taxes on dividend distributions or interest payments. If the decision to organize the holding country in the favorable treaty country is not supported by significant commercial reasons, the treaty benefits may be denied.

The French GAAR, contained in article L64 of the Code of Tax Procedure, which appeared in its current form in 2008, accords the taxing authority the power to disregard as an abuse of law transactions which are

[24] Of the 867 cases referred to the GAAR Committee as of November, 2009, the GAAR was found applicable in 614. The Finance Minister has been successful in 9 of the 18 cases heard by the courts.

[25] See Section 103 of the South African Income Tax Law.

either fictional or designed to meet the literal terms of a statute or favorable decisions. These transactions may be disregarded if it appears that the steps were taken with the single goal of reducing the tax liability which would exist if the steps taken were disregarded and effect given to the substance of the real arrangement.

The terms of article L64 remain ambiguous and, consequently, susceptible to a myriad of interpretations. Yet support for the legitimacy of such an approach is found in the general principle of abuse of right which justifies opposition to skillful tax-minimizing transactions by reliance on the constitutional tenet of equality among taxpayers. Concerns that the GAAR would be applied to nullify legitimate transactions were alleviated in 2009 when the Conseil d'Etat issued two decisions requiring that the government make a two-part demonstration. It held that the taxing authority must show not only an absence of a fiscal reason for the transaction but also that a literal application of the statute would frustrate the intention of the legislature.[26] Finding that the statute evinced no intention to require a minimum holding period, the Court allowed a foreign tax credit to a taxpayer acquiring stock temporarily for the purpose of obtaining the credit.

Austria, Hungary, and Slovenia have enacted a GAAR. The Netherlands enacted a GAAR in 1925 which has fallen out of use. Currently there is reliance on the substance over form approach, adopted by the Netherlands Supreme Court in 1985. The principle applies when there is an arrangement contrary to the objective and purpose of a tax statute and the taxpayer's primary objective is to reduce tax liability substantially.

The Swedish GAAR appeared in its current form in 1995. Originally enacted in 1980, it was abolished between 1993 and 1995. Like others referenced above, the Swedish GAAR applies where: (1) an action in which the taxpayer participates results in a considerable tax benefit, (2) obtaining the tax benefit was the predominant reason for the transaction, and (3) respecting the transaction would be in conflict with the general objectives of the statute. The administrative courts determine whether to apply the GAAR.

The Italian GAAR applies only if the transaction is 1 of 17 listed. If such a transaction lacks a sound business purpose, is intended to circumvent tax law limitations, and is intended to obtain a tax savings or refund otherwise inapplicable, the taxing authority has the right to disregard any steps or parts of the transaction.

The narrow focus of the Italian GAAR has led the courts to resort to more general principles in denying tax benefits to abusive transactions. As the Italian report indicates, the doctrine of "fraus legis" has been resurrected to deal with impermissible tax avoidance arrangements. The difficulty in applying *fraus legis* to tax statutes, which are intended to be read literally, has led the legislature to consider amending the GAAR so that it may applied by the taxing authority and the courts to a broader group of transactions.

Under rules effective in March, 2010, the U.S. Congress shocked the tax world by clarifying the economic substance doctrine, codified in new Code section 7701(o).[27] The new rule is not expected to radically alter U.S. anti-avoidance law. By contrast, legislators in countries lacking activist courts have intended to effect significant change by adopting general anti-avoidance rules.

The legislation targets tax benefits sought to be gained in so called "tax shelters," by requiring that a business transaction change a taxpayer's economic position in a meaningful way and that a taxpayer have a substantial purpose for undertaking the transaction other than federal income tax effects. The new provision mandates that courts find that a transaction has economic substance only if the present value of "reasonably expected pre-tax profit" is substantial in relation to the present value of expected net tax benefits.[28] An additional dictate, seemingly aimed at reversing an approach adopted by the court in *Compaq Computer Corp*,[29] is that foreign taxes be treated as expenses in

[26] See report on France.

[27] IRC § 7701(o) provides:

(o) CLARIFICATION OF ECONOMIC SUBSTANCE DOCTRINE:

(1) Application of Doctrine. – In the case of any transaction to which the economic substance doctrine is relevant, such transaction shall be treated as having economic substance only if:–

(A) the transaction changes in a meaningful way (apart from Federal income tax effects) the taxpayer's economic position, and

(B) the taxpayer has a substantial business purpose (apart from Federal income tax effects) for entering into such transaction.

[28] IRC §7701(o)(2)(A).

[29] *Compaq Computer Corp. v. Comm'r*, 113 T.C. 214 (1999).

determining pre-tax profit, if the IRS issues regulations so providing.[30] Moreover, in determining whether a taxpayer has a substantial purpose for entering a transaction, other than federal income tax reduction, financial accounting benefits linked to tax reduction must be disregarded.[31]

Noting a lack of uniformity concerning proper application of the economic substance doctrine, the Joint Committee on Taxation, a tax-writing arm for Congress, indicated that the new provision "provides a uniform definition of economic substance, but does not alter the flexibility of the courts in other respects" and that it does not change the standard to use in determining whether an economic substance approach is warranted.[32] The IRS had long opposed codification of an economic substance doctrine, in part, because of its success in convincing the courts of its view of unacceptable tax avoidance. It perhaps for this reason, noted by a prominent tax practitioner, that estimated revenue gain from the new provision was reduced from $14 to $4.5 billion.[33]

Accordingly, even after codification of anti-avoidance doctrine, the Joint Committee on Taxation anticipates that the role of the courts largely will remain unchanged. The codification does, however, remove from the judiciary, the discretion to confer tax benefits in a case in which the taxpayer does not meaningfully change its economic position, even if the company has a substantial business purpose for undertaking the transaction.[34] One prominent tax practitioner predicted no impact on "certain basic business transactions," but he was uncertain whether other transactions would be treated differently.[35] He foresaw, however, the legislation's imposition of a penalty equal to 40% of the understated tax for undisclosed transactions lacking economic substance to be a potential deterrent to entry into bona fide transactions.[36]

The new standard incorporates a "facts and circumstances" inquiry, no different than the one employed by the courts when applying common law doctrines.[37] Perhaps because the codification provides little guidance for the courts that will apply it, the legislative history allows that basic business transactions are to be respected even where there is a choice between meaningful economic alternatives based primarily on comparative tax advantages. Examples in the Joint Committee Report include: the choice between capitalizing a business with debt or equity, the choice to use a foreign corporation instead of a domestic one in making a foreign investment, the choice to enter into corporate organization or reorganization in tax-free transactions, and the choice to use a related party in a transaction as long as transfer pricing and other requirements, such as anti-treaty shopping rules, are satisfied.

The U.S. legislature's codification of the economic substance doctrine places it with 13 (out of 21) other countries discussed in this Overview that have adopted statutory anti-avoidance rules. Unlike the statutory rules enacted by the other reported countries, the U.S. rule is tailored to meet a particular concern – assuring that federal courts, choosing to employ a "substance over form" analysis, apply the economic substance doctrine when appropriate in the way advocated by the government in a series of tax shelter cases.[38]

---

[30] IRC §7701(o)(2)(B). Expenses and other transaction costs must also be treated as expenses in determining pre-tax profit.

[31] IRC §7701(o)(4).

[32] Staff of the Joint Committee on Taxation, "Technical Provisions of the Revenue Provisions of the Reconciliation Act of 2010," *JCX-18-10* at 152 (2010) (hereinafter Jt. Comm. Report).

[33] Richard M. Lipton, "'Codification' of the Economic Substance Doctrine – Much Ado About Nothing?," 112 *Journal of Taxation* (June, 2010): 325, 328 (hereafter Lipton, 'Codification' of the Economic Substance Doctrine).

[34] Internal Revenue Service ("IRS") Associate Chief Counsel, William Alexander, suggested that codification of the economic substance doctrine will not vary the way in which the agency will deal with tax avoidance schemes, presumably because Congress enacted the standard advocated by the Service. *See*, Stephen Joyce, "Official Says Codifying Doctrine Will Not Materially Affect IRS's Enforcement Views," 132 *BNA Daily Tax Report* G-1 (July 13, 2010).

[35] Lipton, 'Codification' of the Economic Substance Doctrine, *supra* note 33, at 328. The IRS issued Notice 2010–62, 2010–2 C.B. 411, clarifying the prominent role of the common law economic substance doctrine, but failing to publish a so-called "angel list" that would have removed noncontroversial transactions from the purview of the new statute.

[36] Lipton, 'Codification' of the Economic Substance Doctrine, *supra* note 33, at 328. Lipton notes that "it is possible that this new legislation will have little effect (other than for scoring revenue for purposes of passing the health care bill) and, in hindsight, will simply be viewed as a continuation of the status quo." *But see* Brett Wells, "Economic Substance Doctrine: How Codification Changes Decided Cases," 10 *Florida Tax Review* (2010): 411, 452 ("[S]ection 7701(o)...does significantly alter the landscape with respect to the taxpayer's ability to benefit from many of the types of mistakes that were available in the past.")

[37] Jt. Comm. Report, *supra* note 32, at 153.

[38] *Compaq Computer Corp. v. Comm'r*, *supra* note 29.

GAARs have not resolved many questions of interpretation and approaches to abusive schemes vary widely. For example, two countries with general anti-avoidance rules, the U.S. and France take different positions concerning the tax consequences of similar transactions. The practice of dividend stripping, for example, which involves the temporary purchase of corporate stock in order to receive a dividend, claim a foreign tax credit, and a capital loss upon immediate re-sale, in a transaction primarily motivated by the prospect of a tax advantage and not economic profit became the basis for one of the most famous tax shelter cases in the U.S. The court in that case, *Compaq Computer Corp.*, sided with the taxpayer and allowed the tax benefits sought.[39] The U.S. responded to the decision in two ways. First, it amended the statute to require more than a temporary holding of the stock in order to be eligible for a foreign tax credit. Second, it attacked the court's reasoning by enacting ultimately a codification of the economic substance rule that would directly reverse the result. On the other hand, the result would differ under the French GAAR. As Professor Gutmann's report indicates, a similar transaction would not violate the abuse of right principle in French tax law because there was no indication that the legislature did not intend to accord tax benefits to the owner of the shares at the time of distribution.

27.4 Disclosure and Penalty Rules

Whether a court scrutinizes a tax avoidance scheme by application of a set of judicially-developed principles (common law regimes), by reference to values embedded in a constitution or administrative code (civil law) or by interpretation of a codified rule of general application (GAAR), one cannot predict with absolute certainty whether it will disallow benefits for any given transaction. There remains an incentive to press the written law to its limits in the hope that the arrangement will either escape detection or ultimately will be blessed as not abusive by the adjudicatory authority. Legislatures have acted to offset the play-the-lottery mind-set of some taxpayers, especially those entering into schemes that offer substantial tax benefits, by enacting disclosure and penalty rules. These contribute to the taxing authority's ability to uncover and target transactions that attempt to exploit a tax advantage in a manner not intended or anticipated by the legislature. The South African Revenue Service describes its disclosure regime – the reportable arrangements provisions – as an "early warning system for detecting potential impermissible avoidance arrangements."[40]

A relatively small number of the jurisdictions covered in this report have enacted special disclosure or penalty rules for abusive tax arrangements. The U.S., the latest country to enact a GAAR, has actively sought to deter tax avoidance through a panoply of disclosure and penalty provisions, including rules aimed at tax advisors. This reflects a strategy to deter entry into unacceptable tax-minimizing arrangements, allowing early detection of these transactions. Early detection may allow resolution of these matters administratively and result in reduced opportunities for a court to reject the government's view of the case. At a minimum, the threat of serious penalties may result in self-restraint on the part of taxpayers that might otherwise pursue the benefits of a tax shelter. Among the countries reported the U.K., Canada, South Africa, and the U.S., have extensive disclosure regimes.

In connection with enactment of the GAAR, the U.S. strengthened existing disclosure and penalty provisions. Pre-GAAR, there was a penalty equal to 20% of the underpayment of tax when the taxpayer substantially understates income tax.[41] This penalty is abated if the taxpayer has "substantial authority" for taking the position on the tax return or if the taxpayer both adequately disclosed the relevant facts to the IRS, the tax authority, and had a reasonable basis for such tax treatment.[42] If the taxpayer had reasonable cause for the position taken on the return and acted in good faith, the 20% penalty was abated. For tax shelters, there is no abatement of the penalty even if the taxpayer has substantial authority for its position or discloses the transaction and has a reasonable basis for taking the position.[43]

[39] *Compaq Computer Corp. v. Comm'r*, *supra* note 29.

[40] South African Revenue Service, Draft Comprehensive Guide to the General Anti-Avoidance Rule (2010) at 4 (hereinafter "South African Revenue Service, Draft Comprehensive Guide").

[41] IRC §6662(a),(d),(i).

[42] IRC §6664(c).

[43] IRC §6662(d)(2)(C). A tax shelter is any partnership or other entity, plan, or arrangement where a significant purpose is the avoidance or evasion of federal income tax.

While the above rules remain in place for underpayments attributable to negligence, valuation misstatements, overstatements, and undisclosed foreign financial assets, for any transaction lacking economic substance, the penalty is increased under the new GAAR to 40% of the underpayment of tax.[44] In addition, there is strict liability for non-disclosed noneconomic substance transactions, because a showing of reasonable cause and good faith in failing to report the transaction, does not prevent imposition of the penalty. A showing of reasonable cause and good faith on the part of the taxpayer regarding other non-disclosed transactions normally blocks the penalty. Despite requests by tax practitioners, the IRS has declined to issue a safe-harbor list excluding specified transactions from the purview of the new rules.

In addition to the new rules accompanying the GAAR, the U.S. legislature has enacted penalties applicable to promoters of abusive tax shelters that can rise as high as 50% of the gross income derived from the activity.[45] This provision can catch tax advisors and others who render advice regarding the allowability of a deduction, an exclusion from gross income, or any other tax benefits, if the advisor has reason to know that the advice is false or fraudulent or that there are gross overstatements of value regarding any material matter. For aiding and abetting an understatement of tax liability, there are additional monetary penalties of $1,000 for each document, claim, return, or affidavit provided.[46]

The IRS's adoption of a controversial disclosure provision relating to large corporations indicates the U.S.'s commitment to this modern approach to defeating tax avoidance. Announcement 2010–9 2010–1 C.B. 408 (Jan. 26, 2010) will require large corporate taxpayers to report uncertain tax positions. These are positions taken on the tax return which are required for financial accounting purposes to be reflected in a reserve in the taxpayer's books and records or financial statements. FASB Interpretation No. 48 requires such taxpayers to identify and quantify any uncertain tax position in those accounts. Disclosure will also be required of other tax positions which the taxpayer has not disclosed because it intends to litigate or it has determined that the IRS has a general administrative practice not to examine the issue. The announcement is controversial because it would require disclosure of transactions which are not reportable under the general rule which excuses disclosure, except for tax shelters and non-economic substance transactions, when there is substantial authority for a position taken on a return or the taxpayer believes its reporting position is more likely than not correct. The Commissioner of Internal Revenue indicated that the announcement was "consistent with the Service's 'policy of restraint' in requesting tax accrual work papers."[47]

Taxpayers failing to disclose certain reportable or listed transactions or to file the requisite returns are subject to penalties as high as $200,000.[48] These are transactions which the IRS has either determined to have a potential for tax avoidance or evasion or are listed as such in a periodic publication.

Attorneys and others seeking to represent clients before the IRS must comply with the requirements of the controversial Circular 230. In part, those provisions require disclosure to clients of the potential penalties resulting from taking various positions on the tax return when the attorney cannot indicate that success on the merits is more likely than not.

The UK lacks a GAAR, but it has adopted substantial disclosure rules regarding tax avoidance schemes. The disclosure obligation falls on the promoter (including the taxpayer in certain cases) in cases in which a tax arrangement will, or may be expected, to enable a person to obtain a tax advantage where it is the main benefit of the transaction. Failure to disclose is subject to an initial penalty of £5,000 and up to £600 per day.

Disclosure must be made on the date the tax avoidance scheme is ready for implementation. The reference number received by the promoter upon disclosure must be included in the tax return of each client-participant in the transaction. The Treasury has listed eight areas in which it has announced an intention to challenge schemes in court.

The UK provisions appear to have achieved the desired effect. While nearly 2,000 disclosures had been made by 2009 (the reporting regime began in full force in 2006), the rate of disclosure has decreased in subsequent years. The Treasury feels

[44] IRC §6662(b)(6).

[45] IRC §6700.

[46] IRC §6701.

[47] Richard M. Lipton, "Reporting Uncertain Tax Positions Under Ann. 2010–9: Transparency or Overkill?," *Journal of Taxation* (May, 2010): 260.

[48] IRC §§6707, 6707A.

that the disclosure regime has "changed the economics of tax avoidance."[49]

Australia and Canada have enacted tax shelter promoter penalties. Apart from the federal rules in Canada, Québec has enacted disclosure rules concerning tax avoidance transactions, with penalties of 25% for those failing to comply.

Germany has no disclosure regime for tax shelters. It has enacted loss disallowance rules that target certain tax deferral schemes. This provision is credited with the elimination of the private market for film funds in Germany.

In France, abuse of the tax law may result in a penalty of between 40% and 80% of the tax avoided.

27.5 Prescriptions for Future Developments

One of the beauties and mysteries of a tax statute is that it may present the conundrum of precise, detailed, and technically complex language which may be interpreted in many different ways. The unavoidable lack of precision that results when legislators drafting a statute are not able to anticipate inherent ambiguities in terms may be exploited by taxpayers hoping to order their affairs as they choose so as to minimize their tax liability. Legislators have an interest in encouraging tax-minimizing behavior by eligible taxpayers when they wish to provide incentives. However, some taxpayers may undertake self-help tax reduction by arranging schemes that exploit statutory ambiguity or silence in a way that enables them to gain an advantage over others.

Legislatures are challenged to determine how to address unacceptable tax planning that allows some taxpayers to manipulate tax statutes in unintended ways. Reliance on judicially-developed substance over form, business purpose, and economic substance doctrines, or statutory interpretation that looks to legislative purpose has given way to incorporation of anti-avoidance provisions in specific statutes (TAARs) or codification of general anti-avoidance rules (GAARs). Yet codification of anti-avoidance prescriptions has not led to consistent, predictable results for taxpayers or legislators.

The recent strategy of employing disclosure and penalty regimes holds promise. When countries use different standards to evaluate tax avoidance schemes, taxpayers have an incentive to flock to those countries that not only feature lower rates, but also avoidance-friendly tax systems. While mass harmonization of law across different jurisdictions is not feasible, disclosure regimes which alert authorities to the existence of aggressive planning and advise taxpayers of the abusive features of specified transactions provide opportunities to curtail unacceptable tax planning. Disparities in jurisdictional approaches to tax avoidance may not be eliminated, but information disclosure (and a robust penalty regime to ensure compliance) also offers the prospect of international cooperation in combating abusive schemes through information sharing.

[49] See report on the UK.

	Type of legal system	Branch responsible for enforcement	Does the country acknowledge tax evasion, tax mitigation, and tax avoidance?	Is there a judicial economic substance doctrine?	Is there a GAAR?	When was a GAAR adopted or considered?	Is there an anti-tax shelter program?	Are there special penalties for tax shelters?	Are there disclosure requirements for tax shelters?
Australia	Common law	Executive	The code only distinguishes between tax avoidance and tax evasion	No	Yes; There are three component elements of the GAAR: a scheme, a tax benefit and the dominant purpose of obtaining the tax benefit.	1936 (as modified in 1981)	No	No	No
Austria	Civil law	Executive	Yes (evasion = illegal; mitigation = legal; avoidance is proscribed by generally applicable laws)	Yes: The courts utilize a substance over form approach	Yes	–	No	No	No
Canada	Quebec follows civil law, the rest of Canada follows common law	Canadian Revenue Agency	(not mentioned in report)	Courts are reluctant to develop judicial economic substance doctrine	Yes	1988	Yes	Yes	Yes
China	Civil law	State Administration of Taxation	Tax mitigation is not recognized; Tax evasion and avoidance are	No: The SAT is responsible for regulating tax avoidance	Yes	2007, effective 2008	No	No	No
Croatia	Civil law	Executive	Not as such, but the differences are understood by scholars	Yes	No	N/A	No	No	No
France	Civil law	French Tax Administration	Abuse of law	Yes: Substance over form	Yes, Art. L64	2008	No	Yes	No
Germany	Civil law	Federal Ministry of Finance	Yes	Yes	Yes	1919, revised in 2008	Yes	Yes	No
Greece	Civil law	Executive	Tax commentators make similar distinctions	No – but substance over form (tax legal realism)	No	N/A	No	No	For offshore activities
Hungary	Civil law	Cabinet (HMRC)	Yes: Tax avoidance and evasion	No	Yes	1991	No	No	No

Italy	Civil law	Tax Authorities	Yes	Valid business purpose test	Yes, but the GAAR only applies with respect to a specific, but extremely broad array of transactions	1990	No	No	No
Japan	Civil law	Executive	Yes	Yes: Substance over form	No	1950s	Yes	No	No
Netherlands	Civil law	Tax Administration	There are no general definitions of these terms	Yes, but not styled as such	Yes, although it has largely been superseded by judicial doctrine and special anti-avoidance rules	First enacted in 1925, but the government ceased using the provision in 1987	No	No	No
New Zealand	Common law	Inland Revenue Department	These are no terms of art, but tax avoidance is defined for purposes of the GAAR	Yes	Yes	1878, but not in regular use until 1960s	No	No	No
Poland	Civil law	Tax Administration	Not defined by law	Business purpose is addressed seldomly	No	A GAAR was enacted in 2003, but found unconstitutional in 2005	No	No	No
Russia	Civil law	Federal Tax Service	Tax evasion is proscribed by law	Substance over form approach is utilized by the arbitration courts	(not mentioned in report)	–	Yes	No	No
Slovenia	Civil law	Organ under Ministry of Finance	Acknowledges difference between evasion and avoidance	anti-avoidance, anti-abuse approach is codified	General anti-abuse rule short of GAAR	N/A	No	No	No
South Africa	Common law	South African Revenue Service	Yes	Yes	Yes	1941, amended in 2006 and 2008	No	No	Yes, if covered by GAAR
Sweden	Civil law	Swedish Tax Agency	Avoidance and evasion	Yes	Yes	1980	No	No	No
Taiwan	Civil law	Executive Yuan	Acknowledged, but only "tax evasion" appears in the code	Yes, similar to substance over form criteria in the US	There is a new provision similar to GAAR	GAAR-like statute adopted in 2009	No	No	No

(continued)

(continued)

	Type of legal system	Branch responsible for enforcement	Does the country acknowledge tax evasion, tax mitigation, and tax avoidance?	Is there a judicial economic substance doctrine?	Is there a GAAR?	When was a GAAR adopted or considered?	Is there an anti-tax shelter program?	Are there special penalties for tax shelters?	Are there disclosure requirements for tax shelters?
United Kingdom	England and Wales are common law; Scotland is a mix of common and civil law	HMRC	Tax evasion is distinguished on the basis that it is illegal (tax avoidance is not per se prohibited)	This is sometimes considered when judiciary employs purposive approach to statutory interpretation	No	Currently under consideration	No	No	Yes: Required of promoter and sometimes user
United States	Common law	Executive	Yes	Yes	Yes	2010	Yes	Yes	Yes

Corporate Criminal Liability* 28

Mark Pieth and Radha Ivory

28.1 Corporate (a)Morality and Corporate Risk

Criminal law traditionally focuses on personal guilt. Criminal law is, it seems, intricately linked to notions of culpability, blame, and the infliction of loss on an offender. Its offenses commonly require proof of an accused person's mental state.[1] And its fundamental principles hold that criminal sanctions should address the individual responsibility of the wrongdoer without harming innocent third parties.[2] With these considerations in mind, lawmakers around the world traditionally adhered to the principle societas delinquere non potest.[3] Corporations could, like human beings, hold rights and duties under private law but they could not be regarded as possessing the moral faculties that would enable them to be addressees of the criminal law.[4]

It is, however, equally obvious that corporations can cause substantial harm.[5] They have been drivers of industrialization and the globalization of the economy. Their negligence has resulted in severe injury to individuals, groups, and the natural environment (consider the catastrophe at Bhopal)[6] and their deliberate abuses of power have highlighted their apparently privileged position relative to other persons and entities. The power of some modern corporations,[7] especially **multinational enterprises** (MNEs), may make it difficult for public authorities to apply mechanisms of legal control. The difficulties typically go beyond the simple application of political influence to decision-making processes. Increasingly, decentralized corporate structures and complex internal procedures may prevent law enforcement agencies and criminal justice authorities from identifying the individual wrongdoer(s) within a corporation. Further, though such harm may result from the acts or omissions of individual "rogue employees," it may also be the expression of a corporate culture that tacitly condones, or at least tolerates, wrongdoing. When corporate systems or cultures are to blame, sanctions against lone – possibly low-level – employees seem an inadequate response.[8] Moreover, as systems for the provision of goods and services become more varied and complex, these problems are being replicated outside the commercial sector in entities like trusts and partnerships, and even in nonprofit, governmental,[9] and non-governmental

* V.A., La responsabilité pénale des personnes morales

[1] Allens Arthur Robinson 2008, 1; Hasnas 2009, 1329 et seq.; Weigend 2008, 938 et seq.

[2] Hasnas 2009, 1335 et seq., 1399 et seq., 1357. Cf Beale 2009, 1484 et seq., 1500 et seq.

[3] Böse (2011); Perrin (2011).

[4] Hasnas 2009, 1333; Weigend 2008, 936.

[5] Beale 2009, 1482 et seq.

M. Pieth (✉)
University of Basel, Basel, Switzerland
e-mail: mark.pieth@unibas.ch

R. Ivory
Basel Institute on Governance, Basel, Switzerland

[6] See, e.g., Waldman 2002.

[7] Beale 2009, 1483.

[8] See generally, Weigend 2008, 932 et seq.

[9] Organization for Economic Cooperation and Development (OECD) Working Party on Export Credits and Credit Guarantees, OECD Council Recommendation on Bribery and Officially Supported Export Credits TD/ECG (2006) 24, December 18, 2006, Paris.

K.B. Brown and D.V. Snyder (eds.), *General Reports of the XVIIIth Congress of the International Academy of Comparative Law/Rapports Généraux du XVIIIème Congrès de l'Académie Internationale de Droit Comparé*, DOI 10.1007/978-94-007-2354-2_28, © Springer Science+Business Media B.V. 2012

organizations.[10] These considerations explain the increasing willingness of lawmakers in many jurisdictions to impose criminal liability on corporations and other enterprises, particularly in the area of economic crime and particularly on the basis of devious corporate culture rather than individual wrongdoing.

28.2 Theories of Corporate Personality and Models of Corporate Liability

If corporate liability evolved historically as a response to the changing role of corporations, it evolved doctrinally from the recognition of corporations as legal persons capable of holding rights and obligations separate from those of their human stakeholders (owners, employees, managers, etc.). Private law offered two opposing explanations of corporate personality, both of which relied heavily on anthropomorphic imagery[11] and each of which has given rise to models of **corporate criminal liability** (CCL):

First, according to the **fiction (or "nominalist") theory** of corporate personality,[12] the corporation is nothing more than a legal construct, a term used to describe a group of individuals constituted at any one time.[13] The corporation, on this view, can only act through its human representatives, its operational staff being its "limbs," its officers and senior managers its "brains" or "nerve centre."[14] The corporation may bear criminal guilt on the nominalist view but only because it can be identified with a human being who serves as its "directing mind and will."[15] This is known as the **identification (or "alter ego") model** of corporate criminal liability.[16]

Second, the **reality theory** recognizes the corporation as possessing a distinct personality in its own right, as well as being a person under law.[17] Early on, this view of corporate personality allowed legal entities to be held **vicariously liable** for the civil wrongs of their servants.[18] Eventually, in some jurisdictions, it was extended to allow the imputation of criminal wrongdoing and states of mind to the corporation.[19] Elsewhere, it has given rise to **holistic (or "objective")** and **aggregative models** of liability. Holistic models, unlike the identification and vicarious liability models, do not require the imputation of human thoughts, acts, and omissions to the corporation. Rather, they regard corporations as themselves capable of committing crimes through established internal patterns of decision-making (**corporate culture** or **corporate (dis) organization**).[20] Aggregative approaches also treat the corporation as the principal offender but they do so by adding together the different acts, omissions, and states of mind of individual stakeholders, particularly corporate officers and senior managers.[21] They are something of a compromise between the vicarious and holistic approaches.[22]

National CCL rules, as they have been pronounced or enacted throughout the world, reflect these models of liability. Though the two imputation doctrines are still most widely represented, there are signs that the logic of holistic liability, with its emphasis on corporate (dis)organization and culture, is increasingly popular.

28.3 The Development of Corporate Criminal Liability Rules in Common Law Jurisdictions: The UK, the Commonwealth, and the US

The first steps towards corporate criminal liability were taken in common law jurisdictions, common law sources having been early to talk about ethics in corporations and the deterrent effect of sanctions on company behavior.[23] Both in the United Kingdom (UK)[24] and in

[10] Humanitarian Accountability Partnership International 2008, 7 et seq.; Lloyd/Warren/Hammer 2008, 5, 9.

[11] Heine 2000, 5.

[12] Deckert (2011); Wells 1999, 120 et seq.

[13] Wells 2001, 84 et seq.

[14] *HL Bolton (Engineering) Co. Ltd.* v. *TJ Graham & Sons Ltd.* [1957] 1 QB 159 at 172 (Denning LJ).

[15] *HL Bolton (Engineering) Co. Ltd.* v. *TJ Graham & Sons Ltd.* [1957] 1 QB 159 at 172 (Denning LJ). Wells 2000, 5; Wells 2001, 84 et seq., 93 et seq.

[16] Pieth 2007a, 179 et seq.; Wells 2000, 5.

[17] Wells 2001, 85.

[18] Wells 2001, 132 et seq.

[19] See Deckert (2011); Nanda (2011).

[20] Wells 2000, 6.

[21] Pinto/Evans 2003, 220; Wells 2000, 6; Wells 2001, 6.

[22] Wells 2001, 156.

[23] Coffee 1999a, 13 et seq.; Weigend, 2008, 928; Wells 2001, 81 et seq.

[24] Wells 2001, 63, 86 et seq.

the United States (US),[25] the **industrial revolution** and the attendant expansion of the railroads[26] led courts to apply the civil law doctrine of vicarious liability in criminal cases. In **US federal law**, in particular, the doctrine of respondeat superior allowed courts to impute to corporations the misbehavior of employees acting within the scope of their responsibilities and for the (intended) benefit of the company.[27] The theory was first developed on the basis of specific statutes and was rapidly generalized to crimes with a mental (fault) element. The strict form of vicarious liability, which emerged in the US, enabled corporations to be charged with crimes that they had attempted to prevent, e.g., by issuing instructions or implementing compliance systems. Only much later were prosecution and sentencing guidelines amended to allow decision-makers to take compliance programs into account.[28]

In the **UK**, vicarious liability was gradually limited to regulatory or so-called "objective" offenses created by statute; for traditional mens rea **(or fault-based) offenses**, the acceptance of nominalist theories of corporate personality by the British courts led to the application of the identification model of liability.[29] Hence, from the 1940s, corporations under English, Welsh, and Scottish law could be held responsible for the acts, omissions, and mental states of individuals who served as their alter egos.[30] Over the next 50 years, the identification theory was maintained,[31] though it was interpreted so as to apply in a very narrow range of cases.[32] Only in the 1990s, after several severe accidents[33] and considerable international pressure,[34] did British parliament introduce new rules for corporate manslaughter[35] and bribery.[36] The Law Commission of England and Wales (LCEW (UK)) is not undertaking a general review of CCL rules,[37] despite earlier indications that it would.[38] And, though its August 2010 consultation paper included number of proposals on CCL,[39] the commission seemed to take a general view that the criminal liability of corporations should be more limited than it is at present, at least in "regulatory contexts."[40]

The evolution of criminal corporate liability in **Commonwealth countries** has been far more dynamic: courts in Canada[41] and New Zealand (as affirmed by the Privy Council)[42] have **reinterpreted the concept of the "directing mind"** to go well beyond the concept recognized by English and Welsh courts.[43] Furthermore, at the federal level, Australia has passed legislation to supplement its traditional identification model of liability with a holistic approach. The Criminal Code Act 1995 (Commonwealth) (Criminal Code Act 1995 (Australia)) puts **deficient corporate culture centre stage**, thereby shifting away from the imputation of individual guilt to the corporation and focusing more objectively on the fault of the corporation – as a collective – itself.[44]

---

[25] Coffee 1999a, 14; Nanda (2011).

[26] DiMento/Geis 2005, 162 et seq.; Wells 2001, 87 et seq.

[27] Coffee 1999a, 14 et seq.; DiMento/Geis 2005; Nanda (2011); Wells 2000, 4.

[28] Coffee 1999a, 27, 37; Nanda (2011). See further below, Sect. 28.11.1.2.

[29] Stark (2011); Wells 2001, 93 et seq., 103 et seq.

[30] *HL Bolton (Engineering) Co. Ltd.* v. *TJ Graham & Sons Ltd.* [1957] 1 QB 159 at 172 (Denning LJ). See further, Law Commission of England and Wales (LCEW (UK)) 2010, paras. 5.8 et seq.; Stark (2011); Wells 2001, 93 et seq.

[31] *Tesco Supermarkets Ltd.* v. *Nattrass* [1972] AC 153.

[32] Wells 2001, 115.

[33] Such as the loss of the Herald of Free Enterprise and the Southall Railcrash. See further, Wells 2001, 41 et seq.; below, 0.

[34] OECD 2005b, paras. 195 et seq.; OECD 2008b, paras. 65 et seq.

[35] Corporate Manslaughter and Corporate Homicide Act 2007 (CMCH Act (UK)). See further, Wells 1999, 119; Wells 2001, 105 et seq.; Wells (2011).

[36] Bribery Act 2010 (Bribery Act 2010 (UK)). See further, Wells (2011).

[37] Law Commission of England and Wales (LCEW (UK)) (February 19, 2010), 'Personal Email Correspondence from Peter Melleney, Criminal Law Team'. Cf. LCEW (UK) 2008a, paras. 3.13 et seq.

[38] LCEW (UK) 2008b, para. 6.39.

[39] LCEW (UK) 2010, Proposals 13–16, paras. 8.13 et seq.

[40] LCEW (UK) 2010, Parts 3, 4, 7. See further Wells (2011). A "regulatory context" is "[a context] in which a Government department or agency has (by law) been given the task of developing and enforcing standards of conduct in a specialized area of activity": LCEW (UK) 2010, para. 1.9

[41] *Canadian Dredge & Dock Co. v R.* [1985] 1 SCR 662. See further, Coffee 1999a, 19; Ferguson 1999, 170 et seq.

[42] *Meridian Global Funds Asia Ltd.* v. *Securities Commission* (1995) 2 AC 500. See further, Pinto/Evans 2003, paras. 4.24 et seq.; Wells 2001, 103 et seq.

[43] See further below, Sect. 28.9.1.4.

[44] Criminal Code Act 1995, Act No. 12 of 1995 as amended (Criminal Code Act 1995 (Australia)), s. 12.3; Coffee 1999a, 30; Heine 2000, 4; Wells 2000, 6; Wells 2001, 136 et seq. See further below, Sect. 28.9.1.5.

28.4 The Recognition of Corporate (Criminal) Liability in Civil Law Jurisdictions of Europe and the Americas

28.4.1 CCL in the Civil Law Jurisdictions of Europe and the Americas

Recent extensions of CCL principles in common law countries have paralleled the emergence of corporate liability rules in civil law jurisdictions in Europe and the Americas. Long hostile to notions of corporate mind, morality, and guilt,[45] lawmakers on the Continent found themselves under increasing pressure to sanction corporate wrongdoers in the decades after World War II. The **post-War economic boom** in Western Europe had increased the visibility of industrialization's pitfalls, e.g., the environmental hazards, the harms to public health, and the unscrupulous exploitation of natural resources, particularly in the Third World. The emergence of the **risk society**, as it has been termed,[46] motivated the introduction of CCL rules in Belgium,[47] Denmark,[48] and France.[49]

International political developments set off a much more radical extension of corporate criminal liability principles in civil law countries from 1989. The **fall of the Berlin Wall** and East-West détente increased the pace of globalization,[50] facilitated the **expansion of the European Union** (EU)[51] and generated more fears about the risk posed by transnational (economic) crime.[52] States expressed these concerns over the next two decades with an entirely new system of **international treaties and non-binding standards** against organized crime,[53] money laundering,[54] corruption,[55] and the financing of terrorism.[56] These instruments typically required signatories to introduce criminal or equivalent forms of non-criminal liability or sanctions for legal persons or similar entities.[57] In many

[45] Cf. Böse (2011).

[46] Beck 1986; Giddens 1991; Giddens 1999; Prittwitz 1993; Wells 2001, 42.

[47] Faure 1999.

[48] Nielsen 1999, 321.

[49] Deckert (2011).

[50] Beck 1998.

[51] McCormick 2009, 218 et seq.

[52] Passas 1999.

[53] United Nations Convention against Transnational Organized Crime, November 15, 2000, in force September 19, 2003, 2225 UNTS 209 (UN Convention on Transnational Organized Crime).

[54] Financial Action Task Force (FATF), *FATF 40 Recommendations*, adopted June 20, 2003, as amended October 22, 2004, Paris (FATF Recommendations), Recommendation 2(b).

[55] See e.g., Inter-American Convention against Corruption, March 29, 1996, in force March 6, 1997, Treaty B-58; OECD Convention on Combating Bribery of Foreign Public Officials in International Business Transactions, November 21, 1997, in force February 15, 1999 (OECD Convention on Foreign Bribery); Convention drawn up on the basis of Article K.3 of the Treaty on European Union, on the Protection of the European Communities' Financial Interests – Joint Declaration on Article 13(2) – Commission Declaration on Article 7, July 26, 1995, in force October 17, 2002, OJ No. C 316, November 27, 1995, 49 (EU Convention on the Protection of the ECs' Financial Interest); Convention made on the basis of Article K.3 (2)(c) of the Treaty on European Union, on the fight against corruption involving officials of the European Communities or officials of Member States of the European Union, May 26, 1997, in force June 25, 1997, OJ No. C 195, June 25, 1997, 2; Second Protocol drawn up on the basis of Article K.3 of the Treaty on European Union, to the Convention on the Protection of the European Communities' Financial Interests, June 6, 1997, in force May 16, 2009, OJ No. C 221, July 19, 1997, 12 (Second Protocol to the EU Convention on the Protection of the ECs' Financial Interest); Criminal Law Convention on Corruption, January 27, 1999, in force July 1, 2002, 173 ETS (COE Criminal Law Convention on Corruption); Protocol Against Corruption to the Treaty of the Southern African Development Community, August 14, 2001, in force July 6, 2005 (SADC Protocol against Corruption); African Union Convention on Preventing and Combating Corruption, July 11, 2003, in force August 5, 2006, (2004) XLIII ILM 1 (AU Convention on Corruption); Council Framework Decision 2003/568/JHA of July 22, 2003 on combating corruption in the private sector, in force July 31, 2003, OJ No. L 192, July 22, 2003, 54 (EU Framework Decision on Private Sector Corruption); United Nations Convention against Corruption, December 9 to 11, 2003, in force December 14, 2005, 2349 UNTS 41 (UN Convention against Corruption). See further Pieth 2007b, 19 et seq.

[56] International Convention for the Suppression of the Financing of Terrorism, January 10, 2000, entry into force April 10, 2002, 2178 UNTS 197 (Terrorist Financing Convention); FATF, *FATF IX Special Recommendations*, adopted October 2001, as amended February 2008, Paris (FATF Special Recommendations), Special Recommendation II; FATF, *Interpretative Note to Special Recommendation II: Criminalizing the financing of terrorism and associated money laundering*, Paris, paras. 12 et seq.

[57] OECD Convention on Foreign Bribery, Arts. 2, 3(2); COE Criminal Law Convention on Corruption, Art. 18; Second Protocol to the EU Convention on the Protection of the ECs' Financial Interests, Art. 3; Terrorist Financing Convention, Art. 5; EU Framework Decision on Private Sector Corruption, Arts. 5(1), 6(1); UN Convention on Transnational Organized Crime, Art. 10; SADC Protocol against Corruption, Art. 4(2); AU Convention on Corruption, Art. 11(1); FATF Recommendations, Recommendation 2(b); FATF Special Recommendations, Special Recommendation 6; UN Convention against Corruption, Art. 26.

cases, their implementation at the national level is monitored by peer review bodies. So, it happens that the Organization for Economic Cooperation and Development's Convention on Combating Bribery of Foreign Public Officials in International Business Transactions (OECD Convention on Foreign Bribery), requires state parties "... to establish the liability of legal persons for the bribery of a foreign public official," to ensure "effective, proportionate and dissuasive" punishment and to participate in evaluations by the OECD Working Group on Bribery (WGB).[58] Later instruments from the EU and Council of Europe (COE) repeated the sanctioning requirement in the OECD Convention,[59] calling on state parties to impute to legal persons the wrongdoing of "leading persons" and to treat a lack of supervision by a leading person as triggering corporate responsibility.[60] Austria,[61] Hungary,[62] Italy,[63] Luxembourg,[64] Poland,[65] and Switzerland[66] were motivated by these developments to enact new corporate liability statutes. Some of these statutes closely reflect the EU and COE rules, as we will see below,[67] whereas others adopt "open"[68] or holistic models of liability, at least for serious economic and organized crimes.[69]

[58] OECD Convention on Foreign Bribery, Arts. 2, 3(1) and (2), 12. See further, Pieth 2007a.

[59] COE Criminal Law Convention on Corruption, Art. 19(2); Second Protocol to the EU Convention on the Protection of the ECs' Financial Interests, Art. 4(1); EU Framework Decision on Private Sector Corruption, Art. 6(1). See also, Terrorist Financing Convention, Art. 5(3); FATF Recommendations, Recommendation 2(b); FATF Special Recommendations, Special Recommendation 6. See further, Weigend 2008, 928 et seq.

[60] COE Convention on Corruption, Arts. 18, 19(2); Second Protocol to the EU Convention on the Protection of the ECs' Financial Interests, Arts. 3, 4(1); EU Framework Decision on Private Sector Corruption, Art. 5(1).

[61] Verbandsverantwortlichkeitsgesetz 2006; Hilf 2008; Zeder 2006.

[62] Santha/Dobrocsi (2011).

[63] De Maglie (2011); Manacorda 2008; Sacerdoti 2003.

[64] Braum 2008.

[65] Kulesza 2010.

[66] Heine 2008; Perrin (2011); Pieth 2003, Pieth 2004.

[67] See generally, below Sect. 28.9.2.

[68] Belgium and the Netherlands. On Belgium, see Bihain/Masset 2010, 2 et seq.; on the Netherlands, see Keulen/Gritter (2011). See further below, Sect. 28.9.2.3.

[69] Switzerland. See Heine 2008, 307 et seq.; Perrin (2011); Pieth 2003, 356 et seq., 362 et seq.; Pieth 2004, 603 et seq. See further below, Sect. 28.9.2.2.

28.4.2 Non-criminal Solutions in European and American Civil Law Jurisdictions

Several civil law countries, whilst maintaining that corporations can do no wrong, have recognized **quasi-criminal forms of responsibility**. German,[70] Italian,[71] Chilean,[72] Russian, and (to a more limited extent) Brazilian[73] laws are **hybrids** of this nature. They are frequently portrayed as compromise solutions[74] or as a "third track"[75]: their nominally "administrative" sanctions are handed down by criminal judges; however, they are considered "criminal" for the purpose of mutual legal assistance and they may result in the corporation being ordered to pay considerable sums of money, cease operations, or undergo deregistration.[76]

28.4.3 European and American Civil Law Jurisdictions Without CCL

Finally, for all the rapid change in civil law jurisdictions during the last decade, one should not neglect to mention that a **large group of European and American countries still objects** altogether to the notion of corporate liability – criminal or quasi-criminal. Within Europe, Greece,[77] the Czech Republic,[78] and the Slovak Republic[79] have found it especially difficult to take the step, as has Uruguay in Latin America.[80] In Turkey, CCL rules were abolished and only reintroduced in draft form under intense international pressure.[81]

[70] Böse (2011); Weigend 2008, 930 et seq.

[71] De Maglie (2011); Manacorda 2008; Sacerdoti 2003.

[72] Salvo (2011).

[73] OECD 2007b, paras. 149 et seq.

[74] Böse (2011).

[75] De Maglie (2011). See generally, Manozzi/Consulich 2008.

[76] Böse (2011); Pieth 2007a, 183. See further below, Sect. 28.11.2.2.

[77] Mylonopoulos 2010.

[78] Jelínek/Beran (2011). For criticism, see OECD 2009a; OECD Working Group on Bribery in International Business Transactions (July 20, 2009), 'Letter to His Excellency, Ing. Jan Fischer CSc., Prime Minister of the Czech Republic'.

[79] For criticism, see OECD (July 20, 2009), 'Letter to His Excellency, Mr. Robert Fico, Prime Minister of the Slovak Republic'; OECD 2010.

[80] Langón Cuñarro/Montano 2010.

[81] OECD 2009c, paras. 49 et seq.

When justifying decisions not to criminalize corporate wrongdoing, many of these countries argue on principle; frequently, however, **political and economic considerations** are impeding the introduction of corporate liability from the background.

28.5 CCL Beyond Europe and the Americas: Asia, Southern Africa, and the Middle East

The social, economic, and international legal developments that precipitated the introduction of CCL laws in Europe and the Americas have also prompted law reforms in other countries and regions. Countries around the globe have come under significant pressure to ensure that corporate entities involved in money laundering, corruption, illegal trusts, or embargo-busting are taken to court. **Asian jurisdictions**, such as Japan,[82] Korea,[83] Hong Kong,[84] and Macau,[85] which are well-integrated into the global economy and the international financial regulatory system, have adopted general corporate liability principles along the lines of the imputation models used in other parts of the world. **New Asian economic powers**, the People's Republic of China[86] and India,[87] have also recognized corporate criminal liability, though in China probably only for economic crimes[88] and in India only as a result of a recent controversial Supreme Court decision.[89] According to international monitoring reports, moreover, CCL rules figure in the laws of Israel,[90] Qatar,[91] and the United Arab Emirates[92] in the **Middle East**, and in the law of **South Africa**.[93]

[82] Cf. Pieth 2007a, 182, n. 43. See generally, OECD 2005a, paras. 158 et seq.; Shibahara 1999.

[83] OECD 2004b, paras. 101 et seq.

[84] FATF 2008, paras. 119 et seq.

[85] Godinho 2010.

[86] See generally, Chen 2008, 274 et seq.; FATF 2007; Jiachen 1999.

[87] Asia/Pacific Group on Money Laundering 2005, para. 66.

[88] Chen 2008, 275; Coffee 1999a, 24 et seq.; Jiachen 1999, 76.

[89] *Standard Chartered Bank & Ors.* v. *Directorate of Enforcement & Ors.* (2005) AIR 2622 cited in APG on Money Laundering 2005, para. 66.

[90] OECD 2009b, paras. 47 et seq.

[91] Middle East and North Africa Financial Action Taskforce (MENAFATF) 2008a, para. 154.

[92] MENAFATF 2008b, para. 92.

[93] OECD 2008a, paras. 38 et seq.

28.6 Conclusions

Therefore, CCL rules are a common – if not universal – feature of domestic criminal laws. The risks associated with industrialization and the challenges of globalization have prompted lawmakers of the civil and common law traditions to impose criminal or quasi-criminal sanctions on corporate wrongdoers. They have used three models to enable findings of corporate "guilt": (1) attributing the collective with the offenses of its employees or agents; (2) identifying the collective with its senior decision-makers; and (3) treating the corporation as itself capable of being a criminal (and moral) actor either through the aggregation of individual thoughts and behaviors or an assessment of the totality of the deficiencies in its corporate culture and organizational systems. The points of similarity and convergence between these models becomes apparent as we consider the substantive conditions and the defenses to CCL, the procedures for imposing CCL, and its attendant sanctions in European and American common law and criminal law jurisdictions.[94]

28.7 Entities That May Be Criminally Liable

In describing the substantive conditions for corporate criminal liability, a threshold question is "What **type of collective** may be held criminally or administratively responsible?" As noted above, **privately-owned commercial corporations** (companies) are not the only collective entities with the capacity to harm communities and confound traditional methods of regulation. Jurisdictions may impose liability on **entities without legal personality** which operate an "enterprise," they may impose liability on **publicly as well as privately-owned corporations**, and they may criminalize the acts and omissions of **non-government, non-profit organizations**.

[94] We received reports on Belgium, Chile, France, Germany, Greece, Hungary, Italy, Macau (SAR), Poland, Portugal, Scotland, Spain, Switzerland, the Czech Republic, the Netherlands, the United States (US), and Uruguay, as well as a chapter on England and Wales. Our additional research was concentrated on the common law jurisdictions of Australia and Canada.

28.7.1 Common Law Jurisdictions

28.7.1.1 The UK and the Commonwealth

In the surveyed British and Commonwealth jurisdictions, legal persons are the traditional addressees of CCL rules. **General law identification doctrines**, which apply to non-statutory offenses, were developed to address the problem of whether, and, if so how, groups with fictional personality could assume moral responsibility under law.[95] Even Australia's otherwise innovative codification of CCL rules is expressed to apply to "bodies corporate."[96] For **statutory offenses**, rules of statutory interpretation in many common law jurisdictions deem references to "persons" to include partnerships and unincorporated bodies,[97] as well as bodies corporate.[98]

British and Commonwealth jurisdictions do, however, consider a **wide variety of entities** as **capable of possessing legal personality**. Aside from companies established by individuals to engage in trade and commerce, some recognize partnerships,[99] municipalities,[100] charitable and incorporated non-profit or voluntary associations,[101] and corporations established as vehicles for public-private partnerships[102] as legal persons in their own right. The Crown itself has legal personality, though at common law it is immune from prosecution.[103] Crown immunity may also benefit crown bodies (e.g., government departments or agencies) but whether this extends to fully or partially **government-owned corporations** (GOCs) will depend on the jurisdiction and the offense in question.[104]

Furthermore, some **common law legislatures** are taking a **broader view** of the objects of CCL rules, shifting their focus from legal personality to qualities of "enterprise" and "organization." As a result of 2004 reforms, the **Canadian Criminal Code** now applies to "organizations", defined to mean "(a) a public body, body corporate, society, company, firm, partnership, trade union or municipality or (b) an association of persons that (i) is created for a common purpose, (ii) has an operational structure and (iii) holds itself out to the public as an association of persons."[105] Likewise, the **UK's Corporate Manslaughter and Corporate Homicide Act 2007** (CMCH Act (UK)) applies to "organisations," including listed government departments, police forces and other unincorporated employers.[106] Also, with the **Bribery Act 2010** (Bribery Act (UK)), the UK criminalizes the facilitation of bribery by defined "commercial organisations."[107]

28.7.1.2 The US

Whereas British and Commonwealth jurisdictions have traditionally focused on the liability of corporations *qua* legal entities, US federal lawmakers have been willing to apply CCL rules to **unincorporated entities and individuals**. On the one hand, the **interpretative provisions of the United States Code** (USC) define the words "person" and "whoever" to include "corporations, companies, associations, firms, partnerships, societies, and joint stock companies, as well as individuals."[108] Other undertakings could, presumably, be covered if it were consistent with the statute. On the other hand, the US courts developed the doctrine of *respondeat superior* from **principles of vicarious liability**, which rendered individual masters liable for their servants' civil wrongs.

[95] Wells 2001, 81 et seq.

[96] Criminal Code Act 1995 (Australia), s. 12. See also, Interpretation Act 1987 (New South Wales) (NSW) (Australia), s. 21; Occupational Health and Safety Act 2000 (NSW) (Australia), s. 32A(2).

[97] See, e.g., Interpretation Act 1978 (UK) s. 5 and Schedule 1; Interpretation Act 1996 (British Columbia) (Canada), s. 29. See further, Pinto/Evans 2003, paras. 2.14 et seq.; Stark (2011).

[98] See, e.g., Acts Interpretation Act 1901 (Comm.) (Australia), s. 22(1)(a) and (aa).

[99] See, e.g., Limited Liability Partnership Act 2000 (UK); Stark (2011) (Scotland).

[100] See, e.g., Local Government Act 2002 No. 84 (New Zealand).

[101] See, e.g., Associations Incorporation Act 1981 and Regulation 1999 (Queensland) (Australia); Charities Act 2006 (UK).

[102] E.g., Partnerships UK plc, a company established to invest in public sector projects, programs, and businesses. 51% of its equity is owned by private sector institutions. The remaining shares are owned by HM Treasury. See further, Partnerships UK 2010.

[103] Sunkin 2003.

[104] Cf. CMCH Act (UK), s. 11(1) and (2)(b). See further, Sunkin 2003.

[105] Criminal Code RSC 1985 c. C-46 (Canada) (Criminal Code (Canada)) ss. 2, 22.1, 22.2. See further, Allens Arthur Robinson 2008, 25 et seq.

[106] CMCH Act (UK), s. 1(1) and (2).

[107] Bribery Act 2010 (UK), s. 7(1) and (5).

[108] Nanda (2011), citing 1 United States Code (USC) 1.

28.7.2 Civil Law Jurisdictions

Generally, civil law jurisdictions apply corporate criminal liability rules to legal persons and to organizations that **lack (full) legal personality but carry on an enterprise**. The German Regulatory Offenses Act 1987 (Regulatory Offenses Act (Germany)), § 30 refers, for example, to legal persons and to associations with partial legal capacity (such as unincorporated associations and some partnerships).[109] The Portuguese Criminal Code, art. 11, is also specifically addressed to legal persons and their equivalents (e.g., civil societies and de facto associations).[110] Provisions to similar effect are found in Italian,[111] Dutch,[112] Belgian,[113] Polish,[114] Chilean,[115] and Spanish law,[116] as well as in the law of Macau.[117] Provisions of French[118] and Hungarian[119] law refer only to legal (or "moral") persons. However, these concepts are broadly defined to include all persons established under public and private law with or without profit goals (France) and all legal persons with commercial goals established under private law (Hungary).[120] **Switzerland** alone expressly abandons the dichotomies between individuals and groups, legal persons, and persons without legal personality: art. 102 of its Criminal Code applies to **enterprises**, i.e., legal persons in private law, legal persons in public law, societies, and sole traders.[121]

As to the state/non-state and profit/non-profit distinctions, civil law jurisdictions generally provide **some measure of immunity to governments**, their organs, and agencies,[122] some extending this protection to **non-state actors** that are highly integrated into national or international political processes.[123] The French Criminal Code, for instance, **expressly excludes the state itself** from the category of moral persons which may be criminally liable and imposes special restrictions on proceedings against local authorities.[124] It does, however, permit prosecutions against non-profit organizations.[125] The Belgian,[126] Italian,[127] and Hungarian[128] laws contain similarly broad exclusions for the state and public agencies, Italy also exempting organizations that carry out **functions of constitutional significance** (e.g., political parties, unions, and non-economic public authorities)[129] and Hungary[130] and Belgium,[131] **entities without commercial goals** (i.e., non-profit organizations). Polish[132] and Swiss[133] laws would seem to exclude a narrower range of state organizations, though Switzerland may well exempt charitable or public interest organizations, at least for offenses perpetrated in the execution of their humanitarian mandates. It follows that the liability of GOCs and non-profit organizations under civil law CCL rules will generally depend on the scope of any express exclusions and any explicit or implicit requirement that the alleged corporate offender be commercial in orientation.

28.8 Offenses for Which Corporations May Be Liable

Just as states may limit CCL to certain entities, so they may limit CCL to certain offenses. In fact, concerns that corporations cannot, or should not, be held liable

[109] Böse (2011).

[110] De Faria Costa/Quintela de Brito 2010, 26 et seq.

[111] Decree No. 231 of 2001 (Italy), art. 11; de Maglie (2011).

[112] Criminal Code (Netherlands), art. 51; Keulen/Gritter (2011).

[113] Criminal Code (Belgium), art. 5; Bihain/Masset 2010, 1 et seq.

[114] Collective Entities' Legal Responsibility for Acts Forbidden under Penalty Act 2002 (Poland) (Liability of Collective Entities Act (Poland)); Kulesza 2010, 2 et seq.

[115] Law No. 20.393 (Chile); Salvo (2011).

[116] Criminal Code (Spain), art. 31*bis*; Boldova/Rueda (2011).

[117] Godinho 2010, 1 et seq.

[118] Criminal Code (France), art. 121–2; Deckert (2011); OECD 2000b, 11.

[119] Act CIV of 2001 on the Criminal Measures Applicable to Legal Persons (CMALP Act (Hungary)), art. 1(1); Santha/Dobrocsi (2011).

[120] See above, nn. 119, 120.

[121] Perrin (2011); Pieth 2003, 359; Pieth 2004, 603.

[122] On France, Deckert (2011); on Hungary, Santha/Dobrocsi (2011); on Italy, de Maglie (2011); on the Netherlands, Keulen/Gritter (2011); on Poland, Kulesza 2010, 2 et seq.; on Portugal, de Faria Costa/Quintela de Brito 2010, 16 et seq.

[123] On Italy, de Maglie (2011); on Portugal, de Faria Costa/Quintela de Brito 2010, 26 et seq.

[124] Deckert (2011).

[125] OECD 2000b, 48.

[126] Bihain/Masset 2010, 1.

[127] De Maglie (2011).

[128] Santha/Dobrocsi (2011).

[129] De Maglie (2011).

[130] Santha/Dobrocsi (2011).

[131] OECD 2005d, 37.

[132] Kulesza 2010, 2 et seq.

[133] Pieth 2003, 359. Cf. Perrin (2011).

for offenses that **require proof of** mens rea, that apparently **protect "private" interests** and that are **regulated only at the national level** have characterized judicial and political debates about CCL in many countries.[134] Hence, the question, "What is the scope *ratione materiae* of CCL rules?" can be broken down into, "Can corporations be held liable for offenses that require evidence of the mental state of the accused?" and "Can corporations commit all offenses or only those that are typically associated with the economic, environmental, or social impact of the modern (multinational) corporation, especially as reflected in international instruments?"

28.8.1 Common Law Jurisdictions

Though common law jurisdictions have struggled with both these questions, the imputation of **offenses with a mental element** has historically been the **greatest point of difficulty**. Initially, corporations were only regarded as capable of committing offenses of strict liability, i.e., offenses without a fault element.[135] This changed, as mentioned, with the extension of vicarious liability principles by US federal courts and the recognition of the identification doctrine in Britain and the Commonwealth.[136] Both models now allow organizations to be imputed with the states of mind of their human stakeholders.

The **type of conduct** that can be imputed to corporations has been **less controversial** in common law jurisdictions than in some civil law jurisdictions. As a rule, whether corporations may commit a particular crime is a **matter of interpretation** – of the statute or the common law norm.[137] And, to the extent that early authorities suggested corporations could not be liable for certain crimes involving **deceit and assault** (e.g., perjury, rape, and murder),[138] modern legislators in Canada,[139] the US,[140] and the UK[141] have taken a different view, at least to the extent that such offenses can be committed by officials "in the **scope** of their employment."[142] The LCEW (UK) has also recently recommended the restriction of criminal laws in regulatory contexts to "seriously reprehensible conduct" for which prison terms for individuals or unlimited fines would be appropriate punishments.[143] If its proposals are adopted, many low-level criminal offenses frequently applied to corporations in England and Wales would be repealed and replaced with "civil penalties or equivalent measures."[144] Ironically, Australian "corporate culture" principles apply to the narrowest range of offenses (generally, those which are matters of international concern).[145] However, this is more likely due to the scope of the federal government's law-making power in Australia than to opposition in principle to the "corporatization" of some criminal acts and omissions.[146]

28.8.2 Civil Law Jurisdictions

By contrast, amongst civil law jurisdictions, the **type of act or omission has assumed greater importance**

[134] Jelínek/Beran (2011); Pieth 2003, 360; Wells 2001, 3 et seq.

[135] Wells 2001, 89 et seq.; Pinto/Evans 2003, 15 et seq.; Nanda (2011).

[136] Wells 2001, 93 et seq.; Pinto/Evans 2003, 39 et seq.; Nanda (2011).

[137] Nanda (2011); Wells 2000, 9.

[138] *R.* v. *Great North of England Railway Co.* (1846) 115 ER 1294; *New York Central & Hudson River Railroad Co.* v. *United States* 212 US 481 (1909); *Dean* v. *John Menzies (Holdings) Ltd.* [1981] SLT 50; *Canadian Dredge & Dock Co.* v. *R.* (1985) 1 SCR 662. See further, LCEW (UK) 2010, Pt. 5; Nanda (2011); Stark (2011); Wells 2001, 89.

[139] See e.g., Criminal Code (Canada), Pt. V (Sexual Offenses, Public Morals, and Disorderly Conduct), Pt. VI (Invasion of Privacy), Pt. VII (Disorderly Houses, Gaming, and Betting), Pt. VIII (Offenses against the Person and Reputation), Pt. IX (Offenses against Rights of Property), Pt. X (Fraudulent Transactions relating to Contracts and Trade). See also, Crimes Against Humanity and War Crimes Act, SC 2000, c. 24.18.

[140] See e.g., USC Ch. 7, s. 116 (Female genital mutilation), s. 117 (Domestic assault by habitual offenders), s. 641 (Theft etc. of public money, property, or records). Cf. LCEW (UK) 2010, para. 5.10.

[141] Bribery Act 2010 (UK); CMCH Act (UK), s. 1; the Sexual Offenses (Scotland) Act 2009 (Sexual Offenses Act (Scotland)), s. 57.

[142] Crown Prosecutions Service of England and Wales (CPSEW (UK)) 2010, para. 12.

[143] LCEW (UK), Proposals 1 and 2, see further paras. 1.28 et seq., Parts 3, 4.

[144] LCEW (UK) 2010, Proposal 3. See further, LCEW (UK) 2010 paras. 1.28 et seq., 1.61, 3.1 et seq., 6.5.

[145] See e.g., Criminal Code Act 1995 (Australia), s. 70.2 (Bribery of foreign public officials), s. 71.2 (Murder of a UN or associated person), s. 103.1 (Financing terrorism), Ch. 8, Div. 268 (Genocide, crimes against humanity, war crimes, and crimes against the administration of the justice of the International Criminal Court).

[146] Criminal Code Act 1995 (Australia), ss. 2, 12.3. See further, Allens Arthur Robinson 2008, 15.

than the presence or absence of fault as an element of a crime. For, in displacing the traditional principle of *societas delinquere non potest*, they explicitly acknowledged the possibly of corporate fault (or administrative liability for criminal offenses, as a substitute). However, since many civil law states introduced CCL rules to combat specific risks and/or to comply with specific international obligations, they were forced to deal with the questions of whether corporations should only be held liable for **stereotypically "corporate" crimes**, for conduct subject to an **international criminalization obligations**, or **all crimes** on the books.

28.8.2.1 The "All-Crimes" Approach

French, Dutch, Belgian, Hungarian, and German legislators opted for the broadest "all-crimes" approach: in France[147] and the Netherlands[148] corporations may be held liable for any crime, in Belgium[149] and Hungary[150] for all crimes of intent and, in Germany, for all "crimes and regulatory offenses."[151]

28.8.2.2 The "List-Based" Approach

Czech,[152] Italian,[153] Polish,[154] Portuguese,[155] and Spanish[156] lawmakers chose to **restrict** corporate criminal and quasi-criminal liability **by reference to lists**. The listed offenses reflect concerns about typically "corporate" risks, as well as the influence of international and regional crime control initiatives, as these have changed over time. For example, Italy's Decree No. 231 of 2001 was once limited to bribery, corruption, and fraud but, after amendments at the turn of this century, now applies to financial and competition offenses, terrorism, slavery, money laundering, and handling stolen goods, female genital mutilation, involuntary manslaughter, and offenses involving serious workplace injuries; it may be extended to environmental crimes in the future.[157] Some speculate that the Czech Corporate Criminal Liability Bill of 2004 may have succeeded had it likewise contained a more limited list of crimes.[158]

28.8.2.3 The Dual Approach

Alone among the civil law states surveyed, **Switzerland** incorporates both the all-crimes and list-based approaches, creating **one basis of liability for economic crimes** addressed in international instruments and **another for the remaining domestic offenses**.[159] Hence, by art. 102(2) Criminal Code (Switzerland), an enterprise may be liable for organized crime,[160] the financing of terrorism,[161] money laundering,[162] and various forms of corruption[163] simply by virtue of the fact that it failed to prevent the offense through necessary and reasonable organizational measures. For other offenses, art. 102(1) provides that the enterprise may be liable when the individual offender cannot be identified, and hence prosecuted, due to the enterprise's state of disorganization.[164]

28.9 Natural Persons Who Trigger Liability

All models of corporate criminal liability depend on the attribution of individual acts, omissions and states of mind to a corporation or enterprise,[165] though each attributes the corporation or enterprise with the thoughts and actions of **different natural persons**. These **differences are not merely academic**: how a jurisdiction describes the category of person who can trigger corporate criminal or administrative liability determines, to a large extent, the types of organizations

147 Criminal Code (France), art. 121–2 ("in the cases provided for in the law"). See further, Deckert (2011).

148 Keulen/Gritter (2011).

149 Bihain/Masset 2010, 1. See also OECD 2005d, para. 123.

150 Santha/Dobrocsi (2011).

151 Böse (2011).

152 Jelínek/Beran (2011).

153 De Maglie (2011).

154 Kulesza 2010, 3 et seq.

155 De Faria Costa/Quintela de Brito, 27 et seq.

156 Boldova/Rueda (2011).

157 De Maglie (2011).

158 Jelínek/Beran (2011).

159 See generally, Pieth 2003, 360 et seq.

160 Criminal Code (Switzerland), art. 260*ter*.

161 Criminal Code (Switzerland), art. 260*quinquies*.

162 Criminal Code (Switzerland), art. 305*bis*.

163 Criminal Code (Switzerland), arts. 322*ter* (bribery of Swiss public officials), 322*quinquines* (abuse of influence of Swiss judicial and military officials), 322(1)*septies* (bribery of foreign public officials); Federal Law of December 19, 1986, on Unfair Competition (Switzerland), art. 4a(1) (active and passive bribery in the private sector).

164 Perrin (2011); Pieth 2003, 365 et seq.; Pieth 2004, 604.

165 Pieth 2003, 360.

to which the criminal law applies. **Narrow rules**, which only impute to corporations offenses by corporate officers, organs, and senior executives, will rarely result in convictions against large companies in which lower-level agents, consultants, and employees collectively execute corporate operations.[166] However, **broad rules**, which impute to the organization any agent's or employee's misconduct may render corporations disproportionately liable for the misdeeds of lone individuals who contravene well-established rules and internal cultural norms of good behavior (so-called "rogues").[167]

Thus, a key issue is, "Which natural persons in which circumstances are capable of triggering the criminal liability of the corporation?" The surveyed jurisdictions dealt with this issue in one of three ways:

- by imputing to the corporation offenses by any corporate agent or employee – no matter what steps others in the corporation had taken to prevent and respond to the misconduct (**strict vicarious liability**) or if others had not done enough to prevent the wrongdoing (**qualified vicarious liability**);
- by identifying the corporation with its executive bodies and managers and holding it liable for their acts, omissions, and states of mind (**identification**); and
- by treating the collective as capable of offending in its own right, either through the aggregated thoughts and deeds of its senior stakeholders (**aggregation**) or though inadequate organizational systems and cultures (**corporate culture**, **corporate (dis) organization**).

A similar schema is used in a 2009 OECD recommendation on the implementation of the Convention on Foreign Bribery.[168]

As to the **conditions for attribution**, these would seem to play a greater role in jurisdictions that regard corporations as vicariously liable for offenses by non-executive stakeholders. They have, however, been recognized as part of common law identification doctrines in the Commonwealth and they are embedded in holistic corporate liability principles. Moreover, all the jurisdictions surveyed seemed to require some degree of **connection between the offense and the corporation's objectives**, whether that connection is established by reference to the **scope** of the individual offender's powers or duties, the corporation's perceived **interests**, or the actual or intended corporate **benefit**.[169]

28.9.1 Common Law Jurisdictions

28.9.1.1 Strict Vicarious Liability: US Federal Law

Vicarious liability principles, as they have been developed in US federal law, allow legal entities to be charged with offenses by **all agents and employees**, regardless of their individual functions within the corporation, their status in the organizational hierarchy, or the organization's attempts to prevent the individual wrongdoing.[170] Once the prosecutor establishes that the person is a corporate agent or employee, the issue becomes whether the person was **acting, at least in part, for the corporation's benefit** and **within the scope of his/her duties**; if so, the agent's or employee's offense is imputed to the corporation,[171] even if it had developed and implemented appropriate corporate compliance systems.[172] In this way, vicarious corporate criminal liability norms in US federal law have assumed a **uniquely strict form**.[173] Corporate liability principles under US **state law** tend to be less strict, many state legislatures and courts having adopted rules similar to those set out in the **US Model Penal Code**.[174]

[166] Pinto/Evans 2003, para. 4.20; Wells 2001, 115.

[167] Cf. Beale 2007, 1488.

[168] OECD, Recommendation of the Council for Further Combating Bribery of Foreign Public Officials in International Business Transactions, November 26, 2009, Paris (OECD 2009 Recommendation), Annex I, para. B.

[169] Pieth 2003, 361 et seq.

[170] Hasnas 2009, 1342.

[171] Coffee 1999a, 14 et seq.; Nanda (2011).

[172] Cf. American Law Institute 1962, para. 2.07; *United States* v. *Ionia Management SA* 555 F. 3d 303 (2009) at 310 (McLaughlin, Calabresi, and Livingston JJ). See further, Nanda (2011). Note also that the LCEW (UK)'s provisional proposals include a suggestion that Parliament create a generic due diligence defense to all statutory strict liability offenses in England and Wales: LCEW (UK) 2010, Proposal 14 and Pt. 6. See further below, Sect. 28.10.1 and Wells (2011).

[173] Nanda (2011).

[174] American Law Institute 1962, para. 2.07. See Nanda (2011); Wells 2001, 131.

28.9.1.2 Qualified Vicarious Liability: UK Regulatory Offense Legislation

The UK uses a **milder version** of vicarious liability to impute some statutory offenses to corporations.[175] Typically, these statutes deem a "person" guilty of an offense without requiring evidence of intent, negligence, or another state of mind. In other words, they employ principles of **strict liability**. However, they are also typically accompanied by a **due diligence defense**, which allows the offender to avoid liability if he/she can prove that he/she took all reasonable precautions to prevent the commission of the criminal act or omission.[176] Therefore, such regulatory offense statutes are better regarded as examples of **qualified vicarious liability** than a strict vicarious liability approach.

28.9.1.3 Identification: The Narrow UK View

Such legislation was at issue in Tesco Supermarkets Ltd. **v.** Nattrass (*Tesco Supermarkets*),[177] ironically the leading case on who acts as the directing mind and will, under general law identification principles in England and Wales. In *Tesco Supermarkets*, the House of Lords asked whether the criminal negligence of its employee could be imputed to the corporate owner of a supermarket chain. A supermarket store manager had failed to correctly display a sale item and the company was charged with a breach of the Trade Descriptions Act 1968. The company defended the charges, arguing, first, that it was a different person from the store manager and, second, that it had exercised due diligence to prevent the store manager's offense. The House of Lords agreed.[178] For slightly different reasons, each of the law lords found that the **store manager was not the corporation's** "directing mind and will" and so did not offend as the company. *Tesco Supermarkets* became authority for the proposition that companies are criminally responsible for the offenses of their **corporate organs, corporate officers, and other natural persons who have been delegated wide discretionary powers** of corporate management and control.[179]

28.9.1.4 Identification: The Broader View from the Commonwealth

Tesco Supermarkets is the leading case on the concept of the alter ego in England and Wales and has been extremely influential throughout Great Britain and the Commonwealth. However, the House of Lords **did not take a clear view on the nature of the power** that makes a person the directing mind and will. As a result, it is not clear whether it is necessary that the directing mind and will is a person **formally empowered** to manage the corporation's general affairs under general or specific rules of association or whether it is sufficient that he/she **controls** a relevant aspect of the corporation's operations (in law or in fact). Subsequent English courts tended to adopt a narrower view in criminal contexts,[180] whilst some Commonwealth courts have adopted broader interpretations.

First, since Canadian Dredge & Dock Co. **v.** R. (*Dredge and Dock*),[181] the Supreme Court of Canada has treated a person's capacity for decision-making in a particular operative sector of a corporation as determinative of his/her capacity to act as the corporation. So, in that case, the defendant companies could be charged with bid-rigging by non-executive managers as those managers were acting within the scope of their

[175] See generally, Wells 2001, 85 et seq.

[176] LCEW (UK) 2008, 118 et seq.

[177] [1972] AC 153 at 1 (Reid LJ).

[178] Pinto/Evans 2003, para. 4.14.

[179] *Tesco Supermarkets Ltd.* v. *Nattrass* [1972] AC 153 at 171 et seq. (Reid LJ), 179 et seq. (Morris of Borth-y-Gest LJ), 187 et seq. (Dilhorne LJ), 192 et seq. (Pearson LJ), 198 et seq. (Diplock LJ). See generally, Pinto/Evans 2003, paras. 4.12 et seq.; Wells 1999, 120 et seq.; Wells 2001, 98.

[180] *Attorney General's Reference (No. 2 of 1999)* [2000] QB 796; [2000] 2 Cr. App. R. 207; [2000] 3 All ER 182; *R.* v. *P&O European Ferries (Dover) Ltd.* [1991] 93 Cr. App. R. 72. Cf. *El Ajou* v. *Dollar Land Holdings Ltd.* [1993] EWCA Civ. 4; *Director General of Fair Trading* v. *Pioneer Concrete (UK) Ltd.* [1995] 1 AC 456; *Stone & Rolls Ltd. (in liq.)* v. *Moore Stephens (a firm)* [2009] 1 AC 1391 at paras. 39 et seq. (Phillips of Worth Matravers LJ), paras. 221 et seq., 256 et seq. (Mance LJ). See generally, LCEW (UK) 2010, paras. 5.48 et seq.; Pinto/Evans 2003, paras. 4.23 et seq., paras. 13.9 et seq.; Wells 2001, 112 et seq. Cf. CPSEW (UK) 2010, para. 20 (requiring prosecutors to consider the purpose of a certain regulatory offenses and referring to *Meridian Global Funds Asia Ltd.* v. *Securities Commission* [1995] 2 AC 500, discussed next).

[181] [1985] 1 SCR 662, paras. 29, 32 (Estey J). See further, Allens Arther Robinson 2008, 24 et seq.; Wells 2001, 130 et seq.

duties and to benefit the corporation, at least in part.[182] The companies could not avoid liability on the basis that they had issued "general or specific instructions prohibiting the conduct."[183]

Second, in Meridian Global Funds Asia Ltd. **v.** Securities Commission (*Meridian*), the Privy Council upheld a New Zealand court's decision to determine the directing mind and will "... by applying the usual canons of [statutory] interpretation [to the norm in question], taking into account the language of the rule (if it is a statute) and its content and policy."[184] The legislation in that case required disclosure of share purchaser information in fast-moving financial markets.[185] The Privy Council found that only senior operative personnel could effectively act as the company for those purposes.[186]

28.9.1.5 Corporate Culture: Australian Federal Law

At the federal level, Australia relies on both identification and holistic models of corporate criminal liability. **Section 12.2 Criminal Code Act 1995** provides that the **physical elements** of an offense committed by an employee, agent or officer of a body corporate must be attributed to the corporation if the individual was acting within the actual or apparent scope of his/her employment or authority. **Section 12.3** then elaborates that the **fault elements** of intention, knowledge, or recklessness must be attributed to a body corporate that expressly, tacitly, or impliedly authorized or permitted them. The code also contains special rules for establishing corporate criminal negligence.[187]

Under Australian federal law it is permissible but not necessary to prove that an offense was committed by a human stakeholder whose thoughts, acts, and omission were attributable to the body corporate. If the prosecution relies on corporate culture, it will look more broadly for evidence of **attitudes, policies, rules, general, or localized patterns of behavior or practices.**[188] Evidence of the high-level individual's acts, omissions, and states of mind remains relevant to the question of fault since s. 12.3(4) authorizes the court to consider, in assessing corporate culture, whether a **high managerial agent authorized** the act or lower-level offender reasonably believed that he/she would have received the high managerial agent's authority or permission. However, until these provisions are judicially considered, it is not possible to know exactly how much weight individual managerial (in)action will be given by the Australian courts.

28.9.1.6 UK Law Reforms

The particular narrowness of the British identification doctrine has prompted **criticism and calls for reform.**[189] Unsuccessful attempts to introduce aggregation principles before the courts prompted **legislative action by Parliament** in relation to specific high-profile "corporate" offenses and **LCEW proposals** in relation to statutory offenses more generally.

The capsizing of the *Herald of Free Enterprise* on its way from Zeebrugge in 1987 resulted in the deaths of almost 200 people and the prosecution of **P&O European Ferries (Dover) Ltd.** (P&O Ferries) for reckless manslaughter.[190] For Lord Justice Bingham (Justices Mann and Kennedy agreeing) aggregation of individual acts and states of mind was inconsistent with the local doctrine of identification.[191] Notably, such an approach had been regarded as consistent with corporate criminal liability principles under US federal law.[192] Parliament subsequently enacted two laws that appear to depart from the narrow identification doctrine and, at least at first blush, to introduce

---

[182] *Canadian Dredge & Dock Co.* v. *R.* [1985] 1 SCR 662 at para. 21 (Estey J).

[183] *Canadian Dredge & Dock Co.* v. *R.* [1985] 1 SCR 662 at para. 45 (Estey J).

[184] *Meridian Global Funds Asia Ltd.* v. *Securities Commission* [1995] 2 AC 500 at 507 (Hoffman LJ).

[185] *Meridian Global Funds Asia Ltd.* v. *Securities Commission* [1995] 2 AC 500 at 511 (Hoffman LJ).

[186] *Meridian Global Funds Asia Ltd.* v. *Securities Commission* [1995] 2 AC 500 at 506, 511 et seq. (Hoffman LJ).

[187] Criminal Code Act 1995 (Australia), ss. 5.5, 12.4(2). See further, Beale 2007, 1499 et seq.

[188] Criminal Code Act 1995 (Australia), s. 12.3(6).

[189] See e.g., Drew/UNICORN 2005, 3; LCEW (UK) 2010, paras. 5.81 et seq.; OECD 2005b, paras. 295 et seq.; OECD 2008b, paras. 65 et seq.

[190] *R.* v. *HM Coroner for East Kent; Ex parte Spooner* (1989) 88 Cr. App. R. 10; *R.* v. *P &O European Ferries (Dover) Ltd.* [1991] 93 Cr. App. R. 72. See further, LCEW (UK) 1996, para. 6.05; Wells 2001, 106 et seq.

[191] *R.* v. *HM Coroner for East Kent; Ex parte Spooner* (1989) 88 Cr. App. R. 10 at 16 et seq. (Bingham LJ). See Wells 2001, 108. See also, Crown Prosecution Service of England and Wales 2010, para. 25.

[192] *United States* v. *Bank of New England NA* 821 F. 2d 844 (1987) at 856 (Bownes J) cited in Podgor 2007, 1541.

elements of a holistic approach into UK law. First, to broaden the range of circumstances in which legal entities may be held criminally liable for an individual's death,[193] the **Corporate Manslaughter Act (UK)** creates the offense of **"corporate manslaughter"** ("corporate homicide" in Scotland).[194] The act removes the requirement of an offense by a company officer, organ, or senior manager and enables the **jury to consider** "the extent to which … there were **attitudes, policies, systems or accepted practices** within the organisation that were likely to have encouraged [a failure to comply with health and safety legislation] …, or to have produced tolerance of it."[195] The Corporate Manslaughter Act (UK) is thus said to depart from the identification model, even to approach an aggregative[196] or a corporate culture model of responsibility.[197] Still, the prosecution must show that "… the way in which [the corporation's] activities [were] managed or organised by its **senior management** [was] a **substantial element** in the breach …."[198] So, successful prosecutions will depend, in practice, on evidence of the acts, omissions and knowledge of senior corporate figures.[199]

Second, to address bristling domestic and international criticism,[200] the **Bribery Act 2010 (UK)** creates an offense of **"Failure of commercial organisations to prevent bribery"** in England, Wales, Northern Ireland, and Scotland.[201] In line with the OECD's anti-bribery convention and 2009 recommendations, the act deems relevant commercial organizations guilty of an offense if a person associated with them bribes someone else with the intention of obtaining or retaining specified benefits for the organization.[202] The offense is one of **strict liability**, a parliamentary joint committee having rejected a recommendation that the offense include an element of negligence on the part a natural person employed or connected with the company and responsible for ensuring corporate compliance with anti-bribery laws.[203] Nonetheless, the act's "**adequate systems defense**" allows the organization to avoid liability by proving "… [it] had in place adequate procedures designed to prevent [associated persons] from undertaking such conduct."[204] It would seem that the reference to the commercial organization's procedures was intended to allow the courts to look at the practical measures that had been implemented throughout the company to prevent bribery.[205] On this basis, it could be regarded as akin to a requirement that organizations accused of bribery demonstrate the existence of an adequate "corporate culture."

Finally, if the preliminary proposals of the LCEW (UK) are any guide, some British jurisdictions will adopt a more open, "context-sensitive, interpretative" approach to attribution of liability for statutory offenses.[206] In its August 2010 consultation paper, the LCEW (UK) called on Parliament to specify principles of attribution for statutory offense and, in the absence of such provisions, on the English and Welsh courts to use general rules of statutory interpretation to determine how corporate liability for particular offenses is to be established.[207] It saw "… no pressing need for statutory reform or replacement of the identification doctrine,"[208] as, in its view, there was already authority for the proposition that the courts should select the most appropriate approach to liability for the statutory offense in question.[209] It would seem, moreover, that it considered holistic ("corporate culture") models of liability to figure among the approaches available to

[193] Explanatory Notes: Corporate Manslaughter and Corporate Homicide Act 2007 (July 27, 2007), 8 et seq.; Wells 2001, 106 et seq.

[194] CMCH Act (UK), s. 1(1).

[195] CMCH Act (UK), s. 8(3).

[196] LCEW (UK) 2010, para. 5.92; Cartwright 2010, para. B.31.

[197] Belcher 2006, 6; Gobert 2008, 427.

[198] CMCH Act (UK), s. 1(3).

[199] Gobert 2008, 428.

[200] Parliament 2009, para. 72; OECD 2005b; OECD 2008b.

[201] Bribery Act 2010 (UK), s. 7(1).

[202] Explanatory Notes: Bribery Act 2010, paras. 50 et seq.

[203] Parliament 2009, para. 89. Cf. LCEW (UK) 2008b, paras. 6.100 et seq.

[204] Bribery Act 2010 (UK), s. 7(2).

[205] Parliament 2009, para. 92.

[206] LCEW (UK) 2010, paras. 5.7, 5.013 et seq.

[207] LCEW (UK) 2010, Proposal 13 ("Legislation should include specific provisions in criminal offenses to indicate the basis on which companies may be found liable, but in the absence of such provisions, the courts should treat the question of how corporate fault may be established as a matter of statutory interpretation. We encourage the courts not to presume that the identification doctrine applies when interpreting the scope of criminal offenses applicable to companies.") See further, LCEW (UK) (2010), 1.60 et seq., Pt. 5.

[208] LCEW (UK) 2010, para. 5.104.

[209] LCEW (UK) 2010, para. 5.104 and the discussion of the case law in Pt. 5 generally.

the court, in addition to the vicarious and identification models for liability they have traditionally used.[210]

In so doing, the LCEW (UK) has arguably attempted to recast the Privy Council's approach in *Meridian* as the basic approach to attribution of individual acts and omissions to corporations in English and Welsh law. It would seem, moreover, to have taken a broad and quite "open" view of the individuals or collections of individuals through whom a corporation may think or act in accordance with the *Meridian* doctrine. Whether English and Welsh lawmakers courts are willing to accept the commission's flexible but uncertain approach to liability remains to be seen, however. And, having completed its consultations in late 2010, the LCEW is not itself expected to issue its final report until Spring 2012.[211]

28.9.2 Civil Law

28.9.2.1 Jurisdictions with Imputation Models: Identification and Vicarious Corporate Liability

Of the civil law jurisdictions which employ imputation models of corporate criminal or quasi-criminal liability, all enable the corporation to be identified with its **organs, officials, and senior executives** and most enable it to be held vicariously liable for the offenses of its junior **employees, agents, and (in some cases) third parties**. Placing these laws on a **continuum**, the French provisions are triggered by the narrowest range of stakeholders (corporate organs and representatives), Polish and Hungarian rules by the widest (leading persons and persons under their supervision, as well as third parties), and German, Italian, Portuguese, Spanish, and Chilean laws occupy positions between the two extremes, being triggered by varying assortments of individuals and bodies. In all cases, express **conditions of liability**, such as the requirement of a connection between the corporation's aims and the offense, limit the types of individual acts imputable to the collective.

28.9.2.1.1 Identification with Senior Corporate Organs and Representatives: France

At one end of the continuum, French law attributes to corporations only offenses by their **organs and representatives**, "organs" being individuals and bodies who act as the corporation under its rules of association in law or in fact[212] and "representatives" being those who have been delegated executive powers within a certain area of corporate operations.[213] A further condition – that the organ or representative was **acting on behalf** of the legal person in committing the offense – has been interpreted broadly to capture acts in the name of the legal person and activities intended to advance "the organization, operations, and objectives of the [legal] person."[214]

28.9.2.1.2 Identification and (Indirect) Vicarious Liability: Germany

Like France, Germany enables corporations to be charged with offenses by senior managers, and, somewhat indirectly, with offenses by junior personnel that result from an omission by senior corporate figures.

First, **§ 30 Regulatory Offenses Act (Germany)** allows courts to impose administrative sanctions on corporations for offenses by a **broad range of senior managerial stakeholders**:

- representative organs of a legal person or a (human) member of such an organ;
- the chairperson or a board member of an unincorporated association;
- a partner authorized to represent a partnership;
- a person with general authority to represent a legal person, unincorporated association or partnership, or who is a general managerial agent or authorized representative of one of these entities; and
- other persons responsible for the management of the business or enterprise of one of the above entities, including those who supervise the management of the entity or are involved in other ways in controlling it at the executive level.[215]

Once it is established that the human offender was acting in one of these capacities, the prosecutor must

[210] LCEW (UK) 2010, paras. 5.103 et seq. See further, Wells (2011).

[211] LCEW (UK) (2010), iii.

[212] Criminal Code (France), art. 121–2. See further, Deckert (2011).

[213] Deckert (2011).

[214] OECD 2000b, 13.

[215] Regulatory Offenses Act (Germany), § 30(1). See further, Böse (2011).

demonstrate either that the entity's duties were violated through the commission of the offense or that the entity was enriched, or should have been enriched, through the commission of the offense.[216] The corporation's duties (and the range of offenses for which it can be liable) are determined having regard to its objectives, these indicating in turn the **scope of its corporate risk** (*Unternehmensrisiko*). Given the ancillary nature of the corporate sanction, the conviction of an individual is a de facto criterion as well.

Second, under **§ 130 Regulatory Offenses Act (Germany)**, a corporation may be (indirectly) punished for any breach of corporate duties when such a breach resulted from a **failure** by a corporate representative to faithfully discharge his/her **duties of supervision**.[217] In this second provision, the corporation is not made liable for the breach *per se* but for a natural person's intentional or negligent failure to carry out his/her supervisory duties,[218] including careful selection, appointment, and oversight by corporate representatives.[219]

28.9.2.1.3 Identification and Vicarious Liability: Italy, Portugal, Spain, and Chile

Italian, Portuguese, Spanish, and Chilean CCL rules go a step further than the German rules by allowing corporations to be charged with offenses by **senior managers and persons under their supervision**. For example, **art. 5(1) of Italy's Decree No. 231 of 2001** provides for the imposition of administrative penalties on organizations for offenses by "persons performing functions as representatives, directors, or managers of the said corporation or of an organizational unit … and by persons exercising [de facto] management and control of the corporation." They may also be liable for offenses by persons "subject to the authority" of a representative, director, or manager. In any case, the offense must have been committed in the interest of the organization or to its advantage and not solely in the interests of the individual or a third party.[220]

Portuguese, Spanish, and Chilean criminal liability provisions also allow the corporation to be held liable for the acts and omissions of leading persons. By **art. 11(2), the Portuguese Penal Code** provides that a corporation may be criminally liable for offenses by natural persons who occupy leadership positions or by other persons who act under a leading person's authority.[221] Persons with leadership positions are those within the entity's organs, those who represent the organization and those with authority to exercise control over the entities' activities.[222] To offend for the corporation, the leaders or subordinates must have acted in the collective name and interest of the entity and due to a breach of the leader's duties of supervision and control.[223] Likewise, **the new art. 31bis(2) Spanish Criminal Code** establishes the criminal liability of certain entities for offenses committed by their legal representatives, administrators (de jure and de facto), and employees with power of agency, as well as other persons who act under the authority of such senior figures.[224] Managers trigger art. 31*^bis^* when they commit an offense on behalf of the entity or for its benefit; for anyone else, liability arises when the offense is committed in the exercise of the entity's "social activities," on its behalf, for its benefit, and due to a lapse in control by senior figures.[225] **Chilean law** also attributes to corporations offenses by their owners, controllers, responsible persons, chief executives, representatives, administrators, or supervisors, and persons who are under direction or supervision of one of those people.[226]

28.9.2.1.4 Identification and Vicarious Liability: Poland and Hungary

At the other end of the continuum, Poland and Hungary are prepared to impute to corporations offenses by **leading persons, persons under the supervision of leading persons, and third parties**. Article 2 **Polish Act of October 28, 2002** on the Liability of Collective Entities for Acts Prohibited under Penalty (Liability of Collective Entities Act (Poland)) distinguishes between natural persons who act under the authority or duty to

[216] OECD 2003, 32.

[217] Böse (2011).

[218] Ibid.

[219] Ibid.

[220] De Maglie (2011).

[221] De Faria Costa/Quintela de Brito 2010, 28 et seq.

[222] De Faria Costa/Quintela de Brito 2010, 30.

[223] De Faria Costa/ Quintela de Brito 2010, 30 et seq. esp. 33.

[224] Boldova/Rueda (2011).

[225] By contrast, art. 129(1)(a) Spanish Criminal Code, which allows for the imposition of administrative sanctions on entities, does not identify a particular person as the primary author of the offense, nor does it set out conditions for the imposition of liability, except to require a hearing between the prosecutor and the owners of the undertaking and its representatives.

[226] Salvo (2011).

represent the entity, natural persons who are allowed to act by such leading persons, and natural persons who act with the consent or knowledge of leading persons.[227] The Hungarian **Act CIV of 2001 on the Criminal Measures Applicable to Legal Persons** similarly imputes to entities offenses by members or officers authorized to represent the legal person or participate in its management; members or agents of the supervisory board; members and employees of the corporation; and other people.[228] Had it succeeded, the **2004 Czech Corporate Criminal Liability Bill** would have provided for CCL in similar situations.[229]

The apparent breadth of the Hungarian and Polish provisions is qualified by their **extensive conditions for liability**.[230] In both states, criminal proceedings may only be brought against the corporation when a **human offender** has been **convicted first** – a potential impediment to corporate prosecutions according to international monitoring bodies.[231] Other conditions for imputation depend on the human offender's proximity to senior management; they repeat the concepts of **representation** ("behalf of"), **authority** ("scope" of activities or power), **mismanagement** and **knowledge** familiar from other civil law jurisdictions.[232]

28.9.2.2 Corporate (dis)Organization: Switzerland

Alone among the surveyed civil law jurisdictions, Switzerland takes an **overtly holistic approach** to the question of corporate liability.[233] Under **art. 102(1) Criminal Code (Switzerland)**, an enterprise is liable for offenses committed within the framework (scope) of its entrepreneurial objectives and in the execution of its business activities provided that the offense cannot be attributed to a particular individual because of organizational deficiencies in the enterprise itself. Under **art. 102(2)**, an enterprise is liable for listed economic crimes "… if [it] may be accused of not having taken all necessary and reasonable organizational measures to prevent such an offense."

Corporate liability is subsidiary to individual liability under art. 102(1) and primary under art. 102(2); however, in neither case is it strict.[234] Each paragraph should be read as making corporate liability **conditional on proof of corporate fault, i.e., deficiencies in organization**.[235] Specifically, each requires proof, not only that an offense was committed, but also that it was reasonably foreseeable for an enterprise with the aims, objectives, and characteristics of the accused enterprise and that it was allowed to occur – in the case at hand – because of the absence or inadequacy of systemic preventative measures.[236] In addition, the subsidiary nature of liability under paragraph 1, means that there must be a connection between the enterprises' organizational deficiencies and the fact that an individual offender cannot be identified.[237]

In determining what **standard of organization** is required of the enterprise it has been submitted elsewhere that the courts will look at the general law of agency and negligence, industry-specific statutory regulations, private or non-binding standards, and the particular **risk profile** of the enterprise (its size, operations, aims, customers, and geographical presences, etc.).[238] Moreover, in assessing the **sufficiency of the level of organization** in the accused enterprise, it would seem that courts should have particular regard to the decisions of corporate organs, the existence, scope, and enforcement of compliance policies or systems, the knowledge, acts, and omissions of corporate officers and senior executives, and the patterns of behavior amongst individuals connected to the organization as employees or otherwise.[239]

28.9.2.3 "Open" Models: Imputation, Aggregation, and/or Holistic Approaches

Two civil law jurisdictions under review dispense with the need to prove the commission of an offense by an

[227] Kulesza 2010, 4 et seq.

[228] Santha/Dobrocsi (2011).

[229] Jelínek/Beran (2011).

[230] Kulesza 2010, 4; Santha/Dobrocsi (2011).

[231] Group of States against Corruption (GRECO) 2004, 56; OECD 2005c, paras. 43 et seq.; OECD 2007a, 155 et seq.; OECD 2009 Recommendation, Annex I, para. B. See also, GRECO 2006, para. 84.

[232] On Hungary, see Santha/Dobrocsi (2011); on Poland, see Kulesza 2010, 5.

[233] Heine 2000, 4; Perrin (2011). See further, Pieth 2003; Pieth 2004.

[234] Perrin (2011); Pieth 2003, 362 et seq.; Pieth 2004, 604 et seq.

[235] Pieth 2003, 363 et seq.; Pieth 2004, 603 et seq.

[236] Perrin (2011); Pieth 2004, 604 et seq.

[237] Perrin (2011).

[238] Perrin (2011); Pieth 2003, 365 et seq.; Pieth 2004, 604 et seq.

[239] Perrin (2011); Pieth 2004, 606 et seq.

identified human stakeholder without committing to a single alternative model of imputation. In so doing, they invite the application of holistic principles, aggregative models, and traditional imputation doctrines of liability.

First, in the **Netherlands**, a corporation will be regarded as having committed an offense when this is **"reasonable" in the circumstances**. For Dutch courts, imputation is reasonable when the offense was committed **"within the scope"** of an entity having regard to certain **"guiding principles."**[240] The courts ask (amongst other things) whether the person worked for the entity, whether the conduct was part of the everyday business of the entity, whether the entity profited through the criminal act or omission, and whether the entity controlled and accepted the criminal acts or omissions given its relationship with the alleged individual offender and its managers' acts and omissions.[241] The Dutch **open model**, while not expressly holistic or aggregative, enables the courts to attribute to corporations the acts of potentially all employees taking into account the conduct of other individuals in the organization.[242]

Second, in **Belgium**, art. 5(1) Criminal Code deems legal persons "… criminally liable for offenses that are intrinsically connected with the attainment of their purpose or the defense of their interests or for offenses that concrete evidence shows to have been committed on their behalf." Insofar as art. 5(1) does not mention a person (or persons) who offends as or on behalf of the corporation, it signals that liability is not contingent upon proof of the commission of an offense by a certain type of human stakeholder. Hence, the Belgian law **leaves open the question of how corporations incur criminal liability**, particularly for offenses that include an element of *mens rea*.[243] Belgian authorities are yet to take a clear position on whether – as a **matter of fact** – a corporation is liable whenever an offense is intrinsically connected to its purpose or was committed in defense of its interests or whether imputation presumes some element of **corporate fault**.[244]

[240] Keulen/Gritter (2011).

[241] Ibid.

[242] Ibid.

[243] OECD 2000a, 8.

[244] Bihain/Masset 2010, 2 et seq.

28.9.3 Liability of Corporations for Acts of Related Entities

The 2010 environmental catastrophe in the Gulf of Mexico and the subsequent attempts at "blame shifting" between the drilling platform's corporate owner, operator, and contractor[245] have highlighted further issues relating to the question of who can trigger CCL: can corporations be criminally liable for acts or omissions committed by, or in association with, other collective entities, particularly their own subsidiaries, contractors, and agents? Other recent academic surveys[246] have found that states are generally willing to hold corporations liable in civil law for damage caused by their foreign subsidiaries, at least where there is evidence of parent-company control.[247] Moreover, it would seem that, in most states, corporations may be liable in criminal law for complicity in another company's offense[248] and (in the US, at least) through imputation of their offense.[249] Though a detailed examination of these principles is beyond the scope of our general report, we observe that many of the same issues relating to the identification of a single (corporate) perpetrator arise[250] and that objective ("enterprise") liability[251] and due diligence[252] models are being suggested as alternatives to imputation between corporations.

28.10 Special Defenses to Liability for Corporate Offenders

Given the peculiarities of corporate personality, **explicit exculpatory rules are unexpectedly rare.** Even the (in)effectiveness of compliance measures is generally considered as **part of the substantive conditions for liability**.

[245] Fifield 2010, 6.

[246] Thompson/Ramasastry/Taylor 2009, 873 et seq.; Zerk 2006, 215 et seq.

[247] Zerk 2006, 235 et seq.

[248] Ruggie 2007, 831 et seq.

[249] Clough 2008, 916 et seq.

[250] Zerk 2006, 229.

[251] Pitts 2009, 421 et seq.

[252] Clough 2008, 917 et seq. (suggesting parent companies be required by law to take reasonable steps to prevent criminal violations by their subsidiaries).

28.10.1 Common Law Jurisdictions

On the one hand, appeal courts in common law jurisdictions have failed to recognize a general "corporate compliance" excuse or defense. In the UK, a **narrow interpretation of the identification doctrine makes evidence of corporate good practice irrelevant**: the corporate defendants will only avoid liability if its alter ego could rely on a general defense or excuse to avoid personal liability.[253] Even Canada, which takes a broader view of the directing mind and will, does not regard one employee's or officer's good conduct as cancelling another's criminal act or omission.[254] The US approach to vicarious liability is stricter still, though the existence and effectiveness of corporate compliance programs are highly relevant factors at other points in the proceedings and at sentencing.[255]

The general position is **modified by statute in some jurisdictions**. In the UK, due diligence is already a defense to many strict liability statutory offenses (e.g., the Bribery Act (UK)). Further, if the LCEW's 2010 provisional proposals are accepted, it will be available in broader form in relation to *almost any* statutory offense that does not include fault as an element (this to ensure fairness to the accused corporation).[256] In Australian federal criminal law, meanwhile, a body corporate may avoid liability for the conduct of a high managerial agent by proving that it "exercised due diligence to prevent the conduct or the authorization or permission."[257] The traditional excuses of mistake of fact and intervening conduct or event are also modified to accommodate the special features of corporate criminal liability.[258]

28.10.2 Civil Law Jurisdictions

Equally few civil law jurisdictions have been willing to consider corporate compliance as capable of removing liability. Exceptionally, **Italy, Portugal, Spain, and Chile** have created or are contemplating **express defenses** that allow the court to assess corporate compliance programs. Article 6 Decree No. 231 of 2001 (Italy) sets out the "defense of organizational models." It allows companies which have "... adopted and effectively implemented appropriate organizational and management models ..." to avoid liability for offenses of senior managers or junior employees when other listed conditions are met.[259] Article 11(6) Portuguese Penal Code excludes liability for junior employees and senior figures when "the actor has acted against the orders or express instructions of the person responsible," though it is uncertain whether "instructions" may be given as part of a general corporate compliance program and if so whether they must be credibly monitored and enforced.[260] Spain's Art. 31*bis* also allows entities to avoid liability if they confess after the fact, collaborate with authorities, make reparations, and take preventive measures.[261] **Switzerland**, by contrast, takes the opposite approach, imputing the corporation with **liability only when deficiencies in organization are positively established** by the prosecutor.

28.11 Sanctions and Procedure: Charging, Trying, and Punishing Corporate Offenders

Recognizing corporations as capable of committing offenses is the first step in making them objects of criminal law. The issue then becomes whether to treat corporations the same as human offenders during the investigation and trial and at sentencing and, if not, how to treat them, for example, with respect to **procedural rights** and[262] **appropriate sanctions**. Is deterrence the only legitimate goal for sanctioning corporate offenders or could corporations, like human beings, be rehabilitated or otherwise prevented from committing further crime?[263]

---

[253] *Canadian Dredge & Dock Co.* v. *R.* [1985] 1 SCR 662 at para. 43 (Estey J).

[254] *Canadian Dredge & Dock Co.* v. *R.* [1985] 1 SCR 662 at paras. 48 et seq., esp. 65 et seq. (Estey J).

[255] Nanda (2011).

[256] LCEW (UK) 2010, Proposals 14 and 15 and Questions 1 and 2; paras. 1.68 et seq.; Pt. 6, esp. paras. 6.19 et seq, 6.67 et seq., 6.70 et seq., 6.95 et seq.; Wells (2011).

[257] Criminal Code Act 1995 (Australia), s. 12.3(3).

[258] Criminal Code Act 1995 (Australia), ss. 12.5, 12.6.

[259] De Maglie (2011); OECD 2004c, para. 43.

[260] De Faria Costa/Quintela de Brito 2010, 32.

[261] Boldova/Rueda (2011).

[262] See generally, Pieth 2005, 603 et seq.

[263] Henning 2009, 1426 et seq.

28.11.1 Common Law Jurisdictions

28.11.1.1 The UK and the Commonwealth

28.11.1.1.1 Procedure

The general rules of criminal procedure in the UK and the Commonwealth **treat corporations in much the same way as individuals.**[264] In **England and Wales**, a joint guidance on corporate prosecutions for offenses other than manslaughter[265] sets out **additional factors** to be considered in determining whether a corporate prosecution is in the public interest; these factors look to such matters as corporate compliance, self-reporting of wrongdoing, and the availability of civil remedies.[266] Further, the UK **Serious Fraud Office** published a guidance, in which it indicated it would consider pursuing **"civil outcomes" and "global settlements"** with "corporates" that **self-report overseas corruption**. The first such global settlement between American and British prosecutors and a corporate defendant (Innospec Ltd.) was considered *ultra vires* by the UK courts[267] and practitioners speculate that the Serious Fraud Office (UK) may revise its policy.[268] Nonetheless, the guidance is remarkable for its apparent similarity to CCL procedures and sanctions under US federal law and for the comments on corporate sentencing options and principles it drew from the UK courts.[269]

Further, the fact that corporations are often charged under **regulatory statutes** may raise special procedural issues in practice. Simplified procedures without evidence of the mental state, a reversed burden of proof for due diligence,[270] and required cooperation[271] arguably violate the **presumption of innocence** and the **privilege against self-incrimination**, such as those in the Art. 6 ECHR as incorporated into the UK's own Human Rights Act 1998.[272] If so, the question is whether such potentially powerful inhuman actors are entitled to claim these protections.[273] As it stands, the European Court of Human Rights and many common law courts have accepted that corporations may claim at least some procedural rights, such as those mentioned in Art. 6.[274] Moreover, in our view, it is **good policy to preserve basic procedural rights** in criminal proceedings against corporations. Fair procedure rules are not merely mechanisms for equalizing power imbalances between governments and defendants nor are they merely reflective of the need to preserve human dignity in a situation of coercion; equally, they respond to the **nature of the adversarial criminal proceeding** as a mechanism for negotiating competing versions of the truth and allocating legal responsibility.[275] In any case, when **small private corporations** are the subject of criminal prosecutions, it may be difficult to distinguish, in fact, between individual and corporate economic interests.[276]

28.11.1.1.2 Sanctions

When it comes to punishing corporate offenders, **fines are still the primary sanction** in the UK and the Commonwealth, though other financial and non-financial penalties are also available depending on the jurisdiction, the organization, and the offense in question.[277] The significance of fines is explained, at one level, by the **inapplicability of custodial sentences** to corporate offenders. At another level, it reflects the **dominant conception of corporate personality and corporate liability** in British and Commonwealth criminal law: if the corporation is a legal fiction which facilitates commercial collaborations, a monetary sanction may be regarded as the most appropriate punishment and incentive for corporate reform.[278] Similarly, if corporate guilt is derived from a senior individual's

---

[264] CPSEW (UK) 2010, paras. 1, 4 ("A company … should not be treated differently from an individual because of its artificial personality."); Pinto/Evans 2003, paras. 8.1 et seq.; Stark (2011).

[265] CPSEW (UK) 2010.

[266] CPSEW (UK) 2010, para. 32.

[267] *R.* v. *Innospec Ltd.* [2010] EW Misc. 7 (EWCC).

[268] Cleary/Candey 2010; Eversheds Fraud Group 2010.

[269] *R.* v. *Innospec Ltd.* [2010] EW Misc. 7 (EWCC) at paras. 39 et seq. (Thomas LJ).

[270] See above, 28.9.1.2.

[271] Pinto/Evans 2003, paras. 12.39 et seq.

[272] See generally, Pinto/Evans 2003, paras. 12.9 et seq.

[273] Arzt 2003, 457; Nijboer 1999, 317. See further, Pieth 2005, 603 et seq.; Pieth 2009, 201 et seq.

[274] Emberland 2006, 56; Pinto/Evans 2003, paras. 12.57 et seq.; van Kempen (2011); Woods/Scharffs 2002, 552. Cf. Australia, Evidence Act 1995, Act No. 2 of 1995 as amended, s. 187.

[275] Pieth 2005, 605 et seq.; Pieth 2009, 202 et seq.

[276] LCEW (UK) 2010, para. 7.10; van Kempen (2011).

[277] For the UK, see Pinto/Evans 2003, 133 et seq.; Wells 2001, 32. For Australia, see Crimes Act 1914, Act No. 12 of 1914 as amended (Crimes Act (Australia)), s. 14B; Australian Law Reform Commission (ALRC) 2006, Pt. H.30. For Canada, see Criminal Code (Canada) s. 735(1).

[278] Wells 2001, 34.

wrongdoing, there is no logical reason to require corporate cultural reform.

Given the importance of corporate fines in British and Commonwealth corporate criminal law, it is somewhat surprising that **the level of fines has been low historically**, at least in the UK.[279] For Wells, this is due primarily to the **type of offenses** for which corporations are convicted: most successful corporate prosecutions are for regulatory offenses, which do not include an element of harm and are generally tried in the lower courts.[280] At the same time, it may be symptomatic of the relative **lack of statutory or judicial guidance** on how to impose fines large enough to restrict corporate profits without endangering the entity's financial viability – and with it the livelihoods of "innocent" creditors, employees, contractors, and agents. Australian and Canadian federal legislation deals with the calculation of the maximum fine for corporate offenders but not the principles for determining which level of fine is appropriate[281]; they are vulnerable to the same criticism.

The **emphasis on fines** in the UK and the Commonwealth **may be changing**. Regulatory **statutes** already enable courts to impose a wider range of non-financial sanctions than is available under general law[282] and Commonwealth jurisdictions have identified corporate sentencing options and principles under general law as in need of reconsideration and possibly **reform**.[283] Further, in our view, the expansion of CCL rules to cover non-profit and public sector **agencies** will, in due course, prompt lawmakers to reconsider the appropriateness of fines and deterrence in punishing corporations. Also, and perhaps most significantly, the **guidances** discussed above indicate that UK prosecutors and regulators are keen to apply US-style enforcement strategies, particularly in relation to economic crimes.[284]

28.11.1.2 The US

28.11.1.2.1 Procedure

Of all the jurisdictions surveyed, the US has made the most substantial adjustments to its criminal procedure rules for corporations. Recognizing that an indictment may itself seriously threaten a corporation's financial viability, the federal government has empowered prosecutors to defer charges or forestall an investigation against a corporation by means of **deferred and non-prosecution agreements (DPAs and NPAs)**. In exercising their discretion to conclude such agreements with corporations, prosecutors are to have regard to factors determined by the US federal Department of Justice (USDOJ). The memorandum, "Bringing Criminal Charges Against Corporations," issued by **US Deputy Attorney General Holder** in 1999 (**Holder Memo**) initially listed eight company-specific and offense-specific factors, including voluntary disclosure, remedial efforts, and collateral consequences of indictment (e.g., on innocent shareholders and employees).[285]

The Holder Memo was made stricter still in 2003 by **Deputy Attorney General Thompson**.[286,287] The Thompson Memo was **criticized** for encouraging prosecutors to make adverse decisions on the basis of a corporation's refusal to **waive privileges**, to pay **large sums in settlement** and to undertake extensive (and expensive) administrative, operational, and personnel **changes**[288] often under the supervision of an **external "monitor"** with powers and functions sometimes akin to those of a probation officer.[289] Others have noted the lack of objective and well-researched **criteria** for determining the terms and measuring the effectiveness

[279] Black 2010, paras. A.15 et seq. (on fines for regulatory offenses generally); Clarkson/Keating/Cunningham 2007, 260; Wells 2001, 32 et seq.

[280] Wells 2001, 33.

[281] Crimes Act (Australia), s. 4B(3); Criminal Code (Canada) s. 735(1). See also, Crimes Legislation Amendment (Serious and Organized Crime) Act No. 2 of 2010 (Australia), Sch. 8 (increasing the maximum penalty for bribery offenses for bodies corporate without introducing principles for the application of such penalties).

[282] See, e.g., Regulatory Enforcement and Sanctions Act 2008 c. 13. See further Allens Arthur Robinson 2009, 11, n. 17; Black 2010, A.45 et seq.; Department of Justice Canada (DOJ (Canada)) 2002.

[283] ALRC 2006; DOJ (Canada) 2002; New South Wales Law Reform Commission 2003, para. 5.17.

[284] Cotton 2009.

[285] United States Department of Justice (USDOJ), Office of the Deputy Attorney General 1999, points 4, 6, 7 (emphasis added). See further, Nanda (2011).

[286] "Principles of Federal Prosecution of Business Organizations," USDOJ, Office of the Deputy Attorney General 2003.

[287] USDOJ, Office of the Deputy Attorney General 2003, Principle VIB.

[288] Hasnas 2009, 1353 et seq.; Nanda (2011). Cf. Beale 2009, 1492 et seq.

[289] Khanna/Dickinson 2007; Nanda (2011).

of such arrangements[290] and hence their **mixed effectiveness** in practice.[291]

Reform bills on deferred and non-prosecution agreements are currently before US legislators.[292] Meanwhile, Sixth Amendment arguments have been accepted by US courts in United States **v.** Stein & Ors.[293] and (implicitly) by the **successors to Deputy Attorney General Thompson**. They amended the rules relating to the conclusion of DPAs and NPAs[294] and clarified the primary responsibilities of monitors and principles for negotiating their appointment, duties, and terms in office.[295] **Commentators** have also called for the recognition of a **good faith affirmative defense** to CCL[296] or a requirement that the prosecution **prove a lack of due diligence** to prevent the offense by the corporation.[297] All the same, deferred and non-prosecution agreements remain a common means of obtaining financial payments, admissions of wrongdoing, and commitments to reforms from suspected corporate offenders in the US – all without conviction or charge.[298]

28.11.1.2.2 Sanctions

Presuming the corporation is indicted and convicted, US federal law also provides a **particularly wide range of sanctioning options**. US federal courts may impose large fines and may order corporate offenders to make restitution to identified victims of crime, to otherwise remedy the harm, to eliminate or reduce the risk of future harm (e.g., through the introduction of corporate compliance and monitoring systems) and to undertake community service.[299] The appointment of compliance monitors and advisors is particularly in vogue. The **United States Sentencing Commission's Guidelines Manual** (USSC Guidelines) includes the most detailed corporate sentencing guidelines of any jurisdictions considered here.[300] They set out general principles for corporate punishment and state how specific factors are to be weighed in determining the level of fine.[301] Amongst other things, they empower courts to make **substantial reductions** for companies that had in place **effective compliance and ethics programs** at the time of the offense.[302] For Wells, these rules on mitigation of sentence effectively provide an affirmative defense to strict vicarious corporate liability under US federal law.[303] At the very least, they evidence the deterrent and rehabilitative function of US CCL rules.

28.11.2 Civil Law Jurisdictions

28.11.2.1 Procedure

Civil law jurisdictions take a **middle road** between the minimalist or assimilationist approach of Australia and Canada and the exceptionalist approach of the United States and (to a more limited extent) England and Wales. France,[304] Germany,[305] the Netherlands,[306] Switzerland,[307] Hungary,[308] and Poland[309] have all introduced special rules for criminal proceedings against corporations. These enable individuals not only to appear for the corporation but also to exercise certain **rights on the corporation's behalf** during the proceedings. They clarify, in addition, the **competence and compellability** of other corporate "insiders" to testify against the corporation and the interaction between **charges against corporations and individuals**.

For example, an enterprise charged under **Swiss law** appears in the proceedings through a **representative** of

290 Coffee 2005; Ford/Hess 2009; United States Government Accountability Office (USGAO) 2009, 21 et seq.

291 Ford/Hess 2009, 728 et seq.

292 Nanda (2011).

293 435 F. Supp. 2d 330 (2006); aff'd 541 F. 3d 130 (2008); remedy 495 F. Supp. 2d 390 (2007). See further, Nanda (2011).

294 USDOJ, Office of the Deputy Attorney General 2006; USDOJ, Office of the Deputy Attorney General 2008b. See further, Nanda (2011).

295 USDOJ, Office of the Deputy Attorney General 2008a; USDOJ, Office of the Deputy Attorney General 2010; USDOJ, US Attorneys 1997, §§ 9–28.000 et seq. and Criminal Resource Manual, Title 9, §§ 163 and 166. See further, Nanda (2011).

296 Nanda (2011), 33; Podgor 2007.

297 Hasnas 2009, 1356 et seq.; Weissman/Newman 2007, 449 et seq.

298 Nanda (2011); USGAO 2009, 13 et seq.

299 Nanda (2011).

300 United States Sentencing Commission (USSC) 2009, Ch. 8. See further, Nanda (2011).

301 USSC 2009, Introductory Commentary and § 8 C.

302 USSC 2009, §§ 8B2.1, 8 C2.5(f).

303 Wells 2001, 35.

304 Deckert (2011).

305 Böse (2011).

306 Keulen/Gritter (2011).

307 Perrin (2011). See further, Pieth 2005.

308 Santha/Dobrocsi (2011).

309 Kulesza 2010, 6 et seq.

its choice. The representative must be an individual with unlimited power to represent the enterprise under private law and may not be a person who is him/herself accused of an offense on the same or related facts.[310] The representative has the same rights and obligations as the accused,[311] including the enterprise's privilege against self-incrimination (**the** nemo tenetur **principle**).[312] The enterprises' other human representatives are similarly non-compellable (i.e., they cannot be required to give evidence as witnesses against the enterprise), however, they may be asked to give information in another capacity (as Auskunftspersonen, i.e., informants).[313] All other employees and agents are competent and compellable – including individuals who do not exercise formal power but are nonetheless extremely well informed about executive decisions and corporate operations (e.g., **personal assistants to company officers**).[314] Similarly, a corporation defending administrative proceedings in **Germany** has the right to be heard and be represented by **one or more legal representatives** provided those individuals have not been charged in relation to the matter. Except for the representative/s, any natural person may be called as a witness against the corporation, even if his/her conduct could have been attributed to the corporation.[315]

Further, there is little to suggest that **prosecutorial discretion** has been used to obtain waivers or admissions or secure concessions from corporations without indictment or trial in civil law jurisdictions. This may be due simply to the lack of prosecutorial discretion not to charge suspects in some civil law jurisdictions (**the legality principle**) or to the failure of prosecutors to seriously consider corporate charges in exercising the discretion they are given. Responding to the latter criticism, **Hungarian legislators curtailed** prosecutorial discretion in 2008, requiring investigative authorities to "notify the prosecutor without delay" of information incriminating a legal entity.[316] Following the amendments, prosecutors lost their power to discontinue an investigation, though they retained discretion to later discontinue proceedings.[317] German officials responded to similar criticisms by announcing that they would consider introducing prosecutorial guidelines.[318] It remains to be seen whether they draw on the American (and now British) approach.

28.11.2.2 Sanctions

The sanctioning options and principles for corporate offenders in civil law jurisdictions are also broadly similar to those in common law jurisdictions. All the jurisdictions surveyed enable their courts to impose **fines** on corporate offenders[319] and many enable (or require) them to **confiscate or forfeit the proceeds and/or instrumentalities** of offenses.[320] The rules for calculating the fine and determining the things liable for confiscation and so the possible quantum of financial penalties, differ considerably between the jurisdictions and, within jurisdictions, between offenses. Some jurisdictions specify a minimum and/or maximum,[321] whilst others multiply the penalty for individual offenders.[322]

As to **sentencing factors**, in addition to general considerations relating to the offense, the offender, the investigation, and the proceeding, courts in a number of civil law jurisdictions may have regard to the economic capacity of the corporation, the impact of the fine on third parties, and the actual or intended

310 Pieth 2005, 609.

311 Art. 100 *quinquies*, paragraph 2, first sentence. See Pieth 2005, 610.

312 Pieth 2005, 610.

313 Pieth 2005, 611 et seq.

314 Pieth 2005, 612 et seq.

315 Böse (2011).

316 Santha/Dobrocsi (2011).

317 GRECO 2006, para. 85; Santha/Dobrocsi (2011).

318 OECD 2003, paras. 122 et seq.

319 The exception was Spain. Until reforms to its criminal code were enacted, Spanish courts could only fine individuals as a result of which corporations would be jointly liable. See Boldova/Rueda (2011).

320 Belgium, France, Germany, Hungary, Italy, the Netherlands, Poland, Switzerland, and Portugal. On Belgium, see Bihain/Masset 2010, 20; on France, see Deckert (2011); on Germany, see Böse (2011); on Hungary, see Santha/Dobrocsi (2011); on Italy, see de Maglie (2011); on the Netherlands, see Keulen/Gritter (2011); on Poland, see Kulesza 2010, 5; on Switzerland, see Perrin (2011); on Portugal, Faria Costa/Quintela de Brito 2010, 40 et seq.

321 Chile, Belgium (crimes punishable with life imprisonment), Germany, Hungary, the Netherlands, and Poland. On Chile, see Salvo (2011); on Germany, see Böse (2011); on Hungary, see Santha/Dobrocsi (2011); on the Netherlands, see Keulen/Gritter (2011); on Poland, see Kulesza 2010, 5.

322 France and Portugal. On France, see Deckert (2011); on Portugal, see de Faria Costa/Quintela de Brito 2010, 35 et seq.

financial benefit to the corporation from the offense.[323] Recalling the American approach, **Italy** has enabled its courts to **reduce a fine by up to half** if the corporation makes restitution to victims, otherwise attempts to remedy the consequence of the offense and undertakes **preventative reforms** to its organizational model.[324] Corporate compliance systems and subsequent remedial or reparative actions are also considered in the German administrative penalty regime, though some argue that this is inconsistent with the imputation of liability.[325]

In addition, many of the civil law jurisdictions surveyed provided **alternative non-financial penalties** for corporations. **France** pioneered this approach, developing an elaborate system of restraint orders for corporate offenders, which was later the blueprint for the penalties recommended in the **EU Second Protocol** to the Convention on the Protection of the ECs' Financial Interests.[326] Thus, when financial sanctions (alone) are inappropriate,[327] French courts may enjoin corporations from performing specific professional or social activities, from tendering for public contracts and from engaging in certain types of financial transactions; they may also order the closure of one or more of its establishments or the dissolution of the corporation itself (the corporate death sentence).[328] French courts may also appoint a mandataire de justice who, like the US corporate monitor, supervises the measures taken by the corporation to prevent the repetition of the breach.[329] Other jurisdictions similarly provide for temporary injunctions on trade, business, and other related activities,[330] exclusion from eligibility for public contracts and funding,[331] license restrictions or cancellations,[332] supervision or corporation probation orders,[333] publication of the sentence,[334] and dissolution or deregistration.[335] Some of these penalties are ordered as part of the criminal or quasi-criminal proceeding, others may be imposed as an ancillary consequences by regulatory bodies.

28.12 Conclusions

28.12.1 Historical Concepts

At the beginning of this chapter, we introduced three models of corporate criminal or quasi-criminal liability: **vicarious liability**, which developed from *respondeat superior*; the **identification of the corporation with its directing mind and will**; and a **holistic or objective** model that emphasizes the corporate structure itself. These, we noted, emerged around the world in response to historical events and changing attitudes towards corporate risk and regulation, and these theories shape the substantive and procedural treatment of the corporation.

[323] France, Italy, Germany, Hungary, Poland, and Portugal. On France, see OECD 2004a, para. 150, Deckert (2011); on Italy, see OECD 2004c, para. 204; on Germany, see OECD 2003, para. 124, Böse (2011); on Poland, see Kulesza 2010, 6; on Portugal, see de Faria Costa/Quintela de Brito 2010, 37. Cf. Hungary, see further Santha/Dobrocsi (2011).

[324] De Maglie (2011); OECD 2004c, para. 204.

[325] Böse (2011).

[326] Second Protocol to the EU Convention on the Protection of the ECs' Financial Interests, Art. 4(1).

[327] Deckert (2011).

[328] Ibid.

[329] Ibid.

[330] Chile, Belgium, Italy, Hungary, Poland, and Portugal. On Chile, see Savlo 2010; on Belgium, see Bihain/Masset 2010, 21; on Hungary, see Santha/Dobrocsi (2011); on Italy, see de Maglie (2011); on Poland, see Kulesza 2010, 5 et seq.; on Portugal, see de Faria Costa/Quintela de Brito 2010, 40.

[331] Chile, Poland, and Portugal. On Chile, see Savlo 2010; on Poland, see Kulesza 2010, 5; on Portugal, de Faria Costa/Quintela de Brito 2010, 40. Belgium and Germany indirectly exclude companies with criminal records from public contracting and licensing: on Belgium, OECD 2005d, para. 134; on Germany, see Böse (2011).

[332] Italy and Portugal. On Italy, see de Maglie (2011); on Portugal, see de Faria Costa/Quintela de Brito 2010, 40.

[333] Belgium, Italy, and the Netherlands (for some economic crimes). On Belgium, see Bihain/Masset 2010, 21 et seq.; on Italy, see de Maglie (2011); on the Netherlands, see Keulen/Gritter (2011);

[334] Chile, Belgium, Italy, the Netherlands, Poland, Portugal, and Switzerland. On Chile, see Salvo (2011); on Belgium, see Bihain/Masset 2010, 21; on Italy, see de Maglie (2011); on the Netherlands, see Keulen/Gritter (2011); on Poland, see Kulesza 2010, 6; on Portugal, see de Faria Costa/Quintela de Brito 2010, 40; on Switzerland, see Perrin (2011). Cf. Hungary and Germany, see further on Hungary, Santha/Dobrocsi (2011); on Germany, see Böse (2011).

[335] Chile, Belgium, Germany, Hungary, and Portugal. On Chile, see Salvo (2011); on Belgium, see Bihain/Masset 2010, 21; on Germany, see Böse (2011); on Hungary, see Santha/Dobrocsi (2011); on Portugal, see Faria Costa/Quintela de Brito 2010, 35 et seq.

28.12.2 Convergence

To summarize these developments in Europe and the Americas in the last two decades is to observe the **adoption and extension** of CCL and equivalent non-criminal liability rules and their **apparent convergence** around the notion of organizational systems and culture as the loci of corporate fault.[336] Our survey of national corporate criminal liability rules in selected common and civil law jurisdictions enables us to draw the following **specific conclusions**:

First, it would seem that corporate criminal liability rules generally apply to **legal persons and unincorporated groups that carry out an enterprise**. Though a number of civil law jurisdictions restrict CCL rules to enterprises with commercial goals, all surveyed common law countries and some civil law countries are prepared to apply criminal law norms to non-profit non-government entities, at least when they are engaged in trade and commerce, with some exclusions for the state.

Second, as to the offenses for which organizations may be liable, all jurisdictions that recognize corporate criminal or quasi-criminal liability allow corporations to be held liable for crimes of *mens rea*. There is some discomfort, particularly in civil law jurisdictions, with the notion that corporations may be liable as principals for all crimes, especially those that do not reflect "typical" corporate risks. That said, legislators in common law and civil law jurisdictions alike have been willing to recognize corporate liability for a variety of offenses that protect "private" interests under domestic law. On this basis, we observe a general if sometimes tentative **expansion of the notion of corporate crime** – from crimes committed in the context of industrial and commercial activity, to crimes committed in the context of a group, which facilitates or at least stands to benefit from the individual wrongdoing.

Third, corporations can be charged with the misconduct of an **increasingly broad group of human beings**. An emerging issue is the scope and basis for **corporate-to-corporate liability** under national law.

[336] See generally, Heine 1995, 248 et seq.; Pieth 2007a, 181 et seq.; Wells 2001, 140 et seq. On Australia, see Wells 2001, 137; on Switzerland, see Pieth 2004.

Fourth, the vast majority of jurisdictions consider the **adequacy of corporate compliance systems** and the **relationship between the corporate offense and objectives** at some point. American criminal lawyers have taken the most innovative – and controversial – approach to the issue, imposing liability without fault but allowing corporations to mitigate their punishment or to avoid indictment on the basis of their compliance systems. Courts in Britain and the Commonwealth have generally been less receptive to evidence of compliance systems, though recent law reforms and reform proposals, prosecutions guidelines, and civil actions indicate that UK lawmakers and prosecutors may see some merit in the US approach. In civil law jurisdictions, these considerations are usually embedded in criteria for determining whether a natural person's offense can be attributed to the company or (as in Switzerland) the company can be treated as having behaved "criminally" itself. A minority of civil law jurisdictions have provided adequate systems defenses.

Fifth, the adoption of CCL rules has precipitated **modifications to principles of criminal procedure and punishment** in many jurisdictions. To accommodate corporate defendants, many states have refashioned their rules on representation, the competence and compellability of witnesses, the role of the parties in the proceeding, and the privileges of the accused. Some have gone to considerable lengths to provide appropriate alternatives to imprisonment and probation, which are available in relation to individual offenders. Again, in both respects, US federal law stands out even though it is not uniformly admired by American legislators and scholars.

28.12.3 Implications

The **adoption, extension, and convergence** of European and American CCL rules is **significant for stakeholders** in, and observers of, corporate regulatory processes:

For **company promoters and managers**, the frequency of CCL or equivalent administrative rules in diverse jurisdictions **reduces the scope for "forum shopping,"** i.e., the selection of home and host states less likely to prosecute corporate wrongdoing. In this way, CCL laws **complement extraterritorial**

jurisdictional rules, which enable host states to prosecute crimes committed abroad, and **voluntary corporate social responsibility initiatives**, which encourage legal actors to adhere to governance standards throughout their groups and operations. At the same time, as CCL models converge around notions of defective corporate systems or culture, and corporate penalties and prosecution strategies around corporate compliance reforms, it becomes **possible for MNEs to standardize their internal compliance strategies** internationally, potentially **reducing compliance costs and actual incidence of wrongdoing**. Such cost savings may support other incentives for corporations to adopt more exacting governance standards.[337]

For **regulators and commentators**, the spread of CCL rules based on notions of corporate culture or organization is likely to lead to **greater interest in the actual impact of the criminal or quasi-criminal liability norms** on corporate behavior. Do such liability rules reduce the likelihood that individuals, communities, and natural environments will be put at risk by corporate operations?[338] And, in any case, do they adequately reflect community condemnation of such events when they occur? In answering these questions, academics and policy makers alike will face **other difficult questions**, including the appropriateness of public-*cum*-moral condemnation as a goal of the corporatized criminal law; the means for measuring the effectiveness of CCL rules; and the place for normative checks-and-balances in an increasingly future-oriented and rehabilitative criminal law.[339]

28.12.4 Outlook

The **continued extension, expansion, and convergence of CCL rules** in Europe and the Americas depends on a number of factors, among them, the willingness of national legislators and judges to embrace the regulatory/preventative dimension of criminal law and to recognize the legitimacy of collaborations between public prosecutors and corporate defendants as mediated by technical experts and standards. A further and related question is whether CCL or comparable rules are likely to be introduced and/or extended and enforced in **states with growing markets and corporate groups**,[340] such as Brazil, the Russian Federation, India, and the People's Republic of China (**BRIC**). On the one hand, if the European and American experience is any guide, industrialization, economic globalization, and international regulation may prompt BRIC lawmakers to make greater use of CCL rules in controlling corporate risks and power. Moreover, the proliferation and enforcement of legal rules in European and American states may make it politically more difficult for them to refuse to recognize and punish corporate wrongdoing, regardless of any international legal obligation to do so.[341] On the other hand, CCL rules are only one means of approaching corporate control. They are not yet a universal feature of national criminal laws and, where they exist, they are often new and/or sporadically enforced. Furthermore, factors peculiar to the BRIC states and the international economic and political system of the early twenty-first century, may militate against the adoption, expansive interpretation or aggressive enforcement of criminal or quasi-criminal corporate liability laws in emerging markets. This could, in turn, affect the willingness of lawmakers and enforcers in Europe and the Americas to extend and/or enforce their own CCL rules, as well as their conceptions of the regulatory alternatives.

[337] Coffee 1999b, 663 et seq., 692.

[338] Laufer 2006, 184 et seq.; Pitts 2009, 379.

[339] Henning 2009, 1419 et seq., 1426 et seq.

[340] The Economist 2010, 3 et seq.; Wagstyl 2010, 7.

[341] Cf. Bismuth 2010, 226.

List of References

Allens Arthur Robinson. 2008. *"Corporate Culture" as a basis of the criminal liability of corporations: Report for the United Nations Special Representative of the Secretary General on Human Rights and Business*, available at www.reports-and-materials.org/Allens-Arthur-Robinson-Corporate-Culture-paper-for-Ruggie-Feb-2008.pdf.

American Law Institute. 1962. Model penal code: Changes and editorial corrections in 4 May 1962: Proposed official draft, Philadelphia.

Arzt, G. 2003. Schutz juristischer personen gegen selbstbelastung. *Juristenzeitung* 58: 456.

Asia/Pacific Group on Money Laundering (APG on Money Laundering). 2005. APG Mutual Evaluation Report on India against 2003 FATF 40 recommendations and 9 special recommendations, Sydney.

Australian Law Reform Commission. 2006. *Same crime, same time: Sentencing of federal offenders*, Report 103, Sydney.

Beale, S.S. 2009. A response to the critics of corporate criminal liability. *American Criminal Law Review* 46: 1481.

Beck U. 1986. *Risikogesellscaft: auf dem Weg in eine andere Moderne*. Frankfurt am Main.

Beck U. 1998. *Was ist Globalisierung?*. Frankfurt am Main.

Belcher, A. 2006. Imagining how a company thinks: What is corporate culture? *Deakin Law Review* 11: 1.

Bihain L., and Masset A. 2010. *La responsabilite penale des personnes morales en droit: Report to the XVIIIth International Congress of Comparative Law*, Washington, DC.

Bismuth, R. 2010. Mapping a responsibility of corporations for violations of international humanitarian law sailing between international and domestic legal orders. *Denver Journal of International Law and Policy* 38: 203.

Black J. 2010. Appendix A: A review of enforcement techniques. In: *Law Commission of England and Wales (LCEW (UK)), Criminal liability in regulatory contexts: a consultation paper*, Consultation paper no. 195, London, 150.

Boldova, M.A., and M.A. Rueda. 2011. La responsabilidad de las personas jurídicas en el derecho penal español. In *Corporate criminal liability: Emergence, convergence, and risk*, ed. M. Pieth and R. Ivory. Dordrecht: Springer.

Böse, M. 2011. Corporate criminal liability in Germany. In *Corporate criminal liability: Emergence, convergence, and risk*, ed. M. Pieth and R. Ivory. Dordrecht: Springer.

Braum, S. 2008. Le principe de culpabilité et la responsabilité pénale des personnes morales, remarques relatives au projet de lois luxembourgeois. In *Corporate criminal liability in Europe*, ed. S. Adam, N. Colette-Basecqz, and M. Nihoul. Brussels: Projucit. 227.

Cartwright, P. 2010. 'Appendix B: Corporate criminal liability: Models of intervention and liability in consumer law'. In *LCEW (UK), Criminal liability in regulatory contexts: A consultation paper*, Consultation paper no. 195, London, 187.

Chen, J. 2008. *Chinese law: Context and transformation*. Leiden: Martinus Nijhoff Publishers.

Clarkson, C.M.V., H.M. Keating, and S.R. Cunningham. 2007. *Clarkson and Keating criminal law: Text and materials*, 6th ed. London: Sweet & Maxwell.

Cleary, S., and Candey, L. 2010. *'Who's watching you? Rise of corporate monitoring'*, available at <www.inhouselawyer.co.uk>.

Clough, J. 2008. Symposium: Corporate liability for grave breaches of international law. *Brooklyn Law Journal of International Law* 33: 899.

Coffee, J.C. 1999a. Corporate criminal liability: An introduction and comparative survey. In *Criminal responsibility of legal and collective entities*, ed. A. Eser, G. Heine, and B. Huber, 9. Freiburg im Breisgau: Edition Iuscrim.[cited as Coffee 1999a].

Coffee, J.C. 1999b. The future as history: The prospects for global convergence in corporate governance and its implications. *Northwestern University Law Review* 93: 641.[cited as Coffee 1999b].

Coffee, J.C. 2005. Prosecutorial experiments; federal "Deferred Prosecutions Agreements" with corporations are being tailored to the pet projects of government lawyers. *Boward Daily Business Review* 51(207): 12.

Cotton, J. 2009. 'A new, more American world?'. *International Financial Law Review: Supplement – The 2009 Guide to Litigation*, available at <www.iflr.com>.

Crown Prosecutions Service of England and Wales (CPSEW (UK)). 2010. 'Corporate Prosecutions' (last updated April 21, 2010), available at <www.cps.gov.uk/legal/a_to_c/corporate_prosecutions/#a10>.

De Faria Costa, J.F., and Quintela de Brito, T. 2010. *Criminal and administrative liability of the collective entities in Portugal: Report to the XVIIIth International Congress of Comparative Law*, Washington, DC.

De Maglie, C. 2011. Societas delinquere potest? The Italian solution. In *Corporate criminal liability: Emergence, convergence, and risk*, ed. M. Pieth and R. Ivory. Dordrecht: Springer.

Deckert, K. 2011. Corporate criminal liability in France. In *Corporate criminal liability: Emergence, convergence, and risk*, ed. M. Pieth and R. Ivory. Dordrecht: Springer.

Department of Justice Canada (DOJ (Canada)). 2002. Corporate criminal liability: Discussion paper, available at <www.justice.gc.ca>.

DiMento, J.F.C., and G. Geis. 2005. Corporate criminal liability in the United States. In *Research handbook on corporate legal responsibility*, ed. S. Tully. Cheltenham: Edward Elgar.

Drew, K. for UNICORN. 2005. Complying with the OECD anti-bribery convention: Corporate criminal liability and corruption: Exploring the legal options: Seminar held on the 12th of December 2005 hosted by The Crown Prosecution Service, available at <www.againstcorruption.org>.

Emberland, M. 2006. *The human rights of companies: Exploring the structure of ECHR protections*. Oxford: Oxford University Press.

Eversheds Fraud Group. 2010. Fraud and financial crime E-briefing (2010), available at <www.eversheds.com/uk/home/services/fraud_and_financial_crime/ebriefings.page?>.

FATF. 2008. *Third mutual evaluation report anti-money laundering and combating the financial of terrorism Hong Kong, China*, July 11, 2008, Paris.

Faure, M. 1999. Criminal responsibilities of legal and collective entities: Developments in Belgium. In *Criminal responsibility of legal and collective entities*, ed. A. Eser, G. Heine, and B. Huber, 105. Freiburg im Breisgau: Edition Iuscrim.

Ferguson, J. 1999. The basis for criminal responsibility of collective entities in Canada. In *Criminal responsibility of legal and collective entities*, ed. A. Eser, G. Heine, and B. Huber, 153. Freiburg im Breisgau: Edition Iuscrim.

Fifield, A. 2010. Oil spill: Senators scorn efforts to pass blame, *Financial Times*, May 12, 2010, 6.

Financial Action Task Force (FATF). 2007. *First mutual evaluation report on anti-money laundering and combating the financing of terrorism: People's republic of China*, June 29, 2007, Paris.

Ford, C., and D. Hess. 2009. Can corporate monitorships improve corporate compliance? *Journal of Corporation Law* 34: 679.

Giddens, A. 1991. *Modernity and self-identity: Self and society in the late modern age*. Stanford: Stanford University Press.

Giddens, A. 1999. Risk and responsibility. *Modern Law Review* 62: 1.

Gobert, J. 2008. The corporate manslaughter and corporate homicide Act 2007 – Thirteen years in the making but was it worth the wait? *Modern Law Review* 71: 413.

Godinho, J.A.F. 2010. *Country report Macau SAR: Report to the XVIIIth international congress of comparative law*, Washington, DC.

GRECO. 2006. *Second evaluation round: Evaluation report on Hungary*, March 10, 2006, Strasbourg.

Group of States against Corruption (GRECO). 2004. *Second evaluation round: Evaluation report on Poland*, May 14, 2004, Strasbourg.

Hasnas, J. 2009. The centenary of a mistake: One hundred years of corporate criminal liability. *American Criminal Law Review* 46: 1329.

Heine, G. 1995. *Die strafrechtliche Verantwortlichkeit von Unternehmen*. Baden-Baden: Nomos.

Heine, G. 2000. Corporate liability rules in civil law jurisdictions: Room document DAFFE|IME|BR (2000) 23. OECD, Paris.

Heine, G. 2008. Criminal liability of enterprises in Switzerland – A new programme: Organisational deficiencies. In *Corporate criminal liability in Europe*, ed. S. Adam, N. Colette-Basecqz, and M. Nihoul, 303. Brussels: Projucit.

Henning, P.J. 2009. Corporate criminal liability and the potential for rehabilitation. *American Criminal Law Review* 46: 1417.

Hilf, M. 2008. Section 2 – La Responsabilite Penale des Personnes Morales en Autriche Regime de law Nouvelle Loi Aurichienne sur La Responsabilite des Entreprises. In *Corporate criminal liability in Europe*, ed. S. Adam, N. Colette-Basecqz, and M. Nihoul, 45. Brussels: Projucit.

Humanitarian Accountability Partnership International. 2008. *The 2008 humanitarian accountability report*, Geneva.

Jelínek, J., and K. Beran. 2011. Why the Czech Republic does not (yet) recognize corporate criminal liability: A description of unsuccessful law reforms. In *Corporate criminal liability: Emergence, convergence, and risk*, ed. M. Pieth and R. Ivory. Dordrecht: Springer.

Jiachen, L. 1999. The legislation and judicial practice on punishment of unit crime in China. In *Criminal responsibility of legal and collective entities*, ed. A. Eser, G. Heine, and B. Huber, 71. Freiburg im Breisgau: Edition Iuscrim.

Keulen, B.F., and E. Gritter. 2011. Corporate criminal liability in the Netherlands. In *Corporate criminal liability: Emergence, convergence, and risk*, ed. M. Pieth and R. Ivory. Dordrecht: Springer.

Khanna, V., and T.L. Dickinson. 2007. The corporate monitor: The new corporate Czar? *Michigan Law Review* 105: 1713.

Kulesza, W. 2010. *Corporate criminal liability in Poland: Report to the XVIIIth international congress of comparative law*, Washington, DC.

Langón Cuñarro, M. and Montano, P.J. 2010. *Corporate liability in Uruguay? Report to the XVIIIth International Congress of Comparative Law*, Washington, DC.

Laufer, W.S. 2006. *Corporate bodies and guilty minds: The failure of corporate criminal liability*. Chicago: University of Chicago Press.

LCEW (UK). 1996. *Legislating the criminal code: Involuntary Manslaughter*, Report no. 237, London.

LCEW (UK). 2008. *Tenth programme of law reform*, Law com. no. 311, London. [cited as LCEW 2008a]

LCEW (UK). 2008. *Reforming bribery*, Report no. 313, London. [cited as LCEW 2008b]

LCEW (UK). 2010. *Criminal liability in regulatory contexts: A consultation paper*, Consultation paper no. 195, London.

Lloyd, R., Warren, S., and Hammer, M. 2008. *2008 Global accountability report*, London.

Manacorda, S. 2008. *Imputatione collettiva et responsibiliá personale, Uno studio sui paradigmi ascrittivi nel di rito penale internationale*, Torrino.

Manozzi, G., and F. Consulich. 2008. Criminal liability of corporations in the Italian legal system, an overview. In *Corporate criminal liability in Europe*, ed. S. Adam, N. Colette-Basecqz, and M. Nihoul, 207. Brussels: Projucit.

McCormick, J. 2009. Enlargement and the Meaning of Europe. In *The SAGE handbook of European studies*, ed. C. Rumford, 209. Los Angeles: SAGE.

MENAFATF. 2008. *Mutual evaluation report anti-money laundering and combating the financial of Terrorism United Arab Emirates*, April 9, 2008, Bahrain. [cited as MENAFATF 2008b]

Middle East and North Africa Financial Action Taskforce (MENAFATF). 2008. *Mutual evaluation report anti-money laundering and combating the financial of terrorism Qatar*, April 8, 2008, Bahrain. [cited as MENAFATF 2008a]

Mylonopoulos, C. (2010), *Corporate Criminal Liability and the Greek Law: Report to the XVIIIth International Congress of Comparative Law*, Washington, DC.

Nanda, V.P. 2011. Corporate criminal liability in the United States: Is a new approach warranted? In *Corporate criminal liability: Emergence, convergence, and risk*, ed. M. Pieth and R. Ivory. Dordrecht: Springer.

New South Wales Law Reform Commission. 2003. *Sentencing: Corporate offenders*, Report 102, Sydney.

Nielsen, G.T. 1999. Criminal liability of collective entities – The Danish model. In *Criminal responsibility of legal and collective entities*, ed. A. Eser, G. Heine, and B. Huber, 189. Freiburg im Breisgau: Edition Iuscrim.

Nijboer, J.F. 1999. A plea for a systematic approach in developing criminal procedural law concerning the investigation, prosecution and adjudication of corporate entities. In *Criminal responsibility of legal and collective entities*, ed. A. Eser, G. Heine, and B. Huber, 303. Freiburg im Breisgau: Edition Iuscrim.

OECD (Organization for Economic Cooperation and Development). 2000. *Belgium: Review of implementation of the convention and the 1997 recommendation*, June 27, 2000, Paris. [cited as OECD 2000a]

OECD. 2000. *France: Review of implementation of the convention and the 1997 recommendation*, December 2000, Paris. [cited as OECD 2000b]

OECD. 2003. *Germany: Phase 2 report on the application of the convention on combating bribery of foreign public officials in international business transactions and the 1997 recommendation on combating bribery in international business transactions*, June 4, 2003, Paris.

OECD. 2004. *France: Phase 2 report on the application of the convention on combating bribery of foreign public officials in international business transactions and the 1997 recommendation on combating bribery in international business transactions*, January 22, 2004, Paris. [cited as OECD 2004a]

OECD. 2004. *Korea: Phase 2 report on the application of the convention on combating bribery of foreign public officials in international business transactions and the 1997 recommendation on combating bribery in international business transactions*, November 5, 2004, Paris. [cited as OECD 2004b]

OECD. 2004. *Italy: Phase 2 report on the application of the convention on combating bribery of foreign public officials in international business transactions and the 1997 recommendation on combating bribery in international business transactions*, November 29, 2004, Paris. [cited as 2004c]

OECD. 2005. *Japan: Phase 2 report on the application of the convention on combating bribery of foreign public officials in international business transactions and the 1997 recommendation on combating bribery in international business transactions*, March 7, 2005, Paris. [cited as OECD 2005a]

OECD. 2005. *United Kingdom: Phase 2 report on the application of the convention on combating bribery of foreign public officials in international business transactions and the 1997 recommendation on combating bribery in international business transactions*, March 17, 2005, Paris. [cited as OECD 2005b]

OECD. 2005. *Hungary: Phase 2 report on the application of the convention on combating bribery of foreign public officials in international business transactions and the 1997 recommendation on combating bribery in international business transactions*, May 6, 2005, Paris. [cited as OECD 2005c]

OECD. 2005. *Belgium: Phase 2 report on the application of the convention on combating bribery of foreign public officials in international business transactions and the 1997 recommendation on combating bribery in international business transactions*, July 21, 2005, Paris. [cited as OECD 2005d]

OECD. 2007. *Poland: Phase 2 report on the application of the convention on combating bribery of foreign public officials in international business transactions and the 1997 recommendation on combating bribery in international business transactions*, January 18, 2007, Paris. [cited as OECD 2007a]

OECD. 2007. *Brazil: Phase 2 report on the application of the convention on combating bribery of foreign public officials in international business transactions and the 1997 recommendation on combating bribery in international business transactions*, December 7, 2007, Paris. [cited as OECD 2007b]

OECD. 2008. *South Africa: Phase 1 review of implementation of the convention and 1997 revised recommendation*, June 20, 2008, Paris. [cited as OECD 2008a]

OECD. 2008. *United Kingdom: Phase 2* bis *report on the application of the convention on combating bribery of foreign public officials in international business transactions and the 1997 recommendation on combating bribery in international business transactions*, October 16, 2008, Paris. [cited as OECD 2008b]

OECD. 2009. *Czech Republic: Phase 2 follow-up report on the implementation of the phase 2 recommendations: Application of the convention on combating bribery of foreign public officials in international business transactions and the 1997 revised recommendations on combating briber in international business transactions*, February 13, 2009, Paris. [cited as OECD 2009a]

OECD. 2009. *Israel: Phase 1 review of implementation of the convention and the 1997 revised recommendation*, March 19, 2009, Paris. [cited as OECD 2009b]

OECD. 2009. *Turkey: Phase 2* bis *report on the application of the convention on combating bribery of foreign public officials in international business transactions and the 1998 recommendation on combating bribery in international business transactions*, June 18, 2009, Paris. [cited as OECD 2009c]

OECD. 2010. OECD *demands the Slovak Republic establish corporate liability for foreign bribery* (press release), January 18, 2010, available at <www.oced.org>.

Parliament. 2009. *Joint committee on the Draft Bribery Bill: First report of session 2008–09: Volume 1 together with formal minutes*, HL Paper 115-I, HC 430-I, July 28, 2009, London.

Partnerships UK, 'Home' and 'About PUK: Shareholders', available at <www.partnershipsuk.org.uk>.

Passas, N. 1999. Globalization, criminogenic asymmetries and economic crime. *European Journal of Law Reform* 1(4): 399.

Perrin, B. 2011. La responsabilité pénale de l'entreprise en droit suisse. In *Corporate criminal liability: Emergence, convergence, and risk*, ed. M. Pieth and R. Ivory. Dordrecht: Springer.

Pieth, M. 2003. Die strafrechtliche verantwortung des unternehmens. *Schweizerische Zeitschrift für Strafrecht* 121: 353.

Pieth, M. 2004. Risikomanagement und strafrecht: Organisationsversagen als vorraussetzung der Unternehmenshaftung. In *Festgabe zum Schweizerischen Juristentag 2004*, ed. T. Sutter-Somm et al., 597. Basel: Helbing and Lichtenhahn.

Pieth, M. 2005. Strafverfahren gegen das Unternehmen. In *Menschengerechts Strafrecht: Festschrift für Albin Eser zum 70*, ed. J. Arnold et al., 599. Munich: Geburtstag.

Pieth, M. 2007a. Article 2. The responsibility of legal persons. In *The OECD convention on bribery, a commentary*, ed. M. Pieth, L.A. Low, and P.J. Cullen, 173. Cambridge: Cambridge University Press.[cited as Pieth 2007a]

Pieth, M. 2007b. Introduction. In *The OECD convention on bribery, a commentary*, ed. M. Pieth, L.A. Low, and P.J. Cullen, 3. Cambridge: Cambridge University Press.[cited as Pieth 2007b]

Pieth, M. 2009. *Schweizerisches strafprozessrecht: Grundriss für studium und praxis*. Basel: Helbing Lichtenhahn.

Pinto, A., and M. Evans. 2003. *Corporate criminal liability*. London: Sweet and Maxwell.

Pitts, J.W. 2009. Corporate social responsibility: Current status and future evolution. *Rutgers Journal of Law & Public Policy* 6: 334.

Podgor, E.S. 2007. A new corporate world mandates a "Good Faith" affirmative defense. *American Criminal Law Review* 44: 1537.

Prittwitz, C. 1993. *Strafrecht und Risiko*. Frankfurt am Main: V. Klostermann.

Ruggie, J.G. 2007. Business and human rights: The evolving international agenda. *American Journal of International Law* 101: 819.

Sacerdoti, G. 2003. La Convenzione OCSE del 1997 e la sua laboriosa attuazione in Italia. In *Responsabilità d'impresa e strumenti internazionali anticorruzione: Dale Convenzione* OCSE 1997 al Decreto no. 231/2001, ed. G. Sacerdoti, Milano.

Salvo, N. 2011. Principales aspectos de la nueva de responsabilidad penal de las personas jurídicas en Chile (Ley No. 20.393). In *Corporate criminal liability: Emergence, convergence, and risk*, ed. M. Pieth and R. Ivory. Dordrecht: Springer.

Santha, F., and S. Dobrocsi. 2011. Corporate criminal liability in Hungary. In *Corporate criminal liability: Emergence, convergence, and risk*, ed. M. Pieth and R. Ivory. Dordrecht: Springer.

Serious Fraud Office (UK). 2009. *Approach of the serious fraud office to dealing with overseas corruption* (July 21, 2009), available at <http://www.sfo.gov.uk/media/107247/approach%20of%20the%20serious%20fraud%20office%20v3.pdf>.

Shibahara, K. 1999. Le droit japonais de la responsabilité pénale, en particulier la responsabilité pénale de la personne morale. In *Criminal responsibility of legal and collective entities*, ed. A. Eser, G. Heine, and B. Huber, 39. Freiburg im Breisgau: Edition Iuscrim.

Stark, F. 2011. Corporate criminal liability in Scotland: The problems with a piecemeal approach. In *Corporate criminal liability: Emergence, convergence, and risk*, ed. M. Pieth and R. Ivory. Dordrecht: Springer.

Stratenwerth, G. 2005. *Schweizerisches Strafrecht, Allgemeiner Teil I: Die Straftat*. Bern: Stämpfli.

Sunkin, M. 2003. Crown immunity from criminal liability in English law. *Public Law*, 716.

The Economist. 2010. A special report on banking in emerging markets: They might be giants, *The Economist* 395, May 15, 2010.

Thompson, R.C., A. Ramasastry, and M. Taylor. 2009. Transnational corporate responsibility for the 21st century: Translating Unocal: The expanding web of liability for business entities implicated in international crimes. *George Washington International Law Review* 40: 841.

USDOJ (United States Department of Justice), Office of the Deputy Attorney General. 1999. *Memorandum from the Deputy Attorney General Eric Holder to all component Heads of Department and United States Attorneys, 'Bringing Criminal Charges Against Corporations'*, June 16, 1999, available at <http://www.justice.gov/criminal/fraud/documents/reports/1999/charging-corps.PDF>.

USDOJ, Office of the Deputy Attorney General. 2003. *Memorandum from Larry D. Thompson, Deputy Attorney General, to Heads of Department Components, United States Attorneys, 'Principles of Federal Prosecution of Business Organizations'*, January 20, 2003, available at <www.justice.gov/dag/cftf/corporate_guidelines.htm>.

USDOJ, Office of the Deputy Attorney General. 2006. *Memorandum from Paul J. McNulty, Deputy Attorney General, to Heads of Department Components, United States Attorneys, 'Principles of Federal Prosecution of Business Organizations'*, December 12, 2006, available at <www.justice.gov/dag/speeches/2006/mcnulty_memo.pdf>.

USDOJ, Office of the Deputy Attorney General. 2008. *Memorandum from Craig S. Morford, Acting Deputy Attorney General, for Heads of Department Components, United States Attorneys, 'Selection and Use of Monitors in Deferred Prosecution Agreements and Non-Prosecution Agreements with Corporations'*, March 7, 2008, available at <www.justice.gov/usao/eousa/foia_reading_room/usam/title9/crm00163.htm>. [cited as USDOJ, Office of the Deputy Attorney General 2008a]

USDOJ, Office of the Deputy Attorney General. 2008. *Memorandum from Mark Filip, Deputy Attorney General, to Heads of Department Components, United States Attorneys, 'Principles of Federal Prosecution of Business Organizations'*, August 28, 2008, <www.justice.gov/dag/readingroom/dag-memo-08282008.pdf>. [cited as USDOJ, Office of the Deputy Attorney General 2008b]

USDOJ, Office of the Deputy Attorney General. 2010. *Memorandum from Gary G. Grindler Acting Deputy Attorney General, 'Additional Guidance on the Use of Monitors in Deferred Prosecution Agreements and Non-Prosecution Agreements with Corporations'*, available at <www.justice.gov/usao/eousa/foia_reading_room/usam/title9/crm00166.htm>.

USDOJ, US Attorneys. 1997. *United States Attorney's Manual (USAM)*, as revised and amended, available at <www.justice.gov/usao/eousa/foia_reading_room/usam/title9/28mcrm.htm#9-28.800>.

United States Government Accountability Office (USGAO). 2009. *Report to congressional requesters, corporate crime: DOJ has taken steps to better track its use of deferred and non-prosecution agreements but should evaluate effectiveness GAO-10-110*, available at <www.gao.gov>.

United States Sentencing Commission (USSC). 2009. *Guidelines manual*, September 15, 2009, in force November 1, 2009, and as amended November 1, 2010, available at <www.ussc.gov>.

Van Kempen, P.H. 2011. The recognition of legal persons in international human rights instruments: Protection against and through criminal justice? In *Corporate criminal liability: Emergence, convergence, and risk*, ed. M. Pieth and R. Ivory. Dordrecht: Springer.

Wagstyl, S. 2010. A change in Gear: Fast-recovering emerging world companies form a growing number of the largest global groups, changing the corporate landscape and posing stiff competition for Western Rivals. *Financial Times*, May 12, 2010, 7.

Waldman, A. 2002. Bhopal seethes, pained and poor 18 years later. *New York Times*, September 21, 2002, available at <www.nytimes.com>.

Weigend, T. 2008. Societas delinquere non potest? A German perspective. *Journal of International Criminal Justice* 6: 927.

Weissman, A., and D. Newman. 2007. Rethinking corporate criminal liability. *Indiana Law Journal* 82: 411.

Wells, C. 1999. Developments in corporate liability in England and Wales and a new offense of corporate killing – The English Law Commission's Proposals. In *Criminal responsibility of legal and collective entities*, ed. A. Eser, G. Heine, and B. Huber, 119. Freiburg im Breisgau: Edition Iuscrim.

Wells, C. 2000. Criminal responsibility of legal persons in common law jurisdictions: Room document DAFFE|IME|BR (2000) 22. OECD, Paris.

Wells, C. 2001. *Corporations and criminal responsibility*. Oxford: Oxford University Press.

Wells, C. 2010. Appendix C: Corporate criminal liability: Exploring some models. In LCEW (UK), *Criminal liability in regulatory contexts: A consultation paper*, Consultation paper no. 195, London, 187.

Wells, C. 2011. Corporate criminal liability in England and Wales: Past, present, and future. In *Corporate criminal liability: Emergence, convergence, and risk*, ed. M. Pieth and R. Ivory. Dordrecht: Springer.

Woods, S., and B. Scharffs. 2002. Applicability of human rights standards to private corporations: An American perspective. *The American Journal of Comparative Law* 50: 531.

Zeder, F. 2006. *VbVG: Verbandsverantwortlichkeitsgesetz Unternehmensstrafrecht: Textausgabe mit Materialien und Anmerkungen samt einer Darstellung der Rechtslage in 27 europäischen Staaten und den Bestimmungen über die Verbandsverantwortlichkeit im Finanzstrafgesetz.* Wien: Neuer Wissenschaftlicher Verlag.

Zerk, J. 2006. *Multinationals and corporate social responsibility: Limitations and opportunities in international law.* Cambridge: Cambridge University Press.

29 The Exclusionary Rule[1]

Stephen C. Thaman

29.1 Introduction

The notions of "truth" and "evidence" have been inextricably intertwined in the history of Western criminal procedure since the ascension of inquisitorial criminal procedure on the European Continent in the late middle ages. The justice achieved by early customary and lay courts in pre-inquisitorial times often had little to do with either truth or evidence. The only criminal evidence that was accepted as being "true," were the hard facts produced by the flagrant crime, when "hand-having" thieves or "redhanded" assailants were caught in the act and either summarily killed,[2] or hurriedly sentenced to death by *ad hoc* courts where the victim or his or her family might act as executioners.[3] Restoring the peace between victim (or victim's family or clan) and culprit enjoyed priority over the meticulous determination of "what happened" [4] in the era of duels,[5] swearing contests among compurgators[6] and divine ordeals.[7] Even when juries or *Schöffengerichte* replaced these primitive procedures, their roles had more to do with appraising whether the accused should be accepted back into the community and on what terms, than with evidence analysis and truth determination.[8] There was little truth in these procedures, but also little punishment, because punishment triggered anger, feud and blood revenge. Compensation to the victim was the rule, if the suspect was not finished off in flagrancy.[9]

[1] V.B., L'exclusion de certains moyens de preuve.

[2] Thomas Weigend, *Deliktsopfer und Strafverfahren* (Berlin: Duncker and Humblot, 1989), 36. This rule applied to murderers, adulterers, and thieves. A.S. Diamond, *Primitive Law Past and Present* (London: Methuen, 1971), 295. In Mesopotamia, adulteresses caught in the act were thrown bound into the river. Russ VerSteeg, *Law in the Ancient World* (Durham: Carolina Academic Press, 2002), 70.

[3] For such procedures in medieval Germany, *see* A. Esmein, *History of Continental Criminal Procedure with Special Reference to France* (Boston: Little, Brown, 1913), 302 and Weigend, *Deliktsopfer*, *supra* note 1, at 36–37.

[4] H. Patrick Glenn, *Legal Traditions of the World,* 3rd ed. (Oxford: Oxford University Press, 2007), 68–9. Use of punishment or death penalties always risked stoking a feud. Diamond, *supra* note 1, at 293.

[5] Also called "trial by battle." Robert Bartlett, *Trial By Fire and Water* (Oxford: Clarendon, Press, 1986), 103.

[6] According to one Tibetan proverb: "[If the case is] clear, [decide it] by law; [if the case is] unclear, [decide it] by oath." Rebecca Redwood French, *The Golden Yoke. The Legal Cosmology of Buddhist Tibet* (Ithaca: Cornell University Press,1995), 132. Cf. Diamond, *supra* note 1, at 270. According to § 131 of the Code of Hammurabi, if a man accuses his wife of adultery, and she is not caught *in flagrante*, she can cleanse herself by oath. VerSteeg, *supra* note 1, at 66.

[7] Ordeals were usually used in the absence of proof, but among some European tribes the ordeal was used to deter lying under oath. Diamond, *supra* note 1, at 228, 296.

[8] Customary law courts were often presided by a tribal chief, a king or heads of local communities, but leading members of local families had a right and duty to serve as members of the court, and anyone present could participate. These courts then gave way to trials by sworn neighbors in places as diverse as England and Ethiopia. Diamond, *supra* note 1, at 273, 391.

[9] Paid in livestock, trinkets or money. Diamond, *supra* note 1, at 228. On the usefulness of the remedy of compensation, *Tacitus* wrote: "enmities are very dangerous for a free people." Montesequieu, *De L'Esprit des Lois.* Vol. II. 152 (Paris: GF-Flammarion 1979).

S.C. Thaman (✉)
Saint Louis University, St. Louis, MO, USA
e-mail: thamansc@slu.edu

K.B. Brown and D.V. Snyder (eds.), *General Reports of the XVIIIth Congress of the International Academy of Comparative Law/Rapports Généraux du XVIIIème Congrès de l'Académie Internationale de Droit Comparé*,
DOI 10.1007/978-94-007-2354-2_29, © Springer Science+Business Media B.V. 2012

It was with the "scientization" of criminal procedure[10] and the displacement of lay judges and primitive decision making by professional judges with "truth-seeking" inquisitorial powers of evidence gathering and preservation that the link between "evidence" and "truth" was soldered and took priority over more humane concerns of smoothing over the conflict the alleged wrongful act caused in the community.[11] Of course, the ascension of inquisitorial procedure was dictated by the needs of the central powers of church and state which sought to subjugate local government and systems of dispute-resolution. The "truths" the governments sought to prove through their courts were often self-perpetuating myths or fictions upon which the central powers' domination rested: the crimes which arguably gave rise to this system were crimes against the state or religion, which could not be proved adequately by mere witnesses or victims (there were none), but needed to be proved by judges learned in the science (or was it witchcraft) of the law secretly, without being nettled by victims, accuseds, lawyers or the public.[12]

But the dominance of inquisitorial procedure on the European continent did not, despite the advances in evidence-taking and the greater predictability of professional decision making, mean a humanization of the resolution of criminal disputes. Enlightenment thinkers complained that more terror and inhumanity resulted from the administration of the law in these times than from all crimes committed by common criminals.[13] Many innocent persons were convicted and sentenced to death in this era, often based on confessions extorted through legalized torture or the threat thereof.[14] This certainly made up for the amount of guilty persons who were probably exonerated pursuant to the irrational procedures of earlier customary law administered by representatives of the community.

Thankfully, those days are long past (in most countries). Official torture in Europe disappeared by the end of the eighteenth and beginning of the nineteenth Centuries.[15] Continental Europe, however, experienced political convulsions throwing most countries between the extremes of the absolute monarchist police state and liberalism.[16] All pretenses of a state under the rule of law were then erased with the rise of Bolshevism in Russia, Nazism in Germany and its allied states, Fascism in Italy and Francoism in Spain.[17]

It was in reaction to these state crimes that the human rights movement was launched after 1945, resulting in the International Declaration of Human Rights, the European Convention on Human Rights (ECHR) and the International Covenant on Civil and Political Rights (ICCPR). The countries emerging from Fascist domination after World War II, Germany and Italy, enacted new constitutions which reflected the priority given to the protection of citizens against the threat of violence and arbitrariness by the state. Spain followed in 1978. A similar explosion of new constitutions and criminal procedure reform was produced in the 1990s as Latin America emerged from decades of American-sponsored dictatorships which no longer served one of their prime purposes, the brutal elimination of leftist movements, following the end

[10] The "right solution" was based on "textual analysis and logical penetration of its meaning." Law "came increasingly to be regarded as a self-contained, or closed system—a "science." Mirjan R. Damaska, *The Faces of Justice and State Authority* (New Haven: Yale University Press, 1986), 31. This science "needed no illumination" because it was a science of text. Niklas Luhmann, *Das Recht der Gesellschaft* (Frankfurt am Main: Suhrkamp, 1995), 48.

[11] On this transition, Diamond, *supra* note 1, at 339; Uwe Wesel, *Geschichte des Rechts. Von den Frühformen bis zur Gegenwart,* 3rd. ed. (München: Beck, 2006), 54.

[12] On the secret victimless crime of heresy and how it required a new procedure. Richard Vogler, *A World View of Criminal Justice* (Burlington, VT: Ashgate, 2005), 25. The procedure in ecclesiastical courts for heresy and magic was the most "ferocious" and required the forced cooperation of the accused. Luigi Ferrajoli, *Diritto e ragione: teoria del garantismo penale,* 5th ed. (Rome: Laterza, 1998), 577.

[13] *Id.* at 339,382. On criminal procedure of this epoch as a "science of horrors," *Id.*, at 578.

[14] On the conviction of the innocent, Cesare Beccaria, *Dei Delitti e Delle Pene*, 4th ed (Milan: Feltrinelli 1995), 62. *La Bruyere* said: "Torture is a wonderful invention and may be counted upon to ruin an innocent person with a weak constitution and exonerate a guilty person born robust." And further: "I might almost say in regard to myself, 'I will not be a thief or a murderer'; but to say, 'I shall not some day be punished as such,' would be to speak very boldly." Esmein, *supra* note 2, at 352, 380.

[15] John H. Langbein, *Torture and the Law of Proof* (Chicago: University of Chicago Press, 1977), 10.

[16] In Spain, the periods of liberalism invariably coincided with attempts (some more successful than others) to introduce trial by jury, those of monarchic reaction with the abolition thereof. See Ley Orgánica 5/1995, de 22 de Mayo, del Tribunal del Jurado, BOE de 23 de mayo de 1995, "Exposición de Motivos" I.

[17] On the horrendous number of death penalties imposed for the most trivial of offenses during the 12 years of Nazi rule in Germany, *see* Ingo Müller, *Furchtbare Juristen* (Munich: Kindler, 1989): 135–74.

of the cold war. The collapse of the Soviet Union and Yugoslavia also produced reforms in the 15 new post-Soviet republics and the new Yugoslav republics, fruits of which were a host of new codes of criminal procedure and constitutions reflecting the modern notions of human rights.

The experience in Common Law countries was different. Of course England had no experience of Fascism and, due to its unique tradition, no written constitution or Bill of Rights listing specific protections for its citizens. Police lawlessness did not, generally, affect the admission of evidence in the Common Law tradition. In Britain, the courts did not worry about the methods used to acquire evidence if it was otherwise relevant and material.[18]

The U.S., on the other hand, though sharing the Common Law heritage, had its Bill of Rights of 1791, the purpose of which was to restrict the new federal government against passing any laws which would impact on the freedoms of the citizens of the thirteen states which made up the new Union. But nearly all criminal cases in the U.S. were handled in the state courts, governed by state laws and constitutions. Until the end of the Civil War in 1865, African-American slaves were granted little protection under the laws of the states or the federal government. The enactment of the 14th Amendment to the U.S. Constitution in 1865, however, granted the freed slaves "due process of law" rights in relation to the States, yet it was only in the 1930s that the U.S. Supreme Court (USSC) began overturning state criminal convictions based on torture and the use of other coercive tactics which undermine the freedom of will of the accused as "violations of due process."[19]

Already in 1914 the USSC adopted an exclusionary rule which prevented the use of evidence seized by Federal officials in violation of the Fourth Amendment.[20] The problems this rule addressed were made abundantly clear:

> The tendency of those who execute the criminal laws of the country to obtain conviction by means of unlawful seizures and enforced confessions, the latter often obtained after subjecting accused persons to unwarranted practices destructive of rights secured by the Federal Constitution, should find no sanction in the judgments of the courts which are charged at all times with the support of the Constitution and to which people of all conditions have a right to appeal for the maintenance of such fundamental rights.[21]

But the USSC only became a true constitutional court for the entire country, when, influenced by the civil rights movement in the 1950s and 1960s, it decided that the Fourth, Fifth[22] and Sixth Amendments[23] to the US Constitution, were binding on the states, thus enabling it to change racist practices in many, mainly Southern, states which deprived African-American citizens of the protection of the law in criminal cases.

But we should not think that exclusionary rules are American inventions based in the forward-thinking wisdom of the USSC during the years that Earl Warren was Chief Justice.[24] The landmark decisions in this respect were, of course: (1) *Mapp v. Ohio*,[25] which made the Fourth Amendment exclusionary rule, binding on the States; (2) *Wong Sun v. United States*,[26] which re-articulated the exclusionary rule in relation to derivative evidence causally linked to preceding constitutional violations[27]; (3) *Massiah v. United States*,[28] which provided for exclusion of confessions or admissions made to government agents by charged defendants, in violation of the Sixth Amendment right to counsel; and, of course (4) *Miranda v. Arizona*,[29]

---

[18] Blackstone's *Criminal Practice 1974,* 13th ed. (London: Blackstone, 2003).

[19] One of the most notorious of the dozens of cases decided in this area prior to the incorporation of the Fifth Amendment in 1964, was Brown v. Mississippi, 297 U.S. 278 (1936), which involved the torture of Black suspects in a murder case and their hurried sentence to death 3 days later in a kangaroo jury court.

[20] The Fourth Amendment of the U.S. Constitution reads: "The right of the people to be secure in their persons, houses, papers and effects against unreasonable searches and seizures shall not be violated, and no Warrants shall issue but upon probable cause, supported by Oath or affirmation, and particularly describing the place to be searched and the persons or things to be seized."

[21] Weeks v. United States, 232 U.S. 383, 392 (1914).

[22] The Fifth Amendment of the U.S. Constitution provides, *inter alia*, that: "No person…shall be compelled in any criminal case to be a witness against himself…"

[23] The Sixth Amendment provides, *inter alia*, "In all criminal prosecutions, the accused shall have the Assistance of Counsel for his defense."

[24] From 1953 to 1969.

[25] 367 U.S. 643 (1961).

[26] 371 U.S. 471 (1963).

[27] The term "fruit of the poisonous tree" was originally coined by Justice Frankfurter in Nardone v. United States, 308 U.S. 338 (1939), but the idea that the government could not use derivative evidence was articulated 19 years earlier by Justice Holmes in Silverthorne Lumber Co. v. United States, 251 U.S. 385 (1920).

[28] 377 U.S. 201 (1964).

[29] 384 U.S. 436 (1966).

which provided for exclusion of confessions and admissions made during custodial interrogation, where the suspect was not advised of the right to silence and the right to counsel or did not effectively waive those rights, in violation of the Fifth Amendment privilege against self-incrimination.

These landmark decisions, especially *Mapp* and *Miranda*, have been very influential overseas, but so have some of the limitations placed on the exclusionary rule by the Burger court,[30] foremost of these being the exceptions to the doctrine of the "fruits of the poisonous tree" known as "inevitable discovery"[31] and "independent source,"[32] and the "good faith" exception to violations of the Fourth Amendment.[33]

Inquisitorial systems on the European continent had a developed system of exclusion of evidence at a time when Common Law courts never questioned the provenance of evidence brought to it.[34] Continental European codes of criminal procedure prescribed rather strict rules for the gathering of evidence and the performance of other acts during the preliminary criminal investigation and nullified the efficacy of these acts if they were performed in violation of the rules. So-called "nullities" could and did lead to exclusion of evidence. The legalistic approach of early inquisitorial codes mirrored the pedantic nature of the formal rules of evidence which informed the judgment in criminal trials in pre-nineteenth Century Europe.[35] In fact, one of the most influential treatises on exclusionary rules was written in Germany even before the U.S. Supreme Court's decision in *Weeks*, and represents perhaps the first scholarly fashioning of a balancing test for the introduction of illegally gathered evidence.[36]

Despite the gains made in the U.S. to combat inequality and racially disparate treatment within the administration of justice, one can still make the argument that the criminal justice system causes more suffering and misery than the totality of the crimes committed by those who are processed by it. The U.S. has the largest prison population in the world, perhaps the largest *per capita* in history,[37] yet has far from the highest crime rate. Life imprisonment is possible for recidivist thieves[38] and even first-time drug dealers.[39] Normal street crimes are punished around three-times more severely in the U.S. than, for instance, in Germany.[40] This fact is never included in the balancing tests created by the USSC in deciding whether or not to exclude evidence, which is often illegal narcotics that is gained in violation of important constitutional rights. It is the process of balancing human rights against "truth," a code word for a more effective obtainment of criminal convictions, which this general report will address.

All lawmakers and courts "balance," i.e., make value judgments, when navigating between the Scylla of human rights and the Charybdis of accuracy ("truth") and efficiency in criminal trials. The most critical question in this balancing is: what kinds of official law violations are serious enough to trigger non-use of the

---

[30] Warren Burger was Chief Justice of the USSC from 1969 to 1986.

[31] Nix v. Williams, 467 U.S. 431, 444–50 (1984).

[32] First articulated in Silverthorne Lumber Co., *supra* note 26, at 392, but then reaffirmed in Murray v. United States, 487 U.S. 533, 537–9 (1988).

[33] United States v. Leon, 468 U.S. 897, 918–25 (1984).

[34] On this early approach in the U.S., *see* United States v. The La Jeune Eugenie, 26 F. Cas. 832, 844 (Cir. Mass.,1822). The only remedy for violations of the Fourth Amendment was a civil suit.

[35] On the statutory system of proofs derived from the Roman canon law of evidence, Langbein, Torture, *supra* note 14, at 3–5. On how inquisitorial Europe developed "extrinsic" exclusionary rules relating to "values unrelated to the pursuit of truth" at a time when the Common law only knew "intrinsic" rules relating to the probative value of evidence. Mirjan R. Damaska, *Evidence Law Adrift* (New Haven: Yale University Press, 1997), 12–7.

[36] Ernst Beling, Die Beweisverbote als Grenzen der Wahrheitserforschung im Strafprozess (Breslau: Schletter'sche Buchhandlung, 1903).

[37] Circa 2.3 million persons, 751/100,000 of the citizenry, are incarcerated in U.S. prisons. In second place is Russia with around 657/100,000. For comparison, Germany locks up 88/100,000 of its population. Adam Liptak, *Inmate Count In U.S. Dwarfs Other Nations*, New York Times, Apr. 23, 2008, at A1, A14, *available at* http://www.nytimes.com/2008/04/23/us/23prison.html?_r=1&hp&oref=slogin (last visited Feb. 19, 2010).

[38] Ewing v. California, 538 U.S. 11 (2003); Lockyer v. Andrade, 538 U.S. 63 (2003).

[39] Harmelin v. Michigan, 501 U.S. 957 (1991).

[40] 80% of Germans convicted of crimes are fined and only 3% do more than 1 year deprivation of liberty. On the other hand, all convicted in the U.S. federal courts are sentenced to deprivation of liberty. Marcus Dirk Dubber, "American Plea Bargains, German Lay Judges, and the Crisis of Criminal Procedure," *Stanford Law Review* 49 (1997): 547, 560, 596–7.The average sentence is Germany is one-third of that in the U.S. for a similar crime. Jenia Iontcheva Turner, "Judicial Participation in Plea Negotiations: A Comparative View," *American Journal of Comparative Law* 54 (2006): 199, 234–5.

evidence resulting therefrom? This value judgment is sometimes made at the level of international law, as with the prohibition of torture, sometimes in constitutions and codes, and sometimes by the courts. The prevailing view, is that the violations must be "serious," or of "fundamental rights," i.e., of constitutional rights. But even the decision to limit exclusion to constitutional violations requires courts to decide, whether the violation *was* of constitutional magnitude.

But even if a constitutional violation has been identified, which could trigger exclusion or "non-use" of evidence, judges must again decide whether the evidence the prosecution seeks to use is the "fruit of the poisonous tree," i.e., does it derive inexorably from the constitutional violation? But even if one agrees that a constitutional violation has been committed and the evidence sought to be admitted is the fruit thereof, some jurisdictions still require the judge to engage in a balancing of other important interests before deciding on admissibility.

If further balancing is required, then the courts may or must take into account some or all of the following: (1) the seriousness of the constitutional violation (was it intentional, reckless, negligent, etc.); (2) the gravity of the crime which is before the court; (3) the character of the evidence subject to exclusion (its credibility, importance for proving guilt, whether it constitutes the *corpus delicti* of the crime or is "mere evidence," etc.); (4) whether use of the evidence would violate the defendant's right to a fair trial; (5) whether it would bring the court into disrepute; (6) or whether its use or non-use would cause alarm in the community.

This report will explore these issues concentrating mainly on what I thought were the two most critical areas in which exclusionary rules do their work: (1) where police acquire evidence by violating the constitutionally protected right to privacy in one's home or in one's private conversations and (2) where police violate the law in obtaining confessions. After I was chosen as general rapporteur on the subject of exclusionary rules or use-prohibitions relating to illegally gathered evidence, I prepared a questionnaire which was submitted to the various country reporters who were either nominated by their country's section of the International Academy of Comparative Law, or were recruited by me from friends and colleagues. The further organization of this report will follow that questionnaire which will be attached as Appendix One to this report.

In discussing the various areas included in the questionnaire I will refer to the wealth of information and analysis provided by the 24 country reports and the report on the jurisprudence of the European Court of Human Rights (hereafter ECtHR) which have been submitted. I intend to refer to the reports, most of which were temporarily published on the website of the XVIII Congress of the International Academy of Comparative Law, using a two-letter abbreviation for the country (or European Court) and the page number of the report submitted to me: Belgium (BE), written by Marie-Aude Beernaert, of the Catholic University of Louvain and Philip Traest, of the University of Ghent; Brazil (BR), written by Ana Paula Zomer Sica, State Procurator in São Paulo and Leonardo Sica, a lawyer in São Paulo; Czech Republic (CZ), written by Jaroslav Fenyk of Masaryk University in Brno; England and Wales (EW), written by Andrew Choo, University of Warwick; Finland (FI), written by Hannu Kiuru, Helsinki, Vice-President of the Finnish Section of the Comparative Law Association; France (FR), written by Jean Pradel, Professor Emeritus of the University of Poitiers; Germany (GE), written by Sabine Gless, University of Basel, Switzerland; Greece (GR), written by George Triantafyllou, University of Athens; Ireland (IR), written by Yvonne Daly, Dublin City University and Arnaud Cras, University College Dublin; Israel (IS), written by Rinat Kitai Sangero, Academic Center of Law and Business, Jerusalem and Yuval Merin, College of Management School of Law, Rishon LeZion; Italy (IT), written by Giulio Illuminati, University of Bologna; Macao (MA), written by Paulo Martins Chan, Public Prosecutor, University of Macao; the Netherlands (NE), written by Lonneke Stevens and Matthias J. Borgers, Free University of Amsterdam; Norway (NO), written by Runar Torgersen, Public Prosecutor, Oslo; Poland (PL), written by Maria Rogacka-Rzewnicka, University of Warsaw; Portugal (PO), written by Maria João da Silva Baila Madeira Antunes, University of Coimbra; Russia (RU), written by Vladimir I. Rudnev, Institute of Legislation and Comparative Law, Moscow; Scotland (SC), written by Fiona Leverick, University of Glasgow and Findlay Stark, Ph.D Candidate, University of Edinburgh; Serbia (SE), written by Snežana Brkić, University of Novi Sad; Slovenia (SL), written by Ana Pauletič, University of Ljubljana; Spain (SP), written by Lorena Bachmaier Winter, Complutense University, Madrid; Taiwan (TA), written by Jaw-perng Wang, National

Taiwan University, Taipei; Turkey (TU), written by Adem Sözüer and Öznur Sevdiren, Istanbul University; United States (US), written by Mark Cammack, Southwestern School of Law, Los Angeles; and European Court of Human Rights, written by Pinar Ölcer, University of Leiden, the Netherlands.

I would also like to acknowledge, that the country reporter for Croatia, Professor Ivo Josipović, University of Zagreb, graciously excused himself for being unable to submit his report. His excuse was rather compelling: he was elected President of Croatia in the meantime! We wish him the best of luck!

29.2 The General Theory of Admissibility of Illegally Gathered Evidence

29.2.1 Introduction

Exclusionary rules come in a variety of forms and all implicate a kind of balancing of interests, primarily, the interest in ascertaining truth in a particular criminal case, against the respect for the rights of criminal defendants and, indirectly, of the entire civilian population, which have been declared to be so important to the legal order that they have been enshrined as such in human rights conventions and national constitutions. There is a noticeable trend since the 1990s to make exclusion of illegally gathered evidence a constitutional command. Thus, constitutions either require exclusion of any evidence gathered "in violation of law," which could mean through any methods which are criminal, or otherwise violate requirements laid out in the code of criminal procedure (CCP),[41] or might limit the constitutional command to violations of constitutional or "fundamental" rights. In such countries, the constitutional lawgiver has apparently "pre-weighed" conflicting interests and decided that legality and due process will always trump truth in a criminal case.

Occasionally, however, a constitution will require exclusion of illegally gathered evidence but will require, or allow the judge to use his or her discretion to weigh conflicting interests on a case-by-case basis before deciding whether or not to exclude the evidence. In such a system, exclusion would have relative constitutional status which could give way to truth-finding in particular types of cases.

Both the absolute and the discretionary model of exclusionary rules are also found in statutes or CCP's, often in countries where exclusion is not specifically mentioned in the constitution. These statutory rules or commands are sometimes phrased in terms of "exclusion," but are also often articulated as creating "nullities" which invalidate the procedural act and may or may not lead to exclusion of the fruits of this act. As noted in the introduction, nullities existed in continental European inquisitorial CCP's long before Common Law jurisdictions began articulating exclusionary rules. This general report will attempt to distinguish between the functioning of "nullities" and "exclusionary rules" both of which exist in several jurisdictions.

Finally, we will discuss the fate of evidence which only indirectly derives from the initial violation of the law or constitution, so-called "fruits of the poisonous tree." Again, reference is sometimes made to the exclusion of derivative evidence in national constitutions and sometimes in statutes or codes.

If it is constitutional lawgivers or legislators who have struck a preliminary balance for exclusion and against truth-finding in certain cases, it is also the high courts of many countries who, in the absence of direct guidance in the constitution or the codes, have fashioned either absolute or discretionary exclusionary rules. Besides crafting exclusionary rules where none expressly existed, high courts can often be seen to dismantle seemingly clear, absolute exclusionary rules, or at least to carve out exceptions to their functioning. This is often the case in the area of "fruits of the poisonous tree" where many national courts are reluctant to extend a use-prohibition which might apply to a confession, wiretap or other type of search to evidence indirectly gathered as a result of the initial violation. Or, even where the doctrine of the "fruits of the poisonous tree" is recognized, courts will often recognize exceptions to its application.

In this section, however, we will only treat general exclusionary rules. In the following sections we will concentrate on exclusionary practices in relation to violations of the right to privacy and then those related to improper interrogation methods.

[41] I will refer to all codes of criminal procedure with the abbreviation of CCP. Appendix One will include a list of the Codes of Criminal Procedure and sources where they can be found, either in the original language, or in English or another *lingua franca*.

29.2.2 The Principle of Material Truth and Its Importance in the National Legal System

1. *Importance in the Jurisprudence of the High Courts*
Post-inquisitorial jurisprudence, by and large, still pays tribute to the "principle of material truth," i.e., that all evidence that is relevant to prove the truth or untruth of the charges is admissible and that executive investigative and prosecutorial organs, and indeed, even the courts, have a duty to ascertain the truth.[42] But the increasing importance of human rights declarations in international conventions and modern constitutions, as well as the recognition of exclusionary rules, have led courts to qualify the search for truth with the *caveat* of "not at any cost."[43]
Yet, despite the lack of a recognized truth-finding principle in the jurisprudence of common law countries, the rules of evidence have traditionally operated in a similar fashion: any relevant evidence was admissible to prove the truth of the charges, even if gathered in violation of the law.[44] Even following the introduction of exclusionary rules in the U.S. and other countries, the "search for truth" is still invoked by courts to limit the reach of the court-sanctioned exclusionary rules.[45]
There has been a trend, however, even in formerly inquisitorial systems, to strip the trial judge of the inquisitorial duty to ascertain the truth, and make him or her the guarantor of the fairness of the trial, i.e., that the playing field for the prosecution and defense parties is even and both have broad freedom to admit evidence either to prove the truth of the charges or undermine the credibility of the prosecution's evidence.[46]
2. *Statutory Articulations*
The principle of material truth is listed in the general part of many codes of criminal procedure.[47] But it also finds articulation in the special part when referring to the powers of the trial judge. A classical articulation of the inquisitorial duty of the trial judge to determine the truth is found in § 244(2) CCP-Germany, which provides: "In order to establish the truth, the court shall, *proprio motu* [of its own accord], extend the taking of evidence to all facts and means of proof relevant to the decision."[48]
3. *Constitutional Status*
The principle of material truth is not explicitly mentioned in any national constitutions to my knowledge. However, the high courts of some countries have derived its constitutional status from other sections of the constitution. For instance, in Portugal it is deemed to be part of the guarantee of a democratic state,[49] and in Greece it is derived from the state's duty to punish crimes.[50]

29.2.3 Constitutional Provisions Relating to Exclusion of Illegally Seized Evidence

1. *Absolute Exclusionary Rules Not Restricted to Constitutional Violations*
A number of modern constitutions adopted by democratizing countries which have emerged from the clutches of totalitarian, authoritarian, dictatorial or military regimes have given constitutional status to the prohibition of the use of evidence illegally seized by law enforcement officials. Some of the

---

[42] The German Constitutional Court has recognized the search for truth as a core principle of German law. GE, 5. On the *descoberta da verdade material* in Macao, MA, 5. On the duty of the courts to do anything necessary to determine the truth, *see*, BE, 1–2; BR,9; NE, 1; PO, 3; §§.

[43] The groundwork for this famous quote from a 1960 German Supreme Court decision was actually laid in *Beling*'s 1903 treatise, *supra* note 35. GE,2,5. Cf. BE, 1; PL, 5; GR, 2.

[44] EW, 20. A similar approach has traditionally been applied in Israel, as well. IS, 1–2.

[45] Thus, in Leon, *supra* note 32, the US Supreme Court said: "an unbending application of the exclusionary sanction to enforce ideals of governmental rectitude would impede unacceptably the truth-finding functions of judge and jury." US, 15. In a similar vein, the court, in Herring v. United States, 120 S.Ct. 695 (2009), said that the exclusionary rule's "costly toll upon truth-seeking and law enforcement objectives presents a high obstacle for those urging [its] application." US, 27.

[46] Thus, in Finland, the task of the trial judge is to ensure that the procedure is fair, rather than to determine the truth. FI,2. On Taiwan's move in 2002 from an inquisitorial judge with a duty to ascertain the truth, to an adversarial judge whose only duty is, if at all, to help the defense. TA, 2.

[47] Such as §17 CCP-Slovenia, SL, 8.

[48] GE, 5. Cf. §§ 268–9 CCP-Belgium, BE, 1–2; § 5(2) CCP-CZ, CZ, 9; § 321 CCP-Macao, MA,5; §17 CCP-Serbia (2001), SE, 4; §§ 289(3), 329(5), 351(1) CCP-Slovenia, SL,9; § 729 CCP-Spain, SP,8; § 294 CCP-Norway, NO, 2; § 249(2) CCP-Greece, GR,1.

[49] PO, 5.

[50] Found in Arts. 25(1), 96(1) Const.-Greece. GR, 2.

provisions make no distinction between evidence gathered in violation of constitutional (human rights) protections or that gathered in violation of other codified criminal procedure rules that lack constitutional status. For instance, Art. 50(2) of the Const.-Russia of 1993 provides: "In the administration of justice the use of evidence gathered in violation of federal law is not permitted."[51] Art. 5(LVI) Const.-Brazil provides that evidence obtained by "illegal means" will be inadmissible in the proceedings.[52] Similarly, Article 38(para. 8) Const.-Turkey provides that "findings obtained through illegal methods shall not be considered as evidence."[53]

2. *Absolute Exclusionary Rules Limited to Constitutional Violations*
   Other constitutional provisions limit the mandate of exclusion to evidence gathered in violation of constitutional protections. Thus, Art. 29 Const.-Colombia states quite simply: "Evidence obtained in violation of due process is null in the full sense of the law (*nulo en pleno derecho*)." Art. 32(6) Const.-Portugal provides that "Any evidence obtained by torture, force, violation of the physical or moral integrity of the individual, wrongful interference in private life, the home, correspondence, or telecommunications are of no effect."[54]
3. *Discretionary Exclusionary Rules*
   The categorical pronouncements seen in the above sections are different than the constitutional exclusionary rule in Art. 24(2) of the Canadian Charter of Rights and Freedoms, which necessarily implies a discretionary weighing of factors: "where…a court finds that evidence was obtained in a manner that infringed or denied any of the rights or freedoms guaranteed by this Charter, the evidence shall be excluded if it is established that, having regard to all the circumstances, the admission of it in the proceedings would bring the administration of justice into disrepute."[55]

Originally, Canadian courts developed two separate tests to determine whether exclusion was appropriate under Art. 24(2). Under the first test, exclusion would result, regardless of the seriousness of the violation, if it had as a consequence that a suspect-defendant was "conscripted" to produce evidence against himself, such as through a confession or by extracting bodily fluids, etc., and this was, more or less categorically, considered to affect the fairness of the trial. The second test focused exclusively on the seriousness of the violation such that a failure to exclude would bring the administration of justice into disrepute. Important factors here would be the intentionality of the violation and whether police acted in "good faith," but not whether there might have been a hypothetical clean path to the evidence (i.e. inevitable discovery).[56] Apparently the Canadian courts have now moved to a more simple balancing test which weighs three factors: (1) the severity of the violation; (2) whether the admission of the evidence would bring the administration of justice into disrepute from the perspective of society's interest in respect for Charter rights; and (3) the effect of admitting the evidence on the public interest in having the case adjudicated on its merits.[57]

Patterned after the Canadian Charter provision is Art. 35(5) Const.-South Africa, which provides that evidence "obtained in a manner that violates any right in the Bill of Rights must be excluded if the admission of that evidence would render the trial unfair or otherwise be detrimental to the administration of justice."[58]

29.2.4 Statutory General Exclusionary Rules

1. *Absolute Rules Not Limited to Constitutional Violations*
   The statutory exclusionary rule articulated in § 75(1) CCP-Russia includes the same absolute language

[51] RU-1. For similar language, *see* Art. 42(7) Const.-Georgia; Art. 71(3) Const.-Azerbaijan; Art. 27(2) Const.-Belarus; Art. 77(3)(9) Const.-Kazakhstan. English translations of all world constitutions are available at *Constitutions of the Countries of the World*, http://www.oup.com/online/us/law/oceanalaw/?view=usa#ccwo

[52] BR-6.

[53] TU-7

[54] PO-4.

[55] Canadian Charter of Rights and Freedoms, Enacted by the Canada Act 1982 [U.K.] c.11; proclaimed in force April 17, 1982. http://www.efc.ca/pages/law/charter/charter.text.html

[56] Kent Roach, "Canada," in *Criminal Procedure: A Worldwide Study*, ed. Craig M. Bradley, 2d. ed. (Durham: Carolina Academic Press, 2007), 71–2. German courts have also broadly interpreted the notion of "hypothetical clean path" in applying the exception of "inevitable discovery." GE, 11.

[57] *See* R. v. Grant, 2009 SC 32; R. v. Harrison, 2009 SC 34.

[58] PJ Schwikkard and SE van der Merwe, "South Africa," in *Criminal Procedure: A Worldwide Study*, *supra* note 56, at 487.

contained in Art. 50(2) Const.-Russia.[59] § 191 CCP-Italy (1988) provides for a sanction of *inutilizzabilità* ("non-usability") in relation to "evidence acquired in violation of the prohibitions established by the law."[60] § 15 CCP-Serbia of 2006 is even more extensive in its use-prohibition: "Court decisions may not be based on evidence which *per se*, or by method of collection are contrary to the provisions of the present Code, any other law, or have been collected or presented by virtue of violating human rights and fundamental freedoms envisaged by the Constitution or ratified international treaties."[61]

§ 38.23 CCP-Texas (U.S.) similarly provides: "(a) No evidence obtained by an officer or other person in violation of any provisions of the Constitution or laws of the State of Texas, or of the Constitution or laws of the United States of America, shall be admitted in evidence against the accused on the trial of any criminal case."

Occasionally these broad exclusionary rules will even extend to derivative evidence. Thus, § 83 CCP-Slovenia (1994), provides that a court may not base a decision on evidence acquired in violation of constitutional rights and liberties, nor of other explicit norms of criminal procedure, nor on evidence derived from such violations.[62] Recently, codes are also making express reference to exceptions to the exclusionary rule developed in U.S. jurisprudence. For instance, § 157 CCP-Brazil, added in 2008, provides: "Illicit evidence, understood to be that obtained in violation of constitutional and legal norms, is inadmissible and should be removed from the trial: (1) the evidence derived from the illicit evidence is also inadmissible except where there is no obvious or causal nexus between the one and the other or where the derived evidence could be obtained from a source independent of the former; (2) An independent source is considered to be such, that when following the normal procedures used in practice which are proper in criminal investigation, it would be capable of leading to the facts which are the objects to be proved."[63]

The wording of § 254-2 CCP-Turkey, introduced in 1992, appears to indicate an absolute exclusionary rule: "Evidence obtained *unlawfully* by investigative authorities cannot be taken as a basis for the judgement." Nevertheless the courts interpreted "unlawful" not to mean "illegal" and have ruled that suppression is not obligatory just because of a relation to an unlawful act.[64] However, § 202(6)(a) CCP-Turkey prohibits the introduction of any evidence unlawfully obtained, which means it cannot be used for purposes of formulating an indictment or ordering pretrial detention, much less to provide the basis for a guilty judgment.[65]

The first Greek statutory exclusionary rule not formulated as a "nullity" denies probative value to any evidence obtained through "criminal acts."[66] This formulation leaves it unclear whether any violation of statutory rules would lead to exclusion, for their violation might also not constitute a criminal act. Even a search of a dwelling by a police official without probable cause, which would be a constitutional violation, might not be punished as a crime by the penal code.

2. *Absolute Rules Limited to Constitutional Violations*
Statutes may also limit exclusion or "non-use" to violations of constitutional magnitude.[67] For instance, § 11.1 of Spain's Law on the Judicial Power (hereafter LOPJ-Spain) limits its general exclusionary rule in this way, and also extends its coverage to derivative evidence: "Evidence obtained, directly or indirectly in violation of fundamental rights and liberties is without effect."[68]

[59] § 7 CCP-Russia also provides: "Violation of norms of the current Code by the court, prosecutor, investigator, organ of the inquest or inquisitor during criminal proceedings results in declaration of the inadmissibility the evidence gathered thereby."

[60] IT, 1. The concept of "non-usability" had been recognized in Italian jurisprudence even before the enactment of the 1988 Code in the area of wiretapping and interrogations without counsel. (IT, 1–2).

[61] § 18(2) CCP-Serbia (2001) also had a similar provision. SE, 3–4.

[62] Zvonka Fišer et al, "La legislazione processuale penale della Repubblica di Slovenia," in *Le Altre Procedure Penali: Transizioni Dei Sistemi Processuali Penali,* ed. Berislav Pavišić and Davide Bertaccini (Torino: G. Giappichelli, 2002), 1:385.

[63] *See* BR 6–7, noting that the legislation appears to have confused the doctrine of "independent source" with that of "inevitable discovery."

[64] TU, 4.

[65] TU, 7–8.

[66] GR-7.

[67] Cf. § 136.4320 Or.Rev.Stats. which limits exclusion of evidence to situations when required by the constitutions of Oregon or the U.S.

[68] § 11.1 Ley Orgánica del Poder Judicial, Ley Orgánica 6 (July 1, 1985), available at http://noticias.juridicas.com/base_datos/Admin/lo6-1985.html. This restriction to a violation of "fundamental" rights reflects a landmark Spanish Constitutional Court decision of 1984 which clearly required exclusion of evidence if constitutional rights were violated. SP, 5,9.

In a similar manner, § 23 CCP-Colombia provides: "All evidence obtained in violation of fundamental guarantees is null within the full meaning of the law and should thus be excluded from the procedure. Evidence which is the consequence of the excluded evidence, or can only be explained by reason of its existence, receives the same treatment." Like the aforementioned 2008 amendments to the CCP-Brazil, §455 CCP-Colombia, which is entitled "nullity derived from illicit evidence," explicitly provides for exceptions for "attenuated connection, independent source, inevitable discovery, and others provided by law." These "derivative" exclusionary rules will be discussed, *infra*, under the section dealing with "fruits of the poisonous tree."

3. *General Exclusionary Rules Allowing Discretion and Balancing of Factors*

In England and Wales, § 78 of the Police and Criminal Evidence Act 1984 (hereafter PACE) provides: "(1) In any proceedings the court may refuse to allow evidence on which the prosecution proposes to rely to be given if it appears to the court that, having regard to all the circumstances, including the circumstances in which the evidence was obtained, the admission of the evidence would have such an adverse effect on the fairness of the proceedings that the court ought not to admit it. (2) Nothing in this section shall prejudice any rule of law requiring a court to exclude evidence."[69] The discretion given the judge by § 78 PACE has been described in the literature as "broad and unstructured" due to the plethora of factors which may be weighed in addition to the legality of the police actions: the seriousness of the offense, good faith of the officers, type of evidence and its reliability, existence of corroborative evidence, type of illegality and type of right infringed.[70]

§ 359a(1) CCP-Netherlands, which appears to be an adaptation of traditional nullity rules, gives the court discretion to exclude evidence and obligates it to take account of the interest that the breached rule serves, the gravity of the breach and the harm it causes.

(1) If procedural rules prove to have been breached during the preliminary investigation, which breach can no longer be remedied, and the legal consequences of the breach are not apparent from statutory law, the court may rule that: (a) the severity of the punishment will be decreased in proportion to the gravity of the breach if the harm caused by the breach can be compensated in this way; (b) the results of the investigation obtained through the breach may not contribute to the evidence in the prosecution of the offense charged; (c) the Public Prosecution Service will be barred from prosecuting if the breach makes it impossible to hear the case in compliance with the principles of due process.

(2) In applying the first subsection, the court must take account of the interest that the breached rule serves, the gravity of the breach and the harm it causes.[71]

The rules in England and Wales and the Netherlands are not explicitly limited to violations of a constitutional magnitude,[72] yet the judge, in assessing the factor relating to the gravity of the breach, will often be focusing on violations of fundamental rights. § 158-4 CCP-Taiwan has introduced a discretionary test for exclusion, according to which the judge must balance the protection of human rights against the "public interest."[73] In interpreting this section, the Taiwan Supreme Court required that a trial court shall consider the following factors in deciding whether to exclude evidence: the seriousness of the violation, whether the officer acted intentionally, or in "good faith," the seriousness of the criminal offense charged, the deterrent effect if the evidence were to be excluded, the possibility of inevitable discovery of the evidence, and the effect on the defendant's defense.[74]

4. *Statutory "Nullities" and Their Interpretation by the Courts*

Many countries in Europe and Latin America still provide for "nullities" when there is a violation of procedural norms. In some countries, such as France, procedural "nullities" are still the only

[69] Police and Criminal Evidence Act 1984, citations from Michael Zander, *The Police and Criminal Evidence Act* 1984, 5th ed. (London: Thomson/Sweet & Maxwell, 2005), cf. EW, 1.

[70] David Ormerod, "ECHR and the Exclusion of Evidence: Trial Remedies for Article 8 Breaches?," *Criminal Law Review* (2003): 61,64.

[71] NE, 2.

[72] NE, 3

[73] TA, 1.

[74] TA, 3.

statutory grounds for excluding evidence. In others, such as Italy, Brazil, Colombia, Portugal, Spain, Greece, or Macao (China), the code has maintained the doctrine of "nullities" and yet added modern statutory or even constitutional prohibitions on the use of illegally gathered evidence in the form of exclusionary rules or rules of "non-usability."[75]

It is sometimes difficult to understand the relation between the modern rules of exclusion or "non-usability," which were likely inspired by the American jurisprudence of the last 50 years, and the more venerable "nullities," which originally related to procedural acts and not necessarily to the evidence these acts might have produced.[76] In fact, one category of nullities, called "nullities of general order" relates to defects in the procedure which do not necessarily touch on the collection of evidence, yet these are treated as grave violations which could even lead to a dismissal of the prosecution.[77]

§ 170 CCP-France allows for the parties to move for the "annulment of an act or a document of the procedure." But § 171 CCP-France provides: "There is a nullity when a failure to recognize a substantial formality contained in a provision of the present Code or any other provision of criminal procedure has infringed on the interests of the party to which it applies."[78] This formulation appears close to limiting France's nullity-based exclusionary rule to constitutional violations, at least when the "party to which it applies" is the defendant. § 174(3) CCP-France further provides that the annulled act will be removed from the case dossier.

In civil law systems the withdrawal of the document memorializing an investigative measure from the dossier traditionally meant that no use could be made of it or its contents at the trial.[79] Since the document is excluded before the case reaches the trial court, the trial judge will be as insulated from the tainted evidence as would be a jury following a successful pretrial motion to exclude evidence in the U.S.[80]

According to § 177 CCP-Italy, the only nullities are those specifically provided in the code, what the French would call "textual" nullities.[81] The Italian code distinguishes between "relative nullities," which must be raised by the parties and, if recognized, may be "sanitized" or cured by waiver by the affected party or by the official who violated the law,[82] and "absolute nullities," which are usually of constitutional magnitude, which may be raised at any stage of the proceedings, may not be "sanitized" and may lead to exclusion of evidence.[83]

As in French law, § 238 (3) LOPJ-Spain provides for a "nullity" when: "the essential rules of procedure are not respected and this may have caused an

[75] IT, 7, MA, 5; PO, 4; GR, 5,7. In Spain, the provisions relating to nullities and exclusion are located in the LOPJ-Spain and not in the CCP. SP, 7.

[76] On the confusing relation of "non-usability" to "nullities" in Italy, *see* IT, 8.

[77] On nullities of "general order" in Italy, *see* § 178 CCP-Italy. On "general order" nullities in France, *see* Richard Frase, "France," in *Criminal Procedure: A Worldwide Study, supra* note 56, at 213, and FR, 4. The Serbian statutory exclusionary rule in the 2001 code smacks of a rule of nullity, inasmuch as any reference to illegally gathered evidence in the judgment will lead to a reversal, whether or not there was other sufficient evidence to justify the guilt finding. The 2006 code will permit, however, a finding of harmless error. SE, 4. § 289(i) CCP-Turkey also holds that the introduction of unlawfully obtained evidence contaminates the whole trial and must therefore lead to dismissal of the charges, thus following the remedies traditionally applied to absolute nullities. TU, 7.

[78] Similar language is contained in § 802 CCP-France. FR, 4. Similarly, in Brazil nullities are limited to violations which infringe on the interests of prosecution or defense (§ 563 CCP-Brazil) and impact on the ascertainment of the truth or the outcome of the trial (§ 566 CCP-Brazil). BR, 7–8.

[79] However, nullities must be raised before trial, in France before a three-judge *chambre de l'instruction* or they are "sterilized," FR, 5. In systems where the written trial still dominates, such as in the Netherlands or the French trial in the correctional courts, the documents in the dossier could historically be read at the trial if they were prepared according to the rules laid out in the code of criminal procedure. This is now changing as a result of case law of the ECtHR which has held that the use of written statements may violate Art. 6(3)(d) ECHR which guarantees the right to confrontation. See Delta v. France, 16 E.H.R.R. 574 (1993) and discussion in Stephen C. Thaman, *Comparative Criminal procedure: A Casebook Approach,* 2d. ed. (Durham: Carolina Academic Press, 2008), 125–35.

[80] In Serbia the suppressed or "nullified" evidence is also removed from the dossier for this precise reason. SE, 2.

[81] For similar provisions, *see* § 171 CCP-Argentina-Federal; §§ 191, 195 CPP-Venezuela; § 572 CCP-Brazil, BR, 7–8; § 105 CCP-Macao, MA, 4. In addition to "textual nullities," § 171 CCP-France also recognizes "substantial" nullities. Frase, *supra* note 77, at 212. Cf. FR, 4. The only "textual nullities" in Belgium relate to use of anonymous witnesses, and wire-tapping. BE,6.

[82] §§ 183, 184 CCP-Italy. IT, 8. Cf. § 170 CCP-Greece, GR,6.

[83] § 179 CCP-Italy. For the purposes of this study, the most important "absolute nullity" mentioned is the "absence of defense counsel in the cases in which his presence is obligatory." § 179 (1) CCP-Italy; cf. § 106 CCP-Macao, MA, 4–5; § 171 CCP-Greece, GR, 5. Absolute nullities lead to exclusion of evidence as does a finding of "non-usability." IT, 8. Any illegally gathered evidence in Brazil is also referred to as an "absolute nullity." BR, 3–4.

actual restriction of defense rights." Although the Spanish courts, in general, view "nullities" as "irregularities" which do not necessarily lead to exclusion of evidence, as opposed to "illegalities" which would lead to exclusion under the general exclusionary rule in § 11.1 LOPJ-Spain, which provides for exclusion in cases of violation of fundamental rights, it also appears that some grounds for a "nullity" could be of constitutional magnitude, such as acts performed under compulsion, in violation of defense rights, or in the absence of counsel per § 238(2-4) LOPJ.[84]

§ 130(2-4) CCP-Latvia provides for an exclusionary rule in cases of violations of "basic principles of criminal procedure" and lesser violations. It is articulated in terms typical of nullity statutes: "Information or facts, gathered while allowing other procedural violations, are admissible in a limited manner and may be used as evidence only in cases, where the procedural violation allowed is not substantial or may be eliminated."

Some nullity provisions also explicitly refer to derivative evidence. Thus, according to § 174(para. 3) CCP-France: "the annulled acts or documents are withdrawn from the investigative dossier and filed with the clerk of the Court of Appeal" and it is "prohibited to derive any information against the parties from the annulled acts or documents or parts of the acts or documents, upon the pain of disciplinary proceedings against the lawyers or judges."[85] §185(1) CCP-Italy also provides that: "The nullity of an act renders the subsequent acts invalid which depend on that declared to be annulled."[86]

In Italy, the term "nullity" usually refers to acts, whereas the term "non-usability" (§ 191 CCP-Italy) refers to evidence.[87] "Non-usability," on the other hand, has been limited in the literature to cases where there is a statutory prohibition on the gathering of the evidence, what the Germans would call a *Beweiserhebungsverbot*, whereas "nullities" arise, in the context of the gathering of evidence, when legal formalities are violated in the gathering of what would otherwise be admissible evidence.[88] The wording of the CCP-Italy of 1988, however, has left the difference between "non-usability" and "nullities" a bit murky, and the case-law has used the term "non-usability" to apply both to evidence gathered in violation of explicit evidence-gathering prohibitions, as well as otherwise admissible evidence gathered in an impermissible way.[89] Oddly enough, the Italian courts, while recognizing the statutory mandate to exclude derivative evidence in relation to "nullities," have refused to recognize the doctrine of "fruits of the poisonous tree" in relation to the more serious constitutional violations which fall under the rubric of "non-usability."[90]

29.2.5 Court-Made General Exclusionary Rules

1. *Absolute Exclusionary Rules*

The Czech Constitutional Court has ruled that all evidence gathered in violation of the law may not be used in a criminal case.[91]

In Belgium, the Court of Cassation has fashioned exclusionary rules which have gradually replaced the tradition reliance on statutory nullities. As early as 1923, it prescribed exclusion for evidence seized in violation of the law and concretized this approach in a more recent case in 1986, where it mandated exclusion in the case of "acts irreconcilable with the substantial rules of criminal procedure or with general principles of law, and particularly with the respect of the rights of the defense."[92] Belgian courts distinguish between evidence gathered following patently illegal acts, and evidence gathered in the course of an otherwise lawful investigative act where the rules have been violated.[93]

2. *Exclusionary Rules Allowing Discretion, Balancing*
   a. Must the violation be of constitutional magnitude? While Germany has no general constitutional or statutory exclusionary rule or use-prohibition,

[84] SP,6–7, 13–4.

[85] French courts have based exclusion of "fruits" on these sections. Jean Pradel, *Procédure pénale,* 9th ed. (Paris: Cujas, 1997), 604–05.

[86] For similar language, *see* § 573(1) CCP-Brazil, BR, 7–8; § 172 CCP-Argentina-Federal; § 196 (para.1) CCP-Venezuela; § 122 CCP-Portugal, PO,4.

[87] IT, 2.

[88] IT, 7.

[89] IT, 8.

[90] IT, 8.

[91] CZ, 11.

[92] Cass., 13 mai 1986, *Pasicrisie*, 1986, I, 1107, BE,3,6.

[93] An example of the latter would be a promise to induce a confession. BE, 3.

the German Supreme Court has developed a multi-step balancing process to be used by the trial court which focuses in its first step on the type of law enforcement violation:

> The decision as to whether or not there will be a prohibition on use is made on the basis of a comprehensive balancing (…). The weight of the procedural violation as well as the importance for the legally protected sphere of the affected party must be considered and placed in the balance as well as the consideration, that the truth may not be investigated at any price (…). On the other hand, one must consider that prohibitions on use impede the possibilities of determining the truth (…) and that the State according to the case law of the Constitutional Court must constitutionally guarantee an administration of justice which is capable of functioning without which justice cannot be realized (…) If the procedural provision which has been violated, does not, or not primarily, serve to protect the defendant, then a prohibition on use will be unlikely; On the other hand, a prohibition on use is appropriate, when the violated procedural provision is designed to secure the foundations of the procedural position of the accused or defendant in a criminal prosecution.[94]

The exclusionary rules fashioned by the USSC are all based on constitutional violations, be it of the Fourth, Fifth, or Sixth Amendments. *Mapp*, *Massiah*, and *Miranda* required exclusion, once the court determined that the respective constitutional amendments had been violated.[95] This is no longer true, however, for the USSC now treats exclusion following any of the aforementioned violations as a "last resort"[96] and since *Leon*,[97] withholds its decision until it has engaged in a (rather superficial) "cost-benefit" analysis to see whether the need for exclusion trumps the single remaining reason for exclusion, deterrence of unlawful police conduct.[98]

The Irish courts traditionally distinguished between evidence gathered in violation of the law, where the judge had much discretion to weigh various factors before deciding whether to admit or exclude the evidence, and constitutional violations. But, up until 1965, a judge could still refuse to exclude evidence gathered in violation of constitutional rights in the case of "extraordinary excusing circumstances."[99] But then, in 1990, the Irish High Court recognized a categorical exclusionary rule in cases where police clearly violate the constitutional rights of citizens, rejecting the "good faith" doctrine of *Leon*. According to Judge Finlay: "[t]he detection of crime and the conviction of guilty persons, no matter how important they may be in relation to the ordering of society, cannot, however, in my view, outweigh the unambiguously expressed constitutional obligation as far as practicable to defend and vindicate the personal rights of the citizen."[100] The Israeli High Court will only consider exclusion if the violation was of a major statutory rule designed to protect substantial rights of the accused.[101]

§ 158-4 CCP-Taiwan (as amended in 2003), gives the judge discretion in deciding whether to admit evidence gathered in violation of the statutory provisions: "The admissibility of the evidence, obtained in violation of the procedure prescribed by the law by an official in execution of criminal procedure, shall be determined by balancing the protection of human rights and the preservation of public interests, unless otherwise provided by law."[102]

In 1950, the Scottish High Court developed a test which balanced: "(a) the interest of the citizen to be protected from illegal or irregular invasions of his liberties by the authorities, and (b) the interest of the State to secure that evidence bearing upon the commission of crime

[94] BGHSt 38, 214, 218–22. English translation in Thaman, *Comparative Criminal Procedure*, *supra* note 78 at 111. This "balancing approach" (*Abwägungstheorie*) is one of three approaches used by German courts. The other two, the "protective purpose" theory (*Schutzzwecktheorie*) and that of the "right to control information" will be discussed, *infra*. GE, 7–8. German courts have also crafted a new exception to the exclusionary rule in cases where the defendant (or his lawyer) did not quickly object to the illegal methods and move to exclude. This exception has been roundly criticized in the literature. GE, 10.

[95] US, 1–2.

[96] Herring, *supra* note 44, at 700.

[97] Leon, *supra* note 32, at 906–07. US, 27.

[98] *See* Leon, *supra* note 32, at 921, where the USSC abandoned "judicial integrity" as a reason for having a strong exclusionary rule. US, 2.

[99] *See* People (A.G.) v. O'Brien (1965) I.R. 142, 160–61. IR, 14.

[100] People (D.P.P.) v Kenny, (1990) 2 I.R. 110, 134; (1990) I.L.R.M. 569, 579, IR, 7.

[101] IS, 4–5.

[102] TA-1.

and necessary to enable justice to be done. It thus held that evidence shall not be withheld from Courts of law on any merely formal or technical ground."[103] Although the approach of the Scottish High Court has been described as "conspicuously malleable," commentators seem to think that the courts take into account the typical factors used in other balancing tests, such as the seriousness of the violation, the "good faith" of the officers and whether they were acting under emergency circumstances, the seriousness of the criminal offense, and the "fairness" to the accused.[104]While the Scottish courts have struggled for decades in applying this test, the High Court, in 2006, simply equated the Scottish test with that articulated by the ECtHR in interpreting the Art. 6 fair trial right.[105]

Finally, there is a certain hierarchy among constitutional rights. The protection against torture and cruel, inhuman and degrading treatment is well-nigh absolute. Close behind is the right to counsel, which, if completely denied could result in reversal of a conviction or exclusion of evidence.[106] A confession without admonitions as to the right to silence, even when the *Miranda* rule has been recognized as being of constitutional stature,[107] does not, however, bring with it the Draconian exclusionary remedies which result from involuntary confessions. All democratic legal systems, however, allow the privacy of the home and confidential communications to be violated upon probable cause with judicial authorization.[108] But even when the rules are violated, especially in relation to the privacy of the home, exclusionary rules, as we shall see, are relatively weak. The ECtHR, for instance, has, to my knowledge, never found a violation of the right to a "fair trial" following a violation of the right to privacy under Art. 8 ECHR. On the other hand, the ECtHR has found the violation of the right to a "fair trial" and a violation of Art. 6 ECHR in cases involving entrapment or undue incitement by the police in the commission of the crime.[109] In a sense, this could be deemed to be the suppression of the evidence of the commission of the crime due to the excessive involvement of law enforcement authorities in the conception of the criminal offense. We will explore the hierarchization of constitutional rights in further detail in the sections, *infra*, dealing with violations of the right to privacy and interrogation practices.[110]

b. Determining Whether the Violation Was of Constitutional Magnitude

Although exclusionary rules in some jurisdictions apply to non-constitutional violations, I will focus on the judicial determination as to whether the police conduct constituted a serious violations of fundamental rights, for this is the first step in the balancing process in the majority of systems.

c. Was the "Constitutional" Violation Serious or Forgivable?

The first, and perhaps most important attempt at balancing constitutional rights against other considerations undertaken by the USSC, was in *United States v. Leon*,[111] which introduced the "good faith" exception to the theretofore categorical exclusionary rule for Fourth Amendment

[103] Lawrie v. Muir, S.L.T. (1950) 37, at 39–40, 1950 JC 19, at 26. SC, 2.

[104] SC, 3.

[105] HM Advocate v. Higgins, S.L.T. (2006), 946, 950, SC, 9.

[106] Even the ECt.HR will not engage in a weighing process when torture, statements in absence of counsel, or perhaps entrapment are involved. EU, 9.

[107] This is clear in Germany, where the right to silence is seen as protecting human dignity and the personality rights of the accused, and the admonitions are "designed to secure the foundations of the procedural position of the accused." BGHSt 38, at 218–22, 224–5 (1992), English translation in Thaman, *Comparative Criminal Procedure*, *supra* note 78, at 111.

[108] Art. 8 ECHR provides, on the one hand, that: everyone has a right to "respect for his private and family life, home and correspondence," but allows exceptions that are "in accordance with law" and "necessary in a democratic society in the interests of national security, public safety or the economic well-being of the country, for the prevention of disorder or crime, for the protection of health or morals, or for the protection of the rights and freedoms of others."

[109] For a discussion of several ECtHR decisions finding a violation of Art. 6 ECHR, *see* EU, 60. For a similar decision in Italy involving the suppression of child pornography, *see* Cass. 29 aprile 2004, Bonaiuti, in *Rivista penale* (2005), 636, IT, 9. *See* also MA, 7.

[110] For a three-part hierarchy of rights in ECtHR case law, one for non-grave privacy violations, another for grave but relative norm violations, and finally for extremely gave violations not subject to balancing. EU,23.

[111] *Supra*, note 32.

violations. Whereas in *Mapp*, the USSC had based the necessity for the exclusionary rule in deterrence of police lawlessness *and* in preserving judicial integrity, the *Leon* court collapsed the two tests and simply stated that they were the same: if exclusion would not deter lawless police conduct, then the integrity of the courts would not be violated by admitting and using unconstitutionally acquired evidence to prove guilt.[112] The so-called "cost-benefit" analysis of the court was similar to the rationale of the German Supreme Court when it balanced the gravity of the violation against the duty to determine truth in the criminal trial. The *Leon* court pronounced truth-finding, a classically inquisitorial value, to be a cardinal value of US criminal procedure,[113] yet had to abolish the judicial integrity basis for the exclusionary rule, because it was a judge who issued the search warrant which lacked probable cause. *Leon* limited the "good faith" exception to intentional or reckless violations, where the allegations of probable cause were clearly inadequate, thus preventing a sneaky police officer from presenting a clearly inadequate affidavit of probable cause to one of the many rubberstamp U.S. judges.[114]

The USSC has also extended the "good faith" exception to cases where the search warrant itself contained erroneous or inadequate descriptions of the things to be seized or the places to be searched,[115] to searches based on unconstitutional statutes,[116] and illegal detentions based on erroneous court records.[117] Finally, the court has recently lowered the bar to allow admission of evidence which was gathered when the police officer was guilty of "isolated negligence" in believing there was probable cause.[118]

Many courts which "balance" constitutional violations against other interests or values, including the "seriousness" of the constitutional violation, have specifically provided that a non-intentional or "good faith" violation would weigh in favor of using the evidence. For instance, the Australian High Court has fashioned a general balancing test to determine the excludability of illegally seized evidence, which emphasizes consideration of whether there was bad faith on the part of the police, the importance of the evidence, the seriousness of the offense, and the ease with which the law might have been complied with.[119] The Scottish courts also occasionally refer to whether there was bad faith on the part of the police in deciding whether to exclude.[120] The ECtHR has also been known to take into account "good faith," and lack of standing.[121]

§ 359a(1) CCP-Netherlands gives the court discretion to exclude evidence and obligates it to take account of the interest that the breached rule serves, the gravity of the breach and the harm it causes.[122] In 2002 the New Zealand Court of Appeal adopted a multi-factor "fairness" test which gives the trial judge broad discretion based on a list of criteria including the "seriousness of the offense" and the "importance of the evidence" and replaced a stricter *prima facie* test, in place since 1992, which recognized a rebuttable presumption that illegally seized

[112] *Id.*, at 918. On *Leon*'s "good faith" exception and its basis in deterrence, US, 15–6.

[113] *Leon, supra* note 32, at 907.

[114] For a case recognizing "good faith" despite a rubberstamping judge, *see* McCommon v. Mississippi, 474 U.S. 984 (1985) (Brennan, J., *dissenting*). *See also* United States v. Breckenridge, 782 F.2d 1317, 1321 (5th Cir. 1986), where it was held that "good faith" could still be applied when the judge did not even read the affidavit. The Israeli Supreme Court will balance "good faith" in its discretionary equation, but has rejected "deterrence" as a grounds for its exclusionary practice. IS, 3–5.

[115] Massachusetts v. Shepard, 468 U.S. 981, 988–90 (1984), decided on the same day as *Leon*.

[116] Illinois v. Krull, 480 U.S. 340, 349–50 (1987).

[117] Arizona v. Evans, 514 U.S. 1, 14–5 (1995).

[118] *Herring, supra* note 44, at 702.

[119] Bunning v. Cross, (1978) 141 C.L.R. 54 (Austl.), cited in Craig M. Bradley, "Mapp *Goes Abroad*," *Case Western Reserve Law Review* 52 (2001): 375, 380. The Israeli High Court also looks at whether the illegality affected the quality of the evidence. IS, 5–6. For a similar weighing of factors, see GR, 3.

[120] *See* Edgley v. Barbour, 1994 SCCR 789, 792, cited in Peter Duff, "Admissibility of Improperly Obtained Physical Evidence in the Scottish Criminal Trial: the Search for Principle," *Edinburgh Law Review* 8 (2004): 152, 165.

[121] EU, 32. Germany also takes standing into consideration in its balancing, according to the so-called *Rechtskreistheorie*. GE, 10.

[122] NE, 4.

evidence was inadmissible.[123] The reason for exclusion, both according to the overruled *prima facie* test and the new "fairness" test, is the "vindication of the right that has been breached"[124] and not, as with the U.S. Fourth Amendment exclusionary rule, the deterrence of the police.[125]

d. Balancing the Quality or Importance of the Evidence

(1) Introduction

Clearly the "importance" of the evidence in proving guilt depends on its probative value and the extent to which other evidence corroborates that which was obtained in violation of fundamental rights. In this respect, statements induced by torture or cruel, inhuman and degrading treatment should be considered with caution. Physical evidence, on the other hand, speaks for itself. Even if the fruit of an illegal search, wiretap or confession, the antecedent illegality does not affect its credibility.

(2) Evidence of Questionable Reliability

Coerced or otherwise involuntary confessions were traditionally excluded in the U.S. due to their lack of credibility, rather than on constitutional grounds.[126] Even potentially probative evidence may be excluded if the judge decides that its prejudicial nature outweighs its probative value.[127]

A number of post-Soviet codes have exclusionary rules which limit exclusion to situations where the violation affects the credibility of the evidence. For instance, § 105 CCP-Armenia, limits exclusion to situations where there is a "substantial violation in collecting evidence," that is, "a violation of constitutional rights and freedoms of the person and citizen or any other requirement of this code in the form of limitation or restriction of rights guaranteed by law to the participants of the trial that influenced or could have influenced the reliability of the facts."[128]

Similar weak exclusionary rules are applied in the International Criminal Tribunals for the Former Yugoslavia (ICTY) and Rwanda (ICTR) and the International Criminal Court (ICC). Rule 95 of the ICTY Rules of Procedure and Evidence provides: "No evidence shall be admissible if obtained by methods which cast substantial doubt on its reliability or if its admission is antithetical to, and would seriously damage, the integrity of the proceedings."[129] Identical language was incorporated into § 69(7) of the Rome Statute for the International Criminal Court.[130]

(3) Physical Evidence That Proves *Corpus Delicti*

As a general rule, courts have a hard time excluding physical evidence, even when they recognize it is the fruit of a serious constitutional violation. For instance, even if a confession is suppressed as being the product of "oppression," per § 76(2) PACE-England and Wales, § 76(4-6) PACE provides that this shall not have any influence on the admissibility in evidence of "any facts" discovered by utilizing the suppressed confession.[131] Thus, even when the object of a dwelling search is found in gross violation of a warrant requirement, courts

[123] *Shaheed, New Zealand Law Reports* 2 (2002): 377, CA , cited in Richard Mahoney, "Abolition of New Zealand's Prima Facie Exclusionary Rule," *Criminal Law Review* (2003): 607.

[124] *Id.* at 610.

[125] On the development of the deterrent rationale of the U.S. Fourth Amendment exclusionary rule, US, 7–8.

[126] Hopt v. Territory of Utah, 110 U.S. 574, 585 (1884).

[127] Fed. Rule of Evidence 403, § 352 Cal. Evidence Code.

[128] Similar language is used in § 125(2)(1) CCP-Azerbaijan; § 94(2) CCP-Moldova; and § 125 CCP-Turkmenistan. This language appears to be taken from § 143(2) of the Model Code of Criminal Procedure for the Commonwealth of Independent States, which greatly influenced the code-writing in many post-Soviet republics.

[129] United Nations, IT/32/Rev.40, July 12, 2007.

[130] The Rome Statute of the International Criminal Court. July 17, 1998. U.N. GAOR, 53d Sess, U.N. Doc.A/CONF. 183/9 (1998).

[131] § 76(5) PACE provides, albeit, that the jury shall not be told that the "facts" were derived from the statements of the defendant. Alleging that there are no English cases upholding the suppression of physical evidence, Duff, *supra* note 119, at 152.

will often let the evidence in just due to its probative value.[132]

In Italy the police duty to seize contraband, fruits and instrumentalities of crime, i.e., the *corpus delicti*, breaks the nexus between a patently unconstitutional search and its intended fruits, and allows the use of the evidence collected.[133] The other side of this equation, is that "mere evidence" discovered in a patently illegal search would be "non-usable," much as it was in the U.S. up until the 1960s.[134] Since *Warden v. Hayden*, there appears to be no item which may not be seized if it can be used, even as "mere evidence" to circumstantially prove criminal guilt.[135]

This unwillingness to suppress physical evidence is justified by some courts in employing their balancing tests, by asserting that the admission of physical evidence can never violate the right to a fair trial because it is not really the "fruit" of the violation, nor dependent thereon, having pre-existed the violation.[136]

e. The Gravity of the Crime Which Is Being Prosecuted
Balancing tests often consider the seriousness of the crime allegedly committed by the defendant. *Beling* in his treatise on evidentiary prohibitions is clearly more generous when it comes to admissibility of evidence of capital crimes, than less serious ones: "the interest in the solving of high treason or a murder – is infinitely greater than the interest in investigating and punishing a cyclist who drives on the wrong side of the road, or a sassy young man who gives his desire for singing too long a rein during nighttime hours."[137] *Beling's* approach has been adopted by the German courts. Thus, even if the court finds that the violation is important enough to give rise to a prohibition on use – German courts, for instance, views the use of diary entries to prove guilt as a grave violation of the right to develop one's personality – the court must still weigh the seriousness of the crime charged before deciding whether to exclude.

> If the accusation is less weighty, then the personality interest of the author of the writings will often prevail. In cases of probable cause that a serious attack on life, other important legal interests or the state or other serious attacks on the legal order have been committed, then the protection of the private life-sphere must give way. The balancing must be undertaken while taking into consideration the interest in criminal prosecution in light of the importance of the constitutional right, whereby the alleged wrongful act, to the extent it can be judged, must also be considered.[138]

In a 2003 decision, the Belgian Court of Cassation has switched from a categorical exclusionary rule for violation of certain important constitutional rights, to a balancing approach which takes into account the seriousness of the offense. This approach has been criticized in the literature.[139] The Dutch High Court, in applying the statutory discretionary exclusionary rule in § 359(a)(1) CCP-Netherlands, has also indicated that exclusion may not be warranted if the prosecution is for a serious crime.[140]

Andrew Ashworth has, in my view correctly, asserted that the seriousness of the charges facing the defendant should never go into the balancing process, because the more serious the charge, the more detrimental will be the

[132] *See* the English case of R.v. Sanghera *Criminal Appeal Reports* 1 (2001): 20, 299, 305–06, in which police search a robbery suspect's home without a warrant or consent and the loot is allowed into evidence due to its unimpeachable probative value and the "good faith" of the officers, who figured the suspect would have consented.

[133] § 271(3) CCP-Italy, which requires that all documentation of illegally intercepted conversations should be destroyed, makes an exception for physical evidence which can prove *corpus delicti*.

[134] *See* Boyd v. United States, 116 U.S. 616, 628 (1886). The "mere evidence" doctrine was only repealed in Warden v. Hayden, 387 U.S. 294, 310 (1967).

[135] *See* Andresen v. Maryland, 427 U.S. 463, 473 (1976); Fisher v. United States, 425 U.S. 391, 420 (1976).

[136] This approach is used in South Africa, Schwikkard & Van der Merwe, *supra* note 57, at 488.

[137] Beling, *supra* note 35, at 35.

[138] BGHSt 19, 325,331. English translation in Thaman, *Comparative Criminal Procedure*, *supra* note 78, at 113. Thus, the German Supreme Court allowed use of a diary in a brutal rape-murder case, but not in a perjury case. *Id.*

[139] On the so-called *Antigone* case, BE, 9.

[140] NE, 6.

introduction of the evidence to the defendant, presuming that the punishment will be commensurately more severe.[141]

f. The "Fair Trial" Assessment

The ECHR contains no express exclusionary rules and the ECtHR traditionally defers to domestic exclusionary practices. In *Schenk v. Switzerland*, a case involving an unlawful recording of a telephone conversation, the ECtHR stated: "While Article 6 of the Convention guarantees the right to a fair trial, it does not lay down any rules on the admissibility of evidence as such, which is therefore primarily a matter for regulation under national law."[142] This doctrine was followed in a number of English cases dealing mostly with illegal wiretaps or secret tape-recordings. In *Allan v. United Kingdom,* the court cited *Schenk* in holding: It is not the role of the Court to determine, as a matter of principle, whether particular types of evidence – for example, unlawfully obtained evidence – may be admissible or, indeed, whether the applicant was guilty or not. The question which must be answered is whether the proceedings as a whole, including the way in which the evidence was obtained, were fair. This involves an examination of the "unlawfulness" in question and, where violation of another Convention right is concerned, the nature of the violation found.[143] The ECtHR will also look at the effect of the violation on the credibility of the evidence, whether there are domestic remedies for the violation short of exclusion, and whether exclusion would be in the public interest.[144]

It was only in 2006 that the Israeli Supreme Court upheld the suppression of otherwise relevant evidence. And while the case involved a confession, the court generally recognized the power of the trial judge to suppress evidence, on a case-by-case basis, if the evidence was unlawfully gathered and its admission would violate the defendant's right to a fair trial.[145] The Israeli high court called this the "preventative" approach, allegedly adopted by most common law countries, and differentiated it from the "deterrent-educational" approach used in the U.S.[146]

As mentioned, *supra*, § 11.1 LOPJ-Spain clearly requires exclusion of evidence and its fruits gathered in violation of "fundamental" rights. This statute was enacted on the heels of a landmark decision of the Spanish Constitutional Court which required exclusion of both direct and derivative evidence only when the violation touched on the constitutional rights of the citizens. Unlike the USSC in *Leon*, however, the court did not mention deterrence of the police as a rationale, but grounded the prohibition of use on: (1) the violation of a fair trial with all the guarantees established by law (Art. 24 Const.-Spain); (2) a denial of equality of arms, in the sense that the defense may not violate the law in order to produce evidence; and (3) a violation of the presumption of innocence, which in Spanish law restricts the prosecutor to the use of legally gathered evidence to rebut the presumption.[147]

Thus, whereas Spain finds a categorical violation of the right to a fair trial if a violation of constitutional magnitude is ascertained, English law gives the court discretion in every case to make the ultimate decision. We can see here, that the "fair trial" criterion, also adopted by the ECtHR, is flexible enough to include a plethora of factors. In a sense, each judge can give her

[141] Andrew Ashworth, "Excluding evidence as protecting rights," *Criminal Law Review* (1977), 723, 732, discussed in Duff, *supra* note 119, at 169–71.

[142] Schenck v. Switzerland, 13 E.H.R.R. 242, 265–6 (1988), ¶ 46. *See* EU,6.

[143] Allan v. United Kingdom, 36 E.H.R.R. 12, 144, 156 (2003), ¶ 42. The courts in England and Wales have by and large accepted that the test used by the ECt.HR is the same as that used under § 78 PACE, discussed, *supra*. EW, 6.

[144] EW,8. These factors will be discussed, *infra*. This is a two-step test, first to find whether a Convention right was violated, and then a "careful balancing" to determine whether the evidence must be excluded. There must be at least "minimal" legally gathered evidence to support a conviction before illegally gathered evidence may be used. EU, 7–8.

[145] *Issacharov Case* (2006), IS, 2–3.

[146] IS, 3–4.

[147] STC 114/1984 of November 29, RTC 1984. SP, 3–5. *See* Eduardo de Urbano Castrillo and Miguel Ángel Torres Morato, *La Prueba Illícita Penal. Estudio jurisprudencial,* 3rd ed. (Navarra: Thomson/Aranzadi 2003), 41–2, and Marien Aguilera Morales, "Regla de exclusión y acusatorio," in *Proceso penal y sistemas acusatorios*, ed. Lorena Bachmaier Winter et al. (Madrid: Marcial Pons 2008), 84–8, for commentary.

own stamp on what is a "fair trial" with so many factors in the balance.[148]

Courts, like those in England and Wales, which balance factors in deciding whether to admit illegally gathered evidence, are engaging in an exercise of discretion not unlike those involved in deciding the admissibility of otherwise relevant evidence, which might be excessively prejudicial or inflammatory.[149] Yet where it is the trial judge who does the weighing, such as in England and Wales, and that trial judge is also a trier of the fact, as in the Netherlands, then, even if the judge decides to exclude the tainted evidence, it will be very difficult for the judge to banish that evidence from his or her mind when deciding the issue of guilt. Although the evidence may not be referred to in the judgment reasons, it cannot but psychologically influence the decision which the judge eventually reaches.[150]

g. Preserving the Integrity of the Courts

Duff correctly notes that, if exclusionary rules are to have any meaning they must be "extrinsic," and not anchored in the "intrinsic" emphasis on probative value/credibility. The notion of "judicial integrity" is such an "extrinsic" justification for exclusion, yet scholars differ as to its theoretical underpinnings. *Duff* points to: (1) the "disciplinary" model adopted by the U.S. which focuses on deterrence of unconstitutional police conduct; (2) the "vindicatory" model, which focuses on protecting citizens' constitutional rights and would tend to automatic exclusion once a significant violation has been ascertained[151]; and (3) the "moral legitimacy" approach, which is more aimed at proportionality balancing of the seriousness of the constitutional violation and the harm to the public if a dangerous criminal were to go free.[152]

For the *Mapp* court, of course, the "imperative of judicial integrity" was vindicatory, and meant that "the criminal goes free, if he must, but it is the law that sets him free. Nothing can destroy a government more quickly than its failure to observe its own laws, or worse, its disregard of the charter of its own existence."[153] The court in *Leon*, of course, abandoned this high ground by equating judicial integrity with an exclusively disciplinary rationale,[154] while at the same time Canada elevated judicial integrity to constitutional status in Art. 24(2) of its Charter. The Israeli Supreme Court in its seminal 2006 decision in *Issacharov*, decided that its "preventative approach" was really geared at guaranteeing a fair trial *and* judicial integrity, but not at vindicating the right or deterring unlawful police conduct.[155]

It is thus evident, that even an insistence that the courts not launder dirty evidence does not mean that, in the end, one will not end up with a vague balancing test where constitutional violations can be weighed out of the picture.

h. The Public Impact of the Admissibility Decision

But what is the "public interest?" This could mean that the public would be appalled if evidence resulting from torture or pervasive warrantless wiretapping were used in the courts.[156] The Australian High Court has also mandated exclusion when "the public interest in maintaining the integrity of the courts and in ensuring the

[148] According to *Ashworth*, "if courts are allowed simply to pick and choose the guiding principle(s) in the circumstances of any individual case, there is unlikely to be a consistent approach and a danger of the question of admissibility being left to the "whim of the particular court." *Supra* note 140, at 733–74, cited in Duff, *supra* note 119, at 159. Cf. EW, 10, indicating that this is "not an apt field for hard case law and well-founded distinctions between cases."

[149] For instance, pursuant to Rule 403 of the Federal Rules of Evidence.

[150] This problem has been addressed in the literature in the Netherlands. NE,2–3. A judge who becomes acquainted with illegally gathered evidence which has been suppressed may not sit as trial judge per § 39(a)(4) CCP-Slovenia, SL,7. On how this "dilemma" dilutes exclusionary rules in Germany, GE, 6.

[151] The New Zealand courts have rejected the deterrent rationale and focus exclusively on "vindication of the right" that has been breached, though they still balance. Mahoney, *supra* note 122, at 610.

[152] Duff, *supra* note 119, at 160–74.

[153] *Mapp*, *supra* note 24, at 659.

[154] The *Leon* court simply proclaims that if exclusion is not justified by its deterrent effect on *police* misconduct, not misconduct or errors of judges, then judicial integrity is not compromised. *Supra* note 32, at 916.

[155] IS, 3–4.

[156] *See* Duff, *supra* note 119, at 155, for examples.

observance of the law and minimum standards of propriety by those entrusted with powers of law enforcement" requires it.[157]

In *Leon*, the USSC proclaimed: "The substantial social costs exacted by the exclusionary rule for the vindication of Fourth Amendment rights have long been a source of concern. Our cases have consistently recognized that unbending application of the exclusionary sanction to enforce ideals of governmental rectitude would impede unacceptably the truth-finding functions of judge and jury." The court continued: "particularly when law enforcement officers have acted in objective good faith or their transgressions have been minor, the magnitude of the benefit conferred on such guilty defendants offends basic concepts of the criminal justice system."[158]

Thus, the USSC posits a "public interest" in "having juries receive all probative evidence of a crime."[159] More recently, the court bemoaned the exclusionary rule's "costly toll upon truth-seeking," which consists in "letting guilty and possibly dangerous defendants go free."[160] The same logic is used in confession cases where the court weighs the benefits of exclusion in terms of deterring future *Miranda* violations against the exclusion of reliable evidence.[161] The Israeli Supreme Court, in *Issacharov*, has hooked its balancing test to a cost-benefit evaluation, which is tied to the considerations of the "public interest." Thus, in cases where the evidence is crucial to a finding of guilt and the crime charged is serious, the Israeli court has indicated that the principle of truth-finding will trump the violation of human rights because a failure to convict will undermine public confidence in the administration of justice.[162]

With the U.S. disciplinary, cost-benefit approach, it appears that intrinsic emphasis on probative evidence is pushing back the vindicatory interest in protecting constitutional rights and that there is a danger of a return to old Common Law presumptions of admissibility of relevant evidence, or its old inquisitorial counterpart which prioritized truth over rights.

29.2.6 General Rules Relating to "Fruits of the Poisonous Tree"

As was noted, *supra*, the CCP-Brazil was amended in 2008 to introduce an absolute exclusionary rule which explicitly extends to fruits of the poisonous tree, and recognizes the doctrines of inevitable discovery and independent source developed by the USSC. A similar provision was introduced into the CCP-Slovenia in 1994, which provides that a court may not base a decision on evidence acquired in violation of constitutional rights and liberties, nor of other explicit norms of criminal procedure, nor on evidence derived from such violations.[163]

The provision in § 11.1 LOPJ-Spain which provides for exclusion of all "derivative evidence,"[164] has over the years also permitted several exceptions, most recently by a series of Spanish Constitutional Court decisions, which will be discussed in more detail later. However, a good summary of the new Spanish doctrine is presented in a decision of the Spanish Supreme Court of 2004: (1) The general rule is that evidence derived directly or indirectly from a violation of fundamental rights is inadmissible, as long as there is a causal nexus; (2) An exception exists, even when there is a factual causal nexus between the illegality and the evidence, if the causal link is not based in the illegality (is not "anti-juridical"); (3) In order to assess the existence of a legally relevant connection, the following elements should be taken into account: (a) The significance of the constitutional infringement; (b) The importance of the evidence for proving guilt; (c) whether there was a hypothetical clean path to discover the

[157] Ridgeway v. the Queen, (1995) 184 C.L.R. 19,38, cited in Bradley, *Mapp Goes Abroad*, *supra* note 118, at 380.

[158] *Leon*, *supra* note 32, at 907–08.

[159] *Murray*, *supra* note 31, at 537.

[160] *Herring*, *supra* note 44, at 697.

[161] Michigan v. Tucker, 417 U.S. 433, 450–51 (1974) This case dealt not with a statement of often questionable reliability, but the testimony of a witness discovered through a *Miranda*-defective interrogation.

[162] IS, 7.

[163] Fišer et al, *supra* note 61, at 385. This rule does not except the usual exceptions of independent source, inevitable discovery or attenuation of the taint. SL, 8.

[164] SP, 4.

evidence (i.e. inevitable discovery); (d) whether the right violated requires special protection; and (e) whether the violating officers acted intentionally, or erred in good faith, and thus whether exclusion is necessary for deterrent purposes.[165] In the Netherlands, the courts basically have concluded that the discovery of the evidence must have been *exclusively* the result of the antecedent illegality – that the discovery was *largely* the result of the illegality is insufficient.[166] In Greece, both a traditional nullity rule and a modern "exclusionary rule" explicitly apply to derivative evidence.[167]

Some courts, however, have expressly rejected the doctrine of "fruits of the poisonous tree" even while allowing for suppression of the primary evidence seized as a result of a violation of the defendant's rights.[168] The ECtHR has also generally rejected the doctrine of "fruits of the poisonous tree" though it does refer to the exceptions of attenuation, independent source and inevitable discovery.[169]

Some courts will admit evidence that has been discovered through an illegal "search" if it is actually "seized" by independent legal means.[170] The courts will also admit evidence which is seized illegally, if it would have inevitably been discovered through legal means.[171] Both of these doctrines have been recognized and applied by the Spanish courts despite Spain's categorical exclusionary rule in relation to derivative evidence.[172] In 1997, the court even proclaimed that the use of derivative evidence would constitute an incitement to utilize unconstitutional procedures which, indirectly, produce results. The court continued, that "the expansive effect provided in § 11.1 LOPJ only allows evaluating independent evidence, that is, which has no causal connection to that gathered illegally." In the analysis, one should not confuse "different evidence" derived from the illegality, from "independent" evidence without causal connection.[173]

29.2.7 Remedies Other Than Exclusion

The USSC relied on exclusionary rules in the 1960s and 1970s because of the fact that other methods of discipline of police lawlessness, such as criminal prosecutions, civil suits, discipline etc. had all proved to be ineffective. An interesting aspect of the Dutch exclusionary rule is that it gives the judge a range of sanctions, reaching to dismissal of the charges, in the case of extremely serious violations, to exclusion of the evidence, or a discount in punishment in cases where the court deems that exclusion would not be warranted after balancing the various factors mentioned in the statute or where no evidence was gathered as a result of the violation.[174]

---

[165] STS 9/2004 of January 19, available at http://sentencias.juridicas.com/index.php. SP, 11–3.

[166] NE, 7.

[167] §§ 175, 177(2) CCP-Greece, GR, 17.

[168] Cf. TA, 5. "Fruits" are also seldom excluded as a result of Norway's "vague" balancing test. NO, 2–4. The case law and the literature in Germany also overwhelmingly reject the doctrine of "fruits of the poisonous tree." GE, 16–7.

[169] EU, 32. The ECtHR has never ruled that the violation of the right to privacy brings with it exclusion of evidence. EU, 5, 8.

[170] The doctrine of "independent source" is applied in cases where there have been two searches, an illegal one and a legal one, independent of the illegality. It is applied, for instance, when police discover the presence of evidence illegally, but actually seize it pursuant to a search warrant based on information they possessed before the illegal search. Segura v. United States, 468 U.S. 796, 805 (1984); *Murray*, *supra* note 31, at 537.

[171] This doctrine of "inevitable discovery" is applied where there is only one search and seizure, but other investigative procedures independent of the illegality *would have* discovered the evidence legally. Nix v. Williams, *supra* note 30, at 444. The Germans call this the "hypothetical independent source" or "hypothetical clean path." Thomas Weigend, "Germany," in *Comparative Criminal Procedure: A Worldwide Study*, *supra* note 55, at 253.

[172] *See* Decision of June 5, 1995 (Spanish Supreme Court), RJ 1995. no. 4538, 6058, at 6060, English translation in Thaman, *Comparative Criminal Procedure*, *supra* note 78, at 118–9. For instance, in STC 81/April 1, 1998, the Spanish Constitutional Court refused to suppress drugs found pursuant to a search incident to arrest of a person that followed an unlawful wiretap, because the suspect was under heavy surveillance before the wiretap and the arrest would have been made anyway. SP, 11–2.

[173] STS of April 18, 1997 (RJ 1997, 3611), cited in De Urbano Castrillo and Torres Morato, *supra* note 146, at 49–50.

[174] § 359(a)(2) CCP-Netherlands, NE, 6–7. For a voice in the American literature suggesting punishment discounts, instead of exclusion: Guido Calabresi, "The Exclusionary Rule," *Harvard Journal of Law and Public Policy* 26 (2003): 111, 116.

29.3 Rules of Admissibility/Exclusion in Relation to Violations of the Right to Privacy

29.3.1 General Provisions Protecting the Right to Privacy and/or to Develop One's Personality

1. *Constitutional Provisions*

   Art. 8(1) ECHR, which is binding on all members of the Council of Europe, provides: Everyone has the right to respect for his private and family life, his home and his correspondence. Section 29.2, also sets the standards for official interference in this right: "There shall be no interference by a public authority with the exercise of this right except such as is in accordance with the law and is necessary in a democratic society in the interests of national security, public safety or the economic well-being of the country, for the prevention of disorder or crime, for the protection of health or morals, or for the protection of the rights and freedoms of others."[175] Since the ECHR only sets minimum guidelines for the countries subject to its commands, countries can provide greater protection than provided by the ECHR.

   The Const.-U.S. does not explicitly refer to a right to privacy, yet several states have added a constitutional right to privacy in their constitutions.[176] The Const.-Brazil provides that "the intimacy, privacy, honor and image of a person are inviolable.[177] Private life and honor, along with the sanctity of the home are protected by the Const.-Finland.[178] Art. 2(1) of the Const.-Germany (*Grundgesetz*) protects the "free development of the personality."[179] The Preamble and Art. 5 of Const.-Turkey proclaim that it is the "birthright" of every Turk to have the ability to develop his or her "spiritual and material assets."[180] The Basic Law of Macao protects the right to personal reputation and the privacy of their private and family life.[181] Art. 47 Const.-Poland reads: "Everyone shall be entitled to a legal protection of his private life, of his honor and good reputation and to make decisions about his personal life."[182] Art. 26 Const.-Portugal protects the right to one's likeness, as well as the privacy of personal and family life.[183] The right to "privacy" is also protected in a general sense in several other national constitutions.[184]

   Art. 19 Const.-Greece was amended in 2001 to provide for a strict exclusionary rule for all violations of the right to privacy in the home, in one's communications or in one's personal data which brooks of no balancing.[185]

2. *Statutory Provisions*

   Occasionally, statutes explicitly provide for exclusion of evidence gathered in violation of the general right to privacy.[186]

3. *High Court Jurisprudence Interpreting the General Right*

   The right to privacy is often given express constitutional protection, and is defined in a much broader manner than in the U.S. The right to privacy is

[175] The emphasis on individual and family life has also found its imprint in many national constitutions as well. Cf. Art. 20 Const.-Turkey, TU, 9.

[176] Alaska Constitution, Art. I, § 22: "The right of the people to privacy is recognized and shall not be infringed;" Arizona Constitution Art. II, § 8: "No person shall be disturbed in his private affairs…;" Florida Constitution, Art. I, § 23: "Every natural person has the right to be let alone and free from governmental intrusion into the person's private life except as otherwise provided herein;" Montana Constitution, Art. II, § 10: "The right of individual privacy is essential to the well-being of a free society and shall not be infringed without the showing of a compelling state interest;" Washington Constitution, Art. I, § 7: "No person shall be disturbed in his private affairs, or his home invaded, without authority of law." *See* Michael J. Gorman, "Survey: State Search and Seizure Analogs," *Mississippi Law Journal* 77 (2007): 417–64. Each of the 50 U.S. states has its own constitution and laws relating to criminal law and procedure, and they may give more protection than that accorded by the Const.-US as interpreted by the U.S. Supreme Court. US, 2.

[177] Art. 5(X) Const.-Brazil, BR, 18. Similar language is used in the Const.-Spain. SP, 14.

[178] Art. 10, Const.-Finland, FI, 4.

[179] GE, 13. Art. 24 Const.-Serbia also protects the right to develop one's personality. SE, 24. Cf. Art. 5(1) Const.-Greece, which, however, is seldom applied in criminal cases. GR, 12.

[180] TU, 9.

[181] Art. 30 (2) Const.-Macao, MA, 8.

[182] PL, 6.

[183] PO, 4.

[184] Art. 10(1) Const.-Netherlands, NE, 7. Cf. Art. 35 Const.-Slovenia which includes protection of "mental and physical integrity." SL, 10.

[185] GR, 4.

[186] Thus, § 126 CCP-Portugal provides for a "nullity" whenever evidence is obtained in violation of the right to privacy, as well as the more specific right to privacy in one's home and communications. PO, 4–5.

related to the right to human dignity (also never mentioned in the U.S. Constitution) and most importantly to the "right to develop one's personality."[187] This approach has made certain items non-seizable, even where the government has probable cause that they would be material to prove guilt in a criminal case. In Germany and some other countries this protection extends to personal diaries[188] and a person's right to confidentiality in their spoken words.[189] Thus it is impermissible for a participant in a conversation to secretly tape-record the words of a conversation partner, and such evidence is usually not usable in a criminal prosecution. This doctrine is reminiscent of the old "mere evidence" doctrine of the USSC which was overruled in 1967.[190] According to that doctrine, the government only had a right to seize the *corpus delicti* of crime, that is, objects to which it had a superior title: such as fruits and instruments of crime, and contraband. Personal papers were protected, unless they were instruments of crime.[191] In fact, to search for and seize a person's words, even where put to paper or uttered under no compulsion, was considered to be tantamount to compelling self-incrimination. As the *Boyd* court noted: "And we have been unable to perceive that the seizure of a man's private books and papers to be used in evidence against him is substantially different from compelling him to be a witness against himself."[192]

Thus, the now overruled "mere evidence" rule and the current German limitations on using highly personal evidence to prove guilt, constitute *prima facie* intrinsic prohibitions on the seizure of what may be highly probative evidence, not merely prohibitions on "use" due to the irregular or illegal methods of seizure.[193] German doctrine and case-law provide for a nearly absolute prohibition when the most intimate sphere of privacy and personality-development is violated, such as by seizing a diary, secret-taperecordings in the home and violations of privacy of the dwelling, and a relative prohibition when there is an invasion of privacy in an otherwise public realm (such as overhearing a private conversation in a restaurant), and observations made of public conduct.[194]

The ECHR recently decided a case where Russian police contrived to have a detective invited into a defendant's home and once inside, he secretly recorded a conversation in which the defendant made inculpatory statements which were simultaneously transferred outside the house to other officers who were monitoring the conversation. Although the Russian courts found the practice to be legal,[195] the ECtHR found a violation of Art. 8 ECHR, yet, as in nearly all privacy cases, did not deem that the use of the tape-recording violated the defendant's right to a fair trial, because it was not the only evidence of guilt.[196]

Although some constitutions, like the American, do not expressly protect a general right to privacy, the high courts will often read this protection into other more general constitutional provisions. Thus, the Supreme Court of Taiwan has found a right to privacy and to develop the personality in that country's constitution.[197] In the U.S., the Supreme Court has fashioned a test which looks at whether the disputed investigative act violated a "reasonable expectation of privacy" of the person affected.[198]

[187] Art. 2(1) Const-Germany. GE,3.

[188] *See* Decision of German Supreme Court of Feb. 21, 1964, BGHSt 19, 325, 326–8 (1964), English translation at Thaman, *Comparative Criminal Procedure*, *supra* note 78, at 82. GE, 3–4. The Portuguese Constitutional court also decided that evidence from a diary legally seized in a home cannot be used in an unrestricted manner, but only after a balancing of the seriousness of the privacy invasion against the need to know the truth. PO, 6.

[189] *See* Decision of German Supreme Court of June 14, 1960, BGHSt 14, 358, 359–60, 364–5 (1960), English translation at Thaman, *Comparative Criminal Procedure*, *supra* note 78, at 72–3.

[190] See note 133, *supra* and accompanying text.

[191] *Boyd*, *supra* note 133, at 628; *Weeks*, *supra* note 20, at 391–2.

[192] *Boyd*, *supra* note 133, at 633. Note the similarity with the now outdated Canadian exclusionary rule based on constitutional violations which "conscript" the defendant to give evidence against himself. *See* Section II.C.3, *supra*. For a similar comparison of a subpoena *duces tecum* with an involuntary confession, *see* Beling, *supra* note 35, at 14.

[193] On the distinction between *Beweiserhebungsverbot* (evidentiary gathering prohibition) and *Beweisverwertungsverbot* (evidentiary use-prohibition), *see* Claus Roxin, *Strafverfahrensrecht,* 24th ed. (Munich: Beck 1995), 164.

[194] On this "three-sphere approach," *see* GE, 9. On the importance of the diary and tape-recording cases in Germany. GE, 12–4.

[195] RU, 3. It would also be legal in the U.S. *See* United States v. White, 401 U.S. 745 (1971). US, 4.

[196] Bykov v. Russia ¶¶ 69–105 (March 10, 2009), http://cmiskp.echr.coe.int/tkp197/view.asp?item=1&portal=hbkm&action=html&highlight=bykov%20|%20v.%20|%20russia&sessionid=56241174&skin=hudoc-en (accessed July 2, 2010). RU,3.

[197] TA, 3.

[198] The landmark case in this respect is United States v. Katz, 398 U.S. 347 (1967). US, 3.

Both in the U.S. and in the jurisprudence of the ECtHR privacy rights are not seen to be intrinsically related to criminal procedure. The USSC has held that once the right to privacy has been violated, it is not again violated by introducing the evidence seized as a result of the primary violation. The ECtHR has similarly held that the violation of privacy rights does not require a remedy "within criminal procedure."[199]

29.3.2 Protection of Privacy in One's Home

1. *Constitutional Provisions*

   Many democratic constitutions explicitly require judicial authorization for searches of dwellings.[200] The inviolability of the dwelling and of one's private communications rank among the most cherished rights of citizens in democratic countries. They are enshrined in all major human rights conventions.[201] The inviolability of the home and private communications may, of course, be "violated,"[202]in the investigation of criminal cases if it is "necessary" "in a democratic society…to defend order, prevent punishable acts…, etc.[203] Democratic constitutions usually require that a judge decide if this "necessity" exists[204] and without judicial authorization, searches of dwellings are *prima facie* illegal.[205]

   Some national constitutions also include explicit exclusionary rules relating to violations of the constitutional provisions protecting the home.[206]

2. *Statutory Provisions*

   Most democratic countries have also enacted legislation requiring judicial authorization for searches and seizures.[207] Constitutional and statutory provisions

[199] EU, 22.

[200] Art. 15 Const.-Belgium, BE, 1, 12; Art. 5(XI) Const.-Brazil, BR, 23; Art. 18 Const.-Georgia; Art. 12 Const.-Czech Republic, CZ, 12; Art. 13(1,2) Const.-Germany, GE, 15; Art. 9(1) Const.-Greece, GR, 2, 13–4; Art. 14 Const.-Italy; Art. 21 Const.-Lithuania ; Art. 34 Const.-Portugal, PO, 6; Art. 25 Const.-Russia; Art. 40 Const.-Serbia, SE, 9; Art. 36 Const.-Slovenia, SL, 10; Art. 18(2) Const.-Spain, SP, 16; Art. 21 Const.-Turkey, TU, 10; Art. 30 Const.-Ukraine (Art. 30 Const.); United States (Const. IV Amend.).

[201] Cf. Art. 8, ECHR; Art. 17, IPCPR; Art. 12(1) Universal Declaration of Human Rights; Art. 11, American Convention on Human Rights.

[202] As to the "violability" of the so-called "inviolable" rights, *see* Andrés de la Oliva Santos, "Sobre la ineficacia de las pruebas ilícitamente obtenidas," *Tribunales de Justicia*, no. 8–9 (Aug-Sept. 2003): 1, at 5.

[203] Art. 8(2) ECHR. Necessity is, in the criminal law, a weighty standard. Another's life may only be taken in defense of one's own if there is a necessity to do so. If that necessity is not shown, the slayer is guilty of murder or manslaughter. The same holds for commission of a crime under the necessity defense, where it is clear that the person claiming necessity cannot have brought about the necessity with his or her own acts.

[204] Art. 18 Const.-Georgia; Art. 13(1,2) Const.-Germany; Art. 14 Const.-Italy; Art. 21 Const.-Lithuania; Art. 25 Const.-Russia; Art. 18(2) Const-Spain; Art. 30 Const.-Ukraine; IV Amendment, Const.-U.S.. Art. 14 Const.-Italy refers back to the CPP-Italy which allows searches of dwellings pursuant to a reasoned judicial authorization based upon "reasonable cause" (*fondato motivo*) that a person or things related to a crime are to found in a place. § 247 CPP-Italy.

[205] Although the ECHR does not explicitly require judicial authorization, its case law has tended to impose such a requirement. In three cases involving searches authorized and carried out by French customs officials, the Eur. Ct. HR ruled that Art. 8 was violated due to the absence of judicial authorization. *Funke v. France*, 16 EHRR 297, 329 (1993); *Miailhe v. France*, 16 EHRR 332, 354 (1993) and *Cremieux v. France* , 16 EHRR 357, 376 (1993). The Eur. Ct.HR, however, failed to find a violation of Art. 8 when an official of the SwissTelecommunications Service authorized and carried out a search of a home for unauthorized telephone equipment, where a reasoned order was required and the search was very carefully delimited. The Court held, that "it must be particularly vigilant where, as in the present case, the authorities are empowered under national law to order and effect searches without a judicial warrant. If individuals are to be protected from arbitrary interference by the authorities with the rights guaranteed under Article 8, a legal framework and very strict limits on such powers are called for." Camenzind v. Switzerland, 28 EHRR 458, 475–6 (1999). The Fourth Amendment also allows searches of homes under administrative search warrants issued and carried out by regulatory officials if the searches are limited to enforcing adherence to administrative regulations and are strictly limited by a plan. Camara v. Municipal Court, 387 US 523 (1967). In the area of wiretaps and bugging, the Eur. Ct. HR has also stressed that judicial authorization is a normal prerequisite for ordering such measures, though it did approve, prior to the promulgation of Germany's modern wiretap provisions, a procedure requiring the approval of a parliamentary committee. Klass v. Germany, 2 EHRR 214, 235 (1978).

[206] An example is Greece, which amended Art. 19 Const.-Greece to provide for strict exclusion. GR,4.

[207] *See* for instance: §§ 87–8 CCP-Belgium, BE, 12; § 8 PACE-England and Wales; § 56(1), 76(3) CCP-France, FR, 9–10; §§ 98, 105 CCP-Germany, GE, 15; §§ 253–9 CCP-Greece, GR, 14; §§ 244, 247, 253 CCP-Italy; § 168 CCP-Latvia; § 159(2) CCP-Macao, MA, 10; § 219 CCP-Poland, PL,8; § 126(3) CCP-Portugal, PO, 6–7; §§12, 177(5), 182(3) CCP-Russia; § 214 CCP-Slovenia, SL, 11; §§ 546, 550 CCP-Spain; § 116 CCP-Turkey, TU, 10.

regulating dwelling searches will also typically require a certain strength of suspicion before a judge can authorize a search, sometimes called "probable cause"[208] or "reasonable suspicion" or "some evidence." Exceptions will usually be allowed for emergency situations or "exigent circumstances."[209]

The regulatory laws will also usually govern the times during which searches may take place, and the persons who have a right to be present, or must be present during the search. For instance, in those countries which still use an investigating magistrate, the magistrate or his/her secretary or clerk must often be present.[210] In many countries, the person who owns the searched property must be present, or, in default thereof, a member of the community government or a neighbor.[211] His or her lawyer or defense counsel may also have a right to be present.[212] Many codes also provide for civilians to be present who have no relation to the case to be witnesses as to the propriety of the way the search was carried out.[213]

Some statutes provide directly for the exclusion of evidence gathered in dwelling searches in violation of their dictates.[214]

3. *High Court Jurisprudence Interpreting the Effect of the Violations of the Aforementioned Provisions on the Admissibility of Evidence*
   a. The Requirement of Probable Cause

   If a dwelling search or wiretap is based on probable cause and is judicially authorized, then the constitutional underpinnings of the search are normally guaranteed. If the violation relates to a lesser statutory requirement this is often considered to be an "irregularity," rather than an "illegality," i.e., like a "relative nullity" which cancels the evidentiary value of the documentary evidence memorializing the investigative measure but does not prevent proof of the search using other means.[215] In one Spanish case, for instance, the police conducted a search which was authorized by the investigating magistrate based on sufficient suspicion, but neither the investigating magistrate nor his secretary were present during the search, violating a statutory requirement found in § 569(4) CCP-Spain. The Spanish Supreme Court held that this error did not impact upon a fundamental right, and therefore the sanction was merely the annulment of the act documenting the search, making it inadmissible at trial. But this did not prevent the police who conducted the search from testifying in court to prove the seizure of the drugs and the *corpus delicti* of the crime.[216] Here is a good example of the use of the term "nullity" to refer to the cancelation of a procedural act, but not its fruits. The fruits may be proved independent of the annulled record.[217]

   In principle, the USSC has also categorized certain violations of the laws regulating wiretaps and search warrants as being of sub-constitutional status, the violation of which does not require suppression. Thus, mistakes in the execution of an otherwise valid search warrant,[218] will not lead to exclusion. By refusing to suppress the fruits of an otherwise constitutionally valid warranted search in *Hudson v. Michigan*[219] despite a violation of the "knock and announce" requirement of Fed. R. Crim. P. 41, the USSC

[208] *See* IV. Amendment, Const.-US.

[209] The exception for "exigent circumstances" is found in: Art. 13(2) Const.-Germany, §§ 98, 105 CCP-Germany, GE, 15; Art. 14 Const.-Italy.; Cf. MA, 10; PO, 6–7; SE, 12; TU, 1. *See* Thaman, *Comparative Criminal Procedure*, *supra* note 78, at 56.

[210] *See* NE, 8. Magistrate or secretary must be present in Spain, SP, 2.

[211] SE, 10 (either the affected party or a neighbor in Serbia). In Taiwan, either subject, neighbor or representative, TA, 1. Two municipal officers or two neighbors in Turkey, TU, 11.

[212] SE, 10

[213] SE, 10, SL, 11.

[214] § 177(2) CCP-Greece, GR, 15.

[215] On the notion that "illicit evidence" is suppressible under § 11.1 LOPJ-Spain and that "irregular" evidence falls under § 238 LOPJ-Spain and does not lead to suppression of fruits of the violation, *see* Aguilera Morales, *supra* note 146, at 93.

[216] Supreme Court of Spain, Decision of July 9, 1993, English translation in Thaman, *Comparative Criminal Procedure*, *supra* note 78, at 106–08. Cf. SP, 14.

[217] *See* De Urbano Castrillo and Torres Morato, *supra* note 146, at 47–52.

[218] *See* the following two cases in which aspects of Fed. R. Crim. P. 41, regulating serving of search warrants, were violated: United States v. Schoenheit, 856 F.2d 74 (8th Cir. 1988)(violation of prohibition of night service); United States v. Charles, 883 F.2d 355 (5th Cir. 1989) (serving officer did not have warrant in hand).

[219] Hudson v. Michigan, 547 U.S. 586, 589–90 (2006).On the *Hudson* case, *see* US, 17–8.

has come to a result similar to that of the Spanish Courts, but had to resort to contorted reasoning because of a previous decision in which the "knock and announce" rule was declared to be constitutionally mandated.[220]

In the U.S., some Fourth Amendment violations are more serious than others. A search without probable cause or judicial authorization would nearly always trigger exclusion, but searches with judicial authorization that lack probable cause may in the presence of "good faith" not result in loss of evidence.

For a home to be searched for evidence (or suspects) related to crime there must first be "necessity" expressed by a sufficient amount of suspicion that particularly described objects or persons will actually be found in a particular dwelling. Some statutes attempt to articulate a sufficiently substantial level of suspicion "that a crime has been committed and that particular evidence related to the crime" can be found in a particular place. An example of this is the American use of the term "probable cause."[221] On the other hand, in Spain and Germany it appears that almost any suspicion, however slight, will suffice to authorize a search of a dwelling. The requirements for securing judicial authorization for conducting a wiretap or bugging a private space are often stricter. Italy, for instance, requires "grave indicia"[222]of the commission of a particularly serious offense and the measure must be "absolutely indispensable" to the investigation.[223]

Even if law enforcement officials acquire judicial authorization for a search in a country without a requirement of a strong suspicion, such as in Germany, there will, in many cases, be no "necessity" to infringe on the privacy rights of persons because the suspicion is too minimal to guarantee a predictable likelihood of success in the search. Where the investigating official authorizes his or her own search, as in the investigating magistrate systems of Spain or France, we do not have a neutral detached official not "engaged in the often competitive enterprise of ferreting out crime"[224] to dispassionately evaluate the request.

The requirement of a significant level of suspicion before violating the constitutional rights of citizens, coupled with independent judicial verification of this suspicion should be the two indispensable requirements for a finding of "necessity" required to authorize the government's search of a private home or the interception of private communication. In countries where the level of suspicion is not spelled out in sufficient detail, the role of judicial control becomes even more urgent.[225] Not only should

[220] *See* Wilson v. Arkansas, 514 U.S. 927 (1995). The court had to base its decision on the fact that the seizure of the evidence was not a "fruit" of the unlawful entry due to inevitable discovery, and that any taint was attenuated. *Hudson*, *supra* note 221, at 586–87.

[221] U.S. Const. IV. Amend. This has been interpreted to mean "a fair probability" that a crime has been committed (or is in the process of being committed) and that evidence, fruits, instrumentalities of the crime may be found in a particular place. Illinois v. Gates, 462 U.S. 213 (1983). In England "reasonable grounds" are required, § 8 PACE-England, which is similar to the Italian *fondato motivo* . § 247(1) CPP-Italy.

[222] § 267(1) CPP-Italy. Although the U.S. Supreme court once indicated that the "probable cause" standard for wiretaps was higher than that for normal searches, Berger v. New York, 388 U.S. 41 (1967), courts now tend to apply the same standard. Wayne R. Lafave et al., *Criminal Procedure,* 5th ed. (St. Paul: Thomson/West 2009), 265–6.

[223] § 267(1) CPP-Italy. In Germany, "certain facts must justify the suspicion" that the defendant has committed certain serious crimes and that "the investigation of the case or the determination of the whereabouts of the accused would be unsuccessful or made substantially more difficult by using other means." § 100a StPO-Germany. U.S. law requires the order for interception to appraise "whether or not other investigative procedures have been tried or failed or why they reasonably appear to be unlikely to succeed if tried or to be too dangerous," 18 U.S.C. § 25 18(l) (c),(e), an added protection not required in search warrants.

[224] Johnson v. United States, 333 US l0 (l948).

[225] A warrant for a search or seizure of a dwelling may issue "when it is suspected that the search will lead to finding evidence." § 102 StPO-Germany. In Spain for such a search the investigating magistrate need only have "indications that the defendant or effect or instrumentalities of crime, or books, papers or other object which can serve to solve and prove it" will be found. § 545 LECr-Spain. On the almost non-existent requirement of probable cause in Germany, *see* Weigend, *supra* note 170, at 193. Cf. The CPP-France tersely expostulates: "Searches are effectuated in all places where objects may be found which would be useful in ascertaining the truth." Investigating magistrates need not articulate any level of suspicion and there is no requirement to particularly describe the places to be searched or things to be seized. Frase, *supra* note 76, at 153.

the magistrate require more than a "mere" suspicion or hunch, but he or she should have sufficient detail from the police or prosecutor to be able to adequately describe the things to be seized and the places to be searched and should provide reasons why the information gives rise to a "strong suspicion" that the things will be in the described places.[226] Thus, even when a judge authorizes a search warrant, if there was no necessity to do so due to a lack of the requisite level of suspicion, then the search still violates the constitutional right.[227] Where the level of suspicion required is very low or non-existent, the requirement of a judicial warrant is still important to document the fact that there was some evidence, some articulation by the searching officers and that the search is not seeking to validate itself retroactively based on what was actually turned up.[228]

b. The Exception for Exigent Circumstances
Where there is more room for abuse, however, is in the universally accepted exception to the warrant requirement in cases of emergency, "exigent circumstances," or as the Germans say, "danger in delay."[229] To adequately protect the constitutional right of privacy, the exception for exigent circumstances should be narrowly construed to prevent large-scale evasion of the requirement of judicial authorization. It was well-known that German law enforcement officials seldom if ever acquired search warrants,[230] and always (successfully) defended their searches retrospectively,[231] with a perfunctory incantation of the words "danger in delay," often attributed to the fact that there were no evening duty judges to issue warrants. Despite this fact, the appellate courts winked at this sleight of hand, holding that the trial judge had such a broad discretion that it could not be reviewed on appeal.[232] The German Constitutional Court finally took note of this situation in 2001 and has attempted to rectify it by limiting the exception for "danger in delay" to cases that are clearly documented, and by requiring judges to be on duty 24 h for the purposes of issuing warrants.[233]

In this respect, it is suggested that "danger in delay" and "exigent circumstances" should be limited to two types of fact situations, the "flagrant crime,"[234] and the real "emergency situation" involving threat to human life or health. The "flagrant crime" situation would apply to "hot pursuit" cases,[235] or where probable cause develops suddenly upon commission of a crime in the presence of searching officers and where destruction of evidence is likely. If the suspicion of the presence of drugs, however, comes as a result of an investigation, then in principle a warrant must be obtained. The police should not be able to create the need for exigent circumstances by, for instance, walking up to the target house and announcing they are present so as to create the possibility of imminent destruction of evidence.[236] Where there are true emergency circumstances such as danger to life or limb, then, of course, warrantless searches should be permitted.[237]

---

[226] On use of the term "reasonable suspicion," *see* TU, 10; SL, 11.

[227] Where a judge erroneously issues a search warrant based on insufficient evidence in the U.S. the search violates the Fourth Amendment. But if the police officer who requested the warrant "in good faith" believed there was sufficient evidence, then the evidence seized is still usable at the trial. If the police officer misled the magistrate with false or reckless information, or if there was obviously insufficient evidence that should have been apparent to the police officer, then the evidence will be suppressed. *Leon*, *supra* note 32.

[228] Andreas Ransiek, "Durchsuchung, Beschlagnahme und Verwertungsverbot," *Der Strafverteidiger* 10 (2002): 565, at 569.

[229] This exception is widely applied in Scotland. SC, 67.

[230] BVerfGE 103, 142,152 (2001). Weigend, *supra* note 170, at 250, estimated that only 10% of searches were conducted with warrants.

[231] In Germany and many other countries, police must acquire judicial validation of exigent searches within 2 or 3 days after the search. *See* § 98(2) CCP-Germany.

[232] Ransiek, *supra* note 227, at 566. In effect, only the most arbitrary searches led to exclusion of evidence. *Id.*

[233] BVerfGE 103, 142 (2001).

[234] Exception specifically provided in Art. 18(2) Const.-Spain.

[235] *See* Warden v. Hayden, *supra* note 133, at 310; US, 5.

[236] United States v. Timberlake, 896 F.2d 592, 597 (D.C. Cir. 1990); Dunnuck v. State, 786 A.2d 695, 699–700 (Md. 2001) (knocking on door without warrant). Decision of Dec. 12, 2002 (German Constitutional Court), NStZ, Vol. 6 (2003), at 319. But see United States v. MacDonald, 916 F.2d 766, 772 (2d Cir. 1990), allowing creation of the exigent circumstances if done without violating the law.

[237] For the U.S. test in this regard, *see* Brigham City, Utah v. Stuart, 547 U.S. 398, 403 (2006).

c. Limitations Based on Standing or Lack of a Personal Right to Privacy
Many courts have limited exclusion of evidence gathered in violation of the right to privacy in the home to those whose own privacy was compromised by the search. This limitation to those with "standing," as the U.S. courts were wont to call it,[238] has been followed in many countries.[239] However, the U.S. limitation of standing seems to contradict the avowed reason for the exclusion of evidence, the deterrence of illegal police conduct.[240] California abolished the "standing" limitations to its exclusionary rule in 1955 but this rule was then abrogated and California began to strictly follow the jurisprudence of the U.S. Supreme Court following a popular referendum in 1985.[241]

d. Searches in the Absence of Required Persons
In Serbia, courts have excluded evidence, thus preventing the court from relying on it in its judgment reasons, where even one, not to speak of two of the civilian witnesses were not present.[242]

The predominant trend, however, is to treat the presence of civilian witnesses,[243]or other required persons as a minor error not of constitutional status, which will not lead to suppression of the fruits of the search, as long as it was conducted with probable cause and a warrant.

e. Admissibility of Evidence Seized Without a Warrant or Probable Cause
(1) Courts Where There Is a Presumption of Suppression
In some countries, there is a presumption that evidence may not be used if it is the product of a dwelling search without judicial authorization or probable cause.[244] This was definitely the case when the U.S. Supreme Court decided its landmark cases of *Weeks*,[245] relating to the federal courts, and *Mapp,* relating to the state courts.[246]

(2) Courts Where the Probative Value of Physical Evidence Trumps Privacy
In Belgium, a search conducted without written authorization by an investigating magistrate was originally considered to be a nullity, resulting in a prohibition on the use of any evidence gathered. In 2004, however, the Belgian Court of Cassation decided that such evidence would nevertheless be admissible despite the constitutional violation.[247]

In England and Wales, the Court of Appeals has held that, despite the police's failure to get judicial authorization for a home search, the evidence was admissible because there was no doubt as to the reliability of the physical evidence found, and thus, the failure to allows its use would "interfere with the achievement of justice" by letting a guilty man free.[248] Polish courts also do not suppress physical evidence which is the fruit of an unlawful search.[249]

(3) Indirect Evidence (Fruits of the Poisonous Tree)
Some courts sever the causal connection between a constitutional illegality and its "fruits" in ways unknown in the U.S. There is, for instance, the notion that seizures are conceptually independent of searches, and that if the seizure is "legal" then the nexus of illegality has been attenuated. Another, is that a seizure which is a causal result of an illegal search, can nevertheless be attenuated by judicial balancing of other factors.

---

[238] The seminal case on "standing" in the home is Jones v. United States, 362 U.S. 257, 261 (1960), US, 10.

[239] *D.P.P. v Forbes,* (1994) 2 I.R. 542, IR, 18. Cf. NE, 4.

[240] US, 11.

[241] US, 11–12.

[242] SE, 12–13.

[243] See TU, 11–12.

[244] Thus, in the Netherlands, if the investigating magistrate did not authorize the search, and was not present, the evidence is usually not usable. NE, 8. This is clearly the case in Spain, SP, 18. In Greece, any search conducted by police before the formal initiation of criminal proceedings is an absolute nullity and all evidence is non-usable, GR, 15.

[245] *Supra* note 20.

[246] *Supra* note 24. *See* US, 1,6.

[247] BE, 6–7.

[248] *Sanghera, supra* note 131, at 299, EW, 5.

[249] PL, 8. Serbian courts are divided about whether evidence derived from an illegal search should be suppressed, or not. SE, 6, 13. Turkish courts have also resoundingly refused to apply the "fruits" doctrine. TU, 25.

(a) Seizure Is Not a Fruit of an Unlawful Search

It is a doctrine firmly entrenched in Italy and accepted by courts in Germany, that the seizure of drugs, for instance, is not the fruit of a clearly unconstitutional search, even where the express object of the search was to find those very same drugs.

The Italian courts reason, that since § 253(1) CPP-Italy requires the police to seize the *corpus delicti* of a crime, that is, fruits, instrumentalities and contraband, then this *legal* seizure cannot be vitiated by an antecedent unconstitutional search, be it without probable cause or judicial authorization.[250] The courts have held that searches and seizures have different juridical presuppositions and functions and cannot be viewed as linked due to their convergence in reality.[251] Although § 191 CPP-Italy seems quite straightforward in prohibiting the use of any evidence collected in violation of prohibitions established by law, the courts hyper-technically construe the language to defeat its very goal by saying that "non-usability" only applies in relation to evidence gathered in violation of an "express or implicit prohibition" and not to evidence "where a mere formality of acquisition has not been observed."[252] Finally, in 2001, the Italian Constitutional Court made it clear that the "fruits of the poisonous tree" apply only to "nullities," because it is expressly provided by statute, whereas § 191 CCP-Italy, providing for "non-usability," has no language referring to derivative evidence.[253] This doctrine is rather ludicrous, because the Italian literature, like the Spanish, has pronounced that "nullities" relate only to non-constitutional violations in the gathering of evidence, whereas "non-usability" applies only to violations of fundamental rights.[254]

German courts also do not recognize an inexorable link between illegal search and the seizure of the object at which it was aimed.[255] German courts will suppress the item seized if there was an independent prohibition on seizing it, for instance, because it is protected by a privilege.[256] In separating an unlawful search, which is a tool to find evidence to use in a criminal case, from its object, the evidence sought, is an example of the courts either ignoring the plain meaning of constitutional or statutory law or intentionally subverting it in order to achieve a goal, the conviction of a guilty person at any cost, which is no longer the purported goal of criminal procedure. It is clear that the constitutional protection of the dwelling is not only rooted in the protection of privacy, but also constitutes a limitation

[250] Cass. (3.27.96), Giustizia Penale 1997, 138, 140, 144–5, English translation in Thaman, *Comparative Criminal Procedure*, *supra* note 78, at 122–4.

[251] Dec. 4.24.91, Cassazione penale 92, 1879, cited in Giovanni Conso and Vittorio Grevi, *Commentario Breve al Nuovo Codice di Procedura Penale,* 4th ed. (Padua: CEDAM 2002), 550. This decision also provides that any illegality in the means of acquisition of the seizable object (the search) should be punished by disciplinary or penal means. *Id.* For an explanation of the predominant approach, denying a causal link between illegal search and "legal seizure" and some dissenting opinions. IT, 9.

[252] Conso and Grevi, *supra* note 250, at 392.

[253] IT, 8. Decision no. 332/2001, Italian Constitutional Court, Gazzetta Ufficiale, no. 38 (Oct. 3, 2001), available at http://www.cortecostituzionale.it/giurisprudenza/pronunce/schedaDec.asp?Comando=RIC&bVar=true&TrmD=&TrmDF=&TrmDD=&TrmM=&iPagEl=1&iPag=1 (last visited Feb. 22, 2010); Cf. Conso and Grevi, *supra* note 250, at 339.

[254] Giuseppe Luigi Fanuli, *Inutilizzabilità e nullitá della prova nel giudizio abbreviato, nel "patteggiamento" e nell'istituto della acquisizione degli atti su accordo delle parti* (Milan: Giuffrè 2004), 5–6.

[255] The German Constitutional Court has made it clear that use-prohibition will not be the regular, "normal" result of an unconstitutional search. BVerfG NJW 1999, 273, 274. BVerfG NStZ 2000, 488, 499; StV 2000, 233, 234. The German Supreme Court in 1989 held that legal errors in the search do not lead to non-use. BGH NStZ 1989, 375, 376. It postulated: "...when no legal hindrances to the issuance of a search warrant would have existed and the seized objects as such were legally accessible for use as pieces of evidence" there will be no exclusion. Cited in Ransiek, *supra* note 227, at 566; Weigend, *supra* note 170, at 252.

[256] *Id.*

on the ability of the state to gather information or seize evidence in those spaces. Search and seizure cannot be logically separated into different actions with different motivations.[257] In Poland, violation of the constitutional protections against unlawful home searches are punished by disciplinary measures and not exclusion of evidence.[258]

In a limited sense, the U.S. Supreme Court has held that the seizure of incriminating evidence is not a "fruit" of an unlawful search, if the search was only unlawful due to the way it was carried out, for instance, by the police not properly knocking and announcing their presence before entering the home, and not due to lack of probable cause or a judicial warrant.[259]

(b) The Magistrate Would Have Issued a Warrant

The doctrine of "inevitable discovery," however, can serve as a gaping loophole in the constitutional protections if interpreted in too broad a manner. Some American courts have recognized this exception if the police were already in the process of getting a search warrant (and the judge would hypothetically have issued it) when they searched under insufficiently exigent circumstances.[260] However the most dangerous extension of this notion of a "hypothetical independent source" is when the court allows the introduction of evidence because probable cause existed and a judge would have approved a warrant application had it been submitted.[261] The German Courts, however, have used this latter rationale to justify their refusal to enforce the privacy requirements of Art. 13 Const-Germany with an exclusionary remedy. Clearly such a justification would completely undermine the constitutional requirement of a judicial warrant.[262]

(c) Attenuation of the Taint

(i) Subsequent confession cleansing the illegality

One finds a number of cases where the privacy of a citizen is violated through a warrantless search or wiretap, yet where the defendant confesses or admits to the truth of the evidence discovered subsequent to the illegality. Many courts find that such a subsequent confession will attenuate the taint by, in a sense, providing an independent source for the conviction, unless, of course, the accused is immediately confronted with the illegally seized evidence or the illegal wiretap and confesses under immediate influence of the illegality.[263]

4. *Effect of International Human Rights Jurisprudence*

The ECHR is directly applicable nearly all European countries. The reluctance of the ECtHR, however,

[257] Ransiek, *supra* note 227, at 568. At least one section of the Italian Supreme Court has rejected the prevailing approach and recognized a strict functional relationship between the act of searching and the seizure. Dec. of March 13, 1992 (Cass. Pen. 93, 393 and Dec. of 12.10.90; 2.28.94, 5.12.94, (Annuale nel Proc. Pen. 95, 711). Cited in Conso and Grevi, *supra* note 250, at 550. On the admissibility of the fruits of illegal searches, GE, 16–7.

[258] PL, 8.

[259] *Hudson, supra* note 218. *See* US, 14–5.

[260] United States v. Cabassa, 62 F.3d 470, 473 (2d Cir. 1995); United States v. Whitehorn, 829 F.2d 1225, 1232–3 (2d Cir. 1987) (search warrant signed after the search); United States v. Curtis, 931 F.2d 1011, 1013 (4th Cir. 1991).

[261] Although this has been recognized in the U.S., *see* United States v. Buchanan, 910 F.2d 1571, 1573–4 (7th Cir. 1990), the overwhelming majority of U.S. courts have rejected this argument, for it would make the warrant requirement meaningless. United States v. Johnson, 22 F.3d 674, 680 (6th Cir. 1994); United States v. Echegoyen, 799 F.2d 1271, 1279 (9th Cir. 1986); State v. Handtmann, 437 N.W.2d 830, 838 (N.D. 1989); United States v. Brown, 64 F.3d 1083, 1085 (7th Cir. 1995).

[262] *See* GE, 11. *See* also, Ransiek, *supra* note 230, at 566. *See* BGH NJW 1989, 1741, 15 1744, which held that the evidence found in an unconstitutional search will be admissible as long as it is otherwise legally seizable (i.e., contraband, fruits, instrumentalities—and not a protected diary) and a judge would have issued a search warrant had the police sought one. Cited in Weigend, *supra* note 173, at 252.

[263] *See* TU, 12 (confession after illegal search and seizure of marijuana).

to take a stand on the evidentiary consequences of violations of Art. 8's right to privacy in the home has had a negative influence on the development of the law in this area. The Belgian Court of Cassation has used this as a reason to allow the use of evidence gathered as result of an illegal search of a home, overturning its earlier stricter approach based in the doctrine of nullities.[264] But in many countries, the protection given by their legislation and high courts is greater than that accorded by the ECHR as interpreted by the ECtHR.[265]

29.3.3 Protection of Privacy in One's Communications

1. *Constitutional Provisions*
   Many modern constitutions expressly protect privacy in one's private communications.[266]
   Some of these constitutions also include express exclusionary rules when the right to privacy in one's communications is violated.[267]
2. *Statutory Provisions*
   Most countries have passed legislation regulating the interception and seizure of private communications.[268] The ECtHR has been very strict in requiring that the procedures for wiretapping be clearly authorized by law and that they apply only to serious offenses. Judicial authorization is required and the measure must be strictly limited in time.[269] Each extension of a wiretap must be accompanied by a new judicial authorization.
   Finally, statutory exclusionary rules are often provided as remedies for violation of laws regulating wiretapping and bugging.[270] 18 U.S.C. § 2515 provides for the exclusion of all derivative evidence in the U.S. Once the intercepted communication has been deemed to be in violation of the law: "no part of the contents of such communication and no evidence derived therefrom may be received in evidence in any trial, hearing, or other proceeding in or before any court, grand jury, department, officer, agency, regulatory body, legislative committee, or other authority of the United States, a State, or a political subdivision thereof."[271] The broad sweep of the exclusionary rule of § 2515 would certainly prevent use of evidence even against third parties, thus giving more protection than the general Fourth Amendment rule for searches.[272]
   In some countries there exists a statutory requirement that judicial authorization be acquired before gathering information about the telephone numbers a suspect has called or about the telephones from which a suspect has received calls.[273] The devices used to gather such information in the U.S. are called "pen registers" for the former, and "trap and trace devices" for the latter.
3. *High Court Jurisprudence Interpreting Effect of Violations of the* Above *Provisions on Admissibility of Illegally Seized Evidence*
   a. Relating to Exclusion of Evidence in General

---

[264] BE, 10–13. The seminal case in this area is the so-called "Antigone" case of 2003. BE, 5–6.

[265] Such as in Greece, GR, 17.

[266] Art. 5(XII) Const.-Brazil, BR, 25; Art. 10(3) Const.-Finland, FI, 4; Art. 10 Const.-Germany, GE, 13; Art. 20 Const.-Georgia; Art. 19(1) Const.-Greece, GR, 18; Art. 15 Const.-Italy, IT, 14; Art. 22 Const.-Lithuania; Art. 32 Const.-Macao, MA, 12; Art. 49 Const.-Poland, PL, 6; Art. 34(1) Const.-Portugal, PO, 7; Art. 23 Const.-Russia; Art. 41 Const.-Serbia, SE, 14; Art. 37 Const.-Slovenia, SL, 12; Art. 18(3) Const.-Spain, SP, 21; Art. 12 Const.-Taiwan, TA, 6; Art. 22 Const.-Turkey , TU, 12–13; Art. 31 Const.-Ukraine.

[267] An example is Art. 19(3) Const.-Greece which applies a strict, non-balancing exclusionary rule to violations of the right to privacy in one's communications. GR,4, 18.

[268] *See* for instance: §§ 259*bis* et 314*bis* CCP-Belgium, BE, 13–14; § 100 CCP-France, FR, 11; §§ 100b(2), c, d, h CCP-Germany, GE, 13–16; § 267(1–3) CCP-Italy; § 136 CCP-Latvia; § 172(1) CCP-Macao; §§ 126la–126nb, 126t–126ub and 126zg-zja CCP-Netherlands, NE, 9; §§ 187–90 CCP-Portugal, PO, 8; §§ 13, 185, 186 CCP-Russia; §§ 149–50 CCP-Slovenia, SL, 13; § 579 CCP-Spain, SP, 21; §§ 135–6 CCP-Turkey, TU, 13–5; 18 U.S.C. § 2510 ff. Cf. FI, 7; PL, 9; SE, 15.

[269] 15 days: BR, 26; 30 days: BE, 15, SL, 14; 90 days: SE, 15, TU, 15, IR, 14–15; 120 days: FR, 11.

[270] § 177(2) CCP-Greece, GR, 19; § 13 Secret Monitoring Law-Israel (1997), IS, 1; § 271 CCP-Italy, IT, 14; § 190 CCP-Portugal, PO, 8; SE, 16; SL, 14. §§ 5–7 Act of Communication Protection and Surveillance (Taiwan), hereafter ACPS, mandates suppression for "serious" violations of the wiretapping law and extends to "fruits of the poisonous tree." TA, 6.

[271] Identical fruit-of-the-poisonous-tree language is contained in the Foreign Intelligence Surveillance Act, as well. 50 U.S.C. § 1805(e)(5).

[272] Since Title III has preempted state law in the area of wiretapping and bugging, this comprehensive exclusionary rule is binding on the states and must be replicated in state law. One such example is § 77-23A-7 U.C.A.,CCP-Utah.

[273] BE, 14.

The jurisprudence of the USSC has limited exclusion to those violations of the wiretap statute that are of constitutional magnitude. Thus, mistakes in the execution of an otherwise valid Title III wiretap will not lead to exclusion.[274] The Turkish Court of Appeal has also ruled that evidence gathered in violation of their wiretap statute may not be used as a basis for a judgment of guilt.[275]Although German doctrine on exclusion is not consistent, the courts have refused to exclude evidence gained pursuant to an initially valid wiretap warrant, which, however, was extended beyond the 3 month limit without additional judicial authorization.[276] The German courts have, however, excluded evidence in other circumstances involving the warrantless bugging of a hospital room and an apartment.[277]

In some countries, courts will allow use of evidence gathered through unconstitutional wiretaps if it is used against third parties whose rights were not violated by the intervention.[278]

Sometimes the high courts interpret seemingly absolute exclusionary rules and turn them into balancing tests which will allow use of unconstitutionally gathered communications in some circumstances. Much as the Italian courts have nullified the general exclusionary rule of § 191 CCP-Italy and the Spanish Constitutional Court has turned the absolute rule of § 11.1 LOPJ-Spain into a balancing test, the Greek courts have also ignored a clear statutory-constitutional exclusionary rule relating to illegally intercepted communications.[279] The Irish courts will also engage in balancing when the dictates of the wiretapping legislation are violated, by taking into account the intentionality of the violation, the interests of justice, whether the violation was of a technical rule or a fundamental right, whether there were exigent circumstances, and the probative value of the evidence.[280]

Finally, there are countries which have no clearly delineated policy on exclusion,[281] and others in which the courts, apparently, never exclude illegally gathered evidence in this area.[282]

b. Relating to Installing Pen Registers/Trap and Trace Devices

Although the U.S. has codified rules for installing pen registers and trap and trace devices to ascertain the external aspects of telecommunications, the USSC has ruled that this procedure does not impact upon constitutional values and thus is not subject to the Fourth Amendment exclusionary rule.[283] On the contrary, several European countries' high courts have insisted that the identity of one's communication partners and, in relation to cell or mobile phones, their location, is included within the constitutional protections.[284] However, other countries follow the U.S. approach.[285]

c. Admissibility of Indirect Evidence (Fruits of Poisonous Tree)

Another area where the lawmaker has determined the appropriate balance in mandating the exclusion of fruits, is in the U.S. wiretap statute, where 18 U.S.C. §2515, expressly prohibits the use of derivative evidence in any manner whatsoever, including against third parties.[286] In Germany, however, the testimony of witnesses who were discovered through an illegal interception has been admitted.[287] Although the CCP-Italy mandates "non-usability" of illegally intercepted conversations, there is no restriction

[274] The Title III provision must "directly and substantially implement" the congressional intention to restrict the use of electronic surveillance or be "intended to play a central role in the statutory scheme." United States v. Giordano, 4 16 U.S. 505, 527 (1974); United States v. Chavez, 4 16 U.S. 562, 574 (1974). For a similar approach, CZ, 11.

[275] Decision of April 8, 2003, TU, 16.

[276] BGHSt 44, 243, 248 (1998), GE, 16.

[277] GE, 13, 16.

[278] *See* NE, 3–4; SP, 11.

[279] Art. 19(3) Const.-Greece, § 177(2) CCP-Greece, GR, 10–11, 19–20.

[280] IR, 15. This balancing seems to overturn the strict exclusionary rule set in *Kenny*, *supra* note 99, which was the rule for over 20 years. IR, 16.

[281] *See* SC, 11–12.

[282] NO, 10.

[283] Smith v. Maryland, 442 U.S. 735 (1979), US, 4.

[284] Sentence 486/2009, in:www.tribunalconstitucional.pt, PO, 9. Cf. SL, 13.

[285] SE, 18; TU, 16.

[286] This appears also to be true in Brazil, where a flagrant arrest based on an unlawful wiretap was deemed to be a nullity. BR, 11.

[287] BGHSt 32, 68 (1983), see Weigend, *supra* note 170, at 253. GE, 16. Cf. *Tucker*, *supra* note 160, at 450, which refused to suppress testimony of a witness found through a *Miranda*-defective confession.

on using the contents of those conversations to further the investigation, discover new crimes, etc.[288] In Italy, a new wiretap may also be based on information gleaned from illegal wiretaps.[289]

(1) The "Contra-legality" of the Causal Nexus

In 1998 the Spanish Constitutional Court announced a new approach to "fruits of the poisonous tree" which departed radically from the categorical approach which was adopted in 1984, and which led to codification in § 11.1 LOPJ-Spain. It made the nice distinction between "natural" and "juridical" causation. The court was definitely influenced by the doctrine of the ECtHR[290] and analyzed the extent an illegal wiretap tainted the other evidence in terms of the right to a "fair trial." It analyzed whether the violation was of a required "intensity" and then used a balancing test to determine whether there was an "anti-juridical" nexus between illegality and the derivative evidence. The Court determined, that the violation was not so "intense" due to the fact that the police did get a wiretap order, and the violation was based on a lack of probable cause. The court also noted that such an "error" was not intentional and not grossly negligent, and that under the totality of the circumstances, the derivative evidence could be used.[291] Thus we see an incorporation of the "good faith" rule articulated in *Leon* in relation to wiretaps, a step even the USSC has not yet taken.[292]

Up until this new jurisprudence of the Spanish Constitutional Court, physical evidence found as a result of an unconstitutional wiretap or bugging was routinely suppressed per § 11.1 LOPJ-Spain as being "fruit of the poisonous tree" and not usable during the trial.[293] For example, in one case police used a scanner to intercept cell phone conversations without having obtained judicial authorization. The information gathered led to an arrest on a beach and a search incident thereto uncovered drugs. The Supreme Court held that the drugs were fruit of the poisonous tree and could not be used.[294] Since the new case law, however, the decision depends on the new balancing test developed by the constitutional court. In the seminal 1998 case in which the Spanish Constitutional Court altered its theretofore strict exclusionary rules, the court used the doctrine of inevitable discovery to dissociate the arrest of the defendant in possession of drugs from an unconstitutional wiretap, by arguing that the defendant was already under heavy police surveillance and the arrest was therefore not sufficiently tainted by the antecedent illegality.[295]

Several jurisdictions, however, have found that a confession by a suspect following an unlawful wiretap may, in certain circumstances, attenuate the taint of the original illegality. Thus, while a confession induced through confrontation with an illegal wiretap might lead to exclusion, the German courts have allowed the confession if it took place a few days after the confrontation with the tainted evidence.[296] This has also been an area where the Spanish courts have applied the new balancing test developed by the constitutional court and have allowed confessions by persons arrested as a result of an unlawful wiretap.[297]

[288] Franco Cordero, *Procedura penale* 804 (Milan: Giuffrè, 5th ed. 2000).

[289] Conso and Grevi, *supra* note 250, at 399.

[290] Citing Schenk v. Switzerland, *supra* note 141, at. 265–6.

[291] STC 81/Feb. 4, 1998, available at http://www.boe.es/aeboe/consultas/bases_datos/doc.php?coleccion=tc&id=SENTENCIA-1998-0081.

[292] *See* United States v. Rice, 478 F.3d 704, 711–12 (6th Cir. 2007) which finds there is no "good faith" exception to the exclusionary rule under Title III.

[293] *See* Juan-Luis Gomez Colomer, "La intervención judicial de las comunicaciones telefónicas a la luz de la jurisprudencia," *Revista Jurídica de Catalunya,* no. 1 (1998): 145, at 162–3. SP, 10.

[294] STS 137/1999 Feb. 8, 1999, available at http://sentencias.juridicas.com/index.php. For cases showing the application of a strong doctrine of "fruits of the poisonous tree" prior to the new approach of the Constitutional Court, SP, 25.

[295] *See* STC 81/1998, *supra* note 290. For cases explaining application of the doctrine of "inevitable discovery" under the new Constitutional Court approach, SP, 26.

[296] GE, 16–17. The Italian courts have also allowed such confessions and witness statements taken under similar circumstances. IT, 9.

[297] STC 6/June 6, 1995; STC 54, March 26, 1996, SP, 11. Cf. STC 136/May 8, 2006, where the in-court confession was sufficiently attenuated from the illegal wiretap, SP, 26.

4. *Effect of International Human Rights Jurisprudence* The ECtHR has found violations of Art. 8 ECHR in relation to the lack of wiretap legislation or its inadequacy against several countries.[298] These important opinions have led to enactment of new legislation in France, England and Wales, Scotland,[299] and Turkey.[300]

   The ECtHR, however, with its weak exclusionary jurisprudence in cases involving the violation of privacy rights, has not been influential in the development of the exclusionary rule in its relation to the violation of wiretap laws.[301] Though Spain's wiretap law still does not comport with the requirements of ECtHR case law, its decisions have greatly informed the jurisprudence of the Spanish high courts so that Article 8 is not violated.[302]

29.3.4 Other Actions Invasive of Privacy Which Could Lead to Suppression of Evidence

1. *Rules Relating to Search of Personal Effects: Automobiles, Private Containers and Related Jurisprudence*
   In most countries, automobiles and other private containers are provided less protection than dwellings or other private premises. In the U.S., for instance, the mobility of automobiles has led to a court-made rule that no search warrant is required to search them, as long as there exists probable cause.[303] A host of exceptions, however, make automobile searches very common, even without probable cause, based on exceptions related to inventory searches or searches incident to arrest.[304]

   Some countries, however, have passed legislation regulating automobile searches and sometimes will require the presence of the suspect or his or her lawyer, when practicable, or the search will be unlawful and evidence could be suppressed as a result.[305] If an automobile is used as a home, however, or is located on the premises of a home, a warrant requirement might be imposed.[306]

   The search of the person, or containers carried on the person, such as purses, or briefcases, also require judicial authorization in certain situations. However, the power of the police to "stop and frisk," especially for drugs, [307] but also for other evidence of crime,[308] or for weapons,[309] and to search a person and his or her effects incident to arrest creates a wide exception to this rule.

   Intrusive searches of the body will often require judicial authorization, and other forceful or humiliating searches of the person frequently trigger an automatic exclusion of evidence.[310]
2. Rules Relating to Data Mining and Other Collection of Semi-Private Information and Related Jurisprudence

[298] For instance, the French scheme was ruled in violation of Art. 8 ECHR in Kruslin v. France, ¶ 34, 12 EHRR 547, although the French investigating magistrate was held to be a sufficiently independent magistrate to issue such warrants. France then amended its law, adding § 100 CPP-France. FR, 10. The Spanish law has also been held to violate Art. 8, Valenzuela Contreras v. Spain, 28 E.H.R.R. 43 (1998) even though the Eur. Ct. HR has conceded that its highest courts have corrected many of its deficiencies in their jurisprudence. See also Prado Bugallo v. Spain (Feb. 18, 2003). http://cmiskp.echr.coe.int/tkp197/portal.asp?sessionId=56968978&skin=hudoc-en&action=request, SP, 26–27. The U.K. was condemned in Khan v. United Kingdom (2001) 31 EHRR 45, at 1016. which led to the passage of Regulation of Investigatory Powers Act in 2000. EW, 3.

[299] On the influence of the *Khan* decision on new Scottish legislation, SC, 11.

[300] TU, 13.

[301] For discussions of *Khan*, *supra* note 297, and *Allan*, *supra* note 142, and how they dovetail with the discretionary exclusionary rule in England and Wales, EW, 2–5.

[302] SP, 22.

[303] Carroll v. United States, 267 U.S. 132 (1925). For a similar rule, *see* SE, 20.

[304] South Dakota v. Opperman, 428 U.S. 364 (1976); New York v. Belton, 453 U.S. 454 (1981).

[305] In France, permission of the investigating magistrate is necessary, except in cases of flagrancy. New laxer rules were introduced in 2003 to deal with terrorist cases. FR, 12. For a case finding a violation of Art. 6 ECHR based on an automobile search conducted without the presence of the accused when the accused was arrested and available. Lisica v. Croatia ¶¶ 47–62 (ECtHR, Feb. 25, 2010)

[306] *See* BE, 17. On the requirement of a warrant for campers, etc.: GR, 22; SE, 15. On the requirement of a warrant and civilian witnesses where private compartments in an automobile are searched, SE, 15. In the U.S. the mobile home would have to be attached to utilities in a campground to be treated as a home. California v. Carney, 471 U.S. 386 (1985).

[307] On the power to "stop and frisk" upon reasonable suspicion, without judicial authorization: *O'Callaghan v Ireland*, (1994) 1 I.R. 555, IR, 16. Cf. Terry v. Ohio, 392 U.S. 1 (1968).

[308] SC, 7 (but if no reasonable grounds exist, the evidence gained as a result will be suppressed); SE, 12–13.

[309] On a "cacheo" for weapons, SP, 15.

[310] Such as forcing a person to squat and expel drugs, SP, 15–16.

Data mining usually refers to the filtering by government of a reservoir of data collected from the citizenry for the purposes of crime investigation or detection. This data consists usually of quasi-private information that has already been transmitted to some other person or entity through the voluntary activity of a citizen. The U.S. Supreme Court has generally determined that one does not have a "reasonable expectation of privacy" as to such information in Fourth Amendment terms, so no exclusionary rule will inhere if rules regulating the gathering of such information are violated.[311] In other countries, however, judicial authorization may be required in order for government officials to gather such information for purposes of criminal investigation.

Data mining can also be aimed at electronic communications that are stored with an internet service provider. In the U.S., the Stored Communications Act regulates government access to such stored information, requiring a search warrant for communications that have been stored for less than six months, and only the equivalent of a court order or subpoena, based on less than probable cause, for communications stored for longer than that time.[312] Only the communications protected by the Fourth Amendment requirement of a search warrant based on probable cause, are subject to being suppressed if the procedures are violated. Other countries have enacted similar legislation, sometimes requiring formal judicial authorization.[313]

Another area of semi-private evidence gathering would be the secret tape-recording of conversations by a person with whom a suspect is willingly communicating. Such information, again, is not protected by the Fourth Amendment in the U.S., and, thus, no exclusionary rule applies.[314] In some European countries, however, secret taperecording might be deemed to violate Art. 8 ECHR, yet the Art. 6 ECHR balancing test to determine whether or not the defendant's right to a fair trial was violated, usually balances out in favor of the ascertainment of truth over the suspect's right to privacy.[315] In others, however, most notably in Germany, secret tape-recording is illegal, thus constituting a prohibition on gathering evidence, and such evidence will normally be excluded, unless the crime charged is of such gravity that the interest of protecting the public outweighs the privacy interest.

29.3.5 Invasion of Privacy as an Indirect Fruit of a Violation of a Different Constitutional Right

1. *Search as Fruit of Unlawful Arrest or Seizure*
   In the U.S., a search which follows an unlawful arrest or detention is usually deemed to be "fruit of the poisonous tree" and the evidence discovered in the search will be suppressed.[316] This also holds true when the unlawfully arrested or detained suspect subsequently "consents" to the search. In some countries, however, the subsequent consent attenuates the taint of the initial unlawfulness and the evidence may be used in determining guilt.[317]

29.4 Rules of Admissibility/Exclusion in Relation to Illegal Interrogations

29.4.1 The General Right to Remain Silent/Privilege Against Self-incrimination

1. *Constitutional Provisions*
   The privilege against self-incrimination is guaranteed by the Fifth Amendment to the U.S. Constitution and is also included in many modern constitutions.[318]

[311] Examples are telephone numbers given to a phone company, *Smith v. Maryland*, *supra* note 282, and financial transactions revealed to a bank, California Bankers Ass'n v. Schultz, 416 U.S. 21 (1974); United States v. Miller, 425 U.S. 435 (1976).

[312] 18 U.S.C. § 2703.

[313] *See* SE, 21–22, for a procedure related to organized crime cases. In Spain, service providers must store communications for up to 1 year, but a judicial warrant is required to compel the providers to turn it over to law enforcement authorities. SP, 28. A warrant is also required in Turkey, TU, 17.

[314] The suspect is deemed to have "assumed the risk" when speaking to the undercover agent. United States v. White, *supra* note 194. US, 4.

[315] In general, *see* EU, 57. As to England and Wales, *see R v. Loveridge*, (2001) EWCA Crim 973, (2001) 2 Cr App R 29 (p 591), relating to secret taperecording in a jail cell, EW, 5 and BE, 17.

[316] For similar approaches, *see* GR, 24.

[317] NE, 6–7 (man illegally arrested throws bag down and tells police "see for yourself" after being asked whether he had burglar's tools).

[318] Art. 37 Const.-Czech Republic, CZ, 8; SE, 22; Art. 29-Const.-Slovenia, SL, 17–18; Arts. 17(3), 24(2) Const.-Spain, SP, 29; Art. 38(5) Const.-Turkey, TU, 19.

Though it is not mentioned in the ECHR, the ECtHR has recognized it as part of the right to a fair trial under Art. 6 ECHR.[319] In some countries, the privilege, while not explicitly enumerated as a basic right, is presumed to be incorporated under the "right to a defense" [320]or the presumption of innocence.[321]

2. *Statutory Provisions*
   If the right to remain silent, or not to make a declaration against oneself, is not given express constitutional stature, it is usually guaranteed by statute.[322] There are a few exceptions, however.[323] The right to remain silent is considerably weaker, however, in countries in which the prosecution may comment on the accused's silence when he/she is confronted by the police,[324] or remains silent at trial, and such silence may be used by the jury to convict, or by a judge or mixed court as a judgment-reason supporting conviction.[325]

29.4.2 The Protection Against Involuntary Self-incrimination: Torture, Coercion, Threats, Promises, etc.

1. *Constitutional Provisions*
   The protection against torture and other cruel, inhuman or degrading treatment is recognized as *jus cogens* in international law and finds reflection in the Convention Against Torture (hereafter CAT), Art. 3 ECHR, and Art. 7 of the ICCRP. It is also incorporated in the bills of rights of many national constitutions.[326] The Eighth Amendment of the Const.-U.S. prohibits "cruel and unusual punishment."
2. *Statutory Provisions*
   The CAT has been ratified by most countries of the world and thus codified in their CCP's or other statutes along with CAT's exclusionary rule.[327] But not every country has codified Art. 15 CAT, which requires that evidence which results from torture must be excluded.[328]

   § 136a CCP-Germany prohibits the use of maltreatment, fatigue, physical intervention, the administration of substances, torture, deception, hypnosis, threats to apply measures not applicable according to the rules, or promises of a benefit not provided by law during questioning and provides for a mandatory exclusionary rule if the prohibitions are violated.[329] A less categorical exclusionary rule is found in § 76(2) PACE-England and Wales, which provides that evidence "may" be rendered inadmissible under subsection (a) "where it has been obtained by oppression."[330] Some statutes simply prohibit conduct by interrogators which render a statement "involuntary," regardless of whether the conduct amounts to torture or cruel, inhuman or degrading treatment.[331]
3. *High Court Jurisprudence with Respect to Admissibility of Statements Induced by Torture, Cruel, Inhuman or Degrading Treatment or Otherwise Involuntary Statements*
   Art. 15 CAT clearly indicates that statements acquired by torture may not be used, yet CAT is

[319] Murray v. United Kingdom, (1996) 22 EHRR 29.

[320] PL, 15.

[321] *See* PO, 9; MA, 14.

[322] § 24 CCP-Finland, FI, 9; §§ 31(2), 105, 273(2) CCP-Greece, GR, 26; §§ 50, 119(2) CCP-Macao, MA, 15; § 29 CCP-Netherlands, NE, 11; § 175 CCP-Poland, PL, 16–17; § 61(1)(d) CCP-Portugal, PO, 11; § 89(2) CCP-Serbia(2001), SE, 22.

[323] For instance, in France, FR, 12.

[324] *See* §§ 18, 19 Criminal Justice Act 1984, IR, 21. Cf. § 116 CCP-Israel, IS, 8.

[325] *See* § 19A Criminal Justice Act 1984, IR, 21.

[326] Art. 7, Charter of Basic Rights and Freedoms-Czech Republic, CZ, 8; Art. 5(III) Const.-Brazil, BR, 32; Art. 7(2) Const.-Greece, GR, 3, 27; Art. 28(4) Const.-Macao, MA, 17; Art. 96 Const.-Norway (prohibiting "interrogation by torture," NO, 13; Art. 40(1) Const.-Poland, PL, 1; Art. 23 Const.-Serbia, SE, 24; Art. 18 Const.-Slovenia, SL, 20; Art. 15 Const.-Spain, SP, 31; Art. 17 Const.-Turkey, TU, 19.

[327] § 113(1) CCP-Macao, MA, 17.

[328] §§ 417bis-417 quinquies CCP-Belgium, BE, 18.

[329] GE, 6, 20–21. Similar rules may be found in § 64(3) CPP-Italy; § 171(7) CCP-Poland, PO, 2–3 (including built-in exclusionary rule); § 126(1) CCP-Portugal, PO, 4; § 9 CCP-Russia¸§ 89 CCP-Serbia, SE, 2, 24; §§ 98, 156(1) CCP-Taiwan, TA, 1,7; § 135(A) CCP-Turkey, TU, 20.

[330] § 76(8) PACE provides that "oppression" includes 'torture, inhuman or degrading treatment, and the use or threat of violence (whether or not amounting to torture)'. EW,9. *See* §§11, 227 CCP-Slovenia, prohibiting extortion, coercion, threat and other means, SL, 20. § 389 CCP-Spain prohibits compulsion or threats, and provides for an exclusionary rule. SP, 2, 30–31.

[331] § Evidence Ordinance (1971)-Israel, which also includes a built-in exclusionary rules like § 136a CCP-Germany, IS, 10. Cf. § 188 CCP-Italy, prohibiting "methods or techniques that influence the liberty of auto-determination or alter the capacity to remember or evaluate the facts." IT, 11. Cf. § 29(1) CCP-Netherlands, NE, 9.

silent with respect to statements induced by cruel, inhuman or degrading treatment. Nevertheless, there are few jurisdictions which would allow the use of a statement which was the product of torture or cruel, inhuman or degrading treatment to prove guilt. Many of the statutory exclusionary rules mentioned, *supra*, also reach even lesser "involuntary" statements induced by deception, threats, promises, fatigue, etc.

The jurisprudence is nearly unanimous with respect to statements induced by torture[332] and only slightly less so in relation to cruel, inhuman and degrading treatment[333] and other involuntary statements.[334] The ECtHR has also refused to put standing limitations on the use of statements that were arguably the results of torture or even assess whether the use of the statements was necessary for the finding of guilt. Thus, in *Harutyunyan v. Armenia*, the Court found a violation of the Art. 6 ECHR fair trial guarantee when the trial court referred to the torture-induced confession of the defendant and the torture-induced testimony of two witnesses, even though the defendant and witnesses corroborated the veracity of their statements at a later time to different officials and the court did not rely on them in making its judgment.[335]

However, in England and Wales when "oppression" has been found, courts, influenced by the "fair trial" approach of the ECt.HR, will still admit the confession where the balancing falls to the detriment of the accused.[336] A similar approach exists in Israel and the Netherlands.[337] This is not the case, however, in Ireland, Scotland, Poland and Taiwan, where an "involuntary" confession or one acquired through "oppression" may not be used.[338] In the U.S., involuntary confessions have been inadmissible since the late nineteenth Century under various theories: originally, due to their unreliability,[339] later as a violation of the 5th Amendment privilege against self-incrimination,[340]and, more recently, as a violation of due process under the 5th and 14th Amendments to the Const.-U.S.[341]

A last type of deception used by state officials to induce suspects to make incriminating statements is through the use of undercover police officers or informants, either in the field, or in jail in the guise of "jail plants." This common practice could be seen as violating the right to a "knowing" statement in the sense that the person covertly interrogated has not been advised of the right to silence or counsel,[342] or as undermining the free will of the suspect through the inherent deception of the practices and their subtle use of the pressures of

[332] BE, 18; *A v Secretary of State for the Home Department* (2005) UKHL 71, (2006) 2 AC 221, EW, 6–7; GR, 28–9; *see* ATC 970/1987, decision of Spanish Constitutional Court, SP, 32.

[333] CZ, 11 ("coerced statements").

[334] BE, 18 (statements induced by deception). In England and Wales, "oppression" has been described as: "Exercise of authority or power in a burdensome, harsh, or wrongful manner; unjust or cruel treatment of subjects, inferiors, etc; the imposition of unreasonable or unjust burdens." R v Fulling, (1987) QB 426, 432. EW, 9.

[335] 49 E.H.R.R. 9, 202, 217–8 (2009).

[336] I.e., no exclusion if the defendant would have confessed anyway. Exclusion is not aimed at deterring police misconduct. EW, 11.

[337] While the case law points to five factors that will render a confession involuntary – violence or threat thereof, unfair methods of interrogation, psychological pressure, deceit and temptation or promises – Israeli courts rarely suppress due to the importance of the principle of material truth. The undermining of the accused's free will during the interrogation must be serious for exclusion to ensue. IS, 10–12. In the Netherlands, there must be a "considerable breach," which directly led to a statement which harmed the procedural position of the suspect, NE, 13. In Turkey, though involuntary confessions are generally inadmissible, they can be used if there is other substantial incriminating evidence, TU, 2,21.

[338] In Ireland and Scotland, an "involuntary" statement is one acquired through "threats or inducements." IR, 23–5. In Scotland the seminal case is *Chalmers v HM Advocate,* 1954 JC 66, which also talks of general inadmissibility where "bullying, pressure or third degree methods" are used. SC, 15. Cf. PL, 19–20. For the Taiwan case law, TA, 7.

[339] Hopt v. Territory of Utah, *supra* note 125, at 585.

[340] Bram v. United States, 168 U.S. 532 (1897), US, 1, 18.

[341] Brown v. Mississippi, *supra* note 18. US, 1, 18. The test is whether the will of the suspect has been overborne as a result of official coercion. The courts apply a "totality of the circumstances" approach, which focuses on the object aspects of police conduct but also the subjective attributes of the suspect. Spano v. New York, 360 U.S. 315 (1959). If threats of violence are used, exclusion is usually automatic. Arizona v. Fulminante, 499 U.S. 279 (1991), US, 19.

[342] See discussion, *infra*, IIIC.

police custody.[343] In the U.S. and in other countries, the practice is tolerated.[344]

4. *Admissibility of Indirect Evidence (Fruits of Poisonous Tree)*
Although CAT does not mention exclusion of the "fruits" of tortured confessions it is presumed that the use of derivative evidence would violate international law as well. The Grand Chamber of the ECtHR recently made this clear in the case of *Gäfgen v. Germany*.[345] In *Gäfgen*, the Grand Chamber found that police threats of torture directed at a kidnapping suspect did not amount to torture under Art. 3 ECHR, but only "inhuman and degrading treatment" but it was not willing to extend the exclusionary rule to physical evidence derived from the torture threats, that is, the body of a kidnap victim and the tire tracks linking the disposal of the victim's body with defendant's car.[346] The ECtHR found that Gäfgen's right to a fair trial was not violated, under the totality of circumstances, because the trial court only used the physical evidence to corroborate the in-court confession, and not as the main evidentiary basis for the judgment of guilt.[347] In a strong dissent in *Gäfgen*, however, it was argued that the consequences of both the use of torture and cruel, inhuman or degrading treatment should be the same: strict exclusion of the confessions and any fruits.[348]

Many confessions found to be "involuntary" by the USSC would likely not rise to the level of cruel, inhuman or degrading treatment,[349] yet they are all inadmissible in court. Regarding fruits of involuntary confessions, the USSC intimated in *Oregon v. Elstad*, that a confession which otherwise comports with *Miranda* would be subject to exclusion if it follows on the heels of a confession deemed to be involuntary under the due process analysis.[350] In England and Wales, when an initial confession is found to be inadmissible due to "oppression," a subsequent non-coerced and otherwise legal confession may be suppressed as a fruit of the poisonous tree. The courts look to see whether the "blight persists" and/or the earlier confessions continues to exert a "malign influence" over the succeeding one.[351] Courts will thus exclude the subsequent confession where the initial breach was flagrant or substantial, and depending on whether it was "continuing," or whether, for instance, the interrogators clearly let the suspect know that the initial confession could not be used, therefore giving her a clear chance to freely decide whether to talk to the police thereafter.[352]

In *United States v. Patane*, the plurality clearly stated said that physical evidence would be excluded if found as a result of a "coerced" confession.[353] Because the USSC based its reluctance to apply the fruits-of-the-poisonous-tree doctrine to violations of *Miranda* on the then popular (and still breathing) doctrine that the required warnings as to the right to silence and counsel were merely "prophylactic," and not required by the Fifth Amendment, the

---

[343] For an Israeli case where the tactics used by the undercover agents were held to be sufficiently serious to warrant exclusion, IS, 15. A combination of both approaches was evident in the case of *Allan v. UK* , *supra* note 142, at 143, in which the defendant had invoked his right to silence when interrogated by police, but was then encouraged by a police jail plant to confess and was coached by the police as to what questions to ask. EU, 54.

[344] For the U.S., *see* Illinois v. Perkins, 496 U.S. 292 (1990). For the Netherlands, NE, 11.

[345] ¶ 166, Gäfgen v. Germany (Application 22978/05), Grand Chamber Judgment (June, 1, 2010), available at http://cmiskp.echr.coe.int/tkp197/view.asp?item=1&portal=hbkm&action=html&highlight=g%E4fgen%20%7C%20v.%20%7C%20germany&sessionid=56764895&skin=hudoc-en4

[346] *Id.*, ¶¶ 67, 74. The court also noted that there was no clear consensus among the states of the Council of Europe as to the application of the "fruits of the poisonous tree" doctrine to statements induced by conduct that did not rise to the level of torture. In *Gäfgen*, the police threatened a kidnap suspect with torture if he did not reveal the location of the kidnapped boy.

[347] *Id.*, ¶179. The Grand Chamber found that the in-court confession attenuated the taint of the illegality. On the idea of waivability of even absolute rights that are not subject to balancing (through the in-court confession), EU, 50. The Grand Chamber followed the approach of the German courts in the case, which, after finding that cruel and inhuman treatment was used under §136 CCP-Germany, found that admission of the physical evidence was appropriate due to the seriousness of the crime. GE, 23. Some German courts, however, will never exclude the fruits even of coerced statements, and will strain to find a "hypothetical clean path" to the otherwise tainted evidence. GE, 23.

[348] ¶ 2 *Gäfgen* (partly dissenting opinion of Judges Rozakis, Tulkens, Jebens, Ziemele, Blanku and Power). For a similar approach: GR, 29.

[349] *Inter alia*, Haynes v. Washington, 373 U.S. 503 (1963) (not allowing defendant to call wife, friends or an attorney until he talks); Ward v. Texas, 316 U.S. 547 (1942) (isolating prisoner from friends to prevent him being bailed).

[350] 470 U.S. 298, 340 (1985). For a discussion, US, 22.

[351] *R v Glaves* (1993) Crim LR 685. *Y v DPP* (1991) Crim LR 917, EW, 12. The Taiwan Supreme Court took a similar approach in a 2006 case. TA, 7–8.

[352] *R v Singleton* (2002) EWCA Crim 459, EW, 12.

[353] 542 U.S. 630, 632 (2004). For a discussion, US, 24.

consequence would be, of course, that a clear constitutional violation of due process resulting in an involuntary confession would clearly require exclusion of the "fruits," whether they be subsequent confessions or physical evidence.[354]

In England and Wales, on the other hand, the law clearly states that information and evidence found as a result of an involuntary confession (i.e. one induced by "oppression") are admissible in court as long as the prosecutor does not present evidence to the trier of fact linking the derivative evidence to the antecedent illegality.[355] Fruits of involuntary confessions are also usable in other countries.[356] The Argentine courts have also allowed use of information from involuntary confessions to further the investigation.[357]

5. *Effect of International Human Rights Jurisprudence*
   As can be seen, most countries provide for a strict exclusionary rule for statements induced by torture, cruel, inhuman or degrading treatment, or even those deemed to be involuntary because of the use of techniques, such as deception, promises, threats not relating to violence, etc. Clearly the CAT has been instrumental in unifying countries in strictly prohibiting torture.

   The ECtHR has also, in *Harutyunyan* and to a lesser extent in *Gäfgen*, spoken out strongly in relation to the use of torture-induced statements, albeit to a lesser extent when it comes to "threats of torture" or cruel and degrading treatment. On the other hand, the prevention of torture and cruel and degrading treatment pronounced in Art. 3 ECHR has certainly had an effect in changing practices in Turkey,[358] the European ex-Soviet republics, and other former socialist countries,[359] where torture was, and sometimes still is, a nagging problem, even after those countries submitted to the dictates of the ECHR. As we know from the stories from Abu Ghraib, Guantánamo Bay and elsewhere,[360] torture and cruel, inhuman and degrading treatment also occurs in the "old democracies" of the West.

29.4.3 The Protection Against Unknowing Self-incrimination: The *Miranda* Paradigm[361]

Most European and Latin American jurisdictions now require that persons subject to police interrogation be admonished of their right to confer with counsel and their right to remain silent before being interrogated.[362] Yet lawmakers have not typically provided for an explicit exclusionary rule when the so-called *Miranda* warnings are omitted nor does a failure to deliver the required admonitions normally prevent use of the "fruits" of the violation.

1. *Constitutional Provisions Requiring Admonition of the Right to Silence/Counsel*
   Despite the prevalence of the so-called *Miranda* warnings in the democracies of Western and Eastern Europe and the Americas they are seldom expressly included in the text of the constitution itself. Thus, their incorporation in the constitutions of Serbia and Slovenia can be seen as exceptional.[363]
2. *Statutory Provisions Requiring Admonition of Right to Silence/Counsel without Reference to and Exclusionary Rule*

---

[354] US, 19 (indicating that inevitable discovery and independent source exceptions would still apply, however). Supporting this interpretation, LaFave et al., *supra* note 221, at 543. In *Chalmers*, *supra* note 337, the leading Scottish case, the defendant gave an involuntary confession and then led the police to where he had hidden the deceased's purse. The High Court ruled that the discovery of the purse was "part and parcel" of the same transaction as the confession and should be thus suppressed. SC, 16.

[355] §§ 76 PACE-England and Wales, EW, 13.

[356] PL, 22. The same was true in Taiwan before 1998 when the exclusionary rule was adopted and no case has arise since to test whether the old approach still holds. TA, 8–9.

[357] Alejandro D. Carrió and Alejandro M. Garro, *Argentina*, *in* Criminal Procedure: A Worldwide Study, *supra* note 75, at 32–3. In Germany, illegally seized evidence may also be used to further the investigation, the so-called *Spurenansatz*. GE, 17.

[358] On the influence of ECtHR decisions on practices in Turkey, TU, 22.

[359] Slovenia was twice condemned for violations of Art. 3 ECHR, SL, 21.

[360] For condemnations of France, *see* FR, 14.

[361] Perhaps the most famous decision of the USSC in the area of criminal procedure was Miranda v. Arizona, *supra* note 28, in 1966, in which the court found that the Fifth Amendment privilege against self-incrimination required that all in-custody suspects be advised of their right to remain silent and their right to consult with counsel before being interrogated by police. US, 19–20.

[362] *See* Thaman, *Comparative Criminal Procedure*, *supra* note 78, at 85–96, discussing some European countries and case law. *see also* Stephen C. Thaman, "Miranda in Comparative Law," *Saint Louis University Law Journal* 45 (2001): 581.

[363] Art. 27(2) Const.-Serbia, SE, 25; Art. 19(2) Const.-Slovenia, SL, 17.

Most modern CCP's provide explicitly that a suspect must be advised of the right to silence[364] and the right to consult with counsel before being interrogated by the police or other law enforcement officials.[365] The more protective of these codes require that a defendant consult with counsel before any interrogation may take place, and the most protective require that counsel actually be present when the suspect is interrogated.[366] In many countries, however, interrogators do not have to allow the lawyer to be present during interrogation.[367]

There still exist, however, CCP's which maintain an inquisitorial approach to the interrogation, even if the practice has changed under pressure from international norms and human rights conventions. Thus, in Belgium and France the suspect is not advised of the right to silence and in Belgium may not speak to counsel before being interrogated during the *garde à vue*.[368] In France, the lawyer may speak with his client for 30 min before the *garde-à-vue* but may not be present during the interrogation.[369] *Miranda* rights are also not recognized in some other countries.[370]

Finally, it has long been the rule in the U.S. that a suspect's right to silence when confronted by police interrogation cannot be used against him or her as evidence of guilt at trial.[371] This rule is included in many modern CCP's and has been recognized by the high courts of many countries.[372] In Italy, all suspects must be advised of the right to counsel and counsel must be appointed and present during the interrogation or any ensuing statement is inadmissible at trial. Even spontaneous statements, which are admissible in the U.S., may not be used in Italy, if no counsel was present. Suspects must also be advised of the right to remain silent, of course.[373]

There is a trend, however, in common law countries, especially in the British Isles, to allow use of silence to prove guilt. This began with special legislation in Northern Ireland to deal with terrorist cases arising from the "troubles" there. Once the Northern Irish legislation was deemed not to violate Article 6 ECHR,[374] England and Wales promulgated legislation which closely followed that of Northern Ireland.[375] The Republic of Ireland has followed suit. Comment has also been traditionally allowed in some civil law countries.[376]

The admonition in England and Wales now provides: "You do not have to say anything. But it may harm your defense if you do not mention when questioned something which you later rely on in Court. Anything you do say may be given in evidence."[377] Although the ECtHR upheld comment on exercise of the right to silence in *Murray*, which involved a court trial before a single judge, subsequent decisions of the ECtHR have found, in the context of jury trials, that it violated Art. 6 ECHR (fair trial right) to allow comments in situations when the defendant may have been relying on sound advice by his/her lawyer.[378]

---

[364] Although § 29 CCP-Netherlands, requiring admonition of right to silence, was introduced in 1926, it was ignored from 1935 until 1974. NE, 10. Cf. § 232 CCP-Norway, NO, 17.

[365] BR, 30. §§ 136 (1), 163(a)(3,4) CCP-Germany, GE, 25; §§ 31(2)(2), 100(1), 105 CCP-Greece, GR, 29–30; MA, 20; §§ 59, 61 CCP-Portugal, PO, 11–12. § 5 CCP-Serbia, SE, 23, 25; § 4(1) CCP-Slovenia, SL, 18–19; § 520 CCP-Spain, SP, 29; §§147(c,e) CCP-Turkey, TU, 19, 23.

[366] The right to have counsel present exists in: CZ, 5; § 100(1) CCP-Greece, GR, 29; § 13(3) CCP-Serbia, SE, 25–26; § 245(2) CCP-Taiwan, TA, 10; § 147(c) CCP-Turkey, TU, 23.

[367] IR, 28–29; IS, 13; NE, 15.

[368] §§ 47bis, 70bis CCP-Belgium, BE, 20. 63–1 CCP-France, FR, 12–13. In practice, the various exceptions allowed in Israeli law for allowing suspects to consult with counsel amount to a denial of the right before interrogation, like in Belgium. IS, 13–14. A system similar to *garde-à-vue* is used in Scotland, where the police have 6 h to interrogate and the suspect has no right to see counsel during that time. § 150 Criminal Procedure (Scotland) Act 1995, SC, 13.

[369] § 63–4 CCP-France, FR, 15.

[370] Such as Finland, FI, 12. In Ireland, a suspect has no right to see counsel before being interrogated. IR, 29–30.

[371] Doyle v. Ohio, 426 U.S. 610 (1976); Griffin v. California, 380 U.S. 609 (1965).

[372] Cf. BGHSt 38, 214, 218 (1992), GE, 19.

[373] §§ 63, 64 CCP-Italy (also prohibiting use of statements against third parties). IT, 12. A similar provision has been recently adopted in Greece: § 31(2)(3) CCP-Greece, GR,30 (even statements taken when a suspect was questioned as a witness without counsel cannot be used when the person eventually becomes an accused).

[374] *Murray v. United Kingdom*, *supra* note 318.

[375] For a discussion of §§ 34 Criminal Justice and Public Order Act of 1994-England and Wales, EW, 13–14.

[376] § 198 CCP-Brazil, BR, 30.

[377] §10.5 Code of Practice C-PACE-England and Wales, EW, 14.

[378] Condron v. United Kingdom, 31 E.H.R.R. 1 (2001). Thaman, *Comparative Criminal Procedure*, *supra* note 78, at 171–7. Cf. Beckles v. United Kingdom (2003) 36 EHRR 13, 162. The courts of England and Wales have also balanced several factors in determining in particular cases whether comment on silence would be allowed. EW, 15–16.

3. *Statutory Provisions Which Provide for Exclusion of Statements Taken in Violation of the Miranda Rules*

§ 75(2)(1) CCP-Russia prevents use of any statement made by a suspect-defendant to police or criminal investigators pre-trial in the absence of counsel, even if the suspect waived the right to counsel, if he or she retracts that statement at trial.[379] A similar rule has been codified in Spain[380] and Turkey.[381] In Italy, the denial of the right to consult with counsel constitutes a nullity of general order and requires suppression of any subsequently obtained confession.[382]

Statutory "nullities" also play an important role in this area is where there has been a violation of the right to counsel. Of course, if the violation takes place at trial, or during a hearing on pretrial detention, it does not concern us here. But clearly, where it involves the taking of a confession, or even the conduct of search without the presence of the defendant, it could influence the collection of evidence.[383]

A statutory exclusionary rule for failure to advise of the right to counsel and silence also applies in other countries.[384]

4. *High Court Jurisprudence Interpreting the Effect of Violations of the Above Provisions on the Admissibility of Illegally Seized Evidence*

In the U.S. there is no violation of *Miranda* if a defendant knowingly and intelligently waives his right to counsel, without ever having spoken with one, and then speaks to the police. The USSC long ago said that the police need not secure counsel for a jailed defendant who wants to consult with counsel, as long as they did not interrogate him before he renounced that right.[385] However, if a suspect invokes his right to counsel after having been given the *Miranda* admonitions, then the police may not again try to talk to him until he has conferred with counsel, or until he voluntarily initiates further discussions with the police.[386] In Israel, the police may ignore a suspect's request for counsel and continue interrogating.[387]

After a defendant is charged and has counsel in the U.S., a much stricter rule applies which prevents interrogation altogether unless the defendant and counsel specifically agree.[388] This strict rule used to also apply to defendants who had been charged, arraigned in court and advised of the right to counsel,[389] but this restriction was overruled in a recent case.[390] Despite the clear constitutional foundation of the Sixth Amendment right to counsel, the USSC also recently changed course and allowed

---

[379] RU, 1. This provision was introduced due to the prevalent use of coercion by Russian criminal investigators, not only in inducing confessions, but also in inducing waivers of counsel prior to interrogation. On the problems with the implementation of the rule, *see* Stephen C. Thaman, "The Nullification of the Russian Jury: Lessons for Jury-Inspired Reform in Eurasia and Beyond," *Cornell International Law Journal* 40 (2007): 375–8.

[380] SP, 30; de Urbano Castrillo and Torres Morato, *supra* note 146, at 78. Indeed, no statements taken by police or prosecutor under any circumstances are admissible if the suspect later retracts the confession or does not confirm its veracity before the investigating magistrate or the court. SP, 30.

[381] § 148(4) CCP-Turkey, TU, 24.

[382] Marilena Colamussi, "In tema di deducibilitá della nullitá derivante dalla violazione del diritto dell'imputato in stato di custodia cautelare di conferire con il proprio difensore," in *Percorsi di Procedura Penale. Dal garantismo inquisitorio a un accusatorio non garantito,* ed. Vincenzo Perchinunno (Milano: Giuffrè, 1996), 37.

[383] In § 167(3) CCP-Argentina (Federal), nullities of "general order" include those related to a violation of the defendant's right to counsel. § 238 (4) LOPJ-Spain provides for a nullity "when the act is done without the assistance of a lawyer, in the cases where the law prescribes it as mandatory."

[384] § 89(2) CCP-Serbia, SE, 26; § 4 CCP-Slovenia, SL, 19; §§ 98, 158(2) CCP-Taiwan, TA, 1,6.

[385] California v. Prysock, 453 U.S. 355 (1981); Duckworth v. Eagan, 492 U.S. 195 (1989). The U.S.S.C. has never required the presence of lawyers in the jails, as is required in England and Wales under the system of "duty solicitors." PACE-England and Wales, Code of Practice (C) § 6.6 (a–c), lays out the right of a prisoner to see a solicitor or duty solicitor before being questioned.

[386] Edwards v. Arizona, 451 U.S. 477 (1981); Oregon v. Bradshaw, 462 U.S. 1039 (1983). In Germany, on the other hand, the police may return to try to question a suspect after he or she has attempted to speak with, or has spoken with counsel. BGHSt 42, 170, 171, 173–4, English version in Thaman, *Comparative Criminal Procedure*, *supra* note 78, at 87–8.

[387] IS, 13. The same is true in Taiwan, TA, 9.

[388] Any interrogations of a charged defendant in the absence of counsel violate the Sixth Amendment right to counsel, whether conducted out of custody by an informant, *Massiah*, *supra* note 27, at 204–06, or in custody by police officers. Brewer v. Williams, 430 U.S. 387, 400–01 (1977).

[389] Michigan v. Jackson, 475 U.S. 625, 632 (1986).

[390] In Montejo v. Louisiana, 129 S.Ct. 2079, 2091 (2009), police acquired a confession to capital murder after the defendant was charged and arraigned.

prosecutors to use a statement elicited behind the back of defense counsel in violation of *Massiah* to impeach the defendant when he testified.[391]

At least on paper, the right to counsel pre-trial is stronger in civil law countries, because the preliminary investigation is a formal, statutorily regulated affair which increasingly allows the suspect-accused broad participation rights.[392] On the contrary, the investigation in the U.S. is largely inquisitorial and counsel is not required by the Sixth Amendment until formal charging.[393]

In the last couple of years the E.Ct. HR has taken steps to strengthen the pretrial right to counsel during interrogations. In 2008, in *Salduz v. Turkey*, the court held that the right to counsel guaranteed in Art. 6(3)(c) ECHR applies during the first police interrogation and any conviction based on an admission or statement taken in violation of this right constitutes a violation of the general right to a fair trial guaranteed under Art. 6(1) ECHR. The language is tantamount to that of fashioning a court-made exclusionary rule for any such statements:"The rights of the defense will in principle be irretrievably prejudiced when incriminating statements made during police interrogation without access to a lawyer are used for a conviction."[394]

Violations of the right to a fair trial based on denial of counsel have been found in cases from Turkey, Ukraine and other countries[395] and this case law should bring change to European countries, like France, where the right to pre-interrogation counsel is limited.[396]

The USSC in *Miranda* limited the requirement of such admonitions to cases in which the suspect was in "custody," explaining that "without proper safeguards the process of in-custody interrogation of persons suspected or accused of crime contains inherently compelling pressures which work to undermine the individual's will to resist and to compel him to speak where he would not otherwise do so freely."[397] In Ireland, if police intentionally prevent a suspect from consulting with counsel, then any statement taken in absence of counsel may not be used.[398]

In Germany, if police interrogate a person they have probable cause to arrest for a crime, a failure to advise a suspect of his/her *Miranda* rights usually lead to exclusion of the statement.[399] This is true whether or not the suspect is in "custody."[400] For the German Supreme Court it is not only the coercion of police custody which requires such admonitions.

> The principle, that no one must testify against himself in a criminal proceeding, that is, that everyone has a right to remain silent, belongs to the recognized principles of criminal procedure (…). It has found a positive expression in Art. 14(3 g) of the International Covenant on Civil and Political Rights (…). The recognition of this right to remain silent reflects the respect given to human dignity (…). It protects the

[391] Kansas v. Ventris, 129 S.Ct. 1841, 1846–7 (2009). US, 26.

[392] *See* Thaman, *Comparative Criminal Procedure*, *supra* note 78, at 36–42.

[393] On the inquisitorial nature of the American grand jury, *see* Blair v. United States, 250 U.S. 273, 281–3 (1919). On the inquisitorial nature of the investigation in general, *see* McNeil v. Wisconsin, 501 U.S. 171, 181 (1991).

[394] 49 E.H.R.R. 19, 421, 435–9 (2009). EU, 1. For a similar decision, *see* Panovits v. Cyprus (Dec. 11, 2008), in which a 17 year-old defendant was convicted on the basis of a confession taken after the police advised him of the right to silence, but not to counsel, and where the conviction played a central role in the guilty judgment,.¶ 69–85. All decisions of the ECt. HR available at http://www.echr.coe.int/ECHR/EN/Header/Case-Law/HUDOC/HUDOC+database/

[395] *See, inter alia*, Ibrahim Öztürk v. Turkey (Feb. 17, 2009); Shabelnik v. Ukraine (Feb. 19, 2009); Gülecan v. Turkey (Apr. 28, 2009); Öngün v. Turkey (June 23, 2009) Cimen Isik v. Turkey (July 16, 2009); Özcan Colak v. Turkey (Oct. 6, 2009); Güvenlir v. Turkey (Oct. 13, 2009); Oleg Kolesnik v. Ukraine (Nov. 19, 2009).

[396] It should also have an impact in Scotland, where there is no right to consult with counsel before interrogation. While the courts, there, have held that a suspect must be advised of the right to silence, the case law is inconsistent with respect to whether the penalty for failing to do so is exclusion. SC,14.

[397] *Supra* note 28, at 467. In Spain, admonitions also appear to be required only when the suspect is in custody. § 520(1)(a–c) LECr-Spain. The same is true in Taiwan, TA, 9.

[398] People (D.P.P.) v Healy, (1990) 2 I.R. 73; (1990) I.L.R.M. 313, IR, 27–28. For comparison, *see* Moran v. Burbine, 475 U.S. 412 (1986), in which jail officials intentionally interrogated the suspect without telling him counsel had been appointed and wanted to talk to him. The Israeli courts have reached a a similar decision, IS, 14.

[399] BGHSt 39, 349, 352 (1993). GE, 25.

[400] BGHSt 38, 214, 218 (1992) (person suspected of drunk driving was questioned as a suspect while walking on the street). For a similar case, where the courts found a violation, but did not suppress the suspect's statements, no. 18. For other German cases, *see*: BGH NStZ 2007, 653, 654; BGHSt 37, 48 (1990); BGHSt 40, 211 (1994). GE, 25. For a similar expansive interpretation, BR, 29–30.

personality rights of the accused and is a necessary component of a fair trial (…).[401]

Although the *Miranda* Court clearly held that the admonitions were required by the 5th Amendment to the U.S. Const. the USSC gradually began stripping the *Miranda* warnings of their constitutional status and once having such delegitimized them, it began crafting exceptions which would allow statements acquired in violation thereof to be admissible.[402]

In 1986 the U.S. Supreme Court recognized a "public safety" exception to the need to inform arrested suspects of their *Miranda* rights,[403] and this exception has recently been used in terrorism investigations to justify initial interrogations aimed at discovering whether an alleged terrorist has dangerous associates, or has already planted a bomb, etc.[404]

Although Italy will exclude statements given in the absence of counsel, even when made spontaneously, and require admonitions as to the right to silence, the police, are permitted to gather "summary information" and tips from suspects, even those arrested *in flagrante*. Although "no record or use may be made of the information and tips gathered in the absence of defense counsel,"[405] the "information and tips" may be freely used in ways that do not prejudice the declarant, for instance, against third parties,[406] but may also be used for the purpose of justifying a search or seizure or an order of pretrial detention.[407] The information gleaned from a non-usable statement may also be used without restriction to develop leads in an investigation[408] and may be used to impeach the defendant if he testifies at trial in a contrary manner.[409]

In England and Wales, the courts will on occasion suppress confessions, but primarily when the defendant is denied the right to consult with counsel before being interrogated.[410] For instance, in one case the English Court of Appeal suppressed a confession obtained properly because it was the fruit of a previous confession obtained in violation of the right to consult with counsel.[411] Canadian courts have also suppressed the "fruits" of confessions obtained in violation of the right to counsel.[412] While Australia now recognizes *Miranda* rights, failure to abide by them does not necessarily even lead to exclusion of the statement taken.[413]

Clearly if bad faith is shown by the police in failing to give proper admonitions, then all fruits of statements thus acquired should be suppressed, regardless of how important the case is or there will be nothing to deter police from undermining the constitutional fabric of the political and social system. Yet it is the rare police officer who will admit that his ignoring of *Miranda* warnings was intentional, and it is the rare judge who will reject

[401] BGHSt 38, at 224–5. English translation in Thaman, *Comparative Criminal Procedure*, *supra* note 78, at 111. Since police custody is inherently coercive, *Miranda*, *supra* note 28, at 467, and since admonitions need only be given when a person is in custody, *id*, at 444, U.S. law has distanced itself from the theory that the decision on whether to talk to police in general is linked to constitutional protection of important personality rights. This approach has also been adopted in England and Wales, Thaman, *Comparative Criminal Procedure*, *supra* note 18, at 92, in Italy, § 63 CPP-Italy, as well as in Australia, Van der Meer v. The Queen, (1988) 82 A.L.R. 10, 18, cited in Bradley, *Mapp*, *supra* note 118, at 381.

[402] For instance, in Harris v. New York, 40 1 US 222 (1971), the Supreme Court held that statements acquired in violation of *Miranda* could be used to impeach a defendant if he testifies contrary to the content of the illegally acquired statement. US, 21.

[403] New York v. Quarles, 467 U.S. 649, 655–6 (1984). US, 22.

[404] Federal officials did not *Mirandize* Umar Farouk Abdulmutallab, the so-called "Christmas Bomber" after his arrest on an airplane in Detroit, based on the "public safety exception." Charlie Savage, "Nigerian Indicted in Terrorist Plot," *New York Times*, Jan. 7, 2010, at A 14, http://www.nytimes.com/2010/01/07/us/07indict.html?ref=us Indeed, President Obama has recently suggested that legislation should remove the requirement of giving *Miranda* warnings to terror suspects. Anne E. Kornblut, "Obama administration look into modifying Miranda law in the age of terrorism," *Washington Post*, May 10, 2010, http://www.washingtonpost.com/wp-dyn/content/article/2010/05/09/AR2010050902062.html. This has already been done in Israel, IS, 15.

[405] § 350(5–6) CPP-Italy

[406] Conso and Grevi, *supra* note 250, at 143, 387.

[407] *Id.* at 390.

[408] *Id.* at 400.

[409] §§ 350(7), 503(3) CPP-Italy. Rachel VanCleave, *Italy*. in Criminal Procedure. A Worldwide Study, *supra* note 55, at 264.

[410] § 58 PACE-England guarantees the suspect a right to consult with counsel before being interrogated.

[411] R. v. McGovern, (1991) Crim. L. R. 124, 124–5, EW, 12, reprinted in Thaman, *Comparative Criminal Procedure*, *supra* note 78, at 121–2.Cf. Bradley, *Mapp*, *supra* note 118, at 386.

[412] *Id.*,at 383.

[413] *Id.*,at 381.

a claim of inadvertence by a police officer if given under oath at a motion to suppress evidence.[414]

Of course, the easiest way for the authorities to avoid advising a suspect of his/her right to silence and counsel is to interrogate the person by using undercover agents or "jailplants" who pretend to be a friend or confidant of the suspect in wheedling incriminatory information from them. Though many courts treat this practice under the rubric of "involuntary confessions,"[415] the practice is sometimes treated as circumventing the requirement of giving the *Miranda*-type admonitions."[416]

The solution which will best prevent the undermining of important personality rights of citizens in the investigation of criminal offenses would be to make *all* confessions of suspects-accuseds-defendants and the fruits derived from them inadmissible *per se*, unless they were made in the presence of defense counsel, following proper *Miranda*-type warnings.[417] I would further recommend that confessions be used only to the benefit of the person giving them.[418]

[414] On the problem of police lying in American suppression hearings and the willingness of judges to base their rulings on obvious prevarications, *see* Christopher Slobogin, *Why Liberals Should Chuck the Exclusionary Rule, University of Illinois Law Review* (1999): 363, 388; Donald Dripps, *The Case for the Contingent Exclusionary Rule, American Criminal Law Review* 38, no.1, (2001): 20–22.

[415] *See supra*, III.B.3.

[416] Thus, in Germany, confessions have been suppressed if the undercover agent purposely questions a suspect to avoid informing him of his rights. BGHSt 31, 304 (1983); BGH NJW 2007, 3138; BGHSt 33, 217 (1985); BGHSt 34, 362 (1987). GE, 26–27. For similar case law, no. 18–19.

[417] In regimes like the U.S. where the suspect may waive his right to counsel, the voluntariness of such waivers, especially when given in custody, are suspect for the same reasons that the voluntariness of statements taken in custody are considered to be. Progressive in this respect is a provision in the new Russian CCP which makes any statement given by the defendant to pretrial investigators in the absence of defense counsel inadmissible, whether or not the suspect purportedly waived the right to counsel, if the defendant recants the confession in court. § 75(2)(1) UPK-RF. This is a welcome innovation in a country otherwise known for the brutality of its police interrogators. See in general *Confessions at any Cost*. Police Torture in Russia (Human Rights Watch 1999).

[418] In Italy, the defendant's interrogation is considered to be only a tool in his or her defense, *see* § 65(2) CPP-Italy, Thaman, *Comparative Criminal Procedure*, *supra* note 78, at 103.

5. *Admissibility of Indirect Evidence (Fruits of Poisonous Tree)*

Occasionally a statute will explicitly require exclusion of evidence derived from a confession taken in the absence of admonitions as to the right to silence or to counsel.[419]

In *Michigan v. Tucker* the USSC maintained that the *Miranda* warnings were mere "procedural safeguards" and "not themselves rights protected by the Constitution" and held that, because of this, the "fruits" of confessions obtained in violation of *Miranda* could be used at trial to convict the confessor.[420] In *Oregon v. Elstad*, the Court allowed use of a confession obtained after proper warnings even though it was arguably the "fruit" of a previous confession made in violation of *Miranda*, claiming that: "[t]he Miranda exclusionary rule sweeps more broadly than the Fifth Amendment itself. It may be triggered even in the absence of a Fifth Amendment violation."[421]

In 2000, the USSC, despite its previous assertions that *Miranda* was not constitutionally required, beat back a challenge to the rule and reversed its position.[422] Once this decision was reached, defendants who had been convicted based on the "fruits" of confessions gained in violation of *Miranda*, appealed, claiming that the rule in *Tucker* was no longer valid. A plurality of the USSC, however, recently held that the "fruit" of a negligent *Miranda* violation would still be admissible in court.[423] Some state courts, however, have ruled that physical evidence found as a result of a *Miranda* violation, whether negligent or intentional, must be suppressed.[424]

[419] *See* SL, 19.

[420] *Supra* note 162, at 444. The police gained knowledge of the identity of a witness from the unlawful confession who later testified against the defendant at trial. For a discussion, *see* US, 21.

[421] *Supra* note 349, at 306. For the second confession to be admissible, neither confessions could have failed under the "voluntariness" due process test, i.e., have been the product of coercion, deception, threats, etc. *Id.* at 318.

[422] Dickerson v. United States, 530 U.S. 428 (2000). US, 23. The challenge sought to return USSC jurisprudence to a time when the presence or absence of admonitions as to one's rights was only one factor in determining whether a confession was voluntary. The Israeli Supreme Court has recently excluded evidence in the *Issacharov* case in which the suspect was not admonished, but treated the admonitions as just one factor in the analysis. IS, 11–2.

[423] *Patane, supra* note 352.

[424] Commonwealth v. Martin, 827 N.E.2d 198 (Mass. 2005); State v. Knapp, 700 N.W.2d 899 (Wis. 2005); State v. Peterson, 923 A.2d 585 (Vt. 2007)

In the context of cases with two interrogations, where the first is in violation of *Miranda* and the second following proper admonitions, the USSC in *Missouri v. Seibert*,[425] elaborated on the precedent established in *Elstad*. While it still did not determine that the second confession was a "fruit" of the confession obtained by police who had a policy of intentionally omitting the required warnings to soften up criminal suspects, it did find that the subsequent waiver of *Miranda* rights was not "knowing and intelligent," coming as it did directly on the heels of an interrogation without warnings, and without an accompanying explanation that the first confession would be inadmissible in court.[426] It was intimated in *Seibert* that, had the defendant been advised that the first confession was not usable as evidence, the second one would have been admissible.[427]

In dealing with the repercussions which ensue from failing to advise a suspect of the right to remain silent and the right to counsel before an interrogation, the issue of the constitutional stature of the so-called *Miranda* warnings appears to be crucial. The German Supreme Court has recognized the constitutional stature of the warnings and has concluded that the statements themselves may not be used because of the importance of the warnings in protecting the procedural status of the accused. But it has not extended this evidentiary prohibition to the "fruits" of the confession, whether in the form of physical evidence or subsequent confessions.[428] Thus, even where the German courts might suppress a confession induced by an undercover police agent, the information gathered from the confession can be used for investigative purposes and even be funneled into the trial.[429]

§ 11.1 LOPJ-Spain would clearly exclude both a confession and the "derivative evidence" if those courts find the warnings to be constitutionally rooted.[430] In Spain, no pretrial statement by a suspect to police or prosecutor may be used if not reaffirmed before the investigating magistrate. In the same vein, an unknowing statement, taken without counsel and/or without the suspect having been advised of the right to silence, will not render inadmissible a subsequent statement given with the proper guarantees before the investigating magistrate, not to speak of at trial.[431]

In Canada police are not constitutionally required to advise detained suspects of the right to silence before questioning them, but § 10(b) of the Charter does accord arrested persons the right to attempt to contact counsel before being interrogated.[432] If the right to counsel has been violated, however, and derivative evidence is found that could not have been found but for the violation, the Canadian courts consider this to be "conscripted" evidence and have traditionally suppressed it. Thus, if a suspect points out incriminating evidence in his own house, which would have been searched anyway, this would be admissible, but if the accused, while being denied the right to counsel, informs police that the murder weapon is at the bottom of a frozen river, this must be suppressed.[433] Whether the "conscription" doctrine is still viable is questionable, since the Canadian Supreme Court adopted a new approach to exclusion in two 2009 cases.[434] The Spanish courts will also suppress physical evidence found as a result of a confession obtained in violation of the right to counsel.[435]

6. *Effect of International Human Rights Jurisprudence*
The ECtHR's decision in *Salduz v. Turkey*[436] is already having a big impact on the practices in the

[425] 542 U.S. 600, 614–5 (2004). For a discussion, US, 24.

[426] The German trial court in *Gäfgen* intimated that the statements made by the defendant after the coerced confession might have been admissible had the police advised him of the inadmissibility of the first confession. 48 E.H.R.R. at 261.

[427] *Seibert, supra* noe 424, at 612.

[428] Theodor Kleinknecht et al, Strafprozeßordnung 469 (note 20b) (Munich: Beck, 43rd ed. 1997).

[429] BGHSt 34, 362 (1987), GE, 28. The information gleaned from an unlawful confession can also be used to further the investigation in Spain, SP, 34.

[430] However, some voices in the literature find that, despite *Miranda* violations, the fruits would still be admissible, but not if they were the only support for a conviction. Vicente Gimeno Sendra et al., Derecho Procesal Penal 507 (1996).

[431] SP, 34.

[432] Roach, *supra* note 55, at 75–77.

[433] *Id.*, at 71.

[434] *See Grant, supra* note 56, at ¶61 where the court balanced a non-egregious unlawful detention and questioning, by virtue of which the defendant was "conscripted" to admit possession of a gun, against the admitted importance of the rights impinged on thereby, and the importance of the physical evidence to determine the truth of the charges and admitted the gun.

[435] STS of 25 October 1991, SP, 34.

[436] *Supra*, note 393.

European countries which are members of the Council of Europe.[437] Already in 2009, the Dutch High Court stated that the denial of the right to council before an interrogation will inevitably lead to exclusion of any statements acquired unless the suspect clearly waived his right to counsel or there are exigent circumstances.[438] Clearly, the *Salduz* decision will compel many countries to provide for appointed counsel pre-trial if their legislation did not previously guarantee this right.[439]

29.4.4 Derivative Exclusion of an Otherwise Valid Confession as Fruit of an Unlawful Arrest/Seizure or Search

In the U.S. a confession which is causally related to an unlawful arrest will be considered the "fruit of the poisonous tree" and will be suppressed.[440] This is even true if the defendant was advised of his right to remain silent and his right to counsel and still decided to speak to the police.[441] The Irish courts have also excluded a confession which resulted from an illegally prolonged detention.[442] If, however, sufficient time separates the unlawful arrest from the confession, and especially if the defendant has been released from custody following the unlawful arrest, then courts have found that the taint of the unlawful arrest has been attenuated and the confession may be used in court.[443] Many courts also require that there be not just a temporal connection with the illegality, but also real causation.[444] Thus the mere fact of an unlawful detention will not make a confession of a person while unlawfully detained a fruit thereof, without a further showing of direct causation.[445] For those countries with statutory "fruits of the poisonous tree" legislation, an unlawful arrest certainly is a substantial constitutional violation which will lead to suppression of a subsequent confession.[446]

Despite the meager use of exclusionary rules in France, the application of the French nullity doctrine has led to the exclusion of a confession which came on the heels of an illegal search.[447] Yet, in Spain, where the defendant was aware of the illegality of a search and still testified at trial in a way that corroborated the essence of the illegal search, then the "anti-juridical" nexus between search and confession has been broken and the fruits of the search will be admissible.[448] In Taiwan courts have excluded fruits of unlawful searches, such as where the search led to an arrest and the taking of a urine sample. The urine sample was suppressed.[449]

29.5 Conclusion

Courts have always engaged in value judgments in determining whether to exclude evidence. "Balancing" of the seriousness of a law violation against the protections of human rights conventions and constitutions to determine whether exclusion would be a proper remedy, and then "balancing" exclusion against other interests.

Once the legislator or the high courts have determined that conduct of law enforcement officials violates fundamental rights of a citizen, and that recognized exceptions such as those for exigent circumstances (suitably restricted as advocated, *supra*), do not apply, then it is my opinion that the evidence should simply not be used, nor should its "fruits." The right should be vindicated in what has proved to be the most effective manner. International consensus has approximated

[437] Violations have already been found in cases emanating not only from Turkey, but also from Cyprus, Poland, Russia and Ukraine, EU, 2.

[438] Decision of June 30, 2009, NE, 16.

[439] EU, 2. Cf. NE, 16.

[440] The Taiwan Supreme Court has suppressed such a confession, but only after finding that the unlawful arrest had rendered the confession "involuntary." TA, 12.

[441] Brown v. Illinois, 422 U.S. 590 (1975), US, 14. For a similar ruling, *see* D.P.P. v Madden, (1977) I.R. 336, IR, 4.

[442] People (D.P.P.) v Shaw, (1982) I.R. 1, IR, 5 (in rape-murder case, suspect held longer to encourage him to lead authorities to the victim who was still thought to be alive).

[443] Wong Sun v. United States, *supra* note 25. Cf. US, 14.

[444] IR, 32.

[445] NE, 6. § 156(1) CCP-Taiwan specifically provides for suppression of a confession which resulted from an unlawful detention, TA.

[446] Such as in: SL, 19.

[447] FR, 6.

[448] STC 161/ (Sept. 27, 1999), SP, 18–9. The Spanish Supreme Court, however, in a similar case, has ruled that the confession in court may only be accepted if the evidence of the illegal search is completely excluded from the trial. STS March 13, 1999, SP, 19.

[449] TA, 5.

this position in relation to involuntary confessions and interception of confidential communications carried out without probable cause or judicial authorization and is heading in that direction in relation to confessions obtained in violation of the right to counsel. But this budding consensus should extend to "fruits," even physical evidence.[450] Although the right to privacy in one's dwelling has clearly been recognized as a human right, and judicial authorization and probable cause are required to infringe thereupon, courts have been reluctant, with the exception of the U.S. and Spain, to suppress physical evidence obtained in violation of these minimal requirements, and those two countries are balancing away more of the protection they once firmly protected.

The seriousness of the alleged criminal conduct should only play a role in whether there are exigent circumstances, i.e., danger to life or limb, to extreme damage of property or loss of evidence of serious crime, not in relation to the admissibility question. The area of "good faith" of the violating official should be limited to cases where the officer's conduct was in accordance with standards that, while once accepted by the courts, had since been declared to be unconstitutional. It should never encompass a negligent mistake of law, either by the police or the magistrate who issues a search warrant or wiretap order, or mistake of facts caused by systemic negligence of state officials. Finally, the importance of the evidence to convict the defendant should never be a factor. If the evidence were not important, the violation would likely be harmless error anyway.

The only exception should be based in a narrow interpretation of what U.S. courts call "inevitable discovery" or "independent source." If the evidence is the direct causal fruit of the illegality and would not have been found but for this illegality, it should be excluded, even if it is physical evidence which is of unimpeachable credibility and damning, if admissible, for the defendant.

Similarly, though *Miranda* rights now exist in most democracies and are considered to be included in the right to personal dignity and the right to silence, the courts, while suppressing the words spoken in violation thereof, still balk at extending protection to the fruits derived therefrom. The best way to prevent abuses during interrogations, would be to introduce a strict exclusionary rule which would apply to all statements or confessions as well as their fruits, if they were not given in the presence of defense counsel after an appropriate waiver of the right to silence. In addition, confessions should be treated exclusively as *defense evidence*[451] and should be negotiated with the public prosecutor as are plea bargains in the U.S. Furthermore, they should *always* bring about a reduction of the maximum sentence, as would a plea bargain.

If the law enforcement violation is not considered to be of constitutional magnitude, such an error in the execution of an otherwise valid search or wiretapping warrant, then I think the courts should apply their balancing tests and weigh the proportionality of the violation, the seriousness of the crime being investigated, the nature of the evidence, etc., and then decide on admissibility.

It appears as if the principle of material truth, which I believe nowhere has constitutional status, still holds sway in the criminal courts. Yet, a legal system, which employs explicit loopholes or vague balancing principles in order to use evidence gathered directly or indirectly by means of unconstitutional acts of its investigative organs, can only with difficulty be considered to be a state under the rule of law in the strict sense. As long as such loopholes exist, constitutional rights will be routinely violated by state officials. This is especially the case in systems where the trial judge is considered to be an investigator of the material truth of the charges, no different than the prosecutor or investigating magistrate at the pretrial stage. An inquisitorial judge will intentionally or instinctively give priority to the principle of material truth in exercising his or her Herculean balancing act and neglect his/her role as guarantor of freedom. Therefore, if judicial balancing is to persist, it should be carried out by a neutral judge of the investigation, or liberty judge, and not the trial judge.

[450] The presumptive inadmissibility of illegally gathered evidence was clearly proclaimed in *Mapp*, and *Miranda*, and in early New Zealand jurisprudence. Mahoney, *supra*. note 122, at 610. The Australian Law Reform Commission in its Uniform Evidence Law has also provided for presumptive inadmissibility, but it has apparently not yet become law. Mark Findlay et al, Australian Criminal Justice 197 (Melbourne: Oxford 3rd ed. 2005).

[451] This approach finds theoretical articulation in § 65(2) CCP-Italy), and in some South American codes.

A dismissal or acquittal in a criminal proceeding, even when the evidence seems to point to the guilt of the accused, violates no fundamental human rights. The victim of an act of violence remains a victim, even when the defendant is convicted! In the case of victim-less drug crimes, for instance, which constitute the overwhelming majority of cases involving illegal searches and a large number of those with illegal wiretaps, a dismissal does not prevent future surveillance and legal apprehension of the offender, and, in the U.S., may constitute a lesser of two evils: an escape from lifelong incapacitation in the nation's archipelago of prisons.